Pedro de Ribadeneyra's *Ecclesiastical History of the Schism of the Kingdom of England*

Jesuit Studies

MODERNITY THROUGH THE PRISM OF JESUIT HISTORY

Edited by

Robert A. Maryks (*Boston College*)

VOLUME 8

The titles published in this series are listed at *brill.com/js*

Pedro de Ribadeneyra's *Ecclesiastical History of the Schism of the Kingdom of England*

A Spanish Jesuit's History of the English Reformation

Edited and translated by

Spencer J. Weinreich

BRILL

LEIDEN | BOSTON

Cover illustration: The Calling of Saint Peter. Pedro de Ribadeneyra, *Historia ecclesiastica del scisma del reyno de Inglaterra: En la qual se tratan las cosas mas notables q[ue] han sucedido en aquel reyno, tocantes à nuestra santa religion, desde que començo hasta la muerte de la reyna de Escocia* (Madrid: en casa de Pedro Madrigal, 1588). *SC5 R5207 588hc, Houghton Library, Harvard University.

The Library of Congress Cataloging-in-Publication Data is available online at http://catalog.loc.gov
LC record available at http://lccn.loc.gov/2016052768

Typeface for the Latin, Greek, and Cyrillic scripts: "Brill". See and download: brill.com/brill-typeface.

ISSN 2214-3289
ISBN 978-90-04-32395-7 (hardback)
ISBN 978-90-04-32396-4 (e-book)

Printed by Printforce, United Kingdom

For my parents, Gadi and Caren,
the authors of my own historia

"Of course that is not the whole story, but that is the way with stories; we make them what we will. It's a way of explaining the universe while leaving the universe unexplained, it's a way of keeping it all alive, not boxing it into time."

JEANETTE WINTERSON, *Oranges Are Not the Only Fruit* (1994)

Contents

The Ecclesiastical History of the Schism of the Kingdom of England

BOOK 2
*The Second Book of the Schism of England, Concerning
King Edward, and the Queens Doña Mary and Elizabeth,
His Sisters*

BOOK 3
*The Third Book of the Schism of England, Recounting Various
Martyrs and Other Things that have Occurred in that Realm Since
the First Part of this History was Published*

Acknowledgments

This book owes its existence to conversations with two learned men. It was Carlos Eire who first told me about the *Historia eclesiástica del scisma del reyno de Inglaterra*. His passion, encyclopedic knowledge of early modern Europe, and friendship have shaped me as a historian in ways I am only beginning to comprehend.

It was Robert A. Maryks who kindly indulged my enthusiasm for Ribadeneyra, and who bravely took a chance on an undergraduate's ambitions to translate a book. Ever since, he has been beyond generous with his time and expertise, as supportive and insightful an editor and friend as one could wish for.

These were but the first of many debts accumulated in the preparation of this translation, to which colleagues from around the globe gave of their time, expertise, and wisdom. It pains me not to be able to thank each of them with the effusiveness they deserve; I trust they will understand that my gratitude is not as limited as my words.

First, I wish to thank the staffs of the libraries at Yale and Oxford, as well as the British Library and the Archivum Britannicum Societatis Iesu. Particular thanks are owed to the Woodstock Theological Library at Georgetown University, which in the summer of 2015 graciously opened its doors to a temporarily independent scholar between institutional homes. My studies at Oxford have been immeasurably enriched by a Mica and Ahmet Ertegun Graduate Scholarship in the Humanities, and the space—physical and intellectual—of Ertegun House was instrumental in actually bringing this project to a close. Grateful mention must also be made of the Burns Library at Boston College and the Houghton Library at Harvard University for their assistance with the illustrations.

My thinking about Ribadeneyra has benefited enormously from the opportunity to deliver papers at the first International Symposium on Jesuit Studies, held at Boston College in June 2015; at the fifth Annual Meeting of Postgraduates in the Reception of the Ancient World, held at the University of Nottingham in December 2015; and at "Emotions: Movement, Cultural Contact and Exchange, 1100–1800," jointly sponsored by the Freie Universität Berlin and the Australian Research Council Centre of Excellence for the History of Emotions, Europe 1100–1800, and held at the Freie Universität Berlin in June–July 2016. My colleagues at the *Journal of Jesuit Studies*, especially Emanuele Colombo and Christopher Staysniak, provided invaluable support throughout.

This book would have been much the poorer were it not for the remarkable squadron of scholars and friends who offered thoughts, bibliographic and historiographic assistance, and critiques: Phil Booth, David J. Collins, S.J., Anne K. Dillon, Freddy Cristóbal Domínguez, María de Fátima Gomes, Bruce Gordon, Anthony Grafton, Yasmin Haskell, Gerard Kilroy, Andreu Martínez d'Alòs-Moner, Owen McKnight, John W. O'Malley, S.J., Tim Page, Claude Pavur, S.J., Kevin R. Poole, Rady Roldán-Figueroa, Stuart B. Schwartz, José Solís de los Santos, Corinna Streckfuss, Rebecca Volk, Claire I. Walker, Alexandra Walsham, Bryan Ward-Perkins, and Anders Winroth. Special mention must be made of Tom McCoog, S.J., who in many ways made this project possible, in his patient answers to my questions, and even more in his scholarship, which has led the way for me and for countless others.

Arjan van Dijk, Francis Knikker, Ester Lels, and the rest of the staff at Brill have made my first book project a true delight, something I know to be a rare piece of good fortune. I must also thank the two anonymous peer reviewers for their insightful, constructive critiques.

Any errors that remain are my own.

Finally, there are some debts of a more personal nature. It has been my privilege over the past five years to have several extraordinary scholars as my mentors. To Carlos, Paola Bertucci, Diarmaid MacCulloch, and Paul Freedman, I owe so much—not least the very possibility of undertaking a project such as this.

My friends, who have endured conversations about sixteenth-century historiography, Jesuit Studies, Tudor history, and the agonies and ecstasies of translating early modern Spanish: Hugh Binnie, Simon Brewer, Rivkah Brown, Malina Buturović, Tyler Carlisle, Clifford Carr, Charlie Clegg, Molly Corlett, Chiara Giovanni, Joey Goldman, Thea Goldring, Dylan Hosmer-Quint, Daoud Jackson, Anik Laferrière, Alec Pollak, Michael Thorne, and, most of all, Jason Parisi.

In a sense, this book was undertaken both to annoy and to amuse Douglas Plume. I do not expect him to read the entire thing, but I trust he will appreciate the joke.

I have been blessed with parents, sisters, and grandparents who have supported, indeed embraced, my dreams of entering academia. Whatever I have done and whatever I will do in future, it is upon their shoulders.

Spencer J. Weinreich
Harris Manchester College, Oxford
24 July 2016

List of Figures

List of Bibliographic Abbreviations

AASS *Acta sanctorum quotquot toto orbe coluntur, vel a catholicis scriptoribus celebranter, quæ ex Latinis et Græcis, aliarumque gentium antiquis monumentis.* 68 vols. Antwerp and Brussels: Société des Bollandistes, 1643–1940.

AHSI *Archivum historicum Societatis Iesu*

CSPS Bergenroth, Gustav Adolf, Pascual de Gayangos y Arce, Martin A. Sharp Hume, Royall Tyler, and Garrett Mattingly, eds. *Calendar of Letters, Despatches, and State Papers Relating to the Negotiations between England and Spain Preserved in the Archives at Simancas and Elsewhere.* 13 vols. London: Her Majesty's Stationery Office, London, 1862–99.

LP Brewer, John S., James Gairdner, and Robert H. Brodie, eds. *Letters and Papers, Foreign and Domestic, of the Reign of Henry VIII: Preserved in the Public Record Office, the British Museum, and Elsewhere in England.* 35 vols. London: Her Majesty's Stationery Office, 1862–1932.

CSPV Brown, Rawdon Lubbock, George Cavendish Bentinck, Horatio F. Brown, and Allen Banks Hinds, eds. *Calendar of State Papers and Manuscripts, relating to English Affairs Existing in the Archives and Collections of Venice, and in Other Libraries of Northern Italy.* 38 vols. London: Her Majesty's Stationery Office, 1864–1947.

CH *Church History*

EHR *English Historical Review*

Concertatio Gibbons, John, and John Bridgewater, eds. *Concertatio Ecclesiae Catholicæ in Anglia adversus Calvinopapistas et Puritanos sub Elizabetha regina quorundam hominum doctrina & sanctitate illustrium renouata.* Trier: Henricus Bock, 1588.

HJ *Historical Journal*

HR *Historical Research*

TRP Hughes, Paul L., and James F. Larkin, eds. *Tudor Royal Proclamations.* 3 vols. New Haven: Yale University Press, 1964–69.

CSPSE Hume, Martin A. Sharp, ed. *Calendar of Letters and State Papers Relating to English Affairs: Preserved Principally in the Archives of Simancas; Elizabeth, 1558–1603.* 4 vols. London: Her Majesty's Stationery Office, 1892–99.

HLQ *Huntington Library Quarterly*

JEH *Journal of Ecclesiastical History*

JJS *Journal of Jesuit Studies*

SR   Luders, Alexander, Thomas Edlyne Tomlins, John France, William Elias Taunton, and John Raithby, eds. *The Statutes of the Realm: Printed by Command of His Majesty King George the Third; In Pursuance of an Address of the House of Commons of Great Britain.* 9 vols. London: Dawsons of Pall Mall, 1810–28.

ODNB   Matthew, Colin, and Brian Harrison, eds. *Oxford Dictionary of National Biography.* 60 vols. Oxford: Oxford University Press, 2004.

CHRC   Miranda, Salvador. *The Cardinals of the Holy Roman Church.* 2016. http://webdept.fiu.edu/~mirandas/cardinals.htm. Accessed April 21, 2016.

Philopater   Persons, Robert. *Elizabethae, Angliae reginae haeresim Calvinianam propugnantis, saevissimum in Catholicos sui regni edictum, quod in alios quoque reipub. christianae principes contumelias continet indignissimas: Promulgatum Londini 29. Nouemb. 1591; Cum responsione ad singula capita: qua non tantum sœuitia, & impietas tam iniqui edicti, sed mendacia quoque, & fraudes ac imposturæ deteguntur, & confutantur; Per D. Andream Philopatrum presbyterum ac theologum Romanum, ex Anglis olim oriundum* (Augsburg: Apud Ioannem Fabrum, 1592)

CRP   Pole, Reginald. *The Correspondence of Reginald Pole.* Edited and translated by Thomas F. Mayer. 5 vols. Farnham: Ashgate, 2002–08.

RH   *Recusant History*

Rey   Ribadeneyra, Pedro de. *Historias de la Contrarreforma.* Edited by Eusebio Rey. Historia y hagiografía. Madrid: Biblioteca de Autores Cristianos, 1945.

MHSIR   Ribadeneyra, Pedro de. *Patri Petri de Ribadeneira, Societatis Jesu sacerdotis: Confessiones, epistolae aliaque scripta inedita ex autographis, antiquissimis apographis et regestis deprompta.* 2 vols. Monumenta Historica Societatis Iesu 58, 60. Rome: Monumenta Historica Societatis Iesu, 1969.

CSPR   Rigg, James Macmullen, ed. *Calendar of State Papers, relating to English Affairs, Preserved Principally at Rome, in the Vatican Archives and Library.* 2 vols. London: His Majesty's Stationery Office, 1916–26.

SCJ   *Sixteenth Century Journal*

List of Textual Abbreviations

b.	born
c.	circa
d.	died
fl.	*floruit*
n.p.	no pagination
r.	reigned
sig.	signature (sigs. plural)
s.j.	Societatis Jesu (of the Society of Jesus)

Notes on the Translation

In keeping with my interest in Ribadeneyra's use of the vernacular and engagement with popular audiences, this translation is based on the published editions of the *Historia*. For Books 1 and 2, the base text is the *editio princeps*, published in 1588 by Pedro Madrigal (d. *c*.1594) in Madrid, supplemented by the second 1588 printing (I used the Antwerp edition, published by Christophe Plantin [*c*.1520–89]). The basis for Book 3 is likewise the *editio princeps* of the *Segunda parte*, the 1593 Alcalá de Henares edition. All three books were then compared with the 1594, 1595, and 1605 editions, as well as with the critical editions of Fuente and Rey.[1] Text that differs between editions (save for corrections of minor errors in spelling and the like) has been printed in a different color font, with footnotes indicating the nature of the changes and variant readings where appropriate.

Like many early modern authors, Ribadeneyra is irregular about citing his sources. When outside texts are acknowledged, it is generally through marginal annotations or, somewhat less often, in the body of the text itself. The annotations themselves are equally inconsistent: some include the author, some do not; some include the title of the work, some do not; some include references to specific books, chapters, verses, or page numbers, some do not. I have translated the marginal annotations in the footnotes, signposted by "In the margin." Wherever Ribadeneyra names his source, I have provided a citation: book, chapter, section, or verse numbers in standard works, page numbers of the relevant early modern editions in more recondite sources. Where he does not specify a source, I have attempted to supply the gaps; some of this is necessarily speculative, but it has been my intention at least to offer suggestions of what might have influenced Ribadeneyra (and here I must acknowledge a debt to the rich annotations in David Lewis's translation of Nicholas Sander's *De origine ac progressu*). Throughout the volume, the footnoted text is in English: all translations are my own, save where otherwise noted. In both premodern primary sources and in critical editions thereof, diverse norms of spelling, orthography, and typography obtain; I have endeavored to preserve each source and each editor's usage.

All biblical references follow the Vulgate, both in terms of numbering and of nomenclature. This is significant primarily in the numbering of the psalms and in some of the historical books—what many readers will know as 1 and 2 Samuel are cited here as 1 and 2 Kings, while the books commonly known as

---

1 For the full publication history of the *Historia*, see bibliography.

1 and 2 Kings are given as 3 and 4 Kings. I have done this not out of any desire to confuse, but to match as closely as possible Ribadeneyra's own system of citation. The exception is "Paralipomenon," which I have eschewed in favor of "Chronicles," both because "Paralipomenon" is now thoroughly obscure as a term and because Ribadeneyra never explicitly cites either of the two books in the *Historia*.

Much of the first two books of the *Historia* are relatively straightforward translations of Nicholas Sander's *De origine ac progressu*. To footnote each passage of this translation with the corresponding pages of *De origine ac progressu* would be both overwhelming and pointless. Accordingly, I have placed a footnote at the beginning of each chapter indicating the relevant pages of the 1586 edition of *De origine ac progressu*. There are also substantial passages, even entire chapters, that are similarly faithful renderings of other texts; I have followed the same practice in these instances.

I have translated sense-for-sense, while trying to preserve, wherever possible, the structure and flow of Ribadeneyra's prose. Like many early modern authors and orators, Ribadeneyra extends his sentences far beyond the standards of modern prose, often in impressive displays of Ciceronian periods. I have tried to reproduce something of this rhythm, recognizing the limits of doing so in a language without a full set of gendered pronouns and articles and with very different grammatical norms.

Following the translation are five documentary appendices. The first three are translations of materials relevant to the *Historia*: Ribadeneyra's writings on the Spanish Armada and a letter by Luis de Granada praising the work. The latter two are transcriptions of materials housed at the Archivum Britannicum Societatis Iesu in London: a partial copy of a now-lost letter from John Cecil to Joseph Creswell (or Cresswell, 1556–1623); and a printed catalog of martyred seminarians, of which ABSI holds the only extant copy.

Introduction

If the Bible allots threescore years and ten as the length of a human lifetime, Pedro de Ribadeneyra[1] (1526–1611) spent more than a lifetime as a member of the Society of Jesus: admitted on September 18, 1540, just before the order received papal approval, he died on September 22, 1611, a few weeks shy of his eighty-fifth birthday. Ribadeneyra's may not be the longest tenure in the Society's history, but it must certainly rank somewhere near the top.

True to the spirit of the Society, those seventy-one years were immensely productive. Ribadeneyra had served as provincial of Tuscany (1560) and Sicily (1562), superintendent of the Collegio Romano (1565), visitor of Lombardy (1569), and assistant of Spain and Portugal (1571). He had moved in the highest political circles, advising grandees, ambassadors, inquisitors, superiors general, and emperors. He had worked all over Western Europe, from Palermo to London, from Toledo to Antwerp. Above all, however, he had generated a truly prodigious literary output: biographies (including the first official biography of Ignatius of Loyola [c.1491–1556]), letters, devotional treatises, policy memoranda, a spiritual memoir, histories, works of political philosophy, bibliographies, translations of Augustine of Hippo (354–430) and Albertus Magnus (c.1200–80), and a bestselling hagiography collection. Ribadeneyra's mastery of language and extensive *oeuvre* won him "the title of a standard of the Castilian tongue,"[2] "an established position in Spanish letters from which no one can dislodge him."[3]

Yet, impressive though Ribadeneyra's accomplishments are, they cannot but pale alongside the extraordinary period of European history through which he lived. His were interesting times. Born a few months before the Sack of Rome, he lived to see the fall of the Incan Empire, the Council of Trent, the battle of Lepanto, the French Wars of Religion, and the publication of Galileo Galilei's (1564–1642) *Sidereus nuncius* (1610). In Iberia alone, his contemporaries included Miguel de Cervantes (c.1547–1616), Lope de Vega (1562–1635), Luis de Góngora (1561–1627), and Luís Vaz de Camões (c.1524–80). Between 1526 and

---

1   Numerous spellings have been given for Ribadeneyra's surname: Ribadeneira, Rivadeneyra, Rivadeneira. He himself employed "Ribadeneyra," which is used here, save when other scholars are quoted. Rey, xxxviii.

2   "el titulo de clásico de la lengua castellana." Cándido de Dalmases, "Origenes de la hagiografía ignaciana: Pedro de Ribadeneyra biógrafo de S. Ignacio" (PhD diss., Universidad de Madrid, 1944), 38.

3   "en las letras españolas un puesto fijo que nadie podrá arrebatarle." Rey, xxxv.

FIGURE 0.1 *Pedro de Ribadeneyra, with an image of Ignatius of Loyola*
Pedro de Ribadeneyra. *Della religione del prencipe christiano* (Bologna: Per Pietro
Paulo Tozzi, 1622). BX1793 .R47 1622 JESUITICA, John J. Burns Library, Boston
College.

1611, three kings ruled Spain, and fifteen popes sat upon the throne of Saint Peter. And, for the order so dear to Ribadeneyra's heart, those eighty-five years saw the Society of Jesus grow from an informal circle of university graduates to a religious order of truly global reach.

Of the many challenges facing sixteenth-century Catholicism, few so preoccupied Ribadeneyra as that of England. England's confessional careening—Henry VIII's (r.1509–47) rejection of papal authority, the full-throated evangelical program of Edward VI (r.1547–53), Mary's (r.1553–58) restoration of Roman obedience, the reversion to Protestantism under Elizabeth I (r.1558–1603)—troubled many early modern Catholics. But Ribadeneyra, who had visited England in 1558–59, and remained close to prominent English Catholics for the rest of his life, felt spiritually, intellectually, and emotionally invested in the kingdom's religious destiny. Invested enough, certainly, to produce a lengthy history of what he called "the schism of the kingdom of England" (*el scisma del reyno de Inglaterra*), and to expand, revise, and rework that history over two decades.

That text, the *Historia eclesiástica del scisma del reyno de Inglaterra*, first published in 1588, found readers across the Habsburg dominions—including within the royal family—and inspired no less a dramatist than Pedro Calderón de la Barca (1600–81). Moreover, "for the space of two centuries, it was through this book that Spain learned of the bloody events" of the English Reformation.[4] The *Historia*'s sources and influences stretch from Spain's American empire to the Jesuit missions in Japan, embracing myriad languages, periods, and genres, and offering a snapshot of the rich textual networks of early modern Catholicism.[5] The *Historia*, both taken on its own terms and placed within this broader context, is fascinating evidence of how the English Reformation was perceived, interpreted, and depicted by the rest of Europe.

For all that, however, the *Historia* has won little attention in Anglophone scholarship, and that little has generally been unfavorable. The first English-language article dedicated to the *Historia* appeared in 2015, and its author, Freddy Cristóbal Domínguez, rightly notes the "severe critical neglect"

---

4 "por espacio de dos siglos fue precisamente el libro por donde se conocieron en España las sangrientas escenas de aquella revolucion." Pedro de Ribadeneyra, *Obras escogidas del padre Pedro de Rivadeneira, de la Compañía de Jesús, con una noticia de su vida y juicio crítico de sus escritos*, ed. Vicente de la Fuente, Biblioteca de Autores Españoles (Madrid: M. Rivadeneyra, 1868), 177.

5 Cf. Paul Nelles, "*Cosas y cartas*: Scribal Production and Material Pathways in Jesuit Global Communication (1547–1573)," *JJS* 2, no. 3 (2015): 421–50.

that continues to plague the book.[6] In addition to making a text available to English-speakers, and more thoroughly excavating the *Historia*'s textual genealogy, this translation hopes to prompt a reconsideration of Ribadeneyra's work as a historian—work hardly unimpeachable, but not without importance for the cultural and intellectual history of the Protestant Reformation and the Catholic Counter-Reformation.

This introduction will explore the *Historia*'s composition, publication, and reception, attempting to understand the text's significance for Ribadeneyra, for readers, and for contemporary scholars. The first section sets the stage for what follows with a biographical sketch of our author, before introducing the *Historia* itself and its principal source, Nicholas Sander's (*c.*1530–81) *De origine ac progressu schismatis anglicani* (1585, rev. 1586). Far from a straightforward translation, the *Historia* involves dramatic departures from *De origine ac progressu*, reflecting real differences in their respective authors' historical contexts and intellectual concerns.

We then turn to the publication history, starting with the *editio princeps* of 1588. Ribadeneyra encountered significant difficulties in securing permission to publish: early modern histories were always politically fraught; a vituperative, confessionalized history of England on the eve of the Spanish Armada was downright explosive. This naturally leads into the *Historia*'s connection to the Armada; read in conjunction with Ribadeneyra's other literary contributions to the planned invasion, the *Historia*, with its explicit calls to arms, has clear value as propaganda for marshaling anti-English sentiment in Spain. The failure of the Armada swiftly deflated this militaristic spirit, but the catastrophe was in no small part the reason behind the 1593 publication of the second volume of the *Historia*. The *Segunda parte de la historia eclesiástica del scisma de Inglaterra* can be read as using historical narrative to process the trauma of the Spanish defeat, as well as calling for a renewed commitment to supporting English Catholics. The textual history concludes with an overview of the various editions published in Ribadeneyra's lifetime, together with a consideration of his major sources.

The discussion then shifts to thematic questions, asking first how Ribadeneyra used the *Historia* to intervene in debates within the Society of Jesus and to promote the English mission as an integral part of the Jesuits' providential destiny. A close reading of the *Historia*'s gender politics follows, interrogating Ribadeneyra's conflicted and uncomfortable treatment of Catholic and

---

6   Freddy Cristóbal Domínguez, "History in Action: The Case of Pedro de Ribadaneyra's *Historia ecclesiastica del scisma de Inglaterra*," *Bulletin of Spanish Studies* (September 2015): 1–26, here 2.

Protestant women in power. Finally, Ribadeneyra's historiography is subjected to similar scrutiny, as refracted through the problem of whether he can be considered a "modern" historian.

The last part of the introduction concerns the *Historia*'s afterlife, beginning with its early modern reception. In addition to its influence on Spanish perceptions of England, the book inspired Pedro Calderón de la Barca's masterful history play *La cisma de Inglaterra* (1627). Given Calderón's radical reworking of Ribadeneyra, a detour is warranted to analyze the historiographical work performed by the play's new version of English history. Placing *La cisma* against the background of early seventeenth-century Anglo-Spanish relations, specifically the Spanish Match (the proposed marriage of a Habsburg princess to the prince of Wales), I suggest that Calderón uses this material to think through the potential for a royal marriage to reclaim England for Catholicism. The introduction closes with scholars' generally negative assessments of the *Historia*, and my own attempt to establish its value as a subject of historical study, both for its innovative use of historiography for emotional and intellectual ends, and as a witness to the interconnections of England, Europe, and the world in the late sixteenth century.

The Life and Times of Pedro de Ribadeneyra

Pedro de Ribadeneyra was the first to tell the story of his life, writing his *Confesiones*, a spiritual memoir modeled on Augustine's *Confessions* (397–401), in 1611. The following year, an adoring biography was produced by his secretary of thirty-three years, Cristóbal López (1552–1617). Neither text was published until the twentieth century.[7]

Since Ribadeneyra's death, numerous scholars have penned accounts of his life, of varying lengths and in different languages. In the introduction to his edition of Ribadeneyra's historical writings, Eusebio Rey, S.J. (b.1901) offers an invaluable review of these efforts to 1945;[8] consequently, here we need only note those treatments that have appeared since 1945. Rey provided his own substantial account of the Jesuit's life.[9] In an article in *Sefarad* in 1976, José

---

7   For the *Confesiones*, see MHSIR, 1:1–93. There is also a more recent scholarly edition: Pedro de Ribadeneyra, *Confesiones: Autobiografía documentada*, ed. Miguel Lop Sebastià, Manresa 41 (Santander: Sal Terrae, 2009).

     For López's *Vida*, see MHSIR, 2:429–88.

8   Rey, xxxvi–xli.

9   Ibid., xlvi–lxxiii.

Gómez Menor amassed considerable data on Ribadeneyra's family, in addition to establishing his *converso* ancestry.[10] Jodi Bilinkoff's 1999 article in *Renaissance Quarterly* interpreted the Jesuit's various works of life-writing against the background of his own life.[11] Manuel Ruiz Jurado, S.J. wrote a succinct, informative entry on Ribadeneyra for the *Diccionario histórico de la Compañía de Jesús* (2001).[12] Finally, Robert Aleksander Maryks discusses Ribadeneyra's life and work in his monograph on Jesuits of Jewish origin.[13]

Our story begins in Toledo, where on November 1, 1526[14] Pedro de Ribadeneyra was born, the fourth of five children of Alvaro Husillo Ortiz de Cisneros (d. *c.*1536) and Catalina de Villalobos y Ribadeneyra (d.1574).[15] His adolescence "coincided almost exactly with Toledo's most brilliant period of the modern era," a time of political and cultural flowering.[16] Both of the boy's parents came from well-connected Toledo families, and Alvaro was one of the city's *jurados* (municipal officers with fiscal and executive responsibilities, regarded as representatives of the people).[17] Gómez Menor has convincingly demonstrated that Ribadeneyra's father had *converso* ancestry, a fact the Jesuit understandably never acknowledged (Maryks evocatively calls him a "closet-converso").[18] This family secret notwithstanding, their local prominence, and a certain amount of happenstance, would soon lead to the young Pedro's departure from Toledo, and from Spain altogether.

---

10   José Gómez Menor, "La progenie hebrea del Padre Pedro de Ribadeneira s.i. (Hijo del jurado de Toledo Alvaro Husillo Ortiz de Cisneros," *Sefarad* 36, no. 2 (1976): 307–32.

11   Jodi Bilinkoff, "The Many 'Lives' of Pedro de Ribadeneyra," *Renaissance Quarterly* 52, no. 1 (Spring 1999): 180–96, here 192.

12   Manuel Ruiz Jurado, "Ribadeneira, Pedro de," in *Diccionario histórico de la Compañía de Jesús: Biográfico-temático*, ed. Charles E. O'Neill and Joaquín Maria Domínguez, 4 vols. (Rome: Institutum Historicum Societatis Iesu, 2001), 4:3345–46.

13   Robert Aleksander Maryks, *The Jesuit Order as a Synagogue of Jews: Jesuits of Jewish Ancestry and Purity-of-Blood Laws in the Early Society of Jesus*, Studies in Medieval and Reformation Traditions 146 (Leiden: Brill, 2010), *passim*.

14   The year of Ribadeneyra's birth is sometimes given as 1527, attested by at least one early modern source. The preponderance of the evidence, however, points to 1526, the date more commonly used. See *MHSIR*, 1:vi, note 3.

15   The following paragraphs are based primarily on Ribadeneyra's *Confesiones*, López's *Vida*, and the biographical accounts by Dalmases and Rey. *MHSIR*, 1:1–93; 2:429–88. Dalmases, "Orígenes de la hagiografía ignaciana," 1–18. Rey, xlvi–lxxiii.

16   "coinciden casi matemáticamente con la época más brillante de Toledo en la edad moderna." Rey, xlvii.

17   Gómez Menor, "Progenie hebrea," 316.

18   Ibid. Maryks, *Jesuit Order*, xxvii.

When Pedro was ten years old, his father died. It was at this point that Catalina revealed how, years before, having had three daughters, she made a vow to the Virgin Mary that if she gave birth to a son, he would become a cleric. Though she insisted that her son was not bound by her vow, she did say that such a decision would be a comfort to her. Pedro answered simply, "I will grow and I will see."[19] Catalina arranged for her son to receive the beginnings of a thorough humanist education, first from Alonso de Cedillo (1484–1564), and then from Alejo Venegas (c.1497–1562), both celebrated professors at the University of Toledo.

On May 1, 1539, Isabella of Portugal (1503–39), Holy Roman empress, queen of the Germans, queen consort of Italy, Spain, Naples, and Sicily, and duchess of Burgundy and many other places, died. The wife of Charles V (r.1516–56)— the ruler of all those lands—Isabella was carried off by the complications of her sixth pregnancy, which had ended in a stillbirth on April 21.[20] The tragedy brought nineteen-year-old cardinal Alessandro Farnese (1520–89) to Toledo, bearing the condolences of his grandfather, Pope Paul III (r.1534–49). One night, Farnese happened to be served at table by the young Pedro de Ribadeneyra; taken with the boy's graceful comportment, the cardinal offered to take him into his service. Catalina de Villalobos was prevailed upon to permit her son to return with the powerful churchman to Rome, as he did in due course.

Ribadeneyra arrived in Rome in July 1539, taking his place as a page in the Farnese household. As an old man, he piously recalled of this period,

> I entered a bottomless ocean of opportunities to offend you [God], and the abyss of evils that the court carries with it, where what one sees and what one hears poison, and the habits and words of the wicked corrupt, and the intercourse of one's peers and companions perverts and deforms the heart—and, what is worse, where those who ought to be masters are seated in the throne [*cátedra*] of pestilence and teach a pestilent doctrine, and not only do not punish the evil they see in their vassals and followers, but instead favor and encourage them by their authority.[21]

---

19   "y creçería y vería." *MHSIR*, 1:6.

20   Geoffrey Parker, *Imprudent King: A New Life of Philip II* (New Haven: Yale University Press, 2014), 12.

21   "entré en vn piélago profundíssimo de ocasiones de offenderos, y vn abismo de maldades que la corte trae consigo y adonde lo que se vee y lo que se oye inficiona, y los exercicios y palabras de los malos corronpen, y la conuersación de los otros yguales y compañeros peruierte y trueca el coraçón; y lo que es peor, donde los que debrían ser maestros,

His first months were not without incident, in the form of quarrels with the other serving-boys. One such conflict prompted Ribadeneyra to flee the cardinal's residence, finding refuge in the house shared by Ignatius of Loyola and the other members of the fledgling Society of Jesus.

Here the youth found a home, and in Ignatius a father-figure who was to shape the rest of his life. Clever, headstrong, temperamental, Ribadeneyra became the first pupil to be immersed in Jesuit pedagogy; in Rey's phrase, he was "a unique product of the school of Saint Ignatius."[22] Ignatius personally oversaw his formation and felt an intense affection for the young man—so much so that he eventually entrusted all decisions regarding Pedro to Diego Laínez (1512–65) and Juan Alfonso de Polanco (1517–76), for he feared that he could not be impartial. For his part, Ribadeneyra would always feel an intense loyalty to this second father. In his *Confesiones*, Ribadeneyra wrote,

> But you, Lord, in your paternal providence gave me the blessed Father Ignatius as a father and a guide, so that he might instruct me as a teacher, and discipline, admonish, and rebuke me as a father; and you endowed him with a love for me so extraordinary and so zealous that he could endure all the irritations and trials that must of necessity come about in raising me. And from the hour I met him and spoke with him, you gave me love for him in return, and a delight in seeing him, an inkling of his sanctity, and so great a trust committing all my affairs to him that although the temptations and torments that arose in the space of the twenty months or so I was in our house in Rome before going to study in Paris were numerous and dire, with such a pilot and master the little boat preserved itself and came into port.[23]

---

sentados en la cátedra de pestilencia enseñan doctrina pestilente, y no solamente no castigan el mal que veen en sus súbditos y discípulos, antes les fauorecen, y se alientan con su autoridad." *MHSIR*, 1:7.

22   "un producto especialísimo de la escuela de San Ignacio." Rey, lvi.

23   "Mas vos, Señor, con vuestra paternal prouidencia me distes por Padre y guía al beato Padre Ignacio para que me enseñase como maestro, y me reprimiesse, amonestasse y reprehendiesse como padre; y le infundistes vn amor tan extraordinario y tan cuydadoso para conmigo, que pudiesse suffrir las molestias y pessadumbres que necessariamente hauía de passar en criarme; y a mí, desde la hora que le conoçí y hablé, me distes vn amor recíproco con él, y vna alegría quando le veía, y vn concepto de su sanctidad, y vna confiança tan grande para acudir a él en todas mis cossas, que aunque fueron muchas y graues las tentaciones y tormentos que passé por espacio de casi veinte messes que estuue en Roma en nuestra cassa antes de yr a estudiar a París, con tal piloto y maestro esta nauecilla se defendió y llegó a puerto." *MHSIR*, 1:13–15.

He also received no small prestige from his self-declared status as "Ignatius's Benjamin."[24] Later scholars have likewise defined Ribadeneyra by this relationship: the subtitle of Jean-Marie Prat's biography, for example, is "disciple de saint Ignace," while Benito Sánchez Alonso called him Ignatius's "discípulo predilecto" (beloved disciple).[25] Under such tutelage, it is hardly surprising that Ribadeneyra joined the Society, doing so on September 18, 1540, a little more than a week before the order received papal approbation from Paul III. He was not yet fourteen.

Two years later, Ignatius sent Pedro to the University of Paris to continue his studies. Ribadeneyra arrived in the French capital on June 20, 1542, but was forced to leave only a few days later. War had broken out between Francis I (r.1515–47) and Charles V, necessitating the departure of all imperial subjects from French territory. Accordingly, the Society relocated its students, including Ribadeneyra, to Leuven. After a mere seven months in the Low Countries, however, Ribadeneyra was headed back to Rome. In Leuven, he had been tormented by a "deep despair [*tristeza profunda*]," which he and his fellow Jesuits hoped might be dispelled by Ignatius's presence.[26] Ribadeneyra and several companions set out at the beginning of February 1543; his recollections of the journey are harrowing—all the more so when it is remembered that he was a teenager, far from home and in a precarious mental and emotional state:

> The road was long, the season harsh, the cold fierce; we saw nothing but the sky, snow, and ice. We had to pass through the heretics' territories, where during Lent they would have us eat meat, which we could not eat. We went on foot with few provisions, without rest, whatever sort of travail, discomfort, or difficulty we might encounter [...]. You [God] ordained that the road should be steep, mountainous, and so devoid of villages or people that we met no one. We were forced to travel at a good pace almost the entire day without eating, and as I had not had dinner the night before, and I was of so few years and fewer virtues, I began to fall, and—wracked with hunger—to moan pitifully, and to cry in a miserable,

---

24   Rady Roldán-Figueroa, "Pedro de Ribadeneyra's *Vida del P. Ignacio de Loyola* (1583) and Literary Culture in Early Modern Spain," in *Exploring Jesuit Distinctiveness: Interdisciplinary Perspectives on Ways of Proceeding within the Society of Jesus*, ed. Robert Aleksander Maryks, Jesuit Studies 6 (Leiden: Brill, 2016), 156–74, here 160.

25   Benito Sánchez Alonso, *Historia de la historiografía española: De Ocampo a Solís (1543–1684)*, vol. 2 of 3 vols., Publicaciones de la Revista de filología española (Madrid: J. Sánchez de Ocaña, 1944), 88.

26   *MHSIR*, 1:25.

weak voice, "I'm dying of hunger!" And distraught and unable to walk any farther, I sat down and threw myself upon the ground, repeating, "I'm dying of hunger!" After the fathers my companions had encouraged me, and I was forced by necessity itself, having no other remedy, I got up, and walked, and ran, until I was again exhausted, and once more threw myself on the ground and returned to my miserable song, repeating, "I'm dying of hunger!"[27]

Ribadeneyra finally reached Rome on April 20, now once more under the paternal eye of Ignatius. He describes the reunion in moving terms: "The joy I felt at the sight of our blessed father was unbelievable; I felt I had come into port from a long and perilous storm, and that I had nothing more to fear."[28]

Though the depression he had struggled with at Leuven abated, Ribadeneyra was soon to face a yet greater temptation, in the form of a fierce resentment of Ignatius and a rejection of his vocation. He writes in the *Confesiones*,

when those first days of peace and happiness had passed, I began to feel sad and tormented, and lose that love and affection for our saintly father, and not to look upon him with the eyes of a son, as was my wont, nor to feel pleasure in being with him. And little by little this grew until I came to hate him, and he seemed to me a painted devil.[29]

---

27 "El camino era largo, el tiempo áspero, el frío recio, no víamos sino cielo y nieues y yelos. Hauíamos de passar por tierra de hereges, que en quaresma pretendían que comiéssemos carne, y nosotros no la hauíamos de comer. Yuamos a pié con poco viático, sin reparar en algún género de trabajo o de incommodidad e impossibilidad [...] vos ordenastes que el camino fuesse áspero, montuoso, y tan dessierto de pueblos y de gente, que no topáuamos ninguna, y nos fué necessario andar a buen passo casi todo el día sin comer, y como yo no hauía çenado la noche antes, y era de tan poca hedad y de menos virtud, comencé a desfallecer, y aquexado de la hambre a dar lastimossas vozes, y con vn triste y descaecido alarido a clamar '¡que me muero de hambre!'; y desmayado, y no pudiendo mas andar, me sentaua y arrojaua en el campo, y repetía '¡que me muero de hambre!' Después animado de mis Padres compañeros y forzado de la misma necessidad que allí no tenía otro remedio, me lebantaua y andaua y corría, hasta que tornándome a cansar, de nueuo me echaua en el suelo, y voluía a mi lastimera canción y repetia '¡que me muero de hambre!'" *MHSIR*, 1:26–28.

28 "fué increíble el gozo que recebí con la vista de nuestro beato Padre, pareciéndome que de vna larga y peligrossa tempestad hauía ya llegado al puerto, y que no tenía más que temer." Ibid., 1:33.

29 "Passados, pues, los primeros días de contento y alegría, comencé a andar triste y affligido, y a perder aquel amor y cariño a nuestro santo Padre, y a no mirarle con aquellos ojos de

In the end, Ignatius's pastoral care proved equal to the challenge, and Ribadeneyra overcame his temptation in the course of several days of spiritual exercises and a general confession. His subsequent enthusiasm for and firmness in his vocation, so he tells us, lasted until the day he died. Ribadeneyra took his first formal vows as a member of the Society of Jesus on September 30, 1545, just before his nineteenth birthday.

His young charge now on firmer spiritual ground, Ignatius once more turned to the question of his education. One week after being ordained, Ribadeneyra was sent to the Jesuit college at Padua, where he was to remain for four years. There is some debate over the content and progression of his course of study, but we know that Latin, Greek, rhetoric, and logic formed the core—Ignatius put special emphasis on his grounding in the humanities—and that he later moved on to philosophy and theology.[30] A gifted student, Ribadeneyra is reported to have excelled in prose and verse composition, an early harbinger of his future literary prowess.

In 1549, Ignatius transferred Ribadeneyra to Palermo to teach rhetoric at the Society's new Sicilian college. The young professor, a mere twenty-three years of age, won praise for his oratorical skills, especially for the address he delivered at the college's inauguration. When in 1552 the Society opened the Germanicum, a college at Rome for German Catholics, Ribadeneyra was the natural choice as professor of rhetoric. In Rome, in addition to his teaching duties and a regular schedule of preaching, he completed his philosophical and theological studies, and was ordained on December 8, 1553. "At the age of twenty-nine, by now ordained a priest, Ribadeneyra appears to us a characteristically Renaissance figure within the humanist mode of the first half of the sixteenth century."[31]

At this point, the Society of Jesus had not as yet received permission to expand into the Habsburg territories in the Low Countries. Ignatius chose the Germanicum's young professor of rhetoric as his emissary to Brussels, then the residence of the future Philip II (r.1556–98), to seek his assent for a Jesuit presence and the foundation of several colleges. Ribadeneyra was to make a distinct impression in imperial circles in the Low Countries, once again attracting attention for his eloquent preaching. Philip himself was reported to

---

hijo que antes solía, ni recibir gusto de estar con él. Y poco á poco fué esto creçiendo de tal manera, que vine a aborrecerle, y a parecerme vn demonio pintado." Ibid.

30   See Rey, lix–lxi. Cf. Dalmases, "Origenes de la hagiografía ignaciana," 4–6.

31   "A los veintinueve años de edad, ordenado ya sacerdote, Ribadeneyra se nos presenta como un producto típicamente renacentista dentro de la modalidad humanista de la primera mitad del sigo xvi." Rey, lxiii.

have remarked, after hearing Ribadeneyra speak, "One can easily see that this father is an orator!"[32] He also impressed the University of Leuven, including its distinguished rector and chancellor, the Dutch theologian Ruard Tapper (1480–1559). In a letter to Ignatius, the courtier Pedro de Zárate (d.1563) captures the atmosphere: "I tell Your Reverence [...] that all Leuven is awestruck, and that the Holy Spirit spoke through his mouth, and that his behavior was not that of a mere man. [...] He is one to expound the word of God with zeal and learning."[33]

Not least among Ribadeneyra's admirers in the Low Countries was Gómez Suárez de Figueroa y Córdoba, fifth count—and later first duke—of Feria (c.1520–71). An influential courtier close to Philip, the count's connections proved invaluable in securing the desired permissions, which the king granted on August 3, 1556. In the *Confesiones*, Ribadeneyra recalls how Feria "embraced, supported, and sustained me as though I had been his own son, acting as my advocate, lawyer, and attorney, with as much solicitude and diligence as any member of the Society could have done."[34] The friendship formed in Brussels was only the beginning of a relationship that lasted decades, as Ribadeneyra became a protégé and trusted confidant first of Gómez and his wife, and then of their son.[35] We shall return to the count shortly, for he was also to be instrumental in the Jesuit's enduring connection with England.

Any satisfaction at the success in Brussels was almost immediately stifled by the news that Ignatius had died in Rome a few days before (July 31). Laínez, who as vicar general would govern the order until the election of a new superior general, summoned Ribadeneyra and several of his confrères back to Rome. The fathers left Brussels in November and arrived in Rome on February 3, 1557. They found the city in turmoil and the general congregation delayed, open hostilities having erupted between the Habsburgs and the ferociously anti-Spanish pope Paul IV (r.1555–59). When peace was restored several months later, Cardinal Carlo Carafa (1517–61), the pope's nephew, was sent to Brussels to confirm the settlement, and Ribadeneyra was one of the Jesuits deputed to accompany him. Leaving Rome in the company of Alfonso Salmerón (1515–85),

---

32 "¡Cómo se ve que este Padre es orador!" Rey, lxv.

33 "Digo a V.R. [...] que toda Lovaina está espantada y que el Espíritu Santo habló por su boca y que su proceder no era de hombre [...] él es persona para proponer la palabra de Dios con espíritu y doctrina." Quoted in Rey, lxvi.

34 "me abraçó, amparó y sustentó como si fuera mi proprio padre, haziendo por mí en los negocios offiçio de abogado, de procurador y soliçitador, con tanta solicitud y cuydado como lo pudiera hazer qualquiera de la Compañía." *MHSIR*, 1:63.

35 Henry Clifford, *The Life of Jane Dormer Duchess of Feria*, ed. Joseph Stevenson (London: Burns and Oates, 1887), 184–85.

one of the founding members of the Society, Ribadeneyra was back in Brussels by December 1557; when negotiations concluded the following March, Salmerón returned to Rome, while on Laínez's orders Ribadeneyra stayed where he was, "on account of certain secret and serious issues that had arisen."[36] He spent eight months in residence at Philip's court in Brussels, occasionally visiting Leuven to preach at the university.

Ribadeneyra made his first and only journey to England in November 1558. His *Confesiones* record the five months he spent there in fewer than three hundred words:

> In the month of November, I traveled to England at the insistence of the duke of Feria, who, because Queen Mary was sick and King Don Philip was wholly occupied with the war in France, was going in his name to wait upon her during her illness, and wished to find an occasion to bring a college of the Society to that kingdom, where none of ours had yet come. But it pleased God that Queen Mary should die on the seventeenth of that same month of November in the year 1558, and that her sister Elizabeth should succeed her, and that the matters of our sacred religion should be altered and perverted, in chastisement of that realm, which to this day feels and laments its affliction, and thus there was no opportunity to achieve anything concerning the Society. I was in London, and there I preached to the duke of Feria and his household several times, and had a serious sickness of the chest, which exhausted me, and from which you [God], my wholeness, freed me and restored me to health. And although I then received an order from Father Master Laínez (who was by then the general) to travel to Spain for certain matters in your service, yet since the time had not yet come when you had determined that I should come there, the journey did not come about, and instead you commanded me to return to Rome. And so I left London for Flanders on March 7, the feast of St. Thomas Aquinas, in year 1559, and on the fourteenth of the month I reached Brussels.[37]

---

36 "por algunos negoçios secretos y graues que se ofrecieron." *MHSIR*, 1:69.

37 "por el mes de Nouiembre passé a Inglaterra a instancia del duque de Feria, que por estar mala la reyna María, y el rey don Phelippe muy occupado en la guerra de Francia, yua por assistirla en su nombre en aquella enfermedad, y desseaua tener occassión para introducir en aquel reyno donde no hauía entrado alguno de los nuestros, colegio de la Compañía. Pero Dios fué seruido que la reyna María muriesse a los 17 del mismo mes de Nouiembre deste año de 1558, y que le succediesse Ysabel su hermana, y se alterassen y trocassen las cossas de nuestra sancta religión, para castigo de aquel reyno que hasta agora siente y llora su afflicción; y assí no huuo lugar de tratar cosa de la Compañía. Estuue

What these stoic lines do not convey is the effect of those five months on Ribadeneyra himself. Mere days after he arrived in London, the two pillars of English Catholicism, Queen Mary and Cardinal Reginald Pole (1500–58), passed away. For the next five months, he and the rest of Feria's household were effectively marooned in a city of hostile "heretics." He neither spoke the language nor understood the customs. He witnessed a Protestant (for Ribadeneyra, read "heretic") queen ascend the throne and begin to destroy all the progress made toward the restoration of Catholicism. Thomas M. McCoog, S.J., the leading historian of the Society in England, points out that Elizabeth's accession would also have represented "the final destruction of any hope for [official] Jesuit involvement" in English affairs.[38] To understand the depth of anguish entailed by that "final destruction" requires a certain personal context. At the end of his life, Ignatius had become determined to bring the Society into England, to assist in the Marian restoration of Catholicism. He had proposed to send Ribadeneyra to England as early as 1555, but the journey never materialized, as the requisite permission was not forthcoming from Pole. Polanco conveys the personal dimension of the mission: "Ignatius was anxious about bringing the Society into England *and had laid upon Fr Ribadeneira the task of seeking for an opportunity of doing so.*"[39] Ignatius died several months later, and two years later, Ribadeneyra did become the first Jesuit to reach England, with the task of securing "an occasion to bring a college of the Society to that kingdom."[40] He must have felt himself to be fulfilling Ignatius's final wishes. To have those

---

en Londres, y allí predique algunas vezes al duque de Feria y a su familia, y tuue vna enfermedad de pecho, grande, que me fatigó mucho, de lo qual vos, salud mía, me librastes, y me restituístes la sanidad. Y aunque allí tuue orden del Padre maestro Laynez (que ya era general) de passar a España para çiertos negoçios de vuestro seruicio, pero como aun no hauía llegado el tiempo en que vos hauíades determinado que yo viniesse, no tuuo effecto entonzes aquella venida, antes me mandastes voluier a Roma; y assí me partí de Londres para Flandes a los siete de Março, día de Sto. Thomás de Aquino, del año de 1559, y a los 14 del mismo llegué a Bruselas." Ibid., 1:70–71.

38   Thomas M. McCoog, *The Society of Jesus in Ireland, Scotland, and England 1541–1588: "Our Way of Proceeding?"* Studies in Medieval and Reformation Thought 60 (Leiden: Brill, 1996), 35, 37–38.

39   Quoted in Joseph Crehan, "Saint Ignatius and Cardinal Pole," *AHSI* 25 (1956): 72–98, here 90. Italics mine.

    Crehan suggests that Pole's reluctance stemmed from apprehension about Ribadeneyra, whom he conjectures to have "been in some way indiscreet while at the court of Brussels." Ibid., 91.

40   Ibid., 72.

hopes so abruptly dashed must have taken an immense emotional toll on the young Jesuit (struggling throughout with a chronic chest complaint).[41]

I do not believe that, as Thomas McNevin Veech wrote, in composing a history of England Ribadeneyra was contending with "a country which he felt by reason of his sojourn there had no secrets for him."[42] Any analysis of how the *Historia* was written shows this to be untrue: Ribadeneyra knew full well that there was much he did not understand about England. But Veech is not wrong about the importance of the Jesuit's months in England. The trauma of that stay in London surely had something to do with his decision to undertake the *Historia* in the first place. Given all he had witnessed, can there be any doubt that news from England—of Elizabeth's latest anti-Catholic policy, of a Jesuit martyred in London, of an émigré safely arrived on the Continent—would have meant more to him than to his peers?

The despondency and frustration with which he must have returned to Rome notwithstanding, the 1560s represented the apogee of Ribadeneyra's career within the Society of Jesus. At Laínez's direct command (and over his own strenuous objections), he took his vows as a professed member of the Society of Jesus on November 3, 1560, and was immediately named provincial of Tuscany. This was only the first in a string of appointments over the course of the decade: provincial of Sicily in 1562, superintendent of the Collegio Romano in 1565, visitor of Lombardy in 1569, and assistant of Spain and Portugal in 1571. His colleagues and superiors lauded his performance in each position: early on, Laínez wrote, "Father Ribadeneyra is presently the provincial of Tuscany, and has an excellent aptitude [*muy buenas partes*] for the post."[43] And then in 1574 Ribadeneyra suddenly retired to Spain, where he remained for nearly forty years, never again holding office within the Society.

Various explanations have been offered for Ribadeneyra's abrupt return to his native land and withdrawal from active life in the Society. He himself wrote in the *Confesiones*,

> In the end, I left Rome for Spain on June 18, 1574, in obedience to our father general and on the advice of the physicians, who on account of

---

41   It is perhaps significant that he wrote to his mother twice and his brother once in the space of three months. See *MHSIR*, 1:307–08, 314–18.

42   Thomas McNevin Veech, *Dr Nicholas Sanders and the English Reformation, 1530–1581*, Recueil de travaux publiés par les membres des Conférences d'Histoire et de Philologie 32 (Leuven: Bureaux du Recueil, Bibliothéque de l'Université, 1935), 237.

43   "El Padre Ribadeneyra es al presente Provincial de Toscana y tiene muy buenas partes para tal oficio." Quoted in Rey, lxvii.

my continual and serious ailments determined that I should return to my native and more healthful climes [*los ayres naturales y más sanos*] in Spain.[44]

Ribadeneyra always insisted that the newly elected superior general, Everard Mercurian (1514–80), had ordered him to leave Italy out of concern for his health. In 1577, he wrote flatly, "I came to Spain for the sake of my health."[45] When in 1594 Mercurian's successor, Claudio Acquaviva (1543–1615), requested he take charge of the professed houses at Toledo and Valladolid, Ribadeneyra replied that he had "neither the virtue, nor the health, nor the age, nor the strength, nor the inclination, nor the condition to do this."[46] Among modern scholars, Rey is willing to take Ribadeneyra at his word, noting his longstanding kidney complaints (among others), which had been exacerbated by the difficulties of early modern travel.[47] Others have been more skeptical, observing that Ribadeneyra's departure for Spain came hard on the heels of Mercurian's election as superior general. Amid complaints about excessive Spanish influence in the Society, the victory of Everard Mercurian, a native of Marcourt in modern-day Belgium, was secured by direct papal intervention to prevent a fourth Spaniard being chosen.[48] Mercurian immediately began to "cleanse the house." Though usually characterized as a "de-Hispanization [*desespañolización*]," Maryks has demonstrated that his target was primarily *converso* Jesuits—"Spanish" often being used as a euphemism for accusations of Jewish origin—who were removed from positions of authority in Italy and elsewhere.[49] The atmosphere in Rome becoming distinctly uncongenial for a Spanish *converso* Jesuit, Ribadeneyra might well have been willing, even eager, to decamp to Toledo. Certainly, there were rumors of his "strained relations" with Mercurian—although Cándido de Dalmases points out that the

---

44   "Finalmente a los 18 de Junio de 1574 salí de Roma para España por obediencia de nuestro Padre general, y con consejo de los médicos, que por mis continuos y grandes achaques juzgauan deuía voluer a los ayres naturales y mas sanos de España." *MHSIR*, 1:81.

45   "Yo vine a España for causa de mi salud." Ibid., 1:782.

46   "ni tengo virtud ni salud ni hedad ni fuerças ni inclinación ni condición para acertar en esto." Ibid., 2:178.

47   Rey comments, with some justice, "reading his letters, we come to the conclusion that Ribadeneyra is a man obsessed with the *idée fixe* of health [*Leyendo su Epistolario sacamos la conclusión de que Ribadeneyra es un hombre obsesionado por la idea fija de la salud*]." Rey, lxxiv.

48   Dalmases, "Origenes de la hagiografía ignaciana," 13–15.

49   Rey, lxix. Maryks, *Jesuit Order*, 121–25.

general lamented being deprived of so able a subordinate.[50] Maryks goes so far as to speak of Ribadeneyra being "sent back" to Spain.[51] Rady Roldán-Figueroa, emphasizing Ribadeneyra's unease in a country he had left almost forty years before, notes that in 1577 the Toledan asked Mercurian for permission to return to Rome.[52] To some extent, it remains a matter of interpretation: Does one read "in obedience to our father general" as Mercurian exercising paternal care by ensuring compliance with medical advice, or as the superior general forcing out a Spanish *converso*?

In another possibly significant coincidence, it was just at this moment that the *memorialistas* controversy exploded. In the wake of Mercurian's election, several Spanish Jesuits began composing *memoriales* (policy papers) to Philip II urging him to secure a certain measure of autonomy for the Spanish provinces of the Society—and thus shield them from Mercurian's anti-Spanish, anti-*converso* policies.[53] The extent of Ribadeneyra's involvement with the *memorialistas* is unclear. Bilinkoff comments only that he was accused of participating.[54] Dalmases emphatically denies any connection;[55] Rey concurs, averring smoothly, "It was Ribadeneyra's bad luck that his arrival should coincide with the contentious dispute of the *memorialistas*."[56] Maryks has challenged these categorical dismissals by pointing out Ribadeneyra's many links to the *memorialistas*, though he stops short of including him in their number.[57] Ribadeneyra himself steadfastly denied any involvement, to the extent of including a lengthy rebuttal in his *Confesiones* (long after the affair was over), declaring not only his innocence but also that "the provincial, and the visitor, and the general himself made amends for what they had suspected and believed of me, and in their letters attested to my innocence."[58]

Whether or not we believe him, Ribadeneyra's relationship with the hierarchy in Rome was not of the warmest during this period. He never left Spain again, settling first at the Society's retreat house outside Toledo and then, in 1583, moving to Madrid, where he resided on the top floor of the Jesuit college

---

50 Bilinkoff, "Many 'Lives,'" 191. Dalmases, "Orígenes de la hagiografía ignaciana," 15.

51 Maryks, *Jesuit Order*, 123.

52 Roldán-Figueroa, "Ribadeneyra's *Vida*," 164.

53 Maryks, *Jesuit Order*, 125–28.

54 Bilinkoff, "Many 'Lives,'" 191.

55 Dalmases, "Orígenes de la hagiografía ignaciana," 16.

56 "Mala fortuna fue para Ribadeneyra el que coincidiera su venida con el engorroso pleito de los 'Memorialistas.'" Rey, lxx.

57 Maryks, *Synagogue of Jews*, 125–28, 187–89.

58 "el prouincial y el visitador y el mismo general me dieron satisfación de lo que de my auían sospechado y creydo, y con sus cartas testificaron mi innocencia." *MHSIR*, 1:88.

until his death in 1611. To the end, though, he remained indefatigably active: it was in "retirement" that his prodigious career as an author began. Rey and Dalmases have both furnished detailed overviews of Ribadeneyra's *oeuvre*, which it would be superfluous to rework here.[59] All we need note here is that in 1587 he began to translate and expand a Latin history of the English Reformation, Nicholas Sander's *De origine ac progressu*. The end result, the *Historia*, was published in the summer of 1588, with a second volume produced in 1593 and frequent reprints over the next decade and a half. The narrative spans roughly a century, from the marriage between Henry VIII's older brother, Arthur (1486–1502), and Catherine of Aragon (1485–1536) at the beginning of the sixteenth century to the persecution of English Catholics at its end. In broad outline, Ribadeneyra tells the same story found in any contemporary survey of Tudor England, variously discussing diplomacy, warfare, economic and religious policy, and the personal and political lives of his many characters. His narration and commentary do, of course, have a pronounced Catholic slant—one would hope the contemporary historian would refrain from describing the reformer Hugh Latimer (c.1485–1555) as a "diabolical and blaspheming heretic" (332), for example—but much of his factual content is relatively accurate. (We shall discuss farther on what this means for our assessment of Ribadeneyra *qua* historian, a question that has invited diverse views.)

As a man and as a writer, Ribadeneyra devoted his life to the Society of Jesus, and took seriously his responsibilities to the order and to the memory of Ignatius. He died on September 22, 1611, the last of the first generation of Jesuits. His last years were ones of increasing isolation as his friends and family passed away. And yet, he had seen the order he loved spread to every corner of the earth, and take its place in the very forefront of the Catholic (Counter-)Reformation. The militant spirit in which the Society understood this role, the urgent drive to carry its mission to Catholic, heretic, and pagan alike, was in no small part Ribadeneyra's creation.[60] One can think of few more fitting legacies.

While he lived, Ribadeneyra was widely acclaimed for his eloquence and his oratorical prowess. It seems only just, then, to close this biographical sketch with a description of his speaking style by his fellow Toledan and fellow Jesuit, Bartolomé de Alcázar (1648–1721):

---

59   Rey, lxxviii–lxxxii. Dalmases, "Origenes de la hagiografía ignaciana," 18–28.
60   Spencer J. Weinreich, "The Distinctiveness of the Society of Jesus's Mission in Pedro de Ribadeneyra's *Historia ecclesiastica del scisma del reyno de Inglaterra* (1588)," in Maryks, *Exploring Jesuit Distinctiveness*, 175–88, here 179–82.

[Ribadeneyra] had a clear voice; he spoke Latin in pure, suitable [*propias*], and well-chosen tones; he made use of numerous, cogent, and forceful arguments; he was naturally eloquent; with his modest, agreeable exterior presence and his measured gestures and movements, his talent waxed yet greater [*subía su talento de punto*]. And because his ideas proceeded from a sharp intellect, and his emotions from a heart afire with the love of God, his sermons were as moving as they were incisive. Through them he persuaded and affected his hearers, with wonderful command, charisma, and benefit to [their] souls, that he won them for God and also gained them for the Society.⁶¹

Ribadeneyra, of course, died several decades before Alcázar was born. The latter does not give his source for this account of his confrère; he may well have made it up. Nevertheless, to quote another Jesuit in a very different context, "If that is not the truth, it certainly is very much like it."⁶²

From *De origine ac progressu* to the *Historia*

It has been observed that Ribadeneyra occludes himself as narrator in some of his writings, particularly the biography of Ignatius;⁶³ not so in the *Historia*. To the contrary, he is a visible and vocal author, editor, and translator. The prefatory letters to each volume are merely the first and most explicit places where Ribadeneyra speaks in his own voice. His authorial presence pervades the narrative: he offers commentary ("And thus I believe" [722]), cites his own experiences ("I was in London at this time" [412]), and reminds the reader of

---

61   "Tenia la voz clara, y flexible: hablaba la lengua Latina con voces puras, propias, y escogidas: vsaba de frequentes, vivas, y efficazes sentencias: era naturalmente facundo: con su exterior presencia modesta, y agradable, y con las proporcionadas acciones, y movimientos, subìa su talento de punto. Y, como los conceptos procedìan de vn entendimiento muy agudo, y los affectos de vn corazon muy inflammado en el amor de Dios: eran sus Sermones tan patheticos, como ingeniosos; en los cuales persuadìa, y movìa à sus oyentes, con tan maravilloso dominio, atractivo, y fructo de las almas, que las ganaba para Dios, y las grangeò también para la Compañia." Bartolomé de Alcázar, *Chrono-historia de la Compañia de Jesus, en la provincia de Toledo. Y elogios de sus varones illustres, fundadores, bienhechores, fautores, è hijos espirituales*, 2 vols. (Madrid: Por Juan Garcia Infançon, 1710), 1:287.

62   Giulio Cesare Cordara, *On the Suppression of the Society of Jesus: A Contemporary Account*, ed. and trans. John P. Murphy (Chicago: Jesuit Way, 1999), 14.

63   Bilinkoff, "Many 'Lives,'" 182.

the work of translation and composition ("This I wish to translate here" [307]).
The work of translation in particular is crucial to understanding the *Historia*,
for the core of the text, upon which all else is constructed, is a translation of
Nicholas Sander's *De origine ac progressu*. Thus, we begin with a journey north-
ward, to Surrey, the birthplace of Nicholas Sander.[64]

Nicholas Sander was born around 1530 in Charlwood, Surrey, one of twelve
children. He was educated at Winchester College and then at the notoriously
conservative New College, Oxford, where he received a degree in canon law
in 1551.[65] He remained in Oxford for most of the 1550s, as a fellow of New College and a lecturer in canon law. Sometime after Elizabeth's accession to the
throne in 1558, Sander fled England for Rome, having resigned his fellowship
rather than take the oath of supremacy. Once in Rome, he became a fixture of
the city's English community, and in 1561 he was ordained by his fellow exile,
Thomas Goldwell, bishop of Saint Asaph (1501–85). Sander was moving in exalted circles, becoming an intimate of Cardinal Giovanni Morone (1509–80),
Cardinal Stanisław Hozjusz (Stanislaus Hosius, 1504–79) and Cardinal Giovanni Francesco Commendone (1523–84). As part of Hozjusz's retinue, he traveled
to the Council of Trent (1545–63), where he agitated on behalf of his belea-
guered Catholic countrymen.

By the mid-1560s, Sander had relocated to Leuven, matriculating at the
university (eventually receiving a doctorate in divinity and accepting a place
on the faculty) and once again established himself as a mainstay of the exiled
English Catholic community. He proved extremely prolific, producing influential works of theology, history, and polemic, most famously his tract *De visibili
monarchia* (1571), a strident defense of papal supremacy. He was also something of a firebrand, advocating for a rigorist approach to English Catholics who
wavered in their observance, and for military intervention against Elizabeth.

In the end, Sander proved readier than most to translate his rhetoric
into action: in 1579, he helped lead a small contingent of Irish, Spanish, and

---

64   Sander (sometimes Sanders or Saunder) found an admiring biographer in Veech: see
      Veech, *Nicholas Sanders*.

         Other, briefer treatments include John Hungerford Pollen, "Dr. Nicholas Sander," EHR
      6, no. 21 (January 1891): 36–47; Bertha R. Sutton, "Nicholas Sanders. Controversialist-
      Historian (1530–1581)," *Irish Monthly* 49, no. 582 (December 1921): 504–06; Thomas
      F. Mayer, "Sander [Sanders], Nicholas (c.1530–1581)," in ODNB, 48:859–62; and Gerard
      Kilroy, "'Paths Coincident': The Parallel Lives of Dr. Nicholas Sander and Edmund
      Campion, S.J.," *JJS* 1, no. 4 (2014): 520–41.

65   Christopher Highley, *Catholics Writing the Nation in Early Modern Britain and Ireland*
      (Oxford: Oxford University Press, 2008), 27.

Italian soldiers under the command of the Irish nobleman James FitzMaurice FitzGerald (d.1579) on an invasion of Ireland, sparking what became known as the Second Desmond Rebellion (1579–83). The force landed at Smerwick (now Ard na Caithne in County Kerry) on July 18, 1579; their ships were captured almost immediately, stranding them. FitzMaurice was killed a month into the campaign, and a series of defeats left Sander a fugitive, cut off from the Continent and attempting (with little success) to coordinate the strategies of the fractious rebel leaders. After almost two years of a peripatetic existence in southwestern Ireland, Sander died—of exposure and starvation according to some, of dysentery according to others—sometime in the spring of 1581.[66]

Though his theological writings were deeply respected in Catholic circles, Sander's posthumous reputation has become indissolubly linked to his historical works, particularly his *De origine ac progressu*, composed in the late 1570s.[67] Never published in its author's lifetime, manuscript copies of *De origine ac progressu* circulated widely among Sander's fellow Catholic exiles, part of a collective effort toward a Catholic ecclesiastical history of England, "designed as a counterweight to Protestant 'histories.'"[68] Some years after Sander's death, the manuscript was prepared for publication by Edward Rishton (1550–85), at the suggestion of Robert Persons (1546–1610); the book was printed in Cologne in 1585.[69] Rishton died almost immediately thereafter, and Persons and William Allen (1532–94) oversaw the publication of an expanded edition in Rome the following year—though the book still bore Rishton's name alone.[70] In contrast to Ribadeneyra's self-conscious and declared presence in the *Historia*

---

66 Not only did Sander's military escapade fail to achieve its goals, but it also made life significantly harder for the Catholic priests—especially the Jesuits—working in England. Consequently, many Catholics preferred not to remember his revanchist side, recalling him (as Ribadeneyra does) exclusively as a writer and polemicist. Kilroy, "Paths Coincident," 538–39.

67 Veech, *Nicholas Sanders*, viii–ix.

68 Christopher Highley, "'A Pestilent and Seditious Book': Nicholas Sander's *Schismatis Anglicani* and Catholic Histories of the Reformation," HLQ 68, no. 1–2 (March 2005): 151–71, here 151.

69 Nicholas Sander, *Doctissimi viri Nicolai Sanderi, de origine ac progressu schismatis anglicani, liber: Continens historiam maximè ecclesiasticam, annorum circiter sexaginta, lectu dignissimam; Nimirum, ab anno 21 regni Henrici 8, quo primum cogitare cœpit de repudianda vxore serenissima Catherina, vsque ad hunc vigesimum septimum Elizabethæ, quæ vltima est eiusdem Henrici soboles*, ed. Edward Rishton (Cologne, 1585).

70 Nicholas Sander, *De origine ac progressu schismatis anglicani, libri tres: Quibus historia continetur maximè ecclesiasticam, annorum circiter sexaginta, lectu dignissima; Nimirum, ab anno 21 regni Henrici octaui, quo primum cogitare cœpit de repudianda vxore serenissima Catherina, vsque ad hunc vigesimum octauum Elizabethæ, quæ vltima est eiusdem Henrici*

as translator, author, and observer, Sander is a much more passive element in *De origine ac progressu*, the text being both posthumous and the product of many hands. The great historian of English Catholicism, John Hungerford Pollen, S.J., notes that *De origine ac progressu* "had in its day a larger circulation on the continent than any other book about England whatever"; the text was a "sensation," sparking translations and adaptations in numerous languages.[71]

How are we to characterize the relationship between *De origine ac progressu* and the *Historia*? Veech, though he recognized Ribadeneyra's authorial and editorial contributions, essentially regarded the latter as a translation of Sander's text.[72] More recent scholarship has nuanced this picture, identifying the significant changes to the text's tone, structure, and aims introduced by Ribadeneyra.[73] Christopher Highley speaks of the Jesuit "transforming" his source.[74] (It has also been demonstrated that Ribadeneyra was using the 1586 edition of *De origine ac progressu*, rather than the 1585 version, as Veech had asserted.)[75] Nonetheless, it is beyond question that Sander was Ribadeneyra's principal source for the reigns of Henry, Edward, and Mary, as well as much of the section on Elizabeth. Indeed, Veech's opinion is not without foundation: much of the *Historia*, especially the first book, is a relatively straightforward translation of Sander's Latin into Spanish.

At the same time, Ribadeneyra's fidelity to his source has colored subsequent historiography to an unhelpful degree. I have discussed elsewhere the problems of aligning Ribadeneyra too neatly with the "spaniolized Elizabethans," those English exiles—such as Sander—who found a home and a staging ground in Philip II's dominions.[76] It is true that Ribadeneyra was no stranger to the English Catholic community on the Continent. He was a friend of Sander;

---

soboles, ed. Edward Rishton, Robert Persons, and William Allen (Rome: Bartholomæi Bonfadini, 1586).

71   Pollen, "Nicholas Sander," 41. Felicity Heal, "Appropriating History: Catholic and Protestant Polemics and the National Past," *HLQ* 68, no. 1–2 (March 2005): 109–32, here 114.

72   Veech, *Nicholas Sanders*, 237.

73   E.g., Fátima Cid Morgade, "An Analysis of Pedro de Ribadeneyra's *Historia Ecclesiastica del Scisma de Inglaterra* (1588)" (thesis, Universidad de Valladolid, 2014); Freddy Cristóbal Domínguez, "'We Must Fight with Paper and Pens': Spanish Elizabethan Polemics 1585–1598" (PhD diss., Princeton University, 2011).

74   Highley, "'Pestilent and Seditious Book,'" 154.

75   Veech, *Nicholas Sanders*, 237.

76   See Weinreich, "Distinctiveness," 176–77.
      For examples of this tendency, see Domínguez, "Paper and Pens," and Victor Houliston, "The Missionary Position: Catholics Writing the History of the English Reformation," *English Studies in Africa* 54, no. 2 (2011): 16–30.

a trusted counselor of the English expatriate Jane Dormer (1538–1612), countess of Feria and the wife of his patron; a collaborator of William Allen; and a correspondent of Robert Persons—indeed, his exchanges with Persons may have given him the idea for the *Historia* in the first place.[77] Ribadeneyra also assisted in the publication of an account of the exiled English Bridgettine community of Syon Abbey (intended to help raise money for the displaced convent) and in the dissemination of newsletters about English affairs.[78] But the fact remains that Ribadeneyra was not an Elizabethan, and his changes to his source material highlight the different demands made upon a Spanish author writing in Spanish. As Fátima Cid Morgade straightforwardly puts it, "he turned the English point of view into a Spanish one."[79]

Indeed, it is the act of translation that most marks out the *Historia* as a different project from *De origine ac progressu*; a Spanish-language text spoke to a very different sort of audience from one in Latin. Where *De origine ac progressu* would have been accessible across Europe, but only to those sufficiently well educated as to know Latin, Ribadeneyra's translation would have reached the much broader cross-section of society literate in the vernacular, though confined to Spanish-speakers. Ribadeneyra also eliminates some of the more abstruse segments of *De origine ac progressu*: Sander's painstaking elaboration of the *pro* and *contra* arguments at Henry and Catherine's divorce trial, for instance, is cut. Concomitantly, Sander's manuscript circulated primarily among his fellow English exiles—that is, for readers already familiar with England and English culture—and among well-educated elites. Ribadeneyra, by contrast, must take the time to explain various English customs—trial by a jury of twelve men, for example—to a broader and more demotic European audience. Unsurprisingly, Ribadeneyra—who explains his decision to undertake the translation with two factors: "The first, that I am a Spaniard; the second, that I am a priest of the Society of Jesus" (120)—foregrounds Spain and the Society of Jesus to a greater extent than did Sander or the subsequent editors of *De origine ac progressu*.[80] Ribadeneyra gives Philip II's brief visits to England, for instance, much greater space, detail, and prominence than his source.

---

77 Clifford, *Life of Jane Dormer*, 184–85. Domínguez, "Paper and Pens," 115, 138. Victor Houliston, "Robert Persons's Precarious Correspondence," *JJS* 1, no. 4 (2014): 542–57, here 550.

78 Domínguez, "Papers and Pens," 228. Houliston, "Robert Persons's Precarious Correspondence," 551.

79 Cid Morgade, "Analysis," 13.

80 Ibid., 13, 30. Weinreich, "Distinctiveness," *passim*.

Though Ribadeneyra won renown for the beauty of his Spanish, the signifi-cance of his Castilian prose goes beyond his stylistic abilities. He is remarkable among his contemporaries in the attention he paid to vernacular writing—that is, to broadening the reach of his work and others.'[81] Every single one of Ribadeneyra's published works saw at least one Spanish edition, and he worked extensively as a translator (among his other achievements, he produced the first Spanish-language edition of the *Paradisus animae, sive tractatus de virtutibus*, attributed to Albertus Magnus). It seems reasonable, then, to speak of Ribadeneyra "popularizing" *De origine ac progressu*, creating a text far more accessible to the ordinary reader. As we shall see, there were dangers in (and obstacles to) bringing potentially incendiary content to a wider audience. That Ribadeneyra persevered in so doing might suggest he thought more highly than his contemporaries of the intellectual capabilities of the common people, or that he particularly valued expanding the reach of his historical and theo-logical message.

The difference in language also speaks to two very different historical and cultural moments. Sander was one of the leading lights of the generation of English Catholic exiles that began to write primarily in Latin, rather than English: a reflection of pessimism about the chances of persuading their coun-trymen back to Catholicism and the importance accorded to winning over European elites.[82] By contrast, Ribadeneyra, as Roldán-Figueroa has demon-strated, was at the forefront of a movement *toward* the vernacular in Spanish devotional literature.[83]

Language aside, the substantial differences between the two texts correlate with their respective authors' distinct polemical and intellectual interests. Victor Houliston, noting Sander's training as a canon lawyer, has persuasively read *De origine ac progressu* as a legalistic attack on the legitimacy of Eng-lish Protestantism: Sander "is concerned to prove the break with Rome to be purely a matter of personal expediency to satisfy Henry's lust for Anne Boleyn (c. 1501–36). There is no moral or legal justification for the divorce and no

---

81   Weinreich, "Distinctiveness," 187.

        Ribadeneyra himself wrote of his Spanish translation of his life of Ignatius: "I have now translated and augmented it in our Castilian language, so that our lay-brothers in Spain, and other devout persons who wish to know the origins of our order, who do not know the Latin tongue, may enjoy and benefit from it in their own [*Agora le he traducido y añadido en nuestra lengua castellana, y para que nuestros hermanos legos de España, otras personas devotas y deseosas de saber los principios de nuestra religión, que no saben la lengua latina, puedan gozar y aprovecharse del en la suya*]." Rey, cxii.

82   Highley, *Catholics Writing the Nation*, Chapter 2.

83   Roldán-Figuera, "Ribadeneyra's *Vida*," *passim*.

religious dimension to the secession."[84] Because it is the origins of the schism that are of interest, Sander's history is front-loaded, the treatment of Henry VIII ampler, more detailed, and of greater narrative significance than those of his children. In the edition Ribadeneyra read, however, the edits of Rishton, Persons, and Allen had attenuated this analytic approach: in order to extend the narrative coverage from the late 1570s to the mid-1580s, they reported the events of each succeeding year in an annalistic style, distending the original's tight structure.[85]

Ribadeneyra's changes further shift the narrative center of gravity forward in time. He is comparatively uninterested in the legal and theological *bona fides* of the schism's origins (taking their absence as read): most of his deletions come from the chapters on Henry, including many of the more theoretical passages. His additions are likewise clustered in the latter sections, the product of two, related factors. First and foremost, the passage of time between the two books' publications, though superficially brief, was significant. Both editions of *De origine ac progressu* were printed while Mary Queen of Scots was still alive, an English prisoner just as she had been for nearly twenty years. Ribadeneyra wrote just after her death. As a matter of narrative, the queen's execution at Fotheringhay furnishes a climax of sufficient weight to balance out the divorce and initial schism of Henry's reign. Furthermore, Mary had deliberately staged, and her coreligionists had vigorously embraced, her death as a martyrdom for the Catholic faith, one of superlative polemical value. It is understandable, then, that while Mary makes no more than a few brief appearances in *De origine ac progressu*, Ribadeneyra accords her the single longest chapter in the entire *Historia*, rendered in exuberantly hagiographic colors.

Hagiography brings us to the second and more important factor in Ribadeneyra's insertions—his particular historical and theological interests. Although *De origine ac progressu* and the *Historia* are both nominally ecclesiastical histories, they do not partake of the genre's norms to the same degree.[86] We see this most clearly in their treatment of martyrdom. When he wrote *De origine ac progressu*, Sander was unusual in declaring those English Catholics

84   Houliston, "Missionary Position," 20.
        Cf. Houliston, "Fallen Prince and Pretender of the Faith: Henry VIII as Seen by Sander and Persons," in *Henry VIII and History*, ed. Thomas Betteridge and Thomas S. Freeman (Farnham: Ashgate, 2012), 119–34, here 123–24.
85   Houliston, "Missionary Position," 21.
86   For instance, though *De origine ac progressu* does incorporate extensive quotations from outside sources, these ultimately serve as forensic evidence for Sander's overarching argument, rather than contributing to a "choral" narrative.

executed by the Elizabethan state to be martyrs.[87] Yet, when compared to
Ribadeneyra, Sander seems practically uninterested in martyrs, perhaps because when he wrote in the mid-1570s there had not yet been a great many of
them in England. At that time, Elizabeth's religious policies had only recently
intensified to the point of shedding Catholic blood with any frequency—and it
was only amid the Elizabethan executions that those under Henry VIII took on
full martyrological significance.[88] Ribadeneyra, by contrast, is deeply committed to the idea of martyrdom, harkening back (often explicitly) to the long tradition of Christian martyrs chronicled by Eusebius of Caesarea (c.260–c.340)
and company.[89] Where Rishton et al. allotted the lives of Edmund Campion
(1540–81), Ralph Sherwin (c.1549–81), and Alexander Briant (1556–81) no more
than a few pages, Ribadeneyra gives them several chapters. The stories of individual martyrs are recounted in loving detail, and these were the passages
most frequently expanded and developed in later editions of the *Historia*, adding fresh anecdotes, allusions to ancient forebears, and documentation. This,
too, is a symptom of the historical moment. The discovery of the Roman cata-
combs in 1578 had ignited an explosion of interest in martyrs as the hallmarks
of Catholicism's authenticity. Coinciding as this did with the beginnings of the
English mission and with intensified Elizabeth persecution, England soon took
on a special significance, as the only European country where Catholic martyrs
were actively being made.[90] The English martyrs became icons of the Counter-
Reformation, particularly within the Society of Jesus. In turn, Campion and
the other Jesuit martyrs were integral to the Society's missionary work and its
self-presentation, in England and on the continent.[91] In the *Historia*, the stories
of the Jesuit martyrs receive substantially longer and more detailed treatment

---

87   Thomas M. McCoog, *"And Touching Our Society": Fashioning Jesuit Identity in Elizabethan England*, Catholic and Recusant Texts of the Late Medieval & Early Modern Periods 3 (Toronto: Pontifical Institute of Mediaeval Studies, 2013), 372.

88   John J. LaRocca, "Time, Death, and the Next Generation: The Early Elizabethan Recusancy Policy, 1558–1574," *Albion: A Quarterly Journal Concerned with British Studies* 14, no. 2 (Summer 1982): 103–17. Brad S. Gregory, *Salvation at Stake: Christian Martyrdom in Early Modern Europe*, Harvard Historical Studies 134 (Cambridge: Harvard University Press, 1999), 272.

89   Cf. Anthony Grafton, *What Was History? The Art of History in Early Modern Europe* (Cambridge: Cambridge University Press, 2007), 111–12.

90   Thomas H. Clancy, "The First Generation of English Jesuits 1555–1585," *AHSI* 57 (1988): 137–62, here 144. Anne Dillon, *The Construction of Martyrdom in the English Catholic Community, 1535–1603*, St Andrews Studies in Reformation History (Aldershot: Ashgate, 2002), 15, 83.

91   Dillon, *Construction of Martyrdom*, 109.

than their secular, monastic, and lay fellows. Ribadeneyra was writing at a time when the story of English Catholicism *was* the story of martyrdom.

Before turning to Ribadeneyra's more theoretical interests, there are a few other observations to be made about the two books' comparative structure. Ribadeneyra has consolidated Sander's four books (one for each monarch) into two (the first for Henry VIII, the second shared among his three children). Unlike the uninterrupted streams of (dense) Latin in *De origine ac progressu*, the books of the *Historia* are divided into chapters.[92] While the resulting text is easier to use, it has lost the steady flow of the original, and introduced distinctions where Sander had envisaged a unified (albeit variegated) whole. The chapter titles also allow for brief polemic and didactic interventions, whereby Ribadeneyra can guide the reader.[93] Ribadeneyra's active authorial insertions, noted above, extend to his treatment of Sander: by explaining how he encountered Sander's history and signposting places of direct quotation ("as Doctor Sander says in his history" [398]), he positions his text as a distinct entity from *De origine ac progressu*, which belies how much of the *Historia* is direct translation.

Ribadeneyra's most common interventions vis-à-vis Sander are the insertion of what Rey calls "his characteristic providentialist observations."[94] To be sure, there is a providentialist streak in *De origine ac progressu*: Sander portrays Henry's end as a divine judgment, and the later editors highlight how the king became an instrument of further divine judgments upon others.[95] But these are largely incidental to the broader narrative, while Ribadeneyra is consistently and intensely interested in divine providence and how God's will manifests in history. As Rey explains, "it is common for Ribadeneyra to insert providentialist considerations, by way of a moral, in the emotional moments of the narrative."[96] One such interpolation invites the reader to consider "the punishment our Lord inflicted upon Henry, torturing him in the very things he had most sought to achieve or to get clear of [*desuanecerse*] in this life" (322). Having abandoned his lawful wife, he is cuckolded by two of his subsequent queens, Anne Boleyn and Catherine Howard (c.1521–42). Ribadeneyra clearly takes satisfaction in the (divine) justice of ironic comeuppances—Thomas Cromwell (c.1485–1540) condemned by a law he wrote;

---

92   Highley, "'Pestilent and Seditious Book,'" 156n23.
93   Cid Morgade, "Analysis," 15.
94   "sus típicos considerandos providencialistas." Rey, 1055n.
95   Houliston, "Fallen Prince," 127.
96   "Es corriente en Ribadeneyra intercalar considerandos providencialistas, por via de moraleja, en los momentos emocionales de la narración." Rey, 867–68.

Henry celebrating Anne's death just as she had celebrated Catherine's; the dying Henry desirous of returning to the true path but unable to find any but heretical counselors.[97]

These observations—often no more than a sentence or two—function much like the chapter headings: they guide the reader's understanding. They create and communicate the "meaning" of events. While not arguing so explicit and specific a position as *De origine ac progressu*, the *Historia* is dedicated to identifying the workings of God in history. Indeed, we might read the entire text as an exploration of divine providence: for Ribadeneyra, history and providence could never be separated, and so historiography was always already theology.[98] One formulation offered by Alexandra Walsham in her seminal study of providentialist thought beautifully expresses Ribadeneyra's views: "History was a canvas on which the Lord etched His purposes and intentions, nature a textbook and a laboratory in which He taught, demonstrated, and tested His providence."[99] Similar themes pervade Ribadeneyra's other writings. The *Confesiones* see the will of God in each and every event of the Jesuit's life, from lost travelers finding their way to the village they seek, to the kidney complaint that frees Ribadeneyra of his responsibilities as head of the Collegio Romano.[100] Likewise, *The Life of Ignatius of Loyola* casts the whole of its subject's life and work as the doing of divine providence, asserting that "in a sort of special providential act, he [God] sent Ignatius to help a tottering Church."[101] As the reference to the "tottering Church" suggests, Ribadeneyra's vision of providence was not distinct from history, God's *ex nihilo* interventions into an otherwise separate flow of events. Providence *is* history: witness Ribadeneyra's confident claim to the reader, "Let us take a good look at the mission for which

97   Gabriela Torres Olleta, "Imágenes del poder en el Siglo de Oro: La visión del P. Ribadeneyra en el *Cisma de Inglaterra*," in *La voz de Clío: Imágenes del poder en la comedia histórica del Siglo de Oro*, ed. Oana Andreia Sâmbrian, Mariela Insúa, and Antonie Mihail (Craiova: Editura Universitaria Craiova, 2012), 70–81, here 74, 76.

98   Many contemporaries invested historiography with sacred significance, aligning the moral guidance derived from historical analysis with divine providence. Nicholas Popper, *Walter Ralegh's History of the World and the Historical Culture of the Late Renaissance* (Chicago: University of Chicago Press, 2012), 5, 52.

99   Alexandra Walsham, *Providence in Early Modern England* (Oxford: Oxford University Press, 1999), 2.
       Cf. Rey, cv.

100   *MHSIR*, 1:66, 80.

101   Pedro de Ribadeneyra, *The Life of Ignatius of Loyola*, trans. Claude Pavur, Jesuit Primary Sources in English Translations 28 (St. Louis: Institute of Jesuit Sources, 2014), 116.

the Society was founded. It is precisely the one that is demanded by the historical moment of the Catholic Church."[102]

Rey's observation that providentialist observations tend to appear "in the
emotional moments of the narrative," such as Henry's assault on the monasteries, the death of Catherine of Aragon, or the martyrdom of protagonists like
John Forest (c.1470–1538) and Edmund Campion, is significant.[103] Ribadeneyra
may be reminding his readers (or himself) that all that transpired, shocking,
perplexing, or painful though it might be,

> was intended by that Lord who guides and directs all things, by his eter-
> nal and immutable providence, to his glory and the good of his chosen,
> and takes the injustice and cruelty of tyrants as a means to declare the
> fortitude and patience of the martyrs, and to crown and honor them, and
> by their example, merits, and intercession, to ennoble, inspirit, and de-
> fend his kingdom, which is the holy Catholic Church (486).

Domínguez suggests that these repeated reminders stem in part from
"a prevalent belief that Latinate readers could understand these [lessons] independently while vulgar audiences needed more guidance."[104] For any reader,
providence furnishes a useful pressure-valve, ameliorating the often-troubling
content of the *Historia* and reassuring Catholics that even their worst misfortunes were all part of God's plan. At the same time, the ever-increasing number
and seriousness of these misfortunes, particularly in the aftermath of the Spanish Armada, presented a formidable challenge to any providential interpretation of history, as we shall see.

One final, perhaps counterintuitive observation: the *Historia* is the more
militant and the more militaristic of the two texts. A.A. Parker avers that
"Ribadeneyra's language is much more violent than Sander's, even where he
is following the latter's text closely." It is certainly true that Ribadeneyra is
less measured than Sander when speaking about English Protestants. This is
particularly true of the portrayal of Henry VIII, where Ribadeneyra reproduces
Sander's enumeration of the king's virtues, but adds his own litany of his
vices.[105] More broadly, the discrepancy can be seen in the two histories' distinct endings. The 1586 edition of *De origine ac progressu* closes with a catalog

---

102   Ibid., 117.

103   Rey, 867–68.

104   Domínguez, "Paper and Pens," 159.

105   A.A. Parker, "Henry VIII in Shakespeare and Calderón: An Appreciation of '*La Cisma de
       Ingalaterra*,'" *Modern Language Review* 43, no. 3 (July 1948): 327–52, here 333, 333n1, 351.

of "deeds done for the Catholic religion in the Tower of London," essentially a list of those imprisoned.[106] The *Historia* ends with a fierce peroration urging Spain to military action against England. Any comparison of the two authors' lives would seem to suggest precisely the opposite: Ribadeneyra was living out his peaceful retirement in Toledo while Sander was leading an invasion of Ireland with the intention of overthrowing Elizabeth. But, of course, it was not Sander who published *De origine ac progressu*, and we must remember that the disastrous failure of his expedition was an acute embarrassment to European Catholics, one they airbrushed from his memory whenever possible.[107] English Catholic martyrologists generally sought to depoliticize their stories, so as not to lend support to Protestant accusations that the missionary priests were agents provocateurs.[108] Sander also wrote before Elizabeth's religious policy took its definitively violent turn. By contrast, Ribadeneyra was writing at the high water mark of Catholic executions[109]—and, as Brad S. Gregory reminds us, "Martyrs intensified every other disagreement."[110] What is more, Ribadeneyra's *Historia* came off the presses as the ships of the Spanish Armada were preparing to sail for England. In such circumstances, it could not help being an intensely political text.

The Politics of History, the Politics of the *Historia*

The *Historia* was, and was always intended to be, a text with political significance and political consequences. To a certain extent, this was the product of the historical moment: Francis Drake's (1540–96) devastating raid on Cádiz in

---

106   "Rerum pro religione Catholica in Turri Londinensi gestarum." Sander, *De origine ac progressu*, n.p.

107   Kilroy, "Paths Coincident," 538–39.

108   Susannah Brietz Monta, *Martyrdom and Literature in Early Modern England* (Cambridge: Cambridge University Press, 2005), 217.

109   Peter Lake, *Bad Queen Bess? Libels, Secret Histories, and the Politics of Publicity in the Reign of Queen Elizabeth I* (Oxford: Oxford University Press, 2016), 321.

      "The 1580s was a critical decade in the development of Catholic polemic which, under the pressure of events, was both mutable and ambiguous, depending in part on the audiences being addressed." William J. Sheils, "Polemic as Piety: Thomas Stapleton's *Tres Thomae* and Catholic Controversy in the 1580s," *JEH* 60, no. 1 (January 2009): 74–94, here 92.

110   Gregory, *Salvation at Stake*, 6.

      This phenomenon was driven in no small part by the use of competing martyrologies to define confessional boundaries. Monta, *Martyrdom and Literature*, 1–2.

1587 had spurred Ribadeneyra to complete his history.[111] The project was intimately connected to the Spanish Armada, a subject to which we shall return shortly. Furthermore, as I have argued elsewhere, the *Historia* emerged in, and responded to, a climate of fierce criticism leveled at the Society of Jesus's reputation, within and without Spain.[112]

But anterior to these specific aims, the project itself took on political valences via early modern notions of what history was and what role it should play. Sixteenth-century scholars were well aware that all historiography involves the creation of a narrative, defined by the choices of what to include and what to exclude, how to position cause and effect.[113] There were numerous theories about how these narratives ought to be understood, crafted, and deployed. Two dominant approaches—certainly not mutually exclusive—took their cues from the ancient Roman writers Cicero (106 BCE–43 BCE) and Quintilian (*c*.35–*c*.100), respectively: the former saw history, in the orator's phrase, as "the directress of life [*magistra vitae*]," instructing readers how to behave; the latter as an exercise of rhetoric, often with overtly political objectives.[114] Another strand of historiography, still in formation when Ribadeneyra wrote the *Historia*, was the yet more explicitly political "politic histories," drawing inspiration from Tacitus (*c*.56–*c*.117) and offering often-fraught interpretations of contemporary events. One Spanish exponent of "politic history," the royal chronicler Antonio de Herrera y Tordesillas (1549–*c*.1625), placed histories "among the arsenal of weapons that the monarchy was to deploy against its enemies."[115] A special category of historiographical warfare, especially common in the case of ecclesiastical historiography, was central to the ideological conflicts of the Reformation. Confessional debates were in some senses always

---

111   Houliston, "Robert Persons's Precarious Correspondence," 550.

112   Weinreich, "Distinctiveness," 186–88.

113   Alexander Samson, "Florián de Ocampo, Castilian Chronicler and Habsburg Propagandist: Rhetoric, Myth and Genealogy in the Historiography of Early Modern Spain," *Forum for Modern Language Studies* 42, no. 4 (October 2006): 339–54, here 341.

114   Grafton, *What Was History?*, 31–32. Richard L. Kagan, *Clio & the Crown: The Politics of History in Medieval and Early Modern Spain* (Baltimore: Johns Hopkins University Press, 2009), 88, 102.
        On the importance of the *magistra vita* trope to Jesuit ideas about history, see Paul Nelles, "*Historia magistra antiquitatis*: Cicero and Jesuit History Teaching," *Renaissance Studies* 13, no. 2 (June 1999): 130–72.

115   Richard L. Kagan, "Antonio de Herrera y Tordesillas and the 'Political Turn' in the 'Official History' of Seventeenth-Century Spain," in *Les historiographes en Europe de la fin du Moyen Âge à la Révolution*, ed. Chantal Grell, Mythes, critique et histoire (Paris: Presses de l'Université Paris-Sorbonne, 2006), 277–96, especially 278–79 and 288–89.

already historical, as competing claims on the legacy of the "true" or "Apostolic" Church.[116] Protestants charged that Catholic practices were corruptions and innovations; Catholics retorted with some version of the taunt, "Where was your church before Luther?"[117]

In the course of this introduction, I shall elucidate some of the ways that Ribadeneyra's *Historia* shares in all these currents of thought. His extraordinary erudition allows him to construct a formidable historical lineage for sixteenth-century Catholicism. The text is simultaneously a confident polemical intervention in several contemporaneous discourses, including debates over the Society of Jesus, Anglo-Spanish relations, and Catholic attitudes to heresy, mission, and martyrdom.

But it is to Cicero's didactic vision of history that we must turn first, not least because Ribadeneyra himself foregrounds it. In the introductory material and throughout the text, Ribadeneyra repeatedly stresses the "lessons" and "benefits" readers of all kinds could take from the *Historia*. The conclusion to the first volume even quotes the *magistra vitae* tag. In this, Ribadeneyra is no different from the innumerable other early modern historians who understood their work as "a compendium and source of moral instruction and pragmatic guidance through specific exemplars."[118] Where the *Historia* distinguishes itself—and stakes out an explicitly political territory—is in its dedicatee: Ribadeneyra dedicated the book to the then-*infante* of Spain, the future Philip III (r.1598–1621). What is more, he characterizes the history's educative potential as political, urging the prince to use it to learn "the duties of the good king" (set out in effusive detail in the dedicatory epistle).

With so exalted a dedicatee, Ribadeneyra's message could not but have political valences, even had the content been utterly anodyne. That it was not, but rather touched upon heresy, apostasy, diplomatic intrigue, and ongoing violent conflicts, against the background of rising Anglo-Spanish tensions, the persecution of English Catholics, and the militancy of the "Counter-Reformation,"

---

116   Katherine Van Liere, Simon Ditchfield, and Howard Louthan, *Sacred History: Uses of the Christian Past in the Renaissance World* (Oxford: Oxford University Press, 2012), vii–viii.
      Cf. W.B. Patterson, "The Recusant View of the English Past," in *The Materials, Sources, and Methods of Ecclesiastical History: Papers Read at the Twelfth Summer Meeting and the Thirteenth Winter Meeting of the Ecclesiastical History Society*, ed. Derek Baker (Oxford: Basil Blackwell, 1975), 249–62.

117   S.J. Barnett, "Where Was Your Church Before Luther? Claims for the Antiquity of Protestantism Examined," *CH* 68, no. 1 (March 1999): 14–41.

118   Samson, "Florián de Ocampo," 339.
      Cf. Paulina Kewes, "History and Its Uses: Introduction," *HLQ* 68, no. 1–2 (March 2005): 1–31, here 1.

means that we must read the *Historia* as a self-conscious intervention in contemporary issues of the highest pitch and moment. Furthermore, *De origine ac progressu* bequeathed a certain radicalness to the *Historia*. Sander had sensationally claimed that Anne Boleyn was secretly Henry VIII's daughter, and his history's portrait of Elizabeth as the arch-heretic represented a watershed in English Catholic writing in its willingness to criticize the queen herself.[119] Far from moderating these explosive elements, Ribadeneyra—perhaps, as a Spaniard, free of the ties of patriotism, however faint, that might have restrained his English coreligionists—embraced and extended them, laying the bloodguilt of the Catholic martyrs at the door of Anne's incest and Elizabeth's perversity. All the same, he was aware that his material was sensitive: one of the reasons he so vigorously insists that his is fundamentally an ecclesiastical history, "cutting out all that pertains to political affairs and governance" (555) may have been the potential impropriety of a priest writing on political matters (especially since one of the Elizabethan government's primary accusations against the Society was that the fathers were political agents).[120]

These protestations notwithstanding, Ribadeneyra ran into substantial obstacles in publishing the *Historia*; the leaders of the Society were distinctly wary of allowing one of their number to release so combative a history. Ribadeneyra's direct superior, Francisco de Porres (1538–1621), attempted to block publication of the *Historia*, and Acquaviva shared his misgivings.[121] López records the incident as an example of Ribadeneyra's humility:

> when the then-superior [Porres] said that he would absolutely not give permission for it to be printed, and that he believed he would commit a mortal sin if he did, Father [Ribadeneyra] was neither upset, nor discontent, nor made any complaint, but rather said, very calmly, "So be it [*Pues norabuena*]. All I ask is that Your Reverence assemble the *consultores*, and I will give them my reasons, and if they are content, all to the good, and if not, patience." Thus it was done, and the father gave the committee

---

Highley, "'Pestilent and Seditious Book,'" 166, 171. Domínguez, "Paper and Pens," 24–25.
  Jan Machielsen has questioned whether the anti-Elizabeth animus of *De origine ac progressu* has been exaggerated. Jan Machielsen, "The Lion, the Witch, and the King: Thomas Stapleton's *Apologia pro Rege Catholico Philippo II* (1592)," *EHR* 129, no. 536 (February 2014): 19–46, here 21n8.
120 Domínguez, "History in Action," 7.
121 Permission was eventually granted, after a convoluted process of consultation and review and the intervention of William Allen and Robert Persons. Ibid., 5–6.

his reasons (I believe there were nine), and then he left it to them and departed. And although out of the seven or eight votes, only two were in his favor (one, who had read it in its entirety, said that it was the best thing of that kind he had ever read; the other said that without reviewing it, there was no cause to condemn it), and the decision from the rest was that it should not be published, nevertheless, the father did not protest or turn against the *consultores*. [...] Rather, without showing any frustration, he wrote to our father general with his reasons, and the superior [wrote] with his and with those from the committee, and our father [general], seeing both, deferred the publication to Father Ribadeneyra's judgment: out of weighty considerations he said that although there were certain reasons not to do so, yet he left it to the father. And with this it was printed, and received with amazing enthusiasm.[122]

Bilinkoff speculates that Porres was concerned that so detailed an account of the English schism would disseminate heretical ideas.[123]

It is ironic that Ribadeneyra's superiors might have been concerned about readers imbibing heresy from the *Historia*, because for an explicitly ecclesiastical history, the text has little doctrinal content. That is not to deny that it is a *theological* work, given its reflections on and explorations of the relationship of God and history (to say nothing of the theological valences of all ecclesiastical history during this period). It is equally a *confessional* work, committed to the defense of Catholicism and the undermining of Protestantism. Yet for all that, the treatment of Catholic and Protestant theology is shallow at best. There are

---

122   "Porque diziendo el superior que entonces era, que por ningún caso daría licencia para que se imprimiesse, y que juzgaua pecaría mortalmente si la diesse, el Padre no se turbó ny alteró ny dió quexa; sino con mucha paz dixo: 'Pues norabuena; solo ruego a V.R. que junte los consultores, y yo les daré las razones que tengo, y si les contentare, bien; y si no, paciencia.' Hizose así, y el Padre dió en la consulta las razones que tenía (que creo fueron nueue), y luego los dexó en ella y salióse. Y no obstante que de siete o ocho votos que eran, solos dos eran en su fauor (digo, el vno que la auía leído toda, que dixo era la mejor cosa que en aquel género auía leydo, el otro dixo que sin reuerla no era razón de condemnarla), [y] salió de los demás que no se imprimiesse; con todo el Padre no se quexó ni se alteró contra los consultores, [...] sino sin mostrar pesadumbre, escriuió a nuestro Padre general sus razones, y el superior las suyas, y las que sacó de la consulta; y nuestro Padre, vistas las vnas y las otras, remittió el imprimirla a que se hiziesse lo que al Padre Ribadeneyra le parecía, no obstante que por respectos superiores dixo que algunas razones auía para que no; pero que él lo remitía al Padre. Y con esto se imprimió y se recibió con tal aplauso, que admiró." *MHSIR*, 2:445.

123   Bilinkoff, "Many 'Lives,'" 192.

scattered references to Henry's Six Articles or Elizabeth's Act of Uniformity, to debates over the Mass or papal supremacy, but Reformed theology is never considered as a coherent body of thought. Rather, confessional identity is cast as a moral question: Anne Boleyn is not wicked because she is a Lutheran, she is a Lutheran because she is wicked: "as this woman's religious beliefs could not but correspond to her life and habits, she followed the Lutheran sect" (155). The same is true, *mutatis mutandis*, of the Catholics. Neither side comes to their position out of intellectual conviction, but rather through innate piety on the part of the Catholics, and sinfulness (Anne), ambition (Thomas Cromwell), passion (Henry), or indoctrination (Edward VI) among the "heretics." We shall return to the *Historia*'s connections to the Counter-Reformation; for now, we should simply observe that the text is evidently not intended to convince the "heretics." The *Historia* is addressed to good Catholics.

All this does not detract from the fact that the *Historia* thinks of itself as an ecclesiastical history. Its very first lines explain that it will relate only matters "touching upon our holy religion." Like almost all early modern church historians, Ribadeneyra hews closely to the model set down by Eusebius, the father of the discipline:

> Eusebius interspersed the chapters of his *History* with primary documents: letters, quotations, accounts of the suffering of martyrs [...]. Church history, as Eusebius framed it, was not a smooth narrative—the normal form of ancient historiography—but a choral work, in which the voices of many witnesses were heard, along with that of the author.[124]

Moreover, Ribadeneyra quotes extensively from his forebears, from the Ur-ecclesiastical history that is the Bible, to the earliest exponents of the discipline itself (e.g., Eusebius, Rufinus of Aquileia [*c.*345–410]), to medieval and early modern practitioners (e.g., George Kedrenos [*fl.* eleventh century], Cesare Baronio [1538–1607]). More subtly, he builds references to earlier ecclesiastical histories into the very architecture of his text: as a single example, he repeatedly mentions that the martyrs are punished with the judicial apparatus (chains, prisons, and so on) intended for "adulterers, murderers, and thieves" (219)—a nod to Eusebius's *Ecclesiastical History*, 8.6.

---

124 Anthony Grafton, "Church History in Early Modern Europe: Tradition and Innovation," in *Sacred History: Uses of the Christian Past in the Renaissance World*, ed. Katherine Van Liere, Simon Ditchfield, and Howard Louthan (Oxford: Oxford University Press, 2012), 3–26, here 17–18.

We should not regard Ribadeneyra's erudition as in conflict with his partisanship. In the words of Richard L. Kagan, "Throughout early modern Europe the boundary separating 'polemical' from 'scholarly history' was never well-defined, and few historians [...] wrote history free of ideological influences or polemical concerns."[125] This combination of learned piety and fierce confessional loyalty leads neatly into the immediate polemical project of the first edition of the *Historia*: the promotion of the Spanish Armada.

The Spanish Armada

The Spanish Armada is in some ways the pivot around which the whole of Ribadeneyra's *Historia* turns. This is not simply the accident of chronology, although the preparation, launch, and failure of the Armada doubtless fueled interest in English affairs among Spanish readers. Ribadeneyra, like countless Jesuits throughout the Habsburg dominions, was actively involved in the "enterprise of England." For a year before the expedition sailed, Jesuit provinces across the Iberian Peninsula were praying for its success. Twenty-three members of the Society accompanied the fleet, only eight of whom would survive.[126]

It must be said that to those who conceived, organized, and launched the Armada, moral and theological preparations were just as important as the more quotidian concerns of provisions, weaponry, and the like—indeed, not a few of Philip's projects were undermined by an overemphasis on the divine and an attendant neglect of the logistical.[127] The Jesuits were only a part of the massive religious apparatus, including the entire royal family, marshaled to pray for victory. More than six hundred prostitutes were removed from the fleet to preserve the soldiers' and sailors' moral fiber (a piece of pastoral care for which some were no doubt less than grateful).[128] It is against the background of such priorities that we must reckon with Ribadeneyra's personal contribution to the preparations: in the spring of 1588, he penned an oration addressed to the

---

125   Kagan, *Clio & the Crown*, 4.

126   See Francisco de Borja de Medina, "Jesuitas en la armada contra Inglaterra (1588): Notas para un centenario," *AHSI* 58 (1989): 3–42.

127   Geoffrey Parker, "The Place of Tudor England in the Messianic Vision of Philip II of Spain: The Prothero Lecture," *Transactions of the Royal Historical Society* 12 (2002): 167–221, here 179–80.

128   Robert E. Scully, "'In the Confident Hope of a Miracle': The Spanish Armada and Religious Mentalities in the Late Sixteenth Century," *Catholic Historical Review* 89, no. 4 (2003): 643–70, here 656–57.

departing fleet.[129] This he sent to his friend and patron Ana Félix de Guzmán, countess of Ricla and marchioness of Camarasa (c.1560–1612), with the intention that she would forward it to her first cousin once removed, Alonso Pérez de Guzmán y Sotomayor, seventh duke of Medina Sidonia (1550–1615)—the Armada's commander-in-chief.

In the words of Francisco de Borja de Medina, S.J., "The exhortation constitutes a veritable manifesto, in which Ribadeneyra justifies military action against Queen Elizabeth of England with religious and political arguments."[130] Medina's choice of the word "manifesto" is felicitous: Ribadeneyra's rhetoric has much in common with the official propaganda campaign, organized on an international scale, around the Armada.[131] However easy it is to imagine the Jesuit in serene isolation a decade and a half into his retirement, it should be recalled that he was living in Madrid, "at the time the most sensitive anti-Protestant nerve-center in the Catholic world."[132] He remained well connected and well attuned to the goings-on of the court. In keeping with the official portrayal of the Armada as "a religious crusade," Ribadeneyra argues first and foremost for the expedition's religious mission: the defense of English Catholics and the reclamation of the kingdom for the true church.[133] Simultaneously, he is careful to cast the Armada as a defensive "just war," undertaken in response to the harms done by English power and for the benefit of all of Christendom. Even as he dwells on English attacks on Habsburg imperial possessions and the drain on Spain's resources, he stresses Elizabeth's role as the mainstay of the Protestant cause: "She is the root, the wellspring, the one who continually stokes this fire, feeds this storm, fans up this foul and pestilential vapor, and spreads and extends it through other regions and kingdoms" (745). Significantly, the conviction that England was "the champion and defender of Protestant Europe" was at the heart of both Philip's decision to launch the Armada and

---

129 See Appendix 1.

130 "La *Exhortación* constituye un verdadero manifiesto en que Ribadeneira justifica, con razones religioso-políticas, la acción bélica contra la reina Isabel de Inglaterra." Medina, "Jesuitas," 5.

131 Fernando J. Bouza-Álvarez, "Monarchie en lettres d'imprimerie: Typographie et propagande au temps de Philippe II," trans. Marie-Joëlle Tupet, *Revue d'histoire moderne et contemporaine* (1954–) 41, no. 2 (April 1994): 206–20, here 207.

132 "el centro nervioso antiprotestante más sensible tal vez de toda la Catolicidad en aquellos momentos." Rey, lxxxvi.

133 Robert Bireley, *The Counter-Reformation Prince: Anti-Machiavellianism or Catholic Statecraft in Early Modern Europe* (Chapel Hill: University of North Carolina Press, 1990), 114. Scully, "Confident Hope," 643.

the willingness of other Catholic polities to support the enterprise.[134] Though we do not know what use, if any, was made of the exhortation, its exuberant tone and strident Catholicism and Spanish national feeling speak to the high hopes Ribadeneyra (and others) cherished.

In his covering letter to the countess, Ribadeneyra explains that he wrote the exhortation "as a conclusion to the *Historia de la scisma de Inglaterra*" (739), but chose to delete it for "justos respectos" (good reasons).[135] At least one scholar has interpreted this as evidence that the Jesuit "had reservations about this militancy or at least its public expression."[136] The decision not to incorporate the oration into the *Historia* is significant, but not necessarily an indication of qualms about military action on behalf of the faith. In the aftermath of the expedition's catastrophic failure—when such doubts might reasonably be aired—Ribadeneyra was still insisting "how utterly necessary it remains to prosecute the war and seek out the foe" (757). More to the point, even without the address, the final pages of the *Historia* are suffused with the heady enthusiasm of the Armada. Ribadeneyra reviews the many outrages committed by English Protestantism, and urges Catholic readers to strive with every faculty to effect "the conversion *or destruction* of the heretics."[137] Domínguez has colorfully described this section as "a red-faced, vein-popping call to arms,"[138] and the dedication to the future king puts an even finer point on these geopolitical ambitions.

The peroration is, however, only the most explicitly propagandistic element of the *Historia*. Read against the background of the impending Armada, the entire book can be seen as a piece of confessional agitprop. The dichotomized and sensationalized story, highlighting the alleged moral wickedness of the "heretics" rather than their theological errors, has clear potential for building support for military action against the English. This aspect of the *Historia* has been brilliantly analyzed by Domínguez, whose wheel I have no intention of reinventing.[139] I will note here only his suggestion, shared by other scholars, that the simultaneous publication of Ribadeneyra's history in six cities across the

---

134   Scully, "Confident Hope," 644–45.

135   Carlos Gómez-Centurión Jiménez notes that "it appears rather a text conceived in a distinct mode, given its intrinsic wholeness, and produced for a swifter distribution [*parece más bien un texto concebido de forma independiente, con su entidad particular y destinado a una difusión más ágil*]." Carlos Gómez-Centurión Jiménez, *La Invencible y la empresa de Inglaterra* (Madrid: Editorial Nerea, 1988), 67.

136   Bireley, *Counter-Reformation Prince*, 114.

137   Italics mine.

138   Domínguez, "History in Action," 21.

139   See Domínguez, "Paper and Pens" and Domínguez, "History in Action,"

Habsburg dominions was achieved with royal financial support.[140] Whether or not the *Historia* was an official or semi-official part of the preparations for the Armada, it is hard to disagree with the conclusion of Robert Bireley, S.J. that the text sought to "prepare the Spanish people for the coming Armada."[141]

Despite all these efforts to prepare soldiers, sailors, and Spain itself, the modern reader will know how completely the enterprise of England failed. The Armada set sail as a fleet of 130 ships; roughly half made it back to Spain. A costly but ultimately indecisive battle in the English Channel off Gravelines prevented the Armada from rendezvousing with the Spanish army in the Low Countries; the remaining ships were forced to straggle homeward on a torturous route around Scotland and Ireland. All told, between fifteen and twenty thousand men lost their lives—some in battle, many more in the dozens of shipwrecks over the course of the long retreat. Far from the stormy waters of the Channel, all of Spain eagerly awaited news. In mid-August, there were rumors of victory—the ever-phlegmatic Philip replied only, "I hope it's true," and refused to celebrate without further confirmation. Within a few days, however, more accurate information dispelled any such hopes. Supposedly, Philip met the disastrous news with similar stoicism, saying, "I give thanks to God, whose generous hand has helped me with strength and troops, and will make it possible for me to raise another armada. It does not much matter if the flow of water is cut off, so long as its source is still running."[142] Royal fortitude notwithstanding, it is difficult to exaggerate the shock of the Armada's failure, and the sense of *desengaño* (disillusionment) that began to settle over Spain.[143] Rey is hyperbolic on this point: "In days, almost in hours, an entire nation passed from the joyous optimism and confidence of the Spain of the victories of the Catholic Kings, of Charles V, and of Philip II himself, to the disillusionment of

---

140   Madrid, Valencia, Zaragoza, Barcelona, Antwerp, and Lisbon. For the full publication history, see bibliography. Domínguez, "Paper and Pens," 139. M.J. Rodríguez-Salgado, "The Anglo-Spanish War: The Final Episode of the 'Wars of the Roses'?," in *England, Spain, and the Gran Armada 1585–1604: Essays from the Anglo-Spanish Conferences London and Madrid 1988*, ed. M.J. Rodríguez-Salgado and Simon Adams, 1–44 (Edinburgh: John Donald Publishers, 1991), 37n65.

        Ribadeneyra himself offers some evidence for this conjecture: in his dedicatory epistle to the *Segunda parte*, he mentions to Prince Philip how he published the first volume "under Your Highness's name and favor [*nombre y amparo*]" (551).

141   Bireley, *Counter-Reformation Prince*, 133.

142   Henry Kamen, *Philip of Spain* (New Haven: Yale University Press, 1997), 274–76. MacCaffrey, *Elizabeth I* (London: Edward Arnold, 1993), 238–40.

143   Scully, "Confident Hope," 662. Bireley, *Counter-Reformation Prince*, 111.

the Invincible [Armada]."[144] Ribadeneyra himself had recognized that Spanish military adventures were provoking discontent as early as 1580, a feeling the Armada only intensified.[145]

Whatever the impact on Spain as a whole, for Ribadeneyra the shock of 1588 was profound and enduring. Uppermost in his mind was a basic question of theodicy: if divine providence governed history, how could it be that God had allowed heretics to triumph over Catholics?[146] He himself put it quite acutely:

> What is astounding is that it seems God is abandoning his own in a cause so much his own, that the heretic is left victorious and the Catholic wretched and afflicted. And this gives an opportunity to the weak and the ignorant to imagine that God either has no providence for human events, or that he does not govern them justly, or that what is true is false and what is a life and falsehood is true.[147]

The possibility that God might actually *favor* the heretics was, of course, unthinkable. Confronted with the need to explain this painful defeat, Ribadeneyra turned inward: in a letter-*memorial* addressed to the prominent courtier Juan de Idiáquez y Olazábal (1540–1614), he brooded, "there are weighty reasons for God our Lord having sent us this trial" (756). These he identified with the many sins and abuses embedded in Spanish society and government: the failure to succor the poor, the neglect of religiosity in favor of temporal glory, royal interference in ecclesiastical affairs.[148] These charges are fairly commonplace,

---

144   "En días, casi en horas, todo un pueblo pasa del optimismo alegre y confiado de la España victoria de los Reyes Católicos, de Carlos V y del propio Felipe II, a la desilusión de la Invencible." Rey, cxxv.

145   *MHSIR*, 2:23–28.

    Some have queried how persistent this depression proved: Robert E. Scully, S.J. argues that "a sense of propriety and trust in the ways of God was maintained," and that eventually "the Spanish mood of despair was transformed into one of defiance and renewed confidence in the rightness of their cause." Scully, "Confident Hope," 664.

146   Bireley, *Counter-Reformation Prince*, 111.

147   "Porque lo que mas admira es, que parece que Dios desampara à los suyos en vna causa tan suya, y que se queda el herege como triunfando, y el Catolico lloroso y afligido: y que se da ocasion à los flacos è ignorantes, para que piensen, ò que Dios no tiene prouidencia de las cosas humanas, ò que no las gouierna con rectitud, ò que es falso lo que es verdad, y verdad lo que es mentira y falsedad." Pedro de Ribadeneyra, *Tratado de la tribulacion, repartido en dos libros* (Madrid: Pedro Madrigal, 1589), 142^r–142^v.

148   See Appendix 2.

although the last takes on greater significance in light of the *Historia*'s repeated critiques of Elizabeth's claim to supremacy over the English church, as well as the sensitive issue of royal involvement in the Society of Jesus raised by the *memorialistas* controversy.

In a more explicitly theological and theoretical, but ultimately similar vein, we have Ribadeneyra's *Tratado de la tribulación*, published in Madrid in 1589. A treatise on the spiritual benefits of adversity, the *Tratado* is an attempt to provide a theological solution to the emotional challenge of national trauma, that pervasive sense of *desengaño*. As Ribadeneyra explains, "The trials and calamities of these wretched times are such as have compelled me, for some solace and relief, to write this treatise on tribulation."[149] Though he begins with personal tribulations, the thrust of his argument is in the second book, where he deals with "general tribulations [*tribulaciones generales*]." Here the connection to the Armada becomes patently obvious:

> The greater marvel is that a grand and mighty fleet, which seemed invincible, intended for dedication to the cause of God and his holy Catholic faith and accompanied with so many prayers, vows, and penances from his faithful and his servants, should be undone and lost, in a manner so unusual as to admit of no denial that it was a scourge and severe chastisement from the hand of the Most High.[150]

Throughout, his basic conclusion is twofold: first, that "the Lord would never permit evils in the world except to draw out of them other, greater, and more important goods."[151] Added to this is the well-worn mantra that tribulation is a sign of God's favor, just as a father punishes the child he loves.[152] As Bireley summarizes,

---

149   "Los trabajos y calamidades destos tie[m]pos miserables son de manera, que me han obligado, para alguno consuelo y remedio dellos, à escriuir este tratado de la Tribulacion." Ribadeneyra, *Tratado de la tribulacion*, n.p.

150   "Mayor marauilla es que vna Armada grande, y poderosa, y que parecia inuencible, aprestada para boluer por la causa de Dios, y su santa Fê Catolica, y acompañada de tantas oraciones, y plegarias, y penitencias de sus fieles y sieruos, se aya deshecho, y perdido por vna manera tan estraña, que no se puede negar, sino que es açote y seuero castigo de la mano del muy alto." Ibid., 142ʳ.

151   "el Señor no permitiria males en el mundo, sino fuesse para sacar dellos otros mayores, y mas importantes bienes." Ibid., 19ᵛ. Cf. Ibid., 144ᵛ.

152   E.g., Ibid., 25ʳ.

       Cf. Walsham, *Providence*, 15–16; Houliston, "Missionary Position," 22.

Ribadeneira made a valiant effort to show why God allowed heresy. His power was glorified in the victory over it; his wisdom was manifested in that he raised up teachers to refute the heretics; his goodness was revealed in that he inspired men to die for the faith; the presence of heresy was a test of faith.[153]

Coming hard on the heels of the Armada, this might (perhaps uncharitably) be characterized as one of history's least convincing dismissals of sour grapes.

As Geoffrey Parker puts it, Ribadeneyra "portrayed God's cause, Philip's cause and Spain's cause as all one."[154] In his 2001 Prothero Lecture to the Royal Historical Society, Parker traced the messianic, providentialist strain in Philip II's thought—especially in his approach to geopolitics—a mingling of the political and the theological that finds echoes in Ribadeneyra and in other contemporaries, particularly in the years surrounding the Armada, when spiritual aims seemed inextricably tied to military fortunes.[155] Indeed, balancing the political and the religious proved a persistent problem for the Jesuit mission (and for its historians): Were the fathers simply ministering to the Catholic faithful, as they protested, or did their efforts shade into political agitation, as the regime charged? Scholarship remains divided on this question,[156] but Houliston is right to argue that "the political and pastoral options" were always part of the same conversation.[157] For Ribadeneyra, as for many of his contemporaries, "the political and the theological cannot be separated."[158] Where the Toledan Jesuit differs from his fellows, however, is how important history and historiography would be in his deeper and more visceral responses to the Armada.

The Second Volume of the *Historia*

Some five years after the disaster of the Armada, Ribadeneyra published a continuation of the *Historia*, the *Segunda parte de la historia eclesiástica del scisma*

---

153   Bireley, *Counter-Reformation Prince*, 115.

154   Parker, "Tudor England," 173.

155   Ibid., 174, 179–80, 191, 207–08.

156   E.g., Michael L. Carrafiello, "English Catholicism and the Jesuit Mission of 1580–1581," *HJ* 37, no. 4 (December 1994): 761–74. Peter Lake and Michael C. Questier, "Puritans, Papists, and the 'Public Sphere' in Early Modern England: The Edmund Campion Affair in Context," *Journal of Modern History* 72, no. 3 (September 2000): 587–627; Kilroy, "Paths Coincident."

157   Victor Houliston, *Catholic Resistance in Elizabethan England: Robert Persons's Jesuit Polemic, 1580–1610*, Catholic Christendom, 1300–1700 (Aldershot: Ashgate, 2007), 48.

158   "lo político y lo teológico no se pueden separar." Torres Olleta, "Imágenes," 71.

de Inglaterra.[159] Picking up the narrative just *after* the English victory, this second volume narrates the trials and travails of English Catholics at home and abroad, focusing on Elizabeth's proclamation of October 18, 1591, denouncing Jesuits and other Catholics as traitors and lambasting Philip II and the pope for their aggressive anti-Protestant foreign policy. The Armada itself is mentioned explicitly only once in the whole of the *Historia*, at the beginning of Book 3, Chapter 1, in Ribadeneyra's gloomy observation, "After the queen and her councilors saw themselves free of their fear and anxiety about the Spanish Armada, straightway they turned like lions against the kingdom's Catholics, to persecute and eradicate them" (557). This elision of the Armada has prompted scholars—when they consider the *Segunda parte* at all—to neglect the importance of the naval disaster for Ribadeneyra's continued work on the *Historia*, except insofar as the expedition intensified the persecutions he recounts. I argue that if the first volume sought to lay the ground for the Armada, the second is a logical and fitting counterpart to the letter-memorial and the *Tratado*: part of Ribadeneyra's struggle to exorcise the ghost of the expedition's failure.[160]

To some extent, this is done by retreading familiar ground: even more than the first volume, the *Segunda parte* catalogs the cruelty and sinfulness of the Anglican regime. In this respect, the second volume does no more than reaffirm Ribadeneyra's basic dichotomy between Catholic virtue and heretical vice, and the desperate insistence that defeat was not proof of God's abandonment. And yet, in the aftermath of the Armada, this construction has undergone a subtle shift, a phenomenon observable in the two volumes' distinct uses of Christian history. In the first part, sacred history is marshaled for authentication: the Catholic martyrs are genuine martyrs because they follow a long tradition of martyrs stretching back to the earliest Roman persecutions, right up to the Bible itself. Campion, for example, is paralleled with both Attalus, a second-century martyr described in Eusebius's *Ecclesiastical History*, and Saint Paul. Briant, we are told, "seemed one of those valiant, unconquerable martyrs of the times of Nero, Decius, or Diocletian" (469). Book 2, Chapter 34 counters Protestant claims that the "martyrs" died as traitors with dozens of examples from sacred history of the specious grounds used to put Christians to death. Ribadeneyra here echoes an argument common to all confessions of the Reformation—that persecution proved authenticity. In Gregory's felicitous phrase, Catholics, Protestants, and Anabaptists alike sought to create

---

159 Pedro de Ribadeneyra, *Segunda parte de la historia ecclesiastica del scisma de Inglaterra* (Alcalá de Henares: En casa de Juan Íñiguez de Lequerica, 1593).

160 Bireley regards the *Segunda parte* as the application of the *Tratado*'s general principles to the specific case of England, but his analysis attenuates any particular connection to the Armada. Bireley, *Counter-Reformation Prince*, 115.

"pedigrees of the persecuted," proving the likeness of their martyrs to those of former ages.[161] We have already observed how Ribadeneyra incorporates the long tradition of church history into the *Historia*, both explicitly and implicitly. As I have argued elsewhere, Ribadeneyra was, among other things, using the *Historia* to prove the theological and historical *bona fides* of the Society of Jesus, positioning the order as only the most recent stage in the long history of Catholic martyrdom.[162]

The historicizing of the *Segunda parte*, though it draws on many of the same sources and examples, has a different chronological orientation. It argues that *because* the Catholic martyrs are just like earlier martyrs, they will ultimately achieve the same victory. Here we see at work one of the intellectual underpinnings of providentialist thought, "the assumed interchangeability of past and present"—the mechanics of history do not change over time.[163] Where the claim of the first volume is essentially descriptive, that of the second is predictive, at times even shading into the normative:

> How many persecutions has the Catholic Church suffered hitherto, from the Jews, the pagans, the Moors, the Roman emperors, the barbarian kings, the Goths, the Vandals, the Huns, the Lombards, and from the heretics: the Novatians, the Arians, the Donatists, the Eutychians, the Iconoclasts, the Albigensians, the Hussites, the Calvinists, and innumerable other sects of perdition? They are so many that they cannot be counted, and so extreme that they can hardly be believed. The truth has conquered them all, the Church has triumphed over them all, and has always grown greater, watered by the blood of its blessed defenders—for the more who died, the more were born and multiplied in its defense (713).

As the catalog of foes adduced above indicates, Ribadeneyra ransacks every period of Christian history for parallels to the English persecution of Catholics. The (divine) reason for the existence of and his emphasis on these comparisons, he explains, is

> to teach us the similarity and correspondence between this present persecution and the ancient ones, and we may learn that the author of the past ones is also that of the present one, and *just as they concluded,*

---

161   Gregory, *Salvation at Stake*, 6.
162   Weinreich, "Distinctiveness," 182–85.
163   Walsham, *Providence*, 286.

this will conclude, and the sacred Church triumph over those who now oppress it (614).[164]

The same use is made of his patristic and biblical sources: he cites Augustine's *Creed* (*c*.425), for instance, to the effect that

> this is the holy Church, the one Church, the true Church, the Catholic Church that fights against every heresy. The struggle may be fierce, but it can never be defeated. Every heresy has departed from it, like barren shoots cut off from the vine, while it remains forever firm in its roots, for the very gates of hell cannot conquer it (717).[165]

Similar examples could be produced *ad infinitum*; to get a sense of the sheer omnivorousness at work, it is worth listing the sources cited in just the last paragraph of the *Historia*: Plutarch's (*c*.45–120) *Moralia* (*c*.100); the story of Hezekiah in 4 Kings and 2 Chronicles; Augustine's *The City of God* (426); and Ambrose of Milan's (*c*.340–97) *Hexameron* (*c*.388).

Here we see Ribadeneyra's emphasis on divine providence coming back to haunt him: (theo)logically, he must accept that the failure of the Armada and the continued reign of Elizabeth are willed by God.[166] Simultaneously, these disturbing facts cannot be, *must* not be the Lord's final verdict. His solution is neatly expressed in an aphorism of the Brazilian author and journalist Fernando Sabino: "Tudo neste mundo no fim dá certo. Se não deu, é porque ainda não chegou ao fim" (In the end, all will be right with the world. If it is not, it is because the end has not yet come).[167] Unable or unwilling to question directly the assumptions of heresy, orthodoxy, and divine favor undergirding his worldview, Ribadeneyra turns to history to address them obliquely, by "relocating" the present persecution in the midst (rather than the end) of the cycle of tribulation. He made a similar intellectual move in the *Tratado de la tribulación*, filling an entire chapter with examples from history of enterprises

---

164 Italics mine.

165 Augustine, *Creed*, 1.6.

166 Providentialist interpretations of the Armada have understandably been associated primarily with Protestant countries. However, these modes of thought were ubiquitous in early modern Europe, and Catholic thinkers, too, employed them in attempting to understand the Armada. Scully, "Confident Hope," 660–61. Thomas M. McCoog, *The Society of Jesus in Ireland, Scotland, and England, 1589–1597: Building the Faith of Saint Peter upon the King of Spain's Monarchy*, Biblioteca Instituti Historici Societatis Iesu 73 (Farnham: Ashgate, 2012), 16.

167 Fernando Tavares Sabino, *No Fim dá certo* (Rio de Janeiro: Editora Record, 1998), 217.

that failed repeatedly before succeeding (e.g., Roman invasions of Britain).[168] Multiplying these examples is a way of reinforcing his belief in the eventual vindication of the Catholic Church.[169]

The deployment of ecclesiastical history on display in the first volume of the *Historia* is familiar to any scholar of the Reformation: the past "as legitimation for the present."[170] Each confession constructed its own story of Christian history, intended at once to demonstrate its own legitimacy and disprove others'. Catholicism in particular turned to sacred history to establish the continuity of the Roman church with the earliest days of Christianity—and in the specific case of the British Isles, that what Catholic missionaries intended to do was *restore* the islands' ancient faith, rather than introduce a new one.[171] Such debates drew strength from the foundational principle of Renaissance Christian humanism: "the oldest and most primitive expression of something represented its essential and perfect form."[172] In such an atmosphere, appeals to the history of the Church became commonplace, a crucial intellectual vehicle for advancing and defending confessional claims. Ink-and-paper battles were waged over confessional "ownership" of historical notables like Constantine (r.306–37) or Lucius, the mythical second-century king of the Britons.[173] Legitimacy, whether for a belief, a denomination, or a martyr, was found in claiming links to and similarities with the sacred past.

Understanding the *Segunda parte* as working through the trauma of the Spanish Armada suggests a very different, emotional use for history, unconnected to polemic, whether inter- or intra-confessional. The historically aware Catholic could find solace both in contemplating the conclusion of previous

---

168   Ribadeneyra, *Tratado de la tribulacion*, Book 2, Chapter 14.

169   Compare Giuseppe Antonio Guazzelli's description of Cesare Baronio: "He viewed the successive defeat of these various groups of heretics, in providential terms, as further proof that Rome was the one true Church and that, by implication, it would be victorious over and against the latest, Protestant, heresies." Giuseppe Antonio Guazzelli, "Cesare Baronio and the Roman Catholic Vision of the Early Church," in *Sacred History: Uses of the Christian Past in the Renaissance World*, ed. Katherine Van Liere, Simon Ditchfield, and Howard Louthan (Oxford: Oxford University Press, 2012), 52–71, here 61.

       Consider, too, Persons's use of history to counter Protestant narratives: see Houliston, *Catholic Resistance*, 112–16.

170   Heal, "Appropriating History," 109.

171   Gregory, *Salvation at Stake*, 251. Dillon, *Construction of Martyrdom*, 87. Monta, *Martyrdom and Literature*, 35.

172   Van Liere, Ditchfield, and Louthan, *Sacred History*, 28.

173   Highley, *Catholics Writing the Nation*, 173. Felicity Heal, "What Can King Lucius Do for You? The Reformation and the Early British Church," *EHR* 120, no. 487 (June 2005): 593–614.

persecutions *and* in refashioning current events into a similar narrative. To do so was of course also to reaffirm the historical authenticity of the Catholic faith, but I would argue that the primary motivation here is not intellectual, doctrinal, or polemical, but rather personal and emotional. A possible inspiration here may be Ribadeneyra's lifelong affinity for the Roman philosopher Seneca the Younger (*c*.4 BCE–65 CE) and for Stoic thought more generally. Book 1, Chapter 18 of the *Tratado de la tribulación* consists of excerpts from Seneca's writings, many of them urging readers in despair to compare their situations with those of (less fortunate) others.[174] Whether or not this emotional work of contextualization comes from Seneca, rewriting the narrative of Catholic defeats through historicization was a way of staving off despair.

Quite understandably, the failure of the Armada dampened Spanish enthusiasm for military expeditions to England.[175] The second volume of the *Historia* does not have the first's interventionist agenda, focusing instead on the tenacious faith of the English Catholics and implicitly looking to divine providence for a solution to the kingdom's woes. This is not to say that the *Segunda parte* confines itself to sixteenth-century England—far from it. Ribadeneyra draws on an even wider array of historical and contemporary texts in crafting his narrative of oppression and martyrdom. Freed from (or deprived of) reliance on Sander, Ribadeneyra turned to the copious literary production of the English exiles, whose anti-Elizabethan works circulated widely in English, Latin, Spanish, and Italian. To be sure, the five years between 1588 and 1593 do not offer the widest of historical canvasses, particularly when one is compelled to pass over the Armada in pained silence. Nevertheless, Ribadeneyra finds ample scope in those years to fill his pages.

The centerpiece of the *Segunda parte* is Elizabeth's edict of October 18, 1591, condemning Catholics (with special venom reserved for priests and Jesuits), Philip II, and the pope. The decree also instituted a system of surveillance and investigation to root out such undesirables. Ribadeneyra translates the decree into Spanish, then proceeds to address its various charges systematically. Prosecuting this rebuttal leads him to discuss the wars of Henry IV of

---

174 Ribadeneyra, *Tratado de la tribulacion*, Book 2, Chapter 18.

175 It should be recalled, however, that the disasters of 1588 did not mark a definitive end to Spanish attempts to invade England. Several plans were mooted, including landings at various ports in Ireland, Wales, and England, as well as attacks on Protestant strongholds on mainland Europe. Fleets sailed in 1596 and 1597, with no better success than their predecessor of 1588. See Edward Tenace, "A Strategy of Reaction: The Armadas of 1596 and 1597 and the Spanish Struggle for European Hegemony," *EHR* 118, no. 478 (September 2003): 855–82.

France (r.1589–1610), the arrival of Japanese Christians in Europe in the Tenshō Embassy (1582–90), and a history of miraculous apparitions of crosses. It is ultimately the English martyrs, however, who dominate the *Segunda parte*. In addition to telling many of their stories in detail, Ribadeneyra ends his book with "a brief account of the martyrs who have departed the English colleges and seminaries at Rome and Rheims in France, and suffered in England in defense of the Catholic faith" (728), a catalog of the seminarians martyred between 1577 and 1592.[176] Even to the modern scholar, many of these tales make gripping reading, a mixture of triumphant escapes and heroic martyrdoms, miracles and sheer human grit, pathos and humor, exalted religiosity and gruesome torments. In light of what we have said about Ribadeneyra's efforts to "popularize" history, it is worth observing that many of these stories previously circulated only in Latin, or as private letters, or in erudite forms (and generally lacked the readability with which the *Historia* endows them).

That the second volume of the *Historia* picks up almost exactly where the first left off should not obscure the significant differences in the two volumes' chronologies. Where Books 1 and 2 of the *Historia* cover almost one hundred years between them, Book 3 spans a mere five. Moreover, the relationship between reader and subject has shifted radically. The vast majority of the first volume's narrative occurred a generation or more before its publication: Elizabeth's accession in 1558, for example, comes almost halfway through Book 2. By contrast, the events of Book 3, if not necessarily familiar to Ribadeneyra's Spanish audience, are at least part of the immediate past. To borrow the terminology of modern genre, it is a transition from (recent) history to current events. This was not without its dangers: alterations in European geopolitics could swiftly render such a text embarrassingly inaccurate at best, perilously offensive at worst. Fears of such a fate nearly brought about the suppression of the first volume of the *Historia*, as we saw; the second volume, even more closely tied to contemporary events, ran headlong into the same sort of problem—not once, but twice.

The first mishap came in 1593–94 with the first printings of the *Segunda parte*: specifically, it was Ribadeneyra's treatment of Elizabeth's vitriolic edict that proved troublesome. The details of the incident are unclear, and what

---

176   The catalog is adapted from Juan López Manzano, *Breve catalogo de los martyres que han sido de los dos collegios y seminarios ingleses, que residen en Roma, y en la ciudad de Rhemis de Francia, los quales han padecidos tormentos y muertes en Inglaterra, en estos treze años passados, por la defension de la fee Catholica, por mandado de la Reyna, fuera de otros muchos de todo genero de personas, que tambien han sido martyrizados, aunque no eran destos collegios* (Valladolid: Diego Fernández de Cordova y Oviedo, 1590). See Appendix 5.

follows is a somewhat tentative reconstruction. In July 1593, the *Segunda parte* was published in Alcalá de Henares as a standalone volume. In this version, Chapter 16 ("16a"), "The edict the queen promulgated against our sacred religion, and against the pope, and the Catholic King, who defend it," consisted of a (slightly abridged) translation of the edict, followed by Ribadeneyra's response. Evidently, some at the court in Madrid were concerned about the advisability of the text of the edict, with its scurrilous attacks on the king and the pope, circulating so widely. A letter dated November 18, 1593, from Hernando Lucero (d.1625), the provincial of Toledo, is our primary witness to the consequent royal intervention:

> On the last day of October, in the twelfth hour of the night, I received a courier with a letter from my lord the president of [the Council of] Castile,[177] in which, by order of His Majesty, he commanded the recall of every copy of the *Segunda parte de la historia de Inglaterra* that Father Pedro de Ribadeneyra had printed only a few months ago, because it seems highly inappropriate to those in the government that the edict the queen of England promulgated against the pope, the king, and Catholics should circulate in the Castilian vernacular, to be read by all sorts of people. I received this and obeyed, and arranged to collect the books in the house here, and from the booksellers elsewhere, and I wrote to Father Ribadeneyra and to the father rector of Madrid about what had happened, so that they should do the same and inform me as to which other colleges have books, for the like purpose. I worry lest they demand to have all those sold to laypeople collected by means of the Inquisition, which would be a noisy business and many people would suppose it was done for the sake of wicked doctrine, rather than the other ends at which it aimed. Father Ribadeneyra has written to me that he has already appealed to my lord president with the news I gave him, and that he has hopes that the execution of all this will be suspended. I have learned for a certainty that this mandate was the *motu proprio* of the king, who recently read the book and made the aforesaid intervention.[178]

---

177 Rodrigo Vázquez de Arce (d.1599), president of the Council of Castile from 1591 until his death.

178 "Ultimo de octubre, a las doce horas de la noche tuvo un propio y carta del señor Presidente de Castilla, en que, por orden de Su Majestad, mandaba se recogiesen todos los libros de la *Segunda Parte de la Historia de Inglaterra*, que últimamente, pocos meses ha, imprimió el Padre Pedro de Ribadeneyra, por parecerles en gobierno de Estado mucho inconveniente que aquel Edicto que sacó la Reina de Inglaterra contra el Papa y Rey y

And so the *Segunda parte* was recalled, and the chapter replaced. The revised version of Chapter 16 ("16b") provided only "a summary of the most important things the queen says in her edict," with commentary inserted throughout. Collections of Ribadeneyra's writings published in 1595 and 1605 would also use this redaction.

This relatively straightforward sequence is disturbed by two irregularities. First, there are copies of the *Segunda parte* dated 1593 with the revised chapter (16b). This is hardly irresolvable: it may be that prompt obedience to royal commands had the second redaction coming off the presses before the year was out. Alternatively, the revised version may have been printed in early 1594, but the printers neglected or declined to alter the title page.[179] More puzzling are the 1594 editions from Antwerp and Lisbon, both of which retain Chapter 16a.[180] Here, too, several explanations are possible: Philip may only have been worried about publications within Spain, the passage of a year may have relieved some of the pressure, or the presses outside of Spain may have published the *Historia* unaware of (or unconcerned with) the royal fiat. In any case,

---

católicos ande en vulgar castellano y que lo pueda leer todo género de gente. Yo lo recibí, obedeciendo, e hice recoger los libros que había aquí, en casa, y en los libreros de fuera, y escribí al Padre Ribadeneyra y al Padre Rector de Madrid de lo que pasaba y que ellos hiciesen allí otro tanto y me aviasen en qué otros colegios había libros para lo mismo. Los que están vendidos a seglares, que son muchos, temo no los quisiesen recoger por vía de Inquisición, que sería negocio de mucho ruido y pensarían muchos se hacía por mala doctrina lo que iba por otro término. El Padre Ribadeneyra me ha escrito que ha acudido ya con la nueva que yo le di al señor Presidente y que tiene esperanzas que se suspenderá la ejecución de todo. He sabido por ciencia cierta que ese mandato fué '*motu proprio*' del Rey, que leía aquel libro actualmente y reparó en lo dicho." Quoted in Rey, 885.

Spanish censorship in this period was often driven by the concerns of individual courtiers and officials, as well as royal wishes—Philip II had long been leery of histories of contemporary events, and was only gradually coming to embrace them in the 1580s. See Antonio Domínguez Ortiz, "La censura de obras históricas en el siglo XVII español," *Chronica nova* 9 (1991): 113–21; Kagan, "Antonio de Herrera," 281.

179   Consequently, there are copies of the *Segunda parte* with identical publication details (Alcalá de Henares: En casa de Juan Íñiguez de Lequerica, 1593) but distinct versions of Chapter 16. I have examined two copies, and can attest that the volume held as Österreichische Nationalbibliothek 42.Z.36 contains Chapter 16a, while British Library 704.b.39 contains Chapter 16b.

180   Pedro de Ribadeneyra, *Historia ecclesiastica del scisma del reyno de Inglaterra* (Antwerp: En casa de Martin Nucio a las dos Cyguenas, 1594); Pedro de Ribadeneyra, *Segunda parte de la historia ecclesiastica del scisma de Inglaterra* (Lisbon: En casa de Manoel de Lira, 1594).

the publication history of Ribadeneyra's text is thornier even than its most assiduous scholars have yet acknowledged—and its complexities continued in the years to come.

The second problem arose over Book 3, Chapter 18, in which Ribadeneyra refutes Elizabeth's charge that Philip II's war against Henry IV of France is "utterly unjust." Like all evangelically inclined rulers in the *Historia*, Henry IV is depicted as a "bloodthirsty wolf," a "heretical tyrant" (644, 646). His claims to the throne are specious, his means nefarious, and his ends nothing less than the total subjection of France's Catholics. In 1593, however, Henry converted to Catholicism in order to neutralize Catholic resistance and secure control of France, supposedly quipping, "Paris is well worth a Mass." Ribadeneyra was thus in the awkward position of having written and published a sharp-tongued attack on a Catholic monarch. Yet it was only in the 1605 edition that he appended a "note to the reader" to Chapter 18, explaining that it was written while Henry was still a heretic. Why did the various editions of 1594 and 1595 pass over the matter in silence? The alacrity with which Chapter 16 was revised in accordance with royal instructions makes it difficult to argue that Ribadeneyra did not have the time or ability to change the text—clearly, he could have done so had he so wished. That he did not may stem from his habitual suspicion of Protestant rulers' moves toward Catholicism: consider his dismissal of Henry VIII's Six Articles in Book 1, Chapter 35. Perhaps it was only after more than a decade of solidly Catholic rule that Ribadeneyra felt obligated to add a caveat (and without, it should be observed, removing or altering the vitriolic chapter). I suggest, however, that the timing had more to do with secular considerations: Henry may have become a Catholic in 1593, but his war with Spain continued until the Peace of Vervins in 1598. Tellingly, Ribadeneyra seems to have supported Philip II's controversial decision to abandon the French Catholic League and recognize Henry's claim to the throne.[181] By 1605, Henry was Spain's ally of several years' standing, and so merited greater deference.

Such changes speak to the role Ribadeneyra saw his history playing in contemporary geopolitics. It was alive to changing circumstances, but self-consciously Spanish in its allegiance: Ribadeneyra coordinates his authorial interventions with Spanish diplomatic positions. Above all, he did not see publication, either in 1588 or 1593, as the conclusion of the *Historia*'s intellectual project, continuing to work with and upon his history for nearly twenty years.

---

181   Bireley, *Counter-Reformation Prince*, 122.

A Textual History of the *Historia*

One of the reasons for a translation of the *Historia* is the inadequate appreciation among existing editions of the work's complex textual history. While the progression from Sander to Ribadeneyra and from the first volume to the second are well known, even Eusebio Rey, in preparing an otherwise-excellent Spanish edition, either failed to notice or neglected to note numerous small changes between printings, such as the insertion of additional descriptive clauses or the deletion of a modifier. Such alterations are at first glance insignificant—and it is true that they rarely affect anything more than a sentence or two. They are nonetheless worthy of note, as proof of Ribadeneyra's continuing interest in and commitment to the project over the years.[182]

I hasten to add, however, that in many cases no corrections were made to account for changed circumstances: to take but a single example, Philip Howard, thirteenth earl of Arundel (1557–95), died on October 19, 1595, but the 1605 edition of the *Historia* speaks of him as still languishing in prison. Significantly, the failure of the Armada did not prompt Ribadeneyra to moderate the jingoism of the first volume.

A similarly meaningful omission is the 1605 edition's failure to mention Elizabeth I's death on March 24, 1603. One is tempted to point to Ribadeneyra's advanced age (seventy-six at the queen's death, seventy-eight when the book was published) and the long gap between editions as evidence that Ribadeneyra had neither the energy nor the interest for rewriting the *Historia*. Yet we must remember the disclaimer concerning Henry IV of France—an indication that Ribadeneyra had not closed the book, so to speak, on the *Historia*. Of course, it is one thing to pen a "note to the reader" of fewer than a thousand words, quite another to rework a multi-volume history to insert ten years' worth of new events. The hate-figure of Elizabeth is integral to the structure of the *Historia*: the entirety of the third book is an extended attack on the queen and her government. To remove her from the stage a few pages before the end would unbalance the whole text, leaving the accession of James VI and I (r.1567–1625) an utter anticlimax. Moreover, how much, from Ribadeneyra's perspective, had really changed? One "heretical" ruler had been succeeded by another: the schism from Rome would continue, as would the persecution of Catholics.[183]

---

182   A similar process of edits and revisions took place across the various printing of Ribadeneyra's biography of Ignatius. See Dalmases, "Orígenes de la hagiografía ignaciana," especially Chapter 5.

183   "Robert Parsons had high expectations that the death of Elizabeth and the succession of James VI as king of England would change everything for his persecuted countrymen. In

On the other hand, just as Ribadeneyra may have been adhering to Spanish diplomatic positioning vis-à-vis Henry IV, we might see his elision of James as a nod to the new tone of Anglo-Spanish relations. Soon after his accession, James I indicated his interest in ending his predecessor's war with Spain, culminating in a 1604 peace treaty. For decades to come, Spanish diplomats regarded the relationship with England as integral to imperial fortunes: "Guerra con toda la tierra y paz con Inglaterra" (war with all of the world and peace with England), ran one maxim.[184] Catholics in England and abroad harbored intermittent hopes that James would grant full toleration, and in the event he proved far more lenient than his predecessor.[185] In such an atmosphere, it would hardly do to publish a history subjecting James to the same attacks Ribadeneyra had leveled against Elizabeth. On balance, in 1605 Ribadeneyra probably had good reason to maintain the basic shape of the *Historia* as he had left it in 1595.

To return to the alterations Ribadeneyra *did* make, what occasioned these changes? Some were unexceptional corrections of errata, either by Ribadeneyra or the printer—although, as Rey observes, "many more were let slip."[186] We have already discussed the two political incidents that prompted alterations to the 1594 and 1605 editions. The other significant factor was the availability of new material—whether related to the religious history of England, or simply of interest to Ribadeneyra. Prominent in this regard are a series of texts published just after the *Historia*: Thomas Stapleton's 1588 biography of Thomas More (*c.*1478–1534);[187] the *Concertatio Ecclesiae Catholicæ in Anglia* (also of 1588), a historical and martyrological compendium edited by John Gibbons (1544–89) and expanded by John Bridgewater (*c.*1532–*c.*1596); and the

---

reality, it appeared scarcely a caesura in the long conflict between Catholic and Protestant." Heal, "Appropriating History," 132.

184 Robert Cross, "Pretense and Perception in the Spanish Match, or History in a Fake Beard," *Journal of Interdisciplinary History* 37, no. 4 (2007): 563–83, here 581–82.

185 Kenneth Fincham and Peter Lake, "The Ecclesiastical Policy of King James I," *Journal of British Studies* 24, no. 2 (April 1985): 169–207, here 182–85.

186 "se deslizaron muchas más." Rey, 888.

187 The biography of More was the third part of Stapleton's *Tres Thomae*, a triple life of Thomas the Apostle, Thomas Becket (*c.*1118–70), and More. Thomas Stapleton, *Tres Thomae seu: De S. Thomæ Apostoli rebus gestis; De S. Thoma archiepiscopo Cantuariensi & Martyre; D. Thomæ Mori Angliæ quondam cancellarij vita* (Douai: Ex officina Ioannis Bogardi, 1588).

Interestingly, one of Stapleton's sources was *De origine ac progressu*; he and Sander had been colleagues at Leuven in the 1570s. Sheils, "Polemic as Piety," 89.

1589 edition of Cesare Baronio's revision of the *Martyrologium Romanum*.[188] In the 1595 edition, Ribadeneyra adds an entirely new chapter on More (Book 1, Chapter 30a) that is essentially an epitome of Stapleton's biography, as well as using several of its anecdotes to expand his existing chapter on the knight. In addition to furnishing copious narrative material for Book 3, the *Concertatio* provided Ribadeneyra with primary sources by the martyrs, especially the Jesuits (e.g., Campion's "Brag," Briant's letters), which found their way into later versions of Books 1 and 2. The *Martyrologium Romanum*, with its extensive critical apparatus, proved invaluable to the *Historia*'s work of historicizing the English martyrs.

It is worth asking how many of these changes were Ribadeneyra's doing. Rey sees him as essentially passive: "Ribadeneyra permitted adjustments and additions in the various new editions of his books."[189] No doubt this was the case in at least some of the smaller adjustments—the deletion in 1595 of a single word from the opening paragraph of Book 1, Chapter 40, for example. Yet Ribadeneyra remained an active writer to the end of his life, and so we cannot automatically discount all of the additions, deletions, and changes as purely incidental. Whatever the answer, the text evolved edition by edition over the course of the author's lifetime: multiple printings of the first volume in 1588 and 1589; the second volume, published separately in 1593 and 1594, and together with the first in 1594; and both parts included in collections of Ribadeneyra's works in 1595 and 1605. The textual history came full circle in 1610, when Ribadeneyra's third part was translated into Latin and appended to a new edition of Sander's *De origine ac progressu* (Ribadeneyra's changes to *De origine ac progressu*, however, were not replicated—that text remained as it had in 1586).[190]

It is with Sander that discussion of Ribadeneyra's sources tends to begin and end. The precise relationship between *De origine ac progressu* and the *Historia* has been analyzed with varying levels of sophistication,[191] but it is worth repeating that Ribadeneyra did not simply translate *De origine ac progressu* as he

---

188   Cesare Baronio, *Martyrologium Romanum, ad novam kalendarii rationem, et ecclesiasticae historiae veritatem restitutum: Gregorii XIII pontificis maximi jussu editum; Accesserunt notationes atque tractatio de martyrologio Romano* (Antwerp: Christophe Plantin, 1589).

189   "Ribadeneyra se permitió retoques y añadiduras en las diversas reediciones de sus libros." Ribadeneyra, *Historia de la Contrarreforma*, 888n.

190   Nicholas Sander and Pedro de Ribadeneyra, *Nicolai Sanderi Angli doct. theol. de origine ac progressu schismatis anglicani, libri tres* (Cologne: Sumptibus Petri Henningi, 1610).
      The identity of the translator has not survived, but it was probably not Ribadeneyra. Rey, 886n2.

191   Weinreich, "Distinctiveness," 176.

found it. He deleted material he deemed extraneous, inserted new details, and significantly altered the style and structure of the work. But more importantly, even in the first edition of the first volume of the *Historia*—the printing closest to *De origine ac progressu*—Ribadeneyra's sources extend well beyond Sander. To expand the treatment of Mary's reign, he relied upon several Italian sources (published and manuscript), as well as his own time in England. The stories of the Elizabethan martyrs are drawn, sometimes verbatim, from William Allen's writings, available to Ribadeneyra in Italian translation.[192] Much of the chapter on the queen of Scots comes from various "manuscript reports," as Domínguez notes,[193] but we can also identify several printed sources, foremost among them an anonymous Latin account[194] and the French edition of Adam Blackwood's (1539–1613) biography of the queen.[195] Furthermore, some textual detective work can identify more unorthodox sources: Jane Dormer's reminiscences about Mary, for instance, or manuscripts circulated among Jesuit scholars.[196] In the last analysis, some proportion of Ribadeneyra's "sources" will remain forever unidentified, part of the informal exchange of anecdotes and reminiscences among Catholics on the Continent.

A similar list can be compiled for Book 3, including Robert Persons's *Relaciones de algunos martyrios* (1590), the Spanish Dominican Alfonso Chacón's (1530–99) *De signis sanctissimae crucis* (1591), and the copious controversial literature surrounding Elizabeth's 1591 edict.[197] Ribadeneyra's friendship with

---

192   William Allen, *Historia del glorioso martirio di sedici sacerdoti martirizati in Inghilterra per la confessione, & difesa della fede Catolica, l'anno 1581 1582 & 1583* (Macerata: Sebastiano Martellini, 1583).

193   Domínguez, "History in Action," 11–12.

194   *Mariae Stuartae Scotorum reginæ, principis Catholicae, nuper ab Elizabetha regina, et ordinibus Angliæ, post nouendecim annorum capitiuitatem in arce Fodringhaye interfectæ* (Cologne: Apud Godefridum Kempensem, 1587).

195   Adam Blackwood, *Martyre de la royne d'Escosse douairiere de France: Contenant le vray discours des traisons à elle faictes à la suscitation d'Elizabet Angloise, par lequel les monsonges, calomnies & faulses accusations dressees contre ceste tres uertueuse, tres catholique & tres illustre Princesse sont esclarcies & son innocence aueree* (Antwerp: Gaspar Fleysben, 1588).

196   See Book 2, Chapter 20 and Book 2, Chapter 40, respectively.
        For a discussion of both sources, and of Ribadeneyra's sourcing more generally, see Spencer J. Weinreich, "English Mission, Global Catholicism, Christian History: Providence and Historiography in Pedro de Ribadeneyra's *Historia ecclesiastica del scisma del reyno de Inglaterra*," in *The World is Our House? Jesuit Intellectual and Physical Exchange between England and Mainland Europe*, ed. Hannah J. Thomas and James Kelly, Jesuit Studies (Leiden: Brill, forthcoming).

197   For an overview, see Victor Houliston, "The Lord Treasurer and the Jesuit: Robert Person's Satirical *Responsio* to the 1591 Proclamation," *SCJ* 32, no. 2 (Summer 2001): 383–401.

Persons also kept him supplied with further, unpublished material.[198] We have already mentioned the *Concertatio Ecclesiae Catholicæ* and the letters relating to the Tenshō Embassy (published in Italian in 1593).[199] And in addition to all this, there is the array of classical, patristic, and medieval authors—primarily theologians and church historians—cited, quoted, or alluded to in both volumes. Ribadeneyra was recognized by contemporaries and later scholars alike for his superlative scriptural and patristic learning.[200] To be sure, most early modern Catholic authors turned to ecclesiastical history and historical theology to demonstrate the continuity of Roman doctrine and practice, but Ribadeneyra's range, depth, and diversity of sources outpace even some of his most erudite contemporaries.[201]

Three of these sources in particular are worth singling out: Eusebius, Augustine, and Seneca. As we have noted, the *Historia* self-consciously presents itself as an ecclesiastical history in the tradition of Eusebius, both in its content and in its framing. Eusebius was of course only the first in a long line of church historians—each not only drawing inspiration from their predecessors but often producing self-declared continuations of their work. In citing Eusebius together with many of his intellectual progeny—Rufinus, Socrates Scholasticus (*c.*380–*c.*439), Theodoret (*c.*393–*c.*458), Sozomen (*c.*400–*c.*450)—Ribadeneyra at once reaffirms the essential continuity of (Catholic) church history and claims for himself a position within that lineage.

Among Ribadeneyra's theological sources, pride of place must be given to Augustine. As Rey wrote,

> I do not believe there were many religious writers of the *Siglo de Oro* who internalized certain ascetical aspects of Saint Augustine to a greater degree than Ribadeneyra. [...] From childhood, Ribadeneyra was an enthusiastic reader of the saint, and for the rest of his life there were manifestations of this early influence.[202]

---

198   Houliston, "Missionary Position," 19.

199   Gasparo Spitilli, ed., *Ragguaglio d'alcune missioni dell'Indie orientali, et occidentali, cavato da alcuni avisi scritti gli anni 1590 & 1591* (Naples: Gio. Iacomo Carlino, & Antonio Pace, 1593).

200   Rey, lxiii.

201   This is as true of his political and theological work as it is of his historical work. Bireley, *Counter-Reformation Prince*, 117–18.

202   "No creo existan en el Siglo de Oro muchos escritores piadosos que se hayan asimilado ciertos aspectos ascéticos de San Agustín en grado mayor que Ribadeneyra. [...] Desde su primera juventud Ribadeneyra fué lector asiduo del Santo, y esta influencia mañanera fué tomando a lo largo de su vida manifestaciones tan importantes." Rey, xciii.

Ribadeneyra published Spanish translations of Augustine's *Soliloquies* (386–87) and *Enchiridion* (422), as well as the pseudo-Augustinian *Meditations*.[203] Ribadeneyra's *Confesiones* is transparently an imitation of Augustine's own spiritual memoir, which he also translated into Spanish.[204] Rey has also identified parallels between the structure of the *Tratado de la tribulación* and that of *The City of God*, both attempts to reconcile "heretical" successes with divine justice.[205] It is unsurprising, then, that the *Historia* cites Augustine more frequently than any other theologian, and with an astonishing breadth and depth of knowledge of the saint's *oeuvre*. Alongside familiar works like *The City of God* and *The Confessions*, we find such obscure texts as the *Contra epistolam Parmeniani* (400) and the *Contra Cresconium* (401)—neither of which, tellingly, has even now been translated into English.

As with Augustine, Ribadeneyra's interest in Seneca was deep and lifelong. We have already mentioned the influence of Stoic thought on the *Tratado de la tribulación*.[206] Though Seneca himself is cited only once the *Historia* (Book 3, Chapter 32), reading the *Segunda parte* as a development of the *Tratado* highlights the Stoic element that pervades the history. The *Segunda parte*'s emotional work of deploying history to reframe Catholic defeats bears many resemblances to the Senecan principles adduced in the *Tratado*—Ribadeneyra is here transposing them into a historiographical mode.

Ribadeneyra also assembled an impressive array of sources on recent English history, drawing variously on print, manuscript, and the oral testimonies circulating among Catholic exiles. When new material became available, it was incorporated into the text. In this regard, the *Historia* is not always the most "original" of histories. There are entire chapters that are essentially word-for-word translations or adaptations of other authors' work. At the same time, Ribadeneyra can and does fundamentally repurpose his materials. His attack on Elizabeth's 1591 edict, for example, is mostly an adaptation of Persons's *Philopater*—but where the *Philopater* "is, above everything else, a satirical assault on [William] Cecil [1520–98]" and "begins by dissociating the Edict from the queen,"[207] Ribadeneyra makes every effort to reify that association ("this edict

203 Augustine of Hippo and Pseudo-Augustine, *Libro de las meditaciones y soliloquios y manual*, trans. Pedro de Ribadeneyra (Madrid: Viuda de Pedro Madrigal, 1594); Augustine of Hippo and Pseudo-Augustine, *Meditaciones, soliloquios, y manual del glorioso doctor de la iglesia san Agustin*, trans. Pedro de Ribadeneyra (Madrid: Luis Sanchez, 1597).

204 Augustine of Hippo, *Las confesiones del glorioso dotor de la iglesia san Augustin*, trans. Pedro de Ribadeneyra (Madrid: Juan de Montoya, 1596).

205 Rey, xciv.

206 Ibid., cv–cvii.

207 Houliston, "Lord Treasurer," 393.

of the queen's" [640]) and treats the text as speaking in her voice ("she says" [635]), in keeping with his focus on Elizabeth as the driving force of English "heresy." The *Historia*'s originality lies in combining and reworking so diverse a range of sources, and thus integrating the story of the English Reformation into the broader narrative of European and Christian history. José Solís de los Santos describes the copious supply of early modern printed material as "a trove of facts and subject matter for the royal chronicler and the contemporary historian, into which they also introduced ideological messages to influence the incipient public opinion of the period."[208]

In a forthcoming essay, I discuss how Ribadeneyra's wide-ranging sourcing reflects the textual universe in which he worked and the conceptual framework through which he understood history itself.[209] Here, it suffices to acknowledge the diversity of influences that created the *Historia*, and the extent to which it evolved over time, the mechanics of which I hope will be better elucidated by this volume.

The *Historia* and the Society of Jesus

Ribadeneyra devoted his entire adult life (and a fair portion of his youth) to the Society of Jesus. Bilinkoff has neatly captured how completely he turned his powers to the order's service: "As a priest, educator, and administrator Ribadeneyra dedicated himself to expanding and promoting the Society. As a writer he strove to preserve its history for younger Jesuits and for posterity."[210] The Society permeates almost everything Ribadeneyra wrote, across the many genres and forms he employed. He wrote the first biographies of the first three superiors general of the Society, Ignatius of Loyola, Diego Laínez, and Francisco de Borja (1510–72), as well as a history of the order itself.[211] Not only were these the foundational accounts for the Society's memories of its earliest leaders but, as Claude Pavur, S.J. has written of the life of Ignatius, "His book is [...] not just a biography, nor a 'life and times,' nor an institutional history,

---

208 "un caudal de datos y asuntos para la cronística regia y la historiografía coetánea en que se introduce también un mensaje ideológico para influir en la incipiente opinión pública de la época." José Solís de los Santos, "Relaciones de sucesos de Inglaterra en el reinado de Carlos V," in *Testigo del tiempo, memoria del universo: Cultura escrita y sociedad en el mundo ibérico (siglos XV–XVIII)*, ed. Manuel F. Fernández, Carlos Alberto González, and Natalia Maillard ([Rubí]: Ediciones Rubeo, 2009), 640–98, here 640.

209 Weinreich, "English Mission."

210 Bilinkoff, "Many 'Lives,'" 181.

211 ARSI Hisp. 94.

but also an apologia—an explanation, a justification, and an argument for the Society of Jesus."[212] In an unpublished thesis on Ribadeneyra's hagiography collection, the *Flos sanctorum*, Jonathan Edward Greenwood demonstrates how the work includes revered but as-yet uncanonized Jesuits, such as Ignatius or Francis Xavier (1506–52), to boost the profile of the Society's icons.[213] The *Confesiones* are of course primarily an account of the author's own years as a Jesuit. Ribadeneyra wrote several treatises on the Society's customs and rules, with the express aim of "giving a justification for certain aspects of our Institute that some criticize because they do not properly understand the reasons for the Society has for practicing them."[214] Even the more theoretical works, such as the *Tratado de la tribulación*, are deeply colored by what we would call Ignatian spirituality.

Ribadeneyra long outlived the rest of the first generation of Jesuits, and was acutely conscious of his role as a preserver and transmitter of the Society's communal memory. By the late sixteenth century, he had, in the words of Roldán-Figueroa, "almost unrivaled credentials to act as an interpreter of the identity and mission of the Society of Jesus."[215] I have explored in another forum how the 1588 edition, in addition to its function vis-à-vis the Spanish Armada, was intended to enhance the order's public profile.[216] Accordingly, I shall speak here primarily about the Society's importance to the second volume and in the additions made to the first after 1588.

In large part, Ribadeneyra's rhetoric in Book 3 is no different from that of Books 1 and 2. The Jesuits are the nonpareil of missionaries and martyrs. They come at the urgent request of England's Catholics, and achieve wonderful results through their preaching and pastoral care. They are, moreover, the prime targets of Elizabeth's edict, and Ribadeneyra spends a great deal of time defending them against its charges. "The blessed Father Edmund Campion of the Society of Jesus" remains the standard-bearer for the whole of English Catholicism, a decade and more after his death. Here as elsewhere, Ribadeneyra evinces an explicitly Counter-Reformation view of the Society. In Book 1 of the *Historia*, he rewrites the order's foundation around the anti-Protestant mission, a mission

---

212   Ribadeneyra, *Life of Ignatius*, xviii–xix.
213   Jonathan Edward Greenwood, "Readers, Sanctity, and History in Early Modern History: Pedro de Ribadeneyra, the *Flos Sanctorum*, and Catholic Community" (Master's thesis, Carleton University, 2011).
214   "dar razón de algunas cosas de nuestro Instituto que algunos impugnan, por no saber bien las causas que tiene la Compañía para usarlas." Quoted in Dalmases, "Origenes de la hagiografía ignaciana," 26.
215   Roldán-Figuera, "Ribadeneyra's *Vida*," 159.
216   Weinreich, "Distinctiveness," 187–88.

that is moreover divinely appointed.[217] In the second volume, he addresses one chapter to his "dearest brothers and fathers of the Society of Jesus, and the students and priests of the seminaries, *whom the Lord has chosen* as soldiers and captains in so glorious a campaign."[218] "For Ribadeneyra, Saint Ignatius, the Society of Jesus, and every one of its members had come into the world with the epochal destiny to defend the Catholic faith in a trifold field of action"— namely among Catholics, among heretics, and among pagans.[219]

As the doyen of Jesuit Studies John W. O'Malley, S.J. has demonstrated, such a militant understanding of the Society does not date to the order's foundation. It was only a series of decisions on the part of Ignatius in the Society's early years that "launched the new order as Counter-Reformation *par excellence*," a model that took time to inhere in the Jesuits' sense of themselves.[220] At the time and in the decades to come, the interpretation and application of this mission was not unanimously accepted. Mercurian had been extremely leery of the English mission, and his successor, Acquaviva, also occasionally wavered in his support. To some extent, then, it was not simply a matter of preserving the order's history for younger Jesuits: Ribadeneyra was engaged in making the case for a particular reading of that history. As Rey puts it, "Ribadeneyra never lost an occasion to direct his superiors, by word or in writing, toward the genuine spirit of the governance of the Society."[221]

Ribadeneyra's specific commitment to the English mission may be related to his own life story. His years of travel had given him an unusual level of exposure to living, breathing Protestants. In addition to his harrowing sojourn in England and his struggle to observe the Lenten fast while traveling through non-Catholic territories, he and a companion were once attacked in an inn by evangelicals, surviving only by barricading themselves in their room.[222] For Ribadeneyra, in contrast to Acquaviva and many other Mediterranean Jesuits who had never lived or worked in Protestant lands, the threat of heresy was vividly, viscerally real. England in particular carried a personal weight, as has been discussed, ever since Ribadeneyra's own "English mission," expected to be the fulfillment of Ignatius's hopes, had been shipwrecked so abruptly.

---

217   Ibid., 179–80.

218   Italics mine.

219   "Para Ribadeneyra, San Ignacio, la Compañía de Jesús y cada uno de sus miembros han venido al mundo con el destino histórico de defender la Fe Católica en un triple campo de acción." Rey, lxxxv.

220   McCoog, *Building the Faith*, 1.

221   "Ribadeneyra no perdió nunca ocasión de orientar de palabra y por escrito a los superiores en el genuino espíritu del gobierno de la Compañía." Rey, lxix.

222   *MHSIR*, 1:68–69.

Ribadeneyra might well have worried, seeing the brutal executions of English priests, that the Society's nerve might fail and the English mission be abandoned—all the more so amid the intensified persecution that followed the Armada. In this light, the *Historia* is a reaffirmation that those executed were martyrs, as well as a call to arms urging renewed commitment to the project. It is telling, for example, that the metaphor of the heretics' activities in England as "sowing cockle" (alluding to Matthew 13:24–30) recurs no fewer than five times: the Society's Constitutions provided that "preference [in determining the Society's missions] should be given to the more important countries and *to those places 'where the enemy of Christ our Lord has sown cockle,'* where heresy was undermining the Church."[223]

Rey calls Ribadeneyra "a historian in the service of the idea of the Counter-Reformation."[224] The Toledan Jesuit, he argues, was committed to the intellectual and theological battle against the Protestants, in which "Spain should continue to guard against the Protestant peril at home, and strive abroad to aid those Catholics harmed by its lamentable influence."[225] These two fronts are crucial for understanding Ribadeneyra as a Counter-Reformation writer. He was not a Robert Bellarmine (1542–1621) or a Peter Canisius (1521–97), engaged in theological debates with Protestant interlocutors. Given that the *Historia* was published almost exclusively in Spanish, few Protestants before the modern era would have been able to read it, even had they wished to.[226] If *De origine ac progressu* "was intended not so much to convince as to demoralize the enemy," the *Historia* was not even meant to reach the enemy.[227] But recall Ribadeneyra's emphasis on the Society's threefold mission—to pagans, to Protestants, *and to Catholics.* The *Historia* might not have reached many Protestants, but it reached Catholics, aiming to strengthen their resolve against the "heretics"—of increasing importance as it became clear that reclaiming

223 Nos. 602–32, quoted in McCoog, *Our Way of Proceeding?*, 130. Italics mine.

224 "historiador al servicio de la Idea de la Contrarreforma." Rey, lxxiii.

225 "España debe seguir previniéndose contra el peligro protestante dentro de casa, y colaborar fuera de ella en ayuda de los católicos sometidos a su trágica influencia." Ibid., lxxxvi–lxxxvii.

226 There was a plan to translate *De origine ac progressu*, at least, into English in the mid-1590s, but nothing has survived (if indeed anything came of the idea). Highley argues, "We should not be surprised at the lack of an English translation because, after the excommunication of Elizabeth in 1570, when Catholic activists realized that the re-conversion of England would require foreign intervention, Catholic writers increasingly turned from their native tongue to the lingua franca of Latin in an effort to galvanize transnational support." Highley, "'Pestilent and Seditious Book,'" 155.

227 Houliston, "Missionary Position," 21.

Protestant territory would require aggressive Catholic action. In particular, it could intervene in current debates within the Society of Jesus over the nature of the order itself, pushing for a more militant attitude.

Central to the *Historia*'s account of the Society's role in England are the English seminaries created at Douai (1568, transferred to Rheims in 1578), Rome (1576), Valladolid (1589), and Seville (1592). By the time Ribadeneyra wrote, the Society was responsible for all but the college at Rheims—and even at Rheims there was a distinct Ignatian element.[228] The *Historia* waxes lyrical about how crucial these seminaries are in enabling "our holy religion to triumph over heresy" (551). Certainly, they were entirely dedicated to preparing students for missionary work, and produced impressive numbers of priests for work in England.[229] Ribadeneyra never visited any of the seminaries: he never went north of the Alps after his return from England, and he left Rome in 1574. Though he was in Spain at the time of the two later foundations, he does not appear to have left Madrid after 1583.[230] Nevertheless, as the detailed account in the *Historia* attests, he followed the colleges' progress avidly, not least the exploits of their alumni in England. His alignment with the seminaries (and his insulation from the facts on the ground in England) is equally apparent in his hardline position on conformity and recusancy. Ribadeneyra devotes an entire chapter to proving that Catholics "cannot in good conscience" attend the heretics' "synagogues" (620), a view that characterized the more rigorist seminarians in contrast to their Marian colleagues.[231] Like his friends Persons and Allen, Ribadeneyra was perturbed by English believers' "slide towards conformity, especially the fragmentation of Catholic confession into multiple forms of resistance."[232]

Ribadeneyra's decision to foreground the seminaries in his *Historia* was probably his way of contributing to their work. Like many institutions of higher learning before and since, the English colleges were chronically short of funds.[233] As a longtime friend and adviser to Jane Dormer (a tireless advocate

---

228   Thomas M. McCoog, "'Replant the Uprooted Trunk of the Tree of Faith': The Society of Jesus and the Continental Colleges for Religious Exiles," in *Insular Christianity: Alternative Models of the Church in Britain and Ireland, c.1570–c.1700*, ed. Robert Armstrong and Tadhg Ó hAnnracháin, Politics, Culture, and Society in Early Modern Britain (Manchester: Manchester University Press, 2013), 28–44, here 28–34. Clancy, "First Generation," 140.

229   McCoog, "'Replant the Uprooted Trunk,'" 41–42.

230   *MHSIR*, 1:viii–x.

231   Highley, *Catholics Writing the Nation*, 8.

232   Houliston, *Catholic Resistance*, 26.

233   McCoog, "'Replant the Uprooted Trunk,'" 32–33.

for the exiled English community),[234] Ribadeneyra knew better than most the importance of sustained support, political and financial, from Spanish elites. In addition to highlighting the seminaries' successes, Ribadeneyra stresses that "they need to be encouraged, strengthened, and supported, as the king our lord does, and as Your Highness shall do" (551). In a move still familiar to those seeking funding for expensive projects, he mentions that the royals will not be expected to bear the whole burden: the foundation of Valladolid, for example, was achieved "with further donations from several prelates, lords, and pious, devout persons" (653), while the establishment at Seville is depicted by the *Historia* (not quite accurately) as entirely the city's own doing. If the *Historia* found receptive readers in the future Philip III, his courtiers, and other Spanish elites, it might redound to the benefit of the seminaries. Nor was this message restricted to the upper classes: ordinary Spaniards still needed to be convinced that the seminaries were worth the use of municipal resources and the risk of heretical infiltration.[235]

Of particular interest is Book 3, Chapter 20, in which Ribadeneyra contrasts Elizabeth's hostile reaction to the English seminaries with grateful messages from converted Japanese lords, expressing their delight at the seminaries established in Asia. Some background is required: in 1582, at the urging of the Jesuit visitor in Japan, Alessandro Valignano (1539–1606), four Christian Japanese noblemen—Mancio Itō (1570–1612), Miguel Chijiwa (c.1569–1633), Julião Nakaura (c.1570–33), and Martinho Hara (c.1570–1629) set out for Europe in the so-called Tenshō Embassy. The boys' travels through Portugal, Spain, and Italy (including a visit to the papal court) were an absolute sensation, rapturously reported across Europe. Ribadeneyra's polemical point in reproducing the letters is a keen one: by unfavorably comparing Elizabeth's judgment with that of former pagans, he not only mocks the queen's perversity but also impugns the intellectual integrity of Protestantism. But the letters also touch on the Society more specifically: the Tenshō Embassy was Valignano's brainchild, and the Catholic mission to Japan itself was primarily a Jesuit project.[236]

---

234 See Hannah Leah Crummé, "Jane Dormer's Recipe for Politics: A Refuge Household in Spain for Mary Tudor's Ladies-in-Waiting," in *The Politics of Female Households: Ladies-in-Waiting across Early Modern Europe*, ed. Nadine Akkerman and Birgit Houben, Rulers & Elites 4 (Leiden: Brill, 2013), 51–71.

235 Highley, *Catholics Writing the Nation*, 169. Jenna D. Lay, "The Literary Lives of Nuns: Crafting Identities Through Exile," in *The English Convents in Exile, 1600–1800: Communities, Culture and Identity*, ed. Caroline Bowden and James E. Kelly (Farnham: Ashgate, 2013), 71–86, here 78.

236 See Michael Cooper, *The Japanese Mission to Europe, 1582–1590: The Journey of Four Samurai Boys through Portugal, Spain and Italy* (Folkestone: Global Oriental, 2005).

To early modern Europeans, the Society was perhaps most famous for its missionary work in Asia, with letters from "the Indies" runaway bestsellers of their day.[237] This was a period of intense and intensifying interest in the spread of Catholicism in Asia.[238] Here we see Ribadeneyra's ability to speak to multiple audiences at once. To members of the Society, tying the English schism to the Asian missions evokes a common Jesuit trope of the order's "two wings" (twin missions to Protestant northern Europe and the pagan Indies): it affirms that the English mission is integral to the Society's purpose and character.[239] To the general reader, this was a reminder of the order's most renowned activity—and, of course, a touch of the exotic would do nothing to hurt sales.

We have already mentioned Greenwood's work on the *Flos sanctorum*, which Ribadeneyra used to upgrade the status of beloved Jesuits. Though not hagiography *per se*, the *Historia* performs similar functions, as Ribadeneyra composes, translates, and disseminates stories about Jesuit martyrs, as well as other executed Catholics. Prefiguring his *modus operandi* in the *Flos*, Ribadeneyra accords these still-unofficial martyrs the full apparatus of saints' cults—describing the reverence shown to their corpses and relating their posthumous miracles—and is liberal in his use of terms like "saint(ed)" and "blessed." Repeated descriptions of wonder, sorrow, or inspiration on the part of onlookers model the appropriate devout response to such figures.[240] This is most evident in the *Historia*'s treatment of Edmund Campion, easily the most iconic figure of the English mission. Though Campion was not beatified until 1886 (and canonized only in 1970), soon after his death he became the focus of a cult, not least among his fellow Jesuits.[241] Ribadeneyra not only gives a richly detailed account of Campion's life, work, and martyrdom—emphasizing the

---

237   John Correia-Afonso, *Jesuit Letters and Indian History, 1542–1773*, 2nd ed., Studies in Indian History and Culture of the Heras Institute 20 (Bombay: Oxford University Press, 1969), 32–33, 177–79.

238   Rady Roldán-Figueroa, "Father Luis Piñeiro, S.J., the Tridentine Economy of Relics, and the Defense of the Jesuit Missionary Enterprise in Tokugawa Japan," *Archiv Für Reformationsgeschichte* 101, no. 1 (October 2010): 209–32, here 221.

239   John W. O'Malley, *The First Jesuits* (Cambridge: Harvard University Press, 1993), 70. See also O'Malley, "To Travel to Any Part of the World: Jerónimo Nadal and the Jesuit Vocation," *Studies in the Spirituality of Jesuits* 16, no. 2 (March 1984): 1–21, here 13.

       Intriguingly, Luis Piñeiro (d. 1620) performed the same maneuver in reverse, pressing the claims of the Japanese mission by tying them to the struggles against European Protestantism. Indeed, inspired by Ribadeneyra's *Historia*, he drew explicit links to the "English schism." Roldán-Figueroa, "Father Luis Piñeiro," 210, 225–27.

240   Monta, *Martyrdom and Literature*, 47–48.

241   See McCoog, *And Touching Our Society*, Chapter 4.

links to earlier martyrs, both biblical (Paul) and late antique (Attalus)—but over the course of several editions adds the full complement of hagiographic attributes. The English Jesuit is frequently called both "sainted" and "blessed"; his relics and his likeness become objects of veneration. Ribadeneyra tells a remarkable story of one of the martyred Jesuit's legs being stolen by a Catholic knight, who attempts to secrete the relic out of the country. In tragicomic fashion, the plan is foiled by the wonderful fragrance emitted by the holy remains: the leg is discovered and recovered by the authorities, although the devout knight does escape with his life. The *Historia* also relates how Campion's image has been disseminated and revered (presumably through the Jesuit missions) across the world—using this as a convenient stick with which to beat English Protestants, who do not recognize the sainthood of a fellow-countryman.

Besides the *editio princeps* of the *Historia*, 1588 also saw the revival of papal canonization after a hiatus of sixty-five years, with Sixtus V's (r.1585–90) declaration of the sainthood of the Spanish Franciscan Diego of Alcalá (c.1400–63).[242] The norms of the so-called "canonization *vita*" were of course not yet established, and so it seems unlikely that Ribadeneyra was aiming at official sainthood for Campion. Furthermore, while modern scholarship has outlined how integral a renewed cult of the saints was to Counter-Reformation mission work,[243] and the *Historia* must be seen in this context, Ribadeneyra's Spanish-language text obviously served a different purpose. It seems likely that the *Historia* was intended for more dubious members of the Society (and those outside it), reaffirming the sacred character of the English mission. In subsequent editions, Ribadeneyra supplemented the account of the Jesuit martyrs with translations of their writings, including Campion's Brag and letters from Briant and Sherwin (though Sherwin was not in point of fact a Jesuit, his fierce devotion to the Society indelibly linked him to it, in his lifetime and ever after).[244] This was the first time many of these materials were available in an Iberian vernacular. Bearing in mind Ribadeneyra's long-established interest in making his writings accessible to ordinary readers, this too can be regarded as "an attempt to convey Ribadeneyra's *apologia pro Societate sua*," to raise the profile

---

242   Peter Burke, "How to Be a Counter-Reformation Saint," in Burke, *The Historical Anthropology of Early Modern Italy: Essays on Perception and Communication* (Cambridge: Cambridge University Press, 2005), 48–62, here 49–50.

243   Alexandra Walsham, "Translating Trent? English Catholicism and the Counter Reformation," *HR* 78, no. 201 (August 2005): 288–310, here 303–04.

244   James E. Kelly, "Conformity, Loyalty and the Jesuit Mission to England of 1580," in *Religious Tolerance in the Atlantic World: Early Modern and Contemporary Perspectives*, ed. Eliane Glaser (Basingstoke: Palgrave MacMillan, 2014), 149–70, here 158–59.

of the Society within Spain.[245] We know that one of his preoccupations in later life was "a considerable lack of knowledge in Spain and among Spanish Jesuits about the history of the Society."[246]

More than half of Ribadeneyra's long career in the Society of Jesus was spent in his ostensible retirement in Spain, first in Toledo and then in Madrid. Retirement did not mean withdrawal, as evidenced by his bountiful literary production and frequent correspondence, which engaged actively and vigorously in contemporary debates within and without the Society. When scholars speak of the growth of a Counter-Reformation mentality in "the *evolving* self-understanding of its [the Society's] members,"[247] it can obscure how contested a development this was. Ribadeneyra's *Historia* (and indeed almost all of his writings) is not simply about the preservation of historical memory. It is an intervention, a piece of rhetoric, a bid to shape the direction of the order he so loved. But this is not to say that it was a crass power-play; as Rey reminds us, it was the quintessence of the Society to turn all possible methods to the service of God (however defined): "This entire manner of performing the work of a writer is pure Ignatianism, and a magnificent crystallization of the new method of indiscriminately utilizing every possible means as active instruments for the greater glory of God."[248]

From the *Historia*'s interventions in external debates, we now turn to tensions within the text itself. As we shall see in the section that follows, Ribadeneyra's determination to grapple with contemporary history raised the problem of the exercise of political power by women, both Catholics and Protestants—a problem he was ultimately unable to resolve with perfect consistency.

"O ladies, no ladies at all": Gender and Power in the *Historia*

Quoting from a letter by the English priest John Cecil (1558–1626) in Book 3 of the *Historia*, Ribadeneyra relates the story of several Catholic maidens who, when a judge attempts to intimidate them by merely pronouncing a death sentence without enforcing it, beg to be allowed to die alongside their ghostly father. Cecil gushes, "O ladies, no ladies at all; O manly, valiant hearts" (590).

---

245   Weinreich, "Distinctiveness," 188.

246   Roldán-Figueroa, "Ribadeneyra's *Vida*," 164.

247   McCoog, *Building the Faith*, 1. Italics mine.

248   "Toda esta manera de practicar el oficio de escritor es ingacianismo [*sic*] puro y esplendorosa cristalización del nuevo arte de utilizar indistintamente los medios naturales como instrumentos activos para la mayor gloria de Dios." Rey, xc.

Though Ribadeneyra did not write these lines, they might just as well be his: the figure of the unwomanly woman and the protective penumbra of the male superior are central to the contradictory, conflicted treatment of gender in the *Historia*.

In following the course of sixteenth-century English history, the *Historia* encounters a remarkable series of powerful ladies: Henry VIII's six wives, Jane Grey (1537–54), Mary I, Jane Dormer, Elizabeth, and Mary Queen of Scots (r.1542–67)—among many other, less prominent women. Early modern beliefs about gender and political power presented challenges for female rulers, their subjects, and observers.[249] How could a woman, assumed by her very nature to be subordinate (to say nothing of emotional, inconstant, and irrational), exercise political power? In a seminal study of royal education in early modern Britain, Aysha Pollnitz has demonstrated that the education of elite women, which was restricted to forms, methods, and content thought appropriate for female capacities, was designed to preclude any challenge to male authority.[250] David Loades has argued that Mary Tudor's reign was hampered by the gender norms around the monarchy, not least the queen's own "conviction that government was not woman's work."[251] Endless scholarly ink has been spilled on Elizabeth's deft manipulations of her gender, sexuality, and marriageability. The same tensions manifested in an ambivalence toward female political identity in those, like Ribadeneyra, who wrote about powerful women, as María Cristina Quintero points out.[252]

Quintero takes as her case studies the depictions of Catherine of Aragon, Anne Boleyn, and Elizabeth in the *Historia* and in Calderón's dramatic adaption, *La cisma de Inglaterra*, arguing that both texts evince "the early modern male anxiety and paranoia toward the female body, sexuality, and feminine power."[253] Quintero is undoubtedly correct that the female body was a site of anxiety for Ribadeneyra. However, her focus on these three women occludes critical areas of tension. Specifically, the omission of the two Marys obscures the problem of Catholic queens regnant: Ribadeneyra cannot wholly disavow the positive potential of female rulership. Furthermore, as crucial as the female

---

249   David Loades, *The Reign of Mary Tudor: Politics, Government and Religion in England, 1553–58*, 2nd ed. (London: Longman, 1991), 1.

250   Aysha Pollnitz, *Princely Education in Early Modern Britain*, Cambridge Studies in Early Modern British History (Cambridge: Cambridge University Press, 2015), Chapter 5.

251   Loades, *Reign of Mary Tudor*, 65.

252   María Cristina Quintero, "English Queens and the Body Politic in Calderón's *La cisma de Inglaterra* and Rivadeneira's *Historia eclesiastica del scisma del reino de Inglaterra*," *Modern Language Notes* 113, no. 2 (1998): 259–82, here 260.

253   Ibid., 280.

body was to early modern gendered discourses of power, it was but one axis of that issue. An analysis of *all* the queens of the *Historia*, as well as Jane Dormer and the minor Catholic martyrs, suggests that female autonomy—women outside male control—was equally troubling for Ribadeneyra. What I offer here is not intended to challenge Quintero's work but to broaden it: to suggest aspects of female power beyond corporality that perturbed Ribadeneyra.

Ribadeneyra offers several sometimes-contradictory responses to these anxieties. With remarkable consistency, the *Historia* places elite women in dualities, what Quintero calls "the typical dichotomization of feminine characters into representations of good and evil":[254] Catherine against Anne; Anne of Cleves and Katherine Parr (1512–48) against Mary; Jane Grey against Mary; Mary against Elizabeth; Elizabeth against Mary Queen of Scots. Indeed, at times Ribadeneyra makes the dichotomies explicit, as with Anne and Catherine: "we shall compare lineage with lineage, life with life, and death with death" (262). This presentation partially frees Ribadeneyra of the necessity of examining the problematics of female power. If Mary can be presented as a good queen because she is the anti-Jane and the anti-Elizabeth, the reader need not worry about the difficulties of a queen regnant in the first place. He also seeks to square the supposed contradiction between femininity and power by coding women's achievements as unwomanly ("O ladies, no ladies at all"), although this has the troubling side effect of depicting female protagonists as viragos who might threaten male power. To confront these tensions, Ribadeneyra uses male authority figures to carve out a space of legitimacy for female power. Thus the hierarchy of male over female is preserved, and with it the gendered structure that organized Ribadeneyra's world.

The first of these dualities is "the antithetical inverted relationship between the virtuous and chaste Catherine and the lascivious Anne," a dichotomy that turns on a suspicion of the female body. Ribadeneyra's Catherine is characterized by a denial of her sexuality—witness the umpteen references to her chasteness—and where it must be acknowledged, it conforms to patriarchal authority in the form of a legitimate heir.[255] Contrarily, Anne is defined by her hypersexuality, and an artful, calculated sexuality at that. She shrewdly manipulates Henry, and is disturbingly adept at using her body as a weapon:

> She sported with the king, playing and dancing with him, engaging in every pastime and dalliance ladies use with their gallants, but never straying beyond that. The more warmly she enticed him, the more the

---

254   Ibid., 269.
255   Ibid., 268–71, here 269.

king pined for her; the more untouchable she appeared, the more fiercely
he burned in his love (155).

By means of these wiles she can exercise absolute power over a man ("since I'm
holding the king between my fingers, I'll squeeze him as he deserves and treat
him just as I like" [173])—and not just any man, but a king. Like the witch who
gives herself physically to the devil and uses bodily fluids in her spells, Anne's
body is at once a site of danger to and a weapon against the male power structure. Quintero discusses this primarily in sociopolitical terms: "Anne is thus
presented in Rivadeneira's text as a sexual social outlaw, the disorderly woman
whose fate is a warning of what happens when female carnality escapes the
limits of patriarchal control. [...] Anne represents the erotic body that disrupts
the secular order."[256] Catherine, by contrast, *subordinates* her body both symbolically (in producing a legitimate heir) and physically (repeatedly kneeling)
to her husband.

Disrupt the secular order Anne unquestionably does, but this is not all she
does: she is equally a threat to the religious order. In addition to being an "erotic
body," hers is a "heretical body." Ribadeneyra inherits from Sander the
trope, common in contemporary Catholic writing, of Anne as the physical
embodiment of heresy, from whose sexuality sprang English Protestantism.
Ribadeneyra frequently stresses that Anne has symbolically given birth to
heresy:[257] in one especially vivid moment, he quotes *De origine ac progressu* to
the effect that "Your church does not flow from the sacred breast of Christ [...]
but from the foulness of a whore, her throat justly slashed" (204). In the same
way, Catherine's is not simply the well-controlled body, but also the Catholic
body. Her body is governed by religious observance, the rhythms of prayer,
confession, and divine office ordering her day. She acknowledges the authority of multiple (male) superiors: her husband, her confessor, and the pope. In
the end, Ribadeneyra makes her a saint and martyr for the Catholic Church,
witnessing to her faith with her life.

The terrain is rather different in Edward's reign, as the conversation shifts
away from the body and toward the problem of gendered power dynamics. The
place of Henry's monstrous libido can hardly be taken by his nine-year-old son.
Anne of Cleves (1515–57), Katherine Parr, and Jane Grey take up no more than a
few pages of the *Historia* between them, but taken together they are variations
on the theme of the dangers of women in power. On the one hand, allowing
women influence over men amplifies and disseminates female vices: just as

---

256   Ibid., 271, 276.
257   Highley, "'Pestilent and Seditious Book,'" 163–64.

the Lutheran Anne Boleyn infected Henry, the former queens Anne of Cleves and Katherine Parr exploit their influence to inculcate the young Edward with heresy. More prosaically, women, stereotyped as shallow and vain, subvert men and male politics for their own petty ends. Katherine's feud over precedence with Protector Somerset's wife, Anne Seymour (*née* Stanhope, c.1497–1587), throws the government into chaos and brings about the deaths of both Katherine and her husband. Concomitantly, mental inferiority and natural submissiveness would prevent a woman ever exercising effective authority: she would be the pawn of whatever man had her ear. Ribadeneyra's Jane Grey is a nonentity, bullied into accepting the throne and utterly dominated by her father and the duke of Northumberland. Through her, they attempt to dispossess the rightful heir and establish heretical hegemony in England.

Mary Tudor is a counterpoint to both perils: she is a positive (i.e., Catholic) religious influence, and pointedly rejects male attempts to silence or ventriloquize her. The mirror image of Anne and Katherine, she seeks to reclaim her half-brother for the true church. Though she is unsuccessful, she continually defies pressure to conform on the Mass or the royal supremacy. Her victory over Northumberland is achieved without external support from her cousin, Emperor Charles v; she is not a male powerbroker's puppet. More generally, Mary is, to an even greater extent than her mother, defined by her *lack* of the expected feminine qualities: perhaps the quintessential "lady who is not a lady." She suffers all her misfortunes with "a strong and manly heart" (408). In an encomium to her virtues, Ribadeneyra notes that the queen had "a deep voice, more like a man's than a woman's, a quick wit, a resolute and forceful spirit, and an unerring and thoughtful judgment" (403). With such a formulation, each attribute attached to the same verb, one cannot help feeling that for Ribadeneyra, Mary's wit, spirit, and judgment are in some implicit way tied to a certain masculinity of presence. Mary is no ordinary woman, and so her proximity to political power poses none of the perils represented by Anne, Katherine, or Jane.

And yet, the tension surrounding a woman exercising authority remained—early modern thought construed female virtue as intrinsically passive.[258] While one could praise a woman's manliness to laud her lack of feminine vices, the fear that she might actually usurp masculine agency was real and troubling. Note that Mary's doctrinal role is limited to resisting the heretics around her brother (once again, a good–evil dichotomy to the rescue) and to setting a good example of Catholic praxis: she does not presume to *teach*, a role even

---

258   Quintero, "English Queens," 261.

the more open-minded writers stoutly denied to women.[259] Tellingly, the formula "O ladies, no ladies at all" actually collapses in on itself: however manfully they may have acted, the statement begins by reaffirming that they are, in fact, "ladies." (A contrast, perhaps, with Elizabeth, whose disavowal of marriage and assumption of political power gave her distinctly androgynous characteristics in the eyes of some early modern observers.[260]) Magdalena S. Sánchez perceptively elucidates this delicate balance in a study of depictions of Philip III's wife, Margaret of Austria (1584–1611). Those around her praised Margaret's concern with her salvation as evidence of a *pecho varonil* (manly heart), but framed this behavior within her absolute obedience to her confessor and deference to clergymen more generally.[261] Sánchez analyzes the eulogies produced for Margaret with an eye toward their gendered theology:

> A virtuous woman [...] should be saintly, chaste, charitable, and pious. But a virtuous woman who was truly brave and strong should be married and should be loyal to her husband, and demonstrate strength and justice on all occasions. [...] Espinosa succeeded in defining Margaret of Austria strictly in her position as a wife: *she could be virtuous and strong because she was subordinate to a man.*[262]

Throughout the *Historia*, the foremost virtue of the female protagonists is that they acknowledge that they are, in fact, women, and thus subordinate themselves to a male authority.

Just as Catherine's sexuality was legitimated by submission to her husband, and her asexuality by submission to the Church, the potentially disturbing character of Mary's unwomanliness is defanged first by her extraordinary passivity, and then by her husband. We observed earlier that Mary's triumph comes about without the assistance of her Habsburg kin; as Ribadeneyra tells it, it came about virtually without Mary's assistance, either. Others inform Mary of the plot against her. Thousands spontaneously flock to her banner,

259 Gloria Kaufman, "Juan Luis Vives on the Education of Women," *Signs* 3, no. 4 (Summer 1978): 891–96, here 893.

260 Machielsen, "Lion," 36–37; María Cristina Quintero, *Gendering the Crown in the Spanish Baroque Comedia*, New Hispanisms: Cultural & Literary Studies (Farnham: Ashgate, 2012), 40.

261 Magdalena S. Sánchez, "Pious and Political Images of a Habsburg Woman at the Court of Philip III (1598–1621)," in *Spanish Women in the Golden Age: Images and Realities*, ed. Magdalena S. Sánchez and Alain Saint-Saëns, Contributions in Women's Studies 155 (Westport: Greenwood Press, 1996), 91–107, here 94–95.

262 Ibid., 95. Italics mine.

unsummoned and uncommanded. Northumberland's men defect to her of their own volition, and the duke himself surrenders without taking the field. Far from the considerable coup of planning and execution actually pulled off by Mary and her allies,[263] Ribadeneyra casts the princess's victory as a *deus ex machina*. Quite literally, God is cast as the active subject in the narrative, Mary as the passive object: "our Lord favored his faith and truth, giving the realm to Queen Mary [...]. Queen Mary had received this glorious and unlooked-for victory from heaven" (369).

The pattern holds after the queen has ascended to the throne. Ribadeneyra is keen to make clear the limits to Mary's power ("until parliament assembled the queen's authority could not [...]" [370]) and her eagerness to relinquish illegitimate positions of power (i.e., the royal supremacy). Furthermore, she is swift to seek male authority figures to guide her. As a dutiful daughter, she wants to arrange for the proper ceremonies honoring her father's memory, but desists after conferring "with devout and wise *men*" (371).[264] She immediately implores the pope for Cardinal Pole as a legate and the emperor for his son as a husband (again on the advice of learned *men*). With the arrival of Philip and Pole, reassuringly male faces have been put on royal political power. Much of the narrative either unites Mary and Philip into the single entity, "the monarchs," or shifts entirely to the king's perspective. The official restoration of Catholicism is primarily told in the king's voice, through quotations from his letters. Changes to ecclesiastical policy are conducted by Pole, the reform of the universities by a team of visitors. Ultimately, what distinguishes Mary from Jane Grey is less the difference in power relations (although Mary is by far the more substantial character), so much as the social and religious orthodoxy that legitimates the influence of Philip and Pole. As Mary's husband and spiritual father, respectively—in addition to their unimpeachable Catholicism—they exercise a licit, indeed beneficial, authority over her.

As the *Historia* goes on, Ribadeneyra becomes more and more concerned to neutralize female agency by subordinating it to male authority, likely prompted by the need for a counterpoint to Elizabeth. "Elizabeth represented the inversion, and indeed the perversion, of masculine supremacy and the accepted binomial view of the differences between male and female," the crystallization of every prejudice about women in power.[265] Where Mary had complied with societal expectations by becoming a wife, Elizabeth refuses a husband, instead manipulating men using their desire for her (just as her mother had done).

---

263   See Eric Ives, *Lady Jane Grey: A Tudor Mystery* (Malden: Wiley-Blackwell, 2009), Chapter 22.

264   Italics mine.

265   Quintero, "English Queens," 264; Quintero, *Gendering the Crown*, 124.

She mocks the authority of the pope and usurps his position by making herself the head of the Church. Unsanctioned by a male presence, Elizabeth combines all of the dangers posed by female authority: she is capricious, and controls the lives of the men around her (witness the hapless Hatton). On the other hand, she is easily manipulated herself, particularly by Sir Francis Walsingham's (c.1532–90) stranglehold on information—"she knew nothing more than served his turn" (579). She presumes to dictate to male ecclesiastics, telling her bishops not to elevate the host, and where Anne Boleyn had driven England into heresy, her daughter disseminates it through the world. No wonder, then, that so potent a figure of female wickedness needed an equally forceful rejoinder.

Initially, Mary functions as the intuitive contrast. Juxtaposing the half-sisters creates a series of loaded dichotomies: legitimate and illegitimate, Catholic and heretic, obedient wife and willful virgin. Yet Mary's death makes this difficult to sustain. A stopgap is offered by Jane Dormer—bravely working to shield English Catholics from persecution, but only in conjunction with her husband—but she, too, soon leaves the stage.

A real counterpoint for Elizabeth only appears with Mary Queen of Scots. Elizabeth the heretic is again matched by Mary the Catholic, the queen of Scots positioned as Mary Tudor's logical (and legal) successor. From the first, Ribadeneyra presents her, too, as passive and subordinate to men. He takes liberties with chronology, rendering the teenage Mary "a small child" on Mary Tudor's death, so that it can be her father-in-law, Henry II of France (r.1547–59), who is responsible for her assumption of English heraldry. She is safely married off, not once, but twice (the scandalous third marriage to James Hepburn, fourth earl of Bothwell [c.1534–78], however, is airbrushed out), and, like Catherine of Aragon, fulfills her wifely duty by bearing a child. If Elizabeth is defined by her usurpation of power, Mary is defined by having her power usurped—first deposed, then imprisoned, tried, and executed. In this regard, it should be noted that Ribadeneyra, a prominent anti-Machiavellian political theorist, was especially perturbed by what he saw as Elizabeth's Machiavellian approach to politics.[266] Her treachery and unscrupulousness is potently contrasted with her Scottish cousin's trusting nature.

The bulk of the chapter is given over to Mary's imprisonment and execution—her close confinement the perfect rejoinder to Elizabeth's uncontrolled autonomy. Unable to exercise political power, the queen of Scots

---

266 For a discussion of Ribadeneyra's place in the Catholic anti-Machiavellian tradition, see Bireley, *Counter-Reformation Prince*, 111–35.

Cf. Torres Olleta, "Imágenes," 75.

effectively ceases to be a queen regnant, and thus to disturb the early modern male reader. Where she speaks in her own voice—her frequent letters—it is to declare her submission to God, the Catholic Church, and various male authorities. To the French Jesuit Edmond Auger (1530–91), she writes of her intention to "subject myself in everything to his holy will," and asks the priest to direct her spiritual preparations (514). To Pope Pius V (r.1566–72), she describes herself as "a most devoted and obedient daughter of the holy Roman Catholic Church," and promises to obey the pontiff's commands in all things (516). Even to Elizabeth, she declares that she is "determined to suffer death in *obedience* to the Catholic, Apostolic, and Roman Church" (521).[267] To her almoner, she writes for instruction in how to pray in her last hours. Again and again, her demand to her jailers is for a Catholic priest to counsel and guide her. Deprived of such a spiritual father, Mary administers the Eucharist to herself—and Ribadeneyra cites no fewer than seven authorities to defend the orthodoxy of this assumption of the sacerdotal function.[268] Even at the very end, the queen's last words are a yielding-up of her own autonomy to God's divine providence, down to the Bible verses she quotes: *In manus tuas Domine commendo spiritum meum.*[269]

Mary's execution, like the death of the previous Mary, deprives Ribadeneyra of his foil for Elizabeth. In Book 3, no one suitable protagonist having presented herself, he draws on a medley of Catholic women whose activities are safely regulated by male authority. Lady Allen (dates unknown, *fl.* late sixteenth century), persecuted by Elizabethan officials, goes to extraordinary lengths to save her daughters from the heretics' clutches and is described as "a manful woman, deeply Catholic and experienced" (604). But at each step she is guided or protected by a man: her influential brother-in-law, Cardinal Allen, her late husband, her priest, and the community at Rheims. Similarly, the female martyrs are linked by reverence for their spiritual fathers: the "ladies, no ladies at all" who want to die alongside their priest; the three noblewomen arrested for hearing Mass, along with "the priest who had said Mass for them" (605); the widow imprisoned for life for sheltering priests, and who likewise wishes "to die with her spiritual fathers" (570).[270] And, of course, presiding over all these (and every other Catholic woman) is the legitimating masculine presence *par excellence*: the pope. Perhaps Ribadeneyra's paradigmatic female protagonists

---

267   Italics mine.

268   Moreover, the list in question is formidable: Tertullian (*c.*155–*c.*240); Cyprian of Carthage (*c.*200–58); Clement of Alexandria (*c.*150–*c.*215); Gregory of Nazianzus (329–90); Jerome (*c.*347–420); Ambrose of Milan; and Basil of Caesarea (*c.*329–79).

269   Ps. 30:6 (cf. Luke 23:46).

270   Gregory, *Salvation at Stake*, 95.

are the women religious: desexualized by their chastity, stripped of any challenge to male power by their vows of obedience, they can exercise extraordinary agency (rappelling down castle walls) without threatening the socioreligious power structure. (Incidentally, Ribadeneyra gives both Catherine and Mary monastic attributes: the former is a Franciscan tertiary, the latter's upbringing is compared to a convent.)

That many early modern thinkers were deeply ambivalent about female political agency, and that many believed it was acceptable only when exercised under male guidance, is of course nothing new. What is noteworthy about Ribadeneyra is how the problem of Catholic queens regnant precluded any straightforward condemnation of women in power. The need to accommodate the two Marys led to more complex considerations of the possibility for women to "transcend" their gender—even if the end result was the same recourse to the denial or subordination of female agency.

A Modern Historian?

The preceding section highlighted the rhetorical and historiographical gymnastics forced upon Ribadeneyra in the course of balancing the historical record and his own theological convictions. The inevitable tension between these two commitments leads naturally to a troublingly simple question: how are we to characterize Ribadeneyra as a historian? In the specific case of this translation, the series to which it belongs describes its remit as "modernity through the prism of Jesuit history": a study of the first great Jesuit historian/ biographer can hardly avoid the question of what "modernity" means for the writing of history. Was Pedro de Ribadeneyra a "modern" historian? Was the *Historia* a "modern" history?

Earlier generations of scholars thought the answer was a straightforward "yes." Cándido de Dalmases asserted Ribadeneyra's "right to be considered a modern historian," emphasizing his research, diligent citations of sources, and "critical spirit [*espíritu crítico*]."[271] Eusebio Rey wrote that "the [*Historia's*] flawless interweaving of documentation and narration produces a historical voice of absolutely modern characteristics."[272] In both instances, we appear to have in Ribadeneyra a Spanish instantiation of that much-loved theme

---

271   "derecho a ser considerado como historiador moderno." Dalmases, "Orígenes de la hagiografía ignaciana," 130–36, quotations at 136.

272   "el perfecto engranaje del documento y la narración origina un estilo histórico de rasgos completamente modernos." Rey, cxvii.

of twentieth-century historiography, the "historical revolution": "historians prized accounts of the past that seemed to them to aspire to impartiality, factual accuracy, and a secular outlook—in short, that pointed the way toward modernity."[273] The problems of this heuristic have long been recognized, and need not be reworked here in any detail. Suffice it to say that in attempting to identify forerunners of modern historiography, historians have often distorted or ignored vital details of their subjects' work, especially their religious dimensions.[274]

The issue has recently been reopened, however, in a much more sophisticated form, in a thought-provoking essay by Rady Roldán-Figueroa. Examining the Spanish translation of the *Life of Ignatius of Loyola*, Roldán-Figueroa stresses, as Dalmases did seventy years ago, Ribadeneyra's careful assessment of sources and scrupulous care to include only reliable information. Unlike his predecessor, however, Roldán-Figueroa does not leap to the judgment that Ribadeneyra was therefore a "modern" scholar, offering the more nuanced conclusion that "if the stress on documentary sources was the hallmark of a new, modern style of hagiography, then Ribadeneyra has to be recognized as one of its earliest exponents." In particular, he seeks to reevaluate the primacy given to the Bollandists as the creators of this new, more rigorous discipline of "hagiology."[275] Roldán-Figueroa's essay offers a point of departure for considering Ribadeneyra's methodology as a historian—with an eye not toward determining whether he is "modern," but rather toward situating his historiography within the influences, concerns, and modes of its contextual moment. How did he write his *Historia*? What motivated those choices?

We observed earlier that in its broadest strokes, Ribadeneyra's narrative is not too far removed from any modern survey of Tudor history. Monarch succeeds monarch in the familiar order (albeit with rather heavy-handed commentary), most of the major events of sixteenth-century English history are at least mentioned, and errors of date and place are generally rare and minor (e.g., at the dissolution of her household, Mary was sent to live with her half-sister, not her mother; Christopher Hatton died on November 20, 1591, not October 17). All the same, there is no avoiding the exaggerations, distortions, and outright fabrications that pervade the *Historia*. Among the choicer specimens are the ersatz correspondence between Catherine of Aragon and John Forest, the story of the imperial ambassador shielding Spaniards from taking

---

273   Kewes, "History and Its Uses," 1–2.
274   Joseph H. Preston, "Was There an Historical Revolution?," *Journal of the History of Ideas* 38, no. 2 (June 1977): 353–64.
275   Roldán-Figueroa, "Ribadeneyra's *Vida*," 168–69.

from an anti-papal oath, and, notoriously, the outrageous claim that Anne Boleyn was secretly Henry's daughter. Furthermore, not all "minor" errors were so inconsequential: by stating that Edward VI's evangelically inclined tutors were chosen by Somerset and the other radicals, rather than by Henry VIII (as they were), Ribadeneyra has further evidence for his thesis that "the tender youth of King Edward [...] [was] abused and tyrannized by his tutors and the regents of the realm" (116).

The first observation to be made about these departures from fact is that there is little in the *Historia*—even its most outlandish details—for which the author did not have a source. In all his historical writings, before and after the *Historia*, Ribadeneyra repeatedly emphasized his documentation.[276] As he wrote in the *Life of Ignatius of Loyola*, for example, "I thought that I should not even write down anything that did not have either an identifiable source or sufficiently reliable ones."[277] In many editions of the *Historia*, the title page declares the text to have been "collected from various trustworthy authors" (111). Furthermore, Ribadeneyra will name specific sources to reassure readers about the more incredible elements: he acknowledges that some might be troubled by the lurid stories about Anne, for instance, but reasons that "they were recorded by a man as serious and circumspect as Doctor Sander" (156). As we have seen, Ribadeneyra assembled his *Historia* from a substantial collection of sources, and most of his errors and fictions can be traced to these texts. Sander is responsible for many of them, his tales about Anne's birth being only the most egregious—such stories would win the theologian the nickname "Doctor Slanders" from Protestant polemicists.[278] Even in instances where I have been unable to identify a source for a given anecdote (e.g., the story in Book 3, Chapter 13 of a priest accused of being a demon while striving to repay a dying man's debts), I am reluctant to conclude that Ribadeneyra concocted these stories himself. To do so would have been inconsistent with his lifelong praxis, as well as going against a certain streak of self-doubt and a need for external imprimatur observable elsewhere in his life.[279] Much more likely, I think, that

---

276 Ibid., 170–71.

277 Ribadeneyra, *Life of Ignatius*, 8.

278 Sutton, "Nicholas Sanders," 506.

279 Rey, lxviii.

 Cf. Dalmases's assessment: "Studied chapter by chapter and paragraph by paragraph, it [*sc.* the *Vita*] has brought me to the following conclusion: there will hardly be found one fact mentioned by Ribadeneyra for which we cannot find a documentary source [*Estudiada capítulo por capítulo y párrafo por párrafo, me ha llevado a la siguiente conclusión: no se halla apenas un hecho de los que Rib. refiere, del que no se pueda descubrir la fuente documental*]." Dalmases, "Origenes de la hagiografía ignaciana," 138.

he had a source—a manuscript account, a piece of printed ephemera, an oral recollection—that is now lost to us.

Nor was Ribadeneyra an unthinking scribe or naïve dupe at the mercy of his sources: to the contrary, Dalmases has documented the meticulous vetting and critical eye to which he subjected the data he collected, especially accounts of the supernatural.[280] Roldán-Figueroa in turn stresses Ribadeneyra's "exceptional historical sensibility [...] subjecting traditional accounts and models of telling the lives of saints to scrutiny" and his keen awareness "of the qualitative difference between types of sources"[281] In recent years, researchers from literary scholars like David Womersley to intellectual historians like Anthony Grafton have been at pains to push back the horizon for when historians became "critical" in their use of sources, pointing out that, as early as the fifteenth century, humanists were vigorously interrogating their material's reliability, and that even apparently cut-and-paste jobs were the products of careful thought and analysis.[282] Furthermore, there has been a welcome acknowledgment that even the most polemical early modern historiography often entailed genuine scholarship.[283]

In the specific case of Sander, it should be recalled that "Doctor Slanders" was a Protestant attack, and we need not fault Ribadeneyra for disagreeing. More to the point, bear in mind Pollen's comment on *De origine ac progressu*:

> Let us note the remarkable consensus of writers who have accepted it as an authority. It may briefly be said that practically all writers on the Catholic side, from Bellarmine and Suarez [*sic*] down to Benedict XIV, refer to his name as a sufficient warrant for the facts to be found in his work.[284]

Sander had his own sources, foremost among them a now-lost life of Thomas More and the polemical writings of Nicholas Harpsfield (1519–75). David Lewis,

---

280   Ibid., 148.

281   Roldán-Figueroa, "Ribadeneyra's *Vida*," 169.

282   David Womersley, "Against the Teleology of Technique," *HLQ* 68, no. 1–2 (March 2005): 95–108, here 108. Grafton, *What Was History?*, 22.

       Of the Spanish context, Alexander Samson writes, "Nebrija, Ocampo and Morales all insisted on collating multiple sources and following evidence from reliable eye-witnesses rather than second-hand hearsay or sources writing long after the fact." Samson, "Florián de Ocampo," 350.

283   Dmitri Levitin, "From Sacred History to the History of Religion: Paganism, Judaism, and Christianity in European Historiography from Reformation to 'Englightenment,'" *HJ* 55, no. 4 (December 2012): 1117–60, here 1142–45.

284   Pollen, "Nicholas Sander," 41.

the nineteenth-century translator of *De origine ac progressu*, has exhaustively detailed all the many sixteenth-century accusations, suggestions, and hints about Anne's sordid origins, as well as Sander's other outré material. We need not accept Lewis's bizarre conclusion that this version of Anne's parentage might have some truth to it to recognize that Ribadeneyra had ample reason for trusting Sander.[285]

How then should Ribadeneyra's determination to exclude "anything that did not have either an identifiable source or sufficiently reliable ones" be characterized, and what relation, if any, does it have to "critical" historiography? Roldán-Figueroa rightly points out that when Ribadeneyra scrutinized the traditional norms of hagiography, he did so "without abandoning the moral and spiritual ends of hagiography."[286] I would go further: I believe the critical elements of Ribadeneyra's historiography are themselves *products* of "the moral and spiritual ends" of his writing. His motives for interrogating his sources are theological, not methodological. Lying is always a sin; to lie in telling the lives of the saints is worse yet. He adds, "God, after all, does not have any need of our lies to make his glory shine out. In addition, it is seriously wrong to want to honor the original and supreme Truth with fictional stories and fabrications."[287] The religious significance of critical scholarship is crystallized in Ribadeneyra's explanation for his approach in the *Flos sanctorum*: "To select and pick out things true and attested [*averiguadas*], *and those that can most inspire one to the imitation of these saints.*"[288]

It is in the light of the same concern for the spiritual message of the *Historia* that we must examine Ribadeneyra's willingness to believe and include rather incredible materials. As an example, let us consider his acceptance of the spurious correspondence between Catherine and John Forest. It is not simply that Ribadeneyra did not know what the modern historian knows—that these were the fabrications of the Franciscan historian Thomas Bourchier (d. *c.*1586).[289] Ribadeneyra also operated under very different theoretical and philosophical norms of what could (or ought) be included in a history. It was not a given that historians could not make up details—direct speech in particular—that

---

285   Nicholas Sander, *Rise and Growth of the Anglican Schism*, ed. and trans. David Lewis (London: Burns and Oates, 1877), xxiv–xlvii.

286   Roldán-Figueroa, "Ribadeneyra's *Vida*," 170.

287   Ribadeneyra, *Life of Ignatius*, 8–9.

288   "Escoger y entresacar las cosas ciertas y averiguadas, y las que más pueden mover a la imitación de los mismos Santos." Quoted in Dalmases, "Orígenes de la hagiografía ignaciana," 22. Italics mine.

289   Peter Marshall, "Forest, John (*c.*1470–1538)," in *ODNB*, 20:364.

"should" have transpired but for which the sources had not survived.[290] Nor was this merely the expedient of hacks or amateurs: no less a figure than the celebrated Spanish theologian Melchior Cano (*c.*1509–60) accorded a place in sacred historiography to "verisimilitude," the principle of accepting materials that speak to the realities felt to underlie a historical event, even if their *truth* cannot be definitively established.[291] For Ribadeneyra, further supporting such an approach would be the Jesuits' adherence to a Ciceronian style of moral and epistemic probabilism, whereby they acknowledged limits to certain knowledge of the truth, and accepted what could be reasonably established as resemblance to truth—*veri-similitudo*.[292] Such may well have been Ribadeneyra's reasoning in accepting some of the more eyebrow-raising documentary finds, such as Bourchier's letters. Perhaps queen and friar had not penned these exact words, but the letters portray precisely the sorts of emotional and spiritual "facts" Ribadeneyra believed to have been at play in this instance. They also supply valuable support for his confessional agenda, depicting the strength of the spiritual bond between a Catholic religious and a devout layperson, between a royal woman and her spiritual father.

The importance of Ribadeneyra's religious presuppositions is nowhere more visible than in his account of the basic mechanics of history itself. The reader is by now thoroughly familiar with Ribadeneyra's providentialist view of history: in the *Historia*, everything from Bishop John Fisher's (1469–1535) dining habits to the sudden death of the earl of Essex is divinely ordained. There is also the tricky question of the supernatural. Scholars of the *Life of Ignatius of Loyola* have been keen to point out Ribadeneyra's disdain for "fake miracles intended to aggrandize a saint's profile."[293] Bracketing the question of the motivations for these omissions,[294] we must recall that the *Historia* includes such choice details as levitating corpses, incombustible body parts, and ghostly apparitions.

---

290   Nicholas Popper, "An Ocean of Lies: The Problem of Historical Evidence in the Sixteenth Century," *HLQ* 74, no. 3 (September 2011): 375–400, here 378–79.

291   Van Liere, Ditchfield, and Louthan, *Sacred History*, 138.

292   See Robert Aleksander Maryks, "Rhetorical *Veri-Similitudo*: Cicero, Probabilism, and Jesuit Casuistry," in *Traditions of Eloquence: The Jesuits and Modern Rhetorical Studies*, ed. Cinthia Gannett and John Brereton (New York: Fordham University Press, 2015), 60–72.
        See also Maryks, *Saint Cicero and the Jesuits: The Influence of the Liberal Arts on the Adoption of Moral Probabilism*, Bibliotheca Instituti Historici S.I. 64 (Aldershot: Ashgate, 2008).

293   Roldán-Figueroa, "Ribadeneyra's *Vida*," 171.

294   When one believes, as Ribadeneyra did, that the foundation of the Society was itself the will of God, along with everything else in human history, the methodological significance of deleting obviously supernatural elements is less clear.

Nor can we dismiss this simply as fidelity to the source material: many of these stories originate with Sander, but many others are Ribadeneyra's additions, such as an entire chapter on miraculous apparitions of the cross (without much connection, it must be said, to the rest of the narrative—clearly, Ribadeneyra wanted to include it). His *Tratado de la tribulación* invoked such creatures as the phoenix and the salamander (thought to live amid burning flames) as witnesses to divine truth.[295] Here we must not forget the confessional context: Jesuits were leading exponents of a Counter-Reformation strategy foregrounding the miraculous elements of Catholic devotion.[296] How historians ought to contend with the problem of the supernatural continues to inspire debate, but for Ribadeneyra, and for many of his peers, a critical historical mind also made room for the miraculous and for otherworldly causation.[297]

Turning to the practical side of Ribadeneyra's historiography, our author is not always rigorous in his treatment of his sources. When he reproduces documents, he often does so partially (but without noting this). Book 3, Chapter 11, for example, includes an extended quotation from a letter by Elizabeth Sander (Nicholas Sander's older sister, d.1607)—but what Ribadeneyra represents as a single passage is actually spliced together from a passage at the beginning of the letter and another at its end. (This was hardly unusual, as martyrologists of every confessional stripe abbreviated and altered letters and other texts, often excising material purely personal or pedestrian in character, or attempting to occlude doctrinal disagreements.)[298]

Furthermore, translation is always an act of rewriting, and Ribadeneyra is no exception: his renderings of Sander and other sources, though generally faithful, sometimes alter the sense or implications of the text. In a relatively innocuous instance, he abbreviates a passage from *De origine ac progressu* concerning Elizabeth's crackdown on Anabaptists: Sander describes the exile of a French evangelical community and the execution of certain radicals, while Ribadeneyra condenses the passage to give the erroneous, if ultimately trivial, impression that those put to death had been French. But the translations do at times elaborate substantially on the original sense, and even interpolated new

---

295   Ribadeneyra, *Tratado de la tribulacion*, 148[r].

296   Dillon, *Construction of Martyrdom*, 98–99. Walsham, "Translating Trent?," 303–04.

297   On the historiographical problem of the miraculous, see Carlos Eire, "The Good, the Bad, and the Airborne: Levitation and the History of the Impossible in Early Modern Europe," in *Ideas and Cultural Margins in Early Modern Germany: Essays in Honor of H.C. Erik Midelfort*, ed. Marjorie Elizabeth Plummer and Robin B. Barnes (Farnham: Ashgate, 2009), 307–23.

298   Gregory, *Salvation at Stake*, 23.

material into what are ostensibly quotations. Amusingly, the later editions of the *Historia* endow a letter of Campion's with a citation from the *Martyrologium Romanum*—first published the year after the English Jesuit's martyrdom. Ribadeneyra was clearly willing to adjust the historical material—accepting specious sources, inventing dialogue, omitting unfortunate details—in order to tell the story he *wants* to tell.

The past decade has seen scholarship reject the teleological narrative that insists a critical methodology inevitably entailed disinterested historiography.[299] Ribadeneyra's critical distance "does not exclude the possibility that he could manipulate the narrative to his own ends."[300] One need not consider the *Historia* mere agitprop to acknowledge that Ribadeneyra has concerns other than creating an impartial record of events. Rey speaks of this in terms drawn from Ignatian spirituality: "Ribadeneyra took his apostolic mission as a writer very seriously. The introductions to his books reduce to this: explaining to the reader the apostolic motivations and aims that had placed the pen in his hand to write them."[301] In this regard, the Toledan Jesuit is no more than a product of his time: early modern historiography embraced a far wider range of motivations than its modern-day descendant. We have already discussed the Ciceronian and Quintilianic modes of early modern historiography, as well as the centrality of history in the confessional disputes of the Reformation—all currents of thought informing the *Historia* and its aims.

Ribadeneyra's historiographical method did involve subordinating the completeness and accuracy of his narrative to these didactic and polemic ends. Quintero puts this rather bluntly, stressing Ribadeneyra's concern for exemplarity:

> The author partakes of the humanist notion that history is exemplary and, like many of his contemporaries, he emends and manipulates history in the service of exemplarity. Political and ideological considerations and religious partisanship override any sense of historical accuracy and the historical players are all presented as paradigmatic.[302]

---

299   E.g., Grafton, *What Was History?*; Paulina Kewes, ed., *The Uses of History in Early Modern England* (San Marino: Henry E. Huntington Library and Art Gallery, 2006); Van Liere, Ditchfield, and Louthan, *Sacred History*.

300   Roldán-Figueroa, "Ribadeneyra's *Vida*," 171.

301   "Ribadeneyra toma completamente en serio su misión apostólica de escritor. A eso se reducen las Introducciones de sus libros: a explicar al lector las motivaciones y fines apostólicos que le han puesto la pluma en la mano para escribirlos." Rey, lxxxix.

302   Quintero, "English Queens," 262.

Any number of examples could be summoned to demonstrate how Ribadeneyra reworks the historical facts for the sake of "political and ideological considerations," or the creation of "paradigmatic" figures. Perhaps the most telling are the omissions that permeate the stories of Catholic protagonists; let us take Mary Tudor as a case study.

The preceding section outlined how Ribadeneyra renders Mary first as the entirely passive object of divine providence, and then, when action must be taken, as the properly subordinated partner of Philip, Pole, and the other male exponents of the Catholic restoration—all to mitigate the tensions surrounding a queen regnant. What is more, his treatment of the reign edits out crucial yet inconvenient details. Rather than the obedient daughter of the Church portrayed by Ribadeneyra, Mary "was often as defensive of the royal prerogative against papal interference as her father."[303] Indeed, the accession of the fiercely anti-Habsburg pope Paul IV brought Mary into more or less open conflict with the Holy See.[304] In the political arena, Ribadeneyra mentions neither the queen's endemic disputes with her council nor the unsatisfactory results of most of her parliaments.[305] The same is true of the disastrous loss of Calais to the French in 1558 and the mounting national debt.[306] The most striking omission, particularly in light of Mary's posthumous reputation, is Ribadeneyra's elision of the more than 280 Protestants burned at the stake for their faith.[307] Apart from one throwaway sentence about the justness of executing heretics, the *Historia* mentions only the deaths of "several false bishops" (395), of whom Thomas Cranmer (1489–1556) alone is named, during the reign of a queen "truly merciful and pious, an enemy of all bloodshed" (378).[308]

Parenthetically, given the *Historia*'s consistent concern with the Society of Jesus, it may strike some readers as curious that the Jesuits are barely mentioned in Mary's reign. The fact of the matter was that neither Mary nor her

---

303 Lucy Wooding, "The Marian Restoration and the Language of Catholic Reform," in *Reforming Catholicism in the England of Mary Tudor: The Achievement of Friar Bartolomé Carranza*, ed. John Edwards and Ronald W. Truman (Aldershot: Ashgate, 2005), 49–64, here 64.

304 See Loades, *Reign of Mary Tudor*, Chapter 11.

305 Ibid., 216.

306 John Edwards, *Mary I: England's Catholic Queen*, Yale English Monarchs (New Haven: Yale University Press, 2011), 309–12. Loades, *Reign of Mary Tudor*, Chapter 10.

307 Eamon Duffy, *Fires of Faith: Catholic England under Mary Tudor* (New Haven: Yale University Press, 2009), 7.

308 Ribadeneyra may have felt that too much detail accorded the heretics' deaths might create a false equivalence with the Catholic martyrs, or spark readerly interest in their noxious beliefs.

advisers were especially fond of the Society. Soon after taking the throne, the queen forbade Jesuits from entering England.[309] Although this was soon reversed, neither she nor Cardinal Pole ever agreed to a Jesuit presence in England, despite Ignatius's eagerness. This was a "definite slight to the Society," the product of personal differences, political expediency, and distinct visions of how the English church was to be restored.[310] Hardly the most edifying tale to be told in a Jesuit history.

A similar set of omissions and alterations could be drawn up for any of the Catholic figures in the *Historia*. Thomas More's readiness to send Lutherans to the stake;[311] the rumors of Mary Stewart's adultery with her secretary, David Riccio (or Rizzio, *c*.1533–66) and her controversial third marriage;[312] Edmund Campion breaking under torture and revealing the location of a recusant printing press[313]—all have been edited out. I have chosen to examine Ribadeneyra's rendering of Catholic characters because it is there that the influence of his agenda on his historiography appears in highest relief. Reading primarily, if not exclusively, Catholic sources, Ribadeneyra can be forgiven for not recording (or perhaps even knowing about) Elizabeth's surprisingly lenient policy toward Catholics in the early years of her reign.[314] But it strains credulity that he did not know about the extent of the Marian burnings, or the queen of Scots's third husband. Whatever else there is to say about Ribadeneyra, he was no different from other early modern church historians, the vast majority of whom "doctored the existing evidence to make it prove their points."[315] This by no means invalidates the many aspects of his work that involved a

---

309   McCoog, *Our Way of Proceeding?*, 30.

310   Clancy, "First Generation," 137–38.
        See also Thomas M. McCoog, "Ignatius Loyola and Reginald Pole: A Reconsideration."
        JEH 47, no. 2 (April 1996): 257–73; Thomas F. Mayer, "A Test of Wills: Cardinal Pole, Igna-
        tius Loyola, and the Jesuits in England," in *The Reckoned Expense: Edmund Campion and
        the Early English Jesuits*, ed. Thomas M. McCoog, 2nd ed., Bibliotheca Instituti Historici
        s.i. 60 (Woodbridge: Boydell Press, 2007), 21–37.

311   Christopher Haigh, *English Reformations: Religion, Politics and Society under the Tudors*
        (Oxford: Oxford University Press, 1993), 69.

312   Retha M. Warnicke, *Mary Queen of Scots*, Routledge Historical Biographies (London:
        Routledge, 2006), 114.

313   Stephen Alford, *The Watchers: A Secret History of the Reign of Elizabeth I* (New York:
        Bloomsbury Press, 2012), 109.
        Rumors to this effect were circulating at the time. Dillon, *Construction of Martyrdom*,
        131.

314   LaRocca, "Time," *passim*.

315   Grafton, "Church History," 6.

critical, judicious approach to the historian's task—both are constitutive of his historiography.

In closing, let us return to the question of modernity and "modern" historiography. Roldán-Figueroa persuasively argues for Ribadeneyra's contributions to the development of a critical "hagiology" that would come to fruition in the efforts of the Bollandists. Moreover, he gives Ribadeneyra a central role in the formation of how early modern Spain and the Society of Jesus remembered and recorded their pasts. I agree wholeheartedly that Ribadeneyra's place in Jesuit historiography and in Spanish literary culture has been underrated, and that he is a forerunner of the critical approach to the past that the best of the Society's scholars would exemplify in centuries to come. But I wonder whether the *Historia* also suggests another, more counterintuitive way of seeing modern historiography through the prism of Jesuit history.

Simon Ditchfield has attempted to distinguish early modern practitioners of "sacred history" from contemporary historians of religion:

> Notwithstanding their historical, philological, numismatic, and archaeological bravura when examining both manuscript and material evidence, their mission was different from that of the modern academic historian who, no matter how engaged with contemporary agendas, claims a degree of skeptical detachment that would have been meaningless to his or her early modern predecessor.[316]

Ditchfield here echoes one of the foremost concerns raised about Ribadeneyra's historiography (i.e., his blatant agenda) and the justice of his critique, and its applicability to the *Historia*, cannot be denied. The *Historia* violates almost every norm of the contemporary academy: Ribadeneyra omits inconvenient facts, often fails to cite his sources, hazards assertions and interpretations without evidence, and makes no effort to hide his political and polemical commitments. What is crucial here, however, is Ditchfield's nuance: he specifies that the distinction is between the early modern writer of church history and "the modern *academic* historian." Too often, attempts to define "modern" historiography have been implicitly based on the identification of historiographical praxis that resembles that of the contemporary academy.[317]

---

316   Simon Ditchfield, "What Was Sacred History? (Mostly Roman) Catholic Uses of the Christian Past after Trent," in *Sacred History: Uses of the Christian Past in the Renaissance World*, ed. Katherine Van Liere, Simon Ditchfield, and Howard Louthan (Oxford: Oxford University Press, 2012), 72–98, here 86.

317   Womersley, "Against the Teleology," 95.

It is not simply that copious contemporary historical work is done outside the academy; it must be recognized that a great deal of historical work now in print, academic and otherwise, is explicitly political, emotionally laden, or bound up in the persona and personality of the author. In his important study of Spanish "official histories," Kagan points to contemporary "official histories" that, just as much as their early modern counterparts, have agendas other than the preservation of information.[318] Though Kagan's example is the US Army's official account of the first years of the Iraq War (published in 2008), this is hardly the object-lesson of non-academics presuming to write history. In 2010, two academically trained historians of science, Erik M. Conway and Naomi Oreskes, published an explicitly polemical—and extremely impressive—history of the twentieth century's "debates" over science in the United States.[319] The past century has seen extreme manipulations of historical narratives marshaled for every conceivable political, cultural, and social objective—indeed, if we are looking for a definition of "modern" historiography, the influence of such agendas would not be a bad place to start.

In his thoughtful essay, "Against the Teleology of Technique," Womersley observes that "the establishment of the 'chief topic' of the history of historiography as 'the development of the historical-mindedness peculiar to our culture' has given a teleological slant to the subject, which has resulted in the serious misrepresentation of Tudor historiography."[320] This is absolutely true, but the coin has another side. Telling this teleological narrative of historiographical progress has allowed us to occlude the aspects of modern historiography we are less proud of—its emotionality, its political manipulations, its scope for misinformation. These, too, are part of modern historiography, and they have a history that needs to be traced and analyzed. And while we should never forget that Ribadeneyra was and remains an *early* modern figure—his agendas, concerns, influences, and methods are those of sixteenth-century Catholic Europe—the *Historia* offers glimpses of another kind of "modern" historiography.

La cisma de Inglaterra and the Reception of the *Historia*

Having wandered rather far from sixteenth- and seventeenth-century Spain, let us return to the immediate context of the *Historia*, to consider the book's

---

318   Kagan, *Clio & the Crown*, 299.

319   Naomi Oreskes and Erik M. Conway, *Merchants of Doubt: How a Handful of Scientists Obscured the Truth on Issues from Tobacco Smoke to Global Warming* (New York: Bloomsbury Press, 2010).

320   Womersely, "Against the Teleology," 95.

fortunes in and beyond its author's lifetime. Ribadeneyra dedicated both volumes of the *Historia* to the future Philip III. Whether through the author's many contacts among the Spanish aristocracy or through good fortune, the *Historia* did indeed find its way to the prince. Not only did Philip III enjoy the *Historia* immensely, he also embraced its didactic ambitions, incorporating the text into the education of his own son, the future Philip IV (r.1621–65)—who also counted it among his favorite books.[321] Both kings were avid readers of histories, and shared an eagerness to find in accounts of the past lessons for life and statecraft in the present. As one contemporary wrote, Philip III "read history and meditated about it, as if it were essential for governing well, recognizing that it was teacher of human life, a guide to understanding, and an inspiration for learning about the customs and inclinations of foreigners, as well as to defend himself against them."[322]

The *Historia* found an equally positive reception outside the palace. The Spanish Dominican Luis de Granada (1504–88), a friend of Ribadeneyra and an influential theologian, read the book in the summer of 1588 and wrote the Jesuit an effusive letter of praise, which was printed as a preface to the *Historia* in later editions.[323] On a less exalted level, the *Historia* was shipboard reading on at least one early modern Spanish vessel, according to the researches of Irving A. Leonard.[324] It is to be imagined that many Spanish-speakers across Europe (and perhaps even a few at sea) turned to the *Historia* as they awaited news of the Armada—and all the more so after the dreadful news came. In a 1592 pamphlet, Robert Persons commented on the "greedie acceptaunce" in Spain of books about England, "especiallie the translation of Doctor Sanders booke, *de Schismate Anglicano*."[325] As the years passed, the book proved an enduring favorite among Spanish readers: a nineteenth-century editor of the

---

321   Domínguez, "Paper and Pens," 155. Juan Manuel Escudero Baztán, "La construcción de los caracteres en *La cisma de Inglaterra*: Convención e historia en el personaje de Enrique VIII," in *Actas del V Congreso Internacional de la Asociación Internacional Siglo de Oro (AISO), Münster 20–24 de julio de 1999*, ed. Christoph Strosetzki (Madrid: Iberoamericana, 2001), 479–89, here 487.

322   Kagan, *Clio & the Crown*, 202.
      For Philip IV's interest in history, see R.A. Stradling, *Philip IV and the Government of Spain 1621–1665* (Cambridge: Cambridge University Press, 1988), 309–12.

323   Appendix 3.
      A similar letter from Granada about the *Life of Ignatius of Loyola* was put to similar use: Roldán-Figueroa, "Ribadeneyra's *Life*," 157.

324   Irving A. Leonard, "Spanish Ship-Board Reading in the Sixteenth Century," *Hispania* 32, no. 1 (February 1949): 53–58, here 57.

325   Robert Persons, *A Relation of the King of Spanes Receiving in Valliodolid, and in the Inglish College of the Same Towne, in August Last Past of This Yere 1592: VVryten by an Inglish Priest*

Historia called it "one of Spain's most popular works."[326] The numerous print-ings in Ribadeneyra's lifetime have already been rehearsed; to these should be added editions in 1674, 1781, 1786, 1863, 1868, and 1945, as well as a Portuguese translation in 1732.[327] What is more, the *Historia* swiftly began to provide mate-rial for other authors, just as *De origine ac progressu* had done for Ribadeneyra. Persons drew on it in his polemical writings,[328] and Catholic histories of England cited it, notably the Italian Dominican Girolamo Pollini's (d.1601) *Storia ecclesiastica della riuoluzione d'Inghilterra* (1591)[329] and the Spanish Hieronymite Diego de Yepes's (1530–1613) *Historia particular de la persecucion de Inglaterra* (1599).[330] Recently, Deborah Forteza has tantalizingly suggested that Miguel de Cervantes's "exemplary novel" *La española inglesa* (c.1604) may be a response to the *Historia*, either as a variation on Ribadeneyra's own ideas about exemplarity or as a rejoinder, advocating a more pacific approach to world affairs.[331] Roldán-Figueroa credits Ribadeneyra with popularizing the language of "the English schism" in the Iberian Peninsula, a rhetoric deployed by subsequent writers in the service of their own political and theological agendas.[332] Indeed, with the exception of two minor works, the *Historia* was the first book published in Spain on the English persecutions.[333]

The two King Philips and such luminaries as Granada and Cervantes not-withstanding, the *Historia*'s most prominent reader was neither a Habsburg

---

   of the Same College, to a Gentleman and His Vvyf in Flaunders, Latelie Fled out of Ingland, for Profeßion of the Catholique Religion ([Antwerp]: [A. Conincx], 1592), 58.

326 "una de las obras más populares de España." Ribadeneyra, *Obras escogidas*, 177.

327 See bibliography.

328 Houliston, "Lord Treasurer," 389–90.

329 Pollini's work is usually discussed as an adaptation of Sander, but the Dominican also acknowledged his use of "Pietro di Rebadeira." Houliston, "Missionary Position," 18. Girolamo Pollini, *Storia ecclesiastica della riuoluzione d'Inghilterra: Divisa in cinque li-bri; Ne' quali si tratta di quello che è occorso in quell'isola, da che Arrigo ottavo cominciò a pensare di repudiare Caterina; Raccolta da diversi e graviss. scrittori, dal reverendo padre fra Girolamo Pollini; Divisa in capitoli con una tavola delle cose più notabili* (Florence: Per Filippo II Giunta, 1591), 22.

330 Diego de Yepes, *Historia particular de la persecucion de Inglaterra y de los martirios mas insignes que en ella a avido, desde el año del señor 1570* (Madrid: Luis Sanchez, 1599), 75.

331 Deborah Forteza, "Representaciones del Cisma de Inglaterra en el Siglo de Oro: Ribadeneira y Cervantes," in *"Spiritus vivificat". Actas del V Congreso Internacional Jóvenes Investigadores Siglo de Oro (JISO 2015)*, ed. Maite Iraceburu Jiménez and Carlos Mata Induráin, Colección BIADIG 36 (Pamplona: Servicio de Publicaciones de la Universidad de Navarra: 2016), 33–42.

332 Roldán-Figueroa, "Father Luis Piñeiro," 225–27.

333 McCoog, *And Touching Our Society*, 386.

monarch nor a Dominican divine, but the son of an official in the Spanish treasury: the celebrated playwright Pedro Calderón de la Barca. Sometime around
1627 (although this is disputed),[334] Calderón composed a play loosely based on
the *Historia*, entitled *La cisma de Inglaterra*.[335] Though now considered by scholars "a most impressive example of dramatic art [...], a masterpiece,"[336] the play
is barely known in English (a complete translation only appeared in 1990).[337]

Calderón employed considerable artistic license in adapting the first book of
the *Historia* to write *La cisma* (to distinguish the play from the *Historia*, I shall
employ Calderón's Hispanicized character names).[338] He creates a fictitious
French ambassador, Carlos, the love interest of Ana Bolena. Ana intrigues with
Volseo (Cardinal Thomas Wolsey [c.1473–1530]) to supplant Queen Catalina
(Catherine of Aragon) in King Enrique's (Henry VIII) affections. Ana later be-
trays Volseo and engineers his fall from favor; the cardinal subsequently com-
mits suicide by leaping from a tower after a last confrontation with Catalina.
Ana kills Catalina by poisoning a letter supposedly from the king, while

---

334   Dates proposed have ranged from the 1620s to 1652. See Escudero, "Construcción de los
       caracteres," 479n1.
          I follow the majority of scholars in preferring an earlier date, which, as I will explain,
       seems to make more sense given the play's geopolitical thrust. A cogent argument for
       a post-1649 dating can be found in Gregory Peter Andrachuk, "Calderón's View of the
       English Schism," in *Parallel Lives: Spanish and English National Drama 1580–1680*, ed.
       Louise Fothergill-Payne and Peter Fothergill-Payne (Lewisburg: Bucknell University Press,
       1991), 224–38, here 233–34.
          The first surviving text is Pedro Calderón de la Barca, *Octava parte de comedias del
       celebre poeta español, don Pedro Calderon de la Barca*, ed. Juan de Vera Tassis y Villarroel
       (Madrid: Por Francisco Sanz, 1684), 1–45.
          There appears to have been an earlier *suelto* (standalone) edition, but no specimens
       have survived. Pedro Calderón de la Barca, *La cisma de Ingalaterra*, ed. Juan Manuel
       Escudero Baztán, Teatro del Siglo de Oro: Ediciones críticas 115 (Kassel: Edition
       Reichenberger, 2001), ix.
335   Some scholars prefer the spelling "Ingalaterra," reflecting an early modern variant.
336   Parker, "Henry VIII," 352.
337   Pedro Calderón de la Barca, *The Schism in England (La Cisma de Inglaterra)*, ed. Ann L.
       Mackenzie, trans. Kenneth Muir and Ann L. Mackenzie, Aris and Phillips Classical Texts
       (Oxford: Aris and Phillips, 1990).
          All quotations come from this edition.
338   That Calderón relied specifically on Ribadeneyra is established by three details: Volseo's
       antipathy to Catalina stems from the prediction that a woman will be his downfall, one
       character mocks Volseo's tomb in the same terms as the cardinal's fool does in the *Historia*,
       and a biblical citation of "Judas" rather than "Juda," the precise error Ribadeneyra makes
       in the printed editions. Parker, "Henry VIII," 333. Calderón, *Schism in England*, 15.

her indiscreet conversations with Carlos are overheard by Enrique, who has her beheaded and repents of his schism. The play concludes with a chastened Enrique abdicating the throne to his daughter María, a Catholic zealot ruling somewhat uncomfortably over a nation of heretics. Juana Semeyra (Jane Seymour) is little more than a walk-on role, while Henry's three later wives and two later children are dispensed with entirely, as are such key figures as Cromwell, More, and Cranmer. Conversely, the action is embroidered with bits of stage business without basis in Ribadeneyra. To take only the first scene: the play opens with Enrique asleep at his desk, where he has been writing against Martin Luther (1483–1546). The slumbering king has a vision of a beautiful woman—Ana—who tells him, "I'm going to erase / All you write down."[339] Enrique wakes as Volseo enters bearing two letters, one from Pope Leo X (r.1513–21), the other from Luther. In a moment of ominous foreshadowing, the king confuses the two, trampling the pope's letter beneath his feet and placing Luther's above his head. These may be, as A.A. Parker says, specimens of "consummate dramatic art," but they are wholly Calderón's inventions.[340]

On this subject, Parker does not mince words: "*La cisma de Ingalaterra* is a travesty of history," whether compared with a modern account or Calderón's source material (namely Ribadeneyra).[341] He sensibly opines, "We must presume that he [Calderón] departed from historical fact for a deliberate reason." Rather less sensibly, however, he continues, "this reason must have been more connected with the purposes of his art than with any politico-religious 'thesis,' for his treatment of Henry is so extraordinarily compassionate [...] that any attempt to make propaganda out of his theme can be immediately ruled out."[342] This is symptomatic of scholarly approaches to *La cisma* (especially its freedom in reworking the *Historia*), which have concentrated on questions of dramatic construction, character, and aesthetics. They have simultaneously downplayed political or religious messages, at the expense of more universal statements about humanity.[343]

---

339 Calderón, *Schism in England*, 49.

340 Parker, "Henry VIII," 337.

341 Ibid., 350.

     Cf. Joachim Küpper, "*La cisma de Inglaterra* y la concepción calderoniana de la historia," in *Hacia Calderón: Octavo Coloquio Anglogermano Bochum 1987*, ed. Hans Flasche, Archivum Calderonianum 5 (Stuttgart: Franz Steiner Verlag Wiesbaden GMBH, 1988), 183–202, here 184.

342 Parker, "Henry VIII," 327–28.

343 An important exception is Mario Ford Bacigalupo, "Calderón's *La Cisma de Ingalaterra* and Spanish Seventeenth-Century Political Thought," *Symposium: A Quarterly Journal in Modern Literatures* 28, no. 3 (1974): 212–27.

It is not my intention to embark on a comprehensive analysis of *La cisma*, a task for which I have neither the space nor the expertise. That said, I would like to probe whether "any politico-religious 'thesis'" and "propaganda" are as coterminous as Parker seems to believe. Calderón's play has much to say about religion, politics, and the intersection of the two, but these sentiments do not fit the standard mold of Counter-Reformation propaganda.[344] In what follows, I will hazard a few observations on how Calderón reads and reworks the *Historia*, concentrating on the extraordinary final scene. In the spirit of a stimulating recent collection on how early modern fictions performed historiographical work,[345] I argue that Calderón's modifications of the *Historia* can be read as thinking through Spain's relationship with the English heretics of the early sixteenth century, specifically in the context of the hopes and fears excited by the Spanish Match.

To be sure, many of Calderón's changes respond to aesthetic concerns, but that should not preclude the potential impact of the shifts in Anglo-Spanish relations since Ribadeneyra wrote the *Historia*. For a start, crowns had changed hands several times: in Spain, at Philip II's death in 1598 and Philip III's in 1621; in England, at Elizabeth's demise in 1603 and James I's in 1625. In 1627, when *La cisma* is believed to have premiered, the two thrones were occupied by two relatively new kings, Philip IV and Charles I (r.1625–49). James's accession in 1603 had inaugurated a period of renewed peace between Spain and England and Scotland (an achievement coming undone in the 1620s by both sides' deepening involvement in the Thirty Years' War).[346] A major recurring theme in the two countries' diplomacy was the so-called "Spanish Match," the proposal for Charles, James's second son, to wed Maria Anna (1606–46), Philip III's youngest daughter.[347] The idea had been mooted even before James became king of England, but began circulating in earnest in the 1610s.[348] The urgency of securing a wife for Charles had intensified precipitously in 1612 with the death of his older brother, Henry Frederick, prince of Wales (1594–1612). The negotiations reached their most unusual phase in 1623, when Charles, accompanied by

---

344   It should be noted that Calderón did produce numerous pieces of religious propaganda, which were not merely Catholic but vehemently anti-Protestant. In any event, I concur with Gregory Peter Andrachuk: "the question of religion is not incidental but essential" to *La cisma*. Andrachuk, "Calderón's View," 225.

345   Allison Kavey and Elizabeth Ketner, eds., *Imagining Early Modern Histories* (Farnham: Ashgate, 2016).

346   Brennan C. Pursell, "The End of the Spanish Match," *HJ* 45, no. 4 (2002): 699–726, here 701.

347   See Glyn Redworth, *The Prince and the Infanta: The Cultural Politics of the Spanish Match* (New Haven: Yale University Press, 2003).

348   Cross, "Pretense and Perception," 580. Pursell, "End," 701–02.

George Villiers, first duke of Buckingham (1592–1628), traveled to Spain incognito and spent eight months at the court in Madrid.[349] Though the prince was a sensation in Spain, the Match ran aground over intractable differences on religious policy and disputes over Habsburg control of the Palatinate (Charles's sister, Elizabeth [1596–1662], was the wife of Elector Frederick V [r.1610–23], who had been dispossessed of the Palatinate after his disastrous attempt to claim the crown of Bohemia).[350]

Though in the end nothing came of the negotiations, they were for many years a focus of religious and political anxieties on both sides. One flashpoint was the Spanish demand for toleration (formal or informal) for English Catholics.[351] It was hoped—perhaps not very realistically—that placing a Spanish *infanta* on the throne of England and Scotland might be a first step toward reclaiming the kingdom for the Catholic Church, particularly if the couple's children could be raised in Spain (or at the very least according to Spanish mores).[352] The possibility of Charles's conversion had been floated, although this was not insisted upon. This, of course, raised the troubling specter of a Catholic princess marrying a heretic and ruling over a kingdom of heretics.[353] The *infanta* herself "had said that she would rather become a religious than queen of a kingdom where Catholicism was outlawed"—although her personal objections alone would not have blocked the marriage.[354] Above all, it should be recalled that however the modern historian may assess the Match's viability, contemporary observers had plenty of reason to believe negotiations were proceeding productively, right up until the project collapsed.[355]

---

349   Cross, "Pretence and Perception," 563.

350   See Pursell, "End."

351   Michael C. Questier, ed., *Stuart Dynastic Policy and Religious Politics 1621–1625*, Camden Fifth Series 34 (Cambridge: Cambridge University Press, 2009), 6, 10.

352   Thomas Cogswell, "England and the Spanish Match," in *Conflict in Early Stuart England: Studies in Religion and Politics 1603–1642*, ed. Richard Cust and Ann Hughes (London: Longman, 1989), 107–33, here 112.

       Michael C. Questier has edited a collection of contemporary letters illustrating the hopes excited among English Catholics by the Spanish Match: Questier, *Stuart Dynastic Policy*.

       Similar sentiments were current in the Habsburg domains, too: a manuscript presented to the *infanta* by the English Bridgettine nuns living in exile in Lisbon hoped that "this marriage of Your Highness [has] opened the door for our holy Catholic faith to enter England." Quoted in Lay, "Literary Lives," 79.

353   Cross, "Pretence and Perception," 565–67.

354   Pursell, "End," 719.

355   Questier, *Stuart Dynastic Policy*, 38, 42, 44, 47–48.

Calderón himself may have played a minor role in this chaotic diplomatic drama: it has been suggested that while the prince of Wales was in Madrid, he may have been in the audience when another of the playwright's works, *Amor, honor, y poder*—like *La cisma*, a history play set in England—was performed at court.[356] In any event, Calderón's departures from his source material take on new significance when set against the backdrop of the Spanish Match. Let us begin with one of the more glaring omissions: the deletion of Elizabeth. It is not simply that Henry's Protestant daughter, the primary villain of the *Historia*, does not appear in the play; she seems to have been erased from history altogether. Ana Bolena is executed at the end of *La cisma* (indeed, much of the last scene takes place with her headless corpse onstage), and no mention is ever made of a child from her relationship with Enrique. As a result, besides Ana's brief reign as queen, the only "heretical" monarch in *La cisma* is Enrique himself. This may be related to the fact that for Calderón and his audience, the faces of "heretical" power in England were not, as they had been for Ribadeneyra, female (Elizabeth), but male (James and Charles). Several commentators have observed that Calderón's portrayal of Enrique is noticeably more positive than Ribadeneyra's of Henry.[357] Distressing though James's Protestantism was, the Spanish were rather favorably inclined toward the king of England and Scotland, who had made several gestures of goodwill: attempting (without success) to stem the tide of anti-Spanish sentiment, dissolving parliament in 1621 to prevent open challenges to his alliance with the Habsburgs, and suspending the penal laws against his Catholic subjects the following year.[358] It was Charles

---

356   Don W. Cruickshank, "Calderón's *Amor, honor y poder* and the Prince of Wales, 1623," *Bulletin of Hispanic Studies* 77 (2000): 75–99.

357   Parker, "Henry VIII," 335. Escudero, "Construcción de los caracteres," 483.

   Both Juan Manuel Escudero Baztán and Braulio Fernández Biggs have queried whether this is actually a departure from Ribadeneyra, suggesting that it is faithful to the ambivalent portrait of the king in the last chapters of Book 1 of the *Historia*. Calderón, *La cisma*, 30–31. Braulio Fernández Biggs, *Calderón y Shakespeare: Los personajes en* La Cisma de Ingalaterra *y* Henry VIII, Biblioteca Áurea Hispánica 77 (Madrid: Iberoamericana, 2012), 68.

358   Highley, *Catholics Writing the Nation*, 192–93; Pursell, "End," 706; Brennan C. Pursell, "James I, Gondomar and the Dissolution of the Parliament of 1621," *History* 85, no. 279 (July 2000): 428–45.

   It is essential to differentiate between James's diplomatic policy vis-à-vis Spain and his religious policy vis-à-vis British Catholics, as well as between perceptions of the king's religious and political leanings and his actual intentions. James favored good relations with Spain and was prepared to accept some measure of doctrinal conservatism on the part of his subjects, but was hardly "pro-Catholic." In the wake of the Gunpowder Plot, the king countenanced the passage of harsh anti-Catholic legislation. In particular, Questier has

who in 1624 pushed his father to a declaration of war, and hostilities were not fully entered into until the old king's death in 1625.[359]

The parallel between Enrique and the two seventeenth-century British royals becomes more convincing when one considers the remarkable similarities between the historical Henry VIII's life and the contours of the Spanish Match. Both involved the younger son of an English (British) king, heir to the throne after the sudden demise of his older brother, who marries the youngest daughter of the Spanish king. Though Henry was still within the Catholic fold when he married Catherine in 1509, in the 1620s he would be remembered as a heretic married to a good Catholic—just as Charles might become. For Calderón to give the final political triumph of his play to the child of that first Spanish Match speaks to the hopes that might be invested in *Infanta* Maria Anna's marriage (note, too, the felicitous correspondence of one Catholic María to another). Calderón's María, like her seventeenth-century Habsburg counterpart, expresses serious reservations about the religious and political compromises demanded of her: "I know what is important / That we obey the Church in humbleness, / And I obey it, prostrate on the ground, / Renouncing all the mortal greatness that / They promise me, if the cost that I must pay / Is to renounce the law ordained by God."[360] Henry urges temporary equivocation: "Be silent and dissimulate; the time / Will come when you can carry out your zeal."[361] It is not hard to imagine some combination of Maria Anna's father, Philip III, her brother, Philip IV, or the prime minister, the count-duke of Olivares (1587–1645), giving the *infanta* similar advice. Olivares had personally impressed upon the princess the significance of this opportunity of reclaiming England for Catholicism, enlisting his wife and the *infanta*'s confessor in his efforts.[362]

Quintero argues that the finale's departure from historical reality mars any triumphalism María's staged victory might inspire:

> "Real" historical events surrounding the reign of "Bloody Mary" and her ultimate demise, events well known to Calderón's audience, expose the

---

convincingly argued that the Oath of Allegiance was a fiendishly clever maneuver to sow dissension among British Catholics. James indisputably had a knack for raising Catholic hopes, at home and abroad, about his future actions. Michael C. Questier, "Loyalty, Religion and State Power in Early Modern England: English Romanism and the Jacobean Oath of Allegiance," *HJ* 40, no. 2 (1997): 311–29. Fincham and Lake, "Ecclesiastical Policy," 207.

359   Pursell, "End," 726.
360   Calderón, *Schism in England*, 189.
361   Ibid., 191.
362   Pursell, "End," 714.

staged victory of Catholicism over the heretics as an illusory exercise in wish-fulfillment, as illusory as Henry's dream at the beginning of the play. There is a deep pessimism at the root of this play, as if the playwright himself recognized the futility of his appropriation and rewriting of history.[363]

Certainly no audience member of even the most rudimentary historical awareness could have "believed" the version of events staged by Calderón. And Quintero is probably right insofar as some viewers might well have taken solace in a fantasy of English history as it *should* have unfolded. But to dismiss Calderón's reworking of history (and the *Historia*) as merely "an illusory exercise in wish-fulfillment" is unsatisfying, if only because the triumph of Catholicism Calderón gives us is so patently not all that could be wished for. The playwright makes no secret of the real difficulties confronting María as she prepares to ascend the throne and seek the restoration of the true faith. She is not the perfect Catholic princess, disturbingly ready to swear an oath with every intention of breaking it.[364] At the same time, Quintero's judgment that the play grows out of "a deep pessimism" seems overstated. The play ends with a Catholic princess acknowledged as queen of England, her once-heretical father repenting his sins, and the physical embodiment of heresy, Ana Bolena, lying dead at her feet. However ambiguous the victory, it is a victory nonetheless.

Explaining this curious mixture of triumph and foreboding requires situating Calderón's historical imagination within the tensions of the 1620s, particularly as they crystallized around the Spanish Match. Even before the project had been definitively abandoned, and the more optimistic Catholics could still dream of Charles's conversion, there could be no getting around the fact of the enduring strength of the Protestant interest in England and Scotland. As the María of *La cisma* soon learns, the heretics are too numerous and too influential to be ignored. Tomás Boleno (the fictionalized Thomas Boleyn, c.1477–1539) urges Enrique, "Your Majesty, persuade / The Princess now to moderate her views, / Or else the kingdom will not swear allegiance."[365] What the final scene depicts, then, is a devoutly Catholic princess of Spanish extract compelled to

---

363   Quintero, "English Queens," 278–79.
364   Bacigalupo, "Calderón's *La Cisma*," 224–26.
        Joachim Küpper offers a different reading, citing the widespread Catholic conviction exemplified by Francisco de Quevedo's (1580–1645) dictum that to deceive heretics was "honest treachery against traitors [*traición honesta contra los traidores*]." Küpper, "*La Cisma de Inglaterra*," 197.
365   Calderón, *Schism in England*, 191.

accept religious compromises for the sake of securing the English crown. She must rule over a nation of heretics, but she does so with the firm intention of changing course as soon as possible and for the sake of eventually securing their return to Roman obedience.

Hilaire Kallendorf has convincingly argued that casuistry, that branch of moral reasoning so linked to the Society of Jesus, was fundamental to the theatre of the Spanish Golden Age, as authors, characters, and audiences struggled to answer the ubiquitious question, "What should I do?"[366] (Casuistry attempted to resolve moral issues through "the rhetorical principle of accommodation to times, places, persons, and other circumstances"—an approach aptly suited to the imaginative possibilities of the stage.)[367] Calderón, whose plays are filled with casuistic vocabulary, was an alumnus of the Colegio Imperial, the Jesuit school at Madrid, and had studied canon law for six years:[368] there can be no doubt that he was familiar with this discourse. It does not seem too farfetched to read the final scene of La cisma as an attempt at precisely this kind of moral thinking. Mario Ford Bacigalupo sees the play as condemning María's resort to Machiavellian political expediency;[369] I suggest rather that La cisma points to the fictionalized princess's actions as a workable, imperfect solution to Maria Anna's dilemma. Quintero is right to point out that the play is not necessarily optimistic: Calderón is under no illusions that the process of reclaiming England for Catholicism will be easy. That said, securing positions of power for good Catholics offers the best hope for eventual success.

Although we cannot be certain about the date of composition for La cisma, it seems almost certain that the play was written after 1623, when it became clear that the Spanish Match was a dead letter. This need not invalidate a reading of the play as a meditation on Spain's relationship with England and Scotland, and with heresy more generally. Even several years after the project collapsed, the Match would still have provided the readiest and most iconic template for thinking through the two countries' interactions. More to the point, the basic geopolitical realities remained unchanged. James's realms were too powerfully and too firmly Protestant to make another Armada a feasible suggestion. If the kingdom was to be recovered for the Church, it would be by peaceful means—and to the Habsburgs, famous for winning crowns by

366   Hilaire Kallendorf, Conscience on Stage: The Comedia as Casuistry in Early Modern Spain. University of Toronto Romance Series (Toronto: University of Toronto Press, 2007).

367   O'Malley, First Jesuits, 144–47, here 145.

368   Calderón, Schism in England, 5. John Loftis, "Henry VIII and Calderón's La Cisma de Inglaterra," Comparative Literature 34, no. 3 (Summer 1982): 208–22, here 212.

369   Ford Bacigalupo, "Calderón's La cisma," 224–26.

marriage rather than war, the political idiom of an inter-confessional match was perfectly natural.[370] Rewriting the Match after the fact allowed a freedom of commentary not possible while the sensitive negotiations were ongoing;[371] the original Spanish Match might have failed, but *La cisma* could begin to imagine a successful second attempt. More than one scholar has comment-ed that Golden Age drama is characterized by its efforts at "exploration"—*La cisma* is an instance when that exploration occurred in a geopolitical terrain, in addition to aesthetic or humanistic arenas.[372]

However one interprets the work, *La cisma de Inglaterra* has unquestion-ably been the *Historia*'s most influential legacy. The play proved enduringly popular with Spanish audiences and readers: it saw numerous standalone editions and continued to be performed well into the eighteenth century.[373] And although no full English translation was produced until 1990, there have long been French (1843, 1960), German (partial in 1863, full in 1875, 1911, 1922), and Italian (1949) editions.[374] Political readings aside, *La cisma* is a remarkable work by a consummate master of his art. Calderón's lyrical accomplishments won the admiration of Percy Shelley (1792–1822), who produced a rather in-ept translation of the beautiful monologue put into the mouth of the lovesick Carlos.[375] The French composer Camille Saint-Saëns (1835–1921) even wrote an opera, *Henry VIII* (1883), with a libretto adapted from *La cisma* by libret-tist Pierre-Léonce Détroyat (1829–98) and poet Paul-Armand Silvestre (1837–1901).[376] Inevitably compared to William Shakespeare's (1564–1616) *Henry VIII* (c.1613)—even, incredibly, suggested to be a response thereto[377]—*La cisma* was actually in dialogue with a long tradition of Spanish political, theologi-cal, and historical thought (not least Ribadeneyra's own contributions). "By the 1620s when the play was being written, the English schism still had not been resolved and there were no signs that a solution would be reached in the near

---

370   Pursell, "End," 725.

371   Cf. Jeremy Robbins, "The Spanish Literary Responses to the Visit of Charles, Prince of Wales," in *The Spanish Match: Prince Charles's Journey to Madrid*, ed. Alexander Samson (Aldershot: Ashgate, 2006), 107–22, here 109.

372   Cf. Kewes, "History and Its Uses," 5.

373   Calderón, *Schism in England*, 12.

374   See Kurt Reichenberger and Roswitha Reichenberger, *Bibliographisches Handbuch der Calderón-Forschung: Manual bibliográfico calderoniano*, 4 vols., Würzburger Romanist-ische Arbeiten 1 (Kassel: Thiele & Schwarz, 1979), 1:182–83.

375   Calderón, *Schism in England*, vi.

376   Camille Saint-Saëns, Léonce Détroyat, and Paul-Armand Silvestre, *Henry VIII: Opéra en 4 actes* (Paris: A. Durand & Fils, 1883).

377   Parker, "Henry VIII," 327.

future."[378] Calderón's inheritance from Ribadeneyra extended beyond the raw material of settings and characters: manipulating the *Historia* gave him the tools to think through the contemporary, continuing ramifications of "la cisma de Inglaterra."

Assessing the *Historia*

The picaresque afterlife of the *Historia* has continued into modern academia, where the text has generally not found a favorable reception. In closing, I wish to offer my own perspective, in the context of some of the scholarly responses to Ribadeneyra's history. I have no wish to imitate Lewis or Veech, who in their eagerness to redeem Sander's reputation as a historian made claims for their protagonist that the evidence simply would not bear.[379] Ribadeneyra was not a perfect historian; the *Historia* is not a perfect history. It is, however, a fascinating text, with much to tell us about early modern historiography, the Society of Jesus, and contemporary European reactions to the English Reformation. This translation is my own imperfect attempt to open new conversations along those lines.

The history of the *Historia* extends beyond 1588. Even the most sophisticated analyses of the text usually restrict themselves to the first edition (something I have myself been guilty of).[380] This introduction has been at pains to demonstrate the extent of Ribadeneyra's continued investment in the project after

---

378   Ford Bacigalupo, "Calderón's *La Cisma*," 212.

379   Veech insists, "the publication of public documents in England and abroad have served in great measure to show that Sanders was far better informed and more accurate than many of his detractors." He describes *De origine ac progressu* as "one of the earliest and best-informed contemporary accounts of the schism, from which a reflection of the sentiments and feelings of a large section of the English people at this turning-point in the national history can be gained." Veech, *Nicholas Sanders*, 257–58.

    Distressingly, Rey at times comes close to doing the same for Ribadeneyra. In lauding his erudition and literary style, he claims "his citations are not a headlong and ill-assorted flood of scavenged texts in haphazard arrangement, or in selections at second hand, but rather evidence excerpted from the direct study of the authors [*Sus citas no son aluvión impertinente y abigarrado de textos cazados en cualquier concordancia, o en selecciones de segunda mano, sino testimonios anotados en el estudio directo de los autores*]." As we have seen, the *Historia*'s treatment of its sources and tendency to borrow blocks of text wholesale and unacknowledged do not accord with this rosy assessment. Rey, cxviii.

380   E.g., Cid Morgade, "Analysis," 2; Domínguez, "History in Action," 2n3; Weinreich, "Distinctiveness," 175n2.

1588—in addition to the third volume (usually given no more than a cursory mention), often-substantial changes continued for almost two decades. Above and beyond the textual history, little attention is paid to the *Historia*'s influence after the events of 1588. By thus foreshortening the analytical perspective, scholars have given *De origine ac progressu* and the Spanish Armada an artificially exaggerated prominence in understanding the *Historia*.

The 1588 edition of the *Historia* is the closest—chronologically and in terms of content—to *De origine ac progressu*. Concentrating on the *editio princeps*, then, foregrounds the links between Ribadeneyra and Sander. This is hardly unreasonable, but it tends to lead scholars to treat the *Historia* primarily as an outgrowth of *De origine ac progressu*, discussed within the context of the exiled English Catholics. Two of the most important pieces of scholarship on the *Historia*, Houliston's 2011 article in *English Studies in Africa* and Domínguez's doctoral dissertation of the same year, elucidate how Ribadeneyra reacted to the material he inherited, as well as his engagement with English Catholics on the Continent.[381] (In other cases, the *Historia* is mentioned only as part of the afterlife of Sander's text—sometimes not even by name.[382]) Doing so downplays the distinctness of Ribadeneyra's intellectual projects—the Society of Jesus, the workings of providence in history, making religious and political texts available in the vernacular. Contemporaries certainly saw a difference between the two books: during the debate over the initial publication, Acquaviva suggested that a straightforward Spanish translation of *De origine ac progressu* might be more appropriate.[383] The simple fact is that the political and intellectual environment of the English exiles does not altogether fit Ribadeneyra: their concerns were not always his concerns, nor were their influences necessarily his influences. To be sure, the two worlds were undoubtedly and intricately connected, and the Toledan Jesuit remained passionate about English affairs from the 1550s to the day he died. But to integrate the *Historia* into the tradition of *English* exile writings is to miss a substantial part of what Ribadeneyra was trying to do.[384]

In the same way, the first edition is also the closest to the Spanish Armada. It was Sir Francis Drake's attacks off the coast of Spain in 1587, and the knowledge that a Spanish response must follow, that jolted Ribadeneyra into

381   Houliston, "Missionary Position"; Domínguez, "Papers and Pens," Part 1.

382   E.g., Pollen, "Nicholas Sander," 41. Veech, *Nicholas Sanders*, 237; Highley, "'Pestilent and Seditious Book,'" 154.

383   Domínguez, "History in Action," 6.

384   Weinreich, "Distinctiveness," 176 and *passim*.

finishing his book.[385] The *Historia* may well have been an official part of the propaganda campaign around the Armada, and it certainly echoed many of the themes of those efforts. But by marginalizing the third book of the *Historia*, the jingoistic, interventionist message of the 1588 edition has been allowed to dominate scholarly discussion. This militarism has largely disappeared by 1593, replaced by a more ambiguous providentialism. Moreover, an entire aspect of the Armada, its failure, has been ignored, and with it the complex emotional work performed by *Historia*'s third book. Even the 1588 edition has been ill-served by this emphasis on the Armada: from the first, Ribadeneyra had broader intentions for his *Historia* than simple propaganda.

Beyond the Armada, scholars have been fixated on the *Historia* as anti-English, anti-Protestant polemic, struck most of all by its virulence. Parker's backhanded compliment to the text's importance is representative:

> Ribadeneyra's work still deserves to be read—not because it is full of impassioned invective, but because it is so eloquent a witness both to the intensity of anti-English feeling among the Spaniards of the time and to their ignorance of the nature of the English Reformation. It reads like an account of the excesses of the Anabaptists; and this ignorance fanned legitimate hostility to a quite unwholesome pitch of indignation.[386]

Parker also considered the *Historia*'s invective more intense than that of *De origine ac progressu*, a judgment not shared by Rey, who avers that "Ribadeneyra's exegetical system results in something more moderate."[387]

However one apportions responsibility for the *Historia*'s venom, there can be no denying its presence and its potency. But even venom admits of gradations. Under sustained examination, "the worn tropes, turgid prose and predictability of anti-Elizabethan, anti-heretical vitriol [...] [and] long-established truisms about Anglo-Spanish mutual disdain"[388] reveal substantial nuance. Ribadeneyra is of course unapologetic in his confessional and polemical allegiances, and there is no ambiguity as to who the heroes and villains of the story are. And yet, very few of the "heretics"—even the Catholics' fiercest persecutors—are rendered one-dimensionally; in most cases, Ribadeneyra's righteous condemnations of their sins, heresies, and cruelties are mingled with respect,

---

385   *MHSIR*, 2:77. Domínguez, "History in Action," 5.
386   Parker, "Henry VIII," 333n1.
387   Ibid., 333.
          "El sistema interpretacionista de Ribadeneyra resulta algo más moderado." Rey, 873.
388   Domínguez, "History in Action," 3.

grudging admiration, and even sympathy. No less a Catholic hate-figure than William Cecil receives praise for his administrative skills. Cardinal Wolsey, the archetypal venal clergyman, retains some hope of redemption: "perhaps our Lord punished him in this way so as not to condemn him for all eternity" (192). In a particularly striking passage, Ribadeneyra commiserates with Sir Christopher Hatton's (1540–91) torturous position at court that denies him the family life and religious freedom he craves.

Both Brad Gregory and Jenna Lay have remarked upon the importance of reading polemic sensitively, both for what it can tell us about the religious and intellectual environment in which it moved and for the literary techniques of which it is composed.[389] At the same time, the *Historia* is not *exclusively* polemic, and it is certainly no monotonous, single-minded attack on the heretical foe. Ribadeneyra's text speaks variously to Habsburg royals and Jesuit superiors, ordinary Spaniards and grandees. He intervenes in debates over the Society's mission, promotes martyr cults, publicizes the English seminaries, and engages in sustained theological and historical reflections. The past generation of scholarship has seen a marked rise in the appreciation of the sophistication of Catholic textual practice in the Reformation. There was no one "anti-Elizabethan, anti-heretical" discourse, and though they may have shared a set of tropes, different authors and texts advanced diverse visions of what "Anglo-Spanish mutual disdain" meant and how it should (or should not) be prosecuted.[390] Ribadeneyra has an agenda, to be sure, and as we have seen, he "re-writes and transforms history in order to present historical events as a narrative with a coherent moral message."[391] Throughout his life, he fervently believed that "Spain should continue protecting itself against the heretical threat at home, and collaborate abroad to aid the Catholics harmed by its doleful influence,"[392] but how he understood this mission shifted radically over time. His differences with other Catholic polemicists were no less dramatic, and of no less significance for a full understanding of early modern confessional writing.

---

389   Gregory, *Salvation at Stake*, 12–13. Lay, "Literary Lives," 73.

390   E.g., Alexandra Walsham, "'Domme Preachers'? Post-Reformation English Catholicism and the Culture of Print," *Past & Present* 168 (August 2000): 72–123.
           For various dimensions of the Anglo-Spanish relationship in the late sixteenth century, see Highley, *Catholics Writing the Nation*, Chapter 6; McCoog, *Building the Faith*; Parker, "Tudor England."

391   Quintero, "English Queens," 280.

392   "España debe seguir previniéndose contra el peligro protestante dentro de casa, y colaborar fuera de ella en ayuda de los católicos sometidos a su trágica influencia." Rey, lxxxvi–lxxxvii.

Before moving on, it is worth discussing the *Historia*'s quality *qua* text, separate from its didactic and polemical aims, and from the many critiques of Ribadeneyra's historical method. Put bluntly, is the *Historia* worth reading? It is here that I depart from Domínguez, the *Historia*'s foremost modern scholar. Domínguez makes no secret of his low opinion of the book's quality. He castigates its "thorough unoriginality" and its "ambiguous genre":

> A mix of religion and politics, of "real" history and plain opportunistic propaganda, of ribald titillation and moral posturing, of apology and exhortation, of advice and critique, it does many things but provide the sorts of theoretical reflections attractive to intellectual historians, nor does its confessional cast seem to promise any of the so-called unbiased facts used as grist for the political historian's mill. Although it constitutes an ecclesiastical history, the book does not have much to offer students of early modern historiography or religion either. It is neither an innovative rendering of the genre nor an eloquent participant in theological battles that are of scholarly interest. Moreover, its style is undistinguished. Students of literature avert their eyes.[393]

He continues,

> Here the reader will find no defense of the book's intrinsic value, aesthetic or otherwise. Not even the book's contemporary popularity serves as justification for subjecting readers to what follows. The simple fact that the text's producers intended it to play an important role amidst a complicated political/polemical situation at the end of the sixteenth century should be enough to attract attention. The point is to mine the text for clues of how its author and benefactors tried to employ/deploy the *Scisma* at a critical juncture of war between Spain and England, and more generally, during a period of confessional strife and pervasive malaise.[394]

A few qualifying observations should be made before addressing the broader critique. On the score of unoriginality, Domínguez points out that the *Historia* "was largely an adaptation of English exile Nicholas Sander's 1586 *De origine ac progressu*."[395] Here we return to my earlier comment that too heavy a focus on the *editio princeps* skews the *Historia*'s textual history. Domínguez's statement has much truth to it, particularly in terms of the early printings of the first

---

393   Domínguez, "History in Action," 3–4.
394   Ibid., 4.
395   Ibid., 3.

volume. Moreover, it is equally true of the rest of the *Historia*, *mutatis mutandis*: much of the work originates with authors other than Ribadeneyra. But I suggest that Ribadeneyra demonstrates another kind of originality (perhaps no longer considered such) in how he deploys, manipulates, and repurposes those borrowings.[396] The variegated content of the *Historia* is a characteristically early modern feature, at once a technique for holding the reader's interest and a consequence of more porous boundaries between genres.[397] Moreover, the very fact that we are nonplussed by a cultural phenomenon that was evidently widespread and well received is justification enough for the historian's interest—consider Robert Darnton's famous remark that "when you realize that you are not getting something—a joke, a proverb, a ceremony—that is particularly meaningful [...] you can see where to grasp a foreign system of meaning in order to unravel it."[398]

What is there to say about the work's style? One might plausibly line up various prominent scholars who have lauded Ribadeneyra as a stylist,[399] but that strikes me as at once unproductive and unresponsive to Domínguez's point. It is true that there is a great deal of vitriol in the *Historia*, often rather repetitive—even the most imaginative wordsmith will find it difficult to invent new ways to denounce heresy over the course of several hundred pages. And yet it must be said that there are passages of startling pathos and remarkable verbal creativity. A master orator, Ribadeneyra deploys apostrophes, rhetorical questions, and metaphors to great effect—there is much in the *Historia* that benefits from reading aloud. Finally, I wonder about calling the *Historia* "a bilious book, lacking in charm, but burning with fervor."[400] Is biliousness so antithetical to charm? Is there not a certain allure in a master of prose deploying their talent in single-minded attack? Consider the relish with which we read a truly blistering negative review of a movie, a restaurant, or a book.

Speaking for myself, I enjoy the *Historia*—indeed, I undertook this translation as a labor of love, hoping to see the work better appreciated in Anglophone scholarship—but it can hardly be said to be a neglected masterpiece of Spain's Golden Age. In the last pages of this introduction, then, I will endeavor to defend "the book's intrinsic value," and suggest why it merits more serious study than mining it for a few isolated scraps of historical data.

---

396   Cf. Womersley, "Against the Teleology," 108.

397   Bilinkoff, "Many 'Lives,'" 184.
          Cf. Highley, "'Pestilent and Seditious Book,'" 155.

398   Robert Darnton, *The Great Cat Massacre: And Other Episodes in French Cultural History*, rev. ed. (New York: Basic Books, 2009), 78.

399   Rey has actually done this, for those interested: Rey, cxiv–cxvii.

400   Domínguez, "Paper and Pens," 136–37.

As an initial matter, I posit that the *Historia* is indeed "an innovative rendering of the genre" of ecclesiastical history, specifically the second volume. As I have explained, I read the *Segunda parte* as an extension and development of Ribadeneyra's attempts in his letter-*memorial* and his *Tratado de la tribulación* to process the trauma, theological *and* emotional, of the Armada's defeat. Crucial to this effort is historicization, the marshaling of the past to create a narrative with intellectual room for both present tribulations and a continued belief in divine providence. Church history is cited not (solely) to make claims of authenticity but to visualize the trajectory of future sufferings and so maintain a sense of hope. Bireley sees the *Segunda parte* as simply the application of the *Tratado*'s principles to the specific case of English Protestantism.[401] He is unquestionably correct in terms of the *Segunda parte*'s intellectual genealogy, but he downplays the importance of genre. Explicating these themes in a narrative, rather than a philosophical or theological idiom facilitates and expands the work of historicization. Ribadeneyra is able to assimilate the whole of the text, on a level below content itself, into the tradition of ecclesiastical history. The *Tratado* laid essential groundwork for this exploration, and it is because of the *Tratado* that we can see the emotional contours of the *Segunda parte* in such high relief, but that should not obscure the originality of using ecclesiastical history as a vehicle for emotional work. Furthermore, positioning the *Historia* within this emotional-philosophical project highlights its significance to Ribadeneyra. The man himself acknowledged that writing was a source of pleasure, purpose, and spiritual meaning for him:[402] the *Historia* reminds us that in addition to intellectual and polemical aims, early modern authors could find the writing of history therapeutic, so to speak.

Concomitantly, I am not interested in according or denying Ribadeneyra the title of "popular historian," but the term does underscore his sustained engagement, in the *Historia* and elsewhere, with the challenges and opportunities of broadening the audience for historical writing.[403] Much of the attention given to early modern historiography has focused on elite readerships, whether "official histories" produced for court milieus or works of great erudition composed as volleys in academic and confessional disputes.[404] In the *Historia*, we see Ribadeneyra adapting his material to the interests and capabilities of a non-Latinate Spanish audience. Simultaneously, in the disputes with the Society over its initial publication and with the court over subsequent editions,

401   Bireley, *Counter-Reformation Prince*, 115.

402   Roldán-Figueroa, "Ribadeneyra's *Vida*," 167.

403   Cf. ibid.

404   Kagan, *Clio & the Crown*; Van Liere, Ditchfield, and Louthan, *Sacred History*.

we see concerns over the consequences of making historical and theological controversies accessible to such a readership. It stands to reason that similar debates took place elsewhere and in other forums, as a growing reading public and a flourishing print culture reconfigured access to information. This move toward the vernacular has already been observed and analyzed in Spanish devotional writings, not least in Ribadeneyra's *oeuvre*.[405] Domínguez is correct that the *Historia* is not "an eloquent participant in theological battles that are of scholarly interest," but that argues for the need to broaden what is of scholarly interest. Ribadeneyra did not intend his book to intervene in theological controversies, but rather to speak to a larger, less learned, and above all less *convinced* Catholic audience—not yet persuaded of the necessity of war, or of the seminaries, or of the English mission. Rey describes the project at its most fundamental:

> In the British Isles, the battle [of the Counter-Reformation] is still undecided. Doctor Nicholas Sander has explained it to him [Ribadeneyra] in a certain manuscript, in which he examines the origins and progression of the nascent schism. It is important that these things be understood in Spain.[406]

So long, of course, as they are understood in ways that accord with Ribadeneyra's agenda.

The spread of knowledge about England in Spain leads us to one last, crucial aspect of the *Historia*: its resonance with the ongoing scholarly conversation about the European and global dimensions of the English Reformation. It has been the achievement of the present generation of historians to broaden the story of English Catholicism, particularly that of the Society's English mission, from its former, narrowly insular (in both senses of the word) remit.[407] In 1978, Anthony D. Wright insisted that "the English Catholic community was part of the European Catholic world, not just an insular denomination."[408] Almost fifteen years before, the late, great Reformation scholar John Bossy had made the signal contribution of analyzing "the enterprise of England" "not as an

---

405 Roldán-Figueroa, "Ribadeneyra's *Vida*," 161–62.

406 "En las islas Británicas la lucha anda todavía indecisa. El doctor Nicolás Sander le ha enseñado cierto manuscrito donde estudia los orígenes y progresos del naciente Cisma. Convendría que en España se conocieran estas cosas." Rey, lxxvi.

407 McCoog, *Our Way of Proceeding?*, 3.

408 Anthony D. Wright, "Catholic History, North and South," *Northern History* 14 (1978): 126–51, here 138.

ideological movement but as an organization chiefly occupied, like all other human enterprises, in getting people and objects from one point to another with the lines and methods of communication available."[409] The axes running from England to Rome, through the Low Countries, or France, or Spain, became real networks of people and places, sited in time and space.[410]

This work has continued and continues even now. The English Catholic community remained aware of and engaged with their European coreligionists.[411] Even when they wrote in English, writers like Robert Persons wrote amid European influences and with an eye toward European audiences.[412] Moreover, the scholarly conversation is moving geographically beyond the British Isles. Recent work by Anne Dillon, Highley, Domínguez, and others has investigated the communities of English exiles in Italy, the Low Countries, and Spain, with a particular emphasis on their literary production.[413] McCoog in particular has traced out the many international dimensions of the Jesuit mission to early modern England.[414] Even in studies centered on England and English people, it has become *de rigueur* to stress that "the English story makes no sense viewed outside this European context."[415]

Where the *Historia* has something to add is in the ongoing exploration of how non-Britons participated in the story of English Catholicism. Bossy quite rightly took England and Rome to be the two major nodes of the networks that comprised "the enterprise of England," but they were by no means the only nodes. All roads did not lead to Rome, as it happens. More attention must be paid to the many (sometimes minor) protagonists who were not English. Historians and literary scholars alike are illustrating how the writings of such luminaries as Campion and Persons were disseminated across Europe and translated into Latin and into vernaculars, adapted and deployed by local actors, "in the local context of polemical debate."[416] Besides these networks

---

409   John Bossy, "Rome and the Elizabethan Catholics: A Question of Geography," *HJ* 7, no. 1 (1964): 135–42, here 135.

410   Cf. James E. Kelly, "Panic, Plots, and Polemic: The Jesuits and the Early Modern English Mission," *JJS* 1, no. 4 (2014): 511–19, here 519.

411   Walsham, "Translating Trent?."

412   Stefania Tutino, "The Political Thought of Robert Persons's *Conference* in Continental Context," *HJ* 52, no. 1 (March 2009): 43–62, here 45.

413   Dillon, *Construction of Martyrdom*, 9. Domínguez, "Paper and Pens," 3. Highley, *Catholics Writing the Nation*, 4. Sheils, "Polemic as Piety," 75.

414   E.g., McCoog, *Our Way of Proceeding?*; McCoog, *Building the Faith*.

415   Lake, *Bad Queen Bess?*, 281.

416   Clarinda E. Calma, "Communicating across Communities: Explicitation in Gaspar Wilkowski's Polish Translation of Edmund Campion's *Rationes Decem*," *JJS* 1, no. 4 (2014): 589–606, here 591. Tutino, "Political Thought," 45.

of translation and transmission, much original content was produced by non-Britons, as they reacted to events on the other side of the English Channel.[417] To quote Peter Lake, "events in England were a function of, sometimes a central and sometimes a peripheral part of, a wider dynastic and confessional crisis or conjuncture, one which contemporaries all over Europe viewed, analysed, and tried to operate upon."[418]

The publication and circulation of martyrologies is a special, crucial case. McCoog has pointed out that the sixteenth century saw few accounts of the Elizabethan martyrs published in English. Instead, these texts were printed in mainland Europe,

> in Latin, Italian, French, Spanish, and German for a continental audience. The treatises not only informed continental Catholics of the unjust sufferings endured by their co-religionists for their faith alone, but were *de facto* propaganda intended to arouse Catholic powers to take action either by reaching into their pockets for financial assistance or by fomenting alliances for total liberation.[419]

Hundreds of editions of dozens of texts were printed, such that "by 1590 few literate Catholics, from Seville to Salzburg, from Bruges to Bologna, could have been unaware of the English martyrs."[420] The *Historia* was a part of this floodtide of publications, a further witness to the fact that the "English Catholic community" was not exclusively English—that is to say, that countless Catholics from across Europe were profoundly invested in the Church's struggles in Britain.

In the specific case of sixteenth-century Anglo-Spanish relations, too, the *Historia* can offer a different perspective. This historiography has generally been conceived of through the prism of the "Black Legend," the Protestant mythology casting Spaniards as fanatical, cruel, and bloodthirsty.[421] The difficulty here is that the Legend was largely an English creation, and so scholarship, Anglophone scholarship in particular, tends to look through the lens from the

---

417 Monta, *Martyrdom and Literature*, 235. Anne Dillon, *Michelangelo and the English Martyrs* (Farnham: Ashgate, 2012).

418 Lake, *Bad Queen Bess?*, 281.

419 McCoog, *And Touching Our Society*, 289–90.

420 Gregory, *Salvation at Stake*, 289–90.

421 See J.N. Hillgarth's magisterial *The Mirror of Spain, 1500–1700: The Formation of a Myth*, History, Languages, and Cultures of the Spanish and Portuguese Worlds (Ann Arbor: University of Michigan Press, 2000).

English side, without much acknowledgment that the Spanish looked back.[422] The disparity was obvious as early as 1945, when Rey could speak of "the English Reformation, whose relationship with Spain has not yet been studied from the Spanish point of view."[423]

In a thought-provoking 2001 article in *The English Historical Review*, Peter Marshall posited the existence of "the other Black Legend," namely Spaniards' equally negative perception of England as depraved heretics. Marshall queries (and notes the paucity of academic interest in) "the processes by which England, a traditional ally and trading partner, seems to have come to represent a dire moral warning, an exemplar of national apostasy."[424] As one of the very first texts about the English Reformation published in Spain—and in Spanish— Ribadeneyra's *Historia* is central to this transformation.[425] It was instrumental in publicizing and popularizing knowledge about English Protestantism, and in infusing Spanish perceptions of England with a Counter-Reformation sensibility.[426] By rendering the *Historia* available to non-Spanish-speakers, this translation hopes to offer some answers to Marshall's questions.

Lastly, let us consider the long and varied parade of characters, places, and times Ribadeneyra reviews in the course of writing his *Historia*: Roman emperors and Japanese converts, Jerusalem and the Spanish Main, the days of the patriarchs and the discovery of the New World. This is history conceived of on a global scale, born of a moment when Catholicism was expanding into every corner of the world—an expansion wrought in no small part by the Society of Jesus and applauded by readers across Europe. The *Historia* is thus a witness to the globalization of information. Ribadeneyra wrote—and his readers read— aided by the increasingly availability of information about the far-off and the far-flung.[427] The reader in Toledo or Antwerp could read of fellow Catholics in London, or Paris, or Nagasaki, and feel themselves united in a single Church. This disparate world-picture (and the discontinuities of space and time) could all be brought into focus through the lens of providentialism: *all* was arranged by the divine will, the very image often invoked at the time for the writing and

---

422 Peter Marshall, "The Other Black Legend: The Henrician Reformation and the Spanish People," *EHR* 116, no. 465 (February 2001): 31–49, here 46.

423 "la Reforma anglicana, cuyas relaciones con España no han sido estudiadas todavía desde el punto de vista español." Rey, 855.

424 Marshall, "Other Black Legend," 48.

425 McCoog, *And Touching Our Society*, 386.

426 Roldán-Figueroa, "Father Luis Piñeiro," 225–27.

427 Sanjay Subrahmanyam, "On World Historians in the Sixteenth Century," *Representations* 91, no. 1 (Summer 2005): 43–44. Roldán-Figueroa, "Father Luis Piñeiro," 221.

analyzing of history.[428] Accordingly, the story of English Catholicism must be understood "in relation to wider international initiatives of the rejuvenation of the Catholic faith, for the recovery of territories and peoples temporarily lost to the forces of heresy and for the evangelical conversion of the indigenous peoples of Asia and the Americas to Christianity."[429]

And yet, the book is also filled with less exotic names: Browne and Norton, Winchester and York, the Six Articles and the Act of Uniformity. Sanjay Subrahmanyam has observed that early modern "world histories" are usually not symmetrical or well-ordered in structure, but rather accumulate coverage as necessity demands.[430] It must be remembered that at its most global, the *Historia* is utterly local; this sweeping history is marshaled in response to a specific problem, fixed by a particular place and time. Ribadeneyra's gestures to Christian history and global missionizing were intended to refute Protestant pretensions to apostolicity.[431] As Alexandra Walsham points out, the disparate worlds of global Catholicism were wont to converge:

> The parallels between the situation in that [*sic*] confronted the Catholic clergy in different continents were not lost on contemporaries. Jesuits in Brittany and the kingdom of Naples talked of the "Indians" within their own midst and their colleagues in the British Isles were conscious of the affinities between their endeavours and those of fellow members of the Society abroad.[432]

The *Historia* is a remarkable instantiation of how interconnected the stories of English, European, and global Catholicism are in the early modern period— and of how contemporaries recognized them as such. Global knowledge and global worldviews could and did manifest in ostensibly local texts.

In 1588, a Toledan Jesuit published a history of a distant country he had visited once, thirty years before, whose language he never spoke and whose culture he mistrusted. In some ways, this remains the most extraordinary fact about the *Historia*. The first decade-and-a-half of the twenty-first century has

---

428   Popper, *Walter Ralegh's History*, 5, 52.
        For a fuller discussion of Ribadeneyra's global historiographical vision, see Weinreich, "English Mission."
429   Alexandra Walsham, *Catholic Reformation in Protestant Britain*, Catholic Christendom, 1300–1700 (Farnham: Ashgate, 2014), 2.
430   Subrahmanyam, "On World Historians," 36.
431   Cf. Sheils, "Polemic as Piety," 78.
432   Walsham, *Catholic Reformation*, 43–44.
        Cf. Wright, "Catholic History," 144.

seen renewed and vibrant attention to early modern historiography, sacred and otherwise, spanning the length and breadth of Europe. Yet, a distinct pattern has emerged, with the lion's share of attention going to historians writing the history of their own nation, region or city.[433] That much early modern historical work was inward-looking cannot be denied. The *Historia* is a reminder that even at the height of confessional conflict, early modern individuals remained curious about and invested in other cultures, and that their histories were multidimensional and multidirectional.

---

433   E.g., Highley, *Catholics Writing the Nation*; Kagan, *Clio & the Crown*; Van Liere, Ditchfield, and Louthan, *Sacred History*, especially Part 2.

The Ecclesiastical History of the Schism of the Kingdom of England

Collected from various trustworthy authors by Father
Pedro de Ribadeneyra of the Society of Jesus

*This history, addressed to my lord Philip, prince of Spain, relates the most
noteworthy events that came to pass in that kingdom touching upon our holy
religion, from their beginnings to the death of the queen of Scots*

∴

To Our Lord Prince Don Philip

When the hand of God bestows a pious king, zealous for his glory, patron of the good and persecutor of the wicked, just, peaceable, and moderate, it is so singular a gift to the whole realm that no happiness could be greater than that of its inhabitants. For, just as the king is the head of the kingdom, its life and soul, the path of the king is the path of the kingdom, all depending upon him. For this reason, every subject of our lord the king—and the religious most of all—is obliged unceasingly to beg our Lord to hold Your Highness in his hand, and from this your tender youth to lead you by the righteous paths of his justice and truth.[1] For all the favors and mercies that Your Highness may receive from him will not be received for yourself alone, but rather for all your kingdoms and territories. By their number and magnitude, they have made our lord King Philip the greatest monarch ever seen among Christians—as Your Highness, his heir and successor, shall be, after the long and fortunate years of His Majesty. Together with the rule of so many mighty kingdoms and principalities, he shall leave as Your Highness's principal inheritance the role of defender of our holy Catholic faith, unshakeable pillar of the Church, and glorifier of the name of Jesus Christ. He shall bequeath to you his piety, his faith, his justice, his beneficence, his prudence, his moderation and tranquility in body, soul, and action, and all the other heroic and admirable virtues for which he is renowned throughout the world, so that Your Highness may imitate them and find in them a perfect model. This is the greatest part and the most precious jewel of this prodigious, overflowing patrimony.

And so, in order that Your Highness may perceive how best to imitate the virtues of our lord the king (as His Majesty has imitated those of his father the emperor of glorious memory) and to perform all that your realms need and desire, it behooves Your Highness to hold in your heart that in heaven there is another king, who is the king of kings,[2] before whose reverence and sovereign majesty all other kings are as the worms of the earth—and none of whom can rule rightly, save through him. The more exalted their majesty and the more extensive their power, so much the greater must their submission and humility before him be, for the reckoning he shall demand of them will be stricter and his judgment more severe. For the mighty shall be mightily tormented, if they do not act as they ought, as it says in Holy Scripture.[3] In which, and

---

1 Ps. 22:3.

2 1 Tim. 6:15; Rev. 17:14, 19:16.

3 Wisd. of Sol. 6:6–7.

© KONINKLIJKE BRILL NV, LEIDEN, 2017 | DOI 10.1163/9789004323964_003

in histories both sacred and profane, are found admirable examples of excellent kings, who knew how to combine the awe and majesty of their person and royal state with piety and reverence toward God, devotion and respect toward their counselors, temperance toward themselves, beneficence toward their vassals, gentleness toward the good, severity toward the wicked, mercy toward the poor, and ferocity and abhorrence toward those who trample upon the powerless, good relationships toward friends, valor toward enemies, and, lastly, the staff of justice fair and true toward all, neither turning nor bending for any. For these are the duties of the good king, which Your Highness must strive to learn and to fulfill. And no less, to understand the downfalls of evil kings, the fearful punishments that our Lord has allotted their sins and cruelties, and the disastrous ends they have come to, for thus you shall learn what is to be fled and avoided.

Thus, in hopes of offering some service to Your Highness, as the least of your subjects, I offer you a history of our own times, from which you may take marvelous examples of both the one and the other. For it treats of King Henry VIII of England, who had formerly been a just and valiant prince, a leading defender of the Catholic Church, but who was subsequently blinded with filthy passions, turned his back on God, and became a savage and cruel beast; he devastated his entire kingdom, drowning it in a sea of infinite evils, for which he was abandoned by God (which is the fearful summit of all possible misfortunes). Henry was emulated both by his son and successor, Edward VI, deceived and misled by his tutors, and by his daughter, Edward's sister Elizabeth, who now reigns. Your Highness ought to abhor their examples, for they are truly hateful, and to hold before your eyes the exalted and regal virtues of the illustrious Queen Doña Catherine, daughter of your ancestors, the Catholic Kings, and of our lady Queen Doña Mary, her daughter, the paragons of Christian queens. And no less the zeal, wisdom, and valor with which our lord King Philip restored the Catholic faith in that kingdom. All of this is recounted in this history, so that Your Highness, without departing from your palace, may learn what is to be done, and so become the living image of your father in your deeds, as you are in your features. May God keep Your Highness, as all your realms desire, and as your servants and devoted beadsmen of the Society of Jesus continually beg him. At Madrid, June 20, 1588.[4]

Pedro de Ribadeneyra

---

4   Added in the 1595 edition.

The Author, to the Pious Christian Reader

A book by Doctor Nicholas Sander, an excellent gentleman, English in origin, theologian by profession, and exemplary in character, has come into my hands. In it, he records the origins and progression of the schism begun in England by King Henry VIII, as well as the steps and stages by which it has grown and mounted to that summit of evil where now it stands. Having perused it with no little interest, I though it a book worthy of being read by all. For, besides containing a history of mighty kings, whose deeds, being many and prodigious, men are keen to know, it is also an ecclesiastical history, depicting the alterations and transformations that our holy and Catholic faith has suffered in that kingdom over the course of almost sixty years—and suffers still. And this, moreover, with such great veracity, clarity, and elegance of style, that I dare affirm that no man of conscience [*hombre de sanas entrañas*] can read it without admiration for the book and its author. For in it we find the living image, painted in its true colors, of one of the roughest and direst storms that the Catholic Church has ever endured within one realm. We see a mighty king who desires everything that takes his fancy, and acts upon his every desire: a blind and hopeless passion, armed with fury and power, spilling the blood of saintly men, profaning and ransacking the temples of the Lord and impoverishing itself with their riches, removing the true head of the Church and monstrously proclaiming himself the new head, and perverting all the laws of God and man. We see the constancy and holiness of Queen Doña Catherine, the integrity and justice of the Roman pontiff,[1] the sentiments of other princes, the sins and filthiness of Anne Boleyn, the flatteries and deceptions of the king's courtiers, the patience and fortitude of the sainted martyrs, and, lastly, the chaos, confusion, and devastation of a kingdom, a kingdom once noble, Catholic, and powerful, which had so praiseworthily received the faith from the very earliest days of the primitive Church.[2] And after Pope Saint Gregory (whom the Venerable Bede calls the Apostle of England) replanted it by means of Augustine, it was preserved for the space of almost a thousand years, obedient to

---

1 Pope Clement VII (r.1523–34), born Giulio de' Medici.

2 In the margin: "Polydore Vergil, in Book 2 of his *History*, and Cardinal Pole, in Book 2 of *The Unity of the Church* [*de vnione Ecclesiæ*], say that it was the first kingdom publicly to embrace the faith."

   Vergil, *Anglica historia*, Book 2.

   Reginald Pole, *Pole's Defense of the Unity of the Church*, ed. and trans. Joseph G. Dwyer (Westminster: The Newman Press, 1965), 98.

© KONINKLIJKE BRILL NV, LEIDEN, 2017 | DOI 10.1163/9789004323964_004

the holy Apostolic See.[3] In this book, we see the tender youth of King Edward, King Henry's son, abused and tyrannized by his tutors and the regents of the realm, heresy running wild and unchecked by their hands, until the day Edward died—not without suspicion of poison[4]—and his sister, the illustrious Queen Doña Mary, succeeded him. By the splendor of her saintly life and her zeal for the glory of God, and by the wisdom and strength of her husband, the Catholic King Don Philip, the shadows of heresy were banished and the sun of religion, peace, and justice returned to shine upon the realm in tranquility and joy (a land which, for its sins, did not deserve such happiness). And so, when the Lord carried Queen Doña Mary away to another, better kingdom, with her passed away all the good she had revived. With her sister, Queen Elizabeth, succeeding her, the entire realm was thrown into the troubles and misfortunes recounted in this history.

Those who read it will learn to beware of their passions, to take themselves in hand, and to keep a tight rein on their pleasures and appetites, since a single spark of infernal fire in the heart of King Henry, arising from a perverse lust for a woman of no great beauty, so enflamed him and so deformed him, that from the "defender of the faith" he metamorphosed into its cruelest foe, a savage beast, who set all England ablaze. To this very day the land suffers and bewails

---

3   In the margin: "Book 2, Chapter 1 of his *Ecclesiastical History*."

　　According to the Venerable Bede (*c.*672–731), Augustine of Canterbury (d.604) was dispatched by Pope Gregory I (r.590–605) as a missionary to the British Isles in 582. Bede, *Ecclesiastical History*, I.23.

4   Edward VI died on July 6, 1553, of a chest infection. Rumors alleging that he had been poisoned (with the duke of Northumberland held responsible) circulated widely, both in England and on the Continent. W.K. Jordan, *Edward VI: The Threshold of Power (The Dominance of the Duke of Northumberland)* (London: George Allen & Unwin, 1970), 520n1.

　　The diarist Henry Machyn (*c.*1497–1563) wrote, "The vj day of July [1553], as they say, dessessyd the nobull Kyng Edward the vj. and the vij yere of ys rayne, and une and here to the nobull kyng Henry the viij; and he was poyssoned, as evere body says, wher now, thanke be unto God, ther be mony of the false trayturs browt to ther end, and j trust in God that mor shall folow as thay may be spyd owt." Henry Machyn, *The Diary of Henry Machyn, Citizen and Merchant-Taylor of London, from A.D. 1550 to A.D. 1563*, ed. John Gough Nichols, Works of the Camden Society 42 (London: J.B. Nichols and Son, 1848), 35.

　　As news traveled, the story grew in ghoulishness: by August 16, one Englishman in Strasbourg wrote, "A writer worthy of credit informs me, that our excellent king has been most shamefully taken off by poison. His nails and hair fell off before his death, so that, handsome as he was, he entirely lost all his good looks." Hastings Robinson, ed., *Original Letters Relative to the English Reformation, Written during the Reigns of King Henry VIII, King Edward VI, and Queen Mary: Chiefly from the Archives of Zurich*, trans. Hastings Robinson, 2 vols., Parker Society Publications 53 (Cambridge: Cambridge University Press, 1846), 2:684.

this wildfire, and neither the unending tears of the afflicted Catholics nor the copious blood of the martyrs, shed each and every day, have been enough to quench and extinguish it. At the same time, the wise will learn that because the wellspring of this awful schism is infectious, poisonous, and rooted in incest and sensuality, it can produce nothing but death and corruption.[5] This is a wondrous revelation for the simple and the deluded, who wish to know the truth—that is, to understand the first winds [*causas y vientos*] of the storm, and the consequences, transformations, and disruptions that followed—in order to take shelter in the safe haven of the holy Catholic faith. For light cannot be joined to shadow, nor truth to lies, nor Christ to Belial.[6]

It is likewise a marvelous comfort to all Catholics and good Christians, to awaken and strengthen their hope, for they will here learn that so hateful and abominable an evil can neither endure nor progress further. Not simply because lies and heretical falsehoods are weak in the face of truth and the Catholic religion, but also because this same deceit, which now appears to flourish and reign, and to triumph over the truth in England, is so riddled with fabrications, tricks, and tyrannies that they cannot but destroy it, just as they destroyed and extinguished the idolatries, heresies, and errors that infested and beset our faith in the days of the pagan emperors and the vicious tyrants, those lords of the world, taken and revered as gods upon the earth. They persecuted the faith with all their might and guile, they glutted themselves on our pain and made themselves drunk on the blood of the believers, but all their cunning was ultimately in vain.[7] For the Christian blood they spilled, as Tertullian tells us, was seed, which they sowed in the field of the holy Church: for every Christian that died, a thousand were born, and the pains and torments they suffered for the faith spurred others to embrace it.[8] In the end, it always prevailed; though it has passed through the crucible and the furnace, the gold of its truth suffered no harm, being instead refined and purified,[9] and it shines all the more as all its enemies' tyrannies are brought to nothing, their miserable lives ending in ignominy and humiliation. This is perfect comfort and happiness to all Catholics and servants of God: for as it was, so shall it be;[10] as we read in the histories of the Church, so we see in our own days. For God is the same

---

5   Gal. 6:8.

6   2 Cor. 6:14–15.

7   Job 5:13.

8   In the margin: "At the end of his *Apologeticus contra gentes*."
     Tertullian, *Apologeticus*, Chapter 50.

9   1 Cor. 3:13; 1 Pet. 1:6–7.

10   Luke 17:26.

today as in centuries past, and he is the pilot and captain of the ship of the Church, whom all contrary winds and waves obey—though he seems to sleep and care nothing for our toils, though it seems the night has passed and we are in the fourth watch, let no one despair or doubt[11] that he shall awake in his own time, that he shall calm the commotion of the winds and rebuke the pride of the sea,[12] leaving Pharaoh to drown with all his chariots and horsemen,[13] while one day the children of Israel (the Catholics afflicted and oppressed by the Egyptians) shall, without fear or dread, sing songs of joy and praise to their glorious liberator, to the godly redeemer of their souls and their lives.[14]

The kings and exalted princes of the earth may also benefit from this history, learning out of another's head[15] not to use forbearance or mildness with heretics, to give them neither support nor liberty, imagining thus to preserve their territories and states. For experience has shown us the contrary, and all sound logic teaches us that there is no cancer that spreads so, no fire that catches so, no plague that infects and kills like heresy, and that the remedy is to sever the diseased tree at the root, to cut off the contagion at its inception. Thus, from the discussion of King Henry (who, before he was blinded by lust, was respected throughout the world, renowned in peace and war), princes may learn not to desire all within their power, nor to use their power and authority to ride roughshod over reason and justice, but rather to restrain and moderate themselves by the law of the king of kings, to whom all the might of the world must submit. And it likewise befits princes to learn not to declare their will freely, their likes and dislikes, unless they are quite modest and kept within the limits of sound reason. For there are so many flatterers and men who dissemble in order to please them, that they will fall over themselves in advising things both outrageous and ill-considered, supposing they are in accordance with the princes' desires (though they are not). And once urged, the monarch cannot or will not turn back, as we see in this history in Cardinal Wolsey's advice to King Henry to divorce Queen Doña Catherine, dreaming thus to win his goodwill.

And no less worthy of note is the reverence owed to sacred things and the goods of the Church, for it is certain that after King Henry laid his hands upon the temples of the Lord and despoiled them of their treasures and riches, he

---

11   Matt. 8:23–27, 14:24; Mark 4:37–39; Luke 8:22–25.

12   Mark 4:39; Luke 8:24.

13   Exod. 14, especially 14:28.

14   Exod. 15.

15   This is an inversion of the Spanish proverb, "no one learns out of another's head [*ninguno escarmienta en cabeza ajena*]." "Refranero multilingüe," Centro Virtual Cervantes, 2015, http://cvc.cervantes.es/lengua/refranero/Default.aspx [accessed December 6, 2015].

found himself poorer and his debts larger. He then burdened and afflicted his realm with higher taxes and levies than all the kings before him had exacted in the previous five hundred years. Nor is there any lack of instruction for both the courtiers and confidants of the said kings, and their flatterers, who in the manner of a mirror reflect the prince's semblance and aspect, and like chameleons take their color from him, who praise and exalt his every desire and for their private interests counsel what they think will please him, and destroy themselves seeking means and schemes to facilitate them and put them into action, ravaging everything in their path, though it might be justice, religion, or God himself. For here they will see the end to which all King Henry's leading counselors, all the fomenters of his passions and his vices and all the instruments of his misdeeds and outrages, came, as well as the results of those graces and favors of his they sought and won, to the great harm and degradation of the commonwealth. For in the end they lost the king's favor, and with it their lives, honors, dignities, and estates (their souls being already utterly forfeit), offering the world a lesson in how little those things are to be trusted that have been obtained through bad intentions and worse means, and of how God punishes deeds done in the service of kings but against God, by the hand of those same monarchs.

Now, what am I to say of the other wonderful benefits that we may all take from this history? That is, the compassion (on the one hand) and the blessed envy (on the other) we should have for our brothers in England who, because they would not adore the statue of Nebuchadnezzar[16] and acknowledge the queen as head of the Church, are each day persecuted with exile, imprisonment, insults, false accusations, humiliations, and tortures, and then dispatched in the most atrocious executions. For this we should praise the Lord, who in these times gives us soldiers and captains so courageous and so valiant that, keeping their eyes upon the unfailing truth of his promise and that longed-for, blessed eternity, they despise their lands, kinsmen, friends, houses, estates, reputations, and their very lives. We must shelter, embrace, and support them, and—imitating their devotion—entreat the divine majesty to give them endurance, and victory over his enemies and ours (which is to say, over all the enemies of our holy Catholic faith).

Believing that all these advantages could be derived from this history, I was moved to set to work upon it and to rewrite it in our Castilian tongue—those parts I deemed good for all to know, omitting certain things and adding others that relate to the said schism from various trustworthy authors of our times, and dividing the narrative into two books, and each book into chapters, so that

---

16   Dan. 3.

the reader may have places to rest. And besides those motives for so doing that are common to all nations, two more private and particular considerations have urged me to the work. The first, that I am a Spaniard; the second, that I am a priest of the Society of Jesus. Because I am a Spaniard, I am obliged to desire and to seek all that is honorable and beneficial to my country—as this is, for by it the life of the renowned Queen Doña Catherine, a Spaniard, daughter of the famous Catholic Kings, Don Ferdinand and Doña Isabella, shall be better known and publicized. She was the legitimate wife of King Henry VIII of England, but was repudiated and abandoned by him, with the worst outrages imaginable. These she suffered with unbelievable steadfastness and patience, offering so wonderful an example of holiness that she may very justly (and, indeed, should) be called the mirror of Christian princesses and queens. Just as the life of King Henry may serve as a warning, for rulers to learn what is to be fled and avoided, since it was filled with egregious vices and sins, so too may the life of his wife, Queen Doña Catherine, be the model for all princesses and queens of how they ought to behave, because of the extraordinary, unparalleled virtues that adorned her. My being a priest of the Society is likewise a reason and motive for undertaking this work, for the religious way of life obliges me to support and advance with my feeble powers anything that pertains to our sacred faith (such as this), and membership in the Society all the more so—both because God our Lord has instituted it and sent it into the world in these wretched times to defend the Catholic faith and to combat heretics (as the vicar of that same God says in the bull of its confirmation),[17] and because of the special grace the Lord has bestowed on all its sons, taking as his instrument Elizabeth, queen of England and daughter of King Henry and Anne Boleyn (the germ of this lamentable tragedy, the source and root of such grievous disasters), who, following in the footsteps of her parents while augmenting their methods, persecutes our holy Catholic, apostolic, and Roman faith with extraordinary cruelty and ferocity, and butchers those who profess and teach it, torturing them, abusing them, and murdering them with the most hideous sorts of punishments and executions. And by this means she renders them the greatest good they could possibly wish for. The foremost among those who have perished for their faith during Elizabeth's reign have been certain English

---

17   Ribadeneyra is here referring to the *second* papal bull confirming the Society, *Exposcit debitum*, issued July 21, 1550, which includes the crucial line "for the defense and propagation of the faith." For a comparison of the two bulls, see McCoog, *Our Way of Proceeding?*, 40n117.

      For an English translation of the bull, as reproduced by Ribadeneyra in his *Life of Ignatius*, see Ribadeneyra, *Life of Ignatius*, 210–19.

fathers of our Society, who chose to be persecuted, tortured, tormented, and murdered, rather than separate themselves by so much as a hair from the confession of Catholic truth. And this is so wonderful and so magnificent a gift of our Lord, that every son of this little Society is obliged to acknowledge and to serve him, to wish to follow our brothers in giving our lives for him, and to pray most fervently to the divine majesty, that in his infinite mercy he will take pity on that illustrious realm and end its ills and miseries, and illuminate the queen and her minsters with his light, so that they come to themselves, repent, and find salvation. Or, that he stay their hands, that they may no longer be stained with their brothers' blood. Or, at the very least, that he give the Catholics the fortitude and constancy to shed it—as they have done—for their sacred faith. Let it be as the Lord in his incomprehensible providence determines and ordains to be right and good for his spouse, the holy Church.

The Argument of the Present History, and the Origins of the Lamentable Schism in England[1]

The Britons (whom we now call the English) were converted to the faith of Christ our Lord by Joseph of Arimathea, who planted the first beginnings of our holy religion in that isle.[2] Afterwards, they were secured there by Pope Eleutherius, who was according to some accounts the twelfth, according to others the fourteenth, pope after Saint Peter.[3] It was he who sent Fugacius and Damianus to England, where they baptized King Lucius and much of his realm.[4] So great did the Christian faith grow there that Tertullian, an ancient writer of the time, wrote these words: "The lands of Britain, which the Romans could not reach, have become subjects of Jesus Christ."[5] Subsequently, it came to pass that the Angles and the Saxon peoples of Germany made war upon the Britons, conquering them and driving them into the remotest corners of the island. As they were unbelievers, when they seized the kingdom it fell away from

---

1   Sander, *De origine ac progressu*, 1–4.

2   In the margin: "This is proven by Polydore Vergil; he takes it from Gildas, an ancient author, Books 2 and 4."

     Gildas (*fl.*fifth–sixth centuries) was an early British chronicler, whose best-known work, *De excidio et conquestu Britanniae*, has been variously dated to 479–84 and 515–30. François Kerlouégan, "Gildas (*fl.*5th–6th cent.)," in *ODNB*, 22:223–25, here 223.

     Vergil, *Anglica historia*, Book 2.

3   There is no consensus as to the date either of Eleutherius's ascension (variously 171, 174, and 177) or death (variously 185, 189, and 193). The *Liber Pontificalis* (late ninth century) places him as the fourteenth pope, while Eusebius of Caesarea calls him "twelfth after the Apostles." *Liber Pontificalis*, Chapter 14. Eusebius of Caesarea, *Ecclesiastical History, Books 1–5*, ed. and trans. Roy J. Deferrari, The Fathers of the Church: A New Translation 19 (Washington, D.C.: Catholic University of America Press, 1953), 271.

4   In his *Lives of the Popes* (*c.*1474), Bartolomeo Platina (1421–81) records, "Immediately after starting his pontificate, Eleutherius (who succeeded Soter, as I said) received a letter from Lucius, the king of Britain, in which he petitioned the pope to accept him and his people into the Christian fold. Eleutherius accordingly sent two excellent men, Fugatius and Damianus, to baptize the king and his people." Bartolomeo Platina, *Lives of the Popes*, ed. and trans. Anthony F. D'Elia, vol. 1, The I Tatti Renaissance Library 30 (Cambridge: Harvard University Press, 2008), 91.

     Cf. Raphael Holinshed, *Holinshed's Chronicles: England, Scotland, and Ireland*, ed. Vernon F. Snow, 6 vols. (New York: AMS Press Inc., 1965), 1:511–12.

5   In the margin: "In the book *Adversus Iudaeos*."

     Tertullian, *Adversus Iudaeos*, 7.4.

the faith of Christ. For this reason, Pope Gregory I sent them Augustine, Mellitus, and other saintly Benedictine monks,[6] who converted them from idolatry, made them Christians, and baptized King Æthelberht of Kent.[7] From that day to the twenty-fifth year of the reign of Henry VIII (1534 after the birth of our Lord), for the space of almost a thousand years, there was no other creed in England, no confession but the Roman Catholic—and this with such humility, obedience, and loyalty to the Apostolic See, that from the mighty King Inas, founder of Wells Cathedral and the famous monastery of Glastonbury, to the wretched times of King Henry (more than eight hundred years), each house in England gave the Roman pontiff a sum of money by way of tribute or voluntary offering, in honor of the glorious prince of the Apostles, to demonstrate the entire realm's special devotion to the Holy See. For this reason, the money they offered was known as "Peter's pence."[8] But Henry VIII perverted the faith of Christ and wrenched the kingdom away from the communion and obedience of the Roman Pontiff, though for its ancient loyalty some had called it the firstborn daughter of the Church. What follows is the occasion Henry seized upon to do this.

Henry's elder brother, Arthur, took as his wife Lady Catherine, the daughter of the Catholic Kings of Spain, Don Ferdinand and Doña Isabella of glorious memory, but shortly thereafter he died without issue. What is more, on account of his tender years, feeble health, and sudden death, he left the princess his wife untouched, just as he had found her. With the dispensation of the supreme pontiff, Henry married his sister-in-law, in order to preserve the peace between the Spanish and English. Having taken her as his lawful wife, lived

---

6   "Since Bishop Augustine had advised him that the harvest was great and the workers were few, Pope Gregory sent more colleagues and minsters of the word together with his messengers. First and foremost among these were Mellitus, Justus, Paulinus, and Rufinianus." Bede, *Bede's Ecclesiastical History*, ed. and trans. Bertram Colgrave and R.A.B. Mynors (Oxford: Clarendon Press, 1991), 2.29.

7   Bede's transcription of Augustine of Canterbury's epitaph includes the line "he led King Æthelberht and his nation from the worship of idols to faith in Christ." According to Bede, Æthelberht ruled from 560 to 616. Ibid., 2.3.

8   In the margin: "Polydore Vergil, [*Anglica historia*,] Book 4."

King Inas (or Ine) of Wessex ruled from 688 to 726. His law code ("probably [promulgated] between 688 and 694") required the payment of "church dues" (*ciricsceattas*). It is unclear whether it was Inas, or another king of the period, who began the payment of tributes to Rome that soon acquired the moniker "Peter's Pence." Barry Cunliffe, *Wessex to AD 1000*, A Regional History of England (London: Longman Group, 1993), 298. William A. Chaney, "Anglo-Saxon Church Dues: A Study in Historical Continuity," *CH* 32, no. 3 (September 1963): 268–77, here 268, 271, 276.

with her for twenty years, and fathered children with her (whom he recognized as his heirs), he rejected her. He divorced her, under the pretext that she who had been his brother's wife could not be his. But in truth, it was to wed Anne Boleyn, with whom his kinship was far closer, both through affinity and much stronger impediments, so that if he could not marry Queen Doña Catherine, he could hardly marry her! For Anne was the sister of one of Henry's mistresses (and he had many), and the daughter of another, both of whom were still living at the time. And though it seems a thing incredible and—by reason of its hateful, terrifying nature—unfit to be recorded here, yet I shall relate it, for Doctor Sander has done so, the better to demonstrate (if it is true) the patience and tolerance of God and the abyss of evil in which any man abandoned by his mighty hand falls: Anne was believed, on trustworthy grounds, to be Henry's own daughter, as will be seen hereafter. To wed this woman, he discarded and abandoned his legitimate wife, broke away from the obedience of the Roman Church, and, refusing to align with any ancient sect or the modern ones of Luther or Zwingli, established a new, monstrous one, of which he named himself the sovereign head and demanded to be obeyed as such.[9] And, teaching us the end of the frenzied passions of blind men, he had his beloved Anne (who had always been a Lutheran heretic)[10] publicly beheaded for having betrayed him by sleeping with numerous other men, both before and after wedding the king, including hateful intercourse with her own brother! Among the judges condemning her for adultery and incest was one Thomas Boleyn, who was called her father—though he was not, merely the husband of her mother, as this history will show.

Upon King Henry's hypocrisy and specious pretexts, by which he wished to appear to have repudiated Queen Catherine out of the purest fear of God; upon this diabolical incest, the marriage of a king with his own daughter (or, at least, the daughter of his mistress); upon Anne Boleyn's adultery, which so

---

9   Throughout his doctrinal oscillations, Henry remained wary, at best, of Martin Luther (1483–1546), and implacable in his hatred for the more radical reformers, like Huldrych Zwingli (1484–1531), who denied the real presence. Haigh, *English Reformations*, 125–29, 136.

10   There has been considerable debate over Anne Boleyn's religious identity: most scholars have regarded her as "an evangelical and a patron of radical religious reform," while some argue that she was of a more conservative cast than has been acknowledged. In any case, accounts of Anne penned in the second half of the sixteenth century were unanimous in proclaiming her as a leading evangelical. George W. Bernard, "Anne Boleyn's Religion," *HJ* 36, no. 1 (March 1993): 1–20, here 1–2, 20. See also Eric Ives, "Anne Boleyn and the Early Reformation in England: The Contemporary Evidence," *HJ* 37, no. 2 (June 1993): 389–400; Maria Dowling, "Anne Boleyn and Reform," *JEH* 35, no. 1 (January 1984): 30–46.

offended the king, for, being publicly married to—or, as I should say, sleeping with—him, she had unnatural and hateful intercourse with her own brother; upon this "ecclesiastic supremacy," which Henry was the first of all mortals to seize, is founded that religion and vicious creed professed by the nation of England, under that king and his children Edward and Elizabeth. Let it be clearly understood what buildings and works may be raised upon such foundations.

Yet, because falsehood is protean and heresy a hydra-headed beast, what Henry established with regard to spiritual matters after he had divorced the illustrious Queen Doña Catherine and proclaimed himself supreme head of the Church his children Edward and Elizabeth have transformed and perverted, forcing upon that kingdom a new Gospel, different from that which their father decreed. The wondrous and fearful things that God our Lord has worked in England since the schism began, to recall the hearts of the children to the faith of their fathers, are so numerous, so remarkable, and so varied that they cannot be clearly understood, except in reading the history of the schism and the account of all that came to pass. This I wish to set down here, with all clarity and truth, illustrating it with novelties and various marvelous things taken from the histories of our time, especially that of Doctor Sander, who gathered together documents, public accounts, and the reports, oral and written, of trustworthy men, as well as what he himself saw and observed.

BOOK 1

Here Begins the History of the English Schism

∵

Of the Marriage of the Princess Doña Catherine to Arthur, Prince of England, and of the Marriage She Contracted after His Death with His Brother, Henry[1]

With Emperor Maximilian reigning in the Empire,[2] the Catholic Kings Don Ferdinand and Doña Isabella in Spain,[3] and Henry, seventh of that name, in England, Christianity seemed to flourish and prosper in every way. For Maximilian was a prince noble in peace and war; the Catholic Kings most fortunate in the one and the other; and Henry VII was valiant, wise, victorious in every war he waged, powerful, and rich in cash and in every earthly thing. The superstition of the false prophet Mohammed had fractured and disintegrated into different sects through the new creed of Ismail Sophy, the son of the daughter of Uzun Hasan, who seized the kingdom of Persia and brought its subjects to receive his doctrine with all the majesty of a new empire.[4] The Saracens, who had held Andalusia for some eight hundred years, had been driven out of Spain altogether with the capture of Granada.[5] The New World, discovered—through the Lord's infinite favor—by the Spanish, had begun to submit to the sacred Gospel of Christ, spreading and augmenting the glory of his most holy

---

1 Sander, *De origine ac progressu*, 5–9.

2 Holy Roman Emperor Maximilian I (r.1486–1519).

3 Ferdinand II of Aragon (r.1469–1516) and Isabella I of Castile (r.1469–1504).

4 In 1501, Ismail Safavi (r.1501–04), the grandson of the Aqqoyunlu prince, Uzun Hasan (r.1453–78), seized power in Persia, "imposed his own, mystical form of Shi'a Islam on his new empire, and declared his hostility to the Sunni Ottoman Turks on his western frontier." As Margaret Meserve has documented, many Europeans believed the "Sophy" to be opposed to Islam and harbored hopes of an alliance with this new power against the Ottomans. Margaret Meserve "The Sophy: News of Shah Ismail Safavi in Renaissance Europe," *Journal of Early Modern History* 18 (2014): 579–608, here 580–83.

5 As J.H. Elliott wrote in not-dissimilar terms, "On 6 January 1492 Ferdinand and Isabella made their victorious entry into the city of Granada, wrested after nearly eight centuries from the grasp of the Moors." Ribadeneyra here elides the numerous changes of political and religious regime in Muslim Spain; the Nasrid kingdom of Granada dismantled by Ferdinand and Isabella was merely the last in a long line of distinct polities. J.H. Elliott, *Imperial Spain 1469–1716* (London: Penguin Books, 2002), 45–46.

© KONINKLIJKE BRILL NV, LEIDEN, 2017 | DOI 10.1163/9789004323964_006

faith, with the Castilians claiming the west and the Portuguese the east and south, by the authority of Alexander VI, the supreme pontiff.[6]

In the year 1500, as the Catholic Church was taking this fortunate course, the illustrious monarchs Henry VII of England and Don Ferdinand and Doña Isabella of Spain agreed that Arthur, Henry's firstborn, should wed the princess Doña Catherine, daughter of the Catholic Kings. This they did in 1501, the ceremonies taking place in the church of St Paul's in London, on the day of Saint Erkenwald, which fell upon 14 November.[7] On the night of the ceremony, Prince Arthur and Princess Catherine were brought to their marriage bed with all the pomp and majesty appropriate to such exalted royals. However, King Henry had arranged for a noblewoman of the court to remain there with them,[8] to prevent them proceeding as husband and wife—for besides the fact that the prince was very young (not yet fifteen years of age), he had a chronic fever, of which he died some five months later.[9] After Arthur's death, with the Catholic Kings asking about their daughter, King Henry proposed to them that she should marry his second son, Henry, Arthur's brother and now heir to his throne, who was then twelve years old. To do this correctly, they would seek a dispensation from the Roman pontiff. The Catholic Kings gave ear, and when the greatest scholars of theology and canon law in both kingdoms had been

---

6 In 1493, Alexander VI (born Roderic Llançol i de Borja, r.1491–1503) issued the bull *Inter caetera*, which divided oceanic territories between Portugal and Spain, according to a line of demarcation drawn in the Atlantic (later amended by the 1494 Treaty of Tordesillas). Hamish Scott, ed. *The Oxford Handbook of Early Modern European History, 1350–1750: Volume II: Cultures & Power*, Oxford Handbooks (Oxford: Oxford University Press, 2015), 208.

7 The feast of the Anglo-Saxon bishop Saint Erkenwald (d.693) is actually April 30; November 14 commemorates the translation of the saint's relics, a day long celebrated in English liturgical practice. *AASS*, April III, 781.

8 This ahistorical chaperone seems to originate with Sander, who reports the presence of "a certain honorable lady." Indeed, much subsequent trouble would have been saved *had* there been such a person: the hinge of the matrimonial trial was that no one but Catherine and Arthur (by then long dead) were actually present. Sander, *De origine ac progressu*, 6.

9 In fact, at the time of the marriage, Arthur was a month past his fifteenth birthday. Ribadeneyra has subtly adjusted the words of Sander, who writes that the prince "had by then barely reached fifteen years of age [*decimum quintum ętatis annum vix dum attinget*]." Ibid., 6.

   It is unclear precisely what Arthur died of. Both he and Catherine were stricken with sweating sickness in early 1502, although others have suggested testicular cancer. Catherine's Spanish doctor gave a diagnosis of *tisis*, "a Spanish catchall word covering everything from pulmonary tuberculosis to any wasting, feverish disease that produced ulceration of some bodily organ." Later testimony was to claim that, in the opinion of this doctor, "the prince had been denied the strength necessary to know a woman, as if he was a cold piece of stone... because he was in the final stages of *tisis*." Quoted in Giles Tremlett, *Catherine of Aragon: The Spanish Queen of Henry VIII* (New York: Walker & Company, 2010), 91.

consulted, to scrutinize and examine at length whether such a marriage could legally and morally be contracted, it appeared to all that it could. The monarchs' ambassadors brought the business to the attention of His Holiness, Pope Julius II, who had succeeded Alexander VI and Pius III (who lived only a few days), in whose time the negotiations had begun.[10] On the advice of deeply learned and sagacious men, Julius gave the dispensation for their marriage, removing the impediments and ties of human law, which he disturbed only for the greater good of Christendom and to preserve the alliance and peace between the kings and kingdoms of Spain and England.

The theologians explicitly declared that sacred law was not opposed to such a marriage, as is made clear in Holy Scripture. For, if one looks to the state of natural law, the Patriarch Judah [*Iudas*] ordered Onan, his second son, to marry Tamar, who had been the wife of his older brother Er, who had died without leaving any children, in order to revive the memory and lineage of his brother.[11] And if one considers what the Mosaic Law provides, it commands that the same thing be done, under penalty of malediction and infamy.[12] It is hardly possible that God has commanded, or even permitted, what is against natural law, which he has desired always to be the companion, or—as I should say—the guide and rule of all human nature. But this it could not be, unless he had formed a nature that has never changed or altered; nor does he now change or alter it, for thus he would oppose and contradict himself. The which is so far from God, as Saint Paul says,[13] that there should be no doubt but that a marriage between a man and she who was the wife of his brother, dead without issue, is not contrary or repugnant to divine, eternal, or natural law, but only to human and ecclesiastical law. This the Roman pontiff can and should waive when there are just causes for so doing, as he did in this case. As all the theologians said so, confirming it with the authority of Holy Scripture, the saints, and the most distinguished doctors, without a single person under heaven, throughout the Catholic Church, saying a word to the contrary, Pope Julius (as has been said) gave the dispensation, which Cardinal Cajetan reproduces as follows:[14]

---

10   Alexander VI died on August 18, 1503. Francesco Tedeschini Piccolomini (1439–1503) was elected Pope Pius III on September 22, and died less than a month later on October 18. He was succeeded by Giuliano della Rovere as Julius II (r.1503–13) on November 1.

11   In the margin: "Genesis 38[:6–8]."

12   In the margin: "Deuteronomy 25[:5] and Ruth 3 and 4."

13   In the margin: "2 Timothy 2[:13]."

14   In the margin: "Volume 3, *opusculum* 14."

      Tommaso de Vio (1469–1534), usually known as Thomas Cajetanus or Cajetan (from his birthplace of Gaeta), a noted theologian and exponent of the Counter-Reformation. In his 1534 treatise "On the king of England's marriage to his brother's widow," Cajetan

Pope Julius II, to our beloved son Henry, son of our dearest son in Christ, the illustrious King Henry of England, and to our beloved daughter in Christ Catherine, daughter of our dearest son in Christ Ferdinand and dearest daughter in Christ Isabella, the illustrious Catholic Kings of Spain and of Sicily, blessings in the Lord.

The sovereign authority of the Roman pontiff, through the power given him by our Lord, judges what is expedient before the Lord, according to the considerations of the quality of persons, affairs, and times. For your part, you have presented us with a petition, which states that you, Catherine, our daughter in Christ, and Arthur (then living), firstborn son of our beloved son in Christ, Henry, illustrious king of England, in order to secure peace and friendship between our beloved son in Christ Ferdinand, and our beloved daughter Isabella, the Catholic Kings of Spain and Sicily, and the aforesaid King Henry of England, lawfully contracted marriage *per verba de presenti*. Peradventure having consummated this in carnal copulation, the aforesaid Arthur died, leaving no children by the marriage. In order to preserve this bond of peace and friendship between the aforementioned kings and queen, you wish to marry and bind yourselves in lawful matrimony *per verba de presenti*. Therefore, you have requested of us that we deign to issue a dispensation and in our apostolic beneficence grant you permission to do so. We, who affectionately desire and work toward the peace and concord of all faithful Christians, especially Christian kings and potentates, absolve you of any sort of ecclesiastical penalty whatever. Inclining to your prayers and requests, by the apostolic authority, as per these our present letters, we grant you a dispensation that, the impediment of the said affinity (born of the aforementioned circumstances and the apostolic constitutions and ordinances, and whatever other matters that might be opposed thereto) notwithstanding, you may lawfully contract marriage *per verba de presenti*, and, after having so contracted, you may carry it out. And if, perchance, you have already contracted, whether publicly or in secret, and consummated it with carnal copulation, you may licitly live therein.[15] And, by that same authority, if you have contracted the marriage in this way, we absolve you—any of

---

reproduces the Latin text of Julius II's dispensation. See Thomas Cajetan, *Opuscula omnia nunc primum summa diligentia castigatam et doctissimorum quorundam virorum ope suo nitori accurate restituta* (Lyons: Apud Ioannem Iacobi Iuntae F., 1581), 296.

15   Henry and Catherine had indeed already been officially betrothed, on June 25, 1503; Julius's bull did not arrive in England until 1505. Tremlett, *Catherine of Aragon*, 100. Stella Fletcher, *Cardinal Wolsey: A Life in Renaissance Europe* (London: Continuum, 2009), 128.

you—of this excess, as well as of the sentence of excommunication you might have thus incurred, declaring that the children to be born, or perchance already born, of this marriage, whether now contracted or soon to be contracted, are legitimate—so long as you, Catherine, our daughter in Christ, have not been abducted and seized by force for this purpose. And we desire that if you have contracted your marriage before our dispensation, a confessor chosen by each of you shall impose upon you the penance that seems appropriate to him, which you are obligated to perform. Given in Rome, the first day of January in the year 1504, the first year of our pontificate.

These were the words of the dispensation, by virtue of which the marriage between Henry (for he was still a minor) and the Princess Doña Catherine was performed.

How King Henry VIII Married the Princess Doña Catherine, and of the Children Born to Them[1]

While they waited for Henry to reach the appropriate age for marriage, the illustrious Queen Doña Isabella, mother of the Princess Doña Catherine, died in Spain,[2] and King Henry VII, father of Prince Don Henry, died in England.[3] Henry succeeded him, now a king and eighteen years of age, an accomplished gentleman who in his dignity and beauty of appearance was a perfect picture of royal majesty, a man of sound judgment and one who knew what was proper and who did not have to live in fear of his dead father. Though he had once said that he had no desire to marry the princess, he now thought better of it and, having ordered the papal dispensation to be read out publicly, married Queen Doña Catherine on June 3, 1509, with the consent of his counselors (among whom there was not one who advanced a scruple or showed any opposition).[4] And on the day of Saint John the Baptist the same year, he and the queen his wife were crowned in London at the Benedictine monastery known as Westminster, in the western part of the city, with stupendous celebration and rejoicing.[5] King Henry had three sons and two daughters by Queen Doña Catherine: the eldest of the sons, named Henry like his father, died at nine months, and the others also died very young.[6] Only their daughter Doña Mary lived to

---

1   Sander, *De origine ac progressu*, 9–10, 12–13.

2   November 26, 1504.

3   April 21, 1509.

4   Henry VII forced his son to repudiate the marriage project when he turned fourteen (1505), but a combination of the exigencies of Spanish domestic politics and her own convictions ensured that Catherine remained in England. Almost as soon as he was king, the young Henry decided to marry his sister-in-law. The couple were actually married on June 11, 1509, less than two months after Henry VII's demise. Stella Fletcher characterizes Henry as initially "somewhat reluctant" toward the Spanish match, but this coolness had dissipated by the time the prince became king. J.J. Scarisbrick, *Henry VIII*, Yale English Monarchs (New Haven: Yale University Press, 1997), 8–13. Fletcher, *Cardinal Wolsey*, 15.

5   The new king and queen were crowned at Westminster Abbey on June 24, 1509, the feast of John the Baptist. Eric Ives, "Henry VIII (1491–1547)," in *ODNB*, 26:522–51, here 523.

6   Henry, duke of Cornwall, was born January 1, 1511, and died February 23 of the same year. He was just short of nine weeks old—not months, as Ribadeneyra and Sander have it. Besides this first Henry and the future Queen Mary, Catherine suffered a miscarriage in

maturity, and later became queen of England; she was born on February 18, 1515 [*sic*] at Greenwich.[7] King Henry had the child raised with all the magnificence and pomp befitting the heir to his kingdom, giving her as a governess Margaret, the niece of King Edward IV (the daughter of his brother) and the mother of Reginald Pole, who was later made a cardinal.[8] She was a truly virtuous gentlewoman and a very pious lady. And, as the legitimate heir to his throne, he declared Mary princess of Wales, which is the title in that kingdom given to those next in succession to the crown—what they call in the Empire the "caesar" or "king of the Romans," in France the "dauphin," and in Spain we call the *principe*.[9] To the end that Princess Doña Mary should take possession of this territory and govern it as her own (it being very large, divided into four bishoprics,[10] comprising the western part of England), her father sent her there with a huge retinue of knights and lords.[11]

Since she was the heiress to so great a throne and realm, many a king and prince in Christendom wished to marry her. Among them were King James V of Scotland and Emperor Charles,[12] as well as King Francis of France, who sought her for one of his two sons, the dauphin and the duke of Orleans—and

---

January 1510, as well as giving birth to two sons, both also called Henry, each of whom died within a few hours (October 1513 and December 1514) and an unnamed daughter, who was born on November 10, 1518, and died a few days later. Tremlett, *Catherine of Aragon*, 148, 154, 158, 177, 182, 197, 209.

7   Mary was born at Greenwich on February 18, 1516, but according to Old Style dating, in which the year began on 25 March (Lady Day), it was in 1515. Though Ribadeneyra would have used the Gregorian Calendar, he is here following *De origine ac progressu.* Sander, *De origine ac progressu*, 10.

8   Margaret Pole (1473–1541), countess of Salisbury. The daughter of George, duke of Clarence (1449–78), younger brother of Edward IV, Margaret was appointed Mary's governess in 1520. Her third son, Reginald Pole, was made a cardinal in 1536. Hazel Pierce, "Pole, Margaret, *suo jure* countess of Salisbury (1473–1541)," in *ODNB*, 44:706–09, here 706–08.

9   Although she was often referred to as such, Mary was never formally invested with the title of princess of Wales; doing so would have confirmed her place as Henry's heir, and by the time it had become clear that no more children were forthcoming from Catherine, the king was exploring other options. Loades, *Reign of Mary Tudor*, 3–4.

10   St David's, Llandaff, Bangor, and St Asaph.

11   In the summer of 1525, Mary was sent to Wales with a large household, where she remained in residence for two years. Edwards, *Mary I*, 19, 21.

12   In 1524, representatives of the Scottish crown arrived in London to negotiate a marriage between Mary and James V (r.1512–42) of Scotland, but nothing came of the idea. At the same time, Henry pursued a possible match with Charles V, but the emperor ultimately opted for his cousin Isabella of Portugal. Ibid., 15–18.

because they were both too young, he offered to marry her himself.[13] This is clear proof of how firmly the hearts of all the princes of Christendom believed that the marriage between King Henry and Queen Catherine was legitimate and above suspicion, given how many kings and princes desired and sought to marry the daughter thereof. For she was to succeed to the throne of England, which could not be if she were not the legitimate daughter of a legitimate marriage. In the end, she was betrothed (with certain conditions) to the dauphin of France, and the engagement celebrated with great solemnity at Greenwich in England, while the bishop of Ely traveled to France, where he delivered an elegant speech before King Francis and his court.[14] All this must be noted to understand fully what we are about to discuss.

---

13   In 1518, Francis I negotiated a (short-lived) betrothal between Mary and his firstborn son, Dauphin Francis, duke of Brittany (1518–36). Much later, after the dauphin's death in 1536, his father suggested Mary marry his third son, Charles, duke of Orléans (1522–45). The possibility of a marriage to Francis himself had been mooted under the terms of the 1527 Treaty of Westminster. Edwards, *Mary I*, 15–16, 59. R.J. Knecht, *Francis I* (Cambridge: Cambridge University Press, 1982), 78. Fletcher, *Cardinal Wolsey*, 123.

14   On October 5, 1518, the two-year-old Mary was betrothed at Greenwich to the infant dauphin, as part of a larger set of negotiations, including the English forfeiture of Tournai and massive French indemnities in compensation. The previous month, Nicholas West (d.1553), bishop of Ely, had left for France with an English delegation headed by Charles Somerset, first earl of Worcester (c.1460–1526). Antonio Giustinian (1466–1524), Venetian ambassador to France, reported that West delivered a Latin oration before the French court on December 12. Knecht, *Francis I*, 78. Felicity Heal, "West, Nicholas (d. 1553)," in *ODNB*, 58:233–35, here 233–34. *LP*, 2:4409. *CSPV*, 2:1129–30.

The Title of Defender of the Faith given King Henry by the Apostolic See, and the Reason for This[1]

When Henry was a young and powerful king, well beloved in his realm and esteemed and respected abroad, there arose the hellish madness of Luther, which came into the world for its destruction and the undermining of the Catholic Church, against which he immediately began to wage war. He wrote several books riddled with errors and blasphemies against the pope and the sacraments of the Church, disseminating his heresies and pestilential teachings, which scandalized and horrified the people not a little. Among the Christian princes who opposed this infernal insanity, the one who most distinguished himself was Henry, who not only strove to preserve the purity of our sacred Catholic faith in his kingdom, as other monarchs did, but also did what no one else had, which was to write a very learned and weighty book against Luther,[2] publish it in his own name, and send it to Rome to His Holiness Pope Leo x (in whose pontificate Luther's diabolical sect was spawned). However, this book did not come from the quiver of the king, so much as from that of John, bishop of Rochester, an extremely erudite man, who assisted him and

---

1   This chapter was added in the 1595 edition.

2   The *Assertio septem sacramentorum* was published in the summer of 1521 under Henry's name (precisely how much of the book the king actually wrote is open to dispute, but certainly much of the scholarly legwork was done by others). J.J. Scarisbrick opines, "*The Defence of the Seven Sacraments* is not a piece of theology of the highest order. Estimates of it have varied enormously, but the truth surely is that its erudition is unremarkable [...] its grasp of Lutheranism defective, its exposition of Catholic teaching on the sacraments unimpressive and undoubtedly shot through with that semi- or crypto-Pelagianism against which, essentially, Protestantism protested. [...] In short, it is unlikely to have moved many convinced, informed Lutherans. [...] But this is not to say that it was an ineffective book. On the contrary, it was one of the most successful pieces of Catholic polemics produced by the first generation of anti-Protestant writers." Scarisbrick, *Henry VIII*, 110–12, 116.

   See Henry VIII, *Assertio septem sacramentorum; or Defence of the seven sacraments*, ed. Louis O'Donovan (New York: Benziger Brothers, 1908).

   The *Assertio*, dedicated to the pope, was an important (but not the only) reason for Leo x's grant of the title of *Defensor Fidei* in October 1521. Ludwig Pastor, *The History of the Popes, from the Close of the Middle Ages*, trans. Frederick Ignatius Antrobus, Ralph Francis Kerr, Ernest Graf, and E.F. Peeler, 40 vols. (London: J. Hodges, 1891–1953), 8:442–44.

---

was the principal author.[3] This zeal of King Henry's was wonderfully received by all the world, while the supreme pontiff, Leo x, was so pleased with the service done our Lord, the piety with which the king opposed this infernal monstrosity, the magnanimity and valor with which he had previously aided Pope Julius ii,[4] and the submissiveness, devotion, and obedience he had shown to the Apostolic See in all things, that, with the advice of the sacred college of cardinals, he decided to honor King Henry by giving him the new and glorious title of "Defender of the Faith." This he did, sending him a brief in which he bestowed this title and set out his reasons. I have thought it good to insert a Spanish translation of the Latin, for reasons I shall relate farther on. Accordingly, thus says Pope Leo x in his brief:

> John Clerk,[5] our beloved son and Your Majesty's ambassador, having presented to us, in consistory and in the presence of our venerable brothers the cardinals of the holy Roman Church, the book that Your Majesty, afire with the Catholic faith and burning with the fervor and devotion you have for us and this Holy See, has composed against the errors of various heretics, repeatedly condemned by the Holy See and now recently revived by Martin Luther, so that we might have it examined and approve it with our authority; and having then also declared, in an elegant address, the ready will with which Your Majesty is furnished to persecute the followers and defenders of Luther's errors, no less with all the arms and might of your kingdom as with the true and unanswerable arguments and authorities from Holy Writ and the holy Fathers by which you have confounded their fallacies, we, who are the successors to the prince of the Apostles, Saint Peter, to whom the Lord entrusted the supreme care of his flock,[6] being seated upon this holy throne, whence spring all titles and dignities, having first carefully

---

3   The eminent theologian John Fisher served as bishop of Rochester from 1504 to his death. Though sixteenth-century editions of his works often included the *Defence of the Seven Sacraments*, and Fisher may have assisted Henry in its composition, it is unlikely he was the primary author. Maria Dowling, *Fisher of Men: A Life of John Fisher, 1468–1535* (Basingstoke: Macmillan, 1999), 107.

4   In the first years of his reign, Henry had joined Julius's Holy League (directed against France), in the latter stages of the War of the League of Cambrai. The king had led his armies to several notable—if somewhat inconsequential—victories, including the Battle of the Spurs (1513) and the capture of Tournai (1513). See Scarisbrick, Chapter 2.

5   John Clerk, later bishop of Bath and Wells (c.1481–1541), served multiple stints as Henry's ambassador to Rome. Richard Rex, "Clerk, John (1481/2?–1541)," in *ODNB*, 12:45–47, here 45.

6   John 21:16; Acts 20:28; 1 Pet. 5:2–3.

conferred with our aforesaid brothers, have, by their common opinion and consent, elected to give to Your Majesty the title of "Defender of the Faith," which we bestow in these our present letters. And we command all faithful Christians to address Your Majesty by this title, and when they write to you, to add "Defender of the Faith" after the word "king."

And there is no doubt that we could have found no better title, nor any more worthy and appropriate for Your Majesty's merits—the which, whenever it is heard or read, will call to mind your singular virtue and glorious merits, not to make you conceited with this title, nor to make you arrogant and dissipated, but rather to make you yet humbler, and stronger and more steadfast in the faith of Christ, and in devotion to this Holy See, by which you have been exalted, and to rejoice in the Lord (the giver of all blessings) and take pleasure in leaving to your successors this perpetual and immortal memorial and insignia of your glory, instructing them by your example how they are to follow you and perform other, similar deeds, if they wish to be honored and exalted by a similar title. Given in Rome at St. Peter's, September 27, in the year of the Incarnation of the Lord 1521, the ninth of our pontificate.[7]

The title of "Defender of the faith" left Henry smug and proud, supposing that he could now rival the king of Spain, who possessed the title of "Catholic," and with the king of France, who held that of "Most Christian."[8] He used the mantle of "Defender of the Faith" ever afterwards, and not only he but also all his children and successors have done the same, as his daughter Elizabeth does now in calling herself "Defender of the Faith," though she usurps this title of devotion, given to her father for the merits enumerated by Pope Leo in his brief, and for having defended with books, arms, and all his might the same faith that his daughter now seeks to exterminate and eradicate with such exquisite, extreme methods, with all her violence and cunning.

I have placed this papal bull here for the reader to observe these things and to understand how Catholic, how zealous for our holy faith, how devoted and

---

7   Sander furnishes the text of this brief: see Sander, *De origine ac progressu*, 225–27.

8   The Spanish monarch was known as the "Catholic King" (*Rex Catholicus*), a title first granted to Ferdinand and Isabella in 1494 by Alexander VI, in recognition of their successes against Muslim power on the Iberian Peninsula. The title of "Most Christian King" (*Rex Christianissimus*) had been claimed by French monarchs since the middle ages; Jacques Krynen has identified the reign of Charles V (r.1364–80) as the period when the usage became established. Elliot, *Imperial Spain*, 77. Jacques Krynen, "'*Rex Christianissimus*:' A Medieval Theme at the Roots of French Absolutism," *History and Anthropology* 4 (1989): 79–96, here 81.

obedient to the Apostolic See King Henry was in his youth, and what notable services he did the Church, for which he merited to be adorned with so illustrious a title, of such great glory and majesty. And so that when we see how he was later changed and corrupted, and this same defender of the faith became the cruelest persecutor of that faith, and from a faithful and obedient son was transformed into a fearful tyrant or a savage beast, we may inquire into the cause and origin of so lamentable an alteration, and learn that it was a fierce, blind passion for a woman, which consumed him and transfigured him, causing him to lose the faith whose defender he had been. Let us learn from this that wicked living opens the way to errors, and that a corrupted will also corrupts the understanding. Let us learn, too, how much he who gives rein to his perverted appetites and lives as though he believed none of the teachings of our sacred faith ought to fear to fall and lose that very faith. But let us consider the origins of this change in Henry, and by what steps he came to fall into the abyss of evil that he did, as this history tells.

Of the Dissimilar Habits of the Queen and the King[1]

There was a striking contrast between the behavior and habits of Queen Catherine and King Henry, which gave him the occasion and the urge to pursue other women. For although the queen was no more than five years older than the king, in her life and customs she seemed to have a thousand years on him. This was the sort of life the queen led: whenever she could, she arose in the middle of the night and attended the clerics' Matins. She dressed and readied herself at five in the morning—although she used to say that the only time she thought wasted was that spent beautifying herself. Beneath her royal attire, she wore the habit of the Franciscan tertiaries.[2] She fasted on bread and water every Friday and Saturday, as well as all the vigils of our Lady. Wednesdays and Fridays she confessed, and on Sundays received the sacred body of our Lord Jesus Christ. Each day she prayed the hours of our Lady, spending almost all morning in the church, absorbed in prayer and in hearing the divine office. After eating, she used to read from the lives of the saints for two hours in the company of her attendants and ladies-in-waiting. In the afternoon, she returned to her prayers in the church, before a modest dinner. She always prayed kneeling on the floor, without any cloth-of-state or chair, without any sign of rank or power. This she did all her life. Yet it pleased our Lord that she should be consumed in the flames of the tribulation she endured, so that the sweet fragrance of this saintly queen's heroic virtues should more easily spread throughout the entire world.

On the other hand, King Henry was a spirited youth, given to sports and dalliances. He would take two, sometimes even three of the queen's ladies-in-waiting as mistresses. By one of them, called Elizabeth Blount, he had a son, whom he made duke of Richmond.[3] Though he often marveled at the queen's sanctity, he followed the contrary path, allowing himself to be overcome by his

---

1 Sander, *De origine ac progressu*, 10–11, 13.

2 "It can be said without doubt that Katherine of Aragon was a tertiary [...] the probability is that she had joined the Third Order in Spain before she came to England." D.W. Whitfield, "The Third Order of St. Francis in Mediaeval England," *Franciscan Studies* 13, no. 1 (March 1953): 50–59, here 55.

3 Elizabeth Blount (*c.*1500–*c.*1540), one of Catherine's ladies-in-waiting. She was Henry's mistress for a brief period in the late 1510s. In June 1519, she gave birth to a son, Henry Fitzroy (1519–36). In 1525, the young Henry was created earl of Nottingham, duke of Richmond, and duke of Somerset. Beverley A. Murphy, "Blount, Elizabeth (*c.*1500–1539x41)," in *ODNB*, 6:301.

vices and passions. And so, the lives of the king and queen being so dissimilar, their habits so different, a wild heart like Henry's could never be at peace with a princess so reserved and so pious as his wife. Thus it was that he began to show signs of his discontent, which his servants and intimates soon came to perceive.

Beverley A. Murphy, "Fitzroy, Henry, duke of Richmond and Somerset (1519–1536)," in *ODNB*, 19:935–37, here 935–36.

Of the Cardinal of York's Ambition, and of the Advice He Gave the King Concerning His Marriage[1]

One of the king's confidants who came to know all this was Thomas Wolsey, a man bold and ambitious above all other men, whose life was much more like the Henry's than the queen's. Accordingly, he sought any opportunity to please the king, to harm the queen, and to advance his own interests. Wolsey was a man of low, menial birth, the son of a butcher (so some have written).[2] Having entered the king's household through deceit and cunning, he was initially his chaplain, and then his almoner.[3] Then he made himself rich with the rents of the bishopric of Tournai (which King Henry had taken from the king of France), and until at last he was made bishop—first of Lincoln, then of Durham, then of Winchester and, at the same time, archbishop of York, the two richest sees.[4] In the end, the king also made him chancellor of the realm, analogous to what we call the president of the royal council of Castile, as well as arranging for the pope to make him a cardinal and legate *a latere* in England.[5] Not content with this, he held numerous pensions and rich grants from the emperor and the king of France, as well as wealthy abbacies and church benefices, for King Henry favored him to the point of placing himself and his realm in his hands, neither deciding nor commanding anything without the word or hand of Wolsey. Consequently, both Emperor Don Charles and Francis, king of France—each hoping to keep King Henry on their side, as of great importance

---

1   Sander, *De origine ac progressu*, 13–16.

2   In the margin: "Polydore Vergil, [*Anglica historia*,] Book 27."

    His father's involvement in the meat trade notwithstanding, "both Thomas' parents issued from among east Suffolk's more prominent families." Fletcher, *Cardinal Wolsey*, 6.

3   Wolsey became Henry's chaplain in 1507, and his almoner in 1509. Ibid., 18.

4   Henry attempted to make Wolsey bishop of Tournai in 1514, but encountered difficulties in the presence of an alternative French candidate; Wolsey eventually relinquished his claim to the see in exchange for a handsome pension. An available bishopric (that of Lincoln) was finally found in 1514, but swiftly exchanged for the archbishopric of York, vacated in July by Christopher Bainbridge (*c*.1463–1514). In 1518, the archbishop also became administrator of the see of Bath and Wells, in 1523, that of Durham, and in 1529, that of Winchester. Ibid., 24, 60. "Biographical Dictionary—Consistory of September 10, 1515," in CHRC.

5   Wolsey became cardinal in September 1515, lord chancellor the following December, and papal legate three years later. Ibid. Fletcher, *Cardinal Wolsey*, 38.

in the wars waged between the two—strove to satisfy and win over the cardinal of York, upon whose will they knew the will of the king his lord depended.[6]

All the eminence and favor he possessed seemed but little to the cardinal, insufficient to satisfy his greed and ambition; these rather waxed greater each day as his dignities and influence increased (as they are wont to do). He even lusted and connived to mount to the heights of the supreme pontificate and seat himself upon the throne of Saint Peter.[7] He reckoned what he had to be little, since he could have more; his pleasure at his gains was nothing compared to his anguish at lacking what he craved. Emperor Don Charles caught scent of the cardinal's ambition, and, in order to make it serve his turn and to lure him further upon this path (as is the habit of kings, when it is called for), began to honor him, often writing him elaborate letters in his own hand, full of extravagant courtesies, signing them "Your son, and kinsman, Charles."[8] And to beguile and win him, he implied that if King Henry should, through Wolsey's efforts, ally with him in perpetuity and declare war upon France, he would ensure that when Pope Leo X died the cardinal should succeed to the pontificate.[9] Since men easily credit what they desire, the cardinal instantly believed this: to do himself a good turn, and so as not to lose so excellent an opportunity, he persuaded King Henry to do all the emperor wished. Shortly thereafter, Leo X died,[10] but although it was bruited about all of Italy that the

---

6   Wolsey received a French pension in compensation for relinquishing his claim to the bishopric of Tournai. When Charles V visited England in May 1520, he offered Wolsey the bishopric of Badajoz. The offer was refused (so as not to offend the French), but another pension was supplied. Fletcher, *Cardinal Wolsey*, 67.

7   Wolsey was a prominent candidate in papal elections of both 1521–22 and 1523, but Fletcher argues that he understood how little chance he actually stood of being elected (though diplomatic chatter abounded about Henry and Wolsey's energetic machinations). In 1529, by contrast, when Clement VII briefly fell ill, he exerted every effort to win election, as the only real hope of resolving Henry's matrimonial difficulties. Fletcher also suggests that the 1527 proposal to convene the cardinals in Avignon during Clement's captivity stemmed from "quasi-papal ambition." Ibid., 53, 126, 150–51. Cf. *CSPV*, 3:384; *LP*, 3:3372.

8   A sixteenth-century Latin life of Wolsey noted "For a long time, Emperor Charles sent him letters in no hand but his own, which he signed, 'your son.'" Nicholas Pocock, ed., *Records of the Reformation: The Divorce 1527–1533*, 2 vols. (Oxford: Clarendon Press, 1870), 2:89.

9   In a letter to Wolsey on December 17, 1521, Charles wrote, "I suppose you have heard of the death of the Pope. You remember the conversation we formerly had, and I shall gladly do what I can for you, if you will let me know how I can serve you." *LP*, 3:1877.

10   December 1, 1521.

cardinal of York had been elected pope, this was not so.[11] The emperor, young though he was, arranged for it to be his tutor, Adrian, a most learned and saintly man, different from Wolsey in every way.[12] Wolsey was not surprised that the emperor had advanced Adrian to the pontificate, given his personal obligations, and so he dissembled and had patience—until Adrian died and Clement VII succeeded him.[13] Then, perceiving that the emperor cared nothing for him, and that after he had captured King Francis of France he wrote to him less frequently, by another's hand, without signing more than the name "Charles," the cardinal began to fume and lose control of himself, to rage against the emperor and work against him in any way he could, to aid his enemies and to devote himself to King Francis of France.[14] In this furious rage, stoked by his senseless ambition, he wove himself a web he was later unable to untangle, and it ended badly for him. Now, seeing King Henry disenchanted with the Queen Doña Catherine (who was set against Wolsey because of his ambition) for the reasons we mentioned above, the cardinal cast about for some means of definitively separating the king from the queen, so as to win favor for himself, do her harm, and avenge himself upon the emperor her nephew. Some say that he was also driven to persecute the queen because an astrologer had predicted that a woman would be the cause of his ruin and downfall: giving credit to these words and supposing that the woman was Queen Doña Catherine, he schemed to strip her of her power and separate her from the king.[15] It will be seen hereafter how mistaken he was.

---

11   English observers were overly generous in their estimates of Wolsey's chances in the conclave. Fletcher, *Cardinal Wolsey*, 79.

12   Adriaan Florenszoon Dedel, the Utrecht-born tutor to Charles V who was elected Pope Adrian VI in 1522 (r.1522–23). Although Adrian owed his election primarily to the influence of Cardinal Cajetan, the new pope was widely regarded as Charles's henchman. Pastor, *History of the Popes*, 9:27, 31.

13   Adrian died in Rome on September 14, 1523. Clement was elected on November 19.

14   Francis was taken prisoner by imperial forces in 1525, at the disastrous battle of Pavia, and released the following year. Knecht, *Francis I*, 169–76.

15   This anecdote is derived from the so-called "Spanish Chronicle" (c.1550). "As he rose from base beginnings he rejoiced in having wise people in his train, and amongst them there was an astrologer, who said to him one day, 'My lord, you will be destroyed by a woman.' At the time he had so much power the sainted Queen Katharine was living, and she grieving that so low a man should have so great control, showed but little love towards him, and rather tried that the King should look after the government of his kingdom. The Cardinal knowing this, and remembering what the astrologer had said, made up his mind to invent the diabolical thing we shall tell you of." Martin A. Sharp Hume, ed., *Chronicle of King Henry VIII of England Being a Contemporary Record of Some of the Principal Events of the*

Moved by this or by some other dream of vengeance (as I have said), he summoned the king's confessor, John Longland, bishop of Lincoln,[16] and withdrawing with him in secret told him of his deep obligation to serve the king, on account of the bountiful favors received from his hands, and for having placed him in that state, raising him from the very dust of the earth.[17] To repay what was owed on so many counts, he concerned himself with nothing so much as the king's salvation (besides his own), and he could not remain silent in a matter upon which so much rested, nor speak of it to anyone before him, the king's confessor, who knew the secrets of his soul and had the charge thereof. To make a long story short, he told him that he thought the king's marriage to the queen dubious and dangerous to the king's conscience, as well as his grounds for this. The confessor, imagining that the cardinal spoke in all sincerity and truthfulness, and knowing that the king would not mislike such a suggestion, did not dare contradict a personage so exalted and so powerful. He replied that he thought the king should hear of so serious a matter from nobody but the cardinal, and so the cardinal proposed to broach it with the king.[18] But when the king heard this, he answered the cardinal, "See that you do not place in doubt what has already been determined, nor set in motion a stone you cannot stop when you will."[19]

Three days later, the cardinal returned to the king, bringing the confessor with him, whom he had induced to plead that, whereas the matter was so important and concerned his salvation, His Majesty should at least permit it to be discussed and examined. When the king granted this, the cardinal said, "In France there is Marguerite, the sister of King Francis, who was married to the duke of Alençon and is a lady of extraordinary beauty—she is the one it befits

---

Reigns of Henry VIII and Edward VI Written in Spanish by an Unknown Hand, trans. Martin A. Sharp Hume (London: George Bell and Sons, 1889), 3.

16   John Longland (1473–1547) was bishop of Lincoln from 1522 until his death, and became royal confessor in 1524. A close ally of Wolsey, some contemporaries suggested that the cardinal had prompted Longland to raise the issue of the king's marriage, while others believed Henry brought the matter to his confessor of his own accord. Margaret Bowker, "Longland, John (1473–1547)," in *ODNB*, 34:395–98, here 395–96.

17   Gen. 2:7.

18   The Catholic controversialist Nicholas Harpsfield's *Treatise on the Pretended Divorce between Henry VIII and Catherine of Aragon* (c.1558) related that "The beginning then of all this broil [...] proceeded from Cardinal Wollseye, who first by himself, or by John Langlond, Bishop of Lincolne and the King's confessor, put this scruple and doubt in his head." Nicholas Harpsfield, *A Treatise on the Pretended Divorce between Henry VIII and Catharine of Aragon*, ed. Nicholas Pocock, Works of the Camden Society, New Series 21 (New York: Johnson Reprint Corporation, 1965), 175.

19   The second clause of this sentence was added in the 1595 edition.

Your Majesty to take as a wife."[20] The king responded, "We shall see about that later. For now, keep this a secret, lest we prematurely publish something that besmirches our honor."[21] Because the king knew perfectly well the woman he would take on separating from Queen Doña Catherine.

---

20   Henry was one of many European rulers mooted as potential husbands for Marguerite, the widowed duchess of Alençon (1492–49). As early as 1503, the match had been proposed by King Louis XII (r.1498–1515). Patricia F. Cholakian and Rouben C. Cholakian, *Marguerite de Navarre: Mother of the Renaissance* (New York: Columbia University Press, 2006), 24, 137.

21   "After a few days, the cardinal assaulted the King afresh and with much more vehemency, being with him the said Bishop of Lincolne, who very earnestly, as one which (as he said) had a tender and special regard and charge above all other of the King's soul, for the safeguard of the same, did solicit him that he would suffer that the validity of his said matrimony might be well considered and examined according to right, justice, and equity. [...] The King at length began somewhat to give ear and yield to these persuasions; whereupon, as though the divorce were now concluded and determined upon, the cardinal was in hand with the King that he would cast his fancy for to marry the French King's sister, late wife to the Duke of Alenson, a young virtuous lady. But the King resolved nothing with him at that time." Harpsfield, *Treatise*, 176.

Of the King's Actions Concerning His Marriage to the Queen, and What the French Ambassador Proposed to Dissolve It[1]

And so, once the cardinal and the confessor had sworn themselves to secrecy, the king threw himself into exploring the matter: he gave his nights to it, conferring with various theologians over the arguments in favor propounded by the cardinal, based upon several places in Leviticus and Deuteronomy (badly misinterpreted),[2] as well as scouring the apostolic letters by which Pope Julius II had permitted his marriage to Queen Doña Catherine. Finding nothing to his purpose or satisfaction, neither in the places of Scripture nor in the pope's dispensation, he thought it best to abandon it and proceed no further therein, and all those the king had secretly consulted in the course of a year were of the same opinion. And so he would have done, if, on the one hand, the cardinal had not delved so deeply or been so insistent with the king, or, on the other, if the king himself, weary of the queen's saintly life and stricken with love for Anne Boleyn, had not been overwhelmed with passion and the false hopes she fed him of lawfully dissolving his marriage to the queen.

Around this time, ambassadors came to King Henry from France, asking that his daughter, the Princess Doña Mary, who had been betrothed (as we have said) to the dauphin, marry the duke of Orleans, King Francis's second son. Among the envoys was the bishop of Tarbes.[3] With this opportunity, the king ordered Wolsey—as though on his own initiative and as a friend to the king of France—to inform the bishop of the business: to tell him all that had

---

1 Sander, *De origine ac progressu*, 17–21.

2 In the margin: "Leviticus 18[:16], Deuteronomy 25[:5–6]."

3 The delegation in question, including Gabriel de Gramont, bishop of Tarbes (1486–1534), arrived at the English court in April 1527. Two years later, Henry was to repeat the story of Gramont's speech before the legatine court. J.J. Scarisbrick opines that "It is incredible that an ambassador would have dared to trespass upon so delicate a subject as a monarch's marriage. Nor was it likely that he should have suggested that Mary was illegitimate when her hand would have been very useful to French diplomacy." Salvador Miranda, by contrast, claims that Gramont "was sent as French ambassador to England to secretly try to break the marriage of the English king and Catalina de Aragón and propose to him the hand of Marguerite d'Orléans, widow of Duke Charles d'Alençon." Scarisbrick, *Henry VIII*, 153. "Biographical Dictionary—Consistory of June 8, 1530," in CHRC.

been discussed and that, if lawful means could be found for dissolving the marriage of the king and queen, the king would assuredly marry the king of France's sister. Wolsey did as the king commanded, imparting the matter to the bishop and adding that it would not be proper for any of King Henry's vassals to be the first to raise such an issue, taking so a great burden upon themselves as well as the hatred of the entire realm, such as would befall any who tried to place the king's marriage (a fact accepted by all) in jeopardy or doubt. As for the bishop, he was well placed to do this, as man who looked to the good of his king and desired to firmly establish the tranquility and peace of both kingdoms. Wolsey's arguments seemed sound to the bishop, who, having shared it with his fellow ambassadors, decided to attempt the business. One day, in the presence of King Henry and his council, he said that it was a fact well known among all Englishmen and Frenchmen that there was nothing more desirable or beneficial to all than peace between those two kingdoms; to establish this and tighten it with bonds of loving friendship, it had been agreed that the most serene princess of Wales, Doña Mary, should marry the duke of Orleans—and he did not doubt that this marriage would be of great advantage and glory to both nations. But another path occurred to him, incomparably better suited to achieve what was desired, if he had leave to propose it.

But why—he said—may I not expound it, since I speak in this council, among men who are not only Christian, but exceedingly pious and prudent, who, without any concern for their private interests, always keep the public good as the aim of all their deliberations? How much more advantageous would it be, if persons of mature years (and not children), the heads of kingdoms they have successfully governed (and not other, lesser royals, without experience), and indeed the monarchs themselves made this match and bound themselves together, rather than their children? For our part, it is common knowledge that the duchess of Alençon, the sister of our Most Christian King, has the age and all other attributes for marriage that might be desired in a princess—and that she lacks nothing but a husband, one whose dignity of person and state might add luster to her royal blood, rather than diminish or obscure it. If there were in England such a leading man, or (as I should say) the first, the very head of all nobles and lords, who had no wife—such a one ought to marry that lady, for the universal good, tranquility, and security of both realms. Your Majesty, O Henry, most mighty king, if we are willing to consider the reality and the truth, rather than the false appearances of things, is free of the ties of matrimony and lord of himself, to take any woman he chooses. I say this not only according to my judgment, but also that of all learned men, men of the greatest perspicacity in the world. To be sure, Catherine, that most serene lady, is of an illustrious line and a saintly life, yet having previously been the wife of Your Majesty's brother, I do not know by what argument or with what right, against the commands of the Holy Gospel, you, my lord, have taken to wife the wife of your brother, keeping her and living a married life with her. Truly, I do not doubt that your English vassals have no Gospel but the one we have, nor that they think as we think—but they do not dare speak until Your Majesty gives them license to say freely what they feel. For other nations have always spoken sorrowfully of this business and felt regret for Your Majesty, seeing how in your youth your royal person was beguiled by your counselors and confidants.[4] But now it is time that Your Majesty see for yourself and—if it is true that no one can take his brother's widow as a wife, as per Holy Gospel[5]—find a way to undo it, to free yourself from the wife you have (for she was the wife of your brother), to marry the sister of the Most Christian King, and by said happy marriage, to unite in brotherhood these two mighty kingdoms, their fortunes so tremendous as to strike fear into every other realm and principality. Your Majesty will thoughtfully consider, in your supreme and royal wisdom, what is to be done in this matter. I have only attempted, with a Christian's liberty, to say what occurs to me for the perfect happiness of these kingdoms and the eternal salvation of Your Majesty.

Having heard this disquisition, the king dissembled, pretending that he was troubled by it, and that it was something new and unheard-of. But, because it touched upon his salvation and his honor, he said that he would consent to have it looked into. The bishop, believing he had done an excellent day's work, then returned to France to give King Francis the news of so desirable a prospect (as he thought). But all England, learning what had been said, began to call down wild curses upon the French ambassadors and to speak against the king's intentions and tricks; for there was no one who doubted that all had transpired by his order and wish.

---

4   "From 1514 onwards there was intermittent talk in diplomatic circles of the marriage foundering on the rock of consanguinity." Fletcher, *Cardinal Wolsey*, 128.

5   In the margin: "Matthew 6 [*Matt. 6.*]."
    This is almost certainly a misprint for "Mark 6[:19]."

Of the Other Means Wolsey Used to Achieve His End, and of His Journey to France[1]

At this same time, it was reported that Charles, duke of Bourbon (who paid for this sacrilege and wickedness with his life) and the armies of the emperor had invaded, sacked, and desecrated the holy city of Rome, that he had surrounded Pope Clement VII, and even taken him prisoner.[2] Given this opportunity, Wolsey persuaded the king to come to the pope's aid, both because he could hardly fail to do so, bearing the title of "Defender of the Faith" (which the Holy See had given him for writing a book against Martin Luther), and because this could gain the pope's goodwill, keeping him well inclined and favorable in the matter of the divorce. Simultaneously, he could oblige the king of France by attempting to rescue his two children (who had remained as hostages) from the emperor's hands.[3] The cardinal's arguments impressed the king, who decided to send him to France with 300,000 ducats and two other ambassadors as his colleagues. He gave them all instructions and commissions for the matters they were to conduct jointly, and others separately to the cardinal for those he was to attempt on his own: the divorce from Queen Doña Catherine, the marriage to the king of France's sister, and the liberation of his children from the power of the emperor. And so the cardinal departed for France on this embassy with a huge retinue and amid great fanfare: one author has written that he

---

1   Sander, *De origine ac progressu*, 21–22.

2   In the margin: "In the year 1527."

   Imperial armies, commanded by the renegade French nobleman Charles III, duke of Bourbon (1490–1527), seized and looted Rome on May 6, 1527, in the course of which the duke was killed. Clement VII and his court locked themselves in the Castel Sant'Angelo; after nearly a month of waiting in vain for rescue from his Italian allies, the pope surrendered on June 5, remaining a prisoner until December 6 of the same year. Kenneth Gouwens and Sheryl E. Reiss, eds., *The Pontificate of Clement VII: History, Politics, Culture* (Aldershot: Ashgate, 2005), 30–36.

3   One of the terms of Francis's release was the surrender of the dauphin and his second son, Henry, duke of Orléans and future king, as imperial hostages. They were eventually released under the terms of the treaty of Cambrai, signed on August 3, 1529. Knecht, *Francis I*, 189, 219–20.

brought with him twelve hundred knights,[4] although all this was nothing compared with his ambition.

On arriving at Calais, Wolsey received fresh letters from King Henry, who ordered him to pursue the rest of his commission, but not to speak a word about marriage to the French king's sister (for in his heart Henry had now resolved to marry Anne Boleyn, if he could dissolve the marriage to Queen Doña Catherine). The stunned cardinal felt this blow more than can be imagined, seeing that it marred the schemes of his ambition, for the entire project of the divorce from Queen Doña Catherine and the marriage of King Henry with the duchess of Alençon had been to win her brother, King Francis, and secure his goodwill for all his own aspirations. He well knew that King Henry was blindly, hopelessly stricken with love for Anne Boleyn, but he never imagined that he desired her as a wife rather than a mistress (as her own mother and sister had been, without either having the slightest thought of marriage to the king). But he had deceived himself in this, as in everything else that his insatiable lust for power had treacherously made him believe. One author claims that the cause of Henry's alteration as to marriage with the duchess of Alençon was that, while the cardinal was preparing for his journey to France, the king had dispatched a knight of his court with all speed to bring him a portrait of the duchess—which displeased him the moment he saw it, judging that she was not so beautiful as she had been made out to be or as he desired. And, being a prisoner to his blind passion for Anne Boleyn, he immediately wrote to the cardinal not to pursue the marriage with the king of France's sister, as has been said.[5]

---

4   In the margin: "Guicciardini."

　　Francesco Guicciardini, *Storia d'Italia*, ed. Silvana Seidel Menchi, vol. 3 of 3 vols. (Turin: Giulio Einaudi Editore, 1971), 1876.

5   "The King sent a gentleman to France to bring him a portrait of the lady. This gentleman made such haste that he got back before the Cardinal entered France; and as soon as the King saw the lady's face, which was ugly, his love for Anne Boleyn being more ardent than ever, he sent after the Cardinal, and they reached him in Calais before he had started." Hume, *Chronicle*, 29–30.

Of Anne Boleyn, Her Disposition and Abilities[1,2]

Anne Boleyn was the daughter of the wife of Thomas Boleyn, a leading knight; I say that she was the daughter of his wife, because she could not possibly have been *his* daughter, for his wife conceived and bore Anne while he was away from home for the space of two years as the king's ambassador to France, during which his wife conceived and bore Anne.[3] The reason for this was that, lusting after Boleyn's wife, he sent her husband to France, under the pretext of honoring him with the office of ambassador, in order to enjoy her without danger or suspicion. While he was occupied in his mission, Anne Boleyn was conceived and born in his house, as has been said.[4] Returning to England after two years, Thomas Boleyn learned of his wife's bad faith; demanding a divorce, he met with the magistrates of the archbishop of Canterbury. His wife informed the king, who sent word to Boleyn through the marquess of Dorset[5] not to proceed against her, but rather to pardon her and receive her into his grace again. Boleyn had not the slightest desire to do so (although he saw his peril), until his wife threw herself at his feet and confessed her weakness: how she had tried to conquer the king's importunity, how he had persecuted and beset her, and

---

1   Sander, *De origine ac progressu*, 22–26.

2   In the margin: "William Rastell [*Kastalo*] relates this in the life of Thomas More."
     "Kastalo" is either a misreading of the marginal note "Rastallo," in *De origine ac progressu*, or a printer's error. Ibid., 22.
     The Catholic jurist and printer William Rastell (1508–65) wrote a now-lost *Life* of Thomas More, his uncle (Rastell's mother was More's younger sister), in which he related this story. J.H. Baker, "Rastell, William (1508–1565)," in *ODNB*, 46:92–83, here 83. Eric Ives, *The Life and Death of Anne Boleyn: "The Most Happy"* (Malden: Blackwell Publishing, 2004), 47.

3   Though Thomas Boleyn did serve as ambassador to France, this was not until 1519. His wife, Elizabeth Boleyn (née Howard, *c.*1480–1538), gave birth to Anne *c.*1501. Jonathan Hughes, "Boleyn, Thomas, Earl of Wiltshire and Earl of Ormond (1476/7–1539)," in *ODNB*, 6:470–72, here 470–71.

4   Henry was around nine years of age at the time of Anne's birth, neither king nor even heir apparent.

5   When Anne was born, the marquess of Dorset was Thomas Grey (*c.*1455–1501). It is more likely, however, that Rastell has in mind Grey's son (also Thomas). The elder Grey, one of the few surviving Yorkists, was regarded with suspicion, even hostility, by the Tudors. His son, by contrast, became a leading courtier under Henry VIII. T.B. Pugh, "Grey, Thomas, first marquess of Dorset (*c.* 1455–1501)," in *ODNB*, 23:880–82, here 880, 882. Robert C. Braddock, "Grey, Thomas, second marquess of Dorset (1477–1530)," in *ODNB*, 23:882–84.

© KONINKLIJKE BRILL NV, LEIDEN, 2017 | DOI 10.1163/9789004323964_013

how Anne was his daughter, and none other's. Thus she begged pardon of her husband, for she would thenceforth be loyal to him and keep faith with him, as was right. At this, seeing how fervently the marquess of Dorset and other knights and prominent lords pleaded with him, both in their own names and in the king's, Thomas Boleyn pardoned his wife and arranged to raise Anne as his own daughter.

Before Anne was born, Thomas Boleyn and his wife had had another daughter, called Mary. While visiting her mother's house (her father having returned to France), the king's eyes fell upon Mary. To have her closer to hand, he ordered her brought to the royal palace, where he dealt with her dishonestly.[6] Still not content, though he had already slept with the mother and was at the moment sleeping with one daughter, the king, burning with senseless lust, also wished to possess the other daughter, the sister—Anne Boleyn.[7] Anne was tall of stature, black-haired, long of face, of a complexion rather yellow (as though jaundiced). One of her upper teeth protruded, marring her beauty. She had six fingers on her right hand and a growth like a goiter—to cover this, she took to wearing a high collar, a fashion others followed.[8] The rest of her body was well proportioned and attractive: her lips were most shapely, her dancing and her playing graceful and deft, and her dress utterly singular, full of newfangled contrivances, fashions, and fineries.[9] As to her behavior, she was full of pride, ambition, envy, and dishonesty; while still a girl of fifteen, she slept with two

---

6   Mary Boleyn (c.1499–1543) came to court in 1520, shortly after her marriage to Sir William Carey (c.1500–28). Her term as royal mistress cannot be precisely defined, but the early 1520s may be considered a safe estimate. Jonathan Hughes, "Stafford [*née* Boleyn; *other married name* Carey], Mary (c.1499–1543)," in *ODNB*, 52:58–59, here 58.

7   Rumors to this effect had circulated as early as the 1530s. In 1537, Sir George Throckmorton recalled, "About six or seven years ago [...] I told your Grace I feared if ye did marry Queen Anne your conscience would be more troubled at length, for it is thought ye have meddled both with the mother and the sister." *LP*, 12.2:952.

    Harpsfield (perhaps disingenuously) said the same: "Yea, I have credibly heard reported that the King knew the mother of the said Anne Bulleyne." Harpsfield, *Treatise*, 236.

8   In October 1532, a Venetian diplomat wrote, "Madam Anne is not one of the handsomest women in the world; she is of middling stature, swarthy complexion, long neck, wide mouth, bosom not much raised, and in fact has nothing but the English King's great appetite, and her eyes, which are black and beautiful, and take great effect on those who served the Queen when she was on the throne." *CSPV*, 4:824.

    A French account of Anne's coronation noted, "She wore a violet velvet mantle, with a high ruff [*goulgiel*] of gold thread and pearls, which concealed a swelling she has, resembling gotre." *LP*, 6:585.

9   The backhandedness of Ribadeneyra's praise becomes clearer in the light of his description of actresses in the *Tratado de la tribulación*, where he links their beauty, grace, and skill at

servants of her supposed father, Thomas Boleyn. She was subsequently sent to France, where, having joined the royal court, she conducted herself with such lewdness that she was publicly called "the English nag" or "the English mare." Later, they called her "the royal mule," because she had been intimate with the king of France.[10] And, as this woman's religious beliefs could not but correspond to her life and habits, she followed the Lutheran sect, although she did not cease to hear Mass as though she were Catholic—for since the king was one, she deemed it advantageous for her scheming ambitions.

From France, she returned to England with the reputation I have described, and entered the court, where she soon learned how the king had tired of his wife, and how Wolsey was seeking a separation. Little by little, she came to discover the flames burning in the king's heart: his infatuation for her and the ease with which he tired of his paramours and abandoned them. Besides the numerous other examples, she recalled how her own mother and sister had lost the king's favor.[11] Contemplating all this, even as her sensual nature urged her to acquiesce to the king's will, she was restrained by her ambition and her desire to augment her own wicked pride. Ambition thus conquering lust, she shrewdly determined not to give ear to the pleas and amorous sallies of the king—unless he married her. From the love he showed her and his hatred for the queen, she had no doubt of succeeding. And so, the harder the king pressed her, the more she resisted, swearing that none but her husband should pluck the flower of her virginity. She sported with the king, playing and dancing with him, engaging in every pastime and dalliance ladies use with their gallants, but never straying beyond that. The more warmly she enticed him, the more the king pined for her; the more untouchable she appeared, the more fiercely he burned in his love. And so each day he became more set on the desire of his heart, to leave the queen his wife and marry a maiden as virtuous and pious as Anne Boleyn. When word of this spread in France, the French quipped that the king of England wished to wed the king of France's mule.

---

dancing to their immorality and their power to corrupt. Ribadeneyra, *Tratado de la tribulación*, 70^r–70^v.

10 In 1513, Anne traveled to the French court in the retinue of Mary Tudor (1496–1533), sister of Henry VIII and wife of Louis XII of France. After Louis's death, Anne remained in France for another six years, as a companion to Queen Claude (1499–1524), wife of Francis I. Sander has elided the two Boleyn sisters: it was Mary, in France at the same time, who "seems to have acquired a decidedly dubious reputation." Hughes, "Stafford," in ODNB, 52:58.

11 In the margin: "Cardinal Pole, Book 3, *Defense of the Unity of the Church* [*de vnione Ecclesiæ*]."

      Pole, *Defense*, 185.

I well perceive that I am relating things that, either for their triviality or their character, I might have left out. Yet, considering the matter, it seemed to me that I ought to record them, both because they were recorded by a man as serious and circumspect as Doctor Sander, as integral to the thread of the story and its veracity, and, moreover, because they illustrate the king's blind passion. For Anne's defects, her sinful life and bad repute, were not enough to put him off his wicked intentions and insane obsessions. Not even the fact that Anne was his own daughter, nor all the efforts of his counselors, including Thomas Boleyn (her supposed father), could divert him from his aberrant desire. All these men attempted to restore the king to reason, as will be seen in the following chapter.

What Thomas Boleyn and the Councilors Said to the King Concerning Anne Boleyn, and How He Responded[1]

Thomas Boleyn (who was, as we have said, Anne's putative father) was still in France, commissioned by King Henry on various matters alongside another knight called Anthony Browne.[2] Learning of the king's blind passion and senseless obsession, he took off for England in the greatest haste and without the king's leave (hardly the custom of ambassadors), to reveal to the king now what would endanger him if it subsequently emerged through other means. Thomas begged one of the king's chamberlains to excuse his unceremonious approach to His Majesty and to secure a private audience. This done, as soon as he entered the king's presence he told him (drawing the water from the source) how, being in his service in France, Anne Boleyn had been born in his house. He would have divorced his wife for this, if His Majesty had not commanded him otherwise, and if she had not told him in no uncertain terms that Anne was the king's daughter. The king retorted, "Shut up, you fool [*callad necio*]! A hundred others had to do with your wife: whichever of them is Anne's father, she will be my wife. Go back to your ambassadorship and do not speak a word of this." And so the king departed, his mouth filled with laughter, leaving Thomas Boleyn where he was, still upon his knees. And, lest any perceive the reason for Thomas's sudden journey, it was announced that he had brought the king the portrait of the duchess of Alençon. But, seeing that the final, determined will of the king was to marry Anne Boleyn, Thomas and his wife likewise resolved not to lose so good an opportunity for their advancement, and they advised and supported Anne every way they could to further the business.

However, all the thoughtful, sensible, God-fearing men in England thought and spoke very badly of the affair. In particular, those of the king's council, fulfilling the duties of their office, resolved to speak with him and advise him of his best interests. And because it did not belong to them as laymen to presume to interpret divine law or the grounds for the legitimate dispensation of

---

1   Sander, *De origine ac progressu*, 26–29.
2   Sir Anthony Browne (*c*.1500–48), a close friend of Henry's, frequently dispatched on diplomatic missions. William B. Robison, "Browne, Sir Anthony (*c*.1500–1548)," in *ODNB*, 8:144–46, here 144.

© KONINKLIJKE BRILL NV, LEIDEN, 2017 | DOI 10.1163/9789004323964_014

the king and queen's marriage, they decided to speak only of Anne Boleyn's dissolute and sinful life, or at least her wicked reputation and the kingdom's bad opinion of her. So as not to attempt so grave a matter without foundation, they first sought trustworthy information. At this time, Thomas Wyatt, a knight (raised by the king) and a leading courtier, came to the council: learning of the council's discussions and fearing lest word reach the king by some other route to his harm, he publicly confessed that he had slept with Anne Boleyn, not knowing or even imagining that the king wished to take her for his wife.[3] With these and other reports, the councilors came to the king, telling him that their office and their duty was to advise him on all that pertained not only to His Majesty's life and royal estate, but also his honor and reputation. To fulfill this responsibility, they informed him that Anne Boleyn had an awful reputation in his court as a dissolute and wayward woman, and this of such great note that it would not befit his royal person to marry her; they also told him of what Wyatt had confessed. The king was silent for a moment, finally answering that he was certain that they had been moved to say what they said out of their love and respect for him and their zeal in his service. Yet he firmly believed that everything said of Anne Boleyn was false, fabricated by vile and contemptible people; he dared swear that Anne Boleyn was the most chaste and virtuous of maidens. But Thomas Wyatt, insulted that his words had not been believed, told several councilors that if the king wished to know the truth, he would arrange for the king himself to observe the two of them in secret, because Anne loved Thomas beyond reason. When Charles Brandon, duke of Suffolk,[4] reported this to the king, he replied, "Wyatt is a filthy, deceitful, and insolent man; I have no taste for such sights." And he told Anne everything that had happened, and so she discarded Wyatt. Nevertheless, Wyatt's confession eventually cost him his life, when the king put to death Anne Boleyn and her associates (as will be related later).

---

3   Sir Thomas Wyatt (1503–42), a poet, ambassador, and courtier. Modern scholarship is ambivalent as to whether there was a relationship between Anne and Wyatt, and, if so, whether a confession such as Sander recounts might have taken place. Susan Brigden, *Thomas Wyatt: The Heart's Forest* (London: Faber and Faber, 2012), 52–53, 145–49.

4   Charles Brandon, first duke of Suffolk (c.1484–1545), Henry's lifelong friend and adviser.

What Wolsey Negotiated in France, and His Return to England[1]

In France, the cardinal of York had concluded the other elements of his mission much to his satisfaction, but not the one he most desired, the marriage between his lord the king and the duchess of Alençon, because (as was related earlier) the king had ordered him not to pursue it. He agreed with King Francis on a perpetual peace and alliance with his king, as well as a war in Italy against the emperor to free the pope and the king of France's two children from his power, for the expenses of which Henry would contribute 32,000 ducats each month. It would be commanded by Monseigneur Lautrec, as the king of France's captain general, with Lord Casali present in the name of the king of England.[2] Having concluded these negotiations with King Francis (and having received substantial gifts and grants from his hands), the cardinal wished to leave France for England. He advised the king to send to Rome by the protonotary, Gambara,[3] to inform the pope of what had been done on his behalf and to request him, in recognition of all Wolsey's efforts to secure the liberty and independence of His Holiness and his Holy See, to make him his legate and vicar-general in the kingdoms of France, England, and Germany. But although King Francis publicly showed his support for the cardinal's suit, he opposed it in secret; it was such as could never find favor with the pope, who dissembled because of his present necessity and did not respond until he was at liberty some months later.[4] Meanwhile, as soon as the cardinal had returned to England, the king instructed him to pursue the matter of the divorce. Thinking Wolsey

---

1   Sander, *De origine ac progressu*, 29–31.

2   The 1527 Treaty of Westminster provided for a French force, funded by Henry, to move against imperial forces in Italy. Odet de Foix, vicomte de Lautrec (1483–1528), was made captain-general (at the insistence of the English, according to Francesco Guicciardini [1483–1540]). The Italian nobleman Gregorio Casali (d.1536), Henry's trusted ambassador at Rome, was to accompany Lautrec as commissary. Catherine Fletcher, *Our Man in Rome: Henry VIII and His Italian Ambassador* (London: The Bodley Head, 2012), 8–9. Guicciardini, *Storia d'Italia*, 1873.

3   Uberto Gambara (1489–1549), later a cardinal, served as papal nuncio to France and England in the 1520s. "Biographical Dictionary—Consistory of December 19, 1539," in *CHRC*.

4   "The Cardinal, whose ambitions were limitless, hatched a scheme by which Clement would, in addition to approving the divorce, allow Wolsey to exercise papal powers from Avignon during the Pope's captivity. Clement's reaction to this may be imagined. Even after his release

lukewarm in it, he reproached him and, handling him sharply, said that if he could divorce Queen Catherine (as the cardinal had advised), he could marry a lady of his kingdom just as well as one from abroad. The cardinal, seeing himself all at sea in the business and unable to turn back (though in his soul he wished to), thought it best to suffer, dissemble, and promise to do all His Majesty commanded. To win back his goodwill, he threw a stately, regal banquet for the king and Anne Boleyn at his house in London, York Place.[5]

---

in December, 1527, he refused to cooperate." William Maltby, *The Reign of Charles V* (Basingstoke: Palgrave, 2002), 37.

5   George Cavendish (1497–c.1562), Wolsey's gentleman-usher and first biographer, recalls, "And yet the Cardinal, espying the great zeal that the King had conceived in this gentlewoman, ordered himself to please as well the King as her, dissimuling the matter that lay hid in his breast, and prepared great banquets and solemn feasts to entertain them both at his own house." George Cavendish and William Roper, *Two Early Tudor Lives: The Life and Death of Cardinal Wolsey The Life of Sir Thomas More*, ed. Richard S. Sylvester and Davis P. Harding (New Haven: Yale University Press, 1962), 39.

Of the Other Actions the King Took, the Troubles of His Heart, and Those of Wolsey's[1]

Word of the divorce issue was now spreading through every street and square, with diverse reactions. Thus it was that those who schemed to prosper and advance their interests by the king's new marriage called it a perfectly just proposition, while those who looked only to God and the truth, without respect for anything else, defended the righteous cause of Queen Doña Catherine. Many books were also written, some in favor and some against. The king, however, was not such a fool as not to see the truth, and recognized that those who spoke in favor of the divorce were ignorant, degenerate, wayward folk, while all the serious, learned, and pious men of the realm took the opposite view. Accordingly, in hopes of finding some sort of color or suitable pretext for his plans, he summoned his councilor Thomas More, a man of extraordinary genius, immense learning, and admirable virtue—and recognized as such by the entire kingdom—and asked him what he thought of his marriage to Queen Doña Catherine. More, with the spirit and liberty of a Christian, answered that he saw nothing good in divorce or separation from the queen. The king was deeply chagrined, but pretended otherwise, while offering immense favors and rich rewards if he would acquiesce to his will.[2] To sway him, he had him confer with Doctor Fox, provost [*Rector*] of King's College, Cambridge and the principal promoter of the business and defender of the king's will.[3] More discussed

---

1   Sander, *De origine ac progressu*, 31–35.

2   In October 1527, Henry conferred repeatedly with Sir Thomas More, but was unable to convince him of the validity of the case for the divorce. John Guy, *Thomas More*, Reputations (London: Arnold Publishers, 2000), 149–50.

3   Edward Fox (or Foxe, 1496–1538), provost of King's College, Cambridge from 1528 to 1538, later bishop of Hereford, and the author of several texts defending the king's divorce and the royal supremacy. Andrew A. Chibi, "Fox, Edward (1496–1538)," in *ODNB*, 20:627–29, here 627–28.

  In 1534, More wrote to Thomas Cromwell, "the King's Grace showed it to me himself, and laid the Bible open before me, and there read me the words that moved his Highness and divers other erudite persons so to think, and asked me further what myself thought thereon. At which time not presuming to look that his Highness should anything take that point for the more proved or unproved for my poor mind in so great a matter, I showed nevertheless as my duty was at his commandment what thing I thought upon the words which there I read. Whereupon his Highness accepting benignly my sudden unadvised answer commanded me

it with him as he had been commanded, but after many debates and disputations he was left even more firm and unyielding in his opinion. From then on
he urged the king with even greater conviction not to abandon the queen, to
the extent that the king did not dare mention it to him, though in the highest
affairs of state he valued More more than any other man; the king said publicly
that he prized winning Thomas More to his will above half his kingdom.

At this time, Mary Boleyn, Anne's older sister, seeing that the king showered gifts upon her sister (and not her), and not only the king, but even her
sister took no notice of her, went to the queen and told Her Majesty not to
be troubled, for her husband the king, although he had gone astray with her
sister, could not possibly marry her. "For the laws of the Church prohibit a man
from marrying the sister of one whom he has known carnally—and the king
says he will not deny having been involved with me, and if he does deny it,
I will confess it so long as I live. And since the king shall not marry my sister, Your Majesty may be assured that he will not abandon you."[4] The queen
thanked her and responded that in all things she would proceed by the advice
of her lawyers. But by now Henry did not respect the laws of the Church so
much as he feared the emperor's wrath at seeing his aunt ignominiously cast
off, as well as his subjects and vassals' discontent at abandoning their ancient
friendships and profitable trade with the house of Burgundy to seek new and
dubious alliances with France.[5] Furthermore, he saw that the virtues of Queen
Doña Catherine were well known and well loved in his kingdom, and that she
had won the hearts of all good people, their fervent goodwill and admiration;
that Anne Boleyn was widely regarded as a wicked, infamous woman; that the
cardinal, to whom he had entrusted the government of his kingdom, did not
now press the divorce as he used to; and finally that he would have to render
God a strict reckoning of all he had done before the tribunal of his rigorous
justice. Such thoughts and anxieties so troubled the king's spirit that he found
no rest by day or night, but lived like a soul in torment; not knowing where to
seek advice, lost to sleep, suspicious of his friends, fearful of his enemies, and
condemned by the witness of his own conscience, he led a wretched existence.

---

to commune further with Master Foxe, now his Grace's Almoner, and to read a book with him
that then was in making for that matter." Thomas More, *The Last Letters of Thomas More*, ed.
Alvaro de Silva (Grand Rapids: William B. Eerdmans Publishing Company, 2000), 30.

4 The abrupt shift to direct speech here mirrors the same at Sander, *De origine ac progressu*, 33.

5 The Habsburgs were heirs to the House of Valois-Burgundy through Mary of Burgundy
(1457–82), Charles v's paternal grandmother. Ribadeneyra's "ancient friendships" advert to
the alliance between England and Burgundy against France during the Hundred Years' War,
subsequently revived in Catherine of Aragon's marriages to Arthur and Henry. Loades, *Reign
of Mary Tudor*, 63.

On the other hand, wounded by lust as he was, he believed he could not win Anne Boleyn save by marrying her, and some said that he could do so, since his marriage to the queen had been illegitimate, and that Pope Clement was so indebted to him that he could hope to attain all he sought, and that if there was some resentment at home and abroad, he could quell it with the power of the supreme pontiff. In the end, vanquished by his flesh and battered by the winds and waves of his hopeless obsession, he resolved with implacable obstinacy to abandon the queen and marry Anne, without a thought for the emperor (against whom France, Venice, and Florence were all allied at the time).[6]

Such were the anxieties and cares in which the king found himself, but no better were the torments and sudden perturbations suffered by Wolsey's heart. For now it delighted him that the king disdained the emperor, now it oppressed him that Anne Boleyn was mounting to the royal dignity; sometimes he feared the king would discard him and make use of other ministers to divorce the queen, sometimes he hoped the king would return to himself, shift his affections to the king of France's sister, and marry her. Thus, between joy and sorrow, between hope and fear, he knew not how to escape the passions and wretched cares that gnawed his innards and made him a martyr, having brought himself to such a miserable state by his own evil counsel and blind ambition—so often the hangman and the cross of those who allow them free rein, as Wolsey did.[7] But,[8] in the end, defeated and conquered by his insatiable lust for power, he chose to wrong himself by striving in all things for the king's pleasure and contentment. And soon it shall be told how the king repaid this pleasure.

In all this, we ought to note and carefully consider the torments and troubles suffered by a bad conscience, and the spasms and alterations that beset the heart once the governance of reason has been lost and the winds of passion are allowed to prevail: little by little the land is lost and one enters a raging, bottomless ocean, full of monsters and horrid foes, for not having restrained one's passions earlier, and trimmed the sails of one's desires and vain appetites. To convey all this, we are relating several things that seem insignificant or unworthy of our history, but are necessary or very useful in extracting from it the fruit at which we aim.[9]

---

6 Under the direction of Clement VII, the papacy joined with France, Venice, Florence, and Milan in the League of Cognac (formed in May 1526) to counteract the growing power of Charles V. Maltby, *Charles V*, 36.

7 This clause was added in the 1595 edition.

8 Omitted in the 1595 edition and subsequently.

9 This paragraph was added in the 1595 edition.

Of the Ambassadors the King Sent to the Pope, and of His Holiness's Decision in the Matter of the Divorce[1]

While the king and Wolsey were laboring with these strains and anxieties and pondering what could be done, they decided to send Stephen Gardiner, a jurist of great learning (a former servant of Wolsey's, and now secretary to the king), to the pope, and with him Francis Bryan.[2] These two set out on their mission; along the way, to win the pontiff's goodwill, they negotiated with the Venetians in the king's name for the return of Ravenna (which Venice then held) to the Holy See. This the Venetians refused to do for the time being.[3] From there they went to Orvieto, where the newly freed pope was, having left Castel Sant'Angelo.[4] After they had congratulated His Holiness on his liberation and described the peace of mind it had given their king, they put to him two

---

1 Sander, *De origine ac progressu*, 35–40.

2 Trained in canon and civil law, Stephen Gardiner (c.1497–1555) began his career as an aide to Wolsey and soon graduated to diplomatic assignments, including the 1528 mission to Clement VII. Gardiner's colleague in this embassy was Edward Fox; Sir Francis Bryan (c.1490–1550) does not seem to have been included, but he was one of Henry's most trusted emissaries to the pope throughout the divorce negotiations. Gouwens and Reiss, *Clement VII*, 153. Susan Brigden, "Bryan, Sir Francis [called the Vicar of Hell] (d. 1550)," in *ODNB*, 8:379–83, here 380.

3 "In order to please the pope, English diplomacy from early 1528 put increasing pressure on Venice to relinquish Ravenna and Cervia," which the republic had seized in June 1527 in the aftermath of the Sack of Rome. Henry personally wrote to Doge Andrea Gritti (r.1523–38) requesting the surrender of the two cities. Gouwens and Reiss, *Clement VII*, 32, 37. LP, 4:089.

    An English agent at the papal court informed Wolsey in January 1528, "The Pope seems mad with anger at the refusal of the Venetians to restore Ravenna and Cervia. [...] [He] believes they will not restore the cities unless they are demanded by the kings of England and France. The Pope wishes Wolsey to take the matter up, and that both Kings should send ambassadors to Venice to demand it, and to use strong language if they refuse, and to remind them of their promise to Wolsey when in France." In March, a news bulletin reported, "Can hardly write without indignation of the way the Venetians abuse the patience of these kings, in taking towns from the Pope, who risked his head for their preservation, and refusing to restore them, even at the intercession of this King and Wolsey, to whom they are so much bound." *LP*, 4:3824, 3996.

4 In December 1527, Clement was allowed to leave Castel Sant'Angelo for Orvieto, where he maintained a court-in-exile for six months. Gouwens and Reiss, *Clement VII*, 150.

© KONINKLIJKE BRILL NV, LEIDEN, 2017 | DOI 10.1163/9789004323964_017

proposals. The first, that he should consent to join the league and confederation recently made against the emperor by the kings of England and France.[5]
The second, that by his supreme and apostolic authority he should declare that
the king's marriage to Queen Doña Catherine had been invalid and illegitimate. For although the queen was a truly saintly lady, of illustrious lineage, yet
since she had been the wife of the king's own brother, he could not have taken
her as his wife; in giving the dispensation, Pope Julius II had deceived himself,
for he had no power to grant a dispensation against divine law. Henry could
easily have freed himself from this scruple by a judgment of the bishops of his
kingdom, but he had chosen to turn to the supreme tribunal of the entire Catholic Church, so that neither the emperor (the queen's nephew) nor any other
prince could suggest that the bishops of England followed the will of the king
more than justice in the case.[6] And His Holiness could very easily grant their
requests, since the saintliness of Queen Doña Catherine was so prodigious, her
lifestyle so austere and ascetic, that without doubt she would retire to some
convent, if in her conscience she felt herself free of the ties of matrimony. They
added that to achieve all this with greater propriety and convenience, His Holiness should appoint two judges in England for the purpose, who could be—if
it pleased him—Cardinal Wolsey, because as a native of the kingdom he knew
its affairs well, and Cardinal Campeggio, who, having been Leo X's legate in
England, was not without familiarity and experience in the circumstances of
the nation.[7] The ambassadors concluded their mission by saying that besides
doing justice in this matter, His Holiness would place the king their lord in
his debt by a perpetual and incomparable kindness,[8] and that, lest he fear the

---

5   The Treaty of Westminster (1527), Clement having abandoned the League of Cognac after the
    Sack of Rome. Ibid., 154.

6   The ambassadors' instructions stipulated, "the legatine authority of Wolsey might have been
    sufficient without any reference to the Pope, to avoid all evils that may befal [*sic*] the realm,
    it is indispensable that the commission be couched in the form here devised, as otherwise it
    will not be possible to avoid many inconveniences." *LP*, 4:3913.

7   Lorenzo Campeggio (1474–1539), a Bolognese cardinal of noble background, who became
    Leo's legate to England in March 1518. Wolsey had instructed the ambassadors: "They shall
    therefore study these points, and discuss them with his Holiness, begging him that the dis-
    pensation and commission may be passed without alteration, according to the form here
    devised, and a legate be sent. The commission is to be directed to him and to Wolsey [...]
    Rewards are to be offered, and they are to attempt to procure that Campegius be sent in pref-
    erence to all others, promising that his charge shall be furnished from England." "July 1, 1517,"
    in *CHRC. LP*, 4:3913.

8   Wolsey had told Gardiner and Fox, "This then is the time for the Pope to bind the heart of the
    King for ever." *LP*, 4:3913.

emperor or any other monarch (if by chance they took offense at the decision), from his own purse the king would hire four thousand foot soldiers for the protection and eternal defense of his sacred person.

The pope, after he had acknowledged the king's goodwill with a few solemn words and declared that it was not the right time to join the league, answered that as to the divorce, he would confer with select cardinals and theologians, and that if what the king requested could be lawfully and religiously done, he would agree whole-heartedly, and think himself blessed to have an opportunity to gratify so deserving a king, whose good works had obliged the Catholic Church, both in having written an erudite book against Luther on the seven sacraments of the Church and in having recently aided and defended the Holy See when it was oppressed, freeing his own person from the hands of his enemies and placing him at liberty.

Once the pope had named several cardinals and theologians, and they had scrupulously considered, scrutinized, and discussed all the rationales and arguments put forward by the ambassadors, the unanimous answer was that the marriage of the king and queen was legitimate, valid, and in accordance with divine law, with reasons and responses to all the contrary arguments given with great learning and confidence. Consequently, they declared that in a matter so clear and so certain there was no need to appoint judges—still less in England, where they would do nothing but the king's will. Moreover, the proposed judges, given the considerable favors they had received from the king, were greatly in his debt and could hardly refuse to promote his interests. When this response was given to Ambassador Stephen, he turned to the pope and said that other theologians in Rome thought the opposite of those His Holiness had chosen, and that although the king's marriage was not prohibited by divine law, the king would prove that Pope Julius's dispensation was neither canonical nor legitimate. But, leaving this aside, what astounded him most was that, in delegating the judgment to private persons, he denied so mighty a king, so vigorous a defender of the Church: a different answer, kinder and more gracious, had been hoped for from His Holiness. The pope answered, "I will do for the king all that I may in good conscience do,[9] for here we do not deal with what human law can determine, but rather a marriage between believers, which, being a sacrament instituted by Jesus Christ our Savior, we cannot add to or detract from.[10] It concerns undoing a marriage bound by God, which

---

9   Gardiner and Fox recorded that during their audience with Clement, "The Pope replied
     he would do all that in honor he could do." Ibid., 4:4120.

10   Deut. 4:2, 12:32; Rev. 22:19.

a human being may not put asunder.[11] It concerns a marriage contracted by the authority of our predecessor, confirmed by twenty years of cohabitation and married life and by the birth of many children. Indeed, does it not also concern the honor of Queen Doña Catherine, and of Emperor Charles v? Who can promise that such a declaration would not be followed by war and strife in Christendom? That it would not kindle a fire that we could not later extinguish? It is our duty to avoid such harms and ensure that there are no scandals or disturbances in the Church of God."

With this, the pope named other cardinals and theologians to study the matter again. And although some said that it would be best considered and decided in Rome, where justice would be the only consideration, rather than in England, where nothing would be done against the king's wishes, there were also others who for various deceitful and self-interested motives were of the contrary opinion. They insisted that, while heresy had grown so wildly in Germany and Catholic rulers had shown such timidity in quashing or quelling it, King Henry alone had opposed the storm's fury, with incredible zeal and fervor, and had written a book against it. And for this reason the Holy See should treat him with more indulgence than other monarchs. Especially given that the queen herself wished to enter a monastery, it seemed hard to deny the king the judges he requested, for it might be hoped that while they were conducting their business in England, he would come to himself and return to his senses. At the very least, there could be no danger in trying, since the pope was free to remand the case to himself whenever he liked. The pope inclined to this advice out of his desire to please the king and because he believed what he had been told about Queen Catherine's consent and her entering a convent. Thus, the two cardinals, Bishop Lorenzo Campeggio and Thomas Wolsey, a priest of the holy Roman Church, were appointed as judges.[12]

---

11   Matt. 19:6; Mark 10:9.

12   Clement finally agreed to the appointment of Wolsey and Campeggio as legatine judges in April 1528. "September 10, 1515," in CHRC.

What the Queen Wrote to the Pope, What His Holiness Decreed, and Certain Private Matters That Came to Pass in This Affair[1]

Queen Catherine did not know for certain that ambassadors had been dispatched to Rome, but she suspected it, and so she implored His Holiness not to permit the question of her marriage to be judged in England, for that would make the king judge in his own suit.[2] At the same time, she wrote to her nephew the emperor of Wolsey's schemes and the king's obsession, and affectionately begged him not to abandon her in this predicament and humiliation, which had been brought upon her by his enemies and solely because she was his aunt.[3] The emperor ordered his ambassador at Rome to protest to the pope in his name, both about the ambassadors sent by King Henry, who had handled so a serious matter relating to the queen without her knowledge, and about the judges His Holiness had appointed without hearing her out.[4]

---

1 Sander, *De origine ac progressu*, 40–48.

2 Catherine expressed these concerns to the imperial ambassador to England, Iñigo de Mendoza (1476–1536), who informed the emperor: "The Queen wrote yesterday to say she had heard that this new Legate brought powers and mandates very detrimental to her and to her rights, which powers, she says, have been obtained from the Pope under false pretences, it having been represented to him that in this present case there was no fear of causing scandal, because all the kingdom was in favour of the divorce, and the Queen herself consented to it." *CSPS*, 3.2:562.

3 November 24, 1528, for example, saw an importunate Catherine writing to her nephew to "beg Your Highness to pardon me for being thus importunate, but the truth and justice of my case, and the great injury done unto me by delaying a judgment that must needs turn out in my favour, compel me again to trouble Your Highness upon a point which you must have at heart as much as myself; but knowing, as I do, that, after God, no one but Your Majesty can remedy my troubles, I must needs use with Your Highness the office of the Samaritan with Jesus Christ." Ibid., 4.2:593.

4 On October 9, 1528, Charles wrote to Mendoza, "We consider that the most efficient way of assisting and protecting the Queen, our good aunt, is for us to prevent, by all possible means, the trial of her case coming on in England, and to oppose any mandates of the Pope to particular persons." The emperor added that he had drafted several protests to be sent to the pope. Furthermore, the new imperial ambassador to Rome, dispatched the same month, had express instructions "to assist and help in whatever may be undertaken or done in behalf of our beloved aunt, Queen Katharine of England." Ibid., 4.2:563, 566.

© KONINKLIJKE BRILL NV, LEIDEN, 2017 | DOI 10.1163/9789004323964_018

Though he clearly perceived the misfortunes that could follow from this, he could not fail to support his aunt and defend her against King Henry,[5] even when he contemplated what might well befall England—how all the obsequious, desperate, and soulless men, who sought to gratify the king for their own interests, would be honored and appointed to posts and offices, while all good and wise men who for fear of God alone inclined to the truth and the queen's right would be dispossessed, dismissed, and persecuted.

The supreme pontiff, perceiving that King Henry's excuses were false, dispatched four letters to Cardinal Campeggio by various routes and with all possible speed, ordering him to proceed along his path as slowly as possible; once in England, first to attempt to reconcile the king to the queen; and, if he could not, to persuade the queen to enter some convent;[6] and, if this too could not be accomplished, at least to give no sentence in the king's favor without new, explicit instructions from Rome.[7] He added, *"Hoc summum et maximum sit tibi mandatum*—This you are commanded above all."* And in other letters written from Viterbo, he clearly states that if he were acting only for himself in the matter, he would happily run any risk for King Henry, but as it was he could not satisfy him without an affront to justice and a public scandal in Christendom.[8]

---

5 As Charles explained to Mendoza, "We could not but stand up in this case for the defence of the Queen's honour, she (Katharine) being our most beloved aunt, and our mother's own sister." Ibid., 3.2:483.

6 In December 1528, Giovanni Battista Sanga (d.1532), Clement's secretary and confidant, wrote to Campeggio that "It would greatly please the Pope if the Queen could be induced to enter some religion, because, although this course would be portentous and unusual, he could more readily entertain the idea, as it would involve the injury of only one person." *LP*, 4:5072.

7 Numerous letters from Sanga and Jacopo Salviati (1461–1533), one of Clement's closest advisers, dogged Campeggio as he made his way to England.

   On September 11, for example, Sanga wrote to Lorenzo Campeggio, "As soon as you can do so without scandalising the [French] king, proceed on your journey to England, and there do your utmost to restore mutual affection between the King and Queen. You are not to pronounce any opinion without a new and express commission hence." Ibid., 4:4721.

   Less than a week after his earlier missive (September 16), Sanga sent Campeggio another letter, in which he reiterated: "I am ashamed of repeating the same thing so many times, especially as you were well informed of the Pope's mind on your departure; but every day stronger reasons are discovered which compel the Pope to remind you that you are to act cautiously, and to use your utmost skill and address in diverting the King from his present desire, and restoring him to his former love towards the Queen. Should you find this impossible, you are not to pronounce in any manner without a new and express commission from hence." Ibid., 4:4737.

8 As Sanga wrote to Campeggio on September 16, 1528, "If in satisfying his Majesty the Pope would incur merely personal danger, his love and obligations to the King are so great that he

Campeggio arrived in London on October 7, 1528,[9] and in the company of his colleague, the cardinal of York, he went to the king and on behalf of the pope, the cardinals, the clergy, and the people of Rome offered to do all he could for him, as the liberator of that holy city. After Fox replied in the king's name, the two cardinals remained alone with the king and spoke with him privately and at length.[10] The arrival of Campeggio was totally unwelcome and abhorrent to the whole kingdom, for it was said that he had come to divorce the king from the saintly queen his wife, who passed her days and nights in tears and sighs. Hoping to console her, Campeggio advised her to enter some religious order if she wished to secure her life. With supreme constancy and fervor, she replied that she was determined to defend with her life a marriage lawfully sanctioned by the Roman Church, and that she did not accept him as her judge, since he had not been sent by the pope's will, but by the sheer persistence and pressure of the king, obtained and wrung out (as it were) by lies and slanders.[11] Once Campeggio understood this, he wrote to the pope of the queen's spirit, the king's insistence and haste, and his colleague Wolsey's (who had the first vote) inclination to dissolve the marriage, so that as swiftly as possible His Holiness might instruct him on how to proceed.[12]

---

would content him unhesitatingly; but as this involves the certain ruin of the Apostolic See and the Church, owing to recent events, the Pope must beware of kindling an inextinguishable conflagration in Christendom." Ibid., 4:4737.

9   Actually October 8. Thomas F. Mayer, "Campeggi, Lorenzo (1471/2–1539)," in *ODNB*, 9:871–72, here 871.

10   Campeggio wrote, "I was warmly received and welcomed by his Majesty. The ambassadors and all the prelates and princes of the kingdom were assembled in a large hall. Public audience was given us, and, in the name of us two Legates, my [secretary] Floriano made an appropriate speech. Dr. Fox replied. The King then withdrew with us into another chamber, where I presented the Pope's letter." *LP*, 4:4858.

11   The Venetian ambassador, Sebastiano Giustiniani (1459–1542), reported that "Cardinal Campeggio having tried to persuade the Queen of England to make choice of a monastic life, and consent to the divorce, so that it may be decreed justly, she refused positively, and sent to Flanders for advocates to defend her case." *CSPV*, 4:373.

12   On October 17, Campeggio wrote to Sanga at great length, recounting his interview with Catherine: "Taking leave of his Majesty, the Cardinal and I repaired to the Queen, with whom we conversed alone about two hours. [...] I began by telling her that as the Pope could not refuse justice to any one who demands it, he had sent the cardinal of York and myself hither to understand the state of the question between her Highness and the King's Majesty; but as the matter was very important and full of difficulty, his Holiness, in right of his paternal office and of the love which he bore her, counselled her, confiding much in her prudence, that rather than press it to trial she should of her prudence take some other course which would give general satisfaction and greatly benefit herself and

The pontiff, who imagined that more time would ameliorate the situation, held silent, dissembled, and did not respond to the legate's letters, so that six months passed without any action on his part. But on November 8, 1528, the king, seeing that the people took it amiss that he wished to divorce so exalted and holy a princess as the queen in order to enjoy a harlot, summoned the noblemen and lords of his court, as well as many commoners, and before them all swore that he had not been motivated in this affair by affection for any woman, but only by the pangs and scruples of his conscience.[13] "For," he said, "what woman was there in all the world more pious, of higher birth, or with finer

---

her affairs. I did not further explain the means to her, in order to discover what she would demand. [...] Her Majesty replied that she knew the sincerity of her own conscience; that she wished to die in the holy Faith [and in] obedience to the commands of God and of holy Church; that she wished to declare her conscience [only] to our Lord; and that for the present she would give no other reply, as she intended to demand counsellors of the King her lord and consort, and then she would hear us and make answer. She stated that she had heard we were to persuade her to enter some religion. I did not deny it, and constrained myself to persuade her that it rested with her, by doing this, to satisfy God, her own conscience, the glory and fame of her name, [and to preserve] her honors and temporal goods and the succession of her daughter; that she would lose nothing, 'se non l'uso della persona del Re,' which she had lost already, and which I knew she would never recover; that she should rather yield to his displeasure than submit herself to the peril of a sentence, considering, if that went against her, in what grief and trouble she would be, and in how little honour and reputation; and that she would lose her dowry, because in cases of matrimony it was concluded that on the dissolution, whensoever and howsoever, of a marriage, the dower could not be recovered. I begged her to consider the scandals and enmities which would ensue. On the other hand, instead of all these inconveniences, which should be avoided, she would preserve her dower, the guardianship of her daughter, her rank as Princess, and in short all that she liked to demand of the King; and she would offend neither God nor her own conscience. [...] Thus we left her, resolved, as she assured us, to manifest to our Lord the sincerity of her conscience; to which I replied, that I was sent by the Pope to hear whatever she chose to explain to me, and that I would faithfully tell him my opinion, seeing that I should relate the whole to his Holiness, by whose reply she would be convinced that I had sincerely done my duty. She rejoined that she intended to demand counsellors of the King her consort, as she was a foreigner without any friend; and then she would give us audience." *LP*, 4:4858.

The same day, he begged Salviati for further instructions: "I pray you to solicit for a determinate answer to be given me, either one way or the other; and let the answer be sent with diligence and in duplicate." Ibid., 4:4857.

13   Months later (June 29, 1529), Campeggio would recall that "in a former audience he had heard the king's majesty discuss the cause, and testify before all that his only intention was to get justice done, and to relieve himself of the scruple that he had on his conscience." T.E. Bridgett, *Life of Blessed John Fisher, Bishop of Rochester, Cardinal of the Holy*

qualities than the queen? What in her could possibly dissatisfy me, save that she had been my brother's wife?" O the blindness of man, so complete that he comes to believe others are blind![14]

Those who were present to hear the king's oath looked from one to another, wondering at such shamelessness: familiar with his sinful ways, the rapes, adulteries, and incests he committed at every turn, they knew that he was not so scrupulous as he would have them believe, and that his aims and motives were altogether different.

Campeggio urged the king not to proceed in the matter as a question of law, but rather through mediation and compromise. As the king proved receptive, the two cardinals went to speak with the queen at his command. They had barely begun to explain that they were sent by the pope to examine the validity of Her Majesty's marriage to the king when she interrupted their discourse with no little force, telling them, "You wish to discuss a matter already addressed, and addressed not only in the councils of two of the wisest monarchs, but also in the consistory at Rome; determined by Pope Julius; established by twenty years of cohabitation; confirmed by the succession and our children; and accepted and approved by the world's assent. But these my misfortunes and miseries come to me by your hand, Wolsey, for you hate and persecute me so—whether because I could not suffer your frenzied ambition and wickedness, or because the emperor my nephew did not indulge your insatiable appetites and make you pope!"[15] The cardinals, seeing the queen aflame with agony

---

Roman Church, and Martyr under Henry VIII (London: Burns and Oates, 1888), 170. Gouwens and Reiss, Clement VII, 31.

14   This sentence was added in the 1595 edition.

15   Sander seems to be drawing on Edward Hall's (1497–1547) Chronicle (1548): "And when she had paused a while she answered: Alas my lordes is it now a question whether I be the kynges lawful wife or no? When I haue been maried to him almost xx. yeres & in the meane season neuer questio[n] was made before? Dyuers prelates yet beyng aliue & lordes also & priuie cou[n]sailors with the kyng at that tyme, then adiudged our mariage lawful and honest, and now to say it is detestible and abhominable, I thynke it greate maruell: and in especiall when I consider, what a wise prince the kynges father was, and also the love and natural affeccion, that Kyng Fernando my father bare vnto me; I thynke in my self that neither of our fathers, were so vncercumspect, so vnwise, and of so small imaginacion, but they forsawe what might folowe of our mariage [...] But of this trouble I onely maie thanke you my lorde Cardinal of Yorke, for because I haue wondered at your high pride & vainglory, and abhorre your volupteous life, and abhominable Lechery, and little regard your presu[m]pteous power and tyranny, therefore of malice you haue kindled this fire, and set this matter a broche, & in especial for the great malice, that you beare to my nephew the Emperour, whom I perfectly know you hate worse then a Scorpion, because he would not satisfie your ambicion, and make you Pope by force."

and melting into tears, realized they would make no progress for the moment, and might manage the rest through intermediaries later.

Henry celebrated his birthday with games, parties, banquets, and diversions, to which he invited the cardinals, and led Anne Boleyn before the crowd in magnificent state. Wolsey advised the king for the sake of his honor to stay away from her for the duration of the trial and keep her in her father's house. Very reluctantly, the king agreed that she would leave his house until the end of Lent. Then, in the course of those sacred days, he ordered Thomas Boleyn, whom he had made Viscount Rochford [*Rupe Forte*],[16] to bring her back to the palace in secret, and the king himself wrote love letters pleading and begging her to return.[17] She replied that she would not return having been once cast off: not even her mother could convince her to return to the king, until Thomas Boleyn told her that the king was enraged and would bring about her death and the ruin of her house and her family. And so she said, "If that's the way it is, I will return, but since I'm holding the king between my fingers, I'll squeeze him as he deserves and treat him just as I like."[18] By now, the king was beyond hope; to appease her, he began to indulge and favor her even more, without a thought for his authority or reputation.

Seeing that all the theologians and canonists had agreed that the marriage to the queen would be void but for Pope Julius's dispensation, he decided to undermine the said papal permission by all possible means and methods, to demonstrate that it had been neither legitimate nor canonical. And so he wrote to his ambassadors (who were still in Rome) to take no thought of the cost, but rather to offer enormous gifts and bribes to all the cardinals and theologians involved in the matter. He also implored Pope Clement first to declare Julius's

---

Edward Hall, *Hall's Chronicle: Containing the History of England, during the Reign of Henry the Fourth, and the Succeeding Monarchs, to the End of the Reign of Henry the Eighth, in Which Are Particularly Described the Manners and Customs of Those Periods; Carefully Collated with the Editions of 1548 and 1550* (London: G. Woodfall, 1809), 755.

Cf. Harpsfield, *Treatise*, 181.

16   Boleyn was made Viscount Rochford in 1525. Hughes, "Boleyn, Thomas," in *ODNB*, 6:471.

17   In 1527, Anne left the court for Hever Castle, a reaction to Henry's overly zealous pursuit. The king's love letters from this period are printed in Henry VIII, *The Love Letters of Henry VIII to Anne Boleyn with Notes*, ed. J.O. Halliwell Phillips (London: E. Grant Richards, 1907).

18   Though this particular conversation is Sander's invention, Anne's imperious behavior toward the king did become a source of friction in their relationship. In 1531, Eustace Chapuys (c.1490–1556), Mendoza's successor as imperial ambassador, reported of Anne, "She becomes more arrogant every day, using words and authority towards the King, of which he has several times complained to the duke of Norfolk, saying that she was not like the Queen, who had never in her life used ill words to him." *LP*, 5:216.

dispensation to be dubious and void, and second, to permit Doña Mary, his daughter by Queen Doña Catherine, to marry the duke of Richmond, his own bastard son, so as to establish and secure the royal succession.[19] The wretched man was so blind, he did not see that in this request he made it clear that he sought a divorce from the queen not for a scruple of his conscience, but out of sheer wickedness and the desire to satisfy his own lust: for he considered the marriage of brother and sister lawful under a papal dispensation, but simultaneously denied the legitimacy of a marriage between a brother and his dead brother's wife, contracted under the same dispensation! That the king had requested this of the pope clearly appears in the pope's own letters to his legate, Cardinal Campeggio.[20] What is more, the king wrote to the pope in his own hand, begging that although he had had carnal knowledge of Mary Boleyn, Anne's sister, and according to the ecclesiastical laws he could not marry Anne, His Holiness (to whom it pertained to ease or moderate the rigor of the Church's laws) should grant a dispensation for the union.[21] This comes from what Cardinal Cajetan and Cardinal Pole have written.[22] See how this hapless king, left blinded and deluded by his passion, behaved in an affair of this magnitude: on the one hand, he claimed the pope had no power to grant dispensations, and on the other he requested a dispensation in a similar—indeed, a more complicated—matter. But the heart of the impious, as the Holy Spirit says, is like a raging sea, beaten by contending waves and contrary winds.[23]

The pope was deeply troubled by the king's demands, and rebuked his legate Campeggio for not having forestalled them in England and prevented their reaching Rome, rather than allowing any hope of receiving from the pope that which could not be rightly or justly granted.[24] And because the king's

---

19   Chapuys reported rumors to this effect in the autumn of 1529; John Edwards suggests the
       plan "possibly originated with Anne Boleyn." Edwards, *Mary I*, 32.

20   *LP*, 4:5072.

21   In December 1527, Henry dispatched a draft of a papal bull to Clement VII, by which he
       would be absolved of "affinity arising from illicit intercourse in whatever degree, even the
       first." Such a precaution was necessitated by his previous affair with Mary Boleyn, which
       had rendered Anne related to him within the first degree of affinity. Henry Ansgar Kelly,
       The Matrimonial Trials of Henry VIII (Eugene: Wipf and Stock Publishers, 2004), 46–47.

22   In the margin: "Book 3, *Defense of the Unity of the Church* [*de unione Ecclesiæ*]."
       Pole, *Defense*, 188.
       Cajetan, *Opuscula omnia*, 296–98.

23   In the margin: "Isaiah 57[:20]."

24   In a letter of April 10, 1529, Sanga reprimanded Campeggio: "his Holiness finds himself in
       very great trouble, especially as, owing to your inability to sustain the torrent of the King's
       demands, the whole is referred hither. The Pope is greatly annoyed, and cannot imagine

ambassadors were without shame, and all afire with the letter's postscript, they had threatened the Apostolic See, saying that some grievous misfortune would follow if the king's demands were not granted. Giovanni Battista Sanga, the pope's secretary, described the ambassadors' threats to the legate in the same papal letter.[25] He added, "As though His Holiness would act against his conscience and against the obligations of his office, even if he knew he should thus win the entire world.[26] As though these threats would not fall first upon those who made them, rather than the pope—if the king, to satisfy his desires, chooses the disgrace of separation, not just from his wife in his own kingdom, but also from the Apostolic See, the root and mother of the entire Christian

---

how it has come to pass, that any hope should be entertained there of the revocation by him of the bulls of pope Julius, which stand in the way of the King's desire. His Holiness is told that the ambassadors have been sent here with this hope. He would have wished this hope to be destroyed there, as you could have acquainted them with the causes which restrain him. He is highly displeased that the King and the cardinal of York should entertain hopes of things which he cannot grant; for the more often they do so, the more grievous it seems to them not to obtain what they wish; and it is important to render them less dissatisfied with the Pope's inability to act by not promising them so much at first. You can perform these offices, and thus relieve the Pope of part of his cares, without taking any responsibility upon yourself. The laws and ordinances of the Church, in which you are well skilled, permit of no other course. Your Lordship is prudent, and on the spot; strive, therefore, as much as you can, to subvert any troublesome suits which you find they determine to send to his Holiness." *LP*, 4:5447.

25 Sanga again wrote to Campeggio on April 21, 1529, noting that "the words they use seem very unbecoming,—that if this be not done, great damage will arise from it to the Apostolic See." He continued, "Since then the English ambassadors have been constantly with the Pope, insisting with all possible earnestness on the King's desire. As the Pope is very anxious to satisfy him, it would be unnecessary to importune him so much if we had any means of complying with his wishes. But the demand which these ambassadors make is such that the Pope cannot satisfy them without great consideration. [...] But not even this offer of the Pope's was sufficient for these ambassadors, who, both on account of their King's desire, and because he is aware of the Pope's inclination to gratify him, demand more than his Holiness can do with justice. They wished the Pope to command the Emperor to produce the brief within a limited period, as otherwise it would be pronounced false,—imperious language, which it is not customary to use to any prince, much less to a most powerful Emperor, at whose mercy his Holiness finds himself. Even if the Pope had written such an imperious letter as the ambassadors desired, no more would have been done to compel the Emperor to send the brief than will be accomplished by writing in a more gentle manner." Ibid., 4:5477.

26 Matt. 16:26; Mark 8:36; Luke 9:25.

Church."[27] In this we see how utterly certain the legates were of the king's spirit and determination: they were convinced that he would give up the Catholic faith together with the queen his wife, rather than forego the embraces and delights of Anne Boleyn, who was just as we have described, and as will be described hereafter.

---

27 Sanga wrote to Campeggio, "as if, even to gain the whole world, the Pope ought to do impossibilities; or as if what they menace would not rather prove to their own damage." *LP*, 4:5477.

How the Matter of the Divorce Began to Be Legally Considered, and of the Appeal Lodged by the Queen[1]

When Henry saw that the pope would not accede to his requests, and that peace had been made between His Holiness and the emperor, he began to fear that the emperor, the king of France, and other Christian rulers would establish a universal peace (as was later done at Cambrai);[2] that the pope would thus no longer have such great need of him, and so give less weight to his aid or his promises; that the emperor would become much more powerful; that the king of France, having recovered his children, would no longer seek his friendship; and that, abandoned by all, he would be able neither to repudiate his wife nor to marry Anne without enormous cost to his interests. And so he decided, after first conferring with Wolsey and his advisers, to put pressure on Cardinal Campeggio, who, for very just and weighty reasons, was making excuses and drawing out the matter. At last, by threats, gifts, promises, and bribes, as well as unending importunity, he so hounded the cardinal that—fearing for his life— on May 28, 1529, in the refectory of the Dominican friars, he and his colleague Wolsey convened the tribunal to hear and judge the divorce suit.[3] Before all else, they had the apostolic letters read out; they called first King Henry, in whose name two lawyers appeared, and then the queen, who appeared in person, declaring that she did not recognize them as her judges and that she appealed to the pope.[4] However, they refused to allow any such appeal, showing a certain apostolic rescript that revoked the pope's first instructions.

---

1 Sander, *De origine ac progressu*, 48–51.

2 Clement and Charles were formally reconciled in June 1529, with the restoration of papal territories and Charles's imperial coronation in Bologna the following year. On August 5, a peace treaty was signed at Cambrai between the empire and France, effecting the release of King Francis's captive sons. Gouwens and Reiss, *Clement VII*, 38–39.

3 Giles Tremlett gives the date as May 31, 1529. The hearings were held in the refectory of Black-friars, the London priory of the Dominican Order. Tremlett, *Catherine of Aragon*, 265.

4 "The court being thus furnished and ordered, the judges commanded the crier to command silence. Then was the judges' commission, which they had of the Pope, published and read openly before all the audience there assembled. That done, the crier called the King by the name of 'King Harry of England come into the court etc.' With that the King answered and said, 'Here, my lords.' Then he called also the Queen by the name of 'Catherine Queen of

The following day, once the legates had seated themselves in the court, the queen came forward and, having again lodged her protest and petition, gave her reasons for appealing to the pope, which were as follows. First, that the location of the trial was suspect and prejudicial to her, for she had been born in Spain and was a stranger there, while Henry, the protagonist and author of the trial, was at the same time the king of England.[5] Second, that she deemed the judges questionable, for they were not only indebted to the king, but also his subjects: Wolsey by the bishoprics he held (Winchester and York), as well as his numerous abbacies; and Campeggio by the see of Salisbury, which he had received through the king's favor. Third, she took a solemn oath that nothing had moved her to refuse these judges and appeal to the pope save her justified fear that she could not obtain justice from them.[6] To satisfy the king, the cardinals refused to allow the queen's appeal—but since they had not given a judgment of divorce at his will, nothing they did pleased him. And so the king himself appeared in the court and publicly stated that he had embarked upon this project not out of hatred for or unhappiness with the queen, but purely out of a scruple of his conscience and by the advice of learned men. Though he had the cardinal of York in his kingdom as legate *a latere*, who might have rendered a judgment in the matter by himself, he had asked and implored the pope, as supreme head of the Church, for the judges now present to avoid all suspicion and the baseless doubts of men, and he promised to abide by the sentence they gave, whatsoever it might be.[7]

England come into the court etc.'; who made no answer to the same." Cavendish and Roper, *Early Tudor Lives*, 83.

5 Cavendish avers that Catherine put her protest directly to Henry: "'Sir,' quod she, 'I beseech you for all the loves that hath been between us and for the love of God, let me have justice and right; take of me some pity and compassion for I am a poor woman and a stranger, born out of your dominion. I have here no assured friends, and much less indifferent counsel. I flee to you as to the head of justice within this realm.'" Ibid., 83.

6 Cavendish has Catherine protest to Henry, "for ye may condemn me for lack of sufficient answer, having no indifferent counsel, but such as be assigned me, with whose wisdom and learning I am not acquainted. Ye must consider that they cannot be indifferent counsellors for my part which be your subjects and then out of your own council before, wherein they be made privy, and dare not for your displeasure disobey your will and intent." Ibid., 84.

7 According to Cavendish, Henry explained his conduct thus: "I thought it good therefore in the relief of the weighty burden of scrupulous conscience, and the quiet estate of this noble realm, to attempt the law therein, and whether I might take another wife in case that my first copulation with this gentlewoman were not lawful; which I intend not for any carnal concupiscence, ne for any displeasure or mislike of the Queen's person or age, with whom I could be as well content to continue during my life, if our marriage may stand with God's laws, as with any woman alive. In which point consisteth all this doubt that we go now

When the king had finished, the queen demanded that the judges allow the appeal she had lodged; as they yet hesitated, she rose from her place and crossed to where the king was seated beneath his cloth of state.[8] Upon her knees, she begged him that, as His Majesty was in his own kingdom, while she was a stranger there, he should permit the course of justice to unfold in Rome before the common father of all Christians, the universal judge (and the king's friend). The king stood gazing at her with tender, loving eyes, and answered that he gave her the consent she sought with the greatest willingness. All those present wept profusely and stared avidly at the faces, gestures, and movements of the queen and king, and how the queen departed from the place. As she was leaving, she was called back in the name of the king and of the judges.[9] She replied, "I will obey my husband, but not the judges." However, being advised by her advocates that if she returned she would prejudice the appeal she had made, she wrote to excuse herself and returned to Baynard's Castle, whence she had come.[10] As she was departing, she said to her counselors, "Today is the first time that I have not obeyed my lord the king for the sake of my own interests. When I see him, I shall beg his pardon upon my knees."[11] O sainted lady, worthy of a better husband! But our Lord wished by this cross and this new sort of persecution to purify and perfect her, so that she would receive a more illustrious crown of glory.[12]

---

    about to try by the learned wisdom and judgments of you our prelates and pastors of this realm here assembled for that purpose, to whose conscience and judgment I have committed the charge, according to which (God willing) we will be right well contented to submit ourself, to obey the same for my part." Ibid., 86–87.

8   Catherine, in Cavendish's telling, "rose up incontinent out of her chair whereas she sat and, because she could not come directly to the King, for the distance which severed them, she took pain to go about unto the King, kneeling down at his feet in the sight of all the court and assembly." Ibid., 83.

9   "And the King being advertized of her departure, commanded the crier to call her again, who called her by the name of 'Catherine Queen of England, come into the court etc.'" Ibid., 85.

10   A royal palace along the Thames where Catherine had taken up residence during the hearing.

11   "The Queen would no longer make her abode to hear what the said legates would further discern, albeit the King also requested and commanded her to tarry, wherein afterward she seemed to have some remorse of conscience, as it were for some disobedience toward her husband. And she reported afterward to some that were then of her counsel (by whom I had intelligence of it) that she never before in all her life in any one thing in the world disobeyed the King her husband, neither now would she have done but that the necessary defense of her cause did force her thereto." Harpsfield, *Treatise*, 181.

12   1 Pet. 5:4.

What Rochester and Other Worthy Persons Said in the Queen's Favor, and What Campeggio Answered Concerning the Sentence[1]

It was well understood that Henry had given the queen his consent and permission as a gesture, so as not to appear discourteous; for immediately he was again pressing the legates to give sentence and annul Pope Julius's decision. When the decree was read out, the king's lawyers slandered it with specious arguments, to which the queen's attorneys responded with cogent, forceful logic, demonstrating how firmly her cause was rooted in truth and justice. Those who acted for the queen in this matter were the most esteemed and learned theologians and prelates of the entire realm, including William Warham, archbishop of Canterbury and primate of England,[2] and five other bishops of considerable authority.[3] But foremost among them was John Fisher, bishop of Rochester,[4] a truly exemplary man, the light not only of the kingdom of England, but of all Christendom, a mirror of sanctity, the salt of the people [*sal del pueblo*],[5] a true Doctor of the Church. He stepped forward publicly to present the legates with an erudite book he had written defending the marriage between the king and queen,[6] and to admonish them in a solemn discourse not to look for difficulties

---

1 Sander, *De origine ac progressu*, 61–66.

2 Archbishop William Warham (*c.*1450–1532) was appointed as Catherine's advocate, but was not particularly helpful to her cause. J.J. Scarisbrick, "Warham, William, (1450?–1532)," in *ODNB*, 57:411–15, here 411.

3 In addition to Warham, *De origine ac progressu* names these five as Cuthbert Tunstal, bishop of London (1474–1559); Nicholas West, bishop of Ely; John Clerk, bishop of Bath and Wells; John Fisher, bishop of Rochester; and Henry Standish, bishop of St. Asaph (*c.*1475). Sander also identifies four of the theologians: Thomas Abell (d.1540), Edward Powell (*c.*1478–1540), Richard Fetherston (d.1540), and Robert Ridley (d. *c.*1536). Sander, *De origine ac progressu*, 62.

4 Fisher was a committed and outspoken supporter of Catherine during the divorce proceedings, subsequently becoming "a leading opponent of the Henrician ecclesiastical revolution." Brendan Bradshaw and Eamon Duffy, eds., *Humanism, Reform and the Reformation: The Career of Bishop John Fisher* (Cambridge: Cambridge University Press, 1989), 1, 5.

5 Cf. Matt. 5:13.

6 This is probably *De causa matrimonii*, smuggled out of England and published at Alcalá de Henares in 1530, but by his own admission Fisher penned "seven or eight" tracts on the royal divorce. John Fisher, *De causa matrimonii serenissimie regis Angliae liber* (Alcalá de Henares: Miguel de Eguía, 1530). Bradshaw and Duffy, *Humanism, Reform and the Reformation*, 9–10.

where there were none, nor to allow themselves to pervert the limpid, manifest truth of Holy Writ, nor to weaken the power of ecclesiastical laws, which in this case were perfectly clear and easily understood. Let them carefully contemplate and reflect upon the myriad misfortunes that could arise from this divorce: hatred between King Henry and Emperor Charles, division among the princes who followed them, cruel wars at home and abroad, and, most importantly, dissension in matters of the faith, schisms, heresies, and innumerable sects. "Having spent much time and effort in studying this material," he said, "I dare affirm that there is no power on earth that can dissolve this marriage, nor put asunder what God has joined.[7] Not only have I clearly proven what I say in this book, by the indisputable witnesses of Holy Scripture and the sainted Doctors, but I also stand here to defend it with the shedding of my blood."[8] Thus spoke Rochester, and thus it came to pass. When this man, glorious in the renown of his learning, exemplary in the sanctity of his life, and admirable in his episcopal dignity and his venerable grey hairs, had spoken in this way, four other doctors and three bishops offered their own treatises composed in defense of the queen's marriage. Then, four more distinguished theologians did the same, insisting that nothing would be found in their writings save what was agreeable to the Gospel and holy doctrine, and that they were motivated by nothing save zeal for the truth and fear of God.[9]

At this, seeing that all honest and intelligent men were upon the queen's side, and that each day proclaimed its justice more clearly, the legates knew neither how to bring an end to the matter, nor how to proceed any further. With his customary violence, however, the king was demanding and bullying them to finish up already and give sentence in his favor. And so Campeggio, seeing that on the one hand the king would admit of no excuse, while on the other he could not pronounce the sentence the king desired, it being contrary to the irrefutable proofs that had been presented, to the pope's express will, and to the queen's entirely correct appeal, said with firmness and independence that he had spent many years handling matters of substantial importance, and had

---

7 Matt. 19:6; Mark 10:9.

8 Campeggio wrote that Rochester "presented himself before their reverend lordships to declare, to affirm, and with forcible reasons to demonstrate to them that this marriage of the king and queen can be dissolved by no power human or Divine, and for this opinion he declared he would even lay down his life. [...] He used many other suitable words, and at the end presented the book which had been written by him on the subject." Bridgett, *John Fisher*, 170.

9 *De origine ac progressu* specifies these as Clerk, Tunstal, and West, and Abell, Powell, Fetherston, and Ridley, respectively. Sander, *De origine ac progressu*, 63.

been an *auditor* of the Rota,[10] but he had never seen so much urgency and haste in an affair of any weight whatsoever, still less in one as momentous as this. For it was the custom that an adjournment of several days be taken when a sentence was to be given in a case, to consider the witnesses' statements and weigh their veracity; yet as many days had hardly passed since they had *begun* to discuss the king's suit! "And in a matter," he said, "of such weight and significance? Of such offense and scandal? Unless, perchance, some foolish dolt thinks that to dissolve a sacrament, to undo in a moment a marriage confirmed by twenty years' time, to render a king's daughter a bastard, to provoke the majesty of a mighty sovereign, to denigrate the dispensation and authority of the Apostolic See is nothing at all? I am determined to proceed little by little in so serious a matter, to move forward at a measured, cautious pace, without haste or recklessness."[11] Campeggio said this with great confidence, eliciting diverse emotions and reactions in his hearers: some were pleased with the cardinal's frankness; others were dismayed, thinking another result would have been more profitable to them; still others rejoiced inwardly, but made an outward show of their grief to flatter the king (as is the custom in courts). Among these was Cardinal Wolsey: though it was known he felt the same as Cardinal Campeggio, he fervently urged haste in the matter, to go with the current [*yr al amor del agua*] and please the king.

---

10   Campeggio had been an *auditor* (judge) at the Rota, the highest tribunal of the Catholic Church, since 1511. "July 1, 1517," in *CHRC*.

11   "With that quod the Cardinal Campeggio, 'I will give no judgment herein until I have made relation unto the Pope of all our proceedings, whose counsel and commandment in this high case I will observe. The case is too high, and notable known through all the world, for us to give any hasty judgment, considering the highness of the persons and the doubtful allegations. [...] Wherefore I will adjourn this court for this time, according to the order of the court of Rome from whence this court and jurisdiction is derived.'" Cavendish and Roper, *Early Tudor Lives*, 92–93.

The King Pressures the Legate, the Pope Remands the Case to Himself, and Wolsey is Arrested[1]

Seeing that Campeggio was unwilling to bring the matter to a close, each day finding new excuses and delays, the king sent Charles Brandon, duke of Suffolk, and Thomas Howard, duke of Norfolk,[2] with a huge retinue to where the legates were seated in the tribunal, to beg them in their own names and in the king's to conclude: to dispense and liberate the king, and soothe the tormented royal conscience. Wolsey kept silent, though he was seated in the first place, for he was overcome with terror. Campeggio took charge [*tomò la mano*] and attempted to placate them, but the dukes would have none of it, and forcefully pressed him to render judgment that very day, or the next at the very latest. When the cardinal replied that he could not possibly do so, the infuriated duke of Suffolk pounded the table before the legates and shouted, "By the blessed host, neither legate nor cardinal has ever brought any good to England!"[3] Thus spoke the wretched duke, drunk with wine, or with the venom of his frenzied rage, or with his ambition and his desire to please the king. Yet, how our Lord was to punish the pride and flattery with which these dukes sought to win the king's favor, taking as his instrument the king himself and his children—especially the daughter born to the marriage they so desired—is manifest in the calamities that befell them and their houses. The dukes left the court fuming with rage, and stirred up the king, already scorched in the flames of his lust, feeding the fire with yet more wood.

When the pope learned of what had happened, he accepted the queen's perfectly just appeal and remanded the case to himself, to be heard in the Rota,

---

1 Sander, *De origine ac progressu*, 66–71.

2 Thomas Howard (1473–1554), third duke of Norfolk, a leading proponent of the king's marriage to Anne Boleyn (his niece).

3 Fletcher, following Cavendish, dates this incident to July 31, 1529, when Campeggio announced that, as per the Roman legal calendar, the legatine court would adjourn until October. Fletcher, *Cardinal Wolsey*, 152.

    The wording of Suffolk's outburst varies from writer to writer: Sander seems to be following Harpsfield: "The Duke of Suffolk, giving a great clappe on the table with his hand, did swear that there was never cardinall that did good in England, and forthwith departed in great anger."

    Cf. Cavendish and Roper, *Early Tudor Lives*, 93; Hall, *Chronicle*, 758.

© KONINKLIJKE BRILL NV, LEIDEN, 2017 | DOI 10.1163/9789004323964_021

ordering the legates to proceed no further.[4] As soon as the queen heard of this, she sent to the king through his councilor, Thomas More, a man famous for learning and virtue (as has been said), to inform him of the pope's mandate and to learn whether he wished to be officially notified of the summons, when, and by whom. Though the king was inwardly perturbed, he dissembled for the moment, answering that he was already aware of it; that it was not his will to be personally notified of the summons, but that the legates might be informed; that he was pleased the matter should be heard in Rome, as a place common to all parties and above suspicion; and that he would strive to have it settled there for good. The king said all this most humbly, for he hoped that the pope would revoke his order; with this dream he sustained himself and felt less aggrieved. Notice was given to the legates by several of the queen's lawyers and one of the king's, who publicly stated that the king's will was that the matter should proceed no further in England, but rather be decided and concluded in Rome.

The legates complied with His Holiness's orders and began to hope that King Henry would accept better advice, when the pope suddenly directed Cardinal Campeggio to return to Rome with all speed.[5] The king was dumbfounded, as though he had been struck, and lost all hope of achieving his goal; his fury knew no bounds. Recalling that Wolsey had been the first instigator of the divorce, he began to heap the blame upon him, to rage against him, to abhor him—and to show this openly. There were many in King Henry's court who hated Wolsey (as there are men in every great prince's court who take exception to those with influence and power), some out of envy, others out of their own ambitions or grievances, and others out of chagrin that a lowborn man

---

4 Through the summer of 1529, Clement came under increasing imperial pressure to advoke the divorce case to himself, and equally vigorous pressure from the English ambassadors not to do so. On September 1, the pope wrote to the two legates in England, advoking the matter to Rome. *LP*, 4:5916.

5 Henry wrote to Clement VII on September 30, 1529, protesting Campeggio's peremptory recall: "On the return to your Holiness of cardinal Campeggio, we could have wished, not less for your sake than our own, that all things had been so expedited as to have corresponded to our expectations, not rashly conceived, but owing to your promises. As it is, we are compelled to regard with grief and wonder the incredible confusion which has arisen. If the Pope can relax Divine laws at his pleasure, surely he has as much power over human laws. Complains that he has often been deceived by the Pope's promises, on which there is no dependence to be placed; and that his dignity has not been consulted in the treatment he has received. If the Pope, as his ambassadors write, will perform what he has promised, and keep the cause now advoked to Rome in his own hands, until it can be decided by impartial judges, and in an indifferent place, in a manner satisfactory to the King's scruples, he will forget what is past, and repay kindness by kindness, as Campeggio will explain." Ibid., 4:5966.

should order them about and hold sway over the kingdom. But they had held silent, and dissembled, and flocked to him, attending upon him and serving him (as we see happen with such men every day) out of fear and the hope of pleasing the king. But when they perceived that the king had broken with him, they revealed their true spirit and released the restraint that had imprisoned their indignation by bringing to light all of Wolsey's misdeeds, which had been hidden and buried by the king's favor. And so certain prominent lords came together and, conferring among themselves, drafted a litany of all the wrongs and outrages Wolsey had committed during his tenure; signed by their own hands, they presented it to the king.[6] As much joy and delight as the king showed over it now, he would have been equally pained had they given it him when Wolsey was in favor. He dissembled until Cardinal Campeggio's departure for Rome on September 7,[7] when he ordered his luggage and his rooms ransacked for, perchance, some letter from Wolsey (although none was found).[8] Wolsey entered the king's presence totally unaware of what was being plotted against him; he spoke with him and the council about what needed to be done to pursue the case at Rome. But Stephen Gardiner, the king's secretary and former ambassador to Rome (where he had conducted these negotiations), beginning to fear his own downfall and seeing some of the blame fall upon him, as though the king had begun all this at his urging, implored Wolsey before the king and those present to tell the truth and declare who had been the first instigators of the divorce. Wolsey answered, "I will never deny that I alone was the author; so little do I repent of it, that if I had never begun, I would now begin it all again." Wolsey said these words to please and flatter the king; for it was well known that though he had first counseled the king to divorce the queen, he had come to rue it when he perceived that he would take Anne Boleyn in her stead—but by that time he could not turn back, loving the glory of men more than that of God.[9]

---

6 Under the leadership of Thomas Darcy, first Baron Darcy de Darcy (c.1467–1537), Wolsey's enemies drafted a catalog of his misdeeds, which they presented to the king on July 1, 1529. See ibid., 4:5749.

7 Actually October 7, as per a letter of Eustace Chapuys the following day. CSPS, 4.1:182.

8 As Chapuys related to Charles V on October 25, 1529, "Fears were entertained by some people here lest the Cardinal should contrive to send his valuables out of the country, and therefore a very strict watch was kept at all the ports. It was on this account that when the custom house guards asked to examine Campeggio's trunks, notwithstanding the passport received from the King, that upon his refusing to surrender the keys of them, the locks were forced, the trunks opened, and their contents inspected to that Cardinal's great displeasure." Ibid., 4.1:194.

9 John 12:43.

   The king kept silent while Wolsey spoke, but once Cardinal Campeggio had departed, whenever Wolsey began to address the king, he refused to hear him, and so Wolsey saw that in his anger the king had turned against him. Shortly thereafter, the king ordered the duke of Norfolk to arrest him, and dismissed him from the offices of chancellor and (later) bishop of Winchester. Then he stripped and dispossessed him of his palace and the mansions he had built in London, of his household goods, his jewels, and all the wealth he had piled up. He sent him to a country house, and thence to his diocese of York.[10] The king gave the post of chancellor to Thomas More (possibly hoping to win him over by this favor and honor), and the bishopric of Winchester to Stephen Gardiner.[11]

---

10   Cavendish gives a detailed account of the 1529 confiscation of Wolsey's wealth. The cardinal sojourned for several weeks at Esher in Surrey, before slowly making his way to Cawood in North Yorkshire by September 29, 1529. Cavendish and Roper, *Early Tudor Lives*, 102–03, 125, 148.

11   More was made chancellor almost immediately, while Gardiner was not nominated as bishop of Winchester until September 1531. Seymour Baker House, "More, Sir Thomas [St Thomas More] (1478–1535)," in *ODNB*, 39:60–76, here 68. Glyn Redworth, *In Defence of the Church Catholic: The Life of Stephen Gardiner* (Oxford: Basil Blackwell, 1990), 30.

Of the Other Methods the King Used to Give Color to His Wickedness, and of the Results[1]

Who would have believed that the king, having thus dealt with the one who gave him such bad advice, would not now reject and condemn the advice itself? But with perverse stubbornness and obstinacy Henry persevered in the sin he had punished so severely in Wolsey, thereby putting himself beyond excuse and condemning himself by his own judgment of another—and we know, as Saint Paul says, that against such persons the judgment of God is according to truth.[2]

And so, when the king saw that nothing had come of the legate's visit, he sent his agents and advocates to Rome to pursue the suit (among them was one Thomas Cranmer, subsequently archbishop of Canterbury), diligently assembling all the theologians and legal scholars he could to certify in writing that his marriage to Queen Catherine was invalid.[3] Thus, if the pope (as it now appeared)[4] rendered judgment against him, he could appeal to their authority, as though it were the official view of the universities themselves, imagining thus he could beguile the world. For he wished the ignorant masses to believe that all the various colleges and renowned universities of Christendom were on his side, that they believed and opined the way a few illiterates, with only the name of jurist or theologian, wrote in the king's favor, having been bought with his gold. To this end, the king charged Reginald Pole, an Englishman of royal blood and a young man of notable virtues and prospects, who had received many favors from him, with procuring the signatures of the scholars

---

1   Sander, *De origine ac progressu*, 71–80.

2   In the margin: "Romans 2[:1–2]."

3   Thomas Cranmer was made archbishop of Canterbury in 1533. In 1529, learning of the lackluster progress of the divorce efforts, he had suggested consulting learned opinion across Europe; the campaign was well underway by the beginning of 1530. Cranmer himself was sent to Bologna, where Charles V and Clement VII were meeting for the imperial coronation. Diarmaid MacCulloch, *Thomas Cranmer: A Life* (New Haven: Yale University Press, 1996), 45–49.

4   In the 1605 edition, the adverb *ya* is omitted, so the parenthetical comment would read "as it appeared."

of the University of Paris (where he was then living).[5] But when Pole showed himself tepid in the business—or rather, to speak clearly, when he refused to perform it—the king gave him a man of his council as a colleague, to rouse him and spur him on.[6] When this did not suffice, Pole having rather recused himself in letters to the king, the task was given to Guillaume de Langey, a Frenchman who had more respect for the king's angels [*angelotes*] and[7] coin than for his own honor: with the power of cash, he bought the signatures of some theologians and jurists (as I have said), none of whom knew the first thing about law or theology.[8] This attempt to corrupt and pervert the scholars of Paris with bribes in the king's name provoked a huge scandal and much consternation. Not content with this, the king tried the same thing at the University of Cologne (though he found no one there to support him) and other universities in Germany, France, and Italy. There are authors who record that some of the officials serving the king in this business, and some of the scholars who fawningly sold him their votes and their souls, perished awfully, visibly punished by God.[9] Reginald Pole, who had full knowledge of these projects

---

5   In the margin: "Pole, Book 3, *Defense of the Unity of the Church* [*de la vnion de la Yglesia*]." Pole, *Defense*, 191–92.

    Pole was actually *sent* to Paris by Henry in October 1529 to work toward the university's approval of the divorce, returning the following summer. Thomas F. Mayer, "Pole, Reginald (1500–1558)," in *ODNB*, 44:715–26, here 716.

6   Probably George Boleyn (*c.*1504–36), Anne's brother and a privy councilor, who led an English delegation to France to seek King Francis's support. John Edwards, *Archbishop Pole*, The Archbishops of Canterbury (Farnham: Ashgate, 2014), 26.

7   The specific reference to angels, a English gold coin, is added in the 1595 edition.

8   Guillaume de Bellay, seigneur de Langey (1491–1543), was a prominent French diplomat. While on a mission to England in 1530, he had assured Henry of Francis's support for the divorce. Bellay exerted considerable effort—including bribery—to attain a favorable verdict from the Sorbonne; he was initially unsuccessful, but royal pressure was applied to good effect. Knecht, *Francis I*, 239–40.

9   In the margin: "Peter of Leiden, dedicatory epistle to the commentary of Denis the Carthusian on the four books of *Sentences*. Johann Cochlaeus in a letter to the Englishman Richard Morison."

    The Dutch Carthusian scholar Peter Blomevenna (or Peter of Leiden, 1466–1536) mentions Henry's attempts at bribery in a dedicatory epistle addressed to the faculty of the University of Cologne, prefacing the 1535 edition of Denis the Carthusian's (born Denis Ryckel, 1402–71) commentary on the medieval theologian Peter Lombard's (*c.*1096–1160) *Sentences* (*c.*1150). Denis the Carthusian, *D. Dionysii Carthusiani, de his quae secundum sacras scripturas & orthodoxorum patrum sententias, de sanctissima & indiuidua trinitate semper adoranda, catholice credantur, liber primus*, ed. Peter Blomevenna, vol. 1 of 4 vols. (Cologne: Petri Quentel, 1535), sig. Aiiʳ.

    The Catholic controversialist Johann Cochlaeus (born Johann Dobneck, 1479–1552) wrote his *Scopa Ioannis Cochlaei Germani in araneas Ricardi Morysini Angli* (1538) as one

and schemes, writes that he was astonished at the king's madness: to seek to buy his own shame and dishonor with such waste and expense, and to inform the world that he had spent twenty years in an incestuous marriage.[10] Even in his own kingdom, Henry could not secure the University of Oxford's approval for his intent—although, through certain deceptions and frauds, some proclaimed their assent.[11]

The king was advised to try to win over Reginald Pole, who had by now returned to England from Paris; he made the attempt, offering him, through his kinsmen and friends, either of two vacant bishoprics, among the richest and most esteemed in England. He wanted neither, but his friends begged him at the very least to find some honest means of satisfying the king, lest he destroy him and his entire family, and they pressed him such urgency and force that he was overcome by their pleas, and answered that he would consider it. Now, given how many flatterers there are, people who think only of pleasing rulers for their own self-interest, those who had thus begged him went to the king with only this answer, telling him that Pole was now on his side and that he would soon come to speak with His Majesty on the subject. The king took enormous pleasure in this, thenceforward looking upon him with favorable eyes and eagerly awaiting when he would come as they had promised. Pole commended the matter to God with great insistence and fervor, praying that he show him a path offensive to neither king nor God. When he believed he had found one, resting more upon human cleverness than truth, he went to speak with the king, who received him with warmth and affection and in the highest spirits led him into an inner chamber. Standing there and intending to say what he had come up with, Pole was suddenly troubled—wonderful to relate!—and cut himself short, unable to speak for a good while. After coming to himself, he began to speak, saying the exact opposite of what he had planned: without flattery or artifice, as befits a noble and Christian man, he decorously revealed his heart and his entire opinion to the king. The king was stunned by so sudden a reversal, as though beside himself, colors coming and going from his face; several times he put his hand to his dagger as though to stab him, and he

---

salvo in a polemical battle with the English statesman and scholar Sir Richard Morison (c.1510–56). Johann Cochlaeus, *Scopa Ioannis Cochlaei Germani in araneas Ricardi Morysini Angli* (Leipzig: Nicolaus Vuolrab, 1538), sig. Bi^v.

10   In the margin: "Book 3, *Defense of the Unity of the Church* [*de vnione Ecclesiæ*]."
      Pole, *Defense*, 190.

11   While Cambridge proved amenable to the divorce, Oxford was more troublesome. It took more than a month of pressure from Henry and his agents to produce the desired verdict. Claire Cross, "Oxford and the Tudor State from the Accession of Henry VIII to the Death of Mary," in *The Collegiate University*, ed. James McConica, The History of the University of Oxford 3 (Oxford: Clarendon Press, 1986), 117–49, here 125.

dismissed Pole (as he himself related) with dreadful words. The king later said to his confidants that he had thought of killing Pole then and there, refraining only because of the simplicity and humility with which he had spoken.[12] Pole was thirty years old at the time; by God's grace and the intercession of his friends, he received the king's permission to depart for Padua, as well as a royal pension.[13] Many men, extremely learned and distinguished in holy theology, and in both branches of law, wrote erudite and weighty tomes in support of the marriage between the king and queen, not only in England (as has already been said), but also in the other provinces of Christendom. There was also a monstrous heretic called Philip Melanchthon, who wrote a letter to the king in which he advised him to keep the queen as his wife, but to take Anne Boleyn as his mistress![14] I say this to expose the counsel of the authors of this new and pestilential doctrine, as contrary to the law of God as is the creed they profess.

---

12   This incident was told and retold by Pole and members of his circle: see Thomas F. Mayer, "A Sticking-Plaster Saint? Autobiography and Hagiography in the Making of Reginald Pole," in *The Rhetorics of Life-Writing in Early Modern Europe: Forms of Biography from Cassandra Fedele to Louis XIV*, ed. Thomas F. Mayer and D.R. Woolf (Ann Arbor: University of Michigan Press, 1995), 205–22.

13   Pole left England in the early months of 1532, slowly making his way to Padua, having received a royal subsidy of one hundred pounds. Mayer, "Pole, Reginald," in *ODNB*, 44:716. Edwards, *Archbishop Pole*, 23.

14   The German reformer Philipp Melanchthon (born Schwartzerdt, 1497–1560), one of Luther's closest associates, wrote to Henry on August 23, 1531; his advice was even more explosive than Ribadeneyra makes it out to have been: to *marry* Anne in addition to Catherine, for the sake of producing an heir. See Philipp Melanchthon, *Melancthons Briefwechsel: Kritische und kommentierte Gesamtausgabe,* ed. Heinz Scheible, 15 vols. (Stuttgart: Frommann-Holzboog, 2003), 5:177–83.

Of the Threats the King Made against the Pope, and of the Death of Wolsey[1]

Matters standing thus, the king decided to write to the pope once more, and he ordered some of the nobility of his realm to do the same, too, imploring him that since it was essential for the king to have a male heir for the sake of the succession, he make haste and swiftly bring the matter to an end, so that the king might freely marry another woman and father sons by her.[2] The pope replied that he would fulfill the obligations of his office, but that it was not in his hands whether the king had a son, no matter whom he married![3] Not satisfied with this, the king proclaimed that none of his subjects, English or Irish, should thenceforth engage in, seek, or pursue any business with Rome without his permission, so as to pressure and intimidate the pope.[4]

He learned that Wolsey was at leisure in his bishopric, enjoying parties and banquets, and that he was requesting the return of an ornate, bejeweled pontifical miter of enormous value that the king had seized, because he wished to use it at a certain feast.[5] The king regarded this as an unbearable presumption: he ordered Henry, earl of Northumberland, to arrest him on the day of the feast itself, when all the nobility and crowds of people had assembled, and to bring

---

1 Sander, *De origine ac progressu*, 80–81.

2 This letter, dated July 13, 1530, was signed by two archbishops, four bishops, two dukes, two marquesses, thirteen earls, and assorted lords, abbots, and academics. See Pocock, *Records of the Reformation*, 1:429–33.

3 The pope's reply of September 27, 1530 included the smooth rejoinder, "But the power to grant children belongs to God, not us." See ibid., 1:434–37, here 436.

4 On September 12, 1530, Henry issued a proclamation prohibiting the requesting, receiving, or obeying of bulls from Rome. *TRP*, 1:197–98.

5 "It came into his head to travel to York, and there to take up residence in his episcopal seat like a conqueror, as was his wont, and celebrate the day and many thereafter in ceremonies, celebrations, and games—such that he who had begun to be pitied now sought after hatred. And because he missed his costly sacred vestments, by which he might make himself more distinguished, he did not hesitate to write to Henry to send him the mitre and cope he had used in other services. Seeing these letters, the king could not but wonder at Wolsey's audacity and insolence, saying, 'Is there yet pride in this man, who has clearly fallen?'" Polydore Vergil, *Polydori Vergilii Vrbinatis Anglicæ historiæ libri vigintiseptem: Ab ipso autore postremùm iam recogniti, adq[ue] amussim, salua tamen historiæ ueritate, expoliti* (Basel: Apud Mich. Isingrinium, 1555), 688–89.

him to London. The earl did as he was instructed, but on November 28, while he was escorting the prisoner on the journey, the cardinal died at Leicester.[6] It was rumored that the cardinal had taken certain poisons rather than see himself disgraced;[7] I believe this to be a fabrication. It is true that when the earl arrested him as a traitor to the royal majesty, the wretched man said, "Would to God I had not offended the divine majesty more than the temporal! But having ground out my entire life in the king's service to give him pleasure and peace of mind, I have offended God and lost the king's grace."[8] Some said that during his life Wolsey had erected a sumptuous tomb for himself and one day, as he went to inspect it, his lunatic fool said, "Why do you spend so much money in vain? Do you imagine you will be buried here? Well, I say unto you, when you die, you won't have enough to pay the gravedigger!"[9] And so it was.

This is the reward Wolsey received from the world, perfectly in keeping with his pride and sycophancy—perhaps our Lord punished him in this way so as not to condemn him for all eternity.[10] But it is an excellent lesson for the

---

6   On November 4, 1530, Henry Percy, sixth earl of Northumberland (c.1502–37), arrested Wolsey at Cawood. In the course of his return to London, Wolsey died at Leicester Abbey on November 29. R.W. Hoyle, "Percy, Henry Algernon, sixth earl of Northumberland (c.1502–1537)," in ODNB, 43:717–20, here 717.

7   "It was said that he took some sort of poison to avoid a more shameful death." Hume, Chronicle, 28–29.

8   "But if I had served God as diligently as I have done the King, he would not have given me over in my grey hairs. Howbeit this is the just reward that I must receive for my worldly diligence and pains that I have had to do him service, only to satisfy his vain pleasures, not regarding my godly duty." Cavendish and Roper, Early Tudor Lives, 183.

9   "For this Cardinal had a fool, and one day that the Cardinal went to see a very splendid sepulcher which he was having made for himself, the fool went with him, and said, 'My lord, why are you striving and spending so much money on this? Do you think you will be buried here? I tell you, when you die, you will not have enough to pay the men to bury you.' And so it was as the fool had prophesied." Hume, Chronicle, 29.

10   The possibility that earthly sufferings might mitigate those in the next life was evidently one that interested Ribadeneyra. In his Tratado de la tribulación, he argued, "For after the Lord pardons us, out of his mercy, the guilt of mortal sin, and the obligation to eternal punishment into which we have fallen thereby, he wishes that we render satisfaction, and repay what we owe in temporal pains, either in this life or in the other. And it is a supreme mercy of God when he gives us the time and opportunity to repay this in this [life] [...] Taking [afflictions] with patience, as sent from his blessed hand, let us pay here, to our little cost, what we must pay at such great cost in purgatory. [...] It is a true mercy of the Lord to afflict us in this life, so that we pay for our guilt there, rather than in the other [life], though if it should be in the pains of purgatory." Ribadeneyra, Tratado de la tribulacion, 35ᵛ–37ᵛ.

intimates, officials, and advisors of kings to put God before all else,[11] and not to offend him in gratifying men. Yet the example and miserable fall of Wolsey did not suffice to instruct others, who similarly played their parts in this lamentable, heart-breaking tragedy. Among them was one Thomas Cranmer, of whom we shall speak in the chapter that follows.

---

11   Cf. Matt. 6:31–33.

How the King Named Cranmer as Archbishop of Canterbury, of His Sinful Life, and of How He Deceived the Pope[1]

As the king's crimes and misdeeds had become so hateful, our Lord elected to punish him by allowing him free rein to carry on, without hesitation or fear of anything. God took to himself that excellent man, William Warham, the archbishop of Canterbury, who had aided the queen's cause with such fervor.[2] At the request of Thomas Boleyn and his beloved Anne, the king gave the archbishopric to Thomas Cranmer, who had been Thomas's chaplain, and later the king's agent in Rome.[3] This was the reason he was given the post, and because the king judged that his lifestyle and habits were such as could be useful in his ambitions, if the pope gave sentence in favor of the queen. Thomas Cranmer was a heretic, as will be seen later, for which he was burned in the time of Queen Mary; he was also an immoral man, of such lustfulness that while in Germany, he had seduced a maiden from the house where he was staying and carried her off to England.[4] When he was archbishop, she was publicly carried through the streets in a litter wherever he went, and he kept her as his mistress until Henry's death and the reign of his son, King Edward, when he married her in the sight of the entire world.[5] This was the man the king chose as his minister and named as archbishop and primate of his kingdom, to further his own

---

1   Sander, *De origine ac progressu*, 82–84.

2   On 22 August, just before standing trial for *praemunire*, Warham died of natural causes in Hackington, Kent. Scarisbrick, "Warham, William," in *ODNB*, 57:414.

3   Cranmer had joined Thomas Boleyn's household by the autumn of 1529, subsequently becoming one of Henry's leading diplomats. He was appointed archbishop of Canterbury in 1533 with the Boleyns' backing. See MacCulloch, *Thomas Cranmer*, Chapters 3 and 4.

4   While on a diplomatic mission to Nuremberg in the summer of 1532, Cranmer stayed in the house of the reformed theologian Andreas Osiander (1498–1552). There he met Margarete (d. 1570s), the niece of Osiander's wife; the two married soon after, but the nuptials were kept secret until the accession of Edward VI. Ibid., 71–72, 250.

5   This picaresque story originates in the polemical screed *Bishop Cranmer's Recantacyons* (*c*.1556), probably the work of Harpsfield: "Like a peddler, he carried his goods in secret, so that at each junction, there was a box near at hand with the baggage." Nicholas Harpsfield, *Bishop Cranmer's Recantacyons*, ed. Richard Monckton Milnes and James Gairdner, Philobiblon Society Miscellanies 15 (London, 1877–84), 8.

will—to which Cranmer so entirely conformed, in all that could please him, that years later the king was heard to say, "There is but one in my kingdom—Cranmer, archbishop of Canterbury—who has never strayed from my will."

But even though Cranmer was a man of this sort, to be more sure of him the king gave him the archbishopric on the condition that, if the Roman pontiff ruled in favor of the marriage with the queen, he, as archbishop and primate, would give a contrary sentence and declare against the pope that the king was obligated to divorce her. And because the king had not yet lost all shame before the Apostolic See, nor broken from it, Cranmer had to request papal confirmation of his position,[6] and in the proper manner take the solemn oath used for the consecration of bishops: to adhere to the communion of the Apostolic See and to obey its commands. Lest he offend the king by this oath, or by it fail to attain what he sought, Cranmer searched for some means of serving two masters, though they commanded contradictory things.[7] And because he loved the king from his very heart (as a man like himself), but merely feared the pope, he chose to win the king's favor by a willfully, deliberately false oath—so as to offend the pope all the more. Accordingly, he summons a notary public and tells him that he will swear the customary and canonical obedience to the Roman pontiff, but before doing so he wishes the notary to produce a separate document, in which he protests that he takes the oath against his will and that he will neither keep faith with the pope nor obey him in anything contrary to the king's pleasure. When this codicil and protest had been written and authenticated before witnesses (so as to remove any suspicion of the king's), he swore the solemn oath and took possession of his archbishopric.[8] This was Cranmer's

---

Ribadeneyra may have (deliberately?) misunderstood his Latin source here: he translates Sander's "cista" as "litera," which generally refers to a litter, rather than a box. Sander's implication is one of secrecy, Ribadeneyra's one of brazenness. Sander, *De origine ac progressu*, 84. Cf. Harpsfield, *Treatise*, 275.

6   Cranmer received papal confirmation of his appointment as archbishop on February 21, 1533. Scarisbrick, *Henry VIII*, 310.

7   Matt. 6:24; Luke 16:13.

8   Cranmer was consecrated as archbishop of Canterbury at Westminster on March 30, 1533. Before the consecration oath, Cranmer insisted on making a prior protestation in Latin, which he did in the presence of a notary and three witnesses. This included the stipulation that "I Thomas, bishop-elect of the archbishopric of Canterbury, allege, say and protest, openly, publicly, and expressly with these writings, that [...] it is not nor will it be my will or intention by such oath or oaths, no matter how the words placed in these oaths seem to sound, to bind myself on account of the same to say, do or attempt anything afterwards which will be or seem to be contrary to the law of God or against our most illustrious king of England, the commonwealth of his kingdom of England, or the laws and prerogatives of the

entrance; later we will see his exit and his end, and the reward for his tricks and deceptions. These matters are particularly to be noted, both for our example and instruction and to comprehend the unfathomable providence and justice of the Lord, who, though he permits the wicked to prevail and to attain their desires for a time, in the end punishes them and overthrows them with a force as great as that mildness and patience of his they knew not how to avail themselves of.

---

same." See Jonathan Michael Gray, *Oaths and the English Reformation*, Cambridge Studies in Early Modern British History (Cambridge: Cambridge University Press, 2013), 102–03.

The Conference between the Kings of England and France, and What They Discussed[1]

At this moment, Emperor Don Charles was waging a momentous campaign at Vienna against the Turk, Suleiman, who had come in person with countless formidable battalions, devastating and destroying the lands through which he passed.[2] And if the emperor, trusting in God, had not opposed him with all his prodigious strength, bravery, and cunning, Christendom would have had good cause to lament. Henry did not wish to lose this opportunity. He traveled to Calais (which was his at the time), a place considered impregnable, secretly bringing Anne Boleyn with him. Knowing that King Francis of France was ill-disposed to the emperor, he arranged to confer with him face-to-face, and the two monarchs met at a place between Calais and Boulogne, with huge pomp and ceremony.[3] In these discussions, Henry made every effort to rile up the king of France, to secure an alliance, and to propose a joint attack on the emperor (who was, as we have said, occupied in the war against the Turk). It was not difficult for him to win over the king of France, who felt himself wronged by the emperor, who had refused to return his children as he hoped. Besides this, Henry urged and implored him to threaten the pope, so as to incline him more effectively to his will, and even desired and encouraged King Francis to seize control of his realm's clergy on his own authority and demand that they yield up the tenth part of church incomes, in contempt of the pope. In the end, what he accomplished was that two French cardinals, Tournon[4]

---

1   Sander, *De origine ac progressu*, 84–86.

2   1532 saw Sultan Suleiman I (r.1520–66) lead an invasion of Hungary, capturing no fewer than seventeen towns and castles; as in the more famous campaign of 1529, the Ottomans' target was Vienna. Andrew Wheatcroft, *Enemy at the Gate: Habsburgs, Ottomans, and the Battle for Europe* (New York: Basic Books, 2009), 59.

3   This conference between Henry and Francis, held partly in Calais and partly in Boulogne, took place from October 21 to October 29, 1532. "Although ostensibly directed against the Turks, the real purpose of the meeting between the two kings was to co-ordinate their actions in Germany and Rome." Knecht, *Francis I*, 226.

4   Cardinal François de Tournon (1489–1562), an Augustinian canon and archbishop of Embrun. "Biographical Dictionary—Consistory of March 9, 1530," in *CHRC*.

and Tarbes,[5] were sent to the pope in both kings' names, with severe threats unless he did as they demanded. These were King Francis's public orders to the cardinals for their dealings with the pope—but in secret he instructed them to use more meekness, and to convince him to acquiesce to the kings' desires with the due humility and gentleness, not through harshness and fear. In particular, they were to negotiate the marriage of Catherine de' Medici, the daughter of Lorenzo the Younger (and the pope's niece), to his second son, the duke of Orleans—a marriage that subsequently came to pass.[6] King Henry had decided to marry Anne Boleyn on the spot, during the conferences, with all possible magnificence and ceremony—but he did not do so, because (beyond anything he could have imagined) news arrived that Suleiman the Turk had ignominiously retreated from Vienna and the emperor had returned to Italy in triumph.[7] With matters thus shifted, the news left King Francis much less enthusiastic about friendship with King Henry. For in their friendships, leagues, and alliances, princes generally have their eyes upon nothing but their own interest, and by this they guide their decisions.[8]

---

5   Gabriel de Gramont.

6   Caterina Maria Romula de' Medici (1519–89), the daughter of Lorenzo II de' Medici, ruler of Florence and duke of Urbino (r.1513–19). Catherine and Clement were actually first cousins twice removed (Clement's first cousin, Piero de' Medici [1471–1503] was Catherine's grandfather). Clement VII orchestrated the betrothal between Catherine and Henry of Orléans—subsequently King Henry II—in attempt to play off France against the Empire. The match was made in 1531, but the wedding did not take place until 1533. Leonie Frieda, *Catherine de Medici* (London: Weidenfeld & Nicolson, 2004), 30–31, 41.

7   The Ottomans were deflected from Vienna by the spirited resistance of the small fortress of Köszeg, withdrawing by the end of August 1532. Wheatcroft, *Enemy at the Gate*, 59.

8   This sentence was added in the 1595 edition.

The King's First Attack on the Clergy of England[1]

The king returned from France to England full of rage and frenzy, and so began to wage open war upon the ministers of God and to despoil them of their property through fresh slanders and tricks. In a new, bizarre tyranny, he brought charges against every clergyman in his kingdom, having them cited for the crime of having recognized the authority of the legates of the pope, a foreign power (it was then that this sort of language began to be used),[2] and having obeyed and defended him against the king's will. By this they had fallen into dire straits and forfeited all church property throughout the kingdom; this was to be confiscated by the king and, what is more, they themselves were to be thrown in jail.[3] Every churchman was stunned and bewildered, as though blasted by awful lightning: seeing themselves abandoned by the secular lords, sold out by their own archbishops and metropolitans—Cranmer and Lee (to whom the archbishopric of York had been given)[4]—with whom Henry had colluded, and without any means of resisting, they gave up and submitted to the king's will. They obsequiously begged him to be content with 400,000 ducats and to forgive them the rest, out of his supreme power in his kingdom over clergy and commoner alike, and this was the first time he was spoken of in this manner. This became the excuse for the royal officials to begin calling him supreme head of the Anglican Church.[5] Little by little, evil and reckless men began to say that the Roman pontiff had nothing to do with the realm of England, if the king, by his gracious will, did not choose to allot him some portion

---

1   Sander, *De origine ac progressu*, 86–89.

2   *Praemunire*—the charge of illegal importation of a foreign jurisdiction over and above the king's—was actually a centuries-old legal maneuver, commonly used for at least a generation before the 1530s, primarily in disputes over competency between secular and ecclesiastical courts. Haigh, *English Reformations*, 74.

3   In the autumn of 1530, Henry's government charged first a handful of bishops, then several hundred clergymen, and finally the entire English church with *praemunire*. The penalty was the forfeiture of all property and life imprisonment. Ibid., 88.

4   Edward Lee (*c*.1481–1544) was made archbishop of York in September 1531. Claire Cross, "Lee, Edward (1481/2–1544)," in *ODNB*, 33:56–59, here 57.

5   "On 24 January 1531 Southern Convocation formally submitted to Henry, as the northern body would do soon after, and received royal pardon—at the price of £100,000." Shortly thereafter, Henry demanded "to be styled not just king and Defender of the Faith, but 'protector and only supreme head of the English Church.'" Scarisbrick, *Henry VIII*, 275–76.

of his power. If he did not, all mortals were to be subject to the king, not only in civil and secular matters, but also in ecclesiastical and spiritual ones. All these innovations and outrages arose from the refusal to imagine or admit that the king had divorced the queen without legitimate or valid authority.

These are matters well worthy of note, as things to be cut off at the root. For the flattery of subjects and the ambition of kings, in addition their sovereign might, often bring about horrendous consequences when God, reason, and justice are not their guides. A few worthy and Christian men at the king's court understood this: seeing from afar the fearful storm that menaced the kingdom, they hoped to find a safe port in time, to escape the waves and the perils of the raging sea. First among them was Thomas More, the chancellor of the realm and an exceptional man, as has been said: having held that office for three years now, he begged the king to give him rest in his weary old age, some peace from the heavy task of continually writing against the heretics, and to deign to place that burden upon other shoulders, which might be better able to bear it. The king understood what More was about, and, wanting a chancellor more to his purpose and taste, acceded to his request and appointed as chancellor Thomas Audley, a man of middling rank, but very poor.[6] So that he could honorably maintain this dignity, he gave him a monastery of the Canons Regular in London, called Christ Church, with all its rents and buildings, scattering the religious to other houses of the same order. This was the first sign of the hateful spirit Henry harbored against the religious.[7]

---

6   Thomas More resigned as chancellor on May 16, 1532; four days later, Henry gave the position to Thomas Audley (c.1487–1544). Audley was the son of a local official in Essex. L.L. Ford, "Audley, Thomas, Baron Audley of Walden (1487/8–1544)," in *ODNB*, 2:935–40, here 935–36.

7   "Thomas Fuller, in his *Church History*, said that Audley received the grant of Christ Church in London, the first priory to be suppressed, 'to clear his voice, to make him speak shrill and loud for his master.'" Audley certainly benefited financially from many of Henry's suppressions and dissolutions of religious houses. Ibid., 2:939.

How the King, against the Pope's Mandate, Secretly Married Anne Boleyn[1]

When the pontiff learned of what had happened in England and of the king's hardened spirit, he was distraught and cast about for a remedy. He had already written insistently imploring the king not to be overcome by passion, nor to seek after innovations, nor to do anything against his first marriage with the queen while the suit was still pending. When the pope saw that this had availed him nothing, he wrote further, public letters in the form of briefs, sternly commanding him, by his apostolic authority and under penalty of excommunication, not to proceed any further until the case had been concluded.[2]

But Henry, burning with the savage fires of infernal love, would not abandon his wicked purpose, neither for the advice the pope had given as a father, nor for the warning he now gave as a judge—rather, each day he became yet more enflamed with his sinful desires. Seeing that the only thing lacking to abandon the queen and marry Anne was the decree of divorce, and that he had no hope of obtaining it from the pope, he decided to order Cranmer to provide it. He was sure he would comply, since that was why he had been made archbishop of Canterbury. And so as not to appear to marry a woman without rank or

---

1   Sander, *De origine ac progressu*, 89–99.

2   On December 23, 1530, a secret consistory met at Rome: "The Pope ordered then that the Cardinals should give their votes on the report made by the reverend Paulus de Capisuccis, in the Consistory of the 14th of the same month, concerning the matrimonial cause which was pending between the king and queen of England. The procurators of the Queen had asked that the Pope should forbid the archbishop of Canterbury, by a special brief, to take cognizance of this lawsuit, in case he should be applied to, as it had been reserved for the decision of the Sacred College of Cardinals. The procurators of the queen of England had likewise asked that the Pope should repeat and confirm in a brief all the inhibitions which the auditors of the Rota, to whom this cause was entrusted, had directed to all prelates of England. The same procurators had further petitioned that the Pope should forbid the king of England, whilst the lawsuit was pending, either to cohabit with any other woman, and especially a certain lady Anne, or to contract marriage; and in case that such a marriage should be contracted, to declare it null and void. Lastly, the same procurators had prayed that the Pope should forbid the said lady Anne, and all women in general, to contract, *lite pendente*, marriage with the king of England. After long deliberations it was concluded that all the afore-mentioned petitions were justifiable in law, and that the briefs should be granted." *LP*, 4:6772.

distinction, he first gave Anne Boleyn the title of marchioness, and then married her in secret.[3] The king married her because he could not enjoy her unless he made her his wife, thanks to the resistance she cunningly offered to all of his advances and pleas,[4] and they wed in secret because no judge had pronounced a sentence of divorce against Queen Doña Catherine. There was in the palace a cleric called Rowland (later made a bishop for the service he rendered), whom the king summoned to his chapel one morning before dawn. He told him that Rome had given sentence in his favor, so that he might wed any woman he liked. The churchman, supposing that kings do not lie, believed him and held silent, and then said, "I trust Your Majesty will have apostolic letters from His Holiness." When the king made a sign in the affirmative, the cleric returned to the altar to perform his office, and there and then married the king and Anne Boleyn. But, stricken in his conscience and fearful of doing a deed repugnant to God, he turned once more to the king, saying, "The sacred canons command, and I think it most important, that the letters apostolic be read out before all present, and published." Then the king replied, "I have the pope's letters, but they are kept in my private study, where none but I may find or fetch them; but it is not seemly for me to leave this place at this hour to go for them." The cleric thus reassured, he performed the ceremony, marrying Henry to Anne and giving him a second wife while his first yet lived, the bond to her husband unbroken by any authority.[5]

---

3   Henry made Anne marchioness of Pembroke in September 1532. Eric Ives, "Anne [Anne Boleyn] (c.1500–1536)," in *ODNB*, 2:181–88, here 183.

    Henry and Anne were probably married in secret on January 24 or January 25, 1533, having already cohabited for several months. The question of the date, and whether there might have been a prior ceremony the previous November, is discussed in MacCulloch, *Thomas Cranmer*, 637–38.

4   In the margin: "Chapter 7."

5   Rowland Lee (c.1487–1543), a loyal partisan of the king, was made bishop of Coventry and Lichfield in 1534. The story of Lee officiating at the clandestine marriage originates with Harpsfield, but there is little other evidence for it. Michael A. Jones, "Lee, Rowland (c.1487–1543)," in *ODNB*, 33:106–09, here 108–09.

    "The King was married to Lady Anne Bulleyne long ere there was any divorce made by the said Archbishop [of Canterbury]. The which marriage was secretly made at Whitehall very early before day, none being present but Mr. Norris and Mr. Henage of the Privy Chamber and the Lady Barkeley, with Mr. Rowland the King's chaplain, that was afterward made Bishop of Coventry and Lichfield. To whom the King told that now he had gotten of the Pope a lycence to marry another wife, and yet to avoid business and tumult the thing must be done (quoth the King) very secretly; and thereupon a time and place was appointed to the said Master Rowland to solemnize the said marriage. At which time Mr. Rowland being come accordingly and seeing all things ready for celebration of mass and to solemnize the marriage [...] came

These are the nuptials revered and acclaimed by all the heretics in England—the Lutherans, the Zwinglians, the Calvinists, the Puritans, and all the
other monstrosities that devastate and pervert that kingdom—as the fount of
their gospel, the foundation of their church, the origin and birth of their faith.
The hellish fury of lust and vice assailed King Henry, and he cast himself into
an abyss of innumerable sins and abominations, as we have seen and as we
shall see again hereafter. He wrapped himself in a blind, demented hypocrisy,
by which he would have it believed that he had separated from the queen out
of the scruples of his conscience: she could not be his wife, having been his
brother's (even though she had not contracted any affinity, since she had remained a maiden, as the king himself admitted to the emperor; even if any had
existed, she had been left without children and had been given a papal dispensation), while at the same time, without any sort of dispensation or license, he
married the sister of his mistress, the daughter of his mistress—and what is
more, his own daughter (as she was known to be by numerous and sound reasons)! This was against all natural, divine, and human laws, and Henry had no
scruples about committing so horrible and unthinkable an outrage—he had
one in his marriage to the queen!

> O unthinkable audacity—says Sander—unheard-of hypocrisy, lust infer-
> nal and worthy of eternal fire! But in the end it is no marvel that man sins,
> or that, having come to the depths and the heights of his wickedness, he
> turns his back on God and scorns him. What is astonishing and fearful,

---

to the King and said—'Sir, I trust you have the Pope's lycence, both that you may marry and
that I may join you together in marriage.' 'What else?' quoth the King. Upon this he turned
to the altar and reverted himself, but yet not so satisfied, and troubled in mind he cometh
eftsoones to the King and saith—'This matter toucheth us all very nighe, and therefore it is
expedient that the lycence be read before us all, or else we run all—and I more deep than
any other—into excommunication in marrying your grace without any baynes asking, and
in a place unhallowed, and no divorce as yet promulged of the first matrimony.' The King,
looking upon him very amiably, 'Why, Master Rowland,' quoth he, 'think you me a man of so
small faith and credit, you, I say, that do well know my life passed, and even now have heard
my confession? or think you me a man of so small and slender foresight and consideration
of my affairs that unless all things were safe and sure I would enterprize this matter? I have
truly a lycence, but it is reposed in another sure[r] place whereto no man resorteth but myself, which if it were seen, should discharge us all. But if I should, now that it waxeth towards
day, fetch it, and be seen so early abroad, there would rise a rumour and talk thereof other
than were convenient. Goe forth in God's name, and do that which appertaineth to you. I will
take upon me all other danger.' Whereupon he went to mass, and celebrated all ceremonies
belonging to marriage." Harpsfield, *Treatise*, 234–35.

what bewilders and dumbfounds, is to see numberless people follow (with such peace and confidence) not their own tastes and appetites, but the lust, hypocrisy, and sinfulness of another man, to praise and revere it as the very cornerstone of their faith, their hope, and their salvation. Who will marvel at hearing that in ancient days there were Cainite heretics, who worshipped Cain, the murderer of his own brother, as the progenitor of manly virtue?[6] Or the Ophites, who (as Tertullian says) revered the serpent who deceived our first parents in the terrestrial paradise as the author of the knowledge of good and evil?[7] Or any other sort of delirious madmen? For do we not see in our own days a horde of countless heretics who laud this marriage—or, more accurately, this abominable and frightful incest of a father with his own daughter—and say that by it they have escaped the darkness of Egypt and entered into the light and purity of the Gospel?[8] Truly, by these nuptials they opened the door (what blind, wretched men!) to every misfortune and heresy. But may the immense goodness of the Lord always be blessed and glorified, for it proclaims to us that as these are the children of a damned birth, they are the children of confusion and darkness. Now must the daughter lie down with her father, the sister with her brother (as Anne Boleyn did),[9] so that your unnatural birth may come to light, and upon this are placed the foundation stones of your religion. Your church does not flow from the sacred breast of Christ, as does the Catholic Church, but from the foulness of a whore, her throat justly slashed.[10]

All this comes from Sander.

---

6   In the margin: "Concerning whom, St. Augustine, *De haeresibus*, Chapter 18, and Philastrius; Tertullian's book *On Heresies* calls them Chaldeans."
     Augustine, *De haeresibus*, Chapter 18.
     Philastrius, *Liber de haeresibus*, Chapter 2.
     The reference to "Tertullian" is to the *Adversus omnes haereses*, spuriously attributed to Tertullian, but the text makes no reference to the Chaldeans: Pseudo-Tertullian, *Adversus omnes haereses*, Chapter 47.

7   In the margin: "[Pseudo-]Tertullian, *Adversus omnes haereses* [*lib. de præscript. aduersus hæret.*], and Augustine, *De haeresibus*, Chapter 17, and Philastrius."
     Pseudo-Tertullian, *Adversus omnes haereses*, Chapter 47.
     Augustine, *De haeresibus*, Chapter 17.
     Philastrius, *Liber de haeresibus*, Chapter 1.

8   Exod. 10:21–23.

9   A blackly parodic echo of Isaiah 11:6?

10   Sander, *De origine ac progressu*, 98.

By now, Henry publicly treated Anne like his wife, and banished the saintly queen from his presence—not only from his bed, as he had done before, but from his royal palace and their shared home. Thus, the unfortunate queen found herself in a rural manor, situated in a baleful region, accompanied only by three ladies-in-waiting and a tiny household.[11] Here, she spent day and night in prayer, fasting, penance, and other holy works, begging our Lord above all for the wellbeing of those adulterers she had left in the palace. When this became widely known, and it was understood that Anne Boleyn would undoubtedly become queen, it will hardly be believed (save by one who understands the world's protean and deceptive instability) how people of all sorts began to flock to her, hoping to win her favor: some to preserve and protect their goods (many of them churchmen), others to prosper and rise by alteration.

---

11   In May 1534, Catherine had relocated to Kimbolton in Huntingdonshire, a "rather gloomy and old-fashioned" manor house. Chapuys reported that under pressure from Henry, Catherine had requested a reduction in her household, leaving only three ladies-in-waiting, her confessor, her doctor, and her apothecary. The remainder of the household at Kimbolton was made up of northerners, over whom Catherine had little influence. Tremlett, *Catherine of Aragon*, 346. *CSPS*, 4.2:1081.

Of Thomas Cromwell, and of the Heretics Who Flooded the King's Court, and What They Proposed against the Churchmen[1]

Since it was known that Anne was a Lutheran heretic at heart, countless Lutherans flocked to her, and so the king's court was soon swollen with a pack of heresy-addled degenerates. They spent their time deriding sacred things, jeering at priests, ridiculing and mocking monks, concocting and inventing a thousand fables about them, censuring the wealth and power of the prelates and churchmen, and above all in slandering and insulting the pope, and he who was most brazen and insolent in these things won the palm and Anne's favor (and, through her, the king's). Foremost among them was Thomas Cromwell, a shrewd, cruel, ambitious, and greedy man, a true heretic (and accordingly the fervent enemy of all churchmen), whom—to please Anne and because it served his own turn—the king chose to exalt and make the colleague of Archbishop Cranmer and Chancellor Audley. To this end, he first made him his secretary, then a knight, then a baron, then an earl, then lord chamberlain of the realm and keeper of the privy seal, and finally the leader of his council in secular matters and his vicegerent in spiritual and ecclesiastical matters.[2] And so the entire kingdom seemed to be in the palm of his hand, as it had once been in Wolsey's.

The heretics resolved to lose no time with this opportunity, but rather to throw oil on the fire and stir up the spirit of the king against all the churchmen of his realm, for he already appeared to be enraged against them, lost to any reverence for the pope, and beginning to taste of heresy through Anne. To achieve their goals, they began to circulate numberless pamphlets clandestinely among the people and in the houses of the gentry, and to spread pasquinades filled with lies, deceits, and impieties against ecclesiastics, to make them hated and abhorred. For these are the methods and tricks of the heretics, by which they overthrow those who might resist them, and kill or dispel the dogs lest they

---

1 Sander, *De origine ac progressu*, 99–104.

2 Henry VIII made Thomas Cromwell successively principal secretary (1533), Vicegerent in Spirituals (1535), Lord Privy Seal (1536), Baron Cromwell of Wimbledon (1536), a knight (1536), earl of Essex (1540), and Lord Great Chamberlain (1540). David Loades, *Thomas Cromwell: Servant to Henry VIII* (Stroud: Amberley Publishing, 2013), 10, 97, 108, 132.

bite or bark, so that they, the wolves, may scatter and slaughter the Lord's herd at their leisure. One of these books, entitled *The supplication for the beggars* [*peticion de los pobres mendigos*], was presented to the king.[3] After proclaiming the infinity of the truly poor in the kingdom, and their extreme necessity, it announced that the real cause of the situation was the other "poor," the well-fed, idle churchmen, who by artifice and deceit seized and wasted more than half the kingdom's wealth, allowing actual paupers to die of starvation. It begged His Majesty, as supreme minister of God on earth and father to the poor, to aid the helpless, to provide them with what they needed, to extend his hand to the downfallen, to sustain and gather the abandoned and the lost. This he could easily do, if by redistributive justice he gave to each what was right, stripping from the clergy's rents ninety-nine parts in a hundred and allotting them to his treasury. Thus by his will the true poor would be sustained, with one part remaining for the churchmen, likewise kept under His Majesty's control. It is perfectly clear that this tract was not published without the approval, or at least the permission, of the king.[4]

As no ecclesiastic dared respond to this, lest he seem to do so out of his own interests, Thomas More (a layman of rare talent, as we have said) entered the fray and wrote a learned and thoughtful book.[5] First refuting the tract's slanders uttered against the clergy, and dispersing the heretics' shadows with the light and splendor of the truth, he then clearly demonstrated that the goods and income of the Church did not come to anything near what the deluded misbelievers claimed, and that those who had left such property to the Church had done something not only pious, but also necessary for the preservation of divine worship, without which the commonwealth could not survive. He added that these incomes not only served for the maintenance of the clerics, but also for the numberless laymen who depended upon them, and that every pauper received substantial alms from the churchmen, by whose hands many hospitals, colleges, monasteries, and pious projects (the shelter and refuge of

---

3   In 1529, Simon Fish (d.1531), an evangelical polemicist, published *A Supplication for the Beggars*, in which he urged King Henry to seize the property of the clergy, whom he claimed were despoiling England, for the good of the nation. Simon Fish, *A Supplicacyon for the Beggers* (Antwerp: [Joannes Grapheus], 1529).

4   Far from a government-promoted publication, the *Supplicacyon* was one of several reforming tracts declared "books of heresy, and worthy to be damned and put in perpetual oblivion" in a royal proclamation of June 22, 1530. *TRP*, 1:194.

5   Soon after the 1529 appearance of Fish's text, Thomas More published a rebuttal, *The Supplication of Souls*, contending that the souls condemned to purgatory needed the prayers offered up by the clergy. Thomas More, *The Supplycacyon of Soulys: Agaynst the Supplycacyon of Beggars* (London: William Rastell, 1529).

the poor and wretched) had been established. Finally, that the riches of the churchmen were really the treasures of the poor on earth and in heaven. All this More wrote with great spirit, piety, and eloquence: thus he stopped the mouths of the heretics, none of whom dared open them to respond.

And it should be understood that More wrote an important truth—how important it is for the churches and prelates to be wealthy and powerful—as can be seen in Germany and other northern regions. For the Catholic faith has been preserved in those areas subject to bishops and prelates of the Church, where they were powerful, princes of the Empire, and lords of cities, and thus able to control their subjects and vassals, preserving the Catholic faith in their lands. Where they had not the means or strength for this, there it was lost, as it has been lost in many others for want of the ecclesiastics' vigorous force and power. And besides the fact that this income is generally better employed and spent in the hands of the ecclesiastics than in those of laymen, for the relief of countless poor persons, consider the bequests made in Christendom for the relief of the indigent, orphans, and maidens: it will be found that the best part of them was left by churchmen, with which an infinity of people are even now sustained and without which they would perish.[6]

---

6 Ribadeneyra's stress on the necessity of a strong episcopacy may be a reflection of similar priorities set down by the Council of Trent. Cf. A. Katie Harris, "Forging History: The Plomos of the Sacromonte of Granada in Francisco Bermudez de Pedraza's *Historia Eclesiastica*," SCJ 30, no. 4 (Winter 1999): 945–66, here 966.

What Parliament Decreed Concerning the Clergy, and the Judgment Cranmer Gave in the King's Favor[1]

The king was advised that for Cranmer to give sentence in his favor, it would be best for the parliament of the realm, then in session, to command all church-men to take an oath of obedience to the king, such as they had formerly sworn to the pope, and that to put this forward with authority, he should choose the bishop of Rochester, esteemed throughout the kingdom. If the bishop agreed, it would be accomplished; if not, it would reveal the vicious spirit he harbored against the king. Anne hoped for the latter, for she had wished to see Roches-ter dead ever since he had defended the cause of the queen with such valor. Out of this hatred, she had previously tried to murder him, bribing one of the bishop's cooks, called Richard Roose [*Riseo*], who poured some poison into the pot from which Rochester and his servants usually ate all together, but it was God's will that the bishop did not eat at table that day as was his custom. Almost all the servants who did eat died, and the cook was publicly punished; in consequence, Anne's hatred and fury toward the bishop only grew stron-ger.[2] The king sent Rochester a writ concerning the oath, to the distress and agony of the saintly bishop. For, on the one hand, he saw that what the king

---

1 Sander, *De origine ac progressu*, 104–09.

2 The preface to the 1531 "Acte for Poysoning" recounted how Richard Roose (d.1531), "^ootherwise called Richard Coke^ which of his most wikked and dampnable disposicon did cast a c[er]teyn venyme or poyson into a vessell replenysshed w[ith] yist or barme stondyng in the kechyn of the rev[er]end ffather in god John Bisshop of Rouchest[er] ^at^ his place in Lamebythe mersshe ^w[ith]^ which ^yist or barme and other thynges convenyent^ porrage or gruell ^was forthw[ith]^ made for his ffamylye there beyng whereby not onely the nomber of xvii parsones of his sed famylye ^which did eate of the seid porrage^ were mortally in-fected or pysenned and one of them therof is decessed but also c[er]teyn poor people which resortted to the seid bishops place for almes and were there charitably fed w[ith] the re-maynes of the seid porrage and other vytailles were in likewise infected and one pore woman of them is also therof nowe decessed. [...] And because that detestable offence nowe newely ^comytted^ requyreth condigne punysshment for the same it is ordeyned and enacted that the seid ^Richard Roose^ shalbe therfore boyled to deathe." K.J. Kesselring, "A Draft of the 1531 'Acte for Poysoning,'" *EHR* 116, no. 468 (September 2001): 894–99, here 898–99.

Contemporary rumor speculated that Anne or Henry had been behind the attempt, but Roose only admitted that he had added purgatives to the dish "as a jest." Ibid., 894, 896.

commanded was contrary to God, and, on the other, that the king would not allow delay or excuse of any kind: embattled with conflicting thoughts like contrary winds,[3] in the end he allowed himself to be conquered. He saw that a frightful, cataclysmic storm threatened him and all clergymen if he did not obey; to allay the scruples of his conscience, the king said that he would add to the oath that they swore to the extent licit and permitted by divine law.[4] Fisher also hoped that in time the king would be restored and return to his senses and, tired of his affection for Anne, take better counsel and understand that what he demanded and commanded was neither lawful nor possible. And so, befuddled by fear, vain hopes, and passable arguments, Rochester allowed himself to be borne along, and persuaded other churchmen (hitherto firm and unyielding) to obey the king and swear the oath he demanded, with the condition of its being licit and in accordance with the law of God. Later, Rochester was so distraught and pained at this deceit that he felt he could not expunge the guilt save by his own blood, and he publicly accused and berated himself, saying, "As a bishop, my duty is not to proceed in so grave a matter with double-dealings and dubious reservations, but to instruct others clearly and openly in the truth, the commands and prohibitions of God's sacred law, and to draw the deceived out of their errors."[5]

When the churchmen submitted to the oath, the king's plan had succeeded, and he commanded Cranmer, being now, by the authority of parliament and the ecclesiastical arm, free of the oath of obedience made to the pope, to pronounce the sentence of divorce, which he did in this way. Bringing with him all the bishops, jurists, lawyers, and notaries that seemed suitable, he went to a small town near the queen's residence. Over the course of fifteen days, he had her repeatedly summoned, but she never answered.[6] Then Cranmer warned

---

3 Isa. 57:20.

4 On February 11, 1531, the Convocation of Canterbury approved a formula for Henry's title as supreme head that included the saving clause "insofar as the law of Christ allows," which is generally credited to Fisher. Henry Ansgar Kelly, Louis W. Karlin, and Gerald B. Wegemer, eds., *Thomas More's Trial by Jury: A Procedural and Legal Review with a Collection of Documents* (Woodbridge: Boydell Press, 2011), 23.

   For the document in question, see David Wilkins, ed., *Concilia Magnae Britanniae et Hiberniae a Synodo Verolamiensi AD 446 ad Londinensem AD 1717; Accedunt constitutiones et alia ad historiam Ecclesiae Anglicanae spectantia*, 4 vols. (London: R. Gosling, 1737), 3:735.

5 Pollen suggests that this description of Fisher's remorse may originate with a now-lost life of the bishop available to Sander. The possibility that the scene may be Sander's invention either did not occur to Pollen, or he elected not to voice it. Pollen, "Nicholas Sander," 44–45.

6 On May 10, 1533, Thomas Cranmer opened yet another inquiry into Catherine's marriage(s). These proceedings took place at Dunstable Priory in Bedfordshire, ten miles from Ampthill,

the king (as had been plotted between the pair of them) not to treat as his wife she who had been his brother's wife, for this was contrary to the laws of the Gospel, nor to persist any longer in that frame of mind, for if he did not obey, the archbishop would be forced—though it pained him greatly—to use the weapons of the Church, that is, ecclesiastical censures, against the king.[7] And there was no shortage of flatterers and swindlers, those already infected with heresy, who lauded the false and perverse archbishop in their loudest voices. They said that was clear that he was a true prelate, given by the hand of God, who with such freedom, without reverence or fear of any kind, admonished and reprimanded the king and compelled him to do his duty.[8] Such were the tricks, lies, and devices of the heretics, their shadows so black they imagined they could obscure the truth. In the end, without hearing the queen's side and at the king's pleasure and will (he being a party and actor), Cranmer published his sentence and declared that according to divine justice the king was required to separate from the queen, and free to marry another whenever he wished.[9]

---

where Catherine was staying. Uncharacteristically, Sander is overly generous toward the archbishop: Cranmer pronounced Catherine contumacious a mere two days into the trial. MacCulloch, *Thomas Cranmer*, 92–93.

7   Years later, Reginald Pole would rebuke Cranmer: "Was it anything but an illusion to exhort him repeatedly to that which he himself had attempted in every possible way, to cast off his wife? Then, as though you despaired of swaying him, for a better charade, you added the threat of ecclesiastical censure, when all knew that no fear of divine or human law would force him to keep her any longer?" Thomas Cranmer, *Memorials of the Most Reverend Father in God Thomas Cranmer, Sometime Lord Archbishop of Canterbury*, ed. John Strype, 3 vols., Ecclesiastical History Society Publications 2 (Oxford: T. Combe, 1848), 3:618–19.

8   A pamphlet published in late 1533 in support of Henry's marriage to Anne Boleyn declared, "And this manner of ways only ought every bishop to use [...] for they be bound more to obey God than man, which office and ways (according to his duty) our good bishop of Canterbury (now living) hath begun to shew and follow. For first he apperceiving when he came to his dignity, that his prince and sovereign lived in unlawful and unfitting matrimony (according to his duty) meekly did admonish him and therein also repaved him, exhorting him to leave it, or else he would do further his duty in it, So that at the last, according to Gods laws he did separate his prince from that unlawful matrimony. In which doing, we think that every true subject should much the better esteem him, because he would execute God's commandment and set this realm in the way of true heirs." Pocock, *Records of the Reformation*, 2:529.

9   For the sentence of divorce, issued on May 23, 1533, see Thomas Rymer, ed., *Fœdera, conventiones, literæ, et cujuscunque generis acta publica, inter reges Angliæ, et alios quosvis imperatores, reges, pontifices, principes, vel communitates, ab ineunte sæculo duodecimo, viz. ab anno 110, ad nostra usque tempora, habita aut tractata; Ex autographis, infra secretiores archivorum regiorum thesaurarias, per multa sæcula reconditis, fideliter exscripta*, 2nd ed., 15 vols. (London: J. Tonson, 1726–35), 14:462–63.

But the king, as we have said, had not waited for this judgment to marry Anne (albeit in secret), or to sleep with her as his wife—as the king himself wrote to the king of France! The solemnities of these nuptials were publicly observed on Holy Saturday, in the year 1533, and on June 2 Anne was crowned as queen, with greater pomp and ceremony than any queen before her.[10] She departed the Tower of London in an open litter, so that all could see her. Before her came all the knights, the gentlemen of rank, and the grandees of the realm, every one richly adorned. Then followed the ladies and noblewomen upon their mares. Anne was attired in crimson brocade, studded with numberless gems; at her throat, she wore a collar of pearls, each bigger than a large chickpea, and a priceless chain of diamonds; upon her head, a tiara (really a sumptuous crown), with flowers in her hands.[11] She turned from one side to the other, as though saluting the crowd, perhaps ten of whom hailed her and shouted, "God save you," as they used to do Queen Doña Catherine.[12] This was Anne Boleyn's day of triumph, utterly different from the sad, sorry spectacle of her end, when (just a little while later) she was beheaded—as will be seen farther on.[13]

---

10   On April 12, 1533, Holy Saturday, Anne made her first public appearance as queen, and Henry announced that they had been married the previous November. Anne was crowned on Whit Sunday, June 1, 1533, part of a stunningly elaborate ceremony that spanned several days. During the preparations, Chapuys reported, "it is said that the ceremony will be conducted more sumptuously than on any other like occasion." Eric Ives, *The Life and Death of Anne Boleyn: "The Most Happy"* (Malden: Blackwell Publishing, 2004), 178. CSPS, 4.2:1062.

11   "At ten o'clock Anne left the Tower in an open litter, so that all might see her, but before she came out all the salary preceded her, all in very fine order and richly bedight. Then came the gentlemen of rank, and then all the ladies and gentlemen on horseback and in cars, very brave. The Queen was dressed in a robe of crimson brocade covered with precious stones, and round her neck she wore a string of pearls larger than big chick-peas, and a jewel of diamonds of great value. On her head she bore a wreath in the fashion of a crown of immense worth, and in her hand she carried some flowers. As she passed through the city she kept turning her face from one side to the other; and here it was a very notable thing to see, that there were not, I think, ten people who greeted her with 'God save you!' as they used to when the sainted Queen passed by." Hume, *Chronicle*, 13.

12   On this detail Chapuys confirms the "Spanish Chronicle": "The coronation pageant was all that could be desired, and went off very well, as to the number of the spectators, which was very considerable, but all looked so sad and dismal that the ceremony seemed to be a funeral rather than a pageant for I am told that the indignation of the English against their king is daily increasing, as well as the hope that Your Majesty will one of these days apply a remedy to this state of things." CSPS, 4.2:1077.

13   In the margin: "Book 1, Chapter 34."

What Christendom Thought of the King's Marriage, and Pope Clement's Sentence against Him[1]

Word of this shameful deed escaped from England, spreading through all the provinces of Christendom; the horror, indignation, and distress it roused in the heart of every Christian prince was not to be believed. In particular, the emperor was bitterly insulted and deeply infuriated (as was only reasonable): he begged the pope not to allow King Henry to get away with this shameless outrage, to become an example, so abominable and yet unpunished, from which the direst misfortunes would befall all of Christendom. Although the pope took this to heart, as much for the matter itself as for the justified insistence of the emperor, yet, imagining he might cure Henry with mildness and kindly methods, and hoping to use the king of France as intermediary, he delayed the remedy until they met in Marseilles, when his niece, Catherine de' Medici, married King Francis's second son.[2] But after he witnessed the insolence of King Henry's ambassadors—who in the presence of King Francis had dared to interrupt the pope and allude to a future council,[3] which they urged upon the king of France (who responded with the spirit and voice of the Most Christian King, that in all else he would be Henry's brother, but where he turned against religion, he desired neither his company nor his friendship)—he returned to Rome and examined once more the question of the marriage between King Henry and Queen Catherine. He then pronounced the following judgment, in the year 1533, one year before his death.

Pope Clement VII

Although the suit before us between our dearest children in Christ Catherine and Henry VIII, monarchs of England, over whether the marriage

---

1 Sander, *De origine ac progressu*, 109–13.
2 Catherine de' Medici and Henry, duke of Orléans, were married in Marseilles on October 28, 1533, with both Francis and Clement in attendance. Frieda, *Catherine de Medici*, 44–46.
3 Francis I described this encounter in a memorandum: "When going to the Pope one evening he [*sc.* Francis] found that the English agents had signified to him their appeal, and intimated the Council, which, not without cause, put him in the greatest despair and anger. [...] It is not only strange conduct, but insulting, that they should defy a guest of his, which they confess they would not have dared to do if his Holiness were elsewhere." *LP*, 6:1426.

contracted between them was valid, by us committed, in the consistory of the cardinals, to our beloved son Capizucchi, our chaplain, *auditor* of causes of our sacred apostolic palace, and dean,[4] was yet pending, the said Henry has abandoned the said Catherine, and actually married a certain Anne, against our mandates and decrees, in which we directed and enjoined him not to do so, our letters promulgated as briefs by the advice of our brothers the cardinals of the holy Roman Church, rashly disdaining by his deeds everything we said. Therefore, we, by the sovereign authority conceded to us, in the person of the blessed Saint Peter (and not by our own merit), by Christ, king of kings, seated in the tribunal and throne of justice, holding God alone before our eyes, in accordance with our duty and by the advice of our brothers the cardinals of the holy Church (gathered in consistory in our presence), pronounce and declare that the separation from and abandonment of the said Queen Catherine, and the deprivation of her conjugal rights and royal dignity (which she possessed when first she made this appeal), and the marriage contracted between the said Henry and the said Anne (all these matters being notorious and public, as we have declared) are and have always been invalid, unjust, outrageous, and tainted by the defects of nullity, injustice, and outrage. The children born, or who may be born in future, to this union of Henry with Anne have been and are illegitimate. The said Queen Catherine must be restored to her former estate: the possession of her conjugal rights and the dignity of queen. The said king must expel the said Anne from his person and his abode, and from any claim to the rights of wife and queen—in short, abandon her. And so we proclaim in these our letters apostolic: we decree, declare, restore, replace, discard, and separate. And likewise by this same judgment, by the same advice, and by dint of our office, we affirm that the said King Henry has fallen into and incurred the censures and penalties of the highest excommunication, and the others detailed in our aforementioned letters, as he has not obeyed them, but rather disdained them. Therefore, we command all faithful Christians to shun him. But, wishing to exercise the office of a pious and benign father toward the said Henry, we suspend the promulgation of the aforesaid censures until and through the coming month of September, so that he may more easily comply with our sentence and our orders.

---

4 Paolo Capizucchi (1479–1539), a doctor of civil and canon law, became an *auditor* of the Rota in 1513, and was named dean on July 27, 1528. Gigliola Fragnito, "Capizucchi, Paolo," in Alberto M. Ghisalberti, ed., *Dizionario biografico degli Italiani*, 80 vols. (Rome: Instituto della Enciclopedia Italiana, 1960–), 18:571–72, here 571.

And if in this period he does not obey, neither restoring the said Catherine to the status she held when she lodged her appeal, nor dismissing the said Anne from his bed and the dignities of wife and queen, nor swiftly undo all he has attempted, we will and decree that this our present declaration shall thereafter have effect and force.

Thus we proclaim.[5]

---

5 Ribadeneyra translates from the Latin text provided in Sander, *De origine ac progressu*, 111–13. For a modern text, see Pocock, *Records of the Reformation*, 2:677–78.

What Henry Did When He Learned of the Pope's Sentence[1]

Henry took this judgment as the direst insult and affront; rather than reflecting or taking hold of himself, he resolved on vengeance. And so he commanded, under the gravest penalties, that thenceforth none should call Doña Catherine "queen," or his wife, but simply the widow of Prince Arthur.[2] After Anne told him she was pregnant and about to give birth, he cast aside his daughter Princess Mary, breaking with her as though she were a bastard, and sent her to live in poverty with her mother, stripped of all authority and royal dignity.[3] The princess was by then seventeen years of age, acknowledged as princess of Wales, and recognized as heiress and successor to the kingdom (as has been said). How astonishing that Henry's father, King Henry VII, had ordered the death of Edward Plantagenet—son of the duke of Clarence, nephew to King Edward IV, and brother of Margaret, countess of Salisbury (mother to Cardinal Reginald Pole)—not for any crime, but merely to assure the succession of the crown to his son and his heirs,[4] but Henry VIII came to debase this lineage and became an unnatural father to his daughter, who was defended by Reginald

---

1   Sander, *De origine ac progressu*, 113–19.

2   On June 28, 1533, Eustace Chapuys wrote to Charles V that "the King had resolved for certain considerations, and in order to avoid inconveniences of all sorts, that queen Katharine should henceforwards relinquish that title. For that very reason the King would no longer in future make for the Queen's maintenance such provision as he had made up to this day." *CSPS*, 4.2:1091.

    Less than a week later, a royal proclamation of July 2 declared "the said Lady Catherine should not from henceforth have or use the name, style, title, or dignity of Queen of this realm, nor be in any wise reputed, taken, accepted, or written by the name of Queen of this realm, but by the name, style, title and dignity of Princess Dowager, which name she ought to have because she was lawfully and perfectly married and accoupled with the said Prince Arthur." *TRP*, 1:210.

    For 25 Hen. VIII. c. 28, the law stripping Catherine of the title of queen, see *SR*, 3:484–86.

3   Ribadeneyra (following Sander) errs here: when Mary's household was dissolved in late 1533, she was actually sent to join that of her half-sister, the infant Elizabeth, at Hatfield. Edwards, *Mary I*, 35–37.

4   Edward, earl of Warwick (1475–99), the only surviving son of George, duke of Clarence. His superior claim to the throne threatened Henry VII, who imprisoned and eventually executed him, ostensibly for plotting to overthrow him. Christine Carpenter, "Edward, styled earl of Warwick (1475–1499)," in *ODNB*, 17:806.

© KONINKLIJKE BRILL NV, LEIDEN, 2017 | DOI 10.1163/9789004323964_031

Pole, nephew of the man Henry VII had slain to establish the succession! Who would have believed a father would turn against his own daughter, or that his enemy should defend her? This Pole did in the four books he wrote to Henry VIII on the unity of the Church.[5] Not satisfied with this, Henry replaced the queen's ladies with his own guards and spies, so as know who entered her house and what was done there, whom she trusted, who advised her, who were her friends—all of whom he jailed and harassed on specious pretexts and charges. And to frighten and cow the others, he first seized the queen's confessor, a worthy brother of the Observant Franciscans called John Forest,[6] and then three other priests, learned theologians who had defended the queen's cause before the legates.

And as he waxed ever more audacious and ever more frenzied, our Lord permitted that, on September 7, 1533 a daughter was born to him, named Elizabeth (the present queen), whom, on account of the all the blood she has spilled and all the blood shed in her name, some have justly called "the daughter of blood." Even at the time of the birth, many doubted whether this was King Henry's child, for everyone knew of Anne's sinfulness and her different lovers, with whom she was later sentenced to death. For this reason, the Princess Doña Mary, who knew many secrets through her mother the queen and through her mother's ladies, once queen never consented to recognize Elizabeth as her sister, nor as her father's daughter.[7] He had Elizabeth baptized with enormous

---

5   In the margin: "Pole, Book 3."
     Pole, *Defense*, 196–97.

6   Though Forest was a habitué of the Henrician court and did serve as one of Catherine's chaplains, there is no direct evidence for the tradition that the friar was the queen's confessor. Anne Dillon, "John Forest and Derfel Gadarn: A Double Martyrdom," *RH* 28, no. 1 (May 2006): 1–21, here 3.

7   In 1553, parliament passed an act (1 Mar. St. 2. c. 1) declaring illegitimate any child born to Henry by any woman other than Catherine of Aragon—i.e., Elizabeth. See *SR*, 4.1:200–01.
     During Henry's lifetime, Mary "was prepared, out of courtesy, to call her 'sister,' as she was accustomed to calling the definitely illegitimate Henry Fitzroy 'brother.' For her the two semi-siblings were in the same category." Edwards, *Mary I*, 36.
     Later, however, she dismissed Elizabeth as the "the illegitimate child of a criminal who was punished as a public strumpet." Soon after Mary's accession to the throne, the imperial ambassador reported that "as for the Lady Elizabeth, the Queen would scruple to allow her to succeed because of her heretical opinions, illegitimacy and characteristics in which she resembled her mother." The Venetian ambassador recorded that only Philip's intervention had blocked "opposed and prevented the Queen's wish to have her disinherited and declared a bastard by Act of Parliament, and consequently ineligible to the throne." Jane Dormer recalled, "We see how different were the mothers of these two queens, and of the latter the father might be doubted, for Queen Mary would never call her sister, nor be persuaded she was her father's daughter. She would say she had the face and countenance of Mark Sweton

pomp and majesty in the church of the Franciscan friars at Greenwich:[8] an unhappy omen of the destruction and disaster that the entire Franciscan Order
was to suffer in England, as will be told farther on.

At this time, there was in England a nun called Elizabeth Barton, commonly
taken for a saint.[9] King Henry ordered her put to death, along with two Benedictines, two Franciscans, and two secular priests; the men for treating her as
a servant of God and claiming that she spoke by his Spirit, and the woman for
saying that Henry was no longer king, since he did not rule of God,[10] and that
his daughter Mary (treated like a bastard) would sit upon the royal throne—
which later came to pass, just as she had said.[11] The same day this sentence
was carried out, it was decreed that all the lords and noblemen of the realm
should swear before Archbishop Cranmer of Canterbury, Chancellor Audley,

---

[sic], who was a very handsome man." CSPS, vol. 11, p. 393. Gómez Suárez de Figueroa
y Córdoba, "The Count of Feria's Dispatch to Philip 11 of 14 November 1558," ed. and trans.
M.J. Rodríguez-Salgado and Simon Adams, Camden Miscellany fourth series, 29 (1984):
302–44, here 313. CSPV, 6:884, 1068. Clifford, Life of Jane Dormer, 80.

8   September 10, 1533.

9   Elizabeth Barton (c.1506–34), a Benedictine nun "renowned as a miracle worker and seer"
and famous as the "Holy Maid of Kent," was hanged as a traitor at Tyburn, on April 20,
1534, for her prophecies' criticisms of the king. Diane Watt, "Reconstructing the Word:
The Political Prophecies of Elizabeth Barton (1506–1534)," Renaissance Quarterly 50, no. 1
(Spring 1997): 136–63, here 136, 140.

10   Hosea 8:4.

11   Alongside Barton, the bill of attainder named Richard Master (d.1558), Barton's parish
priest; Edward Bocking (d.1534), a Benedictine monk of Christ Church, Canterbury, and
Barton's confessor; John Dering (d.1534), another Benedictine of Christ Church, who had
written a book in support of Barton; the friar Hugh Rich (d.1534), warden of Richmond
Priory; Henry Risby (1489–1534), warden of Greyfriars, Canterbury; and the priest Henry
Gold (d.1534). The entire group was executed at Tyburn on April 20, 1534, with the exception of Master, who was reprieved. Watt, "Reconstructing the Word," 136, 139n, 140,
154, 156. Diane Watt, "Barton, Elizabeth [called the Holy Maid of Kent, the Nun of Kent],
(c.1506–1534)," in ODNB, 4:201–04, here 203.

The bill of attainder alleged that "the seid Elizabeth subtylly and craftily [...] reveled
and shewed unto the seid Edward that she had knowledge by revelacion from God, that
God was highly displeased with our seid Soveraigne Lorde for the same mater, and in case
he [decisted] not from hys procedyngs in the seid devorse and separacion but pursued
the same and maryd agayn, that then within one moneth after suche marriage he shuld
no lenger be Kyne of this Realme, and in the reputacion of Almyghtie God shuld not be
a Kynge one day nor one houre [...] that the Kynges actes and procedyngs in the same
were ayenst holy scriptures and the pleasure of Almyghty God [...] the seid Elizabeth
shulde have by revelacion of God that the seid Lady Katharyne shuld prospere and do
well, and that her issue the Lady Mary the Kynges doughter shuld prospere and reigne in
this Realme, and have many fryndes to susteyne and maynteyne her." SR, 3:449–50.

Secretary Cromwell, and the king's other councilors that the second marriage was lawful, that Elizabeth, born thereto, was the true heir to the kingdom, and that Princess Doña Mary was excluded as illegitimate.[12] From the day of this order, Queen Doña Catherine began to sicken and waste away markedly, never again enjoying even a day of health. And because the bishop of Rochester and Thomas More refused to swear, they were jailed; and because the Friars Minor publicly spoke out against the second marriage, the king became so infuriated with them that on August 11 he had every friar to be thrown out of their monasteries and placed in various prisons.[13] There were more than two hundred Franciscans imprisoned at one time: the chains and cells wrought to punish adulterers, murderers, and thieves were used to torture and destroy the servants of God. They also arranged for the entire kingdom to take the oath recognizing the king as the sovereign head of the Church: even the foreigners (of whom there were a great many then living in London) were to swear like the rest. When certain Spaniards then resident in the city learned of this, they turned to the imperial ambassador in hopes that he could avert this. By his advice, they fled London and stayed away for several days, until the ambassador came to an arrangement with Cromwell whereby the Spanish would not have to swear. In this way, they were liberated.[14]

---

12   See 26 Hen. 8. c. 2: Ibid., 3:471–74.

13   On August 11, 1534, Chapuys wrote to the emperor, "Out of the five convents of Minor Observant friars, three have already been closed, owing to their respective congregations having refused to swear to the statute against the Pope. The two remaining are every day expecting to be turned out." *CSPS*, 5.1:84.

A few weeks later, the ambassador reported that "All the Minor Observant friars of this kingdom have been expelled from their convents, owing to their having refused to take the oath against the authority of the Apostolic See. They have, moreover, been distributed among the several convents in the provinces, where they are locked up, put in chains, and worse treated than if they were prisoners; indeed they would much prefer being in irons than in the hands of those under whose power they now are." Ibid., 5.1:86.

14   "The Commissioners were thereupon sent all over the kingdom to administer the oaths to the King and everybody swore without hesitation, some through fear and some through inclination. In the city of London there were a great many foreigner of various nations, and they also were sent for. But the Spaniards, when they saw this, went to the Emperor's ambassador, who was called Estacio Capucho, and told him what had occurred, and he answered them, 'Gentlemen, my advice to you would be that you should leave the city for a few days until the fury blows over, and afterwards I will speak to Cromwell about it.' So all the Spaniards went away, some one way and some another, and were about twenty days absent. The Ambassador spoke to Cromwell [...] Then Cromwell sent a gentleman to tell them not to summon the Spaniards, and these returned to their houses. All the other foreigners were summoned, but what they swore need not be told, only that the Spaniards were free." Hume, *Chronicle*, 38.

Of the Parliament Convened to Approve the King's Marriage and to Destroy Religion[1]

Henry saw that his divorce from the queen was not as well received in the kingdom as he would have liked, and that all the pious, thoughtful, and prudent people took it very badly. Hoping to prevent or check the damage at its root, he took an insane course, utterly without measure. He decided to proceed no further in the business by means of edicts, but rather through the public authority and consensus of the entire realm, and, certain that he could succeed in his plan (as kings generally do), he convened a parliament on November 3, 1534. He knew that the foremost churchmen were on his side, that various other bishops would not resist, that Rochester was in prison, and that he could easily exclude from the parliament any others who might object, or bend them to his will by promises, threats, and suasion. Of the lords and knights he likewise controlled a large portion, for he had exalted many of them, and he was certain that they, and those others who were infected with Lutheran heresy (no small number), would not do—or even desire—anything but what he ordered. There were two preeminent noblemen: one was Charles Brandon, duke of Suffolk, the king's brother-in-law (married to his sister, Mary),[2] a degenerate, soulless man, very similar to Henry in his lifestyle—his family and his posterity were devastated and destroyed in divine chastisement. The other was Thomas Howard, duke of Norfolk, a good soldier and a Catholic, yet one who, so as not to lose the king's favor, allowed himself to follow the current. However, our Lord did not permit him to enjoy much of the king's grace won through his double-dealing service, for a little later he was condemned to life imprisonment, while his firstborn son and heir to his house, known as the earl of Surrey, was beheaded at the king's command.[3]

---

1 Sander, *De origine ac progressu*, 119–25.

2 Mary, the fifth child of Henry VII, had been queen consort of France, as the wife of Louis XII. Soon after her husband died, she decided to preclude another royal match by secretly marrying Charles Brandon in February 1515. David Loades, "Mary (1495–1533)," in *ODNB*, 37:68–70.

3 Henry Howard (*c.*1516–47), eldest son of Thomas Howard, third duke of Norfolk, was known as the earl of Surrey, although technically never a peer in his own right. Victims of the aging Henry's paranoia, father and son were arrested as traitors in December 1546, and Surrey was beheaded on January 19, 1547. Susan Brigden, "Howard, Henry, styled earl of Surrey (1516/ 17–1547)," in *ODNB*, 28:361–66, here 361, 364–65.

By such ministers and wicked methods Henry ensured that the parliament enacted everything he desired. First, that his daughter Princess Doña Mary was deprived of her titles, dignities, and claim to the throne, which were given to Elizabeth, Anne Boleyn's daughter.[4] Second, that the pope was permanently stripped of all power and jurisdiction over the English and Irish, and that thenceforth it would be high treason and a breach of *lèse-majesté* for anyone to give the Apostolic See the least honor or respect in the world.[5] Third, that only the king was to be regarded as the supreme head of the Church of England, the errors, heresies, and abuses of which were to be corrected by his limitless authority,[6] and that, as said head, he was to be paid the annuities of all benefices for the first year, as well as a tenth of all income from preferments and ecclesiastical dignities.[7] Fourth, that no Roman pontiff should be called "pope," only "bishop." And he ordered this law to be enforced with such rigor that any person found to have a book in which the name of "pope" had not been erased was condemned to death! From every calendar, index, table of the works of the holy fathers, from the entirety of canon law, from every Scholastic theologian, the title "pope" was expunged. Not content with this, he ordered anyone who possessed the works of Saint Cyprian, Saint Ambrose, Saint Jerome, Saint Augustine, and any other sacred doctor or scholar of the Church—what unbelievable insanity!—to write at the beginning that if anything in those works defended or affirmed the primacy of the Roman pontiff, they renounced and

---

4   "An Acte ratyfienge the othe that everie of the Kynges Subjectes hath taken and shall hereaft[er] be bounde to take for due obs[er]vacyon of the acte made for the suretie of the successyon of the Kynges Highnes in the Crowne of the Realme" (26 Hen. 8. c. 2), though it did not mention Mary by name, demanded an oath of loyalty "to the Kynges Majestye and to his heires of his body of his moost dere and entierly belovyd laufull wyfe Quene Anne begotten & to be." *SR*, 3:492–93.

5   In his *Acts and Monuments* (first edition 1563), John Foxe (*c*.1516–87) reproduces "The King's proclamation for the abolishing of the usurped power of the Pope," issued June 9, 1534, which banned any recognition of papal authority in England. John Foxe, *The Acts and Monuments of John Foxe*. ed. Stephen Reed Cattley, 8 vols. (London: R.B. Seeley and W. Burnside, 1838), 5:69–71.

6   "An Acte conc[er]nynge the Kynges Highnes to be supreme heed of the Churche of Englande & to have auctoryte to refourme & redresse all errours heresyes & abuses yn the same" (26 Hen. 8. c. 1) declared "that the Kyng our Sov[er]aign Lorde his heires and successours Kynges of this Realme shalbe takyn acceptyd & reputed the onely supreme [heed] in erthe of the Churche of England [...] And that our said Sov[er]aigne Lorde his heires and succesours Kynges of this Realme shall have full power & auctorite frome tyme to tyme to visite represse redresse reforme ordre correct restrayne and amende all suche errours heresies abuses offences contemptes and enormyties what so ever they be." *SR*, 3:492.

7   26 Hen. 8. c. 3. See ibid., 3:493–99.

denied that word, sentence, and argument. He likewise prohibited anyone from interacting or communicating by letter with the pope or with his ministers outside England.[8] Besides this, in all oratories, churches, and monasteries where litanies and other prayers were said, he ordered the cessation of the supplication on behalf of the pope, and put in its place a curse against him.[9]

Desiring companions in his wickedness, he sent ambassadors to the king of France to persuade him to do the same; the Most Christian King did not deign to give them ear. They continued on to Germany, in hopes of concluding an alliance with the Lutheran princes. But though they praised the king for having abandoned obedience to the pope, they considered the cause of the break so wicked and so unseemly that they refused join with Henry.[10] Thus despised and deserted by all outside his realm, he ordered those within to produce sermons and books to defend the newfangled ecclesiastical authority he had usurped. Thus it was that he again put pressure on Reginald Pole, sending parliament's decisions to him at Padua, along with amicable, generous letters, warmly asking him to write in favor of the statutes and decrees and of his new authority (as his kinsman and his friend, obligated by the many favors received at his hands). But Pole wrote four truly elegant books on the unity of the Church, which he dedicated and sent to the king, arranging for them to be delivered to his hands, learnedly lambasting the king's false supremacy and his sins,

---

8   25 Hen. 8. c. 19, §4. See ibid., 3:461.

9   Henry's edict of June 9, 1534 required bishops "to cause all manner of prayers, orisons, rubrics, canons of mass-books, and all other books in the churches, wherein the said bishop of Rome is named, or his presumptuous and proud pomp and authority preferred, utterly to be abolished, eradicated and raised out, and his name and memory to be never more (except to his contumely and reproach) remembered, but perpetually suppressed and obscured: and finally, to desist and leave out all such articles as be in the general sentence which is usually accustomed to be read four times in the year, and do tend to the glory and advancement of the bishop of Rome, his name, title, and jurisdiction." Foxe, *Acts and Monuments*, 5:70.

     Cranmer in particular seems to have expended no little effort in enforcing this point. He wrote to Cromwell on June 12, 1538, that he had purged the pope's name from his library at Croydon, and again on January 11, 1539, informing him that "I have committed two priests unto the castle of Canterbury, for permitting the bishop of Rome's name in their books." Thomas Cranmer, *Miscellaneous Writings and Letters of Thomas Cranmer, Archbishop of Canterbury*, ed. John Edmund Cox, Parker Society Publications 16 (Cambridge: Cambridge University Press, 1846), 369–71, 387.

10   In the margin: "So says Cochlaeus in his book against Morison."
     Cochlaeus, *Scopa*, sig. Biv^v.

and exhorting him to repentance.[11] The king took this response deeply to heart: he stormed and raged, roaring like a lion, condemned Pole as a traitor, guilty of *lèse-majesté*, and worked to procure his death by various means.

---

11   In 1535, Pole received letters from Henry seeking his (favorable) opinion on "causes of matrimony and concerning the authority of the Pope." In the autumn of that year, Pole set to work on the book that would become *De unitate*, a copy of which was presented to Henry in early summer 1536. Pole, *Defense*, xv–xvii.

Of the Inhuman Persecution the King Initiated against All Religious[1]

The king's deeds were so beyond all reason or justice that no sane, impartial person could think them anything but awful—and the saintlier and more exemplary their lives, the more they abhorred them. Henry knew this and it tormented him. For, sinful and frenzied though he was in his life and rule (as we have seen), he desired to be so but not to seem so, at least to good men and the servants of God. In those days, there were many religious orders in England, with numerous noteworthy servants of our Lord, renowned in sanctity and learning; but there were three of particular prominence: the Carthusians, the Observant Franciscans, and the Bridgettines. And so Henry resolved to assail and assault these orders, in hopes that when their members were conquered and reduced to obedience, all the others would yield and submit. We see in this the providence of our Lord, who allowed him to exhaust his artillery in attacking the very strongest: unable to breach or overthrow the impregnable force of truth, he would be left all the more abashed and confused, while the holy religious would triumph with yet greater glory, giving in their struggle an illustrious testimony to our true and sacred faith.

And so, on April 29, 1535, three venerable Carthusian priors were summoned, the decisions of parliament were put to them, and they were commanded to acknowledge and swear to the king's supreme headship of the Church. They answered that the law of God commanded the opposite. And Cromwell (who, as we have said, was the king's vicegerent in spirituals) said, with utter disdain, "You must swear, entirely, clearly, and distinctly, whether or not the law of God permits." When they refused, saying that the Catholic Church taught no such thing, the damnable vicegerent retorted, "Don't give me any nonsense about the Church! Will you swear, or not?" As they preferred to displease their king rather than their God, they were sentenced to death, without being defrocked, in the Carthusian habit—as a greater disrespect and insult to religion.[2] Accompanying them were John Hale, a priest and vicar,

---

1   Sander, *De origine ac progressu*, 125–30.

2   Sander takes this story from Maurice Chauncy's (*c.*1509–81) *Historia aliquot nostri saeculi martyrum* (1550). Ribadeneyra draws on other parts of the text, and was probably familiar with its 1583 printing at Burgos. "After they had been imprisoned for a week, many members

full of zeal, and Reynolds [*Reginaldo*], a noted theologian and Bridgettine monk, a man illustrious for his piety and learning.[3] Standing at the foot of the gallows, he urged the crowd to unceasing prayer for the king, lest he who had been a Solomon in piety and wisdom at the beginning of his reign also end like him, deceived and corrupted by women.[4]

He died, as Cardinal Pole writes, with such happiness and steadfastness that when the noose was placed around his neck, it seemed a necklace of precious stones.[5] These five died in the same place, outside the city of London, on May 4; to further intimidate the Carthusians, the quartered remains of one of them, the prior of London, were placed at the monastery gate, while two laymen were made superiors of the house, to pervert the young monks by flattery and threats. These laymen lived in luxury and overabundance, while they murdered several of the monks through starvation, and abused and harassed the rest with blows and insults. Seeing that they defended themselves with the authority of Holy Scripture and the Church Fathers, they stripped them of every book—but the Lord taught them what to do and what to say. Perceiving that nothing came of this, the heretics ordered another three Carthusian priests seized and bound

---

of the king's council came to them, to put to them parliament's decree abrogating the authority of the pope, and falsely, violently, and criminally usurping his supreme power, and abolishing all external powers, jurisdictions, and obediences, to whatever person or entity they may have been owed or promised. Only the king and his people were to be obeyed, and the king himself acknowledged, regarded, and affirmed as supreme head of the Church, in spiritual and in temporal matters. And when our fathers replied that they would confer together as to whether and how far divine law would permit this, he [*sc.* Cromwell] declared, 'I will admit of no exceptions, whether divine law permits or no: you must swear entirely, fully, and sincerely in your heart, and affirm it with a public, spoken oath, and maintain it firmly.' Our most blessed fathers answered that the Catholic Church had always held and taught otherwise. He retorted, 'I care nothing for the Church: will you submit, or not?'" Maurice Chauncy, *Historia aliquot nostri sæculi martyrum cùm pia, tum lectu iucunda, nunc denuo typis excusa* (Burgos: Felipe de Junta, 1583), sigs. Iiiiᵛ–Iiᵛ.

3 In April 1535, three Carthusian priors—John Houghton (*c.*1486–1535), Robert Lawrence (*c.*1485–1535), and Augustine Webster (1488–1535)—along with Richard Reynolds (*c.*1492–1535), a Bridgettine monk and a Cambridge-educated scholar of great renown, were arrested for treason. On May 4, they were hanged at Tyburn, together with John Hale (d.1535), the vicar of Isleworth (the parish responsible for Syon Abbey). Virginia R. Bainbridge notes the "unprecedented step" of hanging them still in their habits, without having been degraded. Virginia R. Bainbridge, "Reynolds, Richard [St Richard Reynold] (*d.* 1535)," in *ODNB*, 46:567–68. See Book 1 Figure 27.1.

4 1 Kings 11:3–4.

5 In the margin: "Book 3, *Defense of the Unity of the Church* [*De unione Ecclesiæ.*]." Pole, *Defense*, 253.

A. Pro primatu Sancti Petri, ciusq, successorum in Sancta Romana ecclesia septem Angli Carthusiani monachi saeuè laniati sunt.

B. Nquem alij eius ordinis carceris paedore et fame enecti. Cum primis passi sunt Reginaldus ordinis S. Brigit ʒ Ioānes Hanlus sacerdos.

C. Duo alij Carthusiani Eboráci catenis ferreis è sublimi trabe uiui pendent, donec ossibus dissolutis dilabuntur et complures alij aliàs eam ob rem dilacerantur, Henrico VIII. Angliae rege iubente Anno M.D.XXXV. 28

FIGURE 27.1   *The martyrdoms of the Carthusians of London and York, Richard Reynolds, and John Hale.*
Giovanni Battista Cavalieri, *Ecclesiae anglicanae trophaea sive sanctorum martyrum qui pro Christo catholicaeque fidei veritate asserenda antiquo recentiorique persecutionum tempore mortem in Anglia subierunt, passiones Romae in collegio Anglico per Nicolaum Circinianum depictae: Nuper autem per Io. Bap. de Cavalleriis aeneis typis repraesentatae* (Rome: Ex officina Bartolomeo Grassi, 1584). NE1666 .C57 1584 OVERSIZE, John J. Burns Library, Boston College.

stiffly upright, with iron rings at the throat, arms, and feet, so that they could not make the slightest movement. They were dragged on hurdles through the main streets and squares of London, then hanged on the gallows by a thick cord so that they did not suffocate too quickly. Before they expired, the rope was cut and they were allowed to fall. The executioner then hacked off their natural parts and pulled out their innards—all while the men were still alive— and threw these in the fire. Lastly, they were beheaded and quartered. After being boiled (to make them last longer), the remains were placed along the major roads.[6] They were killed such that the companion who followed stood watching the tortures and murder of his fellow, who was dispatched before his very eyes—in this way they tried to torment and terrify them even more. But all were so steadfast in the strength and spirit of the Lord that no alteration appeared in their complexion, nor weakness in their words, nor any sign of fear in their countenance or behavior. Two further Carthusian fathers, as a great favor and grace, were hanged without torture on May 12.[7] Not content with this, the savage tyrant also arrested and jailed ten more saintly Carthusians, handling them like bandits, with such brutal and barbarous cruelty that they all died in prison through squalor, hunger, and maltreatment, except for one, who came to the same end as his sainted companions. Cromwell was deeply grieved that so many had died in prison without greater suffering.[8]

---

6   Sander identifies these men as the English Carthusians Humphrey Middlemore (d.1535); William Exmew (d.1535); and Sebastian Newgate (1500–35), all three executed at Tyburn on June 19, 1535.

7   Sander identifies these two as the Carthusians John Rochester (c.1498–1537) and James Walworth (d.1537).

8   In 1535, Cromwell began to press the Carthusians of the London Charterhouse to acknowledge the royal supremacy. Every monk who refused was arrested; six were executed at Tyburn, and the rest left to rot in Newgate prison, dying of starvation and ill-treatment. Loades points out that Cromwell made every effort to effect the monks' submission: "just about the last thing that he needed was martyrs to the Old Faith. Nevertheless that was what he got." Loades, *Thomas Cromwell*, 109–11.

Of the Illustrious Men Thomas More and John of Rochester, and of the Latter's Martyrdom[1]

Throughout the realm, the eyes and hearts of all were turned to the imprisoned bishop of Rochester and Thomas More, to see what the king would do to them and how they would conduct themselves in their struggle and trial. The king, who knew well the reputation of these two renowned men, was extremely keen to win them—especially More, whom he considered more important because he was a layman. Thomas More was born in London to a prominent family, and was learned in all subjects, being especially eloquent in Greek and Latin; he spent almost forty years in the government of the nation and served many times as a royal ambassador. He had borne great responsibilities and held distinguished posts, carrying out each to the highest standards of excellence and integrity.[2] Furthermore, although he had been married twice, with many children, he was so far from covetousness that his property did not amount to a hundred ducats in yearly income.[3] He always took the greatest care to uphold justice and religion and to combat, with all his influence, his learning, and his writings, the heresies that had crept out of Germany to infect the kingdom of England in secret: he had distinguished himself as the foremost among the king's ministers in curbing and controlling them. For this, just as he was loved and respected by all good men, he was hated and attacked by the wicked. While in prison he had been stripped of his offices and goods, but he never showed any sign of sorrow, pain, or loss of spirit; on the contrary, he showed utter joy, saying that the entire world is nothing but a prison and a jail, into which we are cast because of sin and from which each is called at the hour

---

1 Sander, *De origine ac progressu*, 130–37.

2 Ribadeneyra details More's long public career at home and abroad in another chapter added in the 1595 edition, Book 1, Chapter 30a. See also Cathy Curtis, "More's Public Life," in *The Cambridge Companion to Thomas More*, ed. George M. Logan, Cambridge Companions to Religion (Cambridge: Cambridge University Press, 2011), 69–92.

3 In his *Life of Sir Thomas More*, written during Mary's reign, More's son-in-law, William Roper (1496–1578) recalls this admission from his father-in-law: "'Then will I,' said he, 'shew my poor mind unto you. I have been brought up,' quoth he, 'at Oxford, at an Inn of Chancery, at Lincoln's Inn and also in the King's Court, and yet have I in yearly revenue at this present left me little above an hundred pounds by the year.'" William Roper and Nicholas Harpsfield, *Lives of Saint Thomas More*, Everyman's Library (London: Dent, 1963), 27.

© KONINKLIJKE BRILL NV, LEIDEN, 2017 | DOI 10.1163/9789004323964_034

of their death to hear their sentence, and that he gave thanks to our Lord that his cell was neither as harsh nor as cramped as others,' since one was always to choose the least of all evils.[4] Henry sent many of his friends to visit this learned and exemplary man, to bring him to the king's opinion; seeing that all his might and cunning could not overcome him, Henry's heart was filled with anxieties and troubles and he began to ask what would most benefit him: to leave his mortal enemy and the leading critic of his adultery still breathing, or to kill him and incur the displeasure of the entire kingdom.

In the end, Henry decided to begin with eliminating Rochester—for he had learned that Pope Paul III had made him a cardinal while in prison,[5] and he harbored no hope of being able to sway him—and to see if he could shock and weaken Thomas More with his friend's death. With this decision, the bishop of Rochester was summoned to judgment on June 22, 1535, by now hoary with age and nearly moribund. Surrounded by soldiers and hangmen, he was brought from the Tower of London to Westminster, partly by horse and partly by a barge on the river Thames (he could not go by foot on account of his advanced age and weakness).[6] Because he refused to acknowledge the ecclesiastical primacy of the king, he was condemned to be drawn, hanged, and disemboweled, just as the three Carthusian fathers had been (as we related in the previous chapter). But they subsequently mitigated this penalty, fearing (so they say) that given the saintly bishop's weakness, if he were dragged he would die before arriving at the place of punishment.[7] As he was being carried thither, when he could see it from afar, the saintly old man joyously threw away the staff he held and said, "Feet, perform your office, for only a short way remains to you."[8] Once there, he raised his eyes to heaven and spoke a few brief and solemn words to

---

4 The idea of the world as a prison, with God as jailer, is expounded in More's *Dialogue of Comfort against Tribulation*: see Thomas More, *The Yale Edition of the Complete Works of St. Thomas More*, 15 vols. (New Haven: Yale University Press, 1963), volume 12, Chapters 19 and 20.

5 Paul III made Fisher a cardinal in May 1535. "Biographical Dictionary—Consistory of May 21, 1535," in *CHRC*.

6 June 22, 1535 was the date of Fisher's execution; his trial had concluded some five days earlier. Dowling, *Fisher of Men*, 157.

7 "He was so weakly at the period of his execution as scarcely to be able to crawl from his prison in the Bell Tower to Tower Hill, so that a chair was carried at his side on which he rested thrice on the way." John Bruce, "Observations on the Circumstances Which Occasioned the Death of Fisher, Bishop of Rochester," *Archaeologia* 25 (January 1832): 61–99, here 77.

8 Probably following Sander, this detail also appears in Thomas Stapleton's life of Thomas More: see Thomas Stapleton, *The Life and Illustrious Martyrdom of Sir Thomas More, Formerly Lord Chancellor of England (Part III of "Tres Thomae," Printed at Douai, 1588)*, trans. Philip E. Hallett (London: Burns, Oates & Washbourne, 1928), 210.

the crowd, and then prayed to our Lord for the king and the kingdom, and said *Te Deum laudamus, te Dominum confitemur*. Finishing the hymn, he lowered his head to the blade; he gave his soul to God; he received a martyr's crown.[9] His head was placed on a pike at the gates of London, in the view of the whole city, but a miracle occurred: each day it appeared fresher, more beautiful, and of a more venerable aspect—and so the king ordered it removed.

This man was one of the saintliest, most learned, and most diligent pastors, perfect in every virtue, Christendom then possessed. In the days of King Henry VII, he was so esteemed and respected by the entire kingdom that the king's mother took him as her counselor and confessor, and by his advice she founded two leading colleges at the University of Cambridge, where he was later chancellor. There and at the University of Oxford he established lectures in theology, which by his efforts and care flourished throughout England.[10] King Henry VII himself named him bishop of Rochester, solely on account of his virtues and merits, and without favor or conditions.[11] Because that bishopric was not as rich as he deserved,[12] Henry VIII had wanted to transfer him to a more remunerative see, but could never get his consent—for the saintly prelate said that that church had been his first wife, he had labored with her, and he would not trade her for anything.[13] For he deemed it no small mercy of God to be able on the day of his death to render a good account of the little

---

9   For a sixteenth-century depiction of the scene, see Book 1 Figure 29.1.

10   Henry VIII's paternal grandmother, Margaret Beaufort (1443–1509), countess of Richmond and Derby. Fisher became her confessor in the mid-1490s. In 1502, under his direction, Beaufort funded the Lady Margaret professorships in divinity, one at each university. In 1506, she founded Christ's College, Cambridge, while her will provided the impetus for the foundation of St John's College, Cambridge (established in 1511). Fisher was elected chancellor of Cambridge in 1504, serving until his death. Richard Rex, "Fisher, John [St John Fisher] (c.1469–1535)," in *ODNB*, 19:685–93, here 685. Bradshaw and Duffy, *Humanism, Reform and the Reformation*, 6, 28, 58. Michael K. Jones and Malcolm G. Underwood, *The King's Mother: Lady Margaret Beaufort, Countess of Richmond and Derby* (Cambridge: Cambridge University Press, 1992), 208–09.

11   Henry VII wrote to his mother about his plans to appoint her confessor to a bishopric, "For non other cause but for the grate and singular virtue that I know and se in hym as well in conyng and natural wisdom, and specially for his good and vertuouse lyving." Bruce, "Observations," 62.

12   Rochester was "the poorest and one of the smallest of English dioceses." Bradshaw and Duffy, *Humanism, Reform and the Reformation*, 3.

13   A contemporary life of Fisher wrote in a similar vein: "No royal authority could ever sway him to allow himself to be transferred to a greater and richer church. Truly, he refused to desert the spouse that had been his first, and in which he had labored so much for its beautification and augmentation." Pocock, *Records of the Reformation*, 2:553–54.

flock with which he had been entrusted.[14] Truly, in these matters the reckoning will be more severe than anyone imagines; no one will be safer than he who had fewer sheep and fewer pastures to account for. From the responsibilities of his little bishopric, he produced more substance than he would have from a richer and a greater. Henry VIII had loved and respected Rochester above all other mortals, saying publicly (as Cardinal Pole writes) that he regarded him as the most learned theologian he had ever known.[15] But later, spurred by his senseless passion, he had him arrested (as has been said), and when he learned that the pope had given the prisoner a cardinal's hat, he instructed the magistrates to ask whether he had arranged this or known of it. He replied that he had desired neither that honor nor any other in his life—much less at that moment, being the age he was, imprisoned, and at death's door.[16] He wrote superbly against the heretics of the time, with incredible clarity and force, and it is even said that he was the author of the book on the seven sacraments attributed to Henry, which he later defended with the highest skill. He led his church for thirty-three years,[17] and through his saintly decrees and unending vigils, studies, and fasts, the alms and works of a true and holy priest, he so nurtured it that he was loved and revered by all as a genuine prelate and man of God. For he left neither jail nor hospital, beggar nor invalid untouched or unaided by his counsel, generosity, and presence.

Afterwards, when they arrested the bishop, the officers of the law confiscated all his goods. Supposing that an old man, having been bishop so many years, would have piled up a substantial hoard, they eagerly wrenched open his coffers in search of gold. Finding a sealed chest, sturdily shut with bars of iron, they smashed it open to see if they could find what they so desired. What they found was a hairshirt, a scourge, and various other instruments the saintly man used to afflict and punish himself (as old as he was, and weakened by so many labors!), as well as a few pennies he would give to the poor after he had completed his penance. So they were cheated of their vain hopes, at once awed and unnerved. This glorious confessor lived for fifteen long months in an inhuman cell, wasting away though he was with age and the labors, cares, and penances

---

14   Heb. 13:17.

15   In the margin: "Book 1, *Defense of the Unity of the Church* [*de unione Ecclesiæ*]."
        Pole, *Defense*, 43.

16   Interrogated in the Tower on the matter, Fisher affirmed "that yf the Cardinall's hatt were layed at his feete he wolde not stoupe to take it up, he did set so little by it." A transcription of Fisher's interrogation on June 12, 1535 is printed in Bruce, "Observations," 95–99, here 99.

17   Actually thirty-one years (1504–35).

of his long life—well beyond anyone's expectations.[18] It seems that our Lord preserved him by a special miracle, so that his illustrious martyrdom and the spilling of his immaculate blood would defend the rights and preeminence of the Apostolic See against the tyranny and violence of so accursed a king.

---

18   "I judged that he would not have more than a year to live, even if he employed the most admirable care in preserving his health in his own home. But I heard afterward that when he was summoned to London to be confined in prison, his diminishing strength had made him very weak for some time during the journey. Now, however, since it is clear that he was able to remain alive for 15 months in the filth of that offensive jail, does not everyone recognize that it was the hand of God surpassing nature that extended his life in order to make your very great disgrace more evident?" Pole, *Defense*, 285.

Rowland Lee wrote to Thomas Cromwell on April 18, 1534, "Truly the man is nigh going and doubtless cannot continue, unless the king and his council be merciful unto him; for the body cannot bear the clothes on his back, as knoweth God." Bruce, "Observations," 72–73.

Fisher himself wrote to Cromwell on December 22, 1534, "Forthermo[r] I byseche yow to be gode M[r]. unto me in my necessite, for I have nather shert nor shete nor yet other clothes that ar necessary for me to wear but that be ragged and rent to shamefully. Nothwithstandyng I might easily suffer that if thei wold keep my body warm. But my dyet also God knows how sclendar itt is att meny tymes. And now in myn age my sthomak may not away but with a few kynd of meatts, which if I want I decaye forthwith, and fall in to coafes and disseasis of my bodye, and kan not keep myself in health." Ibid., 93–94.

BOOK 1, CHAPTER 29

The Martyrdom of Thomas More[1]

The imprisoned Thomas More soon learned of his holy companion Rochester's death, even though the king had forbidden anyone to tell him. Fearing that his sins would deny him the crown of martyrdom, he turned unto our Lord with a heart full of grief and a face full of tears, saying, "I confess, my Lord, that I do not deserve such glory, I am neither so just nor so holy as your servant Rochester, whom you have chosen, among all those of this kingdom, as a man dear to your heart. Yet, O good Lord, regard not my deserts, but rather your infinite mercy: if it may be, make me a sharer in your cup, in your cross, in your glory." More spoke this with great feeling and anguish.

Those who did not hear his words speculated that he had quailed in the face of the fear of death, imagining that he chose to relent and submit to the will of the king. At the king's command, many people came to his cell to sway him, among them his own wife, Alice, who tried to dissuade him from casting himself and his children into perdition. He asked her, "Madam, how many years do you think I have left to live?" She responded, "Twenty years, my lord, if it please God." Then he said, "And so, madam, you would have me trade eternity for twenty years? If you should say twenty thousand years, you would say much—and yet, you would say nothing at all, for it is nothing, compared with eternity."[2] The servants of Satan, seeing that they could make no dent in that soul, an unshakeable rock in its steadfastness, took away all his books and writing implements, so that he could neither commune with the dead nor communicate with the living. Even so, he wrote two books while in prison: one (in English) on consolation in adversity,[3] and the other (in Latin) on the Passion of Christ our Lord.[4]

On the first day of July, after he had been jailed for approximately fourteen months, he was brought from the Tower of London to his trial. Questioned about the law passed while he had been in prison, which stripped all authority from the pope and gave it to the king,[5] he answered with tremendous deliberation, acuity, and firmness. In the end, he was accused of having written to

---

1 Sander, *De origine ac progressu*, 137–47.
2 This episode also appears in Stapleton, *Thomas More*, 177.
3 *A Dialogue of Comfort against Tribulation.* See volume 12 of More, *Complete Works.*
4 *De tristitia Christi.* See volume 14 of Ibid.
5 The First Act of Supremacy (26 Hen. 8. c. 1), passed in November 1534: see *SR*, 3:492.

Rochester inciting him against the terms of the law,[6] and he was condemned to death. And his sentence was to be drawn, hanged and allowed to fall from the gallows, disemboweled while yet breathing, beheaded, and cut into quarters, which, along with his head, were to be placed wherever the king commanded. This was the sentence given against More for no other crime than having at first kept silent, and then having spoken the truth to the king, for having been a faithful minister and loyal counselor to him, for having honored God and his conscience. However, this harsh, inhuman sentence was later moderated and changed to that of beheading, more because it is the custom of the kingdom of England to behead persons distinguished in blood or rank who are to be executed, rather than because of any clemency and benignity of the king's.[7]

At this he joyfully declared, "By the grace of God, I have always been a Catholic and I have never strayed from the communion and obedience of the pope, whose power I hold to be rooted in divine right, legitimate, praiseworthy, and necessary, though you have rashly sought to curtail and abolish it with your law. I have studied this material for seven years, and turned over many tomes to understand it the better, and to this day I have found no author of sanctity and weight, neither ancient nor modern, who holds that in spiritual matters, which touch upon God, a secular man—even a prince—could be the head and superior of ecclesiastics, who have such things in their charge.[8] What is

---

6   More's indictment read, "And on May 12, More maliciously wrote to Bishop John Fisher, consenting to Fisher's denial of the supremacy, telling him of his own silence, and calling the act a two-edged sword." Kelly, Karlin, and Wegemer, *Thomas More's Trial*, 179.

7   This passage was added in the 1595 edition.

     "'Our sentence is that Thomas More shall be taken back from this place by William Kingston, the Constable, to the Tower and thence shall be dragged right through the City of London as far as the gallows at Tyburn. There he shall be hanged, cut down while yet alive, ripped up, his bowels and the parts set up in such places as the King shall designate.' Such was the noble sentence pronounced against Sir Thomas More as a penalty for keeping silent. Such was the condemnation of one who had rendered the highest services to King and State, because he would not be untrue to his conscience. Such was the honourable reward conferred upon a faithful Councillor who had nobly served his King, because he would not give approval to filthy lust or barter his honor for gain. This ferocious sentence, which was usually carried out upon only the very worst criminals, was indeed afterwards changed to the milder one of simple beheading. But this was rather because the Kings of England are accustomed to choose this manner of execution for those who are illustrious by birth or office, than through any clemency on the part of Henry." Stapleton, *Thomas More*, 195.

8   In a letter of August 12, 1535, Nikolaus von Schönberg, cardinal-priest and archbishop of Capua (1472–1537) described More's declaration to Marino Ascanio Caracciolo, cardinal-deacon and bishop of Catania (1478–1538): "For the past seven years, I have done nothing

more, I say that this decree you have made was vilely done, for it is contrary to the oath you have sworn not to attempt anything against the Catholic Church, which is undivided and unique throughout all of Christendom, and you have no authority to enact laws, decrees, or accords repugnant to the peace and harmony of the universal Church.[9] This is my creed, this is my faith, in which I shall die, by the grace of God."

Barely had More uttered these words when all the judges began to stridently denounce him as a traitor to the king. In particular, the duke of Norfolk demanded of him, "Do you thus declare your ill will toward the king's majesty?" He responded, "My lord, I declare no ill will toward my king—only my faith and the truth. Whereas I have been so dedicated to the service of the king in everything else, I beg of our master that he be no more merciful to me, nor pardon me in the least, save to the extent I have been His Majesty's faithful and loving servant."[10] Then the chancellor challenged More, "Do you think yourself greater or wiser than all the bishops, abbots, and churchmen? Than all the nobility, knights, and lords? Than the entire Council, or, indeed, than the entire kingdom?" To this, the saint replied, "My lord, for each bishop you claim for your side, I have a hundred upon mine, and all of them saints. For your nobles and knights, I have all the lords and nobility of the martyrs and the confessors. For your single council (and God knows full well how you conducted it), one thousand years of ecumenical councils of God's own Church stand in my favor. And for your puny kingdom of England, the realms of France, Spain, Italy,

---

but study this case, and I have found no doctor, neither ecclesiastical nor secular, who holds that the temporal can or should be head over the spiritual." Thomas Wheeler, "An Italian Account of Thomas More's Trial and Execution," *Moreana* 26 (June 1970): 33–39, here 37.

    Cf. The Guildhall Report (a detailed contemporary account of the trial): "And I affirm that I have entirely dedicated the whole of seven years to consideration of this question, and I have found nothing, in any canonical doctor of the Church, to suggest that a layman either can or should be superior to the ecclesiastical order." Kelly, Karlin, and Wegemer, *Thomas More's Trial*, 192. My translation.

9   The Guildhall Report continues, "I add this besides, that your Statute was wrongly made, because you deliberately swore your oaths against the Church, which alone is whole and undivided through the whole Christian world. And you alone have no power to enact anything, without the consent of all other Christians, which is contrary to the unity and concord of the Christian religion." Other accounts modify this, to run "you swore that you would do nothing against the Church." Ibid., 193.

10   The Guildhall Report's account runs as follows: "Then the duke of Norfolk spoke up and said, 'More, now you are plainly revealing your mind's stubborn malice.' But More replied, 'What I say, I say because necessity compels me, for I wish to exonerate my conscience and not weigh down my soul. I call on God, the searcher of hearts, as witness.'" Ibid., 192.

and every other mighty province, principality, and kingdom all defend my honor."[11] Hearing More speak these words before the people, it seemed to the judges that they had achieved nothing, and they ordered him to be removed and sentenced him to death. This done, they returned him to his cell. Along the way, he was met by his beloved daughter, Margaret (whom he himself had taught Latin and Greek),[12] who sought his blessing and the kiss of peace. These father gave daughter with infinite affection and tenderness.[13]

Once back in his cell, More again gave himself up to prayer and contemplation, the Lord refreshing his saintly spirit with many exquisite and divine consolations; sometimes he took a sheet and wrapped himself in it, as though shrouding himself, and while living he contemplated and rehearsed what would befall him after death.[14] On the eve of his martyrdom, he wrote a letter to his daughter, Margaret (using a piece of coal, for he had no pen), in which he told her of his fervent desire to die and to see our Lord the next day, for it was

---

11   In the margin: "From Cardinal Pole, Book 3, and a letter written by the cardinal of Capua concerning the death of More."

       Wheeler, "Italian Account," 37.

       These specific arguments do not appear in Pole's *Defense*, but the cardinal does recount More's trial in considerable detail. See Pole, *Defense*, 217–20.

12   Though he did employ tutors, More took an active role in his children's education. John Guy asserts that Margaret was "the one person in England who knew Latin and Greek to the point where she could correct Erasmus." John Guy, *A Daughter's Love: Thomas & Margaret More* (London: Fourth Estate, 2008), 61–65, 67–71, 159.

13   This encounter is confirmed by the Guildhall Report and many other contemporary accounts: "Now when the trial was over and More was being led back to prison, before he had arrived at the prison, one of his daughters, named Margaret, rushing through the midst of the crowd of guards and soldiers, burning with great desire for her parent, taking no care for herself or the public place or those standing by, she barely broke through at last to her father, and there, embracing his neck with pitiable weeping she bore witness to her extreme grief. And after she held onto him tightly for some time, with sorrow completely overcoming her voice, her father with the guards' permission consoled her thus: 'Margaret, be of strong spirit, and do not torment yourself further; this is God's will. You have long known all the secrets of my mind.' Then, when her father had scarcely been taken away another ten or twelve steps, she again fell upon him and once more threw her arms around his neck. Thereupon More, shedding no tears, and showing no distress of countenance or mind, said only this, 'Farewell, and pray to God for the salvation of my soul.'" Kelly, Karlin, and Wegemer, *Thomas More's Trial*, 193–94.

14   The description of More's final meditations is added in the 1595 edition.

       "During those last days, within the narrow limits of his prison, he would walk up and down clad in a linen sheet, like a corpse about to be buried, and severely discipline himself." Stapleton, *Thomas More*, 208.

the day of the Octave of the prince of the Apostles, Saint Peter, and he was to die for affirming the saint's primacy and apostolic throne, as well as being the eve of the Translation of that glorious martyr Saint Thomas, who had always been his patron in life.[15] And it came to pass just as he desired. For on July 6 he suffered.

He left the Tower of London weak, pale, and wasted with the abuses of the long imprisonment he had suffered, with an overgrown beard and bearing a red cross in his hand, his eyes fixed on heaven, and dressed in the poor, vile clothing of one of his servants. For although he had intended to wear a comely garment of camlet that his friend, the Italian Antonio Bonvisi,[16] had sent him in prison, both to gratify his friend and to give it to the executioner in payment of the good deed he was to receive from him, so great was the jailer's greed or malice that he had taken it, forcing him to set out attired in the aforesaid manner. But for More this servile, shameful garb was utterly precious and gorgeous, as though for a wedding-feast, both because it made him poor like Christ, and because he was drinking the chalice of the Lord,[17] and he rejoiced in that garb for the marriage of the Lamb.[18] When they escorted him to his death, one woman, moved by compassion, offered him a cup of wine: he thanked her,

---

15   On July 5, 1535, More wrote to his daughter, "I cumber you, good Margaret, much, but I would be sorry, if it should be any longer than tomorrow, for it is Saint Thomas' Even and the Vtas [Octave] of Saint Peter and therefore tomorrow long I to go to God, it were a day very meet and convenient for me." More, *Last Letters*, 128.

16   Antonio Bonvisi (d.1558) was an Anglo-Italian merchant, based in London for much of the first half of the sixteenth century. Bonvisi himself was actually born in England sometime between 1470 and 1475, but he came from a distinguished Lucchese family. He remained a close friend and correspondent of Thomas More until the latter's death. C.T. Martin, "Bonvisi, Antonio [Anthony] (1470x75–1558)," rev. Basil Morgan, in *ODNB*, 6:575–76, here 575.

17   Matt. 20:22–23, 26:39; Mark 10:38–39; Luke 22:42; John 18:11; 1 Cor. 10:21.

18   "His beard was long and disordered, his face was pale and thin from the rigour of his confinement. He held in his hand a red cross and raised his eyes to heaven. His robe was of the very poorest and coarsest. He had decided to make his last journey in a better garment and to put on the gown of camlet, which Bonvisi had given him in prison, both to please his friend and to be able to give it to the executioner But through the avarice or wickedness of his gaoler, he, so great and renowned, he who had held such high office, went out clad in his servant's gown made of the basest material that we call frieze. But this was for Thomas More a fitting nuptial garment: by it he was made like to Christ, who willed to be poor: clothed in it he hastened to drink the Chalice of Christ and to celebrate the Nuptial Feast of the Lamb." Stapleton, *Thomas More*, 208–09.

      Cf. Rev. 19:7–9.

but refused to take it, saying that Christ our Redeemer had been offered gall in his blessed passion, not wine.[19]

Standing in the place of execution, having finished his prayers, he called those present to witness that he died in the Catholic faith, charging them to pray to God for the king and declaring that he died as a loyal subject of the king, but even more of God, who is the King of Kings. Then, when the executioner begged his pardon, he kissed him with love and tenderness and, having already commended him to his children and his friends, gave him a certain sum of money (imitating Saint Cyprian in this), and said these words: "Today you will do me a better turn than any man has yet done me, or could ever do me." And with that[20] he exposed his throat to the blade, at which the executioner severed that head of all justice, truth, and piety. All who were present wept; it seemed to them that he had beheaded not More alone, but the entire kingdom as well.[21] Henry, meanwhile, was highly pleased, as though it were the office of the head of the Church to lop off the heads of men renowned for learning and virtue. However, some write that he was gaming when they brought him the news of More's death, and that he turned to Anne Boleyn, seated beside him, and said, "You are the cause of this man's death," and at this rose from the

---

19   This account of the prelude to More's execution is added in the 1595 edition.

"As he was passing on his way, a certain woman offered him wine, but he refused it, saying 'Christ in his passion was given not wine, but vinegar, to drink.'" Stapleton, *Thomas More*, 209.

Cf. Matt. 27:34.

20   More's behavior toward the executioner is added in the 1595 edition.

"For after saying the Psalm and finishing his prayer, he rose briskly, and when according to custom the executioner begged his pardon, he kissed him with great love, gave him a golden angel, and said to him: 'Thou wilt give me this day a greater benefit than ever any mortal man can be able to give me. [...]' But, even before, he had asked his daughter and other friends to do whatever acts of kindness they could to his executioner." Stapleton, *Thomas More*, 210–11.

Though Stapleton does not draw the parallel with Cyprian of Carthage—said to have arranged for his family to give his executioner thirty-five gold pieces—Roper does, though his telling is somewhat different. According to Roper, while still at the prison, More gave the jailer the rich garment sent by Bonvisi, with the words, "Nay, I assure you, were it cloth of gold, I would account it well bestowed on him, as St Cyprian did, who gave his executioner thirty pieces of gold." *AASS*, September IV, 325. Roper and Harpsfield, *Saint Thomas More*, 49–50.

21   Reginald Pole was to berate Henry, "You have killed, you have killed the best of all Englishmen!" Pole, *Defense*, 232. For a sixteenth-century depiction of More's death, see Book 1 Figure 29.1

A. Ioannes Fiſcherus, epús Roffenſis in Anglia Card. declaratus, uitæ et doctrinæ integerr. laude clariſſ. ab Henr. viij, qd Pont. auctem tueretur capite plectitur.
B. ThomasMorus, eques aurat?, ſummo regni magratu perfunct?, prudentia, eruditione, mor innocentia et ſuauitate inſignis, ob eandem cauſam eiuſdem Regis iuſſu ſecuri percutitur.
Ambo Anglicanæ reipub. lumina; alter ſacri, alter laici ordinis decus.
C. Margarita regiæ familiæ fœmina prudentiſſ, Comitiſſa Sar. Card. Poli mr, ob geſtatū inſigne quinq. plagaz Chriſti, eadem morte, ſub eodem Rege, plexa eſt.
27

FIGURE 29.1   *The martyrdoms of John Fisher, Thomas More, and Margaret Pole.*
Giovanni Battista Cavalieri, *Ecclesiae anglicanae trophaea sive sanctorum martyrum qui pro Christo catholicaeque fidei veritate asserenda antiquo recentiorique persecutionum tempore mortem in Anglia subierunt, passiones Romae in collegio Anglico per Nicolaum Circinianum depictae: Nuper autem per Io. Bap. de Cavalleriis aeneis typis repraesentatae* (Rome: Ex officina Bartolomeo Grassi, 1584). NE1666 .C57 1584 OVERSIZE, John J. Burns Library, Boston College.

game, entered his chamber, and wept many tears—as they say the crocodile does, when it has killed and eaten a man.[22]

More's daughter Margaret wished to bury her father honorably, for she knew that Rochester's body had been thrown away, without a priest, without a cross, and without a winding-sheet—none had dared to bury him, on account of the king's wrath.[23] Fearing lest the same fate befall her father, but having brought from her house neither a cloth with which to wrap his corpse, nor gold with which to buy some, she entered a shop and gathered up enough bits of fabric to serve her pious purpose, begging that they be given her on credit. By chance she put her hand to her purse, and found the exact price of the cloth she had taken, neither more nor less by even a single coin. Spurred on by this miracle, she covered her father's body (none dared disturb a lady, the daughter of such a father) and thus fulfilled the duty owed to a father and a holy martyr.[24] By the king's command, his head stood on a pike on London Bridge for a month, and when they came to remove it and throw it in the river, Margaret availed herself of all her cunning to acquire it, so fresh and handsome that it seemed to live, save the hairs of his beard—which, while More lived, had begun to go white, and after his death were somewhat blonde.[25]

---

22   The story of Henry's reaction to the death is added in the 1595 edition.

"For even King Henry himself, when the news was brought to him that the supreme penalty had been exacted of Thomas More—he happened to be playing with dice at the time—was greatly upset. 'Is he then dead?' he enquired. Hearing that it was so, he turned to Anne Boleyn, who was sitting by him, and said: 'You are the cause of that man's death.' And rising at once he retired to another room and shed bitter tears." Stapleton, *Thomas More*, 212.

23   Like More himself, John Fisher was in fact interred, though without any memorial, in St. Peter ad Vincula, the chapel of the Tower of London. "The Chapel Royal of St. Peter Ad Vincula," *Tower of London*, 2015, http://www.hrp.org.uk/TowerOfLondon/Sightsandstories/Prisoners/Towers/ChapelRoyalofStPeter [accessed December 7, 2015].

24   The same story appears in Stapleton, *Thomas More*, 213–14.

In spite of Margaret's best efforts, More's decapitated body remained at St. Peter ad Vincula. His head was placed on a pole on London Bridge, whence Margaret rescued it. The skull was eventually placed in St Dunstan's Church, where Margaret was also buried. Guy, *A Daughter's Love*, 266, 274.

25   The fate of More's head is added in the 1595 edition.

"But now, before we come to relate the laments of others besides ourselves over the death of Thomas More, we will record what happened to the head and the body of the blessed martyr. The former, by order of the King, was placed upon a stake on London Bridge, where it remained for nearly a month, until it had to be taken down to make room for other heads. [...] The head would have been thrown into the river, had not Margaret Roper, who had been watching carefully and waiting for the opportunity, bribed the executioner whose office it was to remove the heads and obtained possession of the sacred relic." Stapleton, *Thomas More*, 213.

Other Details of the Life and Death of Thomas More[1]

So exemplary was the life of Thomas More, and so illustrious his martyrdom, that I decided I ought to supplement what I said in the previous chapter with some things from the many that Thomas Stapleton, an Englishman and a doctor in theology, has compiled in the life of the man that he published after our history saw the light of day.[2] Now, two advantages may be derived from this. The first, that lawyers, judges, ministers, the favorites of princes, and the governors of commonwealths will have a perfect model to imitate; the other, to teach us that the life of this exceptional man made him worthy to die shedding his unspotted blood for that Lord he had served so marvelously, and that it is no wonder that King Henry strove by so many means to win him over and bend him to his will, since the eyes of the entire kingdom were upon him, nor that one so firmly rooted in God should resist so many bitter blows with such valor.

So, Thomas More was born, as we said, in London, of noble stock, although not of the most exalted or influential. His father was named John More, a serious and even-tempered gentleman who had received honorable posts from the king[3] and who raised his son in the fear of our Lord with such diligence that he thought of nothing but the exercises of his studies and of virtue, and this with such great obedience and respect for his father, that he never afforded him displeasure nor disgrace—to the contrary, even when he was an adult, and chancellor of the realm, whenever they met in public he begged his blessing on his knees, so great was the reverence he felt for him.[4] While yet a child, More sought to combine his studies of eloquence with devotion and piety, and he worked harder to be a good Christian than to be a good scholar: he often

---

1   This entire chapter was added in the 1595 edition. Rather than flood the reader with Latin and/or English quotations from Stapleton's *Tres Thomae*, I will place the relevant page references in footnotes at the end of each passage.

2   The Sussex-born and Oxford-educated Thomas Stapleton received his doctorate in theology from Douai University in 1571. His *Tres Thomae* was the first printed biography of More. Highley, *Catholics Writing the Nation*, 26–27. Sheils, "Polemic as Piety," 81.

3   John More (*c*.1451–1530) had received several judicial appointments from both Henry VII and Henry VIII, as well as a knighthood in 1520. Eric Ives, "More, Sir John (*c*.1451–1530)," in *ODNB*, 39:51–53, here 52.

4   Stapleton, *Tres Thomae*, 10, 12–13; Stapleton, *Thomas More*, 3.

mortified his flesh with a hairshirt, or slept on the floor with a piece of wood for a pillow, and his longest slumbers were four or five hours. He fasted and watched frequently, and this with such discretion that as much as possible he kept hidden anything that might win him praise or a good reputation.[5] At this time, he wrote a pious and scholarly treatise on the four last things.[6] He eagerly heard sermons from preachers who spoke from the heart and moved their audience with deeds and words to a holy fear of the Lord.[7] After having been trained in the Latin and Greek languages and achieving true distinction in both, he gave himself up to the study of the other liberal arts, in all of which he excelled. Then he dedicated himself to the study of law, especially the common law unique to the kingdom of England, by which cases are generally decided and judged in that realm.[8] This he read and applied as a lawyer with great integrity. The first thing he advised parties who came to him was to reconcile, and when he could not achieve this, he requested them to explain the matter in detail, and if it seemed unjust to him, he urged them to abandon it, and if they absolutely refused to do so, he would not put his hand to something that he deemed baseless or wicked. But if he though the suit just, he strove to conclude it with the greatest speed and the least harm to all parties possible.[9]

From his youth More had a strong inclination to join the Franciscan Order, but after considering it at length he decided that though the religious state was more perfect and sound in and of itself, and our Lord does a great kindness to those he calls to it and gives perseverance in it, yet for him (moved by private reasons), that of marriage was more suitable and apt. It may be that by this path God chose to set him up as a mirror for married persons and to teach us through More's life and death that there can be martyrs in, and his majesty possesses surpassing servants in, every walk of life.[10] So it was that he first married a most virtuous maiden, by whom he had three daughters and a son, whom he raised in the true fear of God and to whom he taught the liberal arts. When his wife died, he married for a second time, more to have some to look after his children and household than for any other reason. In marriage, More's vigilance and piety was miraculous, governing his house and clan with a gentle Christianity and a Christian gentleness. In his house there was neither

---

5   Stapleton, *Tres Thomae*, 18; Stapleton, *Thomas More*, 9.
6   For More's unfinished treatise *The Four Last Things* (1522), see More, *Complete Works*, 1:128–82.
7   Stapleton, *Tres Thomae*, 20; Stapleton, *Thomas More*, 10–11.
8   Stapleton, *Tres Thomae*, 25–26; Stapleton, *Thomas More*, 15–16.
9   Stapleton, *Tres Thomae*, 26–27; Stapleton, *Thomas More*, 17.
10   Stapleton, *Tres Thomae*, 18–19; Stapleton, *Thomas More*, 9–10.

idler, nor lecher, nor gabbler, no games or immodest contact between men and women. All had to confess and take communion at the proper times and hear divine offices on feast days, and, on the most important and solemn ones, to rise in the night to pray. Almost every night he would summon as much of his household as he could and pray with them, offering them a few words of holy exhortation, and on Good Friday he gathered them all with the utmost care to read to them the passion of the Lord, expounding it and mentioning at appropriate passages various points of greater feeling or significance. At his table, a chapter of Holy Scripture was always read, with some brief exposition, and if some theologian or scholar dined with him, they spoke warmly of the meaning of what had been read, and then of various matters of virtuous and holy recreation.[11]

Now, since More was widely reputed as a man of integrity and learning, he was named a syndic of London, a high judicial office of great importance, which he filled with such distinction that the king, taken with his good qualities, decided to make use of him and deputed him as his ambassador, first to France and then to Flanders. Finally, he called him to his privy counsel and made him a knight, treasurer general, and chancellor of the duchy of Lancaster, relying on his counsel and industry in every matter of weight and import. And all this with so many signs of his confidence that it was said that once, when More was with his family in a town near London, the king suddenly went to see him, eating at his table and remaining there for a day or two relaxing with him, amazed at his wisdom, erudition, and pleasant conversation. The king's favor grew so great that he gave him the position of chancellor (the highest dignity in the realm), with such signs of love and respect for his person that it was a kindness upon a kindness. For besides the fact that More had never sought it or connived at it, but instead refused it out of modesty, he was the first married man, not of exalted or noble lineage, to ascend to that dignity, and when he was given the office and seated in the chancellor's chair, the duke of Norfolk, one of the most important and influential lords in the kingdom, accompanied him and at the king's command made a speech to all present, in which he enumerated the reasons the king had given him that office, all of them rooted in the wonderful prudence, personal integrity, learning, and grace of Thomas More, and in the knowledge the entire realm had of this through the many, varied, and serious matters he had handled at home and abroad. And that on this account, more respecting More's merits than the grandeur of his blood, he had appointed him to that dignity, judging that by this his conscience would rest more securely and more peacefully, and all the realm would

---

11   Stapleton, *Tres Thomae*, 216–220; Stapleton, *Thomas More*, 95–97.

enjoy fairness, justice, and tranquility. More was not carried away by this, but rather, as one who understood that the charge he bore was truly good more in appearance than reality, looked upon the chancellor's chair with a grave and sorrowful countenance, and said that he seated himself as though on a throne of troubles and perils, void of contentment, one he feared and from which the fall was easy. He fulfilled his responsibilities with utter rectitude, saying that in what pertained to justice, there was no difference between friend and foe; he was so solicitous in dispatching the business of the litigants that in the highest tribunal, where there usually more cases than could be contained, it came to pass that when cases were called for none could be found, which has never happened before or since.[12]

Numerous though the obligations of his office were, those of his conscience and piety were not neglected; rather, he devoted hours to these with the utmost diligence and attention, drawing from them the spirit and strength to bear the weight of the others properly. Before all else, he heard Mass every day, putting his hands to other business only when he left that holy occupation. One day while hearing Mass he was urgently summoned by the king, two or three times, but he refused to abandon the service until it was finished, saying that he was more bound to attend upon the king of kings than a king of the earth. Every day he said the divine office, the seven psalms, and the litany. He had an oratory in his house, and a place set apart where he withdrew to pray whenever he emerged exhausted from the council, as to a harbor safe from the turbulent waves of a stormy sea. He was openhanded with the poor and supplied all their wants; it was the same with churches: he gave his parish church many vessels of gold and silver for divine worship, and used to say, "The good give it, the wicked take it away." Despite his great authority and dignity, he was so humble, modest, and pious that he delighted in attending to the priest during Mass and in busying himself with the most servile tasks. However burdened he might be with business, he never allowed anyone to speak with him in church. When he had to deal with something of great pitch and moment, he confessed and received the sacred body of Christ our Lord, imploring him for the light to do right. Sometimes he went, as though on a pilgrimage, to a certain

---

12   Stapleton, *Tres Thomae*, 27–39; Stapleton, *Thomas More*, 17–27.

      More's public career included the offices of undersheriff of the city of London (1510), emissary to Flanders (1515), royal secretary (1518), member of the privacy council (1518), emissary to France (1520), under-treasurer of the exchequer (1521), speaker of the House of Commons (1523), chancellor of the duchy of Lancaster (1525), and lord chancellor (1529). More was knighted in 1521, as part of his appointment as under-treasurer. Curtis, "More's Public Life," 72–79.

house of worship seven miles distant from his own—and this always, out of his deep devotion, on foot—though this is something rarely done in England, even among the common folk.[13] He was quite restrained in food and drink, modest and unexceptional in his dress. Sometimes he wore a hairshirt next to his flesh, and he mortified himself harshly on certain days (Fridays, the vigils of the saints, and the Ember Days). The day before he died, he sent his daughter Margaret Roper his hairshirt and his discipline, with a note written with a coal for lack of a pen—like one who lays down his arms, having fought and conquered.[14] He always fled the honors, ambitions, and vanities of the court and considered it a great cross to live there, even when he was at his height, favored and singled out by the king. Yet, to serve him, to defend the Catholic faith against the heretics through his influence, and to do some service to his homeland, he endured and persevered in his position, until he saw the king transformed and the kingdom menaced by a fearful storm he could not match. Then, preferring to lose the grace of his king than his God, his reputation than his conscience, he entreated the king to permit him to rest, which he did.

When his son-in-law Roper spoke to him about how well-governed the kingdom was, and how loved and respected the king was both at home and abroad, More answered, "So it appears now, but let us pray to God that the king does not change, nor find other counselors, less strong or steadfast." And on another occasion he told Roper, when he had praised the realm's sound customs, fervor, and piety (for to be sure these were once considerable), "For the moment, my son, it is as you say, but within a few days all the goodness that now flowers will wither away, and those who follow it will be despised and trampled like the ants you see here," stepping upon them as he spoke. Returning to his house one day, he found his daughters deep in prayer and told them, "My daughters, you do well to pray and busy yourselves in this holy occupation, for very soon there will be nothing in England more despised than those who devote themselves to this, and you yourselves will think this way, if our Lord does not give you his grace and spirit."[15]

After More had laid down his responsibilities and withdrawn to his corner, he busied himself in writing against the heretics (as we have said), and though he had not then the grandeur he used to, as long as he lived he possessed enormous authority, won through the many distinguished posts he had held and the entire realm's wonderful pride in him. And this was the reason the king tried so hard to win over More in the question of the divorce and to bring him

13   Stapleton, *Tres Thomae*, 85–88; Stapleton, *Thomas More*, 66–69.

14   Stapleton, *Tres Thomae*, 94–96; Stapleton, *Thomas More*, 74–75.

15   Stapleton, *Tres Thomae*, 200–03; Stapleton, *Thomas More*, 80–81.

into accordance with his will, using such exquisite and extraordinary means as would have sufficed to overcome any heart less Christian or less steadfast than that of this saintly man. Now, at first More had handled this business with marvelous delicacy and caution, lest he offend either God or the king, and did not speak of it unless the king himself asked his opinion, which he gave with simplicity and modesty.[16] Yet, as kings generally dislike anyone to dare to differ from their will by a hair, he could not fail to offend King Henry by opposing him in what he so fiercely desired. Since More understood this, and already saw from afar the harms that could befall him, he dismissed numerous servants from his household, sold four hundred ducats' worth of silver, which was all he possessed, and provided his married children with separate houses. Most nights he arose from his bed and passed the entirety in prayer, tearfully entreating our Lord to give him victory over death[17] and to strengthen him with his spirit to die zealously for the truth. So as to be better prepared and armed, and to make a trial, as it were, of what was to come, he agreed with a friend of his, one of the king's officers, that while he was dining with his wife and children he should enter without warning and suddenly summon him in the king's name and demand his attendance. This was done several times, his family weeping with shock and grief: he calmed them all, telling them to place their hope in God and conform themselves to his will, anticipating the blow that he was to receive—just as it came to pass.

For, on Palm Sunday, after hearing a sermon in the great church of St Paul's in London, one of the king's bailiffs came to him and ordered him to appear before the commissioners the following day. At this he went home and took leave of his wife and children; on the following morning he confessed and took communion, and then boarded a barge with his son-in-law Roper, traveling to London by river. When he arrived, he stood for a long moment frozen in contemplation, commending himself utterly to our Lord, and finally, with a joyful and smiling countenance, said to his son-in-law, *Vicimus filij*—we have conquered, my son—which was the result of his prayer and the grace and strength he had received from the Lord thereby. More presented himself before the commissioners, as he had been commanded, and, refusing to swear to Henry as head of the Church or to his daughter Elizabeth as the heir to the

---

16   Stapleton dedicates a chapter to More's attempts to negotiate Henry's insistent demands for a favorable opinion on the divorce. See Stapleton, *Tres Thomae*, 272–79; Stapleton, *Thomas More*, 145–51.

17   1 Cor. 15:55–57.

throne, he was condemned to perpetual imprisonment and sent to the Tower of London,[18] where he wrote his daughter Margaret a letter in these words:

> Dearest daughter, I am well, thanks be to God, healthy of body and tranquil of soul; of the things of this world I desire no more than I have, imploring our Lord to console you with the hope of eternal life, and that he himself instruct you with his divine spirit in those things I have long intended to teach you concerning celestial goods, and I hope in his majesty that he will do this better than I could have done with all my frigid words, and that he keep you and give you his holy blessing. As for me, may God give me a spirit eternally faithful, simple, and plain, and if I have none such, may he not suffer me to live. For a long life I neither expect nor desire, but rather I am prepared to die tomorrow, if our Lord be pleased, and I know of no man (blessed be God) who would give a flick of his fingers [*vn papirote*] for my sake, and I more rejoice in this state of mind than if I were lord of the universe.

While in prison, they grievously tempted and assailed him to conform to the will of the king, but they could never bring him to it. His beloved, precious daughter Margaret first wrote him a heart-wrenching letter, and then spoke with him, offering him, amid fierce and copious tears, many reasons to soften, laying before him the kindnesses and favors he had received from the king, the obligation he had to serve him and satisfy him in all things not contrary to God, such as this, for the entire kingdom had embraced and resolved upon it. She told him not to think himself wiser than so many prelates, doctors, religious, and gentlemen of exemplary life and eminent learning, who had accepted and taken the oath, to which he as a layman could and even should conform himself, especially seeing that the realm in parliament had, by the common consent of all the estates, enacted and decreed this statute, which he was to obey as a subject of the kingdom and a citizen of the commonwealth—the entirety of which had been scandalized by his stubbornness and obstinacy, and could not believe that it sprung from anything but his belief that he was wiser than all the rest, or a hatred and ill will he bore the king, or some vanity, boldness, or wicked counsel. Let him consider well, since he was the father of a family, the desolation of his house, the isolation of his wife, the abandonment and destruction of his children and grandchildren, the affliction and persecution of his kinsmen and friends, and finally the suffering and death of Margaret herself, for her life hung upon his. And the love the father bore his daughter was so great that he could not help but be moved by her and by the fear of the dangers that would

---

18   Stapleton, *Tres Thomae*, 288–91; Stapleton, *Thomas More*, 158–61.

come upon her, and upon his wife, children, and friends, for his sake. And this troubled him more than his imprisonment or the fear of his own death; he said that he overcame it through the fear of hell, the hope of blessedness, and the memory and contemplation of the sacred passion of Christ our Redeemer.[19] And thus the love of God counted more with this saintly father than the love of his children, and the eternal salvation of his soul more than worldly harm to his house, and he answered his daughter steadfastly, undoing with sound and solid arguments the vain and superficial ones she had put to him, as she herself wrote to her sister.[20]

But More's temptations did not end here, for a dear friend of his, a doctor of theology by the name of Nicholas Wilson, a learned and thoughtful man, having been incarcerated for refusing to take the oath, eventually recanted while in prison and promised to swear, and before doing so he wrote More a letter, asking him if he would swear to the same thing.[21] More replied in these words:

> I am not curious as to comprehending the consciences of others: I have a care of my own, and there, on account of my sins, I have more to do than I can manage. It seems to me that I have lived a long time, and I do not hope or wish to live any longer. Since entering prison, once or twice I thought I would die and, if truth be told, the expectation of death gave me joy. Not because I forgot the strict reckoning that I have to give, but because I trust in the goodness of the Lord and in the blood of his blessed son, and I implore him to give me always the desire to be freed of this fragile flesh and to be with him. For I do not doubt but that it is acceptable and pleasing to him when one comes to him who greatly desires to come before his divine majesty and presence—indeed, I hold it certain that in general anyone who is to go to God must desire it greatly before they depart.[22]

Nor was the weakness and fall of this Nicholas Wilson, though he was a churchman and a theologian, capable of sapping More's invincible spirit, nor toppling this unshakeable pillar of the kingdom of England, any more than the terrors

---

19   Stapleton, *Tres Thomae*, 289–98; Stapleton, *Thomas More*, 162–68.
      Cf. More, *Last Letters*, 62–63.

20   For this letter, written in August 1534, see More, *Last Letters*, 72–89.

21   Stapleton, *Tres Thomae*, 298–99; Stapleton, *Thomas More*, 171.
      The theologian Nicholas Wilson (d.1548) was arrested in 1534 as the only London clergyman to refuse to swear the oath of succession. Wilson submitted while imprisoned in the Tower of London, and received a pardon on May 29, 1537. Kenneth Carleton, "Wilson, Nicholas (*d.* 1548)," in *ODNB*, 59:620–21, here 620.

22   Stapleton, *Tres Thomae*, 299–300; Stapleton, *Thomas More*, 172.
      Cf. More, *Last Letters*, 94–95.

and horrors with which they again pressed him in prison, telling him that unless he obeyed parliament, a draconian law would be passed against him and they would kill him brutally, as a rebel and traitor. Of this he wrote to his daughter Margaret thus:

> Of course, I cannot prevent this law being enacted. But I am utterly certain that if I die according to this law, I shall die innocent before God, and that all the harm that could be done me with this law I anticipated and accepted long ago. And in this state of mind, most beloved daughter of mine, I have had considerable struggles with human frailty, and dire battles with my weak flesh (may God pardon me), and greater fears of pain and death than befit a Christian, especially in a cause such as this. But blessed and praised be the Lord that the end of this fierce and perilous battle has been the victory of the spirit, which is strengthened with the light of faith, and also by a fact I have recognized—that no harm can follow from such a death (if it comes) to a man without sin, but only surpassing good. Moreover, this horrid cell helps me not a little in taking no thought of the violent death that would be dealt me by such an undertaking, and if by its sharpness one should be deprived of a few days of life, this little loss is well recompensed with the knowledge that so much the sooner will one enjoy eternal, blessed days. And though the sufferings of those who die healthy are greater, I have never yet seen an invalid die without pain. And likewise I know that at whatever hour a natural death comes—the which hour is uncertain, and might perchance be tomorrow—I would take it for a signal mercy of God to have died earlier in this cause. And thus sound logic teaches me not to fear such a death as later one will wish to have had. Lastly, a violent and cruel death may come upon a man by many paths, with greater danger of losing the soul and less merit before God. And for these well-considered reasons, though at other times the recollection of death has been fearful to me, now it frightens me not at all; I do not on this account fail to recall my wretchedness and, contemplating the fall of Saint Peter,[23] to entreat our Lord each day to protect me and preserve this will until the end of my life. And to conclude, my Margaret, and declare to you the deepest and most secret things of my heart, I have resigned and confided myself entirely to the will of God, so much so that after I entered this prison I have never asked him to free me from it, nor from death, but rather in all and through all to work his holy will in me. For he knows what is best for me, better than I do. Nor have I wished to return home since I came here out of fondness for my house; it is certainly true that sometimes I have wanted to see my friends, and especially the companion God has given me and you my children, out of the

---

23   Matt. 26:69–75; Mark 14:66–72; Luke 22:56–62; John 18:17–27.

care that the same God has charged me with. But even this desire (since the Lord ordains it differently) I yield up and place in his blessed hands, rejoicing and delighting in him, and in knowing that you all live in my house with utter peace, charity, and tranquility in his holy service.[24]

More wrote all this, and I chose to include it here because in addition to having been a martyr of Christ, and thus owed all praise and honor, he was a truly illustrious and valiant martyr, and with so glorious a death sustained the hearts of many and gave life to the kingdom of England, more than any other who died for the faith. For although the Carthusian fathers and the other religious by their steadfast example and the bishop of Rochester by his admirable learning, sanctity, and dignity did much to retain many, yet as they were all churchmen, there was greater opportunity for the malicious to claim that they died in defense of their ecclesiastical estate and their own interests. This could not be said or imagined of More, for he was a layman and married, regarded as an oracle by the entire nation, and layman and clergy alike relied upon his judgment. And so by More's example countless persons were preserved in obedience to the Apostolic See, and many of them died for the Catholic faith. I have also written this so that, moved by this example, neither shall prosperity exalt us, nor adversity cast us down, nor, amid the changes and instability of what is called fortune, shall our hearts fail to remain forever constant. And although our weakness should sometimes feel fear and pain (as this saintly man confesses of himself), let us not despair on that account, nor quail, for in strengthening and sustaining this weakness we see the virtue and grace of the Lord. But it is high time we return to what we have in hand, and proceed with our history.

---

24   Stapleton, *Tres Thomae*, 300–01; Stapleton, *Thomas More*, 173–74.
      Cf. More, *Last Letters*, 101–03.

The Sentence of Pope Paul III against King Henry[1]

At this time, Pope Paul III was ruling over the Church of God, having succeeded the late Clement VII as pontiff.[2] As he was a magnanimous and sagacious man, who knew what had happened in England, how the king had taken no notice of the letters, emissaries, warnings, commands, and threats of his predecessor, but had rather gone from bad to worse each day, he elected, having contemplated the matter and repeatedly commended it to our Lord, stirred by his zeal and justice, to employ sharper remedies, to cure (if possible) the cancerous wound, since it could not be healed by gentle and merciful means. On August 30, 1535, in the first year of his pontificate, he promulgated a bull.[3] Therein, after recounting his obligation as universal shepherd to watch over every church and the soul of every believer, as well as his longstanding affection for King Henry on account of his great merits, he relates with what deep sorrow of soul he had learned that this same Henry, his former piety, the reverence owed to God and his church, and his own honor and salvation all forgotten, had, against divine law and the Church's prohibition, shamefully abandoned the noble and saintly Queen Doña Catherine, his lawful wife, with whom he had lived for many years and fathered many children, and, while she yet lived, contracted a marriage with an English woman, called Anne Boleyn. And that, worsening in his wickedness, he had enacted impious, heretical laws against the supremacy of the Roman pontiff, seizing and usurping for himself (an unheard-of novelty!) the title of head of the Church in his kingdom, and forced his subjects to accept and approve these sacrilegious decrees, and that those who refused, be they laypersons, seculars, or religious of any order, had been killed with exquisite tortures, among them the saintly bishop of Rochester, glorious in the dignity of the cardinalate.

Through these deeds Henry had incurred excommunication and the other penalties and censures of the Church, according to the ancient and sacred canons, and had lost his right to rule, and although—seeing the obstinacy

---

1 Sander, *De origine ac progressu*, 147–54.

2 Clement VII died in Rome on September 25, 1534. Alessandro Farnese was elected Pope Paul III on October 13, 1534.

3 Sander includes the Latin text of this bull, *Eius qui immobilis* (dated August 20, 1535): see Sander, *De origine ac progressu*, 148–53.

and hardness with which this Pharaoh[4] had disdained all the remedies, commands, and judgments of his predecessor, Clement—the pope had little hope of the king's repentance, yet he would delay his punishment, so as to exercise the office of a mild father, compelled until now to proceed with the greatest mercy and kindness that his duty as universal shepherd would permit. And so he begs and entreats him, by the very heartstrings of Jesus Christ, to return to himself, repent his sins and misdeeds, annul his unjust laws (nor force his subjects to approve them), and cease imprisoning and persecuting the innocent— and gravely warns all the king's henchmen, counselors, and accomplices not to support, advise, or aid him any further. And if the king and his minions should refuse to obey, he excommunicates them, strips the king of his crown, places him under interdict, and declares any offspring from the marriage with Anne to be illegitimate and reprobate; he absolves all vassals and subjects of their obedience and of any oaths sworn to the king; he orders all believers to abstain from commerce with Henry or the cities and persons who follow him; he declares null and void all contracts made with them; he commands all prelates and churchmen to leave England, while every man, prince and commoner, is to oppose Henry and strive to expel him from his kingdom; he annuls every league and alliance between Henry and any other king or prince, as well as other matters and penalties, which may be seen in the papal bull.

---

4 Exod. 7–12.

Henry Despoils the Monasteries, and Impoverishes Himself with Their Wealth[1]

But Henry, as a man abandoned by God, each day sunk further into his wickedness. After he had slain these servants of God, he then decided to rob the monasteries of their wealth: to this end, he announced that as supreme head of the Church, he was ordering a visitation, and he appointed for the purpose a lawyer called Legh, an unholy layman.[2] His instructions for the visitation were these: to investigate and inquire in great detail into the misdeeds and sins of all the religious. That anyone younger than twenty-four years should depart the monastery and return to the world, whether or not they wished to; if older than twenty-four, they were not to be compelled, but were free to leave their house. Those who departed were given clerical garb and eight ducats in exchange for their monastic habit, while the nuns were given secular clothing. Lastly, that all the monks and nuns of every order must yield up to the king's officials all the jewels, ornaments, and reliquaries they possessed.[3] All this was to provide the king an opportunity to ruin the monasteries and steal their property. Legh, the damnable visitor, in order to "reform" the monasteries of nuns, those virgins consecrated to God, induced them to every kind of vice and filthiness.

With this, on February 4, having published monstrous accusations against the religious (which his officers had fabricated), the king secured through parliament that all monasteries with less than seven hundred ducats of income

---

1 Sander, *De origine ac progressu*, 154–56.

2 Sir Thomas Legh (d.1545), a diplomat and administrator who became a commissioner in the royal visitation of 1535–36. A harsh enforcer of Cromwell and Henry's instructions, Legh proved unpopular with both court elites and the general populace. Anthony N. Shaw, "Legh, Sir Thomas (*d.* 1545)," in *ODNB*, 33:205–07, here 205–06.

3 "Whereupon, the same year [1536], in the month of October, the king, having then Thomas Cromwell of his council, sent Dr. Lee to visit the abbeys, priories, and nunneries in all England, and to set at liberty all such religious persons as desired to be free, and all others that were under the age of four and twenty years; providing withal, that such monks, canons, and friars as were dismissed, should have given them by the abbot or prior, instead of their habit, a secular priest's gown, and forty shillings of money, and likewise the nuns to have such apparel as secular women did then commonly use, and be suffered to go where they would; at which time also, from the said abbeys and monasteries were taken their chief jewels and relics." Foxe, *Acts and Monuments*, 5:102.

© KONINKLIJKE BRILL NV, LEIDEN, 2017 | DOI 10.1163/9789004323964_038

per year should be surrendered to the king, with all their property.[4] He began with these less substantial houses—so he said—because they were less necessary to the commonweal, and because monastic discipline and order could not be maintained there (since they had only a few religious). But in truth, it was to acquire land little by little, to move from the lesser to the greater with fewer disturbances and difficulties, and to weaken the resistance from the abbots of the richer and better-endowed monasteries, seeing themselves free and their incomes untouched.[5] In this first assault, Henry persecuted and devastated 376 monasteries, from the spoils whereof he reaped some 120,000 ducats in income each year, and from the movable goods 400,000 ducats—not counting everything stolen or embezzled by his officials—while among the brothers and sisters, more than ten thousand persons renounced their habits and returned to the world.[6] From this it may be understood that after he had devastated and desolated them in this way, within the space of three years this accursed king had left not a single monastery standing. No less worthy of note is that after these first robberies and sacrileges, the king became poorer and poorer, with greater and greater necessities, so that to escape from them he was compelled to impose enormous taxes and levy upon his people, for which they took up arms against him. Despite this deepening poverty, it will be seen hereafter how he despoiled every other church and appropriated their wealth.[7]

---

4   27 Hen. 8. c. 28. See *SR*, 3:575–78.

5   "Woe! be even to the great abbots themselves that winked at the matter, yea, and gave their consent to the suppressing of the lesser, thinking to keep and preserve their own still, which they could not do long after, for all the fair and flattering promises made unto them." Harpsfield, *Treatise*, 142.

6   "In a Parliament begoon in the monethe of February [1536], was graunted to the king and hys heires, all religious houses in ye realme of Englande of the value of two hundred pound & under, with all landes and goods to them belonging, the nomber of these houses weare. 376. the value of their lands. 32000. pound & more, the mouable goods 100000. pound, ye religious put out, were more then. 10000." John Stow, *A Summarie of the Chronicles of England from the First Comming of Brute into This Land, vnto This Present Yeare of Christ 1575 Diligently Collected, Corrected and Enlarged, by Iohn Stowe* (London: Richard Tottle, and Henry Binneman, 1575), 436–37.

7   In the margin: "Book 2, Chapter 45."

What the Queen Wrote to Her Confessor, Encouraging Him in the Face of Death, and How He Answered Her[1]

The saintly Queen Doña Catherine now endured unending sorrows and afflictions, caused on the one hand by seeing her husband in so miserable a state and without any remedy, and on the other by the harassment shamelessly perpetrated by Anne Boleyn. Yet she was much more affected by the barbarous and inhuman cruelty with which the king's officials abused that venerable, old, and holy father, the Franciscan John Forest, her confessor. She had heard that he was condemned to death, to be hanged and at the same time burned alive, having been held prisoner for two years in a harsh and awful jail among thieves and felons, with innumerable torments and sufferings.[2] When she heard this, the pious queen could not but be moved, dissolving into tears of compassion for her spiritual father. Risky as it was, her sorrow gave her the strength to write him these words, which clearly show the perfect insight and estimation the Lord had given her of herself and of the perishable things of this wretched world:

> My venerable father, as you have so often counseled others and consoled them in their travails, you will know well what befits you in this moment, when the Lord calls you to fight for him. If with joy you pass through these little, brief pains and the torments that are readied for you, you know that you will receive your eternal reward. He would be a madman and a fool who sought perdition in order to free himself from any sort of tribulation in this miserable life. But to you, my most fortunate father, God has shown the mercy of learning what many men never know, and to finish the course of your saintly life with imprisonment, torture, and a cruel death suffered for Christ's sake. Woe unto me, your miserable daughter, who in a time of loneliness and abandonment, such as this, must lose so treasured a guide, so dear and so beloved a father in Jesus Christ!

1 Sander, *De origine ac progressu*, 156–62.
2 Forest's imprisonment in 1534 is largely a matter of tradition, and has not been reliably verified. Marshall, "Forest, John," in *ODNB*, 20:364.

Truly, if I could speak with you and confess to your goodness the ardent fires of my heart (as I have laid bare to you my secrets and the intimate thoughts of my conscience and my soul), you would see in them the burning desire to die, either with you or before you. And if the Lord, to whom I humbly submit my life and all my desires, is pleased—or is not displeased—with this, I will purchase death with all the pains and torments of this life. For I can neither live nor be at peace in this accursed world, seeing myself deprived of such holy ones (of whom the world is not worthy). But perhaps I have spoken like one of these foolish women.[3] And since it seems that God has so ordained it, go you before,[4] my father, with fortitude and a blessed end, and with your prayers obtain the Lord's grace for me, that I may swiftly and surely follow you by the same path, steep and arduous though it may be, and, in the meantime, in his mercy make me a sharer in your holy torments, travails, and battles. This I will receive as your last blessing in this life, since after your victories and crowns, I hope for greater grace and favor in heaven.

It is not for me to exhort you to run toward the blessed and eternal crown that is prepared for you, nor to yearn for it, though you should suffer every torment and pain that the world can give you. For your noble blood, your wondrous learning, your knowledge and love of heaven, and the life and vocation of so holy an order as that of Saint Francis (which you embraced in your tender youth) teach and instruct you in what to do in a struggle so fierce, and give you the strength to do it. But because it is a great gift of God to suffer for him, I will beg the divine majesty with my unending prayers, tears, and penances to give you the grace to finish the battle with valor and win the glorious crown of immortal life. The Lord be with you, father of my soul, and remember me always, on earth and in heaven before God.

Your inconsolable daughter,
Catherine

The holy confessor took tremendous solace in this letter, and replied to her from prison with these words:

Most serene lady, queen, and my dearest daughter in the heart of Christ, your servant Thomas[5] gave me Your Majesty's letter, which not only offered me solace and joy in this my affliction and continual hope of

---

3   Job 2:10.

4   John 14:3.

5   Probably fictional.

being soon loosed from the fetters of this wretched flesh, but also spirit and strength to endure my torments with patience and perseverance. For although it is true that I see the misery and meanness of all human things, and that all the felicities and adversities of this life are undone in a moment[6] and disappear like smoke,[7] and that in comparison to the immortality and glory we hope for, we are not to regard or take notice of them, yet I cannot deny to Your Majesty that the sweet words of your letter and your love have awakened and truly reinvigorated my soul—which often feels your sorrow, fears for your health, and is anxious and solicitous whenever I think of your disgrace—to disdain for any pain and any death, have raised it up, and ignited it with the hope and contemplation of eternal goods. May Jesus Christ our Lord repay Your Majesty, my lady, my daughter dearer to me than all the things of the earth, for this kindness to me and for this brief consolation; may he give you that peace and joy of his countenance that has no end.[8]

I humbly beg Your Majesty to implore the Lord, with your fervent and continual prayers, to strengthen me in this battle, for with that I will have no need to fear my constancy and strength, nor to think of the torments prepared for me, however terrible they may be. For it would not be decent, or appropriate to my white hairs, for me to be moved by these bugbears and children's terrors in so solemn a matter of God as this; or, having now lived sixty-four years, to flee like a coward from death; or, at the end of forty-three years in the habit of Saint Francis, having learned to disdain all perishable things, not to love and long with all my soul for what is to last forevermore.

Living and dead, I shall always watch over you, my lady, my most loving daughter, and pray to the Father of Mercies[9] that the measure of your sorrows shall be the measure of your triumphs and consolations. Meanwhile, pray to the Lord for this your servant and devoted beadsman, and deign to do so with greater strength and fervor when you learn that I am in the horrible torments prepared for me. I send to Your Majesty my rosary, for they say that no more than three days remain to my life.[10]

---

6   1 Cor. 15:52.

7   Ps. 101:4.

8   Num. 6:26; Isa. 9:7.

9   2 Cor. 1:3.

10   These letters were first printed in 1582 by Thomas Bourchier at Paris; some scholars have accepted their veracity, but the broad consensus considers them "Bourchier's invention." Marshall, "Forest, John" in *ODNB*, 20:364.

The Latin text of the letters was added to Sander's *De origine ac progressu* by the editors of the 1586 edition, whence Ribadeneyra had it: see Sander, *De origine ac progressu*, 157–60.

These were the words of this servant of God. And though a lady-in-waiting to the queen wrote to him of her mistress's unceasing lamentations for his impending death, and urgently begged him to find some way to escape death if he desired the queen to live, he responded with a rebuke, saying that the servant had not learned to write that way from her mistress. "As though," he said, "we were not to be resurrected in glory, as though our crown was not to be so much the greater, the greater was our suffering and the sharper the torments we overcame." And that it befitted the queen that he die for the vindication and sake of her cause—which he would do with the greatest goodwill, at the same time dying for the truth.[11]

For the Bourchier texts, see Thomas Bourchier, *Historia ecclesiastica de martyrio fratrum Ordinis divi Francisci, dictorum de Observantia, qui partim in Anglia sub Henrico octauo rege: partim in Belgio sub principe Auriaco, parim & in Hybernia tempore Elizabethæ regnantis reginæ, idque ab anno 1536 vsque ad hunc nostrum præsentem annum 1582 passi sunt* (Paris: Apud Ioannem Poupy, 1582), 53–61.

11   Like the letters, the story of their reception derives from Bourchier, via the 1586 edition of *De origine ac progressu*. Both sources identify this lady-in-waiting as a certain "Domina Elizabetha Hammonia," whom I have not been able to verify independently. See Sander, *De origine ac progressu*, 160–62; Bourchier, *Historia ecclesiastica*, 61–62.

The Death of Queen Doña Catherine and the Letter She Wrote to the King[1]

This was the saintly father's response, thinking he was soon to die and precede the queen to heaven—but our Lord in his eternal providence ordained differently. For the queen died a few days later from the bad air, her continual ailments, and her sadness at heart (and not without suspicion of poison), on January 6, in the year 1535, the fiftieth of her life and the thirty-third since she had come to England.[2] Her body was interred with moderate ceremony in the city called Peterborough.[3] Beyond all doubt, this queen was wondrous in her sanctity, in her wisdom, and in her steadfastness and patience. For though she was by nature given to seclusion and penance (as we have seen), she could never be brought to enter a convent or to do anything else to the detriment of her marriage. Being cast out of the palace, abused, and persecuted by the king and his ministers, she never consented to flee England and to escape to Spain or Flanders, as her nephew the emperor begged her, where she would have been highly honored and fittingly attended. She bore her travails and disasters with deep patience and acceptance, saying that her sins merited far more and that she believed the principal cause of her disastrous marriage had been the death of the innocent youth Edward Plantagenet, son of the duke of Clarence and nephew to King Edward IV, whom King Henry VII had put to death—not for any guilt of his, but to assure the succession to the throne to his children and to persuade the Catholic Kings to give their daughter in marriage to his son Prince Arthur, as they eventually did.[4] The saintly queen used to say that if it pleased God, she desired neither extreme joy nor extreme misery, for both had their temptations and perils. But if she had to choose between the two,

---

1 Sander, *De origine ac progressu*, 162–65.

2 Catherine died on January 7, 1536, at the age of fifty. Rumors of poison were widespread, but the cause of death was almost certainly cancer. Tremlett, *Catherine of Aragon*, 365–66.

3 Catherine was interred at Peterborough Abbey on January 29 with the ceremonies appropriate to the dowager princess of Wales, not a queen of England. Ibid., 367. Edwards, *Mary I*, 38–39.

4 Christine Carpenter posits of the judicial murders of Edward Plantagenet and the Yorkist pretender Perkin Warbeck (*c.*1474–99), "this double execution may simply have been a precondition for the marriage of Prince Arthur to Katherine of Aragon." Carpenter, "Edward," in *ODNB*, 17:806.

© KONINKLIJKE BRILL NV, LEIDEN, 2017 | DOI 10.1163/9789004323964_040

she preferred an unfortunate lot to a prosperous one, since in her sorrow it would be a wonder to lack any sort of relief and comfort at all, while in joy one usually lacks all sense.[5] When she was on the point of death, she wrote this letter to her husband the king:

> My lord, my king, and my loving husband, the deep love I have for you prompts me to write to you at this hour and in the anguish of my death: to admonish and charge you to have a care for the eternal health of your soul, more than for all the ephemeral things of this life and all the pleasures and delights of your flesh—for the sake of which you have given me so many sufferings and burden, and entered a labyrinth, an ocean of cares and troubles. With a willing heart I forgive all you have done to me, and I beg our Lord that he too pardon you. What I beg of you is that you look after our daughter Mary, whom I commend to you, asking that you deal with her as befits a father. Also, I commend my three ladies to you and request that you give them a year's salary, so that they may marry honorably, and the other servants, lest they fall into poverty, as well as any others who might deserve it. Lastly, I swear and promise, my lord, that there is no mortal thing my eyes long for more than you.[6]

The queen made two copies of this letter; she sent one to the king and the other to the imperial ambassador, Eustache Chapuys (begging him that if the king did not fulfill her requests, he see to them or prevail upon the emperor to do so).[7]

---

5   Sander took this aphorism from the *Satellitium* (1527) of the Spanish humanist Juan Luis Vives (1493–1540), part of Catherine's circle and tutor to Mary: "I remember your mother, that wisest of women, said to me, when we were returning from Syon to Richmond by boat, that she had rather a moderate, middling fortune than either a harsh or an easy one; yet if she was to choose between them, the sorrowful was to be preferred to the blessed, for in affliction we do not lack consolation, but in great felicity we lack our sense." Juan Luis Vives, *Ioan. Lodovici Vivis de recta ingenuorum adolescentum ac puellarum institutione, libelli duo, multa eruditione ac pietate referti: Eiusdem ad veram sapientiam introductio, satellitiu[m] animi, siue symbola principum institutioni potissimum destinata* (Basel: Robert Winter, 1539), 116.

6   As with the correspondence with Forest, this letter is likely a Catholic fiction and probably originates with Nicholas Harpsfield. Ribadeneyra translates from the Latin text in Sander, *De origine ac progressu*, 144.

   Cf. The paraphrased text in Harpsfield, *Treatise*, 199–200.

7   In a letter of January 21, 1536, Chapuys wrote to Charles v, "Knowing that according to English law a wife can make no will while her husband survives, she would not break the said laws, but by way of request caused her physician to write a little bill, which she

When Henry received the queen's letter, he could not but be moved (hard as his heart was) and to weep many a tear,[8] and he asked the imperial ambassador to visit her on his behalf. But as much haste as the ambassador made, by the time he arrived she had already expired. When the king learned of this, he ordered his entire household into mourning and gave her the obsequies of a queen. While all were occupied with this, Anne Boleyn alone showed signs of her joy and delight, dressing herself and her ladies in bright colors and elegant fashions.[9] When some offered her condolences on the queen's death, the evil woman said that she was not grieved that she had died, only that she had died with so much honor. The feelings evoked across Christendom at the queen's death cannot be described, nor the honor, pomp, and expense given by almost every Christian prince in her memory, praising and extolling her virtues while cursing and despising King Henry and his council, who had driven her to her death with such cruel and inhuman treatment.[10]

This was the end of the saintly Queen Doña Catherine, renowned, to be sure, as a queen and as the daughter of kings—and of such great kings as the Catholic Kings of glorious memory—but much more illustrious and fortunate for the extraordinary virtues with which she shone in the world and in which

---

commanded to be sent to me immediately, and which was signed by her hand, directing some little reward to be made to certain servants who had remained with her." *LP*, 10:141.

8   "At the reading of which letter the King burst out a weeping." Harpsfield, *Treatise*, 199–200.

9   According to Chapuys, both Henry and Anne were elated at Catherine's death: "You could not conceive the joy that the King and those who favor this concubinage have shown at the death of the good Queen [...] The King, on the Saturday he heard the news, exclaimed 'God be praised that we are free from all suspicion of war'; and that the time had come that he would manage the French better than he had done hitherto, because they would do now whatever he wanted from a fear lest he should ally himself again with your Majesty, seeing that the cause which disturbed your friendship was gone. On the following day, Sunday, the King was clad all over in yellow, from top to toe, except the white feather he had in his bonnet, and the Little Bastard was conducted to mass with trumpets and other great triumphs. After dinner the King entered the room in which the ladies danced, and there did several things like one transported with joy. At last he sent for his Little Bastard, and carrying her in his arms he showed her first to one and then to another. He has done the like on other days since, and has run some courses at Greenwich." *LP*, 10:141.
Hall states, "Queen Anne ware yelowe for the mournyng." Hall, *Chronicle*, 818.

10   Two weeks after Catherine's death, Chapuys reported that "From all I hear the grief of the people at this news is incredible, and the indignation they feel against the King, on whom they lay the blame of her death, part of them believing it was by poison and others by grief; and they are the more indignant at the joy the King has exhibited." *LP*, 10:141.

she now reigns with Christ.[11] Let us now move on and witness the end of Anne Boleyn, which followed soon thereafter, and we shall compare lineage with lineage, life with life, and death with death. So shall we perceive how secret and incomprehensible are the judgments of the Lord,[12] how little tribulation harms the just, and how much prosperity damages the wicked—for the one purifies and refines the gold of virtue,[13] while the other is a stumbling-block[14] and a knife to the sinner. And although the vices and misdeeds of Anne Boleyn were so foul and hateful that no Christian—much less a religious—could speak of them without covering their face in shame, yet I will set down some few, since they are already well known and written and printed by many distinguished chroniclers. I shall attempt to preserve such moderation as shall neither offend chaste and clean ears, nor mar the truth of my history. Of what I shall say, all may at least take this: to lose late in life the sins and bad habits learned while young, for where there is greater license, there is more peril; where there is more magnificence and power, more brazenness and frailty—if liberty is not restrained by the ties of reason, and power properly subject to the law and spirit of heaven. But let us follow our path and return to the thread of our history.

---

11   Rev. 20:6.

12   Rom. 11:33.

13   Ps. 65:10; Isa. 48:10; Zech. 13:9; Mal. 3:2–3; 1 Pet. 1:7.

14   Ps. 72:2–3; 1 Cor. 8:9.

The King Sentences Anne Boleyn to a Public Death, and the Reason for This[1]

The queen's death left Anne Boleyn so pleased and so smug that she could not contain her delight, for she now saw herself free of competition and securely seated upon her throne, with all addressing her openly as queen, and she could be accepted as such. But by the just judgment and chastisement of God, when they say, "peace, peace," suddenly he raises up war against them, and they fall from their state and repay in torment the grave sins of their pride and vice.[2] Four months after the death of Queen Catherine, the king began to tire of Anne and lust after one of her maids-of-honor, by the name of Jane Seymour; little by little, his affections began to wane, as we shall relate.[3] Anne had miscarried after giving birth to Elizabeth: it began to seem as though, having so far given the king no male children, she never would have any,[4] and since she was the wife of a king, it was only right that she should become mother to a king. To secure the throne for a child doubly born to the house of Boleyn, which should then possess the crown forever, she lay with her brother, George Boleyn

---

1   Sander, *De origine ac progressu*, 166–69.

2   Jer. 6:14–15; 1 Thess. 5:3.

3   The first solid evidence for Henry's interest in Jane Seymour (*c.*1508–37) dates to four months after Catherine's death, in a report from Chapuys on April 1, 1536: "some days ago, the King being here in London, and, the young Miss Seymour, to whom he is paying court at Greenwich, he sent her a purse full of sovereigns, together with a letter, and that the young damsel, to whom he is paying court, after respectfully kissing the letter, returned it to the messenger without opening it, and then falling on her knees, begged the royal messenger to entreat the King in her name to consider that she was a well-born damsel, the daughter of good and honourable parents without blame or reproach of any kind; there was no treasure in this world that she valued as much as her honour, and on no account would she lose it, even if she were to die a thousand deaths. That if the King wished to make her a present of money, she requested him to reserve it for such a time as God would be pleased to send her some advantageous marriage." *CSPS*, 5.2:43.
   Scarisbrick suggests the king's interest may have begun as early as 1534. Seymour had been part of the retinue of both of Henry's previous wives. Scarisbrick, *Henry VIII*, 348, 350.

4   On January 27, 1536, a few months pregnant, Anne suffered a miscarriage. Scarisbrick, *Henry VIII*, 348.

(for more absolute secrecy), and had abominable intercourse with him.[5] But it did not turn out as she had hoped, for she conceived no children. In her desire for a child and out of the wicked ways she had learned as a girl, she was easily prevailed upon and shared herself with others—so much so that she not only lusted after various high-born men and slept with them, but also a musician or dance instructor, known as Mark (the son, so they say, of a carpenter).[6]

Because Anne's lovers were so numerous, and she herself so loose and brazen, her sins could not be kept from the king. But with extraordinary discretion, he held silent, until one day, when certain festivals and sports were held at Greenwich, he saw Anne throw her handkerchief from her window to one of her lovers walking through the yard, for him to wipe the sweat from his face. At this the king arose in high dudgeon, and without a word to anyone left for London with only a few retainers; leaving everyone astonished and Anne perturbed at his sudden departure.[7] The following day, she boarded her barge to travel to London via the Thames, some five leagues away; en route, the constables took her into custody, to bring her captive to the Tower of London (which is along the same river).[8] When she realized she was a prisoner, Anne was first astonished, then began to rage, then to wail and lament, and finally to beg and plead to be brought before the king. He refused, for, being now weary of her and besotted with Jane Seymour, he had resolved to punish Anne and have done with her, which he did in this way. They brought her from her cell and hauled her before a public tribunal, where they presented her before the judges, among whom (by the king's command) sat Thomas Boleyn.[9] Being convicted of adultery and incest with her own brother, she was condemned to death, and on May 19 she was publicly beheaded, not having enjoyed the title of queen more than five months (since the death of the saintly Queen Catherine).

They say she refused to confess before her death, being a heretic, and that she showed signs not so much of remorse as satisfaction at having risen from a

---

5   Among the charges against Anne was the (specious) accusation of incest with her younger brother George. Joseph S. Buck, "Boleyn, George, Viscount Rochford (c.1504–1536)," in ODNB, 6:467–69, here 467–68.

6   Mark Smeaton (c.1512–36) has been "variously described as a musician, a player of the virginals or the spinet, or an organist [...] According to Cavendish, he was the son of a carpenter, but perhaps better evidence suggests that he was a Fleming." Ives, Anne Boleyn, 325.

7   "On May Day, 1536, jousts were held at Greenwich during which Anne is said to have revealed her infidelity by dropping a handkerchief to a lover and thus sent the king stalking off in a rage." Scarisbrick, Henry VIII, 349.

8   On May 2, 1536, the duke of Norfolk, Thomas Cromwell, and Thomas Audley arrested Anne at Greenwich, and brought her by barge to the Tower of London. Ives, Anne Boleyn, 334.

9   After Anne's trial and execution, one Spanish diplomat averred that "Her own father, who was innocent in this case, approved of the sentence." CSPS, 5.2:58.

poor woman to a queen,[10] and that she blamed her disastrous end on her pride and on the abuse perpetrated by the king, for her sake and at her urging, upon Queen Doña Catherine.[11] They also say that the day her sentence was carried out, the king dressed in bright colors—our Lord permitting this to repay her in the same coin for the shamelessness and license with which she had done the same on the day of the obsequies for the saintly Queen Doña Catherine (as has been related).[12] So great was Thomas Boleyn's anguish at the sentence that he died within a few days.[13] Three days after Anne's execution, her lovers and paramours were also punished: her brother George Boleyn, Henry Norris, William Brereton, and Francis Weston—all gentlemen of the king's privy chamber—as well as the musician we mentioned, Mark Smeaton.[14] Furthermore, an old woman of Anne's chamber, her go-between and accomplice, had previously been burned in the courtyard of the Tower of London, before the queen's eyes.[15]

---

10   "'I do not care for all the harm they can do me now,' she said, 'for they can never deny I was a crowned Queen, although I was a poor woman.'" Hume, *Chronicle*, 67.

11   "My fault has been my great pride, and the great crime I committed in getting the King to leave my mistress Queen Katherine for my sake, and I pray God to pardon me for it." Ibid., 70.

12   In the margin: "Chapter 33."

      On the day of Anne's execution, Chapuys reported that "Already it sounds badly in the ears of the public that the King, after such ignominy and discredit as the concubine has brought on his head, should manifest more joy and pleasure now, since her arrest and trial, than he has ever done on other occasions, for he has daily gone out to dine here and there with ladies, and sometimes has remained with them till after midnight. I hear that on one occasion, returning by the river to Greenwich, the royal barge was actually filled with minstrels and musicians of his chamber, playing on all sorts of instruments or singing; which state of things was by many a one compared to the joy and pleasure a man feels in getting rid of a thin, old, and vicious hack in the hope of getting soon a fine horse to ride—a very peculiarly agreeable task for this king. The other night, whilst supping with several ladies at the house of the bishop of Carlion [Carlisle], he manifested incredible joy at the arrest of Anne, as the Bishop himself came and told me the day after." *csps*, 5.2:55.

13   Thomas Boleyn actually outlived his daughter by nearly three years, dying on March 12, 1539. The mistake comes from the Spanish Chronicle, which states, "a few days afterwards her father died of grief." Hume, *Chronicle*, 70.

14   Anne's "accomplices" were actually executed two days before her, on May 17, 1536. They were Anne's brother George Boleyn, three grooms of the privy chamber—Henry Norris (c.1482–1536), William Brereton (c.1487–1536), and Sir Francis Weston (1511–36)—and Mark Smeaton. Ives, *Anne Boleyn*, 352.

15   Bridget Wiltshire, Lady Wingfield (d.1534), was a longtime member of Anne's retinue and a close intimate of the queen. Her age is uncertain, but she died two years before Anne's fall. Ibid., 329–31.

      Cf. "So the gentlemen ordered the old woman to be burnt that night within the tower." Hume, *Chronicle*, 66.

So ended the king's frenzied, reckless love for Anne Boleyn. Such was the conclusion of her vices and her pride. Thus our Lord punished him and her, avenging the death of the saintly Queen Doña Catherine. It is a good lesson in recognizing the end to which all the unbridled appetites of men come, how they drag down those who allow them the upper hand, and how the wicked have no worse tormentor than their own conscience and the knowledge of God's enmity. Let us reflect upon Anne Boleyn's rise to the throne and her fall, her beginning and her end, her triumph and her disgrace, and let us recognize that such a life deserved such a death, such glory such torment and disgrace, and that vice is far costlier than virtue. Throughout the kingdom, the only reaction to Anne's death was universal contentment and joy—for she was universally hated for her notorious, infamous sins of mind and body. Outside of England, there was the same delight. Miserable woman, to be born, grow, marry, and die in such opprobrium and disgrace! Accursed, in ruining her father, her brother, and many others besides, and even more for her arrogance and pride, in wishing to rival a queen renowned in birth and virtues, from whom she could not have been more different. But, above all, wretched and abominable in being the origin and fountainhead of the schism and devastation of her country, and for having left behind a daughter who aped her, filling and overflowing her mother's measure.

The King's Marriage to Jane Seymour, the Sessions of Parliament, the Disturbances That Arose in the Realm, and the Birth of Edward[1]

On the day after Anne's death, the king married Jane Seymour, for he was already so much a captive to his love that he could not wait a single day more—and it was known that he had put the one to death so as to wed the other.[2] He convened a parliament, as well as a synod of the bishops, in which he proposed two things. The first, that all he had done against the Princess Doña Mary in favor of Anne's daughter Elizabeth should be undone and declared null and void.[3] The other, that a form be provided for religious observance in England, because there had been so much confusion and disorder while Anne was alive that many knew not what to believe, do, or affirm. And, lest it seem that he feared the pope or intended to return to his obedience, before everything else he ordered that no one in the synod should dare speak a word concerning his primacy or call it into question.

To carry all this out more efficiently, he declared Thomas Cromwell his vicegerent for all ecclesiastical and spiritual matters, giving him a private seal for dispatching such affairs and instructing him to preside over the synod of bishops and prelates.[4] This he did many times, though a layman and unlettered, and by his authority as vicegerent he enacted certain canons and decrees, sealed with his seal, and ordered the archbishops, bishops, abbots, and all the clergy of England to obey them. Among them, there was one good

---

1 Sander, *De origine ac progressu*, 169–76.

2 "As soon as Henry heard that Anne's execution was accomplished, he entered his barge and visited Jane. Next day [May 20] he was betrothed to her. On 30 May he was married quietly at York Place, in the Queen's Closet." Scarisbrick, *Henry VIII*, 350.

3 "An Acte for the establishment of the succession of the Imperyall Crowne of this Realme" (28 Hen. 8. c. 7), actually removed both Mary and Elizabeth from the order of succession. See *SR*, 3:655–62.

4 "In January 1535 Cromwell had been granted the new office of Vicegerent in Spirituals to enable him in effect to exercise the Supremacy on the king's behalf instead of the Archbishop of Canterbury, who would have been the natural choice for such a position. Henry seems to have been determined to appoint a layman, and since it also carried the right to preside at the convocations, to emphasize the secular superiority to which the Church was now subjected." Loades, *Thomas Cromwell*, 108.

injunction, by which every curate was mandated, under the direst penalties, to start teaching their congregations the Pater Noster, the Ave Maria, the Credo, the commandments of the law of God, and all the other elements of Christian doctrine, in English.[5]

Thereafter, with the public imprimatur of the parliament and the synod, the king created a book mandating what was to be believed and observed, of which there were six catholic [*catolicos*] points. The first, the truth of the holy sacrament of the Eucharist. The second, that it was sufficient for salvation to receive in one kind. The third, that clerical celibacy was to be maintained. The fourth, that vows of chastity and continence made to God were be observed. The fifth, that Masses were to be celebrated, being things ordained by God and necessary for our salvation. The sixth, that the confession of sins to a priest was to be retained in the Church. And he who contravened these points would be severely punished as a heretic.[6] I decided to include these statutes

---

5   The first Henrician Injunctions, promulgated by Cromwell in 1536, provided that "the parsons, vicars, and other curates aforesaid shall diligently admonish the fathers and mothers, masters and governors of youth, being under their care, to teach, or cause to be taught, their children and servants, even from their infancy, their *Pater Noster*, the Articles of our Faith, and the Ten Commandments, in their mother tongue: and the same so taught, shall cause the said youth oft to repeat and understand. And to the intent this may be more easily done, the said curates shall, in their sermons, deliberately and plainly recite oft the said *Pater Noster*, the Articles of our Faith, and the Ten Commandments." See Walter Howard Frere and William McClure Kennedy, eds., *Visitation Articles and Injunctions of the Period of the Reformation*, 3 vols., Alcuin Club Collections 14–16 (London: Longmans, Green and Co., 1910), 2:1–11, here 6–7.

6   Henry's religious settlement veered toward conservatism with the 1539 passage of "An Acte abolishing div[er]sity in Opynions" (31 Hen. 8. c. 14), better known as the Six Articles, enshrined in the so-called "King's Book." Far from Cromwell's brainchild, however, the act represented a significant defeat for the evangelically inclined vicegerent. The articles were as follows: "First, that in the most blessed sacrament of the Aulter, by the strengthe and efficacy of Christs myghtie worde, it beinge spoken by the priest, is p[re]sent really, under the forme of bread and wyne, the naturall bodye and bloode of our Saviour Jesu Criste, conceyved of the Virgin Marie, and that after the consecrac[i]on there remayneth noe substance of bread or wyne, nor any other substance but the substance of Criste, God and man; Secondly, that Comunion in both kinds is not necessary ad salutem by the lawe of God to all p[er]sons; And that it is to be beleved, and not doubted of, but that in the fleshe under the forme of bread is the verie blode, and withe the blode under the forme of wyne is the verie fleshe, aswell aparte as thoughe they were bothe together; Thirdly, that Preests after the order of Presthode receyved as afore may not marye by the lawe of God; Fourthly, that vowes of Chastitye or Wydowhood, by Man or Woman made to God advisedly ought to be observed by the lawe of God, and that it exempteth them from other lib[er]tyes of Cristen people, wch without that they myght enjoye; Fyftly, that it is mete and necessarie that private masses be contynued

and resolutions of the English parliament here to demonstrate how blind and inconstant heresy is, always progressing from bad to worse. For when it began and was yet weak in that kingdom, they affirmed, and published in these decisions, things Catholic and true; later growing in their wickedness, they revoked them and undid what they had once done. For this is characteristic of heretical and deluded men, to weave and unweave, to affirm a thing and then deny it, to be firm and settled in nothing whatsoever. And as the demon grew stronger among them day by day, they tumbled from one error, to another, to those even greater and madder—as the Apostle says, *proficiunt in peius*.[7]

But, to return to our history, they enacted this, though they observed it but little, for the resolutions of men are of no avail without God. No limb can have life apart from the head, nor the vine bear fruit if severed from the root[8]—no more could Henry, his bishops and prelates, and the nobility of his realm preserve the true and Catholic faith while separated from the vicar of Jesus Christ and the successor of Saint Peter, who is the universal pastor and supreme head of the Catholic Church. Let us recognize the great truth of what Saint Cyprian said: "Heresies and schisms are born because there is no single priest obeyed in the Church, a judge who stands in Christ's stead."[9] For this reason, neither the king's laws nor parliament's decrees sufficed to cleanse the realm of heresy— all the more so because the same king who by these laws wished to appear a good and pious Christian also ransacked the churches, profaned the monasteries, and despoiled the altars, sanctuaries, and relics of every treasure and ornament, with such extreme sacrilege and impiety that he appeared to believe nothing at all, or like another Mohammed to be composing another Qur'an out of diverse sects and religions. Thus the king himself, though he made a show of severity toward the Lutherans and Zwinglians, shared many of their errors, and his primate, Cranmer, his vicegerent, Cromwell, and the other bishops and prelates he had created were thoroughly infected with the plague of heresy, and through them many knights and prominent nobles. For their sins they had been abandoned by the true spirit of Jesus Christ and the unity and power of

---

and admytted in this the Kings English Churche and Congregac[i]on as wherby good Cristen people orderinge them selfes accordingly doe receyve bothe godly and goodly consolac[i] ons and benefytts, and it is agreable also to God's law; Sixtly, that auriculer confession is expedient and necessarie to be retained and contynued used and frequented in the Churche of God." *SR*, 3:739–40.

7   In the margin: "2 Timothy 3[:13]."

8   John 15:5; Col. 1:18.

9   In the margin: "Book 1, Letter 3."
    Ribadeneyra is evidently using Desiderius Erasmus's (1466–1536) edition of Cyprian's letters: see Cyprian, *Letters*, 59.5.

his head, so it is no marvel that they fell into various errors and opened the door to the heresies that began then and later grew until they scorched the whole of England. It seemed that in those days there was no God but the will of the king, which was the compass-north to every flatterer and toady.

Seeing all this and despairing of any remedy, across the realm the Catholics rebelled against the king, with more than fifty thousand men taking up arms.[10] To signal that their intent was the defense of the Catholic faith, they adopted as the emblem of their banners and standards the five wounds of our Lord Jesus Christ and the chalice and the host, with the name of Jesus in their midst.[11] The king greatly feared this uprising of the Catholics, and (although he sent men to make war against them) tried to appease them, promising and swearing to rectify everything they wished and not to punish anyone for the insurrection. By this trick, the Catholics laid down their arms, and the king then put to death thirty-two of them, among them several knights, barons, abbots, priests, and friars.[12] As this sentence was carried out, our Lord carried

---

10   The Pilgrimage of Grace, an uprising in the north of England in the autumn and winter
        of 1536–37. The rebels were motivated by a mixture of economic, political, and religious
        grievances. See R.W. Hoyle, *The Pilgrimage of Grace and the Politics of the 1530s*, (Oxford:
        Oxford University Press, 2001).

        Cf. A letter from Eustace Chapuys to Isabella of Portugal, October 14, 1536. "A great
        number of men have risen, some say 30,000, some 50,000, who refuse to pay the taxes
        imposed by the last Parliament, and object to the suppression of churches, wishing eccle-
        siastical matters to be as formerly." *LP*, 11:698.

11   The Pilgrims swore the following oath: "Ye shall not enter into this our Pilgrimage of
        Grace for the commonwealth but only for the love that ye bear unto Almighty God, his
        faith and the Holy Church militant and maintenance thereof, the preservation of the
        king's person, his issue and [...] purifying of the true noble blood to the intent to expel
        all villains' blood and other being [...] against the commonwealth from his grace and the
        privy council of the same. And that you shall not enter into our said pilgrimage for no
        peculiar profit to yourself nor to do no displeasure to any private person but by counsel
        of the commonwealth nor slay nor murder for no envy or malice old or [new] but in your
        hearts put away all fear for the premises of the commonwealth. And to take before you
        the cross of God and in your hearts his faith to the restitution of his church and to the
        suppression of these heretics and subverters of the just laws of God. [...]." Many of the
        Pilgrims wore badges emblazoned with the five wounds of Christ. Hoyle, *Pilgrimage of
        Grace*, 416, 458–59.

12   In December 1536, the duke of Norfolk negotiated a settlement at Doncaster that persuad-
        ed the Pilgrimage to disband (although a second uprising, Bigod's Rebellion, took place
        in Yorkshire the following February). In May 1537, however, Henry carried out reprisals,
        trying and executing seventeen of the rebels, including several minor nobles, a former
        Cistercian abbot, a priest, and a knight of the garter. Ibid., 363, 406–10.

out another against him, taking the duke of Richmond, his bastard son, whom he dearly loved[13]—although a little later he gave him a son by his wife Jane Seymour, called Edward, born October 10, 1537.[14] As his mother was wracked by the pangs of childbirth and in danger of her life, the doctors asked the king which he would rather lived, the son or the mother? Henry chose the son, since it was in his power to take another wife, but not to have another son, and so the son survived and the mother died.[15]

---

13 Henry Fitzroy died on July 23, 1536, of a pulmonary infection.

14 Edward VI was probably born on October 12 or 13, 1537 at Hampton Court. A letter sent in Jane's name to Thomas Cromwell declares, "by th'inestimable goodnes and grace of Almighty God we be delivred and brought in child bed of Prince conceived in moost Laufull Matrimony betwene my lord the Kinges Maiestie and us [...] Yevyn under our Signet at my lordes Manour of Hampton-courte the xij. day of Octobre." Richard L. DeMolen notes, however, that these form notices were often sent out prematurely, and that other contemporary evidence points toward October 13. Richard L. DeMolen, "The Birth of Edward VI and the Death of Queen Jane: The Arguments for and Against Caesarean Section," *Renaissance Studies* 4, no. 4 (1990): 359–91, here 362–65.

15 Jane Seymour did not die in childbirth—indeed, her death came on October 24, 1537, nearly two weeks after Edward was born. Contemporaries recorded that the queen was suffering from "an naturall laxe"; Cromwell blamed Jane's ladies for indulging her cravings for perilous foods. *LP*, 12.2:970, 1004.

Nevertheless, the story of death in childbirth became widespread. One epigraph for Jane lamented, "Here a Phoenix lieth, whose death / To another Phoenix gave breath: / It is to be lamented much, / the World at once ne'r knew two such." Several contemporaries blamed Henry's supposedly aggressive instructions to the doctors: in a contemporary ballad, the midwives ask Henry, "O king, show us thy will, / The queen's sweet life to save or spill?" The king replies, "Then, as she cannot saved be, / Oh, save the flower though not the tree." Jennifer Loach, *Edward VI*, ed. George W. Bernard and Penry William, Yale English Monarchs (New Haven: Yale University Press, 2002), 6–7.

G.R. Elton records a similar witness: "In November 1538, Richard Swann, a young servingman of Hounslow, risked his life by telling of a prophecy touching the birth of Prince Edward, to the effect 'that he should be killed that never was born'; he knew it meant the Prince because a lady had told the King at the time of Edward's birth 'that one of the two must die,' whereupon Henry had ordered the child to be saved by being 'cut out of his mother's womb.'" G.R. Elton, *Policy and Police: The Enforcement of the Reformation in the Age of Thomas Cromwell* (Cambridge: Cambridge University Press, 1972), 59.

There is considerable scholarly debate over whether Edward was born by Caesarean section, and the extent to which the labor was responsible for the queen's death. See DeMolen, "Birth of Edward VI."

Cardinal Pole's Arrival in Flanders, and the Results Thereof[1]

Like a merciful father, Pope Paul III had bided his time, suspending his sentence against the king and harboring high hopes for his amendment and correction. Indeed, seeing that he had punished Anne Boleyn, the origin of so many evils, that he had declared in parliament that he had no wish to follow the opinions of Luther and enacted harsh laws against them, that the entire country had been unsettled by the recent schism, and that, with the saintly Queen Doña Catherine dead, he was now a widower and free to marry whatever lady he liked, who would not have believed that the king must return to himself, be restored, and take other, better counsel?

For these reasons, and at the entreaties of many Christian monarchs, the pope chose to probe the king's attitude once more, and, having conferred with the emperor and the king of France, sent Reginald Pole (whom he had recently given a cardinal's hat) to Flanders as legate *a latere*, to the end that, being close to England, he might beg and importune Henry to examine himself and turn again to God, in the name of the pope and of the said monarchs.[2] The legate traveled to Paris, where he was welcomed with enormous pomp and ceremony. When Henry learned of this, he dispatched Francis Bryan with all speed to ask the king of France to hand over the legate—if he did not, he could consider their friendship at an end.[3] The king of France could not do as Henry asked, because the legate had arrived under his word and bond—but, so as not to

---

1　Sander, *De origine ac progressu*, 176–81.

2　Pole was created cardinal by Paul III on December 22, 1536, and the following February he was named legate *a latere*, but more to promote foreign intervention in England than to effect a reconciliation. "Biographical Dictionary—Consistory of December 22, 1536," in *CHRC*.

3　Henry bombarded Bryan and Stephen Gardiner, his ambassador in Paris, with letters on the problem of Pole's presence in France. On April 8, 1537, he wrote: "Approve of Gardiner's conduct as detailed in his letter sent by Arthur Nowell, in delivering the King's 'letters certificatories' to the French king and demanding the deliverance of Reynold Pole. The French king replied that he had entered his dominions with a safe conduct, but that he would command him to leave them within ten days. Sir Francis on his arrival shall, with or without Gardiner as they may think best, act according to his instructions for Pole's delivery, reminding Francis that there is no exception of safe conduct in the treaty, and if it be admitted in this case the same thing may be attempted again. [...] If the French king makes any overture for Pole's delivery, except in accordance with the treaty, they are to make the same answer that Gardiner made, viz., that they had no commission to demand him in any other way." *LP*, 12.1:865.

irritate Henry (with whom he thought it important to remain friendly), he had the legate discreetly warned to leave his realm the very next day. This he did, leaving for Cambrai at great peril to his life: he found the route thick with soldiers, not only imperial and French, but also English (who had come to fight on France's side).[4] So much so that the retainers who accompanied the legate were so terrified and panic-stricken that none dared bear a cross before him, as is the custom for legates—it was the legate himself who picked it up and carried it with high spirits and steadfastness, until the frightened servants took it from him and performed their office.

When he arrived at Cambrai, Pole learned that Henry had had him proclaimed a traitor and offered fifty thousand ducats to his killer;[5] seeing himself in yet deeper peril, among brazen and well-armed people, he knew not what to do, save to turn to God, whose cause his was. As he never abandons his own,[6] he moved Eberhard von der Mark, cardinal and bishop of Liège (and at that time the president of the council of Flanders) to invite him to that city, receiving him under his guarantee and welcoming and entertaining him most kindly.[7] Henry was deeply pained at this, sending to Flanders to promise that if the legate was handed over, he would abandon the king of France and return to the emperor's party, aiding him with four thousand infantry, with ten months' pay deposited in the hands of the council of those provinces. So great

---

Henry wrote again a week later: "Has received their sundry letters by Francisco and by Gardiner's servant Massy, relating the arrival of Pole at Paris, his solemn reception and departure, the stay of Bryan with the French King, and Gardiner's advice about spreading a report of aid to be given to the Emperor against the French. [...] As Francis told Gardiner in his last conference that he would by no means suffer Pole to have any honour in his realm, they are both immediately to repair to his presence [...] and tell the French King Henry has been much surprised to hear of the pompous receiving of Pole into Paris, especially as Francis had informed the King by Tyndeville, bailly of Troys, of Pole's traitorous purposes. [...] Desires them to enquire by all means into the mystery of Pole's sudden departure from Paris, and to have good spial upon him wherever he be if he remain on this side the mountains. [...] Gardiner is to [...] demand of Francis to make his purgation of that matter, that he may not incur the King's displeasure." Ibid., 12.1:939.

4 Pole's journey came in the midst of the Italian War of 1536–38, between France and the Holy Roman Empire: though the action was confined to Lombardy, Piedmont, and Provence, tensions would have been high in the borderlands between northeastern France and the imperial provinces of the Low Countries. See Knecht, *Francis I*, 274–88.

5 On April 25, 1537, Henry instructed his ambassadors, "And for as much as we would be very glad to have the said Pole by some mean trussed up and conveyed to Calais, we desire and pray you to consult and devise between you there-upon." *LP*, 12.1:1032.

6 1 Kings 12:22; 3 Kings 6:13; Ps. 93:14.

7 Eberhard von der Mark (1472–1538), elected prince-bishop of Liège in 1506 and made a cardinal in 1520, hosted Pole at Liège for six months. "Biographical Dictionary—Consistory of August 9, 1520," in *CHRC*.

was the hatred the king harbored for Cardinal Pole. The pope learned of the danger to his legate and ordered him to return to Rome, sending men to protect him from Henry's rage, and he made the cardinal of Liège his legate in Flanders, in recompense for the good deed he had done Pole and the service rendered to the Apostolic See.[8] But Henry, when he saw that Cardinal Pole had escaped him, turned on his kinsmen and friends with incredible savageness and fury: he ordered the arrest of Cardinal Pole's mother, Margaret, countess of Salisbury and daughter of George, duke of Clarence (the brother of King Edward IV). Advanced in years though she was, and much admired for her holy life and habits, because she was the mother of such a son she was charged with having received letters from him and then publicly beheaded on May 28, 1541.[9] In the same order, the king sentenced to death Cardinal Pole himself; Gertrude, marchioness of Exeter;[10] Adrian Fortescue, a prominent knight; and Thomas Dingley, of the order of Saint John. These last two were beheaded on July 10.[11] Together with Margaret, the cardinal's mother, his older brother, Henry Pole, Baron Montagu; Henry Courtenay, marquess of Exeter and earl of Devon, grandson of King Edward IV (the son of his daughter); and Edward Neville, another important knight, were arrested, and all of them, along with two priests, condemned on the same day for defying the king's impious decrees.[12]

---

8   Von der Mark was made legate *a latere* in the Low Countries in the fall of 1537. Ibid.

9   Margaret Pole was arrested in late 1538 and accused of having "comytted and p[er]petrated div[er]se and sundry other detestable and abominable treasons." She was beheaded on the morning of May 27, 1541, at the age of sixty-seven. Pierce, "Pole, Margaret," in *ODNB*, 44:708–09.

     For a Catholic rendering of the countess's martyrdom, see Book 1 Figure 29.1.

10   Gertrude Courtenay, marchioness of Exeter (d.1558), was arrested in November 1538. Though attainted for treason by parliament in July 1539, the marchioness was eventually released without trial. J.P.D. Cooper, "Courtenay [*née* Blount], Gertrude, marchioness of Exeter (*d.* 1558)," in *ODNB*, 13:677–78.

11   Sir Adrian Fortescue (*c.*1481–1539), a landowner of unstable fortunes, and Sir Thomas Dingley (*c.*1507–39), a knight of the hospital of Saint John of Jerusalem, were both beheaded on Tower Hill on July 9, 1539. Richard Rex, "Fortescue, Sir Adrian (*c.*1481–1539)," in *ODNB*, 20:447–48, here 447. G.J. O'Malley, "Dingley, Sir Thomas (1506x8–1539)," in *ODNB*, 16:244.

12   December 1538 saw the conviction for high treason of Henry Pole, Baron Montagu (1492–1539), Henry Courtenay, marquess of Exeter and earl of Devon (*c.*1498–1538), and Sir Edward Neville (*c.*1482–1538). Courtenay (the son of Katherine of York [1479–1527], sixth daughter of Edward IV) and Neville were beheaded on Tower Hill on December 9. Pole was executed on January 9, 1539. Thomas F. Mayer, "Pole, Henry, Baron Montague (1492–1539)," in *ODNB*, 44:701–03. J.P.D. Cooper, "Courtenay, Henry, marquess of Exeter (1498/9–1538)," in *ODNB*, 13:678–81, here 678–80. Alasdair Hawkyard, "Neville, Sir Edward (*b.* in or before 1482, *d.* 1538)," in *ODNB*, 40:489–90.

The King's Cruelty against the Franciscans, and the Death of Father Brother John Forest[1]

The persecution and oppression of Catholics in England at this time was brutal and horrific, stoked and fomented by the accursed vicegerent, Cromwell. Because he was a heretic and wanted the king to join with the German heretics against the emperor, he incited him against Pole and those of his house, as persons close to the pope and the emperor—by whose advice, he said, the pope had made Pole a cardinal. Cromwell seized an opportunity to rile and inflame the king even more when Charles, duke of Guelders, a thoroughly Catholic prince, died and was succeeded by William, duke of Cleves. Because he secretly favored the heretics, and feared that the emperor would seize the title of Guelders, William had joined forces with the king of France and several German princes opposed to the emperor;[2] for greater security, he wished to include King Henry in the confederation and alliance, and to give him his sister, Anne of Cleves, in marriage, the which idea was pleasing to the king, advantageous to Cromwell, and desirable to the German princes.[3]

With this opportunity, Cromwell persecuted the Catholics with slanders and false accusations, deeming them friends to the pope and the emperor. And so he finished off the saintly Franciscans who had been imprisoned several years before (although some had died in prison, many were yet living). The king wished to have done with all of them, but, fearing the scandal (given their number), he chose a few and had them put to death by various means. They hanged one with the cord of his habit. They killed another in the prison through starvation. They murdered some with filth and maltreatment. Thirty-two were chained in pairs and sent to different regions, so that they would die in prison with less notoriety and consternation among the populace. But because that

---

1 Sander, *De origine ac progressu*, 181–85.

2 Charles II of Egmond, duke of Guelders (r.1492–1538) died in 1538, leaving his duchy to his first cousin once removed, William, duke of Jülich-Cleves-Berg (r.1539–92), a development displeasing in the extreme to Charles V. Retha M. Warnicke, *The Marrying of Anne of Cleves: Royal Protocol in Early Modern England* (Cambridge: Cambridge University Press, 2000), 68.

3 In March 1539, Henry dispatched emissaries to Cleves to discuss a potential marriage to William's older sister, Anne. In September, a German delegation traveled to England to finalize the agreement. Ibid., 62, 93.

blessed father, Brother John Forest, a Franciscan friar (of whom mention has already been made), had been beloved of Queen Doña Catherine and had zealously resisted the king's supremacy, they decided to torture him with greater cruelty and send him to heaven with more atrocious sufferings. Therefore, on May 22, 1538, in a field in the city of London known as Smithfield [*Fabro*], they suspended him from a pair of gallows with chains on his arms and burned him alive on a slow flame, beginning at his feet, until he yielded his spirit to the Lord.[4] To this barbarous outrage against a servant of God they added another, greater impiety against God himself. There was in Wales, near Glastonbury, a wooden statue of Christ, ancient and highly revered, to which the faithful used to flock; the ministers of Satan ripped it from its place and dragged it to London, where they burned it together with the saintly confessor.[5]

And so as not to leave undone any cruelty or outrage against this sainted martyr of Jesus Christ, they wrote poems and songs, which they published and affixed to the corners of the city, mocking and ridiculing him for denying their Gospel and the king's headship of the Church.[6] The king turned his cruelty not only upon the religious and the followers of God, but also against his own officials and servants, no matter how intimate or favored. For if they offended him in the least little thing, or contradicted his appetites and pleasures, he put them to death for it, forgetting their former service. Among these were Nicholas Carew, his Master of the Horse, of the order of St. George and the Garter;[7]

---

4   On May 22, 1538, Forest was burned at Smithfield, before a crowd of thousands, including Cromwell, Cranmer, and other leading nobles and prelates. See Peter Marshall, "Papist as Heretic: The Burning of John Forest, 1538," *HJ* 41, no. 2 (June 1998): 351–74, and Dillon, "John Forest."

5   The statue was not of Christ, but one of Dderfel Gadarn, a sixth-century warrior saint "much loved and revered in Wales." Dillon, "John Forest," 2.

    Ribadeneyra has added this erroneous, incendiary detail, possibly drawn from contemporary illustrations that show a statue of Christ in the flames (see Book 1 Figure 37.1): Sander simply mentions "a certain wooden image or statue of great size." Sander, *De origine ac progressu*, 184.

6   The 1586 edition of *De origine ac progressu* actually reproduces some of these doggerel verses: "Forestus frater, mendacij pater, / Qui mortis author voluit esse suæ; / Per summam impudentiam, negauit Euangelium, / Et Regem esse caput Ecclesiæ." Ibid.

    Edward Hall's *Chronicle* offers the corresponding English: "And Forest the Freer / That obstinate lyer / That willfully shalbe dead. / In his contumacie / The Gospell doth deny / The kyng to be supreme head." Hall, *Chronicle*, 826.

7   The diplomat and courtier Sir Nicholas Carew (*c.*1496–1539) was one of Henry's closest companions, master of the horse since 1522. In 1535, Carew was made a knight of Garter (which order bore the insignia of St. George). He fell victim to one of Cromwell's purges, arrested for treason in December 1538 and beheaded on March 8, 1539. Stanford Lehmberg, "Carew, Sir Nicholas (*b.* in or before 1496, *d.* 1539)," in *ODNB*, 10:53–56.

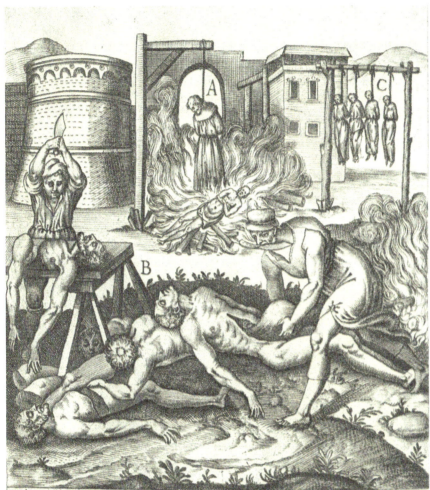

A. *Ob fidem fedi Romanę feruatam Ioannes foreſtus ordinis S. Francisci de*
obseruantia facerdos uenerandus uiuus fuspensus, igneꝗ fubiecto cōbustus
eſt, qui accendebatur ligno facræ Chriſti ſtatuæ.

B. *Sedi funt in quatuor partes poſt fuspendium fpirantes doctor Powelus,*
fetherſtonus, Abelus facerdotes docti, Gardinerus quoꝗ et Larcus Lon-
dini: Stoneus item Auguſtini a nus cantuariæ.

C. *tres Rⁿᵈⁱ Abbates ordinis S. Benedicti necantur. et aliquot ipsorū Monachi laqueis*
ſoffocantur.

and Leonard Grey, lord deputy of Ireland.[8] Even his fellow heretics did not escape his savage rage if they crossed the line by speaking ill of the king's laws. Thus, he burned a certain John Lambert, a Zwinglian, even though he had appealed to the king against Vicegerent Cromwell.[9]

---

8   Leonard Grey, Viscount Graney (c.1490–1541) had been lord deputy of Ireland since 1536. In June 1540, he was charged with treason, and beheaded at Tower Hill on June 28, 1541. Mary Ann Lyons, "Grey, Leonard, Viscount Graney (c.1490–1541)," in ODNB, 23:865–67, here 865, 867.

9   John Lambert (d.1538) was a Norfolk-born religious radical who moved in evangelical circles both in England and the Continent. In 1538, he was arrested for heterodox views on the sacrament of the altar. Foxe, in the most influential account of Lambert's life and death, avers that Lambert (disastrously) appealed to the king himself: Henry, fiercely conservative when it came to the Eucharist, personally participated in the trial on November 16, 1538. Lambert was condemned the same day and burned as a heretic at Smithfield on November 22. See Foxe, *Acts and Monuments*, 5:181–237.

Of Henry's Sacrilege against the Tombs, Relics, and Images of the Saints, and the Pope's Judgment against Him[1]

But because Henry imagined that his authority was not limited to the earth or to his mortal subjects, he also attempted to wage war against the saints in heaven: at the advice and encouragement of his vicegerent, he ordered every image of our Lady and the other saints banished from his realm. To these the people had flocked with zeal and devotion, and the whole kingdom had offered huge donations and precious gifts, because in them our Lord had manifested himself in palpable miracles and clear displays of his mercy through the intercession of his saints—these the king intended to steal by such tricks, and so he did. Indeed, nothing valuable or precious in any holy place escaped the king's hands. Then he turned upon the sepulchers of the sainted martyrs and persecuted their relics.

In England, there were three cults of three English martyrs that were loved and revered more than all others. The first, that of the martyr Saint Alban, who had been the first (that we know of) to shed his blood for the faith of Jesus Christ on that island, in the year of our Lord 300, in the time of Emperor Diocletian. And for this reason, he is rightly known as the protomartyr of England.[2] The second was that of King Saint Edmund, martyred by the pagans in the year 871 for the same faith.[3] The third, that of Saint Thomas, archbishop of Canterbury, who suffered in 1171 in the days of King Henry II for the sake of justice and the defense of the Church's liberties.[4] The tombs of these three martyrs were the most famous shrines in the whole kingdom, and (through the

---

1 Sander, *De origine ac progressu*, 185, 187–93.
2 Bede's *Ecclesiastical History* dates the death of Alban, "protomartyr of Britain," to the persecutions carried out by Emperor Diocletian (r.284–305) in the first years of the fourth century. Bede, *Ecclesiastical History*, 29.
3 Edmund (or Eadmund) was a ninth-century king of East Anglia, who died during the 869–70 Viking invasion. David Farmer, *The Oxford Dictionary of Saints*, fifth edition (Oxford: Oxford University Press, 2011), 136.
4 Thomas Becket, archbishop of Canterbury, was slain on December 29, 1170 by knights in the service of King Henry II (r.1154–89), with whom Becket had clashed over the rights of the Church. W.L. Warren, *Henry II*, The English Monarchs (Berkeley: University of California Press, 1973), 508–11, 518.

© KONINKLIJKE BRILL NV, LEIDEN, 2017 | DOI 10.1163/9789004323964_045

generosity of previous kings and the devotion of the people) the richest. These Henry assailed with all his might, despoiling and ransacking them with such savageness and godlessness that one learned man who was present uttered this lament:

> If you had been present and had seen, as I saw, the temples profaned, the altars overturned, the sanctuaries plundered, the images and relics of the saints abused with injuries and insults, I truly believe you would not have been able to hold back your tears, moans, and sighs, seeing men taken for Christians perpetrate such cruel and barbarous deeds as no history records, neither by enemy of Christ nor by tyrant. What would Henry VII, father of this sacrilegious tyrant, say, if he were resurrected now and saw all the donations and treasures, given to the Church and piously conse-crated to God by so many foreign Christian monarchs and previous kings of England, stolen and profaned by his son? Without doubt, he would curse the day he had fathered him, and the day such a hateful, horrid monster was born.[5]

Thus speaks that author. But although Henry persecuted every saint in the kingdom, he was fiercest against the glorious Archbishop Thomas of Canter-bury, as much because he had died for the Church's liberties as for the infinite wealth of his shrine. The royal treasurer at the time acknowledged that there was so much gold, silver, jewels, precious stones, and sumptuous ornaments that it took no fewer than twenty-six wagons to bear it away.[6] And from this may be extrapolated what they raked in from despoiling all the other churches, oratories, and monasteries of the land.

---

5   In the margin: "Richard Hiliard."

  Richard Hiliard (dates unknown, *fl.* sixteenth century) was an English cleric who fled Britain for the English hospice at Rome. His writings on the English Reformation have only survived in fragments. *The English Hospice in Rome* (Leominster: Gracewing, 2005), 206. Kenneth Pickthorn, *Early Tudor Government: Henry VIII* (Cambridge: Cambridge University Press, 2015), 129.

  For the passage reproduced in the 1586 edition of *De origine ac progressu*, see Sander, *De origine ac progressu*, 188.

  Cf. the fragments of Hiliard's work that survive in BL Arundel MS 152, fol. 312–13.

6   Nicholas Pocock regarded this figure as "perhaps an exaggeration of Sander's," but it has proved an enduring part of the mythos of the shrine's destruction. At the time of the shrine's destruction, Thomas Howard, third duke of Norfolk, would have been lord high treasurer. Nicholas Pocock, "Review of *Letters and Papers, Foreign and Domestic, of the Reign of Henry VIII*," *EHR* 9, no. 34 (April 1894): 373–77, here 373.

This barbaric, irreligious tyrant was not content to have to put his sacrilegious hands upon the treasures of God and his holy martyr, but in a hellish, devilish madness he then ordered the saint to be summoned to appear before his tribunal, almost four hundred years after he had died in the defense of justice and been canonized in heaven and on earth, renowned throughout the world for his numberless miracles. Henry condemned him as a traitor and ordered him erased from the calendar of saints, and in parliament he decreed, on pain of death, that no one should celebrate his day, nor pray to him, nor call him a saint, nor possess a book or calendar in which his name had not been effaced.[7] And to make plain the unbelievable impiety and blasphemy with which this was done, I will insert here part of Henry's decree against that glorious and sainted prelate, whom we may justly call twice-martyred—once in his life, and again after his death. In the edict, having uttered numerous falsehoods and spoken of him despicably, he concludes with these words:

> Therefore, His Majesty expressly ordains and commands that the said Thomas Becket—so he calls the saint in derision—henceforth be neither regarded, nor addressed, nor revered as a saint, and that all his images and portraits be removed from every church, chapel, and site throughout the realm, and that the feasts formerly celebrated and observed in his honor be neither celebrated nor observed, and that all books, divine offices, collects, antiphonies, and prayers created for his commemoration or invocation be obliterated.[8]

---

7   A royal proclamation of November 16, 1538 asserted of Becket, "his canonization was made only by the Bishop of Rome because he had been a champion to maintain his usurped authority and a bearer of the iniquities of the clergy [...] the King's majesty [...] hath thought expedient to declare to his loving subjects that, notwithstanding the said canonization, there appeareth nothing in his life and exterior conversation whereby he should be called a saint, but rather esteemed to have been a traitor to his prince." *TRP*, 1:185–86.

   In early September 1538, Henry had the shrine to Thomas at Canterbury dismantled, a process lasting several days. Robert E. Scully, "The Unmaking of a Saint: Thomas Becket and the English Reformation," *Catholic Historical Review* 86, no. 4 (October 2000): 579–602, here 593.

8   "His grace straightly chargeth and commandeth that from henceforth the said Thomas Becket shall not be esteemed, named, reputed, nor called a saint, but Bishop Becket, and that his images and pictures through the whole realm shall be put down and avoided out of all churches, chapels, and the places, and that from henceforth the days used to be festival in his name shall not be observed, nor the service, office, antiphons, collects, and prayers in his name read, but erased and put out of all the books; and that all other festival days, already abrogate, shall be in no wise solemnized." *TRP*, 1:275.

These are the words of the decree, in which we see such extreme arrogance, brazenness, and more than diabolical godlessness that its like will hardly be found from any tyrant or persecutor of our sacred faith, gentile or heretic, in all centuries past. But Henry's did not stop here, for after these words he adds the following:

> His Majesty also commands that no one should dare celebrate the other feast days that have been abrogated, but rather that the statutes and mandates given by His Majesty concerning this be observed, so that his subjects and vassals be no further deceived, but rather liberated from all the superstition and idolatry that prevailed in times past, and this is ordered under penalty of His Majesty's anger and displeasure, and other penalties according to his will.[9]

What antipope, or, as I should say, what Antichrist could say more than what Henry says in these words? For he casts the saints out of heaven, and commands that they be neither recognized nor honored as saints, they who have always been revered as such by the Catholic Church! And that so glorious a prelate, so illustrious and steadfast a martyr as was Saint Thomas, chancellor and primate, the glory of his nation, a light and model of all sanctity in the Church of God, should be treated like a felon, rebel, and traitor! And in this Henry has been crueler than Henry II himself, whose words were the cause— or at least the occasion—of the sainted priest's death: for Henry II thought himself offended in certain matters (although unreasonably) by Saint Thomas the archbishop, while Henry VIII could not possibly have received any slight or harbor any dislike for him, save that he had died for the liberties of the Church, whose supreme head is the pope. Henry II refused to support or defend those who killed him, instead sending them to the pope to beg pardon and penance for the crime. The king himself was purged of it, gave satisfaction that it had not been done at his order or by his will, and fulfilled with all obedience and humility the penance imposed by the papal legates for merely having given an opportunity for the saint's death through his words. In his decree, Henry VIII justifies the murderers and claims that the saint was the cause of his

---

9 "And that all other festival days, already abrogate, shall be in no wise solemnized, but his grace's ordinance and injunctions thereupon observed, to the intent his grace's loving subjects shall be no longer blindly led and abused to commit idolatry as they have done in times past, upon pain of his majesty's indignation and imprisonment at his grace's pleasure." Ibid., 1:276.

own death.[10] Henry II revered the sainted martyr, prostrating himself before his tomb, often adoring his holy relics with his son, and imploring his forgiveness with many tears. And on the day he first did so, he won a notable victory against his enemies and captured the king of Scotland, as well as achieving other notable successes through the saint's intercession.[11] Four hundred years later, Henry VIII had the same relics burned and scattered to the wind, and persecuted the saint as though he had been some pariah or heretic. Henry II gave many precious gifts to the shrine where Saint Thomas was interred, and for his sake enriched the monastery, which he always held in the highest esteem. Henry VIII devastated the monastery, profaned the shrine, and stole every treasure and valuable that Henry II and all his successors had left for divine worship and the adoration of the sainted martyr. Lastly, Henry II ultimately undid the laws he had passed against the Church's liberties, for the sake of which Saint Thomas had died. Henry VIII revived these very laws,[12] and others yet worse (as appears in this history), to make himself the monstrous head of the Church of England,[13] and he proclaimed other things equally abominable and unbelievable. Pope Paul III recounts these in the bull he promulgated against King Henry in the year 1538, in which, after enumerating the reasons he delayed in proceeding against him, in hopes of his correction and reform, and that he now considers him a lost cause, beyond cure, he says these words:

> For, not satisfied with having put to death, with extreme and cruel tortures, the living priests and prelates, he has not shrunk from perpetrating

---

10   In the margin: "Peter of Blois's letter 66, to Walter [Ophamil, d.1191], archbishop of Palermo."

      In the modern edition, this is letter 227. See Peter of Blois, *Petri Blesensis Bathoniensis archdiaconi opera omnia*, ed. I.A. Giles, 4 vols., Patres Ecclesiæ Anglicanæ (Oxford: John Henry Parker, 1847), 1:195–97.

11   On July 12, 1174, Henry II underwent public penance at Becket's shrine at Canterbury—ostensibly out of contrition for occasioning the saint's death, more realistically to neutralize the possibility of the cult being used against him. The next day, at Alnwick in Northumberland, a Scottish force under King William the Lion (r.1165–1214) was surprised and defeated by a troop of Yorkshire gentry, ending in the king's capture. Warren, *Henry II*, 135.

12   Though it does not appear that Henry VIII specifically revived Henry II's ecclesiastical legislation, J.J. Scarisbrick has noted the Tudor monarch's interest in and use of his Plantagenet ancestor's Constitutions of Clarendon (which Henry II had relinquished in 1172 after prolonged negotiations with the papacy) to buttress his own claim to authority over the Church. Scarisbrick, *Henry VIII*, 264. Warren, *Henry II*, 531.

13   The disquisition on Becket is added in the 1595 edition.

atrocities against the dead—and against those of the dead as for many centuries have been revered as canonized saints throughout the universal Church. Whereas, after having summoned the blessed martyr Thomas of Canterbury to judgment, in mockery and derision of religion denounced him for contempt, and declared him a traitor, he had him disinterred and burned, with his sacred ashes scattered to the wind. This glorious martyr had been honored and adored throughout the kingdom with the deepest reverence, on account of the innumerable miracles the Lord worked through him. In this Henry shows himself more barbarous than the barbarians. For even foes, when they are victorious in battle, do not waste their cruelty on the fallen. This same Henry has stolen the golden sarcophagus that held the holy corpse, and all the gifts and precious things that had been offered there, and despoiled the monastery (rich in jewels) dedicated to the blessed Saint Augustine, the apostle of England, in the same city of Canterbury. Just as he himself has been transformed into an animal, so he has chosen to honor the other brutes, his comrades—for, having expelled the monks of the monastery, he has made it a pen for beasts and wild things, which is a wickedness unheard-of, not only among Christians, but even among infidels and Turks![14]

The pope says all this, and adds that, seeing that the wound was gangrenous and incurable, he has decided to act the part of a good surgeon—that is, to amputate the rotten limb, lest the entire body perish. Therefore, on January 1, 1538, the fifth year of his pontificate, he excommunicated the king, and pronounced and renewed all the censures and penalties contained in the previous bull.[15]

---

14   Soon after his accession, Paul III had drawn up a bull of excommunication, *Eius qui immobilis*, dated August 30, 1535. The bull was suspended, in hopes that Henry would return to obedience. On December 17, 1538, Paul promulgated *Cum redemptor noster*, the bull to which Ribadeneyra refers, confirming the excommunication of 1535. Ribadeneyra works from the text as reproduced by Sander: see Sander, *De origine ac progressu*, 190–93. For a modern text, see Luigi Bilio, Francesco Gaude, Charles Cocquelines, and Luigi Tomassetti, eds., *Bullarum diplomatum et privilegiorum sanctorum Romanorum pontificum Taurinensis editio*, 27 vols. (Turin: Seb. Franco et Henrico Dalmazzo, 1857–72), 6:203–05.

15   There is a discrepancy in the dating here: the bull as reproduced by Sander is dated "the Kalends of January [*calendis Ianuarij*]," that is to say, January 1, while the critical text reads "the sixteenth [before] the Kalends of January [*decimosexto kal. ianuarii*]," that is to say, December 17. As the bull was issued at the end of 1538, rather than the beginning, it is to be surmised that the numeral was omitted from Sander's text. Sander, *De origine ac progressu*, 193. Bilio et al., eds., *Bullarum*, 6:205.

And he ordered the sentence published in various cities in the provinces of Flanders (which belonged to the emperor), France, and Scotland, as a sign that he had conferred with the rulers of these territories and that they approved of what he had done.[16]

---

16   "If the publication of these present letters be accomplished in Dieppe, Rouen, or Boulogne, towns in France in the diocese of Amiens, or in the city of St Andrews, or in the town of Coldstream, of the diocese of St Andrews, in the kingdom of Scotland, or in Tuam and Ardfert, cities or dioceses of the realm of Ireland." Bilio et al., eds., *Bullarum*, 6:205.

The Assault on the Monasteries of England, and the Tyranny with Which it Was Done[1]

But this did not cause Henry to mend his ways; to the contrary, he committed yet further insults, outrages, and attacks. For, after he had expelled every friar of the four mendicant orders from their houses, which he confiscated and took for himself, and had given the monastery of Saint Augustine in London, together with its chapel and all its movables, to his vicegerent, Cromwell (by whose advice all this had been done), who had begun to erect a sumptuous palace on the spot (which God did not permit him to finish),[2] he convened a parliament in the year 1539, which met on April 28. Since none dared resist the king or reject the proposals made by Cromwell, it was declared that every monastery in the realm, of monks and nuns alike, belonged to the king, with all their incomes and lands arrogated to the crown.[3] When this decree was published, you could see gangs of thugs seize the holy religious and drag them from their houses with insults and curses; they broke open the convent doors by force, and molested and raped the consecrated virgins, who were unable to remain in their profession but had nowhere to lay their heads. In London at this time four convents were looted, the nuns thrown out of their houses in a miserable, pitiful spectacle. And because certain clerics and religious spoke with some boldness about the king's impious cruelty, they were imprisoned and later quartered.[4]

---

1 Sander, *De origine ac progressu*, 193–97.

2 Cromwell first occupied a large house at Austin Friars (the neighborhood surrounding the friary of the Augustinian Friars) in London in 1522. Ten years later, he received a ninety-nine-year lease of further holdings formerly belonging to the Augustinian Friars. The friary was dissolved in 1539, and Cromwell appropriated the entire property. Loades, *Thomas Cromwell*, 17. David Loades, *The Life and Career of William Paulet (c.1475–1572): Lord Treasurer and First Marquis of Winchester* (Aldershot: Ashgate, 2007), 58. *LP*, 5:1028.

3 31 Hen. 8. c. 13. See *SR*, 3:733–39.

4 Sander identifies these as "two London priests, one of whom was the rector of the parish of Wandsworth, and a servant who attended to him, along with a certain monk by the name of Waire [*Mairus*]." Sander, *De origine ac progressu*, 194.

   Cf. "The viij of July Griffith Clarke vycar of wandsworth with his chapleine & his seruaunt and fryer Waire, were all fower hanged & quartered at S. Thomas waterings." Stow, *Summarie*, 443.

Not satisfied with having stripped the religious of their possessions, the king found another, even more diabolical scheme to strip them of their souls. He had a public proclamation written in the name of the religious themselves, in which they begged the king, as the highest judge, to free them from the servitude and captivity of the monasteries, at manifest peril of their souls, and give them liberty, and that, receiving this sovereign mercy from his hand, they would cede—and later did indeed cede—to him, freely and unsought, of their own will and without compulsion, promise, duplicity, or pressure from anyone, the monasteries, estates, and incomes they had unjustly possessed hitherto, placing them in the hands of His Majesty, to whom they rightly belonged.[5] All this, to appear to do what he did not out of greed for the goods he plundered, but in acquiescence to the pleas of the religious themselves. For this is the hypocrisy and fraudulence of the heretics in disguising their wickedness, to commit them and place the blame on their victims, and so get away with tyranny and violence. The king sent his minions to every monastery with this impious document to bring the abbots and monastics to sign and seal it, either by pressure or by force. Those who, overcome by terror or weakness, obeyed them were favored and showered with gifts, as godly men, peace-loving and law-abiding, friends to the commonweal. And those who remained constant and firm were abused and slandered, called pharisaical, arrogant, seditious, and rebels against the king. And so at this time there was no creature in England more wretched than the benighted religious, for they could not but lose the goods of their order, unless they lost their souls. When this trick did not fall out as the king had hoped, he martyred three abbots and two clerics for

---

5   The effusive preamble to 31 Hen. 8. c. 13 declared, "Where diverse and sundrie Abbotts Priours Abbesses Prioresses and other Ecclesiasticall Governours and Governesses of diverse Monasteries Abbathies Priories Nonries Colleges Hospitalls Houses of Friers and other religious and ecclesiastical Houses and places within this our Soveraigne Lorde the Kinges Realme of Englande and Wales, of their owne free and voluntarie myndes good willes and assents, without constraynte coaction or compulsion of any manner of person or persons [...] by the due order and course of the comen lawes of this his Realme of Englande, and by their sufficient writings of recorde under their covent and comen seales, have severally geven graunted and by the same their writinges severally confirmed all their saide Monasteries Abbathies Priories Nonries Colleges Hospitals Houses of Friers and other religious and ecclesiastical houses & places, and all their Scites Circuites and precynctes of the same, and all and singuler their Mannors Lordshipps Graunges Meeses landes tenants meadowes pastures rents revercions services woodes tithes pencions porcions churches chappells advowsons patronages annuyties rights entres condicions commons lets courtes libertyes privileges and franchesies appertyning or in anywise belonging to any suche [...] to our saide Soveraigne Lorde his heires and successors for ever." *SR*, 3:733.

refusing to sign the said document; foremost among them was Whiting, the abbot of Glastonbury, a venerable man of whom we shall speak in the following chapter.[6]

---

6   These five ecclesiastics are identified by Sander as Hugh Faringdon (born Hugh Cook, d.1539), abbot of Reading; Richard Whiting (d.1539), abbot of Glastonbury; Thomas Marshall (also known as John Beche, d.1539), abbot of St John the Baptist at Colchester; and the priests John Rugge (d.1539) and William Onion (d.1539). Sander, *De origine ac progressu*, 197. Claire Cross, "Cook [*name in religion* Faringdon], Hugh (*d.* 1539)," in *ODNB*, 13:103–04. Nicholas Doggett, "Whiting, Richard (*d.* 1539)," in *ODNB*, 58:733. Jennifer C. Ward, "Marshall [Beche], Thomas (*d.* 1539)," in *ODNB*, 36:869–70.

For a sixteenth-century Catholic rendering of these martyrdoms, see Book 1 Figure 37.1.

The Death of Whiting, Abbot of Glastonbury; The End of the Religious Orders in England; And the Beginnings of the Society of Jesus[1]

Glastonbury is a place in the western part of England that is regarded, according to tradition and the authority of ancient writers, as that which Joseph of Arimathea (he who buried Christ our Lord,[2] was cast out of his homeland by the Jews, and came to Britain with several companions in the reign of Emperor Nero) received from King Arviragus in the year of our Lord 50, in order to erect a chapel to the God of heaven. So says Gildas, a renowned Christian British author, known as "the wise" on account of his deep learning, who wrote eleven hundred years ago, and all of the later annals of England confirm this.[3] The place was exalted after Lucius, king of the Britons, was washed with the water of holy[4] baptism there.[5] And Inas, the wise and pious prince of the West Saxons [*Vestanglos*], the first to make the kingdom of England a tributary of the

---

1 Sander, *De origine ac progressu*, 197–205.

2 Matt. 27:57–60; Mark 15:43–46; Luke 23:50–53; John 19:38.

3 Venerable traditions held that Joseph of Arimathea first brought Christianity to Britain, and the quasi-mythical ruler Arviragus (or Arwîrac) patronized the new faith. Gildas, however, mentions neither Joseph nor Arviragus, and actually dates the advent of Christianity to the reign of Tiberius (r.14–37). J.G.O. Whitehead, "Arwîrac of Glastonbury," *Folklore* 73, no. 3 (1962): 149–59. Gildas, *The Ruin of Britain, and Other Works*, ed. and trans. Michael Winterbottom, History from the Sources 7 (London: Phillimore, 1978), 18.

   Sander seems to be drawing on Raphael Holinshed's (1529–80) *Chronicles* (1577). "In the daies of the said Aruiragus, about the yeare of Christ 53, Ioseph of Arimathia, who buried the bodie of our savior, being sent by Philip the Apostle (as Iohn Bale following the authoritie of Gildas and other British writers reciteth) after that the Christians were dispersed out of Gallia, came into Britain with diuers other godlie christian men, & preaching the gospell there amongst the Britains, & instructing them in the faith and lawes of Christ, conuerted manie to the true beliefe, and baptised them in the wholsome water of regeneration, and there continued all the residue of his life, obtaining of the king a plot of ground where to inhabit, not past a foure miles from Wells, and there with his fellowes began to laie the first foundation of the true and perfect religion, in which place (or néere therevnto) was afterward erected the abbeie of Glastenburie." Holinshed, *Chronicles*, 1:486–87.

4 The word "holy" (*santo*) is omitted beginning with the 1595 edition.

5 Glastonbury was supposedly the site of Lucius's baptism, *c*.185. Alan Smith, "Lucius of Britain: Alleged King and Church Founder," *Folklore* 90, no. 1 (1979): 29–36, here 29.

Roman pontiff, erected a palatial monastery there around the year of our Lord 740,[6] which many subsequent kings expanded, enriched, and ennobled, calling the spot the first land of the saints.

The abbot of this monastery was one Whiting, a man respected for his advanced age, saintly life, and exemplary holiness (which he preserved in the midst of copious worldly wealth).[7] Now, in his monastery, and in all others in England at the time, all the religious lived in common, diligently attended services, and strictly maintained their seclusion. Cloistered in his monastery Whiting had a community of one hundred religious, and in separate houses roughly three hundred servants and domestics, many of them the sons of gentlemen and knights, whom he later sponsored and supported at university. He offered hospitality to every pilgrim, welcoming them with open arms; once, he hosted five hundred guests—and their horses—in his house, all at the same time.[8] Every Wednesday and Friday he unfailingly distributed bountiful alms to the poor, who flocked there from throughout the region.[9] In those days, the incomes of the richest monasteries and abbeys throughout England were spent on these and similar works. Well, to return to Whiting, since he refused to sign the document the king had sent to all the monasteries, and a treatise against the king's divorce had been surreptitiously found among his papers (which the king's minions had themselves planted in said papers when they rifled through them in secret, hoping to achieve their end by this artifice),[10] by various lies and tricks he was dragged to London by a sizable force, and then made to return to his house. When they were drawing near, a priest approached the litter

---

6   "Moreover, king Ine builded the monasterie of Glastenburie, where Ioseph of Arimathea in times past builded an oratorie or chappell (as before is recited) when he with other christians came into this land in the daies of Aruiragus, & taught the gospell heere to the Britains, conuerting manie of them to the faith." Holinshed, *Chronicles*, 1:639.

7   In point of fact, Richard Whiting was criticized in a 1538 visitation for his rather lordly lifestyle. Doggett, "Whiting, Richard," in *ODNB*, 58:733.

8   "Richard Whiting is recorded to have entertained up to 500 'persons of fashion' at once." Julian M. Luxford, *The Art and Architecture of English Benedictine Monasteries, 1300–1540: A Patronage History*, Studies in the History of Medieval Religion 25 (Woodbridge: Boydell Press, 2005), 55.

9   "He also maintained the tradition of hospitality to all, with the abbey feeding the poor of the neighbourhood twice weekly. His abbacy coincided with a period of general decline for the Benedictines, yet at Glastonbury the number of monks rose from forty-six to fifty-four. During the 1530s, moreover, there was an increase in the number of monks who went from Glastonbury to Gloucester College at Oxford." Dogget, "Whiting, Richard," in *ODNB*, 58:733.

10   Whiting was convicted of only two specific charges: possession of a book against Henry's divorce and having withheld various treasures from royal commissioners. Ibid.

in which the good old man (utterly unaware of what had been plotted against him) was traveling, and told him to confess himself, for he was to die that very hour. The venerable abbot was distraught, tearfully begging and pleading in the name of Christ's passion to be given the space of a day or two to prepare himself for death—at least, to be allowed to enter his monastery, so as to commend himself to the prayers of his monks and bid them farewell. But he could attain neither the one nor the other; instead, he was immediately seized and snatched from the litter, placed in a tumbril, and dragged up to the crest of the mountain that stood above the monastery, where he was hanged, drawn, and quartered, still in his monk's habit.[11]

Having brutalized and killed the shepherd, they then scattered the sheep: after that, there were no more religious who dared bark, like faithful mastiffs, against the bloodthirsty wolves and oppose Henry's tyranny. He, like one triumphing over his foes, looted, ransacked, and devastated every monastery, seizing their property and their goods. And lest his successors try to restore these to the Church, he parceled them out to the knights and gentry of the kingdom—some exploiting them for the income, others selling them for cash—and to force as many as possible to defend his tyrannous cruelty, he compelled many to buy these properties, no matter how much it burdened them. This was the lamentable end of the monasteries and monastics of England, one thousand years after they had planted the faith of Christ in that kingdom, flowered, and been exalted by the liberality of the rulers and the devotion of the people. Henry, to triumph even more in his sin, commanded the bishops and churchmen to celebrate this deed in public sermons, preaching God's

---

11   On November 16, 1539, John Russell, first earl of Bedford (*c*.1485–*c*.1554), wrote to Thomas Cromwell: "My lorde, thies shalbe to asserteyne, that on Thursdaye the xiiijth daye of this present moneth the abbott of Glastonburye was arraynd, and the next daye putt to executyon, wyth ij. other of his monkes, for the robbyng of Glastonburye churche, on the Torre Hyll, next unto the towne of Glaston., the seyde abbottes body beyng devyded in fower partes, and heedd stryken off, whereof oone quarter stondythe at Welles, another at Bathe, and at Ylchester and Brigewater the rest, and his hedd uppon the abbey gate at Glaston." Thomas Wright, ed., *Three Chapters of Letters Relating to the Suppression of Monasteries,* Works of the Camden Society 26 (London: John Bowyer Nichols and Son, 1843), 260.

      Cf. Another letter to Cromwell, also dated November 16, from Richard Pollard (*c*.1505–42), MP for Taunton and an energetic reformer: "the same xv. daye the late abbott of Glastonberye went frome Wellys to Glastonberye, and there was drawyn thorowe the towne apon a hurdyll to the hyll callyd the Torre, wheare he was putto execucion; att wyche tyme he askyd God mercye and the kyng for hys great offensys towardes hys hyghenes." Ibid., 261.

mercy in having freed them from the heavy yoke of the bishop of Rome and the demands of the religious.

But, O ineffable and secret judgments of God[12]—says Doctor Sander— who thus willed by the affliction of England to instruct the religious of every order in all other kingdoms to appease the wrath of the Lord by sincere penance, the reformation of their lives, and faithful observance of their customs and rules, lest they bring upon themselves a like scourge, which, though most just and most rigorous, the Lord softened and restrained with his accustomed mercy and sweetness. For, when in Germany, by the blaspheming tongue of Luther, and in England, by the unheard-of cruelty of this tyrant, it seemed that the ideals of a perfect, monastic life had been discarded, and obedience and honor to the vicar of Christ had been so neglected and abandoned that the name of the pope—so beloved and so revered by the faithful—was abhorred by the wicked, at this very moment, I say, he raised up with his Holy Spirit the soul of Ignatius of Loyola and his saintly companions to enter upon the narrow path to perfection.[13] And besides their other praiseworthy customs and vows, by the special light and inspiration of God they added a fourth vow for their professed to take. By this vow they dedicate themselves to the service of the pope and the Apostolic See, in any duty or ministry pertaining to the faith upon which His Holiness might choose to employ them, to go at his command into any land or region, among the faithful or the infidels, without contradiction or remuneration, as though sent by God, to seek with all their might the health of souls,[14] undoing with their works and their new pledge and obligation the impiety of Luther and the savagery of Henry. These fathers created a congregation and established a new order of religious, given the name of the Society of Jesus by the pope. By the miraculous industry and holy writings of Ignatius, it has extended and

---

12   Rom. 11:33.

13   Matt. 7:14.

14   *Regimini militantis ecclesiae*, the bull founding the Society, states, "We have deemed it to be very helpful to the upon ourselves, beyond the bond common to all the faithful, a special vow. It is meant so to bind that whatsoever the present Roman Pontiff and his successors may command us concerning the advancement of souls and the spreading of the faith, we shall be obliged to obey instantly as far as lies in us, without evasion or excuse, going to whatever country into which they may send us, whether among the Turks or other heathen, and even to the Indies, or among whatsoever heretics and schismatics, or among any believers whomsoever." John C. Olin, ed., *The Catholic Reformation: Savonarola to Ignatius Loyola* (New York: Fordham University Press, 1969), 205.

propagated this sweet name and the Catholic faith, rooted in the communion of the Roman Church, into the most distant lands and regions of India, Japan, and China. Not resting even at this, they have established their houses and colleges in northern parts, valiantly struggling and waging war against the heretics of our miserable days. They have entered England to illuminate those blinded and separated from the obedience of the Catholic Church by the violent tyranny of those who govern them. This they have done with no less effort or danger than in the Indies, for with their own blood they have offered glorious witness to the truth; they have sacrificed their lives for it and for the confession of the faith of Christ, dying in the cruelest torments, even now, in the days of Queen Elizabeth. Blessed be the Lord who has given us another son in the place of Abel, slain by his brother Cain![15]

These were Sander's words,[16] recounting how in the same year that the English orders were eradicated—1540—the Society of Jesus was founded and approved by the Holy See in Rome.[17] But let us return to our history. The ruin and devastation of the monasteries and sacred houses that took place in the days of this English Nebuchadnezzar[18] will not be easily credited. For besides being nearly infinite in number, the monasteries and shrines were, through their ancient memorials, images, and relics, filled with a heavenly piety and fragrance—and no less with great wealth and treasure. These palatial and sublime buildings were torn down by Henry, who barbarously said that he had to remove the crows' nests, lest the birds return.[19] And therefore he spared

---

15   Gen. 4:25.

16   This passage was actually an addition by the editors of the 1586 version of *De origine ac progressu*. See Sander, *De origine ac progressu*, 202–04.

17   On September 27, 1540, Pope Paul III confirmed the Society of Jesus in the bull *Regimini militantis ecclesiae*. O'Malley, *The First Jesuits*, 35.

       For an English text of *Regimini militantis ecclesiae*, see Olin, *The Catholic Reformation*, 203–08.

18   Cf. Dan. 2–4.

19   This savage witticism was attributed to Henry by the editors of the 1586 edition of *De origine ac progressu*: Sander, *De origine ac progressu*, 204.

       The line seems to originate with Gerald of Wales's (*c.*1146–*c.*1226) *Topography of Ireland* (*c.*1188), which relates of Máel Sechnaill mac Máele Ruanaid, king of Meath (r.845–62): "The before-mentioned king of Meath, after he had planned in his mind the treacherous enterprise, having cunningly enquired of Turgesius by what contrivance or art certain birds which had lately migrated into the kingdom, and were very destructive throughout the country, could be got rid of and exterminated, he received for reply, that their nests

neither book nor shelf, nor anything smacking of learning or letters, piety or
devotion. Thus it was that everything accomplished by the piety, faith, reverence, and generosity of every Christian in England, since the day it first entered
into the faith, what they had given, offered, gathered, and piled up for divine
worship in the shrines and monasteries of the monks and nuns in all the past
centuries, all this was destroyed and laid waste in the blink of an eye by the
insatiable greed and tyranny of Henry.

---

should be everywhere destroyed, if it should be found that they had already built them.
The Irish interpreting this of the castles of the Norwegians, rose to a man through the
whole island, on the death of Turgesius, and laid the castles in ruins." Gerald of Wales, *The
Historical Works of Giraldus Cambrensis*, ed. Thomas Wright, trans. Thomas Forester and
Richard Colt Hoare (London: George Bell and Sons, 1894), 151–52.

Henry Marries Anne of Cleves, Exalts Cromwell, and Imposes New Burdens on His Kingdom[1]

We said earlier that the duke of Cleves was eager to give his sister in marriage to King Henry, in order to form an alliance with him.[2] The business progressed rapidly and was concluded. At the beginning of 1540, the time having come to seal the match they had agreed upon, Anne arrived in England.[3] Many reckoned that these nuptials would offer considerable advantages for the German Protestants and for Cromwell, who had been their author—and even more for William, duke of Cleves, who now stood allied with Henry, the German princes, and King Francis of France, to whose niece, the daughter of the queen of Navarre, he was engaged.[4] By these means he imagined he could protect himself from the emperor and retain the duchy of Guilders in spite of all his power. Yet, by divine will, all fell out contrary to their expectations. For the emperor subsequently defeated and subdued the German princes who had taken up arms against him, Henry shifted to his side,[5] and Duke William not only did not wed his fiancée, the king of France's niece, but also lost the territories of Guelders and Jülich. He found himself in such dire straits that he threw himself at the emperor's feet and begged pardon.[6] And thus it was that Cromwell, the instigator of the marriage, fell into the utmost misery, and lost his power and his life, as will be seen hereafter. Yet God permitted him to rise for a certain time and to mount to an even higher rank, so that he would fall farther and with greater

---

1   Sander, *De origine ac progressu*, 205–07.

2   In the margin: "Chapter 37."

3   Anne arrived at Deal in Kent on December 27, 1539. She and Henry were married at Greenwich on January 6, 1540. Warnicke, *Marrying of Anne of Cleves*, 127, 149, 160.

4   In 1541, as part of his alliance with France, Duke William married Francis I's niece, Jeanne d'Albret (1528–72), the daughter of the king's sister, Marguerite de Navarre, and Henry II, king of Navarre (r.1503–55). Ibid., 242.

5   By April 1539, Charles had passed into the Low Countries, where he was preparing military action against the duke of Cleves. The prospect of war with the emperor forced Henry to rethink his commitments to the hapless duke. Loades, *Thomas Cromwell*, 207.

6   By November 1542, imperial troops had overrun Jülich. In September of the following year, William signed the Treaty of Venlo; he yielded Guelders to Charles V, but was allowed to retain his remaining titles. William *had* wed Jeanne d'Albret, but the marriage was annulled. Warnicke, *Marrying of Anne of Cleves*, 251.

© KONINKLIJKE BRILL NV, LEIDEN, 2017 | DOI 10.1163/9789004323964_048

suffering, as he often does with those he wishes to humble. For the king made him earl of Essex and lord chamberlain of the realm, while his son Gregory was given the title of baron.[7] Cromwell—wishing to repay the king's kindness and knowing well both his greed and his poverty—proposed in parliament, and drove through practically by force, that two-fifths of all the goods and property in the realm should be given to the king, so that he who had twenty should give eight, and he who had one hundred should give forty.[8] This was done no more than a year after the king had looted every church in the kingdom and confiscated their wealth: let the dire punishment of God be seen and marked, and let it be well understood that the more the king acquired of the Church's wealth, the more he impoverished himself; nor, having taken more, was he any richer or greater, nor did he relent in further squeezing his subjects. In the same parliament, they abolished the order of the knights of Saint John, which still survived in England, and allotted all its income to the king;[9] the prior of the order, named William Weston [*Bestono*], a man of constancy and valor, died of grief within ten days.[10]

---

7   In 1540, Cromwell was made earl of Essex and lord great chamberlain, while his son, Gregory (*c.*1520–51) became Baron Cromwell. Loades, *Thomas Cromwell*, 10, 238.

8   32 Hen. 8. c. 50. See *SR*, 3:812–24.

9   32 Hen. 8. c. 24. See ibid., 3:778–81.

10   Sir William Weston (1469–1540) was the prior of the hospital of Saint John of Jerusalem. Following Sander, Ribadeneyra has erred as to date: Weston died on May 7, 1540, the very day the act passed in the House of Commons. G.J. O'Malley, "Weston, Sir William (*b.* 1469, *d.* 1540)," in *ODNB*, 58:312–13.

The King Tires of and Divorces His Wife, after Having Cromwell Put to Death[1]

By this time, Henry had begun to tire of his fourth wife, Anne of Cleves, for various reasons. First, having sent his ambassadors to his allies among the Protestant German princes to secure their approval of the religion of England (which he called "Reformed"), he could not obtain it from a single one, and as a prideful man he felt this deeply.[2] Second, the emperor had traveled to Flanders through France (being royally entertained by King Francis), entered his own lands, and severely punished those in Ghent who had begun to revolt; his sudden arrival terrified the duke of Cleves—whereupon Henry, too, was frightened, and sought to be friends with the emperor once more.[3] The third and principal cause was that Anne of Cleves was German, and knew neither the language nor the customs of England, and so could not charm or entertain the king as he wanted.[4] And so Henry wearied of her and turned his eyes upon another lady, named Catherine Howard.[5] In order to marry her, he resolved either to kill or

---

1 Sander, *De origine ac progressu*, 207–14.
2 "Since 1535 the Germans had consistently refused to accept Henry's invitations to send Melanchthon to England as the leader of a major theological delegation. [...] They had insisted throughout that Henry accept all aspects of their doctrine. They had impugned loudly any theological deviation of the king's part, and ignored his interest in a religious compromise." Rory McEntegart, *Henry VIII, the League of Schmalkalden and the English Reformation*, Studies in History New Series (Woodbridge: Boydell Press, 2002), 200–01.
3 In 1539, the city of Ghent revolted against the taxes levied to fund Charles's foreign wars. The following year, after a tour of France at the invitation of Francis I, the emperor personally led an army against the city, which surrendered without a fight. Maltby, *Charles V*, 39, 101.
4 Anne's education, at least in terms of courtly graces, had been lackluster: she could neither sing nor play, and spent most of her time sewing. Henry's emissary to Cleves reported, "Could never hear that she is inclined to the good cheer of this country and marvel it were if she could." Scarisbrick, *Henry VIII*, 373–75.
5 The Protestant activist Richard Hilles (*c.*1514–87) wrote to the Swiss reformer Heinrich Bullinger (1504–75) on February 28, 1541, "Before St. John Baptist's day it was whispered the King intended to divorce his queen Anne, sister of the duke of Gelderland, whom he had married publicly at Epiphany after last Christmas. Courtiers first observed that he was much taken with another young lady, very small of stature, whom he now has, and whom he was seen crossing the Thames to visit, often in the day time and sometimes at night." *LP*, 16:584.

abandon Anne of Cleves—but first of all he intended to punish Cromwell, the matchmaker. At this point, Cromwell was at his peak [*en su trono*], having risen from the child of a poor blacksmith,[6] so they say, to such high estate that across England nothing was done but by his command, and he trampled upon the lords and grandees of the realm, maintaining men in his livery throughout the kingdom, and it was considered a blessing to be (and to be known as) his servant. In the end, he became the second king of the kingdom, perpetrating such vicious cruelties against the Catholics as ordering several knights and bishops arrested and thrown into the Tower of London for no other reason than that they were beloved of the people, or that their alms had supported a few poor Catholics imprisoned for having denied the royal supremacy.[7]

And so, looking to destroy Cromwell and seeking excuses to do it, the king found the one I shall here relate. When the duke of Saxony, the landgrave, and several other German princes decided to take up arms against the emperor, forming the first of the Schmalkaldic Leagues, they begged Henry to join them, which he did. A little later, the emperor gained enough clout with Henry to draw him away, and when the princes of Germany again importuned him to ally with them and renew their league, he did not dare break his word.[8] But Cromwell, either because the king had instructed him in secret, or because as a Lutheran heretic he wished to please the princes of his own sect, or because he knew that his king feared the emperor and would be pleased to see him embattled and engaged in war in Germany, and that his reluctance about allying with the princes stemmed from trepidation rather than inclination, decided to sign the pact in the king's name. The emperor protested to the king about

---

6   Thomas Cromwell's father, Walter Cromwell (dates unknown), was something of a jack-of-all trades. He owned land, ran an alehouse, sheared sheep, and may well have worked as a smith—in addition to several run-ins with the law. Loades, *Thomas Cromwell*, 12.

7   In May 1540, Cromwell brought about the arrest of two prominent conservatives—Richard Sampson, bishop of Chichester (d.1554) and Nicholas Wotton (c.1497–1567)—as well as Arthur Plantagenet, first Viscount Lisle (d.1542), the deputy of Calais, who was accused of colluding with Reginald Pole. Ibid., 226.

8   In late 1530, Protestant princes met at Schmalkalden in Thuringia to coordinate a response to the imperial threat. In February 1531, they finalized a military alliance that became known as the League of Schmalkalden (or Schmalkaldic League). The leading exponents of the project were John Frederick I, elector of Saxony (r.1532–47), and Philip I, landgrave of Hesse (r.1509–67). Over the following decade and a half, numerous delegations would be exchanged between Henry and the League, without the conclusion of a formal alliance. The vacillations mentioned by Ribadeneyra probably refer to the Frankfurt Interim of 1539, which forced a break in Anglo-German relations. McEntegart, *League of Schmalkalden*, 13, 146, 151–52.

this agreement, and the king denied it; when the emperor sent him a copy of the documents, signed in the king's name, he was abashed and, finding no other excuse, threw all the blame on Cromwell, saying that he had signed it against his will.[9] With the occasion of the emperor's fierce complaints against Cromwell—indeed the king could have wished for nothing better—he dispatched him in the manner I shall describe.

On July 8, 1540, Cromwell was with the king, conferring on various matters, with the greatest favor and fortune in the world; at their parting, the king asked him, with loving, amiable words, to arise at dawn the following day and come speak with him at York Place,[10] for he had pressing matters to discuss with him. The next morning, he arrived in high spirits, with a large and elaborate retinue, entered the council, sat down, and began to put forward several proposals. The duke of Norfolk, earl marshal of the realm and uncle to that Catherine Howard whom the king wished to marry,[11] interrupted Cromwell's disquisition, saying, "These issues will be dealt with later; now we must speak about you, whose wickedness and treachery has imperiled the realm, and therefore I, by the mandate of the king and in the name of the kingdom, arrest you and order you to follow me to prison." And the duke touched him with the staff he carried, as is the custom in England. Cromwell was utterly dumbfounded; before a huge crowd of people he was handed over to the captain of the guard

---

9   In a letter to King Francis of June 10, 1540, the French ambassador, Charles de Marillac (*c.*1510–60), described Cromwell's fall: "The substance was that the King, wishing by all possible means to lead back religion to the way of truth, Cromwell, as attached to the German Lutherans, had always favoured the doctors who preached such erroneous opinions and hindered those who preached the contrary, and that recently, warned by some of his principal servants to reflect that he was working against the intention of the King and of the Acts of Parliament, he had betrayed himself and said he hoped to suppress the old preachers and have only the new, adding that the affair would soon be brought to such a pass that the King with all his power could not prevent it, but rather his own party would be so strong that he would make the King descend to the new doctrines even if he had to take arms against him." *LP*, 15:766.

Two weeks later, Marillac wrote, "Next day were found several letters he wrote to or received from the Lutheran lords of Germany. Cannot learn what they contained except that this King was thereby so exasperated against him that he would no longer hear him spoken of, but rather desired to abolish all memory of him as the greatest wretch ever born in England." Ibid., 15:804.

10   Whitehall.

11   Catherine Howard's father, Lord Edmund Howard (*c.* 1478–1539), was Thomas Howard's younger brother.

to be detained.[12] Ten days later, with the king himself as his accuser, he was sentenced to death by parliament on four counts: heresy, *lèse-majesté* (that is, as a traitor to God and the king), felony (which in that kingdom includes robbery, homicide, and other crimes worthy of death), and graft [*peculado*] (that is, defrauding the public purse).[13] The sentence was then carried out: he was publicly beheaded—and as a greater humiliation, a base man, condemned for an unspeakable crime, was punished alongside him at the same time and place.[14] This was the end of the prosperity and ascendancy of Cromwell, who had enjoyed hardly three months since the king had raised him to so lofty a rank. And it should be noted that Cromwell had been the author of a law providing that if anyone was convicted of the crime of *lèse-majesté*, though absent and unheard, it would be held as lawful a condemnation as if delivered by twelve men (which constitutes the highest judgment in England)—and it

---

12   Marillac offers a rather different account: "To commence with the day of his taking in the Council Chamber of the King's house at Westminster:—As soon as the Captain of the Guard declared his charge to make him prisoner, Cromwell in a rage cast his bonnet on the ground, saying to the duke of Norfolk and others of the Privy Council assembled there that this was the reward of his services, and that he appealed to their consciences as to whether he was a traitor; but since he was treated thus he renounced all pardon, as he had never thought to have offended, and only asked the King not to make him languish long. Thereupon some said he was a traitor, others that he should be judged according to the laws he had made, which were so sanguinary that often words spoken inadvertently with good intention had been constituted high treason." Marillac reports that Cromwell's arrest was executed discretely, and only the public seizure of his house at Austin Friars made the news public. *LP*, 15:804.

13   For Cromwell's bill of attainder, see Gilbert Burnet, *The History of the Reformation of the Church of England*, 3 vols. (London: T.H. for Richard Chiswell, 1681), 1:187–92.

14   July 28, 1540 also saw the execution of Walter Hungerford, Baron Hungerford of Heytesbury (1503–40), one of Cromwell's associates, condemned for witchcraft, treason, and buggery. D.J. Ashton, "Hungerford, Walter, Baron Hungerford of Heytesbury (1503–1540)," in *ODNB*, 28:827–28.

      Cf. Marillac's letter to Anne, duc de Montmorency (1493–1567). "With him was beheaded the lord of Hongrefort, aged about 49 years, attainted of sodomy, of having forced his own daughter, and having practised magic and invocation of devils." *LP*, 15:926.

      Cf. "And the x. day of June was arestyd and had unto the tower lorde Thomas Cromewell erle of Essex for grete tresone; and the xxviij. day of July was he and lorde Waltr Hungerforthe be-heddyd at towre hylle, Cromwelle for tresone and lorde Hungerforthe for bockery." John Gough Nichols, ed., *Chronicle of the Grey Friars of London*, Works of the Camden Society 53 (London: J.B. Nichols and Son, 1852), 43–44.

was by this law that he was condemned.[15] God willed that he pay the penalty of his own devilish law, and thus all stood in fear of the Lord, saying with the Prophet, "We saw the wicked exalted, and lifted up above the cedars of Lebanon, and we looked again and he had vanished, we sought him and we did not find his place."[16] Let men learn not to trust in their own greatness, nor think themselves secure when the winds of grace and worldly favor are fruitful and auspicious to them, but learn how to trim their sails and reach a safe port in time, and in their navigations to take no north but the law and will of God.

After Cromwell's death, his goods were seized and auctioned off, and the king summoned all of Cromwell's servants and told them to find a better lord in future.[17] Then he sent word to his wife, Anne of Cleves, that for various reasons it was not fitting for them to be joined in matrimony, and that although he had serious grounds for proceeding harshly against her (one of which was his knowledge that she was not untouched by heresy), yet he wished to be gentle and respectful toward her and toward the princes of Germany, and he accordingly permitted her to find some honest cause for their separation, for he would be most pleased with this, so long as it was done swiftly and well.[18] On receiving the king's ultimatum, this wretched lady understood the risk she ran if she made the slightest protest, and so she appeared before the council the following day and confessed that before she married the king, she had wed another in the deepest secrecy. This was untrue, as she herself later said and proved to Queen Mary (for she lived until she became queen).

---

15   Cromwell was condemned under the terms of the Treason Act of 1534, whose primary author he had been. For these provisions, see 26 Hen. 8. c. 13, §3: *SR*, 3:509.

16   In the margin: "Psalm 36[:35–36]."

17   Marillac recorded that "they saw all the King's archers under Mr. Cheyney at the door of the prisoner's house, where they made an inventory of his goods [...] The money was 7,000 *l.* st., equal to 28,000 crs., and the silver plate, including crosses, chalices, and other spoils of the Church might be as much more. These movables were before night taken to the King's treasury—a sign that they will not be restored." *LP*, 15.804.

18   Thomas Manners, first earl of Rutland (*c.*1492–1543), who was tasked with delivering the news to Anne, reported: "And for that I dyd see her to take the matter hevely, I desired her to be of good comfort, and that the Kynges highnes ys so gracyous and wertues a prince that he wold nothyng but that shuld stond with the law of God, and for the dyscharge of his conscience and hers and the quyetnes of this realme hereafter; and at the sute of all his lordes and commyns which ys the state of the hole realme, his Highnes [is conte] nt to refar the matter to the bysshoppes and the clergye who be as well lerned men and of as good conscience and lyveyng as any be in the world; so that her Grace hath cause to reyose and not to be sory, whiche matter she hard well and sayd nothyng to yt." Ibid., 15:844.

Hearing Anne's confession, the parliament then interposed its authority, enacting a law by which Henry and Anne were separated and Henry could take another wife.[19]

---

19   Following Sander, Ribadeneyra compresses the timeline significantly, and gives Anne a more active role than she in fact played. On July 4, 1540, Anne was informed of parliament's intentions to conduct an inquiry into the validity of her marriage. On July 9, a double convocation of the Church of England declared the marriage null and void, while two days later Anne herself signed a notarial document registering her consent to the divorce. There does not seem to have been any significant contact between Anne and Mary during the latter's reign. See Warnicke, *Marrying of Anne of Cleves*, 229–39, 253–55.

Cf. The parliamentary act for "The dissolution of the pretensed mariage with the Lady Anne of Cleves" in SR, 3:781–83.

Of Catherine Howard, Henry's Fifth Wife, and How, after Ordering Her Put to Death, He Married Katherine Parr[1]

Within eight days, the king married Catherine Howard, the duke of Norfolk's niece (his brother's daughter).[2] But though the king was pleased beyond measure with his new bride, that did not stop him from inflicting his cruelty on Catholics. Thus, on July 30, he put to death three saintly doctors of theology for having defended the cause of Queen Doña Catherine and for now denying the king's pontifical power. Alongside them he condemned three Zwinglian heretics, ordering that they be paraded two by two, a Catholic together with a heretic, as a blacker mockery of religion and a worse torment to the Catholics, who received more pain from this awful company than from their own deaths. When a knight of the king's household saw them borne off to death, companioned in this manner, and learned that some were condemned for being Catholics and the others for not being so, he said, "On this account I will take care henceforth to be of the king's religion—that is to say, none at all!"[3] Then, on August 2, he also dispatched the prior of Doncaster with three other monks and two laymen, on the same grounds, as well as for refusing to acknowledge the royal supremacy.[4]

---

1   Sander, *De origine ac progressu*, 214–19.

2   Henry and Catherine were married on June 28, 1540, several weeks after the finalization of the divorce from Anne.

3   Sander identifies the three Catholics as Thomas Abell, a former chaplain to Catherine of Aragon, Edward Powell, a canon of Lincoln and Salisbury, and Richard Fetherston, archdeacon of Brecon, and the three evangelical activists as Robert Barnes (*c.*1495–1540), Thomas Garrard (1498–1540), and William Jerome (d.1540). All six were executed at Henry's order on June 30, 1540. The Catholics were hanged, drawn, and quartered as traitors, while the Protestants were burnt as heretics. Gary G. Gibbs, "Abell, Thomas (*d.* 1540)," in *ODNB*, 1:69–70. Ethan H. Shagan, "Powell, Edward (*c.*1478–1540)," in *ODNB*, 45:79–80. Ethan H. Shagan, "Fetherston, Richard (*d.* 1540)," in *ODNB*, 19:453. Carl R. Trueman, "Barnes, Robert (*c.*1495–1540)," in *ODNB*, 3:1006–09, here 1009. Susan Wabuda, "Garrard, Thomas (1498–1540)," in *ODNB*, 21:515–16. For a sixteenth-century Catholic rendering of these martyrdoms, see Book 1 Figure 37.1.

4   *De origine ac progressu* identifies three of these men: the Carthusian Lawrence Cook (d.1540); William (whom Sander strangely calls "Eegidio") Horn (d.1540), a laybrother of the London Charterhouse; and Clement Philip (d.1540), a layman. Sander, *De origine ac progressu*, 217.

At this time, the king was continually hounded by the pangs of his conscience and by certain (albeit weak) desires to return to God and the unity of his Church. For he saw that he had proved himself to be neither altogether Catholic nor altogether heretic, and therefore both Catholics and heretics abhorred him, and that in the sects of the misbelievers there were alterations and innovations every day, and only in the Catholic faith certainty, constancy, and safety. On this account, he sent ambassadors to the emperor, who was at the imperial diet of Germany, to discuss some means of being reconciled with the Roman pontiff.[5] But he wanted to preserve his honor, and he would neither publicly admit his error, nor do penance for it, nor restore any property to the churches—all of which was repugnant to the sacred canons and to the eternal salvation of his soul. And so all these good thoughts and intentions ended in smoke and withered away, for they had no roots, being founded more upon the glory of men than upon that of God.[6]

And, just as this accursed king had been disloyal to his first wife and a traitor to God, so his wives were to him—for Catherine Howard had not yet enjoyed two years of marriage to the king when, on his own accusations, she was convicted, condemned, and executed for adultery,[7] and with her the adulterers, Thomas Culpeper and Francis Dereham.[8] Because it was known that these men had been Catherine's lovers not only as queen but well before, and to avoid such a mishap in the future, parliament passed a law stating that any woman the king intended to marry who was taken for a virgin without in fact being so, and did not reveal the truth to the king, had committed the crime of

---

5   In November 1540, Henry sent Gardiner to Regensburg, where Charles V had summoned the imperial diet. Though Henry implied that his break with Rome might be negotiable, the diet collapsed under the weight of theological differences before any real watershed was reached—although an Anglo-Imperial alliance was concluded. Haigh, *English Reformations*, 155–56.

6   Ps. 101:4; John 12:43.

7   Catherine married Henry on June 28, 1540. Less than two years later, in October 1541, Thomas Cranmer was informed of her infidelities and her downfall began. She was condemned by a bill of attainder on February 7, 1542 and beheaded on February 13. David Loades, *Catherine Howard: The Adulterous Wife of Henry VIII* (Stroud: Amberley, 2012), 153, 157.

8   Thomas Culpeper (c.1514–41), a gentleman of the king's privy chamber, had been slated to marry Catherine before Henry chose her. Thomas and the queen began an affair in the spring of 1541. Francis Dereham (c.1513–41) was a courtier and kinsman of the Howard family, with whom Catherine became sexually involved in late 1538. Though their relationship ended when Catherine became a maid of honor to Anne of Cleves late the following year, she made him her secretary in 1541 (probably in an attempt to buy his silence). After the discovery of Catherine's infidelity, both Culpeper and Dereham were convicted of treason on December 1, 1541, and beheaded at Tyburn on December 10. Ibid., 42–43, 115, 123, 149–50.

lèse-majesté and was to die for it. And the same penalty applied to those who had slept with her, unless they disclosed this to the king.[9]

Henry, scorched and burning in the fierce flames of his lustfulness, could not for a second be without a woman, and consequently resolved to take a sixth. So as not to suppose her to be a maiden who was no such thing, he took as wife a widow named Katherine Parr,[10] who was the sister of the earl of Essex (who later became marquess of Northampton)[11] and who had been married to Baron Latimer.[12] Luckily for her, the king died before he killed her, which they say he had decided to do.[13] For of the first two Catherines, he had repudiated one and killed another, and he had done the same to the two Annes—and so it is believed that the third Katherine's fate would have been no different, had God not foiled the king's intentions with his sudden death.

---

9   These provisions were appended to the bill of attainder for Catherine and her lovers (33 Hen. VIII. c.21): see *SR*, 3:859.

10   On July 12, 1543, Henry married the twice-widowed Katherine Parr, daughter of a well-to-do Northamptonshire courtier. Scarisbrick, *Henry VIII*, 456.

11   William Parr, earl of Essex and marquess of Northampton (1513–71), was Katherine Parr's younger brother. In 1527, he married Anne Bourchier (1517–71), daughter of Henry Bourchier, earl of Essex (*d*.1540). When Bourchier died, the earldom was taken by Thomas Cromwell, but Parr eventually received the title when his sister became queen. He became marquess of Northampton for his loyalty to Edward Seymour after Henry's death. Susan E. James, "Parr, William, marquess of Northampton (1513–1571)," in *ODNB*, 43:856–58, here 856.

12   John Neville, third Baron Latimer (1493–1543) married Katherine Parr in the summer of 1534; the marriage ended with his death in 1543. Keith Dockray, "Neville, John, third Baron Latimer (1493–1543)," in *ODNB*, 40:510–11.

13   In the last year of Henry's life, Katherine's position became increasingly precarious. John Foxe relates that Stephen Gardiner unsuccessfully tried to use the queen's outspoken evangelical beliefs (and her habit of arguing with Henry) against her, urging "that the greatest subject in this land, speaking those words that she did speak, and defending those arguments that she did defend, had, with indifferent justice, by law deserved death." Foxe avers that, although Henry did begin to turn on Katherine, she won his favor back in the end. Rumors continued to circulate, however, Katherine was to be disposed of and replaced, possibly by Catherine Brandon (*née* Willoughby), duchess of Suffolk (1519–80). Foxe, *Acts and Monuments*, 5:553–60. Sheryl A. Kujawa-Holbrook, "Katherine Parr and Reformed Religion," *Anglican and Episcopal History* 72, no. 1 (March 2003): 55–78, here 58–59.

How Henry Declared Himself King of Ireland, and the Right the Kings of England Had to Call Themselves Its Lords[1]

For approximately four hundred years, the kings of England had called themselves lords of Ireland (to which the kings of Scotland had also laid claim). But on January 23, 1542, Henry demanded by public edict to be called "King of All Ireland."[2] To understand this, one must know that around the year of our Lord 1170, when Adrian IV, an Englishman by birth, sat upon the throne of Saint Peter (before becoming pope, he had converted the kingdoms of Norway and Sweden to the faith of Christ by his pious life and preaching),[3] the Irish—who, ever since they received the teachings of the holy Gospel, had dedicated themselves and all they had to the Roman pontiff, whom alone they recognized as the sovereign lord of their country—fell into chaos, and suffered grievously amid the wars and atrocities of mighty lords.[4] To free themselves from this and find some peace, a large portion of the people wished to submit to King Henry II of England (he who was later responsible for the martyrdom of Saint Thomas of Canterbury), who had just then landed in Ireland with a formidable army,

---

1 Sander, *De origine ac progressu*, 220–25.

2 The Parliament of Ireland declared Henry king in June 1541, an act he subsequently repudiated and replaced with his own royal proclamation of January 23, 1542. Scarisbrick, *Henry VIII*, 424–25. *TRP*, 1:307–08.

3 Born in Hertfordshire, Nicholas Breakspear was elected Pope Adrian IV (r.1154–59) on December 4, 1154. Though he had not actually converted either Norway or Sweden, Breakspear had served as papal legate to Scandinavia, where he was responsible for establishing much of the region's ecclesiastical infrastructure. He died only a few years into Henry II's reign, well before the Irish invasions of the 1170s. See Brenda Bolton and Anne J. Duggan, eds., *Adrian IV The English Pope (1154–1159)*, Church, Faith and Culture in the Medieval West (Farnham: Ashgate, 2013), Chapters 4 and 7.

4 The 1160s was a period of political turmoil in Ireland, seeing the downfall of Murchetach Mac Lochlainn of Munster (r.1156–66) and Diarmait Mac Murchada of Leinster (r.1126–71). As Pope Alexander III (born Roland of Siena, r.1159–81) wrote in 1171, he had been informed "how great are the enormities of vice with which the people of Ireland are infected, and how they have departed from the fear of God and the established practice of the Christian faith, so that souls have been placed in peril." Warren, *Henry II*, 187–92, 197.

© KONINKLIJKE BRILL NV, LEIDEN, 2017 | DOI 10.1163/9789004323964_051

preferring a single lord to many.[5] Accordingly, Adrian IV (although some say that it was Alexander III, placing the event some years later) was implored in the name of the king and of the bishops and magnates of Ireland to be pleased to grant Henry the lordship of the whole of Ireland,[6] to the end that they might alleviate the perpetual conflicts among the island's elites, conduct divine worship with greater solemnity and reverence, and eradicate some of the abuses that the chaos of the war had introduced in the marriages of the inhabitants.[7] The Roman pontiff acquiesced to their entreaties for these reasons—and because he derived no benefit from that island, nor could he assist it without enormous effort and expense, being so far distant. So it was that lordship over Ireland was given to Henry and his successors—but with certain conditions, to which Henry and the lords and magnates of Ireland swore and assented twice: first in the parliament of Dublin and later at that of Cashel.[8] And it was in this manner that the king of England was declared and acclaimed as lord of Ireland by apostolic authority.

At that time, King Henry II had such respect and reverence for the pope that His Holiness likely had good reason for the decision to transfer sovereign authority over Ireland to him and make him its lord. For, when his own sons had risen up against him, and with them a large part of the realm, Henry had written a letter to Pope Alexander III, informing him of his plight and imploring him for advice and support. This I wish to translate here, to the letter, as proof

---

Sir Anthony St Leger (c.1496–1559), Henry VIII's lord deputy of Ireland, opined, "the Irish have a foolish notion that the bishop of Rome is the king of Ireland." Quoted in McCoog, *Our Way of Proceeding?*, 18n25.

5   After Mac Lochlainn's fall and his own ouster from Dublin, Mac Murchada turned to the English for aid. "On 18 October 1171, King Henry II landed at Waterford and demanded everyone's submission." Warren, *Henry II*, 192–94.

6   In 1171, Alexander III wrote to the Irish bishops, "We have further learned from your letters that Henry, the noble king of the English, our dearest son in Christ, moved by inspiration from God and summoning all his strength, has subjugated this barbarous and uncouth race which is ignorant of divine law; and through his power those forbidden things which used to be practised in your lands, now begin to diminish." Ibid., 197.

7   In the margin: "Polydore Vergil, in the *Anglica Historia*, Book 13."

8   Gerald of Wales's *The Conquest of Ireland* records that in October 1172, "the princes of the north of Ireland, and Roderic of Connaught, made voluntary submission at Dublin," and "a synod of the clergy of the whole of Ireland at Cashel" made provision for "bringing the church of Ireland in all respects into conformity with the English church." Gerald of Wales, *Historical Works*, 230–32.

of that kingdom's utter submission and obedience to the supreme pontiff, as well as the part he played in calming it and restoring it to reason.[9]

> Whereas our Lord has exalted Your Holiness and placed you in the highest pastoral office to instruct the people in the knowledge of salvation, though I am absent in body, I am yet present in spirit, and I prostrate myself at your blessed feet, and beg of you sound counsel. The kingdom of England is under your jurisdiction, and in what relates to feudal obligations, I recognize you alone, and to you hold myself accountable. England knows the power of the papal throne, and as earthly weapons avail not, the patrimony of Saint Peter is defended by the spiritual sword. I could have easily punished my sons' wrongs by force of arms, but I recalled that I am a father; though their disobedience and rashness has given me much pain and fury, yet even so I have not lost a father's feelings, and this consideration and this innate love compels me to cherish them. And so, holy father, let the spirit of counsel awaken your prudence, and seek some means for a father to change the hearts of his sons, for the heart of the father is in your hands, and by Your Blessedness will the hearts of the sons be changed. I give you my word, and I promise Your Greatness upon the faith of that Lord in whom all kings reign, to do whatever you command and ordain. Jesus Christ our Lord, holy father, preserve Your Holiness for the sake of his Church.

In this letter we see that more than four hundred years ago the king of England confessed himself the pope's vassal, affirmed that his realm was under His Holiness's jurisdiction, sought his counsel and favor in returning his sons to obedience, and promised to obey all he might command. But let us return to

---

9   In the margin: "Among the letters of Peter of Blois, letter 162."

  In the modern edition, this is letter 136. See Peter of Blois, *Opera omnia*, 1:19–21.

  Nicholas Vincent has stated that this letter, traditionally dated to the 1173–74 rebellion of Henry II's eldest son Henry the Young King (r.1170–83), was first printed at Mainz in 1600. As Ribadeneyra's use of the letter in 1595 demonstrates, however, the text was available in the sixteenth century, via Jacques Merlin's (d.1541) 1519 edition. Nicholas Vincent, "The Court of Henry II," in *Henry II: New Interpretations*, ed. Christopher Harper-Bill and Nicholas Vincent, 278–334 (Woodbridge: Boydell Press, 2007), 302n3. See Peter of Blois, *Petri Blesensis diuinaru[m] ac humanaru[m] litterar[um] viri admodu[m] copiosissimi insignia opera in vnu[m] volume[n] collecta [e]t emendata authore*, ed. Jacques Merlin (Paris: A. Boucard, 1519), fol. lxxxi^r–lxxxi^v.

our history and continue what we began concerning the dominion of Ireland after it was yielded to King Henry and the rest.[10]

But subsequently, when the kings of England did not observe the conditions imposed by the Apostolic See, especially when Edward II (who was deposed by parliament for his awful rule) mistreated the Irish and oppressed them in various ways, they appealed to the pope as their supreme sovereign and judge, protesting against the king and begging for aid. The pope at that point—around the year of our Lord 1320—the Frenchman John XXII (whom Platina places as John XXIII),[11] wrote to King Edward, warning him in the strictest terms to cease these harassments and abuses against the Irish and abide by the conditions under which that title had been given to previous kings of England. And he sent him the written copy of these, as can be seen in one of his perpetual decrees, the fifth of John XXII.[12]

I decided to discuss this here to show Henry's ingratitude in having received the lordship of Ireland from the Roman pontiff and then turned his back upon him, as well as how wrongly and how insolently he declared himself king of

---

10   This account of Henry II's submission to the pope is added in the 1595 edition.

11   Jacques Duèse was elected Pope John XXII (r.1316–34) on August 7, 1316. The numbering of popes with the name "John" is a vexed matter, owing to misreadings, an antipope, and overzealous attempts at correction.

      Cf. Bartolomeo Platina, *Liber de vita Christi ac omnium pontificum*, ed. Giacinto Gaida. Rerum Italicarum scriptores: Raccolta degli storici italiani dal cinquecento al millecinquecento 3.1 (Città di Castello: S. Lapi, 1900), 267n7.

12   In the margin: "This decree is found in the book of papal bulls printed in Rome."

      In late 1317, a group of Irish chieftains sent a "Remonstrance" to Pope John XXII, protesting Edward II's (r.1307–27) treatment of their island. To this, they appended the papal letter *Laudabiliter*, which they claimed had been sent by Adrian IV to Henry II as part of the grant of dominion over Ireland. The following year, John wrote to Edward, forwarding both the "Remonstrance" and *Laudabiliter*. Anne J. Duggan believes *Laudabiliter* to have been a forgery, but this did not prevent its repeated use in Anglo-Irish disputes. Anne J. Duggan, "The Power of Documents: The Curious Case of *Laudabiliter*," in *Aspects of Power and Authority in the Middle Ages*, ed. Brenda Bolton and Christine Meek (Turnhout: Brepols Publishers, 2007), 251–75, here 255–56.

      For the text of the Remonstrance, see Domhnall Ó Néill, "Remonstrance of the Irish Chiefs to Pope John XXII." trans. Edmund Curtis, Corpus of Electronic Texts (2010), http://www.ucc.ie/celt/published/T310000-001.html [accessed December 6, 2015].

      Though I have not been able to determine which book of papal bulls Ribadeneyra is referring to here, the text of John's letter to Edward II can be found in Augustin Theiner, ed., *Vetera monumenta Hibernorum et Scotorum historiam illustrantia quae ex Vaticani, Neapolis ac Florentiae tabulariis deprompsit et ordine chronologico disposuit Augustinus Theiner* (Rome: Typis Vaticanis, 1864), 201.

Ireland, no longer recognizing—indeed, publicly renouncing and demanding his realm utterly renounce—the supreme spiritual and temporal power of the Roman pontiff, without which he was not lord of Ireland nor could he claim the title of king. To this day, the heretical ministers of that kingdom affirm that the English monarchs' title to Ireland from the Apostolic See is valid and in force, exploiting the pope's authority to tyrannize the island, but denying it in order to carry on without restraint and with the utmost license. It was in this spirit that Henry usurped the title of king. At the same time, to make another ostentatious display of his power, he declared war upon the kings of France and Scotland[13] and renewed the persecution of Catholics in England, putting to death various clerics and priests for denying his ecclesiastical supremacy.

---

13   The so-called "Rough Wooing," a series of wars between England and Scotland from 1543 to 1550, which originated in Henry's aggressive foreign policy of 1541: claiming the kingship of Ireland, initiating new military campaigns, and launching an unprecedented progress through northern England. Given the long-standing "Auld Alliance" between Scotland and France, the wars inevitably involved action against both nations. Elizabeth A. Bonner, "The Genesis of Henry VIII's 'Rough Wooing' of the Scots," *Northern History* 33, no. 1 (1997): 36–53, here 36, 50.

The Poverty Henry Found Himself in after Despoiling the Churches, and the Taxes He Imposed on His Kingdom[1]

Then came the year 1544, the thirty-sixth of Henry's reign, and the just and merciful Lord chose to demonstrate how hateful the king's looting of the Church's goods had been, and how detrimental to king and kingdom. For although the monasteries of England had piled up so many precious treasures and valuables that one would have thought even a small portion would have sufficed to slake and sate the avarice, however insatiable, of the greediest king in the world, yet it all served only to stoke and enflame Henry, as a few drops of water do a roaring fire. He had laid hands upon all the churches' treasures: the crosses of gold and silver, the sacred vessels, the precious ornaments of the altars, the jewels and riches of a thousand monasteries; he had seized every bequest, every estate, every scrap of land, every privilege, every deed, every tenant; he had confiscated the tithes and annates of every benefice in the kingdom, sold the lead, lumber, and even the stones of the monasteries themselves; and, in the end, he had amassed so much gold and silver that he seemed the richest king in Christendom, and he could have quite reasonably exempted his people from every tax and toll—as he had claimed he would when he first laid hands on the monasteries' goods, to secure the people's docile assent.[2] This having been the justification, by God's will and chastisement it fell out so contrarily that a few years after the ransacking and violation of the monasteries, he had been beggared, and found himself in severer necessity than he or any previous king had ever been.[3] And thus it was that he alone forced more exactions and charges upon the people than any ruler of the last five hundred years, as we see in their histories and biographies and the annals of England.

---

1 Sander, *De origine ac progressu*, 227–34.
2 Nicholas Harpsfield reported that in March 1536, Cranmer had preached a sermon that insisted the people "had no cause to be grieved with the evertion of the abbeys," as the king would thereby "gather such an infinite treasure that from that time he should have no need, nor would not put the people to any manner of payment or charge for his or the realm's affairs." Harpsfield, *Treatise*, 292.
3 "By November 1545 the king was virtually bankrupt, living from hand to mouth as funds trickled in." Haigh, *English Reformations*, 163.

© KONINKLIJKE BRILL NV, LEIDEN, 2017 | DOI 10.1163/9789004323964_052

It should be noted that before these robberies, when the religious were flourishing and the monasteries were in possession of their incomes, the king's false
counselors and true deceivers [*verdaderos engañadores*] suggested that if His
Majesty made himself master of those goods, not a single pauper would be
left in England, since he could give to each whatever was needed. What a lie!
Where before there had been one beggar, now there were twenty; where before
there had been many to aid the poor and give them the alms they sought, it
would now be a marvel to find one!

In this regard, consider well the innovations and artifices the king employed
to escape his poverty, after he had brought every monastery in the realm to the
ground and stolen their incomes and their property. First of all, in the same
year he demanded each person yield up more than a third of their wealth,
as has been said—that is, two parts in five—and he imposed exactions of
this sort many times thereafter. Second, he concocted a new form of tribute,
commanding that whoever possessed more than two hundred ducats' worth
of property should offer the king a quantity roughly commensurate to their
wealth.[4] Third, he ordered that each person should give some sign of their willingness to please and serve the king by making an offering and present, which
he called a "benevolence." To secure this hateful "benevolence," he named several collectors of little benevolence, so strict and so cruel that none could prevail against them,[5] for they not only readily and eagerly took what was given,
but also demanded the surrender of anything that struck their fancy, and harassed, persecuted, and jailed those who resisted. The fourth sort of robbery
and tyranny was even worse, and even more important to the king: to debase
and counterfeit the silver coins in England: originally of pure, refined silver,
barely one part copper or tin in eleven (all that was needed to make a useful
alloy), little by little the king falsified it until the coins had barely two ounces
of silver, with eleven of copper or tin. For an even greater profit, he recalled all
the coinage in the realm and then had new, lighter coins struck, of fewer carats,
and with this he paid his officials, administrators, and soldiers, as well as those
who had turned in their older, better money.[6] Since all this did not satisfy the

---

4   34 and 35 Hen. 8. c. 27. See *SR*, 3:938–51.

5   On January 5, 1545, Henry issued writs for commissioners for the collection of benevolences:
    see *LP*, 20.1:16.

6   Henry attempted to raise revenue through debasement of the currency, both by adjust-
    ments to face value and alloying of metals (including reducing the required quantity of silver
    from 11.1 parts per dozen to four). C.E. Challis, "The Debasement of the Coinage, 1542–1551,"
    Economic History Review, New Series, 20, no. 3 (December 1967): 441–66. For the relevant
    proclamations, see *TRP*, 1:261–62, 264–66, 327–29.

king's greed and profligacy, in another session of parliament he decreed that he be paid a tenth, and then another fifteenth, of all the rents in the kingdom, and of movable goods a whole two tenths.[7] Because there was no one to resist his madness, he seized all the hospitals, seminaries, colleges, chantries, foundations, and bequests that the faithful had left for the sake of their souls, and disposed of and exploited them and all their property just as he liked,[8] so that there was nothing in the entire kingdom from which any advantage or profit could be taken that was not in his power, unless they decided to start selling the heads of the living or the tombs of the dead.

---

7   "An Acte concerning the Graunt of one entire Subsidie and two whole Fifteenes and Tenths granted by the Temporaltie" (37 Hen. VIII. c.25). See *SR*, 3:1019–32.

8   37 Hen. VIII. c. 4. See ibid., 3:988–93.

The King's Cruelty, and How the Lord Punished His Ministers for Their Sins[1]

This was Henry's final tyranny against the churches, although he was unable to put it into practice, since death allowed him no space. And it is worth noting that the closer it drew to him, the more he seemed to rage and to show the blades and razors of his cruelty. So it was that not even a month before his death, he banished the duke of Norfolk from the court and sentenced him to life imprisonment. This elderly nobleman had served him in war and peace and in all affairs of state, in advancing the divorce from Queen Catherine and in the condemnation of Rochester and Thomas More, as has been said. He also ordered the duke's eldest son, Henry, the earl of Surrey and a man of great gifts, beheaded.[2] Not so much because they had offended him, as because of the deceptions of the heretics, who could not stomach such powerful lords, so very Catholic, to be so close to the king. But in this as in everything else, our Lord willed to manifest his justice against those who had served Henry in the divorce from Queen Doña Catherine, and in the other injustices perpetrated for his pleasure, for all these men came to a bad end, as has been seen of some in this history already and will be seen of others hereafter. As for the duke of Norfolk and his firstborn son, they were killed off as we have just said, while the earl's son, Thomas, was also beheaded by Queen Elizabeth, though he had done her no small service in the changes she made to religion,[3] while his son and brother remain prisoners to this day.[4] So Cardinal Wolsey, the instigator and promoter of the king's divorce, and Anne Boleyn, its ultimate

---

1 Sander, *De origine ac progressu*, 234–36.

2 Surrey was beheaded at Tower Hill on January 19, 1547. Brigden, "Howard, Henry," in *ODNB*, 28:365.

3 Thomas Howard, fourth duke of Norfolk (1538–72), Surrey's eldest son, was a leading courtier of Queen Elizabeth, eventually executed for treason in 1572. Michael A.R. Graves, "Howard, Thomas, fourth duke of Norfolk (1538–1572)," in *ODNB*, 28:429–36, here 429, 435–36.

4 Philip Howard, thirteenth earl of Arundel, was the son of Thomas Howard, the fourth duke of Norfolk. A known Catholic, he was imprisoned in 1586; though he was condemned to death in 1589, the sentence was never carried out and he died in prison six years later. Henry Howard, first earl of Northampton (1540–1614), was Surrey's second son and the fourth duke's younger brother. Long associated with Catholic circles at court, he was imprisoned throughout the 1580s. J.G. Elzinga, "Howard, Philip [St Philip Howard], thirteenth earl of

© KONINKLIJKE BRILL NV, LEIDEN, 2017 | DOI 10.1163/9789004323964_053

cause, and Thomas and George Boleyn, her supposed father and brother, and Cromwell, the principal instrument of the whole tragedy, have all been seen to pay for their misdeeds with their lives, their punishment meted out by the king they strived to serve and please. Farther on, we shall see how the duke of Suffolk and all his house came to an end, as well as the accursed Cranmer, archbishop of Canterbury, who issued the sentence of divorce and who in the time of Queen Mary was burned at the stake as a heretic and a traitor. Let all mortals, especially ministers of kings, learn from this always to hold justice before their eyes and to place the will of God above that of men, even kings, when it diverges from the divine will—but let us return to Henry.

Arundel (1557–1595)," in *ODNB*, 28:406–09, here 406, 408. Pauline Croft, "Howard, Henry, earl of Northampton (1540–1614)," in *ODNB*, 28:366–74, here 366–67.

BOOK 1, CHAPTER 47

The King's Last Illness and Death, and the Provisions of His Will[1]

The king fell ill with a grave and fatal disease;[2] realizing he could not escape it and tormented by the cruel executioner that was his conscience, he began surreptitiously to confer with certain bishops about how he might be reconciled to the Apostolic See and return to the communion of the Church. But he did not merit to find anyone to tell him the truth, having barbarously and cruelly put so many to death for doing so and speaking freely at his own command. And so he was now left without any who dared tell him what he ought to hear. Instead, one of the bishops, suspecting some trick, that his opinion was asked disingenuously, answered that the king, whose wisdom surpassed all other mortals, had abrogated the supremacy of the Roman pontiff by divine inspiration and the public authority of the entire realm, and therefore he had nothing to fear. They say Stephen Gardiner, bishop of Winchester, spoke with the king in secret and advised him to summon parliament and impart to it this business of such pitch and moment, and if there was not sufficient time, to declare his spirit and intentions in writing, for our Lord is content with our good desires when we cannot put them into practice. But as soon as the bishop finished these words, a troop of scoundrels and flatterers rushed upon the king, banishing such thoughts and removing what scruples he had, for they feared to lose the property they had gained in the dissolution of the monasteries if the king returned to papal obedience. The king abandoned his good intentions lightly, as usually happens with those not founded and rooted in charity and the love of God.

And lest it seem that Henry had performed no good deed in his life and died without any bequest for the poor, he had the church of Saint Francis in the city of London (which had been closed and neglected since the friars were thrown out) reopened and cleansed, and a Mass celebrated there, providing that thenceforth it was to be a parish church. That very day, the king's almoner

---

1   Sander, *De origine ac progressu*, 236–39.

2   The king's health, increasingly precarious in his later years due to a luxurious lifestyle and frequent injuries, took a decided turn for the worse in the autumn of 1546. By the end of the year it had become clear that the king was not long for the world. Scarisbrick, *Henry VIII*, 488, 495.

preached to the people in praise of the king's piety, amplifying in copious words his liberality and magnificence. He read out a royal decree bequeathing to the poor this church, the hospital of Saint Bartholomew, and two other parish churches, with a thousand ducats a year. And above the church, this inscription was to placed: *Ecclesia Christi Ab Henrico Octauo Angliae Rege Fundata*. Which is to say, "The church of Jesus Christ, founded by Henry VIII, king of England."[3] A generous restitution indeed, a magnificent compensation for Henry to make in the hour of his death! A thousand monasteries and ten thousand churches ruined and despoiled in his kingdom, and in recompense he ordered the opening of one church (which wasn't his) and relinquished two others and a hospital (which weren't his either)—proof that his end was in keeping with the course and tenor of his life. A sycophant, heretical preacher was found to laud and magnify the king's supreme liberality, beguiling and deceiving the king himself and blinding the people, so that they did not see what they saw.

Nearing the end and given up for lost by the doctors, the king was informed of his danger. He demanded a goblet of white wine and, turning to one of his intimates, said, *"Omnia perdidimus"*—we have lost all. And with a few anguished words and in mortal agony he died, so they say, with the names of churchmen and monks on his lips.[4] He died on January 28, 1546, having lived to fifty-six, of which he reigned thirty-seven years, nine months, and six days—twenty-one of these as a Catholic in perfect peace, the following five amid dire unrest and disturbances, and the last twelve in open schism and separation from the Church.

---

3 On January 13, 1547 Henry made a "Grant to the mayor and citizens, in fulfilment of an agreement dated 27 Dec. 38 Hen. VIII., of the church of the late Grey Friars in London, the house and site of the said Friars [...] Also grant of the parish churches of St. Nicholas and St. Audoen within Newgate, London [...] Also grant that the church of the said Grey Friars shall be a parish church, to be called the church of Christ within Newgate, and be the parish church of all the inhabitants within the site of the said Grey Friars and within the said parishes of St. Nicholas and St. Audoen, and within that part of St. Sepulchre's parish which lies in and within Newgate. Also grant that the said late hospital of St. Bartholomew shall be a place and house for the poor, to be called The House of the Poor in Westsmythfelde of the foundation of King Henry VIII., and that the church within the site of the said hospital shall be a parish church, called the church of St. Bartholomew the Little, the parish church for all inhabitants within the site and close of the said late hospital." *LP*, 21.2:770.

4 In support of Sander's account, David Lewis cites the "Prevarication of the Holy Church's Liberties, ch. iv., s.31," in the Eyston Manuscript, to the effect that "In his last sickness [Henry was] always muttering out, 'Monks and friars,' and desperately concluding his life with these his last words, 'Bryan, we have lost all!'" Sander, *Rise and Growth*, 164n2.

Just before he died, parliament, to avoid any doubts or confusion, had authorized Henry, with the advice of prudent persons, to provide for the succession to the throne, so that his will might be obeyed in this matter.[5] And so he made his testament, providing that Edward, his son by Jane Seymour, who was nine years of age, should succeed him, and then Mary, his daughter by Queen Doña Catherine, and thirdly Elizabeth, his daughter by Anne Boleyn, and that if they all died without issue, the crown should go to whomever it rightly belonged.[6] In so doing he admitted that he had repudiated Queen Doña Catherine neither for any scruple of conscience nor for not truly being his wife, but only for the satisfaction of his lust and to marry (as he did) Anne Boleyn. It is even written that the day before he died, the king summoned Princess Doña Mary, and told her, with the utmost tenderness and tears in his eyes, "My daughter, fortune has been utterly against you, and it pains me deeply that you have not married as I had wished. But, since it has not come to pass, whether by my neglect or your ill luck, I beg you to strive to be a mother to your brother, who is yet a child."[7]

---

5   Ribadeneyra mistakes the Second Succession Act (28 Hen. 8. c. 7) of 1536 for the Third Succession Act (35 Hen. 8. c. 1) of 1543. Under the terms of the former, Mary and Elizabeth were both declared illegitimate, and Henry was empowered to provide for the succession as he pleased, either by letters patent or his will. The latter statute reinstated Mary and Elizabeth in the order of succession, but without legitimating them. For an overview of Henry's legislation on the succession, see Eric Ives, "Tudor Dynastic Problems Revisited," HR 81, no. 212 (May 2008): 255–79. For the two acts, see SR, 3:655–62 and 955–58, respectively.

6   Henry's will declared, "We will by these Presentes, that immediately after our Departure out of this present Lief, our said Son Edward shall have and enjoy the said Imperial Crown and Realm of England and Ireland [...] to him and to his Heyres of his Body lawfully begotten. And for Default of such Issue of our said Sonne Prince Edwarde's Body laufully begotten, We will the said Imperiall Crown [...] shall holly remain and cum to the Heires of our Body of our entirely beloved Wief Quene Catheryn that now is, or of any other our lawful Wief that We shall hereafter mary; And for lack of such Issue and Heires, [...] the said Imperial Crown [...] shall holly remayn and cum to our sayd Doughter Mary and the Heires of her Body laufully begotten [...] And if it fortune that our said Doughter Mary to dye without Issue of her Body laufully begotten [...] the said Imperial Crown [...] shall holly remayn and cum to our said Doughter Elizabeth, and to the Heyres of her Body laufully begotten." Henry goes on to specify the next heirs, in the event of his children all dying without lawful issue: the children of Lady Frances Grey (1517–59), the eldest surviving child of Henry's sister Mary and Charles Brandon. See Rymer, Fœdera, 15:110–17, here 112–14.

7   "One day before he died he sent for Madam Mary, his daughter, and the good lady on seeing her father so ill, went and knelt before his bed. When he saw her abundance of tears came into his eyes, and he said to her, 'Oh daughter! fortune has been hard against thee, and I grieve I did not have thee married as I wished; but since thy fortune wished it, or my misfortune prevented it, I pray thee, my daughter, try to be a mother to thy brother, for look, he is very little yet.'" Hume, Chronicle, 151.

Of Henry's Natural Gifts and Character[1]

Henry was sharp of mind and sound of judgment—when he deliberately chose to concentrate on some matter of importance, especially in the morning and before eating, for he usually took wine with his meals. In consequence, all the degenerates in his household and those who had business with him waited until after he had eaten, for then he was happier, buoyant with wine, and more inclined to accede to their suits. Others lost intentionally while gambling to please him, and afterwards told him they had lost all they had in playing with His Majesty, and asked him to grant them the estates of such-a-one, who was a wicked man and a traitor, or the rents of this monastery, or the property of that church, or some other thing of value, so that they walked away from their losses with a profit. He was open-hearted in doing kindnesses to strangers and it was rare for a pilgrim to approach him and depart unhappy. He was a friend to learned men, supporting them and augmenting the salaries of the professors at the universities.[2] Generally speaking, he was careful to appoint upright, well-educated men as bishops; many of those he chose endured prisons, dungeons, and tortures for the confession of the Catholic faith in the reigns of his children Edward and Elizabeth. He had the deepest respect for the holy sacrament of the Eucharist: when it was brought to him just before his death, he got up and fell to his knees to revere it, and when he was told that in his weakness he might hurt himself, he replied "Even if I should fall upon the floor and lay myself level with the dust, I could not honor this sacred sacrament as I ought."[3]

After Henry first strayed from the true path of virtue and obedience to the pope,[4] like a runaway horse without reins he ran through every vice and

---

1 Sander, *De origine ac progressu*, 239–45.

2 Between 1535 and 1546, Henry established five regius professorships (in divinity, Greek, Hebrew, law, and physic) at Cambridge and Oxford. See F. Donald Logan, "The Origins of the So-Called Regius Professorships: An Aspect of the Renaissance in Oxford and Cambridge," in *Renaissance and Renewal in Christian History: Papers Read at the Fifteenth Summer Meeting and the Sixteenth Winter Meeting of the Ecclesiastical History Society*, ed. Derek Baker (Oxford: Basil Blackwell, 1977), 271–78.

3 One observer reported of Henry in 1539, "His Grace receives holy bread and holy water every Sunday, and daily uses all other laudable ceremonies. In all London no man dare speak against them on pain of death." *LP*, 14.1:967.

4 Prov. 21:16.

© KONINKLIJKE BRILL NV, LEIDEN, 2017 | DOI 10.1163/9789004323964_055

misdeed, especially lust, avarice, and cruelty. Such was his sensuality that to sate his appetites and vices he committed countless and barbaric injustices and outrages; the older he got, the more it grew and the less he was lord of himself. Rarely did he see a beautiful woman he did not covet; there were few he coveted he did not violate. His greed is manifest in the stories we have told, for there was nothing sacred or profane he had not stolen, neither churchman nor layman he had not despoiled and robbed. He had once been so benign and so quick to pardon that the whole kingdom loved and adored him: indeed, in the days when he ruled with a sound mind, only a few men were executed, and only two knights—one at his father's command[5] and the other at Cardinal Wolsey's instigation.[6] After he separated from Queen Doña Catherine and thus from obedience to the Holy See, he became so cruel that the outrages and butcheries committed in his kingdom could barely be described or conceived. From public documents, we know that he dispatched three—even four—queens; two noblewomen; two cardinals (and a third condemned to death *in absentia*); twelve dukes, marquesses, earls, and sons of lords; eighteen barons and important knights; thirteen abbots, priors, and guardians of monasteries; seventy-seven monks, clerics, and religious; and an uncountable crowd of gentry and commoners. The closer one became to the king, the more trusted a friend, the closer one drew to the knife and death. Accordingly, he was abhorred as a tyrant, his death welcomed by the entire realm and no less by the world. By the emperor and the kings of Scotland and France,[7] because they regarded him with suspicion or enmity. By Pope Paul III and by all the

---

5   On April 30, 1513, Edmund de la Pole, third duke of Suffolk (1471–1513), the Yorkist heir to the throne who had been held prisoner in the Tower since 1506, was beheaded. Henry put him death as a possible rival, especially since Edmund's younger brother, Richard (1480–1525) had taken up arms against him. The French chronicler Martin du Bellay (1495–1559), however, asserted that Henry VII, "having promised the said king, Lord Philip, that he would not put him [Pole] to death, he did not do so; yet at his passing and as his last will, he instructed his son, King Henry VIII, to behead him immediately upon his [Henry VII's] decease, which charge he fulfilled." Martin du Bellay and Guillaume du Bellay, *Mémoires de Martin et Guillaume Du Bellay*, ed. V.-L. Bourrilly and Fleury Vindry, 4 vols. (Paris: Librairie Renouard, 1908), 1:47.

6   Polydore Vergil (c.1470–1555) records that Wolsey, "burning with hatred and ravenously thirsting for human blood, began to plot a means to bring down Edward, duke of Buckingham, as he had already resolved to do, as has been said." Edward Stafford, third duke of Buckingham (1478–1521) was beheaded in May 1521. Vergil, *Anglicæ Historiæ*, 665.

7   Charles V; Mary Stewart; and Francis I, respectively. As Sander notes, Mary was a child of four at the time (and so presumably without strong feelings on the occupant of the English throne). It is possible Ribadeneyra is referring to Scotland's regent at the time, James Hamilton, duke of Châtelherault and second earl of Arran (c.1516–1575). The regent was indeed no

Catholic princes, prelates, and churchmen then gathered in the Council of Trent, because they held out hope that with Henry's death the disasters and misfortunes of the kingdom of England might be at an end.

---

friend of Henry's, having abandoned his former Protestant leanings and championed an alliance with France. Sander, *De origine ac progressu*, 244. Warnicke, *Mary Queen of Scots*, 24, 28.

How God Punished King Henry through His Own Sins[1]

See how God our Lord punishes infamous sinners, even in this life; he does this to manifest his incomprehensible providence, how he, the just and true judge, rewards each according to his deeds,[2] how the wicked begin to taste here and now the punishments of hell, to be tortured in their delight, receiving their pain and chastisement from their own pleasures. In this chapter, as the end and conclusion to the first book, let us discuss the punishment our Lord inflicted upon Henry, torturing him in the very things he had most sought to achieve or to get clear of [*desuanecerse*] in this life. For the pains of hell, which his accursed soul now suffers and shall suffer eternally, together with his wretched corpse, after the day of universal judgment, cannot be explained or understood, and last forevermore, so long as God is God. First of all, our Lord punished King Henry in his body, whose delight and pleasure he so sought that he forgot his soul, and so destroyed himself and his kingdom. Having been a well-disposed, graceful gentleman in his youth, his insatiable sensuality and brutishness made him ugly, deformed, and so obese that he could not mount a stair, and there was scarcely a door wide enough for him to pass through. When he died, he was prepared for embalming, and they say that not a drop of blood was found, all being instead covered by nothing but ghastly humors and fat.[3] He was likewise punished in his body by being denied the honor of a

---

1 Sander, *De origine ac progressu*, 244–45, 247–49.

2 Ps. 7:12, 27:4, 61:13; Matt. 16:27; Rom. 2:6; 2 Tim. 4:8.

3 Cf. Eusebius of Caesarea's account of the death of Emperor Galerius (r.305–11): "From there an innumerable multitude of worms burst forth and gave out a deathly stench, for the entire bulk of his limbs through gluttony, even before the disease, had been changed into an excessive amount of soft fat, which then becoming putrid furnished an unbearable and most horrible sight to those who approached." Eusebius of Caesarea, *Ecclesiastical History, Books 6–10*, ed. and trans. Roy J. Deferrari, The Fathers of the Church: A New Translation 29 (Washington, D.C.: Catholic University of America Press, 1955), 200.

There may also be a link with Harpsfield's description of the fate of Henry's body, supposedly fulfilling a prophecy that, like the biblical Ahab, the king's blood would be licked by his dogs: "For at what time his dead corpse was carried from London to Windsor there to be interred, it rested the first night at the monastery of Syon, which the King had suppressed; at which time, were it for the jogging and shaking of the chariot or for any other secret cause,

royal burial and sepulcher.[4] For in the successive reigns of his three children, none has taken any thought for their father's body. Queen Doña Mary dearly wished to do so, but could not, as a Catholic: he was a schismatic, outside the communion of the Catholic Church. Edward and Elizabeth could do so (being heretics), but without any pang of conscience they attended to nothing in the world so little as the obsequies and memory of their father. And this was God's just punishment. For he should not have the honor of a king's tomb who had sacrilegiously defiled the martyrs' sepulchers, scattering their sacred ashes and relics.

God likewise punished the king's soul, allowing him to fall into so many sins and crimes, and into the pangs and throbs of conscience and the rotting of his heart, all his life long, ever since he first tumbled into the abyss of so many evils.[5] For his cares and troubles were assuredly without number, beating down upon him and overwhelming him like contrary waves and winds:[6] he was often overcome, without knowing how to turn back. He punished his honor, of which he had been so covetous, for not only did he lose the glory and title of defender of the Church, which Pope Leo X had so justly given him for rebutting Luther, but he lost his reputation as a just and peaceable king, instead made infamous as one of the most impious, bloodthirsty, and brutal tyrants ever to assail the Catholic Church. And no less noteworthy is another rebuke to his honor: two of his wives and queens—blinded and deranged by whose love he had committed so many crimes—were unfaithful, living in such degeneracy and sin that they well deserved to be publicly beheaded.

He allowed himself to be so possessed by his own will that he would brook neither advice nor resistance—no less was this a punishment from God, for when, at the end of his life and in his last agonies, he wished to return to his senses and be reconciled with the Church, as we have said, he could find no one to counsel him and tell him the truth. For he was regarded as such an enemy to truth, so utterly set upon his own will, that everyone was terrified to contradict him or breathe a word that might offend him. For they knew that they might pay for it with their lives. Meanwhile, the flatterers and rascals to whom

---

the coffin of lead, wherein his dead corpse was put, being riven and cloven, all the pavement of the church was with the fat and corrupt putrified blood dropped out of the said corpse foul embrued." Harpsfield, *Treatise*, 203.

4   Henry received a solemn funeral, with a Mass in St George's Chapel. He was buried alongside Jane Seymour, as his own sumptuous tomb was as yet unfinished. Scarisbrick, *Henry VIII*, 497.

5   On the idea that God punishes sin with further sins, see Ribadeneyra, *Tratado de la tribulacion*, Book 2, Chapter 2.

6   Isa. 57:20.

he had surrendered in life prevented him in death from doing what might have secured the salvation of his soul. So it was that since he had refused to hear the truth when it was spoken to him, when he wished for it he could find no one to speak it, by the righteous judgment of God.

In the same way, his last will and testament was not fulfilled. In his testament, Henry decreed that his son Edward should have sixteen protectors and guardians of equal power: these he named (most of them Catholics), and provided for his son to be raised in the Catholic faith—except as regards the supremacy—and the realm always to remain free of heresy.[7] But just as he had violated the last wishes of countless men, annulling their wills and demolishing the monasteries, the shrines, the altars, the tombs of the saints, and the bequests of the faithful, hardly had the king breathed his last when several powerful men suppressed his testament and published a counterfeit in his name, by which they perverted his intentions and all he had determined as to the succession to the throne. Excluding, dismissing, intimidating, and even imprisoning some of the sixteen guardians the king had appointed (because they were Catholics), the remainder named a heretic as regent, whom they called the "protector," to govern and administer the kingdom as he chose.[8] In the end, they entrusted the child king to heretical teachers, undid Henry's laws and made new, contrary ones, and little by little destroyed the Catholic faith in the kingdom and introduced the sect of the sacramentarians and the Zwinglians—those Henry hated most. Thus God our Lord, who allots to each according to their deserts,[9] punished Henry's perfidy and wickedness with the perfidy and wickedness of his men. And it is no less to be observed that, having married so many times and taken so many wives in order to father children and perpetuate the succession (as he himself said), after his children Edward,

---

7   The stipulations about preserving Catholicism do not appear in Henry's will, but the king did make substantial provision for Masses, obits, and other bequests for his soul, a distinctly un-Protestant decision. On the other hand, at the time of Henry's death, the evangelical faction was ascendant, and Henry deliberately excluded two leading conservatives, Gardiner and the duke of Norfolk, from the council governing his son. Overall, the council was religiously balanced, with conservatives and radicals in roughly equal numbers, along with a large contingent of "religious 'neuters.'" Rymer, *Fœdera*, 15:110–12. Haigh, *English Reformations*, 167.

8   A scant three days after Henry's death, the will was overturned and Edward Seymour, earl of Hertford (*c*.1500–52), was chosen as lord protector. Far from the minority coup depicted by Sander, thirteen of the sixteen councilors cosigned the decision. Thomas Wriothesley, first earl of Southampton (1505–50), was expelled from the council in March 1547, but more for opposition to Seymour's appointment than for his religious convictions. Loach, *Edward VI*, 25–26.

9   Ps. 27:4, 61:13; Matt. 16:27; Rom. 2:6.

Mary, and Elizabeth had all reigned according to the order he had planned, and reached the age to bear children (to whom they might leave the crown), none has had any. For Edward died as a youth of sixteen years, without having married; Queen Mary had no children, marry though she did; and Elizabeth has declined to marry. All this has come to pass so that neither sapling nor fruit should remain of so bad a root and stem,[10] and he who committed so many excesses, outrages, and acts of violence to secure the throne for his children should be punished with the very things he had desired and wherein he had sinned.

End of the First Book.

---

10   Matt. 3:10, 7:19; Luke 3:9.

BOOK 2

*The Second Book of the Schism of England,
Concerning King Edward, and the Queens
Doña Mary and Elizabeth, His Sisters*

∴

How King Henry's Testament was Disregarded, and How the Earl of Hertford became Protector of the Realm[1]

Those in power concealed King Henry's death for several days,[2] and when the time seemed right, they announced it and at the same time proclaimed his son Edward, a child of nine years, as king of England and Ireland. With the poor boy still subject to his tutors and ruled by others' intentions, they declared him supreme head of the Church of England and Ireland next to Jesus Christ himself—as though he had taken so little care or notice of it.[3] Their first duty being the fulfillment of the dead king's will, they were zealous in nothing so much as doing precisely the opposite. Among the sixteen guardians Henry had left for his son, as we have said, there were several Catholics, dedicated to the good of the realm and a return to union with the Church and obedience to the Holy See (maintaining that Henry had had this intention at the hour of his death). They were ignored by the other guardians, heretics with high hopes for their own glory and profit by advancing the current schism. These men prevailed over the Catholics, whom they terrorized and chased from the government (among them Thomas Wriothesley, whom the king had left as chancellor, and the earl of Arundel),[4] naming Edward Seymour, earl of Hertford (who subsequently made himself duke of Somerset on his own authority), brother to Queen Jane Seymour and uncle to little Edward, as the sole guardian and protector of the realm. He was a Zwinglian heretic and, in order to increase his prestige and marshal the forces of his friends—fellow heretics and adherents of the same sect—he arranged that before the king was crowned, new titles and dignities be given to certain leading knights, among them one John Dudley, Baron Lisle,

---

1 Sander, *De origine ac progressu*, 253–61.

2 Henry's demise was kept secret for three days, largely due to the question mark this placed over the duke of Norfolk's death sentence. Scarisbrick, *Henry VIII*, 496.

3 Edward VI was proclaimed "by the grace of God King of England, France, and Ireland, defender of the faith and of the Church of England and also of Ireland in earth the supreme head" at Westminster on January 31, 1547, and again the following day. See *TRP*, 1:381–82.

4 Henry Fitzalan, twelfth earl of Arundel (1512–80), though never formally dismissed as a privy councilor, was marginalized by the new protector. Julian Lock, "Fitzalan, Henry, twelfth earl of Arundel (1512–1580)," in *ODNB*, 19:758–65, here 758–60.

who was honored with the title of earl of Warwick.[5] Though he, alone among the protector's allies, was a Catholic, he was nevertheless perfectly obedient to the regent's will (this was devious dissimulation, with the intent of destroying him, as will be seen hereafter).[6]

Having thus usurped the title of protector, contrary to Henry's intentions, and named himself duke of Somerset, he then schemed to make himself lord of the entire kingdom in things spiritual and temporal, to be demi-king and demi-pope of England, for all this seemed to him encompassed in the title "protector." Accordingly, he commanded that no churchman presume to exercise any right or jurisdiction of his dignity or title without the king's (which was to say, his) renewed and particular mandate. Thus it was that the bishops and archbishops who had been consecrated first by papal authority and then by Henry's could not ordain anyone or exercise their offices without the license and special commission of the child king. Even Cranmer himself, archbishop of Canterbury and primate of England, could not use his own authority (a marvel!) without a new commission and license from the boy. This was given not once and for all, but at the king's pleasure and only for so long as he willed,[7] This was the form of the license:

> Edward, by the grace of God king of England, France, and Ireland, supreme earthly head of the Church of England and Ireland, to the Reverend Thomas, archbishop of Canterbury, greetings, etc. Although all authority to judge, all jurisdiction, both ecclesiastical and secular, remains with its source, the supreme head of the royal power, etc., we give you the power, by these our present letters, which we desire to last at our pleasure and as long as it accords with our will, so that in your diocese of

---

5   Seymour secured the assent of Henry's executors for his appointment through a liberal dispensing of titles and lands in the late winter of 1547. He himself was made duke of Somerset, Parr became marquess of Northampton, Wriothesley earl of Southampton, and John Dudley, Viscount Lisle (1504–53), became earl of Warwick. Four others were made barons, and thousands of pounds' worth of crown lands was distributed. Loach, *Edward VI*, 26–27.

6   Dudley's religious affiliation is open to debate: in his public career, he was "a committed supporter of protestantism;" imprisoned and condemned to death by Mary, however, he claimed to have recanted and returned to the Catholicism of his forebears, probably in hopes of a pardon that was not forthcoming. David Loades, "Dudley, John, duke of Northumberland (1504–1553)," in *ODNB*, 17:73–84, here 73, 76–77, 82–83. Loades, *Reign of Mary Tudor*, 99.

7   1 Edw. 6. c. 2. See *SR*, 4.1:3–4.

Canterbury you can ordain all those who seem good to you, and raise them to any order, up to that of the holy priesthood.[8]

And as the protector was a Zwinglian and sacramentarian heretic, he was not content with the damage Henry had done, but felt that the form of religion the king had left was not to his liking or taste, and that soon it could be reformed and return to its ancient dignity and glory.[9] He wished, following the example of Jeroboam, to proffer new gods to the people[10]—that is to say, new rites for prayer and the praise of God, a new creed, new priests not ordained in the form commanded by the Roman Church, so that he might completely separate the people from obedience thereto. To achieve this, he seized the wind and ordered it not to blow over the surface of the earth:[11] he forbade the bishops and Catholic priests of every church to preach or teach. Only the Lutheran and Zwinglian heretics were given permission to speak, so that, without a single Catholic preacher to share the bread of sound and true doctrine to those who sought it, when they were hungry they would become ravenous and more readily and willingly eat the poisonous dish of false belief.

To the heretics, the protector's favor and authority seemed to offer the perfect opportunity to emerge from their lairs, remove their masks, and uncover the evil intentions of their hearts with greater freedom than ever before.[12] Among these, Thomas Cranmer, archbishop of Canterbury—who had previously submitted totally to the will of King Henry, and for his sake heard Mass each day (even saying it on certain solemn holidays) to retain the appearance of a Catholic—now began to show himself for what he was. He wrote a pestilential catechism, brimming with heresies, which he dedicated to King Edward,[13] and publicly wed the mistress he had brought from Germany (as we

---

8   Soon after Edward's accession, Cranmer received the letters patent authorizing him to exercise his jurisdiction as archbishop. Ribadeneyra translates from the Latin excerpt provided in Sander, *De origine ac progressu*, 257–58.
     For the full patent, see Wilkins, *Concilia*, 4:2–3.

9   Somerset's religious inclinations have also been the subject of much debate, but recent evidence suggests he was a fairly enthusiastic evangelical. Diarmaid MacCulloch, *The Boy King: Edward VI and the Protestant Reformation* (Berkeley: University of California Press, 2002), 42–44. Loach, *Edward VI*, 43.

10   In the margin: "3 Kings 12[:28–33]."

11   Rev. 7:1.

12   Cf. Luke 6:45.

13   This catechism, dedicated "To the moste excellent prince Edward the VI," was Cranmer's adaptation of the German reformer Justus Jonas's (1493–1555) Latin version of a German

mentioned), whom he had kept hidden out of fear of Henry.[14] Furthermore, another diabolical and blaspheming heretic, called Hugh Latimer, mounted the pulpit—he had been stripped of a bishopric by King Henry for having eaten flesh on Holy Friday.[15] Still more arrived from Germany and other places, like crows and birds of prey to a corpse; they were given benefices, ecclesiastical titles, and bishoprics.[16] With such assistance, the protector began to extirpate the Catholic faith from the kingdom; in furthering such schemes, he used the means that shall now be discussed.

---

catechism. See Thomas Cranmer and Justus Jonas, *Catechismus, That Is to Say, a Shorte Instruction into Christian Religion for the Synguler Commoditie and Profyte of Childre[n] and Yong People: Set Forth by the Mooste Reuerende Father in God Thomas Archbyshop of Canterbury, Primate of All England and Metropolitane* (London: Nycolas Hyll for Gwalter Lynne, 1548).

14   Though there was no second marriage ceremony, after Henry's death Cranmer was able to acknowledge Margarete, as well as their three children. MacCulloch, *Thomas Cranmer*, 361.

15   The pugnacious Protestant divine Hugh Latimer had been made bishop of Worcester in 1535, but was forced to resign in 1539 for his opposition to the Six Articles, specifically their conservative Eucharistic theology. Susan Wabuda, "Latimer, Hugh, (c.1485–1555)," in *ODNB*, 32:632–39, here 635–36.

16   Soon after Edward's accession, Thomas Cranmer dispatched invitations to reformers across Europe, seeking assistance in reforming the English church. As Ribadeneyra describes in the following chapter, many accepted. MacCulloch, *Boy King*, 77–81.

The Means the Protector Employed to Pervert the Faith of the Boy King and that of the Kingdom[1]

To begin with, the protector seized total control over the royal household and filled it with heretical servants, so that while the king was still a child and in his power, he could more easily and effectively extend and disseminate heresy, and so that after Edward had grown and become master of himself, he would approve of what his uncle and guardian had done. First of all, the protector provided two notorious heretics as tutors, a layman and a married priest.[2] From the first rudiments, the very first letters, they taught him dogmas against the pope and against priests, religious, and ecclesiastics, and the poor boy king drank their poison and came to abhor that which offered him life and health.[3] His pages and companions were the sons of knights already infected with heresy, as were his ladies and maids, who were to pervert his faith through gifts and loving blandishments. Among these were Anne of Cleves and Katherine Parr, the former queens; they often visited the palace and, being heretics, vomited up in their words the venom of their hearts.[4]

Having secured the king's upbringing and corruption, which was a stronghold and even more a weapon for his wickedness, Somerset adopted another, more effective means of uprooting and eradicating the Catholic faith in

---

1 Sander, *De origine ac progressu*, 261–72.

2 Sander specifies these two men as Richard Cox (*c.*1500–81), a married clergyman who was later to become bishop of Ely, and Sir John Cheke (1514–57), a lay classical scholar. Felicity Heal, "Cox, Richard (*c.*1500–1581)," in *ODNB*, 13:861–65, here 862. Alan Bryson, "Cheke, Sir John (1514–1557)," in *ODNB*, 11:291–98, here 292.

3 In terms of religion, Cheke and Cox were both reformers, and Edward's French instructor, Jean Belmain (*fl.* mid-sixteenth century), was a fervently anti-papal Calvinist. Pollnitz, *Princely Education*, 141–42, 166.

4 Anne of Cleves's interactions with Edward's court was generally limited to periodic pleas for money. Though "Edward seems to have been fond of her," she does not appear to have exercised a religious influence. Warnicke, *Marrying of Anne of Cleves*, 252–53.

As queen dowager and wife of a leading politician, Katherine was a habitué of the Edwardian court until her death. Though she was a deft advocate for the evangelical cause, this was largely confined to Henry VIII's lifetime. She did play some role in Edward's education, although the precise nature of this has been debated. Kujawa-Holbrook, "Katherine Parr," 55, 73–74.

England: to infect and contaminate the realm's universities, which were like the common wells of the people—all who drank from them would be poisoned, the pestilence spreading and taking hold without remedy. For there is nothing more beneficial than the sound education and training of the young people who frequent the universities—and nothing more harmful than the bad. And although there were certain young libertines in those days, curious and lovers of novelty, who had tasted the books of Luther (brought over from Germany), they were as yet few in number. And as the rectors of the more important colleges and the professors of every discipline were worthy men, dedicated to the ancient faith and the ancient customs, the universities were thus far undamaged, still fortresses and sturdy castles to shelter and protect the Catholic faith. Therefore, to demolish them it was ordered under the king's name and authority that every university and college in the realm should be visited—and the visitors were the persons most apt for their schemes.[5] They undid every ordinance and statute established by the founders for the preservation and promotion of religion, learning, and propriety. They created new laws to bring up the youth without restraint and incline them to their sect; they took the chairs and pulpits from Catholic scholars and churchmen and allotted them to dissolute, foolhardy, chattering youths. They removed the rectors of the colleges and the governors of the universities, either through artifice and slander or through public accusation, and put heretics and pestilential teachers in their place, to corrupt the students in their faith and habits. From every university and every library they banished any book of the theologians we call the Scholastics, such as the Master of the *Sentences*,[6] Saint Thomas, and other holy and learned men, who clearly, succinctly, and steadfastly proclaim the

---

5   1549 saw the Edwardian government carry out a visitation of both universities, ending in the promulgation of new statutes, the first official declarations that the universities were "Protestant." These new regulations required attendance at Protestant services throughout the term, as well as stipulating which books were (and were not) to be taught. Many conservatives left their posts, either forced to resign or flee, or imprisoned for resistance. Cross, "Oxford and the Tudor State," 136–39.

6   Peter Lombard was known as *Magister Sententiarum* ("Master of the *Sentences*") from his *magnum opus*, the *Four Books of Sentences* (*c.*1150).

   Rather puzzlingly, from the 1595 edition onwards, this title is changed from "maestro de las Sentencias" to "maestro de las ciencias" (lit. "master of knowledges"). If this is deliberate, Ribadeneyra's intention seems to be to foreground the great Italian Dominican Thomas Aquinas (1225–74): rather than equating him with his predecessors Peter Lombard and Duns Scotus (*c.*1266–1308) (as Sander had done), the phrase in the later editions reads, "such as that master of [all] knowledge, Saint Thomas."

   Cf. Sander, *De origine ac progressu*, 264.

truths of sacred theology and lend us light to confound the contrary errors.[7] And to ridicule them further, they had certain degenerate and wild youths take a huge number of these books, carry them on catafalques like dead men through the city, and burn them in the public square: making a bonfire with them, they were to weep and lament with dirges and sad songs. This they called the obsequies of Scotus and of all Scotists.[8]

And in place of these wholesome doctors, of this sound and solid learning, of the philosophers and the theologians, they stuffed the universities and the realm's principal cities with jabbering speechifiers, crazed youths, presumptuous poets, and arrogant grammarians, to entice the people to loose living (and so to the eternal perdition of their souls) with cosmetics and comedies, poems and ludicrous songs. Recognizing that there were men outside the realm even more skilled and adept at this sort of wickedness, they summoned from Germany the German Martin Bucer and the Italians Peter Martyr and Bernardino Ochino—all of them apostates from religion—as well as other degenerate heretics, so that by preaching to the people in their synagogues and teaching their errors to the university students, they could more easily deceive everyone else. Accordingly, they were given the regius professorships [*Cathedras de Prima*] of divinity[9] at Cambridge and Oxford, and with them the canonries and prebends that had been given to the previous (Catholic)

---

7   As early as October 1535, injunctions had been issued to the universities stipulating that "That no lectures should be read upon any of the doctors who had written upon the Master of the Sentences, but on the Old and New Testament. [...] That students in arts should be instructed in logic, rhetoric, arithmetic, geography, music, and philosophy, and should read Aristotle, Rodulphus, Agricola, Melanchthon, Trapezuntius, &c. and not the frivolous questions and obscure glosses of Scotus, Burleus, Anthony Trombet, Bricot, Bruliferius, &c." *LP*, 9:615.

8   The ludic atmosphere of the Protestant revamping of the universities, as well as the reformers' low opinion of Duns Scotus, can be glimpsed in a letter from Richard Layton (*c*.1500–44), one of Cromwell's agents, to his master: "We have set Dunce [Duns Scotus] in Bocardo [the Oxford jail], and banished him Oxford for ever, and is now made a common servant to every man fast nailed up upon posts in all common houses of easement. The second time we came to New College we found the quadrant full of leaves of Dunce, and Mr. Grenefelde, a gentleman of Buckinghamshire, gathering them up for sewelles or blawnsherres to keep the deer within the wood, and thereby have the better cry with his hounds." Ibid., 9:350.

    For book-burning as a projection of state power, see David Cressy, "Book Burning in Tudor and Stuart England," *SCJ* 36, no. 2 (Summer 2005): 359–74.

9   Many chairs at Spanish universities were named for the hours at which their holders lectured. The prestigious prime chairs were equivalent to the regius professorships at Oxford and Cambridge.

professors.[10] Lewd and base as these men were, they immediately filled the colleges (which had hitherto been like monasteries of the most secluded monks) with their mistress, prostitutes, and other sordid women of ill-repute, whom they had brought with them from Germany or corrupted while in England,[11] to the end that the wiles and songs of these sirens would lull and weaken the young men, and incline them to embrace and follow their errors and heresies. Furthermore, they began to preach—or, as I should say, to shout—with the greatest cunning and deceitfulness, and ordered that anyone who understood Latin should be present at each day's sermon. What they taught was anything of licentiousness or debauchery, running wild and unrestrained among their lusts and pleasures, and they abominated everything to do with penance, repentance, austerity, or the imitation and cross of Jesus Christ.

To seem more credible and to deceive without resistance of any kind, they strove to strip away the authority of our sacred Fathers and the glorious Doctors of the Church with a thousand lies and slanders. They reworded the Holy Bible in Latin and in English, corrupting it in innumerable places with poisonous glosses and annotations, contrary to the text and to the truth, and foisted it upon one and all to read.[12] In the pulpit, they ridiculed and mocked the pope, as well as the prelates of the Church, religious, and ecclesiastic persons, with stunning shamelessness and to universal derision. Through these and similar means, these accursed new masters sowed and spread their doctrine, which the most deranged and degenerate men of the kingdom drank down.

---

10   Prominent among the European evangelicals Cranmer invited to England were the Alsatian Martin Bucer (1491–1551), the Florentine Pietro Martire Vermigli (known as Peter Martyr, 1499–1562), and the Sienese Bernardino Ochino (1487–1564). All three had formerly been members of religious orders: Bucer a Dominican, Vermigli an Augustinian Canon, and Ochino a Capuchin. Bucer and Vermigli were appointed to the regius professorships of divinity at Cambridge and Oxford, respectively, while Vermigli was tasked with ministering to Italian Protestants in London. See Martin Greschat, *Martin Bucer: A Reformer and His Times*, trans. Stephen E. Buckwalter (Louisville: Westminster John Knox Press, 2004), Chapter 8; Mark Taplin, "Vermigli, Pietro Martire [Peter Martyr] (1499–1562)," in *ODNB*, 56:327–31, here 329; Mark Taplin, "Ochino, Bernardino (c.1487–1564/5)," in *ODNB*, 41:415–18, here 415–17.

11   Both Martyr and Richard Cox, chancellor of Oxford from 1547 to 1552, lived in the colleges with their wives, provoking violent reactions from scandalized locals. Cross, "Oxford and the Tudor State," 138.

12   The Great Bible, an English translation with royal imprimatur, first became widely-available in late 1539; a (by no means radically) Protestant text, it remained the standard English text for at least a generation. S.L. Greenslade, "English Versions of the Bible A.D. 1525–1611," in *The Cambridge History of the Bible* (Cambridge: Cambridge University Press, 1963), 3:141–74, here 150–51.

Many youths barely able to speak mounted the pulpit with hateful presumption, teaching they knew not what, having merely heard it from those new instructors. And in those days the people of England were given to nothing so much as hearing or speaking of novelties, and to discussing and debating the faith, which they did in marketplaces, inns, and taverns with unbelievable shamelessness and liberty.

What Parliament Enacted against Our Sacred Religion[1]

Although religious matters in England were in chaos, as we have seen, and the Catholics were oppressed and beset, the heretics did not make as much progress in expanding their sect as they would have liked. Since they were numerous, and diverse, and contradicted one another, they could not agree or cooperate in anything but distancing themselves from the Catholic Church in every way. As for the heretical masters and teachers, having already sold their souls they wanted to sell their tongues too, to profit in the here and now, teaching whatever pleased the protector and Primate Cranmer—who had not yet clarified their beliefs. Bucer was much inclined to combine the dogma of Zwingli with that of the Jews, for he was of that race.[2] Peter Martyr had once been a Lutheran, but later transformed into a Calvinist to please those in power.[3] And because they could not agree, instead proceeding divergently and doubtfully, they did not have much credit or authority with the people.

Consequently, to advance their position and give strength to their wickedness, in 1547 they convened a fresh parliament in London to debate (laymen though they were) how the realm was to believe and worship. Beginning with the protector's chief priority, it was mandated that the scraps of church

---

1   Sander, *De origine ac progressu*, 272–81, 317–18.
2   There is no evidence for Sander's claim of Martin Bucer's Jewish background, and the Strasbourg reformer's opinions on Judaism were thoroughly antipathetic. However, at least one satire did describe him as "By character a Jew, a false Christian." Greschat, *Martin Bucer*, 157–58, 204.

    It is interesting that Ribadeneyra, a man of *converso* background himself, chooses to repeat this charge. I have suggested that this was an attempt to broadcast his own Catholicism by mimicking the prejudices of the day. Weinreich, "Distinctiveness," 181–82.
3   "This taught peter Martyr, at his first commyng to oxford, when he was but a lutheran in this matter, whose words I, and ma[n]y other mo wrate in the diuynite schole, when he redde lecture there, but when he came ones to the court, and sawe that that doctrine myslyked them, that myghtdo him hurt yn his lyuige, he anon after turned his tipped, and sang an other songe." Richard Smith, *A Confutation of a Certen Booke, Called a Defence of the True, and Catholike Doctrine of the Sacrame[n]t, &c. Sette Fourth of Late in the Name of Thomas Archebysshoppe of Canterburye: By Rycharde Smyth, Docter of Diuinite, and Some Tyme Reader of the Same in Oxforde* (Paris: R. Chaudière, 1550), sigs. Aviii^r–Bi^r.

---

property that had escaped the lion's claws of the dead king should be given to the young cub, the new king. Furthermore, a law was passed declaring that all the shrines, churches, oratories, and chapels established or bequeathed for prayers, alms, offerings, and sacrifices for souls in purgatory now belonged to King Edward. In the same way, all the chapels and foundations with any income, rent, or endowments, as well as the fraternities, brotherhoods, and congregations instituted for any sort of pious works, were confiscated for the king.[4] After this decree, the first and most crucial, they proceeded to matters of belief: they prohibited bishops to be consecrated or priests to be ordained using the forms and ceremonies of the Roman Church (as had been done hitherto, removing only what pertained to obedience to the Roman pontiff), but rather with a new procedure. They made the same provisions for the administration of the sacraments, and published a book on this.[5] After this, since some few precious and beloved images of saints still remained in the kingdom, they had them seized and smashed or burned.

And they sent out nefarious, heartless men, to the end that by royal authority and their own impiety and presumption, not a single image or statue of a saint should remain. At the same time, they sent out heretical preachers to sermonize to the people against the images they had stolen, and so it was that no image of our Lord nor of his blessed mother, no apostle, no martyr, no saint (male or female) was left anywhere in the land.[6] And in place of the cross, which they had demolished in some places, they erected the king's arms: three lions [*Leopardos*] and three fleurs-de-lys, supported by a serpent on one side and a dog on the other.[7] Thus they signaled that they neither worshipped nor

---

4   1 Edw. 6. c. 14. See *SR*, 4.1:24–33.

5   The Edwardian regime's religious program, including new ceremonies for ordaining clergy and the administration of the sacraments, was set out in the *Book of Common Prayer*, first published by Cranmer in 1549: Church of England, *The Boke of the Common Praier and Administration of Ye Sacramentes & Other Rites and Cermonies of the Church: After the vse of the Church of England* (Worcester: In officina Ioanni Oswæni, 1549).

6   Visitations of English churches began in August 1547, with wide powers to enforce changes. Devotional images of any kind came under the strictest scrutiny, with the visitors instigating bouts of iconoclasm. MacCulloch, *Thomas Cranmer*, 375–76.

7   Ribadeneyra follows Sander in calling the big cats in Edward's heraldry "leopards," though they are lions. Sander, *De origine ac progressu*, 277.

   Cf. "Then should you have seen in the place where Christ's precious body was reposed over the altar, and instead of Christ his crucifix, the arms of a mortal King set up on high with a dogg and a lyon." Harpsfield, *Treatise*, 282.

   The only surviving example of the royal coat of arms so displayed are at St Mary the Virgin in Westerham, Kent. MacCulloch, *Boy King*, 163.

regarded as God that Lord whose glorious standard and peerless arms—the cross—they had torn down, but rather the king of England, whose arms they had put in their place. The Zwinglians were not content with these egregious sins, and arranged for parliament to abolish the sacred sacrifice of the Mass, which is the life, sustenance, and salvation of faithful souls, and the honor, glory, and foundation of the Catholic Church. By this means the king confiscated the chalices, crucifixes, candelabras, cruets, censers, lecterns, osculatories, and all the other vessels, gold and silver instruments, and sumptuous ornaments of inestimable worth that existed in the realm for divine worship.[8] Recognizing that the people might miss the solace and holy sacrifice of the Mass, little by little they introduced a new form of Mass, abandoning the canons and the ancient ceremonies; they had it said in English, to make the simple folk believe that nothing had been removed, but only translated from Latin to the vernacular. They ordered the other divine offices to be said in the same way, willing to leave only the word "Amen" to be said and used as before.[9]

This parliament of laymen—as if it were a council of prelates and bishops—legislated spiritual matters, which belong to the ecclesiastical estate, frequently determining the opposite of the age-old customs of the land and the Catholic Church. There was a marriage case about a woman who, having wed a man and had children with him, then married (while the first husband was still alive) another, with whom she also had children. When the suit came before parliament as to which of the two men was the woman's legitimate husband, it was determined that it was the second, because he was an influential man, in violation of the teachings of Scripture.[10]

---

8   In 1552, the Edwardian regime plundered the nation's churches in an effort to raise money for its ongoing wars: Eamon Duffy has called it "the largest government confiscation of local property in English history." Duffy, *Fires of Faith*, 4.

9   See the Act of Uniformity of 1548 (2 & 3 Edw. 6. c. 1): *SR*, 4.1:37–39.

10   Ribadeneyra has drastically abbreviated this episode from Sander: "There was a certain artisan, whose name was Matthew Barre, whose wife (by whom he had also fathered children) used to wash the linen clothes of Cromwell's household, where Ralph Sadler was living at the time, a man of no little renown, now even a member of Queen Elizabeth's council. Now, this Matthew traveled to foreign parts for I know not what reason, although some thought that he was suspicious of his wife's virtue, and accordingly departed, so as not to be forced to see what he could neither bear nor better. And so, when he had been gone for several years, his wife, either hearing or pretending that her husband was death, married Sir Ralph Sadler. Eventually, Matthew returned to his homeland, where he learned that his wife had wed another, and he began to demand her back. On the other side, Sadler, who had fathered children with her, could not bear to be torn from her. The matter was brought before the highest tribunal, that is, to the the parliament of the realm,

in both the reign of King Henry and of King Edward. There, it was determined that the woman who had been the wife first of Matthew, and then of Sadler, and borne children by both, was thenceforth to be regarded as the wife of Sadler, rather than Matthew, her first husband. For Sadler was richer and more powerful, and thus a wife was adjudicated to a second husband, while the first man was yet living, contrary to the truth of the Gospel." Sander, *De origine ac progressu*, 279–81.

Although the details are sketchy, there is some truth to this story. In 1534, Sir Ralph Sadler (1507–87) married Ellen Mitchell (1510–68), ostensibly the widow of Matthew Barre (dates unknown, *fl*. early fifteenth century). In 1545, Barre reappeared, and a commission of churchmen found that his marriage to Ellen had been and was lawful. Sadler was forced to use his influence to secure a secret act of parliament (37 Hen. VIII. c. 30) declaring his children by Ellen legitimate. See Arthur Joseph Slavin, "Parliament and Henry VIII's Bigamous Principal Secretary," *HLQ* 28, no. 2 (February 1965): 131–43.

The Catholics' Sentiments, and the Weakness They Showed[1]

The more learned and thoughtful English Catholics imagined that Henry's death had ended the kingdom's trials and tribulations, but when they realized these were actually worsening, waxing greater greater day by day, they began to feel their injuries more keenly and to berate and reproach themselves for not having resisted the king's will with more spirit and force. Well, on the one hand reading in Saint John Chrysostom that in his day churches had been founded and altars erected to Jesus Christ in England, to the glory of the inhabitants,[2] and on the other seeing how those same altars and temples of their forebears had been torn down, twelve hundred years after Chrysostom's death—not by heathens, Jews, or pagans, but by those calling themselves Christians—what pain must they have felt? What tears must they have shed? What heartbreak, what dejection must they have known? For if the altars had once been proof that the faith of Christ flourished (as that renowned and saintly sage attests), their overthrow is a clear signal of the perfidy and wickedness of the Antichrist. The bishops of Winchester, London, Durham, Worcester, and Chichester [*Licestre*],[3] all distinguished and scholarly men, who had votes in parliament and were Catholics at heart, bewailed this, and made some resistance to the innovations of each passing day. But because they had been ordained bishops outside—or, to speak properly, against—the Catholic Church, by the mandate not of the pope, but of King Henry, to secure his divorce and the royal supremacy, they did not have the strength of spirit to defend the truth, such as our Lord grants those who are ordained and canonically anointed within the unity of the Catholic Church. And so they tardily and feebly resisted the supremacy

---

1   Sander, *De origine ac progressu*, 281–83.

2   In the margin: "Homily that Christ is God."

    John Chrysostom, *Demonstration against the Pagans that Christ is God.*

      See John Chrysostom, *Apologist,* trans. Margaret A. Schatkin and Paul W. Harkins, The Fathers of the Church: A New Translation 73 (Washington, D.C.: Catholic University of America Press, 1985), 173, 239.

3   Stephen Gardiner, Edmund Bonner (*c.*1500–1569), Cuthbert Tunstal, Nicholas Heath (*c.*1501–78), and George Day (*c.*1502–1556), respectively.

    "Licestre" is a misreading or misprint of Sander's "Cicestrensis." Sander, *De origine ac progressu,* 282.

of the boy king, while straightforwardly approving all the decisions and innovations that in their eyes did not contain manifest heresies, so as not to lose their bishoprics, honors, and incomes. And soon enough they paid (all too well) for this sin, for in King Edward's reign they were harassed and persecuted for refusing to acquiesce to his will in all things, as we shall see[4]—and even more in that of Queen Elizabeth, who stripped them of their sees and afflicted them with harsh imprisonment, even unto death.[5] All this they suffered with the utmost patience and steadfastness, on the one hand praising the mercy of the Lord, and on the other his justice, in thus chastising them.

Now, after the bishops had approved these decrees out of fear, as well as others put forward by the boy king's authority, when the time for parliament drew near the heretics abandoned public Masses and the Catholic administration of divine office and the sacraments, hoping thus to cement the decrees and extend them through the entire realm. There were some who said or heard Mass in secret, but did not on this account forebear to attend the heretics' temples and partake of their sacraments, imagining (as Saint Augustine says of some in Africa who followed the Donatists)[6] that it sufficed to revere Christ in any manner at all, ignorant of his desire to be worshipped in the unity of the Church, and of the impossibility of simultaneously drinking the chalice of Christ and that of the demons.[7]

---

4   In July 1548, Gardiner was imprisoned for his resistance to Edwardian religious reforms; he was deprived of the see of Winchester in February 1550. Redworth, *Stephen Gardiner*, 281–87.

    Bonner was deprived in October 1549 and soon thereafter imprisoned in Marshalsea prison. Kenneth Carleton, "Bonner, Edmund (d. 1569)," in *ODNB*, 6:552–56, here 553–54.

    Tunstal managed to navigate these turbulent ecclesiastical waters almost until the end of Edward's reign, but was eventually imprisoned and deprived in October 1552. D.G. Newcombe, "Tunstal [Tunstall], Cuthbert (1474–1559)," in *ODNB*, 55:551–55, here 553–54.

    In March 1551, Heath was committed to the Fleet; he was deprived of his bishopric in October. David Loades, "Heath, Nicholas (1501?–1578)," in *ODNB*, 26:180–82, here 180–81.

    Day was imprisoned in December 1550 and deprived the following October. Malcolm Kitch, "Day, George (c.1502–1556)," in *ODNB*, 15:581–82.

5   By Elizabeth's accession, Gardiner and Day were both dead. In May 1559, Bonner was once again deprived of the bishopric of London, and a year later he was back in the Marshalsea, dying there in 1569. Tunstal's refusal to take the oath of supremacy led to his second deprivation in September 1559; he died a few months later. Heath was deprived in July 1559 and briefly imprisoned, but his relative neutrality and Elizabeth's favor enabled him to live out nearly twenty years of peaceful retirement. Carleton, "Bonner, Edmund," in *ODNB*, 6:555–56. Newcombe, "Tunstal," in *ODNB*, 55:554–55. Loades, "Heath, Nicholas," in *ODNB*, 26:181.

6   In the margin: "Augustine."

    Augustine of Hippo, *Letters*, 93.7.

7   1 Cor. 10:21.

The Princess Doña Mary's Constancy in the Catholic Faith, and the Methods the Heretics Employed to Separate Her from it[1]

Only the most serene Princess Doña Mary, King Henry's daughter and Edward's sister, never consented to shutter the oratory in her house or to end the Masses said for her (or to hear them in secret and out of the public gaze), royal commands notwithstanding (so they say), imitating the faith and steadfastness of her saintly mother, Doña Catherine.[2] The protector and the other heretical regents used every conceivable means to overcome her, entreaties as well as threats, but to no avail. Not only was the saintly maiden firm and unyielding in her resolve, but she also sharply rebuked the protector and her brother's other counselors, in person and in writing, warning them to reflect upon their deeds, for the time would come when they would have to account for the realm's wounds, the grievous abuse of her brother's youth, and the perversion of her father's last will and testament.[3] For this reason, because she was the king's sister, next after him in the succession to the crown, and because in the end Edward loved her as his sister (once he was a little older, she appealed to him and he melted with her tears), none dared lay a hand on the princess's person, much as they wished to.[4] Again and again they tried to compel her

---

1 Sander, *De origine ac progressu*, 283–86.

2 Mary could be dramatic in her defiance of Protestant legislation: "when the new Prayer Book was enacted by statute, Mary moved to challenge the King's authority and even the validity of his laws, at least in so far as they touched the Catholic religion. On Whit Sunday, June 9, 1549, when the new book was supposed to be used for the first time in all churches, Mary organized a particularly splendid Mass of Pentecost, according to the old, Latin rite, in her chapel at Kenninghall." In 1551, she displayed her resistance to the campaign against rosaries by parading through London with a retinue of 130, each openly bearing a rosary. Edwards, *Mary I*, 69. Haigh, *English Reformations*, 205.

3 In the autumn of 1547, Mary wrote a letter (now lost) to Somerset, protesting the regime's religious innovations. See David Loades, *Mary Tudor: A Life* (London: Basil Blackwell, 1989), 142–50.

4 Edward was in fact adamantly opposed to indulging Mary's conservatism, which he regarded as idolatry. The king stubbornly resisted pressure from his lay and ecclesiastical advisers, perfectly willing to risk imperial displeasure. Faced with Edward's determination, Mary was quick to blame his tutors, but in turn refused to capitulate. Far from the fraternal protection

with sweetness and with rigor; seeing that she was as strong as a rock, they decided to persecute her chaplains—so she would have no one to say Mass for her—and so they jailed them and punished them like criminals.[5] Princess Doña Mary informed her cousin the emperor of this outrage; he instructed his ambassador to protest to the king and the regents of the realm in his name and convey his astonishment that while the king was a child, still guided by tutors, they would deny his cousin, the king's own sister, what was conceded to the ambassadors of other kings and princes (that is, to have Mass said in a private oratory), and seek by force to keep from her the means of worship and reverence for Jesus Christ lauded by every Christian in the world and observed by their own ancestors.[6] The council acknowledged the justice of this protest, and ceased to harass the princess about the Mass—all the more because King Edward, though as a child he left governance to the protector and his advisors, had nevertheless shown his grief that his sister should be so cruelly treated without his knowledge. Yet, in truth, it was God our Lord's particular mercy to this pious maiden, in a time of such calamities, to furnish her with the means

---

depicted by Sander, the compromise allowing Mary to hear Mass privately was pressed upon the king over his strenuous objections. Pollnitz, *Princely Education*, 181–85.

5   Mary's two primary chaplains, Dr. Francis Mallet (d.1570) and Dr. Alexander Barclay (c.1476–1552), were imprisoned in December 1550. Pollnitz suggests that this was an attempt by the council to mollify Edward, still frustrated by the compromise over his sister's Masses. Pollnitz, *Princely Education*, 185.

John Foxe reproduces a letter Mary sent to the privy council protesting the pair's incarceration: Foxe, *Acts and Monuments*, 6:13.

6   On May 10, 1549, Charles wrote to François van der Delft (c.1500–50), his ambassador in London, "More particularly, with regard to the answer given you by the Protector when speaking of the innovations and changes made in religion, namely, that he will not inquire into what our cousin may choose to do, it appears to us that this declaration does in no way ensure her safety for the future, for she may be troubled and persecuted whenever they see fit to do so hereafter, with the excuse that she is committing a breach of the law. Put these considerations before the Protector from us, and ask him to give her a written assurance in definite, suitable and permanent form, that notwithstanding all new laws and ordinances made upon religion she may live in the observance of our ancient religion as she has done up to the present; so that neither the King nor Parliament may ever molest her, directly or indirectly by any means whatever. If you see that he makes difficulties about it, and will not agree, make no definite answer but say that you will communicate with us. You may add, as from yourself, that the refusal seems very strange to you, and that you cannot say how we may take it or look upon it." *CSPS*, 9, p. 375.

As the conflict over Mary's religious arrangements perdured and Edward refused to compromise, Charles actually urged the princess to relent, arguing that it would not be a sin if she submitted under duress. Pollnitz, *Princely Education*, 182.

to have his sacred body in her oratory and to enjoy his gift and his presence. Throughout Edward's reign, she kept it in an honorable and secure place, lavishly adorned; she spent a good part of each day and night before it, committing all her tribulations (numerous and formidable) to him, the true consoler of the afflicted. She implored him with devout tears and groans to grant her relief, endurance, and remedy for her miseries and for those of all the realm. And neither her prayer nor her trust was in vain. For in the resistance she offered to the heretics in power, and in the freedom and authority with which she rebuked them and warned them to consider what they were doing, for the time would come when a complete account would be demanded, it seems as though she received numerous and sure signs of what was to come, as will be seen hereafter.

And besides the assurance that our Lord gives a pious maiden and the interior gifts of her heart, Mary could also find solace and strength in the words her saintly mother had written her after they had stripped the princess of the royal dignity and declared her a bastard. Being from such a mother and so saintly a queen, I have elected to place this here, translated from the original English of her own hand.

> Daughter, today they have given me tidings that, if they are true, the time has come in which almighty God intends to test you. And I rejoice in this, for I see that he shows you great love, and I beg you to conform yourself to his holy will with a happy heart, and to know with certainty that he will never abandon you, if you take care never to offend him. I ask you, daughter of mine, to offer yourself to the Lord, and if you should feel any passion or bitterness in your soul, confess yourself straightway and cleanse yourself of all sin, and observe and fulfill the laws of God in every detail as he shall give you the grace to do, and so shall you be well-armed and confident. If that lady[7] should come to you (as it is said) bearing a letter from the king, I believe that missive will instruct you what you must do: see that you respond in few words and that you obey the king in everything he commands that is not contrary to God or your own conscience. Do not waste many words with her, nor in disputing this matter, but rather— whatsoever may come, whatever company the king may give you—speak little and meddle in nothing.

---

7   Lady Anne Shelton (*née* Boleyn, 1475–1556), Anne Boleyn's aunt, had been placed in charge of Mary's household in 1533. Joseph S. Block, "Shelton family (*per.* 1504–1558)," in *ODNB*, 50:216–17, here 216.

I intend to send you two books in Latin for your peace of mind, one a *Vita Christi* with the message of the gospels,[8] and the other the letters Saint Jerome wrote to certain ladies, in which you shall find many good things.[9] From time to time, for your recreation and comfort, play the clavichord or the lute, if you have one. But above all, I beg you, by the love you owe to God and you have for me, to keep your heart pure, with only holy thoughts, and your body chaste and pious, separating yourself from all immoral or loose company, neither seeking nor desiring a husband. And take care, I implore you by the sacred passion of Jesus Christ, not to decide upon any estate nor resolve to adopt any particular mode of life until this tempest and time of storms has passed. For I promise you that you will come to a good end, better than you can desire.

I could wish, O good daughter, that you knew the heart with which I write this letter—truly, never have I written with a better or more loving one. For I go on in the knowledge that God loves you very much, and I entreat him to augment your good and keep you safe. Now, daughter, you must begin, and move ahead amid travails, for I will follow you with a willing heart. I do not deem all that may befall us worth a hair, since when they have done their worst, I believe we shall then be the better. Give my greetings to the good countess of Salisbury, and tell her from me to take heart, for we cannot come to the kingdom of heaven save through the cross and tribulation.[10] Wherever you may be, my daughter, take no thought of sending me messages, for if I have liberty, I will find you or send for you.

Your dear mother,
Catherine, the queen[11]

---

8   The enormously popular *Vita Christi* (1374) by the Carthusian Ludolph of Saxony (c.1295–1378).

9   The Roman noblewomen Paula (347–404) and Eustochium (c.368–c.420), her daughter, exchanged a series of letters with Jerome, their spiritual mentor. These letters were frequently published in Latin and in vernacular translations.

10   Acts 14:21.

11   For the English text of this letter, which is of questionable authenticity, see *LP*, 6:1126. A contemporary copy is held as BL Arundel MS 151, fol. 195.

How the Regents Attempted to Uproot the Catholic Faith[1]

Then the heretics strove to have their laws obeyed and their religious inventions and alterations put into practice; to this end, they ordered the two archbishops of England, those of Canterbury and York,[2] to see to their enactment and instruct their suffragan bishops accordingly. The mandates were as follows:

> Thomas, by the grace of God archbishop of Canterbury and legitimately and fully authorized by that prince renowned in Christ King Edward VI, supreme earthly head of the Church of England and Ireland, to you, Edmund, bishop of London, and all the other bishops our brothers: we order, in the name of our lord the king's majesty and on his behalf and authority, that images be removed from every church in every diocese, that Masses no longer be said, etcetera.[3]

And because the bishops were not negligent, they dispatched visitors and commissioners to execute the orders, along with preachers of pestilent spirit and tongue to provoke and incite the people. They also carried a Holy Bible, misleadingly translated into English, as well as Erasmus of Rotterdam's New Testament paraphrases in the same language, mandating that these be purchased at public expense and placed in the church for all to read (intending to entrap and ensnare the people by these tomes).[4] They also brought certain homilies

---

1 Sander, *De origine ac progressu*, 286–92, 300.

2 Robert Holgate (*c.*1481–1555), archbishop of York since 1545.

3 Ribadeneyra works from the Latin excerpt furnished in Sander, *De origine ac progressu*, 286. Cranmer's "mandate for the removal and destruction of images" is printed in Wilkins, *Concilia*, 4:22–23.

4 The Edwardian Injunctions, published July 31, 1547, stipulated "that they shall provide within three months next after this visitation, one book of the whole Bible of the largest volume in English. And within one twelve months next after the said visitation, the Paraphrasis of Erasmus also in English upon the Gospels, and the same set up in some convenient place within the said church that they have cure of, whereas their parishioners may most commodiously resort unto the same, and read the same." Between 1517 and 1524, the Dutch humanist Desiderius Erasmus produced a series of Latin paraphrases of the New Testament, subsequently translated into English. See Frere and Kennedy, *Articles and Injunctions*, 2:114–30, here 117–18.

and sermons on the gospels, full of blasphemies and errors, to be read out to the people every Sunday.[5] They banned processions and prohibited the invocation of the saints, the holy water and bread distributed in the churches on Sundays, rosaries and pardon beads, the missals and Catholic books, and, in sum, anything that smelled or savored of piety, or might preserve the memory of the ancient and truthful religion.[6]

And because they knew that the more lascivious and carnal, the more enslaved to their own sensuality a person was, the more inclined and receptive they would be to the doctrine of licentiousness they preached (and the more obstinate and steadfast therein), they used unimaginable tricks, ruses, and threats to compel the clergy to marry, harassing and tormenting them until many agreed, some out of weakness, seizing the opportunity, others out of fear—for those who refused were humiliated, denounced as criminals and traitors, dismissed from their positions with various slanders, and imprisoned. But after these marriages had produced a horde of illegitimate children and bastards, the realm swelling with this calamitous baggage [*mercaduria*], and the wives were maintained and treated like prostitutes and women of ill-repute (and their children no less), parliament was implored to declare such children legitimate, and so it did.[7] Afterwards, they sent more royal commissioners and receivers to collect whatever was left of the churches' property, which they did

---

5   The injunctions also mandated the reading of the evangelical homilies published by Thomas Cranmer in 1547. The following year, a royal proclamation prohibited sermons and reiterated the requirement to read out the homilies specified in the injunctions. Ibid., 2:129. *TRP*, 1:432–33.

6   The Edwardian Injunctions ordered that "to the intent that all superstition and hypocrisy, crept into divers men's hearts, may vanish away, they shall not set forth or extol any images, relics, or miracles, for any superstition or lucre, nor allure the people by any enticements to the pilgrimage of any saint of image. [...] and that works devised by men's fantasies, besides Scripture, as wandering to pilgrimages, offering of money, candles, or tapers, or relics, or images, or kissing and licking of the same, praying upon beads, or such like superstition, have not only no promise of reward in Scripture, for doing of them, but contrariwise, great threats, and maledictions of God, for that they be things tending to idolatry and superstition [...] that such images as they know in any of their cures to be or have been so abused with pilgrimages or offerings [...] they [...] shall for the avoiding of that most detestable offence of idolatry, forthwith take down or cause to be taken down and destroy the same [...] Also that they shall take away, utterly extinct and destroy all shrines, covering of shrines, all tables, candlesticks, trindles or rolls of wax, pictures, paintings, and all other monuments of feigned miracles, pilgrimages, idolatry, and superstition: so that there remain no memory of the same in walls, glass-windows, or elsewhere within their churches or houses." Frere and Kennedy, *Articles and Injunctions*, 2:115–16, 126.

7   2 & 3 Edw. 6. c. 21. *SR*, 4.1:67.

with such thoroughness and brutality that there was nothing of gold or silver, brocade or silk, cloth or brass, iron, steel, or tin that they left untouched. Even the bells (which were of the finest metal) were ripped from the churches, leaving only a single one in each for gathering and summoning the people.[8]

I have gone on at such length to convey the heretics' malice and perversity, as well as the means they employ to uproot our sacred Catholic faith and sow the cockles of their damnable sects,[9] and so that Catholic rulers and prelates will watch over their flocks[10] and use the opposite methods to nurture, protect, and increase them in all virtue and holiness. And also to prove by the example of England, among others, that vicious people, those who wish to live without God and without law, stand upon the brink of heresy—the wicked, the lustful, the idle, those who either doubt the existence of another life, or live as though there were none—that they are prone to adopt that sect and creed, which conforms to their loose living. I have also enumerated these matters in detail to explain why our Lord so harshly castigated that kingdom, and why their punishment lasted so long. Indeed, having waged open and bloody war in parliament against the saints and God himself, and banished the holy sacraments—including the sacrament of sacraments, the awesome sacrifice of the Mass—how could the Lord's wrath be appeased, or his mercy secured, once the channels through which God imparts that mercy have been stopped up? The sins they commit are infinite and monstrous, and each day multiply yet more; the remedies (prayers and penance, the intercession of the saints, the use of the sacraments) fall away, and they lack the living host, the sublime sacrifice of the true body and blood of Christ our Redeemer, which alone avails to assuage and calm the heart of the Father. And so what marvel is it that, with their sins mounting and the remedies wanting, the Lord's scourge and chastisement should persist in that kingdom? But let us trust in his ineffable goodness that the martyrs' blood continually shed there, in witness and proof of his truth, will win pardon and mercy from his divine majesty. And to bring us to this consummation, he strengthens and inspires his servants to fight and conquer in glory. And this is no small mercy of God's; and in England and

---

8   Among the other provisions for confiscating church property, the Edwardian royal injunctions stipulated that "all ringing and knolling of bells, shall be utterly forborne at that time, except one bell in convenient time to be rung or knolled before the sermon." Frere and Kennedy, *Articles and Injunctions*, 2:124.

9   Matt. 13:25.

10   Acts 20:28.

elsewhere there are an innumerable number of English Catholics, so pure and constant in their faith that, for the sake of preserving it clean and whole, they have joyously suffered all the pains and degradations its enemies could devise. Let us aid them with our prayers, encourage them by our example, give them relief and solace through our compassion and our charity, and fiercely implore the Lord to end so horrible and barbarous a tyranny.

Now, returning to our story, by these policies and visitations the heretics greatly expanded their party and weakened and enervated that of the Catholic Church. Supposing that the field was theirs and they had triumphed over the truth, they held grandiose celebrations and festivities, not only in that kingdom but also in Germany and the other provinces whither they had spread. And they wrote numerous books praising the child king and his destiny, as well as the strength and spirit of the protector, lauding his "liberty." This was in their own interests, since at that very moment Emperor Don Charles had defeated all the princes and rebels of the Empire who had taken up arms against him, by the singular favor of God and the justice of the cause he defended.[11] Elated though they were, they were soon sobered by events in England, as will be related in the following chapters.

---

11   At Mühlberg in Saxony, on April 24, 1547, Spanish and imperial forces under Charles V won a decisive victory over the Schmalkaldic League, taking prisoner both John Frederick I of Saxony and Philip I of Hesse. Maltby, *Charles V*, 59–60.

The Things that Happened to Check the Heretics[1]

First of all, deep divisions and debates emerged among the heretics, each one seeking to defend his own sect and creed: since these were innumerable and irreconcilable to one another (after all, heresy is a hydra-headed monster), there were of necessity quarrels and disputes among the scholars. This could not but hinder the progress and growth of their false religion. Things proceeded so far that the Zwinglians—who with false gentleness would deceive the simple by preaching that none were to be compelled into faith, but rather should be permitted to believe whatever they liked—burned one George van Parris as an Arian heretic,[2] and a woman called Joan Bocher for following the ancient errors of the misbeliever Valentinus.[3] Moreover, when eminent, thoughtful, and learned Catholics saw the dissensions and conflicts among the heretics, they took heart and took the field, ready to dispute with them. They commenced to challenge their false teachings with the utmost boldness and daring, confounding their lies and rendering them so obvious, patent, and clear that the heretics thought it best to withdraw and to maneuver more discreetly. At Oxford, Peter Martyr, the principal minister of Satan, neither dared to debate Richard Smith, a distinguished doctor of divinity, nor knew how to reply to Tresham and Chedsey, two other Catholic theologians; indeed, the disputation left him so stunned and bewildered that the whole audience jeered and hissed, practically kicking him out of his post,[4]

---

1   Sander, *De origine ac progressu*, 293–94, 299–308, 313–17.

2   George van Parris (d.1551), a Fleming immigrant living in London, was burned at Smithfield on April 24, 1551 as an Arian, having affirmed that "God the Father is only God, and that Christ is not very God." Andrew Pettegree, "Parris, George van (d. 1551)," in *ODNB*, 42:860–61.

3   Joan Bocher (d. 1550), a Kent-based radical "burnt for her Anabaptist view of the Incarnation: that Christ did not take flesh of the Virgin." John Davis, "Joan of Kent, Lollardy and the English Reformation," *JEH* 33, no. 2 (April 1982): 225–33, here 225.

   Valentinus (*c*.100–*c*.160) was a leading Gnostic theologian, whose eponymous movement, according to Irenaeus of Lyon (d.202), held that though Christ appeared to have been born, he merely "passed through Mary just as water passes through a tube." Irenaeus of Lyon, *Against the Heresies (Book 1)*, ed. and trans. Dominic J. Unger, Ancient Christian Writers: The Works of the Fathers in Translation 55 (New York: Paulist Press, 1992), 39.

4   In the autumn of 1548, Peter Martyr's first lecture as regius professor was sabotaged by Oxford conservatives, who flooded the university with their supporters. The Italian reformer refused his predecessor Richard Smith's (1499–1563) challenge to a disputation then and there,

and the same thing happened to Bucer at Cambridge and to others elsewhere.[5]

To stifle the Catholics and cow them with force (since argument was of no use), the heretics turned to attacking and harassing them, throwing many out of the churches and dismissing them from their benefices, locking them in prison and torturing them. The Catholics—partly because of their successes, and partly because of their shame at their former fear and weakness—found new strength and defended the cause of God with firm spirit, as though in satisfaction of their guilt. The leaders were the bishops then imprisoned and deprived of their titles, including those of London, Winchester, Durham, and Worcester. Others, seeing the peril to their consciences on the one hand (if they consented to or approved the royal edicts), and to their lives, houses, and properties on the other (if they did not), fled the kingdom to escape disaster, voluntarily exiling themselves and enduring poverty and want abroad rather than witness what was happening there, at so grievous a risk to their souls. Many distinguished men, renowned for learning and virtue, took this opportunity to leave England for the Low Countries of Flanders, where our Lord provided them solace and succor through the charity and beneficence of a wealthy and influential merchant, Antonio Bonvisi, an Italian by birth and a native of the city of Lucca. Having spent many years in England and conceived a love for the land—and, more importantly, as a god-fearing man—he was horrified at the calamities and miseries suffered by Catholics of that kingdom, and aided them (especially Thomas More, throughout his afflictions) as long as he stayed there. And after he had departed England for Leuven, he gathered and sustained yet others, and from his enormous wealth provided them with relief and assistance, with such readiness and generosity that it pained him that more Catholics had not left England to be welcomed to his house.[6]

---

but a date was fixed for the following May. By that time, Smith had fled Oxford, and it was his fellow conservatives, William Tresham (1495–1569) and William Chedsey (c.1510–c.1577), who confronted Martyr. Unsurprisingly, assessments of the resulting debate vary considerably, but Martyr was sufficiently frustrated with the outcome to warn his colleagues against any future such encounters. Cross, "Oxford and the Tudor State," 135, 137. McCoog, *Reckoned Expense*, 141.

5 Though Bucer tried—with some success—to restrain Peter Martyr's combativeness over the real presence, he was drawn into controversy at Cambridge over the authority of the Bible, the nature of the church, and justification by faith. In the end, Bucer prevailed, but only with the help of his allies at court. Greschat, *Martin Bucer*, 234–36.

6 As mentioned, though Antonio himself was born in England, the Bonvisi were among the most prominent families in Lucca. Bonvisi was a mainstay of conservative opposition to Henry VIII's religious policy since the divorce. Increasingly uncomfortable with the militant

What is more, in this time of so many horrors and such diverse sects and heresies, certain unnatural, fearful things came to pass in the kingdom, to the terror and unease of the people. At every turn, one saw monstrous births from women and animals. The River Thames, which washes and waters the city of London, rose and fell three times in the space of nine hours, ebbing and flowing far outside its wonted course.[7] That same year of 1550 [*sic*], a new malady, unknown to any doctor, appeared in England, striking down count-less people—in the city of London alone, an immense number died within seven days, as well as thousands of others in other parts of the realm. And it was a sort of fatal sweating sickness, which was neither the plague nor the pox, nor looked like them, but ravaged and killed as though it were.[8] Many considered it a portent, reckoning that God our Lord was warning and advising them through this scourge to reform their errors, and the Catholics took heart at this, while the heretics cowered in fear. Furthermore, there were other signs of discontent, with the direst chaos reigning in every corner of government or public affairs.

And since those in power attended only to their own interests and ambi-tions, to oppressing and impoverishing the Catholics, and to robbing and afflicting the populace with unjust taxes and unbearable exactions, the miser-able and abused could do nothing but feel and protest their outrage. This is best seen in one cruelty and tyranny the rulers employed across the kingdom. On July 9, 1551, with the whole country unawares, a public edict seized from each and every person the fourth part of all their silver, and another fourth part forty days later. In this way, one who today possessed one hundred ducats in sovereigns [*Reales*], in forty days would find themselves with fifty, though they had spent nothing, bet nothing, and lost nothing. For it was decreed first that the sovereign should be worth three quarters, and that at the end of forty days it should be worth only half a sovereign, and so it was with the other silver coins of greater and lesser worth.[9] And since those who ruled the land were the

---

Protestantism of Edward's government, in September 1549 Bonvisi fled England for Leuven. There he remained until his death, his house notorious as a haven for exiled English Catho-lics. Martin, "Bonvisi, Antonio," in *ODNB*, 6:575–76.

7 "And the xviij. day [of December 1550] followyng ther agayne; and that same day was too tydes at London brygge within the space of v. howeres, and grett spryngges that dyd moch harme by the watter syde and on the watter." Nichols, *Chronicle of the Grey Friars*, 68.

8 Probably due to Old Style dating, Ribadeneyra has erred as to chronology: it was 1551 that saw a particularly virulent outbreak of the sweating sickness (the precise medical identity of which remains a mystery).

9 Having thoroughly (and profitably) debased the coinage, the royal council announced on May 8, 1551 that, starting August 31 of that year, the shilling (normally worth twelve pence)

ones who concocted these impositions and tricks, and knew when the coinage was to rise and fall, they anticipated it and made haste to pay their debts to their creditors and the salaries to their servants, and to purchase estates and lands with the money that was worth twenty today, but only fifteen tomorrow. And our Lord permitted these sins to teach the people how little they ought to trust the protector and his confederates, and what evil abusers of the grace of God and heaven's gifts they were, who governed earthly matters with such injustice and wickedness. For it is truth everlasting, as Christ our Lord said, that if you have been faithless in managing worldly and vain things, who will trust you with spiritual goods, the true and the eternal?[10] For all these reasons, the joy and content of the heretics was tempered, but much more so by something else, which follows.

---

would be worth only nine pence. On August 16, this number was reduced to six pence. Loach, *Edward VI*, 110–11.

For the two proclamations, see *TRP*, 1:518–19 and 1:529–30, respectively.

10   In the margin: "Luke 16[:11]."

How the Protector Killed His Brother, and How He was Overthrown and Slain by the Earl of Warwick[1]

Such bitter enmity arose between the protector and his brother[2] that the protector put his brother to death, then Dudley killed off the protector, then the same Dudley and the duke of Suffolk poisoned King Edward,[3] and finally the two of them were lawfully condemned and executed, along with their children—and all this in the space of a mere four years, which is a wondrous thing, and well worth understanding, to the praise and dread of the secret and righteous judgments of God. The Protector Edward Seymour had a brother called Thomas Seymour, the lord high admiral, who after Henry's death had married his last wife, Katherine Parr.[4] There was a fierce rivalry and deep discord between the protector's wife and Katherine Parr over precedence: for each wished to come before the other, as the wife of the dead king or the wife of the living regent.[5] This dispute passed from the wives to the husbands, egged on by John Dudley, earl of Warwick, who hoped to use it to overthrow both of them. And with this hatred growing stronger by the day (because the protector's wife, who dominated him, would not let him alone), the protector resolved to rid himself of his brother preemptively, so as to avoid any open conflicts or scandals. Because he had no accusation actually worthy of death to use against him, he looked for a false one, and arranged for Hugh Latimer, that arch-heretic (called

---

1   Sander, *De origine ac progressu*, 294–98, 318–19.

2   Thomas Seymour, Baron Seymour of Sudeley (*c*.1509–49), the younger brother of Edward and Jane Seymour.

3   Henry Grey, duke of Suffolk (1517–54), successively the ally of Thomas Seymour and John Dudley.

4   Thomas Seymour secretly married Katherine Parr in the spring of 1547. George W. Bernard, "Seymour, Thomas, Baron Seymour of Sudeley (*b*. in or before 1509, *d*.1549)," in *ODNB*, 49:896–99, here 897.

5   Anne Seymour (*née* Stanhope), duchess of Somerset, the protector's second wife. A longstanding tradition—which Sander draws from the Spanish Chronicle—holds that she and Katherine Parr feuded over precedence, but modern scholarship has questioned the veracity of this story. It is true that Somerset took Katherine's jewels and give them to his wife. Retha M. Warnicke, "Seymour [*née* Stanhope], Anne, duchess of Somerset (*c*.1510–1587)," in *ODNB*, 49:855–56, here 855.

Cf. Hume, *Chronicle*, 160–61.

© KONINKLIJKE BRILL NV, LEIDEN, 2017 | DOI 10.1163/9789004323964_064

"the Apostle of England" by those like him), to accuse him openly from the pulpit as a traitor to the king.[6] This he did, and thus Thomas Seymour was imprisoned, condemned to death, and beheaded on March 20, 1548, on the orders of his own brother, while his wife, Katherine Parr, died of grief, envy, and anguish practically on the same day.[7] In this way, the protector was freed of his brother, and his wife of her rival.

But this merely resolved the conflicts and dissensions between the brothers, for many people across England had taken up arms for their faith and surrounded the city of Exeter, where they fought the horsemen from the duchy of Cleves who had come against them, whom they put to flight.[8] Elsewhere there were large disturbances and disruptions, causing damage and devastation throughout the kingdom, while the French took this opportunity to seize certain strongholds near Boulogne (which was still held by the English).[9] And when the blame for these humiliations and injuries fell upon the protector's bad governance, John Dudley publicly denounced him for incompetence, with the advice and support of other grandees;[10] for his safety, the protector

---

6   On March 15, 1548, Latimer preached a sermon before Edward VI in which he cast Seymour as Adonijah, the rebellious son of King David. In the weeks after Seymour's execution, several more sermons urged obedience to magistrates' decisions; Latimer even alleged that the imprisoned admiral was still plotting against the king and the protector. Hugh Latimer, *Sermons*, ed. George Elwes Corrie, 2 vols., Parker Society Publications 27, 28 (Cambridge: Cambridge University Press, 1844), 1:112–17, 148, 161–62, 164.

7   The Spanish Chronicle correctly places Katherine's death *before* her husband's. Katherine died on September 5, 1548; Thomas was arrested in January of the following year, swiftly attainted of treason, and beheaded on March 20. Bernard, "Seymour, Thomas," in ODNB, 49:898.
      Cf. "When the Queen saw the small consideration in which she was held, so great was her chagrin that she fell ill, and in a short time died." Hume, *Chronicle*, 161.

8   Risings began in Cornwall, Devonshire, Lincolnshire, Oxfordshire, and Buckinghamshire in the summer of 1549. The rebels' motivations were largely religious: the restoration of doctrines like transubstantiation and the removal of the new Prayer Book. By July 2, Exeter was under siege; it was not until August 6 that a combined force of Englishmen and foreign mercenaries was able to disperse the uprising. Loach, *Edward VI*, 70–76.

9   Keen to avenge the loss of Boulogne, Henry II declared war on England on August 8, 1549 and laid siege to the city. Though the king took personal command of the campaign, the English resistance proved unexpectedly stout, and France only regained the city by treaty. Ibid., 52–53.

10   The extent to which John Dudley was actually the ringleader of the coup against Somerset is open to question. Discontent was widespread, given the protector's incompetent handling of the uprisings in the southwest and the conflicts with France. MacCulloch, *Boy King*, 94–95. Loach, *Edward VI*, 89–91.

withdrew with the king to a certain fortress. But when he saw how few followed him, while practically the whole realm flocked to Dudley, whom he could not resist, he lost heart and gave himself up, being taken prisoner on October 14, 1549.[11] And although he was released within four months and reconciled with Dudley, this was a false and fictitious accord, and as such did not last.[12] For Dudley was not content that the protector no longer possessed the title nor exercised the office and authority of protector (which he had not done since his capture). Moreover, since this deed had won him a reputation as a man of fortitude and valor, as well as the hearts of most of the realm, he decided to make an end of the protector, so as to become master of the field and to rule the kingdom as he chose. To do this with greater authority (as the king also desired), he named himself duke of Northumberland and arranged that many sympathetic knights were honored and exalted with new titles and royal grants; all of which happened in the year 1551.[13] Seeing himself now all-powerful and surrounded by so many friends and influential lords, he ordered Edward Seymour detained once more, along with his wife and several of his allies. It was claimed that on a certain day he had entered Northumberland's house armed to kill him, and for this he was condemned and beheaded.[14] A little later, the same sentence was carried out upon four other knights, as confederates in the same crime.[15]

---

11   On October 6, 1549, Somerset removed the king to the fortified castle of Windsor, where they remained for about a week. The protector surrendered on October 11, and by October 14 was back in London, a prisoner in the Tower. Barrett L. Beer, "Seymour, Edward, duke of Somerset [*known as* Protector Somerset] (*c.*1500–1552)," in *ODNB*, 49:860–68, here 865.

12   Somerset emerged from the Tower on February 6, 1550. Within two weeks, he received a royal pardon, and by April 10, he had been restored to the council. Loach, *Edward VI*, 93.

13   "This attack [on Protector Somerset] was presaged by Warwick's promotion to duke of Northumberland on 11 October 1551. Northumberland bought support through granting titles: Dorset was promoted duke of Suffolk, St John to marquess of Winchester [...] and Herbert to earl of Pembroke." Loades, "Dudley, John" in *ODNB*, 17:81.

14   One of Warwick's associates, Sir Thomas Palmer (d.1553), alleged that Somerset planned to invite his rival to a banquet at which he would be murdered. Somerset was arrested in October 1551, convicted of inciting men to riot, and executed on January 22, 1552. Loach, *Edward VI*, 102.

15   February 26, 1552 saw the executions of four of Somerset's close allies: Sir Thomas Arundell (*c.*1502–52), Sir Miles Partridge (d.1552), Sir Michael Stanhope (*c.*1508–52), and Sir Ralph Vane (*d.*1552). Beer, "Seymour, Edward," in *ODNB*, 49:867.

The Ambition of the Earl of Warwick, Who Named Himself Duke of Northumberland; The Death of King Edward and the Succession of Queen Mary[1]

Having preemptively rid himself of his enemy and put an end to the affair (happily, he believed), Dudley conceived hopes of further, greater successes— and of claiming the throne. With the whole government in his hands, as well as the king himself, who was ill with a chronic sickness that was slowly consuming him,[2] it all seemed within his grasp. And even if it was not, Dudley judged that it could be whenever he pleased, since he had Edward in his power: how easy it would be to snatch away his crown together with his life, as well as those of his sisters and heirs! Now, King Henry had had two sisters: Margaret, the elder, who had married the king of Scotland,[3] and Mary, the younger, who had wed King Louis XII of France, and then the duke of Suffolk, by whom she had a daughter, called Frances, who married Henry, marquess of Dorset, who was given the title of duke of Suffolk through Dudley's favor.[4] By this lady the duke had three daughters, who, as daughters of the king's niece and granddaughters of his sister, appeared to have a very strong claim to the throne—if Henry's children did not interfere.[5] For although they were the granddaughters of the younger sister, and logically the children and heirs of the elder, the queen of Scotland, should have been preferred, Dudley insisted that what was in Scotland did not matter, only what was here in England. Thus, the dukes of Suffolk and Northumberland met and took counsel together, agreeing that the three daughters of Suffolk and his wife (King Henry's niece) should marry as follows: the two younger ones with the firstborn sons of the earls of Pembroke and of Huntington (both very wealthy lords), to secure their loyalty and bind them through kinship, and the eldest, named Jane (who would, if the line of Henry

---

1 Sander, *De origine ac progressu*, 319–22.

2 In early 1553, Edward fell ill with "a chronic infectious disease in the chest [...] almost incapable of treatment in the days before antibiotics." Loach, *Edward VI*, 162.

3 Margaret Tudor (1489–1541) married James IV, king of Scots (r.1488–1513), in 1502.

4 Frances Brandon married Henry Grey, then marquess of Dorset. Grey became duke of Suffolk on October 11, 1551. Retha M. Warnicke, "Grey [*other married name* Stokes], Frances [*née* Lady Frances Brandon], duchess of Suffolk (1517–1559)," in *ODNB*, 23:836–37, here 836.

5 Henry and Frances Grey had three daughters: Jane, Catherine (1540–68), and Mary (c.1545–78).

failed, come to the throne), with Dudley's fourth son, called Guildford, and that once these nuptials were concluded, they would eliminate Henry's heirs. The marriages between Suffolk's two daughters and the sons of Pembroke and Dudley took place in London on the same day with enormous pomp and ceremony; at just that point the king became sick (or sicker) and began slowly wasting away.[6]

To lose neither time nor opportunity, Dudley summoned Princess Doña Mary (whom alone he feared), so as to have her in London, under a strong guard and in his power.[7] Totally unaware, she came at Dudley's request: as she approached London, she was warned by her servants that the king her brother was nearing the end of his life, and that this summons was not well-intentioned, with some treachery or ambush undoubtedly prepared for her. This was a warning from God, for the pious maiden abandoned the path she had taken, and by a long journey reached a (not very strong) fortress of hers.[8]

---

6   At Whitsuntide (late May) 1553, Northumberland helped arrange a series of marriages involving his family, the Greys, and other aristocratic clans. Grey's eldest daughter, Jane, was to marry Lord Guildford Dudley (c.1535–54), Northumberland's fourth surviving son. The second daughter, Catherine, married Henry Herbert (c.1538–1601), eldest son of William Herbert, first earl of Pembroke (c.1501–70). Ribadeneyra, following Sander, elides Mary Grey with Northumberland's daughter, Katherine (c.1538–1620). Mary Grey was betrothed to her cousin Arthur Grey (1536–93), eldest son of William Grey, thirteenth Baron Grey de Wilton (c.1508–62). It was Katherine Dudley who married Henry Hastings (c.1535–95), eldest son of Francis Hastings, second earl of Huntingdon (1514–61). Scholars remain divided as to whether these marriages should be seen as the first stage of the attempt to settle the throne on Jane, or merely a (significantly timed) example of the kinship alliances so common to the aristocracies of every nation. Ives, *Jane Grey*, 152–53. Loades, *Reign of Mary Tudor*, 15–16.

7   This was certainly the surmise of Jean Scheyfve (c.1515–81), the imperial ambassador, who a month before Edward's death had written to the emperor, "It is therefore to be feared, Sire, that the Duke may dissemble with the Princess until the King dies or is very near his end, when he may suddenly arrest the more important men among those who might take her side, throw them into the Tower and keep them there under colour of preventing any possibility of disturbances. He may then send a body of horse, secretly and by night, to the Princess, inform her of the King's death, and summon her to come to London for the Crown. He may urge the advisability of this course for the tranquillity of the realm, and conduct her to the Tower." *CSPS*, vol. 11, p. 49.

    There is some evidence that this was the case. According to a letter of Cecil's, Mary was being enticed to Hunsdon, her estate closest to London, by the royal council. Ives, *Jane Grey*, 173–74.

8   Scheyfve reported on July 4 that Mary "was warned by a friend yesterday that she had better go further away into the country; and it has been decided that it will be wiser for her to retire to her house of Framlingham in Norfolk, sixty miles from London. She is at present at Hunsdon, twenty miles from London, where it would be much easier to seize her. She has confidence in her friends in Norfolk." *CSPS*, vol. 11, p. 70.

King Edward died in 1552 [*sic*], in his sixteenth year and the seventh of his reign, on July 6—the same day on which, years before, King Henry had ordered the beheading of that excellent, saintly man, Thomas More.[9] Let it be understood that the death of the one was vengeance for that of the other, that God our Lord punished King Henry's wickedness and tyranny with the death of his son. Two days after she reached her stronghold, Princess Doña Mary was secretly informed of her brother King Edward's demise, and although she was a woman, alone, abandoned and unprovided for, she trusted in God our Lord, the true protector of justice and innocence, and with the greatest courage, spirit, and strength had herself proclaimed and heralded as queen of England.[10]

Eric Ives points out that Scheyfve has elided Mary's immediate destination, Kenninghall in Norfolk, with her ultimate goal, Framlingham in Suffolk. The latter was more easily defended, but the former was farther from London, allowing more time for raising an army. Ives, *Jane Grey*, 226.

Cf. The account of the Spanish merchant Antonio de Guaras (1520–79), who was based in London during Edward and Mary's reigns: "And two days before the King's death, being the fourth of July, she went by night with great speed forth from her residence for about sixty miles, accompanied only by her servants, feigning that she changed her habitation on account of three or four sick people in her house." Antonio de Guaras, *The Accession of Queen Mary: Being the Contemporary Narrative of Antonio de Guaras, a Spanish Merchant Resident in London*, ed. and trans. Richard Garnett (London: Lawrence and Bullen, 1892), 82. 89.

9   Again, probably thanks to Old Style dating, Ribadeneyra errs as to the year: Edward VI died on the evening of July 6, 1553; More had been beheaded eighteen years earlier to the day.

10   "Within three days her Highness had certain notice of the death of the King. And immediately she caused herself to be proclaimed Queen in her house, and in all the country round about." Guaras, *Contemporary Relation*, 90.

How the Dukes of Northumberland and Suffolk Proclaimed Jane Queen of England, and What Befell Them[1]

Though the dukes of Northumberland and Suffolk were troubled by Edward's death coming sooner than expected, since matters were not quite prepared, yet, so as not to weaken their enterprise with delay, they made haste to the Tower of London, where they secretly summoned the majority of the nobles and persons of influence, and made them swear to accept Jane, Suffolk's eldest daughter, as queen, and the same oath was taken by the mayor [*Gouernador*] and six leading aldermen [*Senadores*] of London. And thus was Jane acclaimed as queen of England.[2] She made her entrance into the castle with much pomp and majesty, her train carried by her own mother—who had a greater right to the throne, if anyone did, than her daughter, who could only make such pretensions as the daughter of such a mother.[3] But, as one author, an eyewitness to this spectacle, says, this was a monstrosity—alongside another, no better: that her own mother (who should have been queen before her daughter, as we have said) and father should flatter her and serve her upon their knees, hoodwinking the wretched lady, pressuring her with abuse and hateful words and actions, forcing her to assume the role of queen against her will and make an entrance with the royal crown and scepter, like an actress in a comedy—which could be nothing but a tragedy for her, and last only a few days.[4]

---

1   Sander, *De origine ac progressu*, 322–27.

2   A delegation of London city fathers, led by the lord mayor, Sir George Barne (*c.*1500–58), came to the Tower to sign the letters patent making Jane queen. Jane was formally acclaimed as queen on July 10, and by the next morning, copies of the proclamation had been posted all over London. Ives, *Jane Grey*, 191–92.

   The circular letter proclaiming Jane queen is printed in John Gough Nichols, ed., *The Chronicle of Queen Jane, and of Two Years of Queen Mary, and Especially of the Rebellion of Sir Thomas Wyat: Written by a Resident in the Tower of London*, Works of the Camden Society 48 (London: J.B. Nichols and Son, 1850), 103–05.

3   In point of fact, Frances Grey had been excluded from the order of succession set out by Henry's will, which mentioned only her *heirs*.

4   An anonymous letter, apparently from an Italian diplomat, stated, "the daughter was compelled by the father, even by beatings [...] Entering the tower with the gentlemen before her, the ladies to the right, with the duke of Northumberland closest to her among the men,

The dukes punished several men who had spoken badly of this business, even cutting off the ears of one man, by the name of Gilbert: on the same day that the sentence was carried out upon this unfortunate fellow, his accuser (his employer, a man named Sander) drowned while sailing on the River Thames.[5] Others were also imprisoned and abused for refusing to sign the dukes' edict and mandate against Queen Mary. Practically the first—and the most important—of these was Francis Englefield, a knight of great integrity: as a Catholic and a vassal of Queen Mary, he preferred to risk his life and rank than to deny justice and truth.[6] Consequently, he was imprisoned together with many others, all of whom regarded their deaths as assured if Northumberland succeeded with his schemes—as all expected, given his high (and, as he thought, certain) prospects, within and without England. For upon his side he had all the nobility of the realm, bound by oath; the support and favor of the people; the forces of the entire kingdom; the dead king's authority; and his last will and testament, displayed in written form and duly sealed. Simultaneously, he appeared to have nothing to fear from Princess Doña Mary, a woman, alone, and abandoned—and still less from the forces and powers outside the kingdom.[7] For he had made peace with King Henry II of France a few days earlier,

---

and among the women, her mother, who, as the most exalted, carried the train of her dress. Now, tell me whether this seems a monstrosity, to see a girl [made] a queen through her mother, with her father and mother yet living and neither king nor queen, and addressed and knelt to—not just by all the others, but by her father and her mother." Girolamo Ruscelli, ed., *Delle lettere di principi, le quali o si scrivono da principi, o a principi, o ragionano di principi: Libro terzo; Di nuovo ricorrette, et secondo l'ordine de' tempi accommodate* (Venice: Appresso Francesco Ziletti, 1581), 136ʳ–137ᵛ.

5 "The leuenth of July, Gylbert Potte, drawer to Ninio[n] Saunders Vintner, dwelling at S. Johns head within Ludgate, was set on the pillory in cheape, with bothe his eares nayled, and cleane cut of, for woords speaking at time of the proclamation of Lady Jane [...] About fiue of the clocke the same daye in the afternoone, Ninion Saunders master to the saide Gilbert Potte, and John Owen a gunner, shootinge London bridge towardes the black friers, were drowned at saint Mary locke." Stow, *Summarie*, 475.

   Cf. Machyn, *Diary*, 35–36.

6 In August 1551, Sir Francis Englefield (1522–96), one of Mary's closest advisers, resisted the council's attempts to prohibit Mary's Catholic practices, for which he was committed to the Tower of London, along with his allies Robert Rochester (c.1519–157) and Edward Waldegrave (c.1516–61). A.J. Loomie, "Englefield, Sir Francis (1522–1596)," in *ODNB*, 18:447–49, here 447–48.

7 "Deeming that he had the King of France for his ally, and held the nobility of the realm captive, and that all had consented to this treason [...] and he deemed that doing as he did he had in his power at any time the Lady Mary." Guaras, *Contemporary Narrative*, 87–88.

giving him Boulogne (a place of the utmost importance to the French);[8] Mary Queen of Scots was now married to Dauphin Francis, Henry's firstborn son;[9] and Emperor Don Charles (to whom alone Queen Mary, his cousin, could look for aid) was just then wholly embattled and surrounded by enemies on every side.[10]

With such expectations of success, the duke arranged matters in London as he thought fit. He proclaimed Jane as queen, placed her in the Tower for greater safety, received the oaths and signatures of the knights and lords, encouraged the populace, distributed titles and offices, chose several preachers to praise and support Jane's party (and undermine that of Queen Mary) from their pulpits; with this, judging that all that remained was to have Mary in his power, he summoned his soldiers and, leaving Suffolk in his stead to maintain things in London, speedily set off in pursuit of the queen, who remained alone and vulnerable in her castle, as we have said.[11] But God our Lord, who ever favors justice and innocence, favored her in that moment. For the people, out of their love and reverence for her, and their hatred for Northumberland, were moved to come to her aid and pledge themselves to her, with such readiness and zeal that within ten days more than thirty thousand armed men had

---

8   Boulogne had actually been surrendered to the French in March 1550 for a large indemnity. This assertion may be related to Guaras's report that "They say that he [Northumberland] made a close league with the King of France, and great promises to deliver Calais and Guines to him in return for his alliance." Ibid., 86.

9   Mary, the child-queen of Scotland, had been betrothed to the French dauphin, Francis (1544–60), eldest son of Henry II, in 1548; raised together in France, they were not actually married until 1558. Jenny Wormald, *Mary Queen of Scots: A Study in Failure* (London: Collins & Brown, 1991), 61–62, 86.

10   The imperial ambassador wrote to Charles v on July 7, 1553 that Dudley "founds his hopes on the present state of affairs in Christendom, on the fact that your Majesty's hands are full, on the troubled condition of Germany, on the disagreement that promises a prolongation of the war between your Majesty and France; and in order to hide his plans and machinations in France he caused my Lord [Andrew] Dudley to be sent to your Majesty, to be followed by the other English ambassadors, and another mission to be sent to France to perform neighbourly offices, endeavour to make peace, and behave in a hypocritical manner, whilst he has been enabled to conduct his plans in the desired direction without arousing suspicions." *CSPS*, vol. 11, p. 73.

11   Guaras records that on July 13, 1553 "Northumberland departed to encounter the Queen with all the cavalry he had, in which his chief strength lay, being more than three thousand horsemen well equipped and about thirty pieces of cannon and ammunition waggons. [...] The Duke left Jane who had been proclaimed queen in the Tower of London, and with her, for her surer custody as he deemed, the Duke of Suffolk her father." Guaras, *Contemporary Relation*, 91.

assembled and marched to her.[12] So abundant were the supplies in her camp that things were practically given away for free! Certain lords and knights outside of London joined the queen, while those within, when they learned of this and saw that Northumberland had left the city with his army, declared him a traitor (though they had not dared to oppose him while he was present) and arrested Suffolk, who had been left in his place, and his daughter Jane—acclaimed as queen only a little before. They restored to Queen Mary her honor, preeminence, and royal authority, and undid by public decrees everything previously done in support of Jane.[13] With news of this sudden, utterly unexpected turn of events, Northumberland despaired, losing all hope when he saw his soldiers deserting and crossing over to Queen Mary's camp.[14] Lest he lose everything, he decided to follow the queen's fortunes and recognize her as such himself (this he did at Cambridge),[15] and to yield himself up to the magistrate, ten days after proclaiming Jane as queen. Five days later, he was brought a prisoner to London, whence he had only just departed in triumph.[16] He was

---

12   Mary was hardly alone at Framlingham: from the first contingent of sixty or retainers, she soon attracted thousands of common and noble supporters. Sander has inflated the size of Mary's force: the princess seems to have assembled roughly ten thousand men—still more than three times the number Northumberland had mustered. As Ives details, the influx of troops to Mary was due less to divine providence or spontaneous popular sentiment than to a carefully planned and well-executed communications system. See Ives, *Jane Grey*, Chapter 22.

13   On July 19, the council in London reversed course—motivated in part by the discouraging news of Mary's successes and in part by growing popular support for the princess—and declared for Mary, proclaiming her queen. Guaras records this as a valiant struggle on the part of the councilors, "who were as though prisoners in the power of Lady Jane and the Duke of Suffolk." Ibid., 219–20. Guaras, *Contemporary Relation*, 95–96.
      For the proclamation of Mary as queen, see *TRP*, 2:3.

14   Though many subsequent accounts claimed Northumberland's army suffered debilitating rates of desertion, Eric Ives argues that the force remained largely intact at the duke's surrender. It is true that key elites, such as John de Vere, sixteenth earl of Oxford (1516–62), did defect to Mary at this time. Ives, *Jane Grey*, 204–05. Loades, *Reign of Mary Tudor*, 19.

15   "These tidings, so dismal for Northumberland and his party, came to him while he was preparing to take the field and go to besiege the Queen [...] He was so thunderstruck that he immediately ordered her Highness to be proclaimed Queen, and took down and tore with his own hands the proclamation of Jane which so few days before he had caused to be published and posted at the corners of the streets of the town wherein he was [Cambridge], and waving with his miserable and treasonous hands a white truncheon [...] he cried, 'Long live Queen Mary!'" Guaras, *Contemporary Relation*, 97–98.

16   "After this her Highness gave commission to the said Arundel to go with armed men and take order that the Duke of Northumberland and his chief partisans should be apprehended and kept in safe custody, which he performed, and bestowed them as was fitting,

condemned as a traitor, together with his four sons, and accordingly beheaded on August 22, 1552 [*sic*].[17]

Before his death, he abjured his heresy and sincerely professed the Catholic faith, which they say he had always professed in his heart as the one true faith, even though, blinded by ambition, he had always shown signs to the contrary, thinking by such stratagems and deceptions to win the kingdom for his family, placing worldly gain above the Catholic faith and the salvation of his soul.[18] Such are the mad ambitions and the deceitful hopes of men, who, according to the righteous judgments of God, lose where they think to gain, and, raised on high, fall into the abyss, cast down by their own lust for power. In retribution for his grave guilt, and for the disabusing of the people, who had gathered from every corner of London for so unusual and wondrous a spectacle, they say the duke, standing on the scaffold, spoke to those present in this manner:

> Honored people who have come to see me die, I beg you that, though my death may be horrible and ghastly to the frailty of flesh, you regard it as just, since it comes by divine will. I am a miserable sinner and I have deserved this death and I am justly and lawfully condemned.
>
> If I have offended any person, I beg their pardon, and I implore you to help me with your prayers, in this, the last hour of my life. For the unburdening of my conscience, I wish to warn about one thing: to preserve

---

in the aforesaid town of Cambridge. And afterwards, on the twenty-fifth of July, they were commanded to be brought prisoners to the Tower, guarded by about three thousand soldiers." Ibid., 99.

17 On August 18, 1553, John Dudley was tried for high treason, and beheaded on Tower Hill four days later. His sons—John, second earl of Warwick (*c.*1527–54), Ambrose, later third earl of Warwick (*c.*1530–90), Robert, later first earl of Leicester (*c.*1532–88), and Guildford—were all imprisoned with their father. All but Guildford were eventually reprieved. Loades, "Dudley, John," in *ODNB*, 17:82–84. Simon Adams, "Dudley, Ambrose, earl of Warwick (*c.*1530–1590)," in *ODNB*, 17:58–62, here 59. G.J. Richardson, "Dudley, Lord Guildford (*c.*1535–1554)," in *ODNB*, 17:69–70, here 69. Simon Adams, "Dudley, Robert, earl of Leicester (1532/3–1588)," in *ODNB*, 17:92–112, here 94.

18 The day before his execution, Dudley was brought to the chapel in the Tower, where he heard Mass and received the Eucharist. The prisoner then addressed the crowd: "My masters, I let you all to understand that do most faithfully believe this is the very right and true way, out of the which true religion you and I have been seduced these sixteen years past, by the false and erroneous preaching of the new preachers, the which is the only cause of the great plagues and vengeance which have light[ed] upon the whole realm of England, and now likewise worthily fallen upon me and others here present for our unfaithfulness. And I do believe the holy sacrament here most assuredly to be our Savior and Redeemer Jesus Christ; and this I pray you all to testify and pray for me." Ives, *Jane Grey*, 117.

yourselves from those false preachers and teachers of new and perverse doctrines. They make a show of preaching the word of God, but in truth they preach nothing but their own dreams and delusions, having neither constancy nor stability in their teachings. Nor do they know what they shall believe tomorrow, since each day and each hour their creeds and dogmas change. Remember the harms and disasters that have rained down on this kingdom since that pestilence invaded, as well as the wrath of God we have brought upon ourselves for separating ourselves from the Catholic Church and that sacred, healthful doctrine, which was preached by the holy apostles of Christ, watered with the blood of the martyrs, and taught by all the saintly doctors of every century, and which even today is preserved and kept by every kingdom in Christendom—in comparison with whom we are but ants. We have suffered war, famine, pestilence, the death of our king, disturbances, uprisings, and strife among ourselves— and what is worse, division within our sacred faith. There has hardly been a plague or misery we have escaped, or which has not arisen from this wicked root and source of all calamities, and you will see the same in the other lands that have been deceived as we. Therefore, I urge you to return home and reunite with the rest of Christendom and with the Catholic Church, so that you may be members of the body of Jesus Christ,[19] who cannot be the head of a monstrous or deformed body.[20]

What I say to you, I say not to please or flatter anyone, nor urged on by anyone, but driven only by my own conscience and by the love and zeal I have for the good of my country. I could say much more to you on this subject, but I have other business, all my own and more pressing, which is to prepare myself for the death God has sent me. For the time flies, and I am already at the last steps, the last moments of life. Yet bear witness that I die in the holy Catholic faith!

I humbly entreat the queen's majesty to pardon me; I confess that, hav- ing taken up arms against Her Majesty, I deserve this death and a thou- sand more. But Her Majesty, well able to put me to death in ignominy, to execute me in the severity of her righteous anger, has deigned, as a pious and merciful princess, to have my cause seen and heard in trial. Though according to the law I must be hanged, drawn, and quartered, she has exercised her clemency and mitigated the just penalties of law. And thus I beg all those present to implore God to preserve her for many years,

---

19   Rom. 12:5; 1 Cor. 12:12, 12:17; Eph. 5:30.

20   1 Cor. 6:15.

and give her the grace to rule in peace and quiet, in the loyalty and obedience of her vassals.

To these words, the people responded, "Amen."[21]

Then the duke knelt, prayed the psalm *Miserere mei*, and then the *De profundis*, and the *Pater noster*, and the psalm *In te Domine speravi*, and concluded with *In manus tuas Domine commendo spiritum meum*;[22] then, making a cross in the straw upon the scaffold and kissing it, he laid himself down and was beheaded.[23]

---

21   Ribadeneyra here draws on the scaffold speech as recorded by Commendone. C.V. Malfatti, ed., *The Accession, Coronation and Marriage of Mary Tudor, as Related in Four Manuscripts of the Escorial*, trans. C.V. Malfatti (Barcelona: Sociedad alianza de artes graficas, 1956), 27–30.

22   Ps. 50; Ps. 129; Matt. 6:9–13 or Luke 11:2–4; Ps. 30; Ps. 30:6 (cf. Luke 23:46), respectively.

23   Like the speech on the scaffold, these details come from Commendone's account: "whereupon he recited the psalms 'Miserere mei Deus' and 'De profundis', the 'Paternoster' in latin and six of the initial verses of the psalm 'In te Domine speravi' making an end with this verse: 'in thy hands o Lord I commend my soul'. When he had finished his prayers, the executioner asked him for his forgiveness and he answered him: 'I forgive you and do your duty without fear'. And bending towards the block he said: 'I have deserved thousand deaths'; and he made the sign of the Cross on the straw and kissed it, placed his head on the block and was beheaded." Malfatti, *Accession*, 30.

What Queen Mary Did on Taking Possession of the Kingdom[1]

In this way, our Lord favored his faith and truth, giving the realm to Queen Mary in a victory illustrious and bloodless, some twenty years after her father, King Henry, had begun the schism in England. God placed her upon the throne, he preserved her from the arms, power, and malice of practically all the nobles of the realm, and he punished those who had disturbed and corrupted it for the sake of their own ambition. Let all mortals know that his divine majesty provides for human affairs, and although he may wait and, to our eyes, delay, in the end he rewards and punishes in his own time, and the good do not despair and the wicked do not prevail.[2]

After Queen Mary had received this glorious and unlooked-for victory from heaven, she entered the city and the Tower of London in supreme triumph and majesty.[3] Without the advice or consent of any, moved only by her Christianity, she renounced and abandoned the sacrilegious title of ecclesiastical primacy, which she ordered erased from all royal letters and proclamations.[4] She liberated the bishops jailed for the Catholic faith, and restored the titles and estates of the duke of Norfolk and the son of the marquess of Exeter, who had been condemned to life imprisonment by her father King Henry.[5] She freed the

---

1 Sander, *De origine ac progressu*, 328–29, 332–35.

2 1 Kings 2:9.

3 "On the thirty-first of July her Majesty the Queen made her entry, amid all imaginable joy of the people. She brought with her about five thousand soldiers on horseback, and more than fifteen hundred courtiers, the least of whom wore a velvet suit and chain, and others were arrayed sumptuously." Guaras, *Contemporary Relation*, 100.

4 Though she was uncomfortable with the title, Mary remained supreme head of the Church of England for at least a year, using it publicly until the end of 1553; ironically, it was in this capacity that she ordered visitations of the universities and the dioceses. In September 1553, Pole's associates in England informed him that "Mary thinks to abandon the headship, but has been persuaded to wait for parliament" and that "She will swear the same oath as her father, and does not want the headship. Parliament will lift all laws about it." Loades, *Reign of Mary Tudor*, 108. *CRP*, 2:187, 194.

5 In August 1553, Mary released Thomas Howard from the Tower, where he had been imprisoned since 1547. The octogenarian duke was restored to his former prominence, dying the following year. Also freed was the nobleman Edward Courtenay (1526–56), a prisoner since 1538.

people from the tribute King Edward had imposed upon them, and mandated a just and fair value for the currency, lest her subjects be burdened or deprived of their property.[6] By this all with eyes to see[7] perceived how monarch had given way to monarch, from a heretic prince to a Catholic princess, and rejoiced at so wonderful a transformation.

And because until parliament assembled the queen's authority could not compel the people to attend the divine offices and other Catholic ecclesiastical rites, while it was being convened she suspended by public edict the execution of her brother's laws supporting the heretics. And she exhorted all to abandon the heretics' temples, company, and communion and return to the rites and communion of the Catholic Church.[8] In the public eye, she practiced what she preached, and by the mere declaration of her will and her example the whole populace was inspired to imitate their queen and lady. Thus it was that the divine offices began to be celebrated once more in Catholic churches across the realm; the pulpits were taken by Catholic preachers and the heretics forced to keep silent, as was confirmed much later by the public authority of parliament, which repealed all the laws passed against the Catholic faith in Edward's reign.[9] Throughout England and Ireland, and all other places subject to the crown, it was ordered that the ancient forms of the divine offices and the Mass be restored.[10]

The heretics took considerable umbrage and offense at this change, but they did not dare protest or resist. Even so, there was one heretic more brash and frenzied than the rest who, when a Catholic churchman mounted the pulpit in Saint Paul's in London for the first time since Queen Mary's accession, and

---

Mary showed him considerable favor, making him earl of Devon and a knight of the Bath, as well as granting him sizable properties. Michael A.R. Graves, "Howard, Thomas, third duke of Norfolk (1473–1554)," in *ODNB*, 28:423–29, here 427–28. Ian W. Archer, "Courtenay, Edward, first earl of Devon (1526–1556)," in *ODNB*, 13:675–77, here 675.

6   One of Mary's first proclamations, issued on August 20, 1553, provided for the issue of new gold (sovereigns and angels) and silver coins (groats, half-groats, and pennies), specifically in response to the "base moneys of late made within her majesty's realms." *TRP*, 2:8–9.

7   Deut. 29:4; Ps. 134:16; Isa. 6:9; Jer. 5:21; Ezek. 12:2; Matt. 13:15; Mark 8:18; John 12:40; Acts 28:27; Rom. 11:8.

8   See *TRP*, 2:35–38.

9   1 and 2 Phil. and Mar. c. 6, provided for the renewal of "the Statute made in the fifthe yere of the Reigne of King Richarde the Seconde, concerning tharresting and apprehenc[i]on of erronious and hereticall Preachers." *SR*, 4.1:244.

10   In December 1553, parliament passed 1 Mar. St. 2. c. 2, which demolished the legislative foundation of the Edwardian church settlement. See ibid., 4.1:202.

began preaching before a huge audience, hurled a sharp dagger in hopes of skewering him—but it did not find its mark, and was left, still quivering, in the pulpit. Tumult and chaos followed among the heretics, and to escape their clutches the preacher chose to leave off his sermon and hide.[11] On another occasion, a different heretic discharged a pistol to murder a preacher in the same spot, but it pleased God that he failed.[12] Because of these two outrages, thereafter a guard was provided for the preachers, until time and the fear of the law restrained and pacified the heretics and the realm knew unbroken peace and quiet.[13] Pious though Queen Mary was, desirous of her father's eternal salvation and of rendering him solemn honors, after taking counsel with devout and wise men she refrained from doing so and did not permit public prayers to be offered for him, because he had been the author and source of so lamentable and horrible a schism—for she cared more for the laws of the Church than for her own wishes and griefs.

---

11   Gilbert Bourne (c.1510–1569), later bishop of Bath and Wells.

"The xiij. of August [1553], master Bourne a Canon of Paules, preaching at Paules crosse, not only prayed for yᵉ dead, but also declared yᵗ doctour Bonner bishop of London (late restored, and there in presence) for a sermon by him made in the same place, upon yᵉ same gospell, was about fiue yeres since, uniustly cast into the vile priso[n] of the Marshalsey, and there kept duringe the reigne of king Edwarde, which saying so offe[n]ded some of the audience, that they breaking sylence sayd, the byshop had preached abhomination, other some cried (meaning of the preacher) pull him out, pull him out; and some being nere the pulpit began to clime, wherewith the preacher stepped backe, and one master Bradford, a preacher of king Edwardes time, stepped into his place, and gently perswaded the audience to quietnes & obedience, alledging saynt Paule to the Romaines, let euerye soule submit himselfe to the authority of the higher powers, &c. neuerthelesse master Bourne standing by master Bradford, one threw a dagger at him, which hit a side post of the pulpit and rebounded backe again a great way, whereupo[n] master Bradford brake his speache and forced himselfe wyth the helpe of John Rogers, an other preacher, to conuey master Bourne oute of the audience, which with great labour they brought into Paules schoole." Stow, Summarie, 479–80.

12   Henry Pendleton (d.1557), an Oxford-educated theologian and noted preacher.

"The x. of June [1554] doctor Pendilto[n] preached at Paules crosse, at whom a gunne was shot the pellet wherof went very neere him, & light on yᵉ church wall. But the shooter could not be found." Ibid., 489.

13   "The xx of August [1553] master watson chapleyne to the Bishop of Winchester, preached at Paules crosse, by the Queenes appointment, & for feare of the like tumult as had been the Sunday last past, certaine lordes of the counsell repayred to the sermon […] sir John Jernigan captaine of the Garde, with two hu[n]dred of the garde, which stode about the pulpyt with halberdes." Ibid., 480.

In those first days of seeking to restore the Catholic faith, many of the clergy erred grievously in one thing: when the queen gave permission for them to practice as they had done before, many clerics who had been unorthodoxly ordained in the days of King Henry and of Edward thoughtlessly leapt to celebrate the mystical sacraments and the divine sacrifice of the Mass, without any regard for the canons or church laws, nor scrutiny as to which bishops had ordained them, or how, or even if they were suspended, irregular, or bound by some ecclesiastical censure. It may be that this was no small part of the reason the kingdom so swiftly lost this blessing, in the just chastisement of God our Lord, who demands holy matters to be handled with the appropriate sanctity and reverence. Yet the kingdom's reconciliation with the Apostolic See was effected thereafter, and all received absolution and benediction (as we will see)—and we must believe that those who had been careless then bitterly bewailed their sin and did penance for it.

How the Pope, at the Queen's Entreaty, Sent Cardinal Pole to England as His Legate[1]

Since the healing of so grievous a rupture and the cleansing of so gangrenous and universal a wound as the entire kingdom had received in separation from and disobedience to the Apostolic See required much time, effort, and divine inspiration, unthinkable without the goodwill and support of the supreme pontiff, the queen implored Pope Julius III, then presiding from the throne of Saint Peter, to send her Cardinal Reginald Pole as his legate.[2] Being a native of the kingdom, so distinguished in blood, and one who, along with his entire family, had suffered so many troubles and disasters for the Catholic faith in the days of her father, King Henry, he seemed, with his great virtue, learning, and wisdom, an apt instrument to restore the realm to the Catholic faith and reduce it to obedience to the pope, as she desired. At first, she spoke of this with a few bishops and several trusted counselors, in the deepest seclusion and secrecy (to avoid the anticipated disturbance and dissension). The pope was highly pleased with the queen's entreaty, and resolved to send Cardinal Pole as legate *a latere.* But because he knew the division and discord the heretics had incited in that kingdom and foresaw the potential obstacles in so arduous a task, before sending the legate he dispatched his chamberlain, Giovanni Francesco Commendone—an able, clever man, who later became a cardinal—with all haste, to observe the state of things and inform him and the legate of all that was happening.[3] Commendone fulfilled his instructions with such diligence and circumspection that in addition to his observations

---

1 Sander, *De origine ac progressu*, 336–41.

2 Pope Julius III (r.1550–55), born Giovanni Maria Ciocchi del Monte, was elected on February 7, 1550, after the death of Paul III on November 10 of the previous year. The initiative in naming Pole legate to England came from Julius (he did so in August 1553, almost as soon as news of Mary's accession was confirmed); it was initially uncertain whether Mary would accept a papal legate. In September 1553, one of Pole's agents wrote of the necessity of "induc[ing] Mary to ask for you," and it was not until November 1554 that letters patent confirmed the cardinal's legatine powers. *CRP*, 2:129–31, 186.

3 Though the pope did express concerns on this score (he wrote to Pole, "delay might be best because of the heretics"), the hesitation in dispatching Pole stemmed more from imperial worries that the cardinal might object to Mary's marriage to Philip, and English fears that he would reopen the question of formerly monastic property. Ibid., 2:195. Rex H. Pogson,

throughout the country, he was able to speak with the queen several times in secret. He brought His Holiness a document in her own hand, humbly begging absolution for the kingdom for the schism and promising obedience to the Apostolic See, as well as the dispatch of ambassadors to offer this publicly, as soon as the realm was at peace and free of the fears then rampant.[4]

With this document and Commendone's favorable report, the pope was perfectly prepared to send the legate, who for his own part had worked to scope out the territory and widen a path that most had deemed totally closed-off. Pole wrote the queen a letter emphasizing the mercy our Lord had shown in giving her the scepter and crown of that kingdom without the support of the emperor or any other prince whatsoever, but only the succor and assistance of heaven—to the end that she acknowledge all as coming from his hand, seek to serve and please him, and understand that his divine majesty is accustomed to try and test his own,[5] to purify them with every sort of affliction, and then, once they have been thoroughly proved, to console and exalt them. That the service she owed our Lord was to sever the roots of chaos in the kingdom and provide for religion, peace, and justice—so long exiled that neither sprig nor trace nor memory of them remained—to flower there anew. And that if she contemplated the causes of so much devastation and disruption, she would find that the beginning and source of all had been disobedience to the Church: for when Henry her father turned his back on Jesus Christ and his vicar and cast off obedience to the pope for offering no support in the divorce from the queen her mother, it was at that very instant that, together with this obedience, true religion, justice, and security fled the realm, and it was transformed into a den of thieves.[6] Consequently, to cleanse this sore it was necessary to return to the ancient and Catholic faith, and to begin at its root and foundations— as her piety, zeal, wisdom, and valor gave hope that she would—acknowledging the Apostolic See and rendering it the obedience due to the supreme

---

"Reginald Pole and the Priorities of Government in Mary Tudor's Church," *HJ* 18, no. 1 (March 1975): 3–20, here 3n4.

Commendone, a papal chamberlain and protonotary apostolic to Julius III, was dispatched to England in 1553 to survey religious affairs in the kingdom. "Biographical Dictionary—Consistory of March 12, 1565," in *CHRC*.

4   In September 1553, Commendone reported to the consistory Mary's favorable attitude and her desire for an absolution for the religious irregularities of her accession and coronation. At the same time, he cautioned that the situation in England was too uncertain to warrant a papal legate just yet. *CRP*, 2:195. David Loades, "The Enforcement of Reaction, 1553–1558," *JEH* 16, no. 1 (April 1965): 54–66, here 54.

5   Isa. 48:10; Heb. 12:6; James 1:12.

6   Matt. 21:13; Luke 19:46.

head, rejoining the unity and the communion of the Catholic Church. And so, through this union and submission, it might receive the inspiration and spirit that God always imparts to the members through the head. That, to serve her in this and in all else, His Holiness had commanded him to travel to England as his legate, and that he set off with a willing heart to see a lady seated upon the throne as queen, for which she had suffered so much, and to follow and assist her in an office of true service to God and the universal good of the whole kingdom. And to that end he had wanted to write that letter first, to learn her intentions regarding obedience to the Apostolic See and the disposition of the realm, and consequently what Her Majesty commanded him.[7] The queen responded to this letter with all love and kindness, informing the legate of her fierce desire to see him and to perform and put into practice all he had written, charging him to make haste, and humbly to ask, in her name and for her sake, His Holiness's blessing.[8]

---

7   Ribadeneyra here summarizes a letter that *De origine ac progressu* quotes at length: see Sander, *De origine ac progressu*, 338–41.

    Cf. *CRP*, 2:161–63 and 171–72.

8   Pole was informed in September 1553: "The queen very pleased by your letters, and would give half her kingdom to have you here. Said you would be happy to come. She replied that she feared the heretics, and had to move slowly. She thought your letter the best she had received in years, and is glad about your broad faculties to dispense." Ibid., 2:193.

How the Queen Negotiated a Marriage with the Prince of Spain, and of the Disturbances This Provoked in the Kingdom, and How They Were Quelled[1]

In addition to the counsel of Cardinal Pole, a wise man, experienced in the public and private affairs of the realm, and his authority as legate of the Apostolic See to reform religion (two considerations of the highest importance), the queen and her advisers thought it likewise meet to have a strong secular arm alongside the spiritual, to quell and restrain the rebellious and the audacious, and to execute with force what had been decided with prudence. Therefore, although the pious queen had lived in chastity into her thirty-eighth year of life, and for her own part wished to persevere in her virginal purity, yet, looking to the greater glory of God and the public good, at the entreaty of the entire realm, and with the advice of thoughtful, Catholic men, she decided to marry, judging that by this route she could better settle and determine religious matters. So, turning her eyes in every direction, in order to choose the husband who could best aid her goals and intentions, after proposals and discussions of many men within and without the kingdom, she ultimately chose to marry the prince of Spain, Don Philip, the son of Emperor Don Charles and the heir to countless sprawling kingdoms and domains. He was the widower of the Princess Doña Maria, the daughter of King Don John III of Portugal and Queen Doña Catherine, sister of the aforesaid emperor.[2] For she felt the need, as we have said, of a strong arm and the valiance of a mighty Catholic prince, such as the prince, to rule the kingdom and to return it to the Catholic faith and the obedience of the Apostolic See. The business was discussed with the emperor, who was then in the provinces of Flanders:[3] seeing the good that could

---

1   Sander, *De origine ac progressu*, 329–31, 341–42.

2   Philip had married Maria Manuela of Portugal (1527–45) in 1543. The princess was the daughter of John III of Portugal (r.1521–57) and his wife, Catherine of Austria (1507–78), Charles v's younger sister. Maria Manuela died on July 12, 1545, killed by a hemorrhage suffered in the birth of her son, Carlos (1545–68). Kamen, *Philip of Spain*, 12, 20.

3   There were only a few potential English husbands for Mary: the only serious candidate was Edward Courtenay (Mary was distinctly uninterested), and though it was suggested that Pole could be dispensed from his deacon's orders, this was not pursued. Outside of England, possible suitors included Luís, duke of Beja (1506–55), the king of Portugal's younger brother.

be done for all of Christendom in reducing that kingdom to the obedience of the Catholic Church—as well as the benefit to his son, and the protection for all his realms and provinces if they were joined with the strength of so large and powerful a nation—he took it as settled. The matter was concluded with a few conditions, asked of him for the sake of the calm, tranquility, and docility of the English.[4] And so the agreement was made and signed by both parties; I will not include it here because it does not really pertain to this history, being ecclesiastical.

The conclusion of the marriage deeply perturbed certain powerful heretic English lords, who attempted to unsettle the realm in order to prevent it and the fruits that must follow.[5] One of these was the earl of Devon, the son of the marquess of Exeter, who hoped to marry the queen himself (because she had initially given some indication of this)—and rebelled after nothing came of it. The queen arrested him and threw him into the Tower of London, later banishing him to Italy.[6] Another was the duke of Suffolk, whose life she had previously spared; seeing him a malcontent, and once more stirring up the kingdom, she had him beheaded.[7] Similarly, Thomas Wyatt, an influential knight who had agitated in several towns, was defeated and subdued not by

---

The Spanish match seems to have been Charles's suggestion to Mary, rather than vice-versa. Charles first instructed his ambassador Simon Renard (1513–73), to raise the idea in August 1553; Mary was immediately receptive, and by October 29 had pledged to marry Philip. Loades, *Reign of Mary Tudor*, Chapter 2.

4   The articles of marriage between Mary and Philip were announced in a royal proclamation of January 14, 1554. See *TRP*, 2:21–26.

   Cf. Loades, *Reign of Mary Tudor*, 72–74.

5   "Theis newes, althoughe before they wer not unknown to many, and very moche mysliked, yit being nowe in this wise pronounced, was not onely credited, but also hevely taken of sondery men, yea and therat allmost eche man was abashed, loking daylie for worse mattiers to growe shortly after. [...] Within vj. dayes after ther was worde brought howe that sir Peter Carowe, sir Gawen Carowe, sir Thomas Dey, and sir [*blank*], with dyverse others, wer uppe in Devonshire resysting of the king of Spaynes comyng, and that they hade taken the city of Exeter and castell ther into their custodye." Nichols, *Chronicle of Queen Jane*, 35.

6   Courtenay was first proposed as a husband for Mary in Henry VIII's lifetime. On his release from prison, the earl conceived new ambitions for the marriage, but the queen never took the prospect seriously. Courtenay's possible involvement in plots against Mary and her marriage to Philip led to several further stints of incarceration and then his dispatch to mainland Europe in 1555. He took up residence in Padua, where he died the following year. Archer, "Courtenay, Edward," in *ODNB*, 13:675–77.

7   By the end of 1553, Henry Grey was plotting with other Protestant nobles to block Mary's marriage with Philip. After several inept attempts at rebellion in January 1554, he was captured, tried as a traitor, and executed on February 23. Robert C. Braddock "Grey, Henry, duke of Suffolk (1517–1554)," in *ODNB*, 23:845–47, here 846.

force of arms or bands of soldiers, but solely through her authority and her
faith in God.[8] The queen pardoned her sister Elizabeth, who went along with
these plots, for she was only a child (and at the entreaty of several influential
persons), and had her imprisoned at Woodstock.[9] The queen chose to pardon
these and many other prominent heretics who had conspired against her because she was truly merciful and pious, an enemy of all bloodshed. And if certain prudent men among her confidants had not dissented, she would have
pardoned Jane and her husband, who had usurped the crown, and Dudley,
who had plotted it all (as she did pardon his four sons, already condemned
to death as traitors). Yet, when she saw how they had abused her clemency
and, presuming upon it, recanted, and that Suffolk and his confederates had
once more proclaimed his daughter Jane as queen, disturbing the realm once
again and threatening peace and religion, she readily agreed to have Jane and
her husband beheaded.[10] For among all the arguments and proofs of Queen
Mary's goodness and piety, one of the chiefest was how easily she pardoned
the injuries and crimes committed against her, and how harshly she punished
those against God.

---

8   In the winter of 1553, Sir Thomas Wyatt (c.1521–54), the son of the aforementioned
     Thomas Wyatt, joined a conspiracy of Protestant soldier-courtiers to thwart Mary's mar-
     riage to Philip, in a rebellion that came to bear his name. In early 1554, he raised troops
     in several Kentish towns, eventually turning his fractious force toward London, where he
     was thoroughly outmaneuvered by the royalists. Wyatt was beheaded as a traitor in April
     1554. Ian W. Archer, "Wyatt, Sir Thomas (b. in or before 1521, d. 1554)," in *ODNB*, 60:591–95,
     here 591–94.

9   At the urging of advisors like Sir William Paget (c.1506–63), Mary did not execute her half-
     sister (actually twenty at the time) for treason, instead imprisoning her at Woodstock in
     Oxfordshire. J.E. Neale, *Queen Elizabeth I* (Harmondsworth: Penguin Books, 1961), 46.

10   None of the rebels mentioned Jane's claim to the throne, and throughout she remained
     imprisoned in the Tower. Even so, at the insistence of Gardiner and Renard, Mary
     consented to the execution of Guilford and Jane (originally condemned as traitors the
     previous November). The couple was beheaded on February 12, 1554; he on Tower Hill in
     the morning, she on the Tower Green in the afternoon. Ives, *Jane Grey*, 265, 274.

     On February 11, Gardiner preached a sermon justifying the execution, in which he
     "axed a boone of the quenes highnes that like as she had before tyme extended hir mercy,
     partyculerly and privatlie, so thoroughe her lenyty and gentylness moche conspyracye
     and open rebellion was growen, according to the proverbe *nimia familiaritas parit con-
     temptum*; which he brought then in for the purpose that she wolde nowe be mercyfull to
     the body of the comonwealth, and conservation therof, which coulde not be unlesse the
     rotten and hurtfull members therof were cutt off and consumed." Nichols, *Chronicle of
     Queen Jane*, 54–55.

Of the Devilish Trick Utilized by the Heretics to Interfere with the Queen's Marriage to the Prince of Spain[1]

Once the rebels were punished and the uprising quelled (as has been said), these renewed commotions and disruptions in the kingdom were quieted. But as the heretics could stomach neither the queen's marriage to a foreign prince, so avowedly Catholic and so powerful, nor the dreaded reconciliation with the Holy See (which they feared, as by nature enemies to all peace and tranquility), they cast about for other ways of inciting the people of London, who were just then ripe for any sort of disturbance or trick, seeking to achieve by craft and treachery what they could not do by force of arms. They induced a poor maiden of eighteen years to hide in an empty space they had made between two walls of a certain house and, through various ingenious rods and pipes, to moan and speak as they instructed her. The girl was called Elizabeth Croft; the author and instigator of this scheme, Drake. He had no difficulty persuading her to cooperate, for this Elizabeth, in addition to being young and dissolute, was both poor and a heretic, and he promised her a large sum of money. She stealthily ensconced herself in the hiding-place prepared for her, and late at night began to give out awful, agonizing shrieks, clear and piercing enough to be heard across the neighborhood. This novelty aroused considerable curiosity and fear. People gathered to see what it was and marvel at the strange occurrence, and the heretics passed in disguise among the crowd, saying that it was no mortal voice, but a heavenly angel. This walled-up "spirit" threatened the city of London, and all of England, if they consented to the queen's marriage with the prince of Spain, or gave their obedience to the bishop of Rome. It thundered that God would send famine, war, plague, and all the calamities and miseries in the world if they acquiesced to these things. What is more, it added many statements against the holy sacrifice of the Mass, against confession and penitence, and against the other articles of our holy Catholic faith—all in so strange a manner and so fearful a voice, that it seemed an oracle or utterance from Delphic Apollo or some sibyl (as the pagans would have said). And the heretics, who as I said were circulating clandestinely, interpreted these prophecies and

---

1   Sander, *De origine ac progressu*, 342–44.

warnings, twisting them in hatred of our holy religion. With this, the people started to riot. The magistrate arrived to see what was happening: he heard the voices, but could not discover the trick. After prolonged discussion, it was decided to tear down the wall from which the voices seemed to emanate, as well as all the surrounding walls. Just as they put hands to the work, the wretched girl emerged from her hiding-place, stunned and distraught; fearful of punishment, she confessed everything. The authors of this wicked device fled, while the girl was only lightly punished, as she had been misled by others, and the matter merely ended in the ridicule, comprehension, and abhorrence of heresy, which can only be sustained through such devilish tricks.[2]

Indeed, this is quite similar to the deception the magi practiced upon Yazdegerd, their king, to draw him away from the Christian faith (to which he had shown himself much inclined). For they had a man hide in a vault beneath the house where the eternal flame that the Persians revered as a god was kept, and cry out when the king was offering his prayers, threatening him that he would lose his kingdom by his trust in the Christian priests. But on the advice of the saintly Bishop Maruthas the ground was excavated and

---

2 "The vj day of Julij was a goodly sermon [by] on of the prebendares of Powlles; and ther was a nuw skaffold mayd ther for the mayd that spake in the wall and wystelyd in Althergat stret; and she sayd openly that yt was on John Drakes ser Antony Knevett servand; and she whept petefully, and she knelyd and askyd God mercy, and the quen; and bad all pepull be ware of false thechyng, for she sayd that she shuld have many goodly thynges gyffyn her." Machyn, *Diary*, 66.

"The xv of July, Elizabeth Croft a wenche about the age of xviij yeres stoode on a scaffold at Paules crosse all the sermon time, where shee confessed that shee being moued by dyuers lewde persons thereunto, had uppon the fourteenth of March laste before passed counterfeited certein speeches in an house without Alders gate of London, through the which, the people of the whole city were wonderfully molested, for that all men might heare the voice but not see her person. Some saide it was an angel and a voice from heauen, some the holy ghoste, &c. This was called the spirite in the wall, shee had laine whistling in a strange whistell made for that purpose, which was geuen her by one Drakes: then was there dyuers companions confederate with her, which putting themselves among the presse, tooke upon them to interprete what the spirit saide, expressinge certaine sedicious wordes against ye Queene, ye prince of Spaine, ye Masse & co[n]fession, &c." Stow, *Summarie*, 624.

"Ther was a mayd that spake in a walle in a howse in Aldersgat stret stode at the Powlles crosse before the precher doctor Wymbsle achedekon of [Middlesex], and there shoyd alle the hole matter and asked God mercy and the quene, and alle the pepulle, for ar evy[ll] insampulle. And the xviij. day of the same monyth stode a man on the pyllery for the same matter, with a paper and a scryptor on hys hed, that was consentynge there-to." Nichols, *Chronicle of the Grey Friars*, 90.

the trick discovered, and the king ordered the magi to be severely punished and the Christians favored yet more, as Socrates recounts in his history, Book 7, Chapter 8.[3]

---

3 Socrates of Constantinople, *Historia ecclesiastica*, 7.8.

The Syrian monk Maruthas, bishop of Maypherkat (or Martyropolis) (d.c.420), served as an emissary between the Roman and Persian Empires, winning the confidence of King Yazdegerd I (r.399–420). See Ralph Marcus, "The Armenian Life of Marutha of Maipherkat," *Harvard Theological Review* 25, no. 1 (January 1932): 47–71.

How the Queen's Marriage to King Don Philip Took Place, and with it the Reconciliation of the Realm with the Apostolic See[1]

Our Lord undid the counsels of the heretics, dispersed their hosts and armies, confounded their hopes, and uncovered their secret tricks and sins, while the queen's justice and truth prevailed. As we have said, the queen had agreed to marry Don Philip, prince of Spain: with an immense fleet and a retinue of countless knights and lords, he landed in England on July 19, 1554, where he was received with the ceremony and dignity befitting so great a prince.[2] Then his marriage to the queen took place with the same pomp and majesty,[3] the emperor his father having first abdicated and transferred to him the kingdom of Naples and the duchy of Milan, so that the prince could marry the queen with greater rank and status, not only as the heir to so many realms and states, but as a true king and lord in his own right.[4] Several months passed in festivities and celebrations, in the encounters and interactions of the Spanish and the English, and in the instruction of the king and his ministers in the affairs of the realm.

Initially, there were deep suspicions and fears among the English: some abhorred the new king because they were infected by heresy, he being so

---

1 Sander, *De origine ac progressu*, 344–48.
2 Philip journeyed to England with a retinue of thousands, escorted by several thousand more sailors and soldiers. The imperial party reached Southampton on July 20, 1554, where Philip was ceremonially welcomed by a delegation of noblemen, including no fewer than four earls, who inducted him into the Order of the Garter. Kamen, *Philip of Spain*, 56. Loades, *Mary Tudor*, 223–24.
3 *The Chronicle of Queen Jane* records that "On saynct James's day, being the xxv. of July, the king and quene weare maried at Winchester," before offering detailed descriptions of the lavish ceremonies, pageants, and displays celebrating the nuptials. Nichols, *Chronicle of Queen Jane*, 78–81.
   Another contemporary account of the ceremony is printed in Ibid., Appendix x.
4 Charles v had designated Philip as heir to the duchy of Milan as early as 1540, and formally confirmed this in 1546. On July 24, 1554, Philip and Mary received word that the emperor had effectively abdicated as duke and as king of Naples, and invested his son with those titles: "Philip was now in his own right a king, and could marry Mary on equal terms." Kamen, *Philip of Spain*, 27, 57.

devout a Catholic prince, while others feared that with his overwhelming power he intended to subdue the kingdom and secure it for himself and his descendants, dismantling the government, transforming the laws, and handing it over to whatever foreigners he pleased. Still others could not bear to see so many illustrious knights and lords of so many nations—Spaniards, Italians, Flemings, Burgundians, and all of them vassals of the king—who dazzled the kingdom with their profligacy, apparel, domestic furnishings, and the number and prowess [*loçania*] of their servants. For these and other reasons, the English were unfriendly, dour, and brusque with the Spaniards, and unhappy with the royal marriage to the king.[5] But he conducted himself with such wonderful thoughtfulness and such extraordinary discretion while in the kingdom, and showed such generosity to its inhabitants, performing singular kindnesses to all those who demonstrated their loyalty or did some service to the queen, as well as preserving the customs and laws of the realm, taking nothing for himself or his men (instead rewarding and enriching them out of his own property), to say nothing of the generosity of the many illustrious persons who came with him, that the English began to lose their fear, and to love and respect (the heretics excepted) the king and his courtiers with the greatest goodwill. And once their spirits had become more tractable and obedient, parliament was convened on November 12 of that year to propose and enact the kingdom's reconciliation with the Apostolic See, so fervently desired by the monarchs.[6] King Don Philip himself described the manner of it in a letter of January 15, 1555 to his sister, Doña Juana, princess of Portugal, whom he had left as regent of Spain.[7] This I wish to insert here, to recount so illustrious and noteworthy a deed in the words of the one God our Lord took as the means of effecting it. And so, he says,

> By what I wrote on September 4 and 18 and November 4 past,[8] you will have understood the beginning the most serene queen and I have made in the affairs of this kingdom, and how we had ordered the convocation

---

5 "At this tyme ther was so many Spanyerdes in London that a man shoulde have mett in the stretes for one Inglisheman above iiij. Spanyerdes, to the great discomfort of the Inglishe nation." Nichols, *Chronicle of Queen Jane*, 81.

  In a proclamation of March 1554, Mary demanded the courteous treatment of her soon-to-be husband's attendants: *TRP*, 2:33–34.

6 1 and 2 Phil. and Mar. c. 8. *SR*, 4.1:246–54.

7 Juana (or Joanna) of Austria (1535–73), Philip's younger sister, had married João Manuel, prince of Portugal (1537–54) in 1552. After João's death a few years later, Juana returned to Spain, where she served as regent in her brother's absence. Kamen, *Philip of Spain*, 56.

8 *CSPS* 13:53, 59, and 88, respectively.

of parliament for the twelfth of the said month of November, in order to pursue them, and it commenced on that day. And as our principal intention was to provide a foundation for religious matters, with the highest hopes that our Lord, whose cause it is, would aid our good intent, we made every effort we thought appropriate with the grandees of the realm—in particular, for their assent to the arrival of the reverend Cardinal Pole, who has been named His Holiness's legate for this purpose. Religious considerations notwithstanding, he is barred entry to this realm, having been banished by law, which may not be revoked save in parliament.[9]

Once his coming was agreed to, we sent two distinguished knights of the realm, councilors both, to bring him over from where he was in Flanders.[10] At his arrival, we commanded that the other prelates and knights receive him: they escorted him to our court on November 23, and he spoke with us and presented us with a brief from His Holiness.[11] On the twenty-eighth of the same, in our presence and that of the houses of parliament, the cardinal declared the purpose of his visit and the end for which he had been dispatched by His Holiness, saying that he brought the keys to open the door shut for so many years and, in the name of the vicar of Christ, to admit and receive those of this kingdom, treating them with piety and love, as well as other apt and holy words on this topic. He requested of us that, as God had placed us in our position, we do as we have always done, out of our goodwill and obedience to the Holy See, and urged the parliament to accept the kindness and mercy offered them by our Lord through his vicar, with many examples and cogent arguments.[12]

Once his speech was finished, we declared in reply: that we greatly rejoiced at his coming and at hearing his commission, and that he should withdraw so that we might confer with parliament on the matter, and that we would shortly give him our answer. After he had gone,

---

9   The parliamentary attainder of Reginald Pole was formally repealed on November 22, 1554 (1 and 2 Phil. and Mar. c. 18). See *CRP*, 2:362–63.

10   In November 1554, two privy councilors, Sir Edward Hastings (c.1512–71) and William Paget, journeyed to Brussels to escort Pole to England. David Loades, "Hastings, Edward, Baron Hastings of Loughborough (1512x1515–1571)," in *ODNB*, 25:736–38, here 737. Sybil M. Jack, "Paget, William, first Baron Paget (1505/6–1563)," in *ODNB*, 42:376–81, here 379–80.

11   Actually November 24. Edwards, *Archbishop Pole*, 140.

12   For the torturous textual history of Pole's address to parliament, and a summary of its content, see *CRP*, 2:366–68. A much longer retelling is provided in a 1555 pamphlet, reproduced in Nichols, *Chronicle of Queen Jane*, 155–59.

we ordered the chancellor of the realm to inform the parliament of our will—specifically, that they consider what our Lord has done for them in thus calling them; how pleased we would be by their examining and discussing it and recognizing what befitted them, their consciences, and the universal good that would come from a good end to all this;[13] and that we should be grateful for their response within three days.

And so they conferred over the next two days, and on the third, which was the day of Saint Andrew the Apostle,[14] being informed that the parliament had reached a decision on the matter, we summoned the cardinal to the palace. When they were all in our presence, they presented us, in their name and that of the entire kingdom, with a memorial in Latin, in which—having recognized the errors into which they had fallen and how they had become schismatics, disobedient to the Church— they fervently begged us to deign to intercede with the legate, so that he might absolve them of what had been done, and they could render their obedience to His Holiness and the sacred Roman Church; all this in many words, as a demonstration that they repented of what had oc- curred. After the memorial had been read aloud, we spoke apart with the cardinal and interceded on their behalf; he agreed to absolve them in His Holiness's name and to admit them into his grace and that of the holy Catholic Church. And then he absolved them, all upon their knees, and this they received with devotion and signs of repentance. Once this act was completed, we descended to the chapel in the company of the legate, to give thanks to our Lord for this sovereign mercy and favor shown to the kingdom—and more especially to me and to the most serene queen, in being employed in a matter of such service and honor to his sacred name. The next Sunday, the cardinal was received in the biggest church in London as the legate of His Holiness, with elaborate ceremonial, the crucifixes and the clergy of the entire city, a huge crowd of people, and demonstrations of universal contentment. A little later, once the Mass was finished, I went with the legate to a balcony of the church that stood above one of the city's squares, where the chancellor preached to a con- siderable audience of knights, citizens, and commoners. In his sermon he proclaimed the mercy our Lord had shown them in drawing them out of

---

13 Stephen Gardiner was made lord chancellor on August 23, 1553. He was instrumental in shepherding both the reconciliation with Rome and the Spanish marriage through parlia- ment. Redworth, *Stephen Gardiner*, 292, 317–18.

14 November 30.

their error, urged them to carry on what they had begun, and everything else appropriate to the theme.

Afterwards, I and the most serene queen, with the assent of parliament, enacted a law providing for the punishment of heretics and those who disobey the commands of holy mother Church, renewing the kingdom's ancient laws on this subject, which are most suitable, and commanding their observance once again—and adding force for all their penalties and execution.[15] Likewise, as per the promise to the legate, they have re-pealed all the previous parliaments' enactments against the authority of the Apostolic See since the separation from the Church, declaring this by public statute. There have also been other laws and decrees passed for the better administration of justice and policy in this kingdom. We trust in our Lord that these things will be bettered each day. I particularly wanted to inform you of all this, and of our contentment in having com-pleted it, for the sake of the satisfaction you will receive from it, and that which will be widely shared across those realms. And thus we lovingly ask you to provide for prayers and sacrifices in every monastery and church, in thanksgiving to our Lord for the good success this enterprise has had, begging him to preserve and advance it.[16]

These have been the king's words, which express in perfect detail what trans-pired in that blessed act of reconciling the kingdom of England with the holy Catholic Church—the which, being a matter of such satisfaction, I have included here. Furthermore, I want to add the form used by the nation in ask-ing absolution, and by the legate in giving it, and it was in this way. The nation submitted a *memorial* or petition in Latin to the monarchs, with a preamble that, translated into Castilian, ran thus:

A petition presented to the most serene lords the king and queen of England, in the name and on the behalf of the same kingdom, that they

---

15   1 and 2 Phil. and Mar. c. 6, reviving medieval heresy statutes: see *SR*, 4.1:244.

16   This letter was included in Alonso Fernández de Madrid's (1474–1559) manuscript collec-tion on the history of Palencia, the *Silva Palentina*. See Alonso Fernández de Madrid, *Silva Palentina*, ed. Jesús San Martín Payo, Pallantia 1 (Palencia: Diputación Provincial D.L., 1976), 612–14.

It is not beyond the realm of possibility that Ribadeneyra knew the *Silva*, but José Solís de los Santos hypothesizes that the letter was printed in a pamphlet or broadsheet *relación* that has not survived (private communication).

Cf. *CSPS*, 13:123, a very similar letter of December 6, 1554, addressed to Francisco de Vargas y Mexia (d.1566), Philip's ambassador in Venice.

should seek absolution for the schism and heresies, etcetera, from the most reverend and most illustrious lord legate.

Within, it said the following:

We, the lords spiritual and temporal and the commons, assembled in this parliament, representing the entirety of the kingdom of England and of all its estates and dominions, in our name and in that of the entire realm do humbly entreat Your Majesties by this our petition, that you deign to show it to the most reverend in Christ Father and Lord Cardinal Pole, sent to this country by our most holy lord, Pope Julius III, and the sacred Apostolic See. By this petition, we declare the pain of our souls at the recent schism, and at having denied obedience to the said Apostolic See in this kingdom and its territories, and at having enacted, passed, or enforced, in word or deed, any law, ordinance, or decree whatsoever against his fundamental and sovereign authority. And, to attest to and proclaim this our repentance and sorrow, we offer our faith and promise by this our plea that we are prepared, and shall be in future, to do all we can, by the authority of Your Majesties, to annul and undo—both in our name and in that of the realm that we represent—the aforesaid laws, decrees, and ordinances in the present parliament. And we humbly beg Your Majesties that, as pure and unsullied persons, stained neither by the deformity of schism nor by the injury this realm has done the Apostolic See, and as pious rulers given us by divine providence, you deign to admit this our humble petition and seek that each of us and the entire kingdom receive from the Apostolic See (by means of the most reverend legate) absolution, release, and discharge from all the censures and penalties we have incurred under the laws of the Church. And that we should be received into the union and unity of the Church of Christ, that this noble kingdom and all its inhabitants may serve God and Your Majesties in union and perfect obedience to the Apostolic See and the Roman pontiffs in time to come, to the greater glory and honor of his divine majesty.[17]

---

17 A Latin text of the petition had been published at Rome at the time of the restoration. Philip II and Reginald Pole, *Copia delle lettere del serenissimo re d'Inghilterra, & del reuerendissimo Card. Polo legato della S. Sede Apostolica alla Santità di N.S. Iulio Papa III: Sopra la reduttione di quel regno alla vnione della Santa Madre Chiesa, & obbedienza della Sede Apostolica* ([Rome], [1554]), n.p.

For a contemporary English version, see Nichols, *Chronicle of Queen Jane,* 160–61.

The legate's absolution was as follows:

> Our Lord Jesus Christ, who redeemed us with his precious blood and cleansed us of all our stains and sins, to beautify us and hold us as a glorious spouse, without defect or wrinkle, whom the eternal Father has ordained as head of the entire Church,[18] by his mercy absolves you. And we, through the apostolic authority invested in us by our most holy lord, Pope Julius III, his vicar on earth, absolve you, and free you from all heresy and schism, and whatever judgments, censures, and penalties you have thus incurred—you, and any one of you, and the entire realm, and its holdings and dominions. And we restore you to the unity of the sacred Mother Church, as is more fully elaborated in our letters. In the name of the Father, and of the Son, and of the Holy Spirit.[19]

Before the legate bestowed absolution, he made a long, learned, and moving speech, discussing with many places from Holy Scripture and wonderful examples the penitence of the sinner, and how agreeable it is to God, and how the angels rejoice at the genuine conversion of a sinner.[20] Then he gave thanks to our Lord, who in his infinite mercy had endowed the kingdom with the spirit and desire to amend itself and return to itself. And at this he rose, as did the king and queen, who then bowed and knelt, along with the entire kingdom, while the legate, with arms upraised and eyes fixed on heaven, humbly implored our Lord to look upon the realm with the eyes of a compassionate father,[21] pardon its crimes, and send down from heaven his sacred benediction. And then he gave the absolution in the aforesaid form. And when he had finished the final words, and said, "In the name of the Father, and of the Son, and of the Holy Spirit," all those present loudly responded, full of piety and peace, "Amen, Amen!" The monarchs and many others wept out of pure joy, lovingly embracing each other and saying, "Today we are reborn in Christ."[22]

---

18   Eph. 1:22, 5:23, 5:25–27; Col. 1:18, 1:22.

19   For a Latin text of the absolution, see Philip II and Pole, *Copia delle lettere,* n.p or *Narratione particolare, del parlamento d'Inghilterra, et in che modo è uenuto quel popolo all'ubbidiena di Santa Chiesa, con l'ordine dell'assolutione, & benedittione data dal reverendissimo cardinale Polo, legato di sua Santità, à tutto il regno: Et appresso le feste, et giuoco delle canne, che si è fatto per allegrezza di tal nuoua* (Venice, 1555), n.p.

20   Luke 15:10.

21   Ps. 102:13.

22   See Cardinal Pole's letter to the pope on November 30, 1554: *CRP,* 2:369–74.
      Cf. "And they all shouted, 'Amen, amen.' As the legate gave the absolution, the queen wept out of devotion and joy, and many in the parliament did the same, and when the

This reconciliation took place on the feast day of Saint Andrew in the year 1554, and afterwards, in the synod celebrated by the same legate (as archbishop of Canterbury), it was ordained that in perpetual commemoration of this incomparable blessing of our Lord, each year the feast of Saint Andrew should be celebrated throughout the kingdom with greater solemnity than before.[23] And that within a certain period, every clergyman and citizen was to kneel, each in his own parish, and request and receive this grace of absolution and reconciliation.[24] This took place across the realm, to the tremendous joy and enthusiasm of the people. Shortly thereafter, ambassadors were sent to Rome to render obedience to the Apostolic See in the name of the monarchs and the nation.[25] Great indeed was the rejoicing in that holy city at the news of the restoration of this noble realm, with public processions, with a plenary indulgence granted for the occasion and circulated throughout Christendom, with a papal Mass celebrated by the supreme pontiff himself, and with the plentiful, overflowing tears of relief that he and the entire college of cardinals shed on reading the letter King Don Philip wrote to His Holiness in his own hand, a word-for-word translation of which I insert here, as follows:[26]

---

absolution was complete they were seen to embrace one another lovingly, saying to each other, 'Today we are reborn! Today we are reborn!" *Il felicissimo ritorno del regno d'Inghilterra alla catholica unione: Et alla obedientia della Sede Apostolica* (Rome, 1555), sig. Biii[v].

23   "We, following the precedent of the so pious enactment of the Cardinal and Legate aforesaid, do decree, in every year in all Cities, Towns, and Villages of this kingdom, on the feast of St. Andrew the Apostle, on which day the peace and reconciliation of this land with God and his Church was effected, that a solemn procession should be performed, assembling in which, not only all the Clergy of every place, but also the faithful members of Christ of the secular order, should renew the memory of so signal a blessing received from God, and shew themselves thankful by alms-giving and other pious works; and that on that very day in the Church whence the procession shall set out, amidst the solemn rites of the Mass, a sermon be addressed to the people in which the reason of this solemnity may be explained." Reginald Pole, *The Reform of England, by the Decrees of Cardinal Pole, Legate of the Apostolic See; Promulgated in the Year of Grace 1556*, ed. and trans. Henry Raikes (Chester: R.H. Spence, 1839), 6.

24   In the months after the reconciliation with Rome, the Marian episcopate, led by Bonner, issued instructions to their dioceses requiring all adult parishioners to be individually absolved of the schism before Easter 1555. Duffy, *Fires of Faith*, 15–16.

25   A delegation, headed by Anthony Browne, first Viscount Montagu (1528–92), Thomas Thirlby, bishop of Ely (c.1506–70), and the Welsh diplomat and lawyer Sir Edward Carne (c.1500–61), left England in March 1555. *CSPV*, 6:23.

26   Julius III learned of the reconciliation on December 14: he ordered the letter read out to as many people as could be packed into the Hall of Consistory, personally participated in

Most Holy Father

Yesterday I wrote to Don Juan Manrique[27] to tell or write Your Holiness of the wonderful conclusion to which the religious issues of this kingdom have come and of the rendering of obedience to Your Holiness—which is the most important. It has pleased our Lord, to whose goodness alone it should be attributed—as well as to Your Holiness, who has taken so many pains to win these souls—that today, the day of Saint Andrew, in the afternoon, the whole of this kingdom, with the unanimous consent of those who represent it and with deep repentance for what has been and contentment at what is to be, has rendered obedience to Your Holiness and the Holy See. And, at the intercession of the queen and myself, the legate absolved them. And as he wrote to Your Holiness all that has happened, I shall not relate it, save that the queen and I, as true and devoted children of Your Holiness, have received a pleasure greater than can be put into words, knowing that besides according with the service of our Lord, it fell to Your Holiness's reign to return such a realm to the communion of the universal Church. And so I have not ceased to thank him for what has come to pass. I trust in him that Your Holiness shall ever know that the Holy See has no son more obedient than I, nor any more desirous of preserving and exalting its authority. May our Lord protect and grace the sacred person of Your Holiness, as is my wish. From London, November 30, 1554.

Your Holiness's most humble son,
The King[28]

---

a thanksgiving Mass, and declared a fortnight of prayers of thanksgiving and a plenary indulgence. Pastor, *History of the Popes*, 13:288.

    The bull of indulgence is reproduced in Wilkins, *Concilia*, 4:111–12.

    See Corinna Streckfuss, "England's Reconciliation with Rome: A News Event in Early Modern Europe," *HR* 82, no. 215 (February 2009): 62–73.

27   The Castilian courtier and administrator Juan Manrique de Lara (d.1570).

28   For the Spanish text of this letter, see Philip II and Pole, *Copia delle Lettere*, n.p.

The Impediments to This Reconciliation, and How They Were Resolved[1]

Thus it was that England's return to the union of the Church was accomplished. It was regarded as a singular grace and gift of God that it had been done with such ease, putting an end to a matter so serious and so full of innumerable and thorny difficulties. For their part, the legate and the king's other loyal servants used all their wisdom to manage these and by gentleness and kindness remove all the impediments that arose—neither few nor insignificant—in the reconciliation. For when King Henry despoiled and seized the realm's monasteries and appropriated their property for himself, many had been sold, or traded, or bestowed upon knights and powerful persons, who had thus augmented their estates and titles. With the reconciliation, these men feared losing the goods they unjustly possessed, that the pontiff would refuse to grant absolution until these were restored to the churches to which they belonged. This troubled them deeply, since besides losing such fat estates, acquired so cheaply and so easily, it was all already mixed and confused with secular properties, so completely absorbed that they could hardly be distinguished or separated. For this reason, those with such holdings (who were numerous and very influential) dreaded and opposed the reunion and reconciliation of the kingdom with the Apostolic See.[2] Their fear grew at seeing the queen's liberality and devotion in relinquishing all the income the royal treasury had collected from the tithes,

---

1 Sander, *De origine ac progressu*, 348–51.

2 A Venetian agent in London reported on January 20, 1555, "On the Legate's arrival the King, before stipulating the union, went in person to Pole, and told him in short that it was impossible to effect the return to the obedience, unless the holders of this Church property were allowed to retain its actual possession. To this, after much discussion, the Legate at length said that should the Pope have to condescend to some indulgence for the removal of the impediments to so holy and necessary a work, this would be done after the completion of the return to the obedience, and that then this indulgence might be used, '*ob duritiam cordis illorum*,' but that with regard to that part of the Church property which was in the hands of their Majesties, they could not in honour allege these reasons; to which the King replied that they would occupy themselves with the conclusion of the union, and that as to the property held by the crown he believed their intention was not to retain any part of it, unless it was deemed that they could do so with a clear conscience, and that they would always refer themselves to the Pope and his Legate, and thus the matter rested." *CSPV*, 6:14.

© KONINKLIJKE BRILL NV, LEIDEN, 2017 | DOI 10.1163/9789004323964_072

first fruits, and other church properties by the command of Kings Henry and Edward into the hands of the legate, for him to dispose of as he saw fit; as well as her concern and eagerness to restore (at the very least) some portion of the property of those ancient and illustrious monasteries, to the glory of God and the honor of the kingdom.[3]

In parliament, the legate was urgently petitioned to produce a public written instrument that, in the name and with the authority of the supreme pontiff, would absolve and free of the canonical penalties and ecclesiastical censures all those who since the beginning of the schism had held and possessed, or now held and possessed, any monastic property or goods whatsoever, and so it was done. Nevertheless, the legate did not refrain from warning such illegitimate possessors to reflect, keep before their eyes the dire penalties God our Lord inflicts upon those who sacrilegiously put their hands upon the goods of the Church (examples of which abound in Holy Writ and ecclesiastical histories), and look to their consciences, even if the Church did not make use of the rigor of the sacred canons or of its rights. This satisfied the unruly and malcontent.[4] In the same document, the legate issued a dispensation for all those who had married within prohibited degrees—for these were innumerable and could not be separated without grave scandal and severe disruption—to continue in matrimony and to have legitimate children.[5]

---

3   See the provisions in 1 and 2 Phil. and Mar. c. 8 relating to confiscated church property: *SR*, 4.1:251.

4   The Venetian report of January 20 noted, "The kingdom having subsequently freely resumed its obedience, as known, promising to abrogate all the laws enacted at the time of the schism against the Pope and the See Apostolic, and whilst occupied with this repeal the Parliament having presented a petition to the King and Queen for that, amongst the other things, they should intercede for the renunciation of the Church property; and the bishops in like manner petitioning apart to the same effect, for the sake of the common weal, although contrary to their own private interest; the Legate having first of all endeavoured by several ways to recover as much as he could for the churches; at length, being unable to do otherwise, in order not to impede the completion of so important a work, and for the public welfare and quiet of England, condescended in such a way to the retention of this property that everybody might very easily perceive that his dispensation was a mere permission *ob duritiam cordis illorum*, as in this dispensation he never would consent to add the clause '*quod absque aliquo conscientiæ scrupulo possent hujusmodi bona relinere*,' although he was several times urged strongly to insert it; and this he did to leave in their minds a goad which in the course of time might move them to make some fitting and due acknowledgment, as some of them have done already." *CSPV*, 6:14.

5   Pole's diligent pastoral care is on full display in the examining of and granting of dispensations for technically invalid marriages; these were not issued in a blanket statement, but rather in more than three hundred individual legatine decisions. Pogson, "Reginald Pole," 13–14.

He confirmed the bishops ordained during the schism who were Catholic of heart, and another six bishops Henry had recreated anew in the same period.[6] Yet the bishops were not satisfied with this general absolution and confirmation: instead, each asked pardon for his own guilt and an individual confirmation of his rank and bishopric, which the Apostolic See granted with the greatest goodwill.[7] Only one, more out of carelessness than malice, did not make this request—the bishop of Llandaff. He alone of all the bishops later relapsed into schism in the time of Queen Elizabeth:[8] witness, recognize, and fear the judgments of God.

The legate's proclamation and document was joined to another from parliament, all published together along with other statutes and decrees; Pope Paul IV confirmed and ratified this in his apostolic letters, and so the unquiet souls were pacified and calmed, as has been said.[9] Some difficulties arose with the secular clerics who controlled the abbey of Westminster (the oldest in London, and the resting place of the kings of England), because King Henry had made it a parish church. They refused to renounce possession and return the monastery to the brothers of Saint Benedict (whose it was), as the queen had commanded. But subsequently, partly though prayers, partly through threats,

---

Thomas F. Mayer, *Reginald Pole: Prince & Prophet* (Cambridge: Cambridge University Press, 2000), 261.

6   Mary inherited an episcopal bench of twenty-three bishops. Within a year, thirteen had been removed from their sees by various expedients—imprisonment, conviction for treason or heresy, or visitations. Ten Edwardian bishops were prepared to support Mary's religious agenda, all of whom had to be formally reconciled with Rome by the papal legate. See David Loades, "The Marian Episcopate," in *The Church of Mary Tudor*, ed. Eamon Duffy and David Loades (Aldershot: Ashgate, 2005), 33–56.

7   Confusion about the validity of Henrician and Edwardian consecrations prompted recourse to Pope Paul IV, who issued the bull *Regimini* (1555), invalidating Edwardian ceremonies of consecration. Paul's predecessor (excluding the brief reign of Marcellus II [r.1555], who died of apoplexy less than a month after his election), Julius III, had given papal approval for five new English bishops on July 6, 1554. Pastor, *History of the Popes*, 14:389.

8   Anthony Kitchin (1471–1563), delightfully—if somewhat uncharitably—described by Eamon Duffy as a "classic timeserver who would doubtless have become a Hindu if required, provided he was allowed to hold on to the See of Llandaff," was the only Marian bishop to acquiesce in the Elizabethan religious settlement. Timeserver or not, Kitchin, who was made bishop in 1545, managed to keep his episcopacy (and his head) for nearly twenty years, through three regime changes. Duffy, *Fires of Faith*, 23.

9   On June 20, 1555, Paul issued the papal bull *Praeclara carissimi*, which confirmed Pole's concessions. Pastor, *History of the Popes*, 14:388–89.

and partly by offering them another place in recompense for that which they relinquished, they deigned to obey.[10]

---

10   In March 1555, a delegation of would-be Benedictines appeared at court, seeking a permanent home; within a month, Westminster had been chosen, but, as Sir John Mason (1503–66), the official responsible for the transition, observed, the dean and chapter had "laid sore law" against the monks' reinstatement, alleging that monasticism had "none institution of Christe." Both Mary and Cardinal Pole brought pressure to bear on the chapter; royal letters patent dissolving the chapter were issued on September 7, 1556, and several weeks later Pole informed the secular ecclesiastics that they would be compensated by the new abbey. The dean and canons had resigned by the end of the month, and the monks were installed by November. The episode is discussed in detail in C.S. Knighton, "Westminster Abbey Restored," in Duffy and Loades, *Church of Mary Tudor*, 77–123.

How the False Bishops were Punished, and Cranmer, Primate of England, was Burned[1]

Once this blessed act had been successfully concluded, it was undertaken to cleanse the realm, to uproot the cockles without damage to the wheat,[2] and to punish those who had sowed it and nurtured it with their malice and their influence. Among these were several false bishops among those selected by King Henry and King Edward and ordained outside the union of the Catholic Church: beyond their heresy, they had conspired against the queen and had been convicted of the crime of *lèse-majesté*.[3] The queen chose not to proceed against them according to the civil law, and instead their cases were heard before an ecclesiastical court. So it was done in the case of Thomas Cranmer, archbishop of Canterbury and primate of England. For, pernicious and pestilential though he was, the queen would not allow him to be interrogated or his case to be heard save by order of the pope and before an apostolic commissioner, with the advocates of the queen and King Don Philip her husband acting as prosecutors, not as judges.[4] Thus the monarchs gave a wonderful example of piety and restraint and demonstrated the respect owed to ecclesiastics, even those as awful as Cranmer, who had been made archbishop of Canterbury by Henry VIII in the manner and for the purpose we have recounted.[5] It was he who rendered the sentence of divorce in the king's favor, against the pope; he who publicly married his mistress; he who, being a heretic, favored the heretics. By now full to bursting with misdeeds, under Mary he was imprisoned, convicted and condemned as a traitor by parliament on his own confession, expelled from the episcopate, and handed over to the secular arm and burned in Oxford

1   Sander, *De origine ac progressu*, 331–32.

2   Matt. 13:28–30.

3   Three of the most prominent evangelical bishops—Thomas Cranmer, Nicholas Ridley, and Hugh Latimer—were tried and convicted of treason or sedition, but their executions were delayed until the restoration of Roman obedience allowed them to be punished as heretics. Edwards, *Archbishop Pole*, 147–49.

4   In March 1555, Mary and Philip sent an embassy to Pope Julius III requesting the deprivation of Cranmer as archbishop. Julius appointed James Brooks (1512–58), newly elected as bishop of Gloucester, as papal delegate to try Cranmer. MacCulloch, *Thomas Cranmer*, 572–73.
     The official account of the trial can be found in Cranmer, *Miscellaneous Writings*, 2.541–62.

5   In the margin: "Book 1, Chapter 18."

© KONINKLIJKE BRILL NV, LEIDEN, 2017 | DOI 10.1163/9789004323964_073

as obstinate and unrepentant.[6] For although he had initially pretended to be a Catholic and a penitent, in hopes of pardon and his life, and had many times affirmed in his own hand that he was prepared to abjure his heresy, this availed him nothing after his charades and hypocrisy were discovered.[7] And so he and many other heretics like him were burned, reviving the ancient, sensible laws, both civil and ecclesiastical, that commanded that all such should be punished. For the sake of order, promptitude, and efficiency, the queen ordered all foreigners who neither held public office nor were considered as natives to leave the kingdom within so many days, under dire penalties. By this mandate alone, more than thirty thousand heretics of various nations and sects, who (as we have said) in Edward's reign had flown to England from every corner, as to a lair and safe haven for their errors and wickedness, departed.[8] Furthermore, the bodies of Bucer and other deceased heretics were disinterred and burned.[9]

---

6   Several months after his arrest, on November 13, 1553, Cranmer was brought to Guildhall to stand trial for treason, on the grounds that he had aided both Jane Grey's seizure of power and the resistance to Mary's accession. Though he initially pleaded not guilty, he changed this before the jury reached a verdict. Parliament passed a bill of attainder against him on December 5, 1553. On March 21, 1555, just outside Balliol College, Oxford—the same spot where Ridley and Latimer had been burned the previous October—Cranmer went to the stake as a heretic. MacCulloch, *Thomas Cranmer*, 554–55, 558, 603–04.

7   Cranmer's ordeal produced no fewer than six recantations, as he, his interrogators, and the Marian regime haggled over the terms of his capitulation. Diarmaid MacCulloch argues that both Cranmer's acceptance and renewed rejection of Catholicism were genuine, understandable products of the physical, mental, and emotional pressure put upon an aging prisoner. Ibid., 584–605.

8   Though many of the European emigres fled of their own volition after Mary's accession, John Foxe reproduces "A Copy of the Queen's Proclamation for the driving out of the Realm Strangers and Foreigners," which gave its targets twenty-four days to leave the country. Foxe, *Acts and Monuments*, 6:429–30.

9   The Marian visitation of Cambridge held a formal inquiry into the heretical teachings of Martin Bucer and Paul Fagius (1504–49). On February 6, 1556, their disinterred remains were burnt in the Market Square. Oxford could furnish no bodies of comparable odiousness, but the remains of Peter Martyr's wife, Catherine Dammartin (d.1553) were cast onto a dungheap (there had not been sufficient evidence to condemn her for heresy, but her violation of a nun's vows of chastity was considered heinous enough to merit this). Cross, "Oxford and the Tudor State," 146–47.

How the Universities were Reformed, and Our Sacred Religion Flourished[1]

After this followed the reform of the universities, which (as we said above) are the springs of the commonwealth;[2] in consequence, the heretics had poisoned them with the venom of their perverted doctrine. To cleanse them, exemplary visitors were dispatched, among them one Niccolò Ormanetto, who later became bishop of Padua and died in Madrid as the nuncio of His Holiness.[3] With great zeal and prudence he visited the colleges of Oxford and Cambridge, reforming and restoring them (as much as was possible) to the splendor of former times and to the rules left by their founders. He dismissed heretics and those suspected of heresy from the professorships, which he entrusted to Catholic scholars, and took over the administration and governance of the universities and the colleges.[4] For the further reformation of the universities, they brought from abroad several men renowned for piety, learning, and wisdom. One of these was Brother Pedro de Soto, a religious of the order of Saint Dominic, a man distinguished for his faith, scholarship, and experience, who had served for many years as Emperor Charles v's confessor and

---

1 Sander, *De origine ac progressu*, 351–53.

2 In the margin: "Book 2, Chapter 2."

   For the Marian reconstruction of the universities, see Claire Cross, "The English Universities, 1553–58," in Duffy and Loades, *Church of Mary Tudor*, 57–76.

3 During Mary's reign, the Veronese cleric Niccolò Ormanetto (d.1577) served as Cardinal Pole's secretary and as papal datary in England. In 1570, he was made bishop of Padua, going on to participate in the Council of Trent and to become papal nuncio to Spain (1572). Ormanetto participated in the 1556 visitations of both universities, joined at Oxford by Bishop Brooks of Gloucester; Robert Morwent, president of Corpus Christi College (d.1558); Henry Cole, provost of Eton (c.1504–c.1579); and Walter Wright, archdeacon of Oxford (d.1561). At Cambridge, Ormanetto's colleagues were John Christopherson, master of Trinity College (d.1558) and Thomas Watson, bishop of Lincoln (1515–84). Veech, *Nicholas Sanders*, 111n1. Duffy and Loades, *Church of Mary Tudor*, 70–71. Duffy, *Fires of Faith*, 37.

4 Less than a month after Mary secured the throne, she nullified any changes to the unversities' statutes made since her father's death. That autumn saw what Claire Cross has called "a near purge" in the universities, as those who resisted the return to Catholic observance either resigned or were forced out. Many of the conservatives driven out by the Edwardian reforms resumed their posts. Duffy and Loades, *Church of Mary Tudor*, 62. Cross, "Oxford and the Tudor State," 142–43.

played a part in the governance of his realms. This father was then in Flanders, and he was summoned to England to cleanse the University of Oxford by his erudition and industry, to repair what Peter Martyr had so recently destroyed, to restore sound scholastic theology, and to banish the heretics' chimeric and fantastical extravagance of speech, by which they had enchanted and dazzled the flighty and ignorant.[5] This good father did with the utmost care, aided by other learned fathers of his order: in a short time, their example and their wisdom had so edified and inspired the students of Oxford that they devoted themselves to solid, Scholastic Catholic teachings with extreme zeal and enthusiasm.[6] And the students, who had so recently heard Peter Martyr, and then heard Father Pedro de Soto, compared the two, just as the glorious Doctor Saint Augustine compared the blessed Saint Ambrose with Faustus the Manichean, who had previously been his master. Saint Augustine relates that in affectations and delights of words, Faustus excelled Saint Ambrose, as a made-up whore excels a modest and dignified matron, but in the knowledge of letters and of sacred matters, and in the interpretation and understanding thereof, there could be no comparison between the heretic and the saint.[7] And the good achieved at Oxford by the good Father Pedro was so enormous that the seed of faith that endures in England to this day is the fruit of what he sowed then, as Doctor Sander says in his history.[8]

After the universities had been reformed and the commonwealth purged of the filth of heresy, the churches began to flourish, new shrines to be established, altars to be erected and consecrated, new colleges to be endowed, and

---

5   The Dominican Pedro de Soto (1493–1563) was a distinguished Spanish theologian who had been Charles's confessor. He was appointed to lecture on Peter Lombard's *Sentences* at Oxford, reinstating the study of Scholastic theology. McCoog, *Reckoned Expense*, 44.

6   The later assessment of John Jewel, the Protestant bishop of Salisbury (1522–71) is a back-handed compliment to the efforts of Soto, Juan de Villagarcia (d.1564), and several other Spanish Dominicans: "Our universities are so depressed and ruined, that at Oxford there are scarcely two individuals who think with us; and even they are so dejected and broken in spirit, that they can do nothing. That despicable friar, Soto, and another Spanish monk, I know not who, have so torn up by the roots all that Peter Martyr had so prosperously planted, that they have reduced the vineyard of the Lord into a wilderness." Ibid., 43–44.

    For the importance of Spanish imports in Mary's restoration of Catholicism, see John Edwards, "Spanish Religious Influence in Marian England," in Duffy and Loades, *Church of Mary Tudor*, 201–24.

7   In the margin: "*The Confessions*, Book 5, Chapter 13."

8   "Truly, these sagacious masters accomplished so much in the universities, that it seems the seed of the Catholic faith, which God preserved for us in the long schism that followed, and so fierce a persecution, came from nowhere else." Sander, *De origine ac progressu*, 352.

monasteries to be constructed—Benedictines, Carthusians, Bridgettines, Dominicans, Franciscans, and all the other orders.[9] For numerous devout persons willingly donated their property for this purpose, and the monarchs led their subjects by their example, assisting all with their favor and their generosity. The people flocked to the divine office, confession, communion, and the sacred sacrifice of the Mass with deep joy and devotion—and particularly to the sacrament of confirmation, which the English customarily attend and revere more than any other nation. So much so that it is considered a disgrace, an impiety, and an offense not to be confirmed by seven years of age. For this reason, the bishops unanimously agree to confirm indiscriminately all children in whatever diocese they find themselves, and parents and godparents are obligated by tradition and law to bring their children for confirmation to the first bishop who, after they have been baptized, comes within seven miles. And since this sacrament had not been legitimately administered in Edward's reign, so many children were brought to the bishops for confirmation from every city, town, hamlet, and village that they were unable to cope. At times, they were so overwhelmed with the infinity of those who rushed to them that it was necessary to minister in the fields, with officers in their midst lest they be suffocated or buffeted by the horde of people. Furthermore, the legate, as archbishop of Canterbury and primate of the realm, published his synodal decrees and the ordinances for the clergy for the restoration of the Catholic faith; these were first sent to the supreme pontiff for His Holiness to see and approve.[10] And the bishops of England wrote to the pope, humbly imploring his pardon for the recent schism and the disasters suffered by that kingdom, promising their obedience to his commands, and begging him to take them into his grace as dutiful sons. Many of them did not know that the clergy had reduced the excess of their tables and the multiplication of benefices, and so this was not observed.

---

9   At Oxford, 1555 saw the London merchants Sir Thomas Pope (c.1507–59) and Sir Thomas White (c.1495–1567) found Trinity College and St John's College, respectively. At Cambridge, John Caius (1510–73) procured the royal re-foundation of Gonville Hall as Gonville and Caius College in 1557. Cross, "Oxford and the Tudor State," 145. Christopher Brooke, *A History of Gonville and Caius College* (Woodbridge: Boydell Press, 1985), 61–63.

Mary's reign saw the (re-)establishment of seven religious houses: the friaries of the Observant Franciscans at Greenwich and Southampton, the Benedictine abbey at Westminster, the Carthusian house at Shene, the Dominican priory at Blackfriars in London, the Bridgettine nunnery of Syon in Isleworth, and the Dominican nunnery at King's Langley. Duffy and Loades, *Church of Mary Tudor*, 23.

10   The 1556 ecclesiastical synod, which met at Lambeth under Pole's leadership, produced a series of decrees for the restoration of Catholicism in England. See Pole, *Reform of England.*

On this account, many god-fearing and prudent men worried that their good fortune could not last long, and they would be punished with yet greater sufferings. What is more, there was also carelessness or excessive leniency in punishing and correcting the priests and religious who, with the earlier license and freedom, had married: they had been ordered to separate from their women and had been deprived of their benefices, but very soon they were admitted to other, even fatter posts, resulting in a dire penury among priests.

The Death of Queen Mary[1]

For these, or for the kingdom's other sins, or because those of King Henry had not been punished sufficiently, our Lord chose to take the queen to himself. With her death, the Catholic faith in that land, which like a mighty ship with brisk winds had sailed on in prosperity, cutting through the ocean's waves—now fierce, now gentle and obedient—suddenly ran aground, and with it peace, justice, and tranquility. The saintly queen died on November 17, 1558, at the age of forty-three years, nine months, and one day, having reigned five years and four months. Without doubt, this lady was blessed: in her magnificent, queenly virtues, in having seen her enemies and those of Jesus Christ beneath her feet and herself seated upon the royal throne, scepter in hand, and in having reduced the kingdom to the Catholic faith and the obedience of the Church. But she was accursed in being the daughter of such a father—and also in having no children to succeed her and leaving the crown to a woman she never regarded as her sister, but only as a bastard and an enemy to herself and the Catholic religion, and whom she always feared would ruin and destroy her. And so for these reasons she wished and attempted to exclude her from the succession to the crown. But because she could not effect this without the assent of parliament, since King Henry's will had been ratified by the authority of parliament (as already mentioned),[2] at the hour of her death she sent to her sister to beg two things. First, that Elizabeth should fulfill all that the queen had undertaken to give her subjects, obliged herself to pay by her royal word or spent for the public good. Second, that she should strive to preserve the Catholic faith, now established and confirmed in the kingdom, and not permit it to be altered or changed. Elizabeth heard out her sister's message and promised to do all she had instructed, but she did not comply.[3] Within a few hours of

---

1 Sander, *De origine ac progressu*, 355–59.

2 In the margin: "Book 1, Chapter 47."

3 Edwin Sandys (1519–88), a future mainstay of Elizabeth's episcopate, wrote to Heinrich Bullinger on December 20, 1558: "Mary, not long before her death, sent two members of her council to her sister Elizabeth, and commanded them to let her know in the first place, that it was her intention to bequeath to her the royal crown, together with all the dignity that she was then in possession of by right of inheritance. In return however for this great favour conferred upon her, she required of her these three things: first, that she would not change her privy council; secondly, that she would make no alteration in religion; and thirdly, that she would discharge her debts, and satisfy her creditors. Elizabeth replied in these terms: 'I am

the queen's death, Cardinal Pole died of a quartan ague, and so all at once any hope of remedy was eliminated and no one was left to resist Elizabeth, nor any skilled pilot to contend with the furious winds and the sea's frightful waves.[4]

---

very sorry to hear of the queen's illness; but there is no reason why I should thank her for her intention to give me the crown of this kingdom. For she has neither the power of bestowing it upon me, nor can I lawfully be deprived of it, since it is my peculiar and hereditary right. With respect to the council, I think myself,' she said, 'as much at liberty to choose my counsellors, as she was to choose her own. As to religion, I promise thus much, that I will not change it, provided only it can be proved by the word of God, which shall be the only foundation and rule of my religion. And when, lastly, she requires the payment of her debts, she seems to me to require nothing more than what is just, and I will take care that they shall be paid, as far as may lie in my power.'" Hastings Robinson, ed., *The Zurich Letters, Comprising the Correspondence of Several English Bishops and Others, with Some of the Helvetian Reformers, during the Early Part of the Reign of Queen Elizabeth*, trans. Hastings Robinson, Parker Society Publications 50 (Cambridge: Cambridge University Press, 1842), 3–4.

4   On November 21, Feria wrote to the emperor: "On the night of the day of the Queen's decease the Cardinal also died. He was very weak and with continual fever, and his servants did not take care to conceal the death of the Queen from him. He was so afflicted by it that it hastened his end." *CSPSE*, 1:1

Ribadeneyra wrote to Diego Laínez from London on January 20, 1559, "the queen died on November 17, and Cardinal Pole fourteen hours later." *MHSIR*, 1:311.

Of the Virtues of Queen Doña Mary

Queen Mary was slight of build, thin (totally different from her father), serious, and restrained; they say she was pretty when she was a girl, and afterwards lost her beauty through maltreatment—though she was never ugly.[1] She was nearsighted, but with very bright eyes, which inspired respect in any she looked at; she had a deep voice, more like a man's than a woman's, a quick wit, a resolute and forceful spirit, and an unerring and thoughtful judgment.[2] She was adorned with numerous extraordinary virtues, the daughter and image of her mother, Queen Doña Catherine. She had been a maiden of such perfect purity, chastity, and wonderful integrity that even when she dwelt in the palace amid the delirious liberty of her father, she seemed not to know or understand anything that had the savor or scent of the court, no more than if she had been raised from her mother's womb in the deepest seclusion among unspotted and saintly maidens. So much so that her own father, not believing what was said about this, decided to make trial of it: this he did, and was amazed, quite dumbfounded, at his daughter's miraculous integrity, which was equal to

---

1 In the words of the Venetian ambassador, "She is not of strong constitution, and of late she suffers from headache and serious affection of the heart, so that she is often obliged to take medicine and is also to be blooded [...] She is of low stature, with a red and white complexion, and very thin; her eyes are white and large and her hair reddish; her face is round, with a nose rather low and wide; and were her age not on the decline, she might be called handsome rather than the contrary, and she had no eyebrows." V.C. Medvei, "The Illness and Death of Mary Tudor," *Journal of the Royal Society of Medicine* 80 (December 1987): 766–80, here 767.

2 A Venetian diplomatic report of May 13, 1557 stated that Mary "is of low rather than of middling stature, but, although short, she has no personal defect in her limbs, nor is any part of her body deformed. She is of spare and delicate frame, quite unlike her father, who was tall and stout; nor does she resemble her mother, who, if not tall, was nevertheless bulky. Her face is well formed, as shown by her features and lineaments, and as seen by her portraits. When younger she was considered, not merely tolerably handsome, but of beauty exceeding mediocrity. At present, with the exception of some wrinkles, caused more by anxieties than by age, which make her appear some years older, her aspect, for the rest, is very grave. Her eyes are so piercing that they inspire, not only respect, but fear, in those on whom she fixes them, although she is very shortsighted, being unable to read or do anything else unless she has her sight quite close to what she wishes to peruse or to see distinctly. Her voice is rough and loud, almost like a man's, so that when she speaks she is always heard a long way off." CSPV, 6:884.

his own brutish vice (which cannot be exaggerated).[3] She had the profoundest devotion and reverence for all sacred things, especially the holy sacrament of the altar: she spent many hours prostrate in prayer before the divine presence, usually hearing two Masses each day with singular dedication and piety. Not a single day passed in which she did not hear Mass—even on the day she died she wanted to hear it, and as the priest finished the consummation, she closed her eyes, never to open them again.[4] Each day, she diligently heard vespers and compline in her oratory. Wondrous to relate, none had ever seen her idle. When she had finished her devotions, or the public business of the nation, she busied herself with her handiwork, which was extremely skillful and neatly done, generally making things for divine worship and the altar service. Likewise, she played the clavichord and the lute wonderfully, and even as a child (for diversion or relaxation in her troubles) with such grace and nimbleness of hand that it amazed the best musicians and instrumentalists.[5] When communion was taken, every Easter and the major feasts—especially those of our

---

3   The tale of Henry's trial of his daughter's virtue, along with several other details in this chapter, appear in the biography of Dormer penned after her death by Henry Clifford (b. c.1570), a member of the duchess's household. Clifford recounts, "She was declared Princess of Wales and heir of the kingdom; so bred as she hated evil; knew no foul or unclean speeches, which when her lord father understood, he would not believe it but would try it once by Sir Francis Brian, being at a mask in the court; and finding it to be true, notwithstanding, perceiving her to be prudent and of a princely spirit, did ever after more honour her." Clifford, *Life of Jane Dormer*, 80–81.

   For further discussion of Dormer's role in the composition of the *Historia*, see Weinreich, "English Mission."

4   "She gave commandment to all, both of her Council, and servants, to stand fast in the Catholic religion; and with those virtuous and Christian advices, still in prayer and hearing good lessons, receiving the holy Sacraments of the Church, left this world, which was the 17th day of November, 1558. That morning hearing Mass, which was celebrated in her chamber, she being at the last point (for no day passed in her life that she heard not Mass) and although sick to death, she heard it with so good attention, zeal, and devotion, as she answered in every part with him that served the Priest; such yet was the quickness of her senses and memory. And when the Priest came to that part to say, *Agnus Dei, qui tollis peccata mundi*, she answered plainly and distinctly to every one, *Miserere nobis, Miserere nobis, Dona nobis pacem*. Afterwards seeming to meditate something with herself, when the Priest took the Sacred Host to consume it, she adored it with her voice and countenance, presently closed her eyes and rendered her blessed soul to God. This the duchess hath related to me, the tears pouring from her eyes, that the last thing which the queen saw in this world was her Saviour and Redeemer in the sacramental species; no doubt to behold Him presently after in His glorious Body in heaven." Clifford, *Life of Jane Dormer*, 71–72.

5   The Venetian report of 1557 noted, "Besides woman's work, such as embroidery of every sort with the needle, she also practises music, playing especially on the claricorde and on the lute

Lady—she dressed in her richest clothes and adorned herself with the most precious jewels she possessed, not only beautifying her soul with virtues, but also her body with attire, and attesting by her ornate exterior the internal care with which she governed herself, so as to receive the Lord worthily, according to the ancient customs of England, observed by lords and commoners alike.[6]

She had a wonderful trust in our Lord and an admirable constancy in all her tribulations, which were numerous and grievous. When parliament ordered that all swear, on pain of death, that King Henry's second marriage with Anne Boleyn was valid and the first with Queen Doña Catherine illegitimate, the king wanted his daughter Doña Mary to swear as well, taking various means, gentle and harsh, to sway her to it—but she never acquiesced. The king was incensed by this, so enraged that, like a man blind and out of his mind, he decided to have her throat cut![7] And he would have carried out this madness, had not Cromwell, who then held the realm in his hand, calmed him—not out of any affection or goodwill for Princess Doña Mary, but because he judged that this unrestrained, barbaric cruelty would damage his projects of planting and establishing his false creed in the kingdom, destroying the monasteries and all holy religion, and bringing other princes to forsake their obedience to the Apostolic See by King Henry's example. The queen demonstrated the same constancy, the same strong and vigorous spirit, in resisting the protector and her brother Edward's other impious ministers when they sought to deny her the Mass and the oratory she maintained in her house, for she never allowed herself to be conquered or to soften at their threats, flatteries, promises, and deceptions, though she saw herself in mortal peril from the wickedness and tyranny of those in power. And no less did she show her fortitude and greatness of spirit when she had herself proclaimed and heralded as queen as soon as she knew her brother was dead, although she was (as has been told) alone, unarmed, and abandoned, her enemies armed and powerful, controlling all the soldiers and fortresses across the kingdom. Yet, having faith in her righteousness and trusting in God, she found the heart and strength to tackle and overcome a challenge well-nigh impossible by the lights of human wisdom.

---

so excellently that, when intent on it (though now she plays rarely), she surprised the best performers, both by the rapidity of her hand and by her style of playing." *CSPV*, 7:884.

6 "When in good health, Mary was fond of music and a good and keen dancer, but a bad dresser, although at the beginning of her reign she did display a certain magnificence of her dress and—like her father—was fond of wearing a great deal of jewellery." Medvei, "Mary Tudor," 767.

7 Mary's refusal to swear to the First Act of Succession (1534) provoked an outraged reaction from her father: at the time, Chapuys wrote that "the King is known to have said that he would have her beheaded for having contravened the laws of the kingdom." *CSPS*, 5.1:45.

In the same way, she showed her valor when the malcontents rebelled and took up arms once again, for she calmed and dispersed them by prayers, rather than soldiers, with authority, rather than force or fear. Throughout, many singular and extraordinary events came to pass, each of which demonstrated her fortitude and steadfastness.

   The queen was always amiable and beneficent, fervently loved by the entire realm, so much so that even when her father and her brother Edward were alive, and she was poor and beset, everyone wished to serve her and join her household, the lords and grandees of the realm importuning her to take their daughters into her retinue and service. So modest was she that she replied, "I marvel at what you ask of me, for my estate is not such as I could do you good; I shall receive service in this, far more than I shall benefit you."[8] When she found herself in the country, before—and even after—she became queen, she sometimes went in disguise, with a pair of maids as companions, to visit her neighbors, the wives of workingmen or paupers though they might be: she asked them various things, and discreetly relieved and aided them as much as she could.[9] And if perchance it was alleged that the queen's servants had committed some injustice, whether seizing beds, or wagons, or coaches in her service, or not having paid for their use, or some similar matter, she strove to understand the reason behind it all, and then saw to restitution and punishment.[10] And out of the goodwill she had won, countless people flocked to her

---

8   "The greatest lords in the kingdom were suitors to her to receive their daughters in her service." Clifford, *Life of Jane Dormer*, 63.

9   "This queen seldom went in progress except it were to the Cardinal's house at Croydon (for Cardinal Pole her kinsman was Archbishop of Canterbury) avoiding by all means to trouble and grieve her subjects in time of hay and corn harvest, when they had use of their horses and carts. And being at Croydon, for her recreation, with two or three of her ladies, she would visit the poor neighbours, they all seeming to be the maids of the Court; for then she would have no difference, and ever one of these was Jane. She would sit down very familiarly in their poor houses, talk with the man and the wife, ask them of their manner of living [...] In the visiting of these poor neighbours, if she found them charged with children, she gave them good alms, comforted them, advising them to live thriftily and in the fear of God, and with that care to bring up their children; and if there were many children she took order they should be provided for, placing both boys and girls to be apprentices in London, where they might learn some honest trade, and be able to get their living. This did she in a poor carpenter's house, and the house of the widow of a husbandman. And in this sort did she pass some hours with the poor neighbours, with much plainness and affability; they supposing them all to be the queen's maids, for there seemed no difference." Ibid., 64–66.

10   "And among others, being once in a collier's house, the queen sitting by while he did eat his supper, on her demanding the like of him, he answered, that they had pressed his

service on her brother the king's death, with thirty thousand armed men coming to her defense (as we have said) for the sake of the love the entire kingdom bore her. She was free, merciful, and humane in pardoning and receiving back into her grace those who had offended her, most severe and rigorous in punishing offenses committed against God our Lord and the Catholic faith, as this history has related. She knew Latin well, and Spanish and French reasonably, such that she could understand those who spoke it and could make clear her own meaning; she also understood Italian.[11]

In her last illness—dropsy[12]—she manifested deep patience and perfect conformity to the divine will. In the last and worst of the fits, her mind now weakening, she became delirious several times and spoke disjointedly—but all her words were of God, or our Lady, or the angels, or the sacred passion of Jesus Christ our Redeemer, or similar matters, revealing what she held in her heart and what she had contemplated while still herself.[13] When they cut her open

---

cart from London, and had not paid him. The queen asked if he had called for his money. He said, yea, to them that set him awork, but they gave him neither his money nor good answer. She demanded; 'Friend, is this true, that you tell me?' He said, 'Yea,' and prayed her to be a mean to the comptroller, that he and other poor men might be paid. The queen told him she would, and willed that the next morning about nine or ten o'clock, he should come for his money. She came no sooner to the Court, but she called the comptroller, and gave him such a reproof for not satisfying poor men, as the ladies who were with her, when they heard it, much grieved. The queen said that he had ill officers who gave neither money nor good words to poor men, and that hereafter he should see it amended, for if she understood it again, he should hear it to his displeasure; and that the next morning the poor men would come for their money, and that they should be paid every penny." Ibid., 64–65.

11 The Venetian report of May 13, 1557 observed, "But whatever may be the amount deducted from her physical endowments, as much more may with truth, and without flattery, be added to those of her mind, as, besides the facility and quickness of her understanding, which comprehends whatever is intelligible to others, even to those who are not of her own sex (a marvellous gift for a woman), she is skilled in five languages, not merely understanding, but speaking four of them fluently, *viz.*, English, Latin, French, Spanish, and Italian, in which last, however, she does not venture to converse, although it is well known to her; but the replies she gives in Latin, and her very intelligent remarks made in that tongue surprise everybody." *cspv*, 6:884.

12 John Edwards attributes Mary's death to the influenza then epidemic in England. Edwards, *Mary I*, 325–27.

13 "She comforted those of them that grieved about her; she told them what good dreams she had, seeing many little children like Angels play before her, singing pleasing notes, giving her more than earthly comfort; and thus persuaded all, ever to have the holy fear of God before their eyes, which would free them from all evil, and be a curb to all temptations." Clifford, *Life of Jane Dormer*, 70.

after her death, they found the liver wasted and dry; piercing it, a green liquid emerged, like the juice of pressed plants, and therefore many believed she had been given poison.[14] And it could be that she had been in the days of her father or brother, but the doctor who opened her told me in London that he did not believe this, and attributed the bad condition of the liver to other causes. They also found the heart withered and consumed: no marvel, as she had suffered so many extreme trials and afflictions of the heart. The only child of the king, the heir to his kingdom and acknowledged as princess, she saw herself robbed of her royal dignity and her mother the queen cast off and shamefully repudiated, and was then declared a bastard—and what is more, compelled to serve and obey a whore with the title and crown of queen, by whom she was ignominiously treated. And after the death of the king her father, she was harassed and hounded by those who governed—or, as I should say, tyrannized—the realm in the reign of King Edward her brother, seeking to deny her the Mass and, after her brother was dead, the kingdom, with the infamous insults and injustices told in this history. All these things, though she suffered them with a strong and manly heart and an invincible patience given her by our Lord, could not but have an effect, battering and consuming her heart with so many fierce blows. It was a great miracle that she was able to endure so long, and a particular grace of our Lord, who preserved her in order to exalt and honor her in this life, and leave her as the paragon of queens, an exemplar of all virtue and sanctity.

---

14   The papal diary for December 22, 1558 recorded, "It was said that the Queen died on the 17th and the Cardinal on the 18 November: so that many, not without reason, suspected that both perished by poison." CSPR, 1:1.

How Queen Elizabeth's Reign Began, and How the King of France Considered Her Unfit to Rule

With Queen Mary dead, her sister Elizabeth, the daughter of King Henry and Anne Boleyn (as has been said), succeeded her to the throne. But King Henry of France, regarding Elizabeth as an illegitimate bastard, ordered Mary Queen of Scots, the wife of his son, Dauphin Francis, and the granddaughter of Queen Margaret of Scotland, the older sister of King Henry VIII—whose line had ended, according to Henry II, with Queen Mary—proclaimed as queen of England and Ireland. Thus he had the arms of England inserted into his daughter-in-law the queen of Scots's cloths-of-state, crests, and plate.[1] The French king was brought to this by Pope Clement's definitive sentence declaring the pretended marriage between King Henry VIII and Anne Boleyn illegitimate, together with any children born thereto. What is more, King Henry himself, once he was calmer and free of passion, had ordered parliament to declare Princess Doña Mary his heir, exempting the kingdom from the oath taken to Anne Boleyn and her daughter Elizabeth.[2] Furthermore, some have written that he insisted to his council that Anne Boleyn had not been, and could not have been, his wife, for a certain reason he had privately shared with the archbishop of Canterbury.[3] And although by the authority parliament had given him at the time of his death, his will provided for his children to succeed in order (Edward, then Mary, then Elizabeth) and this plan was ratified by parliament, yet neither the king her father, nor parliament declared the legitimacy of the marriage

---

1 Sander, *De origine ac progressu*, 365.

   In January 1559, two months after Mary Tudor's death, Henry II had his daughter-in-law proclaimed as queen of Scotland, England, and Ireland, and encouraged her to quarter her arms with those of England as a public demonstration of her claim to the throne. Wormald, *Mary Queen of Scots*, 21.

2 Ribadeneyra is massaging the truth here. It is true that with the passage of 28 Hen. 8. c. 7, Henry voided his marriage to Anne Boleyn and declared illegitimate the children thereof, but the act did not legitimate Mary. It was Henry's future issue by Jane Seymour that the act named as his lawful heirs, and affirmed this by an oath nullifying all previous oaths. See SR, 3:655–62.

3 In the sentence of divorce between Henry and Anne, Cranmer referred to "certain true, just, and lawful reasons recently brought to our attention." For the sentence, see Wilkins, *Concilia*, 3:803–04.

between Henry and Anne Boleyn, and of whatever was born thereto. Earlier, in the first year of Queen Mary's reign, parliament had decreed and established by statute that King Henry's marriage to Queen Doña Catherine had been lawful according to divine and human justice, as were the children born thereto, and annulled and repealed all acts, proceedings, and judgments rendered to the contrary.[4] From this it follows that the other marriage made during Queen Doña Catherine's lifetime, between King Henry and Anne Boleyn, was illegitimate, as was the daughter born thereto. And the common law of England excludes bastard or illegitimate persons from the throne as unfit for the crown of that nation. For these reasons the king of France (as we have said) had his daughter-in-law, the queen of Scots, proclaimed as queen of England, but to no avail: Elizabeth won out and succeeded to the throne. And this was the reason (so they say) that from then on she bitterly hated the queen of Scots, for having usurped the title of queen of England—although she had not usurped it, but had been given it by her father-in-law, she being a small child.[5] To seal up this little chink [*portillo*], and remove all occasion for doubts as to her right to the succession, she has had it decreed that none, on pain of death, should ever dare to affirm that the monarch and the estates of the realm could not name whatever ruler they pleased.[6] Indeed, many desired the ruler to be any native of the kingdom whatsoever, even a heretical, depraved bastard, rather than some foreigner, however legitimate, virtuous, and Catholic they might be. But let us observe the beginnings and the progression of Queen Elizabeth.

---

4   1 Mar. St. 2. c. 1. See *SR*, 4.1:200–01.

5   Ribadeneyra exaggerates: Mary Stewart was a month shy of her sixteenth birthday at Mary Tudor's death.

6   13 Eliz. 1. c. 1 declared it high treason to "in any wyse holde and affyrme or mayntayne that the Co[m]mon Lawes of this Realme not altred by P[ar]lyament, ought not to dyrecte the Ryght of the Crowne of England, or that o[f] said Sov[e]rayne Ladye Elizabeth the Quenes Ma[jest] y that nowe is, with and by the aucthoritye of the Parlyament of Englande is not able to make Lawes and Statutes of suffycyent force and valyditie to lymit and bynd the Crowne of this Realme, and the Descent Lymitac[i]on Inheritaunce and Government thereof." *SR*, 4.1:527.

How the Queen Subsequently Revealed Herself as an Enemy of Catholicism, and What She Did to Destroy it[1]

Throughout her sister Mary's reign, Elizabeth made an outward show of being a Catholic, though it was said that inwardly she was no such thing. But once she had taken the scepter and the throne and began to reign, she revealed herself for what she was and, deluded by her own ambition and several heretical advisers, decided to alter and transform the Catholic religion. For, seeing that she had been born to a marriage condemned by the Apostolic See, and that the sacred canons cast doubt upon her illegitimacy and her right to rule, she chose to disregard them and all church law, so as to avoid any such danger and confusion—accordingly, she attempted to pervert religion itself. To that end, she commanded all Catholic preachers to keep silent,[2] gave permission for

---

1 Sander, *De origine ac progressu*, 366–68.

 Much of this chapter is based on Ribadeneyra's own recollections of his time in England. On January 20, 1559, he wrote to Laínez, "I have already written how the queen died on November 17 and Cardinal Pole fourteen hours later. Since then have followed the acclamation and coronation of this new queen, Elizabeth, who, having been raised from childhood with no such pure milk as her sister, has thus far shown neither the same good will nor the same sincere heart in matters of religion, in which, though as yet there has been no universal alteration, there have nevertheless been such beginnings as we can hope for nothing but a ruinous conclusion. For they have ordered the litany to be said in English, removing the invocation to the saints; they have provided that the Mass be said as it is in the queen's chapel, in which last Sunday, the fifteenth, neither the host nor the chalice was elevated in the solemn Mass for her coronation. She orders that no one should preach anything but the Gospels, the letters of Paul, the Pater Noster, and the Credo—and this said in English and without any further explication. She has confined one bishop to his house because while preaching in honor of Queen Mary he urged the bishops, like good dogs, to bark and chase off the wolves that were to come, and so on. With these winds blowing up, Your Paternity can easily fathom the storm that is to follow if our Lord in his mercy does not prevent it. These things have the heretics here utterly smug, the Catholics utterly downcast—even though they are without comparison more numerous in the kingdom than the heretics. The count of Feria does all he can to prevent harm coming to religion, or at least less than the devil would desire, and in this the Lord's favor is crucial." *MHSIR*, 1:311.

2 On December 27, 1558, a royal proclamation prohibited preaching and public prayer, save in English and on the Gospels, Pauline Epistles, or the Ten Commandments. *TRP*, 2:102–03.

the exiled heretics to return,[3] and, with a bishop standing before her, ready to say Mass, forbade the elevation of the consecrated host.[4] On this account, the bishop of York, to whom it pertained to anoint her as queen (Cardinal Pole, who was archbishop of Canterbury and primate of England, being now dead), refused to do so, as did every other bishop save one, who was weak, the last and the least of all.[5] Yet because she would not be moved, in spite of their scruples, and it was said she had not entered by the proper door, nor observed the ancient ceremonies that law and tradition prescribed for royal coronations, she took a solemn oath to defend the Catholic faith and preserve ecclesiastical privileges and liberties.[6] For the heretics who advised her told her that anything at all could be feigned or dissembled, sworn or perjured for the sake of seizing power. For the same reason, she allowed herself to be anointed with the consecrated oil, although as they anointed her she turned to her ladies and said in mockery and derision, "Keep back, lest the awful smell of this oil offend you."

I was in London at this time, in the house of Don Gómez de Figueroa, then count and later duke of Feria, who had been sent by his lord, the Catholic King Don Philip, to visit, serve, and attend upon his ailing wife, Queen Doña Mary. His Majesty could not do so in person, as he wished, being occupied in the war against France. And as the duke was so zealous for our sacred religion,[7] and so devoted to the Society of Jesus, he desired me, as one thereof, to accompany

---

3 More than three hundred Marian exiles are known to have returned to England with Elizabeth's accession. N.M. Sutherland, "The Marian Exiles and the Establishment of the Elizabethan Regime," *Archiv für Reformationsgeschichte* 78 (1987): 253–86, here 255.

4 Owen Oglethorpe, bishop of Carlisle (c.1503–59). As Suárez de Figueroa wrote to the emperor on December 29, 1558, "On the Sunday of Christmas-tide the Queen before going to Mass sent for the bishop of Carlisle, who was to officiate, and told him that he need not elevate the Host for adoration. The Bishop answered that Her Majesty was mistress of his body and life, but not of his conscience, and accordingly she heard the Mass until after the gospel, when she rose and left, so as not to be present at the canon and adoration of the Host which the Bishop elevated as usual." *CSPSE*, 1:6.

   Cf. *CSPV*, 7:2; *CSPR*, 1:3.

5 Only Oglethorpe, diocesan of one of the poorest sees in England, could be prevailed upon to anoint and crown Elizabeth. William P. Haugaard, "The Coronation of Elizabeth I," *JEH* 19, no. 2 (October 1968): 161–70, here 161.

6 The actual formula of Elizabeth's coronation oath has been lost, but it likely resembled the established wording that had the monarch swear they "would permit the church to enjoy its liberties." William Cooke Taylor, *Chapters on Coronations* (London: J.W. Parker, 1838), 106.

7 This phrase, "zeloso de nuestra santa Religion" is ambiguous: it could be translated variously as "zealous for our sacred religion," with *religion* denoting the Catholic faith, or as "zealous for our sacred order," with *religion* signifying the Society of Jesus. I have opted for the former,

him.[8] He resided in London for several months after the queen's death, representing the king his master with considerable influence, spirit, and prudence. One of the things the duke did, like a Catholic and a valiant knight, was that when he was begged and entreated on Queen Elizabeth's behalf to attend her coronation ceremony and festivities, as he had those of her procession through the city of London and those of her taking possession of the kingdom,[9] he asked whether this coronation would observe all the rites customary in the crowning of other Christian kings of England,[10] according to the practice of our holy mother the Roman Church. And when he learned that there was to be some alteration, nothing could induce him to attend the ceremony, nor enter the church, publicly or privately, neither with the other grandees of the realm nor alone upon a dais (as they had wanted), lest his presence legitimate that impious act, and to offer an example of the proper caution and circumspection Catholics should use in such matters, however trivial they might seem, to avoid contamination.[11]

The new queen filled her household with numerous servants of the new and perverted religion—or, properly speaking, of none at all. One of these was William Cecil, who had been secretary to King Edward VI, a wise man, prompt and able in all affairs, whose genius, cunning, and conscience were all wondrously at his command in whatever he did—and so in the reign of Queen Mary he had made such a show of being Catholic that one could not have asked for a better.[12] He approached Queen Elizabeth with high hopes of favor and wealth:

---

as the second descriptor, "tan deuoto de la Compañia de Iesus," seems to me a more specific modifier of the previous general statement.

8   Cf. The report of the Venetian ambassador Michele Surian (dates unknown, *fl.* mid-sixteenth century), October 29, 1558: "A few days ago his Majesty received news from England that the Queen was grievously ill, and her life in danger, which intelligence, most especially at the present moment, being of very great importance, so disquieted his Majesty and all these Lords that it was immediately determined to send the Count de Feria to visit the Queen in the name of her consort." *cspv*, 6:1274.

9   On November 28, 1558, Elizabeth made her entry into the capital and formally took possession of the Tower of London. On January 14, 1559, the day before her coronation, she ceremonially processed through London to Westminster. Christopher Haigh *Elizabeth I*, 2nd ed., Profiles in Power (Harlow: Longman Group, 1998), 9. MacCaffrey, *Elizabeth I*, 43.

10   The specification of *English* coronation practice is added in the 1595 edition.

11   Suárez de Figueroa escaped the obligation to attend the full coronation on the pretext of ill health, as Philip II later wrote: "In the matter of the Queen's coronation you behaved as was proper since with only accompanying her to the doorway and begging-off the Mass, pleading illness, she should have been satisfied." Haugaard, "Coronation," 165.

12   From 1550, William Cecil, first Baron Burghley, had served as a secretary of state under Edward VI. He went into retirement under Queen Mary, returning to public life under

if she was to uproot the Catholic religion, ignoring the advice of the prelates and nobles of the realm, she might wish to listen to him and have his counsel. Having gained access to the queen, he took as his partner-in-crime the jurist Thomas Bacon[*sic*], his kinsman and a man of the same pernicious inclination as himself, whom he arranged to exalt with honors and endow with riches, to better his hold over him and turn him against the Catholic faith.[13] These two have been the leading ministers in the queen's council and the administration of the realm, although in the royal palace, the foremost favorite has been Robert Dudley, one of the duke of Northumberland's sons, who, condemned alongside his brothers as a traitor, had been pardoned by Queen Mary. He so won Elizabeth's grace and goodwill that he conceived hopes of marrying her, his wife having died quite conveniently in a sudden mishap—plotted and planned by him.[14]

Elizabeth, who relied upon him as one of her foremost advisers and administrators. Wallace T. MacCaffrey, "Cecil, William, first Baron Burghley (1520/21–1598)," in *ODNB*, 10:778–94, here 779.

"We find two William Cecils in Mary's reign: one is a secret critic of the Queen and her government; the other is a loyal subject who is happy to live with a Catholic monarch." Stephen Alford, *Burghley: William Cecil at the Court of Elizabeth I* (New Haven: Yale University Press, 2008), 65.

13 Almost certainly Ribadeneyra's error for Sir Nicholas Bacon (1510–79)—correctly identified in *De origine ac progressu* as "Nicholao Bacono"—Cecil's brother-in-law (their wives were sisters). Bacon, a successful lawyer, became lord keeper of the great seal in 1558, in which capacity he presided over the House of Lords. Robert Tittler, "Bacon, Sir Nicholas (1510–1579)," in *ODNB*, 3:165–70, here 165–67. Sander, *De origine ac progressu*, 367.

14 Robert Dudley, imprisoned in 1553 for participation in his father's attempted coup, was released in October 1554. He subsequently became one of Elizabeth's favorites, and, after the mysterious death of his wife Amy (*née* Robsart, 1532–60), was considered a leading candidate for the queen's hand. Adams, "Dudley, Robert," in *ODNB*, 17:95–97.

The Parliament Convened by the Queen, and How She Made it Decide as She Desired[1]

But because the queen could not undo the statutes parliament had passed in favor of Catholicism in her sister's reign by her own authority, nor alter them or warp them as she wished without the power of parliament, she arranged for it to convene in London soon afterwards. This makes sense only if one understands that in that kingdom they do not handle religious matters through rebellions and uprisings, by fire and blood, as has happened in the kingdoms of France and Scotland and in the provinces of Flanders, but rather propagate and establish their heresies under the cover of laws, royal edicts, decrees, and parliamentary statutes. This has been their subtle, cunning scheme, bolstered by the power of queen and crown, the better to ingrain their wickedness and their sects of perdition.[2] The parliament of the realm is divided into two chambers: in one are gathered the bishops, prelates, lords, and noblemen of the kingdom, and this is called the upper chamber; into the other, which is the lower chamber, enter private gentlemen (usually delegates of the counties) and other men of rank and prominent citizens, who come as advocates for the cities and major towns and who have a vote. Therefore, to realize in this parliament her plots against the Catholic faith, the queen arranged for the cities and provinces to send representatives and delegates who, being tainted with heresy, favored changes to religion. Thus it was that few difficulties were encountered in getting the second, lower chamber to approve all the queen's proposals.[3] But since all the bishops, deeply learned and utterly steadfast, and many of the lords (Catholics bound to Queen Mary) opposed the queen's will, both for the sake of truth and because it seemed a shocking lightness to reverse everything done only a few years ago, sworn to in the kingdom's reconciliation and affirmed by the ambassadors sent to Rome, and she was unable to get away with her scheme, the queen decided to hoodwink a few of the more

---

1 Sander, *De origine ac progressu*, 365–66, 376–80.

2 2 Pet. 2:1.

3 The religious leanings of Elizabeth's first House of Commons have been variously interpreted. Christopher Haigh argues that the strength of its Protestant sentiment has been greatly exaggerated: as he points out, only nineteen Marian exiles were elected, several of whom were still abroad when parliament met. Haigh, *English Reformations*, 241.

influential lords, and get the rest through them.[4] And so she dangled before the earl of Arundel the hope that she might marry him,[5] and before the duke of Norfolk that she would get him the papal dispensation he had been unable to attain,[6] and with these, and other promises and bribes to others, she acquired a majority of the votes and so got her way. Notwithstanding all her determination, cunning, and trickery, there were only three more votes to alter the Catholic faith than to preserve it.[7] As soon as she had won, she spurned the earl of Arundel, just as to this day she has spurned many others who thought to marry her, saying that she wishes to remain a virgin, so that over her tomb it might be written, *Here lies Elizabeth, who was queen so many years, and all her life a maiden*.[8] And she repaid the duke of Norfolk for his service in this way: after many travails, troubles, and slanders, she took his life.[9] However, we may

---

4   Suárez de Figueroa wrote on February 12, 1559, "The Queen has entire disposal of the upper Chamber in a way never seen before in previous Parliaments, as in this there are several who have hopes of getting her to marry them, and they are careful to please her in all things and persuade the others to do the same, besides which there are a great number whom she has made barons to strengthen her party, and that accursed cardinal left twelve bishoprics to be filled which will now be given to as many ministers of Lucifer instead of being worthily bestowed." *CSPSE*, 1:15.

5   Henry Fitzalan entertained hopes of marrying Elizabeth soon after her accession; Suárez de Figueroa wrote home that Elizabeth "joked with me about what had been said of her marriage to the earl of Arundel. She does not get on with him." Lock, "Fitzalan, Henry," in *ODNB*, 19:762.

6   At Elizabeth's accession, Thomas Howard had been negotiating at Rome for months, seeking a dispensation to marry his cousin, Margaret Audley (1540–64). After Mary's death, Thomas broke off his suit at Rome and married Audley; the match received parliamentary sanction in 1559. Graves, "Howard, Thomas," in *ODNB*, 28:430.

7   The first acts passed by Elizabeth's parliament included one reviving the royal supremacy and abolishing papal authority (1 Eliz. 1. c. 1), another undoing the Marian religious settlement and reinstating Edwardian policies, such as the *Book of Common Prayer* (1 Eliz. 1. c. 2), and another reclaiming first fruits, tithes, and rents for the Crown (1 Eliz. 1. c. 4). See *SR*, 4.1:350–64.

     The second of these, the Act of Uniformity, passed through the house of lords by a vote of twenty-one to eighteen; as Christopher Haigh colorfully puts it, "The Church of England was established by the merest whisker, a margin of three votes: a margin achieved by political chicanery, and by keeping the Church rather more Catholic than had been planned." Haigh, *English Reformations*, 241.

8   Pressed by her first parliament to marry, Elizabeth is said to have replied, "And for me it shall be sufficient, that a marble stone declare that a queene, hauing reigned such a time, liued and died a virgine." Holinshed, *Chronicles*, 4:179.

9   Norfolk was executed for treason on June 2, 1572, for his participation in the Ridolfi Plot and his proposed marriage to Mary Queen of Scots. Haigh, *Elizabeth I*, 61, 149.

see this as the just punishment of God, for the duke had persuaded several of his allies in parliament, and by his authority the Catholic faith in England was destroyed and overthrown. During the debate over this shameful alteration, a pious and sober matron of London came to the duke and told him, "When you gave your vote to the heretics to destroy religion, you forgot (as I believe) that your illustrious person and your family have been abused and downtrodden by the heretics, and restored by Queen Mary of sacred memory, exalted and placed in that lofty degree of dignity you now possess. But because you have done this, and loved the glory of men more than that of God,[10] God will take these new men as an instrument to punish you, and with you all the ancient nobility of the realm, for consenting to this sin." These were the good woman's words, and history has proven their truth.

---

10   John 12:43.

How the Queen Named Herself Supreme Governor of the Church, and of the Laws Enacted about This[1]

The first thing the queen wanted was to be acknowledged and addressed as supreme governor of the Church in all spiritual affairs.[2] She took this title of governor because as a woman she could not properly be called supreme head of the Church—which title even Calvin, that arch-heretic and Antichrist, had denounced in her father King Henry.[3] In order to be recognized as governor, she ordered all archbishops, bishops, and prelates of the kingdom, and all clergymen, under the direst penalties, to make a solemn and abominable oath according to this formula:

> I, N., attest and declare in my conscience that the queen alone is the su-
> preme governor of the kingdom of England, and of the other territories
> and states subject to Her Majesty, not less in matters spiritual and eccle-
> siastical than in temporal and civil, and that no foreign monarch, person,
> prelate, state, or power possesses, in deed or in law, any ecclesiastical or
> spiritual jurisdiction, rule, supremacy, preeminence, or authority in this
> realm. Therefore, I renounce and repudiate entirely all such jurisdictions,
> powers, supremacies, and authorities.[4]

---

1 Sander, *De origine ac progressu*, 362, 368–73.

2 Elizabeth opted to forego the title of supreme head, preferring supreme governor as more acceptable to conservative opinion. Haigh, *English Reformations*, 240.

    Cf. a report sent to the Vatican in March 1559. "It is said that the Queen, seeing the great controversy that is raised by this accursed title of Supreme Head of the Anglican Church, is resolved to have no more of it." *CSPR*, 1:16.

3 Though Ribadeneyra has described several figures as "Calvinist," this is the first appearance of the reformer of Geneva himself. In his commentary on Amos (1567), John Calvin (1509–64) wrote, "They who at first extolled Henry, King of England, were certainly inconsiderate men; they gave him the supreme power in all things: and this always vexed me grievously; for they were guilty of blasphemy when they called him the chief Head of the Church under Christ." John Calvin, *Commentaries on the Twelve Minor Prophets*, trans. John Owen, 5 vols. (Grand Rapids: William B. Eerdmans Publishing Company, 1950), 2:359.

4 1 Eliz. 1. c. 1, §9. See *SR*, 4:352.

And because some knights and lords rejected this oath, saying that they could not take it in good conscience, the queen outwitted them by agreeing that lay lords need not swear, so long as the churchmen were obligated, and that it should be thus decreed in parliament. And so it was done. The laymen, imagining they had now escaped, took no notice of what happened to the bishops and pastors, who were thus left abandoned and trapped. And this was God's punishment. For in the days of King Henry, when it was proposed to pillage the monasteries and rob the religious of their property, the bishops had abandoned and deserted them: now, the laymen had forsaken the churchmen. Yet the laymen could not praise all this for long, since many of them had paid for it, and in future all would pay even more.

There were some who hazarded doubts and questions as to what was included within this title of "supreme governor of the Church." The queen had it proclaimed in a certain visitation that it was the same as the title of head of the Church given to her father and brother, nothing more.[5] And lest there be any doubt as what was entailed by her spiritual power, parliament made the following laws and declarations:

1. All privileges and all preeminences, prerogatives, and spiritual supremacies that might stem from any human or ecclesiastical power or law whatsoever for the visitation, correction, or reform of the clergy or any sort of ecclesiastic, and for the identification and punishment of all errors, heresies, schisms, abuses, etcetera, we will henceforth to be annexed and united in perpetuity to the royal crown.[6]

2. We declare that the queen and her heirs and successors to the throne hereafter have, and ought to have, plenary and absolute power to nominate and replace whomever they please for the exercise of the said ecclesiastical jurisdiction, in their name and at their pleasure, for the period they determine. Those so appointed may inspect individuals, punish heresies, schisms, errors, and abuses—that is to say, to exercise every power or authority that any other ecclesiastical magistrate is or has been able to employ.[7]

---

5   A series of royal injunctions issued in 1559 included "An admonition to simple men deceived by malicious," which insisted that "certainly her majesty neither doth, nor ever will, challenge any authority than that was challenged and lately used by the said noble kings of famous memory, King Henry VIII, and King Edward VI, which is, and was of ancient time, due to the imperial crown of this realm." Frere and Kennedy, *Articles and Injunctions*, 3:26.

6   1 Eliz. 1. c. 1, §6. See *SR*, 4.1:352.

7   1 Eliz. 1. c. 1, §8. See ibid., 4.1:352.

3.   We also proclaim that no cleric may attend any synod not convened by the letters and mandates of Her Majesty, nor make or enforce any canon, law, or constitution—synodal or provincial—without Her Majesty's express consent and permission to make, publish, or execute the said canons, under penalty of imprisonment and other punishments at the determination of Her Majesty.[8]

4.   It is further commanded that none shall depart Her Majesty's kingdom or territories for any visitation, council, meeting, or congregation assembled for religious purposes, unless such things are done by royal authority and within the country.

5.   Further, that bishops may not be appointed or ordained by any nomination, election, or authority, save the queen's, and that they neither possess nor exercise the episcopal jurisdiction and power save by the queen's assent, nor in any other manner but through her or through authority derived from Her Royal Majesty.[9]

These were the laws parliament enacted, and the queen accordingly appointed laymen as her commissioners and representatives to exercise power in all spiritual matters and over all ecclesiastical persons and to preside over the meetings of the churches, and to whom appeal might be made against the bishops, as was related in the discussion of King Edward.[10] And it is a frightful thing to see the blindness of men thought to be rational and pragmatic, that they do not see the monstrousness of such deranged decrees and laws, and who desire a woman (who, according to the Apostle, may not preach or speak in the church)[11] as the head of the Church and as judge over the entire ecclesiastical power in her kingdom. As Saint John Chrysostom says, *Quando de Ecclesiae praefectura agitur, universa quidem muliebris natura functionis istius moli, ac magnitudini cedat oportet.* "When the leadership of the church is discussed, all womankind is to be excluded and kept away from the greatness and the burden of so exalted a charge."[12] For as in the beginning God created woman from man

---

8   This specific provision, and the one that follows, do not appear in the texts of either the Act of Supremacy or the Act of Uniformity. They may refer to the former's numerous prohibitions on foreign ecclesiastical authority of any kind, or the reinstatement of 23 Hen. 8. c. 9 and 24 Hen. 8. c. 12, which restricted appeals to other (especially Roman) ecclesiastical jurisdictions. Ibid., 4.1:350–51.

9   1 Eliz. 1. c. 1, §2. See ibid., 4.1:351.

10   In the margin: "Book 2, Chapter 3."

11   In the margin: "1 Corinthians 14[:34–35]."

12   In the margin: "*On the Priesthood*, Book 2."
        John Chrysostom, *On the Priesthood*, 2.2.

and for man, she is naturally subject, just as Christ is the head of man and God of Christ, as Saint Paul says.[13] And to make clear this subjection of the woman, the same apostle commands that she neither pray nor prophesy without covering her head, out of reverence for the angels of heaven,[14] who are present and attendant upon those who pray and upon the priests and ministers of Christ and the dispensers of the divine mysteries, who are likewise called angels in sacred texts, as Saint Ambrose says.[15] But human wickedness corrupts and perverts everything, and makes it so that she who cannot be at the head of a man is acknowledged and treated as supreme and sovereign head of the Church next to Christ, and temporal matters are confounded with ecclesiastical ones, the corporal with the spiritual, Caesar with God.[16] And they remove all order and distinction between the government of souls and that of bodies, between the political, which looks to the peace and tranquility of the commonwealth, and the spiritual and the divine, which is directed toward knowing, loving, and serving the true God and, by these means and rooted in the blood of Jesus Christ, toward achieving the glory that endures forevermore.[17] For they are delirious, monstrous, hateful, terrifying, and horrible, a chaos of confusion and an ocean and abyss without bottom of infinite outrages and crimes. But let us continue with what we have begun.

---

13   Eph. 5:22–24.

14   In the margin: "1 Corinthians 11[:5–6, 10]."

15   In the margin: "Volume 4; Chapter 2 of *The Mysteries*."

  The Mysteries (c.387) appears in the fourth volume of the major sixteenth-century collected edition of Ambrose's works: Ambrose of Milan, *Omnia quotquot extant D. Ambrosii episcopi Mediolanensis opera, primum per Des. Erasmum Roterodamum, mox per Sig. Gelenium, deinde per alios eruditos viros dilingenter castigata: nunc verô postremòm per Joannem Costerium emendata quae singulis tomis contineantur, cum catalogus eorum post vitam D. Ambrosii succedens, tum epistolae Erasmi cuilibet sectioni seorsum praemissae docebunt; Index geminus adiectus est foecundissimus*, ed. Desiderius Erasmus, Sigismund Gelenius, and Johannes Costerius, 5 vols. (Basel: Hieronymus I Froben & Nikolaus I Episcopius, 1555), 4:421–28.

16   Cf. Matt. 22:21; Mark 12:17; Luke 20:25.

17   Ps. 103:31.

The Persecution Initiated against the Catholics for Refusing to Recognize the Queen as Head of the Church[1]

The queen, seeing herself by the passage of these statutes acknowledged and obeyed as supreme governor of the Church, trampling and disdaining the authority of the Apostolic See, began to wield her tyrannical power over spiritual matters. First of all, she arrogated to herself all the ecclesiastical incomes, bequests, and holdings that the queen her sister had relinquished and restored to the churches and monasteries for divine worship and the support of the religious.[2] She appointed deputies and commissioners in spiritual matters, gave them a special seal, annulled all the ancient laws passed for the punishment of heretics, and removed the Mass and the forms of administering the sacraments and reciting divine offices—although out of respect for the duke of Feria she held off from the Mass for several months. She ordained new ceremonies in an utter perversion of divine worship, which she ordered to be celebrated in the vulgar tongue, following in the footsteps of her brother Edward.[3] All this was decided and enacted in parliament, contradicted and opposed with great spirit and zeal by every clergyman and bishop, who alone were the proper judges thereof, as Saint Ambrose wrote to Emperor Valentinian in these words:

> When have you heard, O most clement emperor, that in a matter of faith the laymen have judged the bishops? Is it possible that flattery is so powerful among us that it has perverted us, and we have forgotten the rights of the priesthood? To entrust to others what God has given to us? If the

---

1 Sander, *De origine ac progressu*, 381–85, 390–94.

2 1 Eliz. 1. c. 4 reversed Mary's relinquishment of ecclesiastical incomes. 1 Eliz. c. 24 seized the property of the few monastic houses Mary had managed to reestablish. See sr, 4.1:359–64 and 4.1:397–400, respectively.

3 The Act of Uniformity (1 Eliz. 1. c. 2) resurrected much of the Edwardian church settlement, including English-language services. The deadline for implementation was set for the feast of Saint John the Baptist (June 24), though it is doubtful that this had much to do with the Spanish ambassador. See ibid., 4.1:355–58.

Section 6 of 1 Eliz. 1. c. 1 provided for the repeal of 1 and 2 Phil. and Mar. c. 6, which had revived three medieval statutes against heresy. See ibid., 4.1:351–52.

bishop must be instructed by the layman, what will come of it? Shall the layman discourse and the bishop listen, and then the bishop is to learn from the layman? Truly, if we examine Holy Scripture, or ancient days, we shall find, without the slightest doubt, that in a matters of faith, in a matter, I say, of faith, the bishops have always been the judges of Christian emperors, and not the emperors of the bishops.[4]

These are the words of Saint Ambrose.

Now, as the prelates refused to consent to so manifest a sacrilege, or to acknowledge the queen as supreme governor of the Church, all thirteen of them, learned and distinguished to a man, were deposed from their thrones (except one)[5] and robbed of their titles; with the utmost constancy and sufferance, they ended their pilgrimage in prison cells, giving their lives for the Catholic faith. So influential was the example of these saintly and renowned churchmen that it moved the majority of the clergy to imitate them: thus it was that most of the ecclesiastics who possessed church prebends and dignities either abandoned them and fled the kingdom, or were stripped of them, to be given to heretics. Numerous religious of every order did the same and left England, along with three entire communities of monks and nuns.[6] In this as in the rest, the duke of Feria demonstrated his piety and fortitude. For, when he saw the business coming to a bad end and every means failing to persuade the queen and her council not to deface and pervert the Catholic religion, he implored the queen for the favor of giving him every monk and nun in the kingdom, to send them abroad to places where they might freely observe their vows. He succeeded, to the distress of the heretics and the councilors, who had desired to wash their hands in the blood of the servants of God,[7] and had created many difficulties and alleged many obstacles on the issue. Nevertheless, so effective was the duke's zeal and bravery that he gathered the religious and brought them to his house, where he sustained them and secured their passage to Flanders.

---

4   In the margin: "Book 5, Letter 32."

    Ambrose of Milan, *Letters*, 21.4.

    In the edition Ribadeneyra used, Ambrose's letters are divided into ten books, this one listed as 5.22 (the marginal annotation is probably an error, either on Ribadeneyra or the typesetter's part). Cf. Ambrose, *Omnia*, 3.122.

5   Anthony Kitchin.

6   David Lewis identifies these as "the Friars Observant from Greenwich, the Carthusians from Richmond, and the Bridgettines from Sion." Sander, *Anglican Schism*, 261n2.

    Elsewhere, Ribadeneyra will expand this list to include the Dominican nuns of King's Langley: see Book 3, Chapter 11.

7   Ps. 57:11; Isa. 1:15; 59:3.

And when he departed England, he carried many priests with him in his retinue and that of the duchess his wife. Arriving at the court of King Don Philip, he entreated His Majesty to support, honor, and provide for them, which the king did, and has done ever since,[8] with the generosity and piety befitting so Catholic and so mighty a prince.[9] In addition to the religious, a huge number of the Catholic nobility, men and women, were dealt the same fortunes. The flower of the universities, their most distinguished and renowned men, as though blown by a whirlwind, found themselves in the provinces of Flanders, and thence spread and scattered to different corners of Europe. At this time, more than two thirds of the realm was Catholic, and they bridled at the change in religion—even before they had really experienced the unfathomable calamities that heresy brings in its wake. For, leaving to one side the Catholics among the principal lords and knights (who were numerous), almost all the lesser nobility was Catholic, as well as the common, humble people. In particular, the yeomen, who in that kingdom are prosperous and well respected, abominated these novelties. No one embraced them except in the towns near London and the court, in addition to several port cities, where it was usually the debauched, idle people, the uncontrolled, brash youths, wasteful of their own property and covetous of their neighbors', women of light virtue and heavy sins [*mugeres livianas y cargadas de pecados*], and, in conclusion, the filth and garbage of the entire nation.

For this reason, many Catholics either fled the country or resisted these innovations and alterations, hearkening back to the reconciliation the kingdom had so recently made with the Roman Church. But when the queen began to enforce her sacrilegious laws with dire penalties, and viciously to persecute those who did not obey, many quailed out of fear for their worldly goods. And although they were Catholics in their hearts and believed what our holy mother Church believes, they did not fail to obey the royal and parliamentary mandates: they simultaneously took the sacraments as Catholics in secret and in public as heretics. And they attended the Calvinists' temples, heard their sermons, and polluted themselves with their blasphemous ceremonies, partaking of the chalice of the Lord and that of the demons, joining Christ and Belial, as had been done in the time of King Edward.[10] This weakness and pusillanimity

---

8   This clause is added in the 1595 edition.

9   With no little effort, the count of Feria prevailed upon Elizabethan to allow him to relocate Catholic nobles to the continent, eventually effecting the removal of more than sixty persons. The count and his wife left England in 1559, Gómez in May and Jane in July, each taking several more English Catholics with them. Crummé, "Jane Dormer's Recipe," 58.

10   1 Cor. 10:21; 2 Cor. 6:14–15.

among the Catholics gave the heretics the boldness to carry their enterprise further, in the manner described in the next chapter. Observe and mark all this, and learn the vigilance and care with which heresies must be opposed in their beginnings, and how this infernal fire gathers strength unless it is checked before it catches and grows.

The Form the Queen Provided for Church Governance[1]

And so the queen began to consider the spiritual governance of the realm, and as supreme governor of the Church, to arrange and manipulate all its parts, as per the abominable laws passed in parliament. Before all else, she appointed her visitors, to travel throughout the kingdom and observe how the laws had been observed, and whether any trace or hint of divine worship, piety, or the Catholic faith remained—in the manner of King Edward her brother, as we related, but with even greater rigor and violence.[2] After this, she busied herself with distributing honors, sharing out benefices, providing the formula for the ordination of clerics and the consecration of bishops, as well as the titles and duties each was to hold and the vestments they were to use in the pulpit, in the church, and abroad. She removed some elements of the ceremonies and ancient rites of the Catholic Church and left others, such as she imagined would most win her the reputation of a thoughtful, wise, and experienced woman, and such as would best deceive the Catholics. For the same reason, she ordered the burning of several heretics who had come from France and had not wholly conformed to the heretics of her kingdom, having rather sparked fierce debates and conflicts with one another.[3] She refused to allow her new clerics and ministers to go about in secular clothes, as they wished—instead, she ordered

---

1 Sander, *De origine ac progressu*, 391–404, 406–09.

2 In the first year of her reign, Elizabeth ordered a visitation of English churches to ensure compliance with the Act of Uniformity, including the use of English in ceremonial and the abolition of superstitious images. See Frere and Kennedy, *Articles and Injunctions*, 3:8–29.

3 Ribadeneyra has condensed the text of *De origine ac progressu*: "Afterwards, there were huge conflicts among these churches and new English synagogues, such that several of the French ministers were eventually forced to flee, and some of their compatriots were put to the flames [*Inter quas postea ecclesias, & nouas has Angloru[m] synagogas, magna extitit digladiatio, adeò quide[m], ut ex ministris Gallicanis no[n]nulli sint postea coacti discedere, & ex illis contubernijs aliquot etiam ignibus traditi*]." Sander, *De origine ac progressu*, 398.

David Lewis identifies those burned with two *Dutch* Anabaptists, Jan Wielmacker (d.1575) and Hendrik Ter Woort (d.1575), executed as heretics at Smithfield on July 22, 1575: neither edition of Sander distinguishes the nationality of the expelled clergy and those burned, however, and so we can hardly fault Ribadeneyra for assuming the latter were likewise French. Sander, *Anglican Schism*, 274n3.

that in church they use vestments and surplices, and clerical garb in public, with rochets for the bishops.[4] Nor did she consent to alter the names of the ancient titles and customary offices of the Catholic Church, as they desired: instead, they were called archbishops, bishops, presbyters, deacons, superiors, deans, archdeacons, canons, just as we use, and enjoyed the dignities, titles, and incomes thereof. And she even proposed that the abbot of Westminster Abbey and his monks, who had returned to their house in Queen Mary's reign, should remain there and retain peaceful possession and pray to God for her, so long as they obeyed the laws and decrees of parliament—which they refused.[5] All this she did to preserve the luster and outward pomp of the clergy, whose head she was said to be, and to signal that her creed was not much different from the Catholic faith and that she had a mind to return to thereto, and thereby to delude and deceive various Catholic princes, whom she offered hopes of marriage. And furthermore, to use this official, exterior policy to curb the heretics, who, as though stirred up by Satan, refused to use anything that had any trace of the Catholic Church they so abominated. Thus they disrupted the order and marred the beauty and confounded and perverted all the harmony and sound arrangements of the ecclesiastical hierarchy. She ordered that they use organs, music, crucifixes, tapers, and copes in the churches, and so it was observed for a long time. Indeed, whenever she traveled and entered some city, she delighted in the clergy ceremonially coming forth to receive her, dressed in sacred vestments, and in festivals and celebrations in the churches. For the same reason, she forbade the removal of the bells, thoroughly enjoying when they were rung and played as she passed by a church (for all this she thought of as majesty and greatness), as well as using them to exalt the two festivals of her birth and her coronation, which the whole realm celebrated each year at her command. The day of her birth (September 7) was marked with large, colored letters, and the following day, that of the glorious Nativity of the Blessed Virgin

---

4   Elizabeth's 1559 injunctions stated that, "Her majesty [...] willeth and commandeth that all archbishops and bishops, and all other that be called or admitted to preaching or ministry of the sacraments, or that be admitted into vocation ecclesiastical, or into any society of learning in either of the universities, or elsewhere, shall use and wear such seemly habits, garments, and such square caps, as were most commonly and orderly received in the latter year of the reign of King Edward VI." These provisions proved contentious among the more radical reformers, reigniting the "Vestments Controversy," begun in Edward's reign, over whether a godly church could admit of such finery. Frere and Kennedy, *Articles and Injunctions*, 3:20.

5   John Feckenham (c.1510–84) became abbot of Westminster in 1555. It was rumored that he was offered toleration for himself and the monks at Westminster, if they agreed to accept a Protestant liturgy, but this has been dismissed by modern scholars. C.S. Knighton, "Feckenham [Howman], John (c.1510–1584)," in *ODNB*, 19:228–30, here 229.

Mary, in tiny black letters, for the queen has abolished her principal feasts, those of her Immaculate Conception, Nativity, and sublime Assumption.[6] And some even write (how astounding, how diabolical!) that in the largest church in London—and I do not know about the rest of the kingdom—in place of the antiphony that we Catholics use (and which had been used in England before the invasion of that sect of perdition) to conclude compline by lauding our Lady and imploring her favor, now they sing the praises of Elizabeth! She ordered the observance of fasts or abstinence from flesh on Fridays and Saturdays, adding Wednesday, and at the beginning of each Lent she promulgates an edict forbidding meat to be eaten, under the gravest penalties[7]—not for the sake of penitence, or faith, or devotion, or the fulfillment of God's command, but rather for the prosperity and sound governance of the kingdom, so that the many fishermen may win their bread,[8] and so that during the year there will be a greater supply of meat and greater ease in provisioning her fleets.[9] And she enforces this law, levies punishments on those who disobey, and, as supreme head, grants dispensations from the fasts—but not without a settlement and the payment of a fee.[10]

---

6   December 8, September 8, and August 15, respectively.

7   See, for example, the 1560 proclamation on Lenten fasting, which provided for a penalty of twenty pounds for each offense. *TRP*, 2:139–40.

8   An official homily on fasting explained, "As when any Realme in consyderation of the mainteyning of fissher townes borderyng upon the seas, and for the encrease of fisshermen, of whom do spring Mariners to go upon the sea, to the furnishing of the nauie of the Realme." John Jewel, *Certain Sermons or Homilies Appointed to Be Read in Churches*, 2 vols. (London: Richard Iugge and Iohn Cawood, 1571), 2:185.

9   5 Eliz. 1. c. 5 provided that "Every Wednesdaye in the Weeke through the whole year, w[hich] heretofore hathe not by the Lawes or Customes of this Realme bene used and observed as a Fishe Daye, and w[hich] shall not happen to fall in Christmas Weeke or Easter Week, shalbe hereafter obs[er]ved and kepte as the Saturdays in every Weeke bee or ought to be: And so that no mater of p[er]son shall eate any Fleshe on the same day, otherwise then ought to bee upon the co[m]mon Saterdaye. [...] yt shall not bee laufull to any p[er]son or p[er]sons w[ith]in this Realme, to eate any Fleshe upon any Dayes nowe usually observed as Fishe Days, or upon any Wednesdaye nowe newly lymitted to bee observed as Fishe Daye; upon payne that every p[er]son offending herein shall forfeite Three Powndes for every tyme he or they shall offene, or els suffer Three Monethes close Imprisonement w[ith]out Baile or Mayneprise." *SR*, 4.1:424.

10   One contemporary wrote of the archbishop of Canterbury, "He has also the court of faculties, where, on the payment beforehand of a pretty large sum of money, license are obtained for non-residence, plurality of benefices, dispensations for forbidden meats on the third, fifth, and sixth holiday, the vigils of the saints, Lent, and the ember days at the

King Edward, as has been said, abrogated in parliament all the canons and ecclesiastical laws that prohibited the clergy and religious from marrying and declared their children spurious and illegitimate. Queen Mary revoked everything her brother had done, desiring that the sacred canons on this subject be observed and stand in all force and strength. The heretics have expended their utmost efforts in undoing what Queen Mary did and confirming what Edward decreed, but they have not been able to get away with it. For Elizabeth, who so prides herself as a maiden, who says she will not wed, so as to preserve her virginity, has refused to assent. The truth is that they marry for the first, and second, and third time, usually with fallen women of ill-repute (for no others can be found, even among the heretics themselves, who will have them), but they are not regarded as proper marriages, nor do they seem to be so, but rather like concubinage. Throughout the kingdom the women are taken for and treated like whores and the children like illegitimate bastards.[11] And the preachers of this new gospel are so lustful that they believe they could never observe chastity, but instead like beasts follow their sensuality and appetite.[12] And they are so shameless, being usually gamesome and roguish youths, that they do not mount the pulpit unless ornamented, beautified, and made up, in order to stir up some young woman to senseless, shameful love by their gestures, clothing, words, and expressions, and to trick her into marriage. But such is the Gospel of such preachers, and this is the way it ought to be preached.

---

four seasons; for almost all these are seasons of abstinence from flesh." Robinson, *Zurich Letters*, 271.

11   In 1566, two English evangelicals sent Heinrich Bullinger a list of defects remaining in the Church of England; among them, they complained that "The marriage of the clergy is not allowed and sanctioned by the public laws of the kingdom, but their children are by some persons regarded as illegitimate." Ibid., 239.

12   Rom. 16:18; Phil. 3:18–19; 2 Pet. 2:12; Jude 1:10.

The Means the Pope and Other Christian Monarchs Took to Recall the Queen, and the Sentence Pope Pius V Rendered against Her[1]

Through these methods of the queen's and the rigor and violence of her ministers, heresy made great strides in the country. Hoping to cleanse it and restore the queen to obedience to the Church, and to remove any fear or anxiety (if any she had) of losing her scepter because she was illegitimate, Pope Pius IV, who had succeeded Paul IV,[2] dispatched an apostolic nuncio to England to reassure the queen about the succession if she chose to return to herself, and to beg and entreat her most lovingly not to cast herself and her kingdom into perdition through her hatred and abhorrence for the Apostolic See. But she refused to hear the nuncio, or even to allow him entrance into her realm.[3] What is more, to exercise in all things the office of a merciful father, His Holiness, having ordered the continuation of the Council of Trent, decided to send another nuncio, to tell her at least to send a few of her ministers to the council to discuss with the Catholics the contested points of our holy faith.[4] But her false bishops and ministers, fearing that this would expose their shallowness and ignorance and reveal it to the world, persuaded the queen not to do so.

At the same time, other Catholic monarchs wrote to her not to trust a few unknown, ignorant, malevolent men over all the saints and scholars of Christendom and the ancient princes of her nation. One of their number was Emperor Ferdinand, who also begged her to release the bishops she held prisoner, being

---

1 Sander, *De origine ac progressu*, 412–15, 422–27.

2 Paul IV died on August 18, 1559. Giovanni Angelo Medici (r.1559–65) was elected to succeed him as Pope Pius IV on December 25, 1559.

3 In May 1560, the pope sent the Torinese abbot Vincenzo Parpaglia (dates unknown, *fl.* mid-sixteenth century) as nuncio to England. A former secretary of Reginald Pole's and an intimate of the ultra-Catholic Guise clan, Parpaglia was hardly the most congenial choice, and he was summarily denied admittance to the realm. McCoog, *Our Way of Proceeding?* 50.

4 Pius IV issued the bull *Ad ecclesiae regimen* on November 29, 1560, setting a new session at Trent for the following Easter Sunday, April 6, 1561—although the council did not properly assemble until January 18, 1562. The pope dispatched a nuncio, Girolamo Martinengo (1504–69) to England, but Elizabeth refused him entry, claiming that the presence of a papal nuncio might provoke unrest. John W. O'Malley, *Trent: What Happened at the Council* (Cambridge: Harvard University Press, 2013), 167–68, 170.

men of exemplary life and learning, guiltless of any crime against her, accused and jailed for nothing save wishing to persevere in the ancient faith and communion of all Christians, which the emperor himself followed, and at the very least to allow the Catholics churches in her kingdom, that they might gather to celebrate the divine office according to the practice of the Catholic Church.[5] But she could not be persuaded or softened, either by these letters or by others written by various distinguished persons. Witnessing such intolerable disdain, the Council of Trent contemplated declaring her a heretic and excommunicate, but Emperor Ferdinand himself intervened against this, possibly hoping that she might marry his son the Archduke Ferdinand (for she had given some hope of this) and thereby return and amend.[6] But what the Council of Trent did not do was done some years later by Pius V of holy memory (who had succeeded Pius IV), a brother of the Dominican Order and a saintly man—regarded as such even by the heretics themselves.[7] Like another Phinehas, clad and burning with the zeal and love of God,[8] as he witnessed and lamented the calamities and miseries of a realm so noble, in ages past so Catholic and so

---

5   Holy Roman Emperor Ferdinand I (r.1558–64), Charles V's younger brother.

6   It was actually Ferdinand's third surviving son, Charles II Francis (1540–90) that the emperor intended for Elizabeth—Ferdinand II (1529–95), his second son, was, unbeknownst to much of Europe, already married Philippine Welser (1527–80), daughter of a wealthy merchant family of Augsburg. Paula Sutter Fichtner, *Ferdinand I of Austria: The Politics of Dynasticism in the Age of the Reformation*, East European Monographs 100 (New York: Columbia University Press, 1982), 237–38, 242.

During Sander's attendance at the Council of Trent, he had advocated for a hardline policy on English affairs, arguing that English Catholics must not attend Protestant services and that Elizabeth should be deposed. He is probably the author of a secret memorandum urging the pope to excommunicate the queen. Not unnaturally, Sander has made this out to be a grander affair than it was. As Hubert Jedin recounts, "Militant emigrées in Belgium had been urging since the July session that Queen Elizabeth should be excommunicated by the council as a persecutor of Catholics. The legates had informed Rome of this and had also notified the emperor, who was vehemently against it; Morone had rejected the proposal from the very beginning, as it would involve the council in new difficulties. Such a move, the legates wrote to Rome on June 28, would bring about the 'total ruin' of the remnants of English Catholicism and the deaths of the imprisoned bishops, and indeed the harassment even of those Catholics living in Germany under Protestant rulers might follow. Accordingly, even before the pope had made his position clear, the legates had determined to 'let the matter lie.'" Kilroy, "Paths Coincident," 522. Hubert Jedin, *Geschichte des Konzils von Trient*. 4 vols. (Freiburg: Verlag Herder, 1951–75), 4.2:84–85.

7   Pope Saint Pius V was elected pope on January 8, 1566, after the death of Pius IV on December 9 of the previous year.

8   Num. 25:7–8, 10–11.

pious, as England had been, he hoped, as the universal father and shepherd, to offer a remedy and to restrain the queen. And so he promulgated a bull against her, which, translated from Latin into our Castilian tongue, I have decided to include here, as follows:[9]

> The declaratory sentence of our most holy lord, Pope Pius v, against Elizabeth, pretended queen of England, and the heretics who follow her. In which her subjects and vassals are also freed from any oath, fealty, and obligation of any sort, and those who obey her hereafter are declared excommunicate.
>
> Bishop Pius, servant of the servants of God, as a perpetual memorial.
>
> Jesus Christ our Lord, who reigns on high and has given all power in heaven and on earth[10] to Peter alone, the prince of the apostles, and to Peter's successor the Roman pontiff, has entrusted him with the holy Catholic and Apostolic Church, which is undivided, and given it to the pontiff to be governed with the fullness of his power. He alone has been set as a prince above all nations and above all kingdoms, to uproot and destroy, to ruin and dispel, to plant and build up;[11] preserving the faithful, bound by the chain of charity and the unity of the Spirit, he presents them to the Lord, safe and whole. We, who have been called to the governance of the Church by the benevolence of the Lord, desire to fulfill our obligation and strive with all our diligence and effort to preserve this unity and the Catholic faith (which the Author thereof, to prove the faith of his believers and for our chastisement, has permitted to be oppressed with so many calamities) in its purity.
>
> But the number of the impious has grown so great, and with them their power, that now there is nowhere in the world they have not attempted to infect with their perverse doctrine. Among them, Elizabeth, that slave to sin, the so-called queen of England, has striven with the utmost zeal; to her, as to a safe haven and a secure refuge, have flocked all the cruelest enemies of the Church. As soon as she occupied the throne, she monstrously usurped the position, authority and jurisdiction of supreme head of the Church in England, and has proceeded to destroy and cast down that kingdom, so recently returned to the Catholic faith.

---

9   Sander includes the Latin text of *Regnans in excelsis*: Sander, *De origine ac progressu*, 423–27.

    For a modern text of the bull, see Bilio et al., eds., *Bullarum*, 7:810–11.

10   Matt. 16:18–19.

11   Jer. 1:10.

For she has banned the practice of true religion, which her father, the apostatizing Henry, had devastated, and which Mary, the rightful queen of glorious memory, had restored with the favor of this Holy See. Following and embracing the errors of the heretics, she has thrown her ancient and noble advisers out of the royal council, filling it with lowborn misbelievers. She has oppressed the lovers and devotees of the Catholic faith, exalting false preachers and ministers of wickedness.[12] She has abolished the sacred sacrifice of the Mass, the prayers, the fasts, abstention from flesh, celibacy, and all the other Catholic rites and ceremonies. She has had heretical, pestilential books disseminated throughout the realm, and made the impious mysteries of Calvin, which she has accepted and followed, observed by her subjects and vassals. She has dared to expel the bishops, curates, and other Catholic priests from their churches and deprive them of their benefits; to dispose of these and other ecclesiastical things at her will; to give them to heretics; and to sit as judge in the Church's affairs. She has prohibited the prelates, clergy, and people from recognizing the Roman Church or obeying its mandates and canonical sanctions. She has brutalized many, forcing them to recognize her sacrilegious laws, to abjure the authority and obedience of the Roman pontiff, and to regard her alone as the head of matters temporal and spiritual, and to swear an oath to this effect. She has inflicted grievous punishments and tortures on those who do not obey, which she has meted out upon those who have persevered in the faith and the said obedience. She has imprisoned and oppressed the bishops and Catholic priests, amid such abuse, disease, and pain that many have wretchedly ended the days of their lives. All these things are obvious to every nation, truly infamous, and so fully proven by the most trustworthy testimonies that no space is left to excuse, defend, or deny them. Therefore, seeing that each day the said Elizabeth's sins and misdeeds multiply yet further, and that by her initiative and efforts the persecution of the faithful worsens, as does the destruction of religion, and perceiving too that she is so obstinate and incorrigible that she will neither admit the entreaties and pious advice of Catholic rulers nor permit the nuncios of this Holy See to enter England to discuss some solution with her, we have taken up the arms of justice against her, forced by necessity and not without sharp pain to our soul, considering that we are obliged to chastise one whose ancestors did so much good to the Christian family. And thus armed with the authority of he who, unworthy though we are, has deigned to seat us upon

---

12   Matt. 7:15, 24:24; 2 Cor. 11:13; 2. Pet. 2:1.

this supreme throne of justice, with the plenitude of the apostolic power we declare that the said Elizabeth is a heretic and an abettor of heretics, and that those who follow her in these things have incurred the sentence of excommunication and are cut off from the unity of the body of Jesus Christ. Likewise, she is stripped of her supposed right to the said kingdom, and to any other dominion, title, or privilege. The lords, vassals, and subjects of that realm, and all others who have in any wise taken an oath of loyalty to her, are free of the said oath and of any obligation whatsoever of vassalage, fealty, and obedience, wholly and perpetually. And by the authority of these present letters, we absolve and free them. And we deprive the said Elizabeth of her pretended right to the throne and of all the aforesaid. And we command all lords, subjects, peoples, and aforesaid others, together and individually, forbidding them to presume to obey her or her orders, mandates, or laws and attainting any who do otherwise with the same sentence of excommunication and anathema. And because it will be most difficult to carry these present letters to all necessary parts, we desire that a translation thereof, signed by some public notary and sealed with the seal of a prelate or of his court, shall have the same credit in legal disputes and elsewhere, in any place whatsoever, that the original would have were it exhibited or posted. Given in Rome, at Saint Peter in the year of the incarnation of the Lord 1569, on February 25, in the fifth year of our pontificate.

Caesar Glorierius[13]
H. Cumyn[14]

---

13   Cesar Grolier (b. 1510), generally known as Glorierius, was the illegitimate son of the French courtier and bibliophile Jean Grolier de Servières, viscount d'Aguisy (c.1489–1565). Cesar served as a Latin secretary to three popes, including Pius v. Antoine Le Roux de Lincy, *Researches Concerning Jean Grolier: His Life and His Library*, ed. Roger Portalis, trans. Carolyn Shipman (New York: The Grolier Club, 1907), 4–5.

14   I have not been able to identify this figure, or even to trace his full name, but his signature appears on various papal documents of the mid-sixteenth century.

What Ensued from the Bull's Publication in England[1]

This bull of Pius v was published by being pinned to the doors of the false bishop of London,[2] for which two men died, condemned as traitors. One of them was John Felton, a gentleman of ardent spirit who, seeing the devastation of his homeland, and that so gangrenous a wound could not be cured save by fire and strong medicine, moved by God's zeal affixed the printed bull to the door of the bishop's house on the day of the sacred sacrament in the year 1570, where it remained until eight in the morning of the following day—seen and read by many, and copied out by several. A Spaniard named Pedro Berga, a Catalan by nation and a prebendary in the church of Tarragona, aided John Felton in this business, but he fled, leaving Felton, who refused to run, in the heretics' clutches. They sentenced and punished him as a traitor, with the torments and execution inflicted upon such people in England, as have been described in this book.[3] In the *Martyrologium Romanum*, for February 8, mention is made of several sainted monks who died for having published the apostolic letters of Pope Saint Felix against Archbishop Acacius of Constantinople.[4]

---

1 Sander, *De origine ac progressu*, 427–32.

2 Edmund Grindal (*c*.1519–83), bishop of London since Bonner's deprivation in 1559.

3 On May 25, 1570 (a few days after the feast of Corpus Christi), John Felton (d.1570), a well-born Catholic from Norfolk, nailed up a copy of Pius v's bull *Regnans in excelsis*, thereby publishing it in England and giving it canonical force. According to several contemporary sources, he acquired the bull from Pedro Berga (dates unknown), prebendary of Tarragona and chaplain to the Spanish ambassador. Soon after, Felton was apprehended and confessed, but he was tortured nevertheless, in hopes that he would admit to conspiring with the Spanish. Sentenced as a traitor, he was hanged, drawn, and quartered on August 8, 1570. Julian Lock, "Felton, John (d.1570)," in *ODNB*, 19:282–83, here 282.

4 This sentence is added in the 1595 edition.

The entry for February 8 in Cesare Baronio's 1589 edition of the *Martyrologium Romanum* relates: "At Constantinople, the martyrdom of the sainted monks of the monastery of Dius, who were brutally slaughtered for the defense of the Catholic faith, when they brought letters from Pope Saint Felix against Acacius." Baronio, *Martyrologium Romanum*, 73.

In 484, Pope Saint Felix III (r.483–92) rejected the *Henotikon* (482), a document devised by Acacius, ecumenical patriarch of Constantinople (d.489) and promulgated by Emperor Zeno (r.474–75, 476–91) as an attempted solution to the Chalcedonian controversy. Felix was unable to compel Acacius's submission, though more because the pope's envoys proved

Felton died with the utmost joy and constancy, professing that he perished in the Catholic faith: by this glorious testimony he gave much solace and encouragement to the Catholics, and much dismay to the heretics.[5]

His Holiness's sentence produced diverse effects. The Catholics continued to obey the queen, since they were not strong enough to resist, and because they saw that the bull had not been lawfully and solemnly published (so they said); and that the other Catholic princes and states engaged with the queen exactly as before; and that the pope died a few years afterward, and no one knew whether his successor, Gregory XIII,[6] had renewed and confirmed it; and, lastly, that they would lose their property and their lives if they did anything else. The heretics took care to show outward disdain for the bull, saying that these were bugbears to frighten children, yet inwardly they were perturbed and distraught, all the more so since a pope as saintly as Pius V had pronounced that judgment, and each day the kingdom's Catholics took heart and grew in number. But so deeply did the queen feel this blow that she hardened and grew yet crueler: having summoned parliament, she enacted several ghastly laws against the followers of the Catholic faith, among which were these:

---

feckless than out of any particular brutality on the part of the patriarch. W.T. Townshend, "The Henotikon Schism and the Roman Church," *Journal of Religion* 16, no. 1 (January 1936): 78–86, here 78–80.

5   Ribadeneyra may have drawn on Sander's description of Felton's exploits in his *De visibili monarchia ecclesiae* (1571): "So, by divine providence, a copy of this declaratory sentence was brought to England, to John Felton, a man both of consideration renown for nobility and of even greater renown for his fortitude of spirit. He, driven by zeal and devotion to the Catholic faith, because he observed that the well-nigh hopeless condition of his country could not be cured save by some bitter medicine, refused to allow this sentence of the supreme pastor to remain hidden from his fellows and countrymen. Accordingly, in the year of our Lord 1570, on the feast of Corpus Christi, he affixed the said sentence of Pius V to the bishop's gates, beside the principal church in the city of London. The letter remained on view in broad daylight almost until the eighth hour of the day, and was said to have been seen by many, read by many, and copied out by several more. And another, who was present when Felton posted the letters, when he fled the island, urged Felton to consider his own flight. Felton refused to do so, insisting that whatever happened, it would be determined by God's grace. When they fiercely pursued him for this, and he was finally caught, John Felton showed himself worthy of Jesus Christ and the primate instituted by him. [...] Felton was unanimously condemned by the judges as a notorious traitor. Accordingly, on the eight day of August, being carried to torment, he told those present that he died for the Catholic faith, as he affirmed the primacy of the supreme pontiff and denied the queen's claim to be the supreme head of the Church." Nicholas Sander, *De visibili monarchia ecclesiæ libri octo* (Leuven: Ioannis Fouleri, 1571), 734. For a sixteenth-century depiction of Felton's martyrdom, see Book 2 figure 28.1.

6   Pius V died on May 1, 1572. On May 13, Ugo Boncompagni (r.1572–85) was elected Pope Gregory XIII.

A. *Propter sedis Romanę et fidei catholicæ confessionem, undecim* R^mi *episcopi catholici ex diuturna carceris molestia contabescentes obierunt.*

B. *Plumtreus* Wodhouius *Nelsonus,* Maynus, Hansiusque *sacerdotes in partes dissecantur.*

C. *Storeus* I.V. doctor. *Feltonus etiam nobilis, et* Shir Wodus *idem supplicium subeunt, Regina* Elizabetha Anglię *imperante.*

D. *quidam uir illustris capite plexus est.* 30

FIGURE 28.1   *The incarceration of the catholic bishops and the martyrdoms of several other catholics, including John Nelson, Cuthbert Mayne, Everard Hanse, John Felton, and Thomas Sherwood.*
Giovanni Battista Cavalieri, *Ecclesiae anglicanae trophaea sive sanctorum martyrum qui pro Christo catholicaeque fidei veritate asserenda antiquo recentiorique persecutionum tempore mortem in Anglia subierunt, passiones Romae in collegio Anglico per Nicolaum Circinianum depictae: Nuper autem per Io. Bap. de Cavalleriis aeneis typis repraesentatae* (Rome: Ex officina Bartolomeo Grassi, 1584).
NE1666 .C57 1584 OVERSIZE, John J. Burns Library, Boston College.

1.   That none, on pain of their life, should call Elizabeth a heretic, schismat-
     ic, misbeliever, or usurper of the kingdom.
2.   That none should name any person as, or say they ought to be, successor
     to the throne, neither while the queen lived nor after her days, unless it
     should be a natural son or daughter of the said queen.[7]

These are the very words of the law. And with them, the entire realm is thrown
into peril and confusion, for no one knows who is to succeed the queen. And
saying that she must be succeeded by a natural son or daughter of hers (which
is contrary to the laws of the kingdom) implies that she has such a natural son
or daughter.

3.   That on pain of the loss of property and life imprisonment, none should
     bear, receive, or carry with them any item of devotion brought from
     Rome, such as an *agnus dei*, cross, image, rosary, or anything else what-
     ever blessed by the pope or by his authority.
4.   That on pain of their head, none should bear a bull, brief, or letter of the
     pope's, nor absolve any of heresy or schism, nor reconcile any with the
     Roman Church, nor allow themselves to be absolved or reconciled.[8]

And to further intimidate the Catholics, and prevent them from fleeing the
realm, she confiscated the goods of every Catholic who had departed for religious reasons.[9] And since many had broken these laws, or were falsely accused
of breaking them, a huge tumult broke out against the Catholics: some were
robbed of their property, others imprisoned and persecuted, others cruelly tortured or killed, priests alongside laymen of every rank. But two things came
to pass in this time of need to the solace and inspiration of the Catholics. The
first was that in the city of Oxford, when a commoner named Rowland Jenks
[*Gniseo*] was condemned to have his ears cut off for being Catholic, hardly had
the heretical judge pronounced this sentence when he and all his colleagues,
scribes, and judicial officers were straightway struck down with a malady from
which several died then and there, and others, more than three hundred of
them,[10] within a few hours or days, without the evil spreading to any other

---

7   13 Eliz. 1. c. 1, Sections 1 and 5, respectively. See *SR*, 4.1:526–27.
8   13 Eliz. 1. c. 2. See ibid., 4.1:528–31.
9   13 Eliz. 1. c. 3. See ibid., 4.1:531–35.
10   This clause is added in the 1595 edition.

person or part of the city.[11] And although those of the queen's council made thorough inquiries and investigations to learn whence this sudden infection had come, they found no reason or cause whereby it might be truthfully attributed to nature. And so they proclaimed that the papists were sorcerers and wizards, and born of the same—in the same way that the gentiles attributed to diabolic arts the miracles and marvels worked by our Lord in defense of the martyrs they were tormenting. Furthermore, a doctor of laws named Wright, an archdeacon of Oxford, discussing a certain passage of Saint Paul, concluded by saying, *De Papa hic nullum verbum auditis*; at this he was felled by a grave illness, almost losing his speech altogether, borne from the pulpit not to the table, as he had intended, but to his bed, where he died within a few days.[12] The second event that occurred in this period was a strange division among the heretics. For besides the infinite accursed sects among them, totally contradictory and distinct from each other, there arose the new, pestilential cult of those known as Puritans, who in speeches, sermons, and written texts began to assail

---

11   "The 4. 5. & 6. dais of July [1577], was the assises held at Oxford, wher was arained & condemned one Rowland Jenkes, for his seditious tong, at which time there arose amidst the people such a dampe, y^t that almost al were smouldered, very few escaped y^t were not taken at y^t instant, the iurors died presently, shortly after died sir Robert Bel Lord chief baron, sir Ro. de Olie, sir W. Babington, M. Wenema[n], M de Olie hie shirif, M. Dauers, M. Harcurt, M. Kirt, M. Pheteplace, M. Grenewod M. Fostar, M. Nash, sergea[n]t Bara[m], M. Steuens, &c. there died in Oxford 3.C. persons, and sickened there, but died in other places 2.C. and odde, from the 6. of Julye, to the 12. of August." John Stow, *The Summarie of the Chronicles of England. Diligently Collected, Abridged & Continued vnto This Present Yeare of Christ 1579 by Iohn Stowe, Citizen of London* (London: Richard Tottle, and Henry Binneman, 1579), 442.

      For other contemporary responses to this incident, see Walsham, *Providence*, 234–36.

12   "There was a certain Wright, a doctor of both laws and an archdeacon of Oxford [...] one day, he was preaching among the presbyters who had formerly been subject to his authority, and he came upon the words of Saint Paul, saying to them, 'Christ, in the organization of the Church, gave some apostles and some prophets and other some evangelists and other some pastors and doctors.' Having uttered this, he inserted something of his own [...] saying, 'You heard not a word of the pope here.' Once the sermon had come to its end, he was suddenly struck with a dire illness, such that, having been rendered almost mute, he was borne from the pulpit not to the table, as he had intended, but to the bed, and he departed this life eight days later." Sander, *De visibili monarchia*, 714.

      Walter Wright was an archdeacon of Oxford and a former vice-chancellor of the university. The story of Wright's sudden demise on preaching against the papal supremacy originates with Sander. William Page, ed., *The Victoria History of the County of Oxford*, 16 vols., The Victoria History of the Counties of England (London: Archibald Constable and Company Limited, 1907–), 2:40.

the faith and creed of the queen and her parliament, and to impugn and criticize it as impious and superstitious on more than a hundred counts. And thus
there were, and are to this day, fierce debates and battles among the heretics.
By this, the Catholics each day grow stronger and more steadfast in our sacred
faith, seeing on one side the protection God extended to them, and on the
other, the confusion that prevailed amid the misbelievers.

The Establishment of the English Seminaries in Rheims and Rome, and Their Fruits[1]

But the Catholics have been most benefitted, consoled, and strengthened by the foundations of the seminaries at Rheims in France and at Rome, which began in this way. The horrors of the queen's persecution and the Catholics' troubles were worsening by the day, and certain wise, zealous, and God-fearing men saw that nothing had been able to calm or mitigate the storm. They feared that the English Catholics both in England and abroad would be killed off by age, or abuses in the jails and prisons, or long and arduous exile—or that they would ultimately lose heart, witnessing every day the many savage martyrdoms of their friends and companions. And so they decided that to prevent the Catholic religion from withering on the vine[2] in that land, they ought to create a school or seminary for able young Catholics, who would be nurtured and transplanted, and then grow to replace those passing away. Because they had no doubt that, no matter how this sect of perdition[3] flourished, it must fall (so long as the Catholics did not despair) and come to an end, as all the others that past centuries had raised up against the Catholic Church and God's truth had come to an end. For no heretical cult has yet been able to please men for any length of time, nor endure or persevere in one form, instead always going through drastic changes and alterations. We see this in the heresy of the Arians, who, though they had the might of the princes and monarchs of the world upon their side, ultimately came to an end.

Therefore, since a huge number of accomplished young students had fled England and taken up residence in the provinces of Flanders to live safely as Catholics among Catholics, they gathered in Douai under the discipline and leadership of Doctor William Allen (who later studied theology in the university there and is now a cardinal, on account of his great virtues). Little by little they came to form a bustling college, sustained at first by the alms of several servants of God, and then by the generosity and beneficence of the Apostolic

---

1 Sander, *De origine ac progressu*, 417–21.

2 Isa. 34:4; John 15:6.

3 2 Pet. 2:1.

See.[4] But as the heretics in England were agitating and threatening yet greater evils, it became necessary for the college to relocate to Rheims in France, as our Lord ordained and the Most Christian King of France desired, where it has flourished to the highest profit and benefit to the kingdom of England.[5] And to better this good, His Holiness Pope Gregory XIII (whose name will be lovingly and gloriously recalled in every age for this kindness and for many others like it done for the Church) created another wonderful college for the English at Rome, in the ancient hospice of that nation, which he endowed with ample rents and entrusted to the fathers of the Society of Jesus, for the instruction and governance of the English students, just as they governed and instructed the Germans of the Germanicum [*Colegio Germanico*] and the clerics of the Collegio Romano [*Seminario Romano*].[6] These two seminaries have been like two impregnable fortresses, to this very day giving life and health to the Catholics still in England. For each day countless good-hearted young men of extraordinary abilities arrive to be instructed and educated in the universal and solid truths of our holy religion. After they have absorbed what is needful and have been examined and proved for several years, they return to the kingdom ordained (many of them with further degrees), to teach and preach what they learned in the seminaries. Thus it is that in a few years more than three hundred clerics have been trained in the two seminaries, and transplanted and dispatched to England to cultivate that abandoned vineyard beset with wild beasts,[7] which they have done with so much spirit and effort that many have watered it with their blood. It is a miracle, belonging to the mighty

---

4   William Allen was made a cardinal in 1587. Educated at Oxford, Allen fled England in 1565, establishing the English College at Douai in 1568, to sustain the large number of English Catholics in exile on the Continent. The college received papal confirmation within months of its foundation. Allen received his doctorate in divinity in 1570, and governed the college until 1588. See the "Historical Introduction" to Thomas Francis Knox, ed., *The First and Second Diaries of the English College, Douay: And an Appendix of Unpublished Documents* (London: David Nutt, 1878), xv–cvii.

5   Intensifying anti-Spanish animus in the Low Countries during the late 1570s made the situation of the English College at Douai ever more precarious. In 1578, the English were expelled from the town, and transplanted the seminary to Rheims, where they were welcomed by a French government dominated by the stridently Catholic Guise family. Ibid., xlix–lv.

6   In April 1579, Gregory provided the ancient English pilgrim hospice at San Tommaso as a site for a second English seminary and endowed the enterprise with considerable incomes toward its support. The Collegium Germanicum et Hungaricum, begun in the days of Ignatius of Loyola, was a Jesuit-run college dedicated to training German youths to combat Protestantism in their homelands. The Society also directed the Collegio Romano, the primary Jesuit seminary. Pastor, *History of the Popes*, 19:237–51.

7   Isa. 5:5.

hand of God, that in a time such as this, when it is a wonder to find in other Catholic lands a single man who wishes to become a priest (unless spurred by self-interest), the seminaries should have so many noble youths, some of them well-born and wealthy, who yearn for the priesthood with such fiery devotion and desire, without any hope of gain, but rather the certainty of losing all they have and of enduring dangers, humiliations, and death. Who receive and exercise the priesthood without being dissuaded or hindered in their holy purpose by their misfortunes and worldly perils, or by the prayers and arguments of their parents, kinsmen, and friends. In fact, when they hear that one of their companions or some other English Catholic has been imprisoned, tortured, or cruelly slain for the faith, it seems to strengthen and inspire them, their hearts burning with hotter flames and fiercer desires to spill their own blood for the faith. Just as other colleges are seminaries of orators, philosophers, jurists, theologians, canonists, and physicians, these two are, and truly may be called, seminaries of martyrs.

Initially, the queen and those of her council took no notice of them, reckoning that the English students they reared would, whether out of necessity or self-interest, ultimately return to England to seek benefices and incomes from the queen, serving her according to her laws and religious rites. And if there were some obstinate enough to refuse, they would be few, poor, exiled, and oppressed, and thus hardly able to damage their new church, fortified with the mighty strength of a powerful queen, armed with rigorous laws, supported by diligent, zealous ministers and magistrates, and, to conclude, sustained and defended by methods so exquisitely cruel. But when within a few years they realized that a huge number of gifted youths of rare abilities had left England's colleges and universities and crossed the sea,[8] and then returned as priests, teaching Catholic truth by their examples, sermons, and writings, administering the sacraments in secret, illuminating and inspiring countless persons, absolving them of heresies and errors, and reconciling them to the Church—and so the number of Catholics grew and multiplied day by day, filling the towns, villages, cities, and universities of the realm, even the court and palace of the queen—they acknowledged the disaster and worked to contain it with inhuman edicts and extreme penalties and tortures.

---

8   William Allen wrote in 1583, "Great complaints are made to the Queen's councillors about the university of Oxford, because of the numbers who from time to time leave their colleges and are supposed to pass over to us. This torments them exceedingly." Quoted in McCoog, *Reckoned Expense*, 43.

The Entry of the Fathers of the Society of Jesus into England[1]

Recognizing how the seminary priests were disrupting their sect deeply troubled the queen and her council, but their dismay and concern grew greater still when the fathers of the Society of Jesus entered the kingdom, to wage war against their ministers. The Catholics of England had learned of the foundation of this order, its aims and intentions, and the abundant fruit won by its travails and efforts in every region—most of all in those infected by heresy— and on this account fervently desired to encounter them. This longing burned more keenly with the reports of the Englishmen who had been educated in the seminary at Rome and had gotten to know the fathers, learning from them Catholic virtue and dogma, and returned to their homeland with these weapons to defend—and die for—the truth. And so, out of this desire, the Catholics urgently pressed and lobbied the general of the Society to send some of his soldiers to England on so important a conquest, Englishmen, familiar with the language and the customs of the country.[2] For in the days of their exile many of this nation, men of exemplary life and learning, had entered the Society of Jesus and settled beneath its banner.[3] And it seemed that the Lord had called them, and that he was gathering forces for the war he intended to wage.

The first sent on this glorious enterprise were two English fathers of the Society, Robert Persons and Edmund Campion, and with them several priests chosen from both seminaries.[4] Such was the extraordinary skill, the diligence,

---

1   Sander, *De origine ac progressu*, 433, 436–37, 446–62.

2   Mercurian was extremely reluctant to authorize a Jesuit mission to England. It was after only sustained lobbying on the part of Cardinal Allen and high-ranking members of the Society that he finally agreed in 1579. See McCoog, *And Touching Our Society*, Chapter 1.

3   The language of "banners" or "standards" permeates the earliest documents of the Society of Jesus, including its founding bull and the *Spiritual Exercises*. Olin, *Catholic Reformation*, 204. Ignatius of Loyola, *Ignatius of Loyola: The Spiritual Exercises and Selected Works*, ed. and trans. George E. Ganss, The Classics of Western Spirituality (New York: Paulist Press, 1991), 154–56.

4   Persons reached England on June 16, 1580. Campion, along with the laybrother Ralph Emerson (1553–1604), arrived shortly thereafter. Also included was Ralph Sherwin, "a secular priest with wide philosophical and theological knowledge and facility with Latin, Greek, and Hebrew." McCoog, *Reckoned Expense*, xxvii, 144.

© KONINKLIJKE BRILL NV, LEIDEN, 2017 | DOI 10.1163/9789004323964_086

fidelity, and divine inspiration with which they devoted themselves to the task at hand that in a few months, with the disquisitions and exhortations they delivered in different houses, with sermons and the administration of the sacraments, with the books they wrote, and with other holy ministries, they won countless heretics for God, including many knights and learned men, and reconciled them to the Catholic Church. Their way of proceeding in this arduous, perilous enterprise is evident in a passage of a letter by Father Campion himself, which says this:

> Having arrived in London, a good angel guided me unawares to the very same house that had received Father Robert. Then several young gentlemen came to see me, greet me, clothe me, arm me, prepare me, and send me out of the city. Each day I travel by horse through a different part of the country. Truly, the harvest is most abundant. On the road, I contemplate the sermon, and on arriving at the house I perfect and complete it. After I have spoken a little, and conversed with and listened to those who come to hear me, I receive their confessions, and in the morning when Mass is finished I preach to them and administer the blessed sacrament of the altar. Several clerics, eminent in learning and virtues, assist us, and thus our burden is lightened and the people better satisfied. We will not long be able to escape the clutches of the heretics, for we have infinite eyes, tongues, and ears upon us. Just as Saint Eusebius, bishop of Samosata, did in the days of the Arian Emperor Constantius, when he visited the churches dressed as a soldier, as it says in the *Martyrologium Romanum* for June 21,[5] I travel in secular habit, ragged and wild, which changes at every step, as does my name. I receive many letters, in whose very first line I read, "Campion is imprisoned," and this so often that my ears are already accustomed to it, as a dog to the hammer-blows of the blacksmith, and thus continual fear has displaced this single fear. As I write this, the bloodthirsty persecution worsens: the house is mournful, for nothing is spoken of but death, or prisons, or the loss of property, and of flight from all this. Nevertheless, they press on with good cheer, and the Lord sends us consolations in this enterprise that not only take from us all dread of suffering, but also delight and refresh us with infinite sweetness and calmness. A clean conscience, a valiant, zealous spirit,

---

5 This sentence is added in the 1595 edition. Ribadeneyra also refers to the incognito ministry of Eusebius of Samosata (d. *c.*379), a fervent opponent of Arianism and antagonist of the heretical Emperor Constantius II (r.337–61), in Book 3, Chapter 22.
Cf. Baronio, *Martyrologium Romanum*, 270.

unbelievable fervor, the miraculous fruit—the infinite number who are converted, from every station, age, and rank—are the main reasons for this solace. All sane people recognize the infamy of heresy, and there is nothing coarser or more contemptible than the ministers thereof. We are justly infuriated, seeing that in so miserable a case illiterate, lowborn, vile, criminal, infamous men have their feet upon the neck of, and dictate to, learned, exalted, virtuous men, the glory and ornament of the nation. I cannot continue further, for they come to alert me.[6]

All this says Father Campion. Father Robert Persons includes the following passages in a letter he wrote at London on November 17, 1580, giving news to the fathers of the Society at Rome of his entry and of his companions:

The fury of the present persecution against the Catholics across this kingdom is prodigious, with nobles and commoners, men and women, great and small all carried to prison, even the children bound in chains of iron; their property is seized, they are cast into gloomy dungeons, and they are slandered among the common folk as traitors and rebels, in public edicts, sermons, and everyday speech.

The noblemen imprisoned for Catholicism in the past months are numerous, illustrious, and wealthy, each one mighty in his place, such that the ancient prisons of England have not sufficed, nor even the many new ones built for this. Nevertheless, each day new inquisitors are dispatched to seek out and arrest yet more, whose number, by the grace of God, grows greater every day, so much so that it exhausts those who come to seize them, for we have learned that in one month they discovered the names of more than fifty thousand people in this region who refuse to attend the heretics' churches—and hereafter they shall find many more, as I believe. The enormous masses of secret Catholics may be inferred from the many who publicly offer themselves up, to the peril of their lives and wealth, for refusing to go to the churches or conventicles of the heretics.

It is a miraculous thing to see the constancy and discipline with which the Catholics of this realm flee and abominate the churches of the heretics, and how many willingly offer themselves up to imprisonment rather than even draw near the threshold. It has been recently proposed

---

6   This letter appears in Latin in Sander, *De origine ac progressu*, 436–37. The original manuscript of the undated missive to Mercurian is preserved at the Archivum Romanum Societatis Iesu, Fondo Gesuitico 651/612.

to several nobles that if they consented to attend the heretics' churches once a year—even with a prior declaration that they went not out of faith or an inclination to that creed, but only to demonstrate outward obedience to the queen—they would be set free. To this they replied that it could not be done with a safe conscience.

A boy of ten years (from what I understand) was tricked by his family into walking to the church before the bride on her wedding day (as is the custom). When he was rebuked by those of his own age, who told him that in so doing he had fallen into schism, he began to cry, accepting no consolation until he came to me a few days later; running and throwing himself at my feet, with huge floods of tears, he begged me to hear the confession of that sin, promising that he would rather submit to any sort of torture than again consent to so monstrous a sin. I forebear to relate numberless similar events.

Our situation here is such that, although contact with us is forbidden to all by public edict, yet in every place they support us with fervent affection, and everywhere we go they receive us with the utmost joy. Many make long journeys solely for the opportunity to speak with us and to put themselves and all they have in our hands; everywhere they give us in abundance anything we need, and they entreat us to it. The priests are in harmony with us (or, as I should say, they obey us in everything with great love); in sum, our Society is so highly and so generally esteemed that we must take care to live up to it, especially because we are so far from that perfection they believe of us. And so, more than anyone we stand in need of the prayers of Your Reverences. They seized Father Sherwin by chance four days ago: out in search of another, they fell upon him. He made a noteworthy affirmation and confession of his faith before the false bishop of London[7] and is now committed to prison[8]—but he writes to me that he endures this with pure delight, and when he regards himself as imprisoned for Christ, he cannot restrain his laughter. He is sheer torture to our foes, seeing that all their cruelty cannot separate him—nor any Catholic, even the youngest girls—from his convictions. Indeed, when the pretended bishop of London interrogated a noble maiden about the supreme pontiff and she courageously ridiculed him, the barbaric, brutish man had her openly dragged to the public place for women of

---

7   John Aylmer (c.1521–94), bishop of London since 1577.
8   Sherwin was captured soon after his return to England, in November 1580. Michael E. Williams, "Sherwin, Ralph [St Ralph Sherwin] (1549/50–1581)," in ODNB, 50:343.

ill-repute. But along the route she shouted to all that she was sent to so vile a place not for any vice of hers, but for the sake of the Catholic faith and her own conscience.

We expect that two priests will soon be publicly put to death here: they are called Cottam [*Lotemio*] and Clifton [*Chrytomio*],[9] the latter of whom was dragged through the streets to his interrogation two days ago, loaded with iron chains—he went with so joyous a countenance that the people were astounded, and rushed to see him; he began to laugh with happiness, and the people were yet more awestruck. They asked him how he alone so rejoiced in so miserable a situation, when every other man regarded him with sorrow and compassion? He replied that it was because he was to receive a far greater advantage from the business: "And do you wonder," he said, "that a man should be pleased at his own interests and profit?"

At the beginning of this persecution, there were some in a certain province of the kingdom who out of terror yielded to the insistence of the queen's agents and promised to begin attending the Protestants' churches. When their wives learned of this, they resisted, threatening to abandon them and live with them no longer if for human considerations they separated themselves from obedience to God. Many children likewise estranged themselves from their parents for the same reason.

From early in the morning well into the night, having completed the divine offices and preached (twice on some days), I am busied with an infinity of tasks, but the most important are responses to proffered cases of conscience, giving orders to the other priests, escorting them from place to place, and more apposite efforts: reconciling schismatics to the Church, writing letters to those periodically tempted amid this persecution, arranging temporal assistance to sustain those languishing in prison (for each day brings me someone communicating on their behalf). Briefly, so numerous are these endeavors that if I did not clearly see that what we do is to the greater glory of God, I would easily lose heart with such burdens—but no one should despair in matters of this kind. For I am absolutely convinced that (if my sins do not hinder it) our Lord will,

---

9 Thomas Cottam (1549–82), an English Jesuit, was executed at Tyburn on May 30, 1582. Thomas Clifton (d.1593), trained as priest at Douai, was captured soon after his return to England in January 1580. Sentenced to life imprisonment for affirming the papal supremacy, he died in prison twelve years later. Thompson Cooper, "Cottam, Thomas (1549–1582)," in *ODNB*, 13:579–80. Robert Persons, *Letters and Memorials of Father Robert Persons, s.j.: Vol. I (to 1588)*, ed. Leo Hicks (London: John Whitehead & Son, 1942), 55n38.

as ever, favor our aims. And there is no work of body or soul so great as the consolation we receive from the people's incredible joy at our arrival here. I beg Your Reverences to pray to our Lord for us, and to provide for the prayers of your fellows, so that we may somehow fulfill our obligations and the high expectations of us.[10]

And to demonstrate the fruit produced by these fathers and the other priests their companions, I also wish to include here another passage from a letter by one of these priests, who has labored in that vineyard for the space of a year.[11] This he wrote to the rector of the English College at Rome,[12] as follows:[13]

Our business and our merchandise goes well, with good dispatch; for although there are many who disdain it and more who speak against it, we do not lack many others who buy it and many more who admire it. Nothing is spoken of in England save the fathers of the Society of Jesus, here referred to as "Jesuits," of whom they concoct more fables and fairy tales than did the ancient poets of their monsters. Of the origins, establishment, way of life, customs, and doctrine of these men, of their actions, aims, and intentions, they say so many things, each contradicting the others, that they seem more like dreams and chimaeras than sense. And this is not only broached in conversations and private discussions, but it is even preached in sermons, and published and spread throughout the kingdom in print. The sum of all that is said is that they and the other priests who have arrived with them have been sent by the pope as spies upon this kingdom, and traitors and destroyers of the whole commonwealth. Several Calvinist minsters have written against Campion and against the entire Jesuit Order, especially against the life of its founder, Father Ignatius of Loyola—but they had no success, for within a ten days there was such a reaction that they were left ashamed and abashed.

For our part, numerous books are printed and disseminated throughout the realm, though not without supreme difficulty and mortal peril,

---

10   This letter, written by Persons on November 17, 1580, to Alfonso Agazzari (1549–1602), the rector of the English College at Rome, is printed (with an English translation) in Ibid., 46–64.

11   Cf. Matt. 20:1–16.

12   Agazzari.

13   Ribadeneyra has abbreviated this letter from the fuller Latin version provided in Sander, *De origine ac progressu*, 446–62.

      This letter is also from Persons to Agazzari, composed in August 1581. See Persons, *Letters and Memorials*, 72–90.

for which we have clandestine presses and printers, and a hidden place under the earth, which is frequently changed; the books are distributed with the utmost caution by noble youths. And it is a marvelous thing how they edify and inspire the Catholics, and offend the heretics, who know not how or cannot respond to them. I would never come to an end if I tried to describe the Catholics' zeal and fervor in detail. When any priest comes to them, they first greet him and receive him like a stranger; afterwards, they bring him to their homes and conduct him to some side chamber where there is an oratory. There all prostrate themselves, and upon their knees request a blessing with absolute humility, and seek to know how long he shall be with them (they hope that it will be very long). And if he tells them the following day (for he cannot tarry, on account of the danger of falling into the hands of the law), all prepare themselves to confess on that very afternoon, and the following morning, after hearing Mass, they take communion, and then follows some discourse and sermon from the father to instruct and encourage them. He gives them his blessing once more and departs, generally accompanied along the way by several genteel young men. In their houses, the Catholics maintain (as was the custom in the primitive Church) numerous secret compartments and hiding places, to conceal and protect them when the agents of the law arrive to seek them. If they barge in late at night and the priests are put to flight, they escape to the thickest forests and the jagged cliffs, casting themselves into caves, sometimes into ditches, ponds, and lakes. Sometimes we are seated at table, speaking informally about some element of our holy faith and about devotion (for these are our usual topics and entertainments), in happiness and comfort, and then we hear a call at the door of the house with untoward urgency and noise: at this we are all distraught, thinking that it is the law. Like a stag who hears the baying of the dogs and the shouts of the huntsmen, we are all attention in our hearts and our ears. We abandon our food, commend ourselves to God, and not a one coughs, twitches, or speaks until the servant says what the matter is. If there is no threat, we breathe again and return to our warm conversations, which, with the false fright we have had, is generally brighter and more pleasurable than before.

There is no Catholic in these parts who complains that the Mass is interminable—to the contrary, it will disappoint many if it does not last at least a whole hour. If six or eight Masses are said on the same day (as happens at times when several priests come together), the Catholics hear them all with the greatest willingness. Conflicts or differences among them are a miracle, for they place everything in the hands of the fathers and priests, who decide them as they see fit. There is no desire to marry with heretics, talk with them, or pray with them. When a lady was imprisoned for her faith, and they offered her her freedom if she entered a heretical church just once, she would have none of it, saying that she had entered her cell with a clean conscience, and she desired to leave with it clean, or to die. This is the work of the right hand of him on high.[14] For in the days of King Henry, the entire kingdom, which boasted bishops, prelates, religious, and men of exalted character and learning, abandoned the faith and obedience to the Roman pontiff, obeying the voice of the tyrant. And now, by the mercy of the Lord, when Henry's daughter oppresses the Church with even harsher cruelty, we do not lack boys and girls, men and women who, when hauled to trial, imprisoned, and bound in irons, spiritedly confess the truth, disdaining their pains, torments, and deaths. These days show us more clearly what the spirit of God has achieved in these lands, for after the promulgation of certain edicts and draconian laws against those who recuse themselves from appearing at the heretics' ceremonies and impious rites (who are therefore called "recusants"), more than fifty thousand of the kingdom's most distinguished persons, of the greatest renown and reputation, went and offered themselves up to receive the penalties set out in those laws. This frightened and angered the ministers of Satan,[15] who resolved to enforce the laws against the priests and teachers of the truth, whom they recognized as giving rise to the others' fortitude and spirit.

All this the priest says in his letter.

---

14   Ps. 16:8, 16:11, 17:36, 20:6, 43:4, 59:7, 62:9, 88:14, 97:1, 137:7, 138:10; Isa. 41:10; Acts 2:33.

15   2 Cor. 11:14–15.

The Harsh Laws the Queen Enacted against the Fathers of the Society of Jesus and the Other Catholic Priests[1]

To destroy the fruit these fathers produced and to check the harms inflicted (in her eyes) upon the cult of her false religion, on July 15, 1580 the queen promulgated a cruel and oppressive edict against Jesuits, priests, and the students of the seminaries, declaring them traitors and rebels against her kingdom. Therein, she commanded[2]

1. That all parents, guardians, and persons connected with the care and instruction of children and students are to appear before the bishop within ten days of the publication of the edict and give the names of the children, students, and other persons in their charge outside the realm, and to provide for their return within four months; and that as they return notice thereof is to be given to the same bishop; and that if they do not return within this period, their parents and other persons responsible for them may not send them anything for their support, nor conceal those who send such things.

2. Furthermore, that after this period had elapsed no merchant or any other person may send anything, by exchange or by any other means whatsoever, to support or sustain those who thus remain outside the realm.

3. Likewise, that none are to receive, accept, sustain, support, or offer help of any kind to any Jesuit, seminarian, or priest who has already entered the realm, or shall enter hereafter; and that if at the time of the promulgation of this edict they have any such in their house or know where they are, they are required to produce them and hand them over to justice, to be imprisoned and punished; and that he who does not do so will be held

---

1 Sander, *De origine ac progressu*, 437–45.

2 Following Sander, Ribadeneyra has back-dated this proclamation by half a year: the decree in question was issued on January 10, 1581. Ribadeneyra worked from the Latin translation provided by Sander: Ibid., 439–43.

   For the English text of the proclamation, see *TRP*, 2:481–84.

an abettor, receiver, and aide to such Jesuits and rebellious men, enemies to the country and to Her Majesty.

And all this was mandated with the gravest and cruelest penalties. In response to these edicts and the specious slanders cast upon the servants of God, Cardinal William Allen (in imitation of Saint Justin Martyr, and Saint Athanasius, and other sainted Doctors)[3] wrote an erudite and thoughtful apologia, in which he declared, with perfect moderation and sense, the supreme pontiff's purpose in establishing the seminaries and the aims and holy intentions of the fathers of the Society of Jesus and the other priests in coming to England and laboring there: for the sole purpose of winning souls and bringing them to the true knowledge of God.[4] And he made this argument so cogently that the heretics were at a loss to respond, while the priests were left even more ardent in their endeavors, and the Catholics who received them in their houses do so with the same goodwill and fervor as always, without a thought for the threats and ghastly penalties decreed by the edict. But the queen's fury did not abate, for she saw that in many places the temples and conventicles of the heretics were left deserted; she made further harsh and draconian laws, commanding

1.   That any person whatsoever, man or woman, who shall attain sixteen years of age, is required to attend the churches of the Protestant misbelievers, to pray and hear the sermon, under penalty of twenty English pounds per month (which is approximately seventy ducats).

And by this law she beggared countless Catholics. She declares:

---

3   For the two apologias produced by the early Christian philosopher Justin Martyr (*c.*100–165), see Justin Martyr, *The First Apology, The Second Apology, Dialogue with Trypho, Exhortation to the Greeks, Discourse to the Greeks, the Monarchy, or the Rule of God*, ed. and trans. Thomas B. Falls, The Fathers of the Church: A New Translation 6 (Washington, D.C.: Catholic University of America Press, 1965).

   For the numerous apologias composed by Athanasius (*c.*297–373), the contentious patriarch of Alexandria, see Athanasius, *Historical Tracts of S. Athanasius*, trans. Miles Atkinson, A Library of Fathers of the Holy Catholic Church: Anterior to the Division of the East and West 13 (Oxford: John Henry Parker, 1843).

4   William Allen, *An Apologie and True Declaration of the Institution and Endeuours of the Tvvo English Colleges, the One in Rome, the Other Novv Resident in Rhemes against Certaine Sinister Informations Giuen vp against the Same* (Rheims: Jean de Foigny, 1581).

2.   That it is a crime of *lèse-majesté* to advise or induce any person to depart
       from the present religion of England.

Besides this,

3.   The penalty established in the first parliament to be levied on those who
       hear Mass is doubled.[5]

The Catholics suffered these penalties with utter steadfastness. For the
violent execution of these bloody decrees, the heretics sent agents, spies, and
informants to the houses of Catholic nobles and knights, and after them the
ministers of the law, to seize the priests they found, rob them of their property,
and with the most exquisite tortures torment, dispatch, and murder them.
And to lawless, degenerate men, they promised pardon for their crimes and
misdeeds, and large rewards and favors, if they identified their prey like good
pointer dogs, exposing and capturing priests and Jesuits.[6] By this they stuffed
the prisons (where thieves were usually kept) with a huge number of Catholics and servants of God of every rank, and these were so numerous that they
could not be squeezed into the existing prisons, and so new ones were erected,
with some of the prisoners sent to different regions. Among them, the bishop
of Lincoln[7] and the abbot of Westminster,[8] two venerable old prisoners, were
transferred to another pestilential dungeon and entrusted to a Puritan heretic,
a barbaric man who treated them with extreme cruelty and impiety, taking
away their books (lest they study), insulting and humiliating them, publishing

---

5   These are all provisions of 23 Eliz. 1. c. 1, Sections 4, 1, and 3, respectively. See SR, 4.1:657.
        Cf. 1 Eliz. 1. c. 2, §3. See ibid., 4.1:356.

6   The proclamation of January 1581 added, "And if any other her highness' subjects shall at any
    time certainly know any such persons repaired into this realm for the purpose above named,
    and thereof give knowledge to any of her majesty's officers or ministers whereby either they
    may or shall be taken and apprehended by the said officers, that then the said informer or
    utterer shall have her highness' reward for every such person by him or them disclosed and
    apprehended as in the manner above said, such sum of money as shall be an honorable due
    reward for so good service, besides her majesty's most hearty thanks for the discharge of their
    duty in that behalf." TRP, 2:484.

7   Thomas Watson had been appointed bishop of Lincoln in 1556: he was deprived of his see in
    1559, and imprisoned the following year. He was to remain in custody for the rest of his life.
    Kenneth Carleton, "Watson, Thomas (1513–1584)," in ODNB, 57:665–68, here 666–67.

8   Feckenham was first imprisoned in 1560. He had been released in 1574, under the guarantee
    of Matthew Parker, archbishop of Canterbury (1504–75); after Parker's death, Feckenham was
    taken back into custody. Knighton, "Feckenham," in ODNB, 19:229–30.

a thousand wickednesses of them, and bringing to their cells, in secret and without their knowledge, women of ill-repute, to render his lie and specious slander more credible—and thus those saintly fathers yielded up their souls to God within a few days of one another, with the greatest patience and fortitude.[9]

---

9 Watson and Feckenham were eventually committed to the custody of the bishop of Ely— first Richard Cox and then Martin Heton (1554–1604)—and held at Wisbech Castle in East Anglia, a former episcopal palace converted into a holding center for prominent Catholic prisoners. Both men arrived in August 1580, and both died in early October 1584. Carleton, "Watson, Thomas," in *ODNB*, 57:667–68.

Of the Life, Imprisonment, and Martyrdom of Father Edmund Campion of the Society of Jesus[1]

Among those jailed were many of the priests who (as we have said) circulated through the kingdom, encouraging the Catholics, strengthening the weak, illuminating the blind, and reconciling the converted to the Catholic Church. These men were afflicted with harsh prisons and abuses of every kind, consumed and dispatched with ghastly deaths. Here I will say something about these illustrious martyrs out of all that has been printed in various books. But whereas the foremost of these, the general and captain of all those who in recent years have died in Elizabeth's England for the faith of Jesus Christ, has been Father Edmund Campion of the Society of Jesus, in this chapter I will speak at greater length about his life and martyrdom—and in what follows we shall touch upon something of the rest.

Father Campion was born in London, the capital of England. After the first years of childhood, he entered St John's College, Oxford, where, on account of his singular brilliance and amiable disposition, he was well loved by the founder, Thomas White [*Bukito*], in whose memory he delivered an elegant and eloquent Latin oration.[2] Having completed the course of grades, ranks, and offices that are customarily given to students of his caliber in that university, his friends and confidants, who wished to see him successful and honored, persuaded him to be ordained a deacon, so that he might ascend to the pulpit and preach—though he was never attracted to the errors of our times. So forcefully

---

1 Sander, *De origine ac progressu*, 462–64.

   Most of the description of Campion's life, work, and martyrdom comes from the Italian edition of William Allen's biographies of the Catholic martyrs: Allen, *Historia*, 63–96.

   For an English translation, see William Allen, *A Briefe Historie of the Glorious Martyrdom of Twelve Reverend Priests Father Edmund Campion & His Companions*, ed. and trans. John Hungerford Pollen (London: Burns and Oates, 1908), 1–26.

2 Edmund Campion was born in London on January 25, 1540. "In 1558, a few months before the accession of Elizabeth, Campion entered St John's College, founded barely twelve months earlier by Sir Thomas White, a wealthy merchant, devout Catholic and former Lord Mayor of London." Campion studied philosophy and theology, receiving two degrees and becoming a fellow in 1564. A noted orator, Campion delivered White's funeral address in 1567. McCoog, *Reckoned Expense*, xix–xx. Michael A.R. Graves, "Campion, Edmund [St Edmund Campion] (1540–1581)," in *ODNB*, 9:872–76, here 872.

© KONINKLIJKE BRILL NV, LEIDEN, 2017 | DOI 10.1163/9789004323964_088

did they press him that he allowed himself to be conquered and to be ordained according to the new practice of the land, not fully understanding how odious and displeasing these schismatic dignities were to God our Lord.[3] Anxious to serve him and to become a valiant soldier and defender of his Church, the young man found an occasion to travel to Ireland, where he wrote a history of that island with surpassing eloquence.[4] Then he crossed to Flanders and entered the seminary at Douai, where he studied theology and received his degree, as well as being disabused and instructed in Catholic doctrine and the truths of our sacred faith.[5] Now possessing greater judgment and understanding, greater devotion and zeal, he understood the grave error into which he had fallen in having received the rank of a schismatic deacon. And he was seized by such fierce pangs of conscience and such anxieties that his soul could find neither comfort nor peace until he entered religion, to perform penance for that sin and free himself from that horrible, burdensome scruple, which he bore like a nail embedded in his heart. For this reason, he went to Rome and entered the Society of Jesus, and thence he was sent to Bohemia, where he remained for eight years, being ordained a priest in Prague and teaching, writing, and continually working on behalf of the Church of God with the utmost deftness and skill.[6] Thus it was that of the first two men the general of the

---

3   In 1568, Campion was awarded an exhibition by the Grocers' Company, which came with the stipulation that the recipient preach at St Paul's Cross if asked to do so. Campion was duly ordained a deacon in the spring of the following year. Over the course of 1569, the Company put increasing pressure on the young scholar to fulfill the preaching requirement, driving Campion to resign that autumn. McCoog, *Reckoned Expense*, xxii–xxiii.

4   *Two Bokes of the Histories of Ireland*, composed by Campion during several months in Ireland in the spring of 1571. See Edmund Campion, *Two Bokes of the Histories of Ireland,* ed. A.F. Vossen (Assen: Van Gorcum, 1963).

5   Campion entered the English College at Douai in the late summer of 1571, receiving his degree in 1573. McCoog, *Reckoned Expense*, xxv.

6   Persons relates that Campion "could not tell what better resolution to take for satisfying both God and man and especially his own conscience than to break utterly with the world, and with a penitent heart to repair to the holy city of Rome, there to cast himself at the feet of the blessed Apostles St Peter and St Paul, special patrons of that place, and afterwards by their good help and motion to seek to be received (if he might) into the religion of the Society of the B. Name of Jesus, and therein to lead the rest of his life according of the direction of his Superiors." Arriving in Rome in the spring of 1573, Campion was sent to Prague, thence to Brno, and then back to Prague, where he taught rhetoric in the Jesuit college, the Clementina. He was ordained by the archbishop of Prague in 1578. Campion also produced written work during this period, notably the play *Ambrosia* (1578). Ibid., xxv–xxvi.

   For Campion's time in Bohemia, see McCoog, *And Touching Our Society*, Chapter 3.

Society named for the mission to England, one was Father Campion.[7] En route to Rheims, he asked Doctor Allen what he thought of his going to England and of the the fruit that might be expected from it. Allen told him to be of good cheer, for he might do far more good in his homeland than in Bohemia, for the harvest was more abundant and the value of gathering and securing it would be greater—and in England he might receive the crown of martyrdom, which he could not easily attain in Bohemia.

Campion arrived in England in the year 1580, on the day of the glorious Saint John the Baptist, his protector and advocate, and then began to perform his ministries and to preach every day in secret,[8] some days even two or three sermons, which were attended by huge crowds of listeners and which converted many among the wisest and noblest men of the kingdom, as well as an enormous number of students and genteel youths and other persons of all ranks and classes. After he went to London, he defied the heretical ministers and offered to dispute with them, as well as writing a book setting forth, with supreme erudition, spirit, and eloquence, his reasons for living and dying in the Catholic faith. When the heretics were at a loss to respond to this, their fury and hatred for him grew so great that they expended every effort to capture him and punish him as a traitor and rebel to the nation, hoping to hide their ignorance and stupidity by this pretext and cover. For although Father Campion was but one among a thousand children of the Church, neither foremost nor the leader of those of the Society of Jesus in England, he was so feared by the heretics and so revered by the Catholics that they called him the pope's captain and his right hand. Knowing that they were after him and that he could not escape, given the range and extent of the measures they took to capture him—unless God preserved him by some miracle—Campion addressed the following statements to the queen's council, declaring his reasons for coming to that kingdom and his intentions:[9]

1.   I confess that, although unworthy, I am a cleric of the Catholic Church, and that, by the mercy of God, it has been eight years since I took the

---

7   In light of Mercurian's deep skepticism about the English mission, the choice of men was actually in the hands of Cardinal Allen. McCoog, *Our Way of Proceeding?* 133.

8   Added in the 1595 edition.

9   Campion's famous "Brag," in which he justified the Jesuits' mission to England and challenged the Protestants to public disputation. The "Brag" has been reproduced numerous times: see, for example, E.E. Reynolds, *Campion and Parsons: The Jesuit Mission of 1580–1* (London: Sheed and Ward, 1980), 78–81.

vow and donned the habit of religion in the holy Society of Jesus and entered a new militia under the banner of obedience, casting aside all private interests or honors and separating myself from all vanity or human felicity.

2. Being in Prague, the metropolis and capital of the kingdom of Bohemia, I went to Rome at the command of our general, whom I hold in Christ's stead, and from Rome I came to England with utter joy, as I would to any other part of the world if he so orders me.

3. My office is to preach the Gospel, administer the sacraments, teach the unlearned, disabuse the deceived, take up arms against vices and errors, such as I see so many of my compatriots and my beloved homeland consumed by and well-nigh drowned in.

4. I have never had any intention of meddling in matters of state or the governance of the realm, nor can I do so in any way (being strictly prohibited by the fathers who sent me), for these are foreign to my vocation, and thus I willingly flee them and keep them from my thoughts.

5. By the honor of God our Lord, I ask and entreat Your Lordships to mandate that I be given peaceful and quiet audience, in one of three ways. The first, before Your Lordships alone. The second, before the doctors and scholars of the universities, for I undertake to give an account of myself and to confirm the faith of our sacred Catholic Church, by irrefutable arguments from Holy Scripture, the holy Fathers and Doctors, histories, and natural and moral reasoning. The third, before the lawyers, judges, and canonists, that I may do the same in their presence, and prove my faith by the laws, statutes, and decrees of this realm even now in observance, force, and vigor.

6. I have no intention of saying anything that might seem presumptuous or arrogant, especially having made a vow to place myself beneath the feet of all, and being, as I am and as I wish to be, dead to the world—but yet I have within me a spirit so much of service and praise to the majesty of Jesus my king, such confidence in his divine favor, and such security in this my enterprise that I am emboldened affirm that there is no Protestant whatsoever, nor any minister of any sect, who dares to and can sustain and defend their faith and creed in argument and dispute, if we put our hands to it as I desire.

7. And therefore I fervently beg and entreat you to arm yourselves and take the field, all of you, or each of you, or the leaders and captains among you, for I alone will oppose all, confident in the Lord's grace and his truth, and thus I warn you that the more who come prepared, the more I shall rejoice, and the more shall I welcome them.

8.   And because I know that the queen possesses many natural gifts and that
      God has adorned her with an excellent judgment and intellect, if Her
      Majesty would deign to be present at the disputation or to hear some of
      my sermons, I trust in the divine goodness that her zeal for the truth and
      her love for her people may well prompt her to undo some of the laws
      that are grievous and harmful to her kingdom, and to treat with greater
      kindness and mercy those of us who, without any guilt of ours, are op-
      pressed by them.

9.   Furthermore, I do not doubt but that you, my lords of Her Majesty's privy
      council, being men of such wisdom and experience in matters of the high-
      est import, will, when you have heard these religious controversies faith-
      fully expounded (which our adversaries teach with such great obscurity
      and confusion), perceive how true, how deep, how sure and firm are the
      foundations upon which our Catholic faith is built and, by contrast, how
      weak and fallible are those of the opposing party, though by the evilness
      of the times it seems to prevail against us. And I trust that in the end, con-
      sidering the obligations of your office and the eternal salvation of your
      souls, you will favor those who choose to shed their blood for that faith.
      Many English Catholics and servants of God lift up their hands to heaven
      and continually pray to God for the wellbeing of their homeland. Count-
      less students prepare and furnish themselves with sound doctrine and
      unimpeachable discipline for this enterprise, with the intention never to
      cease until they have achieved victory or they lose their lives in torment.
      All we of the Society of Jesus are of one soul and one heart, and we are
      resolved to die in this conquest, and not to abandon it so long as one of
      us remains alive, and we have the spirit and strength (solely by the grace
      of he who gives it us) to bear with joy any cross, however heavy, you may
      cast upon our shoulders, and to suffer dungeons, prisons, tortures, and
      death for the salvation of your souls. The expense is reckoned, the enter-
      prise is begun, the cause is God's, whom none can resist. The faith of Jesus
      Christ is sown in blood, and in blood must it be reaped.
          If you do not deign benignly to accept what I here tell and offer you,
      and recompense with harshness my efforts and the goodwill and dili-
      gence with which I have traveled so many leagues in coming to this land
      for your sake, I have nothing more to say than to commend this enterprise
      of mine and of yours to God, the searcher of hearts[10] and the righteous
      judge, who rewards each according to their works.[11] To this Lord I pray

---

10   1 Chron. 28:9; Ps. 43:22; 138:23; Jer. 17:10; 20:12; Acts 1:24; Rom. 8:27; Rev. 2:23.

11   Ps. 7:12, 27:4, 61:13; Matt. 16:27; Rom. 2:6; 2 Tim. 4:8.

that he give you light and in his grace unite and reconcile our hearts, before the day of reckoning comes, so that in the end we may be friends in heaven, where there is no discord nor enmity, and all offenses and injuries are forgiven. In the month of October of this present year of 1580.[12]

This is what Father Campion wrote at the time, manifesting his wisdom, bravery, and spirit in the enterprise he was conducting. But our Lord willed that,[13] in the end, he was arrested through the treachery of a damnable man named George Eliot, who had previously been a servant to Thomas Roper and then to the widow of William Petre [de Pedro] (the king's secretary), in whose houses he had lived as a Catholic among Catholics.[14] But having subsequently killed a man and fearing the punishment for his crime, to escape from it, knowing the eagerness of the queen's ministers to apprehend and capture Father Campion, he went to one of them and offered that if he was protected, he would expose Campion and place him in their hands, and so it was done. This he could do because, having the reputation of a Catholic, the Catholics had no suspicions of him, and on the very day of the arrest, July 17, 1581,[15] he heard Mass from Father Campion himself, and a sermon on those words of our Lord addressed to Jerusalem: "Jerusalem, Jerusalem, you who slay the prophets and stone those who are sent unto you."[16]

Now, when Campion was caught and found himself in the hands of his enemies, he treated them with such remarkable restraint, gentleness, patience, and Christian humility in all his words and deeds that all good men were edified and his enemies dumbfounded. They bore him to London along with other priests and Catholic gentlemen, bound hand and foot, and for the greater derision and humiliation, they waited until market day, so that upon his entry there would be a thicker crowd of people, and on the crown of his hat they

---

12   Ribadeneyra probably translated from the Latin text in *Concertatio*, 1ʳ–2ᵛ.

13   The passage on Campion's brag is added in the 1595 edition.

14   George Eliot (dates unknown) had served in the households of both Lady Anne Petre (*née* Tyrrell, d.1582), widow of Sir William Petre (c.1505–72), secretary to Edward VI, and the jurist Thomas Roper (c.1533–98), a grandson of Thomas More. In both situations, Eliot had been taken for a faithful Catholic. Graves, "Campion, Edmund," in *ODNB*, 9:874. C.S. Knighton, "Petre, Sir William (1505/6–1572)," in *ODNB*, 43:912–16, here 913, 915. Richard Simpson, *Edmund Campion: A Biography*, The Catholic Standard Library (London: John Hodges, 1896), 315.

15   Campion was arrested on July 17, 1581 at Lyford Grange in Berkshire. McCoog, *Our Way of Proceeding?* 154.

16   Matt. 23:37; Luke 13:34.

placed a sign with these words in large letters: "This is Campion, the seditious Jesuit." For in this, as in everything else, they imitated the pagan tyrants: we read of the glorious martyr Attalus, whom they led around the amphitheater with a sign upon his breast that said, "This is Attalus, the Christian."[17]

Passing through the silver market, he bowed before a cross with the utmost humility, made a deep reverence, and made the sign of the cross upon his breast as well as he could. The whole crowd was struck with admiration. Three times he was savagely tortured on the rack or *cauallete*; perceiving that they intended to kill him through sheer torment, amid his agony he invoked the favor of our Lord and the holy names of Jesus and Mary with sublime gentleness. Being suspended in the air, his limbs strained and dislocated, his arms and his feet bound to the wheels upon which they tormented him, he forgave his torturers and the authors of his pain with sublime charity,[18] and thanked one of them for having placed a stone beneath his already broken and shattered back, as some little comfort and relief. Not content with these or the many other extreme and horrific torments with which they afflicted and mutilated his body, his enemies tried a thousand diabolical schemes to rob him of his reputation, with preachers barking against him and claiming several times that he had recanted, or else that he had revealed all he knew and been rewarded, or that he had died in prison, and other absurdities of this kind. In other cases, the heretics used first to debate with their Catholic prisoners to try to allure them with words, or at least to convince the people that they had been swayed and agreed with them on some point—and when they could not achieve this, then they turned to torments and brutalized them, avenging themselves with torture upon those they could not conquer with words and arguments. With Father Campion, they did the opposite, because they did not believe they could persuade him without first torturing him; but once they saw him mangled and nearly dead, barely able to force a word past his lips, alone and without books, they dreamed that the sufferings of his body would also oppress his spirit, cloud his judgment, and disturb his memory, and so they conceived some hope of victory. And so the most learned and esteemed heretical ministers came to the jail cell to dispute with him and seize this opportunity to denigrate him—but they were left so abashed and humiliated by the responses that this isolated man, abused and well-nigh dead, gave them, so copious and well shaped, that the judges were forced to order him to keep silent, threatening him with yet greater

---

17   In the margin: "Eusebius, Book 5, Chapter 1."

   The parallel to the story of Attalus in Eusebius's *Ecclesiastical History*, originally implicitly, is set out expressly in the 1595 edition.

18   Luke 23:34.

torments if he did not. These disputations lasted four days, in the morning from eight until eleven and in the afternoon from two to five.[19] Their rules strictly forbade him to ask anything or argue against the others, permitting him only respond to what was asked of him. A huge number of heretics (and disguised Catholics) were present at the debate. Truly incredible was the modesty, sweetness, patience, and gentleness our Lord then gave Father Campion to endure the shouts, insults, injuries, and disrespect with which he was abused by the heretical ministers, to the astonishment and edification of many of his misbelieving hearers. But no less marvelous was the wisdom and force with which our Lord (whose cause he defended) armed him to refute and silence all his adversaries, as has been said—who were so confused and lost that they resolved never again to dispute with a Jesuit. Seeing that all the many sharp and bitter torments they had inflicted on him had proved useless, they tried to sway him with flattery and promises. As though these, and all that there was in the kingdom of England, and in the entire universe, of riches, honor, glory, or rank could be a worthy recompense for the least of his virtues or for that blessed soul, adorned with the singular graces of God, purchased with the precious blood of Christ our Redeemer!

Sentence was passed against Campion and his aforementioned companions on November 20, 1581. And on December 1 they brought Father Campion by himself on one hurdle, with Ralph Sherwin and Alexander Briant together on another; while they were waiting, they lovingly embraced him and spoke a few words of deep tenderness and kindness.[20]

When they hauled Campion before the people, he cried in a loud voice, "Brothers, God keep you, God bless you all and make you Catholics." When they

---

19   In the aftermath of Campion's public challenge in the *Rationes decem*, published on June 27, 1581, the authorities determined that his demands for disputations had become too well known to be ignored. A sequence of Protestant theologians faced Campion and Sherwin in four debates on August 31 and September 18, 23, and 27. While his interlocutors were permitted extensive time and support in preparation, Campion was kept ignorant even of the subject until a few hours beforehand. After the encounter on September 27, the fifth debate was cancelled. McCoog, *Reckoned Expense*, 154, 158–60.

Some onlookers, at least, were impressed with what they saw of Campion: one Oliver Pluckytt (dates unknown) reportedly declared, "Campyon was both dyscrett and learned, and dyd say verie well, and that he thought in his consciens that he was an honest man, And that the said Campyon would have convinced them, yf that he might have bene hard with indifferencye." Quoted in Lake and Questier, "Puritans, Papists, and the 'Public Sphere,'" 621.

20   Campion, Sherwin, and Briant were all hanged, drawn, and quartered together at Tyburn on December 1, 1581. For a contemporary depiction, see Book 2 Figure 32.1.

Qui Summi Pontificis primatum Reginæ in Anglia negant tribui posse,
tanquam Læsæ Maiestatis rei damnantur, et ad supßilicij locum, Cratibus
impositi, ministris interim hæreticis ad fidem Catholicam deserendam
adhortantibus, per mediam Vrbem ignominiosè raptantur. Sic Edmundus
Campianus cum socijs, alijque Catholici tum Sacerdotes tum laici ad
mortem tracti sunt. Anno Domini 1581. 1582. 1583.

FIGURE 32.1   *Edmund Campion, Ralph Sherwin, and Alexander Briant are dragged to the*
                scaffold.
                Giovanni Battista Cavalieri, *Ecclesiae anglicanae trophaea sive sanctorum*
                martyrum qui pro Christo catholicaeque fidei veritate asserenda antiquo
                recentiorique persecutionum tempore mortem in Anglia subierunt, passiones
                Romae in collegio Anglico per Nicolaum Circinianum depictae: Nuper autem
                per Io. Bap. de Cavalleriis aeneis typis repraesentatae (Rome: Ex officina
                Bartolomeo Grassi, 1584). NE1666 .C57 1584 OVERSIZE, John J. Burns Library,
                Boston College.

brought him to the torment, dragging him by the tail of a horse, some heretics harassed him and urged him in shrill screams to recant; others—Catholics— came to him in secret and comforted him as best they could, asking his counsel and washing away the mud that had fallen upon him.[21] On reaching the place of martyrdom, with practically the entire city of London in attendance, he was raised up on the cart; once the crowd had quieted down and he has rested for a moment to gather his strength, with solemn aspect, gentle voice, and fearless spirit he spoke thus: *Spectaculum facti sumus Deo, Angelis et hominibus.* These are the words of Saint Paul, which in the vernacular was to convey, "We are made a spectacle to God, to the angels, and to men—which is today verified in me, who as you see am a spectacle for my Lord, and the angels, and you men." Wishing to proceed, they interrupted him and refused to allow him to speak, telling him to confess his treacheries. And after he had affirmed his innocence with forceful reasons, he gave himself over to calm and profound prayer, preparing himself to drink the last draught of the chalice of Jesus Christ.[22] As he did so, a heretical minister disturbed him, urging him to say, together with him, "Lord have mercy upon me." Campion turned to him with a mild and humble countenance, saying, "You and I are not of one and the same faith, and thus I beg you to be silent. I will keep no one from their prayer, but I desire that only Catholics should pray with me, and that in this moment they should say one Credo—testifying that I die for the Catholic faith, contained therein." They removed the tumbril and let him hang; while he was only half-suffocated and half-alive, they cut the cord;[23] he fell to the earth and they cut him open, severed his natural parts, removed his entrails, pulled out his heart, and carved him into quarters, which were boiled and stuck upon the bridge and other public places in the city. With this, the saintly Father Campion ran his race with joy[24] and effortlessly yielded his spirit to the Lord, always declaring that he died a true and perfect Catholic. The death of Father Campion, his calmness, dignity, and innocence, moved many to sympathy and plentiful tears: to calm these affected souls, the heretics were forced to print books excusing their tyranny and proffering justifications. In this glorious, gracious way, this

---

21   An allusion, perhaps, to the tradition of Saint Veronica, a non-canonical figure who supposedly wiped the sweat from Christ's face as he fell beneath the weight of the Cross. Farmer, *Oxford Dictionary of Saints*, 433–34.

22   Matt. 20:22–23, 26:39; Mark 10:38–39; Luke 22:42; John 18:11; 1 Cor. 10:21.

23   From the 1595 edition onwards, Ribadeneyra shortens this clause slightly, such that it reads "half-alive, they cut the cord."

24   1 Cor. 9:24; 2 Tim. 4:7; Heb. 12:1.

man of God ended his life and conquered in Christ all the miseries of this frail, mortal body, now enjoying the triumphal crown of his blessed confession and the martyrdom he accepted by the singular providence of the Lord, before the entire city of London, where he had been born. Let its citizens, who did not deserve to enjoy the works and life of so illustrious a native son, now at least be converted from their errors and illuminated with the splendor of the truth, by means of the heartfelt prayers he continually makes in the presence of the sovereign majesty and by the merit of that pure blood that he shed for them and before them in testimony of that truth.

Of the Other Martyrs and Persecuted Catholics

After Father Campion had majestically triumphed over the world, the flesh, the devil, and heresy, and received the crown of glory (as has been said), Ralph Sherwin, a virtuous, erudite, and thoughtful priest who had been a student at the seminary in Rome,[1] mounted the hurdle to follow in Campion's footsteps. Ralph was a man so stricken and weakened by fasts, vigils, penances, and other spiritual exercises that all who had met or known him before he was imprisoned were aghast. While in his cell, he was so harsh and rigorous with himself and his body that his astounded guard, heretic though he was, called him a man of God and publicly said that he was the greatest and most devout priest he had seen in his life. He was imprisoned in secret for a year, in which time he frequently debated with the heretical ministers, both in private and in public, before numerous knights and influential persons, to the enormous admiration of the observers and the consternation of his interlocutors. So great was the pleasure and happiness of his soul at seeing himself imprisoned, shackled, and so weighed down with fetters that he could not move, or at hearing the clank of his chain, that he could restrain neither his laughter, which burst form his lips with great force, nor the abundant tears, which his eyes, like two fountains, shed in pure pleasure. He said that never in his life had he heard a song so melodious, nor harmony so sweet, as was the music—to his ears—of the noise of the chains and shackles he wore.

A few days before they martyred him, he wrote a letter to some friends of his, which says, among other points:

> Truly, I had hoped ere now to have left this mortal body and kissed the precious, glorious wounds of my sweet Savior, seated upon the throne of majesty, at the right hand of the Father.[2] And this my desire, or, as I should

---

1 Sherwin resided at the English College at Rome from 1577 to 1580, where he "became the spokesman for those who saw the future of the college to be a place for the preparation of missioners to England rather than a refuge for exiles." Williams, "Sherwin, Ralph," in ODNB, 50:343.

   As with Campion, most of Ribadeneyra's description of Sherwin is a translation of the Italian edition of Allen: see Allen, *Historia*, 97, 103–05; Allen, *Briefe Historie*, 34, 40–41.

2 Matt. 26:64; Mark 14:62; Luke 22:69; Acts 7:55; Rom. 8:34; Col. 3:1; Heb. 1:3, 8:1, 12:2; 1 Pet. 3:22.

© KONINKLIJKE BRILL NV, LEIDEN, 2017 | DOI 10.1163/9789004323964_089

say, God's (for his it is, he having given it me, as I believe), has calmed and exalted my soul such that the sentence of death pronounced against us has not frightened me much, nor has the brevity of life grieved me. True it is that my sins are great,[3] but I commit myself to the mercy of the Lord; my guilt is infinite, but I appeal to the clemency of my Redeemer;[4] I trust in nothing but in his blood; his bitter passion is sweet solace for me, in his precious hands we are written, as the prophet says. O, if he should deign to inscribe himself in our hearts,[5] with what joy we should appear before the tribunal of glory of the eternal Father, whose sovereign and infinite majesty, when I contemplate it, shakes my frail flesh and leaves it awestruck, for so weak a thing cannot bear the presence and majesty of its creator.[6]

And in another letter, written to an uncle of his, on the day before his death, he said:

Innocence is the impenetrable shield and armor with which I am forti-fied against the countless slanders they spread against me and my com-panions: when the sovereign and righteous judge strips away from the faces of men the deceitful mask of treason they thrust upon us, then shall be seen who has a clean and sincere heart, and who an unquiet and sedi-tious one.[7]

After Ralph had run his race with joy,[8] he was followed by the even young-er Alexander Briant, who had been in the seminary at Rheims, a pious and learned priest, of effortless grace in preaching and of marvelous zeal, patience, constancy, and humility.[9] While in prison, they so tormented him with hunger

---

3   Ps. 24:11.

4   In the margin: "Isaiah 49[:16]."

5   Jer. 31:33; 2 Cor. 3:3; Heb. 8:10, 10:16.

6   Ribadeneyra probably translated from the Italian edition of William Allen's account of the English martyrs, which reproduces this letter of Sherwin's. See Allen, *Historia*, 106–07; Allen, *Briefe Historie*, 41–42.

7   William Allen reproduces in full a letter from Sherwin to his uncle, John Woodward (dates unknown), a priest living at Rouen. See Allen, *Historia*, 109; Allen, *Briefe Historie*, 42–43.

8   1 Cor. 9:24; 2 Tim. 4:7; Heb. 12:1.

9   Ribadeneyra's account of Briant is largely a translation of the Italian edition of Allen. See Allen, *Historia*, 112–16; Allen, *Briefe Historie*, 48–51.

that there was little indeed to stop his life ending then and there, for they ordered that he be given nothing to eat or drink. So he remained for many days, until our Lord provided him with some crusts of bread and a bit of hard cheese, which, along with a mouthful of beer and a few drops of water from the gutters that he collected in his hat when it rained, sustained him and saved him from dying of starvation. Among the other tortures inflicted upon him (numerous and extreme), they shoved needles between his fingernails and the flesh—and as they thrust them in, the saint persevered with unbelievable endurance, neither quailing nor flinching, praying the *Miserere mei* with a steady and joyous spirit and imploring our Lord to pardon those who thus tormented him.[10] Seeing this, a certain Hammond, one of the magistrates,[11] was distraught, and as though stricken and deranged began to scream, crying, "What is this? What wonder is this we see? If a man were not well rooted and firm in his faith, the prodigious constancy and firmness of this man would be enough to convert him." They stretched him upon the rack, mangling him with such extraordinary cruelty that they almost tore him apart and dismembered him, for he refused to reveal where Persons or his printing press were. After Briant lost consciousness, unable to stir hand, foot, or any other part of his body, they left him lying on the floor for fifteen days, without a bed or any other comfort, amid grievous pains and sorrows. When they brought him to hear the sentence of his condemnation, he found a way to make a little wooden crucifix, which he carried openly, and to cut himself a tonsure, to show the heretics he prized his holy orders and his faith. In the end, he endured such frightful torments with such admirable steadfastness and joy that he seemed one of those valiant, unconquerable martyrs of the days of Nero, Decius, or Diocletian.[12] All this he could not have humanly endured, save by the special and extraordinary mercy of heaven. And he himself confessed that he had been miraculously consoled in all those pains by the Lord, through the vow he made to enter the Society of Jesus, and other spiritual practices, as he wrote to the fathers of the Society in England, begging them to accept him among them, in a letter that runs thus:

---

10   Luke 23:34.

11   John Hammond (1542–c.1590), a Cambridge-educated jurist, was one of the lawyers tasked with eliciting confessions from Campion and other captured Catholics. P.O.G. White, "Hammond, John (1542–1589/90)," in *ODNB*, 24:957.

12   The Roman Emperors Nero (r.54–68), Decius (r.249–51), and Diocletian, depicted by Eusebius of Caesarea, and by ecclesiastical historians ever since, as the instigators of Rome's most brutal persecutions of the Christians.

Alexander Briant, imprisoned for the sake of Christ, to the fathers of the
Society of Jesus, greetings in the Lord.

When I fully call to mind, most reverend fathers, the miraculous solicitude with which God our Lord seeks the good of his creatures, the eternal
salvation of our souls, and the supreme urgency with which he desires to
possess our hearts in love and take them as his abode,[13] I am left in one
sense awestruck and astonished, and in another ashamed and confused,
to see the villainy of men, who never bring ourselves truly to serve him
and to make ourselves and all we have pure sacrifices and unsullied offerings to his divine majesty, prompted by so many mercies and kindness
received from his free and generous hand, lured on and enticed by the
hope of the prize we are promised, and likewise terrified by the might of
his threats and the fear of his strict and righteous judgments. For, leaving
to one side the immense benefits he has done us, he who has created us
from nothing and preserved us in the existence he gave us, he who has redeemed us at such cost to himself, who has called and justified us after we
were lost, and who has promised us the glory we hope for, how shall I express how, not content with this, he invites and allures us to abandon vanity and to follow him, saying with words of love and tenderness, "Come
to me, all the troubled and burdened, that I may refresh you[14] and that I
may love those who love me, and he who arises at dawn to meet me will
find me without fail,[15] and blessed is the man who hears me and waits
at my doors each day and watches at their shadows, for he who finds me
finds life and receives salvation from the Lord."[16] And he who orders us
to follow him teaches us where we are to find him, saying, "Wherever two
or three are gathered in my name, I am in their midst."[17] There we may
know for certain that Christ is to be found, where many gather, united by
the bond of charity, with the sole end and aim of serving and honoring
the Lord, observing his holy precepts and admonitions, and expanding
and extending, as much as they can, his glorious name and kingdom. And
he who, at this call of the Lord's, having left behind the vanity and falsehood that the world teaches, opens the ears of his soul, such a one shall
learn the truth, and he shall not wander in the shadows and gloom of

---

13   John 14:23; Rom. 8:9; Eph. 2:22, 3:17; 1 John 4:12.
14   Matt. 11:28.
15   Prov. 8:17.
16   Prov. 8:34–35.
17   Matt. 18:20.

error, but walk in safety by the pure springs of the water of life.[18] In such gatherings and meetings, wholly dedicated to the divine service, we find the correct path that brings us to eternal life, not neglected or covered with thorns and thistles, but rather clearly marked and leveled by the feet and the examples of the saint who have trodden it. Nor is it adorned and garlanded with the flowers and novelties of the pleasures and delights of the flesh, which fade away so swiftly and dissolve like smoke,[19] but rather surrounded and filled with laws, precepts, and holy rules, and with sound warnings and counsels, lest the little ones and the untaught stray or lose themselves, casting themselves from the cliffs of vice and sin.[20] Here we find everything arranged with admirable uniformity and harmony, in number, weight, and measure, as a place where divine wisdom truly reigns, whose works are always well-ordered. Here flowers and flourishes religious discipline, here is seen the good of correction and fraternal advice, here is practiced the gentle chastisement of the passions and disordered affections, and here, in the end, is found a fervent and holy emulation, with which each aids, urges, and incites his fellow to brotherly love.

And so, for the sake of these and other things the Lord has shown me inwardly, which I have repeatedly contemplated, after long deliberation over the past two years I have resolved and determined, with a firm and pure intention, to choose this kind of life, if God our Lord is served thereby. To assure myself thereof, I imparted this to a devout and religious gentleman, who was then my spiritual father, asking him to tell me if he knew whether, on my returning to my homeland (whither I had just cause for going), the fathers of the Society of Jesus would receive me into their order, for the Lord was fiercely calling me to it. He answered that if it was a calling from God (as it was) he had no doubt of it, but rather perfect confidence that I would attain it. The strength and spirit I received from such an answer was enormous, and there have also been many other occasions since when before our Lord I again renewed and refreshed that holy intention that God inspired within me, and, finding myself then in England, where I thought my labors and efforts might win some fruit, working to recall some of those souls that wander so far astray from the true path of their salvation, so alien to the knowledge of their Savior, I postponed that intention for some time, until God brought me to a place where I might

---

18   John 4:14; Rev. 7:17, 21:6, 22:1.

19   Ps. 101:4.

20   Matt. 18:6; Mark 9:41; Luke 17:2.

more fittingly complete it. But since it pleases our Lord, according to his divine and secret judgments, that I am now imprisoned and without the freedom to act upon this intent of mine, with this heavenly impulse and calling growing each day within me, as well as the fervent desire for perfection, I have made a vow to our Lord, having considered it for a long time, with the sole aim of better serving God, to his greater glory, of being more assured of my soul's salvation, and of triumphing over the devil, who seeks to hinder me, in a more notable and glorious victory. Thus, I took a vow, as I say, that if and when the Lord wills to remove me from this prison, I would place myself in the hands of the fathers of the Society of Jesus, for them to do in this business what they deem most to the honor and glory of our Lord, and that if (by God's inspiration) they should receive me, I would submit all my freedom to obedience to the Society and the service of our Lord. And it has been this intention and vow that amid all the mighty trials of my imprisonment consoles me and gives me strength to endure the torments I have endured. It is likewise what gave me the confidence to preserve my fortitude and patience amid tortures, when, armed with it and with the intercession of our Lady the Virgin Mary, I came to the throne of the divine majesty to beg for mercy. And without any doubt, it was guided by the hand of the Lord that I came to make this vow and final resolution, when I thought I was before our Lord, having left behind the things of the earth and profoundly contemplating those of the heavens—which came to pass in this manner.

On the first day that the Lord showed me the favor of being tortured for his holy name and faith, before entering the place of torment I managed to sequester myself in prayer for a moment, utterly commending myself and all I had to the Lord, to endure so awful and arduous a trial. My soul received an immense, singular joy and consolation in repeating the holy name of Jesus and Mary and praying the rosary, whence I conceived a steadfast spirit, ready for any sort of peril or combat that the devil should offer me through his ministers. In this spirit, I recalled the former intention the Lord had given me of joining the Society, and it seemed to me a good opportunity to confirm with a vow what I had previously desired, and so, having finished my prayer, I began to consider the matter inwardly. And after long deliberation, I freely swore to enter the Society, if the Lord should be served to free me from that prison. After that it seemed as though our Lord wished to communicate to me that my offering had been accepted, for in every subsequent tribulation and trial I felt his mighty hand was visibly aiding me and comforting me amid the worst agonies and necessities, freeing my soul, as the Prophet says, from unjust lips and the deceiving tongue[21] of those who continually bellowed before me, ready to assay me.

In all this, something happened to me—whether it was supernatural, or miraculous, God alone knows, not I, but that it happened as I shall relate, my own conscience may be my witness before God. In the last torment I suffered, when the cruel torturers again expended their fury upon my flesh, having bound me with cords by the ends of my feet and hands, so stretched that there was no part of my body, no joint however small, that they had not dislocated with the force of the jolts, it happened that, aided by the divine hand, not only did I feel no pain whatsoever, but indeed I felt that in reality I was at rest and relieved from the previous tortures, and so I remained as long as they tormented me, with as much peace and serenity as if nothing had happened. The queen's agents and officials were so shocked at this that they had me removed from the torture; the following day they would find some new, exquisite mode of cruelty with which to afflict me. When I heard this, it made no impression on me, on account of the supreme confidence I had in the almighty hand of the Lord, which in this as in all the rest would give me patience and fortitude, and as they poured out their utmost efforts, I still contemplated the grievous passion of our Redeemer, Jesus Christ, full of infinite sorrows and trials. And what is more, while I was in torment, it seemed to me that one of the tortures had wounded me in my left hand and that blood was flowing from it, but when I came to and looked at it, I found nothing, nor felt any pain there whatsoever. Other notable things happened to me that I omit for the sake of brevity.

And so, to convey to Your Reverences my desire and intention—given that, to speak honestly and realistically, there is at present no hope of liberty from this prison—absent in body and present in soul and the spirit of my heart, I humbly place myself beneath the feet of Your Reverences, imploring you with all the urgency I can muster to consider me entirely present before our Lord, and freely to determine for me what you judge to the greater glory of God and the salvation of my soul, and, if it is possible that in absence I might be received into the Society, I beg Your Reverences by the blood of Jesus Christ to do so, that thus our Lord may make me one of his servants and, aided by the prayers and sacrifices of his many friends, I may go to that reward I have been promised with greater confidence and fortitude. I well know the many tricks and snares of the

---

21   Ps. 119:2.

ancient adversary, who, like a cunning serpent and a coiled snake, seeks with a thousand schemes to deceive and cheat simple souls, who have no one to turn to in their necessity or to unfailingly protect them, by transforming himself into an angel of light,[22] wherefore the Apostle rightly counsels us to test all spirits and movements of the soul and examine carefully whether they are of God.[23] To Your Reverences, as to spiritual men skilled in such battles, I commend this business, imploring you by the merciful heart of the Lord to deign to direct and guide me by your counsel and prudence. And if you should judge it more expedient for divine service, the interests of the Church, and the eternal salvation of my soul hereafter to receive me, as I have said, into the Society of the most holy name of Jesus, I promise before the divine majesty my eternal submission to each and every superior and officer of the Society who governs it now or in future, and to all its rules and statutes, with all my strength, insofar as the Lord assists me to it. Of which intention and vow of mine, I wish my deeds this day and what I have written in my own hand to be a witness on the day of judgment before the righteous tribunal of the judge of the living and the dead.[24]

Of the health and wholeness of my body, Your Reverences have nothing to fear, for I am now, by the goodness of God, as hale and strong as before the tortures, and each day I feel myself to possess yet greater forces. For the moment, nothing else presents itself, save eagerly to ask to be commended in the holy sacrifices and prayers of Your Reverences, that the Lord aid me in these trials of my prison cell, where I remain, awaiting each moment the decision of Your Reverences concerning this business.

The unworthy servant of Your Reverences,

Alexander Briant

Let us now return to our history.[25] All these men were dragged, hanged upon the gallows, allowed to fall while half-alive, cut open, disemboweled, and torn

---

22   2 Cor. 11:14.

23   1 John 4:1.

24   Acts 10:42; 2 Tim. 4:1; 1 Pet. 4:5.

25   Briant's letter is added in the 1595 edition.

While imprisoned in the Tower, Briant requested admission to the Society of Jesus through his contacts with Persons. Thompson Cooper, "Briant, Alexander [St Alexander Briant] (1556–1581)," rev. Michael Mullett, in *ODNB*, 7:543–545, here 543.

Ribadeneyra may have translated from the Latin text included in the *Concertatio* or the Italian text in Allen: see *Concertatio*, 74ᵛ–75ᵛ; Allen, *Historia*, 116–21; Allen, *Briefe Historie*, 51–55.

A. *Edmundus Campianus societatis Iesu sub patibulo concionatur, statimq,
cum Alexandro Brianto Rhemensis, et Rodulpho Sheruiño huius Collegij
alumno suspenditur.*

B. *Illis adhuc tepentibus cor et uiscera extrahuntur, et in ignem proijciuntur.*

C. *Eorundem membra feruenti aqua elixantur, tum adurbis turres et portas
appenduntur, regnante Elizabetha Anno M.D.LXXXI. die prima Decēbris.
Horum constanti morte aliquot hominum millia ad Romanam Ecclesiam
conuersa sunt.* 33

FIGURE 33.1   *The martyrdoms of Edmund Campion, Ralph Sherwin, and Alexander Campion.*
Giovanni Battista Cavalieri, *Ecclesiae anglicanae trophaea sive sanctorum
martyrum qui pro Christo catholicaeque fidei veritate asserenda antiquo recentiorique persecutionum tempore mortem in Anglia subierunt, passiones Romae
in collegio Anglico per Nicolaum Circinianum depictae: Nuper autem per Io. Bap.
de Cavalleriis aeneis typis repraesentatae* (Rome: Ex officina Bartolomeo Grassi,
1584). NE1666 .C57 1584 OVERSIZE, John J. Burns Library, Boston College.

apart, dying as traitors and rebels to the queen, in the same manner as we related of Father Campion.[26]

After these three doughty captains had fought and conquered in glory, the following year, on May 20, 1582, three more priests were martyred in London,[27] and on May 30 of the same year another four of their companions, among whom was one Thomas Cottam of the Society of Jesus, an exemplary, saintly man.[28] And in the same year and in those that followed, many others, clerics and laymen, in London and in other English cities, have shed their precious blood for the confession of Catholic truth with wondrous patience and steadfastness. And there have been many laymen among those who have refused to enter the heretics' churches or attend their profane ceremonies, and for this and for being unable to pay the fines that they owed according to the laws of the land, have been dragged to humiliation and public floggings, abused with extreme opprobrium and derision. The heretics have not been satisfied with persecuting, torturing, and murdering the priests and laymen of middling or low estate, and have also brutalized leading knights and lords and even noblemen of the realm, whom they knew or suspected of having returned to or reaffirmed the Catholic faith, weary of their cruelty and disabused (by the mercy of God) of their errors. Among the lords they have imprisoned or killed have been the earl of Arundel[29] and the earl of Northumberland,[30] who are some of the most illustrious peers of the realm, exalted in gentility, wealth, kin, and dignity. The earl of Arundel, the eldest son of the duke of Norfolk, was fleeing England because he could not stand the atrocities and abuses perpetrated there each day against the Catholics, so that he could live outside the kingdom in peace and security of conscience: he was arrested at sea and thrown into prison with his brothers, uncle, kinsmen, servants, and friends, where he yet remains, waiting for them to do to him what they have done to the earl of Northumberland.[31] Northumberland,

---

26 For a contemporary depiction of the martyrdoms, see Book 2 Figure 33.1.

27 Thomas Ford (d.1582), John Shert (d.1582), and Robert Johnson (d.1582). See Allen, *Briefe Historie*, 57–66.

28 Cottam was arrested less than a month after being sent to England, and executed at Tyburn on May 30, 1582, alongside the priests William Filbie (*c*.1555–82), Luke Kirby (*c*.1549–82), and Lawrence Johnson (known as Lawrence Richardson, d.1582). Cooper, "Cottam," in *ODNB*, 13:579–80. See Allen, *Briefe Historie*, 67–88.

29 Philip Howard, thirteenth earl of Arundel.

30 Henry Percy, eighth earl of Northumberland (1532–85).

31 Unable to endure the pressures of recusancy, Arundel fled in April 1585. Unfortunately, he was overtaken by a privateer and brought back to England. He was committed to the

after his elder brother was killed for having taken up arms for the Catholic faith, and he (at the time a heretic) had profited at the expense of his own brother, was arrested, released for a substantial sum of money, and banished. Later perceiving that he was Catholic at heart, the heretics seized him once again and tried to dispatch him with poisons, but did not succeed (thanks to the interference of a Catholic doctor). Thus it was that while imprisoned in the Tower of London, he was found one night dead in his bed, his body pierced by the bullet of an arquebus.[32] The heretics immediately proclaimed throughout the realm that the earl had lost hope and laid violent hands upon himself, killing himself with that gun because he knew the treacheries he had plotted against the queen and feared the penalties and punishments thereof, together with other false, improbable things, to conceal and camouflage their wickedness.[33] For they are not content with taking the lives of Catholics, but also strive to take their honors, nor does it satisfy them to commit the outrages they commit, but they also cast the blame upon the innocent, as will be seen in the following chapter.

Tower, and condemned to death in 1589, but the sentence was never carried out. He died in prison in 1595. Elzinga, "Howard, Philip," in *ODNB*, 28:406–08.

32   Thomas Percy, seventh earl of Northumberland (1528–72), led the unsuccessful 1569 Rising of the North, in the course of which he was captured by the Scots, who eventually sold him to Elizabeth. Thomas was beheaded at York on August 22, 1572, and his title reverted to his younger brother, Sir Henry Percy, then Elizabeth's ally and (at least ostensibly) a Protestant. Henry became entangled in the Ridolfi Plot to free Mary Queen of Scots, and was briefly imprisoned. A free man, he continued to conspire on Mary's behalf, and was sent to the Tower in January 1584. The earl was found dead on June 21, having ostensibly shot himself through the heart. Almost immediately, however, a pamphlet appeared charging that he had been murdered by the government: *Crudelitatis Calvinianae exempla duo recentissima ex Anglia* ([Cologne], 1585). Julian Lock, "Percy, Thomas, seventh earl of Northumberland (1528–1572)," in *ODNB*, 43:74–45, here 743–44. Carole Levin, "Percy, Henry, eighth earl of Northumberland (1532–1585)," in *ODNB*, 43:709–11, here 710.

33   An official account of Northumberland's death stressed the coroner's ruling of suicide, to the widespread ridicule of the Catholic community. See *A True and Summarie Reporte of the Declaration of Some Part of the Earle of Northumberlands Treasons* ([London]: In aedibus Christopher Barker, 1585).

How the Queen and Her Ministers Claimed that the Holy Martyrs Did Not Die for the Sake of Religion, but Rather for Other Crimes

Whenever they have persecuted Christians and sought by the cruelest tortures and massacres to eradicate our holy religion from the world, it has been the practice of the heathens and the pagans falsely to accuse these oppressed Christians and blame them for innumerable atrocious crimes, so that they would be seen as a pernicious people, hateful and deserving of the direst punishments. Thus, Emperor Nero, having set the city of Rome alight and enjoyed his awful inferno for a few days, when he saw the people's anger begin to turn against him, found false witnesses to cast the blame upon the Christians and denounce them as arsonists, revolutionaries, and enemies of the peace and tranquility of the empire. Under this label he persecuted and afflicted them with unimaginable sorts of tortures and modes of execution.[1] Tertullian laments how the Christians were maliciously accused by pagans who murdered their own children in human sacrifices.[2] And, to defend them against these and other slanders, Justin Martyr penned an *Apologia* to Emperor Antoninus Pius[3]—of whose persecutions Eusebius of Caesarea writes that in Gaul [*Francia*] they claimed that Christians ate human flesh and committed other crimes so hideous and hateful that they cannot be named.[4] Under these pretexts, they slaughtered and exterminated them, as well as rendering them (and with them the faith of Jesus Christ our Redeemer) hateful to the people. In the same way, Julian the Apostate, hoping to extinguish our holy religion and revive idolatry, condemned numerous priests to exile or death under the pretext of having committed countless grievous crimes, especially that of fostering and fomenting sedition against the empire.[5]

---

1 In the margin: "Tacitus, Book 15."
    Tacitus, *Annals*, 15.44.
2 In the margin: "In the *Apologia contra gentes*."
    Tertullian, *Apologeticus*, Chapters 4 and 9.
3 In the margin: "Justin Martyr, *Second Apology* to Antoninus."
4 In the margin: "Eusebius, Book 5, Chapter 1, and [Book] 4."
    Eusebius of Caesarea, *Ecclesiastical History*, 4.16, 5.1.
5 In the margin: "*Tripartite History*, Book 6, Chapter 27."

The heretics have followed in their footsteps, they have walked the very same paths, they have sought to crush the truth by these inventions and slanders. Most of all, when they persecute prelates and priests (the guides, leaders, and shepherds of the Church), they decry their monstrous crimes to render them odious and abhorrent to the people and assert that they are accused and imprisoned as felons on that account, rather than for their faith. So it was that the Arian emperors and their bishops calumniated Saint Athanasius, that mighty and unconquerable champion of the Catholic Church, as a necromancer, a criminal, and a traitor.[6] So it was that the magistrate of Pontus, a servant of the heretic emperor Valens, persecuted Saint Basil, that steadfast column of the Church, for his Catholic faith, under the pretext of other misdeeds—to the astonishment and incredulity of the entire world, he sought to find a woman in Basil's chamber![7] The Vandals (also Arian heretics) persecuted the Catholics of Africa with dreadful ferocity, alleging that they had made secret pacts against them with the Romans.[8] The Empress Theodora, wife of Emperor Justinian, being tainted with the heresy of Eutyches, cruelly hounded Pope Saint Silverius and his priests, deceitfully claiming that she had seized certain letters of theirs, in which they appealed to the Goths to aid them, to overthrow Rome, and to make themselves lords of the empire—though the entire world knew that these were utter falsities, and that she oppressed them for their Catholicism, which she abhorred.[9] Theoderic, the Arian king of the Ostrogoths, did the same in Italy to Pope Saint John, murdering him for his Catholic faith, though he pretended it was for other reasons.[10] For December 16 in

---

6   In the margin: "Rufinus's *History*, Book 10."

       Rufinus of Aquileia, *Church History*, 10.18.

7   In the margin: "Gregory of Nazianzus, in the oration on Basil."

       Gregory of Nazianzus, *Funeral Oration for Basil the Great*, Chapter 56.

8   In the margin: "Victor on the Vandal persecution."

       Victor of Vita, *History of the Vandal Persecution*, 4.4–5.

9   In the margin: "Paul the Deacon, [*Historia Romana*,] Book 16."

       See also Paul's source material, the *Liber Pontificalis*, 60.7–8.

       Eutyches (*c.*380–456), an "aged and muddle-headed archimandrite," became the standard-bearer for a set of Christological beliefs that held that Christ's human nature had been overcome by his divine nature. J.N.D. Kelly, *Early Christian Doctrines*, fifth edition (London: Adam & Charles Black, 1977), 331–32.

10   Ribadeneyra indicates no source, although John I's (r.523–26) death in 526 is related in the *Liber Pontificalis*: "Then the venerable pope John and the senators came home in glory after obtaining everything from the emperor Justin; king Theoderic the heretic received them with great treachery and hatred—namely pope John and the senators—and

the *Martyrologium Romanum*, mention is made of numerous sainted virgins who died in the Vandals' persecutions,[11] of whom Victor says that they died not only for the Catholic faith, but also because they absolutely refused to utter the lies and slanders against the servants of God that the heretics tried to force out of them by coercion and torture.[12] Church history furnishes many more examples.

Yet in all these, there is no more perfect image of such cunning wickedness than the heretics of our own day, especially in the English atrocities of which we are speaking. For all the slanders and miseries that the Catholic Church has suffered hitherto, from pagans, Arians, Goths, Vandals, Lombards, Donatists, Eutychians, Muslims, Hussites,[13] Huguenots, or any other diabolical sect of heretics or heathens, are reflected in this oppression as in a mirror, to such a degree that all others are as nothing in comparison. I have no desire to discuss the viciousness with which they falsely accused the archbishop of Armagh of rape and dragged him through a trial,[14] or how they worked to slander the holy martyr Thomas Cottam with adultery,[15] or the other filth they have piled upon the servants of God, how they have preached it from pulpits, spread it in the marketplaces, and published it in books, all to seduce and delude the common people, who are, by their simplicity, vulnerable to such tricks. All I wish to say is that these servants of Satan have not been content to spill the blood of innocents, saints, and blessed martyrs, but seeing that those who died were learned

---

he wanted to put them too to the sword, but in fear of the emperor Justin's wrath he destroyed them all by maltreatment in prison." Raymond Davis, ed., *The Book of Pontiffs (Liber Pontificalis): The Ancient Biographies of the First Ninety Roman Bishops to AD 715*, trans. Raymond Davis, Translated Texts for Historians 6 (Liverpool: Liverpool University Press, 2004), 48–49.

11   Baronio, *Martyrologium Romanum*, 547.

12   In the margin: "Victor on the Vandal persecution, Book 1 [*vere* 2]."
     Victor of Vita, *History of the Vandal Persecution*, 2.7.
     This citation is added in the 1595 edition.

13   Named for Jan Hus (1372–1415), who challenged many of the mainstays of Roman Catholicism, including papal authority and the withholding of the chalice from the laity at communion. Though burned as a heretic by the Council of Constance in 1415, his followers retained popularity and influence in Bohemia for years to come. See Jennifer Kolpacoff Deane, *A History of Medieval Heresy and Inquisition*, Critical Issues in World and International History (Lanham: Rowman & Littlefield, 2011), Chapter 8.

14   Richard Creagh, archbishop of Armagh (*c*.1523–*c*.1586), was accused of raping the daughter of his jailer, but was subsequently acquitted. Colm Lennon, "Creagh [Creavgh], Richard (*c*.1523–1586?)," in *ODNB*, 14:110–11.

15   William Allen records that Cottam's interrogators pressed him to confess to some unspecified sin of a sexual nature: "And a Minister amongst other thinges, willed him to

men whom their false preachers did not dare to challenge, and so steadfast that all their tortures, no matter how barbaric, could not conquer them, they considered it unwise to admit that they had died for reasons of religion, and so they concocted others, of crimes and treasons. Simple folk might thus be brought to believe they had died not as Catholics, but as felons and traitors. They resorted to this artifice because many heretical sects do not approve of punishing a man for his faith, while others accept it only insofar as it touches upon the prosperity and stability of the commonwealth. Moreover, no sane person could think it just that one should die for professing that faith in which all of their ancestors (ever since they received the faith of Jesus Christ) have been baptized, have lived and died, and have been saved, and which, being obeyed unanimously by all of Christendom, bears the title of the Catholic faith. Thus it was that countless people in England, when they saw the fortitude and endurance of the holy martyrs in their torments, as well as the joyful willingness with which they suffered death, were moved to profess the faith they professed. And yet further crimes and misdeeds were denounced, all the more so because among Catholics such men received the name and honors of martyrs; the heretics hoped to strip the dead of this glorious victory and the living of this example and encouragement. And, in the end, because this route offered the easiest opportunity and clearest occasion to ruin and despoil every wealthy knight and lord who sheltered the said priests and holy martyrs in their houses or aided them in any way as accomplices and abettors of the queen's enemies, and traitors to her royal person and crown. After this, no priest dared enter the kingdom; no one dared harbor them, aid them, write to them, or send their children to be educated at the seminaries at Rome and Rheims. For all these reasons, the heretics of England have proclaimed that none of these blessed martyrs died for their religion, but rather for other, dire crimes, among them attempting to assassinate the queen. But let us see how they proceeded in their courts and tribunals to disguise this fiction and render it more credible.

---

confesse his wicked and leude behaviour which he had committed in Fish-streat about foure yeres since. Cottam. 'What do you meane?' Sherife. 'He would have you to confesse the filthe you committed in Fish-streat.' Cottam. 'O blessed Jesus, Thy name be praised. Is this now laid here to my charge?' The Minister said, 'We do not charge you with it, but we would have you to discharge you thereof if there be any such thing.' Another Minister answered, 'No, it was not he, but his brother.' Cottam. 'You shall heare. You accuse me for filthe committed about four yeres since in Fish-streat, and I was not in London this seven yeres, and if I had done any such thinge, what do you meane to lay it to my charge?' With that ij or iij of them said that it was not he but his brother." Allen, *Briefe Historie*, 79.

The Means the Heretics Employed to Spin Out Their Lies and Make Them Seem Like Truth[1]

The manner in which the queen and those of her council have gone about afflicting the Catholics and the servants of God is worse even than the deaths they inflict. For whereas the reason they died was the confession of the Catholic faith and the refusal to acknowledge the queen as sovereign head of the Church of England, the heretics have proclaimed (as we have said) that this is not the true cause of their torments and deaths, but rather having plotted at Rome and at Rheims the death of the queen, conspired against the nation, urged other princes to invade and conquer it, and other similar matters. They tried to prove this by certain false witnesses, bought and paid for, criminal men of wicked lives, who did not even know how to weave or warp the fabric of their evil. For they accused men they had never seen in their lives of having concocted this conspiracy; others whom they dragged into the dance and made into authors of this rebellion plotted in Rome had never left England, or had not been in Rome when all this had supposedly occurred. And the witnesses themselves had never seen, met, or even heard the voices of many of those against whom they testified, but they said everything the unjust ministers of justice ordered them to in order to receive a pardon for their own serious crimes, as one of them, named John Nicholas, has confessed and written.[2]

This falsehood and artifice was clearly seen in the tribunal and judgment itself. For from the first moment they arrested, jailed, and tortured the saints of God, they asked them about nothing but religious matters. Whom had they reconciled to the Church, where had they said Mass, who had received and sustained them, what had they learned in confession (which cannot, nor should not, ever be revealed under any circumstances), and other, similar points. After this had failed, they sought to disguise their wickedness by sending four doctors of law to examine the martyrs with six questions or articles, so badgering them that if they had not fallen into the guilt of rebellion, it seemed to the ignorant that they had, and they took this opportunity to afflict the souls of the

---

1 Sander, *De origine ac progressu*, 485–87.

2 "After a chequered religious career that veered from Protestant minister to seminarian at the English College in Rome, [John] Nicholas [dates unknown] was arrested upon his return to England and conformed." McCoog, *Our Way of Proceeding?*, 153.

saints, since they could not punish their deeds. For they asked them what they would do, or what they thought ought to be done, when such a thing should come to pass? What would they do if they found themselves in Ireland when the Catholics took up arms against the queen? Was there were any just cause for deposing or depriving the queen, or some other monarch, of the throne? What should be done, or what would they do, if the queen fell into some heresy or apostasy? Or if she were deposed? What would they advise the people in such a situation?[3] In addition to other outlandish things, by which they hoped to discover their hearts and minds, and to punish them, though this belonged to God,[4] to whose eyes actions and deeds are infinitely more open and manifest than to those of men. And what exceeded all tyranny and wickedness: not only did they presume to punish the thoughts wrung out and wrenched from their mouths by force, squeezed out by false suppositions and slanders, but also sins uncommitted, if only they *could* have been committed, or that might probably have been committed had they found an opportunity. And if the martyrs responded that of such hypothetical cases, or of things to come, they could not say anything certain, and that if they erred in anything, they would subject themselves to the laws and their penalties, or with some other general answer, that when what they were asking came to pass, they would do what the Catholic Church or its wisest men should determine in similar cases, the heretics said that these replies, so thoughtful and justified, revealed the malice and disaffection they harbored against the queen and her crown, for which they must die. In the end, they killed them with the cruelty and fierceness we have seen, proclaiming and preaching that they died as rebels and traitors to the queen.

To make this case more convincingly, they wrote a book in English, entitled *The Execution of Justice in England* [*La justicia Britanica, o Inglesa*], which they printed and disseminated throughout the kingdom, in which they attempted to prove that none of the sainted martyrs in England had died for the faith, nor for the sake of religion, but rather as rebels, mutineers, and insurrectionists, and for having conspired against the queen's life.[5] But Cardinal William Allen

---

3   The six so-called "bloody questions" were first put to Campion and his confrères in 1581. The sixth question, put to dozens of individuals throughout Elizabeth's reign, demanded, "If the Pope do by his bull or sentence pronounce Her Majesty to be deprived and no lawful Queen, and her subject to be discharged of their allegiance and obedience unto her, and after, the Pope or any other by his appointment and authority do invade this realm, which part would you take, or which part ought a good subject of England take?" See Patrick McGrath, "The Bloody Questions Reconsidered," *RH* 20, no. 3 (May 1991): 305–19.

4   Deut. 32:5; Rom. 12:19.

5   William Cecil, *The Execution of Iustice in England for Maintenaunce of Publique and Christian Peace, against Certeine Stirrers of Sedition, and Adherents to the Traytors and Enemies of the*

(of whom mention has been made several times in this history) replied to this idiotic, specious book, so thoughtfully and carefully and with arguments of such weight and truth that the ill-constructed lie was overthrown and torn apart.[6]

I ask, what manner of proceeding is this? Who has ever seen or heard such? What tyrant, what barbarian, what pagan, what tiger or wild beast, in all the many persecutions yet suffered by the holy Church, has used this sort of slander? They would torture and mutilate Christians for the mere fact of being such, imagining that they had thus vindicated, pleased, and defended their false gods. Some accursed tyrants thrust guilt upon the guiltless saints to disguise and give pretext to their savagery. But to uncover thoughts through artifice and questions and yet more questions, and to punish them, taking the lives of the innocent not for any misdeed committed, but only for that which their enemy dreams they could commit, or might commit if they found themselves in such a situation—this what these treacherous men do, not punishing treason. This is not to follow the laws, but to pervert them, to confound the commonwealth, and to betray an insatiable thirst for human blood. Who would consent to the examination of wife, children, and the servants of the house, to be asked what they might do if their husband, father, or master conspired against the monarch? If they would follow him? If they would support him in secret, or abet him? If they would give him something to eat? And, on saying yes, to be tortured and killed for this alone? What Catholic monarch or prince is there in the world today who takes as an outrage and punishes with the penalty of death the theologian or jurist who, disputing in the schools, affirms that if that king or prince should fall into heresy or become a schismatic or infidel he might be deposed and deprived of his throne? I say this to show that heresy not only makes a man unfaithful and disloyal to God, but also inhuman, cruel, savage, and barbarous, a breaker of every law, divine and human, a usurper of what belongs to God—that is, to see into and punish hearts—and even to make oneself greater than God himself, for he only ever chastises those sins already committed, while these monsters punish those that might be committed, or those which are no sins but that they think to be so and that others may have committed. With these and other horrid slanders they persecute the

Realme, without Any Persecution of Them for Questions of Religion, as Is Falsely Reported and Published by the Fautors and Fosterers of Their Treasons. Xvii. Decemb. 1583 (London: Christopher Barker, 1583).

6   William Allen, *A True, Sincere and Modest Defence, of English Catholiques That Suffer for Their Faith Both at Home and Abrode against a False, Seditious and Slanderous Libel Intituled; The Execution of Iustice in England* (Rouen: [Robert Persons's press], 1584).

saints, taking their lives as Catholics and their honors as traitors and felons, making them martyrs twice over, in life and in death.

But the Lord has honored them as martyrs, and for the redoubled oppression received from their persecutors, he has given them redoubled glory. First, with the crown of martyrdom in their confession of the faith, the true cause of their deaths, and afterwards by the illustrious renown and glorious reward owed to those who die innocent, as Abel died,[7] and Naboth, who was condemned to death, falsely accused of having uttered words against God and against the king.[8] These valiant martyrs will be blessed forevermore, now free from the cares of this mortal life and safe beneath the hand and protection of God, where comes no torment of human malice, nor falsehood and deceit— but much more blessed are they for having attained this crown and victory with the shedding of their precious blood, by which we hope the just fury of the Lord will be appeased and this universal storm of sin and heresy, fierce and fearful, will abate. Their deaths are priceless before the divine reckoning, their souls are in glory, their memory in benediction, and their names will be eternal. The bodies (which are the lowest and weakest parts of those bold captains), although they have been torn apart, hanged from gallows, stuck upon the city's poles, gates, and towers, and eaten by birds, are highly honored, worthy of greater reverence than the embalmed bodies of the mightiest kings of the earth lying in their regal and sumptuous sepulchers. On the day and in the very hour they stood upon the hurdle to die, they were happier and more fortunate than the comfortable, safe people who stood watching them. And even though such sorrows and fleeting ignominy seem to carnal men the most extreme misery, it was not so, for the tortures concluded in a moment and before their bodies had cooled their better parts had escaped the hands of their tormenters and were rejoicing with God. And many people surreptitiously offered prayers to their glorious souls before their corpses had been quartered. Consequently, in exchange for the honor of this world, which the heretics had sought to take from them, what greater glory could there be than that they have for their valor and virtue, which has spread throughout all of Christendom? In Italy, in Spain, in France, and even in England itself, their sacred relics are held in the highest reverence, and any price would be paid (if they could be bought) for any bit, however small, of their flesh, bones, heads, or clothing, or something stained with a drop of their guiltless blood, as has always been done in the Catholic Church with Christ's martyrs. Their holy relics are revered, kissed, and taken for the dearest and most

---

7   In the margin: "Genesis 4."

8   In the margin: "3 Kings 21[:10, 13]."

precious of treasures: many times the faithful even die for them. Indeed, the *Martyrologium Romanum* includes seven women who died because they had gathered the drops of blood that fell from the body of Saint Blaise while he was tortured.[9] And Saint Julian of Cappadocia, accused and burned over a slow fire because he kissed the dead bodies of the holy martyrs.[10]

From the east to the west, from the north to the south, wherever there are Catholic Christians the fame of these valiant, saintly soldiers will spread, their memory will live, and the exquisite fragrance of their celestial lives and glorious deaths will travel. In England, countless Catholics go in pilgrimage to wherever their heads and quarters are hung, as though coming to guard them, or to ask whose heads and bodies they are. And what traitors were they, whose heads are raised above the rest? And with this excuse they offer a prayer and fulfill their devotion. Thus their enemies do them a greater good through the tortures and cruel deaths they inflict than all their friends and all the princes of the world could have done them, though they should give them the scepter and the crown, leaving the kingdom in their hands. Though the heretics did not intend this, and in fact precisely the opposite, it was intended by that Lord who guides and directs all things by his eternal and immutable providence, to his glory and the good of his chosen,[11] who takes the injustice and cruelty of tyrants as a means to declare the fortitude and patience of the martyrs, and to crown and honor them, and by their example, merits, and intercession, to ennoble, inspirit, and defend his kingdom, which is the holy Catholic Church. And lest we doubt this truth, he has been pleased to give us certain proofs, working wondrous miracles at the deaths of several of his soldiers who shed their blood for his Church in the reigns of King Henry and his daughter Elizabeth, as will be seen in the following chapter.

---

9   In the margin: "February 3."

     Baronio, *Martyrologium Romanum*, 66.

     Saint Blaise (d. *c*.316), bishop of Sebastea in Armenia, is reputed to have been martyred by being beaten with iron combs and beheaded. See *AASS*, February I, 331–53.

10   These citations of the *Martyrologium Romanum* are added in the 1595 edition.

     In the margin: "February, 17."

     Baronio, *Martyrologium Romanum*, 86.

11   Rom. 8:28.

Various Marvels that God has Worked for the Glory of the Martyrs of England

There is no counsel against God, who as Scripture says catches the wise in their craftiness.[1] He has uncovered the heretics' wickedness and duplicity, with which they have tried to oppress the Catholics and the servants of God, not only taking their lives for being such, but also their reputations and honors, defaming them as traitors. For he has performed numberless miracles to vindicate their innocence and truth, some of which I wish to relate here to the glory of the Lord himself who worked them, to the honor of his martyrs, and to the confounding of their persecutors.

The head of the blessed bishop of Rochester was stuck on a pike on London Bridge, where it remained for many days in the sight of all: and it was a wonder that the longer it was there, the fresher, more beautiful, and more dignified it appeared—so much so that King Henry had it removed to prevent the people becoming unsettled by this sight of this novelty, as we have said.[2]

When Margaret, the daughter of the excellent and saintly Thomas More, wished to bury her father, in her sorrow she neglected to bring a cloth in which to wrap him, or money with which to buy one; realizing her carelessness and trusting in God, she entered a shop and gathered together some lengths of cloth that seemed sufficient for that pious duty. Miraculously, she happened upon the fair price of the merchandise, as has been mentioned above.[3]

A citizen of Winchester had long struggled with an agonizing despair and found no means of overcoming it; it pleased God that he should discover one in the advice and prayers of the holy martyr Thomas More, while he was alive and still chancellor of the realm. So much so that as long as the man could turn to him and talk with him, he was free of that burden—but when they seized More, since they could no longer speak together, he again faced the same temptation, with greater force and bitterness, until the day they took More to be martyred, when, breaking through the guards and ministers of the law and the crowd of people accompanying him, the man thrust himself before him, told him of his trials and afflictions, and begged his aid. The saint answered

---

1 In the margin: "Job 5[:13] and 1 Corinthians 3[:19]."

2 In the margin: "Book 1, Chapter 28."

3 In the margin: "Book 1, Chapter 29."

him, "I know you well: pray to God for me, as I will pray for you." The man departed, and he never again experienced that temptation.[4]

The quarters of the saintly Carthusians who died in London for the Catholic faith were placed at the gates of the city and those of their own monastery, and some write that for more than three months they remained perfectly whole, nor had anyone ever seen a crow or rook near them, as we see with the corpses of other dead men, until little by little they dried up.[5] And afterwards, these brothers appeared one night to a monk who, tempted and afflicted and deceived by the devil, thought to give up hope and throw himself into the water: many times they interposed themselves between him and the water into which he wished to hurl himself, until he was spotted and succored by the other brothers, and returned to himself and recognized his guilt, Satan's deceit, and the favor that had come from heaven at the intercession of those saints.[6]

---

4   This episode, drawn from Thomas Stapleton's biography of More—our only source for the anecdote—is added in the 1595 edition. Sheils, "Polemic as Piety," 87.

   "A certain citizen of Winchester was for a long time so troubled by the gravest temptations to despair that prayer and the advice of his friends seemed of no avail. At length by a friend he was brought to see More, who, pitying the man's misery, gave him good and prudent counsel. It was not by his words, however, but by his prayers to God that More at length obtained for the man relief from his grievous temptation. The man remained free from his distress so long as More was at liberty and he had access to him. But when More was imprisoned the temptation returned with still greater force than before. The unhappy man, so long as More was in the Tower, spent his days in misery without hope of cure. But when he heard that More was condemned to death he went up to London in order that, at whatever risk to himself, he might speak to him as he was going out to execution. On More's way, then, from the Tower to the scaffold he burst through the guards and cried out with a loud voice: 'Do you recognise me, Sir Thomas? Help me, I beg you: for that temptation has returned to me and I cannot get rid of it.' More at once answered: 'I recognise you perfectly. Go and pray for me, and I will pray earnestly for you.' He went away, and never again in his whole life was he troubled with such temptations." Stapleton, *Thomas More*, 71–72.

5   A standard trope of hagiography, an inversion of the biblical motif of birds devouring the corpses of the wicked (e.g. Gen. 40:19; Deut. 28:26; 1 Kings 17:44, 46; Jer. 34:20; Rev. 19:21).

   The image suggests that nature itself refuses to acquiesce in the martyr's degradation. Monta, *Martyrdom and Literature*, 68.

6   "At our order's house of St. Anne, near the city of Coventry, there was a certain brother by the name of Richard Croftes, who just after the deaths of our saintly father and of the aforementioned brothers was tormented by various temptations. He fell into the devil's snare and despaired of God's mercy, resolving to drown himself in a pond in the monastery's garden. To carry this out, he left his cell in the middle of the night; close to the ninth hour, he suddenly hurled himself in, but could not do it. Then, walking back and forth around the water's edge until the eleventh hour, he repeatedly attempted to carry out his sinful intention, but he was always prevented. [...] And lo, they [the brothers] suddenly saw a bright light near the pond:

When John Stone, an Augustinian friar, was locked in prison for refusing to recognize Henry as supreme head of the Church, he turned to the arms of all perfect Christians: prayer and penance. He mortified himself with a fast for three days, imploring our Lord with fierce insistence to favor and strengthen him in the bitter battle to the death that he anticipated. After all this he heard a voice from heaven that called him by name and ordered him to hold fervently to his good intentions and die for the truth, as he did, vindicated by this favor from on high.[7]

In Ireland, another doctor of theology, named John Travers,[8] was accused of having penned a book in favor of the papal supremacy; summoned before the judges and asked if this was true, he replied that it was, and extending the three fingers with which he had written the book, he added, "With these three fingers I wrote the book, and hitherto it has never weighed upon me to have done so, by the grace of God, nor do I believe it ever will weigh upon me." He was condemned to death, and his hand cut off and thrown into the fire—but God wished to show that what the saintly man had written was pleasing to him, for the entire hand was burned while those three fingers remained whole,

---

when the abbot pointed it out to his prior and the others, they all hurried thither straightway. Reaching it, they saw the brother walking by one side of the pond, repeatedly trying to drown himself and always forced back, and two of them saw a great light in another corner, in which they confidently affirmed that they saw all of our martyred fathers interposing themselves between the brother and the water, as often as he tried to drown himself or throw himself in. When they drew near him on the shore of the pond, the light disappeared, and they took hold of the brother, his entire body shaking and barely able to speak. They led him back to his cell, where, with a fire lit and his mind calm once more, they asked him what he had been trying to do. He replied that he had gone there to drown himself, to free himself more speedily of this mortal life, knowing that he was damned. 'But I could not,' he said, 'for I was held back by certain ones, who prevented me from advancing and always placed themselves between me and the water. And yet I saw nobody, indeed I know not who they were.' The reverend father of that convent, who had been present at this spectacle, revealed it to several of the brothers in our house, further adding that the brother had immediately been freed of his most dire temptation." Chauncy, *Historia aliquot nostri sæculi martyrum*, sigs. Lii^v–Liii^v.

7   John Stone (d.1538), an Augustinian friar and a doctor of theology, was imprisoned and executed on May 12, 1538 for refusing to support Henry VIII's religious policies. Bede Camm, *Lives of the English Martyrs Declared Blessed by Pope Leo XIII in 1886 and 1895*, 2 vols., Quarterly Series 100, 101 (London: Burns and Oates, 1904–05), 1:269–70.

8   The exact cause of the execution of the Irish divine John Travers (d.1537) is uncertain: different accounts aver that he was put to death as a traitor and fomenter of rebellion in Ireland, others—primarily reliant on Harpsfield—for writing a book supporting papal supremacy. R. Dudley Edwards, "Venerable John Travers and the Rebellion of Silken Thomas," *Studies: An Irish Quarterly Review* 23, no. 92 (December 1934): 687–99, here 690–92.

without any mark, no matter how many times the executioner hurled them into the flames.[9]

When they burned that sainted brother, John Forest, it is written that the fire could not completely burn his body, and that at midday a dove, white as snow, was seen for a long time above his head, to the tremendous wonder and fear of those present.[10]

One night, a Catholic knight resolved to take one of the sainted martyr Campion's legs, which had been nailed to a wall, and so he did, and in his devotion kept it hidden in a chest in his room. But so powerful was the lovely fragrance it gave out that all his guests remarked upon it and asked what beautiful scent that was. Lest it be discovered, he decided to take it to Rome: he placed it in a trunk among his clothing and brought it to the harbor, where he entrusted it to a merchant to be transported with other cargo to a French port, whither he went by another route. Either out of malice or carelessness, the trunk was left in the house of that resident foreigner [*huesped de Inglaterra*]: so strong was the fragrance and sweetness coming from the chest that the merchant opened

---

9   This story and the previous one come from Nicholas Harpsfield's *Sex Dialogi* (1566): "I shall now consider with you two more men: John Travers, a doctor of theology, and John Stone, an Augustinian who was wreathed with the crown of martyrdom at Canterbury. But before he came to this, while still in his cell, overflowing with prayers to God and having fasted for three days without interruption, he heard a voice—though he saw nobody—that addressed him by name, and urged him to be of good heart and not to hesitate to endure steadfastly a sentence of death for him whom he had professed. From this he then derived so much joy and strength that no persuasion or terror could frighten him off from enduring his sentence. I heard this from a thoughtful and trustworthy gentleman, who is yet living, to whom Stone himself revealed this. But Ireland recalls me to itself, giving us, among others, the martyr Travers. He had committed to writing certain things that advanced the preeminence of the supreme pontiff. Hauled before the tribunal and interrogated on this matter, he denied nothing, but, extending his hand, boldly replied: 'With these fingers,' he said, 'I wrote these things, which in so good a cause have never caused me any regret, nor ever shall.' [...] When he was dispatched with the usual tortures, and that hand was cut off by the executioner and tossed into the fire in the sight of the people, the rest of the hand was consumed, but the flames could not harm the thumb and the next two fingers, which are used in writing, however often they were put to the burning." Nicholas Harpsfield, *Dialogi sex contra summi pontificatus, monasticae vitae sanctorum, sacrarum imaginum oppugnatores, et pesudomartyres* (Antwerp: Christophe Plantin, 1566), 994–95.

10   "As soon as the fire was lighted they cast the wooden saint into it and it was burnt. A miracle happened, for the fire had hardly destroyed the body when at midday was seen a dove, as white as snow, over the head of the sainted dead, and remained there for a long time seen by many people." Hume, *Chronicle*, 81.

it, and, finding the cause—the saint's leg—brought it to a London magistrate, where a massive investigation was launched against the man who had removed it from its place. He went to Rome, overjoyed to have carried off—and disconsolate to have lost—such a treasure.[11]

When they tormented Alexander Briant for the second time, a wonder came to pass much like those our Lord worked when the pagan emperors mangled the Christians to force them into idolatry, which Briant himself relates in a letter to the fathers of the Society of Jesus in England, and it was in this way. At first they had racked him, stretching him out in a particular sort of torture, with individual cords so cruelly attached to his fingers and toes that they were nearly ripped off, and leaving him shattered. The following day, when he had lost all feeling, his blood was frozen, and his body had become a veritable altarpiece of pain, they returned to the torture with greater savagery than before. When Briant commended himself to our Lord and implored him for the strength and stamina to pass through that torment for the sake of his love, it was done by his mercy, with such great abundance of his grace that the more frenzied the torturers waxed against him, the more violently they pulled at his feet and hands, the less pain he felt—or, as I should say, he felt no pain at all. Rather, with the renewed torture the pains of the previous torture were healed, leaving him with a calm mind, a peaceful heart, and undisturbed senses, like a man in a comfortable bed. This so enraged and scandalized his judges that they ordered him to be tortured once again on the following day: while they executed their ruthless mandate and the guiltless, saintly priest meditated upon the sacred passion of Christ our Lord, it seemed to him that he had been given a wound in his left hand, that the palm was transfixed and the blood was running out, the effect of the intense meditation in which his soul was absorbed. And with this he felt relief, and so much health and strength that in his letter he asked the fathers of the Society of Jesus to receive him therein, and not to fear his weakness, for the Lord had restored him to perfect wholeness,

---

11   The misadventures of Campion's relic are added in the 1595 edition. I have not been able to find a source for this story in all its particulars, but it probably relates to a detail included in a letter from Persons to Acquaviva of December 28, 1581: "The relics of F. Campion are sought with the greatest eagerness, and large sums of money are offered to the heretics to purchase them. One man was very lucky, for without any expense but his wits he succeeded in stealing a quarter, which he took to a house where several Catholics were assembled. Such was the joy at this unexpected happiness, that many shed tears, and a certain baron who was there fainted." C. W., "On External Devotion to Holy Men Departed," *The Rambler*, new series 1 (1859): 386–90, here 389.

as may be seen more fully in the letter itself, which we have inserted above.[12] It is also written that another miracle occurred in the saintly priest's martyrdom: after they hanged him, ripped him open, removed his heart and entrails, and burned them, the executioners placed his body upon a table, with his chest down, to quarter him. There, before a huge crowd, he rose up into the air, to the utter stupefaction of those around him.[13]

While Cuthbert Mayne, a priest and student of the English seminary at Rheims, was in prison, he was advised to prepare himself for death, for within three days he would be martyred, which he took as the best and happiest news he could receive, giving himself up entirely to prayer and meditation upon his end. On the second night, having applied himself yet more intently to these spiritual exercises, he saw in his cell (a little after midnight) a brilliant, overpowering light; the prisoners in the cells nearby, disconcerted and frightened, called to him to find out what light that was, for they well knew that in his cell he had neither a fire nor a candle, and he gently told them to calm themselves and take no notice of it.[14]

When William Lacy, an illustrious knight, was jailed for his Catholicism, God our Lord revealed his prison, the means, and all the attendant circumstances to

---

12   This comment is added in the 1595 edition, corresponding to the addition of Briant's letter in that printing. See Book 2, Chapter 33.

13   "after his beheading, himself dismembred, his hart bowels and intrels burned, to the gret admiration of some, being layd vpon the blocke his bellye downward, lifted vp his wholy body then remayning from the grounde: and this I adde vpon report of others, not mine owne sight." Thomas Alfield, *A True Reporte of the Death & Martyrdome of M. Campion Iesuite and Preiste, & M. Sherwin, & M. Bryan Preistes, at Tiborne the First of December 1581: Observid and Written by a Catholike Preist, Which Was Present Therat; Wheruuto Is Annexid Certayne Verses Made by Sundrie Persons* (London: R. Rowlands, 1582), sig. Dii[v].

14   Cuthbert Mayne (*c.*1544–77) became a priest at Douai in 1575, and returned to England the following year. He was arrested in June 1577, and hanged, drawn, and quartered on November 30. Raymond Francis Trudgian, "Mayne, Cuthbert [St Cuthbert Mayne] (*bap.* 1544, *d.* 1577)," in *ODNB*, 37:602–03. See Allen, *Briefe Historie*, 104–10.

        For a contemporary Catholic depiction of Mayne's martyrdom, see Book 2 Figure 28.1.
        William Allen relates of Mayne, "After that advertisement he gave himself ernestly to praier and contemplation until his death. The second night after he gave himself to these spiritual exercises, there was seen a great light in his chamber, betweene twelve & one of the clocke, in so much that some of the prisoners that lay in the next romes, called unto him to know what it was, for they knew very well that he had neither fire nor candel, he answered, willinge them to quiet themselves, for it did nothing appertaine unto them." Allen, *Briefe Historie*, 106.

a Catholic priest, his kinsman and dear friend imprisoned for the same faith, in a dream on the night before.[15]

Almost the same thing befell the priest William Filbie in the region called Henley: while sleeping, he had a prophetic vision, in which it seemed that they tore apart his flesh, ripped open his body, and pulled out his entrails, and so extreme was his terror that he cried aloud, awakening and alarming those of his house—and all he had seen in this dream was fulfilled to the very letter when he was martyred for the faith.[16]

The priest Everard Hanse [*Nauo*], having been hanged upon the gallows, allowed to fall while half-alive, and his entrails removed and cast into the flames, spoke, saying "*O felix dies!*" "O blessed day!" And when the hangman ripped out his heart and threw it into a huge bonfire, it leapt up twice; the third time, they hurled it into the flames beneath a bundle of kindling (so that it could not jump), and in a clear and manifest miracle it rose up and parted the wood, until little by little the flesh was consumed with the force of the fire. Many observed this, and were amazed and perturbed.[17] And the Lord has worked other

---

15   William Lacy (d.1582), a Catholic gentleman-turned-priest, was martyred on August 22, 1582.

      "The event and every circumstance of this calamity appeared in a dream, the very same night, to a Catholic priest, his kinsman and dear friend, who was imprisoned for his faith." Allen, *Historia*, 201.

16   "Afterward at Henley M. Filby a Priest and one of the prisoners (not found in the house with the rest, but taken in the watch, as he was comming to the house) had in his sleepe a significant dreame or vision, of the ripping up of his body and taking out of his bowels: the terrour whereof caused him to cry so loud that the whole house was raised therby, which afterward in his owne, F. Campion's, and other his fellowes' Martyrdom was accomplished." Allen, *Briefe Historie*, 11.

      William Filbie became a priest at Rheims in 1581, and returned to England that year. Shortly thereafter, he was arrested at Henley-on-Thames in Oxfordshire, and hanged, drawn, and quartered at Tyburn on May 20, 1582. J. Andreas Löwe, "Filbie, William (c.1555–1582)," in *ODNB*, 19:539.

17   The priest Everard (or Everald) Hanse (d.1581) was martyred on July 31, 1581. See Allen, *Briefe Historie*, 98–103.

      The community at Douai recorded of his martyrdom: "Then, still alive and conscious, his vital parts were severed and thrown into the fire and his stomach opened with the executioner's knife; when his innards had spilled out and the butcher laid his hand upon his beating heart, it is said he spoke with his last breath, 'O happy day!' What is more, the consistent report of many people informs us that when his heart was cast into the fire, it rose from the flames with great force, and when it was thrust back into the fire beneath

marvels like these, to encourage the Catholics, confound the heretics, honor his saints, and affirm his truth.

---

a pile of wood, it ascended once again with such power that it moved from the place and then rested, beating, in the smoke." *Diaries of the English College*, 181.

For a contemporary Catholic rendering of his martyrdom, see Book 2 Figure 28.1.

Ribadeneyra probably got this story from Robert Persons, who included it in his English-language writings. Dillon, *Construction of Martyrdom*, 85.

The Martyrologies and Calendars the Heretics Produced in England

The devil is the ape of God, seeking to usurp the honor and glory due the divine majesty in every way he can: in shrines, altars, sacrifices, offerings, and all that pertains to sacred worship, and to that highest reverence (called *latria*) owed to God alone,[1] the evil one has tried to imitate God, that he might be acknowledged and served as God, deceiving countless men and instructing them to adore stone, and clay, and silver, and gold, and the gods and works of their hands,[2] and him therein, as he did in ancient times, and as the blind pagans do even in our own day. In the same way, the heretics, the sons of the demon,[3] little vipers who emerge from the entrails of a viper, strive to be apes of the Catholics—neither in faith nor in sanctity, but only in usurping the honor owed to them, mimicking in their hypocritical synagogues what the Catholic Church represents in the congregation of the faithful. For this reason, seeing that the Catholic Church has its saints and martyrs, which it reveres as such and honors on their days, to the glory of the saints and the imitation and emulation of their deeds, the heretics have chosen to celebrate as saints and regard as martyrs those heretics who have been justly burned, whether for their crimes or[4] in the name of our faith. The Arian Bishop Georgius died for his crimes in Alexandria, and was venerated and honored as a martyr by the other Arian heretics, as Ammianus Marcellinus says;[5] the Donatist Salvius was killed by other heretics—likewise Donatists, but of another, contrary sect— and those of his sect built a temple to him, and esteemed and revered him as martyr, as Saint Augustine writes.[6] And so, following the example of their

---

1   Beginning with Augustine, theologians had distinguished between *latria*, the worship due only to God, and *dulia*, the reverence that might be accorded the saints. Kelly, *Early Christian Doctrines*, 491.

2   Isa. 2:8; Jer. 1:16; Mic. 5:12; Rev. 9:20.

3   John 8:44; 1 John 3:10.

4   This phrase is added in the 1595 edition.

5   In the margin: "Book 22."
      Ammianus Marcellinus, *History*, 22.11.

6   The citations of Arian and Donatist saints are added in the 1595 edition.
      In the margin: "*Contra Parmeniani*, Book 3, last chapter [6], and *Contra Cresconium*, Book 4, Chapters 48 and 49."

fellow heretics,[7] in England they produce new martyrologies and calendars, erasing the ancient martyrs, confessors, and virgins of the Catholic Church (for these they disdain), and canonizing degenerate men, hateful for every sort of heresy and wickedness, whom they have placed in their calendars, marking their days with large, colored letters.

In this way, they thrust forth as confessors Henry VIII, Edward VI, Erasmus of Rotterdam, Martin Luther, Peter Martyr, and others; Wycliffe,[8] Jan Hus, Cranmer, and other pestilential heretics who died at the stake, they call martyrs; in truth, neither in their synagogues nor in their calendars is there a single virgin, for never have they produced any.[9] But no further proof is needed to perceive what they are, save seeing that they honor and regard as saints these nefarious men, of such foul and abominable lives. Just as the devil, however much as he tries to imitate God and seize by deception the honor due him alone, is not God, nor can be God, but only the ape of God, thus, he who the heretic regards and reveres as a martyr cannot be anything but the mimic and shadow of a martyr. For, as the glorious Doctor, Saint Augustine, says most solemnly, it is not the pain, but the cause, that makes the martyr.[10] And therefore one saintly bishop, imprisoned for being a Catholic and refusing to submit to the Arian Emperor Constantius, wrote to him from his cell, *Interest ex qua causa, non ex quo pendeam stipite*—It matters not that I hang from one pole or another, what matters is the cause for which I die.[11] For if this were not so, we would say

---

7   This phrase is added in the 1595 edition, in keeping with the insertion of the Arian and Donatist examples. Ribadeneyra also changes the precise wording of the sentence's opening—"Pues" replacing "Y para esto"—but the sense remains the same.

8   The English theologian John Wycliffe (*c.*1331–84) was generally regarded as the inspiration for the loose network of heterodox communities and individuals in England known as the Lollards. It has been argued, both by early modern Protestants and by modern scholars, that Wycliffe's thought and the Lollard movement were forerunners of the English Reformation. See Deane, *Medieval Heresy and Inquisition*, 217–46.

9   John Foxe's *Acts and Monuments*, which established a genealogy for Protestant martyrdom reaching back through the Middle Ages to the early church and initially promoted a controversial calendar of new observances commemorating these martyrs.

10   This sentiment appears at least three times in Augustine of Hippo's *oeuvre*: *Contra Cresconium*, Chapter 47; *Letters* 204.4; *Exposition of the Psalms*, 34.II. 13.
     Cf. *Contra epistulam Parmeniani libri tres*, 3.6.
     This idea of Augustine's was universally cited by early modern Christians of every sect and confession to defend their own martyrs and denigrate those of others. Gregory, *Salvation at Stake*, 338.

11   Lucifer, bishop of Cagliari (d. *c.*370), a fierce opponent of Arianism, who fell afoul of Constantius II. Although his Spanish translation is somewhat elaborated, Ribadeneyra quotes the Latin of Lucifer's treatise *Moriendum esse pro dei filio* (*c.*360) to the letter: "It matters for what cause, not from what pole I hang [*interest ex qua causa, non ex quo*

that all the felons and wrongdoers who die for their crimes are martyrs, and the more horrific the torments they suffered and the more savage the deaths they had, the greater the martyrdom! But this title belongs only to those who shed their blood for Jesus Christ and for his faith, in the unity of the Catholic Church; those who are separated from it or are schismatics, are neither saints nor martyrs, nor can they be esteemed as such, as the blessed martyr Saint Cyprian[12] says, thus:

> Does he who has struggled against the priests of Christ think, somehow, to be united with Christ? Does such a one not take up arms against the Church, battle against the will of God, become an enemy to the altar, a rebel against the sacrifice of Christ, an infidel to the faith, sacrilegious in religion, a disobedient servant, an impious son, and a deceitful brother? Disdaining the bishops and priests of God, he dares to erect another altar, and offer up another prayer.[13]

And farther on:

> God did not look at Cain's offering, for he could not have favor from God who had neither peace nor harmony with his brother:[14] what peace is promised the enemies of their own brothers, what sacrifices do these despisers of the priests pretend to offer? Do they think that when they come together they have Christ with them, who come together outside Christ's Church? These are such as, though they be killed and it seems they confess the name of Christ, cannot be freed of this stain by their blood: the guilt of schism and discord is so grievous and so foul that it cannot be expunged by death. There can be no martyr outside the Church: he cannot win the kingdom who has left behind the Church that is to rule with Christ.[15]

Thus far have been the words of Saint Cyprian. But let us leave this, and follow the thread and sequel of our story.

---

pendeam stipite]." Lucifer of Cagliari, *Luciferi Calaritani opuscula*, ed. Wilhelm August Hartel, Corpus Scriptorum Ecclesiasticorum Latinorum 14 (Vienna: Apud C. Geroldi filium, 1886), 313.

12　Cyprian was martyred by beheading at Carthage on September 14, 258. *AASS*, September IV, 331–32.

13　In the margin: "Cyprian, *On the Unity of the Church* [*de simplicitate.*]."
　　　Cyprian of Carthage, *De unitate Ecclesiae*, Chapter 17.

14　Gen. 4:5.

15　Cyprian of Carthage, *De unitate Ecclesiae*, Chapter 13.
　　　Cf. Rev. 20:6.

The False Mercy the Queen Showed Certain Priests in Banishing Them from the Kingdom[1]

The queen saw that her tortures and murders could not overcome the Lord's valiant soldiers, while their constancy yielded only a greater triumph for those who died, deep solace for the remaining Catholics, and awe and dismay for those of her false religion. And that the martyrs' fame, spread throughout the world, had made her infamous, regarded as inhuman and cruel. So it was that she cast about for some artifice to make things seem other than they were, and by a superficial shadow of clemency to ensure that the earlier deaths of the saints be attributed not so much to her gentle and benign spirit, as to the horrific crimes for which they had suffered. This is one of the monstrous, hypocritical evils beloved by the heretics, who, being the bloody wolves that they are, wish to seem sheep, and, slaying like venomous serpents, to be taken for doves.[2] From the old and new jails of London, which were full of Catholics, the queen ordered the removal of twenty men and had them put in a boat to be driven from the realm, commanding them never to return on pain of death; and thus it was done on January 21, 1585.[3] Among these were three fathers of the Society of Jesus, and when one of them, Father Jasper Heywood,[4] protested to the ministers of justice on behalf of himself and all his companions that they had been permanently exiled from their homeland without cause or guilt and without trial, and declared that they would in no wise depart, preferring to die for the faith and shed their blood among their brother Catholics, they ignored him. They did the same when he asked at the very least to be shown the judgment, until two days after their departure, when, by now on the high seas, they again implored the royal agents onboard to produce it. Through the force of their entreaties, it was read out: it said that, having been convicted of

---

1   Sander, *De origine ac progressu*, 476–85.

2   Matt. 7:15, 10:16.

3   On January 21, 1585, the Elizabethan government deported twenty-one Catholic prisoners, chartering a ship to carry them to France. Dennis Flynn, "The English Mission of Jasper Heywood, S.J.," *AHSI* 54, no. 107 (1985): 45–76, here 64.

4   Among those deported was Jasper Heywood (1535–98), a rather erratic poet and translator who had joined the Society of Jesus at Rome in 1562. Sent to England in 1582, he was recalled late the following year after prolonged conflicts with his colleagues. En route, a storm forced his ship back to England, where he was arrested and imprisoned. See ibid.

high crimes and treasons and having merited death, the queen in this instance chose to exercise mercy through their banishment.[5] At this, they all begged the queen's henchmen to return them to England to die there as Catholics, and not to carry them abroad with the reputation of traitors, for what had been imputed to them was false. This they could not attain.[6] When they arrived at Rheims in France, they found that the heretics had reported that they themselves, afraid to die, had arranged to be exiled, and that they had faltered in the faith, even assenting to the heretics in part—at which the Catholics and the students of the seminary at Rheims were not a little distraught. When they learned the full truth and saw the zeal with which their brethren desired to return to England to die there, their joy and relief was inexpressible.

After this group, another twenty-two priests were expelled, plucked from the prisons of York and Hull, most of them old men, some having surpassed sixty or seventy years, and even one past eighty! Many had spent a good part of their lives imprisoned for their Catholicism, some as many as twenty-six years, with marvelous fortitude and steadfastness, suffering the harassments, burdens, and pains that must be endured in so long and so bitter an incarceration at the hand of such cruel foes. Later, they likewise banished another thirty priests and two laymen from several different prisons in the kingdom, imputing grievous crimes to the innocent and lauding and exalting the queen's clemency.[7] As though that was what it was, or could have been, to condemn the guiltless, to banish them for life under pain of death, to force them to abandon their brethren, the sheep in the mouth of the wolf, for whom, like good shepherds, the exiles wished to die.[8] But notwithstanding the utter cruelty of this manner of exile, the heretics did not cease to proclaim the queen's mercy and moderation, which they published and blazoned across the kingdom. They persuaded the simple folk that the papists and traitors' punishment was

---

5   One of the editors of Sander's manuscript, Edward Rishton, was among the twenty-one Catholics forced to leave the country: in *De origine ac progressu*, the narrative shifts into the first person as Rishton recounts his own experiences. Ibid., 64n92.

6   The twenty-one unwilling sailors were forcibly disembarked at Abbeville in Normandy on February 12, 1585. Ibid., 65.

7   "On the fifteenth daie of September, to the number of two and thirtie seminaries, massing priests and others, late prisoners in the tower of London, Marshalsee, Kings bench, and other places, were imbarked in the Marie Martine of Colchester, on the southside of the Thames right ouer against S. Katharines, to be transported ouer into the coasts of Normandie, to be banished this realme for euer, by vertue of a commission from hir maiestie, before specified." Holinshed, *Chronicles*, 4:620.

8   John 10:11.

not nearly so severe (so they claimed), nor the rigor toward them nearly as great as their hateful crimes merited: for the queen had chosen to exercise her natural benignity in pardoning the lives of many who did not deserve it. And the heretics maintained flattering, degenerate men in the courts and palaces of various princes and lords to disseminate these examples of clemency, laud them, and magnify them up to heaven itself.

But to perceive this feigned mercy fully, it should be understood that in parliament at precisely this point (in the year 1585) the queen enacted further laws against the fathers of the Society of Jesus, the priests of the seminaries we have described, and the other Catholics, which prove their own harshness and inhumanity. For, taking as its foundation the lie that the aforesaid Jesuits and priests had conspired against the queen and the kingdom, and had been convicted thereof,[9] it mandates

1. That all persons within the kingdom belonging to the Society or the seminaries are to depart within forty days, and those who are abroad, or any others who have been ordained priests by an authority derived from the Apostolic Roman See are not to enter the realm, under penalty of being regarded as traitors and committing the crime of *lèse-majesté*. And that any who receives them shall be punished with death and the loss of his property.

2. That laymen who are outside the kingdom and do not return within six months are to be treated as traitors.

3. That those who send any subsidy, aide, or relief to Catholics outside the kingdom shall lose their property and their liberty.

4. That he who sends his son or servant outside the realm without the express written permission of the queen shall pay 383 ducats for each infraction.

---

9   27 Eliz. 1. c. 2 began, "Whereas divers Persons called or professed Jesuites, Seminarie Priestes and other Priestes, which have bene and from tyme to tyme are made in the Partes beyonde the Seas, by or according to the Order and Rietes of the Romishe Church, have of late yeres comen and bene sent, and dayly doe come and are sente, into this Realme of Englande and other the Queenes Majesties Dominions, of Purpose, (as hath appeared aswell by sundrie of their owne Examinations and Confessions as by divers other manifest meanes and proofes,) not onely to withdrawe her Highnesss Subjectes from their due obedience to her Majestie, but also to stire up and move Sedition Rebellion and open Hostilitie within her Highnesse Realmes and Dominions, to the greate [daungering] of the safetie of her most Royall Person, and to the utter Ruine Desolation and Overthrow of the whole Realme, if the same bee not the sooner by some good meanes foreseene and prevented." SR, 4.1:706.

5.   That he who does not reveal a priest will be punished according to the queen's pleasure.[10]

And neither knight, nor lord, nor nobleman, nor peer anywhere in the realm was exempt from these laws, which were enforced with such extraordinary severity and heartlessness that they clearly displayed the clemency of the queen and her ministers.

For if they find any priest saying Mass, they treat him worse than a slave, with greater impiety than the cruelest tyrants and foes of Jesus Christ. They carry him, attired in the sacred vestments, through the public places, as an insult to the priestly estate, mistreating some with blows, others with shrieks and yells, others with injuries, shouts, and humiliation, persecuting and ridiculing them, and, after they have had their fill of these abuses and insults, they imprison, torment, and murder them. If ever they need to transfer them to some other city to torture them there, they do so in this way: they mount him upon a weak and feeble mount, which cannot stir without a bridle, spurs, or other equipment, with his arms and legs bound. And before they enter the towns through which they are to pass, a messenger rides ahead to inform the people that they bring a priest, an enemy to the Gospel and to the commonwealth, so they can prepare themselves to receive him. At this news and warning, a crowd gathers from all over the city to welcome the minister of God, jeering, shrieking, and mocking him until he departs or enters a horrid, gloomy cell. In the city of London alone, there are eleven common jails, truly capacious (none more respectable than that for those arrested as debtors) and stuffed with Catholics and servants of God, persecuted for our sacred faith. And in one of these, the Tower, there are so many sorts of torture and so many manners and kinds of suffering that simply to hear of them is sufficient proof of the clemency of the queen's agents, for they are so unprecedented and so diabolical that they compete with the ingenious cruelty of the ancient tyrants, even surpassing them in certain respects. For, leaving apart the fetters, shackles, irons, and other instruments used to torment the body and each of its members with its own particular pain, there are others so horrible and strange, so excruciating and frightful, that only Satan himself could have invented them and inspired the heretics, his ministers. One of these is made of iron, into which they place the person they wish to torture, in such a way that, touching the head to the feet and the knees, they make a man into a ball, and they squeeze and compress him with this device for the space of an hour and a half, so fiercely that

---

10   These are all provisions of 27 Eliz. 1. c. 2, Sections 1 and 2, 3, 4, 5, and 11, respectively. Ibid., 4.1:706–07.

the wretched flesh bursts with the pressure and spews blood from every part, even the extremities of the hands and feet; in this way they tormented the holy martyr Thomas Cottam of the Society of the Jesus, among others.[11]

Thus the treatment meted out in the prisons to those jailed for the faith is often far worse than death itself, for they are not allowed to speak with anyone, nor see their families, friends, or acquaintances, nor write or receive letters, nor can they be given alms or aided in any way without the greatest danger to those who do so. At Lancaster Castle, several Catholic noblemen were allowed nothing to eat but putrid food, nor anything to drink but polluted water, and this as a great kindness.[12] If anyone falls ill from the abuse, starkness, and filth of the prison, the medicine they prescribe and the care they offer is to remove his bed (if he has one), to throw him in an even harsher cell, and in the end to torment him until he perishes, as many have done. And when they see him moaning in agony, the heretics do not on that account soften or relent, but rather laugh at the pains of the miserable one, redoubling them with insulting words. And they frequently spread slanders against their prisoners: either that they had despaired, or had been converted to their sect, or that while debating with their ministers they had been at a loss to respond, or that they had confessed their treacheries and revealed their accomplices and partners in crime, or other things of this sort—but all of them fabrications and lies. When they take Catholics to be executed, they do not treat them with the humaneness men naturally use with other human beings in such circumstances, which is to arrange for them to have some relief or solace (or rather, a little less pain) by dying of asphyxiation before they cut the cord, or by being cut open and disemboweled while they are practically dead, their senses well-nigh senseless. But they abuse the Catholics as they hang, cutting the rope and letting them

---

11   This passage, describing Thomas Cottam's encounter with the gruesome "Scavenger's Daughter" (a form of torture that compresses the body into a ball, forcing blood from the orifices) is added in the 1595 edition. See Book 2 Figure 38.1.

12   The tribulations of Catholics imprisoned at Lancaster Castle were described by Robert Persons: "For indeed, six, I say, or even eight, were confined in the same hole, of distinguished rank though they were, great in themselves and noble in their families. They were given no food, and allowed nothing but what was rotten, and begged for from door to door, nor the use of any but putrid water." Robert Persons, *De persecutione anglicana libellus: Quo explicantur afflictiones, calamitates, cruciatus, & acerbissima martyria, quæ Angli Catholici nu[n]c ob fide[m] patiuntur* (Rome: Ex typographia Georgij Ferrarij, 1582), 38.

Cf. Richard Rex, "Thomas Vavasour M.D.," RH 20, no. 4 (October 1991): 436–54, here 444.

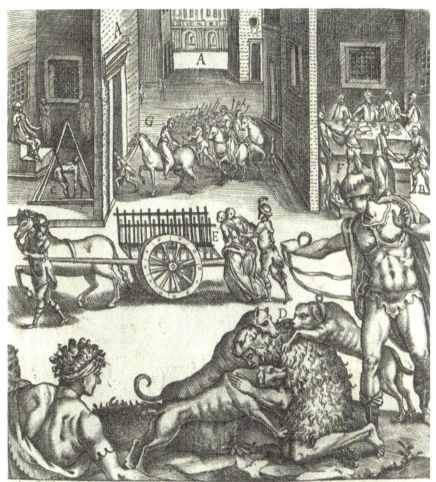

A. Ob fidem Catholicam in Angliā multi carceres cuiusuis conditionis hominibus pleni sunt, in quibus plures
    fame, pædore, et alijs incommodis oppressi obierunt.
B. Varie in catholicos passim animaduertitur. Aliqui ferreis aciculis sub manuum, pedúq; unguibus
    infixis torquentur.
C. Alij inaudito quodam tormenti genere, quo corpus varijs catenis in unum ueluti globum
    redigitur diuexantur.
D. Alij pelle ursina induti canibus exponuntur.
E. Alij uirgis per plateas cæduntur.
F. Alijs candenti ferro aures aduruntur.
G. Ad carceres uero Sacerdotes aliquando Sacris uestibus induti, aut auersi equis
    impositi publicè ducuntur.

FIGURE 38.1   *Various scenes of Catholics enduring persecution. The Scavenger's Daughter is
              depicted in the upper-left corner.*
              Giovanni Battista Cavalieri, *Ecclesiae anglicanae trophaea sive sanctorum
              martyrum qui pro Christo catholicaeque fidei veritate asserenda antiquo
              recentiorique persecutionum tempore mortem in Anglia subierunt, passiones
              Romae in collegio Anglico per Nicolaum Circinianum depictae: Nuper autem
              per Io. Bap. de Cavalleriis aeneis typis repraesentatae* (Rome: Ex officina
              Bartolomeo Grassi, 1584). NE1666. C57 1584 OVERSIZE, John J. Burns Library,
              Boston College.

fall, and opening them and tearing out their hearts while their senses were still intact and alert—and the hangmen does this with such care that it has happened that some sainted martyrs spoke, clearly and distinctly, even as the executioner was already holding their ripped-out, still-beating heart in his hands.

Now, what am I to say of the other mode of punishment in which the queen's clemency and mildness is revealed: the command that respectable, virtuous maidens be dragged to the public places for women of ill-repute, there to be dishonored and humiliated because they refused to speak badly of the pope or to consent to anything contrary to our most sacred faith? Is there a torment crueler, more degrading or horrible for a high-minded and chaste maiden than this? To be meted out at the hands of ministers of a woman who calls herself queen and proclaims that she does not intend to marry, but rather to live a virgin forever! In his *Apologeticus*, Tertullian criticizes the pagan emperors for employing this infamous and detestable wickedness with honest Christian women in these words: "In condemning a Christian woman to the public square, and committing her to the rapist rather than the lion, you prove that among us the loss of chastity is deemed a greater torment than any other torture or sort of death."[13]

Let us proceed no further in discussing this clemency of the queen's—or, properly speaking, of her council's—for we should never make an end of it. Suffice it to say that the name of Christian was never so hateful to the pagans and barbarians as is that of Catholic in England today. And if the strangeness of the tenets, the diversity and contradiction among the sects, the inconstancy and mutability of the doctrine, the license and dissoluteness of the lives, and a thousand other things were not sufficient to perceive and hate the hypocrisy and malice of these heretics, so inhuman a cruelty as this would be enough to make one recognize and abhor. For men naturally benign and loving have been so transformed into panthers and tigers, trading their hearts of flesh for hearts of diamond,[14] since others' humanity, of the same stuff as theirs, moves them not at all; neither being born in the same land and country, nor their probity of lifestyle, nor the dignity of learning, nor the flower of youth, nor the privileges and reverence of sacred orders, nor the compassion owed to children and women; not white hairs, nobility, or famous lineage, not humble words or copious tears, not sighs or sorrowful groans, nor anything else whatsoever is

---

13   This passage is added in the 1595 edition.
       In the margin: "Tertullian, *Apology*."
       Tertullian, *Apologeticus*, Chapter 50.

14   Ezek. 11:19, 36:26; Zech. 7:12.

enough to soften or mollify them, or to mitigate their fierceness against their countrymen and guiltless brothers. This is the queen's clemency, but it will be better understood when we deal with the death of her cousin, the queen of Scots, after an account of how she has plotted to secure herself through the disturbances of neighboring kingdoms.

The Methods the Queen Has Used to Unsettle Neighboring Countries[1]

This is what happened in England. But Queen Elizabeth and her council recognized that as matters were unfolding well for them (according to their lights), their deeds must needs offend the pope and the other Catholic monarchs and princes. And that, being separated from the faith and communion of the Catholic Church, they could have neither peace in their own house nor the security regarding their neighbors they hoped for. And so they decided that to secure the realm and protect the government, they would disturb the peace of neighboring lands, especially those of France, Flanders, and Scotland. By kindling fires there, they would so unsettle them that their princes would be unable to concern themselves with foreign affairs, having so much to do at home. Under this plan, breaking every ancient league and new alliance with the greatest princes and monarchs of Christendom, while merely making a show of observing them, they made pacts and leagues with the rebels against almost every monarch, at once traitors to their homelands and plagues upon Christendom. In Scotland, against Queen Mary; in France, against the three brothers, the Most Christian Kings; in Flanders, against the Catholic King Don Philip. And they so agitated these kingdoms and provinces, dispatching troops and occupying territory, seizing cities and stealing the merchants' wealth, infesting the ocean sea with fleets and inducing their subjects to rebellion, and committing countless other affronts and outrages, that they have ruined the whole realm of Scotland and entangled its king in his present miseries and calamities.[2] They have infected the kingdom of France, endangering the lives of Kings Francis II, Charles IX, and Henry III.[3] They have ravaged and desolated the provinces of Flanders, sustaining the unjust and bloody war waged for so many years against the true and rightful lord, with their money, arms, soldiers, munitions, victuals, schemes, and advice. Nor have they been satisfied

---

1 Sander, *De origine ac progressu*, 410–12, 434–35, 489–94, 497.

2 In addition to Elizabeth's long history of financial support for the Protestant powerbrokers in Scotland, she had encouraged the Ruthven Raid of 1582, which saw the young James kidnapped by Calvinist lords. McCoog, *Our Way of Proceeding?*, 188.

3 1562, for example, saw an English force land in France to assist the Huguenot rebels against Charles IX, with disastrous results, including the loss of Dieppe and Le Havre. Haigh, *Elizabeth I*, 133–34.

with this, but they have also attempted to raise the states against the governor, Lord Don John of Austria, and to drive the Spanish garrison back into Italy.[4] Not thinking themselves safe even with this, they sent from England a high-born gentleman, young and hot-headed, by the name of Egremont Radcliffe, to assassinate Lord Don John through treachery. But it pleased our Lord that this wickedness was discovered and the knight imprisoned: having confessed the truth, he was beheaded at Namur, and with him his brother-in-law (his confederate and companion in treachery).[5]

They have offered and pledged themselves to all heretics, agitators, and disturbers of the commonwealth as comrades, defenders, and soldiers, for the purpose of further kindling and stoking the hellish flames of heresy against the Catholic Church. And this evil desire to spread the venom of perverted doctrine through the world and to embroil Catholic rulers with civil wars and the disobedience of their vassals has waxed so great that to this end they have dispatched ambassadors to Turkey[6] and Muscovy,[7] inciting those princes

---

4   Though Elizabeth was wary of involvement with the Dutch rebellion against Spain, the Treaty of Nonsuch (1585) eventually committed her to 6,400 infantry, one thousand cavalry, and an annual subsidy of 126,000 pounds—that is, to open war on Habsburg forces in the Low Countries. Haigh, *Elizabeth I*, 28, 135.

   Cf. MacCaffrey, *Elizabeth I*, Chapter 17.

5   Egremont Radcliffe (d.1578) was the son of Henry Radcliffe, second earl of Sussex (c.1507–57). A participant in the ill-fated Rising of the North, he spent most the 1570s in exile or in captivity. Upon his release in 1578, he journeyed to the Spanish Netherlands to serve Don John of Austria (1547–78). Even before John's mysterious death on October 1, 1578 (attributed by historians to the plague), an imperial adviser cautioned the governor general "that he is a rash and daring young man, ready for anything, and his sudden liberation and decision to serve us may well engender suspicion." After John died, Radcliffe, along with a confederate by the name of Gray—who does not seem, *pace* Ribadeneyra and Sander, to have been related to him—was arrested on suspicion of having poisoned the governor general. The two were beheaded in Namur in December 1578. Julian Lock, "Radcliffe, Egremont (*d.* 1578)," in *ODNB*, 45:731–33. McCoog, *Our Way of Proceeding?*, 114. *CSPSE*, 2:497.

6   Beginning in the 1570s, Elizabeth began to work toward better relationships with the Ottoman Empire, including proposals for a military alliance against Catholic Europe. See Lisa Jardine, "Gloriana Rules the Waves: Or, the Advantages of Being Excommunicated (and a Woman)," *Transactions of the Royal Historical Society*, sixth series, 14 (2004): 209–22.

7   An Anglo-Russian alliance was first proposed by Ivan IV (r.1547–84) in 1567, and the tsar periodically returned to the project throughout his reign. See Henry R. Huttenbach, "New Archival Material on the Anglo-Russian Treaty of Queen Elizabeth I and Tsar Ivan IV," *Slavonic and East European Review* 49, no. 117 (October 1971): 535–49.

   Russia was a Christian state (albeit not properly so in Ribadeneyra's eyes); equating Muscovy with the Ottomans is more of a political statement—in the sixteenth century, the tsars' polity became a symbol of despotism and tyranny. Scott, *Oxford Handbook*, 397.

against the peace and prosperity of the Catholic religion, employing trickery and deception at first, then open force and violence. Indeed, whereas heresy is a plague, if it is not checked it spreads and grows each day. For this reason, the queen has dared to remove her mask and uncover her face, waging war upon the Catholic King Don Philip with navies and armies, by sea and by land, all while seeking excuses and pretexts for doing so and for aiding the rebels against him. She has extended her support and protection to the rebels of Holland and Zealand, stationed a garrison of Englishmen in their principal cities, and occupied the ports (which are crucial to her intentions); she has given them as governor the earl of Leicester, a man without God, without faith, without law, who, having ravaged his own country, ravages a foreign one.[8] This audacity did not end here: with new spirit and greater heart, she has dared to beset the territories of the Indies, plundering various islands, seizing and sinking ships, and even assailing and assaulting several ports in Spain.[9]

The queen saw that many of her councilors and other wise and thoughtful men were troubled at this, deeming it reckless for a woman, the lady of a realm neither very large nor very powerful, unloved at home and hated and abhorred abroad, to declare war on so mighty a world-monarch without lawful occasion. For, peaceful, mild, and patient though he is—for which reason, and because he took little thought of her (she being a woman), he has sought, like a Christian king, to appease her with kindnesses rather than turning to the clash of arms—yet he is bold and zealous for the Catholic faith, as befits his reputation, and once he has come to a decision, he is firm and unyielding in what he undertakes, and he has ever been victorious in his wars against the most formidable princes of the world. Accordingly, to answer these judgments and criticisms she ordered the publication of a book even worse and even more confused than the war she had begun. After taking as the first cause and foundation something utterly false (but worthy of her faith and creed)—that Christian kings, and she in particular, were not obliged to account for themselves or their

---

8   Under the terms of the Treaty of Nonsuch, Elizabeth dispatched an initial contingent of four thousand soldiers to the Low Countries in late August 1585. Leicester was commissioned to lead the force in October. Unbeknownst to Elizabeth, however, he was subsequently sworn in as governor-general of the Netherlands—a title the queen had been offered in the treaty, but had refused; the queen was furious, demanding his immediate resignation (she eventually relented). His tenure as governor-general was a decidedly mixed bag, seeing towns and fortresses change hands in both directions. See MacCaffrey, *Elizabeth I*, Chapter 17.

9   The exploits of Elizabeth's privateers, most notably the famous Sir Francis Drake, included the seizure of Spanish treasure fleets, the 1585 sack of Santo Domingo, the capture of Cartagena de Indias the same year, and raids on Cádiz in 1587 (in hopes of derailing the preparations for the Armada). MacCaffrey, *Elizabeth I*, 224. Haigh, *Elizabeth I*, 174, 192–93.

deeds to any mortal man, but only to God alone—she proceeds to give the reasons prompting her to succor Holland and Zealand and extend them her protection.[10] But these are so frivolous, specious, and inapposite that there is no need to rehearse them here. In truth, all this did more to expose the injustice and irrationality of this business than to excuse it, and more to exacerbate the earlier injury with new harms than to vindicate it. And what she now practices against the Catholic King, she previously practiced against the Most Christian King of France, claiming several of his cities in Normandy and seeking to justify it with another book to hoodwink the ignorant, to blow smoke in the eyes of the ignorant [*vender humo a los que poco saben*], to mock such mighty kings, and to amuse herself with the travails and disasters of their realms, brought about by her efforts and deceit.[11]

---

10   Elizabeth I, *A Declaration of the Causes Moving the Queen of England to Give Aid to the Defense of the People Afflicted and Oppressed in the Lowe Countries 1585 October 1* (London, 1585).

11   E.g., *A complaint of the churche, against the barbarous tiranny executed in Fraunce upon her poore members: 1562* (London: John Allde for Edmund Halley, 1562).

The Imprisonment and Death of Queen Mary of Scotland[1]

Although every monarch has felt these harms to their kingdoms and territories, and proximity to England has been detrimental to all of them, Elizabeth has turned her wrath and executed her furious rage most of all against her cousin Mary, queen regnant of Scotland, former queen of France, and rightful heir to the throne of England. Elizabeth had her killed, and I shall relate here the form and rationale of the sentence, drawn from reports I have seen from Paris and England, and from the books printed in Latin and French about the martyrdom (as it may be called) of this saintly queen.[2]

To understand all this, it must first be understood that King Henry VIII had (as we have said) two sisters, the daughters of his father, King Henry VII: Margaret, the elder sister, and Mary, the younger. Mary was first married to King Louis XII of France and then to the duke of Suffolk. Margaret married King James IV of Scotland, and by him bore a son, also called James, the fifth of that name in Scotland; he, having wed Mary, the sister of Francis, duke of Guise, had by her a daughter, named Mary Stewart (she of whom we are speaking). After her father died and she became queen of Scots, she married Dauphin Francis, the eldest son of King Henry II of France and heir and successor to his crown.[3] Thus, after the death of his father, Francis succeeded as king of France, and Mary his wife as queen.[4] God our Lord willed that King Francis, a youth of high prospects, died soon thereafter without leaving sons by the queen, and so his brother, Charles IX, succeeded him, and thereafter Henry

---

1 Sander, *De origine ac progressu*, 415–16.

2 The misadventures of Mary Queen of Scots, produced a veritable flood of publications, before and after her death. I have attempted to identify specific sources for Ribadeneyra's information, but an excellent guide to the scope of this literature is John Scott, *A Bibliography of Works Relating to Mary Queen of Scots: 1544–1700*, Publications of the Edinburgh Bibliographical Society 2 (Edinburgh: Printed for the Edinburgh Bibliographical Society, 1896).

3 James V married Mary of Guise (1515–60), elder sister to Francis de Lorraine, second duke of Guise (1519–63). After the deaths of two sons in infancy, Mary gave birth to a namesake daughter at Linlithgow on December 8, 1542. James died six days later, leaving his infant daughter queen of Scotland. Warnicke, *Mary Queen of Scots*, 20, 22–23.

4 Henry II died on July 10, 1559, two weeks after sustaining wounds to his throat and eye in a jousting accident. His son succeeded him as Francis II.

III, now living.[5] Queen Mary returned a widow to her kingdom of Scotland, and although it had no prince equal to her first husband, the king of France, for her to wed, yet to secure the succession of her line and the tranquility and Catholicism of her realm, she married a prominent nobleman named Henry Stewart, Lord Darnley, her kinsman, who came from the ancient lineages of the kings of Scotland and England.[6] By the new king she had a son, named James like his grandfather, who is the present king of Scotland, the sixth of his name.[7] Once this is grasped, it should also be noted that Queen Mary of Scotland was the rightful heir and successor to the throne of England. For with none such to be found in any legitimate children of the present Queen Elizabeth, and the line of her father King Henry VIII ending with her, those called to the throne are the nearest heirs to her grandfather, King Henry VII, whose elder daughter was Margaret Queen of Scots (as we have said): Margaret's granddaughter and her successor to the throne of Scotland—and by rights to that of England— was the Mary of whom we are speaking.

Several prominent lords of her kingdom began to resent and abhor her, because they had committed numerous outrages and crimes during her minority in France, and, at the instigation of the queen of England, robbed the churches and desolated the temples of God, in contempt of his divine majesty and the oppression of his servants. All this they wanted the queen to confirm and approve once she came of age, returned to Scotland, and took full control—but she, a just and Catholic queen, had refused.[8] Driven by their hatred, these lords conspired against her, attempting to kill her even as she was pregnant with her

---

5   Francis fell ill in mid-November 1560, suffering from swelling and pain in his ear and jaw; he died at Orléans on December 5. He was succeeded in turn by his two younger brothers, Charles IX (r.1560–74) and Henry III (1575–89).

6   Mary arrived in Scotland on August 19, 1561, almost a year after her husband's death. After several years of fruitless negotiations with English and continental candidates, on July 29, 1565 the queen wed Henry Stewart, Lord Darnley (1545–67). Henry was Mary's first cousin, the son of Margaret Tudor's daughter Margaret Douglas, countess of Lennox (1515–78). He was also the great-great-great-grandson of King James II of Scotland (r.1437–60). See Wormald, *Mary Queen of Scots*, 102, Chapter 6 *passim*.

7   James VI and I was born at Edinburgh Castle on June 19, 1566.
    The Spanish here, "como su aguelo," is ambiguous—it might equally refer to the young James's grandfather, James V, or to Mary's grandfather, James IV.

8   After the death of Mary's mother in 1560, the balance of power in Scotland had shifted dramatically in favor of the more evangelically inclined Scottish nobles, particularly the association known as the Lords of the Congregation. In July, they concluded the Treaty of Edinburgh with England, which required the withdrawal of all foreign troops from Scotland, Mary's abandonment of English heraldry, and domestic arrangements ensuring the dominance of

son; they seized one of her secretaries, by the name of David, from the queen's very apartments and battered him to death.[9] Furthermore, several powerful nobles killed the king her second husband out of envy and malice,[10] intending to have the queen's bastard brother, James, prior of St Andrews, take power—with the approval and support of the queen of England, so they say, who thus hoped to disturb and destroy the peace and faith of Scotland, and to control the child king and persecute the queen his mother for being a Catholic.[11] All this did indeed happen, for various Scottish knights and lords, the queen of England's allies, seized the young king and imprisoned Queen Mary his mother, abused and falsely slandered by the heretics with the murder of her own husband.

And so, when the wretched and afflicted lady saw herself in this state, a widowed woman abandoned and alone—she who had once seen herself queen of France and of Scotland, and now saw herself the prisoner of heretics and her foes—and with her son, being a child and a captive, unable to assist or succor her, she made a secret escape, commending herself to God in hopes of reaching some other kingdom.[12] She could count upon the support of the king

---

the Congregation. Mary and Francis refused to ratify the treat when it was first concluded, and she continued to resist Elizabeth's pressure to do so. Warnicke, *Mary Queen of Scots*, 54–56.

9   David Riccio was an Italian-born courtier who joined Mary's retinue in 1561 and quickly became a trusted secretary. Rumored to be the father of the queen's unborn son, Riccio was murdered on March 9, 1566 by a coterie of Scottish nobles, including Mary's husband. The future James VI was born two months later. Wormald, *Mary Queen of Scots*, 157–61. John Guy, *Queen of Scots: The True Life of Mary Stuart* (Boston: Houghton Mifflin, 2004), 256.

10   Darnley died at Kirk o' Field near Edinburgh on February 9, 1567: the house itself was devastated by an explosion, and his body was found (visibly unharmed by the blast) in the orchard. Much ink, scholarly and otherwise, has been spilled over what happened at Kirk o' Field and why, but Mary's enemies were not slow to allege her complicity. See Warnicke, *Mary Queen of Scots*, 135–46.

11   James Stewart, first earl of Moray (c.1531–70), an illegitimate son of James V and commendator of the priory of St Andrews. One of several lords intermittently in rebellion against Mary, Moray served as regent for his young half-nephew, and several times sought Elizabeth's backing to seize power in earnest. Mark Loughlin, "Stewart, James, first earl of Moray (1531/32–1570)," in ODNB, 52:685–92, here 690–91.

12   An alliance of Scottish lords joined forces against Mary and her third husband, James Hepburn, fourth earl of Bothwell (c.1534–78). An anti-climactic battle at Carberry Hill on June 15, 1567, left Mary a prisoner at Lochleven, where she was forced to abdicate in favor of her year-old son. The embattled queen escaped the following May; after an abortive attempt to resist Moray, she fled south. Warnicke, *Mary Queen of Scots*, 162–67.

of France, her brother-in-law, and the friendship and solidarity of the dukes of Lorraine and Guise, her cousins by blood.[13] The queen of England knew this, and, reckoning that with the queen of Scots at liberty abroad, she would have less scope for disrupting and undermining Scotland, cunningly and deceitfully wrote her loving letters. She sent her gifts through her ambassadors and invited and implored her to come to her kingdom, offering arms and soldiers to recover Scotland and punish the malcontents and rebels, and giving her word and royal bond to aid and support her. This abused lady trusted her, as a woman to a woman, as a queen to a queen, as a niece to an aunt,[14] as heir and successor to the kingdom of England to the one she thought to succeed, imagining that any one of those claims sufficed as a guarantee—not thinking to trust her as a Catholic to a heretic, which by itself was reason enough not to trust her, and to fear that she would break all other bonds and obligations, however close. And so it was.

For, upon entering England under so many assurances of good faith,[15] the queen of Scots was immediately arrested and held in a castle, and a little later committed to the earl of Shrewsbury for safekeeping.[16] The queen bore this hardship and imprisonment with patience and constancy, like a handmaid of our Lord,[17] and resolved to turn to him in prayer and good works, awaiting from his hand remedy and relief for her sorrows. And when a French father of the Society of Jesus by the name of Edmond Auger, whom she had met in France, wrote her a letter consoling and encouraging her in her affliction, the saintly

---

13   Prominent among Mary's powerful French relatives were her first cousin Henry I de Lorraine, duke of Guise (1550–88), and her second cousin, Charles III, duke of Lorraine (1543–1608). Guy, *Queen of Scots*, xvi.

14   Elizabeth was actually Mary's first cousin once removed (the former's grandfather, Henry VII, was the latter's great-grandfather).

15   "None of her faithfullest subiectes and serwandes councellis did like her minde, sayinge, shee wold truste her selff in the handes of her nearest kinniswoman and cusing Elizabeth, whose amitie and freindshipe shee was sure of, boith in regarde shee caried with her the pledges and gages of her promesed freindshipe and constant lowe which shee had send her, and also the letters which shee had written vnto her, full of honest offers and fauour to succoure her when and as often as neede should require." Adam Blackwood, *History of Mary Queen of Scots; a Fragment*, trans. Alexander Macdonald (Edinburgh: Maitland Club, 1834), 60.

16   In February 1569, Mary was delivered into the keeping of George Talbot, sixth earl of Shrewbury and sixth earl of Waterford (c.1522–90), at Tutbury in Staffordshire. Elizabeth Goldring, "Talbot, George, sixth earl of Shrewsbury (c.1522–1590)," in *ODNB*, 53:692–94, here 692–93.

17   Luke 1:38.

queen answered him with another in French in her own hand.[18] This, because I think it well manifests her piety, sufferance, and steadfastness, I have decided to insert here, translated to the letter into our Castilian tongue, and it goes as follows:

> Master Edmond, I have received your letters as a great solace to my spirit, albeit not without shame or a wound in my heart, confessing myself unworthy and undeserving of your good opinion of me. But I attribute your praises to the mercy of God, who has thus moved you to write to me and to inspire me to strive henceforth to be equal to your estimation. And I trust that you will implore his divine majesty (and that those of your holy Society will aid me), lest I falter in my duty to receive with humble submission all the rebukes it pleases him to send me, to the end that I might subject myself in all things to his holy will, in all the adversities from which hitherto he has mercifully deigned to protect me, endowing me with patience, which I beg him to be content to allow me to the end. Your book has not yet reached my hands, much as I desire it at the moment; I know not who has it, and it would please me greatly to possess a copy.[19]
>
> And as your charity has extended to attend to and consoling a poor woman imprisoned and afflicted for her sins, I beg you, when you are able, to continue, combining in your letters something of salutary admonition with holy comforts, so as to awaken my spirit, befuddled by adversity, to the knowledge of its guilt and to the hope of the true rest and the eternal solace from which this world always separates and distracts us. And if you would take on so much trouble for me, and set out a little guidance or a form of prayer, in which, besides the ordinary prayers, you would include those most appropriate for the highest feast days and for the times of greater necessity, the which might be offered up to God our

---

18   The French Jesuit Edmond Auger was an influential figure at the Valois court of the late sixteenth century. Contrary to Ribadeneyra's account, the two almost certainly did not meet in France, as the Jesuit did not enter court circles until after the widowed queen had returned to Scotland. French scholar Louis Wiesener averred, with some probability, that they first encountered one another when Auger came to Scotland in late 1566 as part of a diplomatic delegation. Louis Wiesener, ed., "Marie Stuart et le P. Edmond Augier: Une lettre inédite de Marie Stuart," *Revue des questions historiques* 2 (1867): 614–18, here 615.

19   Unfortunately, owing to the disappearance of Auger's side of the correspondence, the Jesuit's authorial fecundity, and the difficulty of determining how recent a publication Mary is referring to (it having been more than ten years since she was at liberty to know what was being published, let alone choose her books), it is impossible to identify what book of Auger's it was the queen so desired. Her other letters, however, do speak to her frustration with her limited reading material. Ibid., 616.

Lord by my little household assembly with perfect uniformity, you would perform an office of piety. For here we have no one from whom we might take counsel and are prevented from spending our hours in the service of God as we wish—if there were any good, fitting exercise for the state of one imprisoned, in Latin or in a vulgar tongue, I beg you to prepare it and give it to my emissary to send to me, and to take care to visit my poor students and urge them to pray for me, being sure to do so yourself, and to ensure that the fathers of your college do the same, to whose prayers and sacrifices I entrust myself completely. While I, for my own part, will offer my prayers to God, simple and unworthy as they are, for the preservation of your sacred Society in his service—in the which I entreat his majesty to give me the grace to live and die. At Sheffield [*Ghefild*], June 9.

Your good friend,
Queen Mary[20]

At first, prisoner though she was, they treated the queen with considerable kindness and respect; once they saw her so steadfast in the Catholic faith, each day they pressured her and afflicted her more and more. They changed her guards, putting her in the hands of barbarous, bestial, and heretical men, who harassed and tormented her with insults and other indignities unworthy of her royal person: they forbade her to hear Mass or to retain a priest to say it for her or administer the sacraments—which she in her devotion and piety felt more than the jail cell itself and all the other tortures.

To defame her and to cause other Catholic princes to abandon their devotion and goodwill for her, the heretics claimed that she had broken and converted from Catholicism to their false sect. And to give some plausibility to their wickedness, they had a heretical minister enter the queen's quarters and utter certain prayers in the vernacular in her presence,[21] so that, since the queen

---

20   As I discuss elsewhere, it is not certain how Ribadeneyra acquired his text of this letter (dated June 9, 1578), but it is significant that the only extant French manuscript comes from the papers of his compatriot and close friend, the Spanish Jesuit historian Juan de Mariana (1536–1624). The most likely explanation is either that Mariana lent the manuscript to Ribadeneyra, or that Mariana had it from Ribadeneyra. See Weinreich, "English Mission."

    For the French text, see Wiesener, "Marie Stuart," 616–17. For the Latin, see *Concertatio*, 212ᵛ.

21   Ribadeneyra, anxious for Mary's reputation, has distorted the details of this incident: in late 1568, deprived of Catholic clergy, Mary began to attend Protestant services and listen to sermons in English—a decision, she stressed to her household and her allies abroad, only taken out of necessity. Warnicke, *Mary Queen of Scots*, 172.

had heard them, it would seem that she had communed with the heretic and agreed with what he said. The queen knew the rumor that they had spread and the intentions behind it, and she wrote to Pope Pius V of holy memory a letter on the subject, which runs thus:

Most holy father,

After kissing the feet of Your Blessedness: I have been informed that the rebels against me and those who support and shelter them in their lands have concocted plots and intrigues to make my lord and dear brother the king of Spain believe I have been inconstant in the Catholic faith. Although I have written to Your Holiness these past days, humbly to kiss your feet and commend myself to you, I wanted to write this letter to entreat you to consider me as the most devoted and obedient daughter of the holy Roman Catholic Church, and not to credit the false reports about me that will have come, or perchance will come, to your ears, at the instigation of the said rebels and others of their sect, who declare that I have changed my faith so as to deprive me of the grace of Your Holiness and of other Catholic monarchs. This has so pierced my heart that I had to write once more to Your Blessedness to protest the outrage and injury they do me. I beg that you deign to write in my support to those Christian princes who are Your Holiness's devoted and obedient children, exhorting them to use their authority with the queen of England, in whose power I now languish, to ask her to permit me to depart her kingdom, which I entered confident of her promises and seeking her support against my rebels. And, if she still intends to keep me and absolutely refuses to release me, that at least she allow me to practice my religion, which has been denied and prohibited me since I entered this realm.

And I wish Your Holiness to know the cunning my enemies have used to disguise their slanders against me. They had a heretical minister enter the place where I am so closely confined, and several times recite his prayers in the common tongue, and as I was not at liberty, nor permitted to practice my religion, I took no thought of hearing them, believing that I would not err in this. But if I have erred in this, or in anything else, most holy father, I beg mercy of Your Holiness, and entreat you to pardon and absolve me; truly, I have never had any intention but to live always as the most devoted and obedient daughter of the holy Roman Catholic Church, in which I hope to live and die, according to the advice and instructions of Your Holiness, and I pledge to be so careful and do such penance for my sins that all penitent Catholics, and especially Your Holiness, as the father and lord of all, will be perfectly satisfied with me.

Meanwhile, I kiss the feet of Your Holiness and beg God to keep you many years, for the good of his holy Church. Written at Bolton Castle, the last day of November, 1568.

> The most devoted and obedient daughter of Your Holiness,
> Mary, queen of Scotland and widow of the king of France[22]

How firm in the Catholic faith must the writer of this letter have been? How obedient and devoted to the supreme pontiff, she who humbles herself to him with such reverence? How delicate a conscience did she possess, who asks pardon and absolution for what was no crime, or at most a very slight one?[23]

So the queen remained imprisoned and captive for nearly twenty years, without Queen Elizabeth ever deigning to see her. And in the end, Elizabeth and her council, seeing that Queen Mary was the lawful successor to the throne of England (as we have said) and a Catholic zealous for our sacred faith—so firm and constant that when they had proposed (so they say) to declare her in parliament as the legitimate heir and successor to the kingdom if she promised to maintain the false sect now in power, she had not given them ear, preferring to suffer for the Catholic faith than to rule among heretics[24]—considering that in so many years, with all their many abuses and harassments, they had been unable to weaken her or win her over, and fearing that if she did succeed to the throne, she would restore the Catholic religion and punish the heretics who then ruled and devastated it (as that other Queen Mary of holy memory, the wife of the Catholic King Don Philip, had done), resolved to take the life of the one who would give life to the realm and death to their errors, so as to secure their party and establish their hypocritical and perverted cult. To lessen the loathing, indignation, and horror of the entire world, they sought a pretext (as is their wont) and claimed she had tried to free herself from her cell, and sought to kill the queen of England, and other things specious, shameful, and incredible.[25] And having imprisoned her secretaries with this excuse, and

---

22   This letter was published in Italian in 1586, as part of Girolamo Catena's (dates unknown) biography of Pius v. See Girolamo Catena, *Vita del gloriosissimo papa Pio Quinto* (Rome: Nella stamperia di Vincenzo Accolti, 1586), 278–79.

23   This letter and Ribadeneyra's comments are added in the 1595 edition.

24   In the margin: "Sander, *De visibili monarchia*, Book 7."
      Sander, *De visibili monarchia*, 708.

25   Mary was complicit in several Catholic schemes to secure her freedom, some of which included assassinating Elizabeth. 1571 saw the Ridolfi Plot, masterminded by the Florentine banker Roberto di Ridolfi (1531–1612), whereby the duke of Norfolk would lead a rebellion, aided by a Spanish invasion from the Netherlands, with the endgame of eliminating Elizabeth and marrying the duke to the queen of Scots. Twelve years later, Mary colluded

pressured and badgered and abused her with endless demands and slanders, they finally determined to carry out their wicked intentions and free themselves from their fear and anxiety. In the deepest secrecy, the queen of Scots herself wrote a letter to one of her principal agents and servants,[26] telling him how Elizabeth's commissioners had demanded her confession. Therein (among other matters, which I omit so as not to be overlong) she said a few things I wish to insert here, translated from the French into Castilian, because they reveal much of the truth of the business and unmask the deceitful hypocrisy now reigning in England:

> Queen Elizabeth's commissioners—Lord Buckhurst, my great enemy Amias Paulet, a knight named Dru Drury, and Mr. Beale—came and informed me that parliament has rendered a sentence of death upon me, of which they notified me on the queen's behalf, urging me to admit and confess the sins I have committed against her.[27] They also told me that the queen their mistress had sent me two churchmen, a bishop and a dean, to exhort me to patience and to help me die well and discharge my conscience. They added that the cause of my death was the kingdom's continual demand for it, for the safety of her royal person: for, I being her rival and having long ago appropriated the arms of this realm, and never having consented to abandon them save under with certain conditions, she could not live in perfect peace and safety so long as I lived, especially since the Catholics call me their sovereign lady, and that by this her life has many times been imperiled. The second and most important reason they gave for their sentence and decision, that which they

---

in Sir Francis Throckmorton's (1554–84) namesake plot of 1583, which again envisioned a domestic rising assisted by foreign intervention (this time on the part of France), ending with Elizabeth's murder and Mary's accession to the English throne. It was Mary's apparent consent to a third conspiracy in 1586, associated with and named for Sir Anthony Babington (1561–86), that finally drove the Elizabethan government to execute the captive queen. MacCaffrey, *Elizabeth I*, 136–37, 221, 347–48.

26   James Beaton, archbishop of Glasgow (1517–1603), one of Mary's closest friends and advisers.

27   Sir Amias Paulet (*c*.1532–88) became Mary's jailer in April 1585. Sir Dru Drury (*c*.1531–1617) was added as his colleague in November 1586. Mary was informed of her sentence by Thomas Sackville, first Baron Buckhurst (*c*.1536–1608), and the Puritan courtier Robert Beale (1541–1601), sent as royal commissioners. Michael Hicks, "Paulet, Sir Amias (*c*.1532–1588)," in *ODNB*, 43:150–52, here 151. J. Andreas Löwe, "Drury, Sir Dru (1531/32–1617)," in *ODNB*, 16:1002–03. Rivkah Zim, "Sackville, Thomas, first Baron Buckhurst and first earl of Dorset (*c*.1536–1608)," in *ODNB*, 48:542–48, here 544.

said most pained the queen, was the knowledge that while I live, their faith could not take root or enjoy any security or foundation in this kingdom. I replied that I gave thanks to our Lord, and to them as well, for the honor that they did me in regarding me as a fit instrument to restore the true religion in their land. For although I do not deserve such a sublime lot, I desire to be worthy to be a defender of the Catholic faith, and I shall think myself most fortunate and blessed if that should come to pass. And that I shall shed my blood in testimony and proof of this truth with the greatest willingness, as I have declared. And that if the people think it necessary that I give my life for this isle to have peace and tranquility, I shall be equally generous with that, at the end of the twenty years of imprisonment I have suffered. As to the bishop and the dean, I said that I gave infinite thanks to our Lord that without them I knew my sins and the misdeeds I have committed against my God and against his church, and that I had no desire to assent to their errors or to have anything to do with them whatsoever. But if they would deign to allow me a Catholic priest (as I begged them for the love of Jesus Christ), it would be a true kindness, for I wished to put my affairs in order and receive the holy sacraments, as one departing this world. They told me not to imagine I would die as a saint or martyr, for I should die as a conspirator against the queen, one who sought to wrest her crown from her. I answered that I am not so presumptuous as to wish to aspire to these two crowns of saint and martyr, but that although they held power over my life and body—by divine permission, and not by right and justice (for I was a queen and a sovereign lady, as I have always insisted)—they held none over my soul, nor could they prevent me from hoping in God's mercy and trusting that he who died and gave his blood for me will accept mine and the life I offer up to him for the preservation of his Church, besides which I desired no power, neither here nor anywhere else, nor do I seek a temporal kingdom by the loss of the eternal kingdom. That what I begged of our Lord was that he accept the many pains and sufferings of body and spirit that I suffer, in remittance of my numerous sins. That I had not plotted against the life of the queen, nor counseled or commanded anything whatsoever, nor had what they imputed to me even entered my imagination—and as for what touches me personally, I had had nothing to do with any of it. At this they said, "At the very least you have permitted the English to call you their sovereign lady, and you have offered no contradiction." I responded, "It will not be found that I have usurped this title or made use of it in my letters or in any other fashion; but the rebuking or instructing of ecclesiastics is not my office, being, as I am, a woman and a daughter of the

Church, for the sake of which and in obedience to which I desire to die—but not to kill anyone to seize their power."

To conclude, the day before yesterday Paulet came to me again, with Drury (who is the most moderate of them), and told me that since I had shown no sorrow or regret whatsoever when warned to acknowledge my sins and repent, the queen had ordered them to remove my cloth of state and to inform me that thenceforth I should consider myself a dead woman, with neither the honor nor the rank of a queen. I responded that God by his singular grace had called me to that dignity and I had been rightfully anointed and consecrated, and accordingly I intended to return my majesty to God together with my soul, as from his hand alone had I received it. And that I did not recognize their queen as a superior, nor her councilors as my judges, and that I should die a queen, in spite of them all, for they possessed no further power over me than the highwaymen of the wooded paths possessed over the most righteous prince upon the earth. But that I hoped to God that after he had freed me from this captivity, he would manifest his justice. That it was no marvel that in this isle, where so many kings have died violently, I, who am of their blood, should come to the same fate. Seeing that my servants would not touch the canopy to take it down, my wretched ladies instead shrieking and begging God for vengeance against the queen and her council, the said Paulet summoned seven or eight men of the guard and ordered them to remove it. He seated himself, covered himself and then told me that this was no time of celebration or recreation for me, and therefore he would have to remove my table of state.

Yesterday I gathered my little household together, so that all my servants might be witnesses to my faith, which is the Catholic one, and to my innocence, and I charged them before God to tell the truth concerning everything they knew. I have sent to my lords the dukes of Lorraine and Guise, and to my other kinsmen about the salvation of my soul, the unburdening of my conscience, and the defense of my honor. Commend me to La Rue,[28] and tell him for my sake to recall how I promised to die for the Catholic faith, and that as I see it I am not yet quit of that promise, and that I beg him and all those of his order to commend me to God. I am thoroughly content, as I have always been, to sacrifice myself and offer

---

28   The French Jesuit Henri Samier (dates unknown, *fl.* late sixteenth century), sometimes known by the aliases Jacques La Rue and Hieronymo Martinelli. Samier was an active political operative throughout Europe, working on behalf of Mary as well as other Catholic monarchs. A. Lynn Martin, "The Jesuit Mystique," *SCJ* 4, no. 1 (April 1973): 31–40, here 34.

up my life for the good of the souls of this island. God be with you, for this is the last time I shall write to you: remember the soul of one who has been your queen, lady, and friend. And I implore God, since I cannot, to repay the services you have done me, as the first and oldest of my servants, whom I leave abandoned and orphaned in his blessed hands. From Fotheringhay, Thursday, November 24, 1586.

Your affectionate and good lady
Queen Mary[29]

We see in this letter the spirit and piety of this saintly queen, and how ready and steadfast she was to die for the Catholic faith, which was the true and real cause of her death; the heretics of England, seeing her constancy, feared that if she lived and came to hold the scepter and crown of the kingdom, they would pay with their heads for the corruption and ruination they had wrought. Likewise, we see the inhuman and barbaric cruelty with which they treated this persecuted, blessed lady in the last years of her imprisonment, for they stripped her of the dignity and distinctions proper to her royal person and rank. And no less are revealed the patience, sufferance, and magnanimity she maintained amid her troubles and cares. She also wrote another letter to her aunt Queen Elizabeth, making similar points, as follows:

I have resolved to embrace Jesus Christ alone, he who never abandons the afflicted who call upon him with a good heart, and who renders them justice and consoles them, especially when they have lost all human favor and they turn to his protection. Let the honor and the glory be given him, for I have not been deceived in my hope, as he has given me heart and strength to hope against hope,[30] to endure the injustices, slanders, accusations, and condemnations of my enemies with a spirit resolute and determined to suffer death in obedience to the Catholic, Apostolic, and Roman Church. When they informed me on your behalf of the sentence of the recent parliamentary session and warned me to prepare myself for the end of my long and miserable exile, I begged your agents to thank you on my behalf for such pleasant and agreeable news as this. I do not wish to accuse anyone, but rather pardon all with a willing heart, as I wish each to pardon me if I have offended them,[31] and I desire and implore God most of all to pardon me.

---

29   The French text of this letter was included in Adam Blackwood's life of Mary, first published in 1587: see Blackwood, *Martyre*, 387–97; Blackwood, *History*, 167–74.

30   Rom. 4:18.

31   Matt. 6:12; Luke 11:4.

What I know is that no one is so obliged to look to my honor as you, my lady, for I am of your blood, a sovereign queen, and a daughter of a king. Therefore, madam, for the sake of Jesus Christ (to whose name all the powers of the world attend and kneel), I implore you to consent that after my enemies have sated themselves with my innocent blood, all my poor and friendless servants might carry my body to France to be interred in hallowed ground with some of my ancestors, particularly with the queen my mother and lady, who is in glory.[32] I am moved to ask this of you seeing that in Scotland they have maltreated the bodies of the kings my forebears and despoiled and profaned the shrines,[33] and that, suffering in this land, I cannot be buried with your ancestors (who are also mine). And, most importantly, because according to our sacred faith it is most important to us to be interred in sacred and pure earth. And because I fear the secret malice of some of your counselors, I likewise beg you that the sentence of my death not be executed without your ladyship's knowledge. Not because the torments and pains (which I am prepared to endure) frighten me, but rather because I fear they shall publish and spread throughout the world a thousand lies about it, as they have done to others. For this reason I desire that all my servants be present at my death and be witnesses to my end, that I persevered to the last in the faith of my Savior and in the obedience of his Church. I ask you once more, madam, and again I implore you by the passion of Jesus Christ, and by our kinship, and by the love of King Henry VII, your grandfather and my great-grandfather, and by the obligation and respect owed by a woman to another woman, and by a queen to another queen, that you grant this my last request. And if you concede it to me, let me see your last reply, and let whatever you deign to write to me come to my hands.

To conclude, I humbly entreat God, who is the father of mercies[34] and the righteous judge,[35] to enlighten you with the light of his Holy Spirit, and for myself to give me the grace to end in perfect charity,[36] as I intend to do, forgiving in my death all those who have been the cause of it or

---

32 After her death in Edinburgh in 1560, Mary of Guise's remains had been repatriated to France and interred at Rheims. Warnicke, *Mary Queen of Scots*, 246.

33 In May 1559, pugnacious evangelical preaching in Perth had sparked an outburst of iconoclasm, culminating in attacks on several Stewart royal tombs. Alec Ryrie, *The Age of Reformation: The Tudor and Stewart Realms 1485–1603*, Religion, Politics and Society in Britain (Harlow: Pearson Longman, 2009), 217.

34 2 Cor. 1:3.

35 Ps. 7:12; 2 Tim. 4:8.

36 1 John 4:18.

had any part in it, and this will be my prayer until my last breath and final moment. I count myself most fortunate that our Lord is carrying me off and freeing me of this fragile body before the calamity and dire punishment that I see threatening this island, unless it truly fears and worships God and the temporal governance of the realm takes a better course. Do not interpret it as pride or presumption if, as one who departs this world and prepares for another, I tell you to remember that the day will come when, before the universal and righteous judge, you will render an account of your deeds,[37] as strict and as rigorous as it was for we who came before you. And that I wish that those of my blood and of my country reflect in time, and perceive well that since the light of reason is made manifest to us, we must all take care ourselves to restrain our appetites, such that care for worldly things give place to that of things enduring and true. From Fotheringhay, December 19, 1586.

Your sister and niece, unjustly prisoner,
Queen Mary[38]

And so, determining to execute the sentence against the queen of Scots, Elizabeth dispatched a royal warrant to the earls of Shrewsbury,[39] Kent,[40] Derby,[41] Cumberland,[42] and Pembroke,[43] ordering them to go to the castle of Fotheringhay, where the queen was imprisoned, and put into effect the aforesaid sentence, in the time, place, and manner that seemed best to them. And among other things, the writ said that Elizabeth had thus determined[44]

> to acquiesce to the continual and urgent pleas of her councilors and other worthy persons, to avoid the sure and obvious dangers that could occur if the said sentence were not carried out—not only against her life, but also against those of her advisers and their descendants, and against the public good of the kingdom, both in what related to the Gospel and the true religion of Christ, and for its peace and tranquility.

---

37   Rom. 2:5–6, 14:10, 14:12; Rev. 20:12.
38   The text of this letter appears in Blackwood, *Martyre*, 400–08; see also Blackwood, *History*, 176–81.
39   George Talbot, sixth earl of Shrewsbury.
40   Henry Grey, sixth earl of Kent (1541–1615).
41   Henry Stanley, fourth earl of Derby (1531–93).
42   George Clifford, third earl of Cumberland (1558–1605).
43   Henry Herbert, second earl of Pembroke.
44   For Elizabeth's commission, see Blackwood, *Martyre*, 413–17; Blackwood, *History*, 184–85.

On February 14 of last year, 1587, one Beale, a secretary of the council and a great enemy of the queen of Scots, left London with the royal warrant.[45] And he brought with him the common hangman of London, although disguised by a velvet gown and a gold chain.[46] The officials arrived at the castle where the queen was at three in the afternoon of February 17: they read her the letters patent of their commission and told her to be prepared to die the following morning. Their embassy did not perturb the queen, who just raised her heart and her eyes to heaven, and then with a calm and serious countenance answered that she could not believe this to be the will of the queen her aunt, on account of the royal word and faith given her both before and after she had entered the kingdom, as well as a letter the queen herself had written only a few days earlier, assuring her that she would do no violence whatsoever to her royal person. They replied that regardless of what the queen had said, their lady's will was that she should die. To this the good queen replied that she was astounded to be treated with such harshness, being herself as much a queen as she of England, a sovereign lady and free, in no wise subject to the laws of England, and innocent and guiltless of what was imputed to her, as she would attest to her death, and that this proved that the queen her aunt had a thirst for Catholic blood so deep that it could not be slaked save with that of her niece. But as God our Lord was a father to her, and chose thus to free her from the miseries of this sad life and put an end to her long and wretched captivity and to the maltreatment of the last years of her imprisonment worthy of slave, not a queen, she conformed herself to the will of her Lord and Father, he who takes care of his chosen[47] and leads each to the path that befits them. For she would pay with her life the debt that all we mortals owe, and she hoped in God that

---

45   Beale, then clerk of the privy council, was tasked with delivering Mary's death sentence.
      Gary M. Bell, "Beale, Robert (1541–1601)," in *ODNB*, 4:519–22, here 520.

46   "On the evening of Saturday, February 14, 1587, M. Beale, a close friend of Walsingham,
      was dispatched with a commissioned, signed in the queen of England's hand, to carry out
      the beheading of the queen of Scots, and an order to the earls of Shrewsbury, Kent, and
      Rutland, with a large number of other gentlemen near Fotheringhay, to attend the said
      execution. The said Beale brought with him the executioner of London, dressed entirely
      in black velvet, as it is reported; they departed in secret on the aforementioned Saturday,
      he arrived on the following Monday, the sixteenth, and the aforesaid earls and gentle-
      men were summoned for Tuesday." "Discours de la mort de très haute et très illustre prin-
      cesse Madame Marie Stuard, royne d'Escosse, faict le dix-huitième jour de fevrier 1587," in
      Édouard Fournier, ed., *Variétés historiques et littéraires: Recueil de pièces volantes rares et
      curieuses en prose et en vers* (P. Jannet: Paris, 1856), 5:279–89, here 279–82.

47   1 Pet. 5:7.

since he willed that hers should be so severe, so guiltless of what they claimed of her, it should win pardon for all the other misdeeds she had committed in her life, washed with the blood of Jesus Christ her Redeemer, so that death should be the beginning of true and eternal life and a staircase to heaven. She added further that although she had awaited this blow for many years (for such a queen could not expect any other sentence) and had steeled herself to receive it, because it was so fierce, the most terrible of her life, she would be glad if they gave her a little more time to prepare herself for so dangerous and important a journey, and make provision for some Catholic priest, virtuous and wise, to confess her, assist her, and encourage her, for this would in some measure lighten her sorrow and ease the harshness of their cruel treatment.[48] They denied the queen this delay, and as to the priest, they said that the queen their lady, out of her accustomed clemency and the love of her heart, had sent her someone to assist and comfort her.[49] The queen asked, "Is this person you speak of a Catholic, and shares he the faith and communion of the Roman Church?" And when they answered, "No," the saintly queen said, "It is neither what I desire nor what I need. I am a Catholic, and I am to die as a Catholic, and I die because I am a Catholic, and I consider this a signal mercy of God. My God, who sees my honest desire, who can save without the accustomed means,

---

48   "Shee, newer a white astonished, thanked them for ther goode newes, afferminge that they could bringe none that liked her better, because nowe shee should see an end of all her miseries, and that it was longe since shee had made her selff redie to die, ewer suspectinge, since her detention in England, that shee should newer finde better at ther mistres handes and thers; but shee was sorie shee was not sooner certifeed theroff, that shee might hawe made her will, and giwen order for all her afaires, and to hawe disposed of such litle meanes as they had lefte her, for the better dischardinge of her conscience towardes her poore serwantes, prayinge them to giwe her some time to do it, seeinge they had power to do it without anie checke of the commission." Blackwood, *History*, 186.

    Cf. "She replied that she was prepared for it, and had long expected it, asking when they were resolved to carry it out? They answered that it was left to her judgment, provided that she complied with the commission they had been given, and it would be best if it were done the following day, which was Wednesday, February 18 according to the new style." *Mariae Stuartae*, sig. Aiv[v].

    Cf. "They say that that lady showed herself steadfast, saying that although she would never believe that the queen her sister would ever desire this, but if it was so, seeing that she had brought to such grief in the last three months, she would take death as most welcome, whenever it please God that she receive it." "Discours," 283.

49   One account avers "They were willing to permit her a [Protestant] minister, but she utterly refused." This figure is generally identified as Richard Fletcher (*c*.1544–96), dean of Peterborough and later bishop of London. "Discours," 283.

who saves the souls he himself bought with his own blood, will vindicate me without a priest."

With this, the queen locked herself in her quarters and penned a note to her almoner in these words:

> Today I have been embattled and tempted by the heretics against my religion, to accept solace at their hands. You will learn from others that if nothing else, I have faithfully declared my faith, in which I wish to die. I have sought to have you with me and asked for you, that I might confess and receive the sacred sacraments. They have cruelly denied me this, or that my body should be carried out of this land, or that I should freely make a will or write to anyone, save by their hands and by the assent of their mistress. And so, lacking provision, I humbly confess all my sins in general with deep sorrow and repentance, as I would do in particular if I could, and I beg that this evening you be good enough to keep a vigil and pray with me in satisfaction of my sins, and to send me your benediction. Advise me in writing of the most appropriate and specific prayers I ought to make tonight and in the morning, and of anything else you think I might do to further my salvation. The time is short, and I cannot write more.[50]

After this, having thrown herself upon the floor before the divine presence, she began to resign herself to the hands of God with overflowing tears and heartfelt sighs, and to implore him, since it pleased him that she die thus, to give her strength and steadfastness in that hour. She spent the entire night in prayer,[51] save a few moments when she rose to speak with her steward and commit to him messages for the king her son and others, and then she returned to her devotions. Finally, prostrating herself before the sacred sacrament (which she had had with her throughout her imprisonment by a particular grace of our Lord), moved to the last by the utmost devotion to that sustenance that gives life and strength to those who eat it—and also by fear lest it be abused by the heretics after her death—she herself took it as a viaticum and a protection with all possible humility and the appropriate reverence, since there was no priest to administer it, after the manner of the ancient Christians who, being unable to attend church in times of tyrannical persecutions, received the

---

50   See Blackwood, *Martyre*, 419–21; Blackwood, *History*, 187.

51   "The night preceedinge her death shee spent in praiers, and readinge the passion of Christe, and other spirituall consolatiounes." Blackwood, *History*, 186.

Eucharist in their houses from their own hands, so as to communicate thus.[52] And this practice lasted many years, into the times of peace.[53]

They had made a scaffold of twelve feet square in the great hall of the castle, covered it in black cloth, and placed upon it a cushion of black velvet and the board on which the queen's head was to be cut off.[54] They had locked up all her servants and ladies, leaving only her steward and a doctor, and two ladies who accompanied and waited upon her. These two, when they saw that the hour was now approaching and the author of this tyranny had appeared with his minions to fetch the queen, began to scream and to dissolve into tears, as they had done throughout the night. The queen looked upon them with loving, tearful eyes, and said, "I marvel much that you, who have been for so many years the sharers of my troubles and sorrows and of this wretched captivity should now bewail and lament my freedom and yours. You will go freely to your homes, and I (as I trust in my God), free of the numberless evils of this world, will now begin to have life and rest."[55] It was by then eight in the morning, and her guards hurried her and told her to prepare herself. She replied with a serene and unmoved countenance that she was ready, and that even the two hours of life that remained to her until ten o'clock (the appointed end) she would willingly give them, if that would satisfy or please them. Once more

---

52   In the margin: "This is taken from Tertullian, Book 1 [vere 2], To His Wife; Cyprian, De lapsis; Clement of Alexandria, Stromateis, Book 1."
      Tertullian, To His Wife, 2.5.
      Cyprian of Carthage, De lapsis, Chapter 26.
      Clement of Alexandria, Stromateis, 1.1.

53   In the margin: "Gregory of Nazianzus, oration in praise of Gorgonia; Jerome, in his Apology to Pammachius; Ambrose in the funeral oration for his brother Satyrus; and Basil, to the Patrician Caesaria."
      Gregory of Nazianzus, On his sister Gorgonia, Chapter 18.
      Ambrose of Milan, On the death of Satyrus, 1.43.
      Jerome, Letters, 48.15.
      Basil of Caesarea, Letters, 93.

54   "The place of execution was in a greate parlour, in the middes wheroff a scaffolde was sett vp, twelfe foote square and two foote heigh, spred ower with blacke cotton." Blackwood, History, 188.
      Cf. "In a great hall, a platform had been erected, twelve feet square and two [feet] high, bordered with a rail two feet high, the whole covered with black cloth, and in the middle a single chair with a cushion." Mariae Stuartae, sig. Av^v.

55   "There she found all of her household standing and weeping; she urged all of them to fear God, obey their superiors, and similar sentiments, and then bade them each farewell, kissing the women and extending her hand to be kissed by the men, praying all of them not to lament, but rather to rejoice, and to pray for her." Ibid., sig. Av^v.

she charged her steward to tell her son what she had communicated to him, to serve him, and to bring him her blessing, which she there imparted to him, making the sign of the cross with her hand.[56]

Not one of her servants had the heart to lead her by the hand to the scaffold where she was to die, for they were all pierced and stricken with sorrow, and none wished to be guides and attendants to their lady in so lamentable and doleful a tragedy as this. And because she felt faint, on account of her ill health and having watched the entire night, Paulet gave her two men to help her.[57] The queen was attired in black velvet, bearing a crucifix in one hand and a book in the other; from her breast hung a cross and from her waist a rosary.[58] In this manner she came to the room and mounted the scaffold with miraculous strength and as much joy as if it had been a great festival or a kingly banquet. Having ascended the scaffold, with the utmost gravity and steadiness she turned her eyes to look at the people who were present—perhaps three hundred having been allowed to enter (with many others remaining outside)— and spoke to them in this fashion:

> I trust that some among all you who are present and who see this sorrowful spectacle of a queen of France and Scotland and the heir of England will have some compassion for me, lament this my sad fate, and give a true account to those not present of what transpires here. They have brought me here, an anointed queen and a sovereign lady, not subject to the laws of this realm, to put me to death—because, being a queen, I trusted in the faith and word of another queen, my aunt. As to the crimes they accuse me of, they are that I have worked for the queen's death and my freedom. But, by the circumstances in which I stand and by that Lord who is king

---

56   "On her knees, she spoke at length to her majordomo, and instructed him to seek out her
      son to serve him, as she was assured he would, having always been faithful to her; it would
      be he who rewarded him, for she had little left to do in this life, where she was so troubled,
      and charged him to bring him her blessing, which she then gave." "Discours," 284.

57   "her serwantes, which nowe helde her vp by the armes, beinge amazed, shee conforted
      them, and because they altogether refused to conweie her to her death, which so much
      greiwed them, or to be beholders of so terrible a tragedie, Sir Amias Paulet lent her two
      of his serwinge men to leade her to the place of execution; for thorowe longe lingeringe
      faintnes, and her dailie griewances, she was brought so lowe and weake, that shee was not
      able to go by her self." Blackwood, *History*, 188.

58   "The queen's garb was the same as that in which she had previously appeared before the
      lords and royal officials, of black and costly silk. In one hand she bore a crucifix, of wood
      or bone, with an effigy of Christ hanging upon it, in the other, a book, and a gold cross
      hung from her neck, as well as rosary from her girdle." *Mariae Stuartae*, sig. Avii[r].

of kings and supreme judge of the living and the dead,[59] who first raised me up, never have I sought the death of the queen, neither now nor at any other time. My liberty I have sought, and I do not see that to seek it is a crime, for I am free, and a queen, and a sovereign lady. But, as God our Lord wills that by this death I should pay for the sins of my life, which are numerous and grievous, that I should die for being a Catholic, and that by my example men should learn the end of the scepters and greatness of this life, and comprehend how frightful a thing heresy is, I accept death with the greatest willingness, as sent by the hand of so good a Lord, and I ask and beg that all those present who are Catholics pray to God for me, and be witnesses to this truth and that I die in the communion of the Catholic, Apostolic, and Roman faith. And I declare in this last hour that the principal cause of seeking my freedom has been the desire and zeal to restore and exalt our sacred and Catholic faith in this misfortunate isle, and if I were to live many years, I would not cease to seek this—though they could not be many, given my poor health and great weakness, as you can see. And thus I depart satisfied and joyful, for, having to die a death, I die for so good a cause.[60]

---

59   Acts 10:42; 2 Tim. 4:1; 1 Pet. 4:5.

60   Blackwood describes Mary's last speech thus: "Shee protested, likewise, in all the behold-
      ers presence, that shee newer had attempted anie thinge against the liffe or state of her
      cusinge, nor committed anie [thing] woorthie of blame, either for the owerthrowe of
      religion or the commonewelthe. If they did impute her constancie in her religion as a
      faulte woorthie of deathe, lett them looke [to] it, who never had anie care to instruct and
      informe me otherwise, all the longe time of my tuentie yeares captiuitie. I hope shortlie
      to be in paradice with my deare Sauiour, Jesus Christe, for whose obedience made for me
      I doubte not to shedde my bloode, ewen to the last drope. I counte my selff more happie
      nowe to die in a righte minde to end my miserie, then to liwe longer induringe the dai-
      elie reproches of my ennemies, worse then a bitter death, then to attend anie longer till
      nature, thus faintinge, did finishe the course of her liffe, when shee should not be righte
      in her senses, and perfite remembrance of her duetie towardes God and her neighbour.
      Shee saide, shee hoped in him, of whome that crosse shee caried in her hand put her
      in remembrance, and before whose feete shee prostrated her selff in soule and bodie,
      that he wold receiwe her into eternal glorie. This temporall shee resigned vp hartelie to
      him that gaiwe. Shee protested, as before, in all the auditouris hearinge, that shee was
      innocentlie accused, charged and condemned of such thinges shee newer thought on,
      and hoped the losse of this temporall liffe should be the passage, beginninge and en-
      traunce to liffe eternall, with the holie angelles and the soules of blessed, that should
      recewe her soule and innocent bloode, and represent it before God, for a deduction of
      all her sinnes and offences. Shee besought them all to praie for [her], that God wold
      hear her, and that shee mighte obteine grace and pardon." Blackwood, *History*, 190–91.

Having finished this speech, she prayed with her two ladies, addressing God in Latin. A heretical dean named "Pedro Borungo"[61] came forward, as though to assist her in her prayers and guide her in that moment; she looked at him with a grave and troubled countenance, and did not permit him to approach, saying that she was a Catholic and declaring that she would die in the Catholic faith. The roguish heretic tried to continue, and once more assailed the saintly queen's constancy in her faith, but she became angry and shouted, "Silence, dean, for you disturb me, and I do not wish to hear you, nor have anything to do with you." And so the earls ordered the dean to keep silent, so as not to upset the queen.[62] Although one of them, the earl of Kent, once more attempted to tempt and disturb her, mocking the crucifix the queen bore in her hand, but he did not succeed, for she had it set within her heart. Thus she said to the earl, "It is just that the Christian bear with them at all times, and especially in the hour of death, the sign of their redemption."[63] Once more she made clear her desire

---

61   Ribadeneyra's "Pedro Borungo" is almost certainly a transliteration of his Latin source's "Decanus Petrus Borūgus." *Mariae Stuartae*, sig. Avii[r].

   Ribadeneyra evidently thought this to be the cleric's name, but it is in fact a latinization of "dean of Peterborough," the title of Richard Fletcher, the Protestant divine present at Mary's execution.

62   "Beside her stood a certain doctor, Dean *Petrus Borungus*, who urged her, at the lords' command, to have faith in Christ and to die as a Christian; as he was beginning this oration, she interrupted him, entreating and commanding him in a clear voice to keep silent, declaring that she was well prepared for death. To this he responded that he would say nothing save what he had been ordered to, and what accorded with the truth. Then he uttered much more in this vein, until she exclaimed, "Be quiet, Master Dean, I do not wish to hear you, I have no business with you, you disturb me,' and so as not to upset her, he was ordered to silence." Ibid., sigs. Avii[r]–Avii[v].

63   "The Earle of Kent aunswered, that he was sorie for her to see her so much giwen to the superstitiouns of the times past, and that it wer better for her to carie the crosse of Christe in hearte, not in her hande. To whome shee replied, that it was to litle purpose to carie such a obiect in her hand, if the hearte wer not touched inwardlie with earnest motion and remembrance of his bitter death and passion which he suffered vpon the crosse for miserable mannes sinne, that died vpon the crosse." Blackwood, *History*, 189.

   Cf. "Again, the earl of Kent said, 'I grieve at your plight, my lady, and on the charge of such senseless superstition as I see in your hands.' She answered him that it was proper to have an image of Christ's crucifixion before her eyes, by which she was reminded of him. He averred that it befitted her to carry Christ in her heart, adding (although she refused to hear him) that he would pray for her (although she refused to accept the grace offered from the Most High), that God might forgive her sins, and her. To which she [said], 'Pray you, and I shall pray, too.'" *Mariae Stuartae*, sig. Avii[v].

and anxiety for a Catholic priest, and once again they denied her. Again she repeated that she was innocent, that she pardoned all her enemies, and that she prayed for those who had unjustly condemned her to death, and especially for the queen of England. She encouraged and consoled her ladies, stricken and pierced with grief, urging them to turn their tears into prayers for her soul, which were the last words she spoke to them.[64] Then she presented herself to death, her eyes fixed heavenwards, as though enraptured and ecstatic, with admirable magnanimity and constancy.

O queen unbowed, O queen steadfast, O queen enlightened and strengthened with the spirit of heaven to despise and trample upon the ephemeral things of earth! My lady, do you not recall your distinguished blood or your sovereign majesty? Nor the flower of your youth, beauty, and grace? Nor the throne, nor the royal crown, nor the scepter and lordship? Nor your greatness, command, and authority? Nor the mighty lords and ladies who served you? The guards and soldiers who accompanied you? The peoples and kingdoms that obeyed you and adored you? How does the memory of all that you have lost not trouble you, nor the miserable lot and sorrowful fate that you have not afflict you? Seeing yourself alone and abandoned upon a scaffold, surrounded by executioners, the headsman at your side and the sword at your throat? Being an anointed queen, to die by the hand of another queen, your aunt, whom you had trusted on that account?

None of these things was enough to disturb the saintly queen, for she held her heart and her eyes on fixed on heaven and knew that this life is a comedy, and every living person, king though they may be, is but an actor—and as she loved what is eternal, desired what she loved, and died for the Catholic faith, she did not falter or break, but rather with unconquerable spirit she herself began to lower the collar of her dress to ready her neck for the blow. The executioner wished to help her, but she was so much herself as to take his hand, saying that this was not his office.[65] One of her ladies placed the veil over her

---

64 "Perceiwinge one of them could not holde, but burste foorthe in teares, shee commaunded to holde her peace, and to keepe silence, tellinge her shee had paste her promese that shee and the other maide should not be trublesome to her in her death: shee bid them boith retire themselwes soberlie, and to praie to God for her, now they could do her no more goode." Blackwood, *History*, 191–92.

65 "the two maides together mount vp vpon the scaffolde to do ther mistres the last charitable serwice, and that with watterie eyes and sorrowefull heartes : they began to helpe her to take awaie her maske, her coiffe, and other ornamentes: but the shamelesse executioner could, by no entreatie her Maiestie could make, nor yeet rewarde, be mowed to withholde his helpinge handes." Blackwood, *History*, 189.

eyes,[66] and at this she sank to her knees, uttered certain prayers, and implored God our Lord with deep emotion and loving sighs that since by her sins in life she had not merited to achieve through his divine majesty the remedy and security of that unfortunate kingdom of England, he would at least in that instant accept her death and the blood she shed for his faith and truth, which she offered for the conversion of so many misled and lost people, invoking for this purpose the most serene queen of the angels, our Lady, and all the blessed spirits and saints of heaven, fiercely importuning them to accompany and support her prayer and win from the Lord what she herself was not worthy to attain. Likewise, she offered a prayer for the entire holy Church, for the pope, for the king her son, for the kings of France and Spain, and for the queen of England herself, asking God with an passionate and ardent heart to enlighten and convert her to his sacred faith.[67] With this, she thrice said these words: *In manus tuas Domine commendo spiritum meum.*[68] Then she placed her head upon the block and the executioner severed it with an axe—some say in two, others in three blows.[69] He took it in his hand, saying in a loud voice, "God preserve our Queen Elizabeth, and may this befall all enemies of the Gospel." And he lifted it up and showed it to all those present, and then from a window showed it to

---

66   "One of her ladies covered her eyes, and then she lowered herself to the block." "Discours," 285.

67   "These wer her praiers, beinge vpon her knees vpon the scaffold, prayinge also for the Pope, the kinges of Fraunce, Spaine, the Queene of England, and the Kinge of Scotland, her deare sonne, that God wold enlighten them all with his spirite, and direct them in the truth, and that he wold take pitie vpon his Church militant, and turne awaie his anger from the Isle of Greate Britanne, which shee did perceiwe he threatned with scourges for the abominable, wilfull impietie committed by the inhabitantes." Blackwood, *History*, 191.

68   Ps. 30:6.
       Cf. "She commendes finallie her soule to the tuition of the Almightie, in these woordes of the psalme, sayinge often and reiteratinge the woordes, 'In manus tuas, Domine, commendo spiritum meum,'" Blackwood, *History*, 192.
       Cf. "Crying out in a loud voice, 'Into thy hands, Lord, I commend my spirit.'" *Mariae Stuartae*, sig. Bi[v].

69   "In the meane while, the butcher gaiwe her a greate blowe with the axe, wherbye he pearced the stringes within her heade, which he stroake not of but at the thirde blowe." Blackwood, *History*, 192.
       Cf. "Now, with one of the executioners hellishly restraining her hands, the other took the axe in both hands and struck twice, and so she traded life for death." *Mariae Stuartae*, sig. Bi[v].

those outside.[70] The saintly queen's spirit flew up to heaven, pure, clean, and washed with her blood,[71] leaving her body, its companion, lying upon the floor, soaked in that same blood.

At this spectacle, her servants were left downcast and miserable, the on-lookers astounded, the heretics joyful, the Catholics disconsolate and afflicted, and the king her son and the Most Christian King of France her cousin ob-ligated to avenge this hateful attack upon their mother and sister. The other monarchs of Christendom too, to punish the affront to the royal name and majesty (revered throughout the world) by the death of Mary Queen of Scots. God has permitted this to teach us that there is another life, of certain reward and punishment, since in this one Queen Mary died at Elizabeth's hands. And that there is no security or foundation in crowns, scepters, or territories, for so renowned a queen of Scotland and France died at the hands of the executioner of London. And to leave the entire world at once horrified at so barbarous a cruelty and inspired by this example to die for the Catholic faith, and to make them understand at last how horrid a monster heresy is.

They covered the body with a black cloth and carried it to a side-chamber,[72] and then they rang bells across the province and lit bonfires, and the queen of England ordered the same to be done with the utmost festivity and rejoic-ing in the city of London[73]—and she herself progressed through the city (so they say) upon a white horse, as a manifest sign of her satisfaction and joy.

---

70   "After he had done, he hastelie snatcheth vp the heade in his hande, and shewinge it to the assistantes, saide, 'God saiwe Queene Elizabeth, and so befall all the ennemies of the Gospell.'" Blackwood, *History*, 192.

   Cf. " Then, when the executioner lifted the head and showed it to the onlookers, all cried, 'God preserve our queen, and thus befall all foes of the word of God and enemies of Her Majesty. Amen.'" *Mariae Stuartae*, sig. Bi^v.

71   Rev. 7:14.

72   "The body was immediately covered with a black cloth and withdrawn back into her chamber, where it was opened and embalmed, so they say." "Discours," 286.

73   "The next day, the death of the queen of Scotland having been announced at London, fires were lit in squares across the city, and the bells rang out in token of joy." *Mariae Stuartae*, sigs. Bii^r–Bii^v.

   Cf. "This news was not long concealed, for from three in the afternoon, all the bells in the city of London began to sound, and fireworks were set off in all the streets, with festivities and banquets as a sign of great rejoicing." "Discours," 287–88.

   Cf. "The sentence beinge notifeed to the Queene, is broughte backe to London, and, in signe of ioye, the belles be runge 24 hours, all the greate ordinance in the Toure is shotte, bonefires be made throughout the citie, and finallie, no thinge is lefte vndone to showe ther ioye." Blackwood, *History*, 219.

This was the end of Mary Stewart, queen of Scotland and of France, and this is the history of that lamentable tragedy, recorded briefly and in all simplicity.[74] Yet the heretics (as is their wont), to give some pretext for their impious and barbaric cruelty, offered other reasons for her death (as I have said) and falsely slandered the queen. Her servants could not prevail upon them to give them the corpse to undress with the proper decency and respect before the executioner touched it.[75] Instead, it was he who removed the graying hair, which looked quite white, and then handled the body with his bloody hands just as he pleased, so that the substance, accidents, and circumstances of this deed were all one.[76] The heretics collected all of the holy queen's blood, washed everything it had stained—even to the clothing, boards, and block—and burned the black cloth that had lay on the scaffold and been soaked with the copious blood that she had shed there. All this lest some trace or sign of her martyrdom remain, anything the Catholics might use to revere her,[77] just

---

74   This particular phrase goes through several transformations across editions of the *Historia*. The first edition, reflected in the translation, runs "la historia desta lastimosa tragedia." The 1594 edition does the same. In 1595, the line is somewhat mangled: "la historia lastimosa tragedia" (roughly, "the lamentable and tragic history"). The final edition has "la history y lastimosa tragedia" ("the history and lamentable tragedy").

75   "The tragedie ended, the poore maides, carefull of the honour of ther mistres, humblie besought and prayed Paulett the cruell jealour, that the butcher might hawe no more ado with ther Soweraigne ladies bodie, and that it mighte be permitted them to disatire her bodie when all the people wer departed the place, that no forder indignitie might be offered her sacred Maiesties corpes, seinge all malice, hatred, envie, and contempt of the deade ought to end after ther decesse; they promised him her apparell, and all that was about her, and whatsoewer besides he wold demaunde in reason, so that he wold not anie more come neare or handle her sacred bodie. But cursed Cerberus, Paulet I meane, commaundeth them werie rudlie to departe the chamber; lewinge his hellhounde with the corpes to do with what he wold: he presentlie pulleth of her shoes and all the rest of her apparell, which as yeet was lefte about her bodie, and after, when he had done what he wold, the corpes was caried into a chamber nexte adioninge, fearinge the saide maides should come to do anie charitable goode office." Blackwood, *History*, 193.

76   Ribadeneyra seems here to use self-consciously eucharistic language to describe the treatment of Mary's body, rendering the queen's death a sacrifice along the lines of Christ's.

77   Adam Blackwood is incandescent with rage—for the space of several pages—at the executioner's supposed mutilation of Mary's corpse. Blackwood, *History*, 196–99.
      Cf. "Now, while the axeman thus held up her head, he stripped away the ornaments, and they saw that she was already quite gray, and her hair had recently been shaved almost to the scalp. Nothing of her garments and jewelry was left to the executioner, but their price was given him. Anything whatsoever that her blood had fallen upon, on the axeman or on anyone else, was taken away and washed, even to the wood of the

as was done in France during Emperor Verus's persecution: for they burned everything of the sainted martyrs' and cast their ashes in the Rhône, so that they would not remain as relics, and so that their memory would pass away with the life of the body, as Eusebius relates.[78]

The saintly queen lived forty-four years and almost two months—she was born in the year 1542, to the illustrious house of Stewart and of Lorraine; she died, as we have said, on February 18, 1587 according to the Gregorian Calendar.[79] She was very beautiful. She knew well the Scottish, English, French, Spanish, and Latin tongues.[80] They say that after several months her body was interred at Peterborough, where the body of the sainted Queen Catherine was buried.[81] Now, if this story is true, as it is said and written, *Obstupescite caeli, et desolamini portae eius vehementer*—gape in awe, heavens, and may your gates be utterly desolate.[82] And the reason for awe is that in our own days, among those reputed to be Christian, wise, and politic, there is so heinous and so extreme an exemplar of cruelty as was never yet seen or heard of among barbarians, infidels, or madmen. For what greater inhumanity could there be than for a queen not to support another queen, her neighbor, seeing her abandoned and unjustly assailed by her vassals? What greater coldness, than for an aunt

---

scaffolding. Moreover, the black cloth that had received her blood, and everything else that was stained, was thrown into the fire and burned, lest it serve for any superstition." *Mariae Stuartae*, sig. Bi[v].

78   In the margin: "*Ecclesiastical [History]*, Book 5, Chapter 1."

    The same gloss (including marginal annotation) is offered by a contemporary Latin account, almost certainly one of Ribadeneyra's sources: "In this, the English misbelievers imitate the Gaulish pagans under Emperor Verus fourteen hundred years previous, who burned everything belonging to the martyr, and scattered the ashes in the Rhone. Lest, Eusebius says, any relic remain upon the earth, and so that thus their memories might perish along with their bodies." *Mariae Stuartae*, sig. Bvi[r].

79   According to the Julian Calendar, February 18—the date usually given.

80   Characterizations of Mary's education vary. Retha M. Warnicke offers a generally positive assessment, and suggests that in addition to Scots and French, the queen became fluent in Italian, studied Latin and Spanish, and may even have acquired some Greek and Hebrew. Aysha Pollnitz, by contrast, points out that Mary's early education focused almost exclusively on French, with instruction in other languages erratic at best. She argues that much of the queen's apparent erudition as a child was the product of memorization, and that it was only later in life that she supplemented her lackluster education, particularly in the acquisition of better Latin. Warnicke, *Mary Queen of Scots*, 38–44. Pollnitz, *Princely Education*, 210–16.

81   "Keepinge it seawen monethes ther before it was enterred at Peterborowe, where also Cathrine of Spaine laie buried before." Blackwood, *History*, 194.

82   In the margin: "Jeremiah 2[:12]."

not to extend a hand to her niece, the aunt being seated upon a royal throne to which the niece was rightfully to succeed? What greater faithlessness, than for so many years to seize and imprison a queen—invited, entreated, and importuned by another queen to enter her realm under her royal word and faith? What greater cruelty than for so many years to deny her the dignity of a queen and the reverence of so noble a princess, not even to deign to see or hear her, or to allow her a priest for her comfort and solace? Than not to permit her body to be brought to France, as she herself had written with such passion to beg as a final grace? What greater hypocrisy than to seek some pretext to cover this sacrilege with the veil and cloak of justice? Could one describe this, or believe it? Is there a mind to conceive it, or a tongue to explain it?[83] For this is not even the end of this wickedness; this savage and barbaric cruelty has not yet run its course.[84] Kings have slain other kings, in vengeance or to secure their states and territories, but they have done so in such a way that even in their cruelty there was some trace or sign of humanity, for they have shown some sense of what they had done and some respect for the royal majesty in the manner of the deed. But who has ever seen or heard that an aunt should order the head of her own niece struck off, a queen that of another queen, at the hands of the common executioner, who has bloodied them in tormenting and dispatching thieves, murderers, and criminals against the commonwealth? In the history of the Indians or the barbarians, do we read that they made bonfires, festivities, and revelries for the death of an innocent queen, and that even the very queen who put her to death was seen to celebrate and to parade joyously through the city on horseback, like one who had triumphed over her enemy? Across the world, these things have been done in England alone, and they have been done by the hands of the heretics, and they alone could have done them. For as heresy is a hellish monster, all its offspring are monstrous and hellish. And if the countless previous examples of the brutality, violence, and tyranny the heretics practice in our times do not suffice to make plain this truth, this alone suffices for all, and will suffice in all the centuries to come. For it is such as will not be credited even by the barbarians of Tartary or Scythia, or of any other nation, however savage, fierce, or inhuman.

---

83   Isa. 64:4; 1 Cor. 2:9.
84   Gen. 15:16.

The Happiness That the English Heretics Preach Concerning Their Kingdom

We have already seen the clemency of the queen of England and her ministers. The queen of Scots's cruel death is compelling proof: at this and at the disturbance of other kingdoms and territories (as we have discussed), the heretics have been left so pleased with themselves that, even with England being as it is (and as this history has portrayed), there are several flatterers and men of broken consciences and of degenerate life and belief who write and proclaim that that kingdom has never been more prosperous, taking this as proof that their false religion is true, since they are thus favored by God. But in the one and the other they deceive themselves, for the prodigious profusion and overflow of worldly goods is no true sign that those who possess them are any more beloved or favored by God, for he gives wealth to the good and wicked, to the believers and the infidels, as things indifferent and of little significance. Indeed, Lazarus received evils in this life, while the rich man piled up goods,[1] and Antiochus looted the temple and the Holy of Holies,[2] while those who confessed and adored God were abused and persecuted. And the Lord permitted this so that the good men should either here be purged of what sins they had (being men) through tribulation, or else increase their merits—and lest they serve him for the sake of lowly, cheap things, as are the things of the earth, with which the evil are repaid for their few good deeds, while they are punished for their sins in hell. And so it is that many saints regard the long and continued prosperity in worldly wealth that the wicked possess in this life as a perilous thing and a sign of God's wrath and indignation. For, though the common folk call that one blessed *cuius haec sunt,* the prophet enlightened by heaven says, *Beatus populus cuius Dominus Deus eius.*[3]

But even if it were true (which it is not) that the abundance of temporal goods is a sign of God's special favor, in England the case is entirely the reverse of what they say, for the sun warms no kingdom or province of Christians more wretched or oppressed. This will not be affirmed by the ignorant masses, who judge matters superficially, but rather by sound and thoughtful persons, who

---

1   In the margin: "Luke 16[:19–25]."

2   In the margin: "[1] Maccabees 1[:21–24]."

3   In the margin: "Psalm 143[:15]."

will weigh them in a fair and accurate balance. What happiness could there be in a realm where justice does not reign, by which each is lord of his own and of himself? Where there is no peace and tranquility, which is full of burdens, of outrages, of intrigues and fears? Is there justice in England? Do they rule according to the laws of the kingdom, or according to the desires and whims of the judges, who twist justice to their will? I shall relate only what I have read in the books of serious authors, or what I have heard from trustworthy persons, who are virtuous, thoughtful, and very experienced in the affairs of that kingdom and who know of what they speak. There is no justice but favor, nor any law but grace or disgrace with the queen and her advisers, nor any means of winning this but buying it, nor any witnesses but false ones, and with such degeneracy and corruption that witnesses and perjured oaths are bought and sold, easily found for anything imaginable. And it is no wonder that the heretic, who is faithless to God, should be the same in administering justice to men. For those who possess houses, lands, and estates, or incomes, privileges, and rents, are forced to sell them, whether they will or no, and to give them at whatever price pleases any of the queen's councilors or their favorites. And the firstborn gentleman or the rich noblewoman cannot marry as befits them, but rather as they are commanded, and this without appeal or excuse of any kind, for otherwise they will be harassed and persecuted. It is a dire thing to suffer injustices from anyone, but it is far more grievous to endure them from those who themselves hold the staff of justice, who are obliged by their office to redress the grievances and violations of others. For this is a thing without remedy, when tyranny carries out its outrages and its crimes under the name of justice and armed with power, as is done in England.

Now, the standard gold and silver currency is not as pure or refined as it was before heresy entered the kingdom, for in the reign of Henry VIII, and of his children Edward and Elizabeth, it has been falsified and mixed with other metals, and thus the money is worth much less than it used to be, and this is another injustice, and all the more damaging and harmful, as it is universal, concerning not simply a few persons, but the entire realm. For this reason, the most valuable commodity, of highest price and greatest worth for the English, that which they seek with the greatest eagerness and care, is the pure gold of the *escudos* and the refined, perfect silver of the Spanish *reales*, in order to debase it and mingle it with their own. What am I to say of the taxes, tariffs, and levies with which the entire kingdom of England has been burdened since the beginning of this lamentable schism? But let us pass over what King Henry VIII and his son Edward VI did, since it has already been related in this history in its place, and let us speak of what Queen Elizabeth does and what is happening in England at present. Although there has been no defensive war there, nor has the kingdom been attacked these thirty years,[4] nor has there been any need to impose new exactions for its protection, yet practically every three years the queen enforces a burdensome toll on the entire kingdom. For she has come to demand that the churchmen yield up the third part of their incomes every year, and the nobles a fourth, and the common people a fifth, so that in three collections she gathers to herself the entire church's income, in four that of the nobility, and in five that of the entire realm.

But let us pass over these and other evils, for they are not England's worst. The sins of King Henry, and of Edward and Elizabeth his children, are not so light that they might be expurgated with such light griefs: indeed, they are such as cannot be punished in this life, but only through and in themselves, our Lord permitting them as a scourge and penalty to those who commit them, afflicting the whole realm with consequences born of their own sins and misdeeds, as the bad fruit of a bad tree.[5] So it is that while a few govern and command, do and undo just as they please, and so seem to live with a certain prosperity and contentment (although, being founded upon tyranny and the violation of many, this can be neither true nor lasting), all the rest of the kingdom is so miserably oppressed and afflicted, and perforce must live wretchedly, amid the pains that heresy brings with it. And to understand this more clearly, it should be noted that all of England is divided into two parts: one is that of the Catholics, which is the greater and the better, and the other is that of the heretics, which is the lesser and the worse. Some of the Catholics are true and sound; others, although they are such at heart, outwardly obey the commands of queen and parliament, out of fear of punishment. Some of the heretics (who call themselves "Protestants") are "Calvinists," others "Puritans," which are the two principal sects, besides many others of lesser fame and notoriety. Now let us not regard this business as a closed question, but rather let us proceed to unfold it, examining in particular the felicity or misery possessed by each of these two sorts of people, and so analyze and understand this prosperity of the realm of England that they so laud. For if we should find that every member and part thereof is afflicted and miserable, we must needs confess that the entire body is likewise—for the whole has no other existence but what comes of its parts.

And let us begin with those whom every nation of the world, infidels and barbarians though they may be, always gives the highest esteem and the first place—the priests and prelates. What miseries and calamities has the clergy of England not suffered? Or suffer even now? What Catholic bishop or prelate remains who has not been deposed from his office? Thrown out of his church?

---

4   Ribadeneyra glosses over the small matter of the imminent Armada.

5   Matt. 7:17–18, 12:33.

Despoiled of his goods? Exiled from his homeland? Or afflicted with jails and prisons, and slain with extreme cruelty and violence? There is no need to relate the harassments and torments endured by the other Catholic priests, for this is told in the thread of this history. But to understand it fully, one must see the prisons crammed with priests, Catholics, and servants of God; the shackles, chains, manacles, irons, and newfangled tortures with which they have been ruthlessly mutilated and mangled; the shamelessness, chaos, and inhumanity with which they bear them to the court the midst of degenerates; the slanders with which they are oppressed and the injustice with which they are condemned. How many Catholics, having already been stripped of their property, have been condemned to life imprisonment? How many have died in prison, of hunger, awful filth, and worse abuse? How many have been dragged, hanged, disemboweled, and quartered for our sacred faith? How many distinguished and wealthy men have been reduced to dire poverty and lost their inheritances and estates by the slanders of informers, the lies of accusers, the perjured oaths of godless witnesses, and the wickedness of iniquitous judges? How many have been forced to leave the kingdom and go wandering abroad in the direst poverty and hardship, or to remain there in secret, fleeing from one place to another, hiding amid the scrublands, mountains, forests, and wastes, at times even in swamps and lakes to escape the violence and fury of the heretics? How many married women have been wretchedly separated from their husbands, who have fled or been exiled or imprisoned? How many children have been left orphans? How many virtuous maidens left alone and abandoned? The calamities and miseries endured in England today by the faithful, wealthy, and exalted Catholics are too myriad be recounted nor explained! The Catholic artisans and officials, and the other, lower sorts, since they cannot pay the fines the law imposes on those who hear Mass or who do not come to the heretics' churches, are harassed and tormented on this account, paying with their bodies what they cannot with their purses. Some they drag to humiliation, publicly insulting and scourging them. Others they impale or slice off their ears. Others they give yet harsher punishments. All of these people, who are beyond count, the better part of the realm—we could not say they enjoy this "prosperity."

Now, those others who are Catholic at heart, though outwardly they obey the law out of fear of punishment, are no more fortunate, nor do they enjoy any greater prosperity. For although they dissemble in appearances and go to the heretics' churches, yet, because they cannot so disguise their hearts that certain signs will not betray their contents, they are abhorred and distrusted by the heretics, who remain forever suspicious, scrutinizing their deeds and inquiring and investigating their lives, while the Catholics go on in perpetual anxiety, care, and fear. Yet far worse is the torment of their own consciences, which lacerate and consume them: for on the one hand they deem the articles put to them and to which they swear false, monstrous, and contrary to God and their consciences, while on the other they embrace and obey them so as not to lose their property and their lives. And each day they listen to the ministers of Satan, who read, speak, and preach nothing but blasphemies against Jesus Christ our Redeemer and his vicar, against the Church and the sacraments, and against the saints in heaven and on earth. And not only do they live in this tormented and wretched state, but they often die in it, since, out of love they bear their wives and their dear children, they do not dare reveal themselves, preferring to lose their souls than that those they love should lose their property. These people, who are innumerable, could hardly be called happy either.

As to the heretics, what peace or felicity could they have amid the discord and unrest of their consciences? Amid the diversity of sects and contrariness of opinions, and the changes in their dogmas every day? Among the Calvinists and Puritans, there are such immense differences that every day they write, one against the other. The Puritans, who think themselves the more zealous and virtuous, regard the Calvinists' sect as a chimaera and write publicly against it, and against the queen and her council (because they permit it), and assert that none can be saved by it. In this, they demonstrate that they have no contentment, nor can they have, for they vacillate and shift in their religion, which is the foundation of all prosperity and happiness for the commonwealth, which, this being lacking, must needs fall away and disappear, as experience teaches us. What felicity can a realm have where none may enter without being interrogated, examined, questioned a thousand times, and pressed with a thousand oaths? Nor depart without express written permission from the queen, as though the whole of it were a prison, and she alone possessed the key? What security can there be where there are so many causes for fear? Where they have broken all divine and human laws and waged war against powerful neighboring princes and kings, contrary to ancient leagues, confederations, and friendships? Supported their rebels? Stirred up their people, seized their cities, despoiled the wealth of their subjects, destroyed religion, and scorched their territories, kingdoms, and dominions with infernal fire? What peace and tranquility can there be where upon learning that a poor cleric has come to say Mass, they tremble as though he brought plague and the desolation of the realm with him? Where, upon seeing some ship coming from afar, they fear it comes against the kingdom?[6] Where, upon learning that some Catholic prince is raising men, they assume it is against them? Where, upon the establishment of some seminary or college in some other province to gather and strengthen the English Catholics who wander in exile, to support and sustain

---

6   This sentence is added in the 1595 edition.

them, they dream that it is against their polity and for the destruction of their realm? What blessedness could a realm have that hangs upon the life of one woman, neither young nor particularly healthy, with no idea who is to succeed her, nor to whom the right of succession belongs?[7] Where one cannot mention or discuss this under penalty of life imprisonment and the forfeiture of one's goods, by an express law and decree of the crown itself, as has been explained in this history?[8] What renowned and wealthy man is there in the world whom we should not take for wretched, if he neither knew nor cared to know who was to be heir to his property? Accordingly, how much more justly may one regard a kingdom as wretched that we see in so a dire predicament and necessity, knowing that the last day of the queen's life must be the the last of their tranquility and peace? As the queen's own advisers admit, saying that with her the entire kingdom shall die and be buried, on account of the rebellions that must needs follow, since no successor has been declared, nor can this be discussed. Indeed, the queen herself has no greater happiness than those of her realm, both because the true contentment of good monarchs consists in the felicity of their vassals and because of the trouble and distress that she must have, seeing her kingdom afflicted and malcontent and mighty princes and kings so rightfully offended and enraged against her. And seeing herself in such a position, she has commanded parliament to decree that no one may kill the queen.[9] However, if this law was made to show the queen's real fear of being slain, it is clear proof of the waves and storms of her heart,[10] in light of which her happiness cannot be complete. And if the law was made so that she seemed (falsely) to have such fears and by this means render odious those of the Society of Jesus and the other Catholic priests, as rebels and men plotting some treachery against her life, what greater misery could there be than to have to secure oneself with such fabrications and artifices? But all these, as well as the calamities and miseries that we have related in this history and the dire and innumerable others that might be related, are the fruits of the schism and heresy that now flourishes in England.

---

7   Ribadeneyra is likely drawing here on Persons, who made much of Elizabeth's recklessness in forbidding discussion of the succession. Houliston, *Catholic Resistance*, 12.

8   In the margin: "Book 2, Chapter 28."

9   In the margin: "c. 1, decrees in parliament, March 29, 1585."
        27 Eliz. 1. c. 1. See *SR*, 4.1:704–05.

10   Isa. 57:20.

The Conclusion to This Work

Let us now conclude the history of this bloody, woeful tragedy. We shall not proceed further in enumerating innumerable other related things, dire and strange—as well we might—for they are of the same sort as those we have written, declaring either the queen of England's impiousness against God our Lord, or her cruelty against his servants, or her outrages and audacity against other monarchs, or the deceit and hypocrisy with which all this is done. Accordingly, let us link this conclusion with the beginning of the book. We have seen the wretched beginning of the English schism, how it was planted with incest and lust, has been watered with innocent blood, and has grown and sustained itself with crimes and tyranny. The sin and the comeuppance of King Henry and Anne Boleyn. The weakness of the prelates in not resisting from the start, and how they expiated this guilt, being robbed of their dignities, property, and lives. The flattery and submission of the nobility, who, taken in by Elizabeth's false promises, consented to the deformation of religion and now laments the penalties of that sin. We have seen the passage from queen to queen, from King Henry's first wife, the sainted Queen Doña Catherine, to the five he subsequently took; from his daughter, Queen Doña Mary to the present Elizabeth, the daughter of Anne Boleyn. The devastation of the monasteries, the destruction and looting of the churches, the assault on the orders, the cruelty of the heretics, and the patience and constancy of our sainted martyrs.

Now, what are we to take from this? What are we to learn? What do these examples teach us, but to look well where we put our feet, and whom we follow, and whither we wander, for it is certain that crooked paths[1] will have the same course today as they had in years past, and that in all times he who sows corruption will reap death and corruption.[2] Who will not restrain their disordered passions and take them in hand, seeing how King Henry drowned in an abyss of infinite sins because he had become senselessly infatuated with a crass, vicious, and ugly woman, the daughter and sister of his mistresses—and what is more, his own daughter—and abandoned his lawful wife to marry her? And that she herself paid such a price as a public beheading in punishment of her sins? Who will not set a bound to their ambition, seeing the end of Wolsey's? Who will trust to the intimacy and confidence of their king, recalling the pinnacle of Cromwell's favor and authority, and his miserable fall? Who will set any store in titles and offices won by wicked means and artifice, if they hold

---

1 Prov. 10:9.

2 Gal. 6:8.

© KONINKLIJKE BRILL NV, LEIDEN, 2017 | DOI 10.1163/9789004323964_098

before their eyes Cranmer's entrance into the archbishopric of Canterbury, and his departure? Indeed, what am I to say of the impiety of the protector? And of the mad audacity of John Dudley? And of the flattering wiles of the dukes of Suffolk and Norfolk? And of the disastrous end to which they all came, by the just judgment of God—who, though for a time he endures with mildness and waits with patience, in the end punishes with severity, and makes up for the delay with the awfulness of the penalty? Who will not be struck with admiration at the devotion, patience, and wisdom of the saintly Queen Doña Catherine? And the steadfast and constant faith of her daughter, Queen Doña Mary? And the spirit and fortitude in shedding blood for Christ of the other Mary, the queen of Scots—all of whose lives have been told in this history? What strength shines forth in those sainted martyrs who have suffered for our sacred religion in the days of King Henry and of his daughter Elizabeth? What glorious blazes of virtue did they reveal? What testimonies of their faith and hope? What proofs of their charity, fortitude, and valor? How clearly do we see the power of the Catholic truth, as thus it triumphs over error? And those who teach it, and die for it, being fallen are raised up and being dead live,[3] and from ignominy pass into honor and from the cross to the crown and undying glory?

We should emphasize all these examples, to avoid the wicked and to imitate and follow the good, for this is the fruit that must be taken from this history. For among the other titles and praises given to history, one—and the most important—is *Magistra vitae*, to be the directress of human life, for it teaches what is to be shunned and what is to be done.[4] For this reason we write down the hateful examples of accursed men and the punishments they received, so that we might fear them, and learn, and keep ourselves from falling into them; and we write down the heroic virtues of saintly and exemplary men, so that we might know what has already been accomplished in the path of virtue, that it is not so steep as it appears, and that we might follow the guides who have gone before us with such joy and vigor. And we see this not only in the secular histories composed by so many weighty authors, but also in the ecclesiastical ones, penned by sainted doctors and admirable men, the lights and ornaments of the Catholic Church. And what is more, the same is seen in Sacred Writ, inspired and dictated by the Holy Spirit, which, just as it is records the obedience of Abraham, the sincerity of Isaac, the sufferance of Jacob, the chastity of

---

3   Ps. 144:14; Acts 15:16; Rom. 6:8–9.

4   In his *De oratore* (55 BCE), Cicero declares, "By what other voice than the orator's is history, the witness of time, the light of truth, the life of memory, the directress of life, the messenger of antiquity, committed to immortality?" a sentiment that was to become a much-beloved dictum of early modern historiography. Cicero, *De oratore*, 2.36.

Joseph, the patience of Job, the gentleness of Moses, and the devotion and trust in God of King David, also depicts for us the adultery of that same David, the foolishness of his son, the wise Solomon, the weakness of the mighty Samson, and innumerable examples of bloodthirsty kings and pestilential tyrants, so that we might follow the good and shun the wicked. And for this reason the glorious apostle, Saint Paul, says that everything that is written in Holy Scripture is written for our instruction and learning, for everything therein serves either as a bridle upon vice or as a spur and encouragement to virtue.[5]

But although we may learn from this history all that we have said, two boons among the rest are the most crucial for us to take. The first is to comprehend heresy properly and to abhor it. The second, to nurture in our hearts a living and ardent zeal for the honor of God and for the salvation of the souls of the English, our neighbors, whom we see so thoroughly misled and lost. To fully grasp how pernicious and terrifying a monster heresy is requires divine illumination, by which we penetrate through to what it is, as well as to what a precious jewel faith is, and the inestimable virtues and infinite treasures and riches that surround it. For faith is the root, source, and foundation of all virtues, which cannot exist if it is lacking, and instead wither, as a tree withers if severed from the root upon which it is sustained.[6] And we know that faith is lost through heresy. But leaving this to one side, if we wish to learn something of the calamities that heresy carries with it, let us train our eyes upon those that have befallen the kingdom of England, which are too numerous to be counted and too extreme to be believed. For in this our history we have seen heresy assail a thousand monasteries, profane and destroy ten thousand churches, overturn the ancient monuments of the saints, burn their bodies and scatter their sacred ashes to the wind, cast every religious out of their houses, violate the nuns consecrated to God, and mutilate countless of his servants with inhuman torments. We have seen a woman, daughter and granddaughter to Henry VIII and daughter and sister to Anne Boleyn (as we have said) seated in God's temple like a hateful monster and an idol,[7] usurping the office and title of governor and head of the church, removing, appointing, visiting, correcting, and chastising the bishops, and allowing and denying them the authority to ordain, confirm, and carry out the other priestly functions at her pleasure and will. And for refusing to obey her she has persecuted, abused, deposed, jailed, harassed, and ultimately murdered all the Catholic bishops in England. We have seen a noble, rich, powerful kingdom, the first or one of the first to receive the Gospel

---

5   In the margin: "Romans 15[:4]."

6   John 15:6.

7   2 Thess. 2:3–4.

publicly, which had been a paradise of delights, a garden of lovely and gorgeous flowers, a school of virtues, from which have emerged unconquerable martyrs, saintly bishops, sagacious doctors, renowned confessors, immaculately chaste virgins—among them Saint Ursula and the eleven thousand[8]—made into a den of wild beasts, a refuge of traitors, a haven of pirates, a den of thieves,[9] a nest of serpents, a mother of impiety, a stepmother of every virtue, a fountain of errors, and in the end a frightful rock that has struck and woefully wrecked sanctity and religion. Whither the heretics, those hellish monsters, have not only rushed from every corner, but whence, as from an impregnable castle, they have waged war against the Catholic Church and worked to infect the other provinces and kingdoms, unsettle Catholic monarchs, and disturb the peace of the Church, leaving Scotland ruined, France in turmoil, the states of Flanders beset, and even the realms of Spain and the Indies mired in troubles and woes. We have seen a tyranny so impious and barbaric that under the name of Christianity it has abolished the Mass and exiled God from the realm; summoned and cited in court the saints in heaven, and condemned them as traitors; punished as *lèse-majesté* the possession or bearing of any sacred thing from Rome; poured out its rage and fury upon a queen for being a Catholic, and publicly put her to death, beheaded by the hand of the common executioner of London. If this queen is faithless to God himself, with whom shall she keep faith? If she dares this tyranny against the saints in heaven, who shall be safe upon the earth? What thing of holiness or devotion will she not hate, when she mutilates and murders a person with the most horrid torments for carrying an a*gnus Dei*? If the royal name and majesty is not enough to shield or save a queen—innocent, her niece, her successor, her guest, deceived with sweet hopes and false promises—what Catholic who falls into her hands can escape? What blood will they not drink, who have sated themselves with royal blood, their own blood? But such persons are the supreme enemies of the human race, and heresy, like hellfire and a roaring blaze, and a deadly plague upon the world, should be more hateful to us than death itself.

Therefore, let us benefit from this history, not least in awakening and inspiring in our hearts a holy and ardent zeal for the honor of our Lord and for the good of the kingdom of England. For one of the chiefest signs of being a child of God is that ardor for the honor of the Father eats and consumes one's innards, a fierce and fervent desire that his sacred name be glorified, a care above

---

8　Ursula, a third-century British princess, was supposedly martyred in Rome by pagan Huns, along with her attendants. A misreading of a stone inscription probably produced the unlikely number of eleven thousand for these martyred ladies. See *AASS*, October IX, 73–153.

9　Matt. 21:13; Luke 19:46.

all cares that this great Lord should be known, esteemed, obeyed, and revered by all, his will fulfilled in all things, in heaven and upon the earth.[10] That offenses to him pierce our heart and leave it withered and dry—and all the more so those that are the more universal and grievous, as are those of England, for it spreads and extends its venom and contagion throughout the world. What Christian will not feel and bewail so many atrocious injuries to Jesus Christ? Who would not dissolve into tears, seeing the perdition of the infinite souls that go to Hell each day? Who would not pity the countless Catholics, priests, lords, knights, citizens, youths, and old people, men and women, boys and girls, who are miserably afflicted in England? And if one were in a similarly wretched position, would they not wish to be succored and supported? Who among us will not strive with all their powers to undo so barbarous a tyranny, and remove this blot upon all of Christendom? How can we Spaniards repay our Lord the mercy he has done us in preserving these kingdoms in our sacred Catholic faith, whole, clean, and free of heresy, save with zeal for that same Catholic faith, desire for his glory, and the conversion or destruction of the heretics? And just as, having been exiled, Catholicism was formerly restored to that realm when King Don Philip our lord became its king, let us strive to preserve or recover what once we won. The glory for Spain shall be no less for casting the devil out of England than for having exiled him from the Indies, where he was served and adored before the preaching of the Gospel—especially since in casting him out, he will be driven out of a large portion of the provinces of Christendom, which are sustained in their errors and sins by England's intercourse and the industry of its rulers. And if these tyrants, scorched with infernal fire, stoke this blaze, feed this storm, and spread this corrupt and pestilential air and scatter and extend it through other lands, sending it to Muscovy and the heretical princes and soliciting the Turk to undermine us and take from us (if they can) our faith and the eternal salvation of our souls, why should we allow ourselves to be overcome by their devilish fury, and not do for the sake of God our Lord and of our sacred law what they do against him and it in their prodigious madness and zeal? When some serious Catholic author prints a book against their dogmas, by which they fear some setback to their sect of perdition,[11] there are heretics who collude with the bookseller to buy every copy and burn them, lest they will appear and condemn their errors. Now, what hellish zeal is this? What effort? What care? Who among us does as much again for the sake of the truth as these ministers of Satan do for their lies? Let us keep watch, remain alert, and carry this urgency and pious zeal as though pierced by a nail, and

---

10   Matt. 6:10.

11   2 Pet 2:1.

let us passionately implore our Lord day and night that he show mercy to that kingdom and look upon it with eyes of pity, that he console the numberless disconsolate and oppressed Catholics, that the impiety and tyranny of those soulless, godless people come to an end, that the merits of all the many saints of that isle and of the great store of blood, yet fresh and warm, that so many of his valiant soldiers have shed for his love should prevail. Let us call to the gates of heaven, let us entreat the favor of all those blessed spirits and pure souls that reign with God, let us turn to the sovereign queen our Lady, and with humility and faith invoke through her hands the open heart of the precious Son before the eternal Father. And this not so much that we may have worldly tranquility, nor that the English corsairs not infest our seas nor despoil our armada (important and just a consideration though this is, it is less central), as much as for the glorification of the Lord himself and the prosperity of his holy Church. And to be heard the better, let us amend our lives and show our faith and holy zeal in deeds: if it should be needful, let us give our property, efforts, and lives for so great a thing. Let us hold it a supreme mercy of God (as indeed it is) to shed our blood for his sacred faith, to take part in checking so many abominable outrages as are committed against his divine majesty in England every day, and to ameliorate such irreparable harms to souls as we have seen. And so let us hope in the infinite mercy of the Lord that he will enlighten the blind heretics and give them the grace to return to themselves, or put an end to them and uproot them from the earth, as he has eradicated and disposed of so many of his enemies who have risen in past centuries against his spouse, the holy Catholic, Apostolic, and Roman Church.

The end of this history.

BOOK 3

The Third Book of the Schism of England, Recounting Various Martyrs and Other Things that have Occurred in that Realm Since the First Part of this History was Published

∵

To Our Lord the Prince, Don Philip

Since I published the ecclesiastical history of the lamentable schism of the kingdom of England, under Your Highness's name and favor, many noteworthy things have come to pass, the poisonous fruits of that evil root: it has occurred to me to recount these briefly in this third book, or second part, of my history, and to dedicate it (as I did the first) to Your Highness, so that from this your tender youth you may continue learning what happens in foreign lands, and out of their calamities acknowledge and worship God for the mercy he shows his own, and offer him infinite thanks, not so much for having made you heir to so many grand and mighty kingdoms, as for having given you the king our lord for a father, one whose actions shine with singular piety, justice, valor, prudence, and every other royal virtue, which teach Your Highness what to do preserve these realms. For true it is that all empires and states are sustained, as though upon two columns, by justice and by true religion, and that all the kings of the earth are the deputies of the sovereign king of heaven, through whom they reign: neither their power nor their prosperity will last any longer than it shall please the Lord and they keep their eyes fixed on his mercy above them.

I have also sent this second part of my history to Your Highness to show you how abhorrent a monster heresy is, for it strips a man of his humanity and transforms a woman into a wild and vicious beast. And that you should likewise wonder at the patience and fortitude of our sainted martyrs, and both sorrow for the many noble, wealthy English youths who wander in exile from their home for the sake of our Catholic faith, and envy, support, and sustain them, so that beneath Your Highness's shade and protection they may live securely in the seminaries established for their refuge at Valladolid and Seville by the piety and benignity of the king our lord. For it is primarily against these seminaries and their students and masters that Queen Elizabeth of England rages: against them she writes her bloodstained laws, publishes her barbarous edicts, enforces her horrific, extreme punishments, and pours out all her strength and fury. This tells us that she fears them, that these few and seemingly weak soldiers are waging war upon her—and, since it is a war of the Lord, our victory is certain and assured. But to attain it, for our holy religion to triumph over heresy, virtue over wickedness, and Christ over Satan, they need to be encouraged, strengthened, and supported, as the king our lord does and as Your Highness shall do, as the son and heir to such a father. May God our Lord keep Your

© KONINKLIJKE BRILL NV, LEIDEN, 2017 | DOI 10.1163/9789004323964_099

Highness, as these realms require and as all the religious of the Society of Jesus, your servants and beadsmen, unceasingly implore him in our feeble prayers. At our college at Madrid, in the month of May, in the year 1593.[1]

Pedro de Ribadeneyra

---

1   This sentence is added in the 1595 edition.

To the Benign and Pious Reader[1]

Some years past, kindly reader, I published an ecclesiastical history of the English schism, in hopes of stirring readers' spirits to consider and reflect upon such notable, extraordinary matters relating to our sacred religion as have occurred in that kingdom since the schism's beginning, to the end that, after examining all this, they might marvel at the profound and secret judgments of God,[2] who has permitted so great a realm, formerly so Catholic, to fall into an abyss of infinite evils, and allowed the heretics the power to afflict and persecute the Catholics with such ferocity. And so that we might praise and glorify him for the strength and spirit with which he arms and fortifies those same Catholics, giving them victory over all their enemies. For among the other reasons we have for recognizing and esteeming the truth of our holy Catholic faith (which are innumerable and irrefutable), not the least is that offered us by the glorious martyrs who died for that faith, inscribed in their precious blood and sealed with the seal of their blessed deaths. Nor that of the futility and senselessness of all the tyrants' stratagems and schemes against God, who humbles and confounds them with swarms of flies and mosquitos, as he did with Pharaoh,[3] and by means of frail men and women triumphs over all the power of hell.[4]

We see this clearly in the persecution the holy Catholic Church presently suffers in England: for, this being one of the cruelest and most awful that it has endured since it began, we shall find that it flourishes amid these travails, that amid fierce and contrary winds it comes all the more swiftly into port, that for one who dies for the Catholic faith, a hundred are born who desire to die for it,[5] that there are more who fight for us than against us, and that the greater the wrath of Satan and the fury of his ministers,[6] the more passionate the waves of their persecutions, so much the more will that sturdy rock upon which the Church is founded prove itself strong and unmovable.[7] It can hardly be believed how terrible and fearsome is the storm that the Catholics in

---

1 The address to the reader is omitted in the 1595 and 1605 editions.

2 Rom. 11:33.

3 Exod. 8:21, 8:24.

4 Matt. 16:18.
     Cf. Ribadeneyra, *Tratado de la tribulacion*, 14ᵛ–16ʳ.

5 Cf. Tertullian, *Apologeticus*, Chapter 50.

6 Rev. 12:12.

7 Matt. 7:24–25, 16:18; Luke 6:48.

England endure, so harassed and hounded wherever they go in the kingdom that they can hardly draw breath: they are stripped of their property; they are deprived of their liberty; they are subjected to the harshness and horrors of prisons and dungeons; they are mutilated by the most gruesome tortures; they are defamed as traitors; and they are dispatched by the cruelest of deaths, with the entire kingdom armed against them—and in dying they conquer, and in falling cast down their adversaries, and by the very means that the heretics seek to uproot the Catholic faith, the Lord entrenches and strengthens it yet further. How many times has it happened that the governors of the provinces and the judges—who are often the most obstinate heretics in the entire realm—are converted by the patience and modesty with which they see the Catholics suffer, and support and assist those same Catholics for months and years, until they reveal themselves and are recognized as Catholics? And that the ministers and preachers of heresy themselves, touched by the hand of the Lord, turn to him and embrace the Catholic faith, and by dissimulation defend it and even—favored by divine grace—come to die for it, with fervor as great as was the treachery with which they had previously persecuted it? Indeed, what am I to say of the wardens, jailers, and guards at the prisons who, being fervent heretics and the worst enemies of the Catholic faith (having been chosen for those offices because they were known as such), when they are moved by the life and example of the Catholics they hold prisoner, soften and submit and enter into the path of truth, along with their wives and their servants? And they secretly provide the Catholics with opportunities to say Mass in the prison itself and allow them the freedom to write and receive letters. And not a few times it has come to pass that certain prominent knights and servants of the queen, covert Catholics, have dared to arrange for a Mass to be said within the queen's palace, and even in her own apartments![8] And, in the end, the more the devil rages and strives with all his craft to choke this seed of heaven,[9] the more it takes root and grows in the people and places they least suspect. Even in the young men and women who, given their age and status, have the most reason to delight in the comforts and pleasures of this world, we see so many wondrous effects of divine grace that not even the heretics themselves can

---

8 "Many of the queen's courtiers and intimates are from time to time revealed to be Catholics, and they have dared to have Mass said in the palace, and on occasion in the very room where she sleeps." *Relatione del presente stato d'Inghilterra: Cavata da vna lettera de li 25 di maggio scritta di Londra, et da vn'altra, scritta da vna persona di qualità, venuta di frescho d'Inghilterra, data in Anuersa alli 27 di giugno, & altre* (Rome: Appresso Francesco Zannetti, 1590), 12.

9 Matt. 13:7; Mark 4:7; Luke 8:14.

deny it or refrain from confessing their fear and terror. This is God's gift, these his works, these his miracles, worthy of everlasting wonder and praise.

And so, this my history having been so well received and having borne some fruit by the Lord's mercy, I have elected to add a few things I omitted from the first printing for the sake of brevity, and furthermore to augment it with this third book, or second part, comprising those that have occurred since it was published, the which are of great weight and significance, apt for my purpose, which is to set before the eyes of the reader the persecution and the triumph of the Catholic Church, cutting out all that pertains to political affairs and governance, or that is unnecessary for continuing the thread we were weaving about the schism of the kingdom of England. Nor have I bound myself to include and relate everything, as others shall do this, but rather to choose some of the more noteworthy things that have come to my attention and to render them for the benefit of the pious reader, and so that in the centuries to come some memory shall remain of this truly singular work of the Lord, and of this victory of his spouse the holy Church. The heretics shall be confounded, the Catholics edified and inspirited, and God glorified in his martyrs, who shall be yet more revered and imitated by the faithful. For these same aims of this work of mine, many saintly and erudite men have expended their own efforts in recording the other persecutions that the Church has endured, among which this of England is not the least vicious and frightful, nor the least miraculous and glorious of all.

The Edict Passed against the Catholics by the Advice of the Earl of Leicester, and of His Death, and that of Several Servants of God

After the queen and her councilors saw themselves free of their fear and anxiety about the Spanish Armada, straightway they turned like lions against the kingdom's Catholics, to persecute and eradicate them. Thus it was that an inhuman edict was enacted to seek them out in every corner, apprehend them, and pour out upon them their rage and fury.[1] The principal author of this edict was Robert Dudley, earl of Leicester, a mortal foe of the Catholic faith and all who professed it, so rabid and barbaric that he said he wished to see the entire city of London painted with the blood of Catholics.[2] This accursed man was the son of John Dudley, duke of Northumberland, who had been beheaded as a traitor in the reign of Queen Mary; his four sons had been condemned to the same fate, one of whom was Robert Dudley, who with his brothers was reprieved by the clemency of Queen Mary. After her death he attained such favor and license with Queen Elizabeth that he became the most powerful man in the kingdom, deciding questions of war and peace according to his will. He was governor of Holland and Zealand and captain general of the realm, holding all its forces in his hand—and, not satisfied with these preferments and titles, he sought another, extraordinary and supreme over the entire kingdom.[3] This the queen granted him, but when her council obstructed the decision and refused to sign and seal the new patent for the office of steward of the realm, the earl was so distraught and infuriated (for to great lords and favorites any sort of obstacle to their desires strikes them to the very soul) that he was immediately struck with an illness so grievous that he was swiftly carried off

---

1 This seems to be a reference to a proclamation issued *before* the climax of the Armada crisis: on July 1, 1588, Elizabeth declared martial law against possessors and disseminators of papal bulls and other Catholic documents. See *TRP*, 3:13–17.

2 The earliest reference to this remark I have been able to identify comes in Richard Challoner's (1691–1781) *Memoirs of Missionary Priests* (1741). Challoner almost certainly had it from Ribadeneyra. Richard Challoner, *Memoirs of Missionary Priests, as Well Secular as Regular; And of Other Catholics, of Both Sexes, That Have Suffered Death in England, on Religious Accounts, from the Year of Our Lord 1577, to 1684*, 2 vols. ([London]: [For F. Needham?], 1741), 1:209–10.

3 Ribadeneyra's description of Robert Dudley, first earl of Leicester, follows, in abbreviated form, the defamatory portrait of the earl in *Philopater*, 14–20.

in a horrible, frightful death.[4] Some, however, said that his second wife had killed him, and that this was God's judgment, in punishment for his having murdered his first wife and the earl of Essex, the first husband of his second wife.[5] Nevertheless, whatever happened, the tyrant's death came so promptly that all who knew and recognized his wicked spirit and what he had plotted against the Catholics regarded it as the singular providence of the Lord, who by the punishment of so impious and degenerate a man intended to demonstrate the providence he had for his Church. For, though this man had been the son of a Catholic father—who on the scaffold itself, about to die, had movingly exhorted the people to persevere in the Catholic faith and beware of the heretics ravaging the kingdom (described in the first part of this history),[6] and though God had done him the mercy of freeing him from the death to which he was condemned, he ignored the Lord's gifts and turned his back on him. Deluded by his great intimacy with the queen and deceived by the favorable wind that bore him along, he was so far gone as to become the Catholics' cruelest and fiercest enemy in the kingdom, in order to show himself the queen's most zealous servant. And he gave himself up to a life as dissolute and degenerate as the religion he professed. But our Lord cut short his steps, and after he had raised

---

4 Dudley had served as Elizabeth's master of the horse since her accession. In 1587, he surrendered this office, which was replaced with that of lord steward—which office he did, *pace* Ribadeneyra, enjoy until his sudden death (probably of malaria) on September 4, 1588. Adams, "Dudley, Robert," in *ODNB*, 17:110–11.

 The story that the council opposed Leicester's appointment comes from Persons: "In fact, some believed he had died from rage and fury [...] for, when the queen granted his petition requesting the highest position and extraordinary authority in England, the other councilors refused their assent, nor could he ever prevail upon the chancellor to set the great seal on the writ." *Philopater*, 18.

5 Leicester's first wife, Amy Dudley, died on September 8, 1560, having broken her neck falling down a flight of steps. The murky circumstances surrounding the event and Leicester's known intimacy with Elizabeth prompted swift and enduring speculation that the earl had arranged his wife's demise. Likewise, when Walter Devereux, first earl of Essex (1541–76), died on September 22, 1576, it was rumored that Leicester had had the late earl poisoned, so as to wed the dowager countess, Lettice Knollys (1543–1634)—which he duly did two years later. Though modern historians reject these allegations, such notoriety virtually ensured that at Leicester's own death, foul play was suggested. See Chris Skidmore, *Death and the Virgin Queen: Elizabeth I and the Dark Scandal That Rocked the Throne* (New York: St. Martin's Press, 2010).

 Cf. "Others thought that he had been killed by the just judgment of God, indeed, at the hands of his wife, for the sake of attaining of whom, as we said, he had removed the earl of Essex, her first husband." *Philopater*, 18.

6 In the margin: "Book 2, Chapter 10."

him up, he felled him in the aforesaid manner, for the edification of those who, deceived by prosperity and kindly fortune, forget the wheel upon which it rests and live as though there were no God, or as though he were not a righteous judge, nor provides an eternal reward for the good and punishment for the wicked.[7]

Leicester's death delayed the execution of the pending edict for a time, but as our Lord had determined to render this extraordinary kindness—for such it is to bestow the crown of martyrdom—to some of his servants, whom he had chosen for so exalted a dignity, the queen ordered the deaths of the greater part of those the earl had condemned while he lived, for she imagined the Catholics might take heart and spirit at the earl's death. And so it was that many servants of God were martyred in various parts of the kingdom.

In London, they erected six new gallows to carry out this impious cruelty, and in the nearby towns and villages they martyred many more, all dying with perfect constancy, patience, and joy of spirit.[8] As the saintly martyrs stood at the foot of the gallows, the heretics did not permit them to address the crowd, lest some be converted by their words. When one of the priests, a wise and learned man by the name of Dean, attempted to explain to those present the reasons so much blood is spilled in England in these days, the heretics stopped his mouth with such force and violence that they nearly suffocated him, and he lost consciousness.[9] But even though the martyrs did not speak in that moment, their silence itself spoke for them, and the very sight of the deaths of

---

7 Ps. 7:12, 27:4, 61:13; Matt. 16:27; Rom. 2:6; 2 Tim. 4:8.

8 The anecdotes in this chapter are drawn from a letter printed in Robert Persons's *Relacion de algunos martyrios, que de nueuo han hecho los hereges en Inglaterra, y de otras cosas tocantes a nuestra santa y Catolica religion* (Madrid: Pedro Madrigal, 1590).

   The letter relates, "In London, they erected six new gallows at once." Ibid., 16[r].

   These stories may be compared with a very similar, if somewhat less detailed, letter written by Robert Southwell (*c.*1561–1595) to Claudio Acquaviva. The Latin text is printed, with a translation, in John Hungerford Pollen, ed., *Unpublished Documents Relating to the English Martyrs: Vol. 1 1584–1603*, Publications of the Catholic Record Society 5 (London: J. Whitehead and Son, 1908), 321–28.

9 "One among them was a most reverend and learned priest by the name of Dean, who, when he had come to the place of martyrdom, wished to speak a few words and declare to those present the reason for which so many are nowadays made martyrs in England, but the heretics stopped his mouth with a cloth with such fury and violence that he was left well-nigh suffocated and unconscious." Persons, *Relacion*, 17[r].

   Cf. Pollen, *Unpublished Documents*, 327.

   William Dean (*c.*1557–88), a Yorkshireman trained as a priest at Rheims, was hanged at Mile End Green in Middlesex on August 28, 1588. G. Bradley, "Dean, William (*c.*1557–1588)," in *ODNB*, 15:630.

so many saintly men, innocent and of exemplary character—many of them high-born young men, who, though poised to enjoy the delights of this life, abandoned them with the greatest pleasure—was a forceful sermon in convincing the onlookers that it was the true faith for which they died with such steadfastness and enthusiasm.

Around this time, it happened in London that several blessed martyrs, being dragged to their executions, met a prominent lady whom they knew, who with Christian fortitude and heart encouraged them to die with perfect patience and constancy, as martyrs of Jesus Christ, and begged their blessing at their feet. But at this the heretics seized her and bore her off to prison.[10]

Another Catholic man, horrified at seeing so many, priests and laymen alike, brought to the gallows, crossed himself, as was his custom; at this they laid hands on him and threw him into prison amid great chaos and commotion.[11]

But something of even greater edification came to pass: as one of these martyrs stood on the scaffold to be executed, he urgently begged the people that if there were any Catholics there, they should pray to God for him, for he had need of his favor and aid. The Catholics present, moved by these words, supposed that amid his travails and agonies the servant of God was assailed by the demon with some dire temptation and secretly began to pray to God for him. But one among them was more fervent, who, judging that, since this martyr did not hesitate to die publicly for the confession of the Catholic faith, he was obliged to honor him and aid him with his prayers in the same manner, sank to his knees in the sight of all and prayed to God for him with deep feeling and devotion. And so the martyr was consoled and inspired to die, while the heretics were so distraught and enraged that they immediately arrested the man to punish such audacity.[12]

---

10   "In the streets of London, as they were escorting those who were to die to the place of judgment to put them to death, they met a prominent lady whom they knew. Moved with the strength of the Christian spirit, she encouraged them as martyrs of Christ, and kneeling in the sight of all, she asked their blessing. But at this the heretics seized her and bore her off to prison." Persons, *Relacion*, 17^r–17^v.
      Cf. Pollen, *Unpublished Documents*, 327.

11   "They did the same to a man who—because he was a Catholic and had a custom of making the sign of the holy cross—when he encountered this crowd, frightened at the sight of so many priests and laymen being carried off together to torment, immediately crossed himself, at which the heretics were enraged and thereupon bore him off a prisoner to jail, with many shouts and much confusion." Persons, *Relacion*, 17v.
      Cf. Pollen, *Unpublished Documents*, 327.

12   "But I shall relate another, more notable fact, which is that as one of the martyrs was just about to be executed, he urgently begged the people that if there were any Catholics

Among the others who died for the Catholic faith on that occasion, there was a woman named Margaret Ward and another well-born young man, Thomas Felton by name. The woman was sentenced to death for having helped a priest escape from prison, and before they put her to death they flogged her mercilessly for many days and suspended her in the air, bound by her arms; all the while, she retained so joyous and valiant a spirit that it was astonishing. And they say that those torments were an exercise in which God prepared her for the martyrdom she was to receive by his mercy, and so when the hour of her death had come she embraced it and suffered with wondrous constancy, to the edification of those who saw her die.[13]

---

among them, they should fervently pray to God for him, for he was in need. At this, all the Catholics, supposing that the servant of God must be enduring some serious temptation in his trials, secretly began to pray to God for him. But one among them, more fervent, not content with this, wished also to demonstrate his feelings publicly, judging that as the martyr had not hesitated to die publicly for God and the confession of his faith, he was likewise obliged to honor him and openly to aid him with his prayers. And so, in the presence of all, he knelt and prayed to God for him most devoutly, at which the said martyr was left greatly consoled, although the heretics were infuriated at this boldness and immediately arrested him for punishment." Persons, *Relacion*, 17^v–18^r.

Cf. Pollen, *Unpublished Documents*, 327.

13   Of Margaret Ward (d.1588) and Thomas Felton (*c.*1567–88), the letter in the *Relacion* writes, "This handmaid of God was condemned to death for an utterly frivolous cause, having aided a priest in escaping from prison through a window. On this account, they savagely flogged her for many days before putting her to death, and they hung her up and held her suspended in the air by her arms, but in these torments she never showed despair or weakness, but rather great spirit and joy, saying that these were preambles to prepare her to endure well, with the favor of the Lord, the martyrdom that was to follow. And thus, when the hour of her death had come, she accepted it and suffered it to the wonder and edification of all. The noble youth Thomas Felton, the nephew of the glorious martyr, Felton, whom they had martyred many years before for having published Pius v's bull against the queen in London, did the same. Because the heretics had seen that the young Thomas was spirited and quite determined in matters of the service of God and of his religion, they loaded him with irons and chains to exhaust and break him, and besides this they threw him into a filthy prison, called Newgate, among thieves, where he remained for three and a half months, with great pain and enormous suffering. But he did not quail at this, but was rather sustained by the thought that his uncle had been a valiant martyr of Jesus Christ, and that he too might become one by the grace of the same Lord, and with the fortitude that he is accustomed to give his own, he became resolute and received an unconquerable patience. When the heretics saw this, they took him away to execute him publicly, to the enormous dismay and sorrow of all who saw him die—because he was a beautiful and noble youth, and recognized as such by all, but far more because his interior and exterior virtues, his piety, devotion, zeal, patience, and endurance in his

The young man, Thomas Felton, was nobly born (as we said), very hand-some of face, and nephew to the glorious martyr John Felton, who had been ex-ecuted several years earlier for having published Pius v's bull against the queen in London (as we wrote in the first part of this history).[14] For this reason, and because he was a spirited youth, deeply zealous in anything to the service of God and the Catholic faith, the heretics loaded him with irons and chains to exhaust him, and cast him in a filthy dungeon, alongside thieves, where he was tormented and abused for three and a half months. But he neither wavered nor broke, instead recalling how his uncle had been a valiant martyr of Jesus Christ and holding on to the hope that with the grace of that Lord he, too, might become one. His fortitude and patience were extraordinary, and these the heretics could not endure, and so they bore him off to martyrdom, to the extreme sorrow of all who saw him die—for besides the unique innate quali-ties God had given him, he was adorned with wonderful virtues of piety, devo-tion, fervor, endurance in trials, and a singular gentleness, even toward the very foes who took his life.

---

trials, and his notable meekness toward the enemies who took his life were famous, rare, and worthy of admiration." Persons, *Relacion*, 18ᵛ–19ᵛ.

Cf. Pollen, *Unpublished Documents*, 327.

Margaret Ward was a Catholic laywoman, later canonized, who helped several priests escape from prison, for which she was executed on August 30, 1588. Monta, *Martyrdom and Literature*, 211–12.

14   In the margin: "Book 2, Chapter 28."

Thomas Felton was actually John Felton's son. The Feltons, among the richest fami-lies in Surrey, packed Thomas off to the English College at Douai, and thence to Rheims, where he became a Franciscan. He returned to England in 1583 and spent several years in and out of prison. He was severely tortured, but never recanted his Catholicism or acknowledged Elizabeth's supremacy. He was hanged, drawn and quartered near Brent-ford in Middlesex, on August 28, 1588. Sarah Elizabeth Wall, "Felton, Thomas (1566x8–1588)," in *ODNB*, 19:287.

The Falls of Two Catholics, and What the Lord Worked through Them

Given how horrific are the torments to which the heretics subject the Catholics, how outlandish the tricks they use to corrupt them, God sometimes permits the fall of those who presume upon him and think themselves strong, to the end that such persons' misfortunes should teach us the knowledge of our weakness and edify us, while their victories more clearly manifest the goodness of the Lord and inspire and encourage us. In this persecution, God allowed two to yield to their fear and dread of the torments (just as we read of others in past persecutions), but in such a way that their falls lifted many of the fallen and became a wonderful blessing to them and to all Catholics. One of these was a priest named Anthony Tyrrell,[1] who, at first through fear, and

---

1 Anthony Tyrrell (1552–1615), the scion of a prominent Essex family, was—even by the standards of early modern England—erratic in confessional allegiance. Ordained a priest at Rome and dispatched to England in 1580, he was arrested and imprisoned in London in 1581. By the end of the year, he had escaped, and spent several years traveling in England and on the Continent. Tyrrell returned to England by 1585, and was again arrested in July 1586. Threatened with death, Tyrrell renounced his Catholicism, offered the Elizabethan authorities a fulsome (and not always credible) account of his doings, and informed on other Catholic prisoners. Briefly released, Tyrrell was again imprisoned in 1587: he agreed to preach a sermon at St Paul's Cross describing his recantation, but reversed course and preached in favor of Catholicism. The next year, the Protestant sermon was, in fact, preached, and Tyrrell received a pardon and a rectory in Essex. His Anglican career was not without further incident, including yet another spell in prison, and he eventually abandoned England and ended his days in Naples as a Catholic. Peter Holmes, "Tyrrell, Anthony (1552–1615)," in *ODNB*, 55:800–01.

   Tyrrell's story is related in a somewhat briefer form in a letter printed in Robert Persons's *Relacion*: "One of those who turned back out of weakness was a priest called Anthony Tyrrell. Being a young man, and pressed by the heretics with fears of torture and various offers of rewards, in the end he promised to do all they asked, and began to give some proof of this. And for the greater solemnity and the greater dishonor to the Catholics, they had him prepare to mount the pulpit of St Paul's, the foremost church in London and the most frequented in the kingdom, on a feast-day, so that he might abjure the Catholic faith in the sight of all. But the Lord touched his heart and gave him a spirit totally different from what they imagined. For Anthony Tyrrell went to St Paul's on the agreed-upon day and time, the heretics having gathered the entire populace for so solemn an *auto*, and he mounted the pulpit, as the ministers

then deceived by his ambitions and the promises and hopes they offered him, became a heretic and, at the urging of the queen's ministers, falsely accused many prominent English knights, Doctor William Allen, the fathers of the Society of Jesus, and other priests. He claimed that they had conspired in Rome with Pope Gregory XIII of happy memory to kill the queen and to incite the kingdom; this is the camouflage and cloak with which those in power seek to disguise their impious tyranny.[2] After this wretched priest had fallen into so profound an abyss of wickedness, the Lord in his infinite mercy took pity on him and extended his hand to touch his heart, so that he came to his senses, repented his sins, and returned to the Catholic faith.[3] And thus Tyrrell resolved to flee England and hide himself away to weep and do penance for his sins with some measure of peace and safety. But before leaving he wrote a pamphlet abjuring his errors and declaring the falseness and perjury with which he had accused so many noble, innocent Catholics.[4] He left England and lived as a Catholic abroad for some time, but then, whether tempted by the devil or

---

of hell awaited his abjuration with contentment and joy, so that thereby they might deceive others. He began to reveal to the people the lies and tricks of the heretics and to exhort them all not believe or follow them, since all they said and did was artifice and deceit, and that there was no other true religion, in which one might be saved, save the Catholic, Apostolic, and Roman. Hearing this, the heretics threw him from the pulpit with extreme rage and fury, but he strove to tell the people as much as he could, and what he could not with his mouth, he made up for with his pen, for at his breast he carried many copies of a text he had secretly written in prison, in which he recanted his heresy and professed the true Roman Catholic faith, and with deep emotion asked pardon of God our Lord, and of all Catholics, for his fall and his weakness." Persons, *Relacion*, 14^r–15^r.

Ribadeneyra has expanded this version with details from the *Concertatio*, which includes a lengthy account of Tyrrell's pro-Catholic sermon. *Concertatio*, n.p.

2 "Likewise I confess and wish that all, those now living and those to live hereafter, should know that I falsely accused that most sacred pontiff, Gregory XIII of holy memory, when I affirmed that he had colluded in the murder of our most serene lady, Queen Elizabeth; likewise, Mr. [John] Ballard, when I said that he put a similar question of the queen's murder to Doctor [Owen] Lewis at Milan, and the fathers of the Society of Jesus at Rome, and to him who was then Doctor, but is now Cardinal Allen, and to other persons from the seminaries. In truth, I never knew or heard the subject raised in this fashion, or any other plot or conspiracy against Her Majesty's person. And likewise Mr. Edward Windsor and Mr. Charles Tylney were by me unjustly implicated in crimes, and other men, as illustrious as noble, most falsely accused." Ibid., n.p.

3 1 Kings 10:26.

4 "I wrote private letters to the queen's majesty concerning all of these things, and then, guided by the spirit of God, I clearly refuted and disproved what I had written in a previous book on the aforementioned matters." *Concertatio*, n.p.

moved by his own slackness or some vain consideration, he returned, and because his earlier declaration of his faith and his unjust accusations had by then
been published, the queen's agents seized him and, by flatteries and threats,
by terrors and promises, succeeded in getting him to return to their sect and to
proclaim his faith in another declaration, contrary to the first, attesting that all
he had previously said against the Catholics had been the truth. To do this with
greater solemnity and acclaim, as though he had triumphed over Catholicism,
they ordered him to profess his creed publicly, before the entire populace, to
retract what he had written, abjure the Catholic faith, and confirm his first accusations against the priests and servants of God.[5] He said that he would do it,
but—with his conscience tormenting him and the Lord (who intended to save
him) permitting him no peace, for in his heart he was a Catholic—after he had
thoroughly considered the matter and commended it to God, he resolved to do
what will be related here.

On the day appointed for Anthony Tyrrell to make his declaration, these
ministers of the devil summoned all the people of rank they could to gather
in the square of St Paul's (the most important church in the city of London
and the most frequented in the country), where this abominable *auto* of their
devising was to be celebrated. Many knights, churchmen, and councilors attended, as well as an infinity of other people, who flocked to the event in
hopes of a spectacle and from the reports the ministers themselves had spread
throughout the city. The audience being assembled in utter silence, Anthony
Tyrrell ascended to the pulpit and with a countenance somewhat sorrowful
and distraught began to give an account of himself, to explain the reasons so
many exalted people had gathered there, and to say with deep emotion that he
was the greatest and most wretched sinner; an enemy of God and of his holy
Church, from which he had apostatized; a persecutor of innocent men, against
all reason and justice. Attempting to go on, to declare he was a Catholic and
to expose the tricks of the heretics, they stopped his mouth and ordered him
to keep quiet, furiously rushing at him and laying hands upon him to pull him
from the pulpit. But he had brought with him numerous written statements of
the protestation of his faith, the abjuration of his heresy, and a truthful confession of the lies that at the inducement and instigation of the queen's agents
he had uttered against the pope and against the priests and Catholic gentlemen, together with other excellent discourses. He scattered and tossed these
declarations and pamphlets among the people, shouting, "Since they have not

---

5   "What I wrote before my flight from England was perfectly true and certain, what I have pub-
    lished since was false and foreign to all truth, although I had tried to overturn the former by
    the latter, and reject them as fantasies." Ibid., n.p.

allowed me to speak, you shall read what I believe, what I feel, and the truth of all that has befallen me. My soul I offer to God, and my body to every torment and penalty that the queen's ministers wish to give me; they cannot give me so many that I will not deserve more."[6] The tumult in the crowd was enormous, as was the hue and cry this event provoked in London, the distress for the heretics, the contentment and inspiration for the Catholics, and the fury with which the queen's agents had the priest arrested and thrown into a horrid prison, so as to be avenged by inflicting on him the most gruesome and exquisite of tortures.

The other was a youth, virtuous before his fall, but exceedingly simple, and so he was deceived by the heretical ministers. He was called John Chapman. After he gave in and was set free, he began to feel the torments of his conscience and to repent and bewail his error. He wrote a letter to a Catholic friend of his, whom he had left a prisoner in the jail, in which he says,

> When I was with my companions before the tribunal of judges to receive the sentence of death, and with it the crown of blessed martyrdom that my Lord in his mercy chose to give me (woe is me!), there came to my mind the poisonous words the heretical ministers had said to me the day before, which had unsettled me, and the fear of death and the sweetness of this life perverted my heart and caused me to lose the crown. Now I wander astray, like a lost sheep, and I bear a heart transfixed with a nail of unbearable sorrow.[7] Pray to God for me, and let all learn from my example never trust to their own fortitude nor give ear to the heretics' treacherous speeches, which are like the hisses of a venomous snake.[8]

---

6 "And now I, in the greatest dejection of spirit, upon my knees beg pardon and mercy, first of God and of all the world; my body I leave to the impending torments my sins and transgressions [...] have merited." Ibid., n.p.

7 Luke 2:35.

8 The story of John Chapman (dates unknown) likewise comes from a letter included in Persons's *Relacion*: "The second, named John Chapman, was a very pious and virtuous youth before his fall, but quite simple, and thus he was deceived by the words of the heretical ministers. But, placed at liberty, he thereupon began to repent, and he wrote a letter to a Catholic friend of his whom he had left a prisoner in the jail, urging him to fortitude and perseverance in the faith, and confessing the pangs and utter torments of conscience that he had because he had lost the blessed crown of martyrdom, which God had offered him, and among other things he said the following words: 'When I was with my companions before the public tribunal to receive the sentence of death, and with it the crown of blessed martyrdom, which my Lord in his mercy had prepared for me (woe is me), there came into my mind those poisonous words spoken to me the day before by the heretical ministers, who made me lose that blessed crown with the fear of death and the sweetness of this life, and now I wander like a

When the Catholics learned of the sorrow and anxiety which this miserable young man endured for having fallen in his weakness, they were inspired to beware, offering yet more prayers to God to hold them in his hand and not to permit them to fall.

---

lost sheep, in the unbearable agony of my soul. Pray to God for me, and let all learn from my example not to trust in their own fortitude, nor pay any heed to the deceitful arguments of the heretics.'" Persons, *Relacion*, 15^r–16^r.

The Martyrdom in Oxford of Two Priests and Two Catholic Laymen[1]

The heretics were not satisfied with all the copious Catholic blood they spilled in the year 1588 with the occasion and in the manner we have mentioned, but rather deepened their cruelty, perpetrating further martyrdoms in the year 1589, no less atrocious or glorious than those before. In one of these cases, in the university town of Oxford, they arrested two priests, one named George Nichols and the other Yaxley, both of the seminary at Rheims, from the house of an old Catholic widow, in the middle of the night and with considerable commotion, together with a knight called Belson, who had come to visit Father George, and a domestic of the house by the name of Humphrey, a true servant of God who had tended to Catholics in need for more than twelve years.[2] The agents of the law ordered the widow to keep to her house as though it were a prison, setting large bonds and impounding all her property, while they hauled the four men, the two priests and the two laymen, before the vice-chancellor of the university, who examined them alongside twelve other judges. In the presence of a huge crowd, Father George affirmed in a voice loud and clear and with a steadfast heart, "I confess that, by the grace of God and the Apostolic See, I am a priest of the true, holy Catholic, and Apostolic Roman Church." Nothing more was needed to declare him a traitor, as well as the others, and to afflict and torment them horribly—and all the more so when they saw that the said priest had confounded the heretical ministers who tried to dispute with him, embarrassingly forcing them to silence. And so, after they had been imprisoned and dragged to court several times, chained and loaded with irons, the judges, unable to sway them or force out of them the things they desired, ordered that all four be sent to London, with the greatest possible humiliation. Thus it was done, with the four men suffering countless injuries, insults, and

---

1 Much of the text of this chapter is taken from a letter printed in Persons, *Relacion*, 22^r–41^r.

2 Thomas Belson (c.1563–89), scion of a recusant family, was arrested on May 18, 1589 at the Catherine Wheel Inn in Oxford, together with two priests, George Nichols (d.1589) and Richard Yaxley (d.1589), and Humphrey Pritchard (d.1589), a servant. All four were executed in Oxford on July 5, 1589. Christine J. Kelly, "Belson, Thomas (*bap.* 1563, *d.*1589)," in ODNB, 5:45–46.

abuses all along the route from the cruelty and savagery of the officers who accompanied them.

On reaching London, the shouts, blasphemies, and hateful words with which the Catholics were received by all the city's heretics were beyond belief. Everyone came out to gape at them, as though they were monsters, and to follow them to the prison, but the captives were prepared and armed with patience to suffer with joy all the humiliations and injuries that their enemies chose to give them, for the love of their most sweet savior Jesus Christ, whose cross they bore embedded within their hearts.

After they had been in the dungeons of London for several days, they were brought before Francis Walsingham, secretary to the council of state, a notorious heretic and a dire enemy to all Catholics.[3] He demanded many things of them, in hopes of entrapping them and finding an opportunity to persecute those who had sheltered and supported them. But Father George Nichols did not reply, save that they were all Catholics, and he a priest (although unworthy) of the Roman Church. Here the heretic exclaimed with fierce rage, "If you are a priest, then you are a traitor to the royal crown!" The servant of God replied, "I marvel much, my lord, at your conclusion, for the first to illuminate this kingdom of England and take it from the shadows of idolatry was a priest, those who have subsequently instructed us in the light of the Gospel and the faith we profess were priests, those who have most adorned and honored this realm in every conceivable respect have been priests." The secretary retorted, "Those priests had different offices from yours, which is to disturb the realm and incite it against the queen." "If to preach the Gospel of Jesus Christ," said the priest, "and to teach the true faith and Catholic religion to the ignorant is to disturb the realm, I confess to you that we priests disturb it; but if there is a real difference between the one and the other, why do you commit so great an injury to God and so notorious an outrage to his ministers?"

In the end, when the heretics could not get what they desired, they threw the two priests into an infamous house among criminal and degenerate men and tortured them, keeping them suspended in the air for fifteen hours at a stretch, without being able to extract a word of what they sought, all the while the saintly priests endured their punishments with supreme patience and joy. When torture availed them nothing, the heretics turned to tricks and ruses. They sent a well-trained confederate to pretend to be a Catholic and to confide

---

3 Francis Walsingham served as Elizabeth's principal secretary from 1573 until his death in 1590. The secretary was "the man who sat at the heart of the machine of the Elizabethan state," as well as bearing responsibility for the government's extensive network of spies and informants. Alford, *Watchers*, 53–54.

in them: he was to tell them that he was a Catholic and wished to be instructed the tenets of our sacred faith, and that, given the danger and all the many spies and false Catholics, he had not dared to reveal himself to anyone but them, seeing the extraordinary mercy God had done them in making them martyrs and suffering for their faith, and to implore them to teach him what he was to do and to tell him to whom he might turn in their place, so that his soul might be guided toward eternal life. In addition to being a learned man and a servant of God, Father George was also very prudent, and immediately smelled out this wickedness. He told the man what he suspected and refused to go any further or to name any others. At this the sham Catholic was outfaced, and he caused Father George to be thrown into a deep, filthy hole, full of poisonous vermin, while they bore the others off to London, threatening them with new tortures. There they remained until the council determined that they and the two laymen should be returned to Oxford, where they would be punished to intimidate and edify the students. With this decision they returned them to Oxford, with the same treatment as they had been brought thence—and even much worse.

Before everything else, the heretics condemned the good old woman in whose house the Catholics had been arrested to life imprisonment and the loss of all her property. So good a Catholic and so dedicated a servant of our Lord was she that she took it for a sublime payment for the thirty years of services she had done in harboring Catholics and priests in her house, to see herself despoiled of it and of all her wealth, and her liberty forfeit. What is more, she desired and entreated God that he grant her the mercy to die with her spiritual fathers and sons. This done, sentence was given against the clerics, who were to be drawn, hanged, and quartered as traitors, because they had been ordained by the pope's authority against the queen's command and entered her realm without her permission, for the purpose of disrupting it and spreading false doctrines, and against the two laymen, who were to be hanged for being the companions and accomplices of the said priests.

On hearing their sentence, the servants of God thanked him for the inestimable kindness he had done them, and they embraced each other with the greatest signs of happiness. And on the day they were to be put to death, they greeted the huge crowd that awaited them with countenances devout and joyful, saying, "We come to die for the confession of the Catholic faith, which is the faith of our fathers and of our grandfathers."

The first offered up in sacrifice was Father George, who first offered a prayer to the Lord, and then a declaration of his faith; and though he wished to speak a few words to the people, the heretics did not permit him, and so his life came to its saintly end. After him came the other priest, who, having regarded George as a master and father, embraced his corpse and asked his soul to pray to God for him. Likewise wishing to address the people, he was likewise denied, and after making a profession of his faith he died, greatly moving all those present, for he was a noble youth, of the finest qualities and a pleasing appearance. In the third place came the knight Belson, an upright young man; coming to the gallows and seeing the dead bodies of the priests left in quarters, he kissed them with the utmost tenderness and reverence, entreating their souls (which were already rejoicing in God) to win him the grace to follow them with fortitude and steadfastness, for he held himself most fortunate in having been their spiritual son and in being presented to God in such excellent company, and with this he joyously gave his soul to God.

The last, who completed this glorious *auto*, was the good servant Humphrey, who ascended to the place of martyrdom as though to a feast, with a happy, smiling countenance. Standing on the scaffold, he turned to the crowd and said, "Good people, I call you to witness, in the presence of God and his angels, that today I die for the confession of the Catholic faith." His words stung a heretical minister, who cried, "You wretch, you do not even know what 'Catholic' means, and yet you speak in this fashion?" The martyr replied, "I well know what it is to be a Catholic, although I know not how to explain it with the words of theology, and I know, too, what I should believe—that is, all that the holy mother Roman Church believes—and I shall prove it with my blood." And with this he took his leave of them all, and died holily.

The spectacle of the sentence carried out in Oxford provoked strong feelings among those who were present, and no less wonder, which grew with the novelty of what I am about to relate. The heads and quarters of the two priests and sacred martyrs, according to the tenor of their sentence, were placed upon the old ramparts of Oxford Castle, whither the heretical ministers went to see them with pleasure and pride—but when they saw them still utterly beautiful, the rage and devilish spirit they bore within them drove them to attack the heads, slashing the faces repeatedly to ruin and disfigure them, and for this reason the judges subsequently ordered them to be removed and placed, with the quarters, over the city gates.

There they hung the upper quarters such that all the hands fell downwards—but the right hand of Father George miraculously rose up of its own accord, as though menacing the city. And although certain heretics attempted (as is their wont) to obscure this marvel, proclaiming that it was perfectly natural, some contraction of the nerves, yet all the Catholics—and most of the heretics—understood that this was a work beyond nature, one of the Lord himself. For since the quarters had been boiled in scalding water, how could there be any contraction of the nerves? Especially when one remembers that this father, standing before the judges and seeing the wickedness and injustice with which they condemned them, contrary even to the laws of the kingdom, had told them to bear in mind that there was another, greater, mightier judge, who would investigate them, and would punish that outrage with eternal torment. Now, since they had refused to hear him while he lived, it seems our Lord willed that when he was dead he should threaten them and preach to them.

This opinion was confirmed by the opinion common to all of Father George's holiness, and of the fervor, zeal, charity, and joy with which for six years he had worked unceasingly across the country to win souls for God. They also recalled certain noteworthy and miraculous events that God had worked through him during this holy ministry. One of these was that when a heretical youth named Arcot, an infamous thief and felon, was imprisoned in Oxford Castle, several Catholics in the prison attempted to bring him to recognize his sins and turn to God and the Catholic faith, and convince him that as he must die, he should die as a Catholic, receiving death in requital of his grievous sins. Well, since the young man was bright and well inclined, he opened his heart to this ray of divine light and showed himself prepared to follow the Catholics' advice. By letters, they informed Father George, who furnished them with the method by which to lead that soul to acknowledge and repent its guilt and to prepare itself to confess them at the time he would arrange. Following these instructions, the thief (by divine grace) came to feel his sins so deeply that by day and by night he did nothing but shed tears, wishing to die already to satisfy God. One night, he was informed that he must die on the following morning, and he rushed to the Catholics, throwing himself on the floor and wailing, "I am here, my lords, my fathers, my masters, I am here, I die, and I die without confession!" He spent the entire night bemoaning his sins, doing penance, and praying to God not to abandon him in such necessity. The next morning, they announced the sentence to be carried out, and a huge crowd gathered from throughout the region, for the thief was well known and notorious. Among those who came was the good George (whom the Catholics had alerted), in the guise of a knight, who entered the prison as though a relative of the thief's come to visit and console him. After he had greeted Arcot openly, they went a little apart from the others, under a tree in the courtyard of the jail, and there he talked to him as though consoling and exhorting before death, and the thief confessed himself with copious tears. And Father George discreetly absolved him, embraced him, and bade him farewell, and then left the prison without being recognized. Then the thief declared himself as a Catholic, and however much the heretics beat him, they could never undermine or corrupt him; rather, brought to the gallows he said joyously that if he had a thousand lives, he would happily give them all for the confession of the Catholic faith, and this he said with such emotion and piety that he kissed the instruments of death, the cord, the restraints, the ladder, the gallows, even the hangman himself, provoking admiration for the change the Lord had wrought in the heart of a highwayman; giving hope of pardon for any sinner, no matter how grievous, who chose to convert; and manifesting the power of the Catholic religion—which in this, as in everything else, is divine, and perfectly distinct from all the sects of infidels and heretics and from any other false creed—in winning souls.[4]

---

4   Catholic priests habitually sought out notorious criminals, with an eye toward the propaganda coup to be won through the conversion of such figures. Parallel episodes are also told of Puritan ministers. Peter Lake and Michael C. Questier, "Prisons, Priests and People," in *England's Long Reformation: 1500–1800*, ed. Nicholas Tyacke, The Neale Colloquium in British History (London: UCL Press, 2003), 195–234, here 214–15.

Further Martyrs Who Died in London

In the year 1590, the priests Edward Jones and Anthony Middleton were imprisoned.[1] The former had been in England for many years and reaped a great harvest of souls; because he wore a small beard, and seemed of few years, he was
not taken for a priest, and so he long remained unnoticed.[2] The latter had only
just come to England, but since he was a zealous man and a gifted preacher, he
won great renown among the Catholics, and was therefore fiercely hated and
persecuted by the heretics. Both were captured in London through the trickery of various spies, heretics who pretended to be Catholics with the intent
of exposing and apprehending them. After the pair was arrested, two gallows
were erected in front of the houses where they were held, and without hearing
the case, holding a trial, or giving sentence, they were hanged and quartered,
with a placard placed above the gallows with these words: "For treason, and
for favoring the invasion of this realm plotted by foreigners," in the hope that
this slander would render them hateful to the people. But witness how much
greater is the innocence and constancy of the just than the malice and deceit
of the heretics. For in the city of London, where they had suffered, the crowd
that assembles when any Catholic is executed usually shouts and shrieks and
calls them "traitor"—but in this case they did not do so, instead keeping silent
and returning home sorrowful, sullen, and perturbed.[3]

---

1 Edward Jones (d.1590) and Anthony Middleton (d.1590) were executed in London on May 6,
   1590. Pollen, *Unpublished Documents*, 182–86.

2 The final clause of this sentence was added in the 1595 edition.

3 Ribadeneyra's account of Jones, Middleton, and Christopher Bales (1564–90) is a translation
   of an Italian text, itself based on letters written from England in 1590: *Relatione*, 3–6.
   Cf. A letter from John Curry (c.1552–96) to Robert Persons, dated May 12, 1590, which may
   have been one of the sources for the *Relatione*. "These priests were shortly followed by two
   others (Jones and Middleton), one of whom was in great repute with the Catholics for his
   sermons, by which he moved many to a better life, and filled them with courage to profess the
   faith. [...] Being brought to trial, the only charge against him was that he had acted as a priest.
   His defence was long and bold, showing plainly to all men the cruelty of the heretics and
   his own innocence. After a day or two they are led to the place of execution [in Fleet Street
   near the Conduit], where the populace had gathered in great numbers. Mr. Jones, seeing this
   charge written on top of the gallows, *For Treason And Favouring Of Foreign Invasion*, cried
   out that it was utterly false." John Hungerford Pollen, ed., *Acts of English Martyrs Hitherto
   Unpublished* (London: Burns and Oates, 1891), 315–16.

Father Anthony Middleton, standing on the ladder about to be hanged, begged permission to address four words to the people, and this was denied him. And so he said, "As I cannot speak at length, I say to you only that I call God to witness that they have put me to death for the Roman Catholic faith and for being a priest and preaching the word of God, and I entreat his divine majesty to accept this death in remission of my sins, and for the strengthening of the Catholics in his sacred faith and the converting of the heretics."[4] At these words, a knight mounted on a horse in the midst of the crowd of onlookers called out, "You have spoken well, father, and it is enough." He was immediately arrested and carried off to prison along with another knight, his companion.[5]

In London, at the beginning of Lent, they put to death Father Christopher Bales, a priest, but in a different fashion, for it was with a semblance of justice and by means of a trial: having been ordained by the pope's authority and having been at Rome, he had entered England illegally, and for this alone he was condemned.[6] First they savagely tortured him to learn where he had said Mass, and who had housed and aided him: they hung him up and stretched him for nearly twenty-four hours, but so steadfast was his constancy, endurance, and discretion, that he edified the Catholics in the extreme, and astonished the heretics.

At the time of pronouncing sentence, when the judges asked him if he had anything else to say in his defense, he said, "Only one thing remains for me to ask: would Saint Augustine, who was sent to England by Pope Saint Gregory as a preacher and instructor of the faith, have been a traitor, or not?" And when they answered that he would not, the saint said, "Then why do you accuse me and condemn me to death as a traitor, who have been sent to England by the same Apostolic See that sent Augustine, and have come for the same reason that Augustine came, and have been charged with nothing that could not be charged of Saint Augustine?"[7] But these arguments did nothing to forestall his

---

4   Henry Walpole (1558–95) wrote of Middleton, "He said that he did not doubt but that the shedding of his blood would confirm a great many of Catholics in England." Pollen, *Acts*, 309.

5   Cf. Curry's letter. "In these martyrdoms there is a fact we must not omit to mention. While they were being tried, they had cast friendly glances at their companions and acquaintances. These were forthwith seized and imprisoned in the closest confinement." Ibid., 318.

6   Christopher Bales, a Durham-born priest who had studied at the English College at Rome, was executed in London on March 4, 1590, as a seminary priest. J.T. Rhodes, "Bales, Christopher (1564–1590)," in *ODNB*, 3:486.

7   Cf. a catalog of English martyrs compiled by Richard Barret (d.1599), printed in 1590: "At the beginning of this Lent there was put to death the Reverend Christopher Bales, under pretext of justice and by way of trial, because, after being made priest by the authority of the Pope, he had come into England against the laws, and for this he was condemned. He had been

conviction, alongside a citizen of London named Horner, condemned for having aided several priests. A noteworthy thing befell him on the night before he was to die, which was that while on his knees in the gloomy dungeon, praying with a candle, he saw a crown above the shadow of his head: putting his hands to the top of his head, he found nothing there. He arose and began to move about, to see whether it was his imagination, or some trick of the eye, but as he moved, so moved the crown above the shadow of his head, and this vision lasted an hour, leaving him deeply consoled, for he believed that this was the Lord calling and urging him to martyrdom. And the result was clearly seen the following day, for he died with extraordinary fortitude and joy.[8]

That same year of 1590, two religious of the Bridgettine Order, returning from Spain, whither they had gone to implore His Majesty the Catholic King to aid the exiled convent of English nuns of their order at Rouen in France—with considerable success, His Majesty having doubled his previous support—were seized by the heretics at La Rochelle, through the treachery of the captain of the very ship in which they were traveling.[9] In La Rochelle, they were brought before the prince of Béarn,[10] interrogated on his orders, and so abused for days

---

tortured, and hung up off the ground by the hands for little less than twenty-four hours, in order to make him confess where he had said Mass, and who had kept him. But he stood firm... and answered with a constancy and prudence which edified the Catholics and made the heretics wonder. His piety and faith were especially conspicuous at his death. He was asked by the judge according to custom... when judgment was about to be pronounced, if he had anything to say for himself. He answered, 'This only do I want to know, whether St. Augustine sent hither by St. Gregory was a traitor or not.' They answered that he was not... He answered them, 'Why then do you condemn me to death as a traitor. I am sent hither by the same see: and for the same purpose as he was. Nothing is charged against me that could not also be charged against the Saint.' But for all that they condemned him, and with him a citizen of London called Horner, for having given aid and support to priests." Pollen, *Unpublished Documents*, 179.

8   The layman Nicholas Horner (d.1590), accused of having harbored Bales, was hanged alongside the priest on March 4, 1590. Rhodes, "Bales, Christopher," in *ODNB*, 3:486.

9   Ribadeneyra takes the story of the misadventures of John Marsh (d.1601) and John Vivian (d.1624) from a letter of Elizabeth Sander to Sir Francis Englefield, printed in Spanish translation in Persons, *Relacion*, 42^r–58^r.

     John Bossy notes that English Catholics frequently sailed in and out of the Protestant stronghold of La Rochelle to avoid suspicion. Bossy, "Rome and the Elizabethan Catholics," 139.

10   Henry IV was known as prince of Béarn and duke of Vendôme before his accession to the throne of Navarre in 1572. Ribadeneyra may use these lesser (and outdated) titles as a sign of disrespect for the Protestant monarch.

on end that had it not been for a French Catholic who secretly supplied them with food, they would have starved to death in prison.

After many days, Vendôme ordered that they be handed over to an English heretic to be carried to England as prisoners—for, recognizing that they were both poor and unyielding, so that he could extract neither ransom nor information from them, he decided to curry favor with the queen of England by sending her this present. The captain of the English ship to whom they were entrusted was a savage, barbaric man, such as seemed to have no shred of human nature, who treated them with monstrous brutality. To increase the sufferings and the merits of the servants of God, the voyage from La Rochelle to England, usually only a few days, lasted sixty—and in all this time, in addition to being loaded with irons and chains and exposed, practically nude, in the depths of winter, the fathers were given nothing to eat besides a few salted beans and some water, without bread, and this in such tiny quantities that they were perishing of hunger. Even the heretical passengers in the ship appealed to the captain, but he was so obstinate, so much an enemy to religious, that nothing they said had any impact; instead, he attributed the storms and contrary winds his vessel endured to his carrying those enemies of God (as he called them), and therefore repeatedly attempted to throw them in the sea to drown.[11] Yet, in the midst of some dire peril and necessity, his own conscience brought him to recognize that they were friends of God, and so he spoke kindly to them, begging them to pray to God to save the ship and promising to treat them better. But since that sentiment was born of fear, not virtue, practically extracted by force, as soon as the danger had passed he returned to his natural cruelty. At the end of two months, with countless, serious, and painful travails, they left the sea and were received on land with other, even greater harassments from the heretics, who cast them into prison to abuse and murder them.

---

11   Cf. Jon. 1:4–15.

The Death of Francis Walsingham, the Queen's Secretary

The beginning of 1591 saw the death of Francis Walsingham, the queen's secretary of state, a savage man of harsh and choleric character, and a thorough heretic, unbelievably zealous in extending the sect of Calvin in every direction. With diabolical fervor he dedicated himself to viciously persecuting Catholics, and through his considerable political power—due to his position, the queen's favor, and the earl of Leicester's friendship—he perpetrated numerous awful cruelties against them. But he distinguished himself most in two things. First, in persecuting the seminaries and the priests who lived there. Second, in sowing cockles and discord among princes and kindling fires in foreign realms,[1] so as to preserve peace in England. The hatred and abhorrence that this evil man harbored and displayed toward the seminaries is evident all he did to destroy them, if only he could. At first he attempted to have the Most Christian King of France expel all English Catholics from his realm, and especially those at the seminary in Rheims; when he could not achieve this, he cast about for some way of unsettling and alienating the spirits of the young men who lived in the seminaries, or of sowing division in their midst.[2] This, too, came to nothing: rather, having recognized his guile and his trickery, the youths dedicated themselves all the more to their holy intention and drew even closer one to another, and so from the viper's venom they made theriac.[3] After this, he attempted to poison Doctor Allen, then the rector of the college at Rheims and the principal founder and sustainer of the seminaries, imagining that once this pillar had been toppled, the entire edifice would fall, and for this purpose he sent several men, Englishmen and men of other nations, to France and Italy. And his

---

1 Matt. 13:25.

2 Prov. 6:14, 6:19.

3 "Theriac" was a preparation first theorized by ancient Greek physicians: originally a treatment for snakebite, the term came to refer to a quasi-miraculous panacea, often thought to derive from the venom of various creatures. See Christiane Nockels Fabbri, "Treating Medieval Plague: The Wonderful Virtues of Theriac," *Early Science and Medicine* 12, no. 3 (2007): 247–83.

   Ribadeneyra's source does not make explicit reference to Walsingham: "Other times, they ordered men to Rome and Rheims who secretly sought to create dissension, and sow cockles and conflicts in the souls of the youths, but they did not succeed. Quite the contrary, as from the viper they made theriac." *Relatione*, 13–14.

wickedness progressed even further, for he tried to envenom the water supply at the seminary, to have done with them all at once.[4] But because the Lord was pleased with their service and they had been founded with his blessing, all the craft and malice of men has been powerless to undermine or harm them.

The other thing to which Walsingham devoted himself was (as has been said) kindling and feeding fires in neighboring kingdoms and states, to which he committed the utmost diligence and exquisite means. And to this end he spent and frittered away his wealth on spies, observers, informants, and correspondents, which he maintained in every province, Catholic and heretic, Christian and infidel. With this information and his position as secretary of state, he had the queen's confidence—and he colored things just as he pleased, and she knew nothing more than served his turn. (This is one of the harms princes suffer when their confidants are not all they should be.) But, just as Walsingham was at the height of his power and prosperity, living in the greatest splendor, pride, and magnificence—though he had spent all his wealth, and that of his friends, in serving the queen and persecuting Catholics—God struck him down, visiting upon him a shameful, ghastly abscess in his guts, from which, like another Antiochus or Maximianus[5] he ended his wretched life and began the death without end, leaving every Catholic in the kingdom offering their thanks to our Lord, who had freed them from the hands of so heartless an executioner, and by his death instructed men not to trust so much to temporal felicity, nor to imagine that what is fleeting, brief, and momentary could last forever.[6]

---

4   "Many times they have schemed to poison and murder Mr. Allen, now a cardinal and then the superior of the college at Rheims, as the person upon whom the enterprise rested, and to this end various men were sent, some from England, some from other lands, to Italy and France. And another time, they likewise tried to poison the water, and thus murder all the students." *Relatione*, 14.

     The welcoming atmosphere of the college at Rheims made it facile for English spies to penetrate the community, and the late 1570s saw at least two assassination attempts made against Allen. Eamon Duffy, "Allen, William (1532–1594)," in *ODNB*, 1:824–31, here 826.

5   In the margin: "2 Maccabees 9[:5–10], Eusebius, *History*, Book 3 [*vere* 8], Chapter 28 [*vere* 16]."

     The reference to Eusebius comes from Persons, who gives the citation "Euseb. li. 8. cap 28." It seems likely that Ribadeneyra or someone in the printing process misread the first "8" as "3."

     Walsingham died in London on April 6, 1590, with Catholic writers almost immediately circulating lurid stories about his disgusting condition and agonizing end. John Cooper, *The Queen's Agent: Francis Walsingham at the Court of Elizabeth I* (London: Faber and Faber, 2011), 322–23.

6   "By dint of his office, he dedicated himself to [...] reporting to the queen what was done in parliament, and to keep her informed of things done by others, in other realms throughout the world. He expended extraordinary efforts in this, so as to have countless things to fill the

queen's ears, and for this reason he had enormous hordes of spies in every princely court and every republic, who reported to him by frequent letters what was done, what was said, and even what was thought. When he had received these things, and then fashioned and shaped them to his liking—true or false, but always auspicious—he fed the queen's soul [with them]. […] In these matters, and in maintaining his spies, and in his luxurious and magnificent lifestyle, he poured out such sums of money that he was eventually ruined by his crushing debts. He was also struck by the Lord with a dire abscess and an incurable disease of the lower parts of his body, no different from that of Galerius Maximianus, as Eusebius relates." *Philopater*, 20.

Of the Crosses That Appeared in England[1]

In the same year of 1591, on April 23, the day of Saint George the martyr, the patron saint of England, toward the evening, in the county of Norfolk in the kingdom of England, there appeared in the sky an enormous circle and two smaller ones, with a sun within each of them. The sun in the middle was the clearest and most resplendent; the two on the sides did not shed as much light, though each would have sufficed to light up the night. The sun in the center was surrounded by a small circle, which looked toward the west and intersected the larger circle. Within this larger circle there was another small one, and within that a cross, in the form of a cross of Saint Andrew, between the north and the south. Beyond this smaller circle, toward the eastern part, opposite from the sun in the middle, there was another cross, also like Saint Andrew's, but greater and clearer than the other, which also intersected the larger circle.[2] Many witnessed these circles and crosses, as trustworthy men have written from England. The apparition of the crosses has provoked many debates and competing interpretations.[3] Father Master Brother Alfonso Chacón, of the Order of Preachers, wrote and printed in Rome a treatise on this and other, similar portents, specifically of crosses, such as were seen in May of the same year in Bourges, Amiens, and other towns in France, as well as in the city of Paris, where numerous crosses were seen on different days and in different churches, on the surplices, albs, chasubles, altar cloths, and corporals—and some of them so fixed that they could not be taken out or removed by any means or effort whatsoever.[4] What the Lord wished to signify by these crosses, he alone knows, for although his divine majesty often stirs up men by such marvels, he does not always choose to manifest his will to them, in order that they might submit themselves to him and remain dependent on his ineffable and secret providence.[5] What I can say is that the cross is always a symbol of joy and consolation to its friends, and of sorrow and pain to its foes.

---

1 As Ribadeneyra acknowledges, this chapter is a pastiche of chapters from Alfonso Chacón, *De signis sanctissimae crucis, quae diuersis olim orbis regionibus & nuper hoc anno 1591 in Gallia & Anglia diuinitus ostensa sunt, & eorum expliciatione, tractatus* (Rome: Apud Ascanium, & Hieronymum Donangelos, 1591).

2 See Book 3 Figure 6.1.

3 Cf. Chacón, *De signis*, 65–74.

4 Cf. Ibid., 74–75.

5 Rom. 11:33.

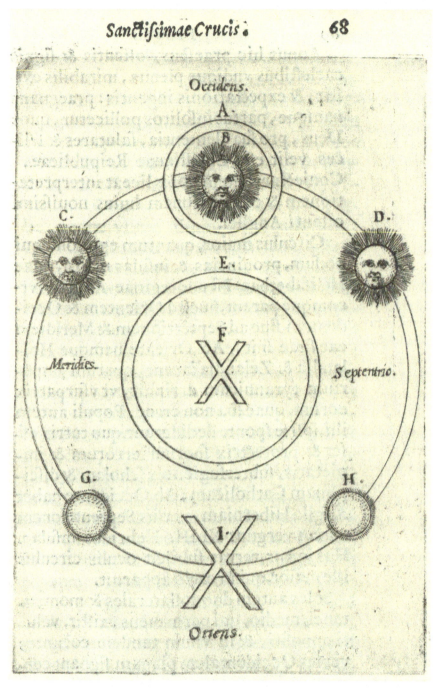

FIGURE 6.1   *A diagram of the apparitions seen in Norfolk on April 23, 1593.*
Alfonso Chacón, *De signis sanctissimae crucis, quae diuersis olim orbis*
regionibus & nuper hoc anno 1591 in Gallia & Anglia diuinitus ostensa sunt,
& eorum expliciatione, Tractatus (Rome: Apud Ascanium, & Hieronymum
Donangelos, 1591). *SC5 C3444 591d, Houghton Library, Harvard University.

We know that the cross Constantine saw in the sky when he was going to war with the tyrant Maxentius was a sign of the victory God intended to give him, which he bestowed by virtue of that same cross, as the voice from heaven told him: "Constantine, in this sign you shall conquer."⁶ And we know, too, that the cross that appeared over the hill of Calvary and extended to the Mount of Olives while Saint Cyril was patriarch of Jerusalem was a portent of numerous glorious victories.⁷ And, since we are speaking of England, in the year 819, when Oengus, king of the Picts, was warring with Æthelstan, king of the Angles [*Ingleses*],⁸ and saw himself in peril, he implored Saint Andrew the Apostle to favor him in the battle he was to fight. And the holy apostle appeared to him and promised that on the following day he would triumph (as he did), in witness whereof a cross of Saint Andrew appeared in the sky over the hosts of the Picts, distinct and glorious.⁹

---

6   In the margin: "Eusebius, *Life of Constantine*, Chapters 22, 23, 24."

   Cf. Chacón, *De signis*, 5–6.

7   In the margin: "Gregory of Nazianzus, fourth oration, against Julian; Nikephoros, Book 7, Chapter 49; Sozomen, [*Ecclesiastical History*], Book 4, Chapter 4 [*vere* 5]; Nikephoros, *Ecclesiasticae historia*, Book 9, Chapter 31 [*vere* 32]."

   Cf. Chacón, *De signis*, 13–14.

   The sheer number of marginal citations here makes it difficult to determine precisely what annotations are meant to gloss which examples. Ribadeneyra has here combined two different marginal annotation from Chacón. Gregory of Nazianzus's orations against Julian and Book 7, Chapter 49 of Nikephoros Kallistos Xanthopoulos's (*fl.* 1320) *Ecclesiastical History* (early fourteenth century) describe apparitions of crosses that Ribadeneyra does not discuss.

   Chacón's chapter on the crosses at Jerusalem also cites the Byzantine historian George Kedrenos's *Synopsis historion* (c.1057), as published in Latin translation: "In the nineteenth year of Constantius's reign, on the day of Pentecost, a shining image of the life-giving cross appeared in the sky, and it extended from Golgotha (where Christ was raised upon the cross) all the way to the Mount of Olives, whence Christ ascended to heaven, ringed by a similar heavenly circle. On the same day, it appeared to both Constantius and Cyril, bishop of Jerusalem." George Kedrenos, *Georgii Cedreni annales, sive historiae ab exordio mundi ad Isacium Comnenum usque compendium*, trans. William Xylander (Basel: Ioannes Oporinus, 1587), 248.

8   Oengus II mac Fergusa, king of the Picts and king of Fortriu (r.820–32), and (probably) Æthelstan, king of the East Angles (*fl.* early ninth century), respectively.

9   In the margin: "Hector Boece, *Historia Scotorum*, Book 10, page 190, and John Leslie, *De gestis Scotorum*, page 179 [*vere* 178]." This citation is taken from Chacón, although the page number for Leslie is incorrect.

   Hector Boece, *Scotorum historiæ prima gentis origine, cum aliarum et rerum et gentium illustratione non vulgari, Libri XIX* (Paris: François Le Preux, 1575), 190.

   John Leslie, *De origine, moribus, et rebus gestis Scotorum libri decem* (Rome: In aedibus populi Romani, 1578), 178.

   Cf. Chacón, *De signis*, 25–26.

And when the redoubtable captain general Afonso de Albuquerque and his Portuguese fleet were near the island called Comorin [*Camarena*], in the western part of the straits of the Red Sea [*mar Bermejo*], adjacent to the kingdom of Prester John, the emblem of the glorious and holy cross appeared in the sky, which he and all the soldiers and sailors revered with the utmost devotion and heavenly consolation. They took this divine portent as a sure sign of the victories the Lord intended to give them against the pagans and barbarians of India, where, on the conversion of the inhabitants, they would plant and worship the cross through which the Lord himself had conquered and defeated his enemies.[10]

And many other examples are to be found in histories sacred and secular, ancient and modern, to declare to us this truth, as well as the mercies our Lord has done for his Church, giving the cross as a pledge of his intentions. And on the other hand, we also read that crosses have often appeared as a terror and rebuke to the wicked, as befell Julian the Apostate when, to oppress the Christians and favor the Jews, he sought to rebuild the Temple of Jerusalem. The foundations had already been opened and all the materials were prepared for commencing the work, when they were consumed by a fire from heaven, and numerous black crosses appeared in the books and on the garments of the Christians, the Jews, and the pagans—which the Jews and infidels could not remove.[11] And all this was a chastisement to the depraved and godless emperor, who with such guile and impiousness had waged war on the cross and the Lord who died thereon for love of us.

---

10   Col. 2:14–15.

    In the margin: "The Annals of Portugal, and Maffei, Book 5, *History of the Indies*." These marginal annotations are taken directly from Chacón.

    Giovanni Pietro Maffei, *Historiarum Indicarum libri XVI: Selectarum item ex India epistolarum eodem interprete libri IIII; Acceßit Ignatij Loiolæ vita postremo recognita; Et in opera singula copiosus index* (Venice: Apud Damianum Zenarium, 1589), 85–86.

    I have not been able to identify the text Ribadeneyra and Chacón identify as "the Annals of Portugal," but the story originated with Afonso de Albuquerque (c.1453–1515) himself: see Afonso de Albuquerque, *Cartas de Affonso de Albuquerque seguidas de documentos que as elucidam*, ed. Raymundo Antonio de Bulhão Pato, 7 vols., Collecção de monumentos ineditos para a historia das conquistas dos Portuguezes em Africa, Asia e America 10 (Lisbon: Typographia da Academia Real das Sciencias, 1884), 1:399.

    Cf. Chacón, *De signis*, 49–50.

11   In the margin: "Socrates, [*Historia ecclesiastica*,] Book 3, Chapter 17 [*vere* 20]; Nikephoros, Book 10, Chapters 32 and 33; Kedrenos, [*Annales*,] page 252; Rufinus, [*Church History*], Book 10, Chapters 38 and 39 [*vere* 38–40]." These marginal annotations are taken from Chacón. From the 1595 edition, "page" is replaced "part [*parte*]," though this makes no sense in the context.

    Cf. Chacón, *De signis*, 35–39.

But it is not my intention to repeat here what is found in these histories as to the crosses that have appeared at various times and with various effects (whoever desires this may find it in the treatise of Father Brother Alfonso Chacón); all I wish to speak of is what recently happened in England, where so much Catholic blood has been spilled, to inspire them and those of France not lose to hope amid the storm they were enduring, however fierce and terrifying it might be, as long as they held fast to the Lord who died upon the cross to give us life[12] and in so doing conquered the earth, dismayed the hearts of the pagans, cast down idolatry, and defeated death, the world, and hell.

In the year of our Lord 529, when Justinian, second of that name [*sic*], was emperor, there was a horrendous earthquake in Antioch that devastated almost the entire city, driving the inhabitants barefoot from their houses, screaming and crying and begging the Lord for mercy. It was revealed to a saintly and religious man that they should write these words above the doors of their houses:[13] *Christus nobiscum, state*; Christ is with us, hold fast and be still. And this alone appeased the wrath of God, and the earth ceased to shake.[14] And the same thing befell Saint Euthymius [*sic*], patriarch of Constantinople, when he was forced from his see. On an island whither a storm had driven him, he saw a cross on a wall, with these words: *Christus nobiscum est, state*, and at this he was consoled.[15] And so ought every Catholic to be, for we know that Christ is with us and will be until the end of the world, as he himself has said and

---

12   John 10:10.

13   Cf. Exod. 12:7; Deut. 6:9, 11:20.

14   In the margin: "Nikephoros, Book 17, Chapter 3, and Book 14, Chapter 34. Kedrenos, [*Annales*,] page 303." These marginal annotations are taken from Chacón.

      Cf. Chacón, *De signis*, 86–87.

      Chacón has incorrectly identified the Byzantine emperor at the time of the earthquake: Justinian II reigned from 685 to 695, and again from 705 to 711. It was Justinian I (r.527–65) who was forced to deal with the aftermath of a devastating earthquake at Antioch—although the event itself actually took place in 526, during the reign of Justin I (r.518–27). Kenneth G. Holum, "The Classical City in the Sixth Century: Survival and Transformation," in *The Cambridge Companion to the Age of Justinian*, ed. Michael Maas, Cambridge Companions (Cambridge: Cambridge University Press, 2005), 87–112, here 99.

15   Both Ribadeneyra and Chacón identify this figure as "Euthymius [*Euthymio*]," but the legend in question attaches to a different patriarch of Constantinople, Eutychius (*c.*512–82). Exiled to the island of Principus (modern-day Büyükada) in the Sea of Marmara, "the blessed man landed there on a Sunday in winter, in the deepest night. When day came, before he did anything else, he saw the image of the cross on a wall, with this maxim: 'Christ is with us, hold fast.' At the sight of this, he was deeply encouraged, and thanked God for affording him this consolation." *AASS*, April 1, 558.

promised us,[16] and by the power of this heavenly symbol the winds will be quieted and the waves will be calmed, and the storm will be changed into prosperity, and a time will come when the sea, as soft as milk [*como vna leche*], will be trampled by the faithful servants of God and the true children of his holy Church.

---

16   Matt. 28:20.

The Arrival in England of Several Priests from the English Seminary at Valladolid, and What Came of This

At this time, eleven or twelve English priests entered England, the first fruits of the seminary at Valladolid sustained by the generosity of the Catholic King, other lords, and pious individuals (as will be related farther on). They came, as they usually do, in disguise; four of them, who were traveling in the guise of sailors and common seamen [*grumetes*], were seized, brought to court, and hauled before the admiral,[1] who set them free because of the full account they were able to give of themselves.[2] But once the deception was discovered and the heretics could not lay hands upon them in spite of all their efforts and they perceived that these were but the first of many such arrivals to come, you would not believe the fear and shock among the queen's council, as if the entire realm had already been conquered and lost to its enemies. To avenge themselves on those already in the country and to frighten those who intended to come, they decided to martyr two priests from the seminary at Rheims whom they had captured. One was named George Beesley, a youth of extraordinary spirit and fortitude, and the other Montford Scott, a man of rare virtue and sanctity who had labored in that vineyard for many years, to the benefit of innumerable souls; he received this reward from the Lord in recompense for his

---

1   Charles Howard, first earl of Nottingham (1536–1624), lord high admiral from 1585 to his death.

2   Twelve priests left Spain in April 1591, disguised as captured English sailors returning home. Though interrogated by the lord high admiral, they were sufficiently convincing to be released. Thomas M. McCoog, "Blount, Richard," in *ODNB*, 6:308–09, here 308.

    Cf. A letter from the priest John Cecil to Robert Persons, November 1, 1591. "the other two Blount and Younger were carried to the Admiral, and after 2 or 3 days examination were rewarded and dismissed. Mr. Fixer and myself were taken by the Queens ships over against Dover by Sir Henry Palmer, and by him sent jointly to the Admiral and Treasurer, who being both out of the way the one at sea the other at Tibalds with the Queen. We were kept at a man's house of his in Westminster, and there had sent us certain interrogatories of martial men and warlike affairs of the K's intentions & preparations and such like. After 5 or 6 days I only was carried to the Treasurer, and by word demanded the same questions, which in writing were tendered us, and so we were dismissed." Pollen, *Unpublished Documents*, 199.

efforts.[3] Both died with utter steadfastness, publicly professing our holy Catholic faith and refusing the queen's proffered pardon and grace.[4]

Other martyrs were made[5] elsewhere in England at this time, which a priest who was there has described in more detail in a letter I have thought it fitting to insert here.[6]

> The commonplace, everyday fruits here—he says[7]—are deaths, martyrdoms, tortures, crosses, and prisons, and all the letters we send you can be nothing but the calamities and miseries suffered by the Catholics, nor speak of anything but the deaths inflicted and the quantities of blood shed. The face and shape of the heretics' fury in England has not changed at all, nor the fierceness with which they persecute the Catholics. But blessed be the Lord, their fortitude and constancy is also as it always has been. Accordingly, let Your Reverence expect no new or unfamiliar theme in my letters, for the times are such that the heretics ask no question about the death or martyrdom of the servants of God, but only what torments they shall inflict, and by what sort of death they shall finish them off.
>
> In the city of York this April, the priest Robert Thorpe [*Thersio*], who was a student at the seminary at Rheims, fought valiantly and ended his race with the greatest joy.[8] And he was accompanied in his sacrifice by the layman Thomas Watkinson [*Batinsono*],[9] his partner in life and death

---

3 Ribadeneyra has taken the reference to the Parable of the Workers in the Vineyard (Matt. 20:1–16) from the letter he quotes below.

4 On July 1, 1591, two seminary priests, George Beesley (1562–91) and Montford Scott (d.1591) were hanged, drawn, and quartered at Fleet Street in London. Peter Holmes, "Beesley, George (1562–1591)," in *ODNB*, 4:821–22, here 821.

5 In the 1593 and 1594 editions, this phrase reads "Otros martyrios se hizieron," which would run, "Other martyrdoms were carried out."

6 This letter, dated September 20, 1591, was sent by John Cecil to Joseph Cresswell. Cecil's letter to Persons of November 1 is almost identical in content, but different in structure and phrasing—Ribadeneyra worked from the earlier letter, though it was the later of the two that circulated in Spanish translation. Pollen, *Unpublished Documents*, 199.

    For the partial transcription of the letter that survives as ABSI Stonyhurst, Collectanea M, fol. 187, see Appendix 4.

7 Added in the 1595 edition.

8 2 Tim. 4:7; Heb. 12:1.

9 Robert Thorpe (d.1591) and Thomas Watkinson (d.1591) were both executed at York on May 21, 1591: the former hanged, drawn, and quartered as a priest, the latter hanged for having harbored said priest. Henry Foley, *Records of the English Province of the Society of Jesus:*

and in the glory of martyrdom, who had greatly aided his labors in the vineyard of the Lord.

Another, similar martyrdom also came to pass in Winchester in July, to the public celebration and praise of every Catholic, for a priest named Roger Diconson and a married layman, Ralph Milner by name, died for the faith with the utmost constancy, and they have gone to rejoice in God.[10] And when the judge warned Ralph to come to his senses and take some thought for his young wife and his eight children, and that if he attended the Calvinists' church—even just once—they would pardon him and release him from the gallows whereon he stood, he responded with great soul and spirit that he was not so deluded as to abandon God for things of as little substance as a wife and children.[11] In him were proved the words of Christ our Redeemer, that he who does not hate his father, and his mother, and his wife, and his children, and even himself for love of him was not worthy of him.[12]

In the same place and court, seven noble maidens were condemned for having received this priest in their houses in order to say Mass. And when the judges, looking at them, did not dare to enforce a death sentence, they decided it would be sufficient to frighten them by announcing this and ordering them back to prison: the women began to shriek and sob, and fervently to implore the judges to execute their sentence, and not to separate them from their most beloved father, for it was right that having been companions in the crime, they should be companions in the death, and they hoped in God that as he had given them the spirit to do what they had done, he would also give it them to die gloriously for their

---

Historical Facts Illustrative of the Labours and Sufferings of Its Members in the Sixteenth and Seventeenth Centuries, 7 vols. (London: Burns and Oates, 1875–83), 3:746–50.

Cf. "In Easter and Whitsun term were martyred at York, to whose executions Toply the torturer went, a priest and a clerk, viz. Robert Thorpe and Thomas Watkinson." Pollen, *Unpublished Documents*, 200.

10   July 7, 1591 saw the execution of the priest Roger Diconson (d.1591) and the layman Ralph Milner (or Miller, d. 1591). Foley, *Records*, 3:297–98.

11   Cf. "At Winchester, Roger Dicconson and Ralph Milner, who, desiring the Judges to be good to his wife and 8 or 9 small children he had, was answered this: 'Go to Church, fool, and look to thy children thyself.' He replied that the loss of his soul was too high a price to pay for so small and vile a commodity, and so he died blessedly *in Domino*." Pollen, *Unpublished Documents*, 200.

12   Matt. 10:37; Luke 14:26.

holy Catholic faith.[13] O ladies, no ladies at all; O manly, valiant hearts; O human frailty and divine strength!

In London in the same month, two other priests died with wonderful joy and constancy, to the edification of their brothers. One was named George Beesley; before they killed him, he was tortured with exquisite torments to make him tell them which Catholics he had met and by whom he had been received and supported. But however much they badgered him, they could never get a thing out of him.[14]

Alongside Beesley, the priest Montford Scott, a wise and holy man, endured his martyrdom with such perfect calmness of spirit and gentleness that even the heretics were frightened, such that the commander of the queen's troops later boasted that he had done the realm a huge service in ridding it of so devout a papist, so worn out with penances, fasts, and vigils.[15]

This August, Thomas Pormort, a student of the Rheims seminary, was imprisoned in the Tower of London, and placed in the torture chamber.[16]

A very distinguished knight, Thomas Fitzherbert [*Fikiharbe*], is also now a prisoner in the Tower. Having made his nephew the heir to his wealth, the wicked nephew accused his uncle of receiving a priest in his

---

13   Cf. "With them were condemned 8 or 9 young damsels but not sentenced, the which with open outcries and exclamations urged the Judges most constantly that, as they were all culpable of the same crime, viz. of hearing Mass, relieving a priest, confessing their sins and serving their Saviour after the rite of the Catholic Church, so they might drink all of the same cup, with such fervour and vehemence that they made the whole assembly astonished." Pollen, *Unpublished Documents*, 200.

14   While he was imprisoned in the Tower, George Beesley was interrogated by Richard Topcliffe (1531–1604), Elizabeth's chief torturer, but revealed nothing. Holmes, "Beesley," in *ODNB*, 4:821.

15   Cf. "At London were martyred George Beesley and Mumford Scott of whom Topley [*sc.* Topcliffe] said that he had that day done the Queen and Kingdom a Singular piece of Service, in ridding the realm of such a praying and fasting papist as had not his peer in Europe." Pollen, *Unpublished Documents*, 200.

16   Thomas Pormort (*c*.1560–92) was briefly a student at Rheims, but received most of his training at the English college at Rome, where he was ordained in 1587. Returning to England at the very end of 1590, he was captured in August 1591; imprisoned at Bridewell, he was then transferred to Topcliffe's home for extended torture. Pormort was eventually martyred on February 21, 1592, at St Paul's churchyard, London. Richard Rex, "Pormort, Thomas (*c*.1560–1592)," in *ODNB*, 44:916–17, here 916. McCoog, *Building the Faith*, 61

Cf. "Mr. Portmort was taken some xx days before I departed, first committed to Bridewell, and then had to Topleys house, and men stood in fear of his confession." Pollen, *Unpublished Documents*, 200.

house so as to enjoy the inheritance. Already eighty years old, every day he wishes and hopes for a blessed death as a martyr.[17]

But just as a troubled river is a blessing to the fishermen[18] from the many fish that gather, so in the midst of these turbulent waters of the persecution of the Catholics, God our Lord consoles us with the abundant catch we win. In London, we have had sixty priests gather together, administering the sacraments, preaching frequently, reconciling several persons each day to the union of the holy Church, and, to be brief, our beloved brother Thomas Stanney [*Estauco*],[19] who was of your college, has won three hundred souls for the Lord in a single province. And when the queen recently came to this region for relaxation, the earl of Hertford,[20] the leader of the Puritans, told her that he could come to receive Her Majesty with twelve hundred papists who refused to attend the churches of their sect, if it should be required.

This is our hope, this our consolation, to see that in spiritual terms we meet with abundant success and that each day the number of the faithful grows, and also to see the dire divisions among the heretics themselves, how the Puritans frightfully persecute the Protestants, and the foremost warlords of the sea and the land are at odds and harbor grudges and mortal hatreds among themselves.

This is the priest's letter.

---

17   Thomas Fitzherbert (*c.*1550–1600) betrayed his father, a Catholic, in the wake of the Babington Plot. His father died in prison, leaving Thomas the only heir to his wealthy uncle, Sir Thomas Fitzherbert (d.1591), by this time also a prisoner in the Tower of London. The old gentleman disinherited his nephew, but this was overturned with the connivance of Topcliffe and Archbishop John Whitgift (*c.*1530–1604). J.E. Mousley and P.W. Hasler, "Fitzherbert, Thomas (*c.*1550–1600)," in P.W. Hasler, ed., *The House of Commons 1558–1603*, 3 vols., The History of Parliament (London: Her Majesty's Stationery Office, 1981), 2:125–26, here 125.

18   A Spanish proverb: "A río revuelto, ganancia de pescadores." "Refranero multilingüe."

19   Thomas Stanney (1558–1617) spent time as a student both in Rheims and Rome, before returning to England in 1581, where he achieved notable successes in winning and keeping converts and penitents. Foley, *Records*, 3:294–95.

20   Edward Seymour, first earl of Hertford (*c.*1539–1621).

Of Three False Puritan Prophets Who Appeared in England[1]

At the same time that in London they were martyring so many priests and Catholic laypeople, three Puritan heretics emerged of quite a different spirit and character. They announced that they were prophets of God, sent by him to relieve that kingdom. The first, called Coppinger, said that he was a prophet of mercy. The second, whose name was Arthington, declared that he was a prophet of justice and vengeance.[2] And the third, called Hacket [*Harqueloto*], that

---

1   I have not been able to identify a specific source for this chapter, but repeated mentions of William Hacket (d.1591) and his confederates in the writings of Robert Persons, Thomas Stapleton, and Richard Verstegan (*c.*1550–1640) indicate that the story was circulating among Catholics on the Continent. Robert Persons, *Elizabethæ, Angliae reginae haeresin Calvinianam propugnantis, sævissimum in Catholicos sui regni edictum, quod in alios quóque reipublicæ christianae principes contumelias continet indignissimas: Promulgatum Londini 29. Nouembris 1591; Cum responsione ad singula capita, qua non tantùm sæuitia & impetas tam iniqui edicti, sed mendacia quóque, & fraudes, & imposturæ dereguntur, & confutantur; Per D. Andream Philopatrum presbyterum, ac theologum Romanum, ex Anglia olim oriundum* (Lyon: Pierre Roussin apud Jean Didier, 1593), 39–40. Robert Persons, *An Aduertisement Written to a Secretarie of My L. Treasurers of Ingland, by an Inglishe Intelligencer as He Passed Throughe Germanie Towardes Italie Concerninge an Other Booke Newly Written in Latin, and Published in Diuerse Languages and Countreyes, against Her Maiesties Late Proclamation, for Searche and Apprehension of Seminary Priestes, and Their Receauers, Also of a Letter Vvritten by the L. Treasurer in Defence of His Gentrie, and Nobility, Intercepted, Published, and Answered by the Papistes* (Antwerp, 1592), 20. Stapleton, *Apologia pro rege Catholico Philippo II Hispaniæ, & cæt. rege. contra varias & falsas accusationes Elisabethæ Angliæ reginæ: Per edictum suum 18 Octobris Richemondiæ datum, & 20 Nouembris Londini proclamatum, publicatas & excusas* ([Leuven]: apud Theodorus Samius, 1592), 209–10. Richard Verstegan, *The Letters and Despatches of Richard Verstegan* (*c. 1550–1640*), ed. Anthony G. Petti, Publications of the Catholic Record Society 52 (London: Catholic Record Society, 1959), 2, 87, 135.

2   Edmund Coppinger (*c.*1555–91) was a scion of a poor, fiercely Protestant Suffolk gentry family. Making his way to London, he entered presbyterian circles, where he befriended the Yorkshire gentleman Henry Arthington (d.1609). The two became associates of the Northamptonshire maltster and self-proclaimed messiah William Hacket. Amid their fervid attempts to reform the Church of England, Coppinger and Arthington became convinced they were "prophets of mercy and judgment, divinely appointed lieutenants of Hacket, the new messiah and supreme king of the earth." Alexandra Walsham, "Coppinger, Edmund (*c.*1555–1591)," in *ODNB*, 13:372–73.

he incarnated Jesus Christ. They ascended some carts in a London square and, summoning the people in loud voices, put to them who they were and why they had come,[3] and denounced the queen's religion and her government, rebuking

---

Cf. The official account of the prophets: "*Coppinger* tolde him, that God (the night before) had enlightned him the said *Coppinger,* who they all three were, saying, that *Arthington* had vnawares prophesied truely: for he was the greatest *Prophet of Gods iudgements* against the whole world, that euer was, but that they both were greater then he: for *Coppinger* himselfe was (he said) the greatest that euer was, and last *Prophet of mercie:* and that he must describe the newe and holie *Ierusalem,* with the seuerall places of ioy, that the elect should enioy after this life, and that they the said *Coppinger* and *Arthington,* were ordained to separate the Lambes from the Goates, before the Lord *Iesus* at the last day. Whereat (it is saide) they were both astonished, considering their owne vnwoorthines and vnfitnes, crying out against themselues and their sinnes: yet submitting themselues to the direction of Gods spirite, which they were assured, should sufficiently furnish them to doe him that seruice, which himselfe did command. Then *Coppinger* proceeded to tell further, that *Hacket* was greater then either of them, and that they two must obey him, in whatsoeuer he commanded, but told not then, what nor howe great he was, other then king of *Europe.*" Richard Cosin, *Conspiracie, for Pretended Reformation Viz. Presbyteriall Discipline: A Treatise Discouering the Late Designments and Courses Held for Aduancement Thereof, by William Hacket Yeoman, Edmund Coppinger, and Henry Arthington Gent. out of Others Depositions and Their Owne Letters, Writings & Confessions vpon Examination: Together with Some Part of the Life and Conditions, and Two Inditements, Arraignment, and Execution of the Sayd Hacket: Also an Answere to the Calumniations of such as Affirme They Were Mad Men: And a Resemblance of This Action vnto the Like, Happened Heretofore in Germanie; Vltimo Septembris. 1591; Published Now by Authoritie* (London: Christopher Barker, 1592), 47.

3   "For after they both had thus come (with mightie concourse of the common multitude as to such a noueltie of hearing two new prophets in these dayes arisen was likely) with an vniforme crye into *Chepeside* neere vnto the crosse: and there finding the throng and preasse of people to encrease about them, in such sort as that they could not well passe further, nor bee coueniently heard of them all, as they desired; therefore they got them vp into an emptie cart which stoode there, and out of that choise pulpit (for such a purpose) made their lewde and trayterous preachment vnto the people: wherein they stoode not onely vpon the wordes of their former crye, but (so neere as I could learne from so common an Auditorie, and in so confused an action) they reading something out of a paper, went more particularly ouer the office and calling of *Hacket:* how he represented *Christ,* by partaking a part of his glorified body: by his principall spirit, and by the office of seuering the good from the bad with his fanne in his hande, and of establishing the Gospell in *Europe* (which as it seemeth they tooke to be all the world, or else supposed, that all *Europe* did professe *Christianitie*) and of bringing in that *Discipline* which they so often bable of, and which they meane by the terme of *Reformation and the holy cause:* that he was now come, and all these things were presently to be performed by him, telling also the people, where they saw him, where he lay and remained: that they were two *Prophets,* the one of *Mercy,* the other of *Iudgement,* sent and

her sharply for trusting the archbishop of Canterbury[4] and the knight Hatton, lord chancellor of the realm,[5] who they said were damned by God and worthy of death, traitors to the queen and the commonwealth, for opposing their Puritan sect. Furthermore, they said that the queen ought to be punished and deprived of her throne and title—although the prophet of mercy added that God had chosen to inflict this chastisement only on the queen's body, while he would save her soul.[6] After this, the sham Christ burned an effigy of the queen, to the profound shock and distress of those present. And since he seemed like the leader of an uprising or disturbance concocted by the Puritans, they arrested him and hanged him on August 7, 1591 in London's main square.[7] They threw the other two into the madhouse, flogging them every day to make them retract and abjure their prophecies against the queen. This they refused to do,

---

extraordinarily called by God to assist him in this great worke, and were witnesses of these things." Cosin, *Conspiracie*, 56.

4   John Whitgift had been installed as archbishop of Canterbury in 1583.

5   Sir Christopher Hatton, one of Elizabeth's favorites, lord chancellor from 1587 until his death.

6   One Catholic observer wrote, "These last few days three fellows made their appearance, who gave out that they were prophets, and wished to be regarded as such. The first, who was previously a Puritan minister, is named Copinger; he now styles himself *Prophet of Mercy,* sent by God (so he says) by an extraordinary mission to proclaim to the world the terrible judgments that will befall it, if it fail to repent and submit itself to the divine will. His followers are 'the elect of God,' and he professes to know these at first sight, and signs them on the forehead with his ring. Others who do not satisfy his wishes, he passes on to his companion, who calls himself *Prophet of Judgment,* his real name being Arthington. This man passes sentence on all whom he lists with as much boldness and self assertion as if he were the counsellor of God. The third, whose name is Hackett, was also once a minister, and declares himself *Jesus Christ,* King of the earth, King of Christendom, descended from heaven to execute judgment on those who refuse his mercy. Two of these prophets appeared in Goldsmiths' Square [Cheapside], a place in London well known and much frequented. There they suddenly mounted a cart and began to fulfil their would-be heavenly commission, and among other things pronounced sentence against the Chancellor and pseudo Archbishop of Canterbury, saying they were traitors to God and to the realm. Finally the *Prophet of Judgment* degraded and deposed the queen, saying she could reign no longer, having rejected the petitions of the faithful and neglected the cause of God and of His church; for which reasons, he averred, she would suffer chastisement, though her soul would be saved. The two prophets with their Christ were forthwith arrested and brought before the [Lord Mayor] of London, and then examined by two counsellors of State, to wit, Secretary Wolley and Mr. Fortescue." Pollen, *Unpublished Documents,* 333.

7   In England, where the Julian calendar remained in force, the date of the execution was reckoned as July 28. Alexandra Walsham, "'Frantick Hacket': Prophecy, Sorcery, Insanity, and the Elizabethan Puritan Movement," *HJ* 41, no. 1 (March 1998): 27–66, here 28.

and so it seems they died in their cells.[8] When they hanged the false Christ, he died blaspheming and calling upon Elias to send fire from heaven, and laid his curse upon them all, saying that the pope and the plague would consume them.[9]

The discord and enmity between the Calvinists and the Puritans is so great that it cannot be believed, and each day it grows yet greater. In the port of Gravesend, they arrested a Puritan by the name of Norton, who was traveling

---

8 "The next day after this (being *Thursday,*) *Coppinger* hauing wilfully abstained from meate (as is said) seuen or eight daies together, died in *Bridewell:* and *Arthington* liueth yet in the Counter in *Woodstreete,* reserued (I hope) vnto sincere and perfite repentance." Cosin, *Conspiracie,* 72.

Arthington was eventually released in 1592, living another seventeen years. Walsham, "'Frantick Hacket,'" 29.

9 "Hee was brought from *Newgate* towards the place of execution, the eight and twentieth day of *Iulie* (being *Wednesday*) after tenne of the clocke in the morning, albeit by reason of the incredible multitude (then in the streetes) but especially in *Chepeside* from one end thereof vnto another (the like whereof at no assemblie in memorie hath bene seene) it was very long ere the Officers (with all they could doe) could get him to the very place. All the way that hee was dragged vpon the hurdle, hee continued his counterfeit vayne that he had then vndertaken: one while crying out *Iehouah Messias, Iehouah Messias:* another while crying out thus: Looke, looke, how the heauens open wide, and the sonne of God commeth downe to deliuer me. Whe[n] he came vnder the gibbet (which was reared hard by the crosse in *Chepeside,* towards the right hand of the streete as you come from *Paules*) and the noise beyng appeased, hee was exhorted to aske God, and the *Queene* forgiuenesse, and to fall to his prayers: but he perseuering in his vnprofitable course of dissimulation, in stead thereof, fell to rayling and cursing of the *Queenes Maiestie,* most villanouslie. But beyng more vehemently vrged to remember his present state, and to giue ouer all hope to doe himselfe good by such dissembling, hee beganne to pray this most passionate, blasphemous, and execrable prayer, videlicet. *O God of heauen, mightie Iehouah,* Alpha *and* Omega, *Lord of Lordes, King of Kings, and God euerlasting, that knowest me to be that true Iehouah, whome thou hast sent: send some miracle out of a cloude to conuert these Infidels, and deliuer me from these mine enemies: If not, I will fire the heauens, and teare thee from thy throne with my handes.* With other words of most execrable blasphemie against the diuine Maiestie of God (not to be rehearsed) by reason that he found not that deliuerance, which he fansied God to haue promised. Then turning towards the *Executioner,* he said vnto him, Ah thou bastards childe, wilt thou hange *William Hacket* thy king? The *Magistrates* and people detesting this subtill, seditious, and blasphemous humour, commanded and cried to the Officers to dispatch with him, or to haue his mouth stopped from blaspheming: but they had much a doe to get him vp the ladder: And when he was vp, he struggled with his head to and fro, (aswel as he could) that he might not haue the fatal noose put ouer his head. Then he asked them (very fearefully) *O what do you, what doe you?* but seeing by the circumstance, what they intended, he beganne to raue againe, and saide, Haue I this for my kingdome bestowed vpon thee? I come to reuenge thee, and plague thee, and so was turned off." Ibid., 71–72.

to Holland to print a book in English against the queen's bishops and their wicked lives. When they seized him, he was carrying a substantial sum of money for the printing.[10] Other ministers and preachers of the Puritan sect, having fled England for Scotland, produced another book against the queen, her governance, and her Protestant creed.[11] This being so, amid so much dissension between the sects, and such deep hatred and enmity between the adherents, with the writing of books and the appearance of prophets against the queen herself, she allows each to live as they please, persecuting only the Catholics with such fierce barbarity, as this entire history has shown.

---

10   This figure is perhaps Thomas Norton (*c*.1532–84), an MP and author who was arrested in 1581, in part for disparaging remarks about the episcopate. P.W. Hasler and Peter Lake consider Norton a Puritan, but others, including G.R. Elton and Patrick Collinson, have disagreed. P.W. Hasler, "Norton, Thomas," in Hasler, *House of Commons*, 3:145–49, here 148.
          Cf. Patrick Collinson, *Elizabethans* (London: Hambledon and London, 2003), 72–74.
          For Norton's career as an anti-Catholic polemicist, see Lake, *Bad Queen Bess?*, Chapter 1.

11   Scotland, more radically evangelical than its southern neighbor, provided a haven for English Puritans dissatisfied with Elizabethan religious governance. Patrick Collinson, *The Elizabethan Puritan Movement* (London: Methuen, 1967), 46.

The Death of Christopher Hatton, Chancellor of the Realm[1]

The false Puritan prophets ended as we have related, and Christopher Hatton, chancellor of the realm—against whom they had most directed their words—also shortly came to the end of his days, for he died on October 17 of the same year.[2] It was the queen's favor that had raised him to so high a rank: when he was still a student, a youth of charming grace and figure, he and some of his fellows had performed a scene before her, and he played his part with so much elegance that the queen became extremely fond of him, and as she began to employ him, he rose from rank to rank through the greater offices and found himself in the highest position in the kingdom.[3]

The chancellor was more moderate than his other colleagues and, so they say, at heart a Catholic and opposed to the shedding of their blood—but, on the other hand, he had so subjected himself to the queen's will, and so desired to please and serve her (lest he fall from her favor and trust) that he did not dare tell her the truth, nor rebuke the other councilors who were more violent and cruel in matters of religion.[4] Well, this is another sort of men, and of the ministers of kings, who judge their actions by the will, good or ill, of their masters, and not by justice and reason, and in fearing to lose the grace of their prince, they lose that of God. They suppose that they have no share of the guilt of their misdeeds, because what they did did not please them. But he who does evil, and he who consents to it, as Saint Paul says, deserve the same penalty;[5] for with God, not to speak the truth is to betray it.[6] Hatton became rich and influential; he wished to marry, in order to have children and leave them the

---

1 Ribadeneyra's account of Hatton is taken from Robert Persons: see *Philopater*, 20–23.

2 Hatton died on November 20, 1591 at Ely Place in London. Wallace T. MacCaffrey, "Hatton, Sir Christopher," in *ODNB*, 25:817–23, here 823.

3 Hatton probably first attracted Elizabeth's attention as one of the members of the Inner Temple performing the play *Gorboduc* for the new year festivities of 1562. Ibid., 25:817.

4 Hatton was (probably unjustifiably) regarded by many Catholics as "inclined to their side and opposed to fire and sword in matters of religion." Ibid., 25:822.

5 Rom. 1:32.

6 "And so, while Hatton might be exonerated by some for so many crimes, yet to me he seems rather worthy of the condemnation of the duplicitous from the words of the Gospels, indeed as one who knew truth and justice, and did the opposite, who received the light and

enormous patrimony he had accumulated, but the queen would never permit it.[7] For this reason, and even more for what I have related, all thinking men thought him accursed and wretched—although the ignorant crowd, which looks only to appearances and the joys that shine in their eyes, called him blessed. In the last days of his illness, the queen often visited and attended to him several times (as some have written), arranging that he be treated with all care and expense, but she could not free him from death (which they say came by poison), nor can she now free his miserable soul from hell.

I have made particular mention in this history of Leicester, Walsingham, and Hatton because they have been the queen's principal ministers, her favorites and intimates, and those who to please her have shown themselves most hostile to our holy religion, whether slandering it as hateful enemies or failing to defend it as false friends. Let the ministers and confidants of kings learn from these examples how they ought first to satisfy God, who placed them in that position, and then their lords, who entrust them with their honor and conscience and the justice and tranquility of their realms. Let them learn from the fates of others what their fate might be, and from the ephemerality and vanity of others' prosperity how briefly theirs will last, that they may live and govern themselves in such a way that when they shall come to their end, their happiness shall not.

---

voluntarily shut his eyes, who saw and praised good men, but chose to take the part of the thieves, and be their confederate." *Philopater*, 20–22.

7   Contrarily, Wallace T. MacCaffrey asserts of Hatton, "Unmarried, he had no family ambitions. Given the special nature of his relationship with Elizabeth, he could not, like Dudley, risk marriage, even had he wished it." MacCaffrey, "Hatton," in ODNB, 25:818.

The Edict the Queen Proclaimed against Priests and Catholics, and Their Deaths

On October 17, the chancellor died, and the next day, the eighteenth, a royal decree was promulgated against Catholics, the fiercest and strictest of all those yet announced.[1] It was believed that the chancellor, being (as we have said) more moderate, and fond of the Catholics in his heart, had blocked its publication, considering it cruel and prejudicial to the whole kingdom, and because he did not wish the lord treasurer, William Cecil, its author, to have so much influence, to take control of the realm's affairs, and to favor the Puritan heretics openly, as he did.[2] But, when the chancellor died, leaving Cecil alone at the helm and without any restraint, the treasurer succeeded with his schemes and published the decree—so extreme, so barbarous, and so filled with lies and absurdities that one need only read it to perceive as such; we shall include a summary of[3] it in due course, after saying a few things to carry on and complete the story.

The queen published her edict and then, to enforce the penalties it prescribed for Catholics, sent her commissioners and inquisitors throughout the kingdom, to search and seek them out with incredible thoroughness and punish them with no less severity. It seemed as though the already horrific persecution and oppression suffered by the Catholics, like a swift and turbulent river, came to maturity with the arrival of this edict and waxed yet worse, to so extreme a point that only those who endure it can fathom it.

One of those martyred in London at that time was Father Patenson, a priest of the seminary at Rheims; on the night before they put him to death, they threw him into a deep dungeon, along with seven thieves who were to die with him on the following day.[4] And our Lord was pleased to give his spirit to this

---

1 Two royal edicts were proclaimed on October 18, 1591: the first "establishing commissions against seminary priests and Jesuits," the second "specifying questions to be asked of seminary priests." See *TRP*, 3:86–95.

2 Throughout his life, Hatton was dogged by rumors of his Catholic sympathies; it is certainly true that he was a dedicated and effective opponent of the Puritans. Nevertheless, Hatton was in fact a close ally of William Cecil, first Baron Burghley, lord high treasurer since 1572. MacCaffrey, "Hatton," in *ODNB*, 25:818–22.

3 Ribadeneyra adds this modifier beginning in the 1595 edition.

4 William Patenson (d.1592) was executed on January 22, 1592. Pollen, *Acts*, 380.

his servant to convert six of them to our sacred faith (for all seven were heretics) and they died protesting that they were Catholics and confessing our holy religion with great patience and joy, to the edification and inspiration of the Catholics who were present, and the fury and rage of the heretics—who avenged themselves on the priest by disemboweling and quartering him with barbaric cruelty. The which is similar to what we read in the *Martyrologium Romanum* of seven condemned thieves who were converted to the faith by Saint Jason and Saint Sosipater, who were imprisoned with them, and were thus inspired to die for Jesus Christ.[5]

Similarly, in the city of Norwich they martyred another priest, seized from the house of a knight called Grey (whom they threw into the Tower of London). And in London they had earlier slain seven at once, three priests of the seminaries at Rheims and Rome and four laymen—two knights and two of their servants—for contact with the said priests.[6]

In the same manner they martyred another priest, very young and of angelic aspect, whose death provoked enormous emotion, not only because of him, but also because they put to death a prominent lady, the daughter of Lord Copley and the wife of a knight of considerable wealth, merely for having sheltered him in her house. This lady was quite young, but of great zeal in religious matters, and so she died with unyielding resolve, rejecting the pardon and reprieve that the queen's agents offered her and the priest if they agreed to

---

5   In the margin: "April 25 [*vere* 29]; and the Greeks mention them in their *Menologium*."
    Baronio, *Martyrologium Romanum*, 189.

6   Ribadeneyra has taken this anecdote and the preceding one from a dispatch of Richard Verstegan, a well-connected Anglo-Dutch Catholic based in London. On March 5, 1592, Verstegan wrote, "There were executed about Christmas 3 priests, and 4 laymen for receiving them: the names of the Priests were Mr Jenings, Mr Eustace Whyte, and Mr. Paul Blasden: 2 of the laymen were gents: the one named Swithin Wells the other Bryan Lacy, the other twain were serving men, whose names I have not. Since which time there hath been a priest executed at Norwich, and one Mr Grey, in whose house he was taken, is sent vnto the tower. The last month was one Mr. Patteson a priest executed at Tyburn, for receiving of whom one of the gents before mentioned is fled away. This Mr. Patteson the night before he suffered being in a dungeon in Newgate with seven prisoners that were condemned for felony he converted and reconciled six of them, to whom also he ministred the sacrament, which the seventh remayning an heretic in the morning vttered. They were all executed together, the six died Catholic, which made the officers to be the more fierce and cruell vnto the priest, who was cut down and bowelled being perfectly alive. No priests are suffered to speak at their deaths, but so soon as they are dead, Topclif in an oration vnto the people faineth the cause to be for the assisting the intended invasion of the realm, and to that end he fixeth also papers upon the gallows or gibbet." Pollen identifies the priest as the aforementioned Pormort. Pollen, *Unpublished Documents*, 208.

attend their synagogues. They quartered the priest and hanged her, to general sorrow.[7] Given the fury of this mighty storm, many knights and prominent Catholics have fled their houses and escaped, some to Ireland, some to Flanders, some to other remote and secure places, while many able Catholic students at Cambridge and Oxford, learning from the queen's decree that there were English seminaries abroad, have left to seek them out, there to live as Catholics and return to their homeland in the manner we shall relate hereafter. All this has given those of the queen's council much to ponder, seeing their schemes undone and their terrors and tortures end in nothing but the victory of the Catholic faith.

Just as the heretics prove what they are by what they do, so the Lord manifests who he is in the virtue he gives to Catholics to resist and defeat them, all the more so to tender, frail women, who in imitation of the ancient saints have shown themselves true daughters of the Catholic Church, in the loss of property, honor, and freedom, in tortures, and in death itself, as we see in the lady of whom we have just spoken, who preferred to die on the gallows than to recognize the queen as head of the Church of England, and in the eight other maidens, who regarded it as a sort of death not to die for the same cause, as has been mentioned. To make the point more clearly, in the following chapter I will discuss the constancy of several other women who, so as not to lose the Catholic faith, deemed the loss of their wealth a profit, their disgrace an honor, their prisons perfect liberty, and a cruel death a gift and the beginning of eternal life.

---

7 Margaret Gage (*née* Copley, d. after 1591), the daughter of Sir Thomas Copley (1534–1584) and the wife of John Gage (1538–1592). Husband and wife were to be executed as Catholics, but were in fact reprieved. Foley, *Records*, 7.2:1357.

Of Several Prominent Women Who Lost Their Wealth, Honors, and Lives for the Catholic Faith[1]

One of the bloodiest persecutors of the Catholics among the queen's ministers is Edmund Trafford, a knight of noble blood, but poor and quite obstinate in his Calvinism. He was made commissioner for the county of Manchester:[2] both because of his hatred for our sacred religion and because he hoped to escape poverty with the Catholics' property, he resolved to fulfill his office such that he would please the queen with his zeal in serving her by oppressing the Catholics, in addition to enriching his house through wealth and favor. For the first concern of the queen's ministers is that the Catholics whom they persecute are persons of substance, from whom they might profit. Commissioner Edmund dearly wished to harass a lady by the name of Allen of Rossall, Cardinal William Allen's sister-in-law; she had married his brother, by whom (now deceased) she had been left three daughters, called Helen, Catherine, and Mary, the eldest of them being sixteen years old. For he knew she was a fervent Catholic and an abettor of Catholic priests—and unable to put his hands upon Cardinal Allen, he would avenge himself on a person so near to him.

Lady Allen was warned of the commissioner's approach and intentions; to arm herself in God against the assault of Satan, she heard Mass and took communion, imploring our Lord to give her the strength to enter into battle with his enemies and to lose wealth and life rather than depart by a jot from what became a Catholic, Christian woman, for she deemed the opportunity to suffer for his holy name a very great mercy. This done, which was the first and most important thing, she decided to hide herself in some safe, unsuspected corner, leaving her three daughters to keep the house and estates, of which she made them a present.

---

1 Most of this chapter is a translation of the account of the travails of Lady Allen, Cardinal Allen's sister-in-law, found in the *Concertatio* under the title "Certamen D. Alanæ" (The struggles of Lady Allen). See *Concertatio*, n.p.

   A briefer account of Lady Allen's sufferings was sent to Ribadeneyra by Robert Persons in a letter of September 10, 1584: see Persons, *Letters and Memorials*, 238–39.

2 Sir Edmund Trafford (1526–90) was described by Joseph Gillow as "the greatest persecutor and despoiler of Catholics in Lancashire." Joseph Gillow, "Lord Burghley's Map of Lancashire, 1590," in *Catholic Record Society Miscellanea IV*, Publications of the Catholic Record Society 4 (London: The Arden Press, 1907), 162–222, here 217.

Thus it was that on the morning of the feast of the Epiphany, the queen's agents entered the lady's house with a large troop of godless men, and demanded all the keys and weapons. They put oaths to the servants to learn where their mistress was, and when they saw a portrait of a certain gentleman in one of the rooms, which they imagined to be of Doctor Allen, so great was the rage that seized them that, uttering a thousand insults and slanders, they began to take their daggers to the picture, leaving it in tatters and throwing it upon the floor to trample with their feet. After they had scoured every corner of the house and seized everything of value, even to the dresses of those three honorable maidens, and from another building some fifteen hundred ducats (which the good mother had hidden for their relief, in case some misfortune should befall them), they remained in the house for a long time, as much to consume and destroy everything in it as because they hoped by this imposition to discover where the noble mother was.

She was informed of all that happened, and when she saw that the soldiers had thoroughly settled themselves in her house, she took no thought of her property, or anything else besides her three daughters, fearing lest some outrage be done them, or that, frightened by the heretics' terrors, they should say or do something contrary to the holy habits in which she had raised them. With such worries and cares, she instructed them to find some way to escape and free themselves from the claws of those lions, among whom they were like lambs, holding always to the advice of their mother and encouraging one another to abandon life before the Catholic faith. As they sought some safe—or less perilous—means of escape, it pleased our Lord, even as they were about to be carried off as prisoners, to furnish them with a perfect moment and a miraculous opportunity: in the middle of the night, as their guards slumbered, the three maidens left through the house's gate without being perceived and, going along the shore, found a boat, which God had held ready for them, by which they passed to the other side of the river, journeying off the path without daring to reveal themselves to anyone, lest they fall into the hands of some heretic. Finally, at the end of fourteen days of travails and toils, they came to the place where their dear mother, more dead than alive, remained suspended between hope and fear of what might become of her daughters—although always steadfastly trusting in the goodness of God, who will never abandon those who confide in him[3] and, out of his love and zeal for his religion, prefer to lose all they have than to depart one jot from his sacred faith.

Great though the mother's joy was to see her three daughters out of danger, it was not enough to dislodge her concern for their sustenance and care, given

---

3   1 Kings 12:22; 3 Kings 6:13; Ps. 93:14.

that they had neither father nor patrimony, neither shelter nor support, besides her. Therefore, she besought several knights, friends of hers, to whom she had made gifts of her wealth on her daughters' behalf, and who were, for these and other considerations, indebted to her, to appear before the magistrates and seek the property that was theirs by the father's will and the mother's gift. But since men are better friends to their own interests than to another's, and are transformed in adversity, forgetting the obligations of virtue and gratitude, and there are precious few who choose to remain friends amid troubles and faithful amid adverse fortune, none was willing to speak on their behalf, because they feared to offend the queen's council, in whose name these estates had been seized, and because it was a matter of religion, so very contentious in England. Several friends advised the mother to send her daughters to appear in court themselves and petition for the restitution of her property: for, as the justice of the suit was so obvious, so in keeping with the laws of England, and the girls maidens of such tender ages, they were sure that they themselves would easily attain what others could not achieve with the greatest effort. But the saintly mother, as a manful woman, deeply Catholic and experienced, understood that her daughters would not be heard in the magistrates' court unless they pledged to attend their synagogues—and that if they did not agree to swear, they would be arrested, thrown in jail, and stripped them of all their property. Lest she jeopardize either her daughters' Catholicism or their liberty, she utterly refused to take this perilous advice, or to permit her daughters to proceed through the courts.

Sentence was given against their property, and the commissioner immediately confiscated everything he could find, even things which were not hers but merely present in her house. Through third parties and friends, the mother appealed to the queen's council to undo the outrage perpetrated upon her daughters by inferior judges. But after all the time she spent, she gained nothing but the knowledge that the more exalted the councilors, the greater scoundrels and heretics they were, the less they cared for the travails and miseries of her daughters, and the greater the thirst with which they coveted her property. Indeed, the highest posts and most prominent offices, unless they fall to persons of extraordinary prudence and virtue, often occasion the wretched downfalls of their holders, matter and fodder for stoking the flame of greed, and ambition, and vice, as we can see in this affair.

In this way, the worthy matron lost her estate, but she did not on this account lose her patience or joy of spirit, but rather offered thanks to the Lord for the mercy he had done her, deeming the poverty of Christ a greater treasure than all the wealth she had possessed in England. Thus it was that she resolved to flee with her two elder daughters, for she preferred to live in an impoverished and secure exile abroad than in her homeland in turmoil and danger. And so she departed and, guided by an angel of the Lord,[4] after enduring extreme trials and perils by sea and by land, often hiding in forests and caves by day and traveling by night, she reached Rheims at the end of two months, safe and sound, to the enormous relief of all the Catholics, especially her brother-in-law Doctor Allen, then the superior and rector of the seminary at Rheims, and now, for his great merits, a most worthy cardinal of the holy Roman Church.

This is an example of a widowed lady and of three young maidens who preferred to lose wealth and home than the Catholic faith. Let us now consider others, from among those who lost liberty, honor, and life for the same faith.

The queen had a certain prominent lady (the wife of a knight called Mordaunt), who had been imprisoned for Catholicism, told that, being who she was, the wife of such a husband, she would order her release, upon her doing one thing only, perfectly simple: passing through one of the heretics' churches a single time, entering by one door and leaving by another at the time when they were celebrating their rites. The lady answered that God would never permit such a thing, and that she would lose the grace of the queen, her husband, and all her family and friends (who were numerous) before she showed any weakness or dissimulation in the profession of her faith and the obedience she owed to her God and Lord. And so she remained a prisoner for many years for refusing to acquiesce to the queen's will.[5]

Three further ladies of illustrious blood, who had been arrested while gathered to hear Mass on Easter Sunday, were carried openly through the streets of London with every imaginable insult, and before them went the priest who had said Mass for them, attired as he had been then. All the heretics were screaming in the streets, shouting a thousand insults and slurs, but they suffered it all with unshakeable patience and fortitude, frightening the heretics and edifying

---

4 Exod. 23:20.

5 "Such was a prominent lady, the wife of a high-born knight, by the name of Mordaunt: imprisoned for the Catholic faith, and being offered her liberty in the queen's name, given that she was so prominent, and the wife of such a man, if only she would once pass through one of the heretics' churches, entering through one door and exiting through another, while they were celebrating their rites. The noble matron refused this with great steadfastness, and preferred to lose the queen's grace, that of her husband, and that of all her kin and friends (who were numerous) than do anything that seemed like weakness or dissimulation in the confession of her God and Lord, and thus she remained a prisoner for many years for refusing what was asked of her." Persons, *Relacion*, 59ʳ–59ᵛ.

   This seems to be Lady Joan Mordaunt (*née* Fermor, d.1592), the widow of John Mordaunt, second Baron Mordaunt (1508–71). C.S. Knighton, "Mordaunt, John, second Baron Mordaunt (1508–1571)," in *ODNB*, 39:24–26, here 25.

the Catholics by the joy with which they endured this affront for the confession of our sacred faith.[6]

Another lady, named Clitherow, also married and nobly born, while standing before the magistrates to be examined, after she had declared that she was a Catholic and prepared to die for her faith, refused to answer any further questions put to her by the judges, so as not to recognize them as legitimate in the case, and so as not in any way to hinder the death she desired to suffer for Jesus Christ. The judges threatened her that unless she answered, they would give her a gruesome death, but she remained unyieldingly firm and steadfast in her refusal, and thus they put her to the death I shall now relate.

They laid the handmaid of the Lord[7] upon the ground, with her face upwards, and tied her down with cords and stretched her by her hands and feet. Below her kidneys, they placed a large, jagged stone, and on her chest a plank, upon which they proceeded to place, little by little, a great weight, until they made blood burst from her mouth, ears, and nostrils, and thus she yielded up her soul to the Lord with perfect patience and joy, her eyes fixed upon heaven and her heart upon that which was all her desire and her good. All those present thought this an extreme atrocity, seeing so horrid and frightful a death for

---

6   Ribadeneyra gives this story with more specifics in Book 3, Chapter 25. Here he draws on
     Persons's *Relacion*; farther on the account is adapted from the *Concertatio*. The ladies in
     question are Elizabeth Parker (*née* Stanley, d. *c.*1590), the wife of Henry Parker, eleventh
     Baron Morley (1533–77), and the daughter of Edward Stanley, third earl of Derby (1509–72);
     Elizabeth Guildford (*née* Shelley, *b.*1533), the wife of Sir Thomas Guildford (*c.*1535–75); and
     Magdalen Browne (*née* Dacre, 1538–1608), the wife of Anthony Browne, first Viscount Montagu. Louis A. Knafla, "Stanley, Edward, third earl of Derby (1509–1572)," in *ODNB*, 52:175–
     77, here 175. S.R. Johnson, "Guildford, Thomas," in S.T. Bindoff, ed., *The House of Commons
     1509–1558*, 3 vols., The History of Parliament (London: Secker & Warburg, 1982), 2:266–67.
     Jacqueline Eales, "Browne [*née* Dacre], Magdalen, Viscountess Montagu (1538–1608)," in
     ODNB, 8:182–83, here 182.
          Cf. "Lady Morley, the daughter of the earl of Derby; Lady Browne; and Lady Guildford—
     all three quite distinguished in blood, and yet more distinguished as steadfast confessors of
     the Catholic faith—having been arrested as they heard Mass together on the day of Easter
     Sunday, were publicly borne to judgment with every imaginable humiliation, with the priest
     who had said Mass for them, attired as he had been [then], and all the heretics hurling a
     thousand attacks and insults through the streets." Persons, *Relacion*, 60ᵛ–61ʳ.
          For the Brownes, and the familial politics of early modern English Catholicism more generally, see Michael C. Questier, *Catholicism and Community in Early Modern England: Politics,
     Aristocratic Patronage and Religion, c.1550–1640*, Cambridge Studies in Early Modern British
     History (Cambridge: Cambridge University Press, 2006).
7   Luke 1:38.

so noble a woman and for such a cause.[8] But heresy is a hellish fury, and knows neither bound nor measure in its sacrilege and cruelty.

Thus far we have spoken of several maiden ladies, wives, and widows who have suffered for Christ. Now, to conclude this chapter, let us say something of certain nuns, brides of the Lord, who have done the same, so as to provide models for ladies of all estates.

Among the religious who left England for the provinces of Flanders, fleeing Elizabeth's persecution, were four entire convents, two of Carthusian and Franciscan brothers, and two of nuns, one of Dominicans and another of Bridgettines, called the monastery of Syon. Two of the houses—the Franciscan friars and the Dominican nuns—dissolved over time, while the others remain standing, having been and being now sustained by the alms of His Catholic Majesty. That of Saint Bridget has endured monstrous storms and tempests, horribly persecuted by the heretics of England, both because therein live chaste virgins, consecrated to God and enemies of their sensuality and filthiness, and

---

8   "But much greater yet was the fortitude and constancy of another noble woman, also married, called Clitherow, who, brought before the public court to be examined and judged by the queen's magistrates, after she had confessed her faith and her determination to die for it, refused to respond to the heretics' other questions—partly so as not to hinder her martyrdom, and partly so as not to acknowledge those heretics as legitimate judges in matters of our sacred Catholic faith. And so, however much the said judges threatened her, and told her of the brutal death they would give her if she did not respond, she always remained silent, and thus they put her to a cruel and frightful death, which was as follows. They stretched the handmaid of the Lord upon the ground with her face upwards, and bound her hands and feet, tying them down with cords, and placed sharp stone beneath her kidneys, so as to pierce the flesh and the bones. On her stomach, they placed a large board, and this they loaded little by little with a great weight, until they made the blood burst from her mouth, ears, and nose, and in the end her soul took flight, to the utter horror and terror of those who were present and saw such a death for such a person and for such a cause." Persons, *Relacion*, 59^v–60^v.

Cf. *Concertatio*, 410^v.

Margaret Clitherow (*née* Middleton, *c*.1553–86) harbored priests and distributed Catholic paraphernalia out of her home in York. Arrested in March 1586, she refused to enter a plea before the assizes, leading to the imposition of *peine forte et dure*—being pressed beneath weights until an answer was given. Clitherow died in the course of this ordeal on March 25, 1586, still refusing to plead. Claire Walker, "Clitherow [*née* Middleton], Margaret [St Margaret Clitherow] (1552/1553–1586)," in *ODNB*, 12:159–60, here 159.

For Clitherow's iconic place as a martyr in late sixteenth-century Catholic writings, see Dillon, *Construction of Martyrdom*, Chapter 6; Peter Lake and Michael C. Questier, "Margaret Clitherow, Catholic Nonconformity, Martyrology and the Politics of Religious Change in Elizabethan England," *Past & Present* 185 (November 2004): 43–90; Peter Lake and Michael C. Questier, *The Trials of Margaret Clitherow: Persecution, Martyrdom and the Politics of Sanctity in Elizabethan England* (London: Continuum, 2011).

because many others, the daughters of knights and important persons, leave England to come and seek them, to follow them and join their community. But as the nuns were too many to be accommodated, it was decided after much prayer and penance to divide: the eldest traveled with the community to Rouen in France, while the younger ones, higher-born and better-connected, returned to England, where they might be supported and assisted by their families and friends, and thus it was done. The nuns arrived in England; as soon as the heretics saw them, they began to lavish gifts upon them, imagining they could easily corrupt them by kindness, since they were young and new to the religious life. But when they failed, they arrested them and sent them to various jails across the kingdom, attempting to frighten them by harshness. Yet neither could lavishness soften them nor severity overcome them. At this, the councilors confined them to the houses of several of the lords of the realm, where the example of these handmaids of the Lord was so great that it moved many of the noble maidens to follow them and embrace Christ our Lord in perfect chastity (so powerful is virtue purified with trials endured for God). What was happening came to the notice of the magistrates, who ordered the sisters removed from these houses and returned to the common jails, with extreme abuse and utter inhumanity.[9] One of them, called Elizabeth Sander, Doctor Nicholas Sander's sister, describes in a letter the many times they seized her and tormented her, in which, among other things, she says,

> The bailiffs arrested me for the second time in my sister's own house, and with the greatest precautions, as though they had captured a notorious bandit, they brought me before more judges than Annas and Caiaphas and Pilate and Herod, for they were not finished until they had presented me before every single magistrate, of which there are a great many in

---

9 The description of the monastics' travails is a slight adaptation of the account found in Persons, *Relacion*, 5ᵛ–8ʳ.

When Elizabeth expelled the various orders in 1559, the brothers of the Franciscan friary at Greenwich scattered, variously to Liège, Antwerp, Lisbon, and Rome. The Carthusian house at Shene re-established itself as Shene Anglorum in the Low Countries. For a time, the Dominican nuns of King's Langley lived a peripatetic existence on the Continent, but they were eventually absorbed into the community at Engelendael near Bruges. As Ribadeneyra goes on to describe, the Bridgettine abbey of Syon relocated first to the Low Countries, then to Rouen, and finally to Lisbon. William Page, ed., *The Victoria History of the County of Kent*, 3 vols., The Victoria History of the Counties of England (London: Archibald Constable and Company Limited, 1908–32), 2:190, 198. Michael Sargent, "Chauncy, Maurice (*c.*1509–1581)," in *ODNB*, 11:268.

that area. They put innumerable, utterly impertinent questions to me, but I answered them all briefly, responding that I was a woman and a nun, and that the first sufficed to assure them that I could not disturb the realm, and the second to tell them that my faith was the Catholic one, since theirs had no nuns. They wanted me to tell them what Catholics I knew in England, and other, similar things.

So it was that in the end, enraged, they threw me in prison in the city of Winchester, where for several days they so abused me and so restricted my food that I expected to die of sheer hunger—but God our Lord relieved me through the charity of the Catholics imprisoned in the same jail, who for the three days I was there willingly provided me with everything I might need.

Many times the heretics implored me to go with them to their churches to hear their sermons, and as I refused, they subjected me to numerous abuses, dragging me from interrogation to interrogation and hauling me before every session of their courts, which meet in the provinces every six months, accusing me of contumacy and obstinacy and sentencing me to pay eighty ducats for each month that I had refused to attend their synagogues, which amounted to around five hundred ducats every six months, the which sums condemned me to life imprisonment, for they all so multiply together among the various courts that payment is beyond me. Countless miseries arise from these courts and tribunals (besides the dishonor and humiliation) through the shamelessness of the sheriffs, bailiffs, and other villainous ministers, to whom we women are subjected, and by the company of degenerate, criminal persons, hearing so many blasphemies and indecencies, that my wretched pain and affliction was only overcome by the contemplation of what our Lord endured in his sufferings for our sins.

And, to be brief, when at one point I was imprisoned in a castle, through his aid and favor one night I lowered myself down the walls with a cord—not out of a desire to flee the prison, but rather to reach Rouen, whither our mother abbess had ordered me to make shift to go. Indeed, the determination to obey my superiors gave me the strength to cast myself into so dangerous a situation, as it was to find myself one black night dangling in the air by that rope, and once I had reached the ground, alone and helpless, without any idea where I was to lay my head, forced to flee through the fields to find safety. In the end, after numerous different incidents and arrests, it pleased our Lord to free me and bring me to the convent at Rouen, to the extreme solace of my spirit and those of the other nuns my sisters, who did not cease in thanking our Lord for the miraculous providence whereby he had plucked me out of so many dangers and trials, may his holy name be blessed forevermore.[10]

---

10   Ribadeneyra only uses portions of this letter, translated into Spanish in its entirety in Persons, *Relacion*, 42^r–58^r.

The letter, one of two extant from Sander to Englefield, is preserved at the Royal English College, Valladolid as Val. Ser. II, L. 5, no. 12. A transcription has been published: "The History of Syon (continued). Englefield Correspondence—English College Valladolid: Sister Elizabeth Saunders 'Second Letter' to Sir Francis Englefield," *Poor Soul's Friend and St. Joseph's Monitor*, April 1966, 43–54.

Cf. Betty S. Travitsky, "The Puzzling Letters of Sister Elizabeth Sa[u]nder[s]," in *Textual Conversations in the Renaissance: Ethics, Authors, Technologies*, ed. Zachary Lesser and Benedict S. Robinson (Aldershot: Ashgate, 2006), 131–46.

The Heretics Seize Four Young Brothers for Their Faith, and are Left Humiliated[1]

Not only do the English heretics persecute the priests and the other Catholics who by their positions, learning, and influence could defend the Catholic faith and hinder the progress of the false sect of Calvin, together with the married women, widows, and maidens, as we have seen, but they also do not exempt the very children, whose tender years have, even among barbarians, customarily been shielded from all harm. Let us set aside all other examples and speak of a single one, for it is most illustrious and teaches us a great deal about the malice of the heretics and the goodness of the Lord, who triumphs over them even through children of few years.

There were four brothers, called Thomas, Robert, Richard, and John Worthington, the sons of a knight and the nephews of a priest, likewise named Thomas Worthington, their father's brother. The eldest was sixteen years old, and the youngest had not reached twelve; all four boys were imprisoned in the province of Lancaster by the ministers of the law, who were looking for their uncle's abode. It was astounding what ruses and tricks the queen's councilors, false bishops, and ministers used to corrupt and deceive these boys, and the constancy, discretion, and spirit the Lord gave them, so that they did not allow themselves to be hoodwinked, nor to stray from the Catholic faith, nor to say anything that could be prejudicial to the priests and Catholics about whom they were interrogated. After the heretics had first separated them, placing the younger two in one place and the elder two in another, they kept John (the youngest of all) without food for an entire day, threatening to starve him to death and forcing him to drink a great deal of wine, so that, his head being addled and unsettled with drunkenness, he would answer the commissioners' questions without judgment. But the Lord deigned to preserve the boy's wit, and so when they interrogated him, he replied that though they had made him drink all that, hoping he would lose his discretion, he was himself, even if his

---

1   Ribadeneyra adapts this account of the brothers Worthington from the Latin version included in the third part of the *Concertatio* under the title "Certamen quatuor nobilium puerorum Vvorthingtoniorum" ("The struggle of the four noble Worthington boys"). See *Concertatio*, n.p.
    Cf. the briefer account in a letter from Robert Persons to Ribadeneyra: Persons, *Letters and Memorials*, 239.

stomach was so troubled that he could barely answer them, or even utter a single word. And so he escaped their clutches. After this, they brought out the eldest of the brothers, whose name was Thomas: the earl of Derby[2] offered him copious gifts and made him extravagant promises, swearing to take him into his household, and exalt and nurture him there, if only he would go to one of their churches or hear some sermon by the heretical ministers, but the Catholic boy could not be moved, repeating always that he prized being Catholic above all the favors and kindnesses the earl could do him. And when they pressed him to answer to their questions—where had he heard Mass, where was his uncle the priest, and other similar matters—under oath, he answered that he could not obey them, nor swear at all, because he did not even know what oath this was, nor in what cases he might swear, nor how he ought to swear according to the law of God. And until he knew this, he refused to burden his conscience. The same thing happened in the interrogation of the two other brothers, whom they likewise sought to entrap with various questions, without being able to get a word out of them that could prejudice or harm a single Catholic. And so as not to be tedious by recounting in detail everything that occurred in the four months the boys were held captive (though they were not always together, or in the same place), I will say only that repeated interrogations, conducted by various powerful lords, prominent royal officials, false bishops, preachers, lawyers, and other judicial officers, as well as the use of every one of the heretics' usual tricks and ruses for corrupting—gifts, promises, threats, beatings, good treatment and bad—they could never weaken or corrupt them, nor move them an inch from their constancy and faith.

Indeed, having forcibly dragged them to the school of a Calvinist master, to the end that there, in the wicked company of the other boys and under the instruction of the misbelieving teacher, they might docilely drink the poison of heresy, they utterly refused to read a single book, or listen to what they said about religion, insisting that they were well-enough instructed in what they ought to believe, and that they had no need of new doctrines or a new master. They were so favored by the Lord, who desires to be praised from the mouths of children,[3] that their example and excellent words sparked in many of the other schoolchildren a desire to become Catholics and to imitate them. And they uttered such sound, thoughtful arguments about the elements of our sacred faith in question that a heretical preacher who had come to sow the cockle of his false creed in the children's hearts[4] knew not how to respond to what God taught them to say.

---

2   Henry Stanley, fourth earl of Derby.

3   Ps. 8:3; Matt. 21:16.

4   Matt. 13:25.

Nor could they elicit their consent to attend the heretics' churches; ordered to do so at the queen's command, the boys replied that they would obey her in temporal and civil matters, but they had no obligation to listen to her in those of religion. And they advanced other arguments like these, with which the heretics were left utterly abashed, and the Catholics edified and inspired to give their lives for the faith and religion for which boys of such tender years had fought with such determination and constancy.

After the Lord had tried them, and by their example shown the force of the truth, even in the mouths of children, and of his divine spirit in the hearts of little, untaught boys, he freed them from the bloody hands of the heretics by diverse means, and a few months later brought them safely to the seminary at Rheims, so that, when they had been instructed there, they could return to England with greater spirit and strength, to fight and defeat his enemies, the misbelievers.

How the English Heretics Accuse the Catholics of being Sorcerers

Among the English heretics' other outrages against the Catholics is to treat them like magicians and sorcerers, just as the pagan emperors and tyrants who persecuted the Christians did: any sort of extraordinary, heroic virtue or miracle that God worked through them they would attribute to some enchantment or witchcraft. If fire did not burn them, if knives did not harm them, if water did not drown them, if their wounds were healed by divine power, the saints were called wizards, enchanters, and witches, as may be seen in the sacred histories of the martyrs. The same thing happens today in England, to teach us the similarity and correspondence between this present persecution and the ancient ones, and we may learn that the author of the past ones is also that of the present one, and just as they concluded, this will conclude, and the sacred Church triumph over those who now oppress it. The Tower of London was scorched by a blast from heaven, and the heretics immediately proclaimed that the papists (as they call the Catholics) had caused the inferno through their pacts with the devil.[1] The heretics punished a Catholic bookseller for having spoken some words in favor of our sacred religion, and they ordered that he himself should cut off his own ears, which they had nailed to a post, and the Lord (who, though he is patient, is also, as he is called, a God of vengeance)[2] punished the iniquitous judges and those who had attended the Catholic bookseller's sentencing, taking their lives almost instantly.[3] This miracle and warning from the

---

1 In 1561, part of the Tower of London was destroyed by lightning. As Robert Persons observed, "Several years ago, the Tower of London was almost miraculously struck from heaven, and caught fire in a furious and inextinguishable blaze: who among our foes did not attribute this to our sorcery?" *Concertatio*, 37^r.

2 Ps. 93:1; Jer. 51:56.

3 This is the Catholic bookseller Rowland Jenks, who has already appeared in the *Historia*.
   "When the court sessions were held in a certain university town, a certain bookseller who had uttered a few words in favor of the Catholic faith was brought before the judges. [...] His ears first fixed to a wooden post in the public square with iron nails, and then a knife put into his hands, the man was to free himself by cutting them off himself. [...] What followed? The wholly miraculous judgement of God. Both judges (for there are usually two present), as well as all the court officials, and many of the most distinguished of all the gathered

Lord, which was quite notorious, the heretical ministers claimed to have been worked by the guile and malice of the Catholics. I could relate other examples besides, but leaving them aside, I shall discuss a single one, which shall better convey this, in addition to how the Catholics benefit the heretics and the reward they receive, for all this shall redound to the greater knowledge and confirmation of our sacred faith.

A leading knight at court, who was Catholic in his heart, fell ill; burdened by the illness, he began to think about the next life. Wishing to put his affairs in order and prepare himself for death, he summoned a priest, to be confessed and to speak with him about his soul. The priest advised him, among other things, that if he possessed anyone else's property, he should restore it, and if he had offended anyone, he should make restitution. To obey this counsel, the sick man, recalling that he owed I know not what sum of money to a Calvinist heretic (although the debt was not public knowledge), instructed that he be repaid, and died shortly thereafter. The dead knight's wife wanted to fulfill her husband's intent and repay that debt, but she found herself in a quandary, for she feared that if she revealed herself by sending the money to the Calvinist, he would accuse her, and she would suffer for being a Catholic. She summoned the priest with whom her husband had discussed the matter, put her distress and difficulties to him, and begged him to take charge of making restitution with his own hands, so she might escape from both scruple and danger. The priest, to do a good deed for the dead husband and the living wife, took responsibility for repaying the debt. For, though he suspected that if he was revealed as a priest, some great trial might befall him, he never imagined that in doing this kindness to the heretic and restoring his property to him, the man would be so accursed as to return evil for good.[4]

And so, commending himself to God, he set out in disguise to seek this man in the city where he lived; leaving his horse at an inn, he entered at the door, took him aside, and gave him his money, the man having first given his word not to inquire or seek to know anything about the person who had sent it, nor about the one who brought it, or the reason he had been given it. At this the priest returned to the inn to retrieve his horse and speedily make his escape. But then the Calvinist exposed him and had him arrested, claiming that he was some devil in the shape of a man, who had come to deceive him with money: for how was it possible, he said, that a man should offer another man

---

persons perished within a few days from an unheard-of sort of disease, some in the city, others elsewhere." *Concertatio*, 37ʳ.

Jenks's story is also related in Persons, *Relacion*, 4ʳ–4ᵛ.

4 Rom. 12:17; 1 Thess. 5:15; 1 Pet. 3:9.

cash and give it him freely, without knowing him? They arrested and confined the priest, locking him in a cell and posting guards, and announced that he was a demon in human form. And they gathered the populace, who came to see this monstrosity and offered money to gawk at him. In the end, after they had abused him in this fashion, they charged him with the crimes of treason and *lèse-majesté*, confiscated his horse and the money he carried, and sent him under heavy guard to London, where they threw him from one prison to another, until they placed him in the Tower, where he remained four four years, expiating with abuse and misery the guilt of so grave a sin, in the heretics' eyes, as repaying a debt.[5] Who will not recognize them by this example? Who will not abhor so diabolical a sect? Who will not marvel at the patience of the Lord in suffering them? Who will not fight against these monsters? Who will not regard victory as certain?

---

5   I have not been able to identify Ribadeneyra's source for this anecdote, but it evinces many of the didactic elements common to Jesuit martyr narratives of the period.

The Benefit the Catholics Have Derived from This Persecution

These are the means the heretics of England use to uproot the Catholic faith from that kingdom, and put an end (if they can), once and for all, to all those who profess it. Measures truly without measure, means impious, cruel, infamous, and fitting for Calvinist heretics, dragged up from hell and learned in Satan's school. But, to prove to us the goodness of the Lord, and how much mightier is his arm than the malice and ruthlessness of his enemies, let every Catholic who reads this history, and so praises the Lord, know that all the queen's ministers have achieved, with all their machinations and plots hatched against our sacred religion in that realm, has been to strengthen, cleanse, and purify the Catholics yet more, bringing them to correct many things that had not been remedied prior to the persecution and to live with greater prudence and caution in the confession of their faith. For, when Queen Mary died and the religion of England was transformed, the Catholic bishops and prelates were put to flight or imprisoned, leaving the people like sheep without a shepherd,[1] in the deepest darkness and shadows as regards the spiritual governance of their souls. So it was that many Catholics practiced all sorts of superstitions and harmful tricks, as well as sacrilegious oaths against the authority of the Apostolic See—and this with little or no scruple of conscience. They went to the heretics' synagogues, heard their sermons, and brought their children and households to listen. They imagined that to be known as Catholics it sufficed not to go to those churches together *with* the heretics, but rather before them, and to return after them. They took communion in the sacrilegious supper of Calvin, or arranged to be noted down as though they had communicated, and heard Mass in secret in their houses, imagining that in this way they had satisfied God. They sent their children to be baptized by the heretical ministers, and also had their marriage ceremonies performed by their hands. And all this they did without scruple, through the ignorance of the remaining Catholic priests, who deemed this licit, or lied out of weakness or fear.

Now, by the mercy of God, every Catholic understands that it does not suffice to believe the Catholic faith in one's heart, but that it is likewise necessary for salvation to confess it with the mouth. It was not only Judas who sinned, in

---

1 Num. 27:17; 3 Kings 22:17; 2 Chron. 18:16; Isa. 13:14; Zech. 10:2; Matt. 9:36; Mark 6:34.

betraying Christ our Lord, but also Saint Peter, in denying him.[2] They refuse to deny that the pope is the universal head of the Catholic Church and vicar of Christ on earth, nor to admit in any way that the queen has any spiritual authority whatsoever in England. They know that they cannot go to the synagogues of the heretics or hear their sermons, and that they have an obligation to prevent their children and households from going, lest those they have borne in Christ[3] be sacrificed to the devil. They maintain the highest veneration for the holy sacraments of the Church, the priests, and all sacred things, and however many draconian laws and death penalties the queen issues against those who carry an *agnus Dei*, crucifixes, medals, or rosaries with them, executing them with such extreme inhumanity, the Catholics' piety is so great that they prefer to risk their lives rather than lose the fruit of their devotions. In the end, we see that this awful persecution has purified and refined the Catholics, and the fire of that tribulation has purged them of the dross of their past sins and made them more resplendent and firmer in the love of the Lord.

---

2   Matt. 26:69–75; Mark 14:66–72; Luke 22:55–62; John 18:17–27.

3   1 Cor. 4:15.

Why the Catholics of England Refuse to Attend the Heretics' Synagogues or to Recognize the Queen as Head of Their Church

Because in most of the martyrdoms recounted in this history, two principal charges were brought against the Catholics by the heretics—refusing to go to their synagogues or hear their preachers, and refusing to acknowledge the queen as supreme spiritual head in the kingdom of England—it is fitting that we set forth in this chapter the specific, forceful reasons the Catholics have for doing as they do.[1] For this, it must first be granted that the impiety and wickedness of any heretic is so great, that, as the illustrious Doctor of the Church Saint Jerome says, there is no man so abominable or impious that the heretic does not exceed him in iniquity.[2] And for this reason, Saint John the Evangelist and numerous saints call the heretics "Antichrists."[3] And Saint Irenaeus, writing against the heretic Valentinus, says that the apostles never consented to interact or speak with the heretics.[4] And Saint Athanasius, in the life of Saint Anthony Abbot, writes that the saint so hated heretics that he urged Catholics not even to approach them.[5] And Saint Cyprian advises us in a letter not to communicate, eat, or speak with them, but rather keep ourselves as far

---

1 "If attendance at church were publicly admitted to be, under certain circumstances, licit, then Catholics who chose to refuse to come to church would be left open to the charge of disobedience and disloyalty. If however they were deemed merely to be following the dictates of divine and ecclesiastical law, they were acting on the promptings of conscience and thus not choosing to be disloyal." Lake and Questier, "Puritans, Papists, and the 'Public Sphere,'" 610.

2 In the margin: "Book 7, *on Isaiah.*"
   Jerome, *Commentary on Isaiah*, 7.18.

3 In the margin: "1 John 2[:18] and 4[:3]; Cyprian, Book 4, Letter 7; Hilary, *Contra Auxentium*; Augustine, *Answer to An Enemy of the Laws and the Prophets*, Book 2, Chapter 2."
   Ribadeneyra again follows Erasmus's organization of Cyprian's letters. In modern editions, see Cyprian, *Letters*, 69.1.
   Augustine of Hippo, *Answer to an Enemy of the Laws and the Prophets*, 2.2.6–7.

4 "Such is the great discretion had by the apostles and their disciples, that they did not communicate even verbally with any of those who adulterated the truth." Irenaeus of Lyon, *Against the Heresies (Book 3)*, ed. Dominic J. Unger and Irenaeus M.C. Steenberg, trans. Dominic J. Unger, Ancient Christian Writers: The Works of the Fathers in Translation 64 (New York: The Newman Press, 2012), 34.

5 Athanasius, *The Life of St. Antony*, Chapter 68.

removed from the heretics as they are from the Church.[6] And Pope Saint Leo says these words: "Flee the conversations and debates of the heretics as the venom of a viper, and have nothing to do with those who, under the name of Christians, make war upon the faith of Christ."[7] And in his history, Theodoret relates that in the church of Samosata, which was Catholic, there was not one man who would consent to hear the bishop when he preached, because he was a heretic, nor to enter the bathhouse with him—or even afterwards, unless they first removed all the water with which he had washed.[8] And Lucifer, bishop of Cagliari in Sardinia, exiled for his Catholicism by Emperor Constantius, wrote a book proving by many citations from sacred writ that Catholics could not in good conscience have any contact with heretics.[9] And there are many other such precepts and examples from among the saints—which, as they have been mentioned in our book on tribulation, we shall omit.[10] And though Catholics ought to use such caution in all things, it is much more needful in what concerns religion and the confession of our most sacred faith, which is perfectly pure and must never be stained with dissimulation or baseness. Given this, the aim of Satan's henchmen in England is to pressure the Catholics into making some acknowledgment of and obeisance to the queen's religious authority as supreme head—and, as a sign of this recognition and obedience, to consent to go to their synagogues and hear their diabolical doctrine. This the Catholics cannot in good conscience do, because in so doing they would imply that they are satisfied with and approve of what the heretics do. No more would it be right for a Christian to wear the garments used by Moors or Jews as the symbols of their sect and their faith, because this would be to proclaim, through such garb, that they were not a Christian.

Saint Eusebius, bishop of Vercelli, banished by the Arian Emperor Constantius on account of his Catholic faith, was handed over to a bishop called Patrophilus, who had been a companion of Arius himself, and was a fanatical, bloodthirsty heretic. He locked the saint in a gloomy, wretched cell, and kept

---

6   In the margin: "Book 3, Chapter 3, Letter 3."
     According to the modern numbering, see Cyprian, *Letters*, 59.20.

7   In the margin: "On the passion of the Lord."
     Leo the Great, *Sermons*, 69.5.

8   In the margin: "Book 4, Chapter 14 [*vere* 13]."
     Theodoret, *Ecclesiastical History*, 4.13.

9   Lucifer of Cagliari penned a treatise entitled *De non conveniendo cum haereticis* ("On not meeting with heretics"). See Lucifer of Cagliari, *Opuscula*, 3–34.

10   In the margin: "Book 2, Chapter 8."
     Ribadeneyra, *Tratado de la tribulacion*, Book 2, Chapter 8.

him there for several days without food, threatening that he would not be given any, unless he took it from his house, from the hands of his servants—with the intent of proclaiming, if he did not take it, that he had starved himself to death in desperation, and if he did take it, that he had conversed with him and was of his faith. The saint resolved to die before eating what the heretical bishop sent from his house, not because he wished to kill himself, but rather because he deemed it better to die than to give the misbeliever an excuse to claim that he had joined and accepted his faith, as he had schemed. But he wrote him a letter, explaining the reasons that moved him not to eat from his hands and that if he died from hunger, it would not be self-slaughter, but rather the false bishop who had murdered him by this artifice. And this resolve vindicated the bishop, for he neither died of hunger nor communed with the heretic, and God was in him and was glorified by him.[11]

All this concerns the Catholics' attending the heretics' churches and listening to their sermons. But the much more perilous and disturbing issue is that the queen demands they affirm and accept her as spiritual head of the kingdom of England—and there are so many unthinkable and horrifying monsters within this monster that they defy description. For, leaving aside that a woman is incapable, by her very nature, of being the head of a man,[12] much less of the Church of an entire kingdom, in this they allow her the authority to confer upon others what she herself neither has, nor can have or give. That is, to give the bishops and priests the authority to preach, to guide souls, and to administer the sacraments—she being unable to preach, or even to speak in the

---

11   In the second of his three extant letters (*c*.355), Eusebius of Vercelli (*c*.283–371) describes his imprisonment by Patrophilus, the Arian bishop of Scythopolis (d. *c*.360): "Lest I eat faithless food from the hands of the faithless, or rather of faithless transgressors (which is worse), as the Apostle says, I wrote a message to them in this fashion [...] I have resolved that my plan is now and will remains in the future not to eat any bread or drink any water until each of you has declared, not only by word but also on paper, that you will not exclude my brothers, who suffer these things with me willingly for the sake of the faith, from the lodgings in which they abide, and now will you prevent them, or those, who have deigned to seek me out, from offering necessary food. [...] But if you decide that you ought to disregard this, not on the grounds that I fear death, but so that after my death you do not say that I wanted to die through a voluntary death and you do not invent some cloud of accusation against us, know that I will assemble the churches [...] And so then on the fourth day they were softened by this letter and compelled us to return famished to these lodgings in which we had been staying." For the letter in Richard Flower's translation, see Richard Flower, *Emperors and Bishops in Late Roman Invective* (Cambridge: Cambridge University Press, 2013), 243–49, here 245–46.

12   1 Cor. 11:3.

church, as Saint Paul says.[13] And not only do they wish her to have this power, in addition to the royal authority, but also to establish and ordain what the preachers ought to preach, with what ceremonies they ought to administer the sacraments, and how God ought to be revered and served, as well as to punish and deprive of their benefices those who do not obey her orders and ecclesiastical laws. This is an ocean of absurdities, confusions, and sacrileges, an abyss of madness and error.

For first they strip the pope, who is the head of the Church and vicar general of Jesus Christ on earth, of his power, so that he cannot control the spiritual affairs of England; though he is the universal shepherd, to whom the Lord entrusted all his sheep,[14] they refuse to acknowledge him as such and to be guided and ruled by him—thus showing that they are not sheep of Christ's flock.[15] From this it follows that they would put two heads on the same mystical body of the Church, one in Rome and another in England—or, properly speaking, make as many heads as there are kingdoms in Christendom, for every monarch has the same claim to be the spiritual head of their realm as this deluded queen asserts in hers. And thus the holy Church would come to have as many heads as it has monarchs and become a horrendous, frightful monster, if it were (as it is) one, or to have as many churches as there are heads, and so divide and dismember the holy communion of the Church that we acknowledge in the Apostles' Creed, multiplying that unity and undoing that knot and tie by which all we Christians across the world, scattered though we may be through diverse regions, with distinct laws and customs, are bound one to another, as members composing a mystical body whose head is Jesus Christ,[16] and in his place, his vicar. Besides this, the door is opened to all the errors and heresies that any sort of obsessed king or deranged, foolhardy man might desire to invent and defend, fencing himself off from the Church's beneficial means of forestalling and punishing them. For general councils would never be convened if the rulers, as spiritual heads of their kingdoms, did not consent, nor, once they had met, would their mandates and decrees be obeyed—as we have seen in England with regard to the Council of Trent, to which the queen declined to send her ambassadors and churchmen, nor, after it had concluded, did she accept its definitions and decrees, because she deems herself supreme spiritual head of her realm, and the source, after Christ, whence all spiritual power must flow there, without acknowledging or accepting any other outside

---

13   1 Cor. 14:34–35.
14   John 21:15–17.
15   Acts 20:28.
16   Rom. 12:5; 1 Cor. 6:15, 12:12, 12:17; Eph. 5:30; Col. 1:18.

her kingdom. Therefore, they have barred from it all bishops, archbishops, and patriarchs who are not Englishmen, or any Englishmen who have not been consecrated through the queen's supremacy, so as not to admit of any other authority, jurisdiction, or power competent to judge and decide religious controversies or errors in England. And finally, they confound and pervert the order of all things divine and human, preferring the body to the soul, temporal rule to the spiritual, and the kingdom of the earth to that of heaven, the inferior to the superior, the sheep to the shepherd, making the head the feet and the feet the head, giving liberty to the subject to pass sentence over the judge, exempting the queen from ecclesiastical censure and discipline, from which no true child of Christ's family can be immune. And there are infinite other outrages in this title of spiritual head or governor that the queen usurps, so many unnatural and hateful monstrosities of errors and crimes that it provokes wonder and fear to see that men of sense do not see them, and that they choose to support so infamous and devilish a tyranny with laws, punishments, and executions. And likewise to witness how, for the sake of undoing this, or of not submitting to it, the Catholics of England must give their lives and for this truth die mutilated and destroyed by the most extreme torments (as die they do).

Saint Athanasius calls Emperor Constantius the Antichrist for having usurped the spiritual power, and says these words: "What deed has he left undone that belongs to the Antichrist? What more will the Antichrist do when he comes? Will he not find the path beaten for his plots and deceptions, for he has raised up his court to inquire into ecclesiastical matters, and made himself sovereign and judge over the cases that emerge from them?" And in another place, he says, "Who, on seeing him rule as a magistrate in ecclesiastical cases, and make himself the head of the bishops, would not rightly judge him to be that abomination of desolation prophesied by Daniel?"[17] And he proceeds to prove that the Church never seized the authority of the emperors, nor were there any flatterers perverse enough to counsel their princes to so base a deed, nor any prince foolhardy enough to attempt it. Bishop Hosius of Córdoba (whose influence at the Council of Nicaea was immense) wrote to the same emperor in these words: "Do not interfere in ecclesiastical matters, nor dictate to us what we ought to do therein, but learn that from us, for God has entrusted the empire to you, and to us what belongs to the Church."[18] Bishop

---

17   Dan. 9:27, 11:31, 12:11.

18   In the margin: "In the letter he wrote to the hermits."

        Athanasius, *Historia Arianorum ad monachos*, Chapters 44, 76.

        Ribadeneyra has copied these sentiments from the *Concertatio*'s reproduction of William Allen's defense of the Catholic martyrs. See *Concertatio*, 257ʳ.

Leontios advised the same thing—and the emperor, as Suidas writes, abashed and ashamed of what he had done, after having been thus warned did it no more.[19] And in the same vein, Saint Ambrose told Emperor Valentinian the Younger, "Do not deceive yourself, O emperor, nor imagine that you have the right to be such over things divine. Do not exalt yourself, but if you wish to rule a long time, subject yourself to God, as it is written, give to God what is God's and to Caesar what is Caesar's.[20] To the emperor belong the palaces, to the priest the churches. The walls of the city are your responsibility, not sacred matters."[21] And so as not to be overlong, I omit what Saint Hilary, Saint Gregory Nazianzus, Saint Chrysostom, and many other holy and sagacious doctors offer against this abominable power claimed by Queen Elizabeth in her kingdom.[22] I will only add that it is so detestable, so beyond all sound judgment and reason, that Calvin himself (whose gospel is embraced with so much impiety in England that they have shed the innocent blood of numerous servants of God to advance it) regarded as blasphemous those who gave Henry VIII, Elizabeth's father, the title of head of the Church (though he was a man, not a woman). It is so monstrous a thing that even so savage a beast, a living portrait of Satan, regarded it as such. And the other Lutheran heretics also condemned it. Even the knights and lords of England itself, when this unheard-of, bizarre outrage was enacted in the first parliament and it was mandated that an oath be taken to affirm the queen as head of the Church in her kingdom, abominated it as an absurdity and exempted themselves from such an oath, while obliging the bishops, prelates, and ecclesiastical persons, as we wrote in the second book of the first part of this history.[23]

Well, although this is the perfect truth, and all English Catholics have such a profound obligation to do as they do, and to give a thousand lives if they had them, lest they condemn their souls to hell by accepting a thing so foul and so monstrous, so contrary to our sacred faith and to the teachings of all the saints,

---

19   In the margin: "Suidas, on Leontios."

   "Suidas" was long supposed to be the compiler of the *Souda*, a tenth-century Greek lexicon of the ancient and late antique world. See "Leontios," trans. Catharine Roth, in "Suda On Line," 2015, http://www.stoa.org/sol/ [accessed September 1, 2015].

   The citation of Suidas likewise comes from Allen, as reprinted in the *Concertatio*, 257ʳ.

20   Matt. 22:21; Mark 12:17; Luke 20:25.

21   In the margin: "Letter 33."

   Ambrose of Milan, *Letters*, 20.19.

   This letter is cited as "Letter 33" in the *Concertatio*, whence Ribadeneyra took his Latin: see *Concertatio*, 357ʳ.

22   All these authors are cited in the same passage from Allen. Ibid., 257ʳ–257ᵛ.

23   In the margin: "Book 2, Chapter 24."

so prejudicial to the union of the holy Church, so abhorred and condemned by all persons who have any use of their reason, the queen's agents (as though they had none at all) nevertheless persecute the Catholics with violence and cruelty, as has been described, for no other crime than seeking salvation. And they are not satisfied with all the laws and edicts that they have promulgated in all the years past, but each day come up with yet more, harsh and barbaric. Among these, the most extreme, and that which most reveals their wickedness, is that issued last year, 1591, of which we made mention earlier. And so that the edict itself will prove what I say, I have decided to include it here, scrupulously translated into our Castilian tongue.[24]

I have decided to include it here, so that from the edict itself the attentive and pious reader may understand the utter truth of what I have said, and how anything of hatred and abhorrence of Catholicism goes unchecked and unbounded in that kingdom. But as it is very long, very extreme, and offensive, I have contented myself with relating its substance, so that he who reads it will not be scandalized by its words, nor be weakened by its arguments or the awful harshness with which they seek to extinguish all who profess our sacred faith. And also so that he may marvel at the wickedness of people so degenerate, at the infinite tenderness of the Lord in enduring this, and at the gravity of our guilt, for the sake of which he permits this, in his righteous judgment punishing the sins of that kingdom with further sins, and such great abominations with other, greater abominations. A terrifying and dire chastisement, more to be feared than any worldly sentence.[25]

---

24   This sentence only appears in the first 1593 edition and the 1594 Antwerp edition—those that included Chapter 16a.

25   This passage appears in the second 1593 edition and all editions from 1595 onwards— those that included Chapter 16b.

The Edict the Queen Promulgated against Our Sacred Religion, and against the Pope, and the Catholic King, Who Defend it[1,2]

The Queen

A declaration of the great disturbances being plotted against the commonwealth by a horde of seminary priests and Jesuits, who have been dispatched in secret and dispersed throughout the kingdom to concoct strange treacheries under the false name of religion, and the provisions and necessary remedies for checking this wickedness, proclaimed by Her Majesty's command.

Although we had good reason to think that at the end of almost thirty-three years of our reign (throughout which Almighty God has preserved us in the peaceful possession of our kingdom) the cruel and violent malice of our enemies would have abated, weakened, and quieted, and especially that of the king of Spain, who for so many years and without just cause has worked to disturb our state (and not only him, but all his clients), that his enmity would have softened and turned to a more gentle and peaceable spirit, that this king would be disposed to live quietly and tranquilly with us and with other Christian monarchs, and that thus a universal peace might be established in Christendom, which is now disrupted and confounded by his wars and conflicts, and by no other cause, yet, observing his present actions, with greater expense and effort than ever before, we clearly perceive the opposite. But we believe that God, who is the Lord of Hosts,[3] is pleased that such men, neither satisfied with what they have nor willing to live in peace, should fall and be ruined

---

1   For the complexities of Chapter 16 across the editions of the *Historia*, see the introduction.

2   The text here is a slight abbreviation of the October 18, 1591 decree: see *TRP*, 3:86–93.

　　Ribadeneyra may have translated from the Latin text provided piecemeal by Robert Persons in the *Philopater*, or the full text appended to Thomas Stapleton's response. See *Philopater, passim*, and Stapleton, *Apologia*, n.p.

　　For the copious Catholic literature attacking Elizabeth's edict, see Houliston, "Lord Treasurer."

3   The Hebrew phrase "יְהוָֹה צְבָאוֹת," translated as "the Lord of hosts," appears frequently throughout the Bible, first used in 1 Kings 1:3.

and overthrown, and for this reason he has permitted this king, in his old age (better suited to peace than war), and in a time when he should be perfectly satisfied with his own territories without wanting to usurp those of others through force of arms (for his empire now commands more crowns, more kingdoms and peoples, greater and more abundant worldly riches than any of his predecessors or any other Christian prince has ever had), in this old age, I say, God has allowed him to initiate a perfidious war, most perilous for all of Christendom, against the reigning king of France; just as for the past two years he has obviously intended to wage against us and invade our realms, all the while treating with us of peace—but God has resisted him, and given him and his entire army cause for repentance and humility.

Therefore, having now learned with certainty that the king of Spain, to provide some pretext for his outrageous, violent actions, has arranged for a Milanese vassal of his to be elevated to the Roman pontificate,[4] and prevailed upon him, without the consent of the College of Cardinals, to exhaust and waste the riches of the Church in raising soldiers in Italy (which had heard no noise of arms in a long time) and many other places, to dispatch them to France under the command of his nephew to invade that kingdom, which has always extended its hand to the Church in all its travails. Furthermore, this war, so broadly and vigorously waged against France, cannot fail to endanger our territories and realms, especially as numerous trustworthy reports inform us that this king's preparations against our crown and lands, by sea and by land, for the coming year are greater than they have ever been.

Besides this, we know that to advance this enterprise the king, availing himself of the power of his henchman the pope (utterly dependent on his will), has negotiated with several conspirators and rabble-rousers, rebellious subjects of this realm (base and common men), who with enormous effort and at the expense of the same king incite a horde of dissolute youths who, partly for lack of wherewithal, partly for the crimes they have committed, have left their homeland and become fugitives, rebels, and traitors.

And whereas certain establishments for the sustenance and support of such persons have been founded at Rome and in Spain, under the name

---

4   The Milanese Cardinal Niccolò Sfondrato (r.1590–91) was elected Pope Gregory XIV on December 9, 1590. Born a Spanish vassal (Philip II was duke of Milan), Gregory was a close ally of the Habsburg monarchy, and owed his election to Spanish influence. Pastor, *History of the Popes*, 22:351–55.

of seminaries, whence, having learned all that is necessary for plotting and advancing their intended treasons and uprisings, they are secretly sent back to our realms with wide powers from the Roman pontiff to persuade all those with whom they dare speak to abandon the obedience they owe to us and our crown, and with the hope of a Spanish invasion, give them to understand that they will be enriched with the wealth and property of others—our loyal subjects.

For this cause, the said priests extract a strict oath from those of our subjects with whom they engage, to abandon the rightful submission they owe to us, to yield their obedience, property, and powers to the king of Spain, and to aid his army when it comes. To do this more efficiently, and to deceive the simple folk more easily, these sowers of treason carry certain papal bulls—some of indulgences, which promise heaven to all those who follow their instructions, and others of malediction, which threaten eternal damnation in hell to those who do not listen to their villainous, perverse arguments.

And though these popish practices have been used of old in various places, yet we have attempted to stop them through the enforcement of the laws we have passed against these rebels, and this solely for their treasons and the crime of *lèse-majesté*, and not on religious grounds, as their supporters falsely claim to find some pretext for their perfidy. And their mendacity is perfectly clear, for in the criminal proceedings brought against them they are not accused, condemned, or executed for anything but the charge of *lèse-majesté*, and because among other things they affirm that if the pope sent an army against us and against our faith, they would follow and aid it. Likewise, it is easily seen that none of them died for matter of religion, for in our kingdom many wealthy men are known to follow a faith contrary to our own, and are not punished or deprived of life or wealth on that account. They are only required to pay a certain financial penalty when they recuse themselves or refuse to go to our churches. And this our manner of governing, so gentle and moderate, manifestly proves how false are the claims of these fugitives from our kingdom and their slanderous pamphlets.

And notwithstanding all this, we know for a fact that some of the heads of these hideouts or sanctuaries, which the traitors call seminaries, or colleges of Jesuits, very recently persuaded the king of Spain that although that mighty Spanish force prepared against us came to an unhappy end, yet if he undertakes this enterprise once more, he shall find within this island many millions of men (thus they color things according to their purposes) who will follow his army as soon as it makes land.

And although prudence and past experience should teach this king not to harbor any such hope or intention of sending his troops to England, yet these reports and promises make him hesitate and vacillate.

These rumors are primarily fed to the king in Spain by a certain scholar by the name of Persons, who does this claiming to be the Catholic King's confessor, and to the Roman pontiff by another scholar, Allen by name, who has been honored with a cardinal's hat for the treasons he has plotted against us. These two have provided the said princes with a list of many men, especially in the ports of our kingdom, who they imagine are, or will be, of their party and supporters and collaborators with the Spanish when their armies arrive. And albeit the pope and the king know well that the greater part of what they say is false, yet seeing that these seminarians, priests, and Jesuits are the ideal agents of their impious projects, and for keeping the people firm in their accursed loyalty, they have sent many of them to England in the utmost secrecy within a few days—that is to say, within the space of ten or twelve months, so that dispersed through the country, they can inform their confederates that the king is determined (as we have learned from those of them taken prisoner) to make another attempt next year, expending all his power against England. But, as some of the king's advisers, more circumspect than the rest, are of the opinion that this shall do nothing but waste the king's time and money, the king has realized that if no progress should be made against us, he can easily turn his forces upon France, or the states of Flanders, or against some part of Scotland, where some of this wicked caste of the seminaries have also penetrated.

Thus, because the king of Spain's intentions have become so clear and obvious that we can no longer harbor any doubt, and though we trust that God, the defender of all just causes, shall undo them and destroy them (as he has always done hitherto), yet, so as not to falter in our duties, having received from his mighty hand the supreme governance of this realm, we consider that we are obligated to use every means that God has given us, combining them with his divine favor, to augment our strength, with the aid and service of our loyal subjects, and to enforce the laws against the seditious through their good diligence, and do and legislate other things to stymie these treacheries.

To this end, before all else we require and charge all our ecclesiastical subjects to make every effort that there be godly ministers in the Church, who by their instruction and the example of their lives may steadfastly preserve the people in the profession of the Gospel, and in what they are obligated to do before God and before us, especially seeing that some few rabble-rousers and instigators among these traitors and turncoats continually watch and work by means of the seminaries to deceive the unlearned and unlettered, and lead them away from sense and justice.

Second, as to maintaining ready forces by land and by sea to break these puffed-up winds [*odres hinchados*] that threaten us from Spain, we hope that with the observance of our previous orders we shall be more powerful than ever in resisting the foe. But we also require our subjects to assist us with their hands, their purses, and their counsels, and plead with God in prayer to aid us and lend his hand to a defense so righteous, honorable, necessary, and beneficial—for it is only to defend our native land, to preserve our wives, families, and children, our honors, our property, our freedom, and our successors, against the rapacious foreigners, and against some few desperate assailants and monstrous traitors.

Third, to provide an effective and timely remedy for the secret, cunning plots of the seminarians, the Jesuits, and the other traitors (without whom we believe the king of Spain would not now be hazarding some new enterprise), as well as those who, with a hypocritical semblance of sanctity, gently worm their way into the souls of our subjects and incline them little by little to their treasons, we have resolved to send our commissioners to all the counties and provinces of our kingdom, and to all the coastal cities, towns, and places thereof, with the broadest mandates to inquire, with the utmost diligence and exquisite means, into all suspect persons, whosoever they may be, who persuade others or allow themselves to be persuaded to give their obedience to the pope or to the king of Spain.

And because it is known that many of the said seminarians enter our kingdom in secret and in sundry garb, so as to seem to be what they are not, and infiltrate the universities and the palaces of the elites, and cunningly insinuate themselves into the families of knights and distinguished ladies, to hide themselves more securely, we command and strictly order each and every person, of whatever sort, estate, sex, condition, or rank, and even the officials of our palace, and our ministers and magistrates, and all the lords of whatever family, and the governors of any society to make a rigorous count of all who have frequented their houses or dwelt therein or presently do something of this sort, or may do in future, for at least these past fourteen months, inquiring especially into the name, condition, and quality of these persons, in what part of England they were born, where they have worked or spent their time for at least a year before they came to their house, how and whence they sustain themselves, what they do and where they are wont to go, with whom they speak, and if at the times stipulated by our laws they go to church to hear the divine offices as they ought.

All these inquiries, with their answers, we order to be written down in detail in books, and that these books be diligently kept, like registers or calendars, by the father of each household, so that our commissioners, when they appear, can thereby understand the character of the persons under suspicion, and recognize the industriousness and loyalty of the said heads of household.

And if anyone should respond to these questions with ill will, or hesitate in their answers, we desire that they should immediately be seized and sent under heavy guard to whatever commissioner is nearest. And we order that the same be done to the fathers of the households or householders who are negligent or remiss in carrying out this inquiry, and that they be punished by the commissioners according to the nature of the infraction. And if any are found who have succored the said suspect persons, or who do not, within twenty days of the publication of this edict in each province, reveal them to the commissioners, we desire that any such person be punished with the same penalty given to the accomplices, abettors, and confederates of traitors and rebels, in which matter we are resolved with utter firmness to allow no leniency or mitigation of the penalty, out of any respect for any sort of dignity or condition whatsoever, nor to admit of any excuse for negligence or omission from those who do not uncover these traitors or do not scrupulously complete the said inquiry for all suspect persons of whatever sort. For this is in no way contrary, but rather highly agreeable to the most ancient laws of our realms and to its laudable customs, for the preservation of subjects' obedience so due to us and to our crown. Given in our palace of Richmond, October 18, 1591, the thirty-third year of our reign.

This is the queen's edict, which I want the pious and thoughtful reader to peruse and examine with care, for this alone shall convey the current state of religion in England as fully as the rest of this history. For, if we look at the intentions it harbors, the reasons it avers, and the purport and content of the edict itself, we shall find that it is sacrilegious before God; false and outrageous in what it says against the supreme pontiff and against the Catholic King of Spain, Don Philip; savage and barbaric against the priests of the seminaries and against the Jesuits; and draconian and intolerable to the entire kingdom of England. And that it is filled with falsehoods, numerous contradictions and incompatibilities, which he who composed it either did not notice or chose to disguise. I well perceive that it does not belong to the historian to respond to such slanders, but rather to tell what came to pass with truth and plainness, in a manner that pleases and improves the reader. But because what we are about is an affair of God and his faith, and my intention in writing this history has been to place before its readers one of the fiercest and most horrific persecutions that the holy Church has yet endured, and to make clear, on the one hand, the impiety of the heretics of our times, and on the other, the artifice and cunning they use in their crimes, for the reasons I set out at the beginning of this book, and because all I could write is contained, as in a cipher, within this edict, I wish to beg the kindly reader's pardon for not examining it at length or responding to its insanities, but for rather expounding at greater length than is my custom the part that touches on our sacred religion. Truly, since this history is not written solely for those now living, who know what has occurred, but also (and much more) for those who do not know this, and for those who will read it in centuries to come (with the Lord's favor), it is right that they should learn the truth as it is, and not as the edict renders it. For, being promulgated by a queen, whose counsels ought to be thoughtful and circumspect, her decrees just and deliberate, and the words thereof truthful and exact, if they believe what it says, they will be seriously deceived and I shall not attain the fruit I seek in this project of mine. And thus it is necessary that, having included the edict, we likewise provide the antidote and the theriac with which it ought to be read, so that this poison does not infect and kill those who read it, imagining that what it says is true and conceiving ideas so contrary to the truth.

The decree contains four principal elements. The first, accusations and slanders against the Catholic King Don Philip of Spain. The second, affronts and outrages against the pope. The third, falsehoods and absurdities against the seminaries. The fourth, provisions against the priests thereof and against the fathers of the Society of Jesus, and new and exquisite means of apprehending them and eradicating them. The thrust of the edict aims at two ends. The first, to render hateful and abhorrent our sacred faith and the Catholic who profess it and the priests who teach it. The second, to terrify the queen's English subjects with made-up fears of invasion and treacheries, so that they will thus come to abominate the students of the seminaries, whom they claim are the cause thereof, and simultaneously yield up their property to the queen for their defense with greater promptitude and generosity.

I wish to speak here only of what concerns our sacred religion, such as belongs to my history and what I have observed from the beginning, omitting all other matters that are not so closely connected or bound up with the said religion as to oblige me to write them down. For this reason, I will not speak here of the edict's absurdities and insanities against the pope and the Catholic King, save on two counts alone, which relate to religion, both so as not to stray from the path I follow and because the things it says are so notoriously false and senseless that one need only read and consider them to see them for what they are. And because it is not right that we should place in dispute or prejudice such thoughtful, just, moderate, famous actions, praised as such by every thinking person, of princes so great and of such majesty, in answer to what one woman, deranged by heresy and badly advised by her ministers, publishes against them, in an edict so idiotic and incoherent as this. Yet what I omit to do here, for the reasons I have explained, has been done by other writers, who have responded to the decree and with the light of truth dissolved the shadows and lies it contains. Of these texts, two have come into my hands; one is the book entitled *Exemplar literarum missarum è Germania, ad dominum Gulielmum Cecilium consiliarium regium*[5]—it is understood that this Cecil is the principal author of this edict. And the other, by a doctor of theology called Andreas Philopater, printed at Lyon, this past year of 1592. To these, I defer.

---

5 Joseph Cresswell, *Exemplar literarum, missarum, e Germania, ad Guilielmum Cecilium, consiliarium regium* (Rome: s.n., 1592).

What is Contained in the Edict the Queen Promulgated against Our Sacred Religion

This is the title of the edict:

> A declaration of the great disturbances that have been plotted against the commonwealth by a horde of priests from the seminaries, and Jesuits, who have been dispatched in secret, and dispersed throughout the kingdom to concoct outlandish treacheries under the false name of religion, and the provisions and necessary remedies for checking this wickedness, proclaimed by Her Majesty's command.

This title, being false, and employed as a pretext for persecuting the seminary priests and the fathers of the Society of Jesus as rebels and disturbers of the kingdom of England, is thus placed as a foundation upon which to raise all that follows, and render hateful those who defend the Catholic faith with their blood, or profess it.

> After having laid—as I said—this false foundation, she proceeds erecting thereon numerous other falsehoods, especially against the pope and the Catholic King for having undertaken a war in defense of the kingdom of France and the Catholic faith, which the prince of Béarn seeks to eradicate. In her edict, the queen calls this war unjust and perilous to the entirety of Christendom. And also because they favor and support the seminaries established at Rheims in France, at Rome, at Valladolid and Seville (as will be seen hereafter) to shelter the English Catholics who wander in exile for the sake of the Catholic faith and intend to return to aid it (as they do) with their sweat and blood. For it is against the students of these seminaries and against the fathers of the Society of Jesus who teach, rear, and encourage them that the queen directs most of the force of the edict, claiming that the Englishmen raised there are base, filthy men, so impoverished and so wicked that, not having wherewithal in England and fearing the penalties for their crimes, they have fled that realm as fugitives, rebels, and traitors. And that, to prevent them returning and to punish those who might return, as they deserve for their great

treasons, she has made certain laws, and it is by these (and for the crime of *lèse-majesté*) alone that she has these men executed, and not for the sake of religion, as their accomplices falsely proclaim to find a pretext for their wickedness.[1]

And to prove the truth of so obvious a lie, she says,

> And the mendacity of those who make such claims is perfectly clear, for in the criminal proceedings brought against them they are not accused, nor condemned, nor executed, save for the crime of *lèse-majesté*, and because among other things they affirm that if the pope sent an army against her, or against her false creed, they would follow and aid it.

And she adds, to further confirm what she says:

> Likewise, it is easily seen that none of them died for matter of religion, for in England many wealthy men are known to follow a faith contrary to the queen's, and they are not punished or deprived of life or wealth on that account, and that they are only required to pay a certain financial penalty when they recuse themselves or refuse to go to their churches. And she concludes that this her manner of governing, so gentle and moderate, manifestly proves how false are the claims of these fugitives from England and their slanderous pamphlets against her.

Finally, after having given a long account of many other false and senseless matters, in order to persuade her kingdom of its peril from the treacheries that the Jesuits and the seminary priests plot and concoct against it, she discusses their remedy, and before all else:

> she requires and charges all her ecclesiastical subjects to make every effort that there be godly ministers in the Church, who by their instruction and the example of their lives may steadfastly preserve the people in the profession of the Gospel, and in what they are obligated to do before God and before the queen, especially seeing that some few rabble-rousers and

---

1 Throughout this chapter, Ribadeneyra sets off passages in italics, just as he does for direct quotations, even though he has substantially altered the text of the edict, and often explicitly speaks in an authorial voice.

instigators among these traitors and turncoats continually watch and
work by means of the seminaries to deceive the unlearned and unlettered, and lead them away from sense and justice—which is the constant
justification and pretext for her guile and cruelty.

Second, she requires her subjects to assist and serve her with their
hands, their purses, and their counsels, and plead with God in prayer to
aid her in a defense so righteous, honorable, necessary, and beneficial—
for it is only to defend their native land, to preserve their wives, families, and children, their honors, property, and freedom against some few
desperate assailants and monstrous traitors.

Third, to provide an effective and timely remedy for the secret, cunning plots of the seminarians, the Jesuits, and the other traitors who, with
a hypocritical semblance of sanctity, gently worm their way into the souls
of the English and incline them little by little to their treasons, she has resolved to send her commissioners to all the counties and provinces of her
kingdom, and to all the cities, towns, and places thereof, with the broadest authorization and mandates to inquire, with the utmost diligence
and exquisite means, into all suspect persons, who persuade others or
allow themselves to be persuaded to give their obedience to the pope—
against whom, and the Apostolic faith, all heretics' hatred is extreme, and
especially those of England.

Besides this, she adds that, because it is known that many of the said
seminarians enter England in secret and in sundry garb, so as to seem to
be what they are not, and infiltrate the universities and the palaces of
the elites, and cunningly insinuate themselves with great artifice into the
families of knights and distinguished ladies, to hide themselves more
securely, she commands and strictly orders each and every person, of
whatever sort, estate, sex, condition, or rank, and even the officials of her
palace, ministers, and magistrates, and all the lords of whatever family,
and the governors of any society to make a rigorous count of all who have
in the past fourteen months prior to the edict frequented their houses;
or dwelt there; or spoken, slept, or eaten; or presently do anything of this
sort, or may do so in future, inquiring especially into the name, condition,
and quality of these persons, in what part of England they were born,
where they have worked or spent their time for at least a year before they
came to their house, how and whence they sustain themselves, what they
do and where they are wont to go, with whom they speak, and if at the
times stipulated by law they go to church to hear the divine offices as they
ought.

And in order that such extraordinary investigations should not be in vain, she commands:

> That all this, with the answers, be written down in detail in books, and that these books be diligently kept in each house, like registers or calendars, by the father of the household, so that the commissioners, when they appear, can thereby understand the character of the persons under suspicion, and recognize the industriousness and loyalty of the said heads of household.

All that we have mentioned thus far does not suffice, but, in order that no Catholic might escape, Elizabeth adds this to her decree:

> That if anyone should respond to these questions with ill will, or hesitate or vacillate in their answers, she desires and commands that they should immediately be seized and sent under heavy guard to whatever commissioner is nearest. And she orders that the same be done to the fathers of families and heads of houses who are negligent or remiss in carrying out this inquiry, and that they be punished by the commissioners according to the nature of the infraction. And if any are found who have succored the said suspect persons, or who do not, within twenty days of the publication of this edict in the provinces, reveal them to the commissioners, it is her will that any such person be punished with the same penalty given to the accomplices, abettors, and confederates of traitors and rebels.

And, in order that all may understand how seriously she takes this business, and how determined the queen is to carry it through to the end without abating her severity one jot, she concludes by saying,

> that she is resolved with utter firmness to allow no leniency or mitigation of the penalty, out of any respect for any sort of dignity or condition whatsoever, nor to admit of any excuse for negligence or omission from those who do not uncover these traitors, or do not scrupulously complete the said inquiry for all suspect persons of whatever sort who might be suspect. For this is in no way contrary, but rather highly agreeable to the most ancient laws of her realms and to its laudable customs, for the preservation of her subjects' obedience so due to her crown, and the tranquility and peace of her realm.

This is a summary of the most important things the queen says in her edict against our sacred religion and those who profess it. Dated at her palace of Richmond, on October 18, in the year of our Lord 1591, the thirty-third year of her reign.

I now ask and implore the pious and thoughtful reader to read and consider carefully the content of this edict, and all that has been included here, for by this alone (to my poor judgment) they shall comprehend the present state of religion in England, just as well as by everything else in this history. For, if we look to the intentions it harbors, the reasons it avers, and the purport and content of the edict itself, we shall find that it is impious against God; false and outrageous in what it says against the supreme pontiff and against the Catholic King of Spain, Don Philip, savage and barbaric against the priests of the seminaries and against the Jesuits; and draconian and intolerable to the entire kingdom of England. And that it is full of falsehoods, numerous contradictions and incompatibilities, which he who composed it either did not notice or chose to disguise. I well perceive that it does not belong to the historian to respond to such slanders, but rather to tell what came to pass with truth and plainness, in a manner that pleases and improves the reader. But because what we are about is an affair of God and his faith, and my intention in writing this history has been to place before its readers one of the fiercest and most horrific persecutions that the holy Church has yet endured, and to make clear, on the one hand, the impiety of the heretics of our times, and on the other, the artifice and cunning they use in their wickedness, for the reasons I set out at the beginning of this book, and all I could write is contained, as in a cipher, within this edict, I wish to beg the kindly reader's pardon for not examining it at length or responding to its insanities, but for rather expounding at greater length than is my custom the part that touches on our sacred religion. Truly, since this history is not written solely for those now living, who know what has occurred, but also (and much more) for those who do not know this, and for those who will read it in centuries to come (with the Lord's favor), it is right that they should learn the truth as it is, and not as the edict renders it. For, being promulgated by a queen, whose counsels ought to be thoughtful and circumspect, her decrees just and deliberate, and the words thereof truthful and exact, if they believe what it says, they will be seriously deceived and I shall not attain the fruit I seek in this project of mine. And thus it is necessary that, having included the edict, we likewise provide the antidote and the theriac with which it ought to be read, so that this poison does not infect and kill those who read it, imagining that what it says is true and conceiving ideas so contrary to the truth.

The decree contains four principal elements. The first, accusations and slanders against Catholic King Don Philip of Spain. The second, affronts and outrages against the pope. The third, falsehoods and absurdities against the semi-naries. The fourth, provisions against the priests thereof and against the fathers of the Society of Jesus, and new and exquisite means of apprehending them and eradicating them. The thrust of the edict aims at two ends. The first, to render hateful and abhorrent our sacred faith and the Catholics who profess it and the priests who teach it. The second, to terrify the queen's English subjects with made-up fears of invasion and treacheries, so that they will thus come to abominate the students of the seminaries, whom they claim are the cause thereof, and simultaneously yield up their property to the queen for their de-fense with greater promptitude and generosity.

I wish to speak here only of what concerns our sacred religion, such as be-longs to my history and what I have observed from the beginning, omitting all other matters that are not so closely connected or bound up with the said religion as to oblige me to write them down. For this reason, I will not speak here of the edict's absurdities and insanities against the pope and the Catholic King, save on two counts alone, which relate to religion, both so as not to stray from the path I follow and because the things it says are so notoriously false and senseless that one need only read and consider them to see them for what they are. And because it is not right that we should place in dispute or preju-dice such thoughtful, just, moderate, famous actions, praised as such by every thinking person, of princes so great and of such majesty, in answer to what one woman, deranged by heresy and badly advised by her ministers, publishes against them, in an edict so idiotic and incoherent as this. Yet what I omit to do here, for the reasons I have explained, has been done by other writers, who have responded to the decree and with the light of truth dissolved the shadows and lies it contains. Of those that have been composed, two three[2] have come to my hands: one, the book entitled *Exemplar literarum missarum è Germania, ad dominum Gulielmum Cecilium consiliarium regium*—it is understood that this Cecil is the principal author of this edict. And the other by a doctor of theology called Andreas Philopater, printed at Lyon in France[3] this past year of 1592. The third is by another, by the name of Didymus Veridico, printed in Germany.[4] To these, I defer.

---

2   From the 1595 edition, Ribadeneyra adds a third book, and thus changes the number.

3   Added in the 1595 edition.

4   Under the pseudonym of Didymus Veridicus Henfildanus, Thomas Stapleton published his own response to the edict, the *Apologia pro Rege Catholico Philippo II*.
    The citation of Stapleton is added in the 1595 edition.

That This Edict is Sacrilegious and Blasphemous against God

Now, to begin with, let me say first of all that this edict of the queen's is sacrilegious and blasphemous against God our Lord, for in it the queen urgently charges her ecclesiastical subjects that there should be pious ministers in the churches, who by their teachings and the examples of their lives should preserve the people in the profession of the Gospel. I ask, what Gospel is this, in which the people of England are to be preserved? Is this the Gospel that Christ our Redeemer left us? The one the Holy Spirit inspired and dictated? The one the Evangelists wrote? The one the Apostles spread? The one the holy Doctors proclaimed? The one the faithful embraced? The one countless hosts of redoubtable martyrs defended with their blood? The one the Roman Church from Saint Peter to Clement VIII,[1] now living, has preserved and taught for nearly sixteen hundred years? Is it the Gospel kept by all nations, provinces, and kingdoms that across the universe bear the name of Catholic? Is it the Gospel that until Henry VIII all the Christian princes and kings of England have followed with such devotion and piety? The one that has been confirmed by so many glorious miracles in every age and corner of the world? Is it that Gospel for which so many knights and lords have left royal palaces and cast aside pomp and luxury, abandoning the cities to fill the wastes and deserts, converting them into gardens, into Paradise itself? For which the monasteries have been stuffed, like beehives, with a numberless number of highborn maidens, infinite citizens of heaven, who have lived the life of the angels in a mortal body? Is it the Gospel that preaches to us the cross, penance, austerity of life, the mortification of our passions, disdain for the world, desire and care for eternity, obedience to God and his ministers, chastity, humility, patience, gentleness, and all other superlative, divine virtues that Jesus Christ taught us through his instruction and his example? This is the Gospel of Jesus Christ our Savior, this the one his masters teach us, these his fruits. But the one that now flourishes in England is the gospel of Calvin and of Satan his master, founded upon incest and the sensuality of King Henry, who, while his lawful wife yet lived, married his whore of a daughter, so filthy and sinful that the king himself had her beheaded by public judgment. It is a gospel taught in England by

---

1 Ippolito Aldobrandini was elected Pope Clement VIII (r.1592–1605) on February 2, 1592.

Bucer and Peter Martyr, two notorious apostates,[2] and the dregs and disgraces of the religious orders, nurtured and supported by Bucer's disciple John Calvin, a Picard by nation, a man without faith, without law, without God, exiled for his crimes, whose teaching was pestilential, his life abominable, and his death frightful and repugnant.[3] The sect is flaming pitch and hellish wildfire, which in a few years has scorched and consumed so many provinces and kingdoms. It is a gospel that strips goodness from God, making him the author of our guilt and sin; free will from men; the sacraments from the Church; merit from good works; efficacy and virtue from divine grace. Blasphemous against our Redeemer, harmful to the redeemed, ignoring the pits of hell and opening the way to every sin and corruption.[4] It is a gospel that has taken innumerable monks and nuns from the monasteries and stained them with hateful baseness and vice, teaching them to lie, perjure themselves, feign, and dissemble, and with a false sweetness and genteel hypocrisy to show themselves first as sheep, and afterwards, looking to their own interests, like bloodthirsty wolves to dismember, slay, drink the blood, and destroy the sheep and herd of the Lord.[5] How many treasons and rebellions has this new gospel of yours raised up in the world since it began? How many cities has it desolated? How many provinces has it ruined? How many kingdoms has it set aflame? How much blood has it spilled?[6] Tell France, tell Flanders, tell Scotland, tell your own kingdom of

---

2   Robert Persons described Martin Bucer and Peter Martyr as "degenerate apostates from mo-
     nastic orders [*sceleratissimi monachorum Apostatæ.*]" *Philopater*, 48.

3   Though it might be stretching matters to call Calvin Bucer's *discipulo*, Bruce Gordon does call
     the Alsatian reformer "Calvin's model churchman, and the greatest influence on his forma-
     tion as a minister and teacher." Calvin was not, in point of fact, exiled from France, but rather
     chose to flee in late 1534, amid rising religious tensions. Calvin's death (probably septic shock
     developed from kidney stones) was quite peaceful, a circumstance seized upon by his follow-
     ers as a sign of having "died well." Bruce Gordon, *Calvin* (New Haven: Yale University Press,
     2009), 42, 54, 333.
         There was a long tradition of English Catholic attacks on Calvin, including allegations
     of a criminal past and an ignominious end: see Peter Marshall, "John Calvin and the English
     Catholics, c. 1565–1640," *HJ* 53, no. 4 (December 2010): 849–70.

4   These are some of the favorite charges Catholic controversialists hurled against evangelical
     belief—charges not entirely without justice. In Alexandra Walsham's felicitous phrase, Cal-
     vinists in particular were forced to "elaborate theological gymnastics" to escape the conse-
     quences of evangelical doctrines of predestination. Peter Martyr himself admitted that God
     was "after some sort [...] the cause of those things which afterward be naughtilie doone."
     Walsham, *Providence*, 14.

5   Matt. 7:15; Acts 20:29.

6   In the 1593 and 1594 editions, these question marks were exclamation points; the passage
     thus originally read: "How many treasons and rebellions this new Gospel of yours has raised

England—for the tyrannies, outrages, and limitless, horrific cruelties now seen there are all the fruits of this gospel of yours. And this being so, do you take it for the gospel of God? What greater impiety could there be? What greater blasphemy against God himself? Just as he is in himself eternal, infinite goodness, so he abhors all wickedness, and as the spring whence it comes is so pure and clear, his teaching cannot be muddy or murky. And the purity of the Gospel that Christ established with his holy life and death does not admit the deformities, stains, and abominations preached to us in this gospel of yours, nor is it possible that two paths so different and incompatible as those of vice and virtue, wickedness and goodness, sin and grace, should arrive at the same end, and that light and shadow, Christ and Belial should run together into one.[7]

Therefore I said that this edict of the queen's is sacrilegious against God, taking for the Gospel of God a teaching so monstrous and irreligious as that of this new gospel of theirs, planted (as has been said) in incest, watered with innocent blood, and sustained with deceit and barbarous cruelty. To preserve this gospel, the queen charges her ecclesiastics to install pious ministers in their churches, to advance it through their instruction and example. These ministers are of a piece with the gospel they profess, the doctrine they teach as pestilential as the spring and fountainhead whence it comes, and the lives of the ministers so profane, sinful, and base that they often end upon the gallows—lest I give offend the souls of those who read this history, I have elected to keep silent on this. This is the first thing Elizabeth commands in her decree, this is the first foundation for everything it ordains, that the gospel of Calvin should be preserved in her kingdom and that of Jesus Christ our Redeemer be eradicated.

---

up in the world since it began! How many cities it has desolated! How many provinces it has ruined! How many kingdoms it has set aflame! What blood it has spilled!"

7   2 Cor. 6:14–15.

The War in France, Which the Edict Calls
Utterly Unjust[1]

She who is so impious toward God (as we said in the previous chapter), is it any wonder that she should be overbold with men? That she should have no respect for the monarchs and kings of the earth, treating thus the king of kings and the sovereign monarch of heaven? But let us set the rest aside, and speak solely of what concerns religion, which is our subject. Such is Elizabeth's slander against the pope and against the Catholic King of having begun a war against France that she calls utterly unjust and dangerous. I consider this a matter of religion, because her entire rationale for deeming the war unjust is that it is against the prince of Béarn, who is a Calvinist heretic, and against his sect and false religion—and Elizabeth thinks it an impiety to impugn it, and a war against it completely illegitimate. And this is why her edict rebukes the pope and the Catholic King for having taking up arms against the prince of Béarn, and not having permitted the land of France to be oppressed and the Catholic faith that has flourished with so much piety and devotion in that most Christian kingdom to this day to be torn from it by the hand of so perverse a heretic.

But why does Elizabeth call defending, assisting, and supporting France in the Catholic faith an invasion and an attack upon it? Why does she claim that that which is against the tyrant who would oppress the kingdom is against the kingdom itself? The most Christian kingdom of France is not the prince of Béarn, nor the handful of deluded knights who follow him, but rather the body of the entire nation, the provinces and cities, the *parlements*, the religious orders, the Catholic universities, the princes, the estates of the realm that, convened in what they call the Assembly or the *cortes generales*, has excluded any heretic whatsoever from the succession to the throne—and consequently the prince of Béarn, who is a relapsed heretic. It is this, the whole body of the kingdom, linked and united in a holy league, yet persecuted and abused, that the pope

---

1 Ribadeneyra's defense of the Catholic coalition against Henry IV draws heavily on Persons's discussion of the same topic: see *Philopater*, 103*ff.*
    Cf. Stapleton, *Apologia*, 100–01, 122–26.

wishes to aid—and rightly so.[2] For if any monarch, any Catholic prince ought to support and assist the Catholics of France, as a limb of the mystical body of the holy Church[3] succoring another, integral, vital limb, if all Catholics and believers, to live up to this name and creed, ought to contribute whatever they can toward this dire necessity, what must he do who is the head of the entire Church, the universal shepherd, and the prince of every prelate and pastor, hearing his sheep bleat and whine and seeing the bloodthirsty wolf, famished and maddened, seeking to devour them? What ought a father to do who sees so many children lost, a farmer who sees his harvest burned, his vines uprooted? How could the pope allow a kingdom like France, so large, so rich, so powerful, so Catholic, so obedient and devoted to the Apostolic See, which has so often supported and defended him in his worst travails, to be devastated, scorched, destroyed, and subjected to a tyrant, an obstinate and relapsed Calvinist, who would extinguish the Catholic faith and strip the pope of his obedience, in that realm and in all the world, if he could? Furthermore, once the said Apostolic See had for all these reasons excluded the prince of Béarn from the crown by its judgment and the severest censures,[4] how could it not execute this, to ensure, through arms and other lawful means, that what was once decided with such sense and reason should obtain and remain in force? Especially as, after sentence had been given, the prince had further demonstrated his perfidy and obstinacy, afflicting the realm and attempting to seize control, oppressing and slaying numerous Catholics, and committing so many abominable crimes that for these alone he deserved to be deprived of the throne.

And we see the frivolousness and senselessness of the allegations in Queen Elizabeth's apparent attempt to smear the pope as an ingrate, for not recalling the benefits the Apostolic See received from France in former times. I ask, who were the kings of France who aided the Apostolic See in its times of need? Were they Calvinists and Huguenots, like the prince of Béarn? Of course not, for then there were neither Huguenots nor Calvinists in the world. They were Catholic kings, who acknowledged, obeyed, and revered the pope as head and

---

2 Over the course of the 1580s, Catholic reactionary elements in France began to coalesce around the Guise clan, forming a confederation variously known as the Holy Union or the Catholic League, a process considerably accelerated by the death of Henry III's younger brother, Francis, duke of Anjou (1555–1584), leaving Henry of Navarre as the heir-apparent. Supported by Spain and the pope, the League proved the major challenge of Henry's IV first years on the throne. See Mack P. Holt, *The French Wars of Religion, 1562–1629* (Cambridge: Cambridge University Press, 1995), Chapter 5.

3 Rom. 12:5; 1 Cor. 6:15, 12:12, 12:17; Eph. 5:30.

4 In September 1585, Pope Sixtus V had excommunicated Henry and declared him incapable of inheriting the throne of France. Holt, *French Wars*, 124.

supreme spiritual monarch of the Church—and as such they aided and supported him, and defended him with the arms and strength of the kingdom of France (which was Catholic, as they were). Now, this being the case, with the Apostolic See desirous of repaying its debt to the kingdom of France and extend a hand to those who had offered theirs in its own difficulties, so often and with such glory, is it not simple gratitude to help the French Catholics, who are the children and heirs of the previous Catholics who aided it, and not the heretics, who would destroy it? Is it not just to strive to preserve in France that religion by which it has flourished, in which its kings became mighty and won the glorious title of Most Christian, to stop the one who seeks to eradicate and eliminate everything to do with Christianity and the Gospel of Jesus Christ? What new logic and manner of argument is this: the Catholics of France have many times aided and succored the Apostolic See in its travails, against the heretics or schismatic princes that afflicted it—therefore, the Apostolic See is obliged to abandon the Catholics of France and leave them in the clutches of the heretics, to be oppressed, extinguished, and annihilated? For this is the obvious consequence that follows from what the queen avers in her edict. This is the great deceit that the Catholic King Don Philip has practiced upon the supreme pontiff, to make him perform the office of father, shepherd, head of the Church, and vicar of Jesus Christ! That the Apostolic See should act according to that faith and creed that is, and is justly called, the Catholic, apostolic, and Roman! That it should not permit a limb so great, so illustrious, and so integral as the kingdom of France to be lost! And that it should extend a hand to France in its wretched oppression and misery, as France was wont to do in its prosperity for the same Apostolic See!

And although there has been no need for the Catholic King to persuade the supreme pontiffs presiding over the Catholic Church to do this, for they were ready to do it of their own accord, as a thing perfectly right, necessary, and befitting their office, yet, if the Catholic King had urged them to it and given the spur to a running horse, promising to join his forces with those of the Apostolic See, what crime or deceit would that be? Elizabeth and all the other heretics will call it trickery, but every Catholic and every thinking person will say that it is the deed of a pious and zealous prince, like the undertaking of the war itself, which Elizabeth has called utterly unjust.[5] But let us examine in what the injustice of this war consists. Is it not just that a Catholic king, one

---

5   "Now, this being so, it clearly follows that it is not an unjust war (as the queen's edict alleges), but rather pious, Christian, and necessary assistance, freely given to the Catholic people of France against the heretic and apostate Navarre by the Catholic King of Spain. Nor is it against the king of France, but rather against the enemy of France, who seized power by

who among all Christian monarchs glories in the title of Catholic King, should defend the Catholic faith? Is it not just that he should extend a hand to a kingdom as Christian and as Catholic as France, which begs it of him and which has no other means of escaping the total slavery of subjection to a heretical tyrant, who torments and flays it, or forces it to abandon the Catholic faith, as Elizabeth now does in England? Is it not just that neighbor should aid neighbor, the mighty the weak and wretched? Is it not just to prevent the heretical foe from gathering their forces, lest they turn them against their own realms and there wage war upon the souls of their vassals and ravage and corrupt the Catholic faith? If Elizabeth does not deem it an unjust war to support the prince of Béarn with cash, weapons, soldiers, munitions, and the equipment of war, by land and by sea, so that he may terrorize the realm of France and devastate the Catholic religion—for, being the Calvinist heretic she is, she feels she has an obligation to advance her diabolical and pestilential sect—why would it be an unjust war to support the Catholics of an entire kingdom in defending themselves against the tyrant and preserving the religion that all the kings of France have observed for the space of twelve hundred years? Could it possibly be lawful for Elizabeth to support a heretical tyrant in destroying so Catholic and illustrious a land, if it is not right for a Catholic prince to contribute to its defense and succor? This holy zeal of the Catholic King is so much the more admirable and worthy of perpetual praise in light of the years of endless, bitter war between the kings of France and Spain, for (in keeping with human nature) he might well have delighted to see the realm of France unsettled.

Note to the Reader[6]

We wrote this in the year 1592, as the prince of Béarn, Henri de Bourbon, was waging cruel war upon the Catholics of France and seeking to subjugate that most Christian and illustrious realm by force of arms, to usurp the crown, and to oppress our sacred Catholic religion, aided by his heretical allies, especially Queen Elizabeth of England, who stoked and fed this fire to burn and consume the kingdom of France with the awful flame of heresy, as she has done in her own kingdom of England. For this reason, she took it ill that the pope and the Catholic King of Spain, Don Philip II, should use their power to rebuff the assault of the prince of Béarn and support the Catholics of France, and so she

---

unlawful tyranny. Nor would it be perilous to the other Christian commonwealths, but rather needful and beneficial to them all, lest heresy penetrate them yet further." *Philopater*, 119.

6   This note to the reader was added in the 1605 edition.

accused and denounced them in her edicts. But after our Lord, by his immense compassion, by the prayers of the many sublime saints who flowered in France and now reign with him in heaven,[7] and by the tears and groans of countless of his servants now living in that kingdom, turned the eyes of his mercy upon it and transformed the heart of the said Henri de Bourbon, so that from a wolf he became a sheep,[8] and from a crow he became a dove; he chose to be a lawful king rather than a tyrant; an obedient son, rather than a persecutor and enemy of the Catholic, Apostolic, and Roman Church; an imitator of Saint Louis[9] and the other ancient Most Christian Kings of France, his forebears.

So it was that he humbly entreated the Holiness of Clement VIII, the supreme pontiff, to absolve him and admit him into the unity of the holy Church, to the kiss of peace and reconciliation, and to the communion of the faithful. Though at first there were various opinions as to what His Holiness ought to do in so complex and thorny a question, yet, after having contemplated, discussed, and confided it entirely to God, with numerous fervent efforts to receive the light and spirit of heaven, and four times showing himself stony and well-nigh unmovable to the ambassadors who implored him on the prince of Béarn's behalf, in the end His Holiness decided to grant him the absolution, both to fulfill the role of a father who does not despise the prodigal son[10] and that of a true shepherd, who searches for the lost sheep through the valleys and the mountains, and carries it on his shoulders,[11] and to avoid the dire, irreparable harms that might be feared from not doing so, frustrating the French Catholics who begged it of him, strengthening the heretics, and giving an occasion for schism—to the ruin of the whole of so noble, powerful, and Christian a kingdom, which has so many times been a refuge and support to the holy Roman Church in its travails. And so on September 16, 1595, the pope absolved the prince of Béarn, who was accordingly acknowledged as the true king of France, Henri de Bourbon, who now reigns as Henry IV.[12] And experience has proved that the Lord inspired his vicar and aided him (as is his wont) in so important a deed, for besides having avoided the harms that threatened without the absolution (which, as we said, were grave and without number), we see that all of

---

7   2 Tim. 2:12; Rev. 20:6.

8   Cf. Isa. 11:6.

9   King Louis IX of France (r.1226–70), canonized in 1297.

10   Luke 15:20–32.

11   Matt. 18:12–13; Luke 15:3–5.

12   In a bid to neutralize Catholic opposition, on July 25, 1593 Henry IV abjured his Protestantism and converted to Catholicism. He was crowned king of France on February 27, 1594.

France is now calm and enjoys order and tranquility, that the heretics are few-er, with less boldness and pride than formerly, while the Catholics are multi-plying and recovering. We see that the king himself shows signs of recognizing God's favor in granting him so powerful a kingdom amid such peace, obedi-ence, and prosperity, after so many bloody wars and storms; the difference there is between the disquiet and disturbance of heresy, accompanied by the torments of a wicked conscience, and the repose and serenity that the Catholic faith brings to the hearts of those who embrace it; and that there is no bet-ter measure for governing and maintaining realms than the true and Catholic faith and the protection of the holy law of God, who is the king of kings and the lord of all nations, which he he gives and takes at his will. I wanted to inform the reader of this, to explain the state of France when I wrote the second part of my history of England, as well as how things now stand in 1604, so that they may praise the Lord who has worked this good and entreat his divine majesty to carry forward what he has begun, so that our sacred and Catholic faith may flourish, and with it justice, peace, unity, and concord among all Christian monarchs, in that most Christian kingdom and throughout the world.

Of the English Seminaries that Have Been Established for the Benefit of the Kingdom of England

But because in her edict Queen Elizabeth directs her greatest force against the seminaries created in France, Italy, and Spain for the many English Catholic youths who wish to dedicate themselves to recalling the heretics of England to our sacred religion, proclaiming that the pope and the Catholic King support and exploit these colleges to undermine her kingdom, and because the young students (whom she calls "seminarians"), the priests, and the fathers of the Society of Jesus who oversee them are the principal targets of her volleys, her machinations, her fury and rage, we ought to give some justification of these establishments and of their customs, before responding to the decree's lies or describing the punishments and tortures inflicted in England upon people so innocent and saintly. For this is Elizabeth's second allegation against the pope and the Catholic King, and it pertains to religion.

Now, in the knowledge that everything to do with the seminaries of Rheims and Rome and their achievements has been recorded in the second book of this history[1] (which for the sake of brevity I do not wish to repeat here), it should be understood that various Roman pontiffs have long provided for certain native children of various Christian lands to be raised apart and instructed in Catholic doctrine and the rites of the Roman Church, so that they might subsequently be dispatched to their homelands to teach the inhabitants what they learned. Of the Roman Pontiff Saint Gregory I (whom the Venerable Bede so justly calls the apostle of England),[2] we read in his *vita* that he had numerous English youths raised in monasteries at his expense,[3] and Gregory VII addressed a brief about such a project to King Olaf of Norway, of the following tenor:[4]

---

1   In the margin: "Book 2, Chapter 29."

2   "We can and should by rights call him our apostle, for though he held the most important see in the whole world and was head of Churches which had long been converted to the true faith, yet he made our nation, till then enslaved to idols, into a Church of Christ." Bede, *Ecclesiastical History*, 123.

3   In the margin: "John the Deacon, in his *Life [of Saint Gregory the Great]*, Book 2, Chapter 46."

4   In the margin: "This brief is found in Johannes Magnus's history of the metropolitan church of Uppsala."

© KONINKLIJKE BRILL NV, LEIDEN, 2017 | DOI 10.1163/9789004323964_120

We wish you to know that we desire to find a means of sending you some of our faithful and learned children to teach and instruct you in every science and in the creed of Jesus Christ, to the end that, having been sufficiently instructed according to the Gospel and the apostolic teachings, you will not waver, but rather, well ordered and rooted in the steady foundation that is Jesus Christ, grow with greater abundance and perfection in the virtue of God, and, conforming your deeds to your faith, receive its fruits and rewards, worthy of eternal recompense. Given the difficulties of the long distance and the lack of those who know your language, we beg you (as we have likewise begged the king of Denmark) to send us some noble youths of your realm, so that under the wings of the apostles Saint Peter and Saint Paul, having diligently learned the sacred and divine laws, they might return to you, bearing with them the mandates of this holy Apostolic See, not as strangers, but as natives and your own. Explicating and preaching the whole of the Christian religion to your realm, with prudence and with faithfulness, with the knowledge of the land and its tongue and with their own virtues, they will be able to cultivate and gather the fruit, through the Lord's favor, of what has been sown in your land.

Thus it was that, following the example of his predecessors the two Gregorys, the first and the seventh, Gregory XIII of happy memory, after having established the English seminary at Douai and transferred it to the city of Rheims in France (as has been mentioned), created the seminary at Rome for other Englishmen, and to entrench and augment it, promulgated a bull on April 23, 1579, the seventh year of his pontificate, in which he declares his intention in the erection and organization of this seminary:[5]

Seeing, to the heartfelt pain of our spirit, that so many enemies have banded together against the holy bride of the Lord,[6] assailing and embattling it upon every side, and that its ancient enemies—the infidels and Turks—have now joined with the heretics and schismatics, and, armed with impiety and wickedness, and stirred by hellish madness, they seek

---

Johannes Magnus, *Metropolis ecclesiae Upsalen, in regnis Suetiae et Gothiae diligentia Iohannis Magnis Gothi Sedis Apost. Legati, primatis & archiepiscopi eiusdem ecclesiæ Upsalen: M.D. XXXVI. Gedani obiter collecta atq[ue] nunc primu[m] M.D. LVII.* (Rome: In aedibus divae Brigidae viduae, 1557), 28.

5   For a contemporary depiction of the foundation, see Book 3 Figure 19.1.

6   2 Cor. 11:2; Eph. 5:25–27; Rev. 19:7–9.

A. *Gregorius* XIII. *Pont. Max. huius Anglorum Collegij fundator, ac parens optimus Alumnos suos Christo commendat: ut quos in Angliam ad fidei defensionem mittit, aduersus hostium insidias, atq, tormenta diuina uirtute confirmet:qua freti iam aliquot pro Catholica Romana ecclesia fortiter occubuerunt.*

B. *Philippus Boncompagnus S.R.E. presb. Card. tit S. Sixti eiusdem Pont. Fr. Fil. Collegij Protector, et Benefactor munificentiss. idé à Deo precatur.*

FIGURE 19.1 *The foundation of the English College at Rome by Gregory XIII.*
Giovanni Battista Cavalieri, *Ecclesiae anglicanae trophaea sive sanctorum martyrum qui pro Christo catholicaeque fidei veritate asserenda antiquo recentiorique persecutionum tempore mortem in Anglia subierunt, passiones Romae in collegio Anglico per Nicolaum Circinianum depictae: Nuper autem per Io. Bap. de Cavalleriis aeneis typis repraesentatae* (Rome: Ex officina Bartolomeo Grassi, 1584). NE1666 .C57 1584 OVERSIZE, John J. Burns Library, Boston College.

to destroy it with all their powers, and considering what our pastoral duties require of us, we will confront the foe's assault with the powers God has given us, and prepare the people that he has entrusted to us to resist the attacks of such cruel and pernicious persons. And as there is no surer remedy nor stronger defense than a Catholic upbringing and education for the youth of the corrupted nations (for by their natural facility and gentleness virtue is more easily imprinted in them), from the beginning of our pontificate we have worked to establish in this city colleges of diverse nations, as seminaries for the Catholic faith.

In the midst of this work, we turned our eyes to the kingdom of England, which in former times was so mighty, and so flourished in piety and zeal for the Catholic religion, and is now beset and consumed by heresy. We were struck with the compassion it warrants, and recalled that it was Pope Gregory the Great who converted that land to the faith of Christ our Lord, that ever since it has been most devoted and respectful to this Holy See and the Roman pontiff, and that even in this dark and shadowy hour there have been many notable and illustrious men in that realm who have shed their blood and given their lives for the authority of the said See and the truth of the Catholic faith. And we held before our eyes the many English youths who, exiling themselves from their homeland and fleeing that miserable kingdom, have abandoned their parents, families, and estates, and, moved by the spirit of the Lord, place themselves in our hands to be instructed in the Catholic religion into which they were born, with the intention first to attain eternal salvation and then, having learned the necessary arts, to return to England to enlighten and redeem the rest. Following in the footsteps of that sainted pontiff, Gregory I, and the paternal affection he had for this nation, to the end that, just as its peoples have him to thank for the establishment of the faith, they may likewise rejoice in the restoration of that same faith that we hope the Lord will work through our means, and embracing these young men's devotion toward the Apostolic See and their desire to learn Catholic doctrine, of our own will and on our certain knowledge, with the plenitude of the apostolic power that we possess, we erect and establish in perpetuity an English college in the buildings of the English hospice in our city, for the glory of Almighty God, the enrichment of the Catholic faith, and the benefit and wellbeing of the English nation, which we so greatly love.[7]

---

7   Gregory XIII issued the bull *Quoniam divinae bonitati* establishing the seminary at Rome on May 1, 1579. For an English translation, see Michael E. Williams, *The Venerable English College Rome: A History, 1579–1979* (London: Associated Catholic Publications, 1979), 210–19.

The fruit of the seminaries at Rheims and Rome has been so abundant that in addition to their many students and sons who have shed their blood for our sacred faith in the kingdom of England, more than three hundred priests are now at work there, illuminating and reconciling the blind heretics, strengthening and sustaining the doubtful, and consoling and encouraging the Catholics, guided by the honor and glory of the Lord. So much so, that the queen and her council fear nothing more than these seminary clerics, and expend their fury and rage upon them more than any other Catholic—for they say that their foreign enemies, numerous and mighty though they are, cannot wage war except upon the bodies of their subjects, but these men proceed against intellects and wills and conquer hearts, planting and sowing the Catholic religion and reverence and obedience to the pope, and this they consider the greatest of their worries. For they see that with the change in religion, there must necessarily be a change in governance, and for this reason they have so oppressed the Catholics of the realm with draconian, inhuman laws, forcing able and good-hearted youths, wealthy and influential knights, and countless other Catholics to flee, exiling themselves from their homeland lest they lose their houses, lives, or faiths.

And as these two seminaries were soon insufficient to support so many English youths, with more leaving England every day, our lord the Catholic King Don Philip, the second of that name, has been pleased, in keeping with his deep piety and great renown, to assist and succor them, not only with his generosity in sustaining them at the seminary at Rheims (as he has always done), but also by ensuring that they have a safe haven and sure shelter in Spain, with another seminary begun in the town of Valladolid, a few years ago in 1589. With the favor of God and His Majesty, and with further donations from various prelates, lords, and pious, devout persons, it has had such excellent progress and growth that we may expect just as copious and fruitful a crop as have come from the two others at Rheims and Rome.[8] And we already have proofs of this in what several students from Valladolid do and endure in England even now, so extraordinary that the church and city of Seville have been moved to embrace and gather these English youths, and offer them houses for their shelter and alms for their sustenance, showing them the generosity of surpassing love in creating another English seminary in that famous and noble

---

8 Ten members of the seminary at Rheims (burdened with more residents than it could support) set out for Spain on May 8, 1589, eventually reaching Valladolid, where they were joined by several other priests and students. Initially housed at the city's Jesuit college, by the end of the year a third seminary was up and running, with some twenty students, and subsidies from the king and wealthy Spanish notables. McCoog, *Building the Faith*, 106–10.

city, this year of 1593, on the octave of the glorious martyr Saint Thomas of Canterbury, primate of England, in the presence of the cardinal-archbishop, Don Rodrigo de Castro,[9] the Church, and the crown, as well as a large number of Seville's nobles and influential citizens.[10]

True it is that the Lord has done a great kindness to our nation in giving it the grace lovingly to embrace the stranger, shelter the abandoned, take into its bosom those who suffer for the Catholic faith, and sustain and encourage those who are tried and tested as martyrs, as well as to demonstrate in action the ancient friendship and good fellowship between these two nations. We are repaying the charity we Spaniards received from the English Catholics in our own times of need, and proving that the hatred and abhorrence that Spain now has for England is not for its people, but only for its heresies, nor for all its inhabitants, but only for those who are foes to Jesus Christ, who hate and persecute his faith and his sacraments, and who have raised their banner against God. And lastly, to follow in this the example of our king and lord, who has embraced the seminaries with such piety and supported them with such beneficence that not content with the gifts he gives them and the other kindnesses he does them, when he was in Valladolid this past year of 1592, he chose to perform and[11] endorse the work of the English seminaries in person, together with his children, the prince our lord and the most serene *infanta*, coming to visit the town and attending certain learned displays enacted there.[12] This English seminary, begun at Valladolid with the assent and authority of the Catholic King, has also been confirmed and instituted by Clement VIII, now living, who that very year, the first of his pontificate, dispatched a bull, at the request and entreaty of the king himself, which runs as follows:

Pope Clement VIII

Whereas there is no fortress firmer, nor remedy more efficacious against those who seek to undermine the Roman Church with their errors and

---

9   The name of Rodrigo de Castro Osorio (1523–1600), cardinal-archbishop of Seville, is added in the 1595 edition.

10   The foundation of the college at Seville was not quite as spontaneous as Ribadeneyra would have it: the project was in large part the work of Robert Persons, though it did enjoy the support of the city, prominent noblemen, and the cardinal-archbishop. The seminary actually opened at the end of 1592, and received papal confirmation two years later. McCoog, *Building the Faith*, 114–15.

11   Omitted beginning in the 1595 edition.

12   Philip, together with the *infante* and *Infanta* Isabella Clara Eugenia (1566–1633), visited the Valladolid seminary in August 1592. See Persons, *Relation of the King*.

false opinions than the Catholic education of the youth of the provinces infected with heresy, since the souls of young people are tractable and apt for the imprinting of virtue, our most beloved son in Christ, the Catholic King Philip of Spain, whose exceeding goodwill and generosity, without question worthy of a Catholic prince, is well known to many exiled English youths, who have fled the afflicted kingdom of England (in former times so prosperous and so devoted to the Catholic faith, and now oppressed and afflicted by extreme miseries, and beset by the destruction and ravages of heresy) and flocked to the realms of Spain, has recognized this and has piously and diligently arranged that in the town of Valladolid, in the diocese of Palencia, an English college should be erected and established for the honor and glory of God Almighty and for the shelter and protection of the said Englishmen, who for the sake of the Catholic faith have voluntarily chosen exile from the said kingdom, and seek in time to return to lead their lost countrymen back to the path of truth, also granting them a certain yearly income for the support of the students and the other members. We have been humbly implored through our beloved son, the noble gentleman Antonio, duke of Sessa and Soma,[13] the king's ambassador to us and to the Apostolic See, that we deign, with the apostolic benignity, to confirm the creation and organization of the said college and provide for everything needful. We, fervently lauding in the Lord this pious project, this most praiseworthy deed of King Philip, accede to their requests by the apostolic authority and our certain knowledge, approving and confirming the creation and organization of the said college, and all the things of whatsoever kind they may be that might follow from this institution, providing for each and every fault, whether of deed or law, that may perchance interfere.[14]

---

13   Antonio Fernández de Córdoba Folch de Cardona (1550–1606), whose many titles included fifth duke of Sessa and fourth duke of Soma, served as Spanish ambassador to Rome from 1590 to 1604. "Fernández de Córdoba Folch de Cardona, Antonio (1550–1606)," in "Censo-guía de archivos de España e Iberoamérica," Ministerio de Educación, Cultura, y Deporte, 2015, http://censoarchivos.mcu.es/CensoGuia/portada.htm [accessed September 14, 2015].

14   It is not clear where Ribadeneyra found the text of this bull. One possibility is that it was contained in *Informacion acerca de la institucion del seminario que por orden de su magestad se ha hecho en Valladolid para los sacerdotes estudiantes ingleses, que vienen huyendo de la persecucion de los hereges de Inglaterra y de las guerras de Francia* (Valladolid: s.n., 1589), which may well have been available to Ribadeneyra, but of which no copies are known to survive.

This is what the supreme pontiffs and the Catholic King have done, and the intention with which they have done it, as is proven by the said bulls and the statutes of the seminaries; not only can no reasonable person fault this, but they should rather laud and praise it on a thousand counts. For—speaking first of the pope—to whom are the Catholics of England to turn, beset and embattled, if not to the head of the Catholic Church? To the one who, as Saint Jerome says, is the surest haven of the communion of the faithful and the touchstone that distinguishes the false doctrine from the true, the tinsel from the purified gold.[15] To the one who is the first shepherd and bishop of our souls, the universal vicar of Jesus Christ. To the one who by dint of his office has received more fully the anointing of the Holy Spirit and a greater abundance of love, mercy, and compassion, who turns away no believer, from whatever corner of Christendom, who comes to him. To the one who has always been the refuge and shelter to every sainted, persecuted bishop who flees to the Apostolic See for support, succor, and solace, like Saint Cyprian to Popes Cornelius and Stephen;[16] Athanasius to Mark and Julius;[17] Chrysostom and Augustine

---

For the Latin text of the bull, see Edwin Henson, ed., *Registers of the English College at Valladolid 1589–1862*, Publications of the Catholic Record Society 30 (London: John Whitehead & Son, 1930), 246–51.

15   In the margin: "Letter 61."

       Jerome, *Letters*, 127.5.

       This citation probably comes from Allen's *apologia* for the seminaries, as reprinted in the *Concertatio*: see *Concertatio*, 249.

16   Cyprian was a close ally of Popes Cornelius (r.251–53) and Stephen I (r.254–57) in the Novatianist Schism. See the Bollandists' "Commentarius Prævius" on Cyprian, in AASS, September IV, 191–325.

17   Attacked by the Arians (with the encouragement of Constantius II), Athanasius fled Egypt in 339, and found refuge at Rome under the protection of Pope Julius I (r.337–52), who convened a synod that vindicated the archbishop. Athanasius was long believed to have corresponded with Julius's predecessor, Mark (r.336), though their letters have been shown to be later forgeries. It is true that an earlier exile had seen the archbishop sojourn in the West during Mark's papacy, and he remained closely allied to the bishops of Rome in years to come. David M. Gwynn, *Athanasius of Alexandria: Bishop, Theologian, Ascetic, Father*, Christian Theology in Context (Oxford: Oxford University Press, 2012), 8, 34–35, 42.

       The 1605 edition changes "Atanasio" to "Anastasio," but whereas Athanasius was a contemporary of Popes Mark and Julius, there is no Anastasius of comparable stature for the period.

to Innocent;[18] Basil to Liberius;[19] Jerome to Damasus;[20] Theodoret to Leo the Great;[21] and other holy men who rested under the wings and protection of other supreme pontiffs, according to the times and circumstances. To whom are the Englishmen wandering in exile on account of their faith to turn, if not to him who holds the position of those who were apostles to England, those who preached the very faith for which they suffer? To him whose throne has always been a comfort and support to every afflicted Christian, the supplier of their wants, the sharer of the Church's goods for the relief and sustaining of those who suffer for Christ, as Bishop Dionysius of Corinth wrote (as Eusebius of Caesarea mentions in his history).[22] All this being so, how dare the Calvinist heretics calumniate either the English Catholics, if, being so abused, harassed, and afflicted, they flock to the Apostolic See as to a gentle and loving mother, or the Apostolic See itself, if it gathers, supports, and sustains them, like beloved children persecuted for defending her?

Now, if we turn our eyes to the Catholic King, what can these monsters allege or aver that would not prove them to be those of whom the prophet says,

---

18   Late in 416, a group of African bishops, Augustine among them, addressed an appeal to Pope Innocent I (r.401–417), seeking his support against what they regarded as the dangerous ideas of Pelagius (*fl.* early fifth century). Peter Brown, *Augustine of Hippo: A Biography* (Berkeley: University of California Press, 2000), 358–60.

John Chrysostom, archbishop of Constantinople (*c.*349–407), had appealed to Innocent in 404, as the eastern patriarch was being outflanked in a power struggle with Theophilus, pope of Alexandria (r.384–412), and Empress Aelia Eudoxia (d.404). J.N.D. Kelly, *Golden Mouth: The Story of John Chrysostom, Ascetic, Preacher, Bishop* (Ithaca: Cornell University Press, 1998), 246–47.

19   Basil of Caesarea, a fierce defender of the Nicene Creed and opponent of the Arians, was an ally of the stridently anti-Arian Pope Liberius (r.352–66). Sozomen and Philostorgius, *The Ecclesiastical History of Sozomen: Comprising a History of the Church from A.D. 324 to A.D. 440, Translated from the Greek with a Memoir of the Author; Also, the Ecclesiastical History of Philostorgius as Epitomized by Photius, Patriarch of Constantinople*, trans. Edward Walford, Bohn's Ecclesiastical Library (London: Henry G. Bohn, 1855), 274–75.

20   Pope Damasus I (r.366–84) was a mentor and protector to the young Jerome, who at one point served as the pontiff's secretary. See the Bollandists' "Commentarius Historicus" on Jerome, in *AASS*, September VIII, 418–688.

21   Dismissed from his see by a fractious council at Ephesus in 449, Theodoret, bishop of Cyrrhus wrote to Pope Leo I (r.440–61), seeking support and protection. Theresa Urbainczyk, *Theodoret of Cyrrhus: The Bishop and the Holy Man* (Ann Arbor: University of Michigan Press, 2002), 10, 26.

22   In the margin: "Book 4, Chapter 23." The first editions of the *Historia* erroneously cite "Book 4, Chapter 29," corrected to "Chapter 23" in the 1595 edition.

"Woe betide you, who call good what is evil, and what is good evil, who make light of the shadows and shadows of the light?"[23] King Don Philip, as a truly Catholic monarch, comes to the aid of those who suffer for the Catholic faith; as a mighty ruler, he sustains so many noble, honored, and persecuted people; and as a compassionate person, he is pained by the grievous trials and calamities of so many of his coreligionists, whom he regards as those whom the Lord of the world calls brother with smiling countenance. And is this deed not[24] worthy of eternal praise and repetition? In every past age, those who suffered for Christ were always honored, revered, and supported—and for this reason Sulpicius Severus's history affirms of the sainted bishops exiled for the Catholic faith by the Arian Emperor Constantius, "True it is, that these saints thus exiled were respected and revered by the entire world, and succored with alms in great abundance, and visited by ambassadors from every nation and region of Christendom."[25] And Saint Ambrose, speaking of those same holy bishops, says, "They wandered throughout the world, like men who had nothing, and they possessed all. Wherever they went, they regarded it as a paradise, and nothing was ever lacking for them, because they were abounding in faith, and they rather enriched others, because though they were poor in money, they were rich to overflowing in divine grace."[26]

---

23   Isa. 5:20.

24   Omitted beginning in the 1595 edition.

25   In the margin: "Book 2." In the 1593 edition of the *Historia*, this citation reads, "Lib. 22." The 1594 edition gives the correct reference of "Lib. 2.", while from the 1595 edition onwards, the number is erroneously expanded to "Lib. 23."
      Sulpicius Severus, *Chronica*, 2.39.

26   In the margin: "Letter 27 to those of Vercelli."
      Ambrose of Milan, *Letters*, 63.69.

How the Heretics of England Criticize the Pope for the English Seminaries He Supports, While the New Christians of Japan Thank Him for Having Done the Same in Their Land

To make clearer what we have just finished saying, to prove that what the pope is doing in aiding the exiled English Catholics and supporting the English seminaries is not subverting that kingdom, as Elizabeth's edict would have it, but rather fulfilling the obligations of his office and the paternal responsibilities that he, as universal shepherd, has for the entire Church, we shall leave aside the other seminaries Gregory XIII of glorious memory founded for the benefit of so many nations. Allow me instead to include here two letters to Pope Sixtus V from two Japanese kings, in which, among other things, they thank him for his generosity toward the fathers of the Society of Jesus and the students of the seminaries of Japan. These letters will also serve to show us the difference there is between the impiety and hatred that the queen of England and her ministers harbor for the Apostolic See, and the devotion and reverence of the Christian princes of Japan. To the end that the accursed heretics might be confounded and bewail their blindness, while the true children of the holy Church are comforted and rejoice in the Lord, offering him infinite thanks for his protection and for his care in extending, augmenting, and expanding the Church to kingdoms and regions so far-off, bringing so many sheep who had wandered astray to his knowledge and love, to be joined with the others he has here, together becoming a single flock under a single shepherd, as the Lord himself said he would.[1] For indeed all the servants of the Lord who are afflicted and consumed by the holy Church's calamities and bewail its troubles and losses will find supreme solace and joy in contemplating how God has expanded our sacred faith in our own times, into so many sprawling, remote realms, and how although with one hand he wounds and lashes us, with the other he heals and comforts us, with the losses among the heretics made up and recompensed with overwhelming profit among the pagans. May he be blessed and praised

---

1   John 10:16.

forevermore for this mercy to his Church. But let us see the letters that manifest this truth to us.[2]

> Transcript of a letter, written in the Japanese language, with a summary in the Portuguese tongue, from Don Protasius, king of Arima,[3] to the blessed memory of Pope Sixtus v, which was headed thus:

> The letter of Don Protasius, king of Arima, to His Holiness, Sixtus v.

The second heading runs thus:

> To the great and saintly Pope Sixtus v, who upon the earth holds the place of the king of heaven, Don Protasius, king of Arima, offers this letter with the utmost reverence.

> Most holy father, supreme among all Christians, upon the sixteenth of the sixth moon, which was July 21, 1590, the father visitor of the Society of Jesus arrived with my cousin Don Miguel Chijiwa, Don Mancio, and the other companions who went to Rome in our name to place their heads beneath the feet of Your Holiness. I have received as much joy at their arrival as if I had won a thousand autumns and another ten thousand years of life. Don Miguel has recounted to me the honors and favors he has received from Your Holiness, King Don Philip, and the other Christian princes of Europe. For these, my thanks to Your Holiness are so infinite that I cannot express them with pen or paper. He has also given me the letter that Your Blessedness has deigned to write to me, in which you do me the grace to place me in honor among the other Christian monarchs. He has likewise brought the sacred splinter of the true cross upon which Christ our Redeemer died, and the sword and hat that Your

---

2   Though this letter was printed in Portuguese in 1593, the one that follows was not. Accordingly, it seems more likely that Ribadeneyra used an Italian translation produced the same year: Gasparo Spitilli, ed., *Ragguaglio*, 22–28.

   For the Portuguese version of the first letter, see *Cartas do Iapam nas quaes se trata da chegada a quellas partes dos fidalgos Iapões que ca vierão, da muita Christandade que se fez no tempo da perseguição do tyrano, das guerras que ouue, & de como Quambacudono se acabou de fazer senhor absoluto dos 66. reynos que ha no Iapão, & de outras cousas tocantes ás partes da India, & ao grão Mogor* (Lisbon: Em casa de Simão Lopes, 1593), 56ᵛ–58ʳ.

3   Arima Harunobu (1567–1612), a *daimyo* (feudal lord) based in Shimabara in Kyushu, who was baptized as Protasius in 1579. "Arima" is actually the name of the clan the *daimyo* headed, rather than that of his domain. Cooper, *Japanese Mission*, 13.

Holiness customarily sends to Christian kings and princes. These are such kindnesses, and I hold them in such high esteem, that I have resolved to preserve them as a perpetual memorial and the foremost treasure and ornament of my house. For, besides the fact that this honor is the greatest I could receive in this world, it likewise produces a benefit to the soul in the life to come. I had intended to welcome these gifts with the greatest celebrations and ceremonies that my power can muster, both because they merit it and to comply with the command of Your Holiness, but, in light of the persecution that the *kampaku* [*Quabacundono*], the supreme lord of Japan,[4] initiated three years ago against the fathers and Christians of these parts, the father visitor[5] judged that this solemn reception be postponed until he returns from Meaco,[6] whither he has gone to visit the *kampaku* with a delegation from the viceroy of India,[7] for he fears that if it should occur earlier, it could provoke considerable ill-will and anger in the heart of the *kampaku*. For this reason, I have not yet been able to carry out my desire. But as soon as the father visitor returns, I will humbly receive the said gifts, and place them upon my head with extreme joy.

I have also learned of the substantial aid Your Holiness has given to sustain the fathers, seminaries, and churches, at which we are so contented and consoled that our hearts delight and leap for joy, for we are persuaded that, Your Holiness having turned your eyes to the Christians of Japan, they cannot fail to progress well, and for my part I kiss Your Holiness's feet, as I trust that by these means the sacred law of the Lord is to grow great in the kingdoms of Japan.

In the extraordinary persecution stirred up by the *kampaku*, we have all seen ourselves in dire troubles and tribulations, and myself in

---

4 Toyotomi Hideyoshi (1537–98) seized power in Japan after the death of his former liege lord, Oda Nobunaga (1534–82). In 1585, Hideyoshi secured appointment as *kampaku* (regent for an adult emperor) for Emperor Ōgimachi (r.1557–86), a title he retained when Ōgimachi abdicated in favor of his son, Emperor Go-Yōzei (r.1586–1611). From the title of *kampaku*, Hideyoshi was sometimes known in Europe as "Quabacondono." In 1587, Hideyoshi promulgated an edict expelling Christian missionaries from Japan, but Mary Elizabeth Berry points out that the order was not rigorously enforced, and was probably intended as a warning to overzealous proselytizers. Mary Elizabeth Berry, *Hideyoshi*, Harvard East Asian Monographs 146 (Cambridge: The Council on East Asian Studies, Harvard University, 1989), 91–93, 178–79.

5 Valignano.

6 Kyoto, sometimes known in the West as "Meaco" (from the Japanese *miyako*, "capital").

7 Manuel de Sousa Coutinho (1540–1591), the Portuguese governor of India from 1588 to 1591. M.N. Pearson, *The Portuguese in India*, The New Cambridge History of India I.1 (Cambridge: Cambridge University Press, 1987.), xiv.

particular, because against his order and mandate my lands receive the better part of the fathers, as I do still, thus placing myself in extreme peril of losing my life and rank. But, as the fathers have no other remedy, and, as servants of God, they have all resolved to die in Japan rather than to abandon these Christians, it seems to me a fitting thing to risk all for the service of our Lord, he who in his paternal providence has thus far not only freed me from every danger, but has exalted and favored me in every instance, while countless pagan lords have been lost and ruined— whence faith and trust in God has been augmented among the Christians of Japan. And now, with the journey of the father visitor to the *kampaku*, we all have the sure expectation that he can bring this persecution to an end: just as it has hitherto been a trial to us newly made Christians, so I hope in our Lord that hereafter will follow a great expansion and the conversion of Japan. And as Your Holiness will learn the rest from the father visitor, I conclude by placing my head beneath the feet of Your Blessedness, and I write the present letter with that reverence and humility due to Your Holiness, in the ninth year of the era called Tenshō,[8] on the tenth of the eighth moon, which is September 22 of the year 1590.

> Prostrated at the feet of Your Holiness.
> *Arimano Sciurino Daibu*
> Don Protasius

Transcript of another letter, from Don Sancho, lord of Ōmura,[9] to the same pope, and written in the same circumstances as the previous one.

The heading thereof:

A letter of Don Sancho, lord of Ōmura, to His Holiness Sixtus V

It has as the second heading:

---

8   "Tenshō" is a *nengō*, a name given to an era in Japanese history. The Tenshō era began in July 1573 and ended in December 1592. See Yachita Tsuchihashi, *Japanese Chronological Tables: From 601 to 1872*, Monumenta Nipponica Monographs 11 (Tokyo: Sophia University Press, 1952), 91–93.

9   In the eight years that elapsed between the Tenshō Embassy's departure and its return home, one of the Christian *daimyo* who had sponsored the mission, Ōmura Sumitada (1533–1587, baptized as Bartolomeu in 1563), had died, leaving his son Ōmura Yoshiaki (1568–1615, baptized as Sancho) as the head of the Ōmura family. Cooper, *Japanese Mission*, 13, 231n1.

The present letter is offered to the great and most holy Pope Sixtus V, whom I humbly revere as the vicar of God.

Most holy father,

This year of 1590, Don Michael Chijiwa, kinsman to King Don Protasius and myself, has returned with his companions, who several years ago had gone with the father visitor to render obedience to Your Holiness in the name of the said king of Arima and of my father Don Bartolomeu, at whose return we have received sublime contentment, hearing the great honors and favor that Your Holiness and—for your sake—all the other princes of Christendom have done them; the protection and fatherly care that Your Blessedness, as vicar of Christ our Lord upon the earth and head of the entire Church, shows all the Christians of Japan; and the aid you have given the fathers of the Society to sustain them, along with the seminaries and colleges, and the extraordinary expenses they incur in Japan—by which we are all so delighted that we believe that no delight could equal this our faith, and that we have received a new light, the knowledge of the truth, and Christian charity. For my part, I render infinite thanks to Your Holiness, and those I want to offer cannot be declared with ink or paper. And as Don Bartolomeu my father is now dead, I am left in his place with an eternal debt to Your Holiness, for the splinter of the true cross and the sword that you sent my father through Don Miguel, which things I regard as the richest treasure that I or any of my descendants could ever possess, and we shall judge it the bottomless ocean and highest summit of so many kindnesses received from your saintly hand, and that through you they have been sent to us from heaven. But, on account of the persecution that the *kampaku*, supreme lord of Japan, has raised against the fathers and against Christianity in these realms, there has been no fitting occasion to receive the aforesaid things with the solemnity and celebrations that I had intended—and thus the father visitor and I decided to omit them for now, until the return of the said father, who goes to wait upon the *kampaku* with a delegation and a gift from the viceroy of India. And we hope that with his journey peace shall be restored to these Christians, as already it seems to be abating and ameliorating because of this mission. And because Your Holiness will learn from the fathers' own letters what I have done in these circumstances to the service of our Lord and the fathers in receiving a large part of them in my lands, and thereby imperiling my person and my estate, as well as everything else that has happened in this persecution, I make an end, humbly placing the feet of Your Holiness upon my head and begging your sacred blessing. I write this present letter with the reverence and humility owed to Your Blessedness, in the ninth year of the era we call Tenshō, on the tenth of the eighth moon, which is September 22 in the year 1590.

With upraised hands and all reverence, I offer this letter at the feet of Your Holiness.

Omura Scim Paciro Nobu Ache Don Sancho

These are the letters of the Japanese monarchs. But let us return to what we were saying about the English seminaries, which have been embraced and favored by the Apostolic See, the Catholic King, and other princes and lords, who take pride in the renown of this, and with their contributions protect and sustain those who dwell there and prepare themselves for martyrdom.

The Qualities Those Entering the Seminaries are to Have, and the Oath They Take, and the Things They Do While There

These seminaries do not indiscriminately admit every Englishman who comes to them, but rather carefully choose those most apt for the end they seek. These are usually youngish men, able, virtuous, well inclined and known to be so. They include many nobles, the children of knights and lords, and several firstborn sons and persons of considerable wealth, among the most distinguished of the realm, who, touched with the hand of God, guided by his spirit, and strengthened by his grace, leave their houses, families, and kin, and all the luxury and comfort that they could have had, so as not to lose—or even risk losing—the Catholic faith.[1] Several learned men also come to perfect their education and their character, and then to return home to sow Catholic doctrine, and uproot the thorns and weeds from that neglected and abandoned vineyard.[2] These men, after having been examined, considered, and tested for many days, are admitted, making a solemn promise to God our Lord to be employed in his service, to receive sacred orders in due course, and to return to England; the oath runs as follows.

The oath of the graduates of the English seminaries.

I, N.N., of such-and-such English college, mindful of the benefits that God our Lord has done me, first and foremost in having removed me from my homeland, which is so beset by heresies, and in having made me a

---

1   "Now, as to the entrants to these seminaries, though the queen says they are children, bought, enticed, and gathered by the king's bribes, yet it is not so; instead, only the worthiest are admitted to the first examination, by a careful selection from those whom God, who gathers the dispersed of Israel, has sent us with a generous hand. Nor is there any great need of conscription to find them, nor have we any necessity of going out to the streets and hedges and highways to compel them to enter—and much less to bring in the good and the bad, the poor and the weak, the blind and the lame [...] to fill the house. Indeed, there are so many from among the most distinguished English youths who, disgusted with personal vanities and delusions, offer themselves to us every day that if the supply of earthly funds were equal to the multitude who rush to us [...] there is no doubt that the English universities would soon be seen abandoned or utterly vitiated by a lack of ready talent." *Philopater*, 152–53.

2   Matt. 13:24–30, 13:40, 15:13.

member of His Catholic Church, wishing not to be ungrateful for so great a mercy of the Lord, have resolved to offer myself entirely to his divine service, to the extent I can, in fulfillment of the aims of this college. And thus I promise and swear by Almighty God that I am prepared in my soul, insofar as his divine grace will aid me, to receive holy orders in good time, and to return to England to seek, win, and convert the souls of my neighbors, as and when the superior of this college, according to its institute, judges it good, commanding me so in the Lord.[3]

This is the oath.

While these English students are in the seminary, they have superiors—who in Rome, Valladolid, and Seville are fathers of the Society of Jesus—whom they obey with utter exactitude. They have rules and statutes, which they observe with great diligence. The hours of every day are divided into exercises in virtue and in letters, such that from the hour they arise to the hour they lay themselves down, no time is wasted or lost. The things they do are usually to improve and perfect their souls, or to learn the skills necessary for winning over the heretics. For their souls, they use spoken and mental prayer, devoutly saying or hearing Mass every day, praying the hours, the rosary, and the litany, the examination of conscience, the reading of some sacred text at table, confession, communion every eight days, preaching during meals on feast days, listening to discourses on topics related to their goals and the means for achieving them, and others things of this kind.[4] And no less care is taken that they be well

---

3 For the oath sworn by the seminarians at Rome, see Wilfrid Kelly, ed., *Liber ruber venerabilis collegii Anglorum de vrbe: I. Annales collegii pars prima; Nomina alumnorum I.A.D. 1579–1630*, Publications of the Catholic Record Society 37 (London: John Whitehead & Son, 1940), 7.

   For the nearly identical oath used at Valladolid, see Henson, *Registers*, 261.

4 "Indeed, out of the twenty-four hours that naturally make up the day, as much as seven (with an interruption), or at most eight are given over to sleep and to the necessities of the night, as well as three in the day for both meals and rest. The remaining thirteen are so precisely apportioned to lectures, meditation, and the study of letters that not even the least of such great treasures is allowed to be cast away. Moreover, each day they begin all their undertakings with meditation on the divine, or inward prayer (as they call it), in which for a set period of time, with a devout posture of body and a deep dedication of soul and spirit, without speaking aloud, in the deep contemplation of their hearts, all together they approach God, and reflect upon the mystery of salvation, and discuss their business. They throb with moans and sighs; they burn with the flames of fervent desire for eternal life and divine love. This divine practice is followed by the eternal worship of the Christian sacrifice, which we call the Mass, which all devoutly attend each day. Then follows their studies, but according to the rule that in quiet moments the duties of prayer and contemplation are resumed morning and evening, consisting now of litanies, now of words addressed to God, by which his majesty

instructed in every sort of letters, human as well as divine, in Latin, Greek, and Hebrew, in every branch of natural and moral philosophy, in Holy Writ and theology, and most especially in those controversial matters that the heretics of England have obscured with their errors and placed in doubt. Thus, being armed and well trained in the sound and solid truths of our sacred Catholic faith, they will more easily answer the heretics' vain arguments, and defeat them. And therefore, they have their particular studies, readings, defenses, debates, disputations, and controversies, and every other literary exercise that might be useful to them. And the Lord is greatly to be praised, seeing how they depart the colleges much improved in virtue and in knowledge—for, since the aim and end of their studies and projects is God, God himself aids and favors them.[5]

When it seems to the superiors of the seminaries that the students are solid and ready for an enterprise so arduous and difficult, they take in hand the most mature and experienced ones, and although all desire to go to their deaths for

---

is revered and the burning zeal of divine love is carefully maintained. [...] Now, while they eat, some apt texts are always read out, by which their food is seasoned, or, some one of the theology students devoutly discourses on some appropriate and improving theme, either in Latin or in English. Further, the hours of rest that follow, though they are free for any honorable and pleasant relaxation of the spirit, yet as a rule no topic of common conversation is admitted among them, save what relates to piety or learning." *Philopater*, 155–56.

5 "So much for the customs—yet the study of letters is almost on an equal footing with them. For, where there is a tranquil mind, a quiet spirit, a serene conscience, a fixed and holy goal, well-apportioned time, good order, appropriate means, careful diligence, and constant, unceasing training, there, though the talent be utterly mediocre, the progress cannot but be great. Yet much more so in those whose wills God has not only apparently purged from all that is earthly or inferior, such that they desire nothing but the very highest, but also whose intellects he has elevated (as it often happens), and illuminated with heavenly light, to comprehend all things. And so, if they are trained in logic, or physics, or metaphysics; if they ascend to theology—whether to the branch called positive, which consists in the interpretation of the texts of Holy Scripture, the explication of controversies, and the knowledge of languages (which particular theology is the only one used among our heretics); or to the moral branch, which instructs the consciences of men, and elucidates the gravest difficulties arising from human actions; or, at last, to the speculative, which is properly called Scholastic, and which, albeit it is the more difficult, is thus the more exalted and the noblest, and wonderfully expounds the majesty, goodness, and other attributes of God, the miracles he has wrought, the mystery of the Holy Trinity, the power of the Sacraments, and the secrets of the life to come with perfect clarity and sublime method; or else to some other part of this sacred learning (indeed, they embrace them all), these youths of ours so apply themselves as to make almost-miraculous progress, and in fact many, I dare say, outstrip in a year seven years in the English universities." Ibid., 157–58.

our sacred faith, what all wish for is not given to all, until their time comes, and in the meantime those judged most fit are dispatched, leaving the rest fiercely envious of their good luck, praying to God for them and taking leave of their sweet brothers with tears and sighs, not because they go to be tortured and cruelly slain in England, but rather because they cannot accompany them, and so swiftly become sharers in their torments, crowns, and triumphs.

The Spirit and Manner in Which These Young Men Return to England

The zeal with which these valiant soldiers and warriors of the Lord go to so glorious and so perilous a conquest is wonderful, a gift of God's own hand—without which it would be unthinkable that so many noble youths, pampered and even spoiled at home, should with such enthusiasm and boldness leap into a frightful abyss of infinite dangers and difficulties, a forest of savage beasts who gorge themselves on human blood, by whom they know they will be torn apart, if God does not miraculously preserve them from their claws.

To convey these young English seminarians' ardor and fervent desire to die for God, and the joy and enthusiasm with which they return to home to shed their blood for the Catholic faith, I wish to include here the words that one of them addressed in Latin, this past year of 1592, to His Holiness Clement VIII, in his own name and in those of his companions when eight of them came from the seminary at Rome, bound for England, to receive his blessing.

> We go—he said—most blessed father, to England, our homeland, which in years past was a true and faithful daughter of the Roman Church, and now, through its great misfortunes, has become its foe and a savage enemy. We go to a forest of beasts and a wilderness of errors and heresies, which in another time was a delightful garden of holiness and religion. We go to England, which is wretched in being lost, and yet more wretched in not perceiving its perdition, and most wretched in that, if it does know, it will neither acknowledge it nor amend, but rather with a perverse and devilish obstinacy brags and sermonizes its misery to us. And even though it abhors us and regards us as traitors for being your sons, and so threatens us with tortures and execution, we acknowledge it and cherish and embrace it as our most loving mother, for if impiety has extinguished her innate love to the extent that she plots our deaths because we are your sons, it is just that piety and divine love should awaken us and inspire us to seek her life and health, though it be at the cost of our travails and our lives. We go, either to restore the Catholic faith in England, if the Lord favors us, or to give our lives for that faith and for the authority of Your Holiness, if God grants us that mercy. We go to certain dangers with uncertain hopes, for we do not know what it shall please God to do—but

howsoever it falls out, we go utterly confident in Your Holiness's blessing, which shall be for us a guide on the journey, strength in peril, and a token of the assistance and favor of the Lord. We humbly entreat Your Holiness to give us this benediction and, as this Holy See has so lovingly sustained us while we have been in exile far from our home, to accompany and strengthen us with your blessing, now that we are returning. And we do not ask this blessing for ourselves alone, but with all our reverence and fervor, we beg Your Holiness not to forget our wretched homeland, nor to omit to consider its remedy. By this right hand of yours, most holy father, the instrument of divine clemency, by the fierce flames of the love of God that burn in Your Holiness's heart, by that benignity that Christ our Redeemer has given you as his vicar for all the souls he bought with his blood,[1] we ask, beg, and implore you, prostrate at your blessed feet, to succor and assist England, though she neither deserves nor asks it, indeed refuses and decries it. It is the nature of the goodness of God to shower its gifts upon the ingrates and the unenlightened. But the will of Your Holiness is capable of what none can conceive; let all know that in piety and goodwill, no less than in authority and dignity, Your Holiness is close to heaven. Few and feeble, we go to fight against a savage, innumerable army of Amalekites: let Your Holiness, like another Moses standing upon the sacred mount, lift up your hands to the heavens and attain for us the valor to struggle and the grace to conquer. And if, perchance, at some point, these hands, weighed down and wearied with the burdens of so many important matters, cannot be raised up on our behalf, there will be no lack of those who, with their prayers, like Aaron and Hur, shall support them in their fatigue, so that by their virtue we may stir our own hands and our spiritual arms, and so achieve victory over our foes.[2] To speak as I feel, may it please the Lord, most holy father, may it please the Lord, I say, that I should be so fortunate and so blessed as to merit to lose my life for my Lord Jesus Christ, for my homeland, and for this sacred Apostolic See, dying for the confession of the Catholic faith! O what a happy day it would be, on which in dying I should begin to live, and how glorious it will be for Your Holiness, if my companions triumph! O, how blessed and divine shall Your Holiness's pontificate be, if in your time England should come to itself, if the lost sheep should return to their shepherd, if the scepter and crown of that kingdom should be cast at those feet that I now humbly kiss; if the faith and devotion that was lost

---

1 Acts 20:28; Gal. 3:13; 1 Pet. 1:18–19.
2 Exod. 17:8–13.

in England under Clement VII should be recovered and flourish again in the days of Clement VIII, to the delight of heaven and earth!

The young man of the English seminary spoke these words with such tenderness and emotion that he drew many tears from the eyes of those present, and he moved the pope himself, to answer in this way:

> We are most envious (if so we may call it) of you, for our Lord has chosen you for so wonderful an enterprise, to labor in his vineyard,[3] your homeland, in the sure hope of martyrdom, and we would regard it as a most blessed lot to be able to accompany you and die with you and be sharers in your happiness and your crown. But as we cannot do this, being detained here with the governance and care of the entire universal Church, nor do we deserve to shed our blood in your homeland, which in another time was truly devoted to this Holy See, we will not fail to accompany you with our will and with our prayers, and to implore our Lord to preserve in you the spirit he has given your hearts. Seek you to kindle and grow, through virtue and through good works, this fervor and devotion that God has sparked in your souls, so that you shall be one who perseveres to the end, to whom the crown is given,[4] and so that you shall be granted the abundant, overflowing fruit we expect from you, through the goodness of the Lord, who has chosen you for this glorious enterprise.[5]

At these words, the supreme pontiff retired to another room, shedding copious tears. And in proof that what the seminary student, whose name was Francis Montford, had said in his audience with His Holiness was the truth, and that those burning words with which he declared his desire to die for Christ had issued from his very heart, within six months of his having uttered them, he put them into action and unhesitatingly died in England for the Lord.[6]

---

3   Matt. 20:1–16.

4   James 1:12.

5   The oration and the pope's reply are printed in Joseph Cresswell's *Exemplum literarum*, 163–66.

6   Francis Montford (*c*.1566–92) entered the English College at Rome in 1590, and was sent to England two years later, being executed in London within months. Francis Aidan Gasquet, *A History of the Venerable English College, Rome: An Account of Its Origins and Work from the Earliest Times to the Present Day* (London: Longmans, Green and Co., 1920), 158.

How the Seminarians Return to England, and What They Do There

In such a spirit do these stout soldiers of the Lord return to England; with such goals they undertake their invasion. They return in disguise, because the laws of the land are so brutal and executed with such extreme rigor; because there are innumerable guards, spies, dogs, and informers; because the reward for exposing this prey is so great, the risk of concealing them so dire, that they cannot enter save in false garb, whether as soldiers, or merchants, or seamen, or something similar, nor travel through the country in any other fashion lest they be recognized and fall into the heretics' hands, forfeiting their own lives and those of the Catholics who have received and sheltered them. Saint Eusebius, bishop of Samosata, did this in the time of the Arian Emperor Constantius, traveling in the guise of a soldier to visit the churches of the Catholics and strengthen and encourage them, and ultimately dying as a glorious martyr of Christ, as is related in the *Martyrologium Romanum*.[1]

One of their principal instructions on arrival in England is not to get involved in the secular politics of the kingdom, whether things go well or ill, so as not to give the heretics their foes an opportunity any shred of evidence for what they presently proclaim with such mendacity: that these men are traitors and rebels, killed and executed for this reason. Accordingly, they busy themselves with edifying the people by their saintly lives, teaching the ignorant, inspiring the weak, supporting the strong, extending a hand to the fallen, confounding the heretics, and consoling and encouraging all Catholics by demonstrating to them that God permits this extreme and barbarous persecution to prove them, to refine them in virtue, and to give them a crown as glorious as their battles and struggles have been fierce and long; that it will soon come to an end; and that in the meantime the same Lord that allows it will give them the strength to endure and overcome it. Since they are the first to expose themselves to troubles and dangers, to torture, to the gallows, and to the knife, their words have considerable force and weight with their hearers. They preach in public when they can, and in secret oratories when they cannot, admonishing and encouraging their listeners with spiritual discourses not to despair, nor, amid

---

1 In the margin: "*Martyrologium Romanum*, June 21."
   Baronio, *Martyrologium Romanum*, 270.

the length and terror of so horrific a storm, to lose the anchor of trust in the Lord. They say Mass for them, hear their confessions, administer communion to them, and bless them; if they have any doubts, these are made clear, and if there are any disputes or conflicts among them, these are straightway resolved, for the Catholics have such love and respect for them that they leave everything in their hands. Besides this, when the Lord enlightens and touches the heretics' hearts, so that they come to themselves and return to the path of truth (as frequently happens), the priests teach and instruct them in what they are to believe and to hold, according to our sacred Catholic, apostolic, and Roman faith, and reconcile them, so that with the favor of the Holy Spirit the servants and slaves of Satan become children of God,[2] incorporated as limbs of the mystical body of Jesus Christ our Savior,[3] which is the holy Church, his bride.[4]

These are the English seminaries that have been established in France, Italy, and Spain. This is the end and aim to which the pope, the Catholic King, and all the other good people who have supported and support them turn their eyes. These are the qualities of the young men received therein, this is the oath they take, these are the occupations in which they spend their time, in the colleges and subsequently in England. This is the spirit with which they go, this the caution and prudence with which they live, this the fruit they have produced, this the war that a few, seemingly weak priests wage against sin, heresy, and hell, to the extreme perturbation and terror of the queen and her ministers, who are trembling and terrified, exhausting themselves in seeking some means of resisting them, and, not finding any in passing bloodstained, barbaric laws against them, vainly hoping to scare them with punishment and force. But let us consider what the queen says in her edict against these assured and proven truths about the seminaries.

First, she claims that to undermine England the Catholic King (against whom the edict is principally directed), exploiting the power of his ally the pope, has negotiated with several seditious rabble-rousers and churlish subjects of hers, low, base men, who have gathered a band of degenerate youths who, partly because they have nothing to eat, and partly because of the crimes they committed, have fled their homeland and become fugitives, rebels, and traitors. That such men, after the seminaries have schooled them in how to subvert the kingdom of England, return with ample powers from the Roman pontiff, to persuade the queen's subjects to abandon their obedience, offering them hopes of fabulous wealth if the Spanish invade England. And they extract

---

2   Deut. 14:1; John 1:12; Rom. 8:14, 8:16, 8:19; Gal. 3:26.

3   Rom. 12:5; 1 Cor. 6:15, 12:12, 12:17; Eph. 5:30; Col. 1:18.

4   2 Cor. 11:2; Eph. 5:25–27; Rev. 19:7–9.

a solemn oath that they will turn against the queen and aid King Don Philip, promising those who do so heaven itself, and threatening those who do not with hell, according to certain papal bulls.

This is what the edict asserts. Consider well all the falsehoods in what it avers of the seminaries, for there will be found more lies than words. Through the truth as set out here, the gentle, scrupulous reader will easily be able to undo the shadows of this perfidious people and perceive how blind they are who imagine that everyone else cannot see at midday. We decline to respond to these inanities or to discuss them in detail, but rather beg the reader to consider them, and marvel that things so false and absurd have been printed in the name of a queen, and that they are believed by the common masses, corrupted by heresy and by hatred and abhorrence for everything that could undeceive them.

The Edict's Cruelty against the Seminarians and the Jesuits

Though the queen's edicts against the seminary priests and the Jesuits are so cruel and inhuman, the rigor with which they are enforced so extreme and barbaric that in content and in deed they exceed every decree and law, however bloody, of every tyrant who has hitherto persecuted the Catholic Church, Elizabeth adds to this proclamation further, ampler procedures for hunting them, sniffing them out, and running them to ground, lest a single one escape her clutches. For, not satisfied with the ordinary judges, courts, and magistrates of the whole kingdom, and the infinity of executioners, jailers, wardens, bailiffs, and other agents who serve her, her edict provides for the designation and creation of special commissioners, to be sent to each and every one of the provinces or counties of the realm (of which there are approximately forty), to seek out, investigate, and apprehend the said priests with the utmost diligence and exquisite means. And these commissioners have not only been instituted and dispatched into every province, but in every city, town, village, and parish of every county they have named and designated persons who vigilantly assist in these inquisitions and inquiries. They have been given secret instructions, commanded to divide among themselves the boundaries and jurisdictions of their commission, to assemble diligently every forty days, at the least, to confer about what they have done and give order for what is to be done. And whenever they get word that some person they suspect has disappeared, they are secretly to alert the commissioners of the other provinces, so as to find and seize them and send them back securely. In these instructions they are given the form they are to use in interrogations and the questions they are to ask the Catholics, and they are commanded to write to the queen and the council every three months about everything they have found, and to substitute or deputize further commissioners as seems good to them, to do in their names all that they themselves do, and this with the most sweeping, generous powers.

Above all and in addition to all the edict's other provisions, the knights and lords and grandees of the kingdom, and the queen's own ministers and attendants, of whatsoever rank or prominence, and all fathers and heads of families throughout the realm, are commanded under the steepest penalties (and under a warrant, which they execute without any exception, mitigation,

© KONINKLIJKE BRILL NV, LEIDEN, 2017 | DOI 10.1163/9789004323964_125

or respect of persons) to make inquiries of every person who has frequented their houses in the past fourteen months, or entered, eaten, drunk, or slept there. And everything they find is to be written down in certain books, marked out for the purpose, which they are to keep for the benefit of the commissioners. Those who do not respond promptly, or hesitate when they are questioned, are to be immediately seized and sent to the commissioners under heavy guard. And the aforesaid fathers of each household are also to be punished if they are negligent in performing this investigation, in writing it down, in keeping it, or in displaying the books. And he who has aided such priests or failed to uncover them is to be punished with the penalties customarily given to the accomplices and abettors of traitors and rebels. Two further details render this draconian mandate yet more terrifying, and the condition of the Catholics of England yet more wretched and miserable. The first, that under the terms of this edict there is no man so downtrodden and base, be he the very dregs of the people, who is not free to harass any Catholic whatsoever, however exalted; the innkeeper, the publican, of any station whatsoever, even to the town crier or the laborer, has the prerogative to investigate, accuse, apprehend, drag to the tribunals and the jails, abuse, and oppress any Catholic he pleases, or to be revenged upon his enemies—even if they are *heretics*—by claiming that they are Catholics and disobey the queen's laws. And it often happens that the most perfidious men, the thieves and murderers, the liars and scoundrels, and the malcontents of the realm, find a way to escape the penalties and punishments deserved by their crimes—the most effective means to be found in the kingdom these days—in investigating and accusing some Catholic. By this means, not only are they not punished, but they even win rewards and favor. The second thing is that, because flattery and the desire to please princes is so common and so strong, and because the queen and her foremost advisers have so openly and vehemently declared the hatred they bear toward our sacred religion and the priests of God who teach and preach it, you would not believe how people appear each day to become inquisitors, investigators, spies, and enforcers of the edict against the Catholics, to curry favor with the queen and her intimates and to show themselves zealous in her service (though it is not their office, nor their affair)—imagining thus to win a reputation as loyal subjects and passionate servants of the queen, and the attendant rewards. And it is not only the common, lowborn folk who do this: some of the most prominent lords of the realm have clamored to perform the office of informant and spy, personally searching and ransacking the corners of their homes to find and arrest a seminary priest, Jesuit, or some other Catholic who had been received in their house. Witness the unbounded hatred they have for the true and sacred religion of the Roman Church, and how heresy renders men (illustrious or noble though they may be) not only flatterers and villains, but also spineless and base.

Perhaps someone will suppose that these are only the queen's words against the seminarians and the Jesuits, and although they are stern, harsh, injurious, and false words, yet in the end, they are no more than threats and words, of which little notice should be taken, and that the fierceness of her edicts, the institution of new commissioners, the horde of investigators and agents, and everything else provided for and decreed against the Catholics is more to frighten them than to execute the ordained penalties. But it is not so, and her fury and fierceness rather advance so far that she seems to have shed all humanity and womanly sweetness, and attired herself in the savageness of a tiger—or, properly speaking, it is those who advise her, the authors of such extreme cruelties as are executed in England upon a people so innocent and well-intentioned. For against these priests they appear to have armed every demon and all their heretical henchmen with every sort of torture, torment, and punishment that hell can devise. For the Catholics are the cells, the fetters, the manacles, the chains, the irons, the shackles, and every other instrument usually used to torment criminal, soulless men. For them is the hunger, the thirst, the nakedness, the fire and the ice, the heat and the cold, and all the abuses that man has ever used upon man. Against them the queen's ministers rage, the preachers scream from the pulpits, the false bishops enforce their harsh inquisitions, the informers expend all their malice, the judges render sentence, and the hangmen execute it, and all the deceived people shout and harass them with slanders, insults, and affronts. They are tormented, mangled, dragged, hanged, and disemboweled while yet alive. They are dismembered and their quarters placed upon the towers, squares, and gates of the cities, as this history has told. In the end, there is no sort of torture or death so shameful and horrific that it has not been perpetrated upon these saintly priests, and upon those who shelter, hide, aid, or support them.

How False it is that None Die in England for the Sake of Religion, as the Edict Claims

This barbaric and savage cruelty does not end here, nor are these hellish monsters satisfied with taking the lives of the Catholics and the servants of the Lord; instead, to strip them of their honor they claim that they do not die for the sake of religion, but rather as rebels and traitors, as the queen bluntly declares in this decree. In the second book of the first part of this history,[1] we discussed at length the falseness of this patent lie, and the queen's ministers' reasons for employing this pretext, thus imitating the pagan tyrants and heretics who in ages past persecuted the Catholic Church on religious grounds. It was their claim that they did all this because the Christians and Catholics were felons, who had committed countless and heinous crimes. To that chapter we refer the gentle and curious reader. This is the greatest outrage and abuse done against those blessed martyrs, but it is not new, nor a recent invention of England's, but rather the custom of the other heretics and savage despots (as we have said), to deny those who die for the Catholic faith the glory and honor of martyrs. For this reason, Saint Hilary called the Arian Emperor Constantius "the deceitful persecutor," and said that he was more awful and brutish than Decius or Nero. And Saint Gregory Nazianzus, writing against Julian the Apostate, says these words: "The godless emperor has raged against us, and, lest we win the honors always given to martyrs (for these he begrudges Christians), his first fiendish move was to have those who suffered for Christ punished as malefactors and felons." And in another place: "This was the apostate's plan, to use force and seem as though he had not, and to torture and slay us, while depriving us of the honor always given to those who suffer for the sacred name of the Lord. O unparalleled madness of a deranged man!" All this from Saint Gregory Nazianzus.[2] Without doubt, this most glorious and eloquent doctor

---

1   In the margin: "Book 2, Chapter 34."
2   In the margin: "First oration against Julian."
    Hilary of Poitiers, *Contra Constantium*, Chapters 5 and 8.
    Gregory of Nazianzus's funeral oration for his brother Caesarius, Chapter 11.
    Gregory of Nazianzus, *First Invective Against Julian*, Chapter 58.
    These quotations come from Robert Persons's response to Elizabeth's edict: see *Philopater*, 173–74.

justly called it unparalleled madness in Julian the Apostate, for he hoped by guile to deny what the entire world saw, and make it seem that the Christians had died as wrongdoers, when everyone knew they perished because they were Christians. We can truthfully say the same of the author of this edict.

O unparalleled madness, O extraordinary insanity of a deranged man, that in a light so clear and so glorious, in a matter so obvious that it can be touched with the hands, proven by so much evidence, you should be so blind as to think that you can blind us, and hoodwink us lest we see what we see with our own eyes and touch with our own hands! First of all, of all the seminary priests or Jesuits who have died at your hands in England in these years, give me one who had taken up arms against the queen? Who had taken the field against her? Who had persuaded her subjects to abandon their obedience in civil matters, such as belong to temporal princes? Give me one who has been accused of murder, of theft, of adultery, or of some other serious crime—as the ministers of your perverted sect are every day, and punished for it. You will not find, nor can you say with any truth, that any of the ministers of God have been accused or punished as criminals. Moreover, to how many of these renowned priests, when you tortured them, and even at the very instant they stood at the foot of the gallows to yield their souls to God, did you offer life and freedom, and even huge rewards, if they confessed the queen to be the supreme head of England? Thus proving that they were to die only for not acknowledging her as such. How many insisted before the entire crowd, at the moment of death itself, that they died innocent and guiltless of the treasons and crimes falsely put upon them, and merely because they were Catholics and because they had not acted against their conscience by recognizing the queen as the spiritual head of the Church of England, invoking God as witness and judge of the truth? How many who wanted to protest and disabuse the people gathered for the sorry spectacle of their death have you commanded to silence and stopped their mouths, lest they reveal the truth and innocence in which they died? And at this moment, do not your dungeons, filled with Catholic laymen, rich and distinguished, with famous knights and noble lords, with venerable priests and prominent gentlemen, raise their voices against you, crying out that these men are imprisoned solely for their religion?

But, to convict this slander and falsehood more clearly, one need only read the secret instructions that the queen gives the commissioners that (as we have said) she has instituted and authorized in every province, city, and town in the kingdom to execute the bloody penalties of the edict against the Catholics. The title of these orders is "Certain secret instructions and mandates of the queen and her council, given to the commissioners or inquisitors, to whom authority has been given to execute the edict recently promulgated against the priests and the other Catholics in every province of England." The second section of the document begins with these words:

> Secondarily, you are to ask the bishop of the diocese of each province, and his secretary, provost, archdeacon, and the public officials and authorities, and the provincial attorneys, legal registrars [*secretarios de las justicias*], notaries, and other ministers and officials of the kingdom, and the mayors and magistrates of whatever city, town, or place, the cause, number, names, and residences of all those than in past years have been discovered, accused, or brought before them or their tribunals for reasons of religion, and for refusing to attend our public churches, be they men or women, and all the proceedings drawn up against them on this account before other judges.[3]

These are the official words of the secret instructions, which God has been pleased to uncover in order to reveal the truth and make manifest the falsehood of this edict, how they so shamelessly affirm that none of the Catholics die for the sake of religion, but only as traitors or offenders against the state and majesty of the queen. Now, because this is of crucial importance to the glory of God, the honor of his martyrs, the edification and example of the faithful, the confounding of the heretics, the vindication of the truth, and the recognition of the cunning deceit of the queen's ministers, who at times reveal themselves (it seems to me) as wolves, and in their deeds veritably attire themselves as wolves, for they are always wolves, and bloodthirsty, savage wolves, I wish to linger a little longer on this point and offer proof from the annals, histories, and the laws of the English *cortes* themselves, which they call acts of parliament.

---

3 At the end of his attack on Elizabeth's edict, Persons includes a transcript of "The secret instructions and mandates of the queen and those of her council, to the commissioners or inquisitors to whom is given authority for enforcing the recently promulgated edict against priests and other Catholics in every province or county in England." The second entry runs: "Second, you will ask of the bishop of the diocese of each province, and from his secretary, provost, and archdeacon, and the other officers and public officials, and also from the provincial attorneys, the registrars of the county, the notaries, and the other ministers and officials of the realm, and of the mayors and magistrates of any city, village, or town whatsoever, the reason, number, names, and residences of all those who have been identified, accused, and brought before their tribunals in the previous year for a question of religion, for having recused themselves from the public churches, whether they be men or women, as well as the legal proceedings or judgments lodged against them by other judges for this reason." *Philopater*, 258–63, here 258–59.

So, in the annals of that kingdom composed by Holinshed and Stow, heretic authors, and written with public imprimatur as a perpetual memorial of the reign and deeds of Elizabeth, for the year 1559 we read these words:

> in the first year of the queen's reign, in the month of July, Nicholas Heath, archbishop of York, and the bishops of Ely and London,[4] and thirteen or fourteen others altogether, having been commanded to appear before the queen's councilors because they had refused to swear that Her Majesty was the head of the Church, and for other points touching religious matters, were deprived of their bishoprics, and the same was done to numerous deans, archdeacons, rectors, vicars, and other churchmen, who were stripped of their benefices and thrown into various prisons.[5]

All this is recounted in the annals of England. And in those of Stow, it says:

> In the twentieth year of the queen's reign, on November 30 [sic], the priest Cuthbert Mayne, a licentiate in theology, was drawn to the gallows, hanged, and quartered, in the town of Launceston in the county of Cornwall, because he placed the ecclesiastical authority of the pope over that of the queen.[6]

And on the same page it says:

> On February 3, in the morning, the priest John Nelson was brought from the prison they call Newgate and drawn to the place of execution and hanged, disemboweled, and quartered, for having denied the queen's ecclesiastical primacy and uttered other, similar sentiments against Her Majesty.[7] And on the seventeenth of the said month, a certain man by

---

4 Thomas Thirlby and Edmund Bonner, respectively.

5 Holinshed, *Chronicles*, 4:184.

   These citations of Holinshed and Stow are taken from the *Concertatio*, 301ʳ–302ʳ.

6 Ribadeneyra miscopies the date (originally November 20) from the account of Mayne's death in the *Concertatio*, 301ᵛ–302ʳ.

   Cf. John Stow, *The Chronicles of England from Brute vnto This Present Yeare of Christ 1580 Collected by Iohn Stow Citizen of London* (London: By Ralphe Newberie, at the assignement of Henrie Bynneman, 1580), 1192.

7 The priest John Nelson (1535–78) was martyred on February 3, 1578, condemned as a traitor for affirming that "If she [sc. Elizabeth] be the setter fourth [...] and defender of this religion now practized in England, then she is a Schismatike and an Heretike." He sought entrance to the Society of Jesus just before his martyrdom. See Allen, *Briefe Historie*, 111–17, here 112.

   For a contemporary Catholic depiction of Nelson's martyrdom, see Book 2 Figure 28.1.

the name of Sherwood was taken from London castle to the gallows and ended his life in the same way and for the same crime of *lèse-majesté*.[8]

Holinshed, in his chronicle for the year 1574, says these words:

> In the sixteenth year of the queen's reign, on April 4, Palm Sunday, three prominent ladies were arrested in London while hearing Mass in their houses: namely the wife of Baron Morley, with her children and many others; and in another part of the city at the same hour, the widow Guildford, who had been the wife of a prominent knight,[9] was seized with numerous other ladies of note; and at the same moment in another neighborhood the wife of another gentleman, by the name of Browne, was taken from her house with several others. They were all imprisoned for the same crime and, being accused and convicted, were condemned according to the letter of the law.[10]

Thus says Holinshed.

Let us buttress this truth yet further. When the parliament and estates of the kingdom of England adjourns, it is the custom to enact a general pardon to all wrongdoers who are imprisoned, however wicked or criminal they might be: only the Catholics are excluded from this pardon, for them alone an exception is made. Thus, in the year 1581, which was the twenty-third of Elizabeth's reign, in the act of parliament for this general pardon, these words were added:

> But it is declared that this concession[11] of a general pardon and grace is in no way to be extended to any person who, on this final day of the present session of parliament is imprisoned or in any other custody for obstinacy or refusing to go to our churches or attend divine offices, or for any other matter or cause relating to obdurate stubbornness on questions of the religion established in this our realm. Wherefore we ordain that all such persons who are for this reason deprived of their liberty may not enjoy

---

8   Cf. Stow, *Summarie* (1580), 1192–93.
     Ribadeneyra describes the martyrdom of Thomas Sherwood (*c.*1564–78) at greater length below.

9   Thomas Guildford was still alive at the time of the incident, dying the following year.

10   *Concertatio*, 301ᵛ.
     Cf. Holinshed, *Chronicles*, 3:324.

11   In the 1605 edition, "conseßion" is altered to "confeßion," rendering the phrase, "this declaration of a general pardon and grace."

the benefit of our general grace, pardon, and remission, so long as they persevere in their said pertinacity and disobedience.[12]

In the year 1585, which was the twenty-seventh of Elizabeth's reign, in the month of March, parliament passed a vicious law against the Catholics, and at the beginning, setting out the contents of the edict, it said that the priests who enter England seek to disturb and unsettle it and to assassinate the queen, taking this as the basis for their law. And, having expatiated on this in fierce words, the author forgot them, and in the ninth paragraph of the same law, includes the following:

> Yet it is understood that this statute and all comprehended in it does not extend to any Jesuit, priest, or seminarian, or any other priest, deacon, religious, or ecclesiastic (as has been said) who in the space of these forty days, or within three days of hereafter entering the realm or any other territory of Her Majesty, subjects himself to any archbishop or bishop of this kingdom, or a justice of the peace in the county he arrives in, and before the said archbishop, bishop, or justice of the peace truly and sincerely takes the oath concerning religion set out in the first year of the queen's reign, signs it in his own hand, and acknowledges and continues to acknowledge and recognize that Her Majesty is to be obeyed in the laws, statutes, and ordinances that have been made or will be made in matters relating to religion.[13]

Could one say in words clearer, more express, or more evident that the very basis for this persecution is religion? For as soon as any priest whatsoever, be it a seminarian or a Jesuit, subjects himself to the queen's religion, the anger ceases and all penalties are foregone! O truth, what power you have, to make even your very enemies confess you! These are the official words of their acts, the proceedings of their estates, their laws, their chronicles, and their annals, faithfully translated from Latin into Castilian. Let us now see how the queen's edict speaks of them.

The decree says that no Catholic dies for the sake of religion. The annals say that several of these men, as well as priests, have been drawn, hanged, disemboweled, and quartered for not recognizing the queen as supreme head of the Church. Is this a question of religion? The annals say that many prominent

---

12   23 Eliz. 1. c. 16, §11. See SR, 4.2:702.

        This detail comes from *Philopater*, 177–78.

13   27 Eliz. 1. c. 2, §8. See SR, 4.2:707.

women have been imprisoned for hearing Mass and condemned according to the purport of the law. Is hearing Mass not a question of religion? The edict says that no one is deprived of their life, nor their possessions, goods, or liberty on account of religion; the annals say that all these bishops, archbishops, prelates, and ecclesiastical persons, raised to such dignities, have been despoiled of their churches, incomes, and benefices, and held and abused in various prisons for charges relating to religion. Is this not to lose liberty, property, and life? That the Catholics are punished, tormented, and slain on religious grounds is proven not only by what we have recounted here, but also by the enactment of an amnesty and pardon for all the heretical criminals in England, with none for the blameless, innocent Catholics, for the parliamentary decree of grace for all imprisoned heretics denied it to the Catholics there for the sake of religion—such that the adulterer, the murderer, the highwayman, the perjurer, the blasphemer, and any other sort of man, however villainous and hateful he might be, could, being a heretic, receive grace and pardon by virtue of these statutes of parliament, while the Catholic, only for being such, is excluded from all grace and pardon. Certain and notorious though all this is, as we have demonstrated, the queen's edict affirms that no one dies or loses their possessions, goods, and liberty for reasons of religion, but only as a traitor and rebel against their rightful monarch and lord. O the shamelessness of the heretic! But let us consider what reasons the edict offers to prop up this obvious falsehood.

The Edict's Proofs that None Die in England for Reasons of Religion

The decree uses three arguments to prove that no one in England suffers because of their faith. The first, that in the criminal proceedings brought against the Catholics, they are neither accused, nor condemned, nor executed for anything but the crime of *lèse-majesté*. The second, that many rich and distinguished men in England follow a different creed than the queen, and they are not on this account deprived of life, property, or liberty. The third, that they proceed in a manner so gentle and so moderate that from even men of a contrary religion who refuse to attend the heretics' churches, no more is mandated to them than the payment of a certain fine. Let us examine these three arguments, and we shall see what weight and truth they possess. For, even though we have demonstrated the falseness of the conclusion, we ought to dissect its assertions, so that they themselves shall testify to our truth.

The first argument is that in the criminal cases no mention is made of religion, but only of the crime of *lèse-majesté*—which is utterly false, as the proceedings themselves attest, for in many of them there is no mention of any crime *but* that of religion. On February 7, 1578, sentence was rendered upon a young man—or, more truthfully, a boy of fourteen years—of genteel aspect, called Thomas Sherwood, whom they hanged at London Castle after they had held him prisoner for six months, tormented with dungeons, chains, hunger, and other tortures.[1] Why? Not for having departed England without permission; not for having been in Rome; not for having been raised in the seminaries, nor having being ordained by the pope's authority; not for having returned to the land (whence he had never strayed) to disturb it; not as a seditious Jesuit nor as a malcontent priest, nor as a traitor. Why, then? Only because, being pressed by the judges with devilish questions, he declared the pope's supreme authority over the entire Church.[2] And the public acts of the judges themselves

---

1   Though this story, and those that follow, appear in the *Concertatio*, the passage is largely a translation of *Philopater*, 182–83.

2   "And so they examined him on the points of the faith: what did he believe and what did he feel? At length, their arguments forced from him that he believed the Roman pontiff to be the supreme authority in England in ecclesiastical matters. [...] Thereupon he was transferred to the Tower of London, and left in an isolated hole next to the torture chamber. [...]

prove this. And at around the same time, also in the Tower of London, another young layman by the name of Copper was martyred, having been accused or convicted of no crime save that of wanting to live in the seminary at Rheims, and having been seized en route.[3] Well, did they not pierce the ears of young Mark Tippet with a hot iron?[4] Did they not cut off those of a bookseller called Rowland Jenks, and another gentleman, Vallenger, for the sake of religion alone?[5] And in the year 1583, John Bodey and John Slade, two learned youths of extraordinary abilities, were martyred, the one in Winchester and the other in Andover, for denying that the queen possessed papal authority in ecclesiastical matters, as the judges' own sentence declares.[6] And in the year 1584, William

---

Finally, after six months of inhuman imprisonment, after chains and starvation, after excruciating torments with the rack, after well-nigh unbelievable constancy, on February 7, 1578 he was piteously offered up as a living and dying sacrifice [*miserandum in modum vivus mortuusq[ue] mactatus fuit*] and carried off to the eternal tabernacle, to receive forevermore the glory and reward of so many travails." *Concertatio*, 79ᵛ–80ʳ.

3 Cf. "Copper was a young man of good parentage and no little training in letters [...] He had resolved to travel to foreign lands for the sake of his religion and his education. When he had made his preparations, and gathered what he had by way of money and belongings, he hastened to the port to depart. But the business being revealed somehow, he was apprehended by the magistrate and sent back to London, where he was first stripped of all his goods, and then thrown into the Tower of London. [...] That holy youth soon came to his end, his strength consumed by cold and hunger." Ibid., 80ᵛ–81ʳ.

4 Cf. "The deranged judge Fleetwood gave Mark Tippet, a virtuous youth born to wealthy parents, raised in a papal seminary for some time, the glory of a confessor, as he was lashed with birches through the city of London, and his ears shockingly bored through." Ibid., 408ʳ.

5 Stephen Vallenger, a Catholic layman (1541–91). See Anthony G. Petti, "Stephen Vallenger (1541–1591)," *RH* 6, no. 6 (October 1962): 248–64.

   Cf. "And first of all, they severely punished those who dared either to write or speak of the deaths of the saints or in condemnation of their iniquity; indeed, for having written of Father Campion's innocence, they forced some to flee both the universities and the kingdom, while they cut off the ears of several others, as befell Vallenger." *Concertatio*, 225ʳ.

   Cf. "Vallenger, a layman and a Catholic, lost his ears, for having made certain statements on the innocence of Fr. Campion." Ibid., 408ʳ.

6 John Slade (d.1583) and John Bodey (1549–1583) were condemned at the Winchester Assizes of 1583: Slade was executed at Winchester on October 30, Bodey at Andover on November 2. Pollen, *Acts*, 49–51.

   Cf. "Add to these, if you will, the two renowned confessors and martyrs John Slade and John Bodey, each of whom was brought to trial and compelled by numerous interrogations to reveal their judgment of the queen's usurpation of the supremacy in ecclesiastical matters [...] because each one declared his faith in the Roman pontiff's universal spiritual primacy, and flatly denied that the queen was the head of the Church of England, or sovereign in the conducting of spiritual affairs, they were condemned to public punishment [...] and so one

Carter in London,[7] and Richard White in Wales, after having been tortured, were slain—the one for having had a Catholic book printed, the other for having confessed his sins to a priest.[8] I have omitted countless other examples, as these suffice to confirm the falseness of the edict's first argument. Those who desire more will find a large number of such cases in the book entitled *Concertatio Ecclesiæ Catholicæ in Anglia, aduersus Caluinopapistas, & Puritanos, sub Elizabetha Regina*, which contains the proceedings themselves and the martyrs' confessions. This was printed at Trier in the year 1588. It includes a petition presented to the queen's council by certain Catholic gentlemen imprisoned for their religion, in which they related the calamities and miseries they endured in their captivity and begged for mercy and the easing of their punishment. At the end, they wrote these words:

> If, with your favor, we might win from Her Majesty what we beg (though we have been imprisoned for a long time, and have been condemned for having refused to go the sermons or the churches of the Calvinists), yet, we will plainly and simply protest that we do not decline to do so out of obstinacy or out of a refusal to obey Her Majesty, but only by the demand of our consciences, and for the sake of religion—for in all else we recognize Her Majesty as our lady, prince, and most merciful queen.[9]

Could it be expressed more plainly, or in words any clearer, that these knights were imprisoned and deprived of their wealth for the sake of religion?

Really, as I have thought to myself at various times, the insistence with which this falsehood is affirmed in the edict and the ease with which it may be

---

of them was put to death at Winchester, the other at Andover in the same province." *Concertatio*, 293ʳ.

7   The printer William Carter (*c.*1549–84) was imprisoned for publishing Catholic texts, and hanged, drawn, and quartered on January 11, 1584. I. Gadd, "Carter, William (*b.* in or before 1549, *d.*1584)," in *ODNB*, 10:377.

Cf. "I would have these foes recall that guiltless workman Carter, who was recently charged for printing the Catholic book *De schismate*, not one word of which could these foes find that related to the condition of the kingdom. Yet these vicious men dragged him to the place of execution, because the author of that book had written that the Catholic faith would eventually triumph over heresy, and pious Judith would cut off the head of Holofernes." *Concertatio*, 295ᵛ.

8   Richard Gwyn (or White, *c.*1537–84), a Welsh poet and teacher, was hanged, drawn, and quartered at Wrexham on October 15, 1584. Daniel Huws, "Gwyn [White], Richard [St Richard Gwyn] (*c.*1537–1584)," in *ODNB*, 24:359. See *Concertatio*, 172ᵛ–203ʳ.

9   Ribadeneyra translates from the Latin provided in Ibid., n.p.

confounded through the very sentences of the judges and the public proceedings, defies belief, unless there is some special meaning or import in England
to these words of "religion" and "treachery," "Catholic" and "rebel," which other
men and other lands beyond this realm neither use nor understand. For in
every other part of the world, religion is a virtue, which teaches honor and
reverence for God with the appropriate worship within and without. And
treachery is a conspiracy against the person or state of a prince—but in England these terms are confounded, and religion and treachery are taken for the
same thing, because there they have some other sense and some other language than that shared by every other nation. Thus it is that they have enacted
laws against those who profess the Catholic religion, as though the mere fact
of being Catholic made them rebels and traitors. Let us provide an example.
The queen orders that no one, on pain of death, should be ordained by the authority of the pope; nor say Mass; neither confess to anyone nor be confessed;
nor carry any bull, brief, or letter of the pope's; nor absolve anyone of heresy
or schism, nor reconcile them to the Roman Church, nor allow themselves to
be absolved or reconciled. She forbids anyone to possess any item of devotion
from Rome, such as an *agnus Dei*, crosses, images, rosaries, and so on. All those
who do so, she deems traitors, allies to the pope, and her enemies, opposed
to her supreme spiritual authority, and as such she persecutes, torments, and
eliminates them. Thus, if a priest says Mass, they say he is a traitor; if he hears
confessions, he is a traitor; if he absolves, he is a traitor; if he reconciles some
heretic, he is a traitor; if he carries with him a relic, or cross, or other object of
devotion, he is a traitor; and as these are all practices of the Catholic faith, they
say that they are rebels and malcontents and enemies of the queen, opposed
to her crown, and as such (as I said) they treat them. For in the vocabulary of
the queen's henchmen, the Catholic religion is the same thing as treason, and
to perform any act pertaining to that faith is the same thing as to commit some
perfidy against the queen.[10] And thus they claim that that they slay no one
for the sake of religion, but only for treason—because for them the greatest
possible treason is to be a Catholic and show any sign of being so, no matter
how small. The which is manifest proof of the hatred and abhorrence these

---

10   Ribadeneyra here echoes the words of Campion's executioners, as reported by William
        Allen: "In your Catholicisme (I noted the worde) all treason is conteined." Allen, *Briefe
        Historie*, 4.
            Many contemporaries noted similar shifts in the connotations of words, contested by
        two opposing sets of moral and political assumptions. Quentin Skinner has analyzed this
        phenomenon through the rhetorical trope of paradiastole. See Lake, *Bad Queen Bess?*,
        84–86.

wretches bear toward God and his holy faith, as among them the most grievous and atrocious crime, punished with the strictest penalties, is to be a Catholic.

But let us proceed to the second reason, which is that there are in England many wealthy persons of the contrary religion who are not punished on that account, nor deprived of their lives, possessions, goods, or liberty. Of this argument, I do not wish to say anything more than what I have said above, when we proved that a great many of them are arrested, robbed of their wealth, their freedom, and their lives for the sake of the Catholic religion. I will only add that this second point contradicts the third, in which, to laud the queen's moderation and mildness in punishing the Catholics, it is said that they are only ordered to pay a certain fine. And I say that this is contradictory, because if the Catholics pay some quantity of money as a penalty, then they are punished for being Catholics, to the detriment of their estates, and thus they are deprived thereof—which is irreconcilable and contrary to the second argument. Yet here we ought to note that the edict does not specify the amount demanded, which is so great that it beggars belief: neither the Turk, nor the Sharif [*Xerife*],[11] nor the prince of the Tartars, nor any other, however barbarous, or inimical to the faith of their subjects, imposed a tribute so steep or a burden so heavy in hatred of religion.

Any Catholic, of any age, condition, status, or dignity whatsoever, male or female, when they reach sixteen years of age is obligated to attend the heretics' churches, or to pay twenty English pounds each month—which is more than sixty-six gold *escudos*.[12] And by this sum they are not then free to worship God in the Catholic faith according to their consciences, but rather they remain captives still, in a never-ending fear and confusion. If they hear Mass, they must pay another fine; if they confess their sins to a priest, they are punished as traitors. And we could offer similar particulars for the other provisions concerning our sacred religion. Moreover, it often happens, a perfectly ordinary occurrence, that having paid the fine for not[13] having attended the heretics' churches, they arrest the Catholics anyway and abuse and afflict them, and confiscate the rest of their property, since they cannot defend it from

---

11   "Xerife," from the Arabic *sharif*, probably refers to the sultan of Morocco.

12   "For neither the Turk, I maintain, nor Persia, nor the Arabs, Moors, or Scythians ever exacted such a tribute from their subjects for the sake of a difference of religion. Truly, every single Catholic, of whatever sex, rank, condition, or class, none excluded and none exempted, if they have reached sixteen years of age, is forced to pay twenty English pounds, which is more than sixty-six French gold coins, each month, for so great a crime as refusing to attend the heretics' churches." *Philopater*, 179.

13   Somewhat puzzlingly, from the 1595 edition onward the "no" in this clause is removed, though the sense remains the same.

such avaricious spirits, nor remove it from the talons of so many birds of prey. And so, in the petition I mentioned above, presented to the queen's council by certain imprisoned knights, it says:

> We turn to Her Majesty's clemency and the mercy of Your Lordships, imploring most humbly that they consider how much less the incomes of our property and the exploitation of our lands amount to than what is necessary to pay the monetary penalties imposed upon us, together with the risk we run of falling ill with some ghastly contagion through the pestilential air and closeness of the cell, and the multitude of prisoners, and the host of deadly diseases that grows greater each day. For all these reasons, we are compelled to entreat Your Lordships to intercede with Her Majesty on our behalf: firstly, that we might win her grace; then, that the monetary penalties be moderated, such that we can pay them and retain some pittance wherewith we may sustain, however poorly, ourselves, our wretched wives, and our destitute children; and lastly, that as we are already imprisoned and fettered, we might have some more liberal captivity, and cells less harsh.[14]

But let us now conclude this chapter, for the most illustrious and reverend Cardinal William Allen has written a learned and thoughtful book on this point, responding to an impudent and arrogant heretic, who dared to write a tract called *The Execution of Justice in England* [*La justicia Britanica*], in which he senselessly and shamelessly seeks to prove that in England no one is punished for the sake of the Catholic faith, as we mentioned in the second book of this history.[15]

---

14   Ribadeneyra again translates from the Latin of *Concertatio*, n.p.

15   In the margin: "Book 2, Chapter 34." In the 1595 edition, this annotation is abbreviated to "Book 2, Chapter 3," and it is deleted altogether in the 1605 edition.

That this Edict is Oppressive and Intolerable to the Entire Kingdom of England

This edict of the queen's is not only sacrilegious against God, slanderous against the pope and the Catholic King, and savage and barbaric against the seminary priests and the fathers of the Society of Jesus—it is also abhorrent to those who govern that kingdom, and intolerable and dangerous to the entire realm, and it is this I wish to explicate here.

What greater infamy could there be for the queen and her council than to be so justly regarded by all the world as inhuman, cruel, and barbarous? For if magnanimity is the proper virtue of mighty princes, for which they are loved, lauded, and revered even by those to whom their clemency does not extend, their cruelty is rightly despised. Now, what cruelty is there in the world that could equal that now practiced in England? Where religion, innocence, saintliness, erudition, nobility, age, youth of either sex and any rank are so brutally persecuted and traduced; where one sees nothing but the deaths of Catholics and servants of God, for no other crime than being so? What nation, what monarch, what region is there today in the world so far from human nature and civilization, where we see what is happening in England? The Turks allow the Christians to live in their faith; the Lutherans in Germany, the Catholics, without force or oppression; in the ravaged parts of France and in Scotland, though the Calvinists have committed many outrages and atrocities, it has been through popular unrest or military excesses, not through sentences and judgments. The Arabs, Scythians, and barbarians do not abuse those who do not offend them, even if they are of some other religion, different from theirs. In England alone there is no honor, neither boundary nor measure against the Catholic faith. There they take for the most loyal to the queen and the most valiant, he who most thrusts in the lance,[1] and most lustily washes his hands in the blood of innocents[2]—and this by those taken for humane, thoughtful, and pragmatic—and proclaim their rule to be moderate, gentle, and in accordance with the ancient laws and praiseworthy customs of their kingdom, as the edict states. What ignorance of the ancient laws, if so they believe, and what unfathomable brazenness, if they do know them yet still seek to persuade us that

---

1   Cf. John 19:34.

2   Cf. Isa 1:15, 59:3.

what they do against God and his saints accords with the venerable laws of the kingdom of England! For what the decree calls the "ancient laws" are those made in the twenty-fifth year of King Edward III, against persons convicted of the crime of *lèse-majesté*,[3] and they specify these cases, among them having plotted against the life of the prince or turned men against him, as is patently obvious. And the politicians of our day now at the helm of the kingdom of England say that everything they do in murdering and destroying so many and such distinguished innocents is founded upon the ancient laws of Edward III, by no other logic than that we outlined above: he is a priest, ergo he is a traitor; he affirms the supremacy of the pope, ergo he is an enemy to the queen; he says Mass, ergo he intends to kill her; he confesses and reconciles, ergo he turns people against the state. Because, as we have said, in their vocabulary, Catholic and traitor are words they consider synonyms, signifying one and the same thing.

Now, if we consider the yoke this edict throws upon the entire kingdom of England, we shall find that it is dire and intolerable, for I know of no greater servitude and misery imaginable than for every head of a household across the land, and many other persons of every sort, class, sex, condition, and rank whatsoever, to be obligated to carry out so rigorous an examination, so meticulous and searching an inquisition and investigation into everyone who has entered their houses—their backgrounds, livelihoods, and creed—to write this all down in a book, maintain this, and present it to the commissioners. And that if they do not do this, or fall short, to be punished by the said commissioners without exceptions and with the most grievous penalties. How grave is this burden for the entire realm? For those who investigate, and for those investigated? For those who question, and for those questioned? If a single inquisitor suffices to afflict a community, how much will all these inquisitors in each community do? And so many commissioners throughout the kingdom, how will they beset and oppress it? Is there a locust that so devours and consumes the crops of the fields as these commissioners and judges lay waste the earth wherever they go? How many will there be who do not know how to write, or cannot do so out of old age, illness, or some other accident? How many who,

---

3   The Treason Act of 1351 (25 Edw. 3 St. 5 c. 2) provided a statutory definition of high treason, which covered the planning or achieving of the death of the monarch or members of the royal family, rebellion, and supporting the monarch's enemies. No less iconic a martyr than Edmund Campion, for one, was condemned to death under Edward III's treason legislation. Alford, *Watchers*, 112.

    For the act, see *SR*, 1:319–20.

    The discussion of Edward III's statute comes from *Concertatio*, 305ᵛ.

even if they do write, will not write to the taste of the commissioners, and will
be punished as careless and negligent? How many, after having written with all
diligence, will lose their books, or have them stolen by someone seeking to do
them harm? How many opportunities are offered by this decree to vengeance,
to greed, to envy, to cruelty, to perfidy? How many guiltless persons will be
stripped of their property and liberty, punished for disobedience and infrac-
tions of the edict, by the whim of the commissioner, and the malevolence of
an enemy, and the false accusations of an informer, and the greed of the notary,
and the wickedness of the other agents of the law? Will not the entire kingdom
become a den of thieves,[4] who steal and destroy with the staff of justice? It is a
grave thing that no one should be able to enter the kingdom of England without being examined a thousand times, questioned again and again, and badgered with a thousand oaths. Graver still, that the entire realm should be sealed
shut like a prison, whence no one may depart save by the express permission
of the queen (as we have explained in this history)[5]—but in the end, he who
neither enters nor leaves is free from these harassments. Yet more, that a poor
traveler who enters an inn or tavern to eat and drink should have to give an account of himself so many times, and be interrogated as to his name, way of life,
and religion; or that when a man is in his own house, he should have neither
quiet nor safety, becoming by this law subject to his enemy's ill-will. That the
brazen wickedness of a godless man should be armed with the queen's authority, to ruin anyone he pleases, and this in every province, city, town, village, and
parish of the whole kingdom! This is the gravest thing of all, it is an unbearable
burden, and an intolerable yoke, and I know not how the queen's councilors
do not see it, or the dangers that might befall them from what they are doing.
So much so that they should not only be regarded as sacrilegious toward God
by all good men, and cruel by all rational men, but also as foolish by all those
knowledgeable about government, statecraft, and the maintenance of kingdoms. Such harsh abuse of the Catholics as is practiced in England could by
itself become the occasion for a revolution: for, with so many Catholics, many
of them wealthy and influential, possessing kin and friends, who see themselves so oppressed and afflicted for no other crime than wishing to maintain
the religion in which their parents lived and died, and in which they were born
(along with many of those who torment them), and that this horrible storm
continues, as it has for so many years, and worsens each day, without any hope
of respite so long as there are those who urge it on and devastate the kingdom,
would it be any wonder that patience should turn to desperation, sufferance

---

4   Matt. 21:13; Luke 19:46.

5   In the margin: "Book 2, final chapter." This annotation is omitted in the 1605 edition.

into fury, and not only among the true Catholics (who are numerous), but also among those who are so at heart (through externally they obey the laws of the land), and among their families and friends who, heretics though they may be, are yet human beings, accessible through reason, and who are disturbed at the injustices done and the savagery and cruelty with which their kinsmen and friends are every day mangled and murdered? We often read that violence has unsettled and even lost kingdoms, and that by a prince's excessive rigor, loyal and obedient subjects are turned against them, and, having lost their respect, they are stripped of their obedience and even their lives. Accordingly, when the Catholics' affliction is joined to the heretics' widespread poverty and the intolerable yoke imposed by the severity of this edict, what might be hoped for, or feared? Let the authors of this decree consider this well, for it is more important that they reflect upon it than that I should keep silent about it [*que mas vale ellos lo consideren, que no que yo lo diga*], and that they recall that no nation in the world has endured more alterations in its government than theirs, and that these have generally arisen as a chastisement to disrespect for religion, as we see in the writings of Gildas the Wise and the Venerable Bede, as well as what other wise and scrupulous historians have observed of English affairs.[6]

---

6 The early British chronicler Gildas composed a three-part sermon, *The Ruin of Britain*, explaining the conquest of England by the Saxons as divine punishment for the Britons' sins. Bede took up many of the same themes, as when he saw the disastrous battle of Nechtans-mere (685) as God's chastisement for the Northumbrians' unjust attack on the Picts. Gildas, *Ruin of Britain*, 13–79. Bede, *Ecclesiastical History*, 427–29.

Why They Publish Such False and Damaging Edicts

Perhaps someone will ask the reason why, if everything we have said is true, such terrible, hateful, and utterly specious and contradictory edicts come from a queen who, as a woman, is by her nature more inclined to peace than to war, and to presents and entertainments more than to tortures and executions—especially given the unbearable yoke she is throwing upon her kingdom and how it might imperil her life and state? Now, one might reasonably hazard this question, but to respond to it properly we must first describe the present state of affairs in England, in whose hands the government rests, and who are the pilots steering this ship with their authority and counsel. For the governance of any kingdom depends upon the leading advisers and ministers of the king, and as they are, so is the government. And it is so crucial that counselors be as they ought that nothing so demands a monarch's utmost diligence and care as choosing the persons they will favor with their confidence and entrust with the affairs of the realm. For if they are certain of this, they are certain of much; and if they err, it is a total error, without remedy. There have been wise men who asked which was the greater or lesser evil, that a king should be good and the counselors wicked, or the reverse, the counselors good and the king wicked. Well, if the king follows the advice of the honest counselors, by this he shall be recalled to himself, however evilly inclined he may be, and will commit no outrages and excesses. But no matter how well-intentioned he may be, however much he strives, if he must trust in ambitious, partial, and prejudiced men, they, to guide the water to their mill, will paint matters with such colors, and dress them up in the respectable guise of justice, piety, and practicality, that, unjust, destructive, and hateful though they may be, the king will embrace them and command them, without perceiving the damage until his own authority will not permit him to turn back. And frequently, the wicked counselors themselves, to advance their interests and to disguise the deceit of their previous advice, each day concoct new snares and new lies, which they conceal and press upon their lord as matters greatly to his service and the good of the kingdom. All this appears in our history, depicted in the examples of Cardinal Wolsey, Cromwell, and others I have omitted for the sake of discussing only what relates to the edicts and the present circumstances of that realm.

At the beginning of her reign, Elizabeth took as her principal ministers several base, avaricious men, Calvinist heretics, who persuaded her, in order to secure her kingdom, to alter the Catholic religion and not to recognize the

Apostolic See.[1] Thus she did, handing over the realm to them, and they, as men of low degree, have undermined the kingdom's nobility. Calvinists that they are, and out of the hate they bear the Catholic religion and the cruelty that is so natural to them (albeit hidden with a false mask of meekness), they have striven to uproot our sacred faith from the land and gorge themselves on the blood of Catholics. And being avaricious and greedy, to enrich themselves with the estates and plunder of so many prominent persons, innocent and rich, whom they torment and persecute under the name of traitor. And so, to advance their project and become the sole rulers, and establish peace in their kingdom through disturbance and conflict in others, they have instigated the queen's outrages and injuries against neighboring monarchs, and the robberies, insults, and arsons in so many different places. It is they who, by means of their friends and protégées the pirates, have infested the sea and enriched themselves by plundering us, both from their share and from the presents and gifts the corsairs themselves give them out of what they have stolen (to keep them supportive and favorable). It is they who, having previously been poor, base, and unknown, have by their power and favor amassed enormous wealth, acquired profitable properties, built sumptuous palaces, and made themselves titled lords. And not content even with this (for their greed knows neither bound nor measure), nor considering themselves sated with what cannot give satisfaction, they seek new sources [*minas*] and new means to possess yet more. And because, being heretics, they deem Catholics unworthy of life and property, they work to strip them of these, the one, so that they will not interfere with their aim of perpetuating their hateful sect in England, and the other, to enrich themselves. And because they cannot accomplish this without substantial resistance if they have given no just or manifest cause, and that of religion (which is uppermost for them) is not accepted or considered as sufficient by some of the more peaceable heretics, they have invented and imagined another, that of rebellion and conspiracy against the queen's life, to compel the queen to employ them and maintain them in their positions, and to devastate and lay waste the entire kingdom. And to give their lies some color and appearance of truth they proclaim that the priests and the Catholics are in league with the pope and the Catholic King, at whose command they have come to England, to win the souls and manipulate the wills of the queen's subjects to ensure a better reception for the armies and fleets they ready against their nation. This is the origin and source of this falsehood, this is the root of this evil, this is the skein from which the thread is taken, this the warp of this charade. From this arise the affronts against the Catholic King, the absurdities

---

1   The last clause of this sentence is omitted beginning in the 1595 edition.

against the supreme pontiff, and the tyrannies against the priests of God. From this arise such idiotic and ruinous edicts as this, an attempt to give some color to their lies and to deceive the wretched people of England, and to pick them clean with fresh obligations, impositions, and taxes, from which the queen's ministers—they who urge the publication of such detestable decrees in order to serve their turn—always take their portion (not the smallest). And she, being a woman, a lover of pleasure and power, seeing herself caught in such dire straits and thrust into such a fierce, turbid current, amid the umbrage of so many mighty princes, leaves the tiller to those she took as the pilots of her ship when first she embarked.

What the Instigators of this Persecution Ought to Consider

But I lovingly beg the authors of these edicts to remember that they are men and Christians, and that they pride themselves on wisdom and prudence, because, as humans, they should not cast off their humanity and wrap themselves in the cruelty proper to savage beasts. Let them recall that the priests and Catholics whose blood they shed are also humans and Christians as they are, as well as their countrymen and compatriots, many of them friends and kinsfolk. For as a like nature teaches even the most ferocious animals not to harm other creatures of their own species, why should they, being humans, forget what they are and butcher their fellow men, their brothers?

And as they are Christians, let them remember the meekness and benignity that Christ taught us in his deeds and words, and that he did not wish his Gospel to be preached or proclaimed through the world by force of arms, nor with severity and harshness, but rather with kindness and gentleness, and with the blood of those who preached it, giving their lives in proof of the truth of what they said. From this and from the patience, endurance, and joy with which Englishmen have died for the Catholic faith, let them learn that this is the true one, the one taught us by the holy apostles, for it is watered with the blood of those who teach it, just as it was planted in blood. And that such heroic and sublime virtues cannot be merely human, or pretended, which shine out from so many servants of God with such light and clarity amid such exquisite torments and atrocious murders, but that they are indeed given by God himself, who strengthens them to die for the truth, while their persecutors are executioners, hangmen, tyrants, and apes of the Neros, Diocletians, Maximians,[1] and the other vicious princes who did to Christians what they now do against the Catholics—except with greater rigor.

And because (as I said) they deem themselves thoughtful and prudent, I ask them to consider how many years it has been since they began to persecute the Catholics of England and afflict the seminary priests and the Jesuits, the

---

1 Three of the most iconic persecutors of Roman Christians: Nero, Diocletian, and Galerius. As before (Book 3, Chapter 5), "Maximino" is probably a reference to Galerius, famous for his hostility to Christianity, rather than the emperor more commonly known as Maximian (r.286–305).

effort they have expended in apprehending them, the interrogations put to them in prison, the slanders and treacheries they have cast upon them, the tortures and deaths they have inflicted on them—and lastly, how they have not neglected anything imaginable to frighten them, to discourage them from entering England, or to eliminate those who have already come. Now, what have they gained in all those years, with so many stringent laws and harsh edicts, with their prisons, with their chains and dungeons, with nakedness and hunger, with humiliation and slanderous infamy, and with all the other weapons they have found and deployed, using all the many godless, zealous, and cruel agents they maintain throughout the realm, to mutilate with atrocious punishments and murder with horrific deaths these priests and servants of the Lord? Have these outrages and excesses put an end to the Catholic faith in England? Has the root that sustains it come to an end?[2] Have the Jesuits and seminarians, perchance, ceased entering your kingdom, or preaching and converting souls to God, frightened off by your edicts and punishments? Not at all—to the contrary, as you yourselves have confessed in this edict of yours, more priests have entered England in this brief span than did in many years before. So, then, what is this?

Do you not clearly see the hand of God here? Do you not see that he fights for the Catholics against you? Do you not see that the Catholic blood you have shed is the seed of yet more Catholics,[3] that for every one you slay, God gives life to a thousand heretics to convert to the Catholic faith, seeing the constancy and confidence with which they die and your impiety and cruelty in putting them to death, and recognizing that these are surefire proofs and unanswerable arguments for the truth of the religion that works such mighty things? For, if it was not thus, how could so many delicate, rich, and tender youths so fervently desire death that it struck fear into the hearts of stout and brave men? How could they retain their courage and joy amid what troubles and weakens even the zealous? How could they strive to return to England and to enter the arena to be tormented by countless thugs and heretical ministers, if the Lord did not stir, guide, and strengthen them with his spirit, as he did with the other martyrs who died for the same faith and sacred religion? Well, and if God fights for them, do you suppose you can overcome them?[4] If God has sent them, do you imagine you can deny them entry? If God multiplies them, do you think to exterminate them? If God strengthens them, do you expect to

---

2   In the 1595 edition, this sentence is altered to "Ha se secado la raiz que la sustenta?" which would read, "Has the root that sustains it withered up?".

3   Tertullian, *Apologeticus*, Chapter 50.

4   Rom. 8:31.

sap their spirit and dismay them with your laws and tortures? Consider how the giants began the tower of Babel [*Babylonia*], but could not complete it,[5] and how God confounded and undid the counsels of Architophel, to the point that he hanged himself;[6] and that Herod could not succeed with his counsels, though he slew the innocents.[7] Nor could the Jews avert the downfall of their city and their temple, as they sought, by the death of Christ, while the impious apostate Julian learned in the end that he could not contend with God, saying, *Vicisti Galiliaee*, "You have triumphed, Galilean" (for so he called Christ our Redeemer, as an insult).[8] For, as Wisdom says, "There is no wisdom, there is no prudence, there is no counsel against the Lord."[9] And it is a hard and pointless thing to kick against the goad, as Saul learned before he was converted,[10] and before him King Pharaoh, who, the more he tried to exterminate the people of Israel, the more God favored them and multiplied them, and at the end of many prodigies, miracles, and plagues, freed them by destroying him and his kingdom.[11] Verily, as Job says, *Quis restitit ei, et pace habuit?*[12] When the seminary began at Douai, you sought to destroy it and you could not. It was transplanted to Rheims in France and you used every possible means to undo it, and not only did you fail, but by its example was created that of Rome. When you saw these two castles erected against your perfidy and madness, you marshaled all your forces against them, and from all your attacks and assaults came the foundation of the third seminary at Valladolid. At which news, you raged and lost your mind, publishing an edict, as hateful as it was false, against all the seminaries and all their priests and executing the decree's penalties with extreme savagery and cruelty. What you have achieved is that by your own edict all of England, and especially the universities, has learned that there are seminaries abroad to raise English Catholics, and so many excellent students, youths of talent and virtue, have left to seek them that these three seminaries of Rheims, Rome, and Valladolid[13] were insufficient, and so a fourth has been started at Seville to welcome and sustain them, and beyond this God will

---

5   In the margin: "Genesis 19 [*vere* 11:6–9]."

6   In the margin: "2 Kings 17[:14–23]."

7   In the margin: "Matthew 2[:16]."

8   In the margin: "Theodoret, [*Ecclesiastical History*,] Book 3, Chapter 20."

9   In the margin: "Proverbs 21[:30]."

10   In the margin: "Acts 9[:5]."
      The preceding passage is taken from William Allen, via the *Concertatio*, 370r.

11   In the margin: "Exodus 1[:12]." This annotation is added in the 1595 edition.

12   Job 9:4.

13   Ribadeneyra specifies the three seminaries beginning in the 1595 edition.

create yet others if needs be, for the plans of his divine majesty cannot be defeated, as Gamaliel said.[14]

Call to mind the examples of all the other tyrants and persecutors of the Church and recall their catastrophic ends, together with the victories, triumphs, and crowns that God ultimately gave those who died for him. That to this day all Catholics honor and revere them, while the memory of those who martyred them is either dead and buried in perpetual oblivion, or living on in eternal ignominy, just as their accursed souls are burning in hell. And have no doubt that the same will happen to you, and that by the same means you employ to torment, murder, and defame as traitors these servants of the Lord, the Lord himself will honor them all the more and render them glorious across the globe. And I have seen the image of the blessed Father Edmund Campion of the Society of Jesus, whom you so furiously slew in London for his Catholic faith, deftly rendered with the pen even in the Indies—that Father Campion, bound and stretched and dismembered with your rack as you tortured him, is held and revered there (as he is here) as a martyr of Jesus Christ, while those who tormented him are hated, abhorred, and despised as tyrants and enemies to God and his Church, your false edicts and interrogations being powerless to strip him of this honor or to cast him as a traitor against your queen and your country.[15]

And if the ancient examples of other tyrants do not frighten or restrain you, at the very least the recent, fresh ones of your own contemporaries ought to warn and call you back. Where is Bacon?[16] Where Walsingham? Where the earl of Leicester, Robert Dudley? Where Hatton, chancellor of the realm? They are all dead and gone, some of them with horrid, frightful deaths, which you should justifiably fear.

So, turn to God, cease to brutalize his servants, and recognize that in taking them for enemies and treating them as such, you give them the opportunity to be honored and revered. Mitigate or revoke your edicts: imitate the ancient persecutors of the Church, who, seeing that they wasted their time and that by

---

14   In the margin: "Acts 5[:39]."
        Cf. Matt. 3:9; Luke 3:8.

15   I am grateful to Gerard Kilroy for the suggestion that Ribadeneyra is referring to the images included in Giovanni Battista Cavalieri, *Ecclesiae anglicanae trophaea sive Sanctorum martyrum qui pro Christo catholicaeque fidei veritate asserenda antiquo recentiorique persecutionum tempore mortem in Anglia subierunt, passiones Romae in collegio Anglico per Nicolaum Circinianum depictae: Nuper autem per Io. Bap. de Cavalleriis aeneis typis repraesentatae* (Rome: Ex officina Bartolomeo Grassi, 1584). See Book 3 Figure 29.1.

16   Nicholas Bacon died of pneumonia on February 20, 1579. Tittler, "Bacon, Sir Nicholas," in *ODNB*, 3:169.

Viri plurimi in Anglia pro fide Catholica retinenda hoc qui expressus
est modo cousq, cruciantur donec uniuersi corporis artus singulatim
luxentur. Sic Edmundus Campianus Societatis Iesu religiosus,
Rodulphus Sheruinus, Alexander Briantus, alijq, Sacerdotes summi
Pontificis Alumni acerbissimè torti fuere. Anno Dñi 1581.1582.et 1583.

3 1

FIGURE 29.1   *The torture and examination of Edmund Campion, Ralph Sherwin, and
Alexander Briant.*
Giovanni Battista Cavalieri, *Ecclesiae anglicanae trophaea sive sanctorum
martyrum qui pro Christo catholicaeque fidei veritate asserenda antiquo
recentiorique persecutionum tempore mortem in Anglia subierunt, passiones
Romae in collegio Anglico per Nicolaum Circinianum depictae: Nuper autem
per Io. Bap. de Cavalleriis aeneis typis repraesentatae* (Rome: Ex officina
Bartolomeo Grassi, 1584). NE1666 .C57 1584 OVERSIZE, John J. Burns Library,
Boston College.

their oppressions the Christians grew greater, undid their laws against them. Emperor Trajan eased the persecution of the Christians on the advice of Pliny.[17] His successor Hadrian wrote in their favor to Proconsul Minucius Fundanus[18] and gave them Jerusalem for their home.[19] Antoninus Pius commended them to the peoples of Asia, admitting that they worshipped a single, immortal God.[20] Marcus Antonius did not wish anyone to be accused for being a Christian.[21]

---

17   In the margin: "Pliny the Younger, *Letters*, Book 10[.97]."

18   In the margin: "Justin Martyr, *Apology*; Nikephoros, Book 9 [*vere* 3], Chapter 27."

      Justin Martyr (100–65) appended a rescript of Emperor Hadrian (r.117–38) to Gaius Minucius Fundanus (dates unknown, *fl.* early second century), proconsul of Asia, to his *First Apology*. It is usually included in editions of the *First Apology* as either Chapter 69 or as Appendix 1.

      The citation of Nikephoros has indicated the wrong book number: Book 9, Chapter 27 of his history concerns the much later events of the Arian controversies of the fourth century. It is Book 3, Chapter 27 that describes Hadrian's orders to Minucius Fundanus, including the text of the rescript. Xanthopoulous, *Ecclesiasticæ historiæ*, 165.

19   In the margin: "Eusebius, Book 4, Chapter 5; Cassius Dio on Hadrian."

      Eusebius of Caesarea, *Ecclesiastical History*, 4.5–6.

      Cassius Dio, *Roman History*, 69.12–13.

20   In the margin: "Justin Martyr, ibid., and Xiphilinus."

      Justin's *First Apology* also reproduces a letter from Antoninus Pius (r.138–61) to the general assembly in Asia, usually listed as Chapter 70 or Appendix 2.

      Cassius Dio, *Dionis Nicæi, reru[m] Romanarum a Pompeio Magno, ad Alexandrum Mamæce filium epitome, Ioanne Xiphilino authore, & Guilielmo Blanco Albiensi interprete*, ed. Joannes Xiphilinus, trans. Guillaume Blanc (Paris: Ex officina Robert Estienne, 1551), 199–200.

      Cf. Cassius Dio, *Epitome della historia Romana di Dione Niceo di xxv imper. Romani da Pompeo Magno fino ad Alessandro figliuolo di Mammea, tradotta per m. Francesco Baldelli*, ed. Joannes Xiphilinus, trans. Francesco Baldelli (Venice: Appresso Gabriele Giolito de Ferrari, 1562), 263.

21   Ribadeneyra cites no source for this statement, but his use of "Marco Antonio" for Marcus Aurelius (r.161–80) parallels that of early modern Latin and Italian editions of the eleventh-century Byzantine monk Joannes Xiphilinus's epitome of Dio Cassius's *Roman History*.

      The text states, "Now, Marcus had one legion of soldiers from Melitene, all of whom worshipped Christ; while he was at a loss which plan to adopt in that battle, the captain of his guards came to him, and told him that there was nothing those known as Christians could not achieve with their prayers, and that there was a legion of such men in the army. On learning this, Marcus asked them to pray to their God. When they had done this, their God straightway heard them, and struck their foes with a thunderbolt, and refreshed the Romans with rain. Utterly awestruck at these things, Marcus honored the Christians by an official edict." Cassius Dio, *Dionis Nicæi*, 204.

      Cf. Cassius Dio, *Epitome della historia*, 268–69.

Gallienus forbade any persecution of them.[22] And lastly, so as not to run on, Maximin, who had been a terrifying beast to the Christians and published savage decrees against them, engraving his laws in metal so as to be eternal, revoked them, recognizing that it availed him nothing and he could not contend with God.[23]

---

[22]   In the margin: "Of his edicts, Eusebius attests, Book 7, Chapters 16 and 25." In the 1595 edition, the citation reads "Chapters 16 and 21;" in the 1605 version, "Chapters 17 and 21."
        In modern editions, Eusebius of Caesarea, *Ecclesiastical History*, 7.13, 23.
[23]   In the margin: "Eusebius, [*Ecclesiastical History*] Book 9, Chapters 7 and 9."

What Ought to Inspire the Seminary Priests and the Other Catholics in this Conquest

But, since I fear my words will not be heard by those who are obstinate and hardened in their blindness, abandoning them I shall turn to you, dearest brothers and fathers of the Society of Jesus, and the students and priests of the seminaries, whom the Lord has chosen as soldiers and captains in so glorious a campaign. Although I had much rather be a sharer with you in the labor and the peril, in your battles and your crowns, yet even if I do not deserve so blessed a lot, I can at least take solace in your fortune, accompany you in spirit, and be present in your travails. You have no need of my encouragement, for the Lord is your guide and your strength, but, to motivate and console myself with the recollection of such praiseworthy favors as you have received from the Lord's hand, I beg and exhort you to keep him ever fresh in your memory, to contemplate and esteem him as is right, and lovingly to embrace and please him. Always remember that while your land of England remains under a profound and gloomy night, like a second Egypt, the Lord has sent his clarity and his light into your hearts as into the land of Goshen.[1] Consider carefully to what exalted dignity he has called you, for he has made you guides to the lost, teachers to the blind, dispensers of his sacraments, preachers of his faith and truth, his soldiers and captains, for an enterprise as admirable and godly as that you bear in hand. Accordingly, prepare your hearts with prayers, penance, and good works, and most of all with a burning desire and zeal for the glory of this great Lord and the salvation of your brothers, and ready and arm yourselves for battle with the shield of faith and the helm of salvation and the double-bladed sword of the word of God.[2]

Do not despair at being so few, while the hosts of your foes are innumerable, nor lose heart at being feeble, poor, and defenseless, while they are strong and mighty, armed with power and malice. Remember that the Lord is most jealous of his glory[3] and, lest man usurp and seize it for himself, often gives to weak

---

1   In the margin: "Exodus 10[:21–23]."

2   Cf. Eph. 6:11–17.

3   Isa. 42:8.

and common people the victory he denies great and mighty armies.[4] Thus he willed that Abraham, with only the retainers of his house, should win the field, victorious over four kings;[5] and that Jonathan, with only one armorbearer, should strike terror into the host of the Philistines;[6] and that the princes' servants or pages alone should defeat the numberless hordes of Ben-hadad and the thirty kings who accompanied him;[7] and that with the jawbone of an ass Samson should slay a thousand foes;[8] and David, with his sling, the proud and well-armed Goliath;[9] and the prophet Elijah alone, 450 prophets of Baal;[10] and one woman, Sisera, the champion of Jabin, king of Canaan[11] and lastly, Saint Judith, Holofernes, loaded with wine, sleep, and pride, thus destroying all the power of the Assyrians.[12] Recall the story of Gideon, who, when God sent him against the vast hosts of Midian, who seemed an innumerable swarm of locust,[13] refused to take more than three hundred soldiers, lest the people of Israel imagine that they achieved victory by their force and valor.[14] And have faith in the Lord that he shall give to the three hundred of you now in England

---

4   The following passage is taken almost verbatim from the *Tratado de la tribulación*: "The
      Lord often undoes the counsels of men, annihilates their power, and causes the many to
      be conquered by the few. He caused Abraham, with only the retainers of his house, to win
      the field, victorious over four kings; and Jonathan, with only one armorbearer, to strike
      terror into the host of the Philistines; and the pages of the princes and lords alone to
      defeat the numberless hordes of Ben-hadad and the thirty-two kings who accompanied
      him; and a thousand foes to die by the jawbone of an ass; and the proud and well-armed
      giant by the sling of David; and the mighty king Sisera to be defeated by one woman and
      killed by another; and Holofernes and all his forces to be destroyed by the hand of Saint
      Judith." Ribadeneyra, *Tratado de la tribulacion*, 190ʳ–190ᵛ.

5   In the margin: "Genesis 14[:14–16]."

6   In the margin: "1 Kings 14[:12–15]."

7   In the margin: "3 Kings 20."

8   In the margin: "Judges 15[:15]."

9   1 Kings 17.

10   In the margin: "3 Kings 18[:22, 40]."

11   In the margin: "Judges 4[:21]."

12   In the margin: "Judith 9 [*vere* 13]."

      Judith 9 contains Judith's prayer before her departure for Holofernes's camp; the cita-
      tion of this chapter rather than Judith 13 may be related to Ribadeneyra's use of Judith 9
      for much the same purpose in the *Tratado de la tribulación*: Ribadeneyra, *Tratado de la
      tribulacion*, 189ᵛ.

13   Judg. 6:5–6.

14   Judg. 7:2–7.

      Ribadeneyra cites the same passage in the *Tratado de la tribulación*, as an example of
      how God teaches mankind not to trust in the strength of numbers. Ribadeneyra, *Tratado
      de la tribulacion*, 188ᵛ.

a total victory over all your foes—at which, like the three hundred warriors of Gideon, you shall carry with you the trumpets of true and clarion doctrine and lanterns alight with charity.[15]

Do not fear to break the earthen vessels of your bodies[16] or to give your lives fighting for the Lord.[17] Nor let the fierceness and fury of your enemies affright you, nor the horrible storms awaiting you, because the Lord will preserve you, as he preserved Daniel in the lions' den,[18] and his three blessed young companions in the furnace of Babylon,[19] and Jonah in the belly of the whale.[20] And when it pleases him that you should suffer, he will give you the strength to suffer. Amid pains, you will be stronger than your pains; imprisoned, freer than your captors; fallen, more exalted than those yet standing; bound, more at liberty than those who bound you; judged, higher than those who passed sentence upon you. Your wounds will be roses and flowers, and the blood that flows from your body will be royal purple. As your body is torn apart, your spirit will remain whole; as the flesh is consumed, your virtue will not be harmed; as the substance gives out, patience will endure yet more, and your death will be a perfect sacrifice to God. The glorious martyr Saint Cyprian, encouraging several saintly bishops, priests, and various others jailed for the sake of Christ, says these words:

They have bound your feet with chains, and constrained the blessed limbs and temples of God[21] in foul prisons, as though the spirit might be imprisoned with the body, or your precious gold could be harmed by the touch of iron. For men consecrated to God, who bear witness to their faith with holy virtue, these are not punishments but ornaments, nor do they tie the feet of a Christian in disgrace, but rather adorn them for a crown. O feet blessedly bound, which will not be loosed by the jailer but by Christ himself. O feet blessedly bound, which go directly to paradise along the path of salvation. O feet constrained for a time in the world, so that they may be free forevermore in the presence of Christ. O feet confined by bars and the enemy's fury, which will nimbly run the glorious path to Christ. The cruelty and malice of the foe may control your bodies,

---

15 Judg. 7:16–22.
16 2 Cor. 4:7.
17 In the margin: "Judges 7[:2–7, 16–22]."
18 In the margin: "Daniel 6[:16–24]."
19 In the margin: "Daniel 3."
20 In the margin: "Jonah 3 [*vere* 2]."
21 Rom. 12:5; 1 Cor. 6:15, 6:19, 12:12, 12:17; Eph. 5:30.

but very soon you will fly from the pains of the earth to the kingdom of heaven. Your body is not spoiled with a soft bed, but rather favored with the delights and consolations of the Holy Spirit. Your limbs, wearied with troubles, have only the earth for a bed, but there is no pain in sleep and rest with Christ. Your bodies are disfigured, wan, and covered with dust— but what befouls the body spiritually washes and purifies the soul. Meager is the ration of bread they have given you, yet man does not live by bread alone, but rather by the word of God.[22] There are no garments for you in times of cold, but he who has clothed himself in Christ is copiously sheltered and adorned.[23] The hair of your head has been well-nigh ripped out, but as Christ is the head of man,[24] of whatever sort it be, in his glory is it beautiful. This ugliness and darkness in the eyes of the pagans, with what splendor will it be recompensed? This fleeting pain of the world, with what illustrious and eternal glory will it be repaid when the Lord, as the apostle says, reforms the body of our humility, and makes it like unto the body of his clarity?[25]

These are the words of Saint Cyprian, translated from Latin into Castilian by Father Brother Luis de Granada,[26] displaying the spirit of this glorious saint and the blessed lot of those who die for Christ.

And rightfully so, for what greater felicity could there be, than to die for that Lord who died for us? To endure torments for him who was likewise tormented for us? And to offer the death we owe to nature as a sacrifice to the author of life? What greater happiness than to purchase heaven and life everlasting with life fragile and ephemeral, which, whether we will or no, must end in a breath? What greater joy than to belong to that company, that mighty squadron of renowned martyrs, who adorn and enrich the heavens? How many servants and menials suffer for their lords and masters, and die for men like themselves, who do not have to be satisfied and who cannot repay them? How many

---

22   Deut. 8:3; Matt. 4:4; Luke 4:4.

23   Rom. 13:14; Gal. 3:27.

24   1 Cor. 11:3.

25   In the margin: "Philippians 3[:20–21]."

26   In the margin: "Part 2, Chapter 16 of *La introduction del symbolo de la fe* [*del Cathe*]."

       Luis de Granada, *Parte primera de la introduction del symbolo de la fe, en la qual se trata de la creacion del mundo para venir por las criaturas al conoscimiento del criador, y de sus diuinas perfectiones* (Barcelona: Iuan Pablo Manescal, Damian Bages, y Hieronymo Genoues, 1584), 61–62.

       The same passage is cited in Ribadeneyra, *Tratado de la tribulacion*, 195ʳ.

       For an English translation of the passage, see Cyprian, *Letters 1–81*, 315–16.

soldiers thrust themselves upon the pikes, the barrels of guns and cannons, to serve their monarch and win renown for valor and courage? How many endure countless, bitter tortures because of their enemies or their crimes—some even more atrocious than those our fortunate martyrs undergo for the Lord? How many invalids bear their prolonged and terrible agonies with patience, and often pains yet sharper to find health, not knowing whether they will find it, nor if they find it, how long it will last, it being so fragile and frail? And so, O soldiers of Christ, O faithful servants of the Lord, let not the torments frighten you, for if they are light, they can be borne, and if they are fierce, they cannot last. This is your enterprise, this is your war, this your conquest. Here there are battles, there are fights, there are wounds, but there are also victories and triumphs—yet with extreme inequality, for the combat is brief and easy, the rewards and crowns immortal.

A Continuation of the Preceding Chapter, and an Exposition of Three Particular Reasons that May Further Inspire the Martyrs

Three things, among all the others, ought to strengthen you in this war. The first, the cause you defend. The second, the manner of your suffering. The third, the certain hope of victory. Now, the first is the cause: it is this, and not the pain, that makes the one who suffers a martyr,[1] for yours is neither to return to England nor to work there for the disturbance and disruption of that kingdom, to take the queen's life and seize worldly power for yourselves—as your enemies proclaim—for your thoughts are not so base. Nor does it befit you to give them any just occasion to slander you, but rather to comport yourselves according to the honor of God; to defend the peace and unity of the Church; to save your souls, and those of your family, kinsfolk, and friends; to preserve the dignity of Christ's priesthood, the majesty of the eternal and holy sacrifice of the Mass and the other sacraments, the uncorrupted, unstained truth of the doctrine God has entrusted to his Church, the pure and proper meaning of Holy Writ, as it has been expounded and interpreted by the sainted doctors; to preserve that inheritance your forefathers received from Saints Pope Gregory and Augustine, the apostles of your homeland, observed, and passed on to you. If to die for the least article of our sacred faith, if to give one's life for the least truth of our holy religion, for the defense of a single sacrament, or for a single word of the law of God, or for the salvation of one soul, is a thing truly glorious, what will it be to die for so many articles, for so many vital truths, for so many sacraments, for the whole of God's law, and for the salvation of every soul of an entire kingdom? Saint John the Baptist so esteemed the preaching of the truth and the reprehension of Herod's vices that he gave his head for it.[2] Saint Matthew preferred to die rather than advise Ephigenia to marry, because she had made a vow of chastity.[3] Saint Peter and Saint Paul did not hesitate to separate several of Nero's lady-friends from his base company and convert

---

1   In the margin: "Augustine, Letter 61."

    In modern editions, see Augustine of Hippo, *Letters*, 204.4.

2   Matt. 14:3–10; Mark 6:17–27.

3   Matthew the Apostle was thought to have been martyred in Ethiopia for refusing to advise Princess Ephigenia, who had dedicated herself to God, to marry. *AASS*, September VI, 196.

them to our sacred faith and most pure religion. For this and other causes, he in his rage took their lives.[4] And, since we are speaking of England, the steadfast martyr Saint Thomas, primate of that kingdom—did he not give his blood for the rights of the Church? Did not the bishop of Rochester and Thomas More, the pride of England and the ornament of our age, and many other religious, scholars, priests, and laymen choose brutal torments and shameful deaths rather than acquiesce to the monstrous marriage of King Henry? Well then, how much greater and more important are the matters at issue now? How much more is there in what is now taught and preached in England? That it is, in short, the gospel of Calvin—sacrilegious, filthy, cruel, diabolical, and a hellfire to engulf the realm and all of Christendom, which you, favored by the Lord, are to extinguish, though it be with rivers of your blood, for in many years no martyrs have had such straightforward and divine occasion to shed it as you now have.

The second thing that ought to inspire you to enter this contest with supreme boldness and confidence is the means they use in England to persecute the Catholics and eradicate, if they can, our holy religion from that kingdom. For, as has been explained in this our history,[5] religious matters are there resolved not by outlawry, uprisings, or riots and popular unrest, but rather by means of trials and sentences, with an appearance and show of false justice. We read that at various points in past centuries the Arian and Donatist and Circumcellion[6] heretics in Italy and in Africa rose up and, armed with impiety and madness, turned suddenly upon the Catholics and slew them. In our own days, we know that in France, Zealand, and Holland, the Calvinists (who are

---

In the *Martyrologium Romanum*, Cesare Baronio notes of Matthew, "We read that Matthew was martyred for the sake of virginity, as indeed the author alludes to the history of Saint Ephigenia, the virgin, of whom we read in her acts that she was dedicated to God." Baronio, *Martyrologium Romanum*, 428.

4   In the margin: "Cesare Baronio takes this from Saint Ambrose, in the first part of his *Annals*."
      Cesare Baronio, *Annales ecclesiastici: Tomus I* (Antwerp: Ex officina vid. Christophe Plantin & Jan I Moretus, 1589), 729.
      Cf. Ambrose of Milan, *Contra Auxentium*, Chapter 13.

5   In the margin: "Book 2." This annotation is deleted in the 1605 edition.

6   The Circumcellions—who called themselves *Agonistici* or *Milites Christi*—were a militant, violent wing of the Donatists, notorious for their excesses against Catholics: "remarkable bands of nomadic terrorists, recruited at haphazard from the dregs of the population, from the discontented of every native race and province, fugitive slaves, ruined farmers, oppressed colons, outlawed criminals, social failures, excommunicated Catholics, and purely religious fanatics [...] the self-appointed defenders of the church of Donatus." R. Pierce Beaver, "The Donatist Circumcellions," *CH* 4, no. 2 (June 1935): 123–33, here 125–26.

the very quintessence of heresy and the firebrands of hell) with yet greater rage and savagery butchered countless Catholics—religious and priests, men and women—without making any accusations or conducting any trials, nor allowing them any time to defend their names, confess themselves, or even draw breath. The fact that they were Catholics was reason enough for a cruel death, such was their hatred for the Catholic faith they so persecuted and abominated. And though we do not deny these dead the name and honor of martyrs, since the Catholic faith was the cause of their death, yet it is nevertheless a more illustrious and a more perfect form of martyrdom that is to be won in England, where there are jails and prisons, torments and tortures, where there are fierce interrogations, questions on end—if one is a priest, if one has said Mass, if one has confessed, if one has absolved, if one has reconciled, if one believes in the supreme power of the pope, if one admits that the queen is head of the Church. Where kin and friends feign kindness with their pleas, and the judges sometimes deceive with false hopes and sometimes terrorize with threats and mutilate with tortures. Where the promise to attend the heretics' churches or to beg pardon of the queen remits the punishment and wins freedom, life, and enormous rewards, even for those at the foot of the gallows, as well as many other things of this kind that prove your martyrdom more voluntary and your constancy greater, as well as the mature judgment and deliberation with which you confess the Lord before men and die for his truth, without any one of the doubts or anxieties of this life being capable of altering or perverting your hearts, nor of dissuading you from this praiseworthy firmness and holy constancy. And I say that these means should move you to join this enterprise with yet fiercer enthusiasm, because, as I have said, your martyrdom will be more perfect and more akin to those of our ancient and blessed martyrs, more glorious before God, more meritorious and honorable for those who die, more edifying for the entire Catholic Church, and more beneficial for the faithful—and even for the heretics, who are often converted by seeing the Catholics die for their faith with such fortitude and meekness, subsequently dying for it themselves.

Well, what shall I say about the assuredness and certainty of our victory? Soldiers, however numerous and valiant they may be, when they assault some city or enter some battle, may always be anxious, and doubt whether they shall conquer or be conquered—for the fortunes of war are uncertain and unfathomable. But in this our spiritual war and conquest, we are assured of victory, not only in the knowledge that if we live, we shall triumph, and if we die, we shall triumph all the more, but also in the certainty that neither the tyrants' cruelty, nor the heretics' malice, nor the persecutors' fury, nor even the very gates and power of hell can ever prevail against the Church and the faith that is founded upon the rock and confession of Saint Peter, as the Lord told and promised us,[7] and that all the waves and winds that arise against this unshakeable stone, however fierce and fearful they may be, must be broken and undone, while it remains forever steadfast and whole. How many persecutions has the Catholic Church suffered hitherto, from the Jews, the pagans, the Moors, the Roman emperors, the barbarian kings, the Goths, the Vandals, the Huns, the Lombards, and from the heretics: the Novatians,[8] the Arians, the Donatists, the Eutychians, the Iconoclasts, the Albigensians,[9] the Hussites, the Calvinists, and innumerable other sects of perdition? They are so many that they cannot be counted, and so extreme that they can hardly be believed. The truth has conquered them all, the Church has triumphed over them all, and has always grown greater, watered by the blood of its blessed defenders—for the more who died, the more were born and multiplied in its defense. We should never come to an end if we wanted to recount these victories and triumphs of the Catholic Church as they deserve, and declare at length the impiety and cruelty of the tyrants, the terror of the torments, the endurance and wondrous constancy of the martyrs, the glorious end they received, and the victory and tranquility the Catholic Church has always won in these unending, bloody battles, by the virtue and grace of Christ our Redeemer. I wish to relate only what Sulpicius Severus wrote concerning one of these persecutions. Speaking of the tyranny of Diocletian and Maximian,[10] which was truly terrible, he says these words:

> In these times, almost the entire world has been watered with the sacred blood of the martyrs, for all these illustrious combatants rushed to the contest and with the utmost zeal sought martyrdom through a glorious death; while now bishoprics are hungered after and bargained for with disgraceful ambition. No war has ever left the world so empty of people,

---

7   In the margin: Matthew 16[:18]."

8   The Novatianist Schism was begun by Antipope Novatian (d.258): Novatianists held to a rigorist view of post-baptismal sin, refusing to readmit Christians who had lapsed under persecution and acquiesced to pagan rites. Kelly, *Early Christian Doctrines*, 436–37.

9   Known by diverse names, the "Albigensians" (from the town of Albi, one of their strongholds) or "Cathars" were a dualist sect of some popularity and influence in Languedoc and Provence from the twelfth to the fourteenth centuries. See Deane, *Medieval Heresy and Inquisition*, Chapter 1.

10   This time, Ribadeneyra *is* referring to the emperor generally known as Maximian (r.286–305), Diocletian's co-emperor.

nor have we ever conquered with greater triumph, as when, with all the destruction and devastation of ten years, we could not be defeated.[11]

And thus Tertullian solemnly declared to the pagans: *Plures efficimur, quoties metimur à vobis, semen est, sanguis Christianorum.*[12] And Saint Jerome: *Persecutionibus Ecclesia crevit, marytrijs coronata est.*[13] And on the same subject Prudentius wrote: *Nec furor quisque sine laude nostrum ceßit, aut clari vacuus cruoris, martyrum semper numerus, sub omni grandine crescit.*[14] So much so that, as Saint Augustine writes, even the princes of this world who were wont to persecute Christians out of devotion to their false gods, having been defeated by the Christians (who had not resisted them, but only perished), turned the page, passing laws and directing their power against the idols for which they had previously killed the Christians, and the highest height of the Roman Empire, removing the imperial diadem from his head, knelt down and prostrated himself before the tomb of Peter, the fisherman.[15] So, then, what am I to say of the heretics who have persecuted the Church, with equal cruelty and greater damage? The victories God has given to the Catholic Church against its enemies the heretics have always been so illustrious that even if there were no other proof that it alone was the legitimate, beloved bride of the Lord, and that all other religions are false sects, the whores and children of Satan, this argument alone would suffice as evidence of this truth. And, to be brief, the Arian heresy is by itself proof enough that the Catholic Church is invincible and unshakeable. Now, they taught that the Son of God was not consubstantial with the Father, which is to say that he was not equal to the Father, nor truly God, but rather a creature, thus overturning the very foundation of the entire Christian religion. Those who disseminated this falsehood were philosophers and learned men, of subtle and acute intelligence, among them many bishops, pastors and teachers. Those who defended it were emperors, princes, and the rulers of the world, and they protected it with all the fierceness and ferocity imaginable, persecuting, torturing, and with bizarre means executing

---

11   In the margin: "*Sacred History*, Book 2."
       Sulpicius Severus, *Chronica*, 2.32.
12   In the margin: "In the *Apology*."
       Tertullian, *Apologeticus*, Chapter 50.
13   In the margin: "Jerome, letter to Theophilus against the errors of John of Jerusalem."
       Jerome, *Letters*, 82.10.
14   In the margin: "Fourth hymn, on the martyrs of Caesarea."
       Prudentius, *Liber Peristephanon* 4.85–88.
15   In the margin: "Letter 42."
       In modern editions, see Augustine of Hippo, *Letters*, 232.3.

and eradicating all the Catholics they could, the priests, prelates, and doctors of the Church, pardoning neither man nor woman, neither elder nor child, neither the poor man nor the rich man, neither the virgin nor the wife.[16] Many were the provinces through which the contagion raged: in the east and the west, in the north and the south. Long indeed was the time the plague endured, but in the end it came to an end and concluded, leaving truth the victor and the holy Church triumphant over its foes, whom the Lord castigated thus: Arius, the inventor and teacher of that blasphemy, died suddenly, his entrails bursting out,[17] while Emperors Constantius[18] and Valens,[19] Theoderic, king of

---

16   Cf. "We see this in the origins, development, and end of past heresies. But so as not to be overlong, I shall speak only of the that of the Arians, which was armed with the might of emperors, with the supposed sophistic wisdom of the philosophers, with the authority of numerous deluded bishops, and with the cunning and tricks of those who professed it, humiliating and butchering the true servants of God and using every sort of deceitful and brutal method to oppress and uproot the true Cathlic Church, but could make no more dent in it than waves upon a tall and sturdy rock. Ribadeneyra, *Tratado de la tribulacion*, 156ᵛ–157ʳ.

17   "It was then Saturday, and Arius was expecting to assemble with the church on the day following: but Divine retribution overtook his daring criminalities. For going out of the imperial palace, attended by a crowd of Eusebian partisans like guards, he paraded proudly through the midst of the city, attracting the notice of all the people. On approaching the place called Constantine's Forum, where the column of porphyry is erected, a terror arising from the consciousness of his wickedness seized him, accompanied by violent relaxation of the bowels [...] Soon after a faintness came over him, and together with the evacuations his bowels protruded, followed by a copious hæmorrhage, and the descent of the smaller intestines: moreover portions of his spleen and liver were brought off in the effusion of blood, so that he almost immediately died." Socrates, *Ecclesiastical History*, 78.

18   "While the emperor Constantius continued his residence at Antioch, Julian Cæsar engaged with an immense army of barbarians in the Gallias, and obtained a distinguished victory over them: on which account having become extremely popular among the soldiery, he was proclaimed emperor by them. Intelligence of this affected the emperor Constantius with the most painful sensations; he was therefore baptized by Euzoïus, and immediately prepared to undertake an expedition against Julian. On arriving at the frontiers of Cappadocia and Cilicia, his excessive agitation of mind produced apoplexy, which terminated his existence at Mopsucrene, in the consulate of Taurus and Florentius, on the 3rd of November, in the first year of the 285th Olympiad. This prince was at the time of his death forty-five years old, having reigned thirty-eight years, for thirteen of which he was his father's colleague in the empire, and during the remaining twenty-five he had the sole administration." Ibid., 166.

19   "On the arrival of the emperor Valens at Constantinople, on the 30th of May, in the sixth year of his own consulate and the second of Valentinian junior's, he finds the people in a very dejected state of mind: for the barbarians, who had already desolated Thrace, were

the Ostrogoths in Italy,[20] and Huneric, king of the Vandals in Africa[21] (the most prominent tyrants to support it, who persecuted the Catholics with the greatest fury and enthusiasm) all came to wretched and miserable ends. For this reason, that glorious father, Saint Augustine, interpreting those words of Psalm 57, "They shall be annihilated, and pass away like flowing water,"[22] said:

---

now laying waste the very suburbs of Constantinople, there being no adequate force at hand to resist them. But when they presumed to make near approaches, even to the walls of the city, the people became exceedingly troubled, and began to murmur against the emperor; accusing him of having been the cause of—bringing the enemy thither, and then indolently wasting his time there, instead of at once marching out against the barbarians. Moreover at the exhibition of the sports of the Hippodrome, all with one voice exclaimed against the emperor's negligence of the public affairs, crying out with great earnestness, "Give us arms, and we ourselves will fight." The emperor, provoked at these seditious clamours, marches out of the city, on the 11th of June; threatening that, if he returned, he would punish the citizens not only for their insolent reproaches, but for having heretofore favoured the pretensions of the tyrant Procopius. After declaring therefore that he would utterly demolish their city, and cause the plough to pass over its ruins, he advanced against the barbarians, whom he routed with great slaughter, and pursued as far as Adrianople, a city of Thrace, situated on the frontiers of Macedonia. Having at that place again engaged the enemy, who had by this time rallied, he lost his life on the 9th of August, under the consulate just mentioned, and in the fourth year of the 289th Olympiad. Some have asserted that he was burnt to death in a village whither he had retired, which the Goths assaulted and set on fire. But others affirm, that having put off his imperial robe, he ran into the midst of the main body of infantry; and that when the cavalry revolted and refused to engage, the foot were surrounded by the barbarians, and completely destroyed. Among these it is said the emperor fell, but could not be distinguished, in consequence of his having laid aside his imperial habit." Socrates, *Ecclesiastical History*, 259.

20   An anonymous sixth-century chronicler recorded of the death of Theoderic, king of the Ostrogoths (r.475–526): "But He who does not allow his faithful worshippers to be oppressed by unbelievers soon brought upon Theodoric the same punishment that Arius, the founder of his religion, had suffered; for the king was seized with a diarrhoea, and after three days of open bowels lost both his throne and his life on the very same day on which he rejoiced to attack the churches." Ammianus Marcellinus, *History, Volume III: Books 27–31. Excerpta Valesiana*, trans. John C. Rolfe, vol. 3 of 3 vols., Loeb Classical Library 331 (Cambridge: Harvard University Press, 1939), 569.

21   "The most wicked Huniric held dominion in his kingdom for seven years and ten months. His death was in accordance with his merits, for as he rotted and the worms multiplied it seemed not so much a body as parts of his body which were buried." Victor of Vita, *History of the Vandal Persecution*, ed. and trans. John Moorhead, Translated Texts for Historians 10 (Liverpool: Liverpool University Press, 1992), 93.

22   Ps. 57:8.

My brothers, let not the waters of the rivers frighten you, for though at times they rush and roar, they are soon finished, and they cannot last. Numerous heresies are dead: their rivers ran as much as they could run, and the streams dried up, and now there is one can barely find a memory of them, though we know what they had been.[23]

And in another place:

This is the holy Church, the one Church, the true Church, the Catholic Church that fights against every heresy. The struggle may be fierce, but it can never be defeated. Every heresy has departed from it, like barren shoots cut off from the vine, while it remains forever firm in its roots, for the very gates of hell cannot conquer it.[24]

The Lord will do this, so we hope, in this persecution of England, if we do not despair, and hold fast and (O most loving fathers and brothers in Jesus Christ) fight on valiantly, steadfast in his divine spirit and promise. And there is no doubting this, for the Lord himself has promised it to us, and experience teaches it to us, and what was, will be—and our own persecutors affirm it in their edicts, showing us that they are afraid, that they are already beaten, and that with all their cunning cruelty and craft they have not been able to scare off our steadfast soldiers. To the contrary, more have entered England in a few months than came in several years previous. Well, and if our enemies are terrified and trembling, what have we to fear? Why should we not trust in that most glorious captain general, our Lord, who tells us, *In mundo pressuram habebitis, sed confidite, quia ego vici mundum?*[25] This is he who has triumphed in his Church over the tyrants, the kings, the emperors, and the monarchs of the world. This is he who has cast down at the feet of his spouse the heretics, the dogmatizers, and the diabolical teachers who have tried to disfigure and infect her. This is he who now fights with us, and having him upon our side, what can we fear? *Si Deus pro nobis quis contra nos?*[26] There can be no doubt of victory

---

23   Augustine of Hippo, *Expositions of the Psalms*, 57.16.

24   Cf. Matt. 16:18.

      In the margin: "*The Creed*, Book 1, Chapter 5 [*vere* 6]."

      Ribadeneyra was intimately familiar with Augustine's works, and it is entirely possible that he chose this quotation independently, but it is worth noting that this passage (cited as 1.5) is included in the *Concertatio*, 234.

25   John 16:33.

26   Rom. 8:31.

with such a guide, with such a shield, with such a protector. Upon our side, the truth fights against falsehood, faith against treachery, justice against injustice, sufferance against cruelty, the Church of God against the synagogue of Satan. For us is the Gospel of Jesus Christ, founded upon his cross, watered with the blood of so many illustrious martyrs, confirmed with countless miracles, declared by so many saintly and sagacious doctors, and obeyed and revered by the entire world without interruption for the space of sixteen hundred years. Holy in the doctrine it teaches, strong and effective in winning and converting souls, one in all places, times, and nations, which, though they are so numerous and so distant, are bound one to another by the link and knot of the Gospel, and united by the visible head, the Roman pontiff, resplendent with the light of prophecy, the cherisher of all who embrace and obey him, and the chastiser, destroyer, and conqueror of all his foes. For us are the power of the Father, the wisdom of the Son, and the goodness and grace of the Holy Spirit, all the blessed hierarchies of the angels and the squadrons of the saints in heaven, especially those who lived or died in England for this same faith, which we now defend against the gospel of Calvin, founded upon incest (as we have said) and watered with blood—not of those who preach it, but of those who challenge it—and sustained with oppression and barbarous cruelty.

Why God Allows the English Catholics to be so Persecuted

As a conclusion to what we have added to this history of the schism of England, it remains for us to offer our judgment of this extreme persecution that the Lord in his ineffable and secret providence permits in that kingdom.[1] For I fear that the common masses, and even some men learned in the wisdom of the world,[2] considering with the eyes of the flesh what is now happening in England, the power God gives his enemies, and the tyranny with which they exploit it, will perhaps be scandalized and say that God abandons his cause, unmoved by his honor or by that of his servants—or, at least, that they shall reasonably come to ask the reason for all this. It is this doubt, this question that I wish to answer here, and satisfy, with the Lord's favor, those who marvel at this work, which is so characteristic of him. And because we discussed this theme at great length in the book we wrote several years ago on tribulation,[3] explaining why God permits heresies and the heretics and infidels' occasional successes against the Catholics and the faithful, and resolving other, related issues, we shall refer the reader to that place and here speak specifically of the persecution in England.

So, I say that, in my poor and weak judgment, the frightful storm now endured by the Catholics of England displays to the fullest the power and mercy of God, who is the master and captain of the ship of his Church, he who steers it by the rudder of his fatherly providence, and however terrible the storms, he shall bring it to the safe and longed-for port of blessed eternity. For he seeks his glory[4] and our good in all things, both of which coincide perfectly in this English persecution, such as could never happen in prosperity. Truly, what greater service can man render God than to give his life for him?[5] And what more honorable or more advantageous event could befall that man, than to die for that Lord who died for him? In the battles and victories of the

---

1 Rom. 11:33.
2 1 Cor. 3:19; James 3:15.
3 In the margin: "Book 2."
  Ribadeneyra, *Tratado de la tribulacion*, Book 2, especially Chapters 5 and 9.
4 John 7:18, 8:50.
5 Cf. John 15:13.

sainted martyrs, the glory of God and the benefit of the martyrs themselves are
so intertwined and bound together that howsoever one increases, the other
increases, and from the greater honor to the Lord, there follows greater honor
and a crown for the martyr. And as the Lord is so jealous of his honor,[6] and so
much a friend to our good, it is no marvel that he permits these conflicts, which
are to glorify him and benefit humanity. Indeed, as Seneca wrote so insight-
fully, "Men delight to see another man contend with a bull or some other beast,
and God to see him contend with brutal torments or great adversity."[7] And the
glory of God shines out in this work not only because he is glorified in the glory
of the man who (as Father Brother Luis de Granada says so well) testifies in
his death to the exaltation of God's majesty and goodness, who chooses to suffer every torment that his fellow men and the demons can invent, rather than
say or do anything contrary to his holy law,[8] but also because it makes utterly
manifest the unconquerable power of the grace of that same God. And this in
two ways: the first, in encouraging and strengthening the sufferer's weakness
and granting them victory over their own pains; the other, in seeing the holy
Church defeat and humiliate all the tyrants and mighty princes, its foes, simply
through the shedding of its blood. Consider, on the one hand, the weapons
the devil uses against the blessed martyrs who are now dying in England for
our sacred and Catholic religion and, on the other, the strength and valor with
which they resist and overcome, and it easily appears how great and how admirable is the force of divine grace. Against the Catholics contend demons and
the human ministers of those demons; against them contend hunger, thirst,
nakedness, humiliation, bribes, hopes, fears, and false promises; against them
contend[9] the torments of the prison—chains, the rack, the wheel, the stake,
the noose, and the knife—and death itself, and not just any death, but a hateful and vicious one; against them contend the weakness of this flesh of ours
and the constitution of humanity (which is the most sensitive and delicate of
all), and the love of self, with all the forces of our nature. Numerous and mighty
though our foes are, and infinite, perilous, and keen though their weapons may
be, greater still is the power of the divine grace that inspires our martyrs, men
and women, children and maidens, giving them prodigious valor and spirit to
resist and conquer—and that with so much fortitude, patience, and joy that
they confound their judges, exhaust the executioners, frighten the heretics,

---

6   Isa. 42:8.
7   Seneca, *De providentia*, 2.8.
        The same passage is quoted in Ribadeneyra, *Tratado de la tribulacion*, 122ᵛ–123ʳ.
8   Granada, *Parte primera*, 65.
9   Omitted beginning in the 1595 edition.

encourage the Catholics, and delight the angels in heaven.[10] And the Lord not only gave this spirit and zeal to those in England itself and unable to escape, but also to the young men and the priests living in the seminaries abroad (and out of danger), enflaming them with such blazing fires of his love that they were dying with their desire to die, and to return to England to do battle against so many mighty enemies, as has been described in this history. And there are even many others who are neither English nor even living in England, but rather dwell elsewhere in perfect peace and tranquility, and who, moved and inspired by the example of all these glorious martyrs of England, desire to go there to accompany them in their tortures and shed their blood for the Lord. On this subject, in confirmation of everything we have said hitherto, I wish to cite here what Cesare Baronio, that most scrupulous author of the *Annales ecclesiastici* [*historia Ecclesiastica*], writes, speaking of Saint Thomas of Canterbury.

> Our age—he says—most blessed in this respect, has merited to see many Thomases, saintly priests and other most noble men of England, crowned (so to speak) with a yet more illustrious crown of martyrdom, such as Saint Thomas had not, exalted with a double title of martyrdom, for they have not died, like Saint Thomas, solely for the Church's liberties, but have also gloriously given their lives to preserve, defend, and restore the Catholic faith. Among them are those the blessed Society of Jesus has nurtured and fed in the sheepfold of its colleges with the grass of its holy teachings, so that like innocent lambs they offer themselves to the Lord, sacrificed as living hosts. Likewise, there are those whom the seminaries at Rome and Rheims, like two unshakeable towers and two firm fortresses of our sacred faith, erected against the north [*Aquilon*],[11] have sent to England to triumph and receive such crowns. Well then, O youth of England, of such extraordinary spirit, take heart, O valiant, steadfast men, run with vigor and joy, for you have rested beneath so glorious a banner, and, in the oath of fidelity you have taken, you have also promised to shed your blood.
>
> The truth is that when I look at you, and see you run toward martyrdom with such prodigious strides, as though garbed in the exalted purple of your blood, I want to follow you, and I cry, "May my soul die the death of the just, and may my last moments be like those of such glorious knights."[12]

---

10   Luke 15:10.

11   Cf. Dan. 11.

12   In the margin: "In the annotations to the *Martyrologium Romanum*, for December 29." Baronio, *Martyrologium Romanum*, 580–81.

All this says Cesare Baronio, and if the spirit God gives to those who die and the desire to die for his love that he imparts to so many of his servants are powerful arguments of the strength and might of his grace, how much greater and more compelling proof of that power will be the victory that his Church wins over all its foes? For it is not just that the martyr lives in dying, conquers in falling, ascends prostrate upon the ground, and is crowned with glory having been dragged and disemboweled, but the holy Church, whose soldier the martyr is, also triumphs in him, and by this death overcomes all the tyrants and heretics, its persecutors, and all the demons and all the power of hell. Besides this, there is considerable benefit in this persecution for the Catholics of England themselves, because thereby they are proved, purified, and cleansed, detached from their earthly affections and borne up to heaven. Hounded, afflicted, and abhorred by the world, without anywhere to set their feet, nor anything to rely upon, each day they make of themselves an exquisite sacrifice. And thus I believe that there are more saints and more sound Catholics in England today than there were in the time of its worldly prosperity—for prosperity generally makes people slack, tepid, and spoiled, while this great tribulation makes them fervent, penitent, and steadfast martyrs. And even though some Catholics fall away through persecution and turn back, they are usually those who lived degenerately and riotously, hardly firm in the faith, while those who are not founded upon sand,[13] but rather upon the sturdy rock that is Jesus Christ, grow in virtue with oppression, like a well-planted tree with frosts and floods. And so, how great a glory for the Catholic Church is the fortitude of our martyrs? Of how much instruction? Of how much edification? How great an example? How great an honor is it to the holy Church to have such illustrious knights for its children? Such valiant warriors for its soldiers? So many zealous captains for its defenders? And not only those it has had, but those it has now, upon whom it prides itself; the present age need not envy ages past in this. Does not what we see render more credible what we have heard, and do not the martyrs who now suffer in England take away our wonder at the martyrs of whom we read in sacred histories? What shall I say of the other benefit to be taken from this persecution—that is, a salutary and needful warning to every province and kingdom of the Catholic Church of how they ought to treat heretics: for who will not learn out of another's head, seeing what is happening in England? How a kingdom that had previously flourished in religion, in virtue, in humaneness, in peace and harmony, in freedom, sweet concord, and honesty with one another, is now become a Babylon in the variety, contrariness, and

---

13   Matt. 7:26–27.

confusion of heresies; a den of thieves[14] in the injustices and outrages common there; a slaughterhouse of God's servants in the blood shed there; war and civil strife in what transpires between the Catholics and the heretics; a slavery and miserable captivity in the oppression and tyranny with which the entire realm is afflicted, most especially those of the ancient, sacred, and apostolic faith—and that this entire blaze arose out of a spark of hellfire in a king's blind infatuation, and grew in the manner we have seen, through the sect of Calvin professed by his daughter, if she professes any at all. And so, what care, what vigilance ought Catholic kings, princes, and states to have in preventing this infernal fire from catching in their kingdoms and territories, when they see that of England engulfed by it? What spirit ought Catholics to have in defending their faith unto death, when they see how their brothers are treated? From what they see in their neighbors' houses, how alert must they be in their own, distrusting the heretics' gentle appearance or feigned promises, with which they are wont to deceive the Catholics (as they deceived the English) and destroy and consume them, as soon as they find themselves with the whip hand? What will become of the kingdom of France, if the French Catholics do not take heed and learn from the English Catholics' sufferings? Truly, though they have seen such sights with their own eyes, and know that a woman who swore to preserve the Catholic faith in her realm in order to become queen later destroyed it, there are those who believe, and persuade others, that they ought to accept as king of France the prince of Béarn,[15] a relapsed Calvinist, so obstinate that he has never wished, nor even pretended, to swear to observe the Catholic faith (something the Calvinists themselves teach may be lawfully done in order to deceive), but rather promised in the estates of Montauban that he would always be a heretic[16] and declared that he would never change religion, though by doing so he would win thirty crowns and thirty Frances! How much more would they follow him, mired in this blind error, if they did not have before them this living, bloodstained, compelling example of England?

---

14   Matt. 21:13; Luke 19:46.

15   In the margin: "See the note at page 216." This annotation was added in the 1605 edition and refers to the note to the reader on Henry IV's conversion added at the end of Book 3, Chapter 18.

16   At an assembly convened in the Huguenot stronghold of Montauban in May 1581, Henry of Navarre and his Protestant allies had sworn an oath not to "do or undertake anything to the prejudice of the union, of the common good, or the peace and tranquility of the said churches, without the command of the said lord king of Navarre, with the counsel and advice of the said churches." For the full text of the oath, see Léonce Anquez, *Histoire des assemblées politiques des réformés de France (1573–1622)* (Paris: Auguste Durand, 1859), 452–53.

The Lord extracts all these benefits from this persecution, not least to teach us that if we wish him to hold us in his mighty hand and preserve us in our sacred Catholic faith, we must, with the gift of his grace, thrust every sin from our hearts, most of all those that open the door to heresy, for a man does not usually fall into extremes of wickedness all at once. He enters into vice gently, proceeding to lose his virtue little by little. And when the soul is utterly imprisoned, he finds and embraces that doctrine with which he can best give some color to his lusts. This should teach our kingdom not to neglect the events of others. And this warning and instruction is no small fruit of this English persecution—no less than awakening and moving us to compassion and the imitation of the English Catholics, who thus suffer for our sacred religion. To compassion, in seeing them so oppressed and afflicted, exiled from their land, driven from their homes, stripped of their property, deprived of their honor and freedom, treated as traitors, tortured and killed as agitators and rebels— for in the end we are all brothers, and members of a single mystical body, whose head is Jesus Christ[17] and, in his place on earth, the supreme Roman pontiff. And it has always been a common, praiseworthy practice among Christians to gather, support, and succor all who suffer for Christ, as this history records. But what we should most strive for, and seek with yet greater zeal, is to imitate the examples of these valiant soldiers, to awaken our tepidity and slackness with the memory of their struggles, summoning new strength and new steel to resist pain, despair, travail, and any other sort of adversity.

Who in their poverty will not be consoled by recalling how many noble, wealthy Catholics are now despoiled of their property and fettered in prison, without a rag to cover their nakedness, or a crumb to sustain themselves? What invalid will not rebuke themselves for being troubled and well-nigh losing hope when wracked by their pain, thinking on the agonies of so many priests and delicate ladies amid horrid tortures? And when toil wearies us, and hunger dispirits us, and the other miseries of this life afflict us, it will be a supreme comfort to bring to mind the life lived by the Catholics of England, and to benefit from this their persecution, which the Lord permits for his greater glory[18] (as we have said) and our greater good, to strengthen our faith, to instruct our hopes, to ignite our love, to impress upon us the power of his divine grace, to encourage our patience, to awaken our devotion, to condemn the indulgence of our flesh, to shame our slackness, and lastly to confound our negligence, seeing what man can do with God's favor—which is denied to none—and how little is done to attain blessedness.

---

17   Rom. 12:5; 1 Cor. 6:15, 12:12, 12:17; Eph. 5:30; Col. 1:18.

18   Perhaps a reference to the Society of Jesus's motto, *Ad majorem Dei gloriam* (To the greater glory of God).

The wonderful benefits all Catholics may take from this English persecution do not end here: there are others, relating to the heretics themselves, our oppressors, by whom the Lord is served, as the bailiffs, attorneys, and executioners of his divine justice, giving them authority and force so long as it pleases him, so that within the scope and limit he allows them, they should test the patience of his faithful, consume the dross of their sins, purify their virtue, and increase their merits and crowns. God gives them this fortune, as they call it (though it is nothing but a punishment) to summon and bring them to knowledge of the truth and his love,[19] and, if they do not convert, to reward them in this life for whatever good deeds they have done, since in the next an eternity of sufferings await them, torments the more terrible, the more grievous their sins have been, and the more generous the patience of the Lord has been in forbearing and waiting for them. For it befits his divine majesty to repay this delay with the severity of the penalty, and to conceal and restrain his arm, so as to wound with greater force; to proceed to punishment with slow and lengthy steps; to teach us patience through our own selves, as Plutarch says, and that we are not to seek to avenge our affronts and injuries; to give the malefactor time to repent; and not least to secure the fruit that is to come from this.[20] From an impious and cruel King Ahab, there is often born a saintly and perfect King Hezekiah,[21] a Saint Peter Martyr from heretical parents, like a rose from thorns.[22] In all of which we see the ineffable mercy and immense goodness of the Lord, which draws the greatest goods from the greatest evils in the world, and permits there to be tyrants, so that there shall be no lack of martyrs, and degenerate men to bear the staff of justice and exercise their cruelty against the bodies of the good, so that these may better demonstrate the patience and virtue of their souls. As he permits the holy Catholic Church to be persecuted, tested, and afflicted, so that, having passed through the crucible, it shall be purer, holier, and more perfect,[23] and so that we may understand that even if like the moon it is sometimes eclipsed and obscured, as Saint Ambrose says, never does its virtue fail or falter.[24]

The end of the history of the schism of England.[25]

---

19   1 Tim. 2:4.

20   Plutarch, *Moralia*, 551C–D.

21   4 Kings 16, 18–19; 2 Chron. 28–29.

22   The first *vita* of the Italian Dominican Peter Martyr (1206–52), assassinated while serving as an inquisitor in northern Italy, states that his parents were heretics. *AASS*, April III, 688.

23   In the margin: "Augustine, *The City of God*, Book 18[.51]."

24   In the margin: "Ambrose, *Hexameron*, on the work of the fourth day."
       Ambrose of Milan, *Hexameron*, 4.8.32.

25   Added in the 1605 edition.

To the Pious Reader

To convey more fully the cruelty of the heretics of our time in the kingdom of England, the constancy and fortitude of our martyrs, and the glory of the Catholic Church, which has so many valiant soldiers for its defense, and is thereby so certain of victory, and to honor the saints who suffered for Christ and edify and instruct the faithful by their example, I wish to place here a brief survey of the martyrs who have suffered and died for our sacred religion in England since the beginning of Elizabeth's reign, especially the priests and students of the seminaries. For they are those most engaged in this war, who dedicate themselves to this conquest with the greatest zeal and fervor. I refer the reader who wishes to see all this at greater length to the book entitled *Concertatio Ecclesiae Catholicæ in Anglia*, printed at Trier in the year 1588, which records how the following persons have been killed, exiled, and despoiled of their property.[1]

Of the ecclesiastics: one cardinal, three archbishops, eighteen bishops, one abbot, four monastic priors, four entire convents of religious. Deans of cathedrals, thirteen. Archdeacons, fourteen. Canons, more than sixty. Priests, for the most part well-born and of noted lineage, 530. Many men of letters, among them fifteen rectors of colleges. Doctors in theology, forty-nine. Licentiates in theology, twelve. Doctors of law, eighteen. Doctors of medicine, nine. Schoolmasters and masters of music, eleven.

Of the laypeople: the most serene Mary Stewart, queen of Scots. Earls, eight. Barons, ten. Prominent knights, twenty-six. Gentlemen, more than 356, and of common people, an enormous number.

Women, more than 110; one among them was Anne Somerset, countess of Northumberland,[2] and many other ladies and women of note, as may be seen in the aforementioned book.

---

1 Just after the title page, the *Concertatio* features a table of the various Catholic martyrs in Elizabeth's reign, from which Ribadeneyra has taken the figures that follow. *Concertatio*, n.p.

2 The *Concertatio* lists Anne Percy (*née* Somerset, c.1526–91) among those who have suffered for the Catholic faith, but as an exile rather than a martyr. The dowager countess of Northumberland, Anne left England after the failure of the Rising of the North, and remained a prominent figure in the Catholic exile community for the rest of her life. *Concertatio*, n.p. Lock, "Percy, Thomas," in *ODNB*, 43:744–45.

   It is worth noting that some Catholic writers characterized exile as a form of "white" or "bloodless" martyrdom, as opposed to the "red" martyrdoms of those executed. Highley, *Catholics Writing the Nation*, 24.

But because, as I said, it is against the seminary priests that the heretics of England most rage, against them that they most pour out their fury, I want to insert here, separately, the number and the names of those who have died for our holy religion, and the year they died. To the end that from it we may take the fruit that, by the toil of those now living and the merits and intercession of those who have already died for the Lord, we may hope for out of his immense goodness.

A Brief Account of the Martyrs Who Have Departed the English Colleges and Seminaries at Rome and Rheims in France, and Suffered in England in Defense of the Catholic Faith[1]

The Year of Our Lord 1577

Cuthbert Mayne, priest and licentiate in theology, was the first martyr of all the English seminaries, a learned and saintly man; he was hanged and quartered for an *agnus Dei* and a printed copy of the universal jubilee for the year 1575 found in his abode.[2]

The Year of Our Lord 1578

John Nelson, a priest, endured the same martyrdom for his steadfastness in affirming that the queen, in following the teachings of Calvin, was a heretic.[3]

Thomas Sherwood, a young student, was martyred in London for the same constancy.[4]

The Year of Our Lord 1581

Edmund Campion, priest of the Society of Jesus, licentiate in theology, noted preacher and excellent scholar, was taken by treachery while preaching in the house of a prominent knight. They tortured him three times, and in the end

---

1   This litany of Catholic martyrs is based on Manzano, *Breve catalogo*. See Appendix 5.

2   Cuthbert Mayne was arrested on June 8, 1577, "endited for having a Bull, holy graines, and an Agnus Dei," and hanged, drawn, and quartered on November 30. See Book 2, Chapter 36, and Allen, *Briefe Historie*, 104–06.

3   See Book 3, Chapter 25.

4   The layman Thomas Sherwood (*c.*1552–78) was "entrapped [...] by enterrogatories of Pius Quintus' Bull, of the excommunication of the Queene's religion, and whether she was an heretike, and of her spiritual soveraignitie, unto all which he answered like a true Christian man." He was hanged, drawn, and quartered in London on February 7, 1578. See Allen, *Briefe Historie*, 118–19.

For a sixteenth-century rendering of Sherwood's execution, see Book 2 Figure 28.1.

sentenced him to death with eleven of his fellow priests, which he accepted with utter joy. And the sentence was executed in London on December 1.[5]

Ralph Sherwin, a priest of the English seminary at Rome, and the first martyr of that college, an educated man, of great spirit and zeal, was likewise taken while preaching in the house of a knight. He died together with Father Campion.

Alexander Briant, a priest, was martyred for having been found in London in the quarters where Father Persons of the Society of Jesus was living. Because he refused to reveal where the said father was, they tortured him three times, and in the last, the most extreme of all, he felt no pain whatsoever, through a vow he made to our Lord to enter the Society of Jesus, as he attests in a letter subsequently published. He was martyred on the same day and in the same place as the previous two.[6]

Everard Hanse, a priest, was martyred in this year for disobeying a new law of the queen's, by which she forbade anyone to persuade anyone to become a Catholic.[7]

The Year of Our Lord 1582

John Paine, a priest, was martyred under the pretext that he sought to kill the queen, the heretics using this fantasy to render the name of priest hateful.[8]

Thomas Cottam, a priest of the Society of Jesus, presented himself in ful-fillment of his solemn word and confessed himself to be a priest—though he knew for certain that, according to the law's harshness, he must die for it, and thus they martyred him.[9]

Thomas Ford, a priest and a licentiate in theology, was imprisoned along with Father Campion, and martyred with numerous companions. The heretics claimed that they had joined with the pope and the king of Spain against the queen of England.[10]

---

5   See Book 2, Chapter 32.

6   For Sherwin and Briant, see Book 2, Chapter 33.

7   Hanse was executed at Tyburn on July 31, 1581, on charges "that the said Haunse, being one of the Pope's scollers, and made Priest beyond the seas, was retorned to seduce the Queene's Maiestie's subjects from their obedience, and that he affirmed the Pope to be his superior here in England, and had as much authoritie in spiritual governement within this realme as ever he had before." Allen, *Briefe Historie*, 100–02.

8   The priest John Paine (1532–82) was executed at Chelmsford on April 2, 1582 on charges of conspiring to assassinate the queen. See Ibid., 89–97 and Book 3 Figure 32.1.

9   See Book 2, Chapter 33. See also *Concertatio*, 93ᵛ–96ʳ and Book 3 Figure 32.1.

10 See Book 2, Chapter 33 and Book 3 Figure 32.1.

Robert Johnson, Richard Kirkman,[11] William Filbie, James Thompson,[12] Lawrence Johnson, John Shert, William Lacy,[13] Luke Kirby,[14] all priests, died for the same cause.

The Year of Our Lord 1583

William Hart,[15] William Chaplain,[16] priests, and Richard Thirkeld,[17] John Bodey, and John Slade,[18] students, were martyred for the same cause, and for having asserted that the pope, not the queen, was the head of the Church in England.

The Year of Our Lord 1584

George Haddock, John Munden, James Fenn, Thomas Hemerford, John Nutter,[19] Thomas Cotesmore, Robert Holmes,[20] Roger Wakeman,[21] James

---

11   Richard Kirkman (d.1582), sent to England in 1579, was martyred alongside William Lacy (Book 2, Chapter 36) on August 22, 1582. Foley, *Records*, 3:43. See *Concertatio*, 100^r–101^r and Book 3 Figure 32.1.

12   The Yorkshireman James Thompson (d.1582) was executed at York on November 28, 1582. Camm, *Lives*, 2:589. See ibid., 101^v–103^r.

13   See Book 2, Chapter 36.

14   For both Johnsons, Filbie, Shert, and Kirby, see Book 2, Chapter 33 and Book 3 Figure 32.1.

15   The Somerset-born William Hart (1558–83), ordained a priest at Rome in 1579, was executed at York on March 15, 1583. Pollen, *Acts*, 218, 252. See also Book 3 Figure 32.1.

16   The priest William Chaplain (d.1583) died in prison in 1583. Thomas Graves Law, *A Calendar of the English Martyrs of the Sixteenth and Seventeenth Centuries* (London: Burns and Oates, 1876), 39.

17   Richard Thirkeld (d.1583) was executed at York on May 29, 1583, on charges of having reconciled the queen's subjects to the Roman Catholic Church. Thirkeld was in fact a priest at the time of his martyrdom, having been ordained at Rheims in 1579. Camm, *Lives*, 2:635–36. See *Concertatio*, 116^v–119^r and Book 3 Figure 32.1.

18   For Bodey and Slade, see Book 2, Chapter 26.

19   On February 12, 1584, five priests—George Haddock (or Haydock, 1556–84), John Munden (or Mundyn, c.1544–84), James Fenn (c.1540–84), Thomas Hemerford (c.1556–84), and John Nutter (d.1584)—were together executed as traitors at Tyburn. Foley, *Records*, 1:471. J. Andreas Löwe, "Fenn, James (c.1540–1584)," in *ODNB*, 19:294–95.
       See *Concertatio*, 133^r–138^r, 139^v–142^v, 143^r–156^r, 156^v, 156^v–160^r, respectively.

20   The secular priests Thomas Cotesmore (d.1584) and Robert Holmes (d.1584) both died in prison at some point in 1584. Law, *Calendar*, 39–40.

21   Roger Wakeman (d.c.1584), a secular priest, died in November of 1583 or 1584 while imprisoned in Newgate. Ibid., 37. Patrick McGrath and Joy Rowe, "The Imprisonment of

Quod S. Romanæ Ecclesiæ fidem tenerent, ac prædicarent in Anglia multi Sacer:
dotes, et laici, hoc mortis genere occisi sunt anno is 8 2. is 83. Inter quos hi fuerūt
Sacerdotes, Ioannes Shertus, Lucas Kirbeius, et Gulielmus Hartus, huius Ro.
Collegij alumni. Robertus, et Laurentius Ionsoni, Gulielmus filbeius, Kircmannus
Threlkelus, et Hudsonus Collegij Rhemensis alumni. Thomas Cottamus, Ioannes
Paynus, Thomas fordus, Gulielmus lacius.   Complures etiam in singulis Regni
prouincijs iam condemnati, talem mortem in horas expectant.
                                                              35

FIGURE 32.1   *The martyrs of 1582 and 1583. The caption mentions John Shert, Luke Kirby,*
William Hart, Robert Johnson, Lawrence Johnson, William Filbie, Richard
Kirkman, Richard Thirkeld, Thomas Cottam, John Paine, and Thomas Ford.
Giovanni Battista Cavalieri, *Ecclesiae anglicanae trophaea sive sanctorum*
martyrum qui pro Christo catholicaeque fidei veritate asserenda antiquo recen-
tiorique persecutionum tempore mortem in Anglia subierunt, passiones Romae
in collegio Anglico per Nicolaum Circinianum depictae: Nuper autem per Io. Bap.
de Cavalleriis aeneis typis repraesentatae (Rome: Ex officina Bartolomeo Grassi,
1584). NE1666 .C57 1584 OVERSIZE, John J. Burns Library, Boston College.

Lomax,[22] priests, were condemned by various courts and executed for the same profession of their faith.

The Year of Our Lord 1585

Thomas Crowther,[23] Hugh Taylor,[24] Edward Pole,[25] Laurence Vaux,[26] priests, suffered for the same cause, despising the pardon and favor the queen offered them all if they abandoned the Catholic religion, as she has offered to many others.

The Year of Our Lord 1586

Edward Stransham, Nicholas Woodfen,[27] Richard Sergeant, William Thomson,[28] Robert Anderton, William Marsden,[29] Francis Ingleby,[30] Robert Dibdale,

---

Catholics for Religion under Elizabeth I," *RH* 20, no. 4 (October 1991): 415–35, here 416. See *Concertatio*, 203ᵛ.

22   James Lomax (*c.*1560–84), a native of Chester, was ordained at Rome in 1582, and was apprehended soon after his return to England later that year. Foley, *Records*, 6:141.

23   The secular priest Thomas Crowther (d.1585) died sometime in 1585 while imprisoned in the Marshalsea. Law, *Calendar*, 40.

24   Hugh Taylor (d.1585), a secular priest, was hanged at York on November 26, 1585. Ibid., 36. See *Concertatio*, 203ᵛ.

25   Imprisoned in the Gatehouse, the priest Edward Pole (d.1585) died sometime in 1585. Foley, *Records*, 3:291. Law, *Calendar*, 39.

26   Though Laurence Vaux (1519–85) was listed in the *Concertatio Ecclesiae Catholicæ* as a martyr, he died of unknown causes while imprisoned in the Clink in 1585. John J. LaRocca, "Vaux, Laurence (1519–1585)," in *ODNB*, 56:217–18.

27   Edward Stransham (*c.*1554–86) and Nicholas Woodfen (born Wheeler, *c.*1550–1586) were executed at Tyburn on January 21, 1586. Pollen, *Acts*, 284. See *Concertatio*, 204ʳ.

28   The secular priests Richard Sergeant (d.1586) and William Thomson (d.1586) were hanged at Tyburn on April 20, 1586. Law, *Calendar*, 22.

29   Robert Anderton (*c.*1560–86) and William Marsden (d.1586) were executed on the Isle of Wight on April 25, 1586. Pollen, *Acts*, 66.

30   Francis Ingleby (*c.*1551–1586) was executed as a priest at York on June 3, 1586. Pollen, *Acts*, 258–59.

John Adams, John Lowe,[31] Stephen Rousham,[32] John Finglow,[33] John Harrison,[34] William Crockett, priests, and Gabriel Everingham,[35] a student, were hanged and quartered for the same reason.

The Year of Our Lord 1587

Thomas Pilchard,[36] John Sandys,[37] John Hambley,[38] Alexander Crowe,[39] Martin Sherson,[40] Edmund Sykes,[41] Robert Sutton,[42] Robert Wilcox,[43] Edward

---

31   October 8, 1586 saw the hanging, drawing, and quartering at Tyburn of three priests: Robert Dibdale (c.1556–86), the former Calvinist minister John Adams (c.1543–86), and John Lowe (1553–86). Law, *Calendar*, 34–35. Pollen, *Acts*, 259.

32   Stephen Rousham (or Rouse, c.1555–87) had been expelled from England in 1585, and after returning was martyred at Gloucester in March 1587. Ibid., 260.

33   John Finglow (d.1586) was executed as a priest at York on August 8, 1586. Thompson Cooper, "Finglow, John (d.1586/7)," rev. Sarah Elizabeth Wall, in *ODNB*, 19:599–600, here 600.

34   John Harrison (d.1586) was a secular priest who died in prison sometime in 1586. Law, *Calendar*, 40.

35   William Crockett only appears in certain Catholic martyrologies, and may have died in 1588, rather than 1586; in any case, little can be said about him with certainty. The same is true of Gabriel Everingham. See Pollen, *Unpublished Documents*, 10n1.

36   Thomas Pilchard (1557–87) was executed at Dorchester on March 21, 1587. Pollen, *Acts*, 261n20.

37   John Sandys (c.1550–86) was actually martyred the previous year, at Gloucester on August 11, 1586. Ibid., 333n18.

38   Sources differ as to the martyrdom of John Hambley (d.1587): Henry Foley, S.J. follows Challoner in placing it at York on September 9, 1587, while Pollen opts for Salisbury "about Easter, 1587." Foley, *Records*, 3:734n7. Pollen, *Acts*, 268n22.

39   Originally a cobbler, Alexander Crowe (c.1551–87) became a priest at Rheims; he was martyred in his hometown of York, on November 30, 1587. Ibid., 270–71.

40   The priest Martin Sherson (1563–88) actually died in February 1588, while imprisoned in the Marshalsea. Ibid., 271n25.

41   Edmund Sykes (d.1587) was executed at York on March 23, 1587. Foley, *Records*, 6:559n34.

42   A former Protestant minister, Robert Sutton (d.1587) became a priest in 1577 at the seminary at Douai; after an eventful ministry in England, he was executed at Stafford on July 27, 1587. Pollen, *Acts*, 323–24.

43   Robert Wilcox (1558–88) actually died the next year, as one of the four "Oaten Hill Martyrs" hanged, drawn, and quartered at Oaten Hill, Canterbury on October 1, 1588. Law, *Calendar*, 34.

Campion,[44] William Way [*Guillermo Vero*],[45] Gabriel Thimelby,[46] priests, suffered in this year for the same confession of their faith.

The Year of Our Lord 1588

John Holford,[47] Thomas Hunt,[48] William Hartley,[49] William Spenser,[50] Robert Morton,[51] George Flower [*Iorge Flouer*],[52] Thomas Morgan,[53] Robert Ludlam,[54] William Wigges, Richard Simpson, Nicholas Garlick, William Dean,[55] William Gunter,[56] Richard Leigh,[57] James Clarkson,[58] Edward Burden,[59] Edward

---

44   Edward Campion (born Gerard Edwards, d.1588) was one of the four Catholics executed at Oaten Hill, Canterbury on October 1, 1588. Pollen, *Acts*, 327.

45   "Guillermo Vero" seems to be William Way (d.1588), martyred at Kingston upon Thames on September 23, 1588. Pollen argues that martyrologists have long erred in differentiating "William Flower *alias* Way" from "William Wigges *alias* Way." each thought to have died at Kingston in the autumn of 1588. Given the appearance of a William Wigges later in this catalog, López Manzano's text seems to be a very early specimen of this error. Ibid., xx.

46   Gabriel Thimelby (d.1587), who seems to have been a lay gentleman rather than a priest, died in prison sometime in 1587. Law, *Calendar*, 40.

47   Almost certainly an error for the secular priest Thomas Holford (1541–88), who was hanged at Clerkenwell on August 28, 1588. Ibid., 32.

48   There is some ambiguity as to the identity of this "Tomas Hunto." Pollen would identify him with the Thomas Hunt (d.1600) executed in 1600, but this is open to question. Pollen, *Unpublished Documents*, 11n4.

49   William Hartley (*c*.1557–88) was executed in London on October 5, 1588. Pollen, *Acts*, 272n26.

50   William Spenser (d.1589) was condemned as a priest and executed at York on September 24, 1588. Foley, *Records*, 3:740–42.

51   Robert Morton (or Mourton, d.1588) was executed in London on August 28, 1588. Pollen, *Acts*, 273n27.

52   Likely an error for Richard Flower (d.1588), a Welsh priested executed on August 28, 1588. Pollen, *Unpublished Documents*, 194.

53   A Thomas Morgan (d.1588) is listed as having been sent to England from the English College at Rome in 1583, and subsequently imprisoned. Foley, *Records*, 3:46.

54   The priest Robert Ludlam (*c*.1551–88) was hanged, drawn, and quartered alongside Richard Simpson (*c*.1553–1588) and Nicholas Garlick (*c*.1555–1588) at Derby on July 24, 1588. Law, *Calendar*, 28.

55   See Book 3, Chapter 1.

56   William Gunter (d.1588), a secular priest, was executed in London on August 28, 1588. Law, *Calendar*, 32.

57   Richard Leigh (*c*.1561–88) was executed at Tyburn on August 30, 1588. Pollen, *Acts*, 306–07.

58   The priest James Claxton (or Clarkson, d.1588) was hanged, drawn, and quartered at Hounslow on August 28, 1588. Law, *Calendar*, 33.

59   Edward Burden (d.1588) was executed as a priest on November 29, 1588. Pollen, *Acts*, 328.

James,[60] Christopher Buxton,[61] John Hewett,[62] priests, and Thomas Felton,[63] a noble youth and the nephew of a martyr, Hugh More,[64] Thomas Lynch,[65] and John Robinson,[66] all four seminary students, were martyred with exceeding cruelty, under the pretext that they had communicated with the Spanish Armada, a charade to render odious the cause of the faith.

The Year of Our Lord 1589

John Amias, Robert Dalby,[67] George Nichols, Richard Yaxley, priests, and Thomas Belson, a young student, after numerous humiliations and abuses, were martyred in this year, at Oxford and elsewhere, for the Catholic faith.[68]

The Year of Our Lord 1590

Miles Gerard, Francis Dicconson,[69] Christopher Bales, Anthony Middleton,[70] Robert Jones [*sic*],[71] priests, were martyred in this year.

---

60   The secular priest Edward James (*c*.1557–88) was hanged, drawn, and quartered at Chichester on October 1, 1588. Law, *Calendar*, 34.

61   Along with Wilcox and Edward Campion, Christopher Buxton (d.1588) was one of the "Oaten Hill Martyrs" executed at Canterbury on October 1, 1588. Ibid., 34.

62   John Hewett (d.1588), who also used the names Weldon and Savell, was executed at Mile End Green in London on October 5, 1588. Pollen, *Acts*, 230n10.

63   See Book 3, Chapter 1.

64   Hugh More (or Moor, d.1588), a student at Broadgates Hall, now Pembroke College, Oxford, was martyred in London on August 28, 1588. McCoog, *Reckoned Expense*, 63n93. Law, *Calendar*, 32.

65   I have not been able to learn anything of Thomas Lynch (d.1588), save that he died in 1588 and was included in several contemporary martyrologies. Pollen, *Unpublished Documents*, 12–13.

66   John Robinson (d.1588) actually was an ordained priest at the time of his execution in Ipswich on October 1, 1588. Law, *Calendar*, 34.

67   Robert Dalby (d.1589), a former Anglican clergyman, was ordained at Rheims in 1588. Returning to England that year, he was quickly arrested, and executed at York in March 1589, alongside John Amias (d.1589). J.T. Rhodes, "Dalby, Robert (*d*.1589)," in *ODNB*, 14:924–25, here 925.

68   For Nichols, Yaxley, and Belson, see Book 3, Chapter 3.

69   Miles Gerard and Francis Dicconson (or Dickinson) were both hanged, drawn, and quartered at Rochester on April 30, 1590. Pollen, *Unpublished Documents*, 291.

70   For Bales and Middleton, see Book 3, Chapter 4.

71   This seems to be Ribadeneyra's error for Edward Jones, also known as Edward Parker, martyred alongside Middleton on May 6, 1590. Pollen, *Acts*, 308. See Book 3, Chapter 4.

The Year of Our Lord 1591

Edmund Gennings, Eustace White, Polydore Plasden,[72] Monford [*Vnfredo*] Scott, George Beesley,[73] Edmund Duke, Richard Holiday, John Hogg, Thomas Hill [*Tomas Hylleo*],[74] priests, suffered similar martyrdoms.

The Year of Our Lord 1592

Thomas Pormort,[75] Richard Williams,[76] Francis Montford,[77] John Thomas [*Thulesio*],[78] Joseph Lampton,[79] priests, with more than twenty others, were martyred in this year in various parts of England, under the queen's new edict against the Catholic faith, and in particular against those from the seminaries in Spain. It has not been possible to uncover even their real names, since, to disguise themselves, the seminary priests are wont to change their names and garments to enter England.

---

72   On December 10, 1591, Edmund Gennings (1567–91), Eustace White (1559–91), and Polydore Plasden (d.1591) were hanged, drawn, and quartered in London. Law, *Calendar*, 37.

73   For Scott and Beesley, see Book 3, Chapter 7.

74   Edmund Duke (1563–90), Richard Holiday (d.1590), and John Hogg (d.1590) were three of the four "Dryburne Martyrs," hanged, drawn, and quartered at Dryburne in Durham on May 27, 1590 (not 1591, as Ribadeneyra has it). It seems likely that "Tomas Hylleo" is an error for Richard Hill (*d.*1590), the fourth of the Dryburne Martyrs. Law, *Calendar*, 24.

75   See Book 3, Chapter 7.

76   A Catholic priest by the name of Williams, almost certainly the Richard Williams of whom Ribadeneyra writes, was reported to have been executed in June 1592. McCoog, *Building the Faith*, 61.

77   See Book 3, Chapter 21.
      Francis Montford's name is deleted from the list beginning in the 1595 edition.

78   This may be John Thomas, a layman executed at Winchester in the summer of 1592. McCoog, *Building the Faith*, 61.
      This name is deleted from the list beginning in the 1595 edition.

79   This name is added in the 1595 edition, replacing Montford and Thomas.
      The priest Joseph Lampton (d.1593) was executed at Newcastle on July 27, 1593. Pollen, *Unpublished Documents*, 231, 293.

The Year of Our Lord 1593

Anthony Page, priest;[80] William Davies, priest.[81]

The Year of Our Lord 1594

John Cornelius of the Society of Jesus;[82] John Ingram, priest;[83] William Harrington, priest;[84] Richard Boste, priest;[85] and others.[86]

These are the martyrs who have departed from the English seminaries, alongside the many laymen of every stripe who, with the encouragement of these priests, have shown the same constancy amid their torments and martyrdoms for the confession of our sacred faith. And beyond the 108 martyrs tallied here, there are as many and more in the prisons, and more than three hundred priests who work constantly at the same enterprise, preaching, confessing, and recalling the deceived people to the knowledge of the truth, and consoling the Catholics in their travails, unremittingly risking their lives out of love for the Lord.

The end.

---

80   The priest Anthony Page (d.1593) was executed at York on April 30, 1593. Ibid., 293.

81   William Davies (d.1593), a Welsh-born priest, was hanged, drawn, and quartered on July 27, 1593, at Baumaris Castle. Daniel Huws, "Davies [Dai], William (*d*. 1593)," in ODNB, 15:418.
       The entries for the year 1593 first appear in the 1595 edition.

82   John Cornelius (*c*.1557–94) expressed interest in joining the Society of Jesus, but was never formally accepted as a member. Of his own accord, he pronounced Jesuit vows before his execution on July 3 or July 4, 1594. Thomas M. McCoog, "Cornelius, John (*c*.1557–1594)," in ODNB, 13:438–39, here 438.

83   The priest John Ingram (d.1594) was hanged, drawn, and quartered at Gateshead on July 26, 1594. J. Andreas Löwe, "Boste, John [St John Boste] (1544–1594)," in ODNB, 6:716–17, here 716.

84   The Yorkshire priest William Harrington (*c*.1566–94) was executed at Tyburn on February 18, 1594. Pollen, *Unpublished Documents*, 293.

85   This is an error for John Boste (1544–94), a priest trained at Rheims who was captured in 1593 and hanged, drawn, and quartered at Durham on July 24, 1594. Löwe, "Boste," in ODNB, 6:716.

86   The entries for the year 1594 first appear in the 1595 edition.

The Exhortation to the Armada

A   Ribadeneyra's Letter to Doña Ana Félix de Guzmán, Countess of
     Ricla and Marchioness of Camarasa,[1] c. May 1588

MHSIR, 2:92–95.

All of us of the Society desire to serve the duke of Medina, to whom we are obligated because of who he is, because of the kindnesses he has always done us, and because it is a thing so dear to Your Ladyship. But I confess to Your Ladyship that for myself, at least, this desire has grown enormously since God our Lord chose him as captain general of the Armada, taking him as his instrument in an enterprise as holy and glorious as that now in hand, which I truly consider to be the most important the Church of God has seen in many ages. Indeed, the greatest kindness his divine majesty could do the duke—after imparting to him his supreme love—is to choose him as his minister in so sublime a business, and I trust that the duke recognizes this and is grateful for it, for they write to us from Lisbon that he is heavily occupied in eradicating offenses to our Lord and public scandals, which is the true path to achieving victory and becoming a faithful servant of God. And so, if it appears to Your Ladyship that His Excellency would receive any service from this exhortation (which I had written as a conclusion to the *Historia de la scisma de Inglaterra*), though I had my grounds for intending to suppress it, I am content that Your Ladyship send His Excellency a copy, if you think it something that might benefit him: though to my mind it is superfluous for the duke, since his excellent judgment will have understood this business better than anyone, and with his zeal, Christianity, and fortitude his heart will be so afire that he will have no need of dead words to enkindle and enflame—with his own lively and forceful ones—the hearts of his soldiers.

I beg Your Ladyship not to reveal the author of this paper, and to tell the duke not to publish it, for I think it unwise for these arguments to come into too many hands.

---

1   Ana Félix de Guzmán, countess of Ricla and marchioness of Camarasa, was the first cousin once removed of the duke of Medina Sidonia, whom Philip II had appointed as commander-in-chief of the Spanish Armada. Francisco de Borja de Medina names Ana Félix de Guzmán as the person to whom the exhortation was sent, but he misidentifies her as the duke of Medina Sidonia's wife (*vere* Ana de Silva y Mendoza, 1560–1610). Though it is entirely possible that Ribadeneyra wrote to the duchess of Medina Sidonia, his established friendship with the countess of Ricla suggests that this is the correct identification. Rey, 1332n. Medina, "Jesuitas," 5.

And so, trusting in this and in what is to come, I send it to Your Ladyship. And with the greatest willingness would I go on this expedition, if such were given to me, and I would consider it a true kindness of our Lord to die therein. But this lack will be supplied by the other fathers of the Society who are going, although I fear not all those sent will arrive in time, the notice having come late, while we who remain will aid those who have left with prayers, and Masses, and penances, and wishes, and sighs. The Lord in heaven, in his mercy, will hear us.[2]

Though I know it is hardly necessary, nevertheless let Your Ladyship write to the duke lest His Excellency omit to remember that, given the number of soldiers, provisions, and munitions that go with the Armada, he should trust as paymasters, captains, and quartermasters only his own people, of the greatest trustworthiness. And that he should see to it that those departing fully understand the importance of the enterprise and set off with the intention of serving God, with a clean conscience and without public scandal. That the knights travel weighed down with weapons, not garments. That no superfluous persons be included, for they will only embezzle and waste the provisions, but rather only those of import. That on arrival in England he distinguish between Catholics and heretics, treating the one with kindness and the other with correction. That the Catholics not be treated worse by our men than they have been by the heretics, nor be scandalized by the wicked habits of our soldiers and so confirmed in their errors and corrupt teachings—albeit unjustly—by the misdeeds and outrages that could arise among them. That great care be taken in not shedding the blood of the weak and oppressed, who have no greater part in the war than to lament their dead, and in not devastating the temples, which, though they now honor the devil in sacrilegious rites, will honor the Lord, as they did in former times, for which purpose they were erected.

B   An Exhortation to the Soldiers and Officers Who Embark Upon This Expedition to England, in the Name of Their Captain General

MHSIR, 2:347–70.

If I did not know, unconquered captains and steadfast soldiers, the zeal and piety, the spirit and valor with which Your Honors have longed for this expedition to England, embark upon it now with trust in God's favor, and hope for a joyous conclusion, I would waste many words and offer many arguments convincing you of its significance. But since these constant hearts and brave souls have no need of words, and since what ought to be said could not be explained in infinite speeches, I have chosen to cut short my thoughts and briefly set before Your Honors some few of the many that

---

2   Ps. 114:1.

occur to me, in confirmation of the joy and satisfaction of the present moment and in thanksgiving to God our Lord, who brought it about for his glory and the honor and singular good of Spain.

This expedition, my lords, incorporates all the grounds for a just and holy war that the world affords. And although it looks like an offensive war, rather than a defensive one, as though we attack a foreign kingdom, rather than defending our own, yet if we consider carefully, we shall find that it *is* a defensive war, in which we defend our sacred religion and the holy Catholic faith. We defend the priceless honor of our king and lord, and of our nation. We defend the land and wealth of all the realms of Spain, and with them our peace, quiet, and tranquility.

No one who did not see or read of them could truly know the outrages England daily perpetrates against God and his saints, for they are so numerous as to be beyond count and so extreme as to be beyond belief. I do not speak of the evils committed there in the time of King Henry, father of this Elizabeth who now rules, or in that of her brother Edward: I pass over a thousand monasteries of God's true servants, male and female, desolated, and ten thousand churches profaned and ravaged; the shrines robbed and the sanctuaries looted; the ancient monuments of the saints cast upon the ground, their bodies burned and their sacred ashes scattered to the wind; the religious violently thrust from their homes; the virgins induced to every baseness and the nuns, consecrated to God, violated; countless servants of Christ mangled by awful and exquisite torments, with such fierce brutality and godlessness that the Catholic Church has endured no greater persecution in any kingdom, of pagans, Muslims, or barbarians. I will not rehearse things past, nor call to mind the catastrophes that have befallen England's Catholics since King Henry VIII separated from the obedience of the Church, for I should never come to an end. I will speak only of its present, wretched state under Elizabeth, the daughter of Anne Boleyn, whom Henry married by divorcing his lawful wife the saintly Queen Catherine, daughter of the Catholic Kings of glorious memory, with whom he had lived in peace for twenty years and had children, while Anne was the sister of one of the king's mistresses and the daughter of another—and even, as some aver with good reason, the king's own daughter (O unnatural, abominable, and unthinkable!), with whom he coupled to produce so horrid and terrifying a monster, to be her mother's daughter and sister and her father's granddaughter, to imitate her father-grandfather in disobedience to the pope and in cruelty and her mother-sister in heresy and vice (for which she was publicly beheaded on the orders of King Henry himself, her father and husband).

Now this Elizabeth, the daughter of such parents, has made herself head of the Church of England; though a woman, by nature subject to a man, as Saint Paul says, and by the mandate of God unable to speak in church,[3] she would have herself

---

3   1 Cor. 11:3, 14:34–35; Eph. 5:23.

acknowledged as spiritual head by the clerics, religious, bishops, and prelates of the Church, whom she installs and removes, examines, corrects, and punishes, allows and denies the faculty of ordination, consecration, and the exercise of all the other priestly functions, at her pleasure and will. And for refusing to obey her, she has persecuted, abused, deposed, imprisoned, oppressed, and ultimately slain all the Catholic bishops in England. It is she who has commanded Catholic preachers to keep silent and the heretics to speak; she who has gathered, supported, aided, and favored all the pestilential ministers of Satan and diabolical teachers of every error and insanity now concocted against our sacred faith; she who has summoned them to her realm, and they have come from France, Scotland, Upper and Lower Germany, and all the other provinces tainted with heresy, flocking to England like the principal university of their doctrine, like a nest of serpents,[4] like a safe haven for thieves and pirates, like a universal exhibition of such poisonous merchandise, from there to spread and extend it throughout the world more easily. It is she who has removed all the images of the saints, persecuted their relics, perverted the use of the holy sacraments, banished the Mass from her kingdom, and commanded that the Roman pontiff, vicar of Jesus Christ and supreme head of the Church of the faithful upon the earth, be neither acknowledged nor obeyed. It is she who harbors such abhorrence for any item of devotion or piety whatsoever from the Holy See that for merely bearing or possessing a rosary, an *agnus Dei*, a cross, an image, or a bull brought from Rome, she mutilates and slays with horrible and ruthless tortures, like traitors, all found to have committed this—in her sight—grave misdeed.

It is she who every day publishes new, inhuman laws against the Catholic faith, executes them with extreme force, and unceasingly sheds the guiltless blood of those who profess it—though they be well-born knights, mighty lords, venerable priests, saintly religious, gentlemen distinguished by lineage, learning, or wisdom. They are dragged to torment, hanged upon the gallows, allowed to fall while yet only half-dead, cut open and their entrails removed and their heart torn out, and then finished off and their quarters stuck on the towers, bridges, and roads of the cities. It is she who keeps the Catholics of her kingdom, who are the greater and the best part of it, so afflicted and oppressed with unjust laws, with new and bitter mandates, with atrocious punishments, with heartless enforcers, with the slanders of informants and perjurers, with the sentences of perfidious, soulless judges, that they can neither speak a word, nor move, nor make a sound, nor even draw breath as Catholic Christians without losing their property, without being exiled in disgrace, or held in some horrid, murky dungeon, or consumed and murdered in some unheard-of, terrible form of death. It is she who, inspired by the heretics whom, as we have said, she maintains in her realm (possessed with the infernal desire of propagating, spreading, and feeding the blaze of

---

4   Matt. 23:33.

their false religious across the world), has sought with all her cunning and artifice to kindle this devastating, scorching fire of heresy throughout the entire world, beginning with the kingdoms and states nearest to her. It is she who has desolated the kingdom of Scotland and put its king in the miseries we see; she who, under the cover of her royal word and faith, arrested his mother Queen Mary, at once the queen of Scotland and France and heir to the kingdom of England, and after twenty years of harsh and bitter captivity had her killed for being a Catholic, beheaded by the hand of the London executioner. It is she who has agitated the realm of France, imperiling the kingdom and the lives of the three brothers, Kings Francis II, Charles IX, and Henry III, and now supports its rebels and pays the heretical soldiers who enter that land for its destruction. It is she who sustains the provinces of Flanders in their long, costly, and bloody war against the king our lord; she who has constantly striven to incite them, to drive out the Spanish soldiers, to murder Lord Don John of Austria, to give new strength and breath to those who were already defeated and overthrown; she who has laid claim to Zealand and Holland, occupying their cities, fortifications, and ports; she who has infested our seas, robbed the merchants of their wealth, and with her money, soldiers, arms, supplies, counsel, and ruses prolonged and expanded the war in those territories, against the ancient ties and modern pacts between the houses of Burgundy and England, against our king, against our sacred faith, and against God. It is she who, drawing renewed courage and boldness from our sufferance and meekness, has dared to attack the provinces of the West Indies, to burn our islands, rob our peoples, seize and sink our ships, enter and sack our cities, overturn justice and royal authority, and throw all the realms of Spain into anxiety and confusion.

And if we thought all this trivial, we have learned how she holds nearby provinces in the palm of her hand and assaults and despoils those farther from her realm. She has had the boldness and audacity (a frightful thing, which ages to come will not believe) to attack the ports of Spain itself, first in Galicia[5] and then at Cádiz—and since part of our Armada was then in the harbor, to assail it, loot it, burn it, and send it to the depths.[6] And the city itself would have been torched, pillaged, and destroyed, if God in his mercy had not prevented it, and the duke of Medina had not come to its aid with

---

5 Brought into a war against Spain by the Treaty of Nonsuch (1585), Elizabeth sent Francis Drake to the Spanish coast, where he raided several Galician villages. Colin Martin and Geoffrey Parker, *The Spanish Armada*, rev. ed. (Manchester: Manchester University Press, 1999), 79.

6 Dispatched on a privateering mission in March 1587, Drake led attacks up and down the western coast of the Iberian Peninsula, as well as the famous "Singeing of the king of Spain's beard"—an astoundingly successful raid on Cádiz, where the English captured four Spanish ships, burning the remainder, and seized provisions stockpiled for the Armada. Harry Kelsey, "Drake, Sir Francis (1540–1596)," in *ODNB*, 16:858–70, here 863–64.

his presence and his men.[7] Elizabeth has done this before our very eyes and in the sight of the whole world, while the marquis of Santa Cruz was readying his fleet at Lisbon,[8] and Andalusia was full of soldiers. Yet in Spain, our most mighty king, the monarch of the world, Don Philip, taking little notice of this Elizabeth, because she is a woman and he intended to win her over through goodwill rather than to come to the clash of arms, has shown sufferance and patience to the point that we see such extreme shamelessness and boldness. It is this same Elizabeth who, reckoning all we have just mentioned but little toward achieving her aims of uprooting our sacred Catholic faith from every kingdom of the faithful, has made alliances with heretical princes and sent her ambassadors to Muscovy and her fleets to Constantinople, to solicit the Turk against us and draw him into our lands to harry and afflict us in our homes, and take from us, if they can, our property and our lives—and, what is more important, the law of God, the Catholic faith, the eternal salvation of our souls!

This is what is at stake in this war, and for this reason I said at the outset that it is a defensive war, defending our sacred religion and most holy Catholic faith. And to whom does it belong to wage it, if not the king our lord and the realms of Spain? To whom does it belong to defend the Catholic faith, if not the Catholic King? To whom does it belong to preserve the Catholic faith in that realm, if not he who once aided in its restoration when it had been cast out? Who has the responsibility to avenge the humiliation and death of the most serene Queen Doña Catherine, one of our Spaniards, the daughter of the illustrious Catholic Kings Don Ferdinand and Doña Isabella, who was abandoned and abominated by King Henry in order to wed the mother of this Elizabeth, if not the king of Spain, the nephew of Queen Doña Catherine herself, and grandson and successor to those same Catholic Kings? What kingdom in all of Christendom has forces capable of taking up arms today against England, if not Spain? How else can Spain repay our Lord for a mercy as enormous as the preservation, by the zeal and vigilance of its king and lord, of our holy Catholic Church and faith whole, pure, clean, and free of falsehoods? Or the fact that, at a time when nearly every land is burning with wars driven by heresy, ours enjoys peace and tranquility? How great will be our nation's glory in not only preserving the purity and power of the Catholic faith in its own realms, but also restoring it abroad; in not only possessing an inquisition to punish the foreign heretics who would come to infect Spain, but also sending

---

7 Drake's forces were prevented from making an incursion into Cádiz itself by the timely arrival of the duke of Medina Sidonia with several thousand of the local militia. Martin and Parker, *Spanish Armada*, 109.

8 The gifted admiral Álvaro de Bazán, first marquis of Santa Cruz de Mudela (1526–88) was the original architect of the Armada, and oversaw much of its preparation at Lisbon. Santa Cruz died on February 9, 1588, replaced as commander-in-chief by the duke of Medina Sidonia. Ibid., 117–23.

out armies of soldiers to smoke out the heretics of other provinces and kingdoms? It is a supreme and sublime honor for Spaniards to have discovered, conquered, and subdued a new world through their valor. But incomparably greater is the honor and glory of those who by their Christianity and zeal have preached the Gospel of Christ our Lord in the New World, so that an infinity of barbarous peoples in exotic lands and mighty kingdoms have been been subjected to the light yoke of the Lord,[9] recognizing and adoring him as the one, true, living God.[10] God has worked these marvels by means of we Spaniards, whom he in his infinite mercy has taken as his instrument for the purpose. Well then, how will we repay the Lord for so glorious a kindness, if not to see that the temples of God, raised by the Christians of old, are not cast down, and that a monster, an idol of a woman, who has made herself head of the Church, reigns no more? The glory to Spain will be no less in casting the devil out of England than in having cast him out of the Indies, nor in restoring the Catholic faith to a mighty and devout kingdom, the first of the first to embrace the faith of Christ openly, than in having first planted it in such far-flung, exotic lands—especially because it will not only be throwing heresy out of England, but also driving and exiling it from practically every other province in Christendom, because, as has been said, the greatest and most perverse heretics have left these places for England, which they have made their lair and stronghold, sustaining themselves by Elizabeth's favor. She is the root, the wellspring, the one who continually stokes this fire, feeds this storm, fans up this foul and pestilential vapor, and spreads and extends it through other regions and kingdoms; and thus, when this root is cut off the branches sustained thereon will wither.[11]

Consider, my lords, if—God forbid—on account of our sins, Spain were afflicted with some tyrannical, heretical king, and Spanish Catholics suffered what the Catholics of England now suffer, how we would wish to be succored and aided, how we would entreat God to move the hearts of the Catholics of other nations to come to our aid and free us, as noble knights and valiant soldiers came from France, Flanders, Germany, and even England to liberate the Spanish Catholics oppressed by the Moors. And so, let us acknowledge the good deed we received then and let us repay it in the same coin; and as we would wish to be helped if we were in a similar predicament or difficulty, let us aid and succor those who are so. Nor is there anyone under heaven who could extend a hand to them, save this unvanquished army of Spaniards, sent like heavenly relief by the Catholic King Don Philip. It is this, then, that pertains to the defense of our Catholic faith, to which the honor and glory of Spain is bound.

Now let us consider the reputation of the king our lord and that of the Spanish nation, which we proffered as the second point and said was entailed in this defensive

---

9   Matt. 11:30.

10   Jer. 10:10.

11   John 15:6.

war. Since Spain was Spain, it has never had the honor it now possesses among every nation of the world, at once because its dominion has never been so broad as now—stretching from the east to the west, from the north to the south—and because of the notable deeds and feats Spaniards have performed in wars in France, Italy, Germany, and Flanders, in Africa, Asia, Europe, and the New World, against Moors and Turks, Christians and pagans, Catholics and heretics. These are so numerous and of such a nature that without question they exceed all those written of the Assyrians, Medes, Persians, Greeks, Latins, Carthaginians, and Romans. And if they were written out—not, I say, with the eloquence and artifice of hyperbolic, mendacious historians, as those of other nations have generally been recorded, but rather with simplicity and truthfulness—they would astound centuries to come and be taken for fables. In this renown and so wide a dominion, our master King Don Philip is the greatest monarch ever seen among Christians: for, setting aside his other kingdoms and territories in Europe—any one of which is enough to exalt any lord, so numerous that they can barely be counted—the borders of his empire are the borders of the world. In his magnificence the east is joined with the west, and the Arctic Pole with the Antarctic (that is, the north with the south), sending his mighty fleets and royal standard to Angola, Congo, Monomotapa,[12] Guinea, Ethiopia, the Arabian Sea, the Persian Gulf, Florida, Santo Domingo, Cuba, Mexico, Peru, Goa, the Malaccas, the islands of Luzon or the Philippines, China, and Japan, encircling the globe [*universo*] without hindrance or obstacle. It it this reputation that has established and preserved peace in Christendom for so many years, that has restrained France, bridled the heretics, beat back the Turks, and pacified the malcontents. And although our nation is not well loved among the others, some because they are subject to us, some because they are troubled that others are so, yet in all these years none has dared to make a move and take up arms against us, fearing their ruin and destruction. Only the states of Flanders have waged war against the king our lord, but less attacking than resisting, not seeking out but struggling and defending themselves against those who seek them in their houses. This they neither would nor could do for any length of time without the backing and support of the queen of England, who, not content to see us expending and pouring out our wealth and capital in this war, is unashamed to seek us at home, loot our ports, and burn our ships, as I have said.

Now, what greater affront or blot to our honor could there be than for it to be said and repeated across the world that a woman who calls herself queen, though she is none, should dare to send a corsair or captain of hers against Spain? That he should ravage our coasts and loot our ports, to burn our ships before our eyes and seize those coming from the East Indies? That he should be lauded and welcomed home in triumph,

---

12   The kingdom of Mutapa in southern Africa, known in Portuguese as "Monomotapa,"
      a quasi-colony of the Portuguese Empire since the mid-sixteenth century.

regaled and feted with celebrations? That comedies should be played in mockery and scorn of us, to his praise and glory—as they have done in England? What will other nations think? What will our own people conclude? What will they say, if this mad and perverse boldness goes unpunished? Perhaps they will say our forbearance is great, or that our timidity is excessive, that we refuse, or are unable, to avenge ourselves! The world is ruled by opinion, and matters of war even more so—by it empires are sustained: while it stands, they do, and as it falls, they fall, and opinion often determines things more than arms and armies. And in nothing at all—after doing what is right as regards God and their realms—should kings and princes be more zealous, more vigilant, or more energetic than in winning, preserving, and increasing that reputation, so that the whole world knows that they will not perpetrate outrages, nor will they allow anyone to perpetrate any against them. For in losing this reputation much is lost, and once lost it is not easily recovered. The entire world fears our power and hates our greatness; we have many outright enemies, and many more hidden ones, as well as false friends. If our reputation is lacking, the outright will find the nerve to attack us, the hidden to reveal themselves and uncover what is in their hearts. Therefore, we must be diligent in punishing the audacious, lest anyone else become audacious, and in curbing the others by punishing Elizabeth, so that in learning out of another's head, they will make no move, nor will the beetles seek to do battle with the eagles,[13] nor the rats with the elephants. Moreover, it will avail us little to have won the name and fame of valiant soldiers, undefeated in previous wars, if we should lose it now, and by removing this restraint that binds and controls all the other states and principalities, to the prejudice of the greatness of our king and lord and that of our nation, give them an opportunity to revolt and rise up against us. It is to prevent this that we have justly waged war in Flanders for so many years, at the cost of so much blood and treasure. For, if the heretics and His Majesty's rebellious subjects should succeed, and the reputation that sustains and subdues our kingdoms should be lost, what hope could we have that the other territories outside Spain would not revolt and abandon their obedience?

Now, what shall I say of the third argument, that of our own advantage and interest—which, though it should not have as much force in Christian hearts as that of religion and zeal for the faith, nor in great-souled ones as that of reputation and honor, such as we have discussed thus far, generally carries a great deal of weight, influencing and moving the majority of men and dominating their counsels and deliberations? It is perfectly just that it should have a place there, and that he who is the protector and defender of the commonwealth (for this is what it is to be a king), attentive to the interests of his vassals, should strive with all his might to divert and stave off all

---

13 An allusion to Aesop's fable of the dung beetle and the eagle (Perry 3): see, e.g., *Aesop's Fables*, trans. Laura Gibbs, Oxford World's Classics (Oxford: Oxford University Press, 2002), 77–78.

that might do them harm, and to consolidate and increase all that is to their good or advantage. First of all, we know well how much the war with the states of Flanders has cost this kingdom, how Spain has been bled dry and consumed to sustain it, preferring to lose its wealth than the obedience of those provinces, together with its reputation, as I said, without which the rest cannot be preserved. Well then, this war: when will it come to an end? When will its calamities and our injuries conclude? Its devastations and our undoing? To abandon what has been begun is not possible, to pursue it and sustain such excessive costs for long is supremely difficult, for there is no hope that the war will end, so long as Elizabeth lives and England urges it on. For the Flemings have now become soldiers through use of arms, and even fortified many towns, having been incited against our nation, and many of them, being heretics, wish to enjoy their liberties and license. It would be wrong to yield to their efforts against the Catholic faith and against God, nor are there any prospects of winning them over with flattery, nor bringing them around with promises, nor convincing them with kindly treatment and compromises, especially as they are light and always find someone to preach to them and persuade them to the contrary. If God is pleased that this business should end—as it is to be hoped he will be—it will be by force of arms, just as it began. But if he does not extend his hand, it does not seem humanly possible that it will end as long as the rebels retain the aid and assistance they presently have. For the Spanish garrison, the principal force with which one must still contend to control those states, is every day depleted and must be continually replenished and reinforced with new men, who must be sent from Spain, which cannot be done without extreme expense and effort, while our foes have assistance ready to hand, since one may pass from England to Zealand and Holland in a few hours: our means of attack are utterly overextended, while they have the means of resistance almost within their very houses. Thus far, we have clearly seen that until they are stripped of these forces, it will be difficult to overcome them. They have no power but that of the English: the empire is quiet; France has already done what it could, and now they could do nothing, even if they wished to; the other monarchs either cannot or will not. Only Elizabeth remains, a heretic and an enemy to God and us, willing and—being so close—able to strengthen them and prolong the war, to our disquiet and the loss of our treasure and our lives. If we wish this war to end, that of England must commence: once this wicked root is cut off, the tree it sustains will fall.[14] So long as the winds blowing from England last, the storm will last, and so long as she throws wood upon the fire, it will burn—like physicians trying to cure a flux [*corrimiento*] that descends from the head to the chest, who work to diminish and evacuate the flowing humor from the weakened and diseased part, but primarily strive to cure the head, which continually produces and distills the humor, in order to sever its root and source, so we, if we want to heal this prolonged and costly

---

14   John 15:6.

sickness of the war in Flanders, must turn to the origin and source whence it feeds, which is the queen of England. For as long as she distills and sends out her forces, her evil humors, there will always be flux and pain, and as long as the cause of the disease lasts, its effects will last, and commonplace though the comparison and analogy may be, nevertheless I offer it because it is true and makes clear what we intend. However much care is taken to clean the house and remove the cobwebs, so long as the spider who wove them lives, there will be more; so long as this wicked spider lives in England, weaving her plots and spinning webs of treason and chaos in Flanders and His Majesty's other realms, we shall perforce have them still. And so, to conclude this argument, I say that Spain will not cease to be consumed and bled dry in sending off fodder for the war in Flanders every year: we must seek new means to bring it to an end, and I see no other, neither stronger nor more efficient, than to bring the war to England, and spend in one year, with hopes of certain successes, what would otherwise be spent over many years.[15] For, deprived of England's strength, Holland and Zealand will soon surrender. This is to do to Elizabeth what she has done to His Majesty and to the other princes her neighbors—that is, to kindle a fire in their houses so that she may have peace in her own; to unsettle theirs to her utter delight, as though watching from the stands while they are on the bull's horns. And thus this war with England is a defensive war, as has been said, for therein His Majesty defends his territories in Flanders, brings so costly a war to a permanent conclusion, and puts an end to the enormous, unending expenses that must continue so long as it lasts—and by this Spain shall have some relief and tranquility, which is all we seek.

But this is not the only benefit to follow from this war. We are not simply seeking to extract His Majesty from necessity and to free him from the obligation to spend outside the realm what the realm gives him, but rather to ensure that the wealth, treasure, and property of the entire kingdom should not be lost and destroyed all at once, as would doubtless be the result if the queen and her council succeed in their plots. For they can do much more than distract the king our lord with uprisings and rebellions in Flanders, or infest the ocean sea, or hinder the merchants' commerce, or seize one or two of the ships that come unprotected from the Indies and steal the property of a few private traders—seeing that the wealth and might of Spain depends on the millions in gold and silver and the inestimable riches in pearls, precious stones, and spices that come each year from both Indies, that the sustenance and life of these realms hangs upon this trade and the regular and safe voyages of the fleets, they seek to take them, [...][16] and to take the Indies themselves from us, or at least to disrupt the

---

15   The Spanish is difficult here; I have followed the emendation offered in MHSIR, 2:361, footnote c.

16   The editors of MHSIR suggest that at least one word is missing here. MHSIR, 2:362, footnote a.

course of the voyages and pillage the fleets, to afflict and devastate these realms and undo at a stroke all their magnificence and wealth. This was their aim a few years ago in entering the Straits of Magellan and stealing an enormous sum of gold and silver in Peru, and now this same thing has again befallen that kingdom.[17] They attempted the very same feat, with even greater boldness and arrogance, two years ago, when they went to the islands of Santo Domingo, seized and looted the island of Cartagena, and spent three days before Havana with the same intention, causing countless disasters and outrages in every part. The fleets themselves would have fallen into their hands, had God not well-nigh miraculously preserved them.[18] And to prove to us that their daring grows by our patience and forbearance and that heresy is shameless and fool-hardy, this year they have raided our Armada in the port of Cádiz and burned or seized part of it, as well as several laden ships from the Indies, and attempted to intercept our fleets and inflict upon us every calamity that can be feared from their senseless schem-ing. And if these evils are not cut off they will doubtless grow, and each year we shall see ourselves amid further cares and new pressures and dilemmas, and what has not happened this year may perchance come to pass in another, and Spain shall have much to lament. And if God, on account of our sins and our negligence, should permit it, the Englishwoman, augmenting her powers through her outrages and her robberies, could unsettle and disturb the territories of the Indies—so distant, unarmed, vulnerable to discontent and unrest, and exposed to any sort of attack. Even if she could not seize or hold them, these facts should give us something to contemplate and consider. This must be stopped, and there is no better way than cutting off the root, as has been said. Thus I say that in this war are defended the wealth and property of the entire kingdom, and its peace, quiet, and tranquility. This is not the affair of the few, but of the many. It does not touch the merchants and businessmen alone—although if it related only to them, that would be sufficient cause to undertake the war, because without them neither the royal patrimony nor the commonwealth can be sustained. Rather, all are concerned in the provision of the maiden, the support of the widow,[19] the protection of the child, the maintenance of the monasteries, the preservation of the hospitals, the feeding of the poor, the security of the workers, the tranquility of the citizens, the honor of the knights and lords. I shall go further: the greatness and honor of our king

17   Late in 1578, Francis Drake passed through the Straits of Magellan and headed north toward Spanish holdings in northwest South America. In the first months of 1579, he seized several rich prizes off the coast of Peru, including the treasure ship *Nuestra Señora de la Concepción*. Kelsey, "Drake," in *ODNB*, 16:862,

18   On January 1, 1586, Drake occupied the city of Santo Domingo, extorting a ransom from the citizens—and then torching the city anyway. A month later, he seized Cartagena de Indias in modern-day Colombia, again receiving a substantial ransom. Sailing to Cuba, the Englishmen looted and burned the fort of San Augustín. Ibid., 16:863.

19   1 Tim. 5:3.

and the peace of the entire realm depend in large part on this trade and commerce and the safe annual fleets from the Indies, which the queen of England wishes to take from us. And so, my lords, do not imagine that in this expedition Your Mercies invade that realm; rather, you defend your own and all I have mentioned here, and much more besides—which there is no need to set out and embellish with words, being likewise grasped by your discernment and prudence. For if this war defends, as we have seen, our sacred and Catholic religion, what Catholic Christian would not embark upon it with joy? If it defends the honor of Spain, what Spaniard will not strive for the fame and glory of his nation? If it defends the reputation of our king, so wise, so just, so moderate and mighty, upon whom depends the wellbeing of all of Christendom, what vassal will not show his loyalty, his zeal, his valor? If our property, if our lives, if our happiness are at risk, and can have no security save through the punishment of this Elizabeth and her ministers, who will not seize the sword and embrace the shield and brandish the lance, and shed their blood to protect and secure the land where he was born, to save the ship on which he sails, for his law, for his kingdom, for his king, and for his God?

Though we are not going to spill our blood, my lords, on this campaign, nor to lose our lives, yet they would be well lost, for these many righteous causes. Instead, we are going to take life from the heretics, and to give it to countless Catholics of the kingdom of England. We shall claim as our prize the riches, the infinite treasures that belonged to the churches and temples of God, now usurped by Elizabeth and her impious ministers. We shall loot and despoil a realm rich with our loot and our spoils, with many years of peace from our many years of war. We go to an easy task, if there is Spanish heart and valor within us, such that to begin it is to end it. In the seventy years since the pestilential sect of Martin Luther began, every time the Catholics have fought the heretics, they have defeated them—in Germany, in Switzerland, in France, in Flanders, and in England itself—God always favoring his truth and his most holy religion. So much so that a few Catholic soldiers have many times put hordes of heretics to flight, and with a small band overcome enormous hosts. For God was fighting alongside them: and it shall be just the same now, since the cause is the same, and even better in many ways. For none of the previous wars occurred in such circumstances, none was waged for God and against wickedness so much as this one. For in this one, we are going to undo a tyranny founded upon incest and lust, fed with the innocent blood of countless martyrs, sustained by outrages and the excessive sufferance of the other princes. We are going to destroy a nest of vipers, a den of thieves,[20] a ditch and cesspit of poisons [*garrulaciones*] and noxious vapors, a university and school of plague, to behead a woman who has made herself the head of the Church, and ordered the beheading of a queen of France and Scotland for being a Catholic, her own niece and successor,

20   Matt. 21:13; Luke 19:46.

who entered her realm under her devilish word. Let no one be frightened to hear someone say "England." We go against a weak women, naturally quite fearful, propped up in
power by her own sins, and exalted to a royal throne so that her fall might be the more
miserable; against a woman who is no legitimate queen, both because she herself is
illegitimate, having been born to an outrageous union condemned by the Apostolic
See, and because she has been deprived of her realm by Pope Pius v of holy memory;
against a heretical, bloodthirsty woman, the daughter of Henry viii, the daughter of
Anne Boleyn, the imitator of such parents. She is surrounded by a pack of councilors
and ministers as impious as she, prompt to kindle wars in unwitting foreign kingdoms
by stealth and deceit, but cowards in any fight of their own. We go against a woman tormented by her own conscience, the foe of every Christian prince and hated by them,
ill loved by her own subjects; who has her forces divided in Holland, Zealand, Ireland,
and Scotland, who can hope for no aid from without her kingdom, and who fears an
uprising within. For the Catholics—who are, without doubt, the majority, oppressed
by her tyranny—upon seeing our banners, upon the appearance of our fleets, will
take up arms for the Catholic faith and their freedom, while the heretics themselves
are so changeable, so fond of novelty, and so wearied of those in power that although
it would be for nothing but to govern themselves and see themselves free of them,
they are pleased with any change or transformation, to which that kingdom has always been subject—we know of no other Christian land that with such great ease and
such little excuse rises up in arms against their king, many times seizing their crowns
and taking their thrones. An English writer known by the name of Gildas, called "the
Wise" on account of his surpassing erudition, wrote of these same English more than a
thousand years ago, *Britani neque in bello fortes, neque in pace fideles*—that the English
are neither valiant in war nor faithful in peace.[21] Their lack of loyalty they have often
shown in rebellions and uprisings against their rulers, as I say, and their lack of spirit in
the wars they have waged against other nations, in which they have always been overcome and subjugated. There is hardly a nation that has ever attacked them that has
not defeated and conquered them. They imagine that they are secure in their realm,
and when no one assails or resists them, they brag and think themselves valiant, and
they lack neither industry nor cunning in robbing like bandits and plaguing the sea.
But when hands are put to it [*se viene a las manos*], then they are revealed for what
they are. Does not experience teach us this? Have the English not lost all they had
in Aquitaine and in Normandy?[22] In our own times, did they not lose the county of

---

21   "In fact, it became a mocking proverb far and wide that the British are cowardly in war
      and faithless in peace." Gildas, *Ruin of Britain*, 18.
22   English holdings in Aquitaine, and in Gascony more generally, were definitively lost to
      the French in 1453, during the chaotic reign of Henry vi (r.1422–61, 1470–71). The duchy
      of Normandy had been reconquered by the French from King John (r.1199–1216) in 1204.

Boulogne? Did they not shamefully surrender to their French enemies Guînes and the fortress of Calais, which they had retained for almost four hundred years and which they deemed impregnable?[23] In our own days, the Spanish have only clashed with the English a few times, but in these few they have always overwhelmed them [*las han llevado en la cabeza*], fighting in the provinces of Flanders, where at the siege of Sluis [*Inclusa*] we have recently seen how little they are worth. When the duke of Parma appeared with the Spanish army—few in men, but very distinguished—the town was defended by its strong position and its large garrison of Walloon and English soldiers, while the earl of Leicester, captain general of the English and their governor in Holland and Zealand, had come to their aid with a huge number of English ships and soldiers. But he lost his nerve, and instead, before his eyes and to his dismay, the place was taken and yielded to His Majesty.[24] Yet, is it any wonder that an Englishman dares not look upon the face of the Spaniard, who has outfaced [*a quien reconocen ventaja*] the mightiest powers? Is it any wonder that the heretic should be weak and cowardly, he who has not the true faith and with it the strength and virtue of God? True religion has always had fortitude and wisdom for companions and sisters, and when religion is lost, they are lost, and when it is preserved, they are preserved, as experience teaches us. For this reason, those who were valiant and invincible when they had the true religion become cowards and turn their backs to the foe once they lose it, and we could say the same of wisdom.

We are going, my lords, we are going, we are going in contentment and joy, we are going upon an enterprise glorious, honorable, necessary, advantageous, and easy. Advantageous to God, to his Church, to his saints, to our nation. To God, who, in chastisement of England, has allowed himself to be exiled thence, and permitted that the holy sacrifice of the Mass no longer be offered there; to his Church, which is oppressed by its foes, the English heretics; to the saints, who have been abused, insulted, and

Ralph A. Griffiths, *The Reign of King Henry VI: The Exercise of Royal Authority, 1422–1461* (Berkeley: University of California Press, 1981), 805. Stephen Church, *King John: England, Magna Carta and the Making of a Tyrant* (Basingstoke: Macmillan, 2015), 119–21.

23   On January 7, 1558, French forces took the city of Calais, an English possession since 1347, followed a few days later by the fall of the garrison at Guînes (or Guisnes). Edwards, *Mary I*, 309–14.

24   In the summer of 1587, Alessandro Farnese, duke of Parma and governor of the Spanish Netherlands (1545–92), besieged the Dutch port of Sluis, which was garrisoned with English troops. The earl of Leicester, governor-general of the United Provinces, failed to relieve the town, hamstrung by difficulties coordinating with his Dutch allies. Following the fall of Sluis on August 4, and a few unsuccessful attacks on nearby cities, Leicester withdrew from the Low Countries in ignominy. Martin and Parker, *Spanish Armada*, 126.

burned there; to our nation, of which our Lord has been pleased to make use in so great a matter. Necessary for the honor of our king; necessary for the security of our realms; necessary for the preservation of the Indies and of the fleets and riches and treasures they send us. Advantageous, so that by God's favor the war in Flanders may come to an end, and with it the need to draw our blood, our lives, our substance from Spain and dispatch it thither to sustain the fight. Advantageous in the spoils and riches we shall win from England, as we return home laden with them and with glory and victory, by God's favor. We are going to an easy undertaking, for God our Lord, whose cause and most holy religion we defend, goes before us, and with such a captain we have nothing to fear. The saints of heaven go in our company, and especially the patrons of Spain and the holy protectors of England itself, who have been persecuted by the English heretics and desire and beg vengeance from God: they will lead the way, and welcome and favor us. And besides the other blessed saints who await us there, who planted our celestial, holy faith there with their lives and their teachings, or who watered it with their blood, we shall find upon our side the blood of the sainted John Fisher, cardinal and bishop of Rochester, of Thomas More, of John Forest, and of innumerable religious—the Carthusians, the Franciscans, the Bridgettines, and the other orders— cruelly shed by Henry and crying out to God from the ground where it spilled, demanding vengeance.[25] And no less the blood of Edmund Campion, of Thomas Cottam, fathers of the Society of Jesus, of Ralph Sherwin [*Corbino*], of Alexander Briant, and of countless other venerable priests and servants of God, whom his daughter Elizabeth has mangled with atrocious and exquisite tortures. And that of the holy, innocent Mary Queen of Scots, which is yet fresh and wet, and with its ardor, heat, and copious abundance demonstrates the cruelty and impiety of this Jezebel and casts volleys against her. There we are awaited by the groans of infinite oppressed Catholics; by the tears of all the widows who lost their husbands rather than lose their faiths; the sighs of innumerable maidens, forced either to give their lives and their wealth or to destroy their souls; the children and youngsters who will be lost, unless there be some remedy, being reared on the poisoned milk of heresy. Lastly, the numberless number of laborers, citizens, gentlemen, knights, lords, priests, of all ranks: the Catholic people, who are afflicted and oppressed and abused by the heretics, and who await us for their liberation. Upon our side go faith, justice, truth, the blessing of the pope, who holds the place of God upon the earth, the wishes of all good people, the prayers and entreaties of the entire Catholic Church. God is mightier than the devil, truth than falsehood, the Catholic faith than heresy, the saints and angels of heaven than all the power of hell, the invincible spirit and puissant arm of Spain than the downcast souls and weak and slack bodies of the heretics. We lack nothing, my lords, but to go with a pure and good conscience and a clean heart, afire with love and zeal for the glory of God, the

25   Gen. 4:10.

honest intention to fight first and foremost for the Catholic faith and for our law and our king and our kingdom. Let us live a Christian life, without scandal or public offense to God; let there be in us devotion toward him, unity and brotherhood among the soldiers, obedience to the captains, Spanish spirit, strength, and valor. For with this there is nothing to fear, and victory is ours.

Ribadeneyra's Letter-*Memorial* on the Causes of the Armada's Failure (Probably to Juan de Idiáquez y Olazábal)[1]

MHSIR, 2:105–11; Rey, 1350–55.

If it should seem unusual or inappropriate to write what I am to say here, I entreat Your Lordship to pardon me, for it is only love and zeal in the royal service that moves me to it, and the belief that, as His Majesty is our king and sovereign lord, all of his vassals are obliged to wish and strive for his happiness and prosperity—and the religious even more so, since the good of all Christendom now hangs upon His Majesty's fortunes.

Though the judgments of God our Lord are most secret,[2] and therefore we cannot know for certain his divine majesty's intentions in the truly extraordinary fate he has given His Majesty's mighty Armada, yet, seeing that in a cause so much his own, undertaken with such holy intentions, embraced throughout these realms, and desired and aided by the entire Catholic Church, he did not deign to give ear to the pious pleas and tears of so many of his own glorious servants, it makes us fear that there are weighty reasons for God our Lord having sent us this trial, and for them lasting, as it may be, as long as they shall last. Now, since he does nothing by chance, nor does a single leaf fall from a tree save by his will[3] (which he often manifests in the variable outcomes of things that depend upon that will alone), it is a perfectly reasonable thing, and quite salutary, to inquire into and reflect upon the reasons God might have had for not granting us this mercy. For my part, I am certain that he does not wish to deny it to us, but rather to put it off for a short time, and in the meanwhile to do us many and greater and more important mercies, of which we have greater need.[4] And that one of these is to sanctify His Majesty, giving him an opportunity to humble himself beneath the Lord's mighty hand; to consider the enormous power he has given him, and how little this strength is worth without him; to be truly zealous for his honor, taking this as the goal of every counsel and placing it before every other interest and aim; not to

---

1 Rey, 1355n.

2 Rom. 11:33.

3 Cf. Matt. 10:29; Luke 12:6.

4 This seems to bear some relation to Ribadeneyra's citation of Augustine in the *Tratado de la tribulación* to the effect "When God delays, and does not immediately give what we beg of him, it is not to deny us his gifts, but to make us esteem them." Ribadeneyra, *Tratado de la tribulacion*, 208ʳ.

despair in adversity, but rather turn to him with renewed spirit and strength, trusting in him and learning that, like a father, he chastises and punishes him in order to reward and encourage him all the more. And so signal is this mercy that, for the sake of His Majesty's soul and also for the true prosperity of his realms, it is of greater advantage and importance than the conquest of the kingdom of England. And at the same time, our Lord has chosen to try our faith, revive our hopes, enflame our prayers, reform our customs, purify our intentions, and cleanse them of the filth of our private interests and worldly security, which many sought in this enterprise—perhaps with greater zeal than the exaltation of our sacred faith and the good of the lost souls of the English.

But, leaving aside the benefits we may take from the Armada's outcome, I wish to place here the things that, after prayer and much reflection, have occurred to me as having possibly been the causes of this universal scourging and chastisement, so that if Your Lordship judges them to have legs [*lleuan camino*], you might convey them to His Majesty in the manner you think best. For I seek only to fulfill my obligation as a subject and a religious (though unworthy) of the Society of Jesus to look to the felicity of His Majesty and of the realm, and the exaltation of our holy Catholic faith. What is more, it has also occurred to me to speak further of how utterly necessary it remains to prosecute the war and seek out the foe, if we do not wish him to seek us out and make war upon us at home.

First, that His Majesty should provide for the relief of the many subjects in his realm, especially in Andalusia, who have been oppressed by his ministers and despoiled of their livelihoods and their children's wherewithal under the name and strength of justice, neither compensated nor heard, but rather harassed and tormented for seeking to defend their property. As I understand it, this came about with such extreme excess and violence that before the Armada departed I heard thoughtful, God-fearing persons say that it could not possibly meet with success, since it left burdened by the sweat and the curses of so many wretched people, whom the Lord always recognizes and hears—especially when it is known that much of what was taken, though taken in the name of His Majesty and of the Armada, was not for his royal service, but rather to enrich those who took it.

Second, that His Majesty, in his great wisdom, should consider and examine, or order to be examined by men of learning, conscience, and zeal in serving the crown, why so enormous and so rich a patrimony as His Majesty's should show so little [*luzga tan poco*] and waste away so much. If indeed the cause is some disservice to God our Lord in some part, or in the means of collecting it, we must remove everything that offends his divine eyes. When Pope Saint Gregory wrote to the empress charging her to request the emperor her husband to take pity on the towns of Sicily and Sardinia, which were deeply oppressed by wars, taxes, and abuses, he said, "Your Majesty will tell me that everything gathered from the taxes of these islands is spent on the wars. I reply, *Idcirco fortasse tantae expensae in hac terra minus ad vtilitatem percipiuntur, quia cum peccati aliqua commixtione colliguntur; retur, quia cum peccati aliqua commixtione colliguntur;*

recipient ergo serenissimi domini, nihil cum peccato."[5] It may well be that this was the cause of the reversal. And even if it was not, but rather the poor administration of the patrimony and the untrustworthiness of those who manage it, it is crucial to find a remedy in an issue of such weight, severely punishing, as public thieves and destroyers of the commonwealth, those who embezzle and favoring those who govern it as they should. From not doing so, the wicked take wings for the one and the good slacken and lose heart for the other. Moreover, we ought to take the utmost care in this because wealth is the sinews of war,[6] while in peacetime it is the bit of kingdoms, making them obey rather than running wild, in the knowledge that the king is powerful. And all the more diligence is called for because His Majesty's wealth is not his alone, but rather that of all his realms, or, properly speaking, of all Christendom, since it is for their benefit, and therefore all this must be thoroughly examined.

Third, that His Majesty should carefully examine and investigate whether in the English affairs that have arisen since our Lord made him king thereof, he has valued the security of his position more than the glory of God and the expansion of the Catholic faith, and whether, so as not to offend the queen of England, he has failed to support those whom, because they are Catholics and loyal to God, she persecutes and harasses. For God our Lord is jealous of his honor,[7] and desires that all Christians—and princes all the more so—strive to further it and be as zealous in this as they are in their power and lordship over other men. He severely punishes any oversight in this, often through the means of those whom they most wished to please and whom they esteemed more than God's honor and the support of his faith. And if there has been any negligence in this, let His Majesty be stricken thereat and strive in all his counsels and deliberations ever to hold the honor and glory of God as his target and chiefest aim, by which everything else that concerns his interests or status is to be regulated and measured.

---

5   On June 1, 595, Gregory I wrote to Constantina (*c.*560–*c.*605), the wife of Emperor Maurice (r.582–602) concerning imperial exactions upon Sicily and Sardinia: "I know that he will say that whatever is collected from the above-mentioned islands is sent over to us for the expenses of Italy. But I suggest that even if less is contributed to expenditure in Italy, yet he should free his empire from the tears of the oppressed. For that reason also, perhaps, all of that expenditure in this land contributes less to its goodness, because the taxes are collected with some admixture of sin. And so let our most serene Lordship order that nothing should be collected through sin." Gregory I, *The Letters of Gregory the Great*, ed. and trans. John R.C. Martyn, 3 vols., Mediaeval Sources in Translation 40 (Toronto: Pontifical Institute of Mediaeval Studies, 2004), 2:354–55.

6   In the fifth *Philippic* (43 BCE), Cicero calls money "the sinews of war [*nervos belli*]." Marcus Tullius Cicero, *Cicero, Philippics 3–9*, ed. and trans. Gesine Manuwald, 2 vols., Texte und Kommentare (Berlin: Walter de Gruyter, 2007), 1:203–04.

7   Isa. 42:8.

Fourth, that greater care should be taken in eliminating sins and public scandals, especially among exalted persons, who must set an example—the bad one they offer infects and corrupts the commonwealth. And as His Majesty is the head and lord thereof, and may so easily amend and correct these excesses with but a single sign of his will, it is clear that our Lord will be able to demand an account of what he does not do.

Fifth, that His Majesty should consider whether it befits his royal person to interfere in the governance of spiritual things as he now does, for it seems to many thoughtful and God-fearing persons that it does not. For, although they assuredly know His Majesty's pious spirit, and that he is moved to this out of zeal for the wellbeing of the religious orders and encouraged by the religious themselves,[8] nevertheless they consider the consequent harms to the religious to be greater, because it foments among them division and a dearth of the charity that is the life and soul of every order, as they bruit among the laity the faults of the religious and besmirch their characters. It furnishes an excuse for other princes and kings, who have not the zeal that God has given His Majesty, to do the same, to imagine themselves to be lords over the orders, empowered to dictate to them, saying that since a king as Catholic and devout as His Majesty does so, they can do likewise. Lastly, we must look to our consciences, and to what may in time befall our Spain, if God our Lord should permit the reign of some headstrong, capricious king, ready to lay his hands upon everything, one who in the name of religion would corrupt the orders, justifying himself with His Majesty's example, though he had neither His Majesty's moderation nor his holy intentions.

The final thing—of no less importance than the rest—is that His Majesty recognize that the greatest treasure of his realm is the abundance, not of gold and silver, nor of revenues, nor of anything else pertaining to the needs, delights, or grandeur of human life, but rather the supply in abundance of valiant and great-hearted men, who can serve as pillars of the commonwealth in war and peace, and that though His Majesty is a mighty king, the greatest monarch there has ever been among Christians, he has a sore lack of such men, as has been demonstrated by the outcome of the expedition. And that these men are not born already fashioned, but rather must be formed through the experience of time, and that this will not happen unless they are given the opportunity, and honored and rewarded by those they serve well. For, although the Spanish are haughty and opposed to learning, and generally want to begin where others end, yet they are deeply loyal and obedient to their king, prompt in diligence and duty. And if His Majesty should support them and give them work, and reward those who serve him well, I know there would be men enough for all His Majesty's realms

---

8 Philip II was an enthusiastic proponent of the Tridentine changes in Catholicism, brooking no resistance to his program of often-drastic reforms to the many religious orders in his domains. Kamen, *Philip of Spain*, 103–04.

and for all the offices of war and peace, for *honos alit artes*, as Tullius says.[9] And this is of even greater importance because the king our lord is now old and wearied, and has need of people to relieve him and to look after his life and health (so crucial for the entire Catholic Church), and because the prince our lord is still too young to possess the strength needed to govern so many kingdoms.

---

9   "esteem nourishes the arts." Marcus Tullius Cicero, *Tusculan Disputations*, ed. and trans. A.E. Douglas, 2 vols. (Chicago: Bolchazy-Carducci, 1990), 1:22–23.

Luis de Granada on the *Historia*

Pedro de Ribadeneyra, *Obras del Padre Pedro de Ribadeneyra de la Compañia de Iesus, agora de nueuo reuistas y acrecentadas* (Madrid: Luis Sanchez, 1605), 2.

Very Reverend Father in Christ,

I know not how to repay Your Paternity the diligence with which you provide me with the fruits of your labors, and especially with this history of England, which I consider akin to those sacred histories where are recounted (as here) the outrages of wicked kings and the devastation of religion in the days of Manasseh,[1] and Zedekiah,[2] and in the first of the Maccabees.[3] I read the entire book from cover to cover, and shed many tears at various places, most of all at the death of the queen of Scotland. The favorites and advisers of princes have here a superb lesson, wherein they shall see that adage fulfilled, *Malum consilium consultori pessimum.*[4] And they shall see how the pretensions of ascending to the heights by artifice and human means, without the fear of God, end in spectacular falls. For that wretched Archbishop Wolsey, not content with the place to which the world had raised him from the dust of the earth,[5] aspired to become pope. May our Lord repay Your Paternity the labor of this book, which must produce considerable fruit in anyone who reads it. I say nothing of the style, for it was born of Your Paternity, and that is all I needed to know to praise this work—and so as to say nothing of it, I conclude, entreating our Lord to remain ever in the soul of Your Paternity. From Lisbon, August 13, 1588.

Fray Luis de Granada

---

1   4 Kings 21; 2 Chron. 33.

2   4 Kings 24:18–19; Jer. 52:2–3.

3   1 Macc. 1.

4   This Latin tag, translated by John W. Rich as "Bad counsel to the counsellor is worst," comes from the Roman grammarian Marcus Verrius Flaccus (*c.*55 BCE–20 CE), whose work survives only in fragments. Flaccus himself seems to have taken it from the Greek poet Hesiod (*fl. c.*700 BCE). T.J. Cornell, ed., *The Fragments of the Roman Historians.* 3 vols. (Oxford: Oxford University Press, 2013), 2:22–23.

5   Gen. 2:7

John Cecil's Letter to Joseph Cresswell, September 20, 1591

ABSI Stonyhurst, Collectanea M, fol. 187ff.

Eboraci mense Aprilis A. 1591. Robertus Thorpus sacerdos Coll. Rhem. alumnus bonum certamen certauit cursum consummauit. neq[ue] v⁰. ad altare sine ministro ascendit felicissimus Martyr habuit enim & vitæ ... et martyrij comitem Ths. Watkinsonum laicum, cuius ope et opera uberrimè et diu in vinea D'ni usus fuerat. Wintoniæ item mense Julij nulla in re dispar, par martyrū pubᶜᵒ. ōnium Catholicorū applausu in Cœlum migrauit. nomina fuerunt Sacerdotis Rogˢ. Dikinsonus, laici Rodulphus Milnerus: et hic quidem cum a Judice iniqua : esset admonitus ut insanie desineret, ut sibi, coniugi adolescentulæ liberisq[ue] octo ... tenellis consuleret, de patibulo descenderet, templumq[ue] Caluinistorum vel semel tantum transiret, respondit stultum esse pro. re tam momentanea et caduca perpetuam a'iæ suæ iacturam facere. Eadem de causa, nimirum quod dᵐ. sacerdotem in ædibus recepissent & in eod. tribunali tanq[uam] læsæ maiestatis reæ declaratæ sunt nobiles quædā virginis num⁰. 7. ac sententiam Judices præ pudore pronunciare noluerunt. illæ autem instare rogare lachrymari, ne a suo dulcissº parte et charissimij socijs abstraherentur. &c. / . Londine eodem mense passi sunt duo sacerdᵉˢ. in plateâ <u>Fleetstreet</u> summâ cum constantia et fratrum suorum ædifico'ne, quorum alter v'r Georgius Beseleyus ante mortem varijs et exquisississimis tormentis exagitatus est, ut nobiles quosdam Cathᶜᵒˢ. proderet, quibus cum tractauerat, a quibus fuerat exceptus, sed frustra. Interrogatus an si iuberet Papa ut reginam interficeret, faceret nec ne? respondit Papam tale aliquid non iussurum, verum si iuberet meritorium esse si exequeretur. / . Mense Augusti captus est Thomas Pormortus Coll. Rom: alumnus et in Bridsuellum ad torturā coniectus. / . Cum Beseleyo passus est grauississimus et sanctiss'. vir Monfordus Scottus qui tanta cū suauitate et modestia mortem obijt ut ipsi et' hæretici obstupescerent; unde gloriari postea solebat Toplife / ... se reginæ et regno illo die maximum praestitisse beneficium, quod papistam ieiunijs orationibus ac vigilijs tam insigniter præ cæteris delictum è medio sustulisset. / .... Charissimus frater nʳ. Thomas Stanney Collⁱ. vestri alumnus in unica Prouᵃ. Hamptoniensi a'ias trecentas Xᵃ. Dr'o luctatus est. / .

Juan López Manzano's *Breve Catalogo*

ABSI Stonyhurst A.1. fol. 53
BREVE CATALOGO DE LOS MARTYRES QUE HAN SIDO DE LOS DOS COLLE-GIOS Y SEMINARIOS INGLESES, QUE RESIDEN EN ROMA, Y EN LA CIUDAD DE RHEMIS DE FRANCIA, LOS QUALES HAN PADECIDOS TORMENTOS Y muertes en Inglaterra, en estos treze años passados, por la defension de la Fee Catholica, Por mandado de la Reyna, fuera de otros muchos de todo genero de personas, que tambien han sido martyrizados, aunque no eran destos Collegios.

Recogido por el Padre Iuan Lopez Mançano, de la Compañia de IESVS, Rector del Collegio Ingles de Valladolid, Conforme a las cartas y informaciones recebidas de los Sacerdotes que andan en aquel Reyno, procurando la conseruacion y augmento de la Fee.

Año del Señor. 1577.
CVTBERTO MAYN Presbitero, y Licēciado en Theologia, Protomartyr de los Seminarios. Fue del Collegio de Rhemis.

Año del Señor. 1578.
IVAN Nelson presbitero, del Collegio de Rhemis.
Thomas Shiruod, mancebo estudiāte, del Coll. de Rhemis.

Año del Señor. 1581.
EVERARDO HANS presbitero del Colle. de Rhemis.
Edmundo Campiano, Licenciado en Theologia. El qual fue primeramente del Collegio de Rhemis. Despues entro en la Compañia de IESVS, y finalmente murio muy gloriosamēte por confessiō de la Fe en Lōdres de Inglaterra.
Rodulpho Shiruino presb. del Colle. de Roma, y protomartir de aquel colleg. y cōpañero en la muerte del P. Cāpiano
Alexander Brianto presbitero, del Collegio de Rhemis, murio juntamente con el Padre Campiano, y Shiruino.

Año del Señor. 1582.
IVAN PAYN presbytero, del Collegio de Rhemis.
Thomas Ford presb. del Coll. de Rhemis, y Licenciado en theologia.
Roberto Ionsono presbitero, del Collegio de Rhemis.

Gulliermo Filbey presbitero, del Collegio de Rhemis. Lorenço Ionsono presbitero, del Collegio de Roma.

Iuan Cotan presbitero, del Collegio de Roma, y despues religioso de la Compañia de IESVS.

Guillermo Lacy, presbitero, del Collegio de Roma.

Ricardo Kirkman presbitero, del Collegio Rhemis.

Diego Tomson presbitero, del Collegio de Rhemis.

Iuan Shirt presbitero, del Collegio de Roma.

Lucas Kirbey presbitero, del Collegio de Roma.

Año del Señor. 1583.

GVILLERMO HARTO presbit. del Colleg. de Roma.

Ricardo Thirkild presbitero, del Collegio de Rhemis.

Iuan Body, y Iuan Slado Estudiantes, del Collegio de Rhemis, y muy Illustes [*sic*] martyres.

Guillermo Chaplē presbitero, del Collegio de Rhemis, murio en la carcel.

Año del Señor. 1584.

IORGE HADOQUE presbitero, del Collegio de Roma.

Iuan Mundin presbitero, del Collegio de Roma.

Diego Fen presbitero, del Collegio de Rhemis.

Thomas Emerford presbitero, del Collegio de Roma.

Iuan Nutter presbitero, del Collegio de Rhemis.

Thomas Cotesmor presbitero, del Collegio de Rhemis.

Roberto Holmis presbitero del Collegio de Rhemis.

Diego Lumax presbitero, del Collegio de Roma.

Año del Señor. 1585.

THOMAS CROVCHER presb. del Colleg. de Rhemis.

Thomas Aufeld presbitero, del Collegio de Rhemis.

Vgo Tayler presbitero, del Collegio de Rhemis.

Duarte Poli presbitero, del Collegio de Rhemis.

Lorenço Vaux pres. del Colleg. de Rhemis murio en carcel.

Año del Señor. 1586.

DVARTE TRANSAMO pres. del Colle. de Rhemis.

Nicolas Vvodfen presbitero, del Collegio de Rhemis.

Ricardo Sergeant presbitero, del Collegio de Rhemis.

Guillermo Tomson presbitero, del Collegio de Rhemis.

Roberto Anderton presbitero, del Collegio de Rhemis.

Guillermo Marsden presbitero, del Collegio de Rhemis.
Francisco Ingelbey presbitero, del Collegio de Rhemis.
Roberto Dibdal presbitero, del Collegio de Rhemis.
Iuan Adams presbitero, del Collegio de Remis.
Iuan Loe presbitero, del Collegio de Roma.
Esteuan Ransam presbitero, del Collegio de Rhemis.
Iuan Finglo presbitero, del Collegio de Rhemis.
Iuan Harrison pres. del Colle. de Rhemis, murio en carcel.
Gullermo Croket presbitero, del Collegio de Rhemis.
Gabriel Embringhã estudiãte, del Coll. de Rhem. murio en (carcel)

Año del Señor. 1587.
THOMAS PILCHARD presbite. del Coll. de Rhemis.
Iuan Sandes presbitero, del Collegio de Rhemis.
Iuan Hamly presbitero, del Collegio de Rhemis.
Alexander Crovv presbitero, del Collegio de Rhemis.
Martin Sherson pres. del Coll. de Rhemis murio en carcel.
Edmundo Sikes presbitero, del Colleg. de Rhemis.
Roberto Sutton presbitero, del Collegio de Rhemis.
Roberto Vvilcokes presbitero, del Collegio de Rhemis.
Duarte Campiano presbitero, del Collegio de Rhemis.
Gulliermo Vvere presbitero, del Collegio de Rhemis.
Gabriel Thimbilby presbitero, del Collegio de Rhemis.

Año del Señor. 1588.
GVLLIERMO HARTLY pres. del Colleg. de Rhemis.
Gulliermo Espenser pres. del Collegio de Rhemis.
Roberto Murton presbitero, del Collegio de Roma.
Roberto Ludlan presbitero, del Collegio de Rhemis.
Gulliermo Vvige Pr. del Col. de Rhemis, murio en carcel.
Ricardo Simsom presbitero, del Collegio de Roma.
Nicolas Garlique presbitero, del Collegio de Rhemis.
Gullermo Dean presbitero, del Collegio de Rhemis.
Vgo Moro mancebo noble, del Collegio de Rhemis.
Gulliermo Guntero presbitero, del Collegio de Rhemis.
Thomas Felton del Collegio de Rhemis, mancebo noble, y hijo de martyr.
Ricardo Lighe presbitero, del Collegio de Roma.
Diego Clarkson presbitero, del Collegio de Rhemis.
Thomas Lynche estudiante, del Collegio de Rhemis.
Duarte Burden presbitero, del Collegio de Rhemis.

Duarte Iames presbitero, del Collegio de Roma.
Christobal Buxton presbitero, del Collegio de Roma.
Iuan Huyt presbitero, del Collegio de Rhemis.
Iuan Robinson estudiante, del Collegio de Rhemis.

Año del Señor 1589.
IVAN ANN presbitero, del Collegio de Rhemis.
Roberto Dalby presbitero, del Collegio de Rhemis.
Iorge Nicolas presbitero, del Collegio de Rhemis.
Ricardo Yaxly presbitero, del Collegio de Rhemis.
Thomas Belson mancebo, del Collegio de Rhemis.

Año del Señor 1590.
MILO GERARD presbitero, del Collegio de Rhemis.
Francisco Diconson presbitero, del Collegio de Rhemis.
Christobal Balis presbitero, del Collegio de Rhemis. Fue martyrizado el dia de la Ceniza,
y cõ el Ioan Hormit lego.
Antonio Mildelton presbitero, del Collegio de Rhemis.
Roberto Ihons presbitero, del Collegio de Rhemis.

El numero de todos es, nouenta y tres.
En Valladolid por Diego Fernandez de Cordoua, y Ouiedo. Impresor del Rey nuestro Señor.
Año M. D. XC.
Cum Licentia Superiorum.

Bibliography

Archival Sources

Archivum Britannicum Societatis Iesu
  Stonyhurst, Anglia A1
  Stonyhurst, Collectanea M

Archivum Romanum Societatis Iesu
  Fondo Gesuitico 651/612
  Hisp. 94

Bodleian Library, Oxford
  e Mus. 56
  Eng. th. b. 1–2

British Library
  Arundel MS 151
  Arundel MS 152

Editions of the *Historia*

Ribadeneyra, Pedro de. *Historia ecclesiastica del scisma del reyno de Inglaterra: En la qual se tratan las cosas mas notables q[ue] han sucedido en aquel reyno, tocantes à nuestra santa religion, desde que començo hasta la muerte de la reyna de Escocia; Recogida de diuersos y graues autores por el Padre Pedro de Ribadeneyra, de la Compañia de Iesus.* Madrid: En casa de Pedro Madrigal, 1588.

Ribadeneyra, Pedro de. *Historia ecclesiastica del scisma del reyno de Inglaterra: Recogida de diuersos y graues autores, por el Padre Pedro de Ribadeneyra, de la Compañia de Iesus.* Antwerp: Christophe Plantin, 1588.

Ribadeneyra, Pedro de. *Historia ecclesiastica del scisma del reyno de Inglaterra: En la qual se trata[n] los cosas mas notables que han secedido en aquel reyno, tocantes a nuestra santa religion, desde que comenco hasta la muerte de la reyna de Escocia; Recogida de diuersos y graues autores por el Padre Pedro de Ribadeneyra, de la Compañia de Iesus.* Barcelona: A costa de Jerónimo Genovés & Jaime Cendrad, 1588.

Ribadeneyra, Pedro de. *Historia ecclesiastica del scisma del reyno de Inglaterra: En la qual se tratan las cosas mas notables q[ue] han sucedido en aquel reyno, tocantes à nuestra santa religion, desde que començo hasta la muerte de la reyna de Escocia;*

Recogida de diuersos y graues autores por el Padre Pedro de Ribadeneyra, de la Compañia de Iesus. Madrid: Pedro Madrigal, 1588.

Ribadeneyra, Pedro de. *Historia ecclesiastica del scisma del reyno de Inglaterra, en la qual se tratan las cosas mas notables que ha[n] sucedido en aquel reyno desde que començo hasta la muerte de la reina de Escocia: Recogida de diuersos y graues autores por el Padre Pedro de Ribadeneyra*. Valencia: Pedro Patricio Mey, 1588.

Ribadeneyra, Pedro de. *Historia ecclesiastica del scisma del reyno de Inglaterra: En la qual se tratan las cosas mas notables que han sucedido en aquel reyno, tocantes a nuestra sancta religion, desde que començo, hasta la muerte de la reina de Escocia; Recogida de diuersos y graues autores por el Padre Pedro de Ribadeneyra*. Zaragoza: En casa de Pedro Puig & la viuda de Juan de Escarrilla, 1588.

Ribadeneyra, Pedro de. *Hystoria ecclesiastica del scisma del reyno de Inglaterra: En la qual se trata[n] las cosas mas notables q[ue] han sucedido en aquel reyno tocantes a nuestra sancta religion, desde que començo, hasta la muerte de la reina de Escocia; Recogida de diuersos y graues autores por el Padre Pedro de Ribadeneyra, de la Compañia de Iesus*. Lisbon: En casa de Antonio Aluarez, 1588.

Ribadeneyra, Pedro de. *Hystoria ecclesiastica del scisma del reyno de Inglaterra: En la qual se tratan las cosas mas notables que han sucedido en aquel reyno tocantes a nuestra santa religion, desde que començo, hasta la muerte de la reina de Escocia; Recogida de diuersos y graues autores por el Padre Pedro de Ribadeneyra, de la Compañia de Iesus*. Lisbon: Manuel de Lyra, 1589.

Ribadeneyra, Pedro de. *Historia ecclesiastica del scisma del reyno de Inglaterra: En la qual se tratan las cosas mas notables q[ue] han sucedido en aquel reyno, tocantes à nuestra santa religion, desde que començo hasta la muerte de la reyna de Escocia; Recogida de diuersos y graues autores por el Padre Pedro de Ribadeneyra, de la Compañia de Iesus*. Madrid: En casa de la viuda de Alonso Gómez, 1589.

Ribadeneyra, Pedro de. *Segunda parte de la historia ecclesiastica del scisma de Inglaterra*. Alcalá de Henares: En casa de Juan Íñiguez de Lequerica, 1593.[1]

Ribadeneyra, Pedro de. *Historia ecclesiastica del scisma del reyno de Inglaterra*. Madrid: s.n., 1594.[2]

Ribadeneyra, Pedro de. *Historia ecclesiastica del scisma del reyno de Inglaterra: Recogida de diuersos y graues autores por el Padre Pedro de Ribadeneyra, de la Compañia de Iesus*. Antwerp: En casa de Martin Nucio a las dos Cyguenas, 1594.

Ribadeneyra, Pedro de. *Segunda parte de la historia ecclesiastica del scisma de Inglaterra*. Lisbon: En casa de Manoel de Lira, 1594.

---

1   As discussed in the introduction, there are two distinct versions of the *Historia* that survive with these publication details.

2   There is no known surviving copy of this edition.

Ribadeneyra, Pedro de. *Historia ecclesiastica del scisma del reyno de Inglaterra: En la cual se tratan las cosas mas notables que han sucedido en aquel reyno, tocantes a nuestra santa religion desde que comenzo hasta la muerte de la reyna de Escocia.* Madrid: Viuda de Pedro Madrigal, 1595.

Ribadeneyra, Pedro de. *Las obras del P. Pedro de Ribadeneyra de la Compañia de Iesus, agora de nueuo reuistas y acrecentadas.* [Madrid]: En casa de la biuda de Pedro Madrigal, 1595.

Ribadeneyra, Pedro de. *Obras del Padre Pedro de Ribadeneyra de la Compañia de Iesus, agora de nueuo reuistas y acrecentadas.* Madrid: En la imprenta de Luis Sanchez, 1605.

Ribadeneyra, Pedro de. *Historia eclesiastica del scisma del Reyno de Inglaterra.* Madrid: Imprenta Real, a costa de Anisson, 1674.

Ribadeneyra, Pedro de. *Historia ecclesiastica do scisma do reyno de Inglaterra: Na qual se tratam as cousas mais notaveis, que succederaõ naquelle reyno tocantes à nossa santa religiaõ, desde que principiou, atè à morte da rainha de Escocia; Tirada de graves authores pelo Padre Pedro de Ribadeneyra da Companhia de Jesus, agora novamente traduzida no idioma Portuguez e offerecida ao gloriosissimo santo Thomas, arcebispo, de Cantuaria, por Pedro Nicolao de Andrade.* Translated by Pedro Nicolao de Andrade. Lisbon: Na Officina de Pedro Ferreira, 1732.

Ribadeneyra, Pedro de. *Historia eclesiastica del cisma de Inglaterra.* Madrid: Manuel Martin, 1781.

Ribadeneyra, Pedro de. *Historia eclesiástica del cisma de Inglaterra.* Madrid: Oficina de D. Plácido Barco López, 1786.

Ribadeneyra, Pedro de. *Historia del cisma de Inglaterra.* Cádiz: Imprenta de la Revista Medica, 1863.

Ribadeneyra, Pedro de. *Obras escogidas del Padre Pedro de Rivadeneira, de la Compañía de Jesús, con una noticia de su vida y juicio crítico de sus escritos.* Edited by Vicente de la Fuente. Biblioteca de Autores Españoles. Madrid: M. Rivadeneyra, 1868.

Ribadeneyra, Pedro de. *Historias de la Contrarreforma.* Edited by Eusebio Rey. Historia y hagiografía. Madrid: Biblioteca de Autores Cristianos, 1945.

Other Printed Primary Sources

Acta sanctorum quotquot toto orbe coluntur, vel a catholicis scriptoribus celebranter, quæ ex Latinis et Græcis, aliarumque gentium antiquis monumentis 68 vols. Antwerp / Brussels: Société des Bollandistes, 1643–1940.

Aesop. *Aesop's Fables.* Translated by Laura Gibbs. Oxford World's Classics. Oxford: Oxford University Press, 2002.

Albuquerque, Afonso de. *Cartas de Affonso de Albuquerque seguidas de documentos que as elucidam*. Edited by Raymundo Antonio de Bulhão Pato. 7 vols. Collecção de monumentos ineditos para a historia das conquistas dos Portuguezes em Africa, Asia e America 10. Lisbon: Typographia da Academia Real das Sciencias, 1884.

Alcázar, Bartolomé de. *Chrono-historia de la Compañia de Jesus, en la provincia de Toledo: Y elogios de sus varones illustres, fundadores, bienhechores, fautores, è hijos espirituales*. 2 vols. Madrid: Por Juan Garcia Infançon, 1710.

Alfield, Thomas. *A True Reporte of the Death & Martyrdome of M. Campion Iesuite and Preiste, & M. Sherwin, & M. Bryan Preistes, at Tiborne the First of December 1581: Observid and Written by a Catholike Preist, Which Was Present Therat; Wheruuto Is Annexid Certayne Verses Made by Sundrie Persons*. London: R. Rowlands, 1582.

L'allegrezza pvblica, et ringratiamenti fatti a Dio dalla Santità di N.S. Iulio Papa III. & dal sacro Collegio, & da tutto il popolo di Roma: Per il felicissimo ritorno del Regno d'Inghilterra alla catholica vnione, & alla obedientia della Sede Apostolica. Milan: s.n., 1555.

Allen, William. *An Apologie and True Declaration of the Institution and Endeuours of the Tvvo English Colleges, the One in Rome, the Other Novv Resident in Rhemes against Certaine Sinister Informations Giuen vp against the Same*. Rheims: Jean de Foigny, 1581.

Allen, William. *Historia del glorioso martirio di sedici sacerdoti martirizati in Inghilterra per la confessione, & difesa della fede Catolica, l'anno 1581 1582 & 1583*. Macerata: Sebastiano Martellini, 1583.

Allen, William. *A True, Sincere and Modest Defence, of English Catholiques That Suffer for Their Faith Both at Home and Abrode against a False, Seditious and Slanderous Libel Intituled; The Execution of Iustice in England*. Rouen: [Robert Persons's press], 1584.

Allen, William. *A Briefe Historie of the Glorious Martyrdom of Twelve Reverend Priests Father Edmund Campion & His Companions*. Edited by John Hungerford Pollen. London: Burns and Oates, 1908.

Ambrose of Milan. *Omnia quotquot extant D. Ambrosii episcopi Mediolanensis opera, primum per Des. Erasmum Roterodamum, mox per Sig. Gelenium, deinde per alios eruditos viros dilingenter castigata: nunc verò postremùm per Joannem Costerium emendata quae singulis tomis contineantur, cum catalogus eorum post vitam D. Ambrosii succedens, tum epistolae Erasmi cuilibet sectioni seorsum praemissae docebunt; Index geminus adiectus est foecundissimus*. Edited by Desiderius Erasmus, Sigismund Gelenius, and Johannes Costerius. 5 vols. Basel: Hieronymus I Froben & Nikolaus I Episcopius, 1555.

Ammianus Marcellinus. *History, Volume III: Books 27–31. Excerpta Valesiana*. Translated by John C. Rolfe. Vol. 3. 3 vols. Loeb Classical Library 331. Cambridge: Harvard University Press, 1939.

Athanasius. *The Life of St. Antony*. Edited and translated by Robert T. Meyer. Ancient Christian Writers: The Works of the Fathers in Translation 10. Westminster: The Newman Press, 1950.

Augustine of Hippo. *Las confessiones del glorioso dotor de la iglesia san Augustin*. Translated by Pedro de Ribadeneyra. Madrid: Juan de Montoya, 1596.

Augustine of Hippo, and Pseudo-Augustine. *Libro de las meditaciones y soliloquios y manual*. Translated by Pedro de Ribadeneyra. Madrid: Viuda de Pedro Madrigal, 1594.

Augustine of Hippo, and Pseudo-Augustine. *Meditaciones, soliloquios, y manual del glorioso doctor de la iglesia san Agustin*. Translated by Pedro de Ribadeneyra. Madrid: Luis Sanchez, 1597.

Baronio, Cesare. *Annales ecclesiastici: Tomus I*. Antwerp: Ex officina vid. Christophe Plantin & Jan I Moretus, 1589.

Baronio, Cesare. *Martyrologium Romanum, ad novam kalendarii rationem, et ecclesiasticae historiae veritatem restitutum: Gregorii XIII pontificis maximi jussu editum; Accesserunt notationes atque tractatio de martyrologio Romano*. Antwerp: Christophe Plantin, 1589.

Bede. *Bede's Ecclesiastical History*. Edited and translated by Bertram Colgrave and R.A.B. Mynors. Oxford: Clarendon Press, 1991.

Bergenroth, Gustav Adolf, Pascual de Gayangos y Arce, Martin A. Sharp Hume, Royall Tyler, and Garrett Mattingly, eds. *Calendar of Letters, Despatches, and State Papers Relating to the Negotiations between England and Spain Preserved in the Archives at Simancas and Elsewhere*. 13 vols. London: Her Majesty's Stationery Office, London, 1862–99.

Bilio, Luigi, Francesco Gaude, Charles Cocquelines, and Luigi Tomassetti, eds. *Bullarum diplomatum et privilegiorum sanctorum Romanorum pontificum Taurinensis editio*. 27 vols. Turin: Seb. Franco et Henrico Dalmazzo, 1857–72.

Blackwood, Adam. *Martyre de la royne d'Escosse douairiere de France: Contenant le vray discours des traisons à elle faictes à la suscitation d'Elizabet Angloise, par lequel les monsonges, calomnies & faulses accusations dressees contre ceste tres uertueuse, tres catholique & tres illustre Princesse sont esclarcies & son innocence aueree*. Antwerp: Gaspar Fleysben, 1588.

Blackwood, Adam. *History of Mary Queen of Scots; a Fragment*. Translated by Alexander Macdonald. Edinburgh: Maitland Club, 1834.

Boece, Hector. *Scotorum historiæ prima gentis origine, cum aliarum et rerum et gentium illustratione non vulgari, Libri XIX*. Paris: François Le Preux, 1575.

Bourchier, Thomas. *Historia ecclesiastica de martyrio fratrum Ordinis divi Francisci, dictorum de Observantia, qui partim in Anglia sub Henrico octauo rege: partim in Belgio sub principe Auriaco, parim & in Hybernia tempore Elizabethæ regnantis reginæ, idque ab anno 1536 vsque ad hunc nostrum præsentem annum 1582 passi sunt*. Paris: Apud Ioannem Poupy, 1582.

Brewer, John S., James Gairdner, and Robert H. Brodie. *Letters and Papers, Foreign and Domestic, of the Reign of Henry VIII: Preserved in the Public Record Office, the British Museum, and Elsewhere in England.* 35 vols. London: Her Majesty's Stationery Office, 1862–1932.

Brown, Rawdon Lubbock, George Cavendish Bentinck, Horatio F. Brown, and Allen Banks Hinds, eds. *Calendar of State Papers and Manuscripts, relating to English Affairs Existing in the Archives and Collections of Venice, and in Other Libraries of Northern Italy.* 38 vols. London: Her Majesty's Stationery Office, 1864–1947.

Cajetan, Thomas. *Opuscula omnia nunc primum summa diligentia castigatam et doctissimorum quorundam virorum ope suo nitori accurate restituta.* Lyons: Apud Ioannem Iacobi Iuntae F., 1581.

Calderón de la Barca, Pedro. *Octava parte de comedias del celebre poeta español, don Pedro Calderon de la Barca.* Edited by Juan de Vera Tassis y Villarroel. Madrid: Por Francisco Sanz, 1684.

Calderón de la Barca, Pedro. *The Schism in England (La Cisma de Inglaterra).* Edited by Ann L. Mackenzie. Translated by Kenneth Muir and Ann L. Mackenzie. Aris and Phillips Classical Texts. Oxford: Aris and Phillips, 1990.

Calderón de la Barca, Pedro. *La cisma de Ingalaterra.* Edited by Juan Manuel Escudero Baztán. Teatro del Siglo de Oro: Ediciones críticas 115. Kassel: Edition Reichenberger, 2001.

Calvin, John. *Commentaries on the Twelve Minor Prophets.* Translated by John Owen. 5 vols. Grand Rapids: William B. Eerdmans Publishing Company, 1950.

Cartas do Iapam nas quaes se trata da chegada a quellas partes dos fidalgos Iapões que ca vierão, da muita Christandade que se fez no tempo da perseguição do tyrano, das guerras que ouue, & de como Quambacudono se acabou de fazer senhor absoluto dos 66. reynos que ha no Iapão, & de outras cousas tocantes ás partes da India, & ao grão Mogor. Lisbon: Em casa de Simão Lopes, 1593.

Cassius Dio. *Dionis Nicæi, reru[m] Romanarum a Pompeio Magno, ad Alexandrum Mamææ filium epitome, Ioanne Xiphilino authore, & Guilielmo Blanco Albiensi interprete.* Edited by Joannes Xiphilinus. Translated by Guillaume Blanc. Paris: Ex officina Robert Estienne, 1551.

Cassius Dio. *Epitome della historia Romana di Dione Niceo di XXV imper. Romani da Pompeo Magno fino ad Alessandro figliuolo di Mammea, tradotta per m. Francesco Baldelli.* Edited by Joannes Xiphilinus. Translated by Francesco Baldelli. Venice: Appresso Gabriele Giolito de Ferrari, 1562.

Catena, Girolamo. *Vita del gloriosissimo papa Pio Quinto.* Rome: Nella stamperia di Vincenzo Accolti, 1586.

Cavalieri, Giovanni Battista. *Ecclesiae anglicanae trophaea sive sanctorum martyrum qui pro Christo catholicaeque fidei veritate asserenda antiquo recentiorique persecutionum tempore mortem in Anglia subierunt, passiones Romae in collegio Anglico per Nicolaum Circinianum depictae: Nuper autem per Io. Bap. de Cavalleriis aeneis typis repraesentatae.* Rome: Ex officina Bartolomeo Grassi, 1584.

Cavendish, George, and William Roper. *Two Early Tudor Lives: The Life and Death of Cardinal Wolsey The Life of Sir Thomas More.* Edited by Richard S. Sylvester and Davis P. Harding. New Haven: Yale University Press, 1962.

Cecil, William. *The Execution of Iustice in England for Maintenaunce of Publique and Christian Peace, against Certeine Stirrers of Sedition, and Adherents to the Traytors and Enemies of the Realme, without Any Persecution of Them for Questions of Religion, as Is Falsely Reported and Published by the Fautors and Fosterers of Their Treasons. Xvii. Decemb. 1583.* London: Christopher Barker, 1583.

Chacón, Alfonso. *De signis sanctissimae crucis, quae diuersis olim orbis regionibus & nuper hoc anno 1591 in Gallia & Anglia diuinitus ostensa sunt, & eorum expliciatione, tractatus.* Rome: Apud Ascanium, & Hieronymum Donangelos, 1591.

Chauncy, Maurice. *Historia aliquot nostri sæculi martyrum cùm pia, tum lectu iucunda, nunc denuo typis excusa.* Burgos: Felipe de Junta, 1583.

Church of England. *The Boke of the Common Praier and Administration of Ye Sacramentes & Other Rites and Cermonies of the Church: After the vse of the Church of England.* Worcester: In officina Ioanni Oswæni, 1549.

Cicero, Marcus Tullius. *Tusculan Disputations.* Edited and translated by A.E. Douglas. 2 vols. Chicago: Bolchazy-Carducci, 1990.

Cicero, Marcus Tullius. *Cicero, Philippics 3–9.* Edited and translated by Gesine Manuwald. 2 vols. Texte und Kommentare. Berlin: Walter de Gruyter, 2007.

Clifford, Henry. *The Life of Jane Dormer Duchess of Feria.* Edited by Joseph Stevenson. London: Burns and Oates, 1887.

Cochlaeus, Johann. *Scopa Ioannis Cochlaei Germani in araneas Ricardi Morysini Angli.* Leipzig: Nicolaus Vuolrab, 1538.

A Complaint of the Churche, against the Barbarous Tiranny Executed in Fraunce upon Her Poore Members: 1562. London: John Allde for Edmund Halley, 1562.

Cordara, Giulio Cesare. *On the Suppression of the Society of Jesus: A Contemporary Account.* Edited and translated by John P. Murphy. Chicago: Jesuit Way, 1999.

Cornell, T.J., ed. *The Fragments of the Roman Historians.* 3 vols. Oxford: Oxford University Press, 2013.

Cosin, Richard. *Conspiracie, for Pretended Reformation Viz. Presbyteriall Discipline: A Treatise Discouering the Late Designments and Courses Held for Aduancement Thereof, by William Hacket Yeoman, Edmund Coppinger, and Henry Arthington Gent. out of Others Depositions and Their Owne Letters, Writings & Confessions vpon Examination: Together with Some Part of the Life and Conditions, and Two Inditements, Arraignment, and Execution of the Sayd Hacket: Also an Answere to the*

Calumniations of such as Affirme They Were Mad Men: And a Resemblance of This Action vnto the Like, Happened Heretofore in Germanie; Vltimo Septembris. 1591; Published Now by Authoritie. London: Christopher Barker, 1592.

Cranmer, Thomas. *The Remains of Thomas Cranmer, Archbishop of Canterbury.* Edited by Henry Jenkyns. 4 vols. Oxford: Oxford University Press, 1833.

Cranmer, Thomas. *Miscellaneous Writings and Letters of Thomas Cranmer, Archbishop of Canterbury.* Edited by John Edmund Cox. Parker Society Publications 16. Cambridge: Cambridge University Press, 1846.

Cranmer, Thomas. *Memorials of the Most Reverend Father in God Thomas Cranmer, Sometime Lord Archbishop of Canterbury.* Edited by John Strype. Vol. 1. 3 vols. Ecclesiastical History Society Publications 2. Oxford: T. Combe, 1848.

Cranmer, Thomas, and Justus Jonas. *Catechismus, That Is to Say, a Shorte Instruction into Christian Religion for the Synguler Commoditie and Profyte of Childre[n] and Yong People: Set Forth by the Mooste Reuerende Father in God Thomas Archbyshop of Canterbury, Primate of All England and Metropolitane.* London: Nycolas Hyll for Gwalter Lynne, 1548.

Cresswell, Joseph. *Exemplar literarum, missarum, e Germania, ad Guilielmum Cecilium, consiliarium regium.* Rome: s.n., 1592.

Crudelitatis Calvinianae exempla duo recentissima ex Anglia. [Cologne]: s.n., 1585.

Davis, Raymond, ed. *The Book of Pontiffs (Liber Pontificalis): The Ancient Biographies of the First Ninety Roman Bishops to AD 715.* Translated by Raymond Davis. Translated Texts for Historians 6. Liverpool: Liverpool University Press, 1989.

Denis the Carthusian. *D. Dionysii Carthusiani, de his quae secundum sacras scripturas & orthodoxorum patrum sententias, de sanctissima & indiuidua trinitate semper adoranda, catholice credantur, liber primus.* Edited by Peter Blomevenna. Vol. 1. 4 vols. Cologne: Petri Quentel, 1535.

du Bellay, Martin, and Guillaume du Bellay. *Mémoires de Martin et Guillaume du Bellay.* Edited by V.-L. Bourrilly and Fleury Vindry. 4 vols. Paris: Librairie Renouard, 1908.

Edgar, Swift, and Angela M. Kinney, eds. *The Vulgate Bible.* 6 vols. Dumbarton Oaks Medieval Library. Cambridge: Harvard University Press, 2010–13.

Eeles, F.C., ed. *The Edwardian Inventories for Buckinghamshire.* Alcuin Club Collections 9. London: Longmans, Green and Co., 1908.

Elizabeth I. *A Declaration of the Causes Moving the Queen of England to Give Aid to the Defense of the People Afflicted and Oppressed in the Lowe Countries 1585 October 1.* London: s.n., 1585.

Eusebius of Caesarea. *Ecclesiastical History, Books 1–5.* Edited and translated by Roy J. Deferrari. The Fathers of the Church: A New Translation 19. Washington, D.C.: Catholic University of America Press, 1953.

Il felicissimo ritorno del regno d'Inghilterra alla catholica unione: Et alla obedientia della Sede Apostolica. Rome: s.n., 1555.

Fernández de Madrid, Alonso. *Silva Palentina.* Edited by Jesús San Martín Payo. Pallantia 1. Palencia: Diputación Provincial D.L., 1976.

Fish, Simon. *A Supplicacyon for the Beggers.* Antwerp: [Joannes Grapheus], 1529.

Fisher, John. *De causa matrimonii serenissimie regis Angliae liber.* Alcalá de Henares: Miguel de Eguía, 1530.

Fournier, Édouard, ed. "Discours de la mort de très haute et très illustre princesse madame Marie Stuard, royne d'Escosse, faict le dix-huitième jour de fevrier 1587." In *Variétés historiques et littéraires: Recueil de pièces volantes rares et curieuses en prose et en vers,* 5:279–89. P. Jannet: Paris, 1856.

Foxe, John. *The Acts and Monuments of John Foxe.* Edited by Stephen Reed Cattley. 8 vols. London: R.B. Seeley and W. Burnside, 1838.

Knox, Thomas Francis, ed. *The First and Second Diaries of the English College, Douay: And an Appendix of Unpublished Documents.* London: David Nutt, 1878.

Frere, Walter Howard, and William McClure Kennedy, eds. *Visitation Articles and Injunctions of the Period of the Reformation.* 3 vols. Alcuin Club Collections 14–16. London: Longmans, Green and Co., 1910.

Gerald of Wales. *The Historical Works of Giraldus Cambrensis.* Edited by Thomas Wright. Translated by Thomas Forester and Richard Colt Hoare. London: George Bell and Sons, 1894.

Gibbons, John, and John Bridgewater, eds. *Concertatio Ecclesiae Catholicæ in Anglia adversus Calvinopapistas et Puritanos sub Elizabetha regina quorundam hominum doctrina & sanctitate illustrium renouata.* Trier: Henricus Bock, 1588.

Gildas. *The Ruin of Britain, and Other Works.* Edited and translated by Michael Winterbottom. History from the Sources 7. London: Phillimore, 1978.

Granada, Luis de. *Parte primera de la introduction del symbolo de la fe, en la qual se trata de la creacion del mundo para venir por las criaturas al conocimiento del criador, y de sus diuinas perfectiones.* Barcelona: Iuan Pablo Manescal, Damian Bages, y Hieronymo Genoues, 1584.

Gregory I. *The Letters of Gregory the Great.* Edited and translated by John R.C. Martyn. 3 vols. Mediaeval Sources in Translation 40. Toronto: Pontifical Institute of Mediaeval Studies, 2004.

Gregory of Nazianzus, and Ambrose of Milan. *Funeral Orations.* Edited and translated by Leo P. McCauley. The Fathers of the Church: A New Translation 22. Washington, D.C.: Catholic University of America Press, 2004.

Guaras, Antonio de. *The Accession of Queen Mary: Being the Contemporary Narrative of Antonio de Guaras, a Spanish Merchant Resident in London.* Edited and translated by Richard Garnett. London: Lawrence and Bullen, 1892.

Guicciardini, Francesco. *Storia d'Italia*. Edited by Silvana Seidel Menchi. Vol. 3. 3 vols. Turin: Giulio Einaudi Editore, 1971.

Hall, Edward. *Hall's Chronicle: Containing the History of England, during the Reign of Henry the Fourth, and the Succeeding Monarchs, to the End of the Reign of Henry the Eighth, in Which Are Particularly Described the Manners and Customs of Those Periods; Carefully Collated with the Editions of 1548 and 1550*. London: G. Woodfall, 1809.

Harpsfield, Nicholas. *Dialogi sex contra summi pontificatus, monasticae vitae sanctorum, sacrarum imaginum oppugnatores, et pesudomartyres*. Antwerp: Christophe Plantin, 1566.

Harpsfield, Nicholas. *A Treatise on the Pretended Divorce between Henry VIII and Catharine of Aragon*. Edited by Nicholas Pocock. Works of the Camden Society, New Series 21. New York: Johnson Reprint Corporation, 1965.

Harpsfield, Nicholas. *Bishop Cranmer's Recantacyons*. Edited by Richard Monckton Milnes and James Gairdner. Philobiblon Society Miscellanies 15. London, 1877–84.

Henry VIII. *The Love Letters of Henry VIII to Anne Boleyn with Notes*. Edited by J.O. Halliwell Phillips. London: E. Grant Richards, 1907.

Henry VIII. *Assertio septem sacramentorum; or Defence of the Seven Sacraments*. Edited by Louis O'Donovan. New York: Benziger Brothers, 1908.

Henson, Edwin, ed. *Registers of the English College at Valladolid 1589–1862*. Publications of the Catholic Record Society 30. London: John Whitehead & Son, 1930.

Holinshed, Raphael. *Holinshed's Chronicles: England, Scotland, and Ireland*. Edited by Vernon F. Snow. 6 vols. New York: AMS Press Inc., 1965.

Hughes, Paul L., and James F. Larkin, eds. *Tudor Royal Proclamations*. 3 vols. New Haven: Yale University Press, 1964–69.

Hume, Martin A. Sharp, ed. *Chronicle of King Henry VIII of England: Being a Contemporary Record of Some of the Principal Events of the Reigns of Henry VIII and Edward VI; Written in Spanish by an Unknown Hand*. Translated by Martin A. Sharp Hume. London: George Bell and Sons, 1889.

Hume, Martin A. Sharp, ed. *Calendar of Letters and State Papers Relating to English Affairs: Preserved Principally in the Archives of Simancas; Elizabeth, 1558–1603*. 4 vols. London: Her Majesty's Stationery Office, 1892–99.

Ignatius of Loyola. *Ignatius of Loyola: The Spiritual Exercises and Selected Works*. Edited and translated by George E. Ganss. The Classics of Western Spirituality. New York: Paulist Press, 1991.

Irenaeus of Lyon. *Against the Heresies (Book 1)*. Edited and translated by Dominic J. Unger. Ancient Christian Writers: The Works of the Fathers in Translation 55. New York: Paulist Press, 1992.

Irenaeus of Lyon. *Against the Heresies (Book 3)*. Edited by Dominic J. Unger and Irenaeus M.C. Steenberg. Translated by Dominic J. Unger. Ancient Christian Writers: The Works of the Fathers in Translation 64. New York: The Newman Press, 2012.

Jewel, John. *Certain Sermons or Homilies Appointed to Be Read in Churches.* 2 vols. London: Richard Iugge and Iohn Cawood, 1571.

John Chrysostom. *Apologist.* Translated by Margaret A. Schatkin and Paul W. Harkins. The Fathers of the Church: A New Translation 73. Washington, D.C.: Catholic University of America Press, 1985.

Kedrenos, George. *Georgii Cedreni annales, sive historiae ab exordio mundi ad Isacium Comnenum usque compendium.* Translated by William Xylander. Basel: Ioannes Oporinus, 1587.

Kelly, Wilfrid, ed. *Liber ruber venerabilis collegii Anglorum de vrbe: I. Annales collegii pars prima; Nomina alumnorum I. A.D. 1579–1630.* Publications of the Catholic Record Society 37. London: John Whitehead & Son, 1940.

Kelly, Henry Ansgar, Louis W. Karlin, and Gerald B. Wegemer, eds. *Thomas More's Trial by Jury: A Procedural and Legal Review with a Collection of Documents.* Woodbridge: Boydell Press, 2011.

Kesselring, K.J. "A Draft of the 1531 'Acte for Poysoning.'" *EHR* 116, no. 468 (September 2001): 894–99.

Latimer, Hugh. *Sermons.* Edited by George Elwes Corrie. 2 vols. Parker Society Publications 27, 28. Cambridge: Cambridge University Press, 1844.

Leslie, John. *De origine, moribus, et rebus gestis Scotorum libri decem.* Rome: In aedibus populi Romani, 1578.

López Manzano, Juan. *Breve catalogo de los martyres que han sido de los dos collegios y seminarios ingleses, que residen en Roma, y en la ciudad de Rhemis de Francia, los quales han padecidos tormentos y muertes en Inglaterra, en estos treze años passados, por la defension de la fee Catholica, por mandado de la Reyna, fuera de otros muchos de todo genero de personas, que tambien han sido martyrizados, aunque no eran destos collegios.* Valladolid: Diego Fernández de Cordova y Oviedo, 1590.

Lucifer of Cagliari. *Luciferi Calaritani opuscula.* Edited by Wilhelm August Hartel. Corpus Scriptorum Ecclesiasticorum Latinorum 14. Vienna: Apud C. Geroldi filium, 1886.

Luders, Alexander, Thomas Edlyne Tomlins, John France, William Elias Taunton, and John Raithby, eds. *The Statutes of the Realm: Printed by Command of His Majesty King George the Third; In Pursuance of an Address of the House of Commons of Great Britain.* 9 vols. London: Dawsons of Pall Mall, 1810–28.

Machyn, Henry. *The Diary of Henry Machyn, Citizen and Merchant-Taylor of London, from A.D. 1550 to A.D. 1563.* Edited by John Gough Nichols. London: J.B. Nichols and Son, 1848.

Maffei, Giovanni Pietro. *Historiarum Indicarum libri XVI: Selectarum item ex India epistolarum eodem interprete libri IIII; Acceßit Ignatij Loiolæ vita postremo recognita; Et in opera singula copiosus index.* Venice: Apud Damianum Zenarium, 1589.

Magnus, Johannes. *Metropolis ecclesiae Upsalen, in regnis Suetiae et Gothiae diligentia Iohannis Magnis Gothi Sedis Apost. legati, primatis & archiepiscopi eiusdem ecclesiæ*

Upsalen: M. D. XXXVI. Gedani obiter collecta atq[ue] nunc primu[m] M. D. LVII. Rome: In aedibus divae Brigidae viduae, 1557.

Malfatti, C.V., ed. *The Accession, Coronation and Marriage of Mary Tudor, as Related in Four Manuscripts of the Escorial.* Translated by C.V. Malfatti. Barcelona: Sociedad alianza de artes graficas / Rucardo Fontá, 1956.

Mariae Stuartae Scotorum reginæ, principis Catholicae, nuper ab Elizabetha regina, et ordinibus Angliæ, post nouendecim annorum capitiuitatem in arce Fodringhaye inter- fectæ. Cologne: Apud Godefridum Kempensem, 1587.

Melanchthon, Philip. *Melancthons Briefwechsel: Kritische und kommentierte Gesam- tausgabe.* Edited by Heinz Scheible. 15 vols. Stuttgart: Frommann-Holzboog, 2003.

More, Thomas. *The Supplycacyon of Soulys: Agaynst the Supplycacyon of Beggars.* London: William Rastell, 1529.

More, Thomas. *The Yale Edition of the Complete Works of St. Thomas More.* 15 vols. New Haven: Yale University Press, 1963.

More, Thomas. *The Last Letters of Thomas More.* Edited by Alvaro de Silva. Grand Rap- ids: William B. Eerdmans Publishing Company, 2000.

Narratione particolare, del parlamento d'Inghilterra, et in che modo è uenuto quel popolo all'ubbidiena di Santa Chiesa, con l'ordine dell'assolutione, & benedittione data dal reverendissimo cardinale Polo, legato di sua Santità, à tutto il regno: Et appresso le feste, et giuoco delle canne, che si è fatto per allegrezza di tal nuoua. Venice, 1555.

Nichols, John Gough, ed. *The Chronicle of Queen Jane, and of Two Years of Queen Mary, and Especially of the Rebellion of Sir Thomas Wyat: Written by a Resident in the Tower of London.* Works of the Camden Society 48. London: J.B. Nichols and Son, 1850.

Nichols, John Gough., ed. *Chronicle of the Grey Friars of London.* Works of the Camden Society 53. London: J.B. Nichols and Son, 1852.

Olin, John C., ed. *The Catholic Reformation: Savonarola to Ignatius Loyola.* New York: Fordham University Press, 1969.

Ó Néill, Domhnall. "Remonstrance of the Irish Chiefs to Pope John XXII." Translated by Edmund Curtis. Corpus of Electronic Texts, 2010. http://www.ucc.ie/celt/published/ T310000-001.html. Accessed December 6, 2015.

Persons, Robert. *De persecutione anglicana libellus: Quo explicantur afflictiones, calami- tates, cruciatus, & acerbissima martyria, quæ Angli Catholici nu[n]c ob fide[m] patituntur.* Rome: Ex typographia Georgij Ferrarij, 1582.

Persons, Robert. *Relacion de algunos martyrios, que de nueuo han hecho los hereges en Inglaterra, y de otras cosas tocantes a nuestra santa y Catolica religion.* Madrid: Pedro Madrigal, 1590.

Persons, Robert. *A Relation of the King of Spanes Receiving in Valliodolid, and in the Inglish College of the Same Towne, in August Last Past of This Yere 1592: VVryten by an Inglish Priest of the Same College, to a Gentleman and His Vvyf in Flaunders, Latelie*

Fled out of Ingland, for Profeßion of the Catholique Religion. [Antwerp]: [A. Conincx], 1592.

Persons, Robert. *An Aduertisement Written to a Secretarie of My L. Treasurers of Ingland, by an Inglishe Intelligencer as He Passed Throughe Germanie Towardes Italie Concerninge an Other Booke Newly Written in Latin, and Published in Diuerse Languages and Countreyes, against Her Maiesties Late Proclamation, for Searche and Apprehension of Seminary Priestes, and Their Receauers, Also of a Letter Vvritten by the L. Treasurer in Defence of His Gentrie, and Nobility, Intercepted, Published, and Answered by the Papistes.* Antwerp: s.n., 1592.

Persons, Robert. *Elizabethae, Angliae reginae haeresim Calvinianam propugnantis, saevissimum in Catholicos sui regni edictum, quod in alios quoque reipub. christianae principes contumelias continet indignissimas: Promulgatum Londini 29. Nouemb. 1591; Cum responsione ad singula capita: qua non tantum sœuitia, & impietas tam iniqui edicti, sed mendacia quoque, & fraudes ac imposturœ deteguntur, & confutantur; Per D. Andream Philopatrum presbyterum ac theologum Romanum, ex Anglis olim oriundum.* Augsburg: Apud Ioannem Fabrum, 1592.

Persons, Robert. *Elizabethœ, Angliae reginae haeresin Calvinianam propugnantis, sœvissimum in Catholicos sui regni edictum, quod in alios quóque reipublicœ christianae principes contumelias continet indignissimas: Promulgatum Londini 29. Nouembris 1591; Cum responsione ad singula capita, qua non tantùm sœuitia & impetas tam iniqui edicti, sed mendacia quóque, & fraudes, & imposturœ dereguntur, & confutantur; Per D. Andream Philopatrum presbyterum, ac theologum Romanum, ex Anglia olim oriundum.* Lyon: Pierre Roussin apud Jean Didier, 1593.

Persons, Robert. *Letters and Memorials of Father Robert Persons, S.J.: Vol. I (to 1588).* Edited by Leo Hicks. London: John Whitehead & Son, 1942.

Peter of Blois. *Petri Blesensis diuinaru[m] ac humanaru[m] litterar[um] viri admodu[m] copiosissimi insignia opera in vnu[m] volume[n] collecta [e]t emendata authore.* Edited by Jacques Merlin. Paris: A. Boucard, 1519.

Peter of Blois. *Petri Blesensis Bathoniensis archdiaconi opera omnia.* Edited by I.A. Giles. 4 vols. Patres Ecclesiæ Anglicanæ. Oxford: John Henry Parker, 1847.

Philastrius. *Sancti Filastrii episcopi Brixiensis diversarum hereseon liber.* Edited by Friedrich Marx. Corpus scriptorum ecclesiasticorum Latinorum 38. Vienna: F. Tempsky, 1898.

Philip II, and Reginald Pole. *Copia delle lettere del serenissimo re d'Inghilterra, & del reuerendissimo Card. Polo legato della S. Sede Apostolica alla Santità di N.S. Iulio Papa III: Sopra la reduttione di quel regno alla vnione della Santa Madre Chiesa, & obbedienza della Sede Apostolica.* [Rome: Valerio & Luigi Dorico], 1554.

Platina, Bartolomeo. *Liber de vita Christi ac omnium pontificum.* Edited by Giacinto Gaida. Rerum Italicarum scriptores: Raccolta degli storici italiani dal cinquecento al millecinquecento 3.1. Città di Castello: S. Lapi, 1900.

Platina, Bartolomeo. *Lives of the Popes*. Edited and translated by Anthony F. D'Elia. Vol. 1. The I Tatti Renaissance Library 30. Cambridge: Harvard University Press, 2008.

Pocock, Nicholas. *Records of the Reformation: The Divorce 1527–1533*. 2 vols. Oxford: Clarendon Press, 1870.

Pole, Reginald. *The Reform of England, by the Decrees of Cardinal Pole, Legate of the Apostolic See; Promulgated in the Year of Grace 1556*. Edited and translated by Henry Raikes. Chester: R.H. Spence, 1839.

Pole, Reginald. *Pole's Defense of the Unity of the Church*. Edited and translated by Joseph G. Dwyer. Westminster: The Newman Press, 1965.

Pole, Reginald. *The Correspondence of Reginald Pole*. Edited and translated by Thomas F. Mayer. 5 vols. Farnham: Ashgate, 2002– 08.

Pollen, John Hungerford, ed. *Acts of English Martyrs Hitherto Unpublished*. London: Burns and Oates, 1891.

Pollen, John Hungerford, ed. *Unpublished Documents Relating to the English Martyrs: Vol. I 1584–1603*. Publications of the Catholic Record Society 5. London: J. Whitehead and Son, 1908.

Pollini, Girolamo. *Storia ecclesiastica della riuoluzione d'Inghilterra: Divisa in cinque libri; Ne' quali si tratta di quello che è occorso in quell'isola, da che Arrigo ottavo cominciò a pensare di repudiare Caterina; Raccolta da diversi e graviss. scrittori, dal reverendo padre fra Girolamo Pollini; Divisa in capitoli con una tavola delle cose più notabili*. Florence: Per Filippo II Giunta, 1591.

Relatione del presente stato d'Inghilterra: Cavata da vna lettera de li 25 di maggio scritta di Londra, et da vn'altra, scritta da vna persona di qualità, venuta di frescho d'Inghilterra, data in Anuersa alli 27. di giugno, & altre. Rome: Appresso Francesco Zannetti, 1590.

Ribadeneyra, Pedro de. *Tratado de la tribulacion, repartido en dos libros*. Madrid: Pedro Madrigal, 1589.

Ribadeneyra, Pedro de. *Flos sanctorum o libro de las vidas de los santos*. Madrid: Luis Sanchez, 1599.

Ribadeneyra, Pedro de. *Della religione del prencipe christiano*. Bologna: Per Pietro Paulo Tozzi, 1622.

Ribadeneyra, Pedro de. *Patri Petri de Ribadeneira, Societatis Jesu sacerdotis: Confessiones, epistolae aliaque scripta inedita ex autographis, antiquissimis apographis et regestis deprompta*. 2 vols. Monumenta Historica Societatis Iesu 58, 60. Rome: Monumenta Historica Societatis Iesu, 1969.

Ribadeneyra, Pedro de. *Confesiones: Autobiografía documentada*. Edited by Miguel Lop Sebastià. Manresa 41. Santander / Bilbao: Sal Terrae / Ediciones Mensajero, 2009.

Ribadeneyra, Pedro de. *The Life of Ignatius of Loyola*. Translated by Claude Pavur. Jesuit Primary Sources in English Translations 28. St. Louis: Institute of Jesuit Sources, 2014.

Rigg, James Macmullen, ed. *Calendar of State Papers, relating to English Affairs, Preserved Principally at Rome, in the Vatican Archives and Library.* 2 vols. London: His Majesty's Stationery Office, 1916–26.

Robinson, Hastings, ed. *The Zurich Letters, Comprising the Correspondence of Several English Bishops and Others, with Some of the Helvetian Reformers, during the Early Part of the Reign of Queen Elizabeth.* Translated by Hastings Robinson. Parker Society Publications 50. Cambridge: Cambridge University Press, 1842.

Robinson, Hastings, ed. *Original Letters Relative to the English Reformation, Written during the Reigns of King Henry VIII, King Edward VI, and Queen Mary: Chiefly from the Archives of Zurich.* Translated by Hastings Robinson. 2 vols. Parker Society Publications 53. Cambridge: Cambridge University Press, 1846.

Roper, William, and Nicholas Harpsfield. *Lives of Saint Thomas More.* Everyman's Library. London: Dent, 1963.

Ruscelli, Girolamo, ed. *Delle lettere di principi, le quali o si scrivono da principi, o a principi, o ragionano di principi: Libro terzo; Di nuovo ricorrette, et secondo l'ordine de' tempi accommodate.* Venice: Appresso Francesco Ziletti, 1581.

Rymer, Thomas, ed. *Fœdera, conventiones, literæ, et cujuscunque generis acta publica, inter reges Angliæ, et alios quosvis imperatores, reges, pontifices, principes, vel communitates, ab ineunte sæculo duodecimo, viz. ab anno 110, ad nostra usque tempora, habita aut tractata; Ex autographis, infra secretiores archivorum regiorum thesaurarias, per multa sæcula reconditis, fideliter exscripta.* Second Edition. 20 vols. London: J. Tonson, 1726–35.

Sabino, Fernando Tavares. *No fim dá certo.* Rio de Janeiro: Editora Record, 1998.

Saint-Saëns, Camille, Léonce Détroyat, and Paul-Armand Silvestre. *Henry VIII: Opéra en 4 actes.* Paris: A. Durand & Fils, 1883.

Sander, Nicholas. *De visibili monarchia ecclesiæ libri octo.* Leuven: Ioannis Fouleri, 1571.

Sander, Nicholas. *Doctissimi viri Nicolai Sanderi, de origine ac progressu schismatis anglicani, liber: Continens historiam maximè ecclesiasticam, annorum circiter sexaginta, lectu dignissimam; Nimirum, ab anno 21 regni Henrici 8, quo primum cogitare cœpit de repudianda vxore serenissima Catherina, vsque ad hunc vigesimum septimum Elizabethæ, quæ vltima est eiusdem Henrici soboles.* Edited by Edward Rishton. Cologne, 1585.

Sander, Nicholas. *De origine ac progressu schismatis anglicani, libri tres: Quibus historia continetur maximè ecclesiasticam, annorum circiter sexaginta, lectu dignissima; Nimirum, ab anno 21 regni Henrici octaui, quo primum cogitare cœpit de repudianda vxore serenissima Catherina, vsque ad hunc vigesimum octauum Elizabethæ, quæ vltima est eiusdem Henrici soboles.* Edited by Edward Rishton, Robert Persons, and William Allen. Rome: Bartholomæi Bonfadini, 1586.

Sander, Nicholas. *Rise and Growth of the Anglican Schism*. Edited and translated by David Lewis. London: Burns and Oates, 1877.

Sander, Nicholas, and Pedro de Ribadeneyra. *Nicolai Sanderi Angli doct. theol. de origine ac progressu schismatis anglicani, libri tres*. Cologne: Sumptibus Petri Henningi, 1610.

Smith, Richard. *A Confutation of a Certen Booke, Called a Defence of the True, and Catholike Doctrine of the Sacrame[n]t, &c. Sette Fourth of Late in the Name of Thomas Archebysshoppe of Canterburye: By Rycharde Smyth, Docter of Diuinite, and Some Tyme Reader of the Same in Oxforde*. Paris: R. Chaudière, 1550.

Sozomen, and Philostorgius. *The Ecclesiastical History of Sozomen: Comprising a History of the Church from A.D. 324 to A.D. 440, Translated from the Greek with a Memoir of the Author; Also, the Ecclesiastical History of Philostorgius as Epitomized by Photius, Patriarch of Constantinople*. Translated by Edward Walford. Bohn's Ecclesiastical Library. London: Henry G. Bohn, 1855.

Spitilli, Gasparo, ed. *Ragguaglio d'alcune missioni dell'Indie orientali, et occidentali, cavato da alcuni avisi scritti gli anni 1590 & 1591*. Naples: Gio. Iacomo Carlino, & Antonio Pace, 1593.

Stapleton, Thomas. *Tres Thomae seu: De S. Thomæ Apostoli rebus gestis; De S. Thoma archiepiscopo Cantuariensi & martyre; D. Thomæ Mori Angliæ quondam cancellarij vita*. Douai: Ex officina Ioannis Bogardi, 1588.

Stapleton, Thomas. *Apologia pro rege Catholico Philippo II Hispaniæ, & cæt. rege. contra varias & falsas accusationes Elisabethæ Angliæ reginæ: Per edictum suum 18 Octobris Richemondiæ datum, & 20 Nouembris Londini proclamatum, publicatas & excusas*. Constance [*vere* Leuven]: apud Theodorus Samius, 1592.

Stapleton, Thomas. *The Life and Illustrious Martyrdom of Sir Thomas More, Formerly Lord Chancellor of England (Part III of "Tres Thomae," Printed at Douai, 1588)*. Translated by Philip E. Hallett. London: Burns, Oates & Washbourne, 1928.

Stow, John. *A Summarie of the Chronicles of England from the First Comming of Brute into This Land, vnto This Present Yeare of Christ 1575 Diligently Collected, Corrected and Enlarged, by Iohn Stowe*. London: Richard Tottle, and Henry Binneman, 1575.

Stow, John. *The Summarie of the Chronicles of England. Diligently Collected, Abridged & Continued vnto This Present Yeare of Christ 1579 by Iohn Stowe, Citizen of London*. London: Richard Tottle, and Henry Binneman, 1579.

Stow, John. *The Chronicles of England from Brute vnto This Present Yeare of Christ 1580 Collected by Iohn Stow Citizen of London*. London: By Ralphe Newberie, at the assignement of Henrie Bynneman, 1580.

Suárez de Figueroa y Córdoba, Gómez. "The Count of Feria's Dispatch to Philip II of 14 November 1558." Edited and translated by M.J. Rodríguez-Salgado and Simon Adams. *Camden Miscellany*, Fourth Series, 29 (1984): 302–44.

"Suda On Line," 2015. http://www.stoa.org/sol/. Accessed September 1, 2015.

Theiner, Augustin, ed. *Vetera monumenta Hibernorum et Scotorum historiam illustran-tia quae ex Vaticani, Neapolis ac Florentiae tabulariis deprompsit et ordine chrono-logico disposuit Augustinus Theiner*. Rome: Typis Vaticanis, 1864.

Theodoret. *Ecclesiastical History: A History of the Church in Five Books from A.D. 322 to the Death of Theodore of Mopsuestia A.D. 427*. Translated by Edward Walford. Greek Ecclesiastical Historians of the First Six Centuries of the Christian Era 5. London: Samuel Bagster and Sons, 1854.

A True and Summarie Reporte of the Declaration of Some Part of the Earle of Northum-berlands Treasons. [London]: In aedibus Christopher Barker, 1585.

Vergil, Polydore. *Polydori Vergilii Vrbinatis Anglicæ historiæ libri vigintiseptem: Ab ipso autore postremùm iam recogniti, adq[ue] amussim, salua tamen historiæ ueritate, expoliti*. Basel: Apud Mich. Isingrinium, 1555.

Verstegan, Richard. *The Letters and Despatches of Richard Verstegan (c. 1550–1640)*. Edited by Anthony G. Petti. Publications of the Catholic Record Society 52. London: Catholic Record Society, 1959.

Victor of Vita. *History of the Vandal Persecution*. Edited and translated by John Moorhead. Translated Texts for Historians 10. Liverpool: Liverpool University Press, 1992.

Vives, Juan Luis. *Ioan. Lodovici Vivis de recta ingenuorum adolescentum ac puellarum institutione, libelli duo, multa eruditione ac pietate referti: Eiusdem ad veram sapien-tiam introductio, satellitiu[m] animi, siue symbola principum institutioni potissimum destinata*. Basel: Robert Winter, 1539.

Wheeler, Thomas. "An Italian Account of Thomas More's Trial and Execution." *Moreana* 26 (June 1970): 33–39.

Wiesener, Louis, ed. "Marie Stuart et le P. Edmond Augier: Une lettre inédite de Marie Stuart." *Revue des questions historiques* 2 (1867): 614–18.

Wilkins, David, ed. *Concilia Magnae Britanniae et Hiberniae a Synodo Verolamiensi A.D. 446 ad Londinensem A.D. 1717; Accedunt constitutiones et alia ad historiam Ecclesiae Anglicanae spectantia*. 4 vols. London: R. Gosling, 1737.

Wright, Thomas, ed. *Three Chapters of Letters Relating to the Suppression of Monasteries*. Works of the Camden Society 26. London: John Bowyer Nichols and Son, 1843.

Yepes, Diego de. *Historia particular de la persecucion de Inglaterra y de los martirios mas insignes que en ella a avido, desde el año del señor 1570*. Madrid: Luis Sanchez, 1599.

Secondary Sources

Adorno, Rolena. "Censorship and Its Evasion: Jerónimo Román and Bartolomé de Las Casas." *Hispania* 75, no. 4 (October 1992): 812–27.

Alford, Stephen. *Burghley: William Cecil at the Court of Elizabeth I*. New Haven: Yale University Press, 2008.

Alford, Stephen. *The Watchers: A Secret History of the Reign of Elizabeth I*. New York: Bloomsbury Press, 2012.

Andrachuk, Gregory Peter. "Calderón's View of the English Schism." In *Parallel Lives: Spanish and English National Drama 1580–1680*, edited by Louise Fothergill-Payne and Peter Fothergill-Payne, 224–38. Lewisburg: Bucknell University Press, 1991.

Anquez, Léonce. *Histoire des assemblées politiques des réformés de France (1573–1622)*. Paris: Auguste Durand, 1859.

Baldwin Smith, Lacey. "The Last Will and Testament of Henry VIII: A Question of Perspective." *Journal of British Studies* 2, no. 1 (November 1962): 14–27.

Bangert, William V. *Jerome Nadal, S.J. 1507–1580: Tracking the First Generation of Jesuits*. Edited by Thomas M. McCoog. Chicago: Loyola University Press, 1992.

Barnett, S.J. "Where Was Your Church Before Luther? Claims for the Antiquity of Protestantism Examined." *CH* 68, no. 1 (March 1999): 14–41.

Bayne, C.G. "The Coronation of Queen Elizabeth." *EHR* 24, no. 94 (April 1909): 322–23.

Beaver, R. Pierce. "The Donatist Circumcellions." *CH* 4, no. 2 (June 1935): 123–33.

Bernard, George W. "Anne Boleyn's Religion." *HJ* 36, no. 1 (March 1993): 1–20.

Berry, Mary Elizabeth. *Hideyoshi*. Harvard East Asian Monographs 146. Cambridge: The Council on East Asian Studies, Harvard University, 1989.

Bilinkoff, Jodi. "The Many 'Lives' of Pedro de Ribadeneyra." *Renaissance Quarterly* 52, no. 1 (Spring 1999): 180–96.

Bindoff, S.T., ed. *The House of Commons 1509–1558*. 3 vols. The History of Parliament. London: Secker & Warburg, 1982.

Bireley, Robert. *The Counter-Reformation Prince: Anti-Machiavellianism or Catholic Statecraft in Early Modern Europe*. Chapel Hill: University of North Carolina Press, 1990.

Bolton, Brenda, and Anne J. Duggan, eds. *Adrian IV The English Pope (1154–1159)*. Church, Faith and Culture in the Medieval West. Farnham: Ashgate, 2013.

Bonner, Elizabeth A. "The Genesis of Henry VIII's 'Rough Wooing' of the Scots." *Northern History* 33, no. 1 (1997): 36–53.

Bossy, John. "Rome and the Elizabethan Catholics: A Question of Geography." *HJ* 7, no. 1 (1964): 135–42.

Bouza-Álvarez, Fernando J. "Monarchie en lettres d'imprimerie: Typographie et propagande au temps de Philippe II." Translated by Marie-Joëlle Tupet. *Revue d'histoire moderne et contemporaine (1954–)* 41, no. 2 (April 1994): 206–20.

Bouza-Álvarez, Fernando J. *Imagen y propaganda: Capítulos de historia cultural del reinado de Felipe II*. Serie Historia Moderna. Madrid: Ediciones Akal, 1998.

Bowden, Caroline, and James E. Kelly, eds. *The English Convents in Exile, 1600–1800: Communities, Culture and Identity*. Farnham: Ashgate, 2013.

Bradshaw, Brendan, and Eamon Duffy, eds. *Humanism, Reform and the Reformation: The Career of Bishop John Fisher*. Cambridge: Cambridge University Press, 1989.

Bridgett, T.E. *Life of Blessed John Fisher, Bishop of Rochester, Cardinal of the Holy Roman Church, and Martyr under Henry VIII*. London: Burns and Oates, 1888.

Brigden, Susan. *Thomas Wyatt: The Heart's Forest*. London: Faber and Faber, 2012.

Brooke, Christopher. *A History of Gonville and Caius College*. Woodbridge: Boydell Press, 1985.

Brown, Peter. *Augustine of Hippo: A Biography*. Berkeley: University of California Press, 2000.

Bruce, John. "Observations on the Circumstances Which Occasioned the Death of Fisher, Bishop of Rochester." *Archaeologia* 25 (January 1832): 61–99.

Burke, Peter. "How to Be a Counter-Reformation Saint." In *The Historical Anthropology of Early Modern Italy: Essays on Perception and Communication*, by Peter Burke, 48–62. Cambridge: Cambridge University Press, 2005.

Burnet, Gilbert. *The History of the Reformation of the Church of England*. 3 vols. London: T.H. for Richard Chiswell, 1681.

Calma, Clarinda E. "Communicating across Communities: Explicitation in Gaspar Wilkowski's Polish Translation of Edmund Campion's *Rationes Decem*." *JJS* 1, no. 4 (2014): 589–606.

Camm, Bede. *Lives of the English Martyrs Declared Blessed by Pope Leo XIII in 1886 and 1895*. 2 vols. Quarterly Series 100, 101. London: Burns and Oates, 1904–05.

Carrafiello, Michael L. "English Catholicism and the Jesuit Mission of 1580–1581." *HJ* 37, no. 4 (December 1994): 761–74.

"Censo-guía de archivos de España e Iberoamérica." Ministerio de Educación, Cultura, y Deporte, 2015. http://censoarchivos.mcu.es/CensoGuia/portada.htm. Accessed September 14, 2015.

Challis, C.E. "The Debasement of the Coinage, 1542–1551." *Economic History Review*, New Series, 20, no. 3 (December 1967): 441–66.

Challoner, Richard. *Memoirs of Missionary Priests, as Well Secular as Regular; And of Other Catholics, of Both Sexes, That Have Suffered Death in England, on Religious Accounts, from the Year of Our Lord 1577, to 1684*. 2 vols. [London]: [for F. Needham?], 1741.

Chaney, William A. "Anglo-Saxon Church Dues: A Study in Historical Continuity." *CH* 32, no. 3 (September 1963): 268–77.

"The Chapel Royal of St. Peter Ad Vincula." Tower of London, 2015. http://www.hrp .org.uk/TowerOfLondon/Sightsandstories/Prisoners/Towers/ChapelRoyalofSt Peter. Accessed December 7, 2015.

Cholakian, Patricia F., and Rouben C. Cholakian. *Marguerite de Navarre: Mother of the Renaissance*. New York: Columbia University Press, 2006.

Chrimes, S.B. *Henry VII*. Yale English Monarchs. New Haven: Yale University Press, 1999.

Church, Stephen. *King John: England, Magna Carta and the Making of a Tyrant*. Basingstoke: Macmillan, 2015.

Clancy, Thomas H. "The First Generation of English Jesuits 1555–1585." *AHSI* 57 (1988): 137–62.

Cogswell, Thomas. "England and the Spanish Match." In *Conflict in Early Stuart England: Studies in Religion and Politics 1603–1642*, edited by Richard Cust and Ann Hughes, 107–33. London: Longman, 1989.

Collinson, Patrick. *The Elizabethan Puritan Movement*. London: Methuen, 1967.

Collinson, Patrick. *Elizabethans*. London: Hambledon and London, 2003.

Cooper, Michael. *The Japanese Mission to Europe, 1582–1590: The Journey of Four Samurai Boys through Portugal, Spain and Italy*. Folkestone: Global Oriental, 2005.

Cooper, John. *The Queen's Agent: Francis Walsingham at the Court of Elizabeth I*. London: Faber and Faber, 2011.

Correia-Afonso, John. *Jesuit Letters and Indian History, 1542–1773*. Second Edition. Studies in Indian History and Culture of the Heras Institute 20. Bombay: Oxford University Press, 1969.

Crehan, Joseph. "Saint Ignatius and Cardinal Pole." *AHSI* 25 (1956): 72–98.

Cressy, David. "Book Burning in Tudor and Stuart England." *SCJ* 36, no. 2 (Summer 2005): 359–74.

Cross, Claire. "Oxford and the Tudor State from the Accession of Henry VIII to the Death of Mary." In *The Collegiate University*, edited by James McConica, 117–49. The History of the University of Oxford 3. Oxford: Clarendon Press, 1986.

Cross, Robert. "Pretense and Perception in the Spanish Match, or History in a Fake Beard." *Journal of Interdisciplinary History* 37, no. 4 (2007): 563–83.

Cruickshank, Don W. "Calderón's *Amor, honor y poder* and the Prince of Wales, 1623." *Bulletin of Hispanic Studies* 77 (2000): 75–99.

Crummé, Hannah Leah. "Jane Dormer's Recipe for Politics: A Refuge Household in Spain for Mary Tudor's Ladies-in-Waiting." In *The Politics of Female Households: Ladies-in-Waiting across Early Modern Europe*, edited by Nadine Akkerman and Birgit Houben, 51–71. Rulers & Elites 4. Leiden: Brill, 2013.

Cunliffe, Barry. *Wessex to AD 1000*. A Regional History of England. London: Longman Group, 1993.

Curtis, Cathy. "More's Public Life." In *The Cambridge Companion to Thomas More*, edited by George M. Logan, 69–92. Cambridge Companions to Religion. Cambridge: Cambridge University Press, 2011.

Darnton, Robert. *The Great Cat Massacre: And Other Episodes in French Cultural History*. Revised Edition. New York: Basic Books, 2009.

Davis, John. "Joan of Kent, Lollardy and the English Reformation," *JEH* 33, no. 2 (April 1982): 225–33.

Deane, Jennifer Kolpacoff. *A History of Medieval Heresy and Inquisition*. Critical Issues in World and International History. Lanham: Rowman & Littlefield, 2011.

DeMolen, Richard L. "The Birth of Edward VI and the Death of Queen Jane: The Arguments for and Against Caesarean Section." *Renaissance Studies* 4, no. 4 (1990): 359–91.

Dillon, Anne. *The Construction of Martyrdom in the English Catholic Community, 1535–1603*. St Andrews Studies in Reformation History. Aldershot: Ashgate, 2002.

Dillon, Anne. "John Forest and Derfel Gadarn: A Double Martyrdom." *RH* 28, no. 1 (May 2006): 1–21.

Dillon, Anne. *Michelangelo and the English Martyrs*. Farnham: Ashgate, 2012.

Ditchfield, Simon. "What Was Sacred History? (Mostly Roman) Catholic Uses of the Christian Past after Trent." In *Sacred History: Uses of the Christian Past in the Renaissance World*, edited by Katherine Van Liere, Simon Ditchfield, and Howard Louthan, 72–98. Oxford: Oxford University Press, 2012.

Domínguez, Freddy Cristóbal. "History in Action: The Case of Pedro de Ribadaneyra's *Historia ecclesiastica del scisma de Inglaterra*." *Bulletin of Spanish Studies* (September 2015), 1–26.

Domínguez Ortiz, Antonio. "La censura de obras históricas en el siglo XVII español." *Chronica nova* 9 (1991): 113–21.

Donnelly, John Patrick. "Antonio Possevino and Jesuits of Jewish Ancestry." *AHSI* 15 (1986): 3–31.

Dowling, Maria. "Anne Boleyn and Reform." *JEH* 35, no. 1 (January 1984): 30–46.

Dowling, Maria. *Fisher of Men: A Life of John Fisher, 1468–1535*. Basingstoke: Macmillan, 1999.

Duffy, Eamon. *Fires of Faith: Catholic England under Mary Tudor*. New Haven: Yale University Press, 2009.

Duffy, Eamon, and David Loades, eds. *The Church of Mary Tudor*. Aldershot: Ashgate, 2005.

Duggan, Anne J. "The Power of Documents: The Curious Case of *Laudabiliter*." In *Aspects of Power and Authority in the Middle Ages*, edited by Brenda Bolton and Christine Meek, 251–75. Turnhout: Brepols Publishers, 2007.

Edwards, John. "Spanish Religious Influence in Marian England." In *The Church of Mary Tudor*, edited by Eamon Duffy and David Loades, 33–56. Aldershot: Ashgate, 2005.

Edwards, John. *Mary I: England's Catholic Queen*. Yale English Monarchs. New Haven: Yale University Press, 2011.

Edwards, John. *Archbishop Pole*. The Archbishops of Canterbury. Farnham: Ashgate, 2014.

Edwards, R. Dudley. "Venerable John Travers and the Rebellion of Silken Thomas." *Studies: An Irish Quarterly Review* 23, no. 92 (December 1934): 687–99.

Eire, Carlos. "The Good, the Bad, and the Airborne: Levitation and the History of the Impossible in Early Modern Europe." In *Ideas and Cultural Margins in Early Modern Germany: Essays in Honor of H. C. Erik Midelfort*, edited by Marjorie Elizabeth Plummer and Robin B. Barnes, 307–23. Farnham: Ashgate, 2009.

Elliott, J.H. *Imperial Spain 1469–1716*. London: Penguin Books, 2002.

Elton, G.R. *Policy and Police: The Enforcement of the Reformation in the Age of Thomas Cromwell*. Cambridge: Cambridge University Press, 1972.

The English Hospice in Rome. Leominster: Gracewing, 2005.

Escudero Baztán, Juan Manuel. "El uso de la historia en Calderón: Tragedia e historia en *La cisma de Ingalaterra*." In *La rueda de la fortuna: Estudios sobre el teatro de Calderón*, edited by M. Carmen Pinillos and Juan Manuel Escudero Baztán, 15–37. Kassel: Edition Reichenberger, 2000.

Escudero Baztán, Juan Manuel. "La construcción de los caracteres en *La cisma de Inglaterra*: Convención e historia en el personaje de Enrique VIII." In *Actas del V Congreso Internacional de la Asociación Internacional Siglo de Oro (AISO), Münster 20–24 de julio de 1999*, edited by Christoph Strosetzki, 479–89. Madrid / Frankfurt am Main: Iberoamericana / Vervuert, 2001.

Fabbri, Demetrios. "Treating Medieval Plague: The Wonderful Virtues of Theriac." *Early Science and Medicine* 12, no. 3 (2007): 247–83.

Farmer, David. *The Oxford Dictionary of Saints*. Fifth Edition. Oxford: Oxford University Press, 2011.

Fernández Biggs, Braulio. *Calderón y Shakespeare: Los personajes en* La Cisma de Ingalaterra *y* Henry VIII. Biblioteca Áurea Hispánica 77. Madrid / Frankfurt am Main: Iberoamericana / Vervuert, 2012.

Fichtner, Paula Sutter. *Ferdinand I of Austria: The Politics of Dynasticism in the Age of the Reformation*. East European Monographs 100. New York: Columbia University Press, 1982.

Fincham, Kenneth, and Peter Lake. "The Ecclesiastical Policy of King James I." *Journal of British Studies* 24, no. 2 (April 1985): 169–207.

Fletcher, Stella. *Cardinal Wolsey: A Life in Renaissance Europe*. London: Continuum, 2009.

Fletcher, Catherine. *Our Man in Rome: Henry VIII and His Italian Ambassador*. London: The Bodley Head, 2012.

Flower, Richard. *Emperors and Bishops in Late Roman Invective*. Cambridge: Cambridge University Press, 2013.

Flynn, Dennis. "The English Mission of Jasper Heywood, S.J." *AHSI* 54, no. 107 (1985): 45–76.

Foley, Henry. *Records of the English Province of the Society of Jesus: Historical Facts Illustrative of the Labours and Sufferings of Its Members in the Sixteenth and Seventeenth Centuries*. 7 vols. London: Burns and Oates, 1875–83.

Ford Bacigalupo, Mario. "Calderón's *La Cisma de Ingalaterra* and Spanish Seventeenth-Century Political Thought." *Symposium: A Quarterly Journal in Modern Literatures* 28, no. 3 (1974): 212–27.

Forteza, Deborah. "Representaciones del cisma de Inglaterra en el Siglo de Oro: Ribadeneira y Cervantes." In *"Spiritus vivificat." Actas del V Congreso Internacional Jóvenes Investigadores Siglo de Oro (JISO 2015)*, edited by Maite Iraceburu and Carlos Mata Induráin, 33–42. Colección BIADIG 36. Pamplona: Servicio de Publicaciones de la Universidad de Navarra: 2016.

Frieda, Leonie. *Catherine de Medici*. London: Weidenfeld & Nicolson, 2004.

Gasquet, Francis Aidan. *A History of the Venerable English College, Rome: An Account of Its Origins and Work from the Earliest Times to the Present Day*. London: Longmans, Green and Co., 1920.

Ghisalberti, Alberto M., ed. *Dizionario biografico degli Italiani*. 80 vols. Rome: Instituto della Enciclopedia Italiana, 1960.

Gillow, Joseph. "Lord Burghley's Map of Lancashire, 1590." In *Catholic Record Society Miscellanea IV*, 162–222. Publications of the Catholic Record Society 4. London: The Arden Press, 1907.

Gómez-Centurión Jiménez, Carlos. *La Invencible y la empresa de Inglaterra*. Madrid: Editorial Nerea, 1988.

Gómez-Centurión Jiménez, Carlos. "The New Crusade: Ideology and Religion in the Anglo-Spanish Conflict." In *England, Spain, and the Gran Armada 1585–1604: Essays from the Anglo-Spanish Conferences London and Madrid 1988*, edited by M.J. Rodríguez-Salgado and Simon Adams, 264–99. Edinburgh: John Donald Publishers, 1991.

Gómez Menor, José. "La progenie hebrea del Padre Pedro de Ribadeneira S.I. (Hijo del jurado de Toledo Alvaro Husillo Ortiz de Cisneros)." *Sefarad* 36, no. 2 (1976): 307–32.

Gordon, Bruce. *Calvin*. New Haven: Yale University Press, 2009.

Gouwens, Kenneth, and Sheryl E. Reiss, eds. *The Pontificate of Clement VII: History, Politics, Culture*. Aldershot: Ashgate, 2005.

Grafton, Anthony. *The Footnote: A Curious History*. Cambridge: Harvard University Press, 1997.

Grafton, Anthony. *What Was History? The Art of History in Early Modern Europe*. Cambridge: Cambridge University Press, 2007.

Grafton, Anthony. "Church History in Early Modern Europe: Tradition and Innovation." In *Sacred History: Uses of the Christian Past in the Renaissance World*, edited by Katherine Van Liere, Simon Ditchfield, and Howard Louthan, 3–26. Oxford: Oxford University Press, 2012.

Greenslade, S.L., "English Versions of the Bible A.D. 1525–1611." In *The Cambridge History of the Bible*, edited by S.L. Greenslade, 3:141–74. Cambridge: Cambridge University Press, 1963.

Gregory, Brad S. *Salvation at Stake: Christian Martyrdom in Early Modern Europe*. Harvard Historical Studies 134. Cambridge: Harvard University Press, 1999.

Greschat, Martin. *Martin Bucer: A Reformer and His Times*. Translated by Stephen E. Buckwalter. Louisville: Westminster John Knox Press, 2004.

Grey, Jonathan Michael. *Oaths and the English Reformation*. Cambridge Studies in Early Modern British History. Cambridge: Cambridge University Press, 2013.

Griffiths, Ralph A. *The Reign of King Henry VI: The Exercise of Royal Authority, 1422–1461*. Berkeley: University of California Press, 1981.

Guazzelli, Giuseppe Antonio. "Cesare Baronio and the Roman Catholic Vision of the Early Church." In *Sacred History: Uses of the Christian Past in the Renaissance World*, edited by Katherine Van Liere, Simon Ditchfield, and Howard Louthan, 52–71. Oxford: Oxford University Press, 2012.

Guy, John. "Henry VIII and the Praemunire Manoeuvres of 1530–1531." *EHR* 97, no. 384 (July 1982): 481–503.

Guy, John. *Thomas More*. Reputations. London: Arnold Publishers, 2000.

Guy, John. *Queen of Scots: The True Life of Mary Stuart*. Boston: Houghton Mifflin, 2004.

Guy, John. *A Daughter's Love: Thomas & Margaret More*. London: Fourth Estate, 2008.

Gwynn, David M. *Athanasius of Alexandria: Bishop, Theologian, Ascetic, Father*. Christian Theology in Context. Oxford: Oxford University Press, 2012.

Haigh, Christopher. *English Reformations: Religion, Politics and Society under the Tudors*. Oxford: Oxford University Press, 1993.

Haigh, Christopher. *Elizabeth I*. Second Edition. Profiles in Power. Harlow: Longman Group, 1998.

Harris, A. Katie. "Forging History: The Plomos of the Sacromonte of Granada in Francisco Bermudez de Pedraza's *Historia Eclesiastica*." *SCJ* 30, no. 4 (Winter 1999): 945–66.

Hasler, P.W., ed. *The House of Commons 1558–1603*. 3 vols. The History of Parliament. London: Her Majesty's Stationery Office, 1981.

Haugaard, William P. "The Coronation of Elizabeth I." *JEH* 19, no. 2 (October 1968): 161–70.

Heal, Felicity. "Appropriating History: Catholic and Protestant Polemics and the National Past." *HLQ* 68, no. 1–2 (March 2005): 109–32.

Heal, Felicity. "What Can King Lucius Do for You? The Reformation and the Early British Church." *EHR* 120, no. 487 (June 2005): 593–614.

Highley, Christopher. "'A Pestilent and Seditious Book': Nicholas Sander's *Schismatis Anglicani* and Catholic Histories of the Reformation." *HLQ* 68, no. 1–2 (March 2005): 151–71.

Highley, Christopher. *Catholics Writing the Nation in Early Modern Britain and Ireland*. Oxford: Oxford University Press, 2008.

Hillgarth, J.N. "Spanish Historiography and Iberian Reality." *History and Theory* 24, no. 1 (February 1985): 23–43.

Hillgarth, J.N. *The Mirror of Spain, 1500–1700: The Formation of a Myth*. History, Languages, and Cultures of the Spanish and Portuguese Worlds. Ann Arbor: University of Michigan Press, 2000.

"The History of Syon (continued). Englefield Correspondence—English College Valladolid: Sister Elizabeth Saunders 'Second Letter' to Sir Francis Englefield." *Poor Soul's Friend and St. Joseph's Monitor*, April 1966, 43–54.

Holt, Mack P. *The French Wars of Religion, 1562–1629*. Cambridge: Cambridge University Press, 1995.

Holum, Kenneth G. "The Classical City in the Sixth Century: Survival and Transformation." In *The Cambridge Companion to the Age of Justinian*, edited by Michael Maas, 87–112. Cambridge Companions. Cambridge: Cambridge University Press, 2005.

Houliston, Victor. "The Lord Treasurer and the Jesuit: Robert Person's Satirical *Responsio* to the 1591 Proclamation." *SCJ* 32, no. 2 (Summer 2001): 383–401.

Houliston, Victor. *Catholic Resistance in Elizabethan England: Robert Persons's Jesuit Polemic, 1580–1610*. Catholic Christendom, 1300–1700. Aldershot: Ashgate, 2007.

Houliston, Victor. "The Missionary Position: Catholics Writing the History of the English Reformation." *English Studies in Africa* 54, no. 2 (2011): 16–30.

Houliston, Victor. "Fallen Prince and Pretender of the Faith: Henry VIII as Seen by Sander and Persons." In *Henry VIII and History*, edited by Thomas Betteridge and Thomas S. Freeman, 119–34. Farnham: Ashgate, 2012.

Houliston, Victor. "Robert Persons's Precarious Correspondence." *JJS* 1, no. 4 (2014): 542–57.

Hoyle, R.W. *The Pilgrimage of Grace and the Politics of the 1530s*. Oxford: Oxford University Press, 2001.

Huttenbach, Henry R. "New Archival Material on the Anglo-Russian Treaty of Queen Elizabeth I and Tsar Ivan IV." *Slavonic and East European Review* 49, no. 117 (October 1971): 535–49.

Iñurritegui Rodríguez, José María. *La gracia y la república: El lenguaje político de la teología católica y el* Príncipe Cristiano *de Pedro de Ribadeneyra*. Estudios de la UNED. Madrid: Universidad Nacional de la Educación a Distancia, 1998.

Ives, Eric. "Anne Boleyn and the Early Reformation in England: The Contemporary Evidence." *HJ* 37, no. 2 (June 1993): 389–400.

Ives, Eric. *The Life and Death of Anne Boleyn: "The Most Happy."* Malden: Blackwell Publishing, 2004.

Ives, Eric. "Tudor Dynastic Problems Revisited." *HR* 81, no. 212 (May 2008): 255–79.

Ives, Eric. *Lady Jane Grey: A Tudor Mystery.* Malden: Wiley-Blackwell, 2009.

Jardine, Lisa. "Gloriana Rules the Waves: Or, the Advantages of Being Excommunicated (and a Woman)." *Transactions of the Royal Historical Society*, Sixth Series, 14 (2004): 209–22.

Jedin, Hubert. *Geschichte des Konzils von Trient.* 4 vols. Freiburg: Verlag Herder, 1951–75.

Jones, E.A. *Syon Abbey 1415–2015: England's Last Medieval Monastery.* Leominster: Gracewing, 2015.

Jones, Michael K., and Malcolm G. Underwood. *The King's Mother: Lady Margaret Beaufort, Countess of Richmond and Derby.* Cambridge: Cambridge University Press, 1992.

Jordan, W.K. *Edward VI: The Threshold of Power (The Dominance of the Duke of Northumberland).* London: George Allen & Unwin, 1970.

Kagan, Richard L. "La historia y los cronistas del rey." In *Philippus II Rex*, edited by Pedro Navascués Palacio, 87–119. Barcelona: Lunwerg Editores, 1998.

Kagan, Richard L. "Antonio de Herrera y Tordesillas and the 'Political Turn' in the 'Official History' of Seventeenth-Century Spain." In *Les historiographes en Europe de la fin du Moyen Âge à la Révolution*, edited by Chantal Grell, 277–96. Mythes, critique et histoire. Paris: Presses de l'Université Paris-Sorbonne, 2006.

Kagan, Richard L. *Clio & the Crown: The Politics of History in Medieval and Early Modern Spain.* Baltimore: Johns Hopkins University Press, 2009.

Kallendorf, Hilaire. *Conscience on Stage: The Comedia as Casuistry in Early Modern Spain.* University of Toronto Romance Series. Toronto: University of Toronto Press, 2007.

Kamen, Henry. *Philip of Spain.* New Haven: Yale University Press, 1997.

Kaufman, Gloria. "Juan Luis Vives on the Education of Women." *Signs* 3, no. 4 (Summer 1978): 891–96.

Kavey, Allison, and Elizabeth Ketner, eds. *Imagining Early Modern Histories.* Farnham: Ashgate, 2016.

Kelly, J.N.D. *Early Christian Doctrines.* Fifth Edition. London: Adam & Charles Black, 1977.

Kelly, J.N.D. *Golden Mouth: The Story of John Chrysostom, Ascetic, Preacher, Bishop.* Ithaca: Cornell University Press, 1998.

Kelly, Henry Ansgar. *The Matrimonial Trials of Henry VIII.* Eugene: Wipf and Stock Publishers, 2004.

Kelly, James E. "Conformity, Loyalty and the Jesuit Mission to England of 1580." In *Religious Tolerance in the Atlantic World: Early Modern and Contemporary Perspectives*, edited by Eliane Glaser, 149–70. Basingstoke: Palgrave MacMillan, 2014.

Kelly, James E. "Panic, Plots, and Polemic: The Jesuits and the Early Modern English Mission." *JJS* 1, no. 4 (2014): 511–19.

Kewes, Paulina. "History and Its Uses: Introduction." *HLQ* 68, no. 1–2 (March 2005): 1–31.

Kewes, Paulina, ed. *The Uses of History in Early Modern England.* San Marino: Henry E. Huntington Library and Art Gallery, 2006.

Kilroy, Gerard. "'Paths Coincident': The Parallel Lives of Dr. Nicholas Sander and Edmund Campion, S.J." *JJS* 1, no. 4 (2014): 520–41.

Knecht, R.J. *Francis I.* Cambridge: Cambridge University Press, 1982.

Knighton, C.S. "Westminster Abbey Restored." In *The Church of Mary Tudor*, edited by Eamon Duffy and David Loades, 77–123. Aldershot: Ashgate, 2005.

Krynen, Jacques. "'Rex Christianissimus': A Medieval Theme at the Roots of French Absolutism." *History and Anthropology* 4 (1989): 79–96.

Kujawa-Holbrook, Sheryl A. "Katherine Parr and Reformed Religion." *Anglican and Episcopal History* 72, no. 1 (March 2003): 55–78.

Küpper, Joachim. *"La cisma de Inglaterra* y la concepción calderoniana de la historia." In *Hacia Calderón: Octavo Coloquio Anglogermano Bochum 1987*, edited by Hans Flasche, 183–202. Archivum Calderonianum 5. Stuttgart: Franz Steiner Verlag Wiesbaden GMBH, 1988.

Lake, Peter. *Bad Queen Bess? Libels, Secret Histories, and the Politics of Publicity in the Reign of Queen Elizabeth I.* Oxford: Oxford University Press, 2016.

Lake, Peter, and Michael C. Questier. "Puritans, Papists, and the 'Public Sphere' in Early Modern England: The Edmund Campion Affair in Context." *Journal of Modern History* 72, no. 3 (September 2000): 587–627.

Lake, Peter, and Michael C. Questier. "Prisons, Priests and People." In *England's Long Reformation: 1500–1800*, edited by Nicholas Tyacke, 195–234. The Neale Colloquium in British History. London: UCL Press, 2003.

Lake, Peter, and Michael C. Questier. "Margaret Clitherow, Catholic Nonconformity, Martyrology and the Politics of Religious Change in Elizabethan England." *Past & Present* 185 (November 2004): 43–90.

Lake, Peter, and Michael C. Questier. *The Trials of Margaret Clitherow: Persecution, Martyrdom and the Politics of Sanctity in Elizabethan England.* London: Continuum, 2011.

LaRocca, John J. "Time, Death, and the Next Generation: The Early Elizabethan Recusancy Policy, 1558–1574." *Albion: A Quarterly Journal Concerned with British Studies* 14, no. 2 (Summer 1982): 103–17.

Law, Thomas Graves. *A Calendar of the English Martyrs of the Sixteenth and Seventeenth Centuries.* London: Burns and Oates, 1876.

Lay, Jenna D. "The Literary Lives of Nuns: Crafting Identities Through Exile." In *The English Convents in Exile, 1600–1800: Communities, Culture and Identity*, edited by Caroline Bowden and James E. Kelly, 71–86. Farnham: Ashgate, 2013.

Leonard, Irving A. "Spanish Ship-Board Reading in the Sixteenth Century." *Hispania* 32, no. 1 (February 1949): 53–58.

Le Roux de Lincy, Antoine. *Researches Concerning Jean Grolier: His Life and His Library*. Edited by Roger Portalis. Translated by Carolyn Shipman. New York: The Grolier Club, 1907.

Leturia, Pietro. "Il contributo della Compagnia di Gesù alla formazione delle scienze storiche." *Analecta Gregoriana* 29, no. 3 (1942): 161–202.

Levitin, Dmitri. "From Sacred History to the History of Religion: Paganism, Judaism, and Christianity in European Historiography from Reformation to 'Englightenment.'" *HJ* 55, no. 4 (December 2012): 1117–60.

Loach, Jennifer. *Edward VI*. Edited by George W. Bernard and Penry William. Yale English Monarchs. New Haven: Yale University Press, 2002.

Loades, David. "The Enforcement of Reaction, 1553–1558." *JEH* 16, no. 1 (April 1965): 54–66.

Loades, David. *Mary Tudor: A Life*. London: Basil Blackwell, 1989.

Loades, David. *The Reign of Mary Tudor: Politics, Government and Religion in England, 1553–58*. Second Edition. London: Longman, 1991.

Loades, David. "The Marian Episcopate." In *The Church of Mary Tudor*, edited by Eamon Duffy and David Loades, 33–56. Aldershot: Ashgate, 2005.

Loades, David. *The Life and Career of William Paulet (c.1475–1572): Lord Treasurer and First Marquis of Winchester*. Aldershot: Ashgate, 2007.

Loades, David. *Catherine Howard: The Adulterous Wife of Henry VIII*. Stroud: Amberley, 2012.

Loades, David. *Thomas Cromwell: Servant to Henry VIII*. Stroud: Amberley Publishing, 2013.

Loftis, John. "*Henry VIII* and Calderón's *La Cisma de Inglaterra*." *Comparative Literature* 34, no. 3 (Summer 1982): 208–22.

Logan, F. Donald. "The Origins of the So-Called Regius Professorships: An Aspect of the Renaissance in Oxford and Cambridge." In *Renaissance and Renewal in Christian History: Papers Read at the Fifteenth Summer Meeting and the Sixteenth Winter Meeting of the Ecclesiastical History Society*, edited by Derek Baker, 271–78. Oxford: Basil Blackwell, 1977.

Luxford, Julian M. *The Art and Architecture of English Benedictine Monasteries, 1300–1540: A Patronage History*. Studies in the History of Medieval Religion 25. Woodbridge: Boydell Press, 2005.

MacCaffrey, Wallace. *Elizabeth I*. London: Edward Arnold, 1993.

MacCulloch, Diarmaid. *Thomas Cranmer: A Life*. New Haven: Yale University Press, 1996.

MacCulloch, Diarmaid. *The Boy King: Edward VI and the Protestant Reformation*. Berkeley: University of California Press, 2002.

Machielsen, Jan. "The Lion, the Witch, and the King: Thomas Stapleton's *Apologia pro Rege Catholico Philippo II* (1592)." *EHR* 129, no. 536 (February 2014): 19–46.

Maltby, William. *The Reign of Charles V*. Basingstoke: Palgrave, 2002.

Marcus, Ralph. "The Armenian Life of Marutha of Maipherkat." *Harvard Theological Review* 25, no. 1 (January 1932): 47–71.

Marshall, Peter. "Papist as Heretic: The Burning of John Forest, 1538." *HJ* 41, no. 2 (June 1998): 351–74.

Marshall, Peter. "The Other Black Legend: The Henrician Reformation and the Spanish People." *EHR* 116, no. 465 (February 2001): 31–49.

Marshall, Peter. "John Calvin and the English Catholics, c. 1565–1640." *HJ* 53, no. 4 (December 2010): 849–70.

Martin, A. Lynn. "The Jesuit Mystique." *SCJ* 4, no. 1 (April 1973): 31–40.

Martin, Colin, and Geoffrey Parker. *The Spanish Armada*. Revised Edition. Manchester: Manchester University Press, 1999.

Maryks, Robert Aleksander. *Saint Cicero and the Jesuits: The Influence of the Liberal Arts on the Adoption of Moral Probabilism*. Bibliotheca Instituti Historici S.I. 64. Aldershot: Ashgate, 2008.

Maryks, Robert Aleksander. *The Jesuit Order as a Synagogue of Jews: Jesuits of Jewish Ancestry and Purity-of-Blood Laws in the Early Society of Jesus*. Studies in Medieval and Reformation Traditions 146. Leiden: Brill, 2010.

Maryks, Robert Aleksander. "Rhetorical *Veri-Similitudo*: Cicero, Probabilism, and Jesuit Casuistry." In *Traditions of Eloquence: The Jesuits and Modern Rhetorical Studies*, edited by Cinthia Gannett and John Brereton, 60–71. New York: Fordham University Press, 2015.

Maryks, Robert Aleksander, ed. *Exploring Jesuit Distinctiveness: Interdisciplinary Perspectives on Ways of Proceeding within the Society of Jesus*. Jesuit Studies 6. Leiden: Brill, 2016.

Matthew, Colin, and Brian Harrison, eds. *Oxford Dictionary of National Biography*. 60 vols. Oxford: Oxford University Press, 2004.

Mayer, Thomas F. "A Sticking-Plaster Saint? Autobiography and Hagiography in the Making of Reginald Pole." In *The Rhetorics of Life-Writing in Early Modern Europe: Forms of Biography from Cassandra Fedele to Louis XIV*, edited by Thomas F. Mayer and D.R. Woolf, 205–22. Ann Arbor: University of Michigan Press, 1995.

Mayer, Thomas F. *Reginald Pole: Prince & Prophet*. Cambridge: Cambridge University Press, 2000.

Mayer, Thomas F. "A Test of Wills: Cardinal Pole, Ignatius Loyola, and the Jesuits in England." In *The Reckoned Expense: Edmund Campion and the Early English Jesuits*, edited by Thomas M. McCoog, 2nd ed., 21–37. Bibliotheca Instituti Historici S.I. 60. Woodbridge: Boydell Press, 2007.

McCoog, Thomas M. "Ignatius Loyola and Reginald Pole: A Reconsideration." *JEH* 47, no. 2 (April 1996): 257–73.

McCoog, Thomas M. *The Society of Jesus in Ireland, Scotland, and England 1541–1588: "Our Way of Proceeding?"* Studies in Medieval and Reformation Thought 60. Leiden: Brill, 1996.

McCoog, Thomas M., ed. *The Reckoned Expense: Edmund Campion and the Early English Jesuits.* Second Edition. Bibliotheca Instituti Historici S.I. 60. Woodbridge: Boydell Press, 2007.

McCoog, Thomas M. *The Society of Jesus in Ireland, Scotland, and England, 1589–1597: Building the Faith of Saint Peter upon the King of Spain's Monarchy.* Biblioteca Instituti Historici Societatis Iesu 73. Farnham: Ashgate, 2012.

McCoog, Thomas M. *"And Touching Our Society": Fashioning Jesuit Identity in Elizabethan England.* Catholic and Recusant Texts of the Late Medieval & Early Modern Periods 3. Toronto: Pontifical Institute of Mediaeval Studies, 2013.

McCoog, Thomas M. "'Replant the Uprooted Trunk of the Tree of Faith': The Society of Jesus and the Continental Colleges for Religious Exiles." In *Insular Christianity: Alternative Models of the Church in Britain and Ireland, c.1570–c.1700*, edited by Robert Armstrong and Tadhg Ó hAnnracháin, 28–44. Politics, Culture, and Society in Early Modern Britain. Manchester: Manchester University Press, 2013.

McEntegart, Rory. *Henry VIII, the League of Schmalkalden and the English Reformation.* Studies in History New Series. Woodbridge: Boydell Press, 2002.

McGrath, Patrick. "The Bloody Questions Reconsidered." *RH* 20, no. 3 (May 1991): 305–19.

McGrath, Patrick, and Joy Rowe. "The Imprisonment of Catholics for Religion under Elizabeth I." *RH* 20, no. 4 (October 1991): 415–35.

Medina, Francisco de Borja de. "Jesuitas en la armada contra Inglaterra (1588): Notas para un centenario." *AHSI* 58 (1989): 3–42.

Medvei, V.C. "The Illness and Death of Mary Tudor." *Journal of the Royal Society of Medicine* 80 (December 1987): 766–80.

Meserve, Margaret. "The Sophy: News of Shah Ismail Safavi in Renaissance Europe." *Journal of Early Modern History* 18 (2014): 579–608.

Miranda, Salvador. "The Cardinals of the Holy Roman Church," 2016. http://webdept .fiu.edu/~mirandas/cardinals.htm. Accessed April 21, 2016.

Monta, Susannah Brietz. *Martyrdom and Literature in Early Modern England.* Cambridge: Cambridge University Press, 2005.

Neale, J.E. *Queen Elizabeth I.* Harmondsworth: Penguin Books, 1961.

Nelles, Paul. "*Historia magistra antiquitatis*: Cicero and Jesuit History Teaching." *Renaissance Studies* 13, no. 2 (June 1999): 130–72.

Nelles, Paul. "*Cosas y cartas*: Scribal Production and Material Pathways in Jesuit Global Communication (1547–1573)." *JJS* 2, no. 3 (2015): 421–50.

Olds, Katrina B. *Forging the Past: Invented Histories in Counter-Reformation Spain*. New Haven: Yale University Press, 2015.

O'Malley, John W. "To Travel to Any Part of the World: Jerónimo Nadal and the Jesuit Vocation." *Studies in the Spirituality of Jesuits* 16, no. 2 (March 1984): 1–21.

O'Malley, John W. *The First Jesuits*. Cambridge: Harvard University Press, 1993.

O'Malley, John W. *Trent: What Happened at the Council*. Cambridge: Harvard University Press, 2013.

O'Neill, Charles E., and Joaquín Maria Domínguez, eds. *Diccionario histórico de la Compañía de Jesús: Biográfico-temático*. 4 vols. Rome / Madrid: Institutum Historicum Societatis Iesu / Universidad Pontificia Comillas, 2001.

Oreskes, Naomi, and Erik M. Conway. *Merchants of Doubt: How a Handful of Scientists Obscured the Truth on Issues from Tobacco Smoke to Global Warming*. New York: Bloomsbury Press, 2010.

Page, William, ed. *The Victoria History of the County of Oxford*. 16 vols. The Victoria History of the Counties of England. London: Archibald Constable and Company Limited, 1907–.

Page, William, ed. *The Victoria History of the County of Kent*. 3 vols. The Victoria History of the Counties of England. London: Archibald Constable and Company Limited, 1908–32.

Parker, A.A. "Henry VIII in Shakespeare and Calderón: An Appreciation of 'La Cisma de Ingalaterra.'" *Modern Language Review* 43, no. 3 (July 1948): 327–52.

Parker, Geoffrey. "The Place of Tudor England in the Messianic Vision of Philip II of Spain: The Prothero Lecture." *Transactions of the Royal Historical Society* 12 (2002): 167–221.

Parker, Geoffrey. *Imprudent King: A New Life of Philip II*. New Haven: Yale University Press, 2014.

Pastor, Ludwig. *The History of the Popes, from the Close of the Middle Ages*. Translated by Frederick Ignatius Antrobus, Ralph Francis Kerr, Ernest Graf, and E.F. Peeler. 40 vols. London: J. Hodges, 1891–1953.

Patterson, W.B. "The Recusant View of the English Past." In *The Materials, Sources, and Methods of Ecclesiastical History: Papers Read at the Twelfth Summer Meeting and the Thirteenth Winter Meeting of the Ecclesiastical History Society*, edited by Derek Baker, 249–62. Oxford: Basil Blackwell, 1975.

Pearson, M.N. *The Portuguese in India*. The New Cambridge History of India I.1. Cambridge: Cambridge University Press, 1987.

Perry, Elizabeth. "Petitioning for Patronage: An Illuminated Tale of Exile from Syon Abbey, Lisbon." In *The English Convents in Exile, 1600–1800: Communities, Culture and Identity*, edited by Caroline Bowden and James E. Kelly, 159–74. Farnham: Ashgate, 2013.

Petti, Anthony G. "Stephen Vallenger (1541–1591)." *RH* 6, no. 6 (October 1962): 248–64.

Pickthorn, Kenneth. *Early Tudor Government: Henry VIII*. Cambridge: Cambridge University Press, 2015.

Pitts, Vincent J. *Henri IV of France: His Reign and Age*. Baltimore: Johns Hopkins University Press, 2009.

Pocock, Nicholas. Review of *Letters and Papers, Foreign and Domestic, of the Reign of Henry VIII*, by James Gairdner. *EHR* 9, no. 34 (April 1894): 373–77.

Pogson, Rex H. "Reginald Pole and the Priorities of Government in Mary Tudor's Church." *HJ* 18, no. 1 (March 1975): 3–20.

Pollen, John Hungerford. "Dr. Nicholas Sander." *EHR* 6, no. 21 (January 1891): 36–47.

Pollnitz, Aysha. *Princely Education in Early Modern Britain*. Cambridge Studies in Early Modern British History. Cambridge: Cambridge University Press, 2015.

Popper, Nicholas. "An Ocean of Lies: The Problem of Historical Evidence in the Sixteenth Century." *HLQ* 74, no. 3 (September 2011): 375–400.

Popper, Nicholas. *Walter Ralegh's History of the World and the Historical Culture of the Late Renaissance*. Chicago: University of Chicago Press, 2012.

Prat, Jean-Marie. *Histoire du pére Ribadeneyra, disciple de saint Ignace*. Paris: Victor Palme, 1862.

Preston, Joseph H. "Was There an Historical Revolution?" *Journal of the History of Ideas* 38, no. 2 (June 1977): 353–64.

Pursell, Brennan C. "James I, Gondomar and the Dissolution of the Parliament of 1621." *History* 85, no. 279 (July 2000): 428–45.

Pursell, Brennan C. "The End of the Spanish Match." *HJ* 45, no. 4 (2002): 699–726.

Questier, Michael C. "Loyalty, Religion and State Power in Early Modern England: English Romanism and the Jacobean Oath of Allegiance." *HJ* 40, no. 2 (1997): 311–29.

Questier, Michael C. *Catholicism and Community in Early Modern England: Politics, Aristocratic Patronage and Religion, c.1550–1640*. Cambridge Studies in Early Modern British History. Cambridge: Cambridge University Press, 2006.

Questier, Michael C., ed. *Suart Dynastic Policy and Religious Politics 1621–1625*. Camden Fifth Series 34. Cambridge: Cambridge University Press, 2009.

Quintero, María Cristina. "English Queens and the Body Politic in Calderón's *La cisma de Inglaterra* and Rivadeneira's *Historia eclesiastica del scisma del reino de Inglaterra*." *Modern Language Notes* 113, no. 2 (1998): 259–82.

Quintero, María Cristina. *Gendering the Crown in the Spanish Baroque Comedia*. New Hispanisms: Cultural & Literary Studies. Farnham: Ashgate, 2012.

Redworth, Glyn. *In Defence of the Church Catholic: The Life of Stephen Gardiner*. Oxford: Basil Blackwell, 1990.

Redworth, Glyn. *The Prince and the Infanta: The Cultural Politics of the Spanish Match*. New Haven: Yale University Press, 2003.

"Refranero multilingüe." Centro Virtual Cervantes, 2015. http://cvc.cervantes.es/lengua/refranero/Default.aspx. Accessed December 6, 2015.

Reichenberger, Kurt, and Roswitha Reichenberger. *Bibliographisches Handbuch der Calderón-Forschung: Manual bibliográfico calderoniano*. 4 vols. Würzburger Romanistische Arbeiten 1. Kassel: Thiele & Schwarz, 1979.

Rex, Richard. "Thomas Vavasour M.D." *RH* 20, no. 4 (October 1991): 436–54.

Reynolds, E.E. *Campion and Parsons: The Jesuit Mission of 1580–1*. London: Sheed and Ward, 1980.

Robbins, Jeremy. "The Spanish Literary Responses to the Visit of Charles, Prince of Wales." In *The Spanish Match: Prince Charles's Journey to Madrid*, edited by Alexander Samson, 107–22. Aldershot: Ashgate, 2006.

Rodríguez-Salgado, M.J. "The Anglo-Spanish War: The Final Episode of the 'Wars of the Roses'?" In *England, Spain, and the Gran Armada 1585–1604: Essays from the Anglo-Spanish Conferences London and Madrid 1988*, edited by M.J. Rodríguez-Salgado and Simon Adams, 1–44. Edinburgh: John Donald Publishers, 1991.

Roldán-Figueroa, Rady. "Father Luis Piñeiro, S.J., the Tridentine Economy of Relics, and the Defense of the Jesuit Missionary Enterprise in Tokugawa Japan." *Archiv für Reformationsgeschichte* 101, no. 1 (October 2010): 209–32.

Roldán-Figueroa, Rady. "Pedro de Ribadeneyra's *Vida del P. Ignacio de Loyola* (1583) and Literary Culture in Early Modern Spain." In *Exploring Jesuit Distinctiveness: Interdisciplinary Perspectives on Ways of Proceeding within the Society of Jesus*, edited by Robert Aleksander Maryks, 156–74. Jesuit Studies 6. Leiden: Brill, 2016.

Ryrie, Alec. *The Age of Reformation: The Tudor and Stewart Realms 1485–1603*. Religion, Politics and Society in Britain. Harlow: Pearson Longman, 2009.

Samson, Alexander. "Florián de Ocampo, Castilian Chronicler and Habsburg Propagandist: Rhetoric, Myth and Genealogy in the Historiography of Early Modern Spain." *Forum for Modern Language Studies* 42, no. 4 (October 2006): 339–54.

Sánchez, Magdalena S. "Pious and Political Images of a Habsburg Woman at the Court of Philip III (1598–1621)." In *Spanish Women in the Golden Age: Images and Realities*, edited by Magdalena S. Sánchez and Alain Saint-Saëns, 91–107. Contributions in Women's Studies 155. Westport: Greenwood Press, 1996.

Sánchez Alonso, Benito. *Historia de la historiografía española: De Ocampo a Solís (1543–1684)*. Vol. 2. 3 vols. Publicaciones de la Revista de filología española. Madrid: J. Sánchez de Ocaña, 1944.

Scarisbrick, J.J. *Henry VIII*. Yale English Monarchs. New Haven: Yale University Press, 1997.

Scott, Hamish, ed. *The Oxford Handbook of Early Modern European History, 1350–1750: Volume II: Cultures & Power*. Oxford Handbooks. Oxford: Oxford University Press, 2015.

Scott, John. *A Bibliography of Works Relating to Mary Queen of Scots: 1544–1700*. Publications of the Edinburgh Bibliographical Society 2. Edinburgh: Printed for the Edinburgh Bibliographical Society, 1896.

Scully, Robert E. "The Unmaking of a Saint: Thomas Becket and the English Reformation." *Catholic Historical Review* 86, no. 4 (October 2000): 579–602.

Scully, Robert E. "'In the Confident Hope of a Miracle': The Spanish Armada and Religious Mentalities in the Late Sixteenth Century." *Catholic Historical Review* 89, no. 4 (2003): 643–70.

Sheils, William J. "Polemic as Piety: Thomas Stapleton's *Tres Thomae* and Catholic Controversy in the 1580s." *JEH* 60, no. 1 (January 2009): 74–94.

Simpson, Richard. *Edmund Campion: A Biography.* The Catholic Standard Library. London: John Hodges, 1896.

Skidmore, Chris. *Death and the Virgin Queen: Elizabeth I and the Dark Scandal That Rocked the Throne.* New York: St. Martin's Press, 2010.

Slavin, Arthur Joseph. "Parliament and Henry VIII's Bigamous Principal Secretary." *HLQ* 28, no. 2 (February 1965): 131–43.

Smith, Alan. "Lucius of Britain: Alleged King and Church Founder." *Folklore* 90, no. 1 (1979): 29–36.

Solís de los Santos, José. "Relaciones de sucesos de Inglaterra en el reinado de Carlos V." In *Testigo del tiempo, memoria del universo: Cultura escrita y sociedad en el mundo ibérico (siglos XV–XVIII)*, edited by Manuel F. Fernández, Carlos Alberto González, and Natalia Maillard, 640–98. [Rubí]: Ediciones Rubeo, 2009.

Stradling, R.A. *Philip IV and the Government of Spain 1621–1665.* Cambridge: Cambridge University Press, 1988.

Streckfuss, Corinna. "England's Reconciliation with Rome: A News Event in Early Modern Europe." *HR* 82, no. 215 (February 2009): 62–73.

Subrahmanyam, Sanjay. "On World Historians in the Sixteenth Century." *Representations* 91, no. 1 (Summer 2005): 26–57.

Sutherland, N.M. "The Marian Exiles and the Establishment of the Elizabethan Regime." *Archiv für Reformationsgeschichte* 78 (1987): 253–86.

Sutton, Bertha R. "Nicholas Sanders. Controversialist-Historian (1530–1581)." *Irish Monthly* 49, no. 582 (December 1921): 504–06.

Taylor, William Cooke. *Chapters on Coronations.* London: J.W. Parker, 1838.

Tenace, Edward. "A Strategy of Reaction: The Armadas of 1596 and 1597 and the Spanish Struggle for European Hegemony." *EHR* 118, no. 478 (September 2003): 855–82.

Torres Olleta, Gabriela. "Imágenes del poder en el Siglo de Oro: La visión del P. Ribadeneyra en el *Cisma de Inglaterra*." In *La voz de Clío: Imágenes del poder en la comedia histórica del Siglo de Oro*, edited by Oana Andreia Sâmbrian, Mariela Insúa, and Antonie Mihail, 70–81. Craiova: Editura Universitaria Craiova, 2012.

Townshend, W.T. "The Henotikon Schism and the Roman Church." *Journal of Religion* 16, no. 1 (January 1936): 78–86.

Travitsky, Betty S. "The Puzzling Letters of Sister Elizabeth Sa[u]nder[s]." In *Textual Conversations in the Renaissance: Ethics, Authors, Technologies*, edited by Zachary Lesser and Benedict S. Robinson, 131–46. Aldershot: Ashgate, 2006.

Tremlett, Giles. *Catherine of Aragon: The Spanish Queen of Henry VIII*. New York: Walker & Company, 2010.

Tsuchihashi, Yachita. *Japanese Chronological Tables: From 601 to 1872*. Monumenta Nipponica Monographs 11. Tokyo: Sophia University Press, 1952.

Tutino, Stefania. "The Political Thought of Robert Persons's *Conference* in Continental Context." *HJ* 52, no. 1 (March 2009): 43–62.

Urbainczyk, Theresa. *Theodoret of Cyrrhus: The Bishop and the Holy Man*. Ann Arbor: University of Michigan Press, 2002.

Van Liere, Katherine, Simon Ditchfield, and Howard Louthan, eds. *Sacred History: Uses of the Christian Past in the Renaissance World*. Oxford: Oxford University Press, 2012.

Veech, Thomas McNevin. *Dr Nicholas Sanders and the English Reformation, 1530–1581*. Recueil de travaux publiés par les membres des Conférences d'Histoire et de Philologie 32. Leuven: Bureaux du Recueil, Bibliothéque de l'Université, 1935.

Vincent, Nicholas. "The Court of Henry II." In *Henry II: New Interpretations*, edited by Christopher Harper-Bill and Nicholas Vincent, 278–334. Woodbridge: Boydell Press, 2007.

W., C. "On External Devotion to Holy Men Departed." *The Rambler*, New Series, 1 (1859): 386–90.

Walsham, Alexandra. "'Frantick Hacket': Prophecy, Sorcery, Insanity, and the Elizabethan Puritan Movement." *HJ* 41, no. 1 (March 1998): 27–66.

Walsham, Alexandra. *Providence in Early Modern England*. Oxford: Oxford University Press, 1999.

Walsham, Alexandra. "'Domme Preachers'? Post-Reformation English Catholicism and the Culture of Print." *Past & Present* 168 (August 2000): 72–123.

Walsham, Alexandra. "Translating Trent? English Catholicism and the Counter Reformation." *HR* 78, no. 201 (August 2005): 288–310.

Walsham, Alexandra. *Catholic Reformation in Protestant Britain*. Catholic Christendom, 1300–1700. Farnham: Ashgate, 2014.

Warnicke, Retha M. *The Marrying of Anne of Cleves: Royal Protocol in Early Modern England*. Cambridge: Cambridge University Press, 2000.

Warnicke, Retha M. *Mary Queen of Scots*. Routledge Historical Biographies. London: Routledge, 2006.

Warren, W.L. *Henry II*. The English Monarchs. Berkeley: University of California Press, 1973.

Watt, Diane. "Reconstructing the Word: The Political Prophecies of Elizabeth Barton (1506–1534)." *Renaissance Quarterly* 50, no. 1 (Spring 1997): 136–63.

Weinreich, Spencer J. "The Distinctiveness of the Society of Jesus's Mission in Pedro de Ribadeneyra's *Historia ecclesiastica del scisma del reyno de Inglaterra* (1588)." In *Exploring Jesuit Distinctiveness: Interdisciplinary Perspectives on Ways of Proceeding within the Society of Jesus*, edited by Robert Aleksander Maryks, 175–88. Jesuit Studies 6. Leiden: Brill, 2016.

Weinreich, Spencer J. "English Mission, Global Catholicism, Christian History: Providence and Historiography in Pedro de Ribadeneyra's *Historia ecclesiastica del scisma del reyno de Inglaterra*." In *The World is Our House? Jesuit Intellectual and Physical Exchange between England and Mainland Europe*, edited by Hannah J. Thomas and James Kelly. Jesuit Studies. Leiden: Brill, forthcoming.

Wheatcroft, Andrew. *Enemy at the Gate: Habsburgs, Ottomans, and the Battle for Europe.* New York: Basic Books, 2009.

Whitehead, J.G.O. "Arwîrac of Glastonbury." *Folklore* 73, no. 3 (1962): 149–59.

Whitfield, D.W. "The Third Order of St. Francis in Mediaeval England." *Franciscan Studies* 13, no. 1 (March 1953): 50–59.

Williams, Michael E. *The Venerable English College Rome: A History, 1579–1979.* London: Associated Catholic Publications, 1979.

Womersley, David. "Against the Teleology of Technique." *HLQ* 68, no. 1–2 (March 2005): 95–108.

Wooding, Lucy. "The Marian Restoration and the Language of Catholic Reform." In *Reforming Catholicism in the England of Mary Tudor: The Achievement of Friar Bartolomé Carranza*, edited by John Edwards and Ronald W. Truman, 49–64. Aldershot: Ashgate, 2005.

Wormald, Jenny. *Mary Queen of Scots: A Study in Failure.* London: Collins & Brown, 1991.

Wright, Anthony D. "Catholic History, North and South." *Northern History* 14 (1978): 126–51.

Unpublished Dissertations

Cid Morgade, Fátima. "An Analysis of Pedro de Ribadeneyra's *Historia Ecclesiastica Del Scisma de Inglaterra* (1588)." Universidad de Valladolid, 2014.

Dalmases, Cándido de. "Origenes de la hagiografía ignaciana: Pedro de Ribadeneyra biógrafo de S. Ignacio." PhD Dissertation, Universidad de Madrid, 1944.

Domínguez, Freddy Cristóbal. "'We Must Fight with Paper and Pens': Spanish Elizabethan Polemics 1585–1598." PhD Dissertation, Princeton University, 2011.

Greenwood, Jonathan Edward. "Readers, Sanctity, and History in Early Modern History: Pedro de Ribadeneyra, the *Flos Sanctorum*, and Catholic Community." Master's Thesis, Carleton University, 2011.

Biblical Index

Index